T0334547

Post-Kyoto International Climate Policy

The **Harvard Project on International Climate Agreements** is a global, multi-disciplinary effort intended to help identify the key design elements of a scientifically sound, economically rational, and politically pragmatic post-2012 international policy architecture for addressing the threat of climate change. It has commissioned leading scholars to examine a uniquely wide range of core issues that must be addressed if the world is to reach an effective agreement on a successor regime to the Kyoto Protocol. The purpose of the project is not to become an advocate for any single policy but to present the best possible information and analysis on the full range of options concerning mitigation, adaptation, technology, and finance. The detailed findings of the Harvard Project are reported in this volume, which contains twenty-seven specially commissioned chapters.

A companion volume summarizing the main findings of this research is published separately as *Post-Kyoto International Climate Policy: Summary for Policymakers*.

JOSEPH E. ALDY is Fellow at Resources for the Future in Washington, DC. He also served on the staff of the President's Council of Economic Advisers, where he was responsible for climate change policy from 1997 to 2000.

ROBERT N. STAVINS is Albert Pratt Professor of Business and Government at the John F. Kennedy School of Government at Harvard University. He is also Director of the Harvard Environmental Economics Program and Chairman of the Kennedy School's Environment and Natural Resources Faculty Group.

Post-Kyoto International Climate Policy:

Implementing Architectures for Agreement

Research from the Harvard Project on International Climate Agreements

Edited by

JOSEPH E. ALDY

and

ROBERT N. STAVINS

CAMBRIDGE UNIVERSITY PRESS

CAMBRIDGE
UNIVERSITY PRESS

University Printing House, Cambridge CB2 8BS, United Kingdom

One Liberty Plaza, 20th Floor, New York, NY 10006, USA

477 Williamstown Road, Port Melbourne, VIC 3207, Australia

314-321, 3rd Floor, Plot 3, Splendor Forum, Jasola District Centre, New Delhi - 110025, India

79 Anson Road, #06-04/06, Singapore 079906

Cambridge University Press is part of the University of Cambridge.

It furthers the University's mission by disseminating knowledge in the pursuit of education, learning and research at the highest international levels of excellence.

www.cambridge.org
Information on this title: www.cambridge.org/9780521129527

First published 2010

A catalogue record for this publication is available from the British Library

ISBN 978-0-521-13785-0 Hardback
ISBN 978-0-521-12952-7 Paperback

Contents

Part IV   Global climate policy and international trade

Part V   Economic development, adaptation, and deforestation

Part VI   Modeling impacts of alternative allocations of responsibility

Harvard Environmental Economics Program
International Advisory Board

The Harvard Project on International Climate Agreements is an initiative of the Harvard Environmental Economics Program, which develops innovative answers to today's complex environmental issues, through research, teaching, and policy outreach.

Harvard Project on International Climate Agreements Faculty Steering Committee

Graham Allison
Douglas Dillon Professor
of Government
Harvard Kennedy School

Jeffrey Frankel
James W. Harpel Professor of
Capital Formation and
Growth
Harvard Kennedy School

Jerry Green
John Leverett Professor in the
University
Harvard Faculty of Arts and
Sciences

James Hammitt
Professor of Economics and
Decision Sciences
Harvard School of Public
Health

William Hogan
Raymond Plank Professor of
Global Energy Policy
Harvard Kennedy School

Dale Jorgenson
Samuel W. Morris University
Professor
Harvard Faculty of Arts and
Sciences

Robert Lawrence
Albert L. Williams Professor
of International Trade
and Investment
Harvard Kennedy School

Richard Peiser
Michael D. Spear Professor
of Real Estate Development
Harvard Graduate School
of Design

Forest Reinhardt
John D. Black Professor of
Business Administration
Harvard Business School

Daniel Schrag
Professor of Earth and Planetary
Sciences
Harvard Faculty of Arts and
Sciences

Steven Shavell
Samuel R. Rosenthal Professor
of Law and Economics
Harvard Law School

Beth Simmons
Clarence Dillon Professor of
International Affairs
Harvard Faculty of Arts and
Sciences

Robert Stavins
Albert Pratt Professor of
Business and Government
Harvard Kennedy School

Richard Vietor
Paul Whiton Cherington
Professor of Business
Administration
Harvard Business School

Harvard Project on International Climate Agreements
Project Management

Robert Stavins
Director

Robert Stowe
Project Manager

Jason Chapman
Project Coordinator

Tyler Gumpright
Project Assistant

Susan Lynch
Webmaster

Matthew Ranson
Research Assistant

Figures

Tables

Contributors

Ramgopal Agarwala is a consultant to the World Bank and Asian Development Bank and a Distinguished Fellow at Research and Information System for Developing Countries in New Delhi. He has worked in various senior positions in the World Bank for 25 years, with his last posting to Beijing as the chief economist of the World Bank in China. His most recent research includes articles on international financial architecture and climate change.

Joseph E. Aldy is a Fellow at Resources for the Future. He served on the staff of the President's Council of Economic Advisers from 1997 to 2000, where he was responsible for climate change policy. Dr. Aldy holds a PhD in economics from Harvard University. His research is on international climate change policy architectures; emissions trading programs and other mitigation policies; and the relationship between economic development and greenhouse gas emissions.

Mustafa H. Babiker holds a BSc in Econometrics and Social Statistics from the University of Kartoum, Sudan, and an MA and PhD in Economics from the University of Colorado-Boulder. He has served as an economist with the MIT Joint Program on the Science and Policy of Global Change and the Arab Planning Institute, and he continues work with the Joint Program on applications of its Emissions Prediction and Policy Analysis model.

Scott Barrett is Lenfest Earth Institute Professor of Natural Resource Economics at Columbia University, in the School of International and Public Affairs. He is the author of *Environment and Statecraft: The Strategy of Environmental Treaty-Making* (2005) and *Why Cooperate? The Incentive to Supply Global Public Goods* (2007). He taught previously at the Johns Hopkins University School of Advanced International Studies and at the London Business School.

Geoffrey J. Blanford currently manages the climate policy research program at the Electric Power Research Institute. His research focuses on energy-economy modeling and the development of integrated assessment tools for application to international climate agreements and technology policy decisions. He has authored several analyses using the MERGE model and holds a PhD in management science and engineering from Stanford University.

Valentina Bosetti holds a PhD in Computational Mathematics and Operations Research from the Università Statale of Milan and an MA in Environmental and Resources Economics from University College of London. At the *Fondazione Eni Enrico Mattei,* in Italy, since 2003, she works as a modeler for the Sustainable Development Program, leading the Climate Change Modeling and Policy initiative. She is currently a visiting researcher at the Princeton Environmental Institute.

Katherine Calvin is a Research Economist at the Pacific Northwest National Laboratory's Joint Global Change Research Institute. Dr. Calvin's research focuses on international climate policy regimes, integrated assessment modeling, and the implications of carbon policy on agriculture and land use.

Jing Cao is an Assistant Professor at the School of Economics and Management, Tsinghua University, in Beijing. She is also an affiliated researcher at The Center for China in the World Economy at Tsinghua, at Environmental Development (China Center), and at the Harvard China Project. She has a PhD in Public Policy from Harvard University. Her research focuses on environmental taxation, climate change economics and modeling, productivity measurements, and economic growth.

Carlo Carraro is Professor of Environmental Economics at the University of Venice and Director of Research of the *Fondazione Eni Enrico Mattei.* He is Vice Chair of IPCC Working Group III and Director of the Climate Impacts and Policy Division of the EuroMediterranean Centre on Climate Change. He holds a PhD from Princeton University and is a Research Fellow of CEPR, CESifo and CEPS.

Wenying Chen is a professor in the Institute of Energy, Environment, and Economy, Tsinghua University. Her research focuses on energy modeling, integrated assessment models in climate change, carbon capture and storage, and energy systems analysis. Professor Chen has led a number of national and international research projects in the field of energy and climate change.

Leon Clarke is a Senior Research Economist at the Pacific Northwest National Laboratory's Joint Global Change Research Institute. Dr. Clarke's research focuses on technology planning for climate change, climate mitigation scenarios, international climate policy, and integrated assessment of climate change.

Richard N. Cooper is Maurits C. Boas Professor of International Economics at Harvard University. He is Vice-Chairman of the Global Development Network and a member of the Trilateral Commission, the Council on Foreign Relations, the Executive Panel of the US Chief of Naval Operations, and the Brookings Panel on Economic Activity. He has served on several occasions in the US Government, most recently as chairman of the National Intelligence Council (1995-97).

Jae Edmonds is a Chief Scientist and Laboratory Fellow at the Pacific Northwest National Laboratory's Joint Global Change Research Institute, Adjunct Professor of Public Policy at the University of Maryland-College Park, and has actively participated in the IPCC. His research in the areas of long-term, global energy, technology, economy, and climate change spans three decades, producing several books and numerous scientific papers and presentations.

A. Denny Ellerman is a Senior Lecturer at MIT's Sloan School of Management and an internationally recognized expert on energy and environmental economics with a particular focus on emissions trading. He is a co-author of the leading book on the US SO_2 trading program, *Markets for Clean Air*, and co-editor of *Allocation in the European Emissions Trading Scheme*. He earned a PhD in political economy and government from Harvard University.

Carolyn Fischer is a Senior Fellow at Resources for the Future in Washington, DC. Her research addresses a variety of environmental policy issues, including climate change mitigation, technological change, international trade and environmental policies, and resource economics. She holds a PhD in Economics from the University of Michigan and a BA in International Relations from the University of Pennsylvania, and she previously served at the White House Council of Economic Advisors.

Jeffrey Frankel is Harpel Professor at Harvard's Kennedy School. He directs the program in International Finance and Macroeconomics at the National Bureau of Economic Research, where he is also on the Business Cycle Dating Committee. He served on President Clinton's Council of Economic Advisers (1996–1999), with responsibility for environmental, international, and macroeconomics. Earlier he was professor of economics at the University of California, Berkeley. His economics PhD is from MIT.

Daniel S. Hall is a Research Associate at Resources for the Future, where his work focuses on climate change policy, including mechanisms for cost containment, the design of offset programs, and legislative analysis. Hall holds a Master of Environmental Science and Management from the Donald Bren School at the University of California, Santa Barbara.

Bård Harstad is an Associate Professor at the Kellogg School of Management, Northwestern University. In recent years he has developed theories for international political economy, with a particular focus on international bargaining and the design elements of environmental agreements. His research has been published in *American Economic Review, Quarterly Journal of Economics,* and *Scandinavian Journal of Economics.*

Jiankun He is the director of the Low Carbon Energy Laboratory at Tsinghua University, China. Professor He's research interests include energy systems engineering and energy modeling, strategic responses to climate change, resource management, and sustainable development. He has been the principal investigator of a number of national key research projects and international collaborative research projects.

Henry D. Jacoby is Professor of Management in the MIT Sloan School of Management and Co-Director of the MIT Joint Program on the Science and Policy of Global Change. He holds a PhD in Economics from Harvard, where he served in the Department of Economics and the Kennedy School of Government. He serves on the Scientific Committee of the International Geosphere-Biosphere Program and on the Climate Research Committee of the National Research Council.

Judson Jaffe is a Vice President at Analysis Group, Inc. He previously spent two years on the staff of the Council of Economic Advisers at the White House, where he provided economic analysis of environmental and energy policy. He received an MPhil in Economics from

Cambridge University, and an AB *summa cum laude* in Environmental Science and Public Policy, and Economics from Harvard University.

Larry Karp is Professor of Agricultural and Resource Economics and the Department Chair at the University of California, Berkeley. His research and teaching interests include environmental economics, trade policy, dynamic methods, and industrial organization. He is Associate Editor of the *Journal of Economic Dynamics and Control* and has served as Co-editor of the *Journal of Environmental Economics and Management*. He is a Fellow of the Agricultural and Applied Economics Association.

Andrew Keeler teaches at the John Glenn School of Public Affairs at the Ohio State University and writes on state, national, and international climate change policy. He served as the Senior Staff Economist for Environment at the President's Council of Economic Advisers (2000–2001) where he was a member of the US negotiating team for climate change and a diplomatic representative to OECD meetings on coordinating national sustainability policies.

Robert O. Keohane is Professor of International Affairs, Princeton University. He is the author of *After Hegemony* (1984) and *Power and Governance in a Partially Globalized World* (2002). He is co-author (with Joseph S. Nye, Jr.) *of Power and Interdependence* (third edition 2001) and (with Gary King and Sidney Verba) of *Designing Social Inquiry* (1994). He is a member of the American Academy of Arts and Sciences, the American Philosophical Society, and the National Academy of Sciences.

Page Kyle is a Research Analyst with the Pacific Northwest National Laboratory's Joint Global Change Research Institute. His research focuses on modeling of greenhouse gas emissions from end-use energy consumption and secondary fuel production, with particular attention to technological development and climate change mitigation.

Michael A. Levi is the David M. Rubenstein Senior Fellow for Energy and the Environment at the Council on Foreign Relations (CFR) and Director of its Program on Energy Security and Climate Change. He was project director for a recent CFR-sponsored independent task force on climate change, and is the author of *On Nuclear Terrorism* (Harvard University Press, 2007) and *The Future of Arms Control* (Brookings Institution Press, 2005).

Warwick J. McKibbin is Professor and Director of the Centre for Applied Macroeconomic Analysis in the College of Business and Economics at the Australian National University. He also holds positions at the Lowy Institute for International Policy and the Brookings Institution. He is a member of the Policy Board of the Reserve Bank of Australia. Professor McKibbin received a PhD in Economics from Harvard University in 1986.

Richard D. Morgenstern is a Senior Fellow at Resources for the Future and has written widely on climate change mitigation policy. His involvement in the issue reaches back two decades and includes his work at the US EPA, where he directed the Agency's climate change activities and, subsequently, as a member of the State Department's negotiating team for the Kyoto Protocol.

Adele Morris is a Fellow and Deputy Director for Climate and Energy Economics at the Brookings Institution. Her economic and natural resource policy experience includes work at the Joint Economic Committee of Congress, the US Treasury, the President's Council of Economic Advisers, and OMB. She was a lead climate negotiator with the US State Department in 2000. She holds a PhD in Economics from Princeton University.

Richard G. Newell is Gendell Professor of Energy and Environmental Economics, Nicholas School of Environment, Duke University; a Research Associate, National Bureau of Economic Research; and a University Fellow, Resources for the Future. He has served as Senior Economist for energy and environment on the President's Council of Economic Advisers and on several National Academy of Sciences committees related to energy, environment, and climate. His PhD is from Harvard University.

Sergey Paltsev is a Principal Research Scientist at the Joint Program on the Science and Policy of Global Change at the Massachusetts Institute of Technology, where he has been working since 2002 as the lead modeler in charge of the MIT Emissions Prediction and Policy Analysis (EPPA) model, a multi-regional computable general equilibrium model of the world economy that has been widely used to study climate change policy.

William A. Pizer is the Deputy Assistant Secretary for Environment and Energy at the US Department of the Treasury. Prior to coming to Treasury, and throughout his involvement with the Harvard

Project, Pizer was a Senior Fellow at Resources for the Future where his research looked at how the design of environmental policy affects costs and environmental effectiveness, often related to global climate change. He holds a PhD in Economics from Harvard University.

Andrew J. Plantinga is Professor of Agricultural and Resource Economics at Oregon State University. He received a PhD in Agricultural and Resource Economics from the University of California-Berkeley and an MS in Forestry from the University of Wisconsin-Madison. His research on the economics of land use is supported by the National Science Foundation, the US Forest Service, and the US Department of Energy.

Eric A. Posner is Kirkland and Ellis Professor of Law, University of Chicago. He is author of *The Perils of Global Legalism* (University of Chicago, forthcoming); *Terror in the Balance: Security, Liberty and the Courts* (with Adrian Vermeule) (Oxford, 2007); *New Foundations of Cost-Benefit Analysis* (with Matthew Adler) (Harvard, 2006); *The Limits of International Law* (with Jack Goldsmith) (Oxford, 2005); and *Law and Social Norms* (Harvard, 2000).

Kal Raustiala is a professor at UCLA Law School and the UCLA International Institute, where he is also Director of the Ronald W. Burkle Center for International Relations. His previous publications include *The Implementation and Effectiveness of International Environmental Commitments* (MIT, 1998), co-edited with David G. Victor and Eugene Skolnikoff.

John M. Reilly is the Associate Director for Research in the Joint Program on the Science and Policy of Global Change and a Senior Lecturer in the Sloan School at MIT. Prior appointments were with the USDA's Economic Research Service and the US DOE National Laboratories. He holds a PhD in economics from the University of Pennsylvania. His research has focused on the economics of energy, agriculture, and climate change.

Kenneth R. Richards is an Associate Professor at the School of Public and Environmental Affairs and an adjunct professor at the Maurer School of Law, Indiana University. He holds a PhD in Public Policy and a JD from the University of Pennsylvania. He is associate director of the Richard G. Lugar Center for Renewable Energy in Indianapolis and the Center for Research in Energy and the Environment in Bloomington, Indiana.

Richard G. Richels is Senior Technical Executive for global climate change research at the Electric Power Research Institute and is Adjunct Professor at the Johns Hopkins School of Advanced International Studies. He has served on a number of national and international advisory panels, including committees of the Department of Energy, the Environmental Protection Agency, the National Research Council, and the Intergovernmental Panel on Climate Change.

Thomas F. Rutherford has been professor of energy economics at ETH Zürich since January, 2008. He earned a PhD in Operations Research from Stanford University under the supervision of Alan S. Manne. He subsequently had academic appointments in economics at the University of Western Ontario and the University of Colorado. Professor Rutherford's main research areas concern the formulation and analysis of computational economic equilibrium models.

Akihiro Sawa is a Senior Executive Fellow, 21st Century Public Policy Research Institute, Keidanren, Tokyo, Japan. He was previously a Director of Environmental Policy (2001–2003) and Director of Resources and Fuel Policy (2003–2004) for the Ministry of Economy, Trade and Industry of the Government of Japan and a Professor at the Research Center for Advanced Science and Technology, University of Tokyo (2004–2008).

Richard Schmalensee is the Howard W. Johnson Professor of Economics and Management at MIT and Director of the MIT Center for Energy and Environmental Policy Research. He has served as the John C. Head III Dean of the MIT Sloan School of Management (1998–2007) and as the Member of the President's Council of Economic Advisers with responsibility for environmental policy (1989–1991).

Alessandra Sgobbi holds a PhD in Analysis and Governance of Sustainable Development at the School for Advanced Studies in the Venice Foundation. She collaborates with the *Fondazione Eni Enrico Mattei,* in Italy, on various projects in the field of natural resources management and climate change. Currently, she works at the European Commission, EuropeAid Cooperation Office, focusing on development interventions in the fields of sustainable consumption and production, energy efficiency, and the "grey" environment.

E. Somanathan received a PhD in economics from Harvard in 1995 and taught at Emory University and the University of Michigan at

Ann Arbor before joining the Indian Statistical Institute, Delhi, where he is Professor in the Planning Unit. His main research interest is in development economics, particularly environmental problems and political economy. He is writing a book on environmental issues in India.

Robert N. Stavins is Albert Pratt Professor of Business and Government, Harvard Kennedy School; Director, Harvard Environmental Economics Program; Director, Harvard Project on International Climate Agreements; University Fellow, Resources for the Future; Research Associate, National Bureau of Economic Research; and Editor, *Review of Environmental Economics and Policy.* He was Chairman, US EPA Environmental Economics Advisory Committee, and Lead Author, Intergovernmental Panel on Climate Change. He holds a PhD in economics from Harvard.

Cass R. Sunstein is the Felix Frankfurter Professor of Law at Harvard Law School. A former attorney-adviser in the Office of Legal Counsel in the Department of Justice, he is author or co-author of more than fifteen books and hundreds of scholarly articles. Sunstein joined the law faculty of the University of Chicago in 1981 and later became the Karl N. Llewellyn Distinguished Service Professor of Jurisprudence at the University.

Massimo Tavoni is a Senior Researcher at the *Fondazione Eni Enrico Mattei,* in Italy, and is now a Post-doctoral Research Fellow at the Princeton Environmental Institute. His research interests include international climate mitigation policies, technological evolution and uncertainty, and tropical deforestation. He holds an MSc in Mathematical Economics from the London School of Economics and a PhD in Political Economics from the Catholic University of Milan.

Fei Teng is an Associate Professor at the Institute of Energy, Environment, and Economy, Tsinghua University. His research interests include climate policy analysis, energy policy analysis, and technology transfer mechanisms in climate regimes. He is a review expert for the CDM DNA in China and also a member of the Chinese delegation to the UNFCCC and its Kyoto Protocol.

Alexander Thompson is Associate Professor of Political Science at Ohio State University. He has research interests in the areas of international organizations and US foreign policy. He is the author of *Channels of Power: The UN Security Council and U.S. Statecraft in Iraq* (Cornell University Press, 2009) and articles in various journals, including *International Organization*, the *Journal of Conflict Resolution*, and the *Journal of Legal Studies*.

Takahiro Ueno is a Researcher at the Socio-economic Research Center of the Central Research Institute of Electric Power Industry, Japan. He was a Visiting Scholar at Resources for the Future in 2006 and 2007. He has researched international negotiations on climate change, energy and environmental technology policy, international cooperation on energy efficiency, and technology transfer to developing countries.

David G. Victor is Professor at the School of International Relations and Pacific Studies, University of California at San Diego; he also serves as Senior Fellow at the Council on Foreign Relations. His current research focuses on the performance of state-controlled oil companies, on global climate protection, and on the emerging global market for coal. His PhD is from the Massachusetts Institute of Technology and his BA is from Harvard University.

Peter J. Wilcoxen is an Associate Professor of Economics and Public Administration at the Maxwell School of Syracuse University and a Nonresident Senior Fellow at the Brookings Institution. He has published extensively on energy and environmental policy and is currently a member of the US EPA's Environmental Economics Advisory Committee. He holds a BA in physics from the University of Colorado and a PhD in economics from Harvard University.

Timothy Wirth has been President of the United Nations Foundation since its founding in 1998. He represented Colorado in the US House of Representatives from 1975 to 1987 and the US Senate from 1987 to 1993. From 1993 to 1997, he served as the first US Under Secretary of State for Global Affairs, leading the US team preparing for the Kyoto climate negotiations. He received a PhD from Stanford University.

Marshall Wise is a Senior Research Scientist at Battelle's Joint Global Change Research Institute at the University of Maryland. He is a longtime member of the MiniCAM integrated assessment model development team with expertise in economic modeling and analysis of energy systems, with experience in both broad-scale energy policy analysis and in detailed analysis of the electric power generation sector.

Jinhua Zhao is an Associate Professor in the Department of Economics and the Department of Agricultural, Food and Resource Economics at Michigan State University. His research interests include applied microeconomic theory, environmental and resource economics, energy economics, dynamic decision making under uncertainty, among others. He was a co-editor of the *Journal of Environmental Economics and Management* (JEEM) and is on the editorial council of JEEM and the *Review of Development Economics*.

Foreword

BY TIMOTHY E. WIRTH

Washington, DC
February 5, 2009

When Charles Keeling began measuring carbon dioxide at Mauna Loa in 1958, the atmospheric concentration was 315 parts per million (ppm). That number represented an increase of 12.5 percent from the pre-industrial level of 280 ppm. Fifty years later, it has reached 385 ppm, and the rate of increase has doubled.

As the Swedish chemist Svante Arrhenius predicted in 1896, those increased levels of carbon dioxide or CO_2 are warming the surface temperature of the Earth. The results are evident all around us. The world's tropical belt has expanded toward the poles by two degrees of latitude—as much as had been predicted for the entire 21st century. The Greenland ice sheet, which holds enough water to raise global sea levels by 20 feet, is melting at an accelerated rate. The Arctic Ocean—engine of the Northern Hemisphere's weather—could be ice-free during the summer within five years.

Civilization was built around the climate we have—along coastlines that may be washed away by storms and rising sea levels; around farmland and forests that will become less productive as water supplies diminish; at elevations cool enough to escape insect-borne disease. Changing the climate puts the very organization of modern societies at risk.

We cannot avoid climate change altogether. The effects of our actions are already clear. For all practical purposes, they are irreversible. We can, however, limit the damage, and toward that end, the world must act—urgently, dramatically, and decisively.

This important new volume, the product of the Harvard Project on International Climate Agreements, recognizes the gravity and complexity of the climate challenge. It attempts to show the way forward with a rich variety of contributions from more than two dozen expert authors. Joseph Aldy and Robert Stavins, as editors, have underscored design elements for a new international climate regime that meet three well-chosen criteria: they must be scientifically sound, economically rational, and politically pragmatic.

Publication could not be more timely. The world is poised at a hinge of history. Civilization's future rests with decisions yet unmade. Hope and fear collide.

Scientists agree that time is running out for concerted action to avert the worst consequences of climate change. The process that was initiated in Rio de Janeiro in 1992, when agreement was reached on the United Nations Framework Convention on Climate Change, must now achieve a new level of commitment. For the essential objective of the Rio treaty—ratified by the United States and nearly every country of the world—was to prevent "dangerous anthropogenic interference with the climate system." Now, physical evidence of climate change suggests that point has already been passed. Some climate scientists say the world must limit atmospheric CO_2 not to 550 ppm (a doubling of pre-industrial levels), or to 450 ppm (the number often associated with a global warming of 2° C), but to 350 ppm—the level passed 20 years ago—to avoid irreversible melting of the Greenland ice sheet and disastrous sea-level rise.

In December 2007, representatives of 187 countries agreed in Bali on a road map to replace the Kyoto Protocol when it runs out in 2012 and more effectively confront climate change over the long term. Ban Ki-moon, the Secretary-General of the United Nations and a new voice of global leadership, has made climate change one of his top priorities at the UN. "Today we are at a crossroads," he said at Bali, "one path towards a comprehensive new climate agreement, and the other towards a betrayal of our planet and our children. The choice is clear." Ban left the talks, but when they threatened to founder, he returned to urge the negotiators on. They listened and adopted a two-year plan for reaching a new agreement.

With the inauguration of Barack Obama as US President in January 2009, the world's largest economy is prepared to participate constructively again. Many countries are hoping that the United States will be the cavalry riding to the rescue; it remains to be seen whether that hope is too audacious.

What are the key elements of an agreement? The Bali road map identifies four: mitigation, adaptation, technology, and finance. In the parlance of climate negotiations, "mitigation" means reducing greenhouse gas emissions and "adaptation" means preparing for climate impacts that cannot be avoided. "Technology" refers to the need, not just to develop cleaner ways of producing and using energy, but also to deploy those technologies on an appropriate scale in rich and poor countries alike. "Finance" encompasses both the mechanisms and investment flows that will enable poor countries to adapt and acquire clean energy technologies.

The UN Framework Convention of 1992 established the principle that countries should engage the climate challenge "on the basis of equity and in accordance with their common but differentiated responsibilities and respective capabilities." Developed countries, especially the United States, were expected to lead because over many years they have contributed the most to the buildup of greenhouse gases in the atmosphere. Meaningful engagement of developing countries, especially of rapidly industrializing economies like China and India, is needed also. All countries must be part of the solution, not just the industrialized countries that caused the problem, but the poorest countries that will feel its effects most acutely.

The questions of who has what responsibility and when obligations will kick in are the central issues in international climate negotiations, and two that will also be critical to the future ratification of any new climate protocol in the United States and around the world. We must be flexible enough to recognize and accept the value of diverse approaches to the climate challenge.

This collection of essays reflects that imperative, drawing on scholars from China, India, Japan, and Australia, as well as Europe and the United States. There are many good ideas here—too many to summarize briefly. Particularly useful is the editors' synthesis in Chapter 29, drawing lessons for policymakers from the many contributions. Aldy and Stavins point to four potential architectures for agreement. In many ways, the four can coexist and support each other:

- Binding emissions caps are needed to bring about reductions from major greenhouse gas sources, although some rapidly industrializing countries may have to step up to that responsibility gradually. Using formulas to allocate reductions is a promising approach for avoiding decisions based simply on politics and power.
- Harmonized domestic policies would facilitate effective implemen-

tation of emissions cuts and reduce both the cost of compliance and the political resistance to carbon limits.

- A system of harmonized carbon taxes would generate revenues equitably to support a comprehensive climate response.
- Linked national cap-and-trade systems, based on permit auctions implemented "upstream," would do the same.

The relationship between these approaches can be seen by considering how best to encourage technology deployment and economic development. Solving the climate crisis will require nothing less than a fundamental transformation of global energy systems. In the United States, transportation and electricity generation are the two largest sources of emissions. In rapidly industrializing nations like China and India, power generation, manufacturing, and transportation are the fastest-growing sources. A new generation of climate-friendly technologies will be needed to reduce emissions quickly and at low cost.

The global recession that began in 2008 as a result of turbulence in world financial markets creates new barriers, as well as new opportunities for major new investments in clean energy technologies. Falling commodity prices, especially for oil, have reduced political pressure for immediate action on energy policy even as capital for new projects has become much more difficult to obtain. The need for substantial government spending to revive the economy, on the other hand, provides a potential stimulus to jump-start the transition to new energy technologies.

In the U.S. presidential election of 2008, both major party candidates made investment in renewable energy a centerpiece of their campaigns, reflecting the breadth of bipartisan support for a change in direction. Research and development are not enough, though—new market signals are essential for this technological revolution to succeed. The most important step is to put a price on carbon, either through a cap-and-trade system or a carbon tax. The purpose is not to penalize consumers with higher energy costs. Rather it is to set the rules of the game so that clean technologies can compete with dirty ones—and indeed, out-compete them over time. This will lead to a great wave of innovation, investment, economic development, and job creation.

Serious action by the United States to significantly reduce its emissions is not only the right thing to do; it is also a precondition for US credibility and global leadership on climate. Without it, other countries will have a convenient excuse for inaction.

Key steps to reduce emissions will include increased efficiency, the transformation of the transportation sector through advanced biofuels and plug-in hybrids, and the phase-out of conventional coal-fired power generation. Such steps could become the basis for harmonized national policies—setting, for example, targets for improvement in energy efficiency and deployment of renewable energy—that could be endorsed globally as confidence-building steps toward a new climate agreement.

The US-China relationship is critical to such progress. These countries are the world's two largest emitters of greenhouse gases, and neither accepted any restrictions under the Kyoto Protocol. China continues to resist the idea of binding targets, but on its own has set a target of improving the energy efficiency of its economy by an extraordinary four percent per year. China has also imposed vehicle fuel economy standards stricter than those of the United States and plans to double its renewable energy capacity (to 15 percent of its overall energy supply mix) by the year 2020. These steps could be a model for other countries and the basis for voluntary targets, globally agreed.

Developing countries, especially China and India, will account for the lion's share of global emissions growth over the coming years. In China alone, as many as 500 million people will join the middle class, gaining access to electricity and motorized transportation, in the next 20 years. In recent years, China has been expanding its coal base at the rate of one large new coal-fired power plant, on average, every week, and India aspires to similar economic growth. Getting these countries to grow cleanly, therefore, is absolutely essential to climate stabilization. The idea of giving handouts to increasingly formidable competitors overseas is politically toxic in many developed countries, but more robust cooperation in areas of mutual interest—such as advancing carbon capture technology for coal plants—would accelerate technology development and deployment to the benefit of all.

Development and clean energy should go hand in hand—the limitations of the dirty energy path are more manifest by the day—but the phrase "technology transfer" has an unfortunate ring. It suggests hand-me-downs from rich countries to poor. Instead, nations that are technology leaders should collaborate on a new international initiative to facilitate cooperation with developing countries on low-cost, clean-energy technologies. Working together through regional innovation centers, researchers would adapt these technologies to their countries and help them "leapfrog" over climate-damaging business-as-usual patterns of development, much as the advent of cell phones averted a massive buildout of telecommunications infrastructure.

Managing the climate crisis requires new forms of international cooperation to reduce global emissions and help vulnerable societies adapt. The UN is the appropriate venue for global negotiation and, in many cases, the right institution to coordinate and deliver international response measures. The United States can lead this global effort by reducing its own emissions, encouraging other nations to implement bold mitigation policies, spurring technological innovation at home and abroad, speeding adoption of clean energy technologies by rapidly developing nations, and providing adaptation assistance to poor nations.

International climate negotiations are complex—to be successful, they will require political resolve, creative negotiating, innovative policy mechanisms, stronger global institutions, and additional financial resources. None of this will be easy, but a flexible and positive approach can yield results if it focuses—as the Harvard Project does—on solutions that are scientifically sound, economically rational, and politically pragmatic. The world can afford no less. If this volume moves negotiators closer to that goal, Aldy and Stavins and their contributors will have provided value indeed.

1 | Introduction

JOSEPH E. ALDY AND ROBERT N. STAVINS[1]

Diverse aspects of human activity around the world result in greenhouse gas (GHG) emissions that contribute to global climate change. Emissions come from coal-fired power plants in the United States, diesel buses in Europe, rice paddies in Asia, and the burning of tropical forests in South America. These emissions will affect the global climate for generations, because most greenhouse gases reside in the atmosphere for decades to centuries. Thus, the impacts of global climate change pose serious, long-term risks.

Global climate change is the ultimate global-commons problem: Because GHGs mix uniformly in the upper atmosphere, damages are completely independent of the location of emissions sources. Thus, a multinational response is required. To address effectively the risks of climate change, efforts that engage most if not all countries will need to be undertaken. The greatest challenge lies in designing an *international policy architecture* that can guide such efforts. We take "international policy architecture" to refer to the basic nature and structure of an

[1] We are indebted to the twenty-six research teams of the Harvard Project on International Climate Agreements who have contributed to this book, as well as the Project's management: Robert Stowe, project manager; Sasha Talcott, communications director; Jason Chapman, project coordinator; Tyler Gumpright, project assistant; Susan Lynch, webmaster; and Matthew Ranson, research assistant. We are particularly grateful to Rob Stowe, who has managed the production of this book—and the overall Harvard Project—from the beginning with inspired leadership and unfailing grace and kindness. Marika Tatsutani edited the manuscript with skill and insight. We also express our sincere gratitude to the Doris Duke Charitable Foundation for providing major funding for the Project and Andrew Bowman for his collaboration beginning with the Project's conception. We greatly appreciate additional financial support from Christopher Kaneb, the James and Cathleen Stone Foundation, Paul Josefowitz and Nicholas Josefowitz, the Enel Endowment for Environmental Economics at Harvard University, the Belfer Center for Science and International Affairs at the Harvard Kennedy School, and the Mossavar-Rahmani Center for Business and Government at the Harvard Kennedy School.

international agreement or other multilateral (or bilateral) climate regime.[2]

The Kyoto Protocol to the United Nations Framework Convention on Climate Change (UNFCCC) marked the first meaningful attempt by the community of nations to curb GHG emissions. This agreement, though a significant first step, is not sufficient for the longer-term task ahead. Some observers support the policy approach embodied in Kyoto and would like to see it extended—perhaps with modifications—beyond the first commitment period, which ends in 2012. Others maintain that a fundamentally new approach is required.

Whether one thinks the Kyoto Protocol was a good first step or a bad first step, everyone agrees that a second step is required. A way forward is needed for the post-2012 period. The Harvard Project on International Climate Agreements was launched with this imperative in mind. The Project is a global, multiyear, multidisciplinary effort intended to help identify the key design elements of a scientifically sound, economically rational, and politically pragmatic post-2012 international policy architecture for addressing the threat of climate change. This book is a product of the Project's research.

By "scientifically sound," we mean an international agreement that is consistent with achieving the objective of stabilizing atmospheric concentrations of GHGs at levels that avoid dangerous anthropogenic interference with the global climate. By "economically rational," we mean pursuing an approach or set of approaches that are likely to achieve global targets at minimum cost—that is, cost-effectively. And by "politically pragmatic," we mean a post-Kyoto regime that is likely to bring on board the United States and engage key, rapidly-growing developing countries in increasingly meaningful ways over time. As Tim Wirth emphasizes in the Foreword to this book, these three criteria are essential for identifying a promising and meaningful path forward.

The Project draws upon leading thinkers from academia, private industry, government, and nongovernmental organizations (NGOs) around the world. It includes research teams operating in Europe, the

---

[2] The need for scholars to focus on the development of a long-term climate policy architecture was first highlighted by Richard Schmalensee: "When time is measured in centuries, the creation of durable institutions and frameworks seems both logically prior to and more important than choice of a particular policy program that will almost surely be viewed as too strong or too weak within a decade" (1998, p. 141).

United States, China, India, Japan, and Australia and has benefited from meetings with leaders from business, NGOs, and governments in many more countries.

The Project originated from a May 2006 workshop at which the Harvard Environmental Economics Program brought together twenty-seven leading thinkers from around the world with expertise in economics, law, political science, business, international relations, and the natural sciences. This group developed and refined six policy frameworks, each of which could form the backbone of a new international climate agreement. These six frameworks, which range from a stronger version of the Kyoto Protocol to entirely new approaches, are the subject of our earlier book, published in September 2007 by Cambridge University Press and titled *Architectures for Agreement: Addressing Global Climate Change in the Post-Kyoto World* (Aldy and Stavins 2007). With these proposals as the starting point, the Harvard Project on International Climate Agreements aims to help forge a broad-based consensus on a potential successor to Kyoto.

The first stage of our work, which focused on establishing the importance of considering alternative architectures for the post-2012 period, featured wide-ranging and inclusive discussions of the six proposed alternatives, as well as others not addressed in *Architectures for Agreement*. It also featured meetings with government officials, business leaders, NGOs, and academics around the world. In the second stage of the Project, we focused on developing a small menu of promising frameworks and key design principles, based upon analysis by leading academics from a variety of disciplines—including economics, political science, law, and international relations—as well as ongoing commentary from leading practitioners in the NGO community, private industry, and government. Economic analysis has been supplemented with political analysis of the implications of alternative approaches, as well as legal examinations of the feasibility of various proposals.

From the beginning, there have been no constraints on what may emerge from the Project. We have maintained from the outset that anything is possible—from highly centralized Kyoto-like architectures for all countries to proposals that are outside of the context of the UNFCCC, such as proposals for G8+5 or L20 agreements.[3] This book

---

[3] The G8 refers to Canada, France, Germany, Italy, Japan, Russia, the United Kingdom, and the United States; in addition, the EU is represented within the

draws upon the findings of our diverse research initiatives in Australia, China, Europe, India, Japan, and the United States.

Learning from experience: the Kyoto Protocol

It is helpful to reflect on the lessons that can be learned from examining the Kyoto Protocol's strengths and weaknesses. Among the Protocol's strengths is its inclusion of several provisions for market-based approaches that hold promise for improving the cost-effectiveness of a global climate regime. We refer, for example, to the well-known flexibility mechanisms such as Article 17, which provides for emissions trading among the Annex I countries[4] that take on commitments under the Protocol. More specifically, this provision allows the governments of Annex I countries to trade some of the assigned emission allowances that constitute their country-level targets. Second, the Protocol's Joint Implementation provisions allow for project-level trades among the Annex I countries. Finally, the Protocol established the Clean Development Mechanism (CDM), which provides for the use of project-level emission offsets created in non-Annex I countries (the developing countries of the world) to help meet the compliance obligations of Annex I countries.

A second advantage of the Kyoto Protocol is that it provides flexibility for nations to meet their national emission targets—their commitments—in any way they want. In other words, Article 2 of the Protocol recognizes domestic sovereignty by providing for flexibility at the national level. The political importance of this provision in terms of making it possible for a large number of nations to reach agreement on emission commitments should not be underestimated.

Third, the Kyoto Protocol has the appearance of fairness in that it focuses on the wealthiest countries and those responsible for a dominant share of the current stock of anthropogenic GHGs in the

Footnote 3 (*cont.*)
> G8, but cannot host or chair. The G8+5 refers to the G8 countries plus the five leading developing countries—Brazil, China, India, Mexico, and South Africa. The L20 refers to the G8+5 nations plus Australia, Argentina, the European Union, Indonesia, Korea, Saudi Arabia, and Turkey.

[4] We use Annex I and Annex B interchangeably to represent those industrialized countries that have commitments under the Kyoto Protocol, though we recognize that a few countries are included in one Annex but not the other.

atmosphere. This is consistent with the principle enunciated in the UNFCCC of "common but differentiated responsibilities and respective capabilities."

Fourth and finally, the fact that the Kyoto Protocol was signed by more than 180 countries and subsequently ratified by a sufficient number of Annex I countries for it to come into force speaks to the political viability of the agreement, if not to the feasibility of all countries actually achieving their targets.

In the realm of public policy, as in our everyday lives, we frequently learn more from our mistakes or failures than from our successes. So, too, in the case of the Kyoto Protocol. Therefore, we also examine some key weaknesses of the Protocol and explore what potentially valuable lessons they may hold for the path forward.

First, it is well known that some of the world's leading GHG emitters are not constrained by the Kyoto Protocol. The United States—until recently the country with the largest share of global emissions—has not ratified and is unlikely to ratify the agreement. Also, some of the largest and most rapidly growing economies in the developing world do not have emission targets under the agreement. Importantly, China, India, Brazil, South Africa, Indonesia, Korea, and Mexico are not listed in Annex B of the Kyoto agreement. Rapid rates of economic growth in these countries have produced rapid rates of growth in energy use and hence carbon dioxide (CO_2) emissions. Together with continued deforestation in tropical countries, the result is that the developing world has overtaken the industrialized world in total GHG emissions. China's industrial CO_2 emissions have already surpassed those of the United States; moreover, China's emissions are expected to continue growing much faster than US emissions for the foreseeable future (see Chapter 26 by Blanford, *et al.*).

These realities raise the possibility that the Kyoto Protocol is not as fair as originally intended, especially given how dramatically the world has changed since the UNFCCC divided countries into two categories in 1992. For example, approximately fifty non-Annex I countries—that is, developing countries and some others—now have higher per capita incomes than the poorest of the Annex I countries with commitments under the Kyoto Protocol. Likewise, forty non-Annex I countries ranked higher on the Human Development Index in 2007 than the lowest ranked Annex I country.

A second weakness of the Kyoto Protocol is associated with the relatively small number of countries being asked to take action. This narrow but deep approach may have been well-intended, but one of its effects will be to drive up the costs of producing carbon-intensive goods and services within the coalition of countries taking action. (Indeed, increasing the cost of carbon-intensive activities is the intention of the Protocol and is fully appropriate as a means to create incentives for reducing emissions.) Through the forces of international trade, however, this approach also leads to greater comparative advantage in the production of carbon-intensive goods and services for countries that do not have binding emissions targets under the agreement. The result can be a shift in production and emissions from participating nations to non-participating nations—a phenomenon known as emission "leakage." Since leakage implies a shift of industrial activity and associated economic benefits to emerging economies, there is an additional incentive for non-participants to free ride on the efforts of those countries that are committed to mitigating their emissions through the Protocol's narrow but deep approach.

This leakage will not be one-for-one (in the sense that increased emissions in non-Annex I countries would be expected to fully negate emission reductions in Annex I countries), but it will reduce the cost-effectiveness and environmental performance of the agreement, and perhaps worst of all, push developing countries onto a more carbon-intensive growth path than they would otherwise have taken, rendering it more difficult for these countries to join the agreement later.

A third concern about the Kyoto Protocol centers on the nature of its emission trading elements. The provision in Article 17 for international emission trading is unlikely to be effective (Hahn and Stavins 1999). The entire theory behind the claim that a cap-and-trade system is likely to be cost-effective depends upon the participants being cost-minimizing entities. In the case of private-sector firms, this is a sensible assumption because if firms do not seek, and indeed succeed in, cost minimization, they will eventually disappear, given the competitive forces of the market. But nation-states can hardly be thought of as simple cost minimizers—many other objectives affect their decision making. Furthermore, even if nation-states sought to minimize costs, they do not have sufficient information about marginal abatement costs at the multitude of sources within their borders to carry out cost-effective trades with other countries.

There is also concern regarding the CDM. This is not a cap-and-trade mechanism, but rather an emission-reduction-credit system. That is, when an individual project results in emissions below what they would have been in the absence of the project, a credit—which may be sold to a source within a cap-and-trade system—is generated. This approach creates a challenge: comparing actual emissions with what they would have been otherwise. The baseline—what would have happened had the project not been implemented—is unobserved and fundamentally unobservable. In fact, there is a natural tendency, because of economic incentives, to claim credits precisely for those projects that are most profitable and hence would have been most likely to go forward even without the promise of credits. This so-called "additionality problem" is a serious issue. There are ways to address it through future restructuring and reform of the CDM; we examine some of these options in several chapters of this book.

Fourth, the Kyoto Protocol, with its five-year time horizon (2008 to 2012), represents a relatively short-term approach for what is fundamentally a long-term problem. GHGs have residence times in the atmosphere of decades to centuries. Furthermore, to encourage the magnitude of technological change that will be required to meaningfully address the threat of climate change it will be necessary to send long-term signals to the private market that stimulate sustained investment and technology innovation (see Chapter 13 by Newell).

Finally, the Kyoto Protocol may not provide sufficient incentives for countries to comply (see Chapter 8 by Barrett). Some countries' emissions have grown so fast since 1990 that it is difficult to imagine that they can undertake the emission mitigation or muster the political will and resources to purchase enough emission allowances or CDM credits from other countries to comply with their targets under the Protocol. For example, Canada's GHG emissions in 2006 exceeded that country's 1990 levels by nearly 55 percent, making it very unlikely that Canada could comply with an emissions target set at 6 percent *below* 1990 levels, averaged over the 2008–2012 commitment period. In short, the enforcement mechanism negotiated for the Kyoto Protocol does not appear to induce policy responses consistent with agreed-upon targets.

Alternative policy architectures for the post-kyoto period

In our earlier book, *Architectures for Agreement: Addressing Global Climate Change in the Post-Kyoto World*, we characterized potential post-Kyoto international policy architectures as falling within three principal categories: targets and timetables, harmonized national policies, and coordinated and unilateral national policies (Aldy and Stavins 2007). The policy architectures that have subsequently been examined as part of the Harvard Project on International Climate Agreements—while falling within the same three categories—move substantially beyond what was articulated in our 2007 book. Nevertheless, an overview of international policy architectures through the lens of these three categories, together with some concrete examples, is helpful.

The first category—targets and timetables—is the most familiar. At its heart is a centralized international agreement, top-down in form. This is the basic architecture underlying the Kyoto Protocol: essentially country-level quantitative emission targets established over specified time frames. An example of an approach that would be within this realm of targets and timetables, but would address some of the perceived deficiencies of the Kyoto Protocol, would be a regime that established emission targets based on formulas rather than specified fixed quantities (see Chapter 2 by Frankel). In lieu of *ad hoc* negotiations over emission caps, this formula approach would establish principles that can be translated into quantitative metrics for determining emission obligations. These formulas could be structured to have some of the appealing properties of indexed growth targets: setting targets as a function of a country's gross domestic product (GDP) per capita, for example. As countries became wealthier, their targets would become more stringent.[5] Conversely, when and if countries faced difficult economic periods, the stringency of their targets would be automatically reduced.

Such an approach does not divide the world simply into two categories of countries, as in the Kyoto Protocol. Rather, it allows for

---

[5] Such a mechanism was proposed by Frankel (2007) and is similar to the graduation mechanism proposed by Michaelowa (2007). As developing countries realize growth in per capita income and per capita emissions on a par with Annex I countries, they would be expected to take on binding emission targets. In the current volume, Chapters 2 (Frankel), 3 (Ellerman), 17 (Karp and Zhao), and 18 (Cao) provide examples of the targets-and-timetables approach.

a continuous differentiation among the countries of the world while including all of them. In this way, it reduces if not eliminates problems of emission leakage, yet still addresses the key criterion of distributional equity and does so in a more careful, sophisticated manner.

The second category—harmonized domestic policies—focuses more on national policy actions than on goals and is less centralized than the first set of approaches. In this case, countries agree on similar domestic policies. This reflects the view that national governments have much more control over their countries' policies than over their emissions. One example is a set of harmonized national carbon taxes (see Chapter 5 by Cooper).[6] With this approach, each participating country sets a domestic tax on the carbon content of fossil fuels, thereby achieving cost-effective control of emissions within its borders. Taxes would be set by nations, and nations would have complete discretion over the revenues they generate. Countries could design their tax policies to be revenue-neutral—for example, by returning the revenues raised to the economy through proportional cuts in other, distortionary taxes, such as those on labor and capital. In order to achieve global cost-effectiveness, carbon taxes would need to be set at the same level in all countries. This would presumably not be acceptable to the poorer countries of the world. Therefore, significant side deals would most likely need to accompany such a system of harmonized carbon taxes to make it distributionally equitable and hence politically feasible. This could take the form of large financial transfers through side payments from the industrialized world to the developing world, or agreements in the trade or development agenda that effectively compensate developing countries for implementing carbon taxes.

The third and final category that we have used to classify potential post-Kyoto climate policy architectures is coordinated and unilateral national policies. This category includes the least centralized approaches that we have considered—essentially bottom-up policies that rely on domestic politics to drive incentives for participation

---

[6] McKibbin and Wilcoxen (2007) advance the idea of parallel, unlinked domestic cap-and-trade programs as a way to move forward in international climate policy. They recommend a harmonized safety-valve price mechanism in their domestic cap-and-trade programs. In this book, Chapters 5 (Cooper), 4 (Jaffe and Stavins), and 7 (Sawa) provide examples of harmonized domestic policies.

and compliance (Pizer 2007).[7] Although these approaches are the least centralized, they should not be thought of as necessarily the least effective. One example of a bottom-up approach—linking independent national and regional tradable permit systems—may already be evolving (see Chapter 4 by Jaffe and Stavins).

The Bali road map and the path ahead

At the December 2007 UN-sponsored climate change talks in Bali, Indonesia (COP 13), the international community reached agreement on the Bali Action Plan, a two-year road map to guide the negotiation of a framework that builds on and succeeds the Kyoto Protocol. This road map identifies many important issues that merit consideration and resolution in the design of an international climate policy architecture. While the Bali Action Plan is intended to yield an international framework at the 2009 climate change talks in Copenhagen, Denmark (COP 15), the road map also provides something of a framework for the international climate policy debate—and thus for actions undertaken domestically by participating countries—for some years beyond the Copenhagen meetings.

The research program pursued by the Harvard Project on International Climate Agreements addresses key issues in the Bali road map with the aim of informing the design and evaluation of various policies that would be included in the next international climate regime. Specifically, Harvard Project research teams have brought their scholarship to bear on each of the five major elements of the Bali Action Plan: a long-term global climate policy goal, emission mitigation, adaptation, technology transfer, and financing.

The Bali road map calls for a "shared vision for long-term cooperative action" that would include "a long-term global goal for emission reductions" as a means to implement the ultimate objective of the UNFCCC. The issue of setting long-term goals has received considerable attention from policymakers around the world. While we believe that the selection of a long-term global climate policy goal does not fall within the domain of scholars but rather should be decided by national leaders, our work can inform the identification and review of various

---

[7] Chapters 4 (Jaffe and Stavins) and 8 (Barrett) describe examples of the third type of architecture: bottom-up, coordinated and unilateral national policies.

long-term emission objectives. The research undertaken for this project and in writing *Architectures for Agreement* identifies a variety of means for constructing a long-term international climate policy architecture—for example, Bosetti, *et al.* in Chapter 23 evaluate the long-term GHG concentration and temperature implications of half a dozen approaches to climate policy. Additional analyses highlight the challenge of achieving long-term, stabilization targets with incomplete participation (Chapter 24 by Jacoby, *et al.*, and Chapter 26 by Blanford, *et al.*) as well as the need to improve the technology options available for achieving ambitious long-term emission-reduction goals (Chapter 25 by Clarke, *et al.*).

The role of emission mitigation continues to be central in international climate change negotiations. The Bali Action Plan calls for "mitigation commitments or actions" by developed countries and "mitigation actions" by developing countries, the latter with support for capacity-building and technology transfer from developed countries. In both cases, mitigation efforts should be "measurable, reportable, and verifiable," a requirement that is addressed by Project research aimed at evaluating various kinds of metrics for assessing mitigation activities (Chapter 10 by Fischer and Morgenstern) and at describing a surveillance institution that can independently review the comparability of effort among participating countries.

The Bali road map provides guidance for these efforts by identifying several specific forms of mitigation, including reducing deforestation and emissions from changes in land use, an issue investigated by Plantinga and Richards in Chapter 22. Sectoral approaches to mitigating emissions also receive attention in the Bali road map; accordingly, Sawa in Chapter 7 and Barrett in Chapter 8, among others, explore the prospects and pitfalls of a sector-specific approach. Finally, the negotiators in Bali also agreed on the general proposition that market-based approaches should be pursued—an issue that receives attention in many contributions to this project (Chapter 6 by Agarwala, Chapter 5 by Cooper, Chapter 3 by Ellerman, Chapter 2 by Frankel, Chapter 4 by Jaffe and Stavins, Chapter 17 by Karp and Zhao, and Chapter 12 by Keohane and Raustiala).

The Kyoto Protocol only mentions the word "adaptation" twice. In contrast, the Bali road map elevates the importance of this issue. Several contributors to this book recognize the need to effectively integrate climate change and economic development in the design of future climate change policy, including Cao (Chapter 18), Hall, *et al.* (Chapter 21), Somanathan (Chapter 19), and Victor (Chapter 20). For example, Barrett (Chapter 8) argues that efforts to transfer resources and facilitate the development of capacity in developing countries should play an important role in the next climate agreement. Newell (Chapter 13) points out that efforts to promote technological innovation can address adaptation needs while also identifying new ways to lower the cost of emission mitigation. Others maintain that promoting economic development, diversifying economic activity, and improving economic resilience, especially in agriculture, should guide climate change policy for the least developed countries.

The Bali road map also focuses on the need to enhance technology transfer to developing countries. Given the rapid growth of emissions in these countries, technology transfer is needed to promote a more climate-friendly trajectory for economic development. The Harvard Project has explored potential reforms of the CDM that would focus on moving more technologies to developing countries (Teng, *et al.* in Chapter 15); it has also examined options for the design of clean technology funds oriented to developing countries (Hall, *et al.* in Chapter 21, Keeler and Thompson in Chapter 14). Of course, the success of technology transfer will depend on the development of new technologies—an issue addressed by Newell in exploring the potential for policy to induce more innovation on climate-friendly technologies (Chapter 13). Along all of these dimensions of action—mitigation, adaptation, and technology transfer—the Project has assessed opportunities to finance a serious and sufficient climate policy program as called for in the Bali Action Plan.

Finally, the Harvard Project has also advanced research on important issues that, while not identified in the Bali road map, are critical to the design of a successful, post-2012 international climate policy architecture. This includes analysis of the equity implications of international climate agreements (Posner and Sunstein in Chapter 11); possible means for promoting compliance with internationally-negotiated commitments (Keohane and Raustiala in Chapter 12); avenues for structuring a dynamic, robust series of negotiations that can facilitate broad participation and agreement (Harstad in Chapter 9); and trade-climate interactions that could enhance an international climate policy agreement (Frankel in Chapter 16).

Implementing architectures for agreement

This book is divided into seven sections: (1) alternative international policy architectures; (2) negotiation, assessment, and compliance; (3) the role and means of technology transfer; (4) global climate policy and international trade; (5) economic development, adaptation, and deforestation; (6) modeling impacts of alternative allocations of responsibility; and (7) synthesis and conclusion.

Part I—alternative international policy architectures

Each of the seven chapters that make up Part I of this book proposes and assesses a specific post-Kyoto international policy architecture. We begin, in Chapter 2, with a proposal by Jeffrey Frankel of Harvard University for "Specific Formulas and Emission Targets for All Countries in All Decades" that builds on the foundation of the Kyoto Protocol, but strengthens it in important ways. Frankel's approach attempts to solve the most serious deficiencies of Kyoto: the absence of long-term targets, the non-participation of the United States and key developing countries, and the lack of motivation for countries to abide by their commitments. Frankel's plan—which reflects political as well as scientific and economic considerations—uses formulas to set emission caps for all countries through the year 2100. The methodology is designed to yield caps that give every country reason to feel that it is only doing its fair share, and it is flexible enough that it can accommodate major changes in circumstances during the course of the century.

In Chapter 3, Denny Ellerman of the Massachusetts Institute of Technology posits that the European Union Emission Trading Scheme (EU ETS) can serve as a prototype for a global policy architecture. Ellerman draws on the first four years of experience with the EU ETS to develop insights about the challenges that can be expected to emerge in a broader program and suggest potential solutions. Interestingly, the problems that are often seen as most intractable for a global trading system—institutional readiness and public acceptance—have not appeared in Europe. Rather, Ellerman finds the greater challenges may lie in developing an effective centralized authority, devising side benefits to encourage participation, and dealing with the interrelated issues of harmonization, differentiation, and stringency. The EU ETS is not perfect, nor does it provide a perfect prototype for a global system, which would surely diverge in important respects from the European model. Nevertheless, Ellerman concludes that the EU example is likely to continue to be highly instructive as policymakers consider the larger and more difficult tasks that lie ahead.

Chapter 4 continues the focus on tradable permit systems, but does so in the context of a potential decentralized, bottom-up global climate policy architecture. Judson Jaffe of Analysis Group and Robert Stavins of Harvard assess "Linkage of Tradable Permit Systems in International Policy Architecture." The authors note that tradable permit systems are emerging as a preferred policy tool for reducing GHG emissions in many countries around the world. Because linking systems can reduce compliance costs and improve market liquidity, there is great interest in doing so. Jaffe and Stavins examine the benefits and concerns associated with linkage and analyze the near-term and long-term roles that linkage may play in a future international climate policy architecture. They find that in the near term, indirect linkages of cap-and-trade systems via a common emission-reduction-credit system could achieve meaningful cost savings and risk diversification without the need for much harmonization among systems. In the longer term, international negotiations could establish shared environmental and economic expectations that could serve as the basis for a broad set of direct links among cap-and-trade systems.

In Chapter 5, we move from global policy architectures based on tradable permit systems to a distinctly different approach, namely a system of harmonized domestic carbon taxes. In "The Case for Charges on Greenhouse Gas Emissions," Richard Cooper of Harvard proposes a world-wide tax on emissions of GHGs from all sources. This approach is premised on the notion that seriously addressing GHG emissions requires a global approach, not one limited to today's rich countries. Levying a charge on CO_2 raises the price of CO_2-emitting activities, including fossil-fuel use, and thus is the most direct method of influencing consumer and industrial behavior around the world. The charge would be internationally adjusted from time to time, and each country would collect and keep the revenue it generates. A carbon tax integrated in an existing tax system may be easier to implement, from an institutional perspective, than alternative mitigation policies in some developing countries with weak regulatory bureaucracies and rule of law.

A developing-country perspective is introduced in Chapter 6 by Ramgopal Agarwala of Research and Information System for Developing Countries in New Delhi, India. Starting from the observation that there has been little progress toward a global consensus on climate policy despite growing awareness of the risks of inaction, Agarwala argues that fundamental differences of perspective between developed and developing countries may impede progress toward a new agreement for quite some time. With this in mind, Agarwala presents an approach intended to reconcile the positions of developing and developed countries. After describing why the Kyoto Protocol satisfies none of the key criteria for a credible global compact, the author posits four fundamentals for a future climate agreement: first, it should set realistic targets designed to stabilize global CO_2 emissions at 2008 levels until 2050 and achieve a 50 percent reduction by 2100; second, it should set appropriate carbon prices by eliminating subsidies to emitters (particularly energy subsidies) and establishing a carbon tax; third, it should support the development and dissemination of carbon-saving technologies; and fourth, it should be negotiated within the United Nations, but should be implemented using institutions such as the International Monetary Fund and World Bank.

Yet another approach to global climate policy is proposed in Chapter 7. Akihiro Sawa of the University of Tokyo describes "Sectoral Approaches to a post-Kyoto International Climate Policy Framework." A number of authors and policymakers from industrialized and developing countries have proposed sectoral approaches to a future international agreement. Though there is significant variation in the details, most of these proposals would determine overall emission targets by estimating and aggregating sector-level reduction potentials based on a technology analysis. This is unlike the Kyoto Protocol, in which economy-wide emission commitments are negotiated from the top down. Sawa reviews the pros and cons of sectoral approaches and proposes a specific example for the post-2012 period. He concludes that a sectoral approach may help solve some of the problems of the Kyoto Protocol, but that some issues—including lower cost-effectiveness compared to an economy-wide approach, the difficulty of collecting the data needed to make a technology-based assessment of reduction potential, and the complexity of sector-level negotiations—remain unresolved.

Part I concludes with an approach that departs dramatically from the tradition of the Kyoto Protocol, namely "A Portfolio System of Climate Treaties," by Scott Barrett of Columbia University. Rather than attempting to address all sectors and all types of GHGs under one unified regime, Barrett argues in Chapter 8 for a system of linked international agreements that separately address different sectors and gases, as well as key issues (such as adaptation and technology research and development) and last-resort remedies (such as geoengineering). Barrett concludes that his proposed multitrack climate treaty system is not perfect, but could nevertheless offer important advantages over the current approach. In particular, by avoiding the enforcement problems of an aggregate approach and by taking a broader view of risk reduction, the portfolio approach could provide a more effective and flexible response to the long-term global challenge posed by climate change.

Part II—negotiation, assessment, and compliance

The remainder of the book focuses on specific issues of design that are important, no matter the climate policy architecture that is ultimately chosen. In fact, the ideas on various design elements in the remaining sections of this volume (Parts II through VII) could be aggregated to serve as the basis for an international agreement. Alternatively, some of these ideas complement the architectures described in Part I and could be integrated with these core proposals. Part II consists of four chapters that examine three closely-related topics: the negotiation process; how to assess commitments and compliance; and how to think about distributional equity and fairness.

In Chapter 9, Bård Harstad of Northwestern University describes "How to Negotiate and Update Climate Agreements," starting from the premise that the outcome of negotiations depends on the bargaining rules. Drawing on a game theoretic analysis, Harstad proposes seven bargaining rules that would facilitate agreement on a post-2012 climate treaty: first, harmonization or formulas should be used to calculate national obligations and contributions; second, a future climate treaty should have a long time horizon; third, the treaty should specify the default outcome if the (re)negotiation process breaks down, and this default outcome should be an ambitious agreement; fourth, investments in R&D, or trade in abatement technology, should be subsidized internationally; fifth, unanimity requirements—where they exist—should be replaced by a majority or a supermajority rule when it comes to treaty amendments; sixth, linkage to international trade agreements makes each of the rules more credible and efficient; and seventh, a "minimum participation rule" can discourage free riding.

Developing effective strategies to address climate change will require collective effort on the part of many countries over an extended time horizon and across a range of activities. Therefore, a key challenge for the international community will be to compare and judge different national commitments. In Chapter 10, Carolyn Fischer and Richard Morgenstern of Resources for the Future take on this topic in "Metrics for Evaluating Policy Commitments in a Fragmented World: The Challenges of Equity and Integrity." Because diverse actions by different nations will be an unavoidable part of future climate policy, it will be critical in international negotiations to have some means of discussing in a coherent and broadly accepted manner about what individual nations are doing to help reduce climate risk. Various metrics for evaluating individual nations' policy commitments and performance are considered by Fischer and Morgenstern, who conclude that no single metric can adequately and fully address the complex issues of equity and the integrity of climate change mitigation measures. Rather, a suite of metrics will inevitably be required.

Clearly, climate change raises difficult issues of justice, particularly with respect to the distribution of burdens and benefits among poor and wealthy nations. Chapter 11, by Eric Posner of the University of Chicago and Cass Sunstein of Harvard University, examines this important topic. In "Justice and Climate Change," these authors focus on the narrower question of how to allocate GHG emission rights within a future international cap-and-trade system. However, the questions they address apply equally to a variety of other mechanisms for allocating cost burdens internationally. They identify shortcomings in an approach that is often advanced on fairness grounds—a per capita allocation in which emissions permits are distributed to nations on the basis of population. Although Posner and Sunstein acknowledge that allocations based on population or on redistributing wealth are generally more equitable than allocations that award permits on the basis of current emissions, they maintain that a per capita allocation would not—in practice—satisfy objectives of fairness and welfare redistribution. Rather, if the goal is a more equal distribution of wealth, an approach that is openly redistributive is better than a per capita allocation.

Ultimately, an international climate agreement will be of no value without sufficient participation and compliance by signatories. This is one of the lessons of the Kyoto Protocol. In Chapter 12, Robert Keohane of Princeton University and Kal Raustiala of the University of California at Los Angeles begin with the proposition that a successful climate change regime must secure sufficient participation, achieve agreement on meaningful rules, and establish mechanisms for compliance. Moreover, it must do so in a political environment of sovereign states with differing preferences and capabilities. In "Toward a Post-Kyoto Climate Change Architecture: A Political Analysis," Keohane and Raustiala address the trade-off between participation and stringency by proposing an "economy of esteem for climate change," in which participation is encouraged by a system of prizes for politicians who take leadership on this issue. They argue that, contrary to provisions in the Kyoto Protocol, only a system of buyer liability (rather than seller or hybrid liability) in an international permit trading regime is consistent with existing political realities and will promote compliance. Drawing analogies to international bond markets, they propose a system of buyer liability that would endogenously generate market arrangements, such as rating agencies and fluctuations in the price of emissions permits according to perceived risk. These features would in turn create incentives for compliance without resorting to ineffective interstate punishments.

Part III—the role and means of technology transfer

Achieving long-term, climate change policy goals will require dramatic progress in the innovation and deployment of energy-efficient and low-carbon technologies (Aldy and Stavins 2008). Policies that directly facilitate technology innovation and diffusion will therefore need to play a central role, alongside policies targeted directly at reducing emissions. This is the focus of the three chapters that make up Part III of this volume.

In Chapter 13, Richard Newell of Duke University takes a broad perspective, proposing a portfolio of "International Climate Technology Strategies" within the context of international agreements and institutions for climate, energy, trade, development, and intellectual property. First, Newell notes that long-term national commitments and policies for emission mitigation are crucial to providing the necessary private-sector incentives for technology development and transfer. Financial assistance to developing countries for technology transfer and capacity building will also be necessary. Tariff and nontariff barriers to the transfer of climate-friendly technologies can be reduced through a World Trade Organization (WTO) agreement on trade in environmental goods and services. To support the upstream supply and transfer of technology innovations internationally, Newell proposes strategies to increase and more effectively coordinate public funding of R&D, as well as strategies to resolve impediments to knowledge transfer. The result is a portfolio of strategies for reducing barriers and increasing incentives for innovation across international agreements and institutions.

An agenda focused on technology transfer is laid out in Chapter 14 by Andrew Keeler and Alexander Thompson of Ohio State University, "Mitigation through Resource Transfers to Developing Countries: Expanding Greenhouse Gas Offsets." Keeler and Thompson propose a more expansive approach to offsets that would meet the different objectives of industrialized and developing countries while providing substantial support for long-term investments and policy changes to reduce GHG emissions in the developing world. Their approach consists of five elements: (1) change the criteria for offsets from "real, verifiable, and permanent reductions" to "actions that create real progress in developing countries toward mitigation and adaptation"; (2) make a significant share of industrialized country commitments achievable through offset payments to developing countries; (3) sell a portion of offset credits up front and put the proceeds in a fund to make investments in projects in the developing world; (4) focus international negotiations on guidelines for an international offsets program; and (5) delegate tasks to new and existing institutions for the purpose of managing the offsets program.

In Chapter 15, titled "Possible Development of a Technology Clean Development Mechanism in the Post-2012 Regime," Fei Teng, Wenying Chen, and Jiankun He, of Tsinghua University in Beijing, offer a proposal that is parallel to the Keeler and Thompson proposal, but that fits within the context of an enhanced CDM. Starting from the premise that it will be essential to transfer climate-friendly technologies from developed to developing countries, the authors propose an enhanced CDM regime with a specific emphasis on technology transfer. This enhanced regime would have three features: first, technology transfer must be identified as a goal before any activities are approved and implemented; second, only projects that use technology transferred under the program can receive credit for emissions reductions; and third, credits would be shared by the technology provider or by the government of the host country if the technology provider or host-country government support or enable the transfer, as well as offer discounted or even free licensing.

Part IV—global climate policy and international trade

Global efforts to address climate change could be on a collision course with global efforts through the WTO to reduce barriers to trade. Such a collision would be terrible news—both for free trade and for climate protection. In Chapter 16, "Global Environment and Trade Policy," Jeffrey Frankel of Harvard University first examines the broad question of whether environmental goals in general are threatened by free trade and the WTO, before turning to the narrower question of whether trade policies that could be included in various national efforts to address climate change are likely to come into conflict with WTO rules. Frankel notes that future national-level policies to address climate change are likely to include provisions that target carbon-intensive products from countries deemed to be making inadequate efforts. These provisions need not violate sensible trade principles and WTO rules, but there is a danger that in practice they will. Frankel describes the characteristics of future national policies that would likely conflict with WTO rules and could provide cover for protectionism—he also describes the characteristics of future national policies that would likely be WTO-compatible. Frankel concludes that in the long term, a multilateral regime is needed to guide the development of trade measures intended to address concerns about leakage and competitiveness in a world where nations have different levels of commitment to GHG mitigation.

In Chapter 17, "A Proposal for the Design of the Successor to the Kyoto Protocol," Larry Karp of the University of California at Berkeley and Jinhua Zhao of Michigan State University examine how international trade mechanisms can be made part of a future climate agreement. In their proposal, nations with mandatory emissions ceilings would have the option to reduce their abatement commitments in exchange for either paying a monetary fine or accepting trade sanctions imposed by other signatory nations. In addition to the potential use of trade sanctions, trade reforms could be used to achieve climate-related objectives. Specifically, these authors support the use of carefully circumscribed border tax adjustments to protect against leakage. They maintain that such adjustments—if thoughtfully and carefully applied—can create effective incentives for countries to participate in a future agreement.

Part V—economic development, adaptation, and deforestation

Developing countries have a key role to play in efforts to address climate change—both because they could be strongly affected by future damages and because they account for an increasing share of global emissions. For this reason, the links between international climate policy and economic development are enormously important. Policies to facilitate adaptation and reduce the rate of deforestation, in particular, are critical for developing countries. Because of the great significance of this set of issues in the post-Kyoto international climate policy debate, we include five chapters on economic development, adaptation, and deforestation in this part of the book.

In Chapter 18, Jing Cao of Tsinghua University provides a Chinese perspective on "Reconciling Human Development and Climate Protection." Describing an approach that shares much with the proposal in Chapter 2 by Jeffrey Frankel, Cao seeks to offer a fair and efficient policy architecture for the post-2012 era, with the hope of breaking through what she characterizes as the current political impasse between developed and developing countries. Cao's proposed approach engages developing countries gradually, through four stages: in the first stage, all countries agree on a path of future global emissions that leads to an acceptable long-term stabilization goal; in the second stage, developing countries focus on "no regrets" mitigation options; in stage three, developing countries take on moderate emission targets; and in the final stage, all countries agree to binding emission targets.

Chapter 19, by E. Somanathan of the Indian Statistical Institute in New Delhi, offers a perspective from India: "What Do We Expect from an International Climate Agreement? A Perspective from a

Low-Income Country." Somanathan recognizes that an effective solution to the climate change problem will require the cooperation of developing countries. However, he argues that it is neither feasible nor desirable to pursue near-term GHG reductions within these countries or emissions trading between developed and developing countries. Arguing that technology improvements are needed to give all countries, including developing countries, a realistic opportunity to cost-effectively cut their CO_2 emissions, Somanathan maintains that a post-2012 international climate agreement should focus on creating incentives for research and development to advance new climate-friendly technologies. Indeed, he indicates that an international agreement involving developing countries should confine itself to promoting technical cooperation.

David Victor of Stanford University, writing in Chapter 20, takes a different approach to engaging developing countries. He proposes "Climate Accession Deals: New Strategies for Taming Growth of Greenhouse Gases in Developing Countries." This approach builds on two premises: first, that developing nations value economic growth far more than they value future global environmental conditions, and second, that many governments of developing nations lack the administrative ability to control emissions. With Victor's proposal, climate accession deals would be negotiated on a country-by-country basis, with an individual accession deal consisting of a set of policies that are tailored to gain maximum leverage on a single developing country's emissions, while still being aligned with its interests and capabilities. Industrialized countries would support each accession deal by providing specific benefits, such as financial resources, technology, administrative training, or security guarantees. According to Victor, accession deals could have several advantages: first, they would be anchored in host countries' interests and capabilities; second, they could yield a significant degree of leverage while minimizing external investment; third, they would engage private enterprise and government ministries other than environmental and foreign affairs ministries; and fourth, accession deals would be replicable and scalable.

Chapter 21, by Daniel Hall of Resources for the Future, Michael Levi of the Council on Foreign Relations, William Pizer, now with the US Treasury Department, and Takahiro Ueno of the Central Research Institute of the Electric Power Industry in Tokyo offers a broad approach to "Policies for Developing Country Engagement." These authors maintain that because no single approach offers a sure path to success for securing developing-country participation, a variety of strategies—including policy reforms, financing approaches, and diplomatic venues—must be pursued in parallel. In their view, post-Kyoto international climate negotiations are likely to focus on a "grand bargain" with developing countries, offering some form of commitments in exchange for further emission reductions and increased financing from developed countries. Developing country commitments could take the form of domestic policy reforms, sectoral targets, or even economy-wide limits (for higher-income developing countries). These authors conclude that forging a new climate agreement that reduces global emissions and provides support to poor countries will be very difficult, but without it there is virtually no chance of stabilizing GHG concentrations at an acceptable level.

Chapter 22 turns to the reality that changes to forests worldwide can have enormous impacts on the global carbon cycle. Because of this, Andrew Plantinga of Oregon State University and Kenneth Richards of Indiana University argue—as do increasing numbers of scholars and policymakers—that forest carbon management ought to be an element of the next international agreement on climate change. In "International Forest Carbon Sequestration in a Post-Kyoto Agreement," they propose a "national inventory" approach, in which nations receive credits or debits for changes in forest cover relative to a measured baseline. Nations would conduct periodic inventories of their forest carbon stock, and the measured stock would be compared with a pre-negotiated baseline to determine offset credits that could be redeemed, or debits that must be covered, in a tradable permit market. With this approach, national governments, rather than project developers, would pursue carbon sequestration activities through the implementation of domestic policies.

Part VI—modeling impacts of alternative allocations of responsibility

Clearly, negotiations on a post-Kyoto international climate regime will be driven in large part by the perspectives of individual countries that are primarily concerned about the impacts of any future agreement on their own economies and societies. Just as no single individual or institution has cornered the market on wisdom regarding the best architecture for a post-Kyoto climate policy, so too has no single economic model captured all dimensions and concerns regarding the consequences of alternative allocations of responsibility. Hence, the sixth part of the book includes five separate chapters that report on the modeling results obtained by research teams on three continents.

In Chapter 23, "A Quantitative and Comparative Assessment of Architectures for Agreement," Valentina Bosetti, Carlo Carraro, Alessandra Sgobbi, and Massimo Tovoni, all of the Fondazione Eni Enrico Mattei in Italy, provide a comparison of eight prominent options: global cap-and-trade with redistribution; global tax recycled domestically; reducing emissions from deforestation and degradation; climate clubs; burden sharing; graduation; dynamic targets; and R&D and technology development. They assess these architectures in terms of four criteria: economic efficiency, environmental effectiveness, distributional implications, and political acceptability, as measured by feasibility and enforceability. The authors conclude, first, that achieving a stabilization target of 450 parts per million (ppm) for the atmospheric concentration of CO_2 only (550 ppm for all GHGs in CO_2-equivalent terms) will be exceptionally difficult to achieve. However, a strategy of progressive commitments—in which consensus is reached on future binding targets for developing countries, but developed countries take action first—can achieve CO_2 stabilization very close to 450 ppm. Second, an extended—possibly global—carbon market, even without global commitments to reduce emissions, will greatly help to reduce costs, as will the inclusion of non-CO_2 gases and credits for avoided deforestation. However, a basic trade-off between economic impact and environmental protection remains.

In Chapter 24, Henry Jacoby, Mustafa Babiker, Sergey Paltsev, and John Reilly of the Massachusetts Institute of Technology write about "Sharing the Burden of GHG Reductions." They use the MIT Emissions Prediction and Policy Analysis (EPPA) model to estimate the welfare and financial implications of various cost and emission-reduction outcomes. They find that a target of reducing global emissions 50 percent by 2050, while it can be done in a way that meets reasonable equity targets, is extremely ambitious and would require large financial transfers from developed to developing countries. The authors conclude that the combination of aggressive targets with expectations of incentives and compensation for the developing countries may not reflect sufficient regard for the difficulty of finding a mutually acceptable way to share the economic burden.

Writing in Chapter 25, Leon Clarke, Kate Calvin, Jae Edmonds, Page Kyle, and Marshall Wise of the Pacific Northwest National Laboratory focus on "Technology and International Climate Policy" to explore interactions between two of the key drivers that determine emissions reductions—technology availability and performance, on the one hand, and international policy architectures, on the other. Four main findings emerge from this analysis: first, technology is more important to reducing the costs of emissions mitigation when international policy structures deviate from full participation; second, near-term carbon prices are inexorably tied to the expected long-term availability of technology; third, the choice of a policy architecture has a larger impact on the distribution of mitigation actions than on the global emissions pathway; and fourth, more rapid technology improvements reduce the relative influence of policy architecture.

Chapter 26 features an analysis by Geoffrey Blanford and Richard Richels of the Electric Power Research Institute and Thomas Rutherford of the Swiss Federal Institute of Technology in Zurich on "Revised Emissions Growth Projections for China: Why Post-Kyoto Climate Policy Must Look East." The authors note that continued growth in developing-country emissions could put stabilization targets effectively out of reach within the next ten to twenty years, regardless of what wealthier countries do. They suggest that a CO_2 stabilization target of 450 ppm is probably no longer realistic, and a target of 550 ppm now appears as challenging as 450 ppm appeared just a few years ago. However, stabilization at 550 ppm may still be feasible if developed countries undertake immediate reductions and developing countries follow a "graduated accession" scenario, in which China and other mid-income countries (for example, Korea, Brazil, Mexico, and South Africa) join global mitigation efforts in 2020, India joins in 2040, and poorer countries delay participation until 2050. On the other hand, their analysis indicates that if developing countries enter into a global regime more gradually—for example, by adopting progressively more stringent targets only as incomes rise—global emissions may continue to grow through 2050, and even the 550 ppm target will begin to look doubtful. These authors conclude that no issue is more urgent for international climate negotiations than that of establishing incentives for timely and meaningful participation by developing countries.

In the final chapter in this part of the book, Chapter 27, "Expecting the Unexpected: Macroeconomic Volatility and Climate Policy," Warwick McKibbin of the Australian National University, Adele Morris of the Brookings Institution, and Peter Wilcoxen of Syracuse University focus on a timely concern: how a future international climate policy architecture may perform in the presence of unexpected macroeconomic shocks, whether positive shocks from economic growth in developing countries or severe financial distress in the global economy. Their premise is that, in the absence of such unanticipated economic shocks, three regimes are similar—in principle—in their ability to reduce emissions efficiently: global carbon cap-and-trade; globally harmonized domestic carbon taxes; and a hybrid system of national long-term permit trading with a globally-coordinated maximum price for permits in each year (that is, a safety valve).[8] However, these three systems differ in how they would transmit economic disruptions from one economy to another. McKibbin, Morris, and Wilcoxen find that whereas a cap-and-trade regime would be counter-cyclical—in the sense that reduced demand for permits would lead to lower permit prices and thereby dampen cost impacts during an economic slowdown—this approach also fails to capture the opportunity for significant additional low-cost emissions reductions during a global economic downturn.

Part VII—synthesis and conclusion

The book closes with two chapters that draw out the key implications of the twenty-six research initiatives of the Harvard Project on International Climate Agreements and provide guidance for the international policy community. In the Epilogue (Chapter 28), Richard Schmalensee of the Massachusetts Institute of Technology steps back and reflects on the factors that make the global dimensions of climate change so difficult and important to manage, the history of climate policy debates, and the key elements of an emerging international policy architecture. He concludes that the most critical and difficult task before the world's policymakers is to "move toward a policy

---

[8] Refer to McKibbin and Wilcoxen (2007) for a detailed description of this type of climate policy architecture.

architecture that can induce the world's poor nations to travel a much more climate-friendly path to prosperity than the one today's rich nations have traveled."

We close the book with Chapter 29, "Lessons for the International Policy Community," in which we begin by highlighting certain principles that the research teams have identified as being important for the design of a scientifically sound, economically rational, and politically pragmatic post-2012 international climate policy architecture. Real progress will require addressing these principles, which constitute some of the core premises underlying various policy architectures and design elements. We also highlight four international climate policy architectures—each of which has advantages as well as disadvantages—because each is promising in some regards and because each raises important issues for consideration. One is within the category of targets and timetables: formulas for dynamic national targets for all countries. Two are within the category of harmonized domestic policies: a portfolio of international treaties and harmonized national carbon taxes. And one is within the category of coordinated and unilateral national policies: linkage of national and regional tradable permit systems.

Regardless of which overall international policy architecture is ultimately chosen, a number of key design issues stand out as particularly important. And so, in the last part of Chapter 29, we identify some of the lessons identified by our twenty-six research teams with regard to five issues and elements for a post-2012 international agreement: burden sharing, technology transfer, CDM reform, addressing deforestation, and making global climate policy compatible with global-trade policy. We infuse all five of these discussions with attention to the relationship between global climate policy and economic development.

The principles, architectures, and design elements proposed and examined in this book and highlighted in the final chapter can serve to illuminate many of the issues facing the international policy community. Our hope is that all those engaged in the ultimate design of climate change policy—from decision makers and diplomats to leaders in the private sector and civil society—will find it useful in reconciling their diverse interests and moving forward with effective solutions to the enormous, collective challenge posed by global climate change.

References

Aldy, Joseph E. and Robert N. Stavins (eds.) (2007). *Architectures for Agreement: Addressing Global Climate Change in the Post-Kyoto World.* New York: Cambridge University Press.

(2008). "Economic Incentives in a New Climate Agreement." Prepared for The Climate Dialogue, Hosted by the Prime Minister of Denmark, May 7–8, 2008, Copenhagen, Denmark. Cambridge, MA: Belfer Center for Science and International Affairs, May 7.

Frankel, Jeffrey (2007). "Formulas for Quantitative Emission Targets," in Aldy and Stavins, (eds.), pp. 31–56.

Hahn, Robert W. and Robert N. Stavins (1999). *What Has the Kyoto Protocol Wrought? The Real Architecture of International Tradable Permit Markets.* Washington, DC: The AEI Press.

McKibbin, Warwick J. and Peter J. Wilcoxen (2007). "A Credible Foundation for Long-Term International Cooperation on Climate Change," in Aldy and Stavins, (eds.), pp. 185–208.

Michaelowa, Axel (2007). "Graduation and Deepening," in Aldy and Stavins, (eds.), pp. 81–104.

Pizer, William A (2007). "Practical Global Climate Policy," in Aldy and Stavins, (eds.), pp. 280–314.

Schmalensee, Richard (1998). "Greenhouse Policy Architectures and Institutions," in W. D. Nordhaus (ed.), *Economics and Policy Issues in Climate Change*, Washington, DC: Resources for the Future Press, pp. 137–58.

PART I

Alternative international policy architectures

2 | An elaborated proposal for a global climate policy architecture: specific formulas and emission targets for all countries in all decades[1]

JEFFREY FRANKEL

This chapter offers a framework of formulas that produce precise numerical targets for emissions of carbon dioxide (CO_2) in all regions of the world in all decades of this century. The formulas are based on pragmatic judgments about what is possible politically. The reason for this approach is the author's belief that many of the usual science-based, ethics-based, and economics-based paths are not dynamically consistent: that is, it is not credible that successor governments will be able to abide by the commitments that today's leaders make.

The formulas proposed here are driven by seven political axioms:

1. The United States will not commit to quantitative targets if China and other major developing countries do not commit to quantitative targets at the same time, because of concerns about economic competitiveness and carbon leakage.
2. China and other developing countries in the very short run will not make economic sacrifices, especially because the United States has not done so.

[1] The author would like especially to thank Valentina Bosetti of FEEM who produced, by means of the WITCH model, all the simulations of the effects of my formula-based proposals, thereby bringing hitherto-abstract ideas to life. This chapter literally could not have been written without her. He would like to thank Joe Aldy and Robert Stavins of the Harvard Project on International Climate Agreements for encouraging and supporting this line of research. For comments and suggestions on the outcome he would like to thank John Deutch, Robert Keohane, Warwick McKibben, Oyebola Olabisi, Rob Stavins, Jonathan Weiner, and an anonymous reviewer. The author would further like to thank for partial support the Sustainability Science Program, funded by the Italian Ministry for Environment, Land and Sea, at the Center for International Development at Harvard University.

3. China and other developing countries, even in the longer run, will not make sacrifices different in character from those made by richer countries that have gone before them.
4. In the long run, no country can be rewarded for having "ramped up" its emissions well above 1990 levels before joining.
5. No country will agree to participate if its expected cost during the course of the 21st century (in present discounted value) is more than Y, where Y is for now set at 1 percent of national income per year.
6. No country will abide by targets that cost it more than X in any individual budget period, where X is for now set at 5 percent of income.
7. If one major country drops out, others will become discouraged and the system may unravel.

The proposed targets are formulated according to the following framework. Between now and 2050, the European Union follows the path laid out in the January 2008 European Commission Directive; the United States follows the path in 2008 legislative proposals associated with Senator Joseph Lieberman; and Japan, Australia and Korea follow statements that their own leaders have recently made. China, India and other countries *agree immediately to quantitative greenhouse gas (GHG) emission targets*, which in the first decades *merely copy their business-as-usual (BAU) paths*, thereby precluding leakage. These countries are not initially expected to cut emissions below their BAU trajectory.

When the time comes for these countries to join mitigation efforts—perhaps when they cross certain thresholds—their emission targets are determined using a formula that incorporates three elements: a Progressive Reductions Factor, a Latecomer Catch-up Factor, and a Gradual Equalization Factor. These factors are designed to persuade the developing countries that they are only being asked to do what is fair in light of actions already taken by others. In the second half of the century, the formula that determines the emissions path for industrialized countries is dominated by the Gradual Equalization Factor. But developing countries, which will still be in earlier stages of participation and thus will have departed from their BAU paths only relatively recently, will still follow in the footsteps of those who have gone before. This means that their emission targets will be set using the Progressive Reductions Factor and the Latecomer Catch-up

Factor, in addition to the Gradual Equalization Factor. The glue that holds the agreement together is that every country has reason to feel that it is only doing its fair share.

We use the WITCH model to analyze the results of this approach in terms of projected paths for emissions targets, permit trading, the price of carbon, lost income, and environmental effects. Overall economic costs, discounted (at 5 percent), average 0.24 percent of Gross Product. No country suffers a discounted loss of more than 1 percent of national income overall from the agreement, nor more than 5 percent of income in any given period. Atmospheric CO_2 concentrations level off at 500 parts per million (ppm) in the latter part of the century. (The next phase of this research will aim for a target of 450 ppm.)

The problem

There are by now many proposals for a post-Kyoto climate change regime, even if one considers only proposals that accept the basic Kyoto approach of quantitative, national-level limits on GHG emissions accompanied by international trade in emissions permits. The Kyoto targets applied only to the budget period 2008–2012, which is now upon us, and only to a minority of countries (in theory, the industrialized countries). The big task is to extend quantitative emissions targets through the remainder of the century and to other countries—particularly the United States, China, and other developing countries.

Virtually all the existing proposals for a post-Kyoto agreement are either based on scientific environmental objectives (e.g., stabilizing atmospheric CO_2 concentrations at 450 ppm in 2100), ethical or philosophical considerations (e.g., the principle that every individual on earth has equal emission rights), or economic cost-benefit analyses (weighing the economic costs of abatement against the long-term environmental benefits).[2] This chapter proposes a path of emission targets for all countries and for the remainder of the century that is intended to be more practical in that it is also based

---

[2] An important example of the science-based approach is Wigley *et al.* (2007). An important example of the cost-benefit-based approach is Nordhaus (1994, 2006). An important example of the rights-based approach is Baer *et al.* (2008).

on political considerations, rather than on science or ethics or economics alone.[3]

The industrialized countries did, in 1997, agree to quantitative emissions targets for the Kyoto Protocol's first budget period, so in some sense we know that it can be done. But the obstacles are enormous. For starters, most of the Kyoto signers will probably miss their 2008–2012 targets, and of course the United States never even ratified. At multilateral venues such as the United Nations Framework Convention on Climate Change (UNFCCC) meeting in Bali (2007) and the Group of Eight (G8) meeting in Hokkaido (July 2008), world leaders have (just barely) been able to agree on a broad long-term goal of cutting total global emissions in half by 2050. But these meetings did not come close to producing agreement on who will cut how much, not to mention agreement on multilateral targets within a near-enough time horizon that the same national leaders are likely to still be alive when the abatement commitment comes due. To quote Al Gore (1993, p.353), "politicians are often tempted to make a promise that is not binding and hope for some unexpectedly easy way to keep the promise." For this reason, the aggregate targets endorsed so far cannot be viewed as anything more than aspirational.

Moreover, nobody has ever come up with an enforcement mechanism that simultaneously has sufficient teeth and is acceptable to member countries. Given the importance countries place on national sovereignty it is unlikely that this will change.[4] Hopes must instead rest on weak enforcement mechanisms such as the power of moral suasion and international opprobrium. It is safe to say that in the event of a clash between such weak enforcement mechanisms and the prospect of a large economic loss to a particular country, aversion to the latter would win out.

---

[3] Aldy, Barrett, and Stavins (2003) and Victor (2004) review a number of existing proposals. Numerous others have offered their own thoughts on post-Kyoto plans, at varying levels of detail, including Aldy, Orszag, and Stiglitz (2001); Barrett (2006); Nordhaus (2006); and Olmstead and Stavins (2006).

[4] The possibility of trade sanctions is probably the only serious idea for penalizing non-participation. Such penalties are not currently being considered at the multilateral level (although they perhaps should be; Frankel 2008b).

Necessary aspects of a workable successor to Kyoto

I have suggested six desirable attributes[5] that any proposed successor-agreement to the Kyoto Protocol should deliver:

- *More comprehensive participation*—specifically, getting the United States, China, and other developing countries to join the system of quantitative emission targets.
- *Efficiency*—incorporating market-flexibility mechanisms such as international permit trading and providing advance signals to allow the private sector to plan ahead, to the extent compatible with the credibility of the signals.
- *Dynamic consistency*—addressing the problem that announcements about steep cuts in 2050 are not credible. The lack of credibility stems from two sources. First, it is known that today's leaders cannot bind their successors. Second, the projected failure of most Kyoto signatories to meet their first-period emission targets makes the lack of seriousness at a global level painfully obvious.
- *Equity*—Taking into account the point made by developing countries that industrialized countries created the problem of global climate change, whereas poor countries are responsible for only about 20 percent of the CO_2 that has accumulated in the atmosphere from industrial activity over the past 150 years (though admittedly this is changing rapidly). From an equity standpoint, developing countries argue they should not be asked to limit their economic development to pay for a climate-change solution; moreover, they do not have the economic capacity to pay for emissions abatement that richer countries do. Finally, many developing countries place greater priority on raising their people's current standard of living (including reducing local air and water pollution). These countries might reasonably demand quantitative targets that reflect an equal per capita allotment of emissions, on equity grounds, even waiving any claims to reparations for the disproportionate environmental damages that can be expected to fall on them.
- *Compliance*—recognizing that no country will join a treaty if it entails tremendous economic sacrifice and that therefore compliance cannot be reasonably expected if costs are too high. Similarly,

[5] Frankel (2007). Similar lists are provided by Bowles and Sandalow (2001), Stewart and Weiner (2003), and others.

no country, if it has already joined the treaty, will continue to stay in during any given period if staying in means huge economic sacrifice, relative to dropping out, in that period.
- *Robustness under uncertainty*—recognizing that the relationship between cost and compliance applies not just to *ex ante* calculations based on current expectations, but also *ex post*, when future growth rates and other uncertain economic and technological variables become known.

Unlike the Kyoto Protocol, the proposal outlined in this chapter seeks to bring all countries into an international policy regime on a realistic basis and to look far into the future. But we cannot pretend to see with as fine a degree of resolution at a century-long horizon as we can at a five- or ten-year horizon. Fixing precise numerical targets a century ahead is impractical. Rather, we need a century-long sequence of negotiations, fitting within a common institutional framework that builds confidence as it goes along. The framework must have enough continuity so that success in the early phases builds members' confidence in each other's compliance commitments and in the fairness, viability, and credibility of the process. Yet the framework must be flexible enough that it can accommodate the unpredictable fluctuations in economic growth, technology development, climate, and political sentiment that will inevitably occur. Only by striking the right balance between continuity and flexibility can we hope that a framework for addressing climate change would last a century or more.

An example of such a framework in another policy area is the General Agreement on Tariffs and Trade, which emerged after World War II and provided the basis for 50 years of successful multilateral negotiations to liberalize international trade, culminating in the founding of the World Trade Organization. Nobody at the beginning could have predicted the precise magnitude or sequence of reforms to various trade barriers, or what sectors or countries would be included. But the early stages of negotiation worked, and so confidence in the process built, more and more countries joined the club, and progressively more ambitious rounds of liberalization were achieved.

Another analogy would be with the process of European economic integration, culminating in the formation of the European Economic and Monetary Union. Despite ambitions for more comprehensive integration, nobody at the time of the founding of the European Coal and Steel Community, or the subsequent European Economic Community, could have forecast the speed, scope, magnitude, or country membership that this path of integration would eventually take. The aim should be to do the same with the UNFCCC thereby establishing credibility.

Political constraints

Let us restore the claims regarding political feasibility to be taken as axiomatic.

1. The United States will not commit to quantitative targets if China and other major developing countries do not commit to quantitative targets at the same time. This leaves completely open the initial level and future path of the targets. Any plan will be found unacceptable if it leaves the less developed countries free to exploit their lack of GHG regulation for "competitive" advantage at the expense of the participating countries' economies and leads to emissions leakage at the expense of the environmental goal.
2. China, India, and other developing countries will not make sacrifices they view as

   a. fully contemporaneous with rich countries;
   b. different in character from those made by richer countries who have gone before them;
   c. preventing them from industrializing;
   d. failing to recognize that richer countries should be prepared to make greater economic sacrifices than poor countries to address the problem (all the more so because rich countries' past emissions have created the problem); or
   e. failing to recognize that the rich countries have benefited from an "unfair advantage" in being allowed to achieve levels of per capita emissions that are far above those of the poor countries.

3. In the short run, emission targets for developing countries must be computed relative to current levels or BAU paths; otherwise the economic costs will be too great for the countries in question to accept.[6] But in the longer run, no country can be rewarded for having "ramped up" emissions far above 1990 levels, the reference year agreed to at Rio and Kyoto. Fairness considerations aside, if post-1990 increases are permanently "grandfathered," then

---

[6] Cuts expressed relative to BAU have been called "Action Targets" (Baumert and Goldberg 2006).

countries that have not yet agreed to cuts will have a strong incentive to ramp up emissions in the interval before they join. Of course there was nothing magic about 1990 but, for better or worse, it is the year on which Annex I countries have long based planning.

4. No country will accept a path of targets that is expected to cost it more than Y percent of national income throughout the 21st century (in present discounted value), where Y is for now set at 1 percent.

5. No country will accept targets in any period that are expected to cost more than X percent of income to achieve during that period; alternatively, even if targets were already in place, no country would in the future actually abide by them if it found the cost to doing so would exceed X percent of income. In this chapter, income losses are defined relative to what would happen if the country in question had never joined. An alternative would be to define income losses in a future period relative to what would happen if the country were to drop out in that period, after decades of participation. For now, we set X at 5 percent.

6. If one major country drops out, others will become discouraged and may also fail to meet their own targets, and the framework may unravel. If such unraveling in a future decade is foreseeable at the time that long-run commitments are made, then those commitments will not be credible from the start. Firms, consumers, and researchers base their current decisions to invest in plant and equipment, consumer durables, or new technological possibilities on the expected future price of carbon: If government commitments are not credible from the start, then they will not raise the expected future carbon price. The reason for this political approach is the belief that many emissions pathways proposed on the basis of scientific or economic analyses are not dynamically consistent: That is, it is not credible that successor governments will be able to abide by the commitments that today's leaders make.

Squaring the circle

Of the above propositions, even the first and second alone seem to add up to a hopeless "Catch-22": nothing much can happen without the United States, the United States will not proceed unless China and other developing countries start at the same time, and China will not start until after the rich countries have gone first.

There is only one possible solution, only one knife-edge position that satisfies the constraints. At the same time that the United States agrees to binding emission cuts in the manner of Kyoto, China and other developing countries agree to a path that immediately imposes on them binding emission targets—but these targets in their early years simply follow the BAU path. The idea of committing only to BAU targets in the early decades will provoke outrage from both environmentalists and business interests in developed countries. But both groups might come to realize that this commitment is far more important than it sounds: It precludes the carbon leakage which, absent such an agreement, will undermine the environmental goal, and it moderates the competitiveness concerns of carbon-intensive industries in the rich countries. This approach recognizes that it would be irrational for China to agree to substantial actual cuts in the short term. Indeed China might well react with outrage at being asked to take on binding targets of any kind at the same time as the United States. But China may also come to realize that it would actually gain from such an agreement, by acquiring the ability to sell emission permits at the same world market price as developed countries.[7] (China currently receives lower prices for lower-quality project credits under the Kyoto Protocol's Clean Development Mechanism [CDM] or joint implementation [JI] provisions.)

In later decades, the formulas we propose do ask substantially more of the developing countries. But these formulas also obey basic notions of fairness, by (1) asking for cuts that are analogous in magnitude to the cuts made by others who began abatement earlier and (2) making due allowance for developing countries' low per capita income and emissions and for their baseline of rapid growth. These ideas were developed in earlier papers (see Frankel 1999, 2005, and 2007 and Aldy and Frankel 2004) which suggested that the formulas used to develop emissions targets incorporate four or five variables: 1990 emissions, emissions in the year of the negotiation, population,

---

[7] Many authors have pointed out that developing countries actually stand to gain economically in the short run by accepting targets and then selling permits, including the Council of Economic Advisers (1998), Keohane and Raustiala (2008), and Seidman and Lewis (2009). Of course this only works when the permits allocated to developing countries are sufficiently generous (i.e., do not reflect a significant abatement obligation), as is reasonable in the short run, but which the developing countries cannot expect in the long run.

and income. One might perhaps also include a few other special variables such as whether the country in question has coal or hydroelectric power, though the 1990 level of emissions conditional on per capita income can largely capture these special variables.

Here we narrow down the broad family of formulas to a more manageable set, and then put them into operation to produce specific numerical targets for all countries, for all five-year budget periods of the 21st century. The formulas are made precise through the development of three factors: a short-term Progressive Reductions Factor, a medium-term Latecomer Catch-up Factor, and a long-run Gradual Equalization Factor. The result is a set of actual numerical targets for all countries for the remainder of the century (presented in Table 2.1). These are then fed into the WITCH model, by Valentina Bosetti, a co-author of that model, to see the economic and environmental consequences. International trading plays an important role. The framework is flexible enough that one can tinker with a parameter here or there—for example if the economic cost borne by a particular country is deemed too high or the environmental progress deemed too low—without having to abandon the entire formulas framework.

Emission targets for all countries: rules to guide the formulas

All developing countries that have any ability to measure emissions would be asked to agree immediately to emission targets that do not exceed their projected BAU baseline trajectory going forward. The objective of getting developing countries committed to these targets would be to forestall emissions leakage and to limit the extent to which their firms enjoy a competitive advantage over carbon-constrained competitors in the countries that have already agreed to targets below BAU under the Kyoto Protocol. (We expect that the developing countries would, in most cases, receive payments for permits and thus emit less than their BAU baseline.) Most countries in Africa would probably be exempted for some years from any kind of commitment, even to BAU targets, until they had better capacity to monitor emissions.

One must acknowledge that BAU paths are neither easily ascertained nor immutable. Countries may "high-ball" their BAU estimates in order to get more generous targets. Even assuming that estimates are unbiased, important unforeseen economic and technological

EUROPE = Western Europe + Eastern Europe
KOSAU = Korea, South Africa + Australia (all coal-users)
CAJAZ = Canada, Japan + New Zealand
TE = Russia and other Transition Economies
MENA = Middle East + North Africa

SSA = Sub-Saharan Africa, excluding South Africa
SASIA = India and the rest of South Asia
CHINA = People's Republic of China
EASIA = Smaller countries of East Asia
LACA = Latin America + the Caribbean

Table 2.1 *Emission targets for each of 11 regions, according to the formulas* (version in which developing countries take on sub-BAU targets somewhat earlier)

	Target Absolute (tons C, thousand millions)	USA	WESTERN EUROPE	EASTERN EUROPE	KOSAU	CAJAZ	TE
2005	1	unlimited	unlimited	unlimited	unlimited	unlimited	Unlimited
2010	2	1.87591	0.88556	0.22849	0.39768	0.57841	0.83501
2015	3	1.94157	0.83051	0.20819	0.42442	0.55573	0.91841
2020	4	1.30761	0.77407	0.18929	0.44852	0.37796	0.86844
2025	5	1.20331	0.69464	0.16579	0.39051	0.33085	0.81847
2030	6	1.16946	0.62428	0.14504	0.34938	0.28811	0.78070
2035	7	0.99089	0.55197	0.12448	0.30825	0.24575	0.74293
2040	8	0.87106	0.47851	0.10454	0.29015	0.20451	0.70293
2045	9	0.70636	0.40449	0.08551	0.27206	0.16478	0.66294
2050	10	0.61066	0.32972	0.06741	0.23973	0.12656	0.61993

Table 2.1 (*cont.*)

Target Absolute (tons C, thousand millions)		USA	WESTERN EUROPE	EASTERN EUROPE	KOSAU	CAJAZ	TE
2055	11	0.47577	0.26596	0.06289	0.20776	0.09307	0.57693
2060	12	0.36873	0.21539	0.05837	0.17718	0.06799	0.53787
2065	13	0.28016	0.17425	0.05385	0.14718	0.04866	0.49881
2070	14	0.21128	0.14247	0.04933	0.11754	0.03470	0.45995
2075	15	0.15125	0.11573	0.04481	0.10556	0.02353	0.42109
2080	16	0.14177	0.11158	0.04029	0.10221	0.02185	0.38258
2085	17	0.13229	0.10742	0.03577	0.09887	0.02017	0.34407
2090	18	0.12280	0.10327	0.03125	0.09552	0.01849	0.32559
2095	19	0.11332	0.09911	0.02673	0.09218	0.01681	0.30711
2100	20	0.10384	0.09496	0.02221	0.08883	0.01513	0.25166

Table 2.1 (*cont.*)

Target per capita: Emi/cap (ton C)	USA	EUROPE	KOSAU	CAJAZ	TE
2005					
2010	5.95988	2.19314	1.91504	2.39863	1.63613
2015	5.90006	2.034108	1.70965	2.55284	1.56933
2020	3.81659	1.88247	1.52749	2.70695	1.06864
2025	3.38963	1.682114	1.31882	2.37698	0.93998
2030	3.19303	1.508378	1.14260	2.15334	0.82547
2035	2.63145	1.333237	0.97673	1.92996	0.71156
2040	2.25701	1.15741	0.82086	1.85037	0.59959
2045	1.79058	0.981416	0.67433	1.77042	0.49047
2050	1.51726	0.803789	0.53520	1.59314	0.38363
2055	1.16172	0.67294	0.50273	1.40777	0.28689
2060	0.88719	0.566716	0.47000	1.22254	0.21299
2065	0.66602	0.478019	0.43706	1.03310	0.15485
2070	0.49756	0.407192	0.40392	0.83854	0.11212
2075	0.35381	0.345552	0.37053	0.76486	0.07719
2080	0.33028	0.331652	0.33680	0.75175	0.07275
2085	0.30776	0.317507	0.30265	0.73761	0.06815
2090	0.28606	0.30306	0.26792	0.72246	0.06339
2095	0.26502	0.288251	0.23247	0.70622	0.05847
2100	0.24445	0.27301	0.19615	0.68884	0.05338

Table 2.1 (*cont.*)

Target relative to 1990	USA	EUROPE	KOSAU	CAJAZ	TE
2005					
2010	1.29911	0.923116	0.98322	0.89166	0.61078
2015	1.34458	0.860684	0.89587	0.95161	0.58683
2020	0.90555	0.798252	0.81453	1.00565	0.39911
2025	0.83331	0.712968	0.71343	0.87559	0.34937
2030	0.80987	0.637466	0.62411	0.78337	0.30423
2035	0.68621	0.560523	0.53567	0.69115	0.25950
2040	0.60322	0.483127	0.44985	0.65057	0.21595
2045	0.48917	0.40602	0.36795	0.60999	0.17400
2050	0.42290	0.32907	0.29009	0.53751	0.13364
2055	0.32948	0.272495	0.27064	0.46583	0.09828
2060	0.25535	0.226842	0.25118	0.39726	0.07179
2065	0.19402	0.189009	0.23173	0.33001	0.05139
2070	0.14632	0.158928	0.21228	0.26354	0.03664
2075	0.10475	0.133029	0.19283	0.23668	0.02485
2080	0.09818	0.125841	0.17338	0.22918	0.02308
2085	0.09161	0.118652	0.15393	0.22168	0.02130
2090	0.08504	0.111463	0.13447	0.21418	0.01953
2095	0.07848	0.104275	0.11502	0.20668	0.01775
2100	0.07191	0.097086	0.09557	0.19918	0.01598

Target relative to BAU	USA	WESTERN EUROPE	EASTERN EUROPE	KOSAU	CAJAZ	TE
2005	1			1	1	1
2010	0.93718	0.82136	1.07575	1	0.90573	0.97
2015	0.58125	0.72218	0.90219	1	0.59071	0.9047
2020	0.49896	0.64149	0.75724	0.83061	0.50236	0.81418
2025	0.45683	0.55440	0.61868	0.71465	0.42927	0.7498
2030	0.36735	0.48348	0.51106	0.61113	0.36202	0.69396
2035	0.30826	0.41717	0.41911	0.5613	0.29957	0.64211
2040	0.23974	0.35443	0.33976	0.51626	0.24096	0.59511
2045	0.19949	0.29457	0.27063	0.44799	0.18517	0.54942
2050	0.15017	0.23665	0.20943	0.38312	0.13622	0.50533
2055	0.1121	0.18851	0.19233	0.32055	0.09942	0.4618
2060	0.0824	0.15067	0.17483	0.26209	0.0711	0.42076
2065	0.06037	0.12053	0.15835	0.20668	0.05067	0.38221
2070	0.04218	0.09764	0.14270	0.18386	0.03436	0.34573
2075	0.03874	0.07874	0.12774	0.17688	0.03191	0.3113
2080	0.03557	0.07550	0.11333	0.17042	0.02947	0.27831
2085	0.03266	0.07241	0.09937	0.16462	0.02708	0.26278
2090	0.0302	0.06960	0.08588	0.16046	0.02494	0.24922
2095	0.02781	0.06766	0.07314	0.15639	0.02273	0.20576
2100		0.06572	0.06049			

Table 2.1 (*cont.*)

Target Absolute (tons C, thousand millions)		MENA	SSA	SASIA	CHINA	EASIA	LACA
2005	1	unlimited	unlimited	unlimited	unlimited	unlimited	unlimited
2010	2	0.51177	unlimited	0.41288	1.83009	0.39464	0.49779
2015	3	0.58766	unlimited	0.51088	2.08354	0.48358	0.58216
2020	4	0.65678	unlimited	0.63579	2.41191	0.57966	0.67417
2025	5	0.72000	0.11618	0.78210	2.78142	0.67840	0.77043
2030	6	0.65952	0.13962	0.94549	2.57781	0.77640	0.86843
2035	7	0.60771	0.16584	1.12277	2.27298	0.87116	0.75977
2040	8	0.60473	0.19496	1.31222	2.11931	0.96049	0.71027
2045	9	0.60176	0.22704	1.50976	1.94741	1.04308	0.66078
2050	10	0.59414	0.25983	1.40956	1.85137	0.86258	0.63716
2055	11	0.58653	0.26227	1.38141	1.79709	0.72852	0.57931
2060	12	0.57226	0.26470	1.35326	1.74282	0.66888	0.51555
2065	13	0.55800	0.26714	1.28759	1.68854	0.61368	0.42716
2070	14	0.52633	0.26957	1.21498	1.63427	0.55429	0.37107
2075	15	0.49466	0.26753	1.11969	1.58000	0.51749	0.36319
2080	16	0.47001	0.24386	0.94502	1.52572	0.48068	0.35531
2085	17	0.44535	0.23956	0.87403	1.47145	0.45211	0.34742
2090	18	0.40085	0.22707	0.73042	1.41717	0.42353	0.33954
2095	19	0.35634	0.22707	0.73042	1.36290	0.38115	0.33166
2100	20	0.35634	0.22707	0.73042	1.30863	0.33877	0.32377

Target per capita
Emi/ cap (ton C)

	MENA	SSA	SASIA	CHINA	EASIA	LACA
2005						
2010	2.36325		unlimited	0.30372	2.65865	0.70466
2015	2.39601		unlimited	0.36574	2.86261	0.81691
2020	2.10619		unlimited	0.44466	3.15812	0.93292
2025	1.86509	0.61237	0.05850	0.53767	3.49364	1.04729
2030	1.68639	0.50976	0.06711	0.64429	3.12618	1.15753
2035	1.53171	0.43006	0.07666	0.76506	2.67853	1.26318
2040	1.39177	0.39474	0.08710	0.90017	2.44300	1.36319
2045	1.26822	0.36505	0.09856	1.04778	2.20932	1.45799
2050	1.15372	0.33747	0.11028	0.99380	2.07893	1.19443
2055	1.05095	0.31442	0.10931	0.98961	2.00366	1.00215
2060	0.96373	0.29188	0.10881	0.98516	1.93479	0.91666
2065	0.88344	0.27300	0.10879	0.95269	1.87182	0.84028
2070	0.80924	0.24903	0.10925	0.91379	1.81427	0.76053
2075	0.73967	0.22822	0.10839	0.85613	1.76170	0.71361
2080	0.67432	0.21319	0.09923	0.73469	1.71366	0.66818
2085	0.61160	0.20025	0.09834	0.69100	1.66976	0.63538
2090	0.58662	0.18015	0.09448	0.58731	1.62959	0.60358
2095	0.56369	0.16138	0.09621	0.59741	1.59275	0.55244
2100	0.47295	0.16396	0.09843	0.60776	1.55886	0.50085

Table 2.1 (cont.)

Target relative to 1990	MENA	SSA	SASIA	CHINA	EASIA	LACA
2005						
2010	2.67631	14.41159	unlimited	0.49685	14.52452	1.33324
2015	2.94363	16.54868	unlimited	0.61478	16.53603	1.63372
2020	2.78346	18.49511	unlimited	0.76509	19.14214	1.95831
2025	2.62330	20.27541	0.57515	0.94116	22.07476	2.29189
2030	2.50224	18.57228	0.69119	1.13777	20.45881	2.62297
2035	2.38119	17.11319	0.82099	1.35111	18.03953	2.94311
2040	2.25299	17.02942	0.96515	1.57909	16.81995	3.24490
2045	2.12480	16.94566	1.12396	1.81680	15.45561	3.52392
2050	1.98697	16.73121	1.28630	1.69622	14.69338	2.91413
2055	1.84914	16.51675	1.29836	1.66234	14.26264	2.46123
2060	1.72395	16.11511	1.31041	1.62847	13.83189	2.25973
2065	1.59877	15.71346	1.32247	1.54945	13.40114	2.07324
2070	1.47421	14.82157	1.33452	1.46207	12.97040	1.87260
2075	1.34965	13.92968	1.32442	1.34740	12.53965	1.74826
2080	1.22622	13.23548	1.20724	1.13720	12.10891	1.62393
2085	1.10279	12.54129	1.18594	1.05178	11.67816	1.52738
2090	1.04355	11.28795	1.12410	0.87897	11.24742	1.43084
2095	0.98431	10.03461	1.12410	0.87897	10.81667	1.28767
2100	0.80660	10.03461	1.12410	0.87897	10.38592	1.14451

Target relative to BAU	MENA	SSA	SASIA	CHINA	EASIA	LACA
2005	1	1	1	1	1	1
2010	1	1	1	1	1	1
2015	1	1	1	1	1	1
2020	1	1	1	1	1	1
2025	1	1	1	1	1	1
2030	0.84599	1	1	0.81467	1	0.78628
2035	0.72519	1	1	0.64230	1	0.66805
2040	0.67434	1	1	0.54438	1	0.57042
2045	0.62911	1	1	0.46150	1	0.50921
2050	0.58430	0.99135	0.82410	0.41023	0.77162	0.43097
2055	0.54408	0.87452	0.72261	0.37592	0.61422	0.35762
2060	0.49920	0.77259	0.63130	0.34285	0.53174	0.2777
2065	0.45884	0.68832	0.54289	0.31506	0.46395	0.22726
2070	0.40912	0.61854	0.46904	0.29151	0.40179	0.21065
2075	0.36464	0.55153	0.40073	0.27137	0.36249	0.1962
2080	0.32977	0.45580	0.31732	0.25398	0.32782	0.18365
2085	0.29861	0.40966	0.27847	0.23879	0.30230	0.17309
2090	0.25850	0.35937	0.22346	0.22562	0.28003	0.16574
2095	0.22461	0.33996	0.21831	0.21508	0.25333	0.15933
2100	0.22041	0.32412	0.21513	0.20550	0.22748	

developments could occur between 2010 and 2020 that will shift the BAU trajectory for the 2020s, for example. Any number of unpredictable events have already occurred in the years since 1990; they include German reunification, the 1997–1998 East Asia crisis, the boom in the BRIC countries (Brazil, Russia, India, and China), the sharp rise in world oil prices up until 2008, and the world financial crisis of 2007–2009. A first measure to deal with the practical difficulty of setting the BAU path is to specify in the Kyoto-successor treaty that estimates must be generated by an independent international expert body, not by national authorities. A second measure, once the first has been assured, is to provide for updates of the BAU paths every decade. To omit such a provision—that is, to hold countries for the rest of the century to the paths that had been estimated in 2010—would in practice virtually guarantee that any country that achieves very high economic growth rates in the future will eventually drop out of the agreement, because staying in would mean incurring costs far in excess of 5 percent of income. Allowing for periodic adjustments to the BAU baseline does risk undermining the incentive for carbon-saving investments, on the logic that such investments would reduce future BAU paths and thus reduce future target allocations. This risk is the same as the risk of encouraging countries to ramp up their emissions, which we specified above to be axiomatically ruled out by any viable proposal. That is why the formula gives decreasing weight to BAU in later budget periods and why we introduce a Latecomer Catch-up Factor (explained below), which tethers all countries to their 1990 emission levels in the medium run.

Countries are expected to agree to the next step, quantitative targets that entail specific cuts below BAU, at a time determined by their circumstances. In our initial simulations, the choice of year for introducing an obligation actually to cut emissions was generally guided by two thresholds: when a country's average per capita income exceeds $3000 per year and/or when its per capita annual emissions approach 1 ton or more.[8] But we found that starting dates had to be further modified in order to satisfy our constraints regarding the distribution of economic losses.

As already noted, this approach assigns emission targets in a way that is more sensitive to political realities than is typical of other proposed

[8] Baer *et al.* (2008) suggest an income threshold of $7,500 per person per year.

target paths, which are constructed either on the basis of a cost-benefit optimization or to deliver a particular environmental and/or ethical goal. Specifically, numerical targets are based (a) on commitments that political leaders in various key countries have already proposed or adopted, as of early 2009, and (b) on formulas designed to assure late-comer countries that the emission cuts they are being asked to make represent no more than their fair share, in that they correspond to the sacrifices that other countries before them have already made.

Finally comes the other important concession to practical political realities: if the simulation in any period turns out to impose on any country an economic cost of more than $X\%$ of income (where X is for the purposes of this analysis taken to be 5 percent), we assume that this country drops out. Dropping out could involve either explicit renunciation of the treaty or massive failure to meet the quantitative targets. For now, our assumption is that in any such scenario, other countries would follow by dropping out one by one, and the whole scheme would eventually unravel.[9] This unraveling would occur much earlier if private actors rationally perceived that at some point in the future major players will face such high economic costs that compliance will break down. In this case, the future carbon prices that are built into most models' compliance trajectories will lack credibility, private actors will not make investment decisions that reflect those prices today, based on them, and the effort will fail in the first period. Therefore, our approach to any scenario in which any major player suffers economic losses greater than $X\%$ would be to go back and adjust some of the parameters of the emission formulas, so that costs are lower and this is no longer the case.

We hope by these mechanisms to achieve political viability: non-negative economic gains in the early years for developing countries, average costs over the course of the century below 1 percent of income per annum, and protection for every country against losses in any period as large, or larger than, 5 percent of income. Only if they achieve political viability are announcements of future cuts credible. And only credible

---

[9] A good topic for future efforts to extend this research is to apply game theory, allowing some relatively less important countries to drop out without necessarily sinking the whole scheme. That is, if the economic damage to remaining members arising from the defections, and the environmental damage, were not too great, remaining countries might continue to participate rather than retaliate by likewise dropping out.

announcements of future cuts will send firms the long-term price signals
and incentives needed to guide investment decisions today.

Guidelines from policies and goals already announced by national leaders

Our model produces country-specific numeric emission targets for
every fifth year: 2012, 2017, 2022, etc. For each five-year budget
period, such as the Kyoto period 2008–2012, computations are based
on the average of the starting year and ending year.

The European Union

The EU emissions target for 2008–2012 was agreed at Kyoto: 8
percent below 1990 levels. In the second 2015–2020 period (for
simplicity we choose the year 2017), the EU target is the one that
Brussels announced in January 2008 and confirmed in December
2008:[10] namely, 20 percent below 1990 levels. On the one hand, as
with other targets publicly supported by politicians in Europe and
elsewhere, skepticism is appropriate regarding EU member countries'
willingness to make the sacrifices necessary to achieve this target.[11]
On the other hand, however, the European Union's commitment to
this number was not conditional on other countries joining in. Indeed
the European Union has said it would cut emissions 30 percent below
1990 levels if other countries joined in. So in this sense we are being
conservative in choosing the 20 percent target.

For the third period (2022–2027), and thereafter up to the eighth
period (2048–2052), the EU targets progress in equal increments to
a 50 percent cut below 1990 levels: In other words, targets relative
to 1990 emissions start at 25 percent below, and then progress to 30
percent, 35 percent, 40 percent, 45 percent, and 50 percent below.

---

[10] *Financial Times*, Jan. 2, 2009, p. 5.

[11] It is not entirely clear to Americans that even Europe will meet its Kyoto targets.
Perhaps the European Union will need to cover its shortfall with purchases of
emission permits from other countries. European emissions were reduced in
the early 1990s by coincidental events: Britain moved away from coal under
Margaret Thatcher and Germany with reunification in 1990 acquired dirty
power plants that were easy to clean up. But Americans who claim on this
basis that the European Union has not yet taken any serious steps go too far.
Ellerman and Buchner (2007, pp. 26–29) show that the difference between allocations and emissions in 2005 and 2006 was probably in part attributable to
abatement measures implemented in response to the positive price of carbon.

Japan, Canada, and New Zealand

These three Pacific countries are assigned the Kyoto goal of a 6 percent reduction below 1990 levels. Of all ratifiers, Canada is probably the farthest from achieving its Kyoto goal.[12] But Japan dominates this country grouping in size. We assume that by 2010 the United States has taken genuine measures, which helps motivate these three countries to get more serious than they have been to date. In a small concession to realism, we assume that they do not hit the numerical target until 2012 (versus hitting it on average over the 2008–2012 budget period).[13]

Japan's then-Prime Minister, Yasuo Fukuda, on June 9, 2008, announced a decision to cut Japanese emissions 60–80 percent by mid-century and successor Taro Aso on June 10, 2009, announced a plan to cut 15 percent by 2020.[14] We interpret these targets as cuts of 10 percent every five years between 2010 and 2050, computed logarithmically. The cumulative cuts are 80 percent in logarithmic terms, or 51 percent in absolute terms (i.e., to 49 percent of the year–2010 emissions level).

The United States

A series of bills to cap US GHG emissions were proposed in Congress in 2007 and early 2008.[15] It is possible that some version of such legislation might pass by 2010.

The Bingaman–Specter bill would have reduced emissions to 2006 levels by 2020 and to 1990 levels by 2030, but with a cap or "safety valve" on the price of carbon. The Lieberman–Warner bill was more aggressive.[16] It would have begun by reducing emissions in 2012 to below 2005 levels and would have tightened the emissions cap gradually each year thereafter, such that by the year 2050, total emissions

---

[12] The current government's plan calls for reducing Canadian emissions in 2020 by 20 percent below 2006 levels (which translates to 2.7 percent below 1990 levels) and in 2050 by 60–70 percent below 2006 levels. ("FACTBOX—Greenhouse gas curbs from Australia to India," Sept. 5, 2008, Reuters. www.alertnet.org/thenews/newsdesk/L5649578.htm.)

[13] In 2007, Japanese Prime Minister Shinzo Abe supported an initiative to half global emissions by 2050. *(Financial Times*, May 25). But ahead of the 2008 G8 Summit, Japan declined to match the EU's commitment to cut its emissions 20 percent by 2020 *(FT*, April 24, 2008, p. 3).

[14] *FT*, June 10, 2008, p. 6; and Associated Press, June 10, 2009, respectively.

[15] The bills are conveniently summarized in Table 1A in Hufbauer, Charnovitz and Kim (2009).

[16] S. 2191: America's Climate Security Act of 2007.

would be held to 30 percent of 2012 levels—in other words, a 70 percent reduction from emissions levels at the start date of the policy.[17] If such a bill were not passed until 2010 or so, the goal of achieving 2005 levels by 2012 (let alone a 4 percent reduction) would for all practical purposes be impossible to achieve. The bill's sponsors would have to adjust 2012 to BAU levels, which are projected to be 39 percent above 1990 levels, or 33 percent logarithmically (i.e., 1990 emissions were 28 percent below current 2012 BAU projections), so the 2050 target would be 42 percent below 1990 levels.[18] A slightly revised "manager's" version of the Lieberman–Warner bill earned significant congressional support in June 2008: though it did not garner a large enough majority to become law, the vote was widely considered an important step forward politically for the activist camp. It was presumed that a new bill in the next session would probably look similar and, with a new president, would have better chances of success.[19]

If taken at face value, with 2012 emissions returned to 2005 levels or lower, then the Lieberman–Warner targets would have shaved off another 13 percent from the target path, so that emissions in 2050 would be 55 percent below 1990 levels.[20] There are three respects in which it might be naïve to accept these political aspirations at face value. First, it is not realistic to think that the United States could go from the steady emission growth rates of 1990–2007 (when emissions increased, on average, by 1.4 percent per year) to immediate rapid cuts, without *passing through an intermediate phase* of slowing, and then peaking or plateauing, before reversing (a trajectory some have

[17] Section 1201, pp. 30–32. (The percentage is measured non-logarithmically.)

[18] See, for example, http://theclimategroup.org/index.php/news_and_events/ news_and_comment/carbon_trading_high_hopes_for_lieberman_warner. (The number is 54 percent, measured logarithmically. This is the preferred way of defining percentage changes. Logarithms are too technical for non-specialist audiences. But measuring changes non-logarithmically has the undesirable property that a 50 percent increase [to 1.50] followed by a 50 percent reduction [to 0.75] does not get you back to your starting point [1.00].)

[19] This chapter was originally written during the 2008 US presidential election campaign, in which both major presidential candidates supported GHG reduction measures along the lines of recent congressional bills. John McCain advocated a 2050 emissions target of 60 percent below 1990 levels, or 66 percent below 2005 levels, close to Lieberman–Warner (*Washington Post*, May 13, 2008, p. A14; and *FT*, May 13, 2008, p.4). Barack Obama endorsed a more aggressive target of reducing 2050 emissions 80 percent below 1990 levels (*FT*, Oct. 17, 2008).

[20] That is 67 percent logarithmically. Or a cut of about 62 percent according to J.R. Pegg, *Environmental News Service*, October 2007.

called "slow-stop-reverse"). Second is the point that many voters and politicians who have supported recent legislative proposals will be unlikely to support the measures that would be needed to attain the targets contained in those proposals in an economically efficient way—that is, by raising the price of fossil fuels through such measures as a carbon tax or tradable permits (without giving away extra free permits). Third, the Lieberman–Warner target is somewhat more aggressive than Europe's goal, measured relative to 1990 emissions, and implies a much more aggressive rate of emissions decline than Europe's over the period 2012–2050. So far, American support for serious action has lagged behind Europe's.

On the other hand, if China and other developing countries accept quantitative targets, as foreseen under this plan, this will boost domestic American support for tough action. In addition, one could argue that because there is more "fat" in US emissions, it should be easier to achieve reductions than in Europe or Japan. The terminal level of emissions in 2050 under the formula would still probably be substantially higher than Europe's, relative to population or GDP.

We assume that the average annual emissions growth rate is cut in half during the period 2008–2012, to 0.7 percent per year or 3.5 percent cumulatively, so that emissions in 2012 are 31.5 percent above 1990 levels.[21] At that point, we assume emissions plateau—growth is held to zero—for the period 2012–2017. These near-term targets are substantially more aggressive than those in the American Clean-Energy and Security Act of 2009 (ACES Act), which was passed by the House of Representatives on June 26, 2009, before consideration by the Senate. The ACES Act specifies that US emission allowances continue to grow at 3 percent per year from 2012 to 2017.[22] *Then* we implement the rest of the Lieberman–Warner formula, such that emissions in 2050 reach a level that is 67 percent below 1990 levels. Using our postponed base this is 98.5 percent below 2012 levels, logarithmically. Spread over 38 years, this implies sustained reductions of 2.6 percent per year on average, or 13 percent every five years. This is a more aggressive rate of reduction over 2017–2050 than Lieberman–

---

[21] That is, 27 percent logarithmically.

[22] Title VII, Part C, Section 721, sub-section (*e*) of HR 2454, also known as the Waxman-Markey bill. The preceding draft of the bill, proposed March 31, 2009, called for emissions targets that increased at about 2 percent per year from 2012 to 2017, peaked in 2021, and hit the same 2050 level as in the version passed by the House in June.

Warner, but substantially less aggressive than the ACES Act (5 percent per year rate of reduction), the reverse ranking of the plans' pre-2017 target paths.

Australia
Canberra has been reluctant to take strong actions because the country is so dependent on coal. In July of 2008, however, Australian Prime Minister Kevin Rudd announced plans to cut emissions to 60 percent below 2000 levels by 2050.[23] In the regional groupings of our model, Australia is classified together with South Korea and South Africa.

Korea and South Africa
Until recently it looked unlikely that any "non-Annex I" countries would consider taking on serious cuts below a BAU growth path within the next decade. But in March 2008, the new president of South Korea, Myung-bak Lee, "tabled a plan to cap emissions at current levels over the first Kyoto period."[24] This was an extraordinarily ambitious target in light of Korea's economic growth rate. He also "vowed his country would slash emissions in half by 2050,"[25] like the industrialized countries—of which Korea is now one. Emissions have risen 90 percent since 1990 and it is hard to imagine any country applying the brakes so sharply as to switch instantly from 5 percent annual growth in emissions to zero.[26] Perhaps President Lee thinks he can offset growth in South Korean emissions by paying North Korea to reforest. We choose to interpret the Korean plan to flatten emissions as covering a period that stretches out over the next fourteen years, so that in 2022 the level of emissions is the same as in 2007.[27]

---

[23] A July 16, 2008, government "green paper," *Carbon Pollution Reduction Scheme*, reported details on implementation via a domestic cap-and-trade program. Rudd's initiative appears to have domestic political support (*The Economist*, July 26, 2008, p. 52). The government went on to set targets of 15 percent above 1990 levels by 2020 (*FT*, Jan. 2, 2009, p. 5) and then 5 percent below 2000 levels by 2020 (*Economist*, June 6, 2009, p. 39).

[24] "South Korea Plans to Cap Emissions," *International Herald Tribune*, March 21, 2008.

[25] "South Korea: Developing Countries Move Toward Targets," Lisa Friedman, *ClimateWire*, Oct. 3, 2008.

[26] This did not stop some environmental groups from criticizing the plan as not sufficiently ambitious. Such criticisms may give political leaders second thoughts about announcing any specific measures at all, as opposed to sticking with banal generalities.

[27] One could note, first, that President Lee came to office setting a variety of ambi-

Meanwhile, South Africa has evidently proposed that its emissions would peak by 2025 and begin declining by 2030.[28]

China

Getting China to agree to binding commitments is the *sine qua non* of any successful post-Kyoto plan. Evidently China has announced plans to start cutting GHG emissions in 2030. Presumably that means relative to BAU, rather than in absolute terms.[29] Of course 2030 is later than industrialized countries would like. The country is expected to cross the threshold of 1 ton of emissions per capita around 2014 and the threshold of $3000 in annual per capita income by 2022. A standard five- or ten-year lag between treaty signing and budget period would point to a first-cuts budget period around 2024–2027. But persuading Beijing to move the 2030 date up by five years is not as critical as persuading it to accept some quantitative target in 2010, even if that target only reflects BAU. The reason is that if China does not adopt some binding target in the near term, the United States and most developing countries will not join, and then the entire enterprise will be undone.

The key questions thus become (1) how to determine the magnitude of China's cuts in its first budget period—that is, for the first period in which it is asked to make cuts below BAU; (2) how to determine Korea's cuts in its second budget period; and (3) how to set targets for everyone else? (The other regions are Latin America—which logically should act after Korea but before China in light of its stage of development—Russia, Middle East/North Africa, Southeast Asia, India/South Asia, and Africa.) Our general guiding principle is to ask countries only to do what is analogous to what has been done by others who have gone before them. To put this general principle into practice, we apply three factors.

---

tious goals beyond his power to bring about, especially for economic growth, and second that his popularity quickly plummeted. At the time of writing, his ability to persuade his countrymen to take serious measures was in question.

[28] *ClimateWire*, Oct. 3, 2008. Statements from environmental or foreign ministries do not necessarily carry a lot of weight, if they have not been vetted by finance or economics ministries let alone issued by heads of government or approved by parliaments. An example would be Argentina's announcement of a target in 1998.

[29] This was China's position in talks near Berlin with five big emerging nations (China, India, South Africa, Brazil and Mexico), ahead of the June 2007 G8 summit in Germany, according to Germany's environment minister (*FT*, Dec. 3, 2007).

Guidelines for formulas that ask developing countries to accept "fair" targets, analogous to those who have gone before

This section discusses the three factors for determining "fair" emissions targets for developing countries. The three factors are additive (logarithmically).

We call the first the **Progressive Reductions Factor**. It is based on the pattern of emission reductions (relative to BAU) assigned to countries under the Kyoto Protocol, as a function of income per capita. This pattern is illustrated in Figure 2.1, which comes from the data as they were reported at that time. Other things equal, richer countries are asked to make more severe cuts relative to BAU, the status quo from which they are departing in the first period. Specifically, each 1 percent difference in income per capita, measured relative to EU income in 1997, increases the abatement obligation by 0.14 percent, where the abatement obligation is measured in terms of reductions from BAU relative to the EU cuts agreed at Kyoto. Normally, at least in their early budget periods, most countries' incomes will be below what the Europeans had in 1997, so that this factor dictates milder cuts relative to BAU than Europe made at Kyoto. In fact the resulting targets are likely to reflect a "growth path"—that is, they will allow for actual emission increases relative to the preceding periods. The formula is:

PRF expressed as country cuts vs. BAU
= EU's Kyoto commitment for 2008 relative to its BAU + .14 * (gap between the country's income per capita and the EU's 2007 income per capita).

The parameter (0.14) was suggested by ordinary least squares (OLS) regression estimates on the data shown in Figure 2.1. Other parameters could be chosen instead, if the parties to a new agreement wanted to increase or decrease the degree of progressivity.

The **Latecomer Catch-up Factor** is the second element in the formula. Latecomers are defined as those countries that have not ratified Kyoto or for which Kyoto did not set quantitative targets. (Perhaps it should also include those like Canada that ratified the treaty but, based on current trends, are not expected to meet the goal.) These countries should not be rewarded by permanently readjusting their targets to a higher baseline. Aside from notions of fairness, such re-basing would give all latecomers an incentive to ramp up their emissions before signing on to binding targets, or at a minimum would undercut any

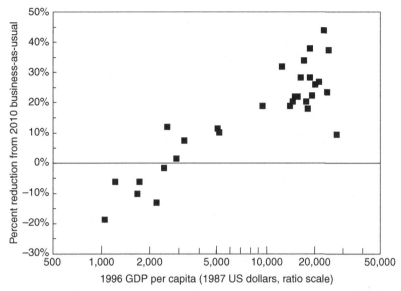

Figure 2.1. The emissions cuts agreed at Kyoto were progressive with respect to income, when expressed relative to BAU
(*Sources:* The World Bank, the US Energy Information Administration, and national communications to the UNFCCC)

socially-conscious incentives they might otherwise introduce to reduce emissions unilaterally in the time period before they join the system. Thus the Latecomer Catch-up factor is designed to close gradually the gap between the starting point of the latecomers and their 1990 emission levels. It is parameterized according to the numbers implicit in the Lieberman proposal to bring US emissions to 70 percent below 1990 levels by 2050 and the Lee proposal to flatten South Korea's emissions over a period beginning in 2008. In other words, countries are asked to move gradually in the direction of 1990 emissions in the same way that the United States and Korea under current proposals will have done before them.

The formula for a country's Latecomer Catch-up Factor (LCF) is as follows. Further percentage cuts (relative to BAU plus a Progressive Reductions Factor) are proportional to how far emissions have been allowed to rise above 1990 levels by the time the country joins in. That is, it is given by:

$$LCF = \alpha + \lambda \text{ (percentage gap between country's lagged emissions and 1990 emissions).}$$

The parameter λ represents the firmness with which latecomers are pulled back toward their 1990 emission levels. The value of λ implicit for Europe at the time the Kyoto Protocol was negotiated was sufficient to pull the EU-average below its 1990 level. But to calibrate this formula, the most relevant countries are not European (since the Europeans are not latecomers), but rather the United States and Korea, since these are the only countries among those that did not commit themselves to Kyoto targets whose political leaders have said explicitly what targets they are willing to accept in the second budget period. The parameters α and λ were chosen as the unique solutions to two simultaneous equations representing the US target in bills sponsored by Senator Lieberman and the Korean target (a flattening of emissions being interpreted here as holding absolute emissions in 2022 equal to 2007 levels). The parameters then work out to

$$\alpha = 0.2115 \text{ and } \lambda = -0.3400$$

Thus:

LCF = 0.2115 − 0.3400 log(country's current emissions / country's 1990 emissions).[30]

The third element is the **Gradual Equalization Factor** (GEF). Even though developing countries under our proposal benefit from not being asked for abatement efforts until after the rich countries have begun to act, and face milder reduction requirements, they will still complain that it is the rich countries that originally created an environmental problem for which the poor will disproportionately bear the costs, rather than the other way around. Such complaints are not unreasonable. If we stopped with the first two factors, the richer countries would be left with the permanent right to emit more GHGs, every year in perpetuity. This seems unfair.

In the short run, pointing out the gap in per capita targets is simply not going to alter the outcome. The poor countries will have to live with it. Calls for the rich countries to cut per capita emissions rapidly, in the direction of poor-country levels, ignore the fact that the economic costs of such a requirement would be so astronomical that no rich country would ever agree to it. The same goes for calls for massive

[30] If Korea were to back away from its president's commitment in light of recent economic difficulties, but some other important middle-income country were to step up to the plate with explicit and specific numerical targets, then the calculation could be redone.

transfer payments from the rich to the poor (as in a proposal by the Group of 77 developing countries).

When one is talking about a lead time of 50 to 100 years, however, the situation changes. With time to adjust, the economic costs are not as impossibly high, and it is reasonable to ask rich countries to bear their full share of the burden. Furthermore, over a time horizon this long some of the poor countries will in any case become rich (and possible vice versa).

Accordingly, during each decade of the second half of the century, the formula includes an equity factor that moves per capita emissions in each country a small step in the direction of the global average. This means downward in the case of the rich countries and upward in the case of the poor countries. Asymptotically, the repeated application of this factor would eventually leave all countries with equal emissions per capita, although corresponding national targets would not necessarily converge fully by 2100.[31]

The parameter (δ) for the speed of adjustment in the direction of the world average was initially chosen to match the rate at which the EU's already-announced goals for 2045–2050 converge to the world average. This number is $\delta = 0.1$ per decade, which is also very similar to the rate of convergence implicit in the goals set by the Lieberman bills for the United States during 2045–2050. Thus:

$$GEF = -0.1 \text{ (percentage gap between country's lagged emissions per capita and the world's)}.$$

We expected to have to adjust the δ parameter, and indeed to add a fourth parameter for the "aggressiveness" of global emissions targets, in order to ensure that no single country was confronted with costs above our threshold constraint while still achieving a relevant global environmental goal in 2100. By lucky coincidence, our initial method of computing δ satisfied the economic objectives and delivered year-2100 atmospheric CO_2 concentrations of 500 ppm. In future extensions of this research—where, for example, we will try to hit a

---

[31] Zhang (2008) and others, motivated by a rights-based approach, propose that countries "contract and converge" to targets that reflect equal emissions per capita. The Greenhouse Development Rights approach of Baer *et al.* (2008), as extended by Cao (2008), emphasizes, from a philosophical standpoint, the allocation of emission rights at the individual level, though these authors apparently recognize that, in practice, individual targets would have to be aggregated and implemented at the national level.

year-2100 goal of 450 ppm—we will have to adjust δ and probably will need to add an aggressiveness parameter, while also adjusting some countries' start dates. One possibility is to write an algorithm that searches over these parameters so as to find values that minimize the threshold of economic cost to any given country for any given year-2100 environmental goal.

The formulas are summarized overall as follows:

$$Log\ Target\ (country_{i,t}) = log\ (BAU_{i,t}) - (PCF_{i,t}) + (LCF_{i,t}) + (GEF_{i,t}),$$

where the three factors (except in periods when set $= 0$ as indicated in Table 2.2) are given by:

$$PCF_{i,t} = log\ (emission\ target\ EU_{2008}/\ BAU\ EU_{2008}) + 0.14\ log$$
$$(country\ i\text{'s income/cap}_{t-1}\ /\ EU\ income/cap_{2007});$$
$$LCF_{i,t} = 0.2115 - 0.3400\ log\ (country\ i\text{'s emissions}_{t-1}\ /\ country\ i\text{'s}$$
$$emissions_{1990});$$
$$GEF_{i,t} = -\ 0.1\ log\ (country\ i\text{'s emissions per capita}_{t-1}\ /\ global$$
$$average\ emissions\ per\ capita_{t-1}).$$

The numerical emission target: paths that follow from the formulas

Table 2.1, above, reports the emissions targets produced by the formulas for each of eleven geographical regions, for every period between now and the end of the century. We express the emission targets in several terms:

- in absolute tons (which is what ultimately matters for determining economic and environmental effects),
- in per capita terms (which is necessary for considering any issues of cross-country distribution of burden),
- relative to 1990 levels, which is the baseline used for Kyoto, and which remains relevant in our framework in the form of the Latecomer Catch-up term, and
- relative to the BAU path, which is important for evaluating the sacrifice asked of individual countries as they join the agreement in the early decades.

Table 2.2 *Years when countries are to commit to targets at BAU and then below BAU*

July 2008 Version (a)-Harvard (500 ppm CO_2)—with later targets for developing countries	USA	EUROPE	KOSAU	CAJAZ	TE	MENA	SSA	SASIA	CHINA	EASIA	LACA
Year when they are assumed to commit to TARGET or BAU	2010	2010	2010	2010	2010	2010	2040	2010	2010	2010	2010
Year when they are assumed to commit to TARGET (PCF & LCF) never above BAU	2015	2010	2025	2015	2015	2030	–	2050	2040	–	2035
year when GEF kicks in	2055	2055	2055	2055	2055	2055	–	2055	2055	–	2055
year when PCF and LCF drop out	2055	2055	2075	2055	2090	2100	–	2095	2095	–	2080

Table 2.2 (*cont.*)

July 2008 Version (a)-Harvard (500 ppm CO2)—with later targets for developing countries	USA	EUROPE	KOSAU	CAJAZ	TE	MENA	SSA	SASIA	CHINA	EASIA	LACA
per cap GDP 2010 K$ per person (2005 USD)	46.679	32.572	17.120	40.110	4.833	4.490	0.636	0.892	2.491	1.935	5.606
per cap GDP year of 1st cut, K$ (2005 $)	51.605	32.572	23.521	44.764	5.995	8.104		6.096	12.907		14.679
per cap GDP 2100 (with policy) K$ (2005 $)	146.634	125.884	71.331	125.499	39.331	38.167	7.9608	22.077	52.048	21.566	63.758
per cap GDP 2100 (without policy) K$ (2005 $)	149.440	126.618	72.337	126.707	39.637	39.021	7.447	22.020	54.288	18.062	65.412

	USA	EUROPE	KOSAU	CAAZ	TE	MENA	SSA	SASIA	CHINA	EASIA	LACA
per capita emissions 2010	5.960	2.541	3.333	3.489	2.362	1.448	0.073	0.252	1.346	0.573	0.889
per cap emissions, year of first cut	6.296	2.541	3.740	3.691	2.551	1.684		0.726	2.671		1.401
per cap emissions 2100 (with policy)	0.775	0.641	0.772	0.942	1.285	0.733	0.101	0.236	0.889	0.290	0.672
per cap emissions 2100 (without policy)	8.789	4.222	5.017	5.162	4.315	3.038	0.322	1.472	5.299	1.774	3.004
January 2009 Version (b)-Poznan (500 ppm CO2 only)—with earlier targets for developing countries	2055	2055	2075	2055	2090	2100	2100	2095	2070	2100	2080
year when they are assumed to commit to TARGET or BAU	2010	2010	2010	2010	2010	2010	2040	2010	2010	2010	2010

Table 2.2 (*cont.*)

January 2009 Version (b)—Poznan (500 ppm CO2 only)—with earlier targets for developing countries	USA	EUROPE	KOSAU	CAJAZ	TE	MENA	SSA	SASIA	CHINA	EASIA	LACA
	2055	2055	2075	2055	2090	2100	2100	2095	2070	2100	2080
year when they are assumed to commit to TARGET (PCF & LCF) never above BAU	2015	2010	2025	2015	2015	2025	2050	2050	2030	2050	2035
year when GEF kicks in	2055	2055	2055	2055	2055	2055	2055	2055	2055	2055	2055
year when PCF and LCF drop out											
per cap GDP 2010 K$ per (2005 USD)	46.679	32.572	17.120	40.110	4.833	4.490	0.636	0.892	2.491	1.935	5.606
per cap GDP year of first cut	51.605	32.572	23.521	44.764	5.995	7.061	2.129	6.096	8.242	9.357	14.679

per cap GDP 2100 (with policy)	146.263	125.936	72.181	125.399	39.086	38.342	7.424	22.062	53.399	18.252	64.298
per cap GDP 2100 (without policy)	149.440	126.619	72.337	126.707	39.637	39.021	7.447	22.020	54.288	18.062	65.412
per cap Emissions 2010	5.960	2.541	3.333	3.489	2.362	1.448	0.073	0.252	1.346	0.573	0.889
per cap Emissions year of first cut	6.296	2.541	3.740	3.691	2.551	1.641	0.149	0.726	2.156	1.255	1.401
per cap emissions 2100 (with policy)	0.717	0.616	0.753	0.922	1.246	0.669	0.095	0.219	0.841	0.27	0.633
per cap emissions 2100 (without policy)	8.789	4.222	5.017	5.162	4.315	3.038	0.322	1.472	5.299	1.774	3.004

The eleven regions are:

EUROPE = Old Europe and   KOSAU = Korea, South Africa,
         New Europe   and Australia (3 coal-
US   = United States   users)
CAJAZ   = Canada, Japan, and   TE   = Russia and other
          New Zealand   Transition Economies
MENA   = Middle East and   SSA   = Sub-Saharan Africa
          North Africa   CHINA = PRC
SASIA   = India and the rest of LACA   = Latin America and
          South Asia   the Caribbean
EASIA   = Smaller countries of
          East Asia

In the first version of this exercise, China sells over a gigaton of carbon in 2040. Its permit sales fall off thereafter, as its target kicks in; but Southeast Asian countries take its place, selling similar quantities in the last two decades of the century. Southeast Asia and sub-Saharan Africa registered rather substantial economic gains toward the end of the century.[32] These gains reflect the benefits of being spared emissions cuts and being able to sell permits to richer countries during the period when those countries are already implementing reductions. Some may judge it appropriate that poor countries register net economic gains from the abatement regime, since these are also the countries that will bear the heaviest burden from climate change in any case (by virtue of the fact that most are located nearer the equator and rely on large agricultural sectors). But we judge the massive international transfers that are implicit in this scenario to be highly unsustainable politically. They are not necessary in any case to satisfy the key economic and political constraints laid out at the beginning of this chapter.

Accordingly, subsequent versions of the exercise assign Southeast Asia and Africa emission targets somewhat below BAU in the latter half of the century, with the result that they do not gain so much for the century as a whole. In addition we move forward by ten years the date at which China is asked to take on below-BAU targets and by five years the date at which the Middle East and North African (MENA) countries are asked to do so. An additional reason for this

---

[32] Tables 2.2a and 2.3a here, and the illustrations in Figures 2.2a–2.5a and 2.7 as in Frankel (2008a), report detailed numerical targets by region and year.

change was to reduce the slackening in global targets—observable as a dip in the price of carbon—that would otherwise occur around 2035. Results for the case where the four developing regions are given more stringent (earlier) targets are given in Tables 2.1 and 2.3b, and in the corresponding figures. Table 2.2 summarizes the dates at which all countries are asked to take on BAU targets and then reductions below BAU as governed by the different formula elements discussed previously (i.e., PRF, LCF, and then GEF).

The United States, even more than other rich countries, is currently conspicuous by virtue of its high per capita emissions.[33] But its target path peaks after 2010 and then begins to decline. Emissions in all the rich regions peak by 2015, and then start to decline. Figure 2.2a reports aggregate targets for member countries of the Organisation for Economic Co-operation and Development (OECD). It also shows actual emissions, which decline more gradually than the targets through 2045 because about 1 million metric tons (equal to 1 gigaton or Gt) of carbon permits are purchased on the world market, as is economically efficient, out of roughly 4 Gt. (Permit sales to the richer countries exceed 1 Gt more often in the version where Southeast Asia and Africa are never asked for targets below BAU, and China and MENA start cutting emissions below BAU only at later dates.) Though the OECD countries buy a substantial amount of reductions in the early decades, it is always less than half their total reductions. The share falls off sharply in the second half of the century. We assume no banking.

Emissions in the non-rich countries, the TE group (transition economies), MENA, China, and Latin America all peak in 2040.[34] Emissions in sub-Saharan Africa and the smaller East Asian economies all remain at very low levels throughout the century. Figure 2.3a shows that among non-OECD countries overall, both emissions targets and actual emissions peak in 2040, with the latter substantially below the former. In other words, the poor countries emit below their targets and sell permits to the rest.

Total world emissions peak in 2045 at a little above 10 Gt, in the case where China and MENA are given the later starting points (Figure 2.4a). They peak ten years earlier, and without exceeding 10

---

[33] As shown in Figure 2 of Frankel (2008a). The figure is omitted here to save space.

[34] Figure 2 of HPICA Discussion Paper 08-08.

Table 2.3a *Implied economic cost of emission targets for each of 10 regions with later targets for developing countries*
PDV at discount rate = 5%. Expressed as per cent of GDP

USA	OLDEURO	NEWEURO	KOSAU	CAJAZ	TE	MENA	SSA	SASIA	CHINA
0.55%	0.18%	0.77%	0.22%	0.31%	0.98%	0.62%	-1.33%	-0.35%	0.50%

Table 2.3b *Implied economic cost of emission targets for each of 12 regions with earlier targets for developing countries*
PDV at discount rate = 5%. Expressed as per cent of GDP

USA	WEURO	EEURO	KOSAU	CAJAZ	TE	MENA	SSA	SASIA	CHINA	EASIA	LACA
0.69%	0.26%	0.84%	0.26%	0.46%	0.57%	0.62%	-0.32%	-0.74%	1.14%	-0.47%	0.57%

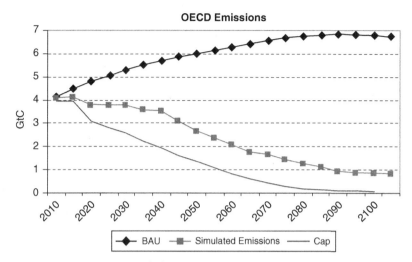

Figure 2.2a. Emissions path for industrialized countries in the aggregate—with later targets for developing countries
Note: Predicted actual emissions exceed caps by amount of permit purchases.

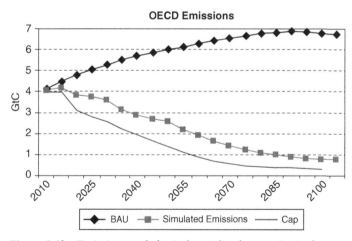

Figure 2.2b. Emissions path for industrialized countries in the aggregate—with earlier targets for developing countries
Note: Predicted actual emissions exceed caps by amount of permit purchases.

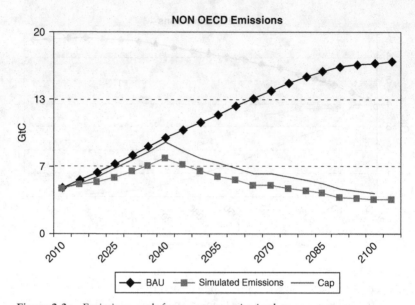

Figure 2.3a. Emissions path for poor countries in the aggregate
—with later targets for developing countries
Note: Predicted actual emissions fall below caps by amount of permit sales.

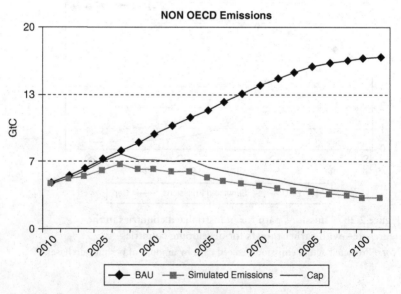

Figure 2.3b. Emissions path for poor countries in the aggregate
—with earlier targets for developing countries
Note: Predicted actual emissions fall below caps by amount of permit sales.

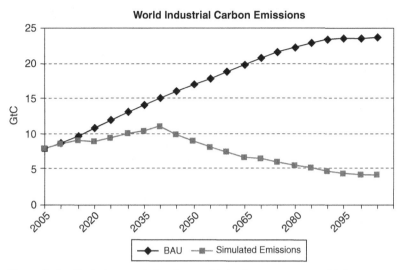

Figure 2.4a. Emissions path for the world, in the aggregate—with later targets for developing countries

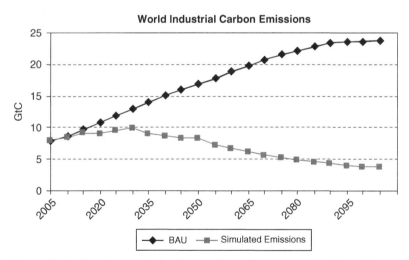

Figure 2.4b. Emissions path for the world, in the aggregate—with earlier targets for developing countries

Gt, in the case where China and MENA are given the earlier starting points (Figure 2.4b). In either case, emissions subsequently decline rather rapidly, falling below 5 Gt by 2090. Thanks to the post-2050 equalization formula, emissions per capita converge nicely in the long run, falling to below 1 ton per capita toward the end of the century.[35]

Economic and environmental consequences of the proposed targets, according to the WITCH model

Estimating the economic and environmental implications of these targets is a complex task. There are many fine models out there.[36] I was fortunate to link up with the WITCH model of FEEM (Fondazione Eni Enrico Mattei, in Milan), as applied by Valentina Bosetti.

WITCH (www.feem-web.it/witch) is an energy-economy-climate model developed by the climate change modeling group at FEEM. The model has been used extensively in the past three years to analyze the economic impacts of climate change policies. WITCH is a hybrid top-down economic model with energy sector disaggregation. Those who might be skeptical of economists' models on the grounds that "technology is really the answer" should rest assured that technology is central to this model. (Economists are optimists when it comes to what new technologies might be called forth by a higher price for carbon, but pessimists when it comes to how much technological response to international treaties will occur absent an increase in price.) The model features endogenous technological change via both experience and innovation processes. Countries are grouped in twelve regions, when Western Europe and Eastern Europe are counted separately, that cover the world and that strategically interact following a game theoretic set-up. The WITCH model and detailed structure are described in Bosetti *et al.* (2006) and Bosetti, Massetti, and Tavoni (2007).

Original baselines in many models have been disrupted in recent years by such developments as stronger-than-expected growth in Chinese energy demand and the unexpected spike in world oil prices

---

[35] Figure 2 of Frankel (2008a).

[36] Researchers have applied a number of different models to estimate the economic and environmental effects of various specific proposed emission paths; see, for example, Edmonds, Pitcher, Barns, Baron, and Wise (1992); Edmonds, Kim, McCracken, Sands, and Wise (1997); Hammett (1999); Manne, Mendelsohn, and Richels (1995); Manne and Richels (1997); McKibbin and Wilcoxen (2007); and Nordhaus (1994, 2008). Weyant (2001) provides an explanation and comparison of different models.

that culminated in 2008. WITCH has been updated with more recent data and revised projections for key drivers such as population, GDP, fuel prices, and energy technology characteristics. The base calibration year has been set at 2005, for which data on socio-economic, energy, and environmental variables are now available (Bosetti, Carraro, Sgobbi, and Tavoni 2008).

Economic effects

While economists trained in cost-benefit analysis tend to focus on economic costs expressed as a percentage of GDP, the politically attuned tend to focus at least as much on the predicted carbon price, which in turn has a direct impact on the prices of gasoline, home heating oil, and electric power.[37]

Based on the WITCH simulations conducted for this analysis, the world price of CO_2 under our proposal surpasses $20 per ton in 2015, as Figure 2.5 shows. It is then flat until 2030, as a consequence of the assumption that major developing countries do not take on major emission cuts before then. The price even dips slightly before beginning a steep ascent, an undesirable feature. It climbs steadily in the second half of the century, as the formula-based targets begin to bite seriously for developing countries. Before 2050 the carbon price has surpassed $100 per ton of CO_2. Only toward the end of the century does it level off, at almost $700 per ton of CO_2 in the case where some developing countries are spared early cuts, and at $800 per ton in the case where they are not spared.

Most regions sustain economic losses that are small in the first half of the century—under 1 percent of income—but that rise toward the end of the century.[38] Given a positive rate of time discount, this is a

---

[37] Frankel (1998). This attitude may seem irrational to an economist; after all, price effects are largely redistributional. But the public's instincts may be correct insofar as predicted price effects are more reliable indicators of the degree of economic dislocation caused by a carbon policy than GDP losses, which are subject to larger modeling uncertainty. Furthermore, distributional effects are key drivers of political support or opposition to a particular policy.

[38] Figure 7 of Frankel (2008a), omitted here to save space, illustrates economic costs, expressed as fractions of income, by region, for the case where the developing countries take on later targets. In this scenario, the highest decade costs are borne by China, just toward the end of the century, reaching 4.1 percent of income in 2100. (On the other hand the PDV of China's cost is less than those of the United States and several other regions.) The maximum income loss for the United States in any decade is 1.9 percent, and for the EU 1.4 percent, both occurring around 2080. Earlier drafts use the term "GDP", but it should really

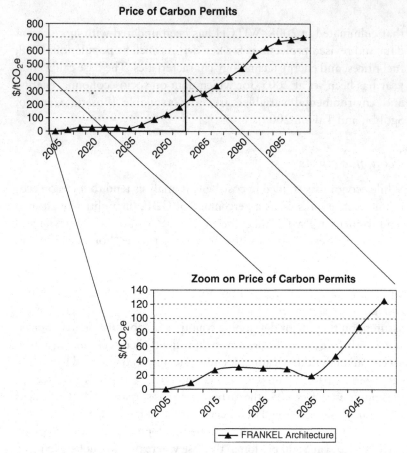

Figure 2.5a. Price of carbon dioxide rises slowly over 50 years, then rapidly—with later targets for developing countries

good outcome. No region in any period experiences costs in excess of our self-imposed threshold of 5 percent of income. The estimated costs of the policy to each country-group, in present discounted value (PDV) terms, are reported in Table 2.3a. No country is asked to incur costs that are expected to exceed 1 percent of income over the century. Only

be "national income," because the value of permit sales is added in, or the value of permit purchases is subtracted out. A theoretical cost–benefit analysis would go one step further, and use consumption in place of income; but our motivation here is political constraints, and our reading of politics is that consumer welfare is not the most relevant measure politically. (In the politics of trade policy, for example, importing so that consumption can exceed income is considered bad.)

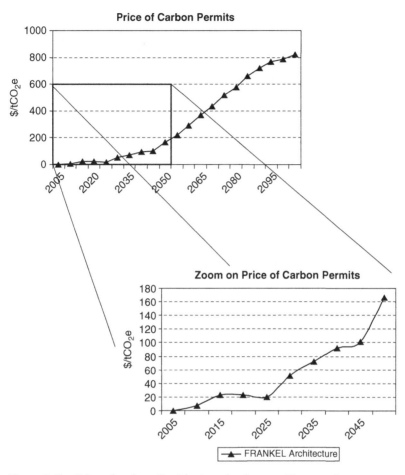

Figure 2.5b. Price of carbon dioxide rises slowly over 50 years, then rapidly—with earlier targets for developing countries

China's costs creep up to 1.1% of income, when it takes on an earlier target, in Table 2.3b. (All economic effects are gross of environmental benefits—that is, no attempt is made to estimate environmental benefits or net them out.)

These costs of participation are overestimated in one sense, and increasingly so in the later decades, if the alternative to staying in the treaty one more decade is dropping out after seven or eight decades of participation. The reason is that countries will have already substantially altered their capital stock and economic structure in a carbon-

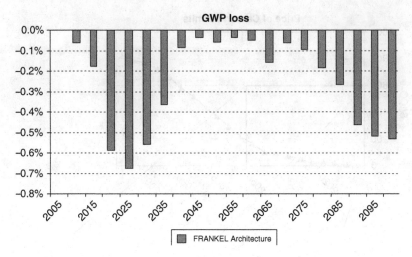

Figure 2.6. Loss of aggregate gross world product by budget period, 2015–2100—with later targets for developing countries

friendly direction. The economic costs reported in the simulations and graphs treat the alternative to participation as never having joined the treaty in the first place. In another sense, however, the costs are underestimated: anyone who drops out can expect leakage to the hilt. Its firms can buy fossil fuels at far lower prices than their competitors in countries that continue to participate.

Figure 2.6 provides Gross World Product loss aggregated across regions worldwide, and discounted to present value using a discount rate of 5 percent. Total economic costs come to 0.24 percent of annual output in the case where China and MENA start later and Southeast Asia and Africa are not given targets below BAU. Overall policy costs come to 0.65 percent in the case where the former two start earlier, the latter two are given targets below BAU, and as a result the price of carbon hits $800 per ton.

Environmental effects

The outcome of this proposal in terms of cumulative emissions of GHGs is close to those of some models that build in environmental effects or science-based constraints, even though no such inputs were used here. The concentration of CO_2 in the atmosphere stabilizes at 500 ppm in the last quarter of the century.

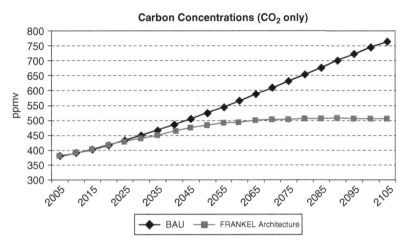

Figure 2.7a. CO_2 concentrations nearly achieve year-2100 concentration goal of 500 ppm—with later targets for developing countries

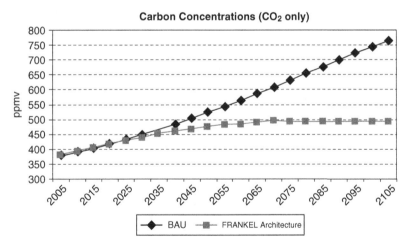

Figure 2.7b. CO_2 concentrations achieve year-2100 goal of 500 ppm—with earlier targets for developing countries

Based on the modeled concentration trajectory, global average temperature is projected to hit 3 degrees Celsius (°C) above pre-industrial levels at the end of the century, as opposed to almost 4°C under the BAU trajectory (Figure 10 in Frankel (2008a)). (Many scientists and environmentalists prefer objectives that are substantially more ambitious.) The relationship between concentrations and temperature is highly uncertain and depends on assumptions made about climate sensitivity. For this reason both figures are reported.

Conclusion

The analysis described here is only the beginning. Several particular extensions are high priority for future research.

Directions for future research

A first priority is to facilitate comparisons by tightening some parameters to see what it would take to hit a 2100 concentration level of 450 ppm or 2°C, which is the goal that G-8 leaders supposedly agreed to in the summit of July 2009.[39] Our first attempts to do this impose costs on some countries, in some periods, as high as 10–20 percent of GDP, which we regard as not practical. But we plan to try tinkering further with model parameters so as to hit the 450 ppm target without any country bearing an unreasonable burden. In the other direction, we could also calibrate the adjustment so as to hit a 2100 target of 550 ppm, again facilitating comparisons.

Second, we could design an algorithm to search over values of some of the key parameters in such a way as to attain the same environmental goal—450 or 500 ppm—with minimum economic cost. To continue emphasizing political feasibility, the objective could be to minimize the expected income loss for any country in any period, so as to minimize the incentive for any country to drop out. Or we could declare that we have already specified a sufficient political constraint (e.g., no loss to any country in any period above 5 percent of income), and proceed to a cost-benefit optimization exercise subject to those constraints.

Third, we could compare our proposed set of emissions paths to other proposals under discussion in the climate change policy

---

[39] *Financial Times*, July 9, 2008, p. 5.

community or being analyzed using other integrated assessment models.[40] Our hypothesis is that we could identify countries and periods in alternative pathways where we believe an agreement would be unlikely to hold up because its targets were not designed to limit economic costs for each country.

Fourth, we could eventually design a user-friendly "game" that anybody could play, choosing different emissions targets for various countries over time, and discovering how easy it is to generate outcomes that are unacceptable, either in economic or environmental terms. It would be a learning tool, hypothetically, for policymakers themselves. Anyone who believes that the GHG abatement targets presented in this chapter are insufficiently ambitious, or that the burden imposed on a particular country is too high, would be invited to try out alternatives for themselves. Perhaps a character from an adversely impacted country would pop up on the screen and explain to the user how many millions of his compatriots have been plunged into dire poverty by the user's policy choices.

Fifth, we could take into account GHGs other than CO_2.

Sixth, we could implement constraints on international trading, along the lines that the Europeans have sometimes discussed. Such constraints can arise either from a worldview that considers it unethical to pay others to take one's medicine, or from a more cynical worldview that assumes international transfers via permit sales will only line the pockets of corrupt leaders. Constraints on trading could take the form of quantity restrictions—for example, that a country cannot satisfy more than Z percent of its emissions obligation by international permit purchases. Or eligibility to sell permits could be restricted to countries with a score in international governance ratings over a particular threshold, or to countries that promise to use the funds for green projects, or to those that have a track record of demonstrably meeting their commitments under the treaty.

The seventh possible extension of this research represents the most

---

[40] For example, the CLEAR path proposed by Wagner *et al.* (2008, Table 2) proposes that by 2050 Russia has cut its emissions 30 percent below 1990 levels, China 46 percent below 2012 levels, India 8 percent above 2012 levels, and the other non-Annex I countries 23 percent below 2012. The Global Development Rights approach of Baer *et al.* (2008) apparently proposes a US emissions target for 2025 that is 99 percent below its BAU path. (These authors might say that their general approaches are more important than the specific parameter values by which they chose to illustrate them. I would say the same of mine.)

important step intellectually: to introduce uncertainty, especially in the form of stochastic growth processes.[41] The variance of the GDP forecasts at various horizons would be drawn from historical data. We would adduce the consequences of our rule that if any country makes an *ex post* determination in any period that by staying in the treaty it loses more than 5 percent of income, even though this had not been the expectation *ex ante*, that country will drop out. At a first pass, we could keep the assumption that if one country pulls out, the entire system falls apart. The goal would then be to design a version of the formulas framework that minimizes the probability of collapse.

A more sophisticated approach would be to allow the possibility that the system could withstand the loss of one or two members. We would try to account for the effect of dropouts on remaining members, with some sort of application of game theory. Ideally we would also try to account from the start for the effect of possible future breakdown on expectations of firms deciding long-term investments. Of course we could try other values of X besides 5 percent.

The ultimate objective in making the model stochastic is to seek modifications of the policy framework that are robust, that protect against inadvertent stringency on the one hand—that is, a situation where the cost burden imposed on a particular country is much higher than expected—or inadvertent "hot air" on the other hand. "Hot air" refers to the possibility that targets are based on obsolete emission levels with the result that countries are credited for cutting tons that wouldn't have been emitted anyway. Three possible modifications are promising. First, we could allow for some degree of re-adjustment to emission targets in the future, based solely on unexpected changes in the evolution in population and income. (Note that adjustments should not be allowed on the basis of unexpected changes in emissions levels, for to do so would be to introduce moral hazard.) Second, when the target for each decade is set, it should be indexed to GDP within that budget period. Perhaps the constant of proportionality in the indexation formula would simply equal 1, in which case it becomes an efficiency target, expressed in carbon emissions per unit of GDP. This approach would be much less vulnerable

---

[41] Among the chapters that introduce uncertainty, McKibbin, Morris, and Wilcoxen (2008) address two of the most recently relevant unexpected developments: growth shocks in Asia and a global housing/equity crash.

to within-decade uncertainty.[42] A third possible feature that would make the policy more robust and that is strongly favored by many economists is an escape clause or safety valve that would limit costs in the event that mitigation proves more expensive than expected, perhaps with a symmetric floor on the price of carbon in addition to the usual ceiling.

A politically credible framework

Our results suggest that the feasible set of emission target paths may be far more constrained than many modelers have assumed. Lofty debates over the optimal discount rate or fair allocation rules might prove fairly irrelevant: For many discount rates or cross-country allocations, an international climate agreement could at some point during the century collapse altogether because it imposes unacceptably high costs on some countries, relative to defecting. Each defection could raise costs on those who remain in the agreement, thereby increasing incentives for further defections and posing the prospect of a snow-balling effect. Commitments to a century-long path that is highly likely to result in a collapse of the agreement after a few decades would not be believed today, and thus might evoke few actual steps in the near term toward achieving long-term emission reductions.

The traditional integrated assessment result is that an economically optimal path entails relatively small increases in the price of carbon in the first half of the century and much steeper ones later. It is interesting that a similar result emerges here purely from political considerations, with no direct input from cost/benefit calculations.[43] This broad similarity of results for the aggregate path does not mean that the difference in approaches does not matter. The framework proposed here specifies the allocation of emission targets across countries in such a way that every country is given reason to feel that it is only doing

---

[42] Lutter (2000).

[43] Integrated assessment models (IAMs) tend to give the result that the optimal path entails shallow cuts in earlier years and deeper cuts coming only later, because (for example) scrapping operating coal-fired power plants today is costly, while credibly announcing stringent goals that will take effect 50 years from now would be cheaper, by giving time to plan ahead. Benefit-cost maximization, though obviously right in theory, is not the most useful logic in practice, because of uncertainty about key model parameters, such as the discount rate, and uncertainty about the credibility of such announcements.

its fair share and in such a way as to build trust as the decades pass. Without such a framework, announcements of distant future goals are not credible and so will not have the desired effects. Furthermore, this framework—in providing for a decade-by-decade sequence of emission targets, each determined on the basis of a few principles and formulas—is flexible enough that it can accommodate, by small changes in the formula parameters, major changes in circumstances during the course of the century.

References

Aldy, Joseph, Scott Barrett, and Robert Stavins (2003). "Thirteen Plus One: A Comparison of Global Climate Architectures," *Climate Policy* 3(4): 373–97.

Aldy, Joseph and Jeffrey Frankel (2004). "Designing a Regime of Emission Commitments for Developing Countries that is Cost-Effective and Equitable," *G20 Leaders and Climate Change*, Council on Foreign Relations.

Aldy, Joseph E., Peter R. Orszag, and Joseph E. Stiglitz (2001). "Climate Change: An Agenda for Global Collective Action," paper prepared for *The Pew Center Workshop on the Timing of Climate Change Policies*, The Westin Grand Hotel, Washington, DC, October 11–12.

Baer, Paul, Tom Athanasiou, Sivan Kartha, and Eric Kemp-Benedict (2008). *The Greenhouse Development Rights Framework: The Right to Development in a Climate Constrained World*. Stockholm: Hendrich Boll Stiftung, 2nd ed.

Barrett, Scott (2006). "Climate Treaties and 'Breakthrough' Technologies," *American Economic Review, Papers and Proceedings* 96(2): 22–5.

Baumert, Kevin and Donald Goldberg (2006). "Action Targets: A New Approach to International Greenhouse Gas Controls," *Climate Policy* 5: 561–81.

Bosetti, V., C. Carraro, M. Galeotti, E. Massetti, and M. Tavoni (2006). "WITCH: A World Induced Technical Change Hybrid Model," *The Energy Journal*, Special Issue on Hybrid Modeling of Energy-Environment Policies: Reconciling Bottom-up and Top-down, 13–38.

Bosetti, V., C. Carraro, A. Sgobbi, and M. Tavoni (2008). "The 2008 WITCH Model: New Model Features and Baseline," Mimeo, August.

Bosetti, V., E. Massetti, and M. Tavoni (2007). "The WITCH Model: Structure, Baseline, Solutions," Working Paper 10, Milan: Fondazione Eni Enrico Mattei.

Bowles, Ian and David Sandalow (2001). "Fundamental of Treaty-Making on Climate Change," *Science* 292: 1839–1840, June 8.

Cao, Jing (2008). "Reconciling Human Development and Climate Protection: Perspectives from Developing Countries on Post-2012 International Climate Change Policy," Discussion Paper 08-25, Harvard Project on International Climate Agreements, Cambridge, MA, December.

Council of Economic Advisers (1998). *The Kyoto Protocol and the President's Policies to Address Climate Change: Administration Economic Analysis*, Washington, DC, July.

Edmonds, J. A., H. M. Pitcher, D. Barns, R. Baron, and M. A. Wise (1992). "Modeling Future Greenhouse Gas Emissions: The Second Generation Model," in Lawrence Klein and Fu-chen Lo (eds.), *Modeling Global Climate Change*, Tokyo: United Nations University Press, pp. 295–340.

Edmonds, J. A., S. H. Kim, C. N. McCracken, R. D. Sands, and M. A. Wise (1997). "Return to 1990: The Cost of Mitigating United States Carbon Emission in the Post-2000 Period," Pacific Northwest National Laboratory, Operated by Battelle Memorial Institute, October.

Ellerman, Denny and Barbara Buchner (2008). "Over-Allocation or Abatement? A Preliminary Analysis of the EU ETS Based on the 2005–06 Emissions Data," *Environmental and Resource Economics*, 41(2): 267–287.

Frankel, Jeffrey (1998). "Economic Analysis of the Kyoto Protocol," *After Kyoto: Are There Rational Pathways to a Sustainable Global Energy System?* Aspen Energy Forum, Aspen, Colorado, July 6.

(1999). "Greenhouse Gas Emissions," *Policy Brief* no. 52, Brookings Institution, Washington, DC, June.

(2005). "You're Getting Warmer: The Most Feasible Path for Addressing Global Climate Change Does Run Through Kyoto," in J. Maxwell and R. Reuveny (eds.), *Trade and Environment: Theory and Policy in the Context of EU Enlargement and Transition Economies*. Cheltenham: Edward Elgar Publishers, pp. 37–55.

(2007). "Formulas for Quantitative Emission Targets," in Joe Aldy and Robert Stavins (eds.), *Architectures for Agreement: Addressing Global Climate Change in the Post-Kyoto World*. New York: Cambridge University Press, pp. 31–56.

(2008a). "An Elaborated Proposal for Global Climate Policy Architecture: Specific Formulas and Emission Targets for All Countries in All Decades," Discussion Paper 2008-08, Cambridge, MA: Harvard Project on International Climate Agreements.

(2008b). "Global Environmental Policy and Global Trade Policy," Discussion Paper 2008-14, Cambridge, MA: Harvard Project on International Climate Agreements.

Gore, Al (1993). *Earth in the Balance.* New York: Penguin Books.

Hammett, James (1999). "Evaluation Endpoints and Climate Policy: Atmospheric Stabilization, Benefit-Cost Analysis, and Near-Term Greenhouse Gas Emissions," *Climatic Change* 41: 447–68.

Hufbauer, Gary, Daniel Esty, Diana Orejas, Luis Rubio, and Jeffrey Schott (2000). "NAFTA and the Environment: Seven Years Later," *Policy Analyses in International Economics* No. 61, Washington, DC: Institute for International Economics.

Hufbauer, Gary, Steve Charnovitz, and Jisun Kim (2009). *Global Warming and the World Trading System,* Washington, DC: Peterson Institute for International Economics.

Keohane, Robert and Kal Raustiala (2008). "Toward a Post-Kyoto Climate Change Architecture: A Political Analysis," Discussion Paper No. 08-01, Harvard Project on International Climate Agreements, Cambridge, MA, July.

Lutter, Randy (2000). "Developing Countries' Greenhouse Emissions: Uncertainty and Implications for Participation in the Kyoto Protocol," *Energy Journal* 21(4): 93–120.

Manne, Alan, Robert Mendelsohn, and Richard Richels (1995). "MERGE: A Model for Evaluating Regional and Global Effects of GHG Reduction Policies," *Energy Policy* 23: 17.

Manne, Alan and Richard Richels (1997). "On Stabilizing CO_2 Concentrations—Cost-Effective Emission Reduction Strategies," Stanford University and Electric Power Research Institute, April.

McKibbin, Warwick, Adele Morris, and Peter Wilcoxen (2008). "Expecting the Unexpected: Macroeconomic Volatility and Climate Policy," Discussion Paper No. 08-16, Harvard Project on International Climate Agreements, Cambridge, MA, November.

McKibbin, Warwick and Peter Wilcoxen (2007). "A Credible Foundation for Long Term International Cooperation on Climate Change," in Aldy and Stavins (eds.), pp. 185–208.

Nordhaus, William (1994). *Managing the Global Commons: The Economics of Climate Change.* Cambridge, MA: MIT Press.

(2006). "Life After Kyoto: Alternative Approaches to Global Warming Policies," *American Economic Review, Papers and Proceedings* 96(2): 31–4.

(2008). *A Question of Balance: Weighing the Options on Global Warming Policies.* New Haven: Yale University Press.

Olmstead, Sheila and Robert Stavins (2006). "An International Policy Architecture for the Post-Kyoto Era," *American Economic Review, Papers and Proceedings* 96(2): 35–8.

Pizer, William (2006). "The Evolution of a Global Climate Change

Agreement," *American Economic Review, Papers and Proceedings* 96(2): 26–30.

Seidman, Laurence and Kenneth Lewis (2009). "Compensations and Contributions Under an International Carbon Treaty," *Journal of Policy Modeling*, in press.

Stewart, Richard and Jonathan Weiner (2003). *Reconstructing Climate Policy: Beyond Kyoto*. Washington, DC: American Enterprise Institute Press.

Victor, David (2004). *Climate Change: Debating America's Policy Options*. New York: Council on Foreign Relations.

Wagner, Gernot, James Wang, Stanislas de Margerie, and Daniel Dudek (2008). "The CLEAR Path: How to Ensure that if Developing Nations Adopt Carbon Limits, Their Early Actions Will Be Rewarded," Environmental Defense Fund Working Paper, October 30.

Weyant, John P. (2001). "Economic Models: How They Work & Why Their Results Differ," in Eileen Claussen, Vicki Arroyo Cochran, and Debra Davis (eds.), *Climate Change: Science, Strategies, & Solutions*. Leiden: Brill Academic Press, pp. 193–208.

Wrigley, Tom M. L., Rich G. Richels, and Jae A. Edmonds (2007). "Overshoot Pathways to CO_2 Stabilization in Multi-Gas Context," in R. G. Richels *et al.* (eds.), *Human-Induced Climate Change: An Interdisciplinary Assessment*, Cambridge: Cambridge University Press, pp. 387–401.

Zhang, Yongsheng (2008). "An Analytical Framework and Proposal to Succeed Kyoto Protocol: A Chinese Perspective," Development Research Center of the State Council, China, Dec 8.

3 | The EU emission trading scheme: a prototype global system?

DENNY ELLERMAN[1]

Introduction

The European Union Emission Trading Scheme (EU ETS) can claim to be first in many respects. It is the first cap-and-trade system for greenhouse gases (GHGs) and it has resulted in by far the largest emissions trading market yet created. These attributes alone make the EU ETS worthy of study, but it is another first that provides the motivation for this chapter: The EU ETS is the world's first multinational cap-and-trade system. As such, it can be seen as a prototype for the multinational GHG emissions trading system that is often advanced as a possible architecture for an eventual global climate regime (Aldy and Stavins, 2008). While the EU ETS is in only its fifth year of existence, experience to date with this program provides a preview of the issues that are likely to appear in a global system, suggests some useful precedents, and offers evidence that some problems may not be so difficult after all.

Two important similarities

Two features make the EU ETS appropriate for study as a prototype for a global emissions trading system: the weak federal structure of the EU and the significant disparities in economic circumstance, institutional development, and political will that exist among its member states. The EU is not a strong federal union like the United States of America. Its member states are independent nations that display and exercise the principal attributes of sovereignty. While some authority in some domains has been ceded to central European institutions,

---

[1] Comments on earlier drafts from Joe Aldy, Barbara Buchner, Henry Jacoby, Richard Schmalensee, Robert Stavins, Peter Zapfel, and an anonymous referee are gratefully acknowledged. The usual disclaimer applies.

the basic decision-making entity in the EU remains the Council of Ministers, which consists of the relevant ministers of the member states with carefully negotiated voting rights. The ETS Directive (European Council, 2003), which provides the legal basis for the EU ETS, can be seen—like all EU directives—as a specialized multinational agreement within the broader framework of the Treaties that established the EU itself. Although surely different in many particulars, a global trading regime can be expected to exhibit a similarly high degree of decentralization.

Just as the EU can mistakenly be seen as possessing a stronger federal structure than what political realities allow, so can the common adjective "European" mask a significant degree of diversity. The demarcation between East and West in Europe is not as marked as that between North and South globally, but there are instructive similarities. The difference in per capita income between the richest and poorest nations in the EU spans a significant part of the difference that would exist among the major emitting countries of the world. The per capita income of Romania and Bulgaria is only a third higher than that of China and one-fifth that of the wealthiest EU nation, Ireland, which has per capita income 5 percent higher than that of the United States.[2]

More than a decade of concerted efforts to transform institutions so that they conform to Western European norms has diminished East–West disparities, but the results have been uneven and remaining differences make participation in the ETS more of a challenge for some EU members than for others. Even greater differences exist in the degree of political will to address climate change and the priority accorded to reducing GHG emissions in different European countries—not only between East and West, but perhaps also between the southern and northern members of the fifteen West European nations. How all of these nations came to adopt a mandatory cap-and-trade system is the question that makes the EU ETS experience interesting and highly relevant in considering how to

---

[2] In contrast, the difference between the US states with the lowest and highest gross state product (Mississippi and Connecticut) is a factor of two. Luxembourg is excluded in the EU comparison because of a high concentration of corporate and financial activity that causes that country's per capita GDP to be 75 percent higher than that of Ireland. Delaware is excluded from the US comparison for the same reason. The international comparisons are based on International Monetary Fund (IMF) statistics for 2005 using purchasing power parity exchange rates.

bridge the economic, institutional and political differences that individual countries will bring to a global regime.

A brief recap of the EU ETS

The EU ETS is a classic cap-and-trade system in that it establishes an absolute limit on covered emissions, along with tradable permits—called European Union Allowances (EUAs)—that convey the right to release those emissions. Under the EU ETS almost all EUAs are distributed for free to affected installations; in turn, affected installations are obligated to report their emissions and to surrender an equal number of allowances annually. The coverage of the EU ETS is partial in the sense that the system includes only carbon dioxide (CO_2) emissions from electricity generation and most industrial activities. Notably, emissions of other types of gases and emissions from transportation, buildings, the service sector, and agriculture are not presently included, although it was envisaged from the beginning that additional GHGs and sectors would be incorporated over time. In its current form, the EU ETS covers about 45 percent of the EU's total CO_2 emissions and a little less than 40 percent of its total GHG emissions.

The EU ETS was conceived in the late 1990s as a means of ensuring that the then fifteen members of the EU (EU15) could meet their commitments under the Kyoto Protocol in the First Commitment Period (2008–2012). In surprisingly short time, this idea matured into a cap-and-trade system featuring a three-year "trial" period (from 2005 through 2007) and a subsequent "real" five-year trading period (2008 through 2012) that would coincide with the Protocol's First Commitment Period. This first "real" period would be followed by subsequent five-year trading periods.

More significantly, the EU ETS has grown from the original fifteen member states to include thirty countries. This expansion was accomplished in three steps: the accession of ten mostly East European member states to the EU on May 1, 2004; the subsequent expansion of the EU to include Romania and Bulgaria at the beginning of 2007; and the inclusion of three of the four nations constituting the European Economic Area (Norway, Iceland, and Liechtenstein) beginning in 2008.

The choice of a cap-and-trade system in Europe and the particular structure that it assumed are the result of four factors. First, European governments came to recognize in the late 1990s that further measures would be needed if the EU15 were to meet their common Kyoto obligations and that these additional measures would need to be adopted at the European level. Second, an EU-wide carbon tax was off the table since proposals to enact one had failed in the 1990s—in part because fiscal matters, unlike regulatory measures, require the unanimous agreement of all member states. Third, early experience with the US trading system for sulfur dioxide (SO_2) and the embrace of trading in the Kyoto Protocol made trading a logical approach. Fourth, the recognition that member states lacked not only experience with trading systems, but also the infrastructure necessary to support such systems prompted the adoption of the trial period to develop these prerequisites.

There is now an abundant literature that reports on, analyzes, evaluates, and criticizes the performance of the EU ETS.[3] For purposes of this discussion, the key accomplishments of the EU approach are that a uniform price for CO_2 exists across the system, that this price is taken into account by most owners of affected facilities when making operating and investment decisions, and that the requisite trading infrastructure—including emissions registries and procedures for monitoring, reporting, and verification—are in place. In short, an effective mechanism for limiting GHG emissions in the covered sectors exists and it is being used to effect progressively more significant emission reductions.

The rest of this chapter addresses five important aspects of the EU ETS as a potential prototype for a multinational system. The first aspect concerns a novel contribution of the EU ETS: the use of a partial, and time-limited, first or "trial" trading period from 2005 through 2007. The second aspect involves the role of a central coordinating entity. The third and fourth aspects concern the related issues of club benefits and appropriate differentiation in the face of increasing stringency. The fifth and last aspect concerns an anticipated problem that hasn't appeared so far in the EU ETS context: public opposition to cross-border financial flows related to emissions trading.

---

[3] For more comprehensive reports, the reader is referred to the Symposium on the EU ETS in the initial issue of the *Review of Environmental Economics and Policy* (Ellerman and Buchner, 2007; Convery and Redmond, 2007; and Kruger *et al.*, 2007); Convery, Ellerman and De Perthuis, 2008; and Ellerman and Joskow, 2008.

The trial period approach

The use of a trial period to launch the EU ETS is a novel feature and one that commends itself for consideration in the context of a global cap-and-trade system. The concept of, and rationale for, a trial period was articulated in an early EU Green Paper on GHG trading (European Commission, 2000).

> As emission trading is a new instrument for environmental protection within the EU, it is important to gain experience in its implementation before the international emissions trading scheme starts in 2008.

Although formulated in the specific context of EU efforts to meet Kyoto Protocol obligations, this statement could apply equally to any nation that is adopting a cap-and-trade system as an instrument for limiting GHG emissions. Furthermore, even those already in a broader system might consider a trial period advantageous for ensuring that the requisite infrastructure and experience are in place before an acceding country becomes a fully participating member.

The EU ETS trial period was defined by two key characteristics. First, it preceded a more serious commitment and, as the name suggests, it was conceived as a rehearsal for the real thing—in this case, reducing the EU's CO_2 emissions sufficiently in 2008–2012 to ensure compliance with the Kyoto Protocol. In a broader context, the same approach could be used to rehearse for full-fledged participation in a global system. Second, the trial period was self-contained in the sense that allowances from the trial period could not be banked for use in the subsequent "real" period. Conversely, allowances could not be borrowed from future real periods for use in the trial phase. The inability to bank or borrow between the two periods virtually assured that the allowance price at the end of the trial period would be either zero (if actual emissions were less than required to meet the EU-wide cap because left-over allowances would have no value in the subsequent trading period), or the penalty price in the opposite case (that is, if emissions exceeded the cap, some firms would have to pay the penalty price for not surrendering enough allowances to cover emissions since they could not borrow from the next trading period).[4]

---

[4] Recall that the final net position is known with certainty only after it is too late to correct any imbalance. The requirement to cover short positions and the

Generally, the inability to bank or borrow would be considered a serious defect; however, if the purpose of a trial period is to gain experience and to establish the requisite monitoring, reporting, and enforcement infrastructure, restricting trading with subsequent compliance periods is more understandable.

The problems that are likely to be encountered in setting up an international cap-and-trade system should not be minimized. Institutionally, EU member states must be considered more prepared and capable of implementing such a system than many of the prospective participants in a global system. Even so, there were numerous difficulties in setting up the European system. The biggest problem was a lack of data at the installation level. Emissions data were needed both for the allocation of allowances to covered installations and, more importantly, to determine the total number of allowances to be distributed by each member state (Ellerman, Buchner and Carraro, 2007). For instance, the EU ETS turned out to have a surplus of allowances in the trial period largely because the baseline used to project future business-as-usual emissions was highly uncertain. In fact, an important benefit of the trial period was that it provided more reliable data on actual emissions for included installations. Verified emission reports for the first year of the trial period, 2005, became the baseline by which the European Commission judged the acceptability of proposed caps for the subsequent (2008–2012) period.

The trial period was even more important for new East European member states where the institutional preparation for participating in an emissions trading system was arguably not as complete as among the EU15. This has rightly been raised as an important issue in considering the feasibility of a global trading system (Kruger *et al.*, 2007). Data deficiencies in Eastern Europe were greater than they were for the EU15 and most of the East European governments required more time to set up the requisite infrastructure for trading and enforcement. Poland's registry did not go on line until 18 months after the start of the EU ETS; Romania and Bulgaria, which became participants in the last year of the trial period, did not have everything in place in time to participate effectively in 2007. One of the most encouraging aspects of

incentive to sell non-bankable surpluses will ensure a price discovery process between the end of the compliance period and the surrender date that will result in this binary outcome.

the EU ETS is the evidence that participants and governments in countries with less institutional capacity can acquire the necessary infrastructure and become full-fledged participants within a few years.

Important lessons from the EU ETS trial period concern not only the creation of the requisite trading infrastructure, but also the issue of program coverage. While an economy-wide, comprehensive system that includes all sources is an ideal that may be practicable in some instances, the more likely reality is that the power sector and large industrial facilities are the most promising candidates for early inclusion in a global system. This was the case in the EU ETS. In keeping with the concept of a trial period and recognizing the problems involved in setting up a system, the European Commission proposed from the beginning to start with those sectors that could most easily implement a trading system. In the EU case, existing directives concerning large combustion plants and integrated pollution prevention and control provided a usable regulatory framework—one that already implied control of GHGs and energy efficiency, albeit by other means (European Commission, 2000).[5] This is not unlike the situation in developing economies where power plants and large industrial facilities are invariably the first sources subject to pollution controls.

Moreover, for those nations already in a global system that seek to extend its reach and to effect large GHG emission reductions in other countries, the arguments for initial partial coverage will be strong. The power sector is often the largest source of emissions in a country, and inclusion of large industrial sources will be highly desirable to avoid leakage and to lessen competitive concerns on the part of nations already participating in the global system. Initial partial coverage need not preclude a later, more comprehensive system, although the issue will be whether an initial partial approach makes it more difficult to arrive ultimately at comprehensive coverage.

Expanding program coverage over time is clearly envisioned in the EU ETS, and indeed, some expansion has already occurred. Opt-in provisions were included in the original ETS Directive, and a number

---

[5] The ETS Directive explicitly amends the Integrated Pollution Prevention and Control Directive to prohibit any member state from establishing a GHG emission limit for any plant included in the EU ETS, and it further stipulates that member states are allowed to forego imposing energy efficiency requirements on plants included in the EU ETS.

of additional sources and even some other gases have been opted in, although the numbers are small. A more significant change will be the inclusion of aviation sources. As of 2012, the EU ETS will expand to include in-flight emissions for all flights originating or terminating in the EU.[6] In addition, the post-2012 amendments to the ETS Directive, which were agreed at the end of 2008, will include chemicals and aluminum, two industrial sectors that were initially excluded from the EU ETS. These two expansions of scope increase the coverage of the EU ETS by about 15 percent and 5 percent, respectively.

Experience with the EU ETS has demonstrated once again that rehearsal has merit. Although not currently envisaged as a feature of a global trading system, similarly constructed trial periods would seem to be a desirable feature, particularly when questions exist concerning the institutional readiness of newly acceding nations. For many of the same reasons as prevailed in the EU ETS, the trading programs implemented by newly participating members in a global system are likely to provide only partial coverage of emissions sources. Expanding coverage to additional sectors will be no easier than expanding the geographic scope of a trading system, but failure to achieve the ideal of full coverage initially is no reason to forego what is practicable.

Defining the center

Kruger *et al.* (2007) note that "the model of decentralization in the EU ETS has broken new ground in our experience with emissions trading regimes across multiple jurisdictions." In that model, cap-setting,[7] allocation, monitoring, reporting, verification, registries, and enforcement are all the responsibilities of the constituent member states, albeit with varying degrees of guidance, review, and approval by the European Commission. Among the most important issues to be decided in the design of a global trading system is the role and identity

---

[6] The aviation sector is not completely integrated into the EU ETS because of the inclusion of emissions for international flights, which are not subject to the Kyoto Protocol. A "gateway" will be established that will allow EUAs to be used for compliance in the aviation sector, but restrict the use of allowances issued to the aviation sector to that sector alone.

[7] The system-wide cap in a decentralized system, such as the EU ETS during the first and second compliance periods, is the sum of the member state "caps" or of the total number of allowances issued by participating countries. Cap-setting is the process of agreeing upon these member state totals.

of a central authority. Again, experience from the trial period of the
EU ETS suggests some potentially workable solutions.

In considering this issue, it is important to avoid the caricature
of the European Commission as an over-staffed and over-bearing
bureaucracy that is slowly but surely snuffing out national pre-
rogative and diversity. While the Commission enjoys the power of
initiative with respect to EU legislation, along with the duty to ensure
that existing EU laws are observed by member states, the ultimate
decision-making institution is the European Council of Ministers,
which represents the governments of member nations.[8] In the end,
the Commission is the agent of the whole, and its success depends on
both the powers granted to it by the still sovereign member states and
on the manner in which those powers are exercised. In the case of the
EU ETS, a careful distinction must be made between the role played
by the Commission in the just-completed trial period and the ongoing
evolution of that role.

The Commission's role in the trial period

The ETS Directive is unusual as an EU directive in endowing the
European Commission with specific and carefully circumscribed
functions that are additional to its general powers as an executive
agent under the European Treaties.[9] The most important of these
specific functions concerns the National Allocation Plans (NAPs) in
which member states determine the total number of allowances to
be issued and how they will be distributed. The ETS Directive gives
the European Commission power to review and reject NAPs within a
limited period of time after the member state notifies the Commission
that its NAP is complete.[10] This power has proved to be important.
Without it, the final EU-wide cap in both trading periods to date

---

[8] A succinct summary of the roles of EU institutions and of the EU's decision-
making processes can be consulted at: http://europa.eu/institutions/decision-
making/index_en.htm.

[9] Most EU directives are simply 'transposed' into national law with the
Commission's role limited to ensuring conformity of the resulting national laws
with the EU directive.

[10] This provision is emblematic of the delicate balance between the power of the
center and the prerogatives of constituent members in the EU. Technically, the
Commission never "approves" a member state's NAP; it is considered approved
unless rejected during the Commission's review.

would have been higher—by about 15 percent in the initial trial period and 10 percent in the subsequent real period. Not surprisingly, the Commission's power to review and reject the allowance budgets developed by member states is carefully circumscribed. NAPs are to be assessed against various provisions and a set of criteria specified in Annex III of the ETS Directive—which is to say, as agreed previously by the member states meeting in Council. The ETS Directive also established a committee of member state representatives to provide the Commission with their opinion on the NAPs submitted by member states.

So far the Commission has exercised its power to review and reject with considerable discretion. In practice, it has focused on three criteria (out of eleven): the total number of allowances member states propose to issue (to guard against cap inflation), the list of installations to be included and their allocations (to ensure inclusiveness), and the absence of *ex post* adjustments in allocation.[11] Equally important has been what the Commission has chosen not to insist upon. Despite appeals for a more "harmonized" approach, allocation to installations was sensibly left to individual member states. The committee process established by the Directive has also proved useful in letting an individual member state know how other member states viewed its NAP, thereby enabling the Commission to perform its role as agent of the whole more effectively (Zapfel, 2007). Finally, no NAP has been formally rejected. Instead an expedient of "conditional approval" and "approval with technical changes" was devised whereby a NAP could be approved conditional on the adoption of certain changes, which have usually been negotiated previously and out of sight. When the NAP process for the first period was over, all of the Commission's required changes had been accepted; and only two member states, Germany and the UK, took the Commission to court on relatively technical matters.

Assessing the NAPs of member states was not the only significant function that the Commission performed in the trial period. Equally

---

[11] What became the Commission's effective ban on *ex post* adjustment presents an interesting use of discretion. At best, this ban is implicit in the ETS Directive and the Annex III criteria. *Ex post* adjustment would have frustrated the creation of an efficient EU-wide emissions market by substituting an *ex post* administrative redistribution of allowances within each member state for trading among installations in an EU-wide market.

important were its efforts to educate member states and to facilitate and coordinate their participation. Zapfel (2007) describes the "active role" that the Commission took "to assist and guide" member states in the preparation of their NAPs and in eliminating "know-how gaps" so as to make informed decisions on technical issues. This involved commissioning studies on various aspects of allocation, issuing an unofficial paper elaborating how to prepare an allocation plan, and developing amplifying guidance on the review criteria. In addition, the Commission was always available and frequently looked to as a source of information, expertise, and informal guidance. These frequent and intense bilateral contacts provided a means for sounding out various NAP features, narrowing differences, and facilitating final agreement.

The evolution of the Commission's role

The first round of NAP development could best be described as a negotiation between individual member states and the Commission in which both sides were trying to agree on an allowance total in the face of large data uncertainties and some confusion over what installations met the definition for inclusion. Moreover, the absence of any international obligation to limit GHG emissions in these years allowed for a more relaxed approach to cap-setting.

All of this would change in the second round of NAP submissions for the 2008–2012 trading period. Decisions about the cap became more serious since the EU now had a legally binding obligation to comply with the limits imposed by the Kyoto Protocol. Also, definitional issues concerning what installations were included had been largely resolved by the time the second-period NAP notifications were due in June 2006. But the most important factor in changing the Commission's approach was the release, in May 2006, of verified emissions data for 2005. These data revealed that EU-wide emissions were lower than previously thought. Despite the significant reductions that the Commission required in the "caps" proposed by member states, it became evident that the finally approved totals for some member states, mostly in Eastern Europe, had involved significant errors in assumed baseline emissions. As a result, the Commission decided that the point of reference for member state caps in 2008–2012 would no longer be the first period totals but 2005 verified emissions.

Additionally, the Commission responded to criticisms about inconsistency and lack of transparency in the negotiation of member state caps for the trial period by adopting a single, carefully calibrated emissions model to project business-as-usual (BAU) emissions in 2010 (the midpoint of the second trading period) based on verified 2005 emissions data combined with expected rates of economic growth and reductions in carbon intensity (European Commission, 2006).

All of these factors caused interactions between the Commission and member states to take on a different tone in the second-period NAP exercise. Caps were no longer set on the basis of a negotiation—rather they were based on an evaluation of whether the totals proposed by member states were consistent with model projections based on verified 2005 emissions. If they were not, and if member states could not present either (a) a good reason for departing from the Commission's methodology or (b) evidence of an error in the Commission's calculations, the totals were adjusted downward. In taking this approach, the Commission effectively put itself in the position of determining member state allowance totals and thereby the EU-wide cap. Member states might challenge Commission decisions, but the burden of proof was shifted heavily against them. This did result in more legal challenges to the Commission's NAP decisions: nine of the ten East European countries have sued the Commission over the caps imposed on them, although one, Slovakia, withdrew its suit after a slight upward adjustment was made to its total.

The trend toward greater centralization of decision making with respect to the ETS was taken much further in the post-2012 amendments that were agreed in late 2008. Under these amendments, the NAP process is largely abandoned—instead, the overall EU-wide cap for the 2013–2020 period and its apportionment among member states are specified centrally in the amended Directive. Auctioning (at the member state level) will become the primary means for distributing national allowance budgets, with some provisions for the transition and for exceptions.

Questions for a global system

Experience with the EU ETS suggests that overarching treaties and agreements, such as the Kyoto Protocol and the European Burden-Sharing Agreement, may not be enough to create an effective cap-and-trade system.[12] Assuming that political will or other motivations are sufficient to support action, some entity must act as agent for the whole and educate, facilitate, and coordinate on behalf of the overall system—hopefully with the vision, ability and political realism that have characterized the European Commission's role in the development of the EU ETS. That experience also raises two questions: is the greater degree of centralization now being pursued in the EU ETS necessary in a global system? And what institution would play the role of a central authority or facilitator in such a system?

Within Europe, the view is that the ETS trial period was deeply flawed and that greater centralization is the remedy. In part this view reflects a vision of a stronger European political structure that could avoid the messiness of decentralized decisions, but it also reflects some of the real problems of the trial period. Yet, despite a high degree of decentralization, the ETS trial period did succeed in imposing a price on slightly less than half of Europe's overall CO_2 emissions and in creating a mechanism for effecting greater reductions in the future. The question for a global system is not so much what degree of centralization is desirable, but what is politically feasible. What may be possible in the EU will likely not be feasible in a broader global system under which participating nations will retain significant discretion in deciding national emission caps, maintain separate national registries, and administer monitoring, reporting, and verification procedures at a national level. For a global system, the trial period of the EU ETS provides a more realistic precedent than the more centralized system to which the EU ETS is evolving.

The more difficult question is this: what institution could assume the functions that the European Commission performed in the ETS trial period on a larger global stage? In many ways, the Commission's role in establishing the ETS was accidental. It was not set up for this purpose; yet it was there when the occasion demanded, and it played its role brilliantly. The Commission can perform the same functions for further accessions within Europe, and it would likely represent the EU in any future international negotiations concerning linkage with

[12] The European Burden-Sharing Agreement, agreed in 1998, redistributes the Kyoto Protocol's common European target of 8 percent emission reductions below 1990 levels among the EU15 in a manner more closely fitting national circumstances. These redistributed targets vary from +27 percent for Portugal to −28 percent for Luxembourg.

trading systems in the United States or elsewhere. Nevertheless, the European Commission cannot serve as the center for an emissions trading system that extends beyond Europe. Perhaps some entity will emerge out of negotiations to link the EU ETS with other national- or regional-level trading systems, much as the WTO grew out of the expansion of trade, but there should be no doubt that some center for a global system will be needed. Otherwise the result will be a system far more disjointed and dysfunctional than the trial period of the EU ETS is sometimes portrayed as being—or the result may be no system at all.

Importance of club benefits

It is not the case that all member states of the EU were equally resolved to address climate change from the beginning and that all are happy with the EU ETS. The UK and Germany, two of the largest EU members, advocated a voluntary trading system for the trial period in order to preserve existing voluntary arrangements in these countries. Spain, Italy, and some other EU15 states agreed to emission targets in the European Burden-Sharing Agreement that seem to have been viewed more as aspirations than as hard numbers to be achieved by later policy commitments. Finally, the East European member states, which joined after the system had been designed, had other priorities and—with the exception of Slovenia—faced no problems in meeting their commitments under the Kyoto Protocol. That the result was a mandatory trial period in which all EU members participated is surprising, not least because, in the EU, various forms of exception are the rule. Club benefits—that is, the advantages that go along with membership in some group—largely explain this result.

The story behind the EU ETS has been told elsewhere (Skaerseth and Wettestad, 2008), but several elements are important from the standpoint of constructing a larger global system. First, it is worth noting that the story of how nations came to participate is a little different for the EU15 and the new member states. For the EU15, a longer experience of working together and a set of prior commitments were important in shaping their participation in the ETS. The EU had taken a prominent position in favor of action on climate change at, and subsequent to, the Rio de Janeiro Conference in 1992. Moreover, this position had wide-spread public support in Europe, especially after the withdrawal of the United States from the Kyoto Protocol in 2001. The governments of the UK and Germany might advocate for voluntary participation in the trial period, in large part due to the strong positions taken by their respective industries, but neither government would have been willing to scuttle the deal given their existing positions on climate change and their broader interests in the EU. As it was, agreement on mandatory free allocation, a temporary opt-out provision, and pooling made mandatory participation more palatable to industry and gave the EU15 governments the excuse they needed to drop their insistence on a voluntary trial period.[13] Southern member states (Spain, Portugal, Italy, and Greece) that could best be characterized as "going along" with the climate policy advocacy of their more northern neighbors up to that point, were too enmeshed in the broad benefits of the EU to give serious consideration to ignoring the EU ETS Directive (although for a while it looked as if Greece and Italy might do so).

The situation was quite different for the new member states. They were not part of the Burden-Sharing Agreement and, with the exception of Slovenia, none faced any problems in meeting its Kyoto Protocol obligation. New members had lower per capita income and faced less public demand for environmental protection, especially for a global problem. Finally and more significantly, these countries were not at the table as voting members when the ETS was negotiated and agreed. When accession became a reality, the common East European reaction to the EU ETS was that it was designed by and for the EU15 and that its provisions did not really fit the circumstances of the new member states (Jankowski, 2007; Chmelik, 2007; Bart, 2007). The Directive was, as characterized by Jankowski, "an ill-fitting suit," which all nonetheless agreed to wear, albeit amid much and continuing protest.

Notwithstanding this discontent, none of the unhappy new member states has pursued their differences to the point of withdrawing from the EU ETS. The first period NAP cuts were accepted without more than complaint, and while the second period cuts have been fol-

---

[13] Pooling refers to an arrangement whereby individual installations would join together to form an entity that would be collectively responsible for reporting emissions and receiving and surrendering allowances on their behalf. It was anticipated that this arrangement would accommodate voluntary agreements in some sectors. In fact, there was little pooling.

lowed by serious legal challenges to the Commission's decisions, these appeals are being pursued through common European institutions. In the meantime, the plaintiff countries are participating in the trading scheme on the Commission's terms, pending the outcome of their legal challenges. How these challenges will play out is anyone's guess, but it is hard to imagine any of the plaintiffs leaving the trading system in the event of an adverse decision. Too much would be called into question. More importantly, the presence of the new member states as voting members when the post-2012 amendments were decided did influence the outcome. The transitional free allocation to electric utilities in most new member states is one result, as is the award of extra emissions rights, all within the EU-wide cap, for new member states with particularly large post-1990 emissions reductions.

The dissonance between the official positions of the governments of new member states and their actions can only be explained by the broader benefits of belonging to the EU. Whatever the perceived disadvantages of mandatory participation in the ETS, those disadvantages pale in significance when compared to the benefits of free flows of labor and capital and access to broader markets that come with being a member of the EU club. As Bart (2007) noted perceptively, the EU ETS was "just another obligation in the long march to the EU." In sum, though the club benefits of EU membership cannot be extended to the world, one lesson of the European experience is that similar side benefits will be needed to induce and maintain participation in a global system.

Stringency, differentiation, and harmonization

Club benefits largely explain how the EU ETS has grown from the initial fifteen member states to the thirty that now participate. The continuing challenge will be to keep everyone in the system when emission reduction targets become more stringent, as any serious policy that attempts to deal with climate change will require. In particular, a conflict has already emerged between the two reasonable objectives of differentiation and harmonization—and it can be expected to get worse as program requirements become more stringent. The same conflict will surely arise in a global system—a prospect that lends particular interest to the resolution found in the EU ETS.

Differentiation and harmonization defined

Differentiation is a well-established concept in climate policy: It originates in the reference to "common but differentiated responsibilities"
among nations in the UN Framework Convention on Climate Change.
"Responsibilities" refers to the burdens or costs that would be assumed
by countries of differing economic and historical circumstances under
the Framework. In a multinational trading system, differentiation
would be expressed by differences in the quantity of allowances
assigned to a nation relative to what that nation's emissions would
otherwise be.[14] Nations assuming greater responsibilities will accept
lower national "caps" and thereby incur a greater cost burden than
nations with less demanding totals.

"Harmonization" entered the climate policy lexicon only with the
implementation of the EU ETS, but this issue will arise in any global
system also. Harmonization refers to the proposed remedy—presumably through a benchmarked allocation—for what is perceived as the
unequal treatment of like facilities as the result of a decentralized free
allocation of allowances. It is intended to address the concern that
awarding more allowances to an installation in one country than to
an identical installation in another country is at the least unfair and
may create a competitive distortion.[15] The concept of harmonization,
which implicitly presumes equality of treatment, calls the whole principle of differentiation into question. If all facilities are to be treated
equally, how can countries be differentiated? And, even if harmonization could be achieved for some particular sector, as several industries
argue should be done in a global system, the burden of differentiation
would then fall more heavily on non-harmonized sectors.

---

[14] A nation's emissions may be higher or lower than its "cap" depending on the
uniform allowance price and the nation's marginal cost of abatement, but the
total cost will be greater or smaller depending on the number of allowances
issued by that country.
[15] The claim of competitive disadvantage ought to lack validity for a fixed, lump-
sum allocation, but it is firmly asserted and believed by many in the political
process. The decision to continue free allocation for installations in trade-
impacted sectors in the post-2012 EU ETS is an example of the efficacy of this
argument.

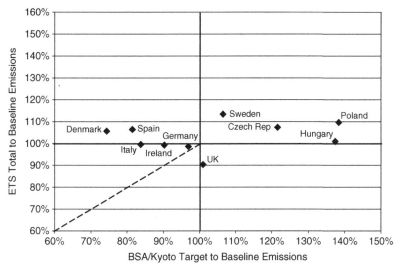

Figure 3.1. Relation of NAP1 totals to baseline emissions and the Kyoto/ BSA targets
Source: Ellerman, Buchner, and Carraro (2007)

The current evolution of differentiation and harmonization in the EU ETS

The EU ETS is evolving from a trial period that could be character-ized as having not very stringent targets, imperceptible differentiation of cost burdens, and no efforts at harmonization, to a post-2012 system that will feature increasing stringency, significant differentia-tion, and near complete harmonization. The lack of stringency in the trial period is well known, but the lack of differentiation is not. In theory, the caps in place for the trial period were to reflect the lesser of predicted BAU emissions or a "Path to Kyoto" trajectory that was consistent with each member state's emissions-reduction commitment under the European Burden-Sharing Agreement (BSA). In reality, the absence of good data, the inherent difficulties of prediction, and press-ing deadlines for implementation frustrated any efforts to differentiate across the burdens imposed on individual member states during the trial period, as shown by Figure 3.1.

Figure 3.1 plots the trial period caps for ten representative member states in relation to their Kyoto/BSA targets (horizontal axis) and to

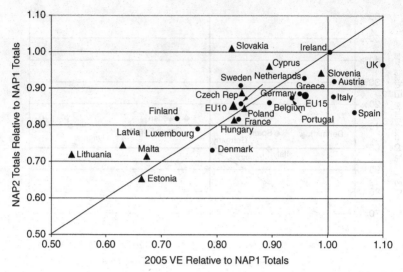

Figure 3.2. NAP2 national totals in relation to NAP1 totals and 2005 emissions

Note: NAP1 and NAP2 refer to the total allowances (EUAs) that each member state could allocate in the first and second trading periods. VE refers to verified emissions.

Source: Compiled by the author.

baseline or recent historical emissions for sectors covered by the ETS (vertical axis). Countries to the left of the vertical axis—that is, those with a constraining Kyoto/BSA target—might be expected to have an EU ETS total that would place them in the lower left-hand quadrant along the dashed diagonal. In fact, the caps of these countries look no different in stringency than those of the countries to the right of the vertical axis.[16] Recent emissions were a more important determinant of member state NAP totals for the ETS trial period than the country's Kyoto/BSA targets.

This lack of differentiation would change with the second NAP round (NAP2) that set member state allowance totals for the 2008–2012 period. For this period, the cap for the original EU15 plus the ten mostly East European countries that joined in 2004 was set at a level 5 percent lower than verified emissions in 2005 and 12 percent lower

---

[16] The UK took an explicit leadership position early in the trial period by adopting a more demanding NAP that it hoped would set an example for others.

than the first period cap. Figure 3.2 shows the relationship between 2005 verified emissions (horizontal axis) and the second period national totals (vertical axis), where both are expressed as ratios of the first period totals.

For nearly all member states, both their 2005 verified emissions and the second period totals are less than in the first period. As is clearly evident from Figure 3.2, the lower a member state's 2005 verified emissions, the lower the quantity of emissions allowances reflected in that state's NAP for the second phase. However, differentiation starts to appear in the graph, as indicated by different countries' perpendicular distance from the diagonal. Spain has the most demanding target with 2005 emissions 6 percent above, and a NAP2 total 17 percent below, its first period total. Slovakia and Lithuania have the least demanding NAP2 totals. More generally, new member states are mostly above and to the left of the diagonal line, indicating less of a burden, while EU15 member states are below and to the right of the line, indicating more of a burden. The separation between the two groups is not complete, but the position of the larger symbols—which aggregate NAP2 emission totals for the ten newer member states and the original EU15, each taken as a group, indicate that some differentiation has occurred. On average, the second period totals for the ten newer members are 3 percent higher than 2005 emissions, while those for the EU15 are 7 percent lower.

Still greater stringency and increased differentiation will result from the recently agreed post-2012 amendments (European Commission, 2008).[17] Starting in 2013, the overall, EU-wide cap is set to decline indefinitely at a rate of 1.74 percent per year such that emissions by 2020 would be 21 percent below 2005 verified emissions. At the same time, the amendments are designed to achieve greater differentiation by assigning the allowances to be auctioned to participating member-state

---

[17] These amendments are part of an "energy-climate package" that includes a series of other measures, some of which, such as the Renewables Directive, overlap with the ETS, while others apply exclusively to sectors not in the ETS. In particular, member state governments are required to take measures to limit non-ETS sector emissions to levels varying from +20 percent to −20 percent from the 2005 baseline so as to achieve an EU-wide reduction for these sectors of 10 percent below 2005 levels by 2020. All of these measures are aimed at ensuring that the EU meets its overall target of reducing total GHG emissions 20 percent below 1990 levels by 2020. The coordination, internal consistency, and efficiency of these measures leave much to be desired.

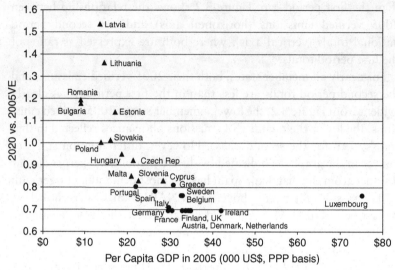

Figure 3.3. 2020 auction rights in relation to 2005 emissions and per capita GDP
Source: Compiled by the author.

governments according to an agreed formula.[18] Eighty-eight percent of the allowances to be auctioned would be allocated to member states in proportion to their 2005 verified emissions. Another 10 percent would be distributed for the purpose of "solidarity and growth within the Community" in amounts that would increase the allowance total for some member states by percentages that range from 2 percent for Italy to 56 percent for Latvia. The remaining 2 percent would be awarded to nine new member states for which 2005 emissions were 20 percent or more below the 1990 level (i.e., all except Slovenia, Cyprus, and Malta).

The amendments state that the basis for most of this differentiation is GDP per capita; the same basis for differentiation has also been proposed for a global system (Jacoby *et al.*, 1999) and, as noted in Frankel (2007), underlies the targets in the Kyoto Protocol. Figure 3.3 shows

---

[18] The differentiation formulas apply to auctioned allowances only, and since the portion to be auctioned expands over time, they should eventually apply to all or nearly all allowances. The number of allowances available for free allocation will depend on the transitional measures in place, the number of trade-exempted sectors, and the allocation rules for those sectors. The discussion in the text assumes full auctioning in 2020 for the sake of illustration.

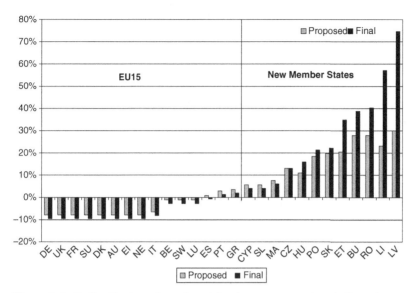

Figure 3.4. Redistribution of auction rights from a proportional allocation
Source: Compiled by the author.

the 2020 allocation of the EU-wide cap, assuming full auctioning, in relation to per capita income on a purchasing power parity basis.

Under the 2008 amendments, most of the East European countries would receive an allocation that would be equal to or greater than their 2005 emissions. Relatively better-off new member states—Hungary, Czech Republic, Slovenia, Malta, and Cyprus—would receive fewer allowances, but still more than any of the EU15. Among the latter group, Luxembourg must be set aside because of the tax-advantaged activity that gives it an artificially high per capita GDP. Otherwise, it is clear that the EU15 states are assuming more of the cost burden of reducing CO_2 emissions. Most of these relatively high-income member states would receive allowances equal to 69.5 percent of their 2005 emissions (or 88 percent of their share, if allowances were simply awarded proportionate to 2005 emissions, of an EU-wide cap designed to reduce emissions 21 percent below 2005 levels by 2020).

The post-2012 amendments represent the first instance in which the beneficiaries of differentiation in a multinational system had a vote in determining the degree of differentiation. Much can and should be written about the role of the new member states in the final agreement, but the net effect is shown in Figure 3.4.

The percentages indicate departures from an apportionment of the EU-wide total that would be strictly proportional (that is, where each state's allocation would be set to 21 percent less than its 2005 verified emissions). The initial Commission proposal contained significant differentiation as indicated by the first column for each member state. Under this proposal, 10 percent of the EU-wide cap would be reserved for redistribution in a manner that would result in a net subtraction for twelve EU15 countries in favor of three, lower-income EU15 countries (Greece, Spain, and Portugal) and all of the new member states. In the negotiation of the final package, the East European new member states prevailed in arguing that member states whose 2005 emissions were at least 20 percent below 1990 emissions should receive some recognition. An additional 2 percent of the EU-wide total was reserved for this "early action" redistribution, which redounded to the benefit of eight of the East European new member states, and particularly to the three Baltic states, plus Romania and Bulgaria.

The post-2012 amendments also present a coherent attempt to deal with harmonization. From 2013 on, installations will fall into either of two categories: those subject to the basic rule of full auctioning and an exceptional category for trade-impacted sectors. There will be no free allocation to the electric utility sector starting in 2013 with some transitional derogation for new member states through 2020. The phase-out of free allocation to other industrial sources will be slower—20 percent auctioning in 2013, 70 percent in 2020, and 100 percent in 2027—with the transitional free allocation based on an EU-wide benchmark. Allocation to all of these installations will be eventually harmonized with zero free allocation. This is not the allocation rule that those advocating harmonization had in mind, but it is an easy and obvious one to administer. Exceptions will continue to apply to installations in sectors or sub-sectors that meet pre-specified criteria for being "trade-impacted"; these installations will receive a free allocation equal to 100 percent of a harmonized best available technology standard. Those sectors or sub-sectors will be determined by the Commission, after consultation with the European Council, by the end of 2009 and every five years thereafter.

The most interesting feature of recent changes in the EU ETS is the coupling of increasing differentiation with increasing stringency. If a global approach is to be "broad then deep" (Schmalensee, 1998), participants will find themselves in a situation not unlike that of the EU member states. An initial broad phase, like the trial period of the EU ETS, may not require much differentiation; however, as the system enters the deep phase (more stringent emission reduction requirements), differentiation will become an increasingly important issue. In its recently completed negotiation of amendments for the post-2012 period, the EU ETS has provided a preview of the magnitude of differentiation that may be required. In this case, 12 percent of the system-wide cap will be redistributed in a manner that will require the "leader" countries to give up 9.5 percent of what they would receive under a proportional entitlement in order to allow the less committed, less wealthy, or otherwise deserving beneficiaries to receive as much as 50 percent more than they would be entitled to under a strictly proportional system.

Financial flows

Before concluding, note should be taken of the absence, in the EU context, of a problem that has commonly been anticipated for a global trading regime. A trading system implies trade among participating entities and accompanying financial flows between participating nations. These flows are likely to be larger to the extent that differentiation creates differences in the apportionment of the system-wide cap that go in the same direction as comparative advantage in abatement. For instance, modeling exercises commonly predict that the cheapest abatement options will be found in the same developing countries that most analyses assume will be the beneficiaries of global differentiation. The concern is that these two factors would combine to create large international flows of capital at a level that is politically or otherwise untenable. A remarkable feature of the EU ETS is that there has been virtually no notice of the cross-border financial flows that have occurred as a result of emissions trading.

Despite all the birthing problems of the EU ETS, the market for EUAs has been very liquid and has resulted in cross-border financial transfers among entities within the participating member states. The 26 x 26 matrix attached as an appendix provides a table of the country of origin of all the EUAs surrendered during the three years of the trial period.

Several points are immediately obvious. First, most of the allowances issued and surrendered were *not* traded outside the member state in which they were issued. Of the total 6.15 billion EUAs surrendered, 5.79 billion (94 percent) were surrendered in the issuing member state, as indicated by the diagonal entries in this matrix. The off-diagonal entries are the international flows, which accounted for only 354 million EUAs or 5.8 percent of the total. The small share of international trading reflects what could be expected and is usually observed with free allocation. That is, most entities that receive free allowances keep them for later surrender against their own emissions. Typically, only the allowances left over after the installation covers its own emissions, or those needed to cover emissions when its allocation is not enough, are traded. The difference between allowances issued and emissions to be covered at installations in different countries can be measured. The sum of the shorts (emissions > allowances) for all installations for the entire trial period was 650 million EUAs, and the sum of the longs (emissions < allowances) at installations with surplus EUAs was 810 million (Trotignon and Ellerman, 2008). At a minimum, 650 million allowances were redistributed from longs to shorts. This figure, slightly more than 10 percent of the total allowances issued, largely explains the relatively small scale of the international transfers.

While the quantity of allowances traded internationally is very modest relative to the total quantity of allowances issued and surrendered, the scale of international transfers is large compared to what would have been required to ensure the compliance of the four member states that were short for the period as a whole: the UK, Italy, Spain, and Slovenia. For all installations to be in compliance in these four countries, EUAs sufficient to cover at least 88 million tons would have had to flow across EU borders. The actual level was four times higher. Even if the many offsetting flows between trading pairs are eliminated, the sum of net flows is 217 million—two and a half times the minimum international transfer required for compliance by all covered sources. If national preferences for keeping allowances within domestic borders had been strictly observed, there would have been only four member states importing allowances. In fact, twenty-two of the twenty-five member states were importers of EUAs in some amount, although only seven were net importers.[19]

---

[19] The net importers were the UK, Spain, Italy, Germany, Austria, Ireland, and Slovenia. Germany, Austria, and Ireland were net importers despite being long for the period as a whole due to a phenomenon that occurred in all member states: some surplus allowances at long installations appear never to have entered the market. See Trotignon and Ellerman (2008) for a more complete discussion.

Another way of looking at this phenomenon is counting how many of the off-diagonal cells in the matrix shown in the appendix are filled. There are 650 such cells of which 470 (72 percent) are occupied and thus indicate a cross border transfer. For most pairings, trade goes both ways, and for many member states the net flows with various trading partners are not all in the same direction. For instance, Germany is a net importer in the aggregate and in trading with most partners, but it is a net exporter to the UK, Italy, and Spain.

Market intermediaries and institutions largely explain the abundance of cross-border transactions. Installations with a deficit or a surplus looked to market intermediaries to obtain needed EUAs, or to dispose of excess EUAs, and these intermediaries operated at a Europe-wide scale. For instance, a UK firm that had a surplus might sell to a broker or at an exchange with the result that the surplus allowances would as likely be sold to a firm that was short in Spain as to a firm that was short in the UK. With EUAs good for compliance regardless of origin and with zero transportation costs, surplus allowances were as likely to cross a border as not.

The absence of any public concern about international allowance flows can be largely attributed to their small scale relative to the total number of allowances in play and to the indifference that buyers and sellers exhibited concerning the national origin of EUAs. The UK was by far the largest importer of EUAs, with net imports totaling 107 million tons for the period as a whole, which was equal to 14 percent of the UK's verified emissions. Placing a value on these imports is difficult given the variability in EUA prices at different points in time, but the year when the allowance import bill was highest in value terms was 2006, when EUA imports would seem to have created a £350 million (≈ €500 million) outflow of funds from the UK. While this might be seen as a large amount, it pales in comparison to payments for other goods and services imported to the UK in 2006, which totaled about £415 billion.[20] Payments to foreigners for allowances were less than one-tenth of 1 percent of the total bill for imported goods and services. The amount in future years could be larger due to higher EUA prices and perhaps higher levels of imported allowances, but this flow would still be a small part of total payments abroad for goods and services. One Euro-skeptic organization in the UK, which regards the EU ETS as emblematic of all that it dislikes about

---

[20] Given as $768 billion in IMF Statistics.

Brussels, has consistently criticized the transfers to the rest of the EU that are implied by the UK's short position in allowances (Open Europe, 2006), but this complaint has failed to find any traction either with the public or the government. Several other aspects of the EU ETS have caught the attention of the public and governments—windfall profits, over-allocation, high initial prices—but not international flows of funds as a result of cross-border allowance trades.[21]

Conclusion

Europe has demonstrated that it is possible to construct a multinational cap-and-trade system that encompasses sovereign nations with considerable disparities in economic circumstance and degrees of willingness to adopt climate change measures. At the same time, the European experience points to the problems that exist in multinational systems and in doing so reveals the distance to be traveled in replicating something similar on a global scale.

The encouraging aspect of the EU ETS experience to date is the evidence it offers that some of the problems often cited as impeding a global system may not be that serious. The institutional disparities between East and West in Europe are not as great as those between North and South on the global scale, but they are still large. It took more time to put the regulatory infrastructure needed to support trading in place in Eastern Europe than it did in the West, but it was done, and companies in the new member states are not only complying, but are increasingly learning to price CO_2 into their operational and investment decisions. The EU's adoption of a multiyear trial period has set a useful precedent for dealing with issues of institutional readiness that could be employed in a global system.

Another problem that did not appear is political or public opposition to the financial flows that accompany international trading. Most of the allowances issued by individual member states were surrendered in the same country, and international transfers were a small percentage of the total, though they were larger than what might have been expected assuming a national preference for avoiding cross-border trades unless absolutely necessary. The widespread use of cross-border

---

[21] For a more complete discussion of these other controversies, see Ellerman and Joskow (2008).

transfers for compliance reflects the role of intermediaries, which operate in an EU-wide market, in redistributing the differences between allocations and emissions that existed for all installations. Surplus allowances were as likely to end up in another member state as in the one in which the selling installation was located; similarly, allowances purchased to cover emissions were as likely to come from surpluses at installations in other member states as from other installations in the same country.

The more problematic question raised by the EU ETS, when seen as a prototype for a global system, is how to reproduce what was essential for success in Europe: namely, a pre-existing central structure and a well-established set of powerful side benefits. The European Commission cannot perform the same role on a global scale, nor can the benefits of participation in the EU be extended beyond Europe. Perhaps a central institution suited for administering a global system will emerge out of bilateral agreements that might link the EU ETS with comparable systems outside of Europe. In any case, some central authority or institution will be needed to review regulatory actions, to coordinate periodic adjustments of the system-wide cap, and to negotiate with new participants. The side benefits for participation may not need to be as powerful as those associated with becoming a member of the EU, but the experience in Europe suggests that something more will be needed than an overarching treaty and an appeal to common concern about climate change. This is not a unique challenge. In diplomacy, issues are inevitably linked, and inducements will be needed if there is to be a global climate regime.

Mechanisms developed to address the differentiation of responsibilities among nations (such as cap setting and allowance allocation) could also serve to deliver incentives for participation, but the EU ETS did not operate this way. The first step was to get everyone in and then to deal with the tensions between stringency, differentiation, and harmonization. In the recently negotiated amendments to the ETS Directive for the post-2012 period, increasing stringency is accompanied by greater differentiation, and harmonization is to be achieved by phasing out free allocation in favor of auctioning with appropriate exceptions for trade-impacted sectors. How well this will work in Europe and whether it could be applied on a global scale have yet to be seen, but at least the problem has been engaged, and a pertinent example is being established.

References

Aldy, Joseph E. and Robert N. Stavins (2007). "Introduction: International Policy Architecture for Global Climate Change," in Joseph E. Aldy and Robert N. Stavins (eds.), *Architectures for Agreement: Addressing Global Climate Change in the Post-Kyoto World*. New York: Cambridge University Press, pp. 1–27.

Bart, Istvan (2007). "Hungary," in A. D. Ellerman, B. K. Buchner, and C. Carraro (eds.), *Allocation in the European Emissions Trading Scheme: Rights, Rents and Fairness*. Cambridge, UK: Cambridge University Press, pp. 246–68.

Chmelik, Tomas (2007). "Czech Republic," in Ellerman, Buchner, and Carraro (eds.), pp. 269–300.

Convery, Frank J. and Luke Redmond (2007). "Market and Price Developments in the European Union Emissions Trading Scheme," *Review of Environmental Economics and Policy* 1: 88–111.

Convery, Frank J., A. Denny Ellerman, and Christian de Perthuis (2008). *The European Carbon Market in Action: Lessons from the First Trading Period: Interim Report*, unpublished special report, available at: www.aprec.fr/documents/08-03-25_interim_report_en.pdf.

Ellerman, A. Denny and Barbara K. Buchner (2007). "The European Union Emissions Trading Scheme: Origins, Allocation, and Early Results," *Review of Environmental Economics and Policy* 1: 66–87.

Ellerman, A. Denny, Barbara K. Buchner, and Carlo Carraro (2007). "Unifying Themes," in Ellerman, Buchner, and Carraro (eds.), pp. 339–69.

Ellerman, A. Denny and Paul L. Joskow (2008). *The European Union's Emissions Trading System in Perspective*. Washington, DC: Pew Center on Global Climate Change, available at: www.pewclimate.org/docUploads/EU-ETS-In-Perspective-Report.pdf.

European Commission (2000). *Green paper on greenhouse gas emissions trading within the European Union* COM (2000) 87, March 3.

(2006). *Communication from the Commission to the Council and to the European Parliament on the assessment of national allocation plans for the allocation of greenhouse gas emission allowances in the second period of the EU Emissions Trading Scheme accompanying Commission Decisions of 29 November 2006* COM (2006) 725 final, November 29.

(2008). *Proposal for a Directive of the European Parliament and of the Council amending Directive 2003/87/EC so as to improve and extend the greenhouse gas emission allowance trading system of the Community.* COM (2008) 16 provisional, January 23.

European Council (2003). *Directive 2003/87/EC, establishing a scheme for greenhouse gas emission allowance trading within the Community and amending Council Directive 96/61/EC,* October 13.

Frankel, Jeffrey (2007). "Formulas for Quantitative Emission Targets," in Aldy and Stavins (eds.), pp. 31–56.

Jacoby, H., R. Schmalensee, and I. Sue Wing (1999). *Toward a Useful Architecture for Climate Change Negotiations,* MIT Joint Program on the Science and Policy of Global Change, Report No. 49, May.

Jankowski, Boleslaw (2007). "Poland," in Ellerman, Buchner, and Carraro (eds.), pp. 301–36.

Kruger, Joseph, Wallace E. Oates, and William A. Pizer (2007). "Decentralization in the EU Emissions Trading Scheme and Lessons for Global Policy," *Review of Environmental Economics and Policy* 1: 112–33.

Open Europe (2006). "The High Price of Hot Air: Why the EU Emissions Trading Scheme is an Environmental and Economic Failure," unpublished paper, available at www.openeurope.org.uk/research/ets.pdf.

Schmalensee, Richard (1998). "Greenhouse Policy Architectures and Institutions," in W. D. Nordhaus (ed.), *Economics and Policy Issues in Climate Change.* Washington: Resources for the Future, pp. 137–158.

Skjaerseth, Jon Birger and Jorgen Wettestad (2008). *EU Emissions Trading: Initiation, Decision-making, and Implementation.* Aldershot, UK: Ashgate Publishing Ltd.

Trotignon, Raphael and A. Denny Ellerman (2008). "Compliance Behavior in the EU ETS: Cross-Border Trading, Banking and Borrowing," MIT-CEEPR Working Paper 2008–12, available at: http://web.mit.edu/ceepr/www/publications/workingpapers/2008-012.pdf.

Zapfel, Peter (2007). "A Brief but Lively Chapter in EU Climate Policy: The Commission's Perspective," in Ellerman, Buchner, and Carraro (eds.), pp. 13–38.

APPENDIX: Origin and disposition of surrendered allowances, 2005–07 (million tons)

Originating from ... (columns); Surrendered in ... (rows)

Phase 1	AT	BE	DK	FI	FR	DE	GR	IE	IT	LU	NL	PT	ES	SE	GB	CY	CZ	EE	HU	LV	LT	MT	PL	RO	SK	SI	Total	Imports	%
AT	91.63	0.20	0.11	0.20	0.52	1.03		0.00	0.05		0.83		0.05	0.05	0.26		0.30	0.00	0.03	0.14	0.13		0.42		0.31	0.02	96.27	4.64	1%
BE	0.21	148.38	0.17	0.12	0.96	0.80		0.04	0.95	0.38	0.23	0.08	0.75	0.03	0.08		0.46	0.17	1.49	0.01	0.66		6.89		0.07	0.07	162.92	14.54	4%
DK	0.00	0.15	72.62	0.06	0.10	0.65			0.01		0.85	0.15	0.15	0.03	0.37		0.43	0.02	0.06		0.02		0.08		0.11	0.11	76.09	3.47	1%
FI	0.20	0.11	0.06	114.34	0.87	0.22	0.25		0.07		0.15	0.14	0.03	0.34	0.78		0.93	0.26	0.02	0.06	0.21		1.09		0.10	0.11	120.24	5.90	2%
FR	0.01	0.07	0.04	0.29	379.71	0.15	0.12		0.07		0.13	0.07	0.43	0.02	0.26		0.25		0.02		0.12		1.73		0.13	0.13	383.67	3.96	1%
DE	0.48	4.02	0.87	2.83	6.72	1391.19	0.08	0.86	1.26	0.27	7.34	0.96	0.96	1.21	8.40			1.35	2.53	0.28	2.39		5.31		1.67		1448.08	56.89	16%
GR	0.02						212.91				0.01	0.02			0.03			0.01					0.84		0.02		213.93	1.03	0%
IE	0.08	0.02	0.06	0.29	0.06	0.00		64.04	0.19	0.01	0.09	0.18	0.02		0.43		0.06	0.56		0.04	0.03		0.06		0.03		66.38	2.33	1%
IT	0.46	1.18	0.66	1.07	6.45	5.42	0.26	0.09	629.12	0.01	1.16	1.19	1.54	0.57	4.13	0.23	3.68	2.05	1.08	0.85	1.14		6.83		2.84	0.05	672.06	42.94	12%
LU										7.88																	7.88	0.00	0%
NL	0.12	2.98	0.27	0.79	2.30	2.84	0.08	0.02	0.15	0.02	216.80	0.08	0.38	0.23	2.72	0.05	1.79	0.58	0.38	0.23	0.75		2.44		0.93	0.00	236.94	20.14	6%
PT	0.01	0.01	0.01	0.01	0.05	0.06	0.08		0.06		0.04	99.44	0.28		0.46		0.22	0.00	0.00	0.00	0.00		0.01		0.02		100.84	1.40	0%
ES	0.27	1.68	2.47	3.77	5.92	3.47	0.13	0.13	1.05	0.10	3.74	3.32	499.67	0.91	4.69	0.01	3.54	1.06	1.13	0.56	0.74		8.21		1.64		548.22	48.55	14%
SE	0.01	0.03	0.07	0.36	0.09	0.19	0.01		0.01		0.01	0.01	0.00	57.05	0.18		0.08	0.15	0.00	0.01	0.08		0.12		0.01		58.46	1.41	0%
GB	0.41	10.09	4.69	5.11	20.59	11.29	1.17	0.16	3.45	0.26	18.52	1.78	2.60	1.20	619.10	0.14	13.83	5.29	2.81	0.75	5.40		17.76		4.33		750.72	131.62	37%
CY																15.73											15.73	0.00	0%
CZ	0.00	0.02	0.07	0.04		0.12			0.12		0.26	0.23	0.03	0.07	0.96	0.01	247.03	0.11	0.48	0.01	0.10		2.02		0.61		252.42	5.39	2%
EE	0.02	0.02	0.00		0.07	0.03							0.03	0.02				39.94					0.04		0.24		40.05	0.11	0%
HU	0.01				0.14	0.03					0.02				0.01		0.15	0.04	78.63						0.02		79.30	0.67	0%
LV																	0.03		0.03	8.55	0.06						8.64	0.09	0%
LT	0.03								0.03								0.00		0.03	0.02	17.98		0.39		0.01		19.13	1.15	0%
MT																						3.96					3.96	0.00	0%
PL	0.04	0.18	0.10		0.26	0.20	0.02	0.00	0.05		0.02	0.02	0.09	0.01	0.62	0.01	0.17	0.00	0.08	0.04	0.02		620.34		0.25		622.53	2.19	1%
RO		0.00	0.03	0.00	0.05	0.04	0.02	0.13	0.08		0.23		0.01	0.18	0.01		0.74	0.04	0.25	0.11	0.07		1.37	55.24	0.03		58.65	3.41	1%
SK	0.00		0.00	0.00	0.22	0.02					0.01				0.05		0.07	0.10	0.01	0.11	0.20		0.17		74.30		75.37	1.07	0%
SI	0.04				0.02	0.40	0.00		0.02		0.09	0.02	0.06		0.19		0.02	0.07	0.01	0.04	0.02		0.19			25.37	26.61	1.24	0%
Total	93.99	169.42	82.36	129.40	425.61	1418.40	215.23	65.47	636.74	8.94	250.53	107.66	507.06	62.14	643.75	16.25	280.83	51.78	89.05	11.73	30.13	3.96	676.55	55.24	87.44	25.49	6145.13	354.16	100%
Exports	2.36	21.03	9.74	15.07	45.90	27.21	2.32	1.42	7.62	1.06	33.73	8.21	7.39	5.09	24.65	0.52	33.79	11.84	10.42	3.18	12.15	0.00	56.22	0.00	13.14	0.11	354.16		
%	1%	6%	3%	4%	13%	8%	1%	0%	2%	0%	10%	2%	2%	1%	7%	0%	10%	3%	3%	1%	3%	0%	16%	0%	4%	0%	100%		

Source: Trotignon and ellerman (2008).
Note: units in million EUAs)

4 | Linkage of tradable permit systems in international climate policy architecture

JUDSON JAFFE AND ROBERT N. STAVINS[*]

As the nations of the world consider alternative international climate policy architectures for the post-2012 period, tradable permit systems are emerging as a preferred domestic instrument for reducing greenhouse gas (GHG) emissions. The two most significant institutions for reducing GHG emissions implemented to date—the European Union Emission Trading Scheme (EU ETS) and the Clean Development Mechanism (CDM)—are tradable permit systems. Furthermore, tradable permit systems are being considered as the primary policy instrument for reducing GHG emissions in Australia, Canada, Japan, and the United States, among other countries.

Due to the increasingly likely prospect of a world with multiple tradable permit systems, attention has focused on how and whether to link these systems. Linking occurs when regulated entities in one tradable permit system are allowed to use emission allowances or emission reduction credits from another system to meet their domestic compliance obligations.[1] These entities can then take advantage of cost savings

[*] Jaffe is Vice President, Analysis Group, and Stavins is the Albert Pratt Professor of Business and Government at the John F. Kennedy School of Government, Harvard University; University Fellow of Resources for the Future; and Research Associate of the National Bureau of Economic Research. This chapter draws, in part, on Jaffe and Stavins (2007), which built upon previous studies by Haites and Mullins (2001), Baron and Bygrave (2002), Blyth and Bosi (2004), Baron and Philibert (2005), Ellis and Tirpak (2006), and Kruger et al. (2007). Exceptionally valuable research assistance was provided by Matthew Ranson, and we benefitted greatly from communications with Scott Barrett, Denny Ellerman, Robert Keohane, and David Victor, as well as valuable comments by Joseph Aldy, Dallas Burtraw, and Peter Zapfel on a previous version of the manuscript, and excellent editorial work by Marika Tatsutani. All remaining errors are our own.
[1] Such linkage of domestic tradable permit systems is completely different from the state-to-state trading envisaged under Article 17 of the Kyoto Protocol, whereby signatories to the Protocol can trade parts of their quantitative

from international trade: just as allowance trading *within* a tradable permit system allows higher-cost emission reductions to be replaced by lower-cost reductions within that system, trading *across* systems allows higher-cost reductions to be replaced by lower-cost reductions from a different system. These cost savings create significant incentives for regulatory authorities to link tradable permit systems.

Despite the benefits of linkage, there are also legitimate concerns about the implications of some linkages. These concerns depend, in part, on the type of linkage involved. One concern is that directly linking two cap-and-trade systems will result in the complete and automatic propagation of cost-containment measures from one system to the other. On the other hand, indirect linkage among cap-and-trade systems via a common credit system could adversely affect global emissions if the credit system suffers from severe additionality problems—that is, the crediting of emission reductions that are not truly "additional" because they would have happened anyway.

Thus, there is an important trade-off between direct linkages, which can require a high degree of harmonization, and indirect linkages via a common credit system, which raise concerns about additionality. This trade-off may suggest a natural progression. In the near term, indirect linkage of cap-and-trade systems via a common credit system could achieve some of the cost savings of direct linkage, but without the need for as much harmonization. In the longer term, international negotiations could lead to a broad set of multilateral, direct links among cap-and-trade systems.

We examine the benefits and concerns associated with international linkage and analyze how linkage may become part—possibly a central part—of the post-2012 international climate policy architecture. Section 2, *Categories of tradable permit systems*, introduces the two general categories of tradable permit systems: cap-and-trade and emission-reduction-credit systems. Section 3, *Greenhouse gas tradable permit systems*, reviews existing and proposed GHG tradable permit systems. Section 4, *Types of linkages*, describes the major types of linkages and provides examples of existing linkages. Section 5, *Implications of linkage*, examines the general implications of linkage,

Footnote 1 (*cont.*)
> national targets or "assigned amounts." Also, the sort of linkage we consider is distinct from agreements between countries or systems for various other forms of collaboration, such as joint funding of research and development.

including potential benefits and concerns. Section 6, *The potential role of linkage in an international climate policy architecture*, discusses the possible roles that linkage might play in future international policy architectures, both in the near term and in the long term. Section 7, *Evaluating the role of linkage in an international policy architecture*, provides an evaluation of linkage in its various roles. In Section 8, *How will near-term climate policy negotiations affect bottom-up linkages?*, we examine how the policy elements of near-term climate negotiations could affect the prospects for linkage. Section 9 concludes.

Categories of tradable permit systems

Because the implications of linkage depend on the type of tradable permit systems that are being linked, it is essential to distinguish between two categories of systems: cap-and-trade and emission-reduction-credit systems.

Cap-and-trade systems

A cap-and-trade system constrains the aggregate emissions of regulated sources by creating a limited number of tradable emission allowances, which emission sources are required to secure and surrender in number equal to their emissions. Faced with the choice between surrendering an allowance or reducing their emissions, firms will choose whichever option is less expensive. As long as trading costs are low and allowance markets are sufficiently competitive, trading will lead firms to put allowances to their highest-valued use—that is, covering those emissions that are most costly to reduce—regardless of how the allowances are initially distributed (Stavins 1995; Hahn 1984). Conversely, the opportunity to trade allowances ensures that the emissions reductions undertaken to meet the cap are those that are the least costly to achieve.

In developing a cap-and-trade system, policymakers must decide on several design elements (Stavins 2008). They must determine how many allowances will be issued, which defines the system's cap. They must also determine the scope of the system's coverage—that is, what emission sources and types of GHG emissions will be subjected to the overall cap. A related decision regards the point of regulation for the trading system. A cap on energy-related carbon dioxide (CO_2) emissions can be enforced by requiring fossil fuel suppliers to surrender allowances for the carbon content of their fuel sales ("upstream" regulation) or by requiring final emitters to surrender allowances for their emissions ("downstream" regulation).

Policymakers also must determine how to distribute allowances. Allowances can be distributed for free or auctioned, or a combination of the two approaches can be employed. If allowances are distributed for free, there are limitless possible methods for determining who receives them and how many allowances go to each recipient. Finally, policymakers must decide on several features of the cap-and-trade system relating to monitoring, reporting, and compliance enforcement.

A key concern for many countries that are developing mandatory climate policies is uncertainty regarding compliance costs. In the context of a cap-and-trade system, this concern is often expressed as concern about the level and volatility of allowance prices. Accordingly, much attention has been given to the potential inclusion of "cost-containment" measures in cap-and-trade systems, such as offset provisions, allowance banking and borrowing, and safety-valve provisions.[2] An offset provision allows regulated entities to offset some of their emissions with credits from emission reduction measures that are outside the cap-and-trade system's scope of coverage. Banking allows firms to save unused allowances for use in future years. Borrowing allows firms to use allowances that will be issued in future years to demonstrate compliance in an earlier year. Both banking and borrowing allow firms flexibility to shift emission reduction efforts over time to minimize costs.

A safety valve puts an upper bound on the compliance costs that firms will incur by offering them the option of paying a predetermined fee (the safety-valve "trigger price") to purchase additional allowances. In its simplest form, a safety valve introduces a tradeoff between avoiding unexpectedly high costs and achieving a system's emissions target. When a safety valve is exercised, firms' emissions exceed the number of allowances that were initially distributed. However, this tradeoff can be mitigated (or potentially eliminated) through provisions such as reducing subsequent years' caps to compensate for any increase in emissions that results from use of the safety valve (Stavins 2008).[3]

---

[2] For a discussion of these and other cost-containment proposals, see Tatsutani and Pizer 2008.

[3] More broadly, a comprehensive, symmetric safety-valve mechanism could provide both a price ceiling and a price floor (Murray, Newell, and Pizer 2009).

Emission-reduction-credit systems

An emission-reduction-credit system brings about emission reductions by awarding tradable credits for certified emissions reductions. Some programs that are described as credit systems can be quite similar to a cap-and-trade system.[4] Therefore, when we refer to credit systems, we are describing systems that have a few key differentiating characteristics. First, participation in the systems is voluntary. Second, the systems serve only as a source of credits that can be used by entities facing compliance obligations in other systems. They do not themselves impose any obligations on entities to hold or surrender credits. Third, the systems grant credits for particular projects based on an estimate of how those projects reduce emissions from some agreed-upon baseline level of what emissions would have been if the projects had not been carried out.

In designing a credit system, policymakers must determine what types of emission sources and actions can be awarded credits. For example, certain emission reduction projects may be excluded from consideration due to concern about the feasibility of measuring results accurately. Also, policymakers must decide on a method for calculating the number of credits that are awarded. These calculations can be performed on a project-by-project basis, or they can be based on standard assumptions applied to all projects of a particular type. In either case, it is necessary to estimate what baseline emissions would have been absent the credited action.

Greenhouse gas tradable permit systems

Although there are only a limited number of existing GHG tradable permit systems, the list of planned and prospective systems is considerably longer. The increasing number and prominence of such systems together with the existence of strong economic and political incentives for linking them provides the motivation for our analysis of linkage as a potential element of the post-2012 international policy architecture. In this section we provide a brief review of some of the major existing, planned, and proposed GHG trading systems.

---

[4] For example, a credit system may set individual emissions limits for firms, and allow them to generate tradable credits if they reduce their emissions below their assigned limit. Such a system would be essentially identical to a cap-and-trade system where each firm is allocated a quantity of allowances that reflects its specific emissions limit.

Cap-and-trade systems

European Union Emission Trading Scheme (EU ETS)

The EU ETS is the world's largest GHG cap-and-trade system. Phase I of the EU ETS, from 2005 through 2007, capped aggregate CO_2 emissions from more than 11,000 industrial facilities and electricity generators in twenty-five European countries (European Commission 2005). Those sources collectively emitted approximately 2 billion metric tons of CO_2 in 2005, about 45 percent of the EU's CO_2 emissions (European Commission 2005, 2007b). The EU ETS cap has been tightened for Phase II, which runs from 2008 through 2012. Also, the scope of the EU ETS has been expanded to cover new sources in countries that participated in Phase I, and to include sources in Bulgaria and Romania, which acceded to the EU in 2007.[5] In 2008, the EU made various revisions to the design of the system that will become effective in 2013 (European Commission 2008).

Norway's emission trading system

Norway began implementing an emissions trading system at the same time as the EU ETS. From 2005 to 2007, the Norwegian program covered a relatively small set of industrial sources accounting for just 10–15 percent of the country's GHG emissions (Norwegian Ministry of the Environment 2005). Norway subsequently agreed to adjust its system to conform to the rules and procedures of the EU ETS, with which it was integrated in 2008. These adjustments included broadening the scope of covered emission sources, such that Norway's system now covers approximately 40 percent of its GHG emissions (Euractiv.com 2007).

Japan's emission trading system

Japan has had a Voluntary Emissions Trading System (JVETS) in operation since April 2006, but participating facilities have accounted for no more than a few million tons of Japan's annual GHG emissions, which exceeded 1.3 billion metric tons in 2004 (Sudo 2006; Japanese

[5] For an assessment of the EU ETS as a model for a potential future international climate policy architecture, see the chapter in this volume by Denny Ellerman. The performance of the EU ETS is analyzed in a symposium of three articles published by the *Review of Environmental Economics and Policy*, Volume 1, Number 1, Winter 2007.

Ministry of the Environment 2006). After considerable national discussion and debate, Prime Minister Yasuo Fukuda announced in June 2008 that the government would employ a cap-and-trade system as its main instrument to achieve ambitious reduction targets of 60–80 percent below current levels by 2050 (ABC News 2008).

Australia's proposed system

Following a change of government in December 2007, Prime Minister Kevin Rudd lent his support for the implementation of a cap-and-trade system by 2010 (and for his country's ratification of the Kyoto Protocol). In July 2008, the Australian government released a green paper with its detailed plan for a national cap-and-trade system to reduce CO_2 emissions 60 percent below 2000 levels by 2050 (Australian Government 2008). Based upon feedback from stakeholders, the government released a white paper later in 2008.

Regional Greenhouse Gas Initiative and other regional efforts in the United States

In 2005, seven northeastern US states agreed to implement the Regional Greenhouse Gas Initiative (RGGI), which three additional northeastern states subsequently joined.[6] The program, which began in 2009, introduced a cap-and-trade system for electricity generators within the ten states. Two auctions of RGGI allowances were completed in 2008. The program places an aggregate cap on covered generators' emissions equal to nearly 190 million tons of CO_2 per year from 2009 to 2014, a level roughly comparable to those generators' recent emissions. From 2015 to 2018, the cap will be reduced by 2.5 percent per year. In addition to RGGI, other regional and state efforts to limit GHGs in the United States have begun. One of the most prominent has resulted from California's enactment of its Global Warming Solutions Act of 2006, which set a statewide GHG emissions limit for 2020 equal to California's 1990 emissions level. In its October 2008 "scoping plan," the California Air Resources Board (2008) included a statewide cap-and-trade system for all energy-related CO_2 emissions as one of the key elements of its proposal for achieving the 2020 target.

---

[6] Participating states include Connecticut, Delaware, Maine, Maryland, Massachusetts, New Hampshire, New Jersey, New York, Rhode Island, and Vermont.

Proposals for a federal cap-and-trade system in the United States
Several bills proposing a federal GHG cap-and-trade system were
introduced in the 110th US Congress. These draft bills differed in many
important respects, including the scope of the system's coverage, the
level of the cap, and the measures included to address cost concerns. It
appears increasingly likely that a meaningful economy-wide cap-and-
trade system will be adopted by the United States in 2009 or 2010.

Proposed Canadian system
In 2008, the Canadian Government announced its intention to
implement a national regulation requiring reductions in the emissions
intensity of major stationary sources of GHG emissions, which together
account for about half of Canada's GHG emissions (Environment
Canada 2008). Regulated sources would be required to achieve an
18 percent reduction in their emissions intensity from 2006 levels by
2010, and an additional 2 percent reduction in each year thereafter.
Among other compliance options, regulated sources could rely on
emissions trading with other sources that have reduced their emissions
intensity by more than the required amount.

Emission-reduction-credit systems

Clean Development Mechanism (CDM)
Established under the Kyoto Protocol, the CDM is the most significant
GHG emission-reduction-credit system to date. Under the CDM, certified emission reductions (CERs) are awarded for voluntary emission
reduction projects in developing countries that ratified the Protocol,
but are not among the Annex I countries subject to the Protocol's commitments to limit emissions. While CERs can be used to meet the emissions commitments of Annex B Parties to the Protocol (where Annex B
refers to the thirty-four industrialized countries and emerging market
economies of central and eastern Europe that took on targets under the
Protocol), they may also be used for compliance purposes by entities
in cap-and-trade systems around the world, including systems in countries that are not Parties to the Protocol, such as the United States.[7]

---

[7] For example, under certain circumstances (and to a limited extent), regulated
   entities could use CERs to meet their compliance obligations under the RGGI
   system (RGGI 2007a).

An Executive Board established under the Kyoto Protocol is responsible for supervising the CDM and for making determinations about CERs issued for particular projects. From project initiation, it can take as long as two or more years to go through that process, and the cost of the process (not including the cost of the actual emission reduction measures) can be substantial (Nigoff 2006; Michaelowa and Jotzo 2005). Nonetheless, as of August 2008, more than 3,000 projects were in the CDM "project pipeline." These projects are expected to generate more than 2.7 billion CERs by the end of 2012 (each CER reflects a reduction of 1 metric ton of CO_2 equivalent). Of these projects, the Executive Board had already registered more than 1,100 that are expected to yield 1.3 billion CERs by 2012. As of August 2008, projects in China accounted for 52 percent of the expected CERs from registered projects; other countries that accounted for a significant share of the total are: India, 14 percent; Brazil, 9 percent; and South Korea, 7 percent. Projects in forty-six other countries collectively accounted for the remaining 19 percent (UNFCCC 2008).

Joint Implementation (JI)

Like the CDM, JI was established as a project-based flexibility mechanism under the Kyoto Protocol. However, unlike the CDM, JI applies to emission reduction projects carried out in an Annex I country (the host country) that has a national emissions target under the Protocol. JI projects generate credits or "emission reduction units" (ERUs) that can be used to cover increased emissions in other countries. When these credits are generated, a corresponding reduction is made in the host country's emissions target under the Protocol. This ensures that the use of ERUs to cover increased emissions in another country is offset by a net reduction in the host country's emissions.

JI projects will likely produce far fewer credits than the CDM. The Joint Implementation Supervisory Committee began accepting proposals in October 2005 (Pointcarbon 2007). By August 1, 2008, it had received submissions for only 163 projects, accounting for an estimated 280 million tons of CO_2-equivalent emission reductions over the five years of the Kyoto Protocol's first commitment period (UNEP Risoe Centre 2008).

Domestic offset programs
In designing domestic cap-and-trade systems, governments can establish offset programs to credit GHG abatement measures involving gases or sources that are not covered by the cap. These offset credits can then be used by regulated entities to meet compliance obligations. For example, electricity generators covered by RGGI can use domestic offsets to cover part of their emissions. RGGI has identified a set of project types that can be implemented to generate offset credits, as well as standards for determining the number of allowances awarded to different projects (RGGI 2007a). Cap-and-trade systems proposed in Australia, Canada, and the United States also include offset programs.

Types of linkages

A linkage between tradable permit systems can take different forms, which in turn can have important implications for how each of the linked systems is affected. Direct linkages between systems can be one-way (unilateral) or two-way (bilateral or multilateral). Also, while an explicit decision is required to establish a direct link between systems, direct links can introduce a set of indirect linkages that were perhaps never explicitly intended (Jaffe and Stavins 2007).

Direct linkages

To establish a direct link between two systems, either one or both systems must accept the other's allowances or credits as valid for use in demonstrating compliance in its own system.

Direct link between a cap-and-trade system and credit system
In this case, regulatory authorities in the cap-and-trade system choose to recognize emission reduction credits from the credit system. Because the credit system does not place requirements on entities to surrender credits or allowances, this linkage is necessarily one-way. If the price of credits is lower than the price of emission allowances, then regulated firms in the cap-and-trade system have an incentive to purchase credits. This will reduce the price of allowances in the cap-and-trade system and increase the price of credits in the credit system until the two prices converge.

Direct link between cap-and-trade systems

Cap-and-trade systems can recognize allowances from other cap-and-trade systems. The resulting linkage can be one-way or two-way, depending on whether the recognition is mutual.

An example of an unrestricted one-way link would be if System A recognizes System B's allowances without restriction, but not vice versa. In that case, if System A's allowance price is higher than System B's, participants in System A will buy allowances from participants in System B, thereby reducing System A's allowance price and increasing System B's price until the prices converge. Such trading will increase emissions in A and decrease emissions in B, as higher cost emission reductions in A are avoided and replaced by lower cost reductions in B. However, if System A's allowance price is lower than System B's, no trading will result from the one-way link. Hence, a one-way link in which A recognizes B's allowances will ensure that A's allowance price never exceeds B's price.

In a two-way direct link, both cap-and-trade systems recognize each other's allowances, making it possible for allowances to flow in either direction. Two-way links can be bilateral or multilateral. In this case, any difference between the systems' allowance prices will lead to sales of allowances from the lower price system to the higher price system until both systems' allowance prices converge at an intermediate level. The result is an increase in emissions in the higher price system and an offsetting reduction in emissions in the lower price system.

If governments place limits on inter-system trading, allowance price convergence may not be complete. A government may limit the quantity of allowances from another system that can be used to demonstrate compliance in its own system. Alternatively, participants in a system may be allowed unrestricted use of another system's allowances, but an "exchange rate" might be applied to their use. Such a requirement might be used to reconcile differences in the denomination of allowances used in the different systems (e.g., metric tons vs. short tons), to reduce inter-system trading, or to ensure that trading leads to a net reduction in emissions.

Indirect linkages

Even if neither system recognizes the other's allowances, two systems can become indirectly linked through direct links with a common third system. As a result of trading between each of the two systems and the common system, developments in one of the indirectly linked systems can affect the supply and demand for allowances in the other system. Hence, changes in the allowance price and emissions level in one system can affect the allowance price and emissions level in another system, even if they are only indirectly linked.

Indirect linkages arising from one-way links between multiple cap-and-trade systems and a common credit system
Indirect links can be created between two cap-and-trade systems if both have one-way links with a common credit system. As a result of such one-way links, the two indirectly linked systems will compete for credits from the third system. This indirect linkage will reduce the difference between the two cap-and-trade systems' allowance prices, as credits will flow to the system with the higher price. In fact, if there is a sufficient supply of credits at a price below pre-linkage allowance prices in the two cap-and-trade systems, linkage will cause prices in all three systems to converge fully.

Indirect linkages arising from links between cap-and-trade systems
A series of bilateral links among several systems can also create indirect links among those systems. This kind of indirect linkage is identical in its effects to a direct multilateral link among all of the systems involved. For example, if System A has a two-way link with System B, which has a two-way link with System C, then trading will lead allowance prices to converge across all three systems even though A and C are not directly linked.

Examples of Existing Linkages

The fact that some linkages have already been established among tradable GHG permit systems reflects the strong incentives that governments face to establish these connections.

One-way linkages
Through its "Linking Directive" (2004/101/EC), the European Union has allowed EU ETS participants to use CDM CERs to meet compliance obligations beginning in 2005, and JI ERUs beginning in 2008 (European Commission 2004). These linkages are subject to

restriction, however. CERs and ERUs generated from nuclear facilities, land-use change, and forestry activities are not recognized, and quantitative limits are placed on the use of CERs and ERUs (European Commission 2007a).[8] The effects of this linkage are already apparent in secondary markets for CERs, where EU ETS allowance prices are considered a major factor influencing CER prices (Carbonpositive 2008).

In the United States, the model rule governing the implementation of the northeastern states' RGGI system allows for several types of one-way links. Covered sources may use emission reduction credits from qualified domestic offset projects, subject to quantitative limits that depend on the prevailing RGGI allowance price (RGGI 2007a). At most, no more than 10 percent of a source's emissions can be covered by offset credits. When and if the RGGI allowance price exceeds a specified threshold, which increases over time, sources have the additional option to use CERs and allowances from other countries' cap-and-trade systems, such as the EU ETS, in meeting their compliance obligations.[9] However, sources are still required to cover at least 90 percent of their emissions with RGGI allowances.

The EU ETS as an example of multilateral two-way linkage

The EU exercised central authority in deciding some aspects of the design of the EU ETS, such as the sectors that are covered by the system. However, to date, EU member states have had significant autonomy and responsibility with respect to many other aspects of the system within their jurisdiction, including: determining how many allowances to allocate; determining how to allocate allowances; and overseeing the monitoring, verification, and reporting of emissions. Thus, the EU ETS can be viewed as an example of multilateral linkage

---

[8] The European Commission has placed limits on the use of CERs and ERUs in each member state at a level necessary to ensure that the total use of CERs and ERUs by each member state—including, but not limited to use in the EU ETS—constitutes no more than half of the reductions necessary to meet that member state's Kyoto target, as modified by the reallocation of its target under the European Union's "bubble." For a description of the method that the European Commission employs to determine these limits, see European Commission (2007a), paragraph 6.

[9] The threshold price is an inflation-adjusted amount that begins slightly below $11 per ton of CO_2 (in 2005 US dollars) and increases by 2 percent per year in real terms.

among individual member states' own systems, where a central authority enforces the harmonization of certain characteristics of each system, and where allowances issued by any member state are recognized by all other member states.[10]

Implications of linkage

Linking tradable permit systems leads to diverse effects that need to be considered in assessing the merits of particular linkages, as well as the merits of linkage more generally as a major design element of the *de jure* or *de facto* post-2012 international policy architecture. These effects depend on the type of linkage established and on the characteristics of the systems being linked.

Benefits of linkage

The most significant benefit of linkage is the opportunity to lower the costs of achieving emission reduction goals by shifting reductions among linked systems in a manner that minimizes total compliance costs. A second benefit is that linkage broadens the market for allowances and credits, which can improve market liquidity, reduce price volatility, and mitigate market power concerns.[11] If one or both of the linked systems is small, the benefits from broadening the market for allowances and credits can be very important. A third benefit of linkage is that it offers the opportunity for nations to establish "common but differentiated responsibilities," consistent with the United Nations Framework Convention on Climate Change (United Nations 1992), without increasing the cost of achieving global emission targets. That is, as long as two systems are linked, they can cost-effectively achieve a particular collective emissions target regardless of how emission reduction responsibilities are initially allocated across those systems. These attributes of linkage are likely to make it an important element

---

[10] In his chapter in this volume, Denny Ellerman makes this point, as well as a broader one—namely, that the EU ETS provides a range of valuable lessons for the development of a post-2012 international policy architecture. In addition to the linkages among EU member states, two-way linkages were recently established between the EU ETS and Norway's emissions trading system, and between the EU ETS and systems in Iceland and Liechtenstein.

[11] Of course, linkage also exposes participants to new sources of price volatility from other linked systems (McKibben and Wilcoxen 2007).

of any cost-effective, long-term effort to reduce GHG emissions in which tradable permit systems feature prominently.

Under certain circumstances, linkage can also decrease global emissions by reducing emissions leakage. For example, linkage between a cap-and-trade system and a credit system reduces the cap-and-trade system's allowance price, and therefore reduces emissions leakage from that system. In some cases, this benefit may be substantial. For example, leakage is a serious concern in the RGGI system in the northeastern United States: analyses have found that nearly half of the projected emission reductions at covered plants could be offset by increased emissions at plants outside the RGGI area (RGGI 2007b). Thus, by reducing leakage, a link between RGGI and a credit system could reduce global emissions.

Concerns about linkage

While linkage may reduce global emissions in some circumstances, a potential concern is that it could increase global emissions under other circumstances. For example, any cap-and-trade system that establishes a one-way linkage with a credit system must confront the problem of "additionality": some emission reduction credits offered by a credit system may not represent truly additional emission reductions because of the difficulty of establishing a baseline against which reductions can be measured. A considerable amount of research on credit systems such as the CDM has focused on this problem.[12] Also, though linkage can reduce overall emissions leakage under certain circumstances, its effect on allowance prices in the linked systems can increase leakage under other circumstances.

In some cases, the distributional implications of linkage also may be a source of concern. Just as international trade changes the prices faced by producers and consumers in different nations, allowance trading across systems raises allowance prices in one of the linked systems and reduces prices in the other system. Hence, while yielding overall cost savings, linkage can create both winners and losers. Impacts on any firm participating in one of the linked systems depend on changes in the allowance price that the firm faces, and on whether

---

[12] See the chapters in this volume by Keeler and Thompson; Teng *et al.*; Plantinga and Richards; Cao; Pizer *et al.*; Somanathan; and Victor.

that firm is a net allowance buyer or seller. Also, because changes in allowance prices affect the prices of energy and other emissions-intensive goods, linkage can have significant effects on firms and households that do not directly participate in trading. Likewise, by changing the production costs of firms that are emissions-intensive or that rely on emissions-intensive inputs, linkage can have significant effects on competitiveness. While these effects may be positive in one of the linked systems, they may be negative in the other.

The ability to trade allowances across systems will lead to capital flows between countries. Because any trading is voluntary, these capital flows are necessarily beneficial to the entities involved in the trading. Others, however, may object—especially if these capital flows are large (Bradsher 2007; Summers 2007). Notably, this has not been a problem in the EU ETS, although the capital flows within that system to date have been relatively small (Ellerman, this volume).

An additional concern related to linkage is that it can reduce national control over the design features and impacts of a domestic tradable permit system. Once one system links to another, its allowance price and emissions consequences are influenced by developments in the linked system(s), including possibly decisions made by the government(s) overseeing the linked system(s). The degree to which linkage reduces a country's control over its domestic system can depend in part on the relative size of the linked systems. While the allowance price in linked systems will fall between the price levels that characterized each system prior to linkage, it will tend to be closer to the larger system's pre-linkage price. For example, prior to linking with the EU ETS, Norway was able to influence the allowance price in its system through its decisions about how many allowances to issue and what sources to include under its cap. Yet, given the size of Norway's system compared with that of the EU ETS, once the link was established, the Norwegian government's decisions ceased to have much impact on the allowance price faced by regulated entities in Norway.[13]

Although linkage can reduce a government's control over the impacts of its tradable permit system, that control already may be

---

[13] At the same time, some of the design elements of even a small cap-and-trade system can have substantial effects on a much larger system, once the systems are linked. An example of such an element is an unrestricted safety valve (that is, the willingness of regulators in the smaller system to sell an unlimited quantity of additional allowances at a pre-determined price).

limited by connections with other systems through trade in emissions-intensive products. The extent of such influences depends, among other factors, on the ease with which emissions generating activity can shift between systems in response to differences between them. For example, if the EU's member states had pursued separate, unlinked cap-and-trade systems instead of creating the EU ETS, those systems nonetheless would have had a significant influence on one another as a result of competition in emissions-intensive product markets within Europe. In contrast, if cap-and-trade systems are established in Australia and the United States, absent a direct or indirect link between them, these systems likely would have very little influence on one another. In such a case, the competitive implications of linkage for the control that each government has over its own system would be more important.

Of course, the concern about linkage reducing a nation's control over its domestic trading system is simply a specific case of the general consequence of being open to international trade of any kind. The only way that a country can maintain complete control over the price of any good it produces is to isolate itself from the world economy, trading off increased control for decreased economic welfare.

A final concern about linkage is that it can alter the incentives that countries face with respect to setting their future caps (Helm 2003; Holtsmark and Sommervoll 2008). In particular, by changing allowance prices in each of the linked systems, linkage alters the trade-off that a government faces between the value it can create by issuing additional allowances and the marginal environmental damage that arises from issuing additional allowances. Moreover, by expanding the scope of the allowance market, linkage reduces the impact that issuing additional allowances would have on allowance prices, and therefore on the value of existing allowances.

Implications of different types of linkage

The degree of control that a government can retain over its domestic trading system depends in part on whether linkage is one-way or two-way. Two-way linkages can increase *or* decrease domestic allowance prices. Also, two-way linkages lead to complete propagation of cost containment measures across the linked systems, including banking, borrowing, and measures that provide for a cost cap or safety valve.

In contrast, one-way linkages can only reduce the price of allowances in the system that establishes the link. Likewise, one-way linkages will allow cost containment measures to propagate in only one direction—from the system with which a link is established to the system that establishes the link.

The effects of linkage also depend on whether a connection is being established between two cap-and-trade systems or between a cap-and-trade system and an emission-reduction-credit system. For example, linkage that involves an emission-reduction-credit system raises the issue of additionality. On the other hand, a link between two cap-and-trade systems can raise other concerns that may be less significant in linking with a credit system. For example, the increase in allowance prices in one of two linked cap-and-trade systems may have more far-reaching economic consequences—such as by increasing domestic energy prices—than would the increase in credit prices resulting from linkage between a cap-and-trade system and credit system.

Even though (unconstrained) two-way linkages are more certain to equilibrate international allowance prices, one-way links between cap-and-trade systems and a common credit system can achieve some and perhaps much of the cost savings and risk diversification that could be achieved by establishing direct two-way links among all of the cap-and-trade systems. In fact, if the common system has a sufficient supply of credits or allowances at a price below the allowance price of the least stringent linked cap-and-trade system, one-way links between cap-and-trade systems and that common system can cause allowance prices in all of the linked systems to converge.

The potential role of linkage in an international climate policy architecture

The potential role of linkage is limited by political and institutional factors. In particular, establishing direct linkages between cap-and-trade systems may require mutual recognition of emission targets, harmonization of certain design elements, and agreement on procedures for making future adjustments to the linked systems, including the setting of future emission caps. Therefore, in the near term, some direct links will be less attractive and more difficult to establish than others. However, indirect linkages among cap-and-trade systems resulting from direct linkages between cap-and-trade systems and a common emission-reduction-credit system may achieve some, and perhaps most, of the cost savings and other advantages of direct links among cap-and-trade systems. As a result, indirect linkages via an emission-reduction-credit system such as the CDM could become an important part of a near-term international climate policy architecture.

Near-term role

Direct and indirect linkages already function as key operational elements of the existing global climate policy architecture and may become increasingly important in the future. In this sense, linkage is emerging from the bottom up as a core element of a *de facto* international policy architecture, which may carry beyond the end of the first commitment period of the Kyoto Protocol in 2012. Moreover, new connections among existing and emerging tradable permit systems will undoubtedly be established in the future.

Pairs or groups of nations, particularly those which are important trading partners, will likely establish direct two-way links between their respective cap-and-trade systems. For example, Norway, Iceland, and Liechtenstein have agreed to link their cap-and-trade systems with the EU ETS (Ellerman, this volume). However, for the reasons discussed above, it may take more time to establish direct links between other cap-and-trade systems. At the same time, many of these cap-and-trade systems may nonetheless become indirectly linked through a common credit system, such as the CDM or some alternative, future protocol for crediting emission reductions achieved in developing countries.

Although a web of mostly indirect links may not result in a maximally cost-effective global market for GHG reductions, particularly in the near term, these indirect links may still yield much of the cost savings and other advantages of a comprehensive system of direct linkages. Moreover, this approach will not require the same degree of harmonization of cap-and-trade design elements as would direct links. However, the efficacy of this scenario depends heavily on an effective and widely accepted international credit system.[14]

---

[14] For further discussion of critical issues associated with credit systems, we refer readers to other chapters in this volume, including those by Agarwala; Teng *et al.*; Cao; Pizer *et al.*; Somanathan; and Victor.

An international policy architecture that consisted solely of linked national-level tradable permit systems would not *guarantee* broad participation. Yet, as we explore in a later section, some forms of linkage may induce participation, encourage compliance, and even lead to more stringent commitments.

Long-term role

It is possible that a comprehensive set of linkages, combined with unilateral emissions reduction commitments by many nations, could function as a stand-alone international climate policy architecture. Such a bottom-up architecture could emerge as more countries establish national cap-and-trade systems and begin to seek gains from linking with other systems. These countries also might use the prospect of linkage as a means of providing incentives to developing countries to participate in an international agreement.

A second possibility is that a collection of bottom-up linkages might serve as a natural starting point for negotiations leading to a top-down agreement. An existing system of linkages may help to develop the experience and mutual trust necessary for global negotiations to succeed. Furthermore, as we discuss below, any future agreement is likely to be heavily influenced by the status quo system of existing linkages and institutional investments.

A third possibility, not mutually exclusive with the second, is that linkage could become an element of a larger, global policy architecture. Because the trade-related cost savings available to linked systems will grow as countries adopt increasingly stringent targets, there are strong economic reasons for policymakers to favor linkage. Thus, a future global architecture could incorporate a set of direct links among domestic cap-and-trade systems as a key design element.

Evaluating the role of linkage in an international policy architecture

We assess three ways in which linkage can contribute to a future international climate policy architecture: (1) as an independent, bottom-up architecture; (2) as a transition to a top-down architecture; and (3) as an element of a larger climate agreement. Our assessment is both positive and normative in the sense that we identify the likely outcomes in each case, and then evaluate these outcomes based on a set of normative criteria.

Linkage as a bottom-up international policy architecture

Linkages among national and regional cap-and-trade systems and with the CDM (or its successor) are likely to continue to evolve. Could such a set of linkages, established without central coordination, function as an effective, stand-alone, bottom-up international policy architecture?

Although such an architecture would need to include certain other design elements, including emissions reduction commitments and participation incentives, its distinguishing feature would be that it would grow organically from pre-existing direct and indirect linkages. Indeed, if international negotiations for a successor to the Kyoto Protocol are unsuccessful, then a set of linkages could well become the *de facto* post-2012 architecture. We assess this architecture in terms of its likely environmental performance, cost-effectiveness, and distributional equity.

The degree to which a system of bottom-up linkages could satisfy our first criterion of meaningful environmental performance depends on whether: (a) participants set sufficiently stringent environmental targets, (b) a sufficient number of key countries participate, and (c) participants comply.

With regard to whether participants will set meaningful environmental targets, commitments to reduce emissions in an architecture of bottom-up linkages would result from unilateral decisions by individual nations, or from negotiations among small groups of nations. In developed countries, internal political support would probably be the driving force behind the adoption of more stringent emission caps (Keohane and Raustiala, this volume), whereas adoption of emission caps in developing nations could depend upon incentives provided by committed developed countries.

As described above, direct linkages between cap-and-trade systems can affect the incentives that countries face in setting future caps. To address the possibility that linkage may create incentives for some countries to adopt less stringent future caps, countries could negotiate cap trajectories as a condition for linkage (Flachsland *et al.* 2008). Another possibility, however, is that cost savings from a system of linkages will allow some countries to adopt more aggressive targets than they otherwise would.

Participation among industrialized countries in an architecture of bottom-up linkages is likely to be high. As emphasized above, many of these countries and regions have begun to move toward setting up meaningful cap-and-trade systems, and some links have already been established. On the other hand, participation by developing countries will most likely be conditional on participation incentives provided by industrialized countries.

Positive incentives for developing-country participation ("carrots") could take at least three forms. One is access to demand for the emission reduction credits that a developing country could produce. In fact, the CDM already provides such incentives. A second form of incentive is the potential gain from becoming a net seller of allowances. Finally, side payments in the form of technical or development assistance can be used to induce participation. In contrast, negative incentives for participation ("sticks") could take two forms. First, industrialized countries could establish border carbon taxes and/or import allowance requirements (Frankel, Trade, this volume; Houser *et al.* 2008; Stavins 2008). Second, access to international markets for permits could be conditioned on participation and graduation to a more demanding set of commitments. No matter what incentives are considered, however, a bottom-up system on its own may not provide the institutional structure necessary to coordinate such participation incentives.

With respect to whether participants would be likely to comply with a policy architecture of bottom-up linkages, the picture is no worse—and indeed may be better—than for some top-down, centralized architectures. In contrast to the Kyoto approach, which leaves the implementation of international targets up to each member state, a bottom-up system would only include industrialized nations where domestic institutions are sufficient to enforce compliance. It would also only include developing nations where international carrots and sticks, such as revenue from permit sales and the threat of loss of access to markets for emissions credits, outweigh the costs of participating. As a result, one advantage of a bottom-up system of linkages, compared with a top-down system, is that it provides no incentive for countries to make commitments they do not intend to keep. Compliance by industrialized countries will probably be enforced by domestic political will. Compliance by developing countries can be enforced by a combination of the carrots and sticks discussed above, such as the threat of loss of access to markets for emissions credits.[15]

The second major criterion by which we can assess an international policy architecture of bottom-up linkage is cost-effectiveness. This is straightforward. Because linking cap-and-trade systems creates gains from trade for the participating countries, such an architecture has the potential to be cost-effective in the sense that it can allow countries to achieve their collective emission targets at minimum cost. This would be the case if the bottom-up system of linkages includes a sufficient set of direct two-way linkages or if there are enough indirect linkages through a common credit system that has an adequate supply of low-cost credits to bring about a convergence of allowance prices.

A third important criterion is distributional equity. As described above, linkage can create both winners and losers within each of the linked systems, along with capital flows from cross-border allowance trades. The political implications of these distributional effects are not obvious. First, the distributional implications of linkage will depend in part on how individual countries choose to allocate allowances in their own cap-and-trade systems. Also, while the political will to participate in a system of linkages will depend in part on the distribution of costs and benefits, it is unclear whether individual political systems will give greater weight to costs and benefits that are concentrated in particular industries or to costs and benefits that are distributed broadly across an entire economy.

A bottom-up system of linkages is already evolving and could function well in the near term if no top-down, post-2012 international policy architecture emerges. However, for a bottom-up system to achieve meaningful long-term environmental performance and a high degree of participation, it will require the major emitting countries—the United States, the European Union, Russia, Japan, China, India, and other key countries—to reach an agreement regarding emissions targets and incentives for participation. Without the cooperation of these countries, it is unlikely that global GHG emissions could be reduced by enough to prevent major climate change.

[15] To ensure compliance, a bottom-up system of linkages would need all trading partners to have comparably effective internal monitoring, reporting, and enforcement mechanisms. Harmonization of such measures is likely to occur during negotiations to establish the terms of linkage between particular systems.

Bottom-up linkage as a step toward a top-down architecture

A collection of linked cap-and-trade and emission-reduction-credit systems could serve as the foundation for a top-down climate agreement. Indeed, a bottom-up system could evolve into a coherent top-down climate architecture, much as the General Agreement on Tariffs and Trade paved the way for the World Trade Organization (Carraro 2007). Questions of interest include whether such a decentralized system of linkages might create momentum towards a top-down agreement, and how existing linkages would then affect any resulting negotiated arrangement.

Any pre-existing links between trading programs, whether direct or indirect, are likely to influence the evolution of a new top-down international agreement because they will function as the status-quo framework. Because linkage creates winners and losers, some constituencies will resist changes, while others may welcome them. Changing the economic, organizational, and political infrastructure that facilitates existing linkages would be time-consuming and costly. More broadly, the existing system is a natural starting point for negotiations. Of course, to the extent that institutional inertia creates a bias towards the status quo it can also impair good decision making and impede negotiations, particularly if the existing system of linkages includes features that are undesirable from the standpoint of reaching a broader climate agreement. This very flaw may also provide some political advantages, however, because nations may be more willing to make commitments to a system in which they already participate.[16]

An existing set of linkages will also have implications for participation in a future international agreement. In particular, it will create constituencies within some developing countries that favor an international agreement if continued demand for credits is conditioned on movement toward such an agreement. If these stakeholders are influential within their own countries, then linkage can

---

[16] Another way in which existing linkages may influence a future climate agreement is by providing a series of experiments to test different approaches (Hahn 1998). Victor *et al.* (2005) argue that such a "Madisonian" approach could provide future climate negotiations with valuable insights about what features of linked trading systems do and do not work.

foster incentives for countries to participate in a future international agreement.

Linkage may also encourage participation in a future international agreement by simplifying the negotiation process. One of the great challenges of international climate negotiations is the necessity of achieving agreement among many parties with exceptionally diverse interests. Linkages can help to mitigate this problem by creating natural negotiating blocks of nations with similar interests. The negotiations necessary to establish bilateral links can contribute to the subsequent negotiation of an international agreement.

There is another way in which linkage can induce participation in a broader international, if not global, regime.[17] Consider a "leader nation" that can accomplish very little to solve the global problem of climate change were it to act on its own. Linkage provides a mechanism by which that nation's emission reduction activities can be extended more widely. Although shunning, shaming, or punishing non-participant nations is one potential route to trying to broaden the coalition of participants (Keohane and Raustiala, this volume), linkage could offer another route.

This is illustrated by the evolution of certain provisions of the EU ETS. The system places "supplementarity" constraints on imports of credits from the CDM and allows for mutual recognition of other cap-and-trade systems established by Kyoto signatories. Amendments to the EU ETS implemented in 2008 introduce two key changes (Ellerman, this volume). First, once a post-Kyoto international agreement has been reached, the ability of countries to sell credits into the EU ETS will be contingent on their ratification of that agreement, leaving the door open for some form of graduation requirement. Second, mutual recognition provisions would no longer require signature of the Kyoto Protocol, but simply the presence of a mandatory cap on emissions in the linked jurisdiction. Thus, while the CDM route is made conditional on future agreements, full mutual recognition would be opened up for any cap-and-trade system. In other words, market access is being used by leader nations to induce participation, and to foster a broader system.

Linkage can also encourage compliance with a future international agreement. This could occur in two ways. First, the "Madisonian

<hr />

[17] We are grateful to Denny Ellerman for this point and for much of the discussion that follows.

workshop" created by many uncoordinated links could provide policy experience with mechanisms for encouraging compliance (Victor *et al.* 2005). Second, existing links might allow countries to demonstrate good faith commitments to emissions reductions.

Linkage may even lead to more stringent environmental commitments. By reducing the cost of emissions reductions, linkage may allow key industrialized countries to make greater emissions reduction commitments than they would have in the absence of linkage. By reducing the allowance price impacts of a more stringent cap, linkage may reduce domestic opposition to more ambitious reduction targets.

Bottom-up linkage as an element of an international architecture

Linkage could play a significant role as one component of a larger international climate policy architecture—a role that would not conflict with the potential near-term role of linkage as the basis for a future agreement. Since not all forms of linkage function in the same way, an international policy architecture could be developed with different near-term and long-term linkage components. For example, in the near term, a system of indirect linkages via a common credit system would provide important cost savings while minimizing negative distributional effects and preserving a high degree of national control over allowance markets. In the longer term, the system could transition to negotiated, multilateral two-way linkages that would create a single, comprehensive market for allowances and credits.

How will near-term climate negotiations affect bottom-up linkages?

If the emergence of a system of linkages would be beneficial to a future (bottom-up or top-down) climate agreement, then it is important to address two questions: what policy elements of a future international climate agreement will facilitate bottom-up linkages? And what policy elements would inhibit or impede such linkages?

A post-2012 international climate agreement could include several elements that would facilitate future linkages among cap-and-trade and emission-reduction-credit systems. First, and perhaps most ambitiously, the agreement could establish an agreed trajectory of emissions caps or allowance prices; specify a harmonized set of cost-containment measures, including offset, banking and borrowing, and safety-valve provisions; and establish a process for making future adjustments to the level of the emissions cap and other key design elements (Jaffe and Stavins 2007). Second, it could create an international clearinghouse for transaction records and allowance auctions (Edenhofer *et al.* 2007). Third, it could provide for the ongoing operation of the CDM or a successor credit system, which could play a central role in indirectly linking existing and emerging tradable permit systems. Fourth and finally, a post-2012 international climate agreement could help developing countries build capacity that would enable and encourage their fuller participation through a system of bottom-up linkages. All of these features would simplify and facilitate the process of negotiating linkages.[18]

There are also potential design elements that would best be avoided by a post-2012 agreement if it seeks to encourage linkage among tradable permit systems. Any global agreement that encourages strategic behavior could impede the development of linkages. For example, an agreement that conditions future commitments on countries' emission levels over the coming years could undermine the ability to achieve a cost-effective distribution of emission reductions across linked systems. Also, depending on the stringency of such restrictions, an international agreement that imposes "supplementarity" restrictions which require countries to achieve some specified percentage of emissions reductions on their own, without trading, could limit the potential benefits of linkage by curtailing the amount of international trading that can occur.

Conclusions

Cap-and-trade systems are emerging as a preferred domestic instrument for reducing GHG emissions in many parts of the world; in addition, the CDM has developed a substantial constituency, despite some concerns about its performance. Because of the considerable political and economic pressure to connect these systems, linkage may

[18] Some of these elements could also emerge *without* a post-2012 multinational climate agreement, through specific bilateral links among systems.

be expected to play a *de facto*, if not *de jure*, role in any future international climate policy architecture.

In the near term, linkage will continue to grow in importance as a core element of a bottom-up, *de facto* international policy architecture. The EU ETS has already established direct links with systems in neighboring countries and the CDM has emerged as a potential hub for indirect links among cap-and-trade systems worldwide. As new cap-and-trade systems appear in countries such as Australia, Canada, and the United States, the global network of direct and indirect linkages will likely continue to spread.

In the longer term, linkage could play a variety of roles. One possibility is that a set of linkages, combined with unilateral emissions reduction commitments by many nations, could function as a stand-alone international climate architecture. Such a system would be cost-effective as long as it included a sufficient number of direct two-way links or indirect links through a common international credit system with an adequate depth of low-cost credits. However, it may be difficult for a system of bottom-up linkages to achieve meaningful long-term environmental results, primarily because it would lack a coordinating mechanism to encourage widespread participation.

A second long-term possibility is that a collection of bottom-up links may eventually evolve into a comprehensive, top-down agreement. In the near term, a system of direct and indirect linkages could build institutional capacity and provide important cost savings; in the longer term, the system could serve as a natural starting point for negotiations leading to a top-down agreement.

A third long-term possibility (and one that is entirely compatible with the second possibility) is that linkage could play a significant role as a component of a larger international climate policy agreement. Such an architecture would use linkage to provide a number of important benefits, including reducing the overall costs of meeting emission reduction targets, improving market liquidity, and providing a framework for the implementation of "common but differentiated responsibilities."

Despite the clear benefits of linkage, there are also legitimate concerns about the implications of some forms of linkage. These concerns depend, in part, on the type of linkage involved. Two-way direct links among cap-and-trade systems reduce the control that the linking countries have over their domestic allowance prices and emissions.

Two-way links also result in the complete and automatic propagation of cost-containment measures from one system to the other. On the other hand, indirect links present a different set of concerns. In particular, indirect linkage via a common credit system could adversely affect global emissions if additionality problems in the credit system are severe. The performance of the CDM to date suggests that this concern deserves serious attention.

Thus, there is a significant trade-off between direct linkages, which can require a high degree of harmonization and international cooperation, and indirect linkages via a common credit system, which raise concerns about additionality. This trade-off may suggest a natural progression. In the near term, linking cap-and-trade systems indirectly, via a common credit system (such as the CDM), could achieve some of the cost savings and risk diversification of direct linkage but without the need for as much harmonization of emerging and existing cap-and-trade systems. Such indirect linkage would also limit potential distributional concerns and preserve a high degree of national control over allowance markets. In the longer term, international negotiations could establish shared expectations about environmental targets and emission reduction responsibilities that would serve as the basis for a broad set of multilateral, direct links among cap-and-trade systems. This progression could promote the near-term goals of participation and cost-effectiveness, while helping to build the foundation for a more comprehensive future agreement.

References

ABC News (2008). "Japan PM Announces Plan to Cut Emissions," June 9, available at www.abc.net.au/news/stories/2008/06/09/2269404.htm.

Australian Government (2008). "Carbon Pollution Reduction Scheme Green Paper," Department of Climate Change, Canberra, July.

Baron, Richard and Stephen Bygrave (2002). "Towards International Emissions Trading: Design Implications for Linkages," COM/ENV/EPOC/IEA/SLT(2002)5, Paris: Organization for Economic Co-operation and Development and International Energy Agency.

Baron, Richard and Cédric Philibert (2005). *Act Locally, Trade Globally: Emissions Trading for Climate Policy*. Paris: OECD and IEA.

Blyth, William and Martina Bosi (2004). "Linking Non-EU Domestic Emissions Trading Schemes with the EU Emissions Trading Scheme," COM/ENV/EPOC/IEA/SLT(2004)6, Paris: OECD and IEA.

Bradsher, Keith (2007). "Clean Power That Reaps a Whirlwind," New York Times, May 9.

California Air Resources Board (2008). "Climate Change Proposed Scoping Plan: A Framework for Change," October.

Carbonpositive (2008). "CER Market Steadies After Price Hit," November 10.

Carraro, Carlo (2007). "Incentives and Institutions: A Bottom-Up Approach to Climate Policy," in Joe A. Aldy and Robert N. Stavins (eds.), _Architectures for Agreement: Addressing Global Climate Change in the Post-Kyoto World_. New York: Cambridge University Press, pp.161–72.

Edenhofer, Ottmar, Christian Flachsland, and Robert Marschinski (2007). "Towards a Global CO_2 Market: An Economic Analysis," Potsdam Institute for Climate Impact Research.

Ellis, Jane and Dennis Tirpak (2006). "Linking GHG Emission Trading Schemes and Markets," COM/ENV/EPOC/IEA/SLT(2006)6, Paris: OECD and IEA.

Environment Canada (2008). "Turning the Corner: Regulatory Framework for Industrial Greenhouse Gas Emissions," available at www.ec.gc.ca/doc/virage-corner/2008-03/pdf/541_eng.pdf.

Euractiv.com (2007). "Norway to Join EU Carbon-Trading Scheme," March 9.

European Commission (2004). _Directive 2004/101/EC of the European Parliament and of the Council Amending Directive 2003/87/EC Establishing a Scheme for Greenhouse Gas Emission Allowance Trading within the Community, in respect of the Kyoto Protocol's Project Mechanisms_, Official Journal of the European Union, L 338/18 L 338/23, November 13.

(2005). _EU Action Against Climate Change: EU Emissions Trading—An Open Scheme Promoting Global Innovation_, Brussels.

(2007a). _Commission Decision of August 31, 2007 Concerning the National Allocation Plan for the Allocation of Greenhouse Gas Emission Allowances Notified by Denmark in Accordance with Directive 2003/87/EC of the European Parliament and of the Council_, Brussels.

(2007b). _Emissions Trading: EU Wide Cap for 2008 2012 Set at 2.08 Billion Allowances after Assessment of National Plans for Bulgaria_, Brussels, October 26.

(2008). _Questions and Answers on the Revised EU Emissions Trading System_, Brussels, December 17.

Flachsland, Christian, Ottmar Edenhofer, Michael Jakob, and Jan Steckel (2008). "Developing the International carbon Market: Linking Options for the EU ETS," Report to the Policy Planning Staff in the Federal Foreign Office, Potsdam Institute for Climate Impact Research.

Hahn, Robert W. (1984). "Market Power and Transferable Property Rights," *Quarterly Journal of Economics* 99(4): 753–65.

(1998). *The Economics and Politics of Climate Change*. Washington, DC: American Enterprise Institute Press.

Haites, Erik and Fiona Mullins (2001). "Linking Domestic and Industry Greenhouse Gas Emission Trading Systems," Toronto: Margaree Consultants Inc.

Helm, Carsten (2003). "International Emissions Trading with Endogenous Allowance Choices," *Journal of Public Economics* 87(12): 2737–47.

Holtsmark, Bjart J. and Dag Einar Sommervoll (2008). "International Emissions Trading in a Non-cooperative Equilibrium," Discussion Paper No. 542, Statistics Norway, Research Department, May.

Houser, Trevor, Rob Bradley, Britt Childs, Jacob Werksman, and Robert Heilmayr (2008). *Leveling the Carbon Playing Field: International Competition and US Climate Policy Design*. Washington, DC: Peterson Institute.

Jaffe, Judson and Robert Stavins (2007). "Linking Tradable Permit Systems for Greenhouse Gas Emissions: Opportunities, Implications, and Challenges," IETA Report on Linking GHG Emissions Trading Systems, prepared for the International Emissions Trading Association, November.

Japanese Ministry of the Environment (2006). *FY 2004 Greenhouse Gas Emissions in Japan*, Tokyo, May 25.

Kruger, Joseph, Wallace Oates, and William Pizer (2007). "Decentralization in the EU Emissions Trading Scheme and Lessons for Global Policy," *Review of Environmental Economics and Policy* 1(1): 112–33.

McKibbin, Warwick J. and Peter J. Wilcoxen (2007). "A Credible Foundation for Long-Term International Cooperation on Climate Change," in Aldy and Stavins (eds.), pp. 185–208.

Michaelowa, Axel and Frank Jotzo (2005). "Transaction Costs, Institutional Rigidities and the Size of the Clean Development Mechanism," *Energy Policy* 33(4): 511–23.

Murray, Brian C., Richard G. Newell, and William A. Pizer (2009). "Balancing Cost and Emissions Certainty: An Allowance Reserve for Cap-and-Trade," *Review of Environmental Economics and Policy* 3, Issue 1, Winter, forthcoming.

Nigoff, Mindy (2006). "Clean Development Mechanism: Does the Current Structure Facilitate Kyoto Protocol Compliance?" *Georgetown International Environmental Law Review* 18(2): 249–76.

Norwegian Ministry of the Environment (2005). *Norway's Report on Demonstrable Progress under the Kyoto Protocol: Status Report as of December 2005*, Oslo.

Pointcarbon.com. (2007). *JI Update: 12 Projects Submitted to UN in October*, November 1.

Regional Greenhouse Gas Initiative (RGGI) (2007a). *Model Rule*, January 5, 2007 version.

(2007b). *IPM Energy Modeling Documents*.

Stavins, Robert N. (1995). "Transaction Costs and Tradeable Permits," *Journal of Environmental Economics and Management* 29: 133–48.

(2008). "A Meaningful U.S. Cap-and-Trade System to Address Climate Change," *Harvard Environmental Law Review* 32(2): 293–371.

Sudo, Tomonori (2006). "Japanese Voluntary Emissions Trading Scheme (JVETS)—Overview and Analysis," Presentation at the US-Japan Workshop on Climate Actions and Co-Benefit, March 22–23.

Summers, Lawrence (2007). "Foreword," in Aldy and Stavins (eds.), pp. xviii–xxvii.

Tatsutani, Marika and William A. Pizer (2008). "Managing Costs in a U.S. Greenhouse Gas Trading Program: A Workshop Summary," Discussion Paper 08–23, Washington DC: Resources For the Future.

United Nations (1992). *Rio Declaration on Environment and Development. Annex 1 of the Report of the United Nations Conference on Environment and Development*, Rio de Janeiro, June 3–14.

United Nations Environment Program (UNEP) Risoe Centre (2008). *Status of JI Projects*, available at www.cdmpipeline.org/ji-projects.htm#1. Accessed August 21, 2008.

United Nations Framework Convention on Climate Change (UNFCCC) (2008). *Expected Average Annual CERs from Registered Projects by Host Country*, August 18.

Victor, David, Joshua House, and Sarah Joy (2005). "A Madisonian Approach to Climate Policy, *Science* 309(5742): 1820–1.

5 | The case for charges on greenhouse gas emissions

RICHARD N. COOPER[1]

The proposal

The proposal discussed in this chapter is to levy a common charge on all emissions of greenhouse gases (GHGs) worldwide. All countries would be covered in principle, but the proposal could be implemented with a much smaller number of countries, provided those countries accounted for most of the global emissions. While all GHGs should in principle be covered, this chapter will address mainly carbon dioxide (CO_2), quantitatively the most important GHG; extending charges to other GHGs could be made with little or (in the case of methane) much difficulty. The charge would be internationally adjusted from time to time, and each country would collect and keep the revenue it generated.

This chapter will discuss the motivation for such a proposal; how it would be implemented; its likely economic effects; its relationship to energy security; the possibility of mixing an emission charge with other schemes to limit emissions, especially "cap-and-trade" schemes; and the negotiability of such an agreement.

Motivation

Table 5.1 reports CO_2 emissions generated by the use of marketable energy (mainly fossil fuels) in 1990, the base year for the Kyoto Protocol. It also presents emission projections to 2010 (the mid-point of the 2008–2012 first commitment period of the Kyoto Protocol), 2020, and 2030. The projections shown in the table were developed by the US Energy Information Administration (US EIA) in its 2008 annual review of the international energy outlook and reflect estimates of future global energy demand based on assumptions about

---

[1] I am grateful to Joe Aldy and Rob Stavins for helpful comments on an early draft.

Table 5.1 *World carbon dioxide emissions[a] (billion metric tons)*

	1990	2010	2020	2030
World	21.2	31.1	37.0	42.3
North America	5.8	7.1	7.6	8.3
USA	5.0	6.0	6.4	6.9
OECD Europe	4.1	4.5	4.8	4.8
OECD Asia	1.5	2.2	2.3	2.4
Japan	1.0	1.2	1.2	1.2
Total OECD	11.4	13.8	14.7	15.5
Total Non-OECD	9.8	17.3	22.3	26.8
Russia	2.4	1.8	2.0	2.1
China	2.2	6.9	9.5	12.0
India	0.6	1.3	1.8	2.2
Brazil	0.2	0.5	0.5	0.6
Other	4.4	6.8	8.5	9.8

[a] From fossil fuels
Source: US Dept. of Energy, EIA, International Energy Outlook (2008), Table A10

economic growth in different parts of the world, energy prices, and the relationship between demand for different types of energy (e.g. electricity, transportation fuels) and economic growth as a function of stage of development. Specifically, the US EIA assumed a price of oil that gradually declines from the high levels of mid-2008 to $70 a barrel in 2015, and then remains roughly unchanged in real terms until 2030. Higher and lower price scenarios are also addressed. The world economy is assumed to achieve an average annual growth of 3.0 percent over the projection period, with countries weighted by their GDP at market exchange rates in 2000. Meanwhile, average world demand for energy is projected to grow by 1.6 percent a year (liquid fuels by 1.2 percent, coal by 2.0 percent).

Table 5.1 shows CO_2 emissions growing steadily over this period, with global emissions reaching double 1990 levels by 2030. Also noteworthy is that by 2020, emissions from non-OECD countries (mostly developing countries) alone exceed the world level of 1990. Put another way, these projections suggest that rich countries could cut their emissions to zero over the next decade and the world would still be back where it started in 1990, with a level of emissions that was even then deemed to be too high. It should be noted that Table 5.1 reports emissions only from the consumption of marketable fuels; importantly, emissions from tropical deforestation, which are significant, are not included (if they were included, projected non-OECD emissions would be higher throughout the timeframe shown). In short, seriously addressing CO_2 emissions requires a worldwide approach, not one limited to today's rich countries. Moreover, if some significant countries are excluded from coverage for any length of time, fossil-fuel-using production will tend to migrate to those countries, thus undermining the efforts of countries that are covered by any arrangement to mitigate GHG emissions.

Decisions to consume goods and services made with fossil fuels are made by over a billion households and firms in the world. The best and indeed the only way to reach all these decision makers is through the prices they must pay. If we are to reduce emissions by discouraging CO_2-emitting activities, we must raise the prices of those activities. Levying a charge on CO_2 emissions does that directly. A cap-and-trade scheme, under which allowable emissions are capped and tradable emission permits are issued, does so indirectly, if less transparently (as emphasized by Williamson, 2008). Lacking perfect substitutes for CO_2-emitting activities—and none are presently or prospectively available in the near future—the permits will have value that will be priced into the CO_2-emitting goods and services, resulting in higher prices.

As noted above, decision makers around the world must be reached, not just those in today's rich countries. A cap-and-trade scheme has two compelling disadvantages on a global scale. First, it will probably be impossible to negotiate meaningful, effective emission limits among all countries. Developing countries will understandably resist any emission ceiling or cap that they believe will limit their economic development—that is, their rate of economic growth. They will argue that the experience of other, more developed countries included a period of rapid growth in demand for fossil-fuel-based energy, and they will not agree to limits on their own potential growth. Emission ceilings could no doubt be negotiated, but the global total would likely be too great to achieve desired environmental results: with developing countries unwilling to accept meaningful caps, developed countries in turn are unlikely to accept emission cuts so deep as to jeopardize current standards of living.

Second, under a meaningful cap-and-trade scheme governments will need to allocate valuable emission permits to domestic firms or residents. This will be an open invitation to favoritism in many countries or, to put it less politely, it will unavoidably foster rampant corruption. Do we really want climate policy to be a handmaiden to corruption around the world? Under an international emission trading regime, ordinary citizens in rich countries will be charged for their consumption of CO_2-emitting activities, or they will (indirectly) purchase emission rights from the often rich cronies of political leaders in developing countries. A universal CO_2 charge would avoid such problematic and politically indefensible transfers.

In short, a global cap-and-trade system is likely to be unachievable because developing countries will not agree to meaningful emission caps and rich countries (at least the United States) will not trade, at least with developing countries.[2]

Implementation issues for a carbon charge

Several practical issues must be addressed in considering a "carbon" charge, including first, what sources, sectors, gases, and geographic areas will be covered and second, what provisions will be made for periodic review, compliance, enforcement, and offset credits.

Geographic coverage should be as broad as possible. Climate change is a global problem, resulting from GHG emissions wherever they occur. The solution also needs to be global. The initial scheme need not cover literally all countries given that three or four dozen countries account for the vast majority of emissions. But key developing countries must be included. As suggested in Table 5.1, China's emissions already exceed those of the United States; India's exceed those of Japan. If deforestation is included, as it should be, Indonesia is the third largest emitting country, followed by Brazil and Russia. The problem of global climate change simply cannot be addressed

---

[2] Experience with Russia and Ukraine is instructive. Both were given generous emission targets to get them to sign the Kyoto Protocol. When the European Union set up its emission trading scheme, Russia and Ukraine were pointedly told they could not expect to participate with their generous emission targets. Concern about the domestic allocation of emission rights in those countries undoubtedly also played a role in their exclusion.

without going well beyond the countries listed in Annex I of the 1992 United Nations Framework Convention on Climate Change.

It is also desirable, insofar as practicable, to cover all the significant GHGs. Six types are listed in the Kyoto Protocol, of which CO_2 is the weakest in terms of its per-ton radiative forcing impact on the atmosphere. Methane, nitrous oxide, some fluorocarbons, and several other GHGs are much more potent warming gases at the molecular level, although much less abundant than CO_2 and less durable (in terms of their residence time in the atmosphere). In the United States, for instance, CO_2 accounted for only 84 percent of the total radiative forcing from all GHG emissions in 2006 (based on CO_2 equivalent global warming potential calculated over 100 years [EIA, 2008]). Wider coverage implies a lower charge to achieve any given level of reduction in overall GHG concentrations, and it is likely to be easier to reduce some non-CO_2 sources of warming faster than CO_2 in the short run. Practical difficulties arise in levying a charge on methane emissions from the agricultural sector. In CO_2-equivalent terms, this category of emissions accounted for only 2.5 percent of the total 2006 GHG inventory in the United States, but the share is probably higher in many developing countries, especially those that grow rice. Thus coverage might exclude the entire agricultural sector (except for marketable energy consumed in agriculture), which also accounts for the bulk of nitrous oxide emissions; or it might reach nitrous oxide emissions through charges on the relevant fertilizers and exclude only agricultural methane.

Deforestation accounts for a significant, although not precisely known, share of global CO_2 emissions. Forestry should be included, both because of the magnitude of emissions involved and because to exclude it would encourage arbitrage around the carbon charge—for example, natural forests could be cleared to plant feedstocks, such as oil palms, for biofuels. Certain practical difficulties arise in covering the forestry sector, both with respect to estimating emissions— although satellite observations make this increasingly possible—and in terms of identifying exactly where the charge should be levied (this issue is taken up below).

An initial charge would be set by international agreement. It should be high enough to affect behavior significantly, but not so high as to lead to unwarranted economic dislocations. I suggest a charge of $15 per ton of CO_2 equivalent (hereafter, references to a "carbon" charge should be understood to mean a charge on all covered GHGs based on their CO_2-equivalent impact on radiative forcing in the atmosphere over 100 years).[3] In the United States, a carbon charge at this level would add about 1.78 cents per kilowatt-hour to the busbar cost of coal-generated electricity and 13 cents to a gallon of gasoline, before allowing for indirect costs (e.g. for distribution [Metcalf, 2007, p.15]).

The charge should be subject to periodic review. An expectation might be that the charge would rise over time, as shown in the optimal scenario described by Nordhaus (2008) and in various scenarios developed by Edmonds *et al.* (2008). But much about the future is highly uncertain: the influence of GHG emissions on climate, the trajectory of GHG emissions, the influence of the charge on GHG emissions, and the pace and shape of new technological developments with regard, *inter alia*, to the development of economical non-carbon sources of energy. As time goes on, we will learn more about the nature and extent of climate change, about its impacts, and about new technological possibilities. We will also learn how responsive firms and households are to the carbon charge. The charge might initially be set for ten years, and then reviewed and adjusted up (or possibly down) at five-year intervals thereafter.

Compliance would be easy to assess. The International Monetary Fund (IMF) has a fiscal division that is well-informed about the tax systems of all member countries, which include all important economies in the world (Taiwan, Hong Kong, Cuba, and North Korea are the significant exceptions). The IMF could be tasked with reporting whether adherents to the carbon charge agreement had in fact passed the required legislation and set up the appropriate administrative machinery. This would be an assignment for the regular Article IV consultations which the IMF holds with all member countries.

From an administrative perspective, the obvious place to levy the charge—at least for energy-related CO_2 emissions—would be at upstream chokepoints in the fuel supply chain: at the refinery for oil (plus bunker fuel and a few other places where crude oil is used directly); at major pipeline collection points for gas; and at mine-heads or rail and barge collection points for coal. The charge would

---

[3] This works out to $55 per ton of carbon, the unit of measurement used by the Intergovernmental Panel on Climate Change (IPCC) and some other analysts. Readers in this field need to pay attention to the units used.

also be levied on imports of fossil fuels and would not be levied on exports (e.g. Canada would levy a charge on fossil fuels consumed domestically, but not on exports of gas to the United States; the United States would levy the charge on its imports of gas from Canada). An alternative, fallback approach would be to levy the charge at power plants and other large direct emitters of CO_2, such as cement plants and steel factories. In general, the charge would be passed into downstream prices. But this is an issue of administration and should be left to the discretion of individual countries, provided the agreed objective was met.

Would countries, especially poor countries, be able to administer a charge on carbon emissions? This should be possible for all but the poorest and least institutionally competent countries, for they do raise significant revenue now—typically 10–25 percent of GDP—and they have a demonstrated capacity to levy duties on imports of goods, which also go through chokepoints such as sea- and airports. Moreover, the countries least administratively capable of imposing a charge are also low emitters.

An issue would arise with respect to pre-existing charges or taxes (or, in some cases, subsidies) on energy. The internationally-agreed charge would go on top of those, without allowance for them. The argument is that the rationale for these pre-existing taxes, whatever it may have been, pre-dated international concern with climate change. Climate change is a new, global concern that requires a global solution. Thus all countries should contribute to mitigation efforts once the concern has been identified and agreement has been reached on needed actions. An exception to this policy of "grandfathering" pre-existing taxes might be made for those (few) countries that imposed energy taxes in response to their obligations under the Kyoto Protocol—i.e. during the past decade, or perhaps in anticipation of Kyoto. Presumably the few actions taken at the sub-national level, e.g. by British Columbia, would be integrated into national systems under the proposal. This incremental approach has the additional practical advantage of avoiding the need to estimate pre-existing taxes (or subsidies) to GHG-emitting activities.

Imposing a carbon charge on deforestation would be more difficult, but could be done using surrogates. For example, estimates could be made of the quantity of waste wood, and associated carbon emissions, generated by the harvest and processing of timber of various kinds.

These estimates could be used to impose an appropriate levy on timber production in the country of origin or, if appropriate, on timber imports by importing countries. Forest clearing for commercial ranching would also be covered. Slash and burn agriculture in very poor societies, where property rights are ill-defined, would be much more difficult to tax, but this type of activity generally accounts for only a small portion of emissions from land-use changes; moreover, the abandoned fields usually revert to heavy vegetative cover in time.

Taking the necessary legislative and regulatory steps and actually collecting the carbon charge, however, are two quite different things. The IMF could be asked to estimate the revenues that should be collected by each signatory country and assess whether they are in fact being collected. Satellite observation of power plants and other large sources of heat, and of deforestation, along with data on imports of crude oil and petroleum products, coal, and gas could help in estimating actual carbon emissions; in addition, large sources could be subject to occasional on-site inspection. The IMF could assess whether significant revenues are being collected, since it routinely reviews government revenues, expenditures, and changes in public debt.

There is some risk that countries could impose the carbon charge, but then weaken its effects through changes in other taxes and/or subsidies to the industries or consumers most affected. Again, careful monitoring of the entire tax/expenditure balance sheet of each country by the IMF could identify and expose the worst abuses. But another point needs to be made: so long as the carbon charge is systematically imposed on all regulated emissions, firms and households would have an incentive, at the margin, to reduce carbon-emitting activities, even if their total burden were mitigated by other tax breaks (which might, for example, keep some firms in business that would otherwise shut down).

If a country were found to be out of compliance, it could be asked in informal consultations, and ultimately in formal international panel reviews, to explain its position. Systematic cheating could of course be possible on a small scale. It would be more difficult on a large scale, and would have to involve the complicity of many officials, something that is increasingly difficult in an age where the internet is ubiquitous and many countries afford protection to whistle-blowers.

If a country were significantly and persistently out of compliance, its exports could be subject to countervailing duties in importing countries. The conceptual and legal basis for such duties—to offset government subsidies to exports—has existed for many years and is embodied in the World Trade Organization (WTO) as well as in national legislation. The new element is that under an international climate agreement the agreed charge on carbon emissions would be considered a cost of doing business, such that failure to pay the charge with government complicity would be considered a subsidy, subject to countervailing duty under existing procedures.

Non-signatory countries could also be subject to countervailing duties. WTO panels have found that imports can be restricted on a discriminatory basis if the originating country is in violation of an international environmental agreement (Webster, 2008; Frankel, 2008). This possibility would provide a potent incentive for most countries to comply with the agreement, whether or not they were formal signatories.

Suitable credits would be given for activities that deliberately withdraw CO_2 from the atmosphere. The most obvious ones concern reforestation (e.g. the regular re-planting of forests that are harvested for paper pulp or other commercial purposes) and carbon capture and sequestration (CCS), which may in the future become an important technique for preventing carbon emissions from entering the atmosphere, particularly at coal-fired power plants.

Economic effects

Imposing a charge on an input to the economy as significant and ubiquitous as energy will have many potential effects. Of course the purpose of the charge is to reduce GHG emissions. In addition, the charge will affect government revenues; may have macroeconomic and inflationary effects; may affect economic growth; and will have potential impacts on the distribution of income, both within countries and between countries.

Emission reductions

How much will a charge of \$15 per ton of CO_2 (or any other particular charge) reduce GHG emissions? The honest answer is we do not know. But we have evidence from empirical research and from model simulations that suggests the short-run response to a \$15 per ton charge will be relatively low, reflecting the fact that energy consumption is deeply embedded in modern economies and not easily changed. The long-run response, however, would be expected to be much larger. A carbon charge will affect emissions through three identifiable channels. First, households can be expected to reduce their spending on energy directly, and on energy-intensive products, both of which will be more expensive after the charge is imposed. Less electricity (than otherwise) will be consumed, less gas or oil for heating, and less motor fuel. More insulation will be installed. Consumers will pay more attention to the lifetime costs of appliances, automobiles, apartments and other long-term purchases as they become conscious of higher energy costs, and shift their purchases to products with lower energy usage.

Second, firms will respond by producing goods that are more energy efficient, and they will alter their production techniques to use less energy—a process that was observed extensively in Europe, Japan, and the United States following the sharp increase in oil prices in the mid-1970s. Developers will use more energy-efficient building materials, will install more insulation, and will orient their buildings to minimize the impact of cold winds and maximize the impact of solar heating in the winter at locations in the northern latitudes, while maximizing the use of breezes and minimizing solar heating in tropical latitudes. Many of these adaptations will involve substituting capital for energy.

Third, low carbon-emitting fuels will, where possible, be substituted for high-emitting fuels in energy-using processes, e.g. wind, hydro, nuclear or gas will substitute for coal and oil in electricity generation.

How sensitive is demand to price? A survey of studies conducted in the 1990s found that the mean long-run price elasticity of energy demand was –0.5; that is, a 10 percent increase in energy prices would reduce demand for energy by 5 percent (Atkinson and Manning, 1995). Cooper (2003) estimated a comparable long-run demand elasticity for crude oil. Simulations using the Emissions Predictions and Policy Analysis (EPPA) model at MIT suggest that GHG emissions would drop by 14 percent in the first five years following the introduction of a \$15 per ton CO_2-equivalent charge in the United States (reported in Metcalf, 2007, p.12), although CO_2 emissions alone dropped only 8 percent in the first five years.

Simulations run on the US Department of Energy's Pacific Northwest National Laboratory (PNNL) model MiniCAM suggest that a \$15-per-ton charge, introduced worldwide in 2012, would reduce global CO_2 emissions from fuel and industrial sources 14 percent below reference case projections by 2020. Estimated reductions would increase to 30 percent below the reference case projection if land-use sources of CO_2 are also effectively covered by the charge. (Land-use sources accounted for 13 percent of estimated global CO_2 emissions in the base year 2005, but become strongly negative—perhaps due to reforestation induced by the policy— following introduction of the carbon charge.)[4]

Not surprisingly, the emission reductions one would expect under a single, common carbon charge differ from country to country. This variation reflects differences in the cost of reducing emissions in different countries, which in turn reflects (at least in part) different initial levels of energy efficiency and differences in the scope of opportunity to install less carbon-intensive processes or devices. Countries that are still developing rapidly may have larger opportunities to substitute more efficient equipment. Thus, the industrialized countries generally show lower percentage reductions in the PNNL simulations—9.3 percent for the United States (which is similar to the EPPA estimate of 8 percent), 11.8 percent for Europe and Japan—than do emerging markets. China, of special interest since its CO_2 emissions by 2020 are nearly twice those of the United States in the reference projection, shows a reduction of 18 percent, while projected industrial and fuel emissions in India fall by 17 percent relative to the 2020 baseline.

Ho and Jorgenson (2007) examine the impact of fuel taxes in China for the purpose of reducing health-damaging pollutant emissions. Their analysis is also applicable to CO_2 emissions. Beginning with a multi-sectoral model of the Chinese economy that accounts for exogenous technical change and savings rates and is calibrated to Chinese data for 1997, Ho and Jorgenson notionally impose fuel taxes set to equal 40 percent of the estimated health damages attributed to pollution caused by burning coal and oil. The result is a tax of 24 percent on coal and about 1 percent on oil. In their simulation, this tax leads to an immediate decline (relative to a baseline projection and abstracting from transitional lags) in coal use of 16.8 percent and a reduction in CO_2 emissions of 13.6 percent. These results indicate a high long-term response to an implicitly low carbon charge (the tax level modeled

---

[4] I am grateful to Jae Edmonds for running these simulations. See also Edmonds *et al.*, 2008.

for coal in this analysis translates to \$1.72 per ton of CO_2 emissions); some of this high response is due to the substitution of untaxed gas for coal, but also to Ho and Jorgenson's assumption of a high long-run substitutability of capital for energy. Higher charges would reduce emissions further, but at a declining rate. An important qualification is that technical change in the model is assumed to be exogenous (not responsive to price incentives), which is surely contrary to reality at the global level if not in China.

An important finding of the Ho and Jorgenson work—indeed its main focus—is that reducing coal consumption in China would have very significant health benefits while also contributing to climate change mitigation.

Revenues

The studies discussed here suggest that energy demand in both the United States and China would respond significantly to a carbon charge. But the response would not be overwhelming at the level of charge suggested, and significant quantities of CO_2 would continue to be emitted. Thus the charge would produce significant revenue. To avoid a significant contractionary macroeconomic effect, this revenue would need to be recycled back into the income stream, either through increased government expenditures or through a reduction in taxes. Ho and Jorgenson, for instance, assume that the revenue collected in China is used to reduce taxes on commodities, labor, and capital in a way that is revenue neutral.

Similarly, this proposal assumes that each country would retain the revenues it collects from a carbon charge, and would be free to use these funds in any combination of additional expenditures or tax reductions it chose, provided that revenues are not recycled in a way that undermines the purpose of the carbon charge, which is to reduce emissions. The macroeconomic impact of the carbon charge could also be kept low by introducing the charge gradually, at a pace consonant with offsetting increases in public expenditures or reductions in taxes.

The introduction of a carbon charge would raise the price of fossil fuels and of energy-intensive goods and services—indeed, that is its principal purpose. It is important that the charge not be undermined by a general rise in inflation. By itself, a levy on carbon would raise the

Table 5.2 *Estimated revenues from carbon charge in 2015, before behavioral response*

	CO_2 Emissions (billion metric tons)	Revenues ($bn)	Revenues/GDP (percent)
World	34.3	515	0.7
USA	6.2	93	0.4
Europe	4.7	70	0.4
Japan	1.2	18	0.2
China	8.2	104	1.3
India	1.6	24	1.1

Note: assumes GDP price increases of 3 percent a year between 2000 and 2015, plus a 20 percent appreciation of the Chinese yuan against the US dollar. Source of underlying data: EIA, International Energy Outlook, 2008.

level of the consumer price index in proportion to the weight of fossil fuels, direct and indirect, implicit in the index. Monetary authorities would need to ensure that this increase does not trigger an inflationary process, whereby workers and capitalists attempt to recoup the loss through higher wages or higher returns. Public discussion of the issues involved, plus a firm hand at the central bank, should contain this potential problem. Using at least part of the revenue generated by a carbon charge for tax reductions would also help.

There is nothing to assure that revenues from a carbon tax will not be misappropriated, or corruptly distributed. But these misappropriations will involve domestic revenues, not funds raised in other countries, and therefore need not be a subject of special concern to other countries, as would be the case under a global trading system. The carbon-charge proposal does not involve large-scale transfers among countries.

The revenues produced by a carbon charge would be substantial, but not overwhelming. If we apply the $15-per-ton CO_2 charge to US EIA's projection for world emissions in 2015 and assume no behavioral response at that time, global revenues from the charge come to $515 billion, or about 0.7 percent of projected gross world product in that year. Table 5.2 shows revenues from this level of carbon charge in absolute terms and as a share of projected GDP, for the United States, Europe, Japan, China, and India—again assuming no behavioral response in that year (as might be the case if the charge were first introduced in that year, with little or no advance notice). For the rich countries, revenue generated is in the tens of billion dollars, but less than one-half of 1 percent of GDP, and perhaps 1 percent of total tax revenue for the United States and Europe, less for Japan. For China and India, revenue from the tax comes to more than 1 percent of GDP, and perhaps over 5 percent of revenue in 2015, augmenting significantly the resource choices those governments could make. Behavioral responses that reduce carbon emissions—the objective of the charge—would of course reduce these revenues, by amounts that depend on the magnitude of the response. Metcalf's report on the MIT simulation, noted above, suggests that a $15-per-ton charge in the United States would reduce that country's CO_2 emissions in the short run by 8.4 percent; applied to the emissions projections noted above, expected US revenues from the charge in 2015 would decline from $93.4 billion to $85.6 billion.

Allowing for behavioral response in the PNNL model reduces projected worldwide revenues by 14 percent, US revenues by 9 percent, and China's revenues (relative to a much higher baseline) by 18 percent.

Gradual reduction of carbon emissions would, of course, reduce the revenue base over time. Whether revenues rose or declined would also depend on the level of the carbon charge over time. In any case, significant revenues are likely to be available for several decades, although not forever. In the PNNL model, fuel and industrial emissions decline by 20 percent relative to the baseline by 2050, but total global emissions continue to rise, suggesting a need (in that model) to raise the carbon charge for several decades.

Growth Effects

Some will be concerned that raising prices on energy will discourage economic growth, especially in developing countries, since energy is a critical input to all modern economies. The impact of a carbon charge on long-term growth is likely to be negligible, however, at least with the right complementary policies, and may even be positive. Four issues must be considered: (1) energy as a direct input to production; (2) use of the revenue from the carbon charge; (3) impact on the cost of capital and hence potentially on the rate of investment; and

(4) impact on international competitiveness and hence potentially on export growth.

Energy is a key input to many sectors of modern economies, including traditional activities such as agriculture. Therefore a first concern is that raising the price of energy will discourage production. Recall, however, that for a variety of reasons energy is used very inefficiently in China, India, and indeed many developing countries, relative to actual practice in rich countries. Thus the possibility exists to produce the same output with a lower input of energy. Sometimes this change simply requires an adequate incentive, such as higher energy prices. Sometimes it requires an incentive plus new knowledge about better practices. Sometimes it requires an incentive plus new investment in more energy-efficient structures or equipment. And of course new investment requires funding. So investments may be diverted from use for other purposes to actions that save energy, and in that way dampen growth. Many energy-saving investments would yield handsome rates of return, however, if energy prices were higher. Moreover, developing countries must make large investments in power generation and distribution to support their growth objectives. Improved energy efficiency could reduce these investment needs, releasing both labor and capital to be used elsewhere in the economy and thereby contributing to growth. According to one estimate, for example, China must spend an average of $67 billion each year over the period 2001–2030, more than 2 percent of GDP, to satisfy its growing requirements for electricity (IEA, 2003, p. 353). Even saving 10 percent of this total would leave $7 billion per year for investment in other activities.

As noted above, a carbon charge will raise revenue. How those revenues are used can influence the rate of growth. If revenues are used to replace growth-inhibiting taxes on capital, the net impact might be to accelerate growth. Thus, Ho and Jorgenson (2007, p. 357) find that when revenues are used to reduce other taxes, GDP is actually higher with a carbon charge than without the charge—that is, the effect of the charge is to (modestly) stimulate growth.

If, as is more likely in many developing countries, revenues from a carbon charge are used to finance expenditures, the impact on growth will depend on the magnitude and the growth-enhancing effects of those expenditures. Expenditures on transport infrastructure would presumably contribute to growth, as would expenditures on under-funded agricultural research and information dissemination, or on education. Expenditures to enlarge or modernize military forces, in contrast, would not contribute much to growth. Thus each government would have substantial discretion over how much revenues from the carbon charge could be directed toward growth-enhancing investments. Certainly revenues can be better used for growth than for subsidizing fossil fuel consumption, as is now done in many countries.

A third channel through which a carbon charge could influence growth would be by changing the cost of capital goods, and hence the real investment that could be undertaken for any given nominal level of spending. Raising the cost of capital goods, other things equal, will reduce growth. Raising the price of energy will increase the cost of those capital goods that are high in direct energy content, such as construction steel and cement. On the other hand, many capital goods are not energy intensive. Moreover, the impact of higher energy prices on capital goods prices would be mitigated to the extent that producers, per the first point above, improve efficiency and reduce energy consumption in response to the carbon charge. It is even conceivable that prices for capital goods would fall, as efficiency improvements outweighed increased energy prices. Furthermore, over a sufficiently long time horizon, technical change can be expected, as in the past, to reduce the prices of many capital goods. There has been no secular decline in the real return to capital over recent decades in rich, technologically advanced countries because capital-saving technical change has compensated, on average, for the declining returns that might have been expected to flow from the tremendous accumulation of capital that occurred during the past half century.

Finally, because higher energy prices, other things being equal, will increase the relative price of energy-intensive products, they could reduce the competitiveness of those products on world markets. A serious loss of competitiveness could, through a variety of channels, have a negative impact on economic growth.

Here the international context in which any country imposes a carbon charge comes into play. Under the proposal outlined in this chapter, all countries would impose a similar carbon charge, so the competitiveness issue would be neutralized for all countries. The relative price of energy-intensive products would rise everywhere, so their consumption would be discouraged, and countries that specialized in the export of such products would experience an impact on their exports. But no country would gain a direct competitiveness advantage, product-by-product, at the expense of other countries—except insofar as they were in a better position to reduce the energy content of their exports or substitute lower-carbon sources of energy.

A charge on carbon emissions can be expected, over time, to stimulate new research and development on low-carbon energy technologies. It is difficult to predict the development and impact of future technology innovations, but in the end this process could provide a significant positive impetus to growth.

Distributional effects

Introducing a carbon charge will have distributional effects across members of each country's population, and between countries. Since countries that levy the charge, under this proposal, would keep the revenues they generate, they could, if desired, use these funds to compensate—in whole or in part—the firms or households that lose the most as a result of the policy. Within countries, distributional effects will occur across sectors of the economy, with carbon-intensive sectors experiencing the main decline in demand (which is the point of the charge); but distributional effects may also occur across income classes, insofar as the carbon-intensity of consumption differs significantly across income classes.

Using MIT's EPPA model to simulate the effects of a $15 per ton charge on CO_2 emissions in the United States, Metcalf (2007) reports that demand for coal would be expected to decline 14.7 percent in the short run (i.e. within the first five years after imposition of the charge). Corresponding short-run demand declines for petroleum and natural gas are estimated to total 5.6 percent and 3.4 percent, respectively. These differing demand impacts reflect differences in the relative price impacts of a carbon charge for each fuel, which in turn reflect the different carbon intensities of the three fossil fuels per unit of useful energy delivered. Both petroleum and gas are imported, so some of the burden of the tax may be absorbed by foreign exporters of these fuels and show up as an improvement in the balance of trade for the United States. This possible effect, which might mitigate the impact on domestic producers' output (though not the impact on their profits), is not reflected in the estimates above. Clearly the main burden would fall on coal miners and on the owners of coal mines. A similar result is likely in many other countries. The economic impact on miners

Table 5.3 *Changes in household disposable income (percent)*

Income Decile	Carbon Tax	With Income Tax Credit to Workers[a]	With Tax Credit to Workers and Social Security Recipients[b]
1	-3.4	-0.7	1.4
2	-3.1	-1.0	1.0
3	-2.4	-0.2	0.6
4	-2.0	0.1	0.3
5	-1.8	0.1	0.1
6	-1.5	0.3	0.1
7	-1.4	0.2	0.1
8	-1.2	0.2	-0.1
9	-1.1	0.0	-0.1
10	-0.8	0.0	-0.2

[a] of $560
[b] of $420
Source: Metcalf (2007), pp. 17–18.

and perhaps mine owners could be mitigated through transitional compensation.

There may also be distributional effects by income class. Metcalf (2007) has calculated how a $15 per ton charge would affect retail prices, and how these prices in turn would affect the disposable income of different income classes in the United States, by income decile. As can be seen in the first column of Table 5.3, the effects of the carbon charge are mildly regressive, hitting the low-income first decile hardest and the high-income tenth decile the least. Metcalf calculates that this regressivity can be reduced by giving flat income tax rebates to all workers. On the basis of revenues calculated to be available, the per-worker rebate comes to $560. The results of this approach are shown in the second column of Table 5.3. The low-income deciles continue to experience some negative impact, in part because they include retirees who would not be eligible for a rebate to workers. Extending the rebate to recipients of social security (the American public pension system) reduces the amount of the rebate, which falls to $420 per recipient, but the overall result is mildly progressive, as shown in the third column of Table 5.3.

The generic point is that a carbon charge will have distributional effects, but that the revenues it generates provide the wherewithal to compensate serious losers, in whole or in part, if the government chooses to do so.

Unlike some other proposals, the approach outlined here does not provide for direct transfers among countries. I believe this is a desirable feature, since the history of unconditional transfers among countries, or even many conditional transfers, is not a happy one (the Marshall Plan is an exception). But there will still be some distributional effects across countries because of the different sectoral impacts noted above. Exporters of coal, in particular, and (to a lesser extent) exporters of oil and of gas, will experience a decline in demand for their products (although due to the possible substitution of natural gas for coal in electricity generation, global demand for gas could conceivably rise), and consequentially some decline in the prices they receive. The terms of international trade will turn against them. By the same token, changes in the terms of trade will benefit net importers of these products. The countries that stand to lose the most from a decline in global demand for coal are the big coal exporters: South Africa, Australia, the United States, and Colombia. The first three, as importers of oil, will be partially compensated by a decline in world oil prices as demand for oil falls; but reduced oil demand will also hit Colombia, as well as many other net exporters of oil. Countries that are large net importers of oil, such as Japan and Korea, will be beneficiaries of these changes. Similar shifts in the terms of trade, it should be noted, would also occur under an effective global cap-and-trade system, or indeed under any effective scheme to limit carbon emissions. In recent years, of course, exporters of all fossil fuels experienced an increase in the prices they receive, and a \$15 per ton CO_2 charge will still leave them with much higher prices than they enjoyed in the early 2000s.

Two further potential objections to a carbon charge

Uncertainty

One objection raised against an emissions charge is that the resulting reduction in emissions will be uncertain: before the charge is imposed, there is no way to know with certainty how extensive the emissions-reduction response will be. This objection is valid, but it bears keeping in mind that the whole domain of climate change and climate policy is replete with uncertainty. As Nordhaus (2008) has pointed out, the presence of uncertainty does not always lead rationally to more stringent action or to a policy that emphasizes quantitative restrictions on emissions. In the policy realm, we need to learn by doing, even as needed research efforts continue to help us better understand changes in the earth's climate and their impacts. Long-term forecasts of energy consumption have been notoriously inaccurate (Abt, 2002; Smil, 2003). Levying a particular carbon charge is only a first step toward addressing the problem of climate change; second and subsequent steps should be clearer and more straightforward to implement than is currently possible under a Kyoto-type agreement with seriously incomplete coverage.

One thing we do know is that other policies—notably a cap-and-trade approach—also involve large uncertainties. Under quantitative emission caps, variability in the price of tradable emission permits is likely to be high. All of the adjustments required by shocks of various kinds will be reflected in prices: for example, a sequence of unusually cold winters could lead to dramatically higher permit prices. Unexpectedly high permit prices will be costly to the economy, as they may cause some plants to shut down or severely curtail output. This in turn will provoke appeals for relief, which governments may (sensibly) provide. But that prospect undermines the apparent quantitative certainty, in terms of expected emissions reductions, that a cap-and-trade approach would seem to provide.

There is a deeper philosophical issue here. A tight and effective cap implicitly places prevention of CO_2 emissions above all other social objectives insofar as, in principle, it requires society to pay any cost to stay within the quantitative target. That feature may recommend a cap approach to some observers. But well-ordered societies do not generally attach infinite economic value to any single objective. Just as individuals do, societies usually make trade-offs among objectives, depending on their incremental costs and benefits. Democratic societies do so through open public debate and political compromise. If some important objectives are threatened, the response frequently is to ease up on other objectives.

Also, it is necessary to look not only to the uncertainties of climate change itself, but also to the uncertainties possibly introduced by our efforts to deal with climate change. Absent a well-functioning global cap-and-trade system, which may be impossible to achieve for the reasons indicated above, we are likely to have disjointed national or regional systems. Inevitably the issue of international competitiveness will be raised, and equally inevitably there will be strong political pressures in countries with more stringent GHG restrictions to (a) restrict imports from countries with less stringent or non-existent restrictions and (b) rebate domestic charges on the embedded carbon content of any export products. The prospect of such trade-influencing national actions, and the ultimate arbitrariness of any actions that are taken, could introduce a high degree of uncertainty into international trade and might, in a worst-case scenario, lead to an unraveling of the WTO-based trading system.[5] Because climate change is a global problem, the solution to it—at least in its broad features—must also be global in scope.

Equity

A second objection to the approach proposed in this chapter is that a carbon charge deals inadequately with "equity." Most of the observed increase in atmospheric CO_2 concentrations over the last two centuries is due to emissions generated by today's rich countries during the course of their development. Therefore, some observers argue, today's rich countries should bear most of the burden of reducing CO_2 emissions and, eventually, atmospheric concentrations. Notions of equity, however, are highly debatable. What looks "equitable" to one person often looks highly inequitable to another. When Englishmen launched the coal-based industrial revolution, they had no idea that climate change three centuries later would be a consequence. Why should their descendants be held responsible? When Americans in the mid-19th century created the petroleum industry with the invention of kerosene—a substitute for increasingly scarce whale oil—they did not know the full long-term implications of this innovation (which probably included saving several species of whales from extinction).

Moreover, according to at least one estimate, the rich countries are not as overwhelmingly responsible for the increased concentration

---

[5] Frankel, 2008, has underlined the difficulties, and the dangers, of allowing widespread rebates on exports. Houser *et al.*, 2008, demonstrate the difficulties in calculating the energy content of goods made in the United States—an easier task than calculating the GHG emissions associated with such goods.

of GHGs in the atmosphere as is commonly believed. If changes in land use are taken into account, this analysis finds that rich countries account for only 55 percent of the increase in atmospheric concentrations since 1890, while today's poor countries account for 45 percent (Mueller *et al.*, 2007). In any case, a debate over past culpability will not help solve the global problem we confront. Economic theory generally holds that optimal decisions require decision makers to take the past as a given, look forward rather than backward, and provide adequate incentives for desired behavior in the future. To focus retrospectively on responsibility for actions in the remote past is to assure continued inaction going forward.

Another reason advanced for having rich countries bear the exclusive, or at least the major, burden of cutting GHG emissions is that they can afford it. "Ability to pay" is a hallowed principle of public finance. But so is the principle that he who benefits should pay the costs. It is widely claimed (though that does not make it correct) that the main burdens of climate change will fall on people living in the tropics—that is, mainly people who today are poor—while populations living at higher latitudes may actually gain, at least in the next few decades, from climate change (see, e.g., Mendelsohn *et al.*, 2006). If this is correct, the tropical countries ought to be those most interested in reducing GHG emissions, and be willing to pay at least their share, and perhaps more.

I conclude that the only equity argument with enduring merit is that everyone who emits GHGs from now on should be discouraged from doing so, insofar as practicable, in proportion to their emissions. Citizens of wealthier nations will—and of course should—pay more because they emit more per capita.

In sum, current efforts to address climate change are predicated on the view that continued GHG emissions will damage the welfare of our descendants, albeit unevenly. Such emissions have a social cost that is not reflected in the current prices of coal, oil, and other sources of GHGs. To correct this market failure, a charge should be added to the prices we would otherwise pay. All emitters, rich or poor, should pay the charge. An analogy would be to compare the use of the atmosphere's absorptive capacity with the use of a common commodity such as copper. All users of copper pay the full current price of copper, regardless of their level of income and regardless of who consumed copper in the past. We need to think of the atmosphere as a scarce resource, like copper, that needs to be rationed by all who use it.

Energy Security

Energy security is a common political theme these days. But achieving energy security and mitigating climate change are only coincidental bedfellows from a policy perspective. Conservation of energy serves both objectives. But energy security really concerns oil and natural gas (the latter especially for Europe, although a growing number of countries will become dependent on imported gas if current trends continue), while mitigation of climate change, at its core, concerns coal (though oil plays an important supporting role). Serious mitigation of climate change might even increase dependence on natural gas, as a lower-emitting fuel for electricity generation. Substitution of electricity and eventually hydrogen for petrol in automobiles and trucks will improve energy security, but it could also put more pressure on the climate insofar as coal and gas are the primary fuels used to generate the electricity. Similarly, liquefying coal to produce substitute fuels for the transport sector would reduce demand for imported petroleum, but would be bad for the climate. To the extent that both enhanced energy security and reduced GHG emissions are desirable, the strong emphasis needs to be on energy conservation and electricity generation with sources of energy other than coal and gas.

Mixed Systems

This chapter has proposed an internationally agreed charge on carbon emissions that in principle all countries would levy. But several economies, most notably the European Union, have already embarked on a cap-and-trade system. The current Australian government also seems committed to this approach, and several bills before the US Congress call for introducing an emissions trading system in the United States. It is worth asking, therefore, whether the two systems can co-exist. The answer is affirmative, provided several conditions are met.

A cap-and-trade country could, if it wished, introduce procedures whereby additional emission permits could be issued if the trading price of permits exceeded the agreed carbon charge by a significant amount for a significant period of time.[6] But it need not do so. It could retain a

---

[6] McKibbon and Wilcoxen in Aldy and Stavins, 2007, proposed a system that mixes short- and long-term emission permits. The price of the short-term

more restrictive arrangement that generated higher carbon prices if it wished. Other countries would only be concerned about the opposite case, in which the price of permits falls significantly short of the internationally agreed carbon charge. Thus, some conditions would need to be met for the two systems to co-exist comfortably.

First, permit prices under the cap-and-trade system over time should average no less than the internationally agreed carbon charge. For example, the average over ten years should be no less than the agreed carbon charge. This would give the cap-and-trade countries an opportunity to tighten their target limits appropriately in a quinquennial review should the permit trading price fall below the agreed charge during the previous five-year period. Second, it might be agreed that if the permit trading price fell below the agreed charge by x percent for more than y months, trading partners could appropriately consider this gap in carbon prices to constitute an export subsidy and levy countervailing duties on their imports from the cap-and-trade countries. The x and y could be negotiated, but a price gap of 10 percent and a time period of six months might be reasonable threshold values for making this determination.

Third, countries could not provide rebates of carbon charges or permit prices on their exports except where the export is a fossil fuel, such as coal, crude oil or refined products, and natural gas, for which carbon charges have already been paid in the exporting country.

Finally, cap-and-trade countries could not give away emission permits to producers of goods and services, or at least to producers of tradable goods and services. These could properly be considered production subsidies in the context of a regime of common carbon charges. A cap-and-trade country would therefore have to auction the emission permits or, if it wanted to give the permits away, could give

Footnote 6 (*cont.*)

permits to be sold by governments on demand would by agreement be the same across participating countries. This is the equivalent of a common carbon charge, where the permit-issuing governments retain the revenue, as in the proposal here. The difference is that each country would initially also distribute long-term emission permits, which would be tradable within but not between countries, and would therefore have (varying) market value. These long-term permits could be allocated according to historical emissions or however the issuing country chooses. In the view of the authors, this would create a constituency for continuing the restraints on carbon emissions over time. Permit allocation is also, however, a mechanism for distributing political favors and, unless under careful control, for corruption.

them directly to households (on a per capita or some other basis). The revenues from selling permits into the trading market would then go directly to consumers, bypassing the treasury. In either case, the larger objective would be to avoid either the appearance or the reality of conferring competitive advantage on certain firms or sectors through the operation of the permit system.

Negotiability

Would it be possible to negotiate an international agreement to impose a carbon charge? Why would countries such as China and India, or the United States for that matter, agree to it? The answer depends on how seriously these countries take climate change and, in particular, whether they view it as a global problem that must be dealt with and that will affect negatively Chinese, Indians and Americans two or three generations from now. The projections in Table 5.1 suggest that any scheme to reduce CO_2 emissions must include the leading developing countries, and include them soon. Because the highest priority in these countries is maintaining an acceptably high rate of economic growth, and because achieving this objective involves increased demand for electricity and motive energy, many developing countries are unlikely to agree on binding emission targets that are effective in mitigating climate change. For this reason, *the framework of international cooperation needs to be altered from one focused on quantitative national emissions targets to one focused on mutually supportive actions.* Since the only way to reach millions of decision makers is through the price system, the natural (although not the only) way to focus on actions would be to levy a common charge on emissions of GHGs, especially CO_2.

The idea of imposing a charge on carbon emissions is in complete harmony with China's official energy strategy, adopted in 2002. In the words of one senior government official, China's strategy "will constantly improve the macro control and power market regulatory system, deepen the power system reform, and try hard to build up *an incentive mechanism for resource conservation, efficiency improvement, environmental protection,* and development promotion." (Wu Yin, Deputy Director-General of the Energy Department of the National Development and Reform Commission, 4/23/04, italics added.) The need to create appropriate incentive systems for efficiency and environmental protection is constantly mentioned by Chinese officials, as is the need to raise the price of coal to reflect its full social costs, including environmental costs (e.g. China Development Forum 2003, p. 93). A charge on environmentally damaging emissions fits perfectly with this objective; moreover, China has already experimented with effluent charges, with some success (Wang and Wheeler, 1999). Limiting growth in the use of coal would also provide significant public health benefits in China, and no doubt in other rapidly growing economies as well. Finally, an international agreement would help to strengthen the position of the central authorities in China vis-à-vis the provinces and municipalities, where most of the problems with enforcing government policies arise.

Saudi Arabia, the world's leading oil producer, has indicated that it would not have a problem with a universal charge on CO_2 emissions, implying that it would not restrict oil production to capture the revenues lost to other countries as a result of imposing a charge on carbon.

A carbon charge will generate significant revenues. Since most governments need additional revenues, a mechanism for raising them in an internationally acceptable way would be welcome, especially to finance ministries. As noted, the revenues could be used in various ways that would enhance growth, including financing research and development. And they could be used to invest in adaptation measures that will help countries cope with those climatic changes that are likely to occur despite efforts at mitigation.

Given that many Americans are highly averse to taxes, revenues from the carbon charge could be used in the United States to reduce taxes, to enhance investment, and/or to neutralize the distributional effects of the carbon charge. Some portion might also be used to finance climate-relevant research and development, such as the development of cellulose-based ethanol or carbon capture and sequestration technology for power plants and other large sources of emissions.

It is not necessary that all countries agree initially to the scheme. A carbon charge could be launched with the major emitters, perhaps three dozen countries in all. But it must include both China and the United States, the two largest emitters of CO_2. Thus, any negotiable scheme must be agreeable to those two countries. Given its perceived reluctance to deal with this issue (although it remains the major source of research on climate change and on many alternative sources of energy), the United States would have to take the initiative, or respond enthusiastically if the initiative were taken by another country.

The likelihood, based on current knowledge, that the major negative impacts of climate change will occur in low latitudes (even though surface temperature is expected to rise more at high latitudes) should provide many developing countries with an incentive to participate, as long as other major emitting areas also participate, and as long as participation was not seen to threaten their development.

If an agreement among a suitable number of relevant countries could be reached, non-participating countries would be encouraged to participate (in practice, even if not through formal agreement) by the possibility that their exports to participating countries would be subject to countervailing duties based on the implicit "subsidy" arising from their failure to impose a carbon charge.

References

Abt, Clark (2002). "The Future of Energy from the Perspective of Social Science," in Richard N. Cooper and Richard Layard (eds.), *What the Future Holds*. Cambridge, MA: MIT Press.

Aldy, Joseph E., Eduardo Ley, and Ian Perry (2008). *A Tax-Based Approach to Slowing Global Climate Change*. Washington, DC: Resources for the Future.

Aldy, Joseph E. and Robert N. Stavins, eds. (2007). *Architectures for Agreement: Addressing Global Climate Change in the Post-Kyoto World*. New York: Cambridge University Press.

Atkinson, J. and N. Manning (1995). "A Survey of International Energy Elasticities," in B. Terry, P. Elkins, and N. Johnstone (eds.), *Global Warming and Energy Demand*. London: Routledge.

China Development Forum (2003). *China's National Energy Strategy and Reform: Background Papers*. Beijing: Development Research Center of the State Council.

Cooper, John C. B. (2003). "Price Elasticity of Demand for Crude Oil: Estimates for 23 Countries," *OPEC Review* 27(1): 1–8.

Edmonds, J., L. Clarke, J. Lurz, and M. Wise (2008). "Stabilizing CO_2 Concentrations with Incomplete International Cooperation," *Climate Policy* 8(4): 355–76.

Frankel, Jeffrey A. (2008). "Addressing the Leakage/Competitiveness Issue in Climate Change Policy."

Ho, Mun S. and Dale W. Jorgenson (2007). "Policies to Control Air Pollution Damages," in Mun S. Ho and Chris Nielsen (eds.), *Clearing the Air: The Health and Economic Damages of Air Pollution in China*. Cambridge, MA: MIT Press.

Houser, Trevor *et al.* (2008). *Leveling the Carbon Playing Field: International Competition and US Climate Policy Design.* Washington, DC: Peterson Institute for International Economics.

International Energy Agency (2003). *World Energy Investment Outlook.* Paris: OECD.

Mendelsohn, R., A. Dinar, and L. Williams (2006). "The Distributional Impact of Climate Change on Rich and Poor Countries," *Environment and Development Economics* 11: 158–78.

Metcalf, Gilbert E. (2007). *A Proposal for a U.S. Carbon Tax Swap: An Equitable Tax Reform to Address Global Climate Change.* Washington, DC: Brookings Institution.

Mueller, Benito, Niklos Hoehne, and Christian Ellerman (2007). "Differentiating (Historic) Responsibilities for Climate Change," October, available at www.oxfordclimatepolicy.org/publications/DifferentiatingResponsibility.pdf.

Nordhaus, William (2008). *A Question of Balance: Weighing the Options on Global Warming Policies.* New Haven, CT: Yale University Press.

Smil, Vaclav (2003). *Energy at the Crossroads: Global Perspectives and Uncertainties.* Cambridge, MA: MIT Press.

US Department of Energy, Energy Information Administration (EIA) (various years, latest 2008). *International Energy Outlook.*

Wang, Hua and David Wheeler (1999). "Endogenous Enforcement and Effectiveness of China's Pollution Levy System," Washington, DC: World Bank, mss.

Webster, D. G. (2008). *Adaptive Governance: The Dynamics of Atlantic Fisheries Management.* Cambridge, MA: MIT Press.

Williamson, John (2008). "Charging versus Cap-and-Trade as Techniques to Curb Climate Change," Washington, DC: Peterson Institute for International Economics.

6 | Towards a global compact for managing climate change[1]

R. AGARWALA

The year 2007 witnessed a major surge in interest in controlling the damage that can be done to the global economy due to the accumulation of greenhouse gases (GHGs) in the atmosphere. The *Stern Review* (Stern 2006) published in October 2006 and publicized in 2007 drew attention to the seriousness of the economic consequences potentially associated with a continuation of present trends in human-induced climate change. In an in-depth cost-benefit analysis (subject to the usual caveats for such analyses), Stern demonstrated that about 1 percent of Gross Domestic Product (GDP) invested in controlling GHG emissions can save an annuitized loss on a broad measure of consumption (that includes nonmarket goods and services) equivalent to 5–20 percent of GDP by mitigating the negative impacts of climate change. In February 2007, the latest assessment report of the Intergovernmental Panel on Climate Change (IPCC 2007a) articulated a growing consensus among climate scientists about the devastating effects of human-induced climate change, particularly for low-income regions and low-income people of the world. Al Gore, the former Vice-President of the United States, in his powerful documentary, *An Inconvenient Truth,* which won two Academy Awards, demonstrated in a graphic manner the high costs of climate change for the world, including developed countries. Since then, and also under the leadership of Al Gore, a series of *Live Earth Concerts* around the world have continued raising global consciousness about the dangers of climate change. On June 7, 2007, the communique issued by the Group of Eight (G8) Summit (G8 2007)—which also had inputs from five major emerging economies, the Group of Five (G5)[2]—devoted a considerable amount of attention to the issue of climate change and strategies for

---

[1] The chapter was prepared by Dr. Ramgopal Agarwala, formerly a Senior Adviser at the World Bank.

[2] The five emerging economies are Brazil, China, India, Mexico, and South Africa.

reducing GHG emissions. Finally, the Nobel Peace Prize awarded to Al Gore and the IPCC in 2007 further raised the public profile of climate change issues.

While the year 2007 began with a bang on climate change discussions, however, it ended with a whimper on climate change agreements. The heated, and even tear-inducing, debates at the Bali Conference in December 2007 only produced a road map for further discussion leading up to the Copenhagen Conference in 2009 along with an agreement for *consideration* of enhanced national/international action on mitigation, adaptation, technology development and transfer, and provision of technical support and new and additional resources, including official and concessional funding for developing countries. There was no agreement even on broad principles to guide these deliberations. Not surprisingly, the follow-up meetings in Bangkok (in April 2008) and Bonn (in June 2008) did not make any real progress towards consensus.

Perhaps the most dramatic demonstration of the differences in perspectives of developed and developing countries[3] on climate change came out at the recent (July 2008) summit meetings of G8 and G5 countries in Hokkaido Toyako, Japan. The G8 declaration (G8 2008) called for adopting the goal of achieving at least a 50 percent reduction in global emissions by 2050 while emphasizing the need for "contributions from all major economies"—code words for including major economies such as China and India in the compact. But the declaration did not specify the base from which this reduction was to be achieved. Nor did it specify targets for developed countries for 2050 or 2020. It also asserted that "all major economies will need to commit to meaningful mitigation actions *to be bound* in the international agreement to be negotiated by the end of 2009" (italics added). The need for resource transfer to developing countries for adaptation and mitigation and for technology development and dissemination was recognized in broad, general terms without any commitment to numerical targets.

By contrast, the G5 declaration (G8 2008a) stated that a shared vision on climate change must be "based on an equitable burden-sharing paradigm that ensures equal sustainable development potential for all citizens of the world and takes into account historical responsibility and respective capabilities as a fair and just approach."

---

[3] In this chapter, the words, "developed countries" and the North and "developing countries" and the South are used interchangeably.

The G5 leaders did not mention a global target for mitigation, but called for quantified emission targets for the developed countries under the Kyoto Protocol of at least 25–40 percent below 1990 levels by 2020 and between 80–95 percent by 2050. The G5 did not call[ed] for any commitments on mitigation by developing countries, either in aggregate or per capita terms, or in terms of emissions per unit of GDP. Instead, they "call[ed] upon the international community to work towards a strengthened scheme for technology innovation, development, transfer and deployment, and a comprehensive review of intellectual property rights regimes for such technologies in order to strike an adequate balance between rewards for innovators and global public good." They also called upon developed countries "to commit clearly to significant additional funding for both mitigation and adaptation in developing countries." The commitment to additional resources should obtain not only in relation to current programs of Official Development Assistance (ODA), but also to existing financial arrangements under the Kyoto Protocol. The G5 leaders "welcome[d] for further exploration, *inter alia*, the proposal by China for setting up a climate financing goal for all developed countries such as 0.5% of GDP (in addition to ODA) for climate action in developing countries as well as the Mexican initiative for a World Climate Change Fund."

Clearly, if the Hokkaido G8 Summit is any indication, the developed and developing countries are not on the same page for managing climate change. In this chapter, we make some proposals to bring them together. In Section II, we argue for a frank discussion of the factors that are behind the slow progress in climate change negotiations and present what may be called some "inconvenient truths." Section III presents five criteria that a global compact must satisfy to reconcile the views of both developed and developing countries and to meet global climate change goals. Section IV discusses how the Kyoto Protocol and Indian policy paper on climate change fail to meet the necessary criteria proposed in the chapter. Section V presents our proposal for a climate change compact that we believe satisfies the five criteria discussed in Section III. Section VII takes up the difficult issue of finding resources to finance adaptation and mitigation programs in developing countries and refers to some proposals for restructuring the global financial architecture in ways that can also generate resources for funding global public goods, including climate change mitigation. Section VI makes some concluding remarks.

Factors behind slow progress in climate change negotiations

In order to make some real progress towards an international agreement on climate change, we must be frank about the problems underlying past and current negotiations on this issue. In fact, there are some "inconvenient truths" that both the developed and developing countries must face up to if there is to be a global compact on climate change.

First, there is the issue of the historical responsibility for the current stock of GHGs in the atmosphere and its implications for the funding of adaptation and mitigation programs. What matters for climate change is not the flow of GHG emissions, but the stock of GHGs in the atmosphere. According to most calculations, developed countries are responsible for more than 50 percent of the current stock of GHGs (see Muller *et al.* 2007). The concept of carbon debt and the responsibility for servicing that debt must be fully accepted. The present value of this debt needs to be quantified and mechanisms for servicing it must be explored. A few calculations can help to illustrate the enormity of developed-country responsibility. Since the dawn of the Industrial Revolution, the concentration of GHGs in the atmosphere has increased from about 280 parts per million (ppm) to about 430 ppm. This increase was the result of GHG emissions estimated to total more than 1 trillion tons in carbon dioxide (CO_2)-equivalent terms over the same period. Estimates of the social cost of carbon emissions today vary from $3 per ton to $130 per ton with an average value of $12 per ton in 2005 mentioned by Working Group II in the Fourth Assessment Report of the IPCC (IPCC 2007b). Even if one uses a low value for the social cost of emissions, the present value of carbon debt would be in the trillions of US dollars. Any reasonable figure on debt service obligations would indicate payments of hundreds of billions of dollars—a major part of which should come from the developed countries—that should be paid to compensate the people of present and future generations (most of whom will reside in developing countries).

Second, the developed countries must accept that there cannot be an international apartheid in lifestyles. If the Western lifestyle is not replicable for the world as a whole, it must be modified in both the developed and developing countries. The emerging middle class in developing countries is by and large trying to replicate the Western lifestyle, and it must be recognized that this middle class will accept departures from current Western norms only if the West itself is likewise changing to more sustainable ways of life (see Naim 2008).

Third, there is suspicion in the South that, first, the economic rise of the South is not acceptable to the North because it could end the North's global dominance and second, that climate change discussions may be one instrument for slowing down the rise of the South. There must be more research in developing countries on the impact of climate change on their economies and an internal conviction that the effects of climate change will be devastating for the South.

Fourth, the developing countries must stop hiding behind the poor. The burgeoning middle class in developing countries is set to exceed the population of the developed countries and their lifestyle and per capita GHG emissions are basically similar to those in the developed countries. Unless the carbon emissions of this group are reduced, developed-country efforts to mitigate emissions will go in vain.

Fifth, present discussions of climate change impacts concentrate too much on very long-term impacts and on impacts with respect to *global* GDP. It is difficult to be terribly worried about what may happen in a hundred years given all the uncertainties that apply, including uncertainties about future technological progress. Something more convincing is needed. Among the possibilities are the following:

i. We need to demonstrate that even though overall global effects may not be large, climate change can wipe out the livelihoods of millions of people—equivalent to the impact of x number of major tsunamis. Utter disaster even for 2 percent of the world population may affect the survival of up to 200 million people, more than the number affected by all the major disasters of the twentieth century, including the World Wars.

ii. The effects of global warming work in tandem with other effects which operate in the short and medium term. For example, the risks of exploding numbers of cars on the world's roads come in the form of pollution and congestion in the near term. Acid rain due to coal burning in China is a problem now. Promoting energy efficiency is good for energy security now, apart from its climate change benefits. In short, the discussion of climate change impacts must put more emphasis on the near term, and on the other adverse effects associated with activities that generate carbon emissions, than is done currently. Or to put it in another way, these discussions must highlight more forcefully the "co-benefits" of mitigating carbon emissions, as has been done in India's climate change paper (Government of India 2008).

iii. Researchers in affected countries need to elaborate on the nature of catastrophic changes that could be caused by climate change, such as changes in monsoon patterns in South Asia or weakening of the Gulf Stream to Europe. These consequences need to be publicized separately rather than being relegated to a footnote in a thick report.

Necessary criteria for a credible global compact

The above discussion may suggest that the positions of developed and developing countries are basically irreconcilable. However, in this chapter we argue that a compromise solution is possible—provided both sides are prepared to show some flexibility. More specifically, we suggest five criteria that have to be satisfied by a credible global compact on climate change:

- First, it has to be *comprehensive*. What matters for the global climate is the global stock of emissions and the global increment in that stock. If a compact leaves out major sources of the emissions, it cannot be effective. In this respect, the developing countries have to agree to be part of the emissions compact, though, as we note below, that does not have to mean that they commit to a "reduction" in CO_2 emissions.[4]
- Second, it has to be *equitable*. Any hint of an analog to the Nuclear Non-Proliferation Treaty, where past and present high levels of emissions become a basis for future entitlements to high levels of emissions, will jeopardize a global compact. It is clear that on ethical grounds, any concept of intragenerational and intergenerational equity will focus on emission rights on a per capita basis. The ethical argument is considerably strengthened by the economic argument that in the 50–100 year horizon relevant for climate change discussions, per capita incomes of major

---

[4] In this chapter, unless otherwise mentioned, figures on CO_2 emissions as given in World Development Indicators 2007 of the World Bank are used as proxies for all GHG emissions.

developing countries may converge towards those of the developed countries. India's per capita income in purchasing power parity (PPP) terms was $3,072 in 2005, an order of magnitude lower than the developed countries' average of $29,114. However, if India's per capita GDP grows at only 5.2 percent per year between 2005 and 2050, its per capita income in PPP terms in 2050 will be slightly higher than that of the developed countries in 2005. For China this catching up may take place sooner. In other words, by 2050, per capita emissions for India and China could be expected to be similar to those of the developed countries today, if these countries replicate the current relationship between carbon emissions and per capita incomes in developed countries. The reduction that these countries can achieve in CO_2 emissions has to be seen in relation to this *potential* level rather than in relation to the *actual* level today. On both ethical and economic grounds, equality in per capita emission rights has to be a fundamental principle of a global compact on climate change.

- Third, emissions targets have to be *realistic*. Unless there is a technological breakthrough, reducing emissions on the scale needed to address climate change is going to be a costly and slow process—and as noted below, progress in the implementation of the Kyoto Protocol does not inspire optimism. Unrealistic targets will reduce the credibility of the compact.
- Fourth, the program has to be *efficient*. It should minimize the global welfare loss associated with achieving emissions reductions and also minimize the risks of corruption in meeting the targets.
- Fifth, the program has to develop an institutional mechanism for *effective* implementation. Unless there are institutions which can, through incentives and/or disincentives, ensure compliance with global agreements, progress is likely to be limited. For developing countries, international assistance has to be massive, but it should be made contingent on the design and implementation of a credible program for adaptation and mitigation. For developed countries, there is a need for clear commitment to mitigation, backed by national legislation.

Limitations of the Kyoto Protocol approach

At present, the Kyoto Protocol is the main international mechanism for managing climate change. That mechanism, however, seems to satisfy none of the five criteria mentioned above.

First, the Kyoto Protocol does not provide a comprehensive mechanism for controlling global emissions. Annex I countries that agreed to emission targets accounted for only 30 percent of global CO_2 emissions in 2003. If transitional economies, which are operating well below their production levels in 1990, are left out, then the percentage of emissions in 2003 covered by the Kyoto Protocol is only 20 percent of the global total.

Second, the Kyoto Protocol does not deal with the issue of equity. The targets it defines in relation to emissions levels in 1990 seem to be the products of political bargaining. There is no effort to demonstrate how the targets are linked to any principle of equity, even though exempting the developing countries from emission reduction targets may be regarded as an implicit recognition of the equity principle.

Third, the Kyoto Protocol does little to indicate, even in broad terms, the programs of technological dissemination, incentives, and resources needed for achieving its emission targets.

Fourth, with respect to efficiency considerations, the Kyoto Protocol uses a cap-and-trade system to achieve carbon reductions. This system is rooted in the basic insight that the marginal cost of reducing emissions beyond the allowable caps may be higher for some entities than the marginal cost of reducing below the caps for some other entities. In this form, an emissions-trading system could in principle work within countries and groups of countries with an aggregate cap. However, there are severe problems in practice. First, the allocation of caps to millions of individual units is a complex process subject to political and administrative manipulations. It has been difficult to implement cap-and-trade systems even in developed countries. It would be nearly impossible in developing countries with weak governance and administrative capacity. Second, there are major uncertainties about the future demand and supply of carbon allowances, and permit prices in existing trading systems have shown large fluctuations. These uncertainties do not provide a stable basis for long-term investments in carbon mitigation. Moreover, when trading with developing countries where there are no limits on carbon emissions, the logic of a cap-and-trade system breaks down completely. A developing country may sell Certified Emission Reductions (CERs) through the Clean Development Mechanism (CDM) with its carbon-saving projects while increasing carbon emissions through other projects. Thus, there is no assurance that extra carbon emissions allowed for the emitter in developed countries is being compensated by a net reduction in overall emissions elsewhere. Thus, the system may not achieve overall emission reductions at all. Finally, in the CDM, neither the buyer nor the seller has an incentive to be honest about the actual carbon savings achieved by the project. The certifying agencies thus face a temptation to avoid due diligence in issuing CERs. The loser when this happens is the global environment, which does not have a seat at the certification table.

Fifth, the Kyoto Protocol does not provide an effective implementation mechanism. The Protocol's enforcement mechanism for Annex I countries, whose targets are supposedly mandatory, is weak insofar as the noncompliant party is only asked to make up for the shortfall in future commitments and to submit a compliance action plan. (Also, the eligibility of a noncompliant party to make transfers under emissions trading is suspended until the party is reinstated.) In addition to weak enforcement provisions, the Protocol allows a country to withdraw from the agreement without specifying any penalty.

In view of the limitations of the Kyoto Protocol, it is not surprising that the objective of reducing carbon emissions is not being achieved. Between 1990 and 2003, global emissions of CO_2 (a principal GHG) increased by 18.9 percent, with the increase shared almost equally between the developed and developing countries. What is surprising is that carbon intensity, in emissions per unit of GDP, declined more sharply in developing countries (28.5 percent) than in high-income countries (12.6 percent). Even more surprising is the fact that CO_2 emissions on a per capita basis, which were already relatively high in developed countries, increased by a further 8.5 percent between 1990 and 2003 in the North, but declined marginally (by 1 percent) in developing countries. Clearly, despite all the hype about climate change in developed countries, the trend in those countries is one of retrogression rather than progress when it comes to reducing their carbon footprints.

Given recent trends, the Kyoto Protocol target of reducing CO_2 emission between 1990 and 2012 is unlikely to be realized even by signatory nations, much less by the world as a whole (IMF 2007).

Table 6.1: *Trends in CO_2 emission, 1990–2003*

	1990	2003	% change 1990–2003
1. CO_2 emissions (billion tons)			
World	22.50	26.8	18.9%
High income	10.65	12.7	19.59%
Low and middle income	10.66	12.6	18.68%
2. CO_2 emissions (kg per 2000 PPP $ of GDP)			
World	0.628	0.507	–19.24%
High income	0.522	0.456	–12.59%
Low and middle income	0.801	0.572	–28.52%
3. CO_2 emissions (metric tons per capita)			
World	4.3	4.3	0
High income	11.79	12.79	8.49%
Low and middle income	2.41	2.39	–0.80%

Source: WDI, World Bank, 2007.

India's 2008 "National Action Plan on Climate Change" (NAPCC), which was the product of a high-level Council chaired by the Prime Minister of India (Government of India 2008), highlights the nature of the problems underlying the international dialogue on climate change. The Action Plan begins with a clear statement about the historical responsibilities of developed countries for current levels of GHGs in the atmosphere and calls for the transfer of new and additional financial resources and climate-friendly technologies to support both adaptation and mitigation in developing countries. At the same time, the report shows agnosticism with respect to the potential adverse effects of global climate change in India.

The report highlights the need for low-carbon growth but avoids— to an even greater extent than other government documents on energy policy—any effort to quantify targets for energy efficiency or carbon efficiency. There is obviously a concern that any mention of quantitative targets may be seized upon by the international community as national commitments, irrespective of the availability of resources and technology to achieve these targets. The only target mentioned in the 2008 plan is that India is determined that its per capita GHG emissions will at no point exceed that of developed countries. Since that is not a likely outcome for decades, this approach could become an alibi for inaction for the foreseeable future. So far as a global climate change architecture is concerned, the Indian position is that the Kyoto Protocol does not expire in 2012; only a new phase of the Kyoto Protocol is to be discussed for the period beyond 2012. The implications of this position are that mitigation commitments will continue to be made by developed countries only and that developing countries will benefit from resources made available under CDM and funds for adaptation.

The Indian climate policy report is a good example of how the developing countries are not on the same page as the developed countries when it comes to a post-2012 agreement on climate change.

An alternative framework for managing climate change

Defining targets for CO_2 emissions that are comprehensive and equitable

As mentioned above, we believe that emission targets that are comprehensive and equitable should be defined on a per capita basis for the world as a whole. It can be argued that defining emission targets on a per capita basis will encourage pro-natal population policy. However, family planning has now become embedded in household behavior and is based on considerations of individual family welfare; the advantages of increased population in terms of expanded emission rights at a national level will be too small a matter to change household behavior. In any case, most other international assistance programs, such as ODA also use per capita allocation as the basic criterion without any demonstrated evidence that this approach encourages pro-natal national policies.

Table 6.2 works through the implications of allocating the G8 emissions target for 2050 on a per capita basis. It suggests that, to achieve the targeted 50 percent reduction proposed in the G8 communique, the developed countries will have to reduce their per capita emissions by 90 percent from 2003 levels, while the developing countries will have to reduce per capita emissions by 40 percent from their already low levels. Such targets do not seem to be realistic. Even countries such as the United Kingdom that are committed to serious emission reduction efforts do not propose 90 percent reductions. Similarly, for

Table 6.2 CO_2 emissions (billion tons), 2003 and 2050

	2003 total emissions (billion tons)	2003 emissions per capita (tons)	2050 total emissions (billion tons) with:		Population (billion) 2050	CO_2 emissions per capita in 2050 with:	
			50% reduction	Stabilization at 2003 level (with equality in per capita emissions).		50% reduction in total emissions from 2003 level	Stabilization in total emissions at 2003 level
High-income countries	12.74	12.79	–	3.44 (–73%)	1.25	1.45	2.75
Developing countries	12.65	2.39	–	21.86 (73%)	7.95	1.45	2.75
World	25.39	4.30	12.70	25.39	9.2	1.45	2.75

Note: Figures in parentheses are changes between 2003 and 2050.
Source: WDI, 2007, World Bank, UN Population Projections and author estimates.

developing countries, a 40 percent reduction in emissions also does not seem realistic—either technologically or in political economy terms—considering the enormous needs of growth over the next few decades. In sum, though the 50 percent reduction target by 2050 is gaining currency, its validity would seem to be questionable.[5]

An alternative target would aim to stabilize CO_2 emissions at 2003 levels by 2050, with a possible target of 50 percent reduction by 2100.[6] Apportioned on an equal per capita basis, this will require reductions in per capita emissions in developed countries of about 80 percent by 2050 and allow an increase in developing countries' per capita emissions of about 20 percent. For countries like India, where per capita emissions in 2003 came to only 1.20 tons; this will allow total emissions in absolute terms to increase by more than 100 percent. If stabilization of emission levels until 2050 is accepted as a more realistic target, it will mean a greater focus on adaptation. In aggregate terms, the approach suggests the following targets:

Between 2003 and 2050, developed countries will reduce CO_2 emissions by no less than 73 percent and developing countries will increase CO_2 emissions by no more than 73 percent.

These targets do not mean that developing countries will not be making efforts to reduce emissions, only that their cuts should be seen in relation to potential emissions after taking into account their growth needs and not in relation to current emission levels. So far as reducing the carbon intensity of growth is concerned, the developing countries will be making the same degree of effort as the developed countries. In 2003, CO_2 emissions per unit of GDP in 2000 international $ (i.e., in PPP terms) were 0.51 kg for the world, 0.46 kg for developed countries, and 0.57 kg for developing countries. Assuming 2 percent annual growth in GDP for developed countries over the period 2005–2050 and 6 percent annual GDP growth over the same

---

[5] If the base level is 1990 rather than 2003, the task will be even more difficult.

[6] As per the *Summary for Policymakers of the Synthesis Report of the IPCC Fourth Assessment Report* (November 2007), this corresponds to a Category III Scenario which has the following characteristics: CO_2 stabilization at a concentration of 440–485 ppm; a peak year for CO_2 emissions in the 2010–2030 timeframe; a change in global CO_2 emissions in 2050 of between –30 to +5 percent of 2000 emissions; a global average temperature rise, relative to the preindustrial equilibrium, of 2.8 to 3.2°C; and global average sea-level rise, again relative to the preindustrial level, 0.6–1.9 meters.

Table 6.3 *Targets for reducing carbon intensity of GDP*

	GDP in trillions of 2000 PPP$		CO2 emission (kg per 2000 PPP$ of GDP)	
	2005	2050	2003	2050
Developed countries	29.4	71.7 (2%)	0.46	0.048 (–5.0%)
Developing Countries	25.3	348.5 (6%)	0.57	0.063 (–5.0%)
World	54.7	420.2 (4.6%)	0.51	0.060 (-5.0%)

Note: Figures in parentheses are annual growth rates between 2005/2003 and 2050.
Source: WDI and author calculations.

time period for developing countries,[7] the above allocation of CO_2-emission rights leads to an average carbon intensity (in PPP terms) of 0.048 kg per unit of GDP for the developed countries and 0.063 for the developing countries in 2050. This translates to an annual reduction in carbon intensity per unit of GDP of about 5 percent per year for both developed and developing countries (see Table 6.3). Thus, this scheme implies parity between developed and developing countries in terms of their efforts to reduce the carbon intensity of future economic growth:

Both developed and developing countries will aim to reduce carbon intensity per unit of GDP by 5 percent per year between 2003 and 2050.

Carbon intensity targets can in turn be divided into targets for reducing the energy intensity of GDP and the carbon intensity of energy. The former may be cost effective in purely economic terms while the latter will require subsidies to compensate for externalities.

---

[7] The assumptions made here are consistent with those of the World Economic Outlook (IMF, 2008), which estimates an average annual GDP growth rate of 2.3 percent for developed countries and 6.5 percent for developing countries over the period 2000–2013. Even though it is difficult to make GDP projections over the long term (up to 2050), it is useful to assume some realistically optimistic numbers as aspirational targets, which is what these assumed growth rates are. The achievement of such growth rates will require, within the emissions quota specified here, 5 percent per year reductions in carbon-intensity per unit GDP. If, however, the developing countries can only achieve annual reductions in carbon intensity of 3 or 4 percent, they can, within the emission quotas, only achieve GDP growth rates of 4 or 5 percent per year, respectively.

The above approach will imply a clear definition of common but differentiated responsibilities for developed and developing countries. The commonality will obtain in targets for reducing the carbon intensity of different economies. However, within the efficiency targets, developing countries, which are at early stage of development, will be allowed to maximize their growth performance, while the developed countries, which are at a mature stage of development, will constrain their growth within the allowable carbon emission targets.

Thus for developed countries, with an economic growth rate of 2 percent per year, CO_2 emissions will be reduced by about 3 percent per year, leading to a 73 percent reduction in total emissions between 2005 and 2050. This target will be mandatory.

For developing countries with a 6 percent per year economic growth rate, CO_2 emissions will increase by about 1 percent per year with an increase in total emissions of 73 percent between 2005 and 2050. For developing countries, commitments to these targets will be conditional on receiving transfers of funds and technology from the developed countries in recognition of the limited capabilities of developing countries and the ecological debt owed by the developed countries for their past emissions.

Getting carbon prices right for efficiency

The Kyoto Protocol and the programs associated with it have been dominated by a planning mindset. Targets are determined by an administrative/political process and countries (and production units) are required to fulfill the targets with the option to buy out emissions above the target through trading mechanisms. As noted above, the trends that characterized 1990–2003 do not present an encouraging picture of success in achieving these targets. Perhaps more attention should be given to articulating the instruments—in particular, market-based instruments such as pricing—to achieve emission-reduction goals.

For a generalized impact on carbon use with a minimum of bureaucratic intervention, the first step is to get the carbon prices right. This in turn would be done in two steps.

The first step will be to eliminate (or at least substantially reduce) the subsidies currently given to emitters, which are estimated to total $250 billion per year by the *Stern Review*. Whatever else is done, the phasing down of subsidies should be a priority; negotiating this should be no more difficult than negotiating on subsidies in the World Trade Organization (WTO) framework. Resulting savings in carbon emissions could be substantial. According to estimates in a study published in 1999 by the International Energy Agency (IEA 1999), eight countries outside the Organisation for Economic Co-operation and Development (OECD) (China, India, Indonesia, Iran, Kazakhstan, Russia, South Africa, and Venezuela) provide an average subsidy of 20 percent in energy pricing. Removing these subsidies could reduce primary energy consumption by 13 percent and lower CO_2 emissions by 16 percent. Studies like this need to be updated to cover major economies in both the developed and developing countries.

The second step will be to explore the mechanism for taxing carbon emitters. The theoretical rationale for such a tax is clear. It is interesting to note that eminent economists with differing views on many development issues, such as Jagdish Bhagwati, Joseph Stiglitz, Lawrence Summers, Jeffrey Sachs, Paul Krugman, all seem to agree that the sources of a negative externality (in this case climate change) should be taxed to compensate for the damage done by GHG emissions. If one takes a conservative estimate of the average social cost of emissions at $10 per ton of CO_2, a carbon tax equivalent to that cost will yield about $260 billion per year. This amount would go a long way toward meeting the costs of mitigation which the *Stern Review* has estimated at 1 percent of world GDP.

Development and dissemination of carbon-saving technologies

Over the longer term, technological breakthroughs will perhaps provide the real solutions to the climate change problem. How can the international community support such activities? What was done in the past for agricultural research activities under the Consultative Group on International Agricultural Research (CGIAR),[8] for example, could provide a model of what international institutions can do for carbon-saving technologies.

There are many examples of carbon-saving technologies and practices at the micro- and macro-level around the world. These "success stories" need to be publicized. Perhaps international institutions can

[8] www.cgiar.org

create a web page for ready access to such success stories. They could also launch a program for social marketing that would convey the importance of carbon-emission reductions to the masses. The massive programs popularizing family planning in developing countries, which seem to have made a dent in a very sensitive area, can provide an example of what could be done for climate change.

For the widest possible dissemination of existing and new technologies, WTO regimes should be made sensitive to climate change issues. As recommended by the *Stern Review*, the reduction of tariff and nontariff barriers for low-carbon goods and services within the Doha Development Round of international trade negotiations could provide further opportunities to accelerate the diffusion of key technologies. Among the nontariff barriers to technology transfer, intellectual property rights are an important barrier. Although technology transfer is one of the objectives of trade-related aspects of international property rights (TRIPS), progress on this front has been inadequate and demands to opt for stronger intellectual property rights in developing countries, irrespective of their technological capability, continues to hinder technology transfer. In the case of global climate change, access to Environmentally Sound Technologies (ESTs) should not be withheld on account of weaker intellectual property rights in developing nations.

The Doha Declaration came out with a solution to facilitate access to drugs and pharmaceuticals, particularly in the case of Human Immunodeficiency Virus/Acquired Immune Deficiency Syndrome (HIV/AIDS). In view of the negative impacts, and particularly the negative health impacts, of global climate change, parties to the WTO should extend a similar approach to facilitate the transfer of low-carbon technologies and ensure that intellectual property rights do not become a barrier. The Montreal Protocol provides a successful example where the global community came together to ensure that all countries could get access to technologies to control and eliminate ozone-depleting substances. It provided for an integrated mechanism to take care of the technology needs of developing nations and provided incentives for technology transfer. In view of the public goods nature of the global climate problem and to ensure that developing nations do not suffer from the negative impacts of climate change due to a lack of technology, the global community should formulate a similar mechanism to promote the development, transfer, and use of environmentally sound technologies to mitigate global climate change.

This mechanism should complement the various multilateral and bilateral initiatives to encourage technology transfer in the context of global climate change.

The development and transfer of technologies can be stimulated through many measures including patent buyouts for important technologies, reduction of tariffs on the sale and transfer of technologies, a global venture capital fund to commercialize clean energy technologies, transfer of technologies to the public domain, licensing schemes that reduce the duration of intellectual property rights to enable technology transfer, and flexible mechanisms for climate technology transfer taking into account the need for long-term climate stabilization.

A global institutional framework for effective implementation

Climate change is now widely recognized as perhaps the greatest market failure in human history and a perfect example of a negative global public good. As mentioned above, the difficulties in making progress in this area should not to be underestimated. Just as providing for national public goods requires national governmental intervention, providing for a global public good may require a breakthrough in global governance structures. And just as at the national level, the imperative of providing for certain national public goods drove the formation of bigger and bigger governance units (in for example the United States and Australia), the imperatives of providing for global public goods such as controlling climate change will require more and more public policy interventions at the global and regional levels. Theories and practices developed in the context of federal states for the allocation of functional responsibly and fiscal resources to meet public goods responsibilities may be increasingly relevant for the challenge of delivering global public goods such as addressing climate change. The massive task of redistributing resources from the minority who owe most of the carbon debt to the majority who are the victims of climate change will require a global compact and global authority to implement it. And that requires a breakthrough in global governance. Without such breakthrough, effective action just will not happen in this area. The TINA (there is no alternative) theme applies here as strongly as anywhere else.

Primary responsibility for helping to meet the challenge of providing for a truly global public good such as coping with climate change should go to global institutions. In this context the UN system is the appropriate forum for *negotiations and agreements* on a global program for climate change.

However, the implementation of the agreed programs is likely to require substantial financial resources as well as the formulation of concrete projects and programs. For that purpose, multilateral financial institutions (MFIs) will have to play a crucial role. The Bretton Woods Institutions, which seem to be losing their traditional business, may be restructured to deliver on this new global mission. The traditional tasks of macroeconomic stability, balance of payments support, infrastructure development, and poverty reduction—which are more national or regional public goods than global public goods—could be increasingly left to regional development banks while the global institutions concentrate on truly global public goods such as emissions control. The International Monetary Fund (IMF) could be an ideal agency for reviewing the issues of carbon subsidies and carbon taxation at national and global levels and the World Bank could serve as an ideal agency for supporting projects and programs for carbon reduction. In particular, the IMF's Article IV Consultation Reports could be restructured to become a vehicle for surveillance on taxes, subsidies, and other carbon reduction programs in both developed and developing countries. The World Bank can build upon its experience with development policy loans to help developing countries design and fund programs aimed at reducing the carbon intensity of their economies. Participation by developing countries in a climate treaty and in its effective implementation could be encouraged by making the receipt of international assistance conditional on such participation and effective implementation.

Mobilizing funding for carbon reduction efforts

If reducing global CO_2 emissions by 50 percent by 2050 is not realistic, global warming of more than 2°C may be unavoidable. Thus, adaptation has to be given a more serious place in global discussions on climate change than has been the case until now. Country-by-country assessments should be made to assess resource needs for both mitigation and adaptation. However, the United Nations Framework Convention on Climate Change (UNFCCC) estimate of an annual bill of $200 billion for activities related to climate change seems a good enough figure to start with. A large part of this expenditure on adaptation and mitigation measures will have to be directed to developing countries that do not have adequate resources of their own. Thus, as part of their historic responsibility for the buildup of GHG emissions to date, developed countries should be willing to transfer resources to help developing countries meet their adaptation and mitigation costs.

While the principle justifying the global transfer of resources to provide for a global public makes eminent sense, however, it may not be realistic to expect this transfer to occur in the current atmosphere when developed countries are facing a resource crunch and are afraid of competition from developing countries. There is a need to explore alternative avenues for mobilizing resources—a process that may in fact be facilitated by the current financial crisis in the United States. One proposal (Agarwala 2008) suggests creating a global currency to replace the US dollar as the main reserve currency. The seigniorage from global finance that is now accruing to the United States will, in the proposed scheme, accrue to the global community and can be used to fund global public goods such as managing climate change. This merely extends to the international level the widely accepted principle that the seigniorage created by national currency should contribute to the funding of national public goods (including defense).

Concluding remarks

Discussions on a post-Kyoto compact to address climate change are not going well. This poor performance is not so different from what has occurred with several other current multilateral negotiations, such as the Doha Round on international trade, multilateral surveillance on global imbalances and exchange rates, and the management of sovereign wealth funds. The basic factor behind this near-paralysis in multilateral negotiations is the changing power equation in the global economy. Until recently, the United States was the undisputed leader in international negotiations and under US leadership, the North basically wrote the rules of the game at the multilateral level. But now the South has stood up and is determined to make its voice heard. In climate-change discussions, there are some basic differences of perspectives between the North and the South. The North is unwilling to face up to its historical responsibilities for climate change and to admit that its lifestyle in basically not sustainable at a global level and must therefore be changed. The South is unwilling to agree that as the center of gravity of the world economy is shifting to developing countries, so is the global distribution of GHG emissions and that unless there is a reduction in emissions per unit of GDP in the South, all the efforts of the North to reduce emissions will come to naught so far as global warming is concerned. The South is also preoccupied with the technicalities of the UNFCCC agreement, which was reached in a different global economic environment in 1992 and is suspicious of any new international commitment on carbon emissions and of whatever mechanisms may be devised to enforce that agreement. In view of the serious risks that humanity faces if global warming trends continue at the present pace, paralysis in coming to agreement on an effective global approach to managing climate change will be most unfortunate.

This chapter makes some bold proposals for breaking the current logjam on climate change discussions. It argues that a global compact has to satisfy five criteria: it has to be comprehensive, equitable, realistic, efficient, and effective. In a departure from the conventional discussion, which puts the UN system center stage, this chapter proposes that the Bretton Woods Institutions should be utilized as the principal instruments for effectively implementing a global compact on climate change. This chapter also suggests some bold proposals for mobilizing resources to manage climate change. These are undoubtedly ambitious ideas—but with the fate of humanity at stake, the world needs nothing less.

References

Agarwala, Ramgopal (2008). "Towards an Asian 'Bretton Woods' for Restructuring of the Regional Financial Architecture," Discussion Paper # 133. New Delhi, India: Research and Information System (RIS) for Developing Countries.

CGIAR. Washington, DC: Consultative Group International Agricultural Research, available at www.cgiar.org/index.html.

G8 (2007). "Growth and Responsibility in the World Economy," Summit Declaration (7 June), Heiligendamm, Germany: Group of Eight.

(2008). "Environment and Climate Change," Summit Declaration (8 July), Hokkaido, Japan: Group of Eight, available at www.g8.utoronto. ca/summit/2008hokkaido/2008-climate.html.

(2008a). "G5 Statement," G5 Documents (8 July), Sapporo, Japan: Group of Eight, available at www.g8.utoronto.ca/summit/2008hokkaido/ 2008-g5.html.

Government of India (2005). *Draft Report of the Expert Committee on Integrated Energy Policy, Planning Commission*, New Delhi: GOI.

(2008). *National Action Plan on Climate Change, Prime Minister's Council on Climate Change*, New Delhi: GOI.

Green, Kenneth P., Steven F. Hayward, and Kevin A. Hesset. (2007). "Climate Change: Caps vs. Taxes," No. 2. Washington, DC: American Enterprise Institute for Public Policy Research, June.

International Energy Agency (1999). *World Energy Outlook. Looking at Energy Subsidies: Getting the Prices Right*. Paris, France: OECD Publishing.

International Monetary Fund (2007). *World Economic Outlook*, Washington, DC: IMF.

(2008). *World Economic Outlook*, Washington, DC: IMF.

IPCC (2007a). *Climate Change 2007: The Physical Science Basis. Contribution of Working Group I to the Fourth Assessment Report of the Intergovernmental Panel on Climate Change*. Cambridge and New York: Cambridge University Press.

(2007b) "Summary for Policymakers," in IPCC (2007), pp. 1–18.

Müller, B., N. Höhne, *et al.* (2007). *Differentiating (Historic) Responsibilities for Climate Change: Summary Report*. Oxford: Oxford Climate Policy.

Naim, Moises (2008). "Can the World Afford a Middle Class?" *Foreign Policy* (March/April).

Stern, Nicholas (2006). *The Economics of Climate Change: The Stern Review*, available at www.hm-treasury.gov.uk/sternreview_index.htm.

7 | Sectoral approaches to a post-Kyoto international climate policy framework

AKIHIRO SAWA

Introduction (Background)

This chapter explores the potential for sectoral approaches to a post-Kyoto international climate policy framework. A number of sector-based proposals have already been put forward; they share the concept that instead of the Kyoto-type, top-down approach of negotiating caps on economy-wide emissions for individual countries, a bottom-up approach should be taken in which technology assessments would be used to establish aggregate emission-reduction targets for different sectors of the world economy. Many surveys have been conducted on sectoral approaches and similar architectures (Bodansky 2003; Philibert 2005 and 2005b; The Pew Center 2005; Siikavirta 2006; IPCC 2007).

Sectoral approaches have not only been a subject of in-depth study in the academic community in recent years, they have also attracted growing interest in political circles as an option for multinational negotiations. Reference to a "cooperative sectoral approach" first appeared in the Bali Action Plan; since then, the Japanese government has led the world in developing specific proposals for making this approach the basis for negotiations on a framework to follow the Kyoto Protocol.

This chapter provides an overview of previous findings on sectoral approaches and presents options for using this concept as the basis for a next international climate policy architecture. It differs from previous studies in that it (1) clarifies the role of national governments in making legally binding commitments under international law to adopt domestic policies and measures for achieving sector-based mitigation targets; (2) categorizes emitting sectors into three groups in an effort to simplify and smooth negotiations; and (3) suggests a way forward for proceeding with negotiations.

Specifically, Section 2 reviews previous studies and practical efforts to apply sectoral approaches and provides a summary of current understanding and thinking on this subject.

Section 3 presents a specific proposal for applying a sectoral approach to establish the next international climate policy framework. This approach focuses on industrial sectors and analyzes sectoral reduction potentials in each country based on technology data to determine reduction targets and implementation measures through international negotiation. Section 3 also discusses methods for deriving national reduction targets by applying this approach to a wider range of sectors, such as the household/commercial and transport sectors, as needed.

Section 4 reviews some ideas for generating incentives for developing country participation in the context of a sector-based approach, including expanding or revising the current Clean Development Mechanism (CDM) scheme, or developing a new crediting system with corrective measures to resolve cost-effectiveness issues.

Finally, Section 5 identifies the challenges in implementing a sectoral approach.

Theoretical analysis and practical application of sectoral approaches

Studies on sectoral approaches to date

The term "sectoral approaches" has appeared in a number of previous studies but still remains without an established definition. Nonetheless, various surveys and reviews have attempted to develop a categorization or typology of sectoral approaches (e.g., Siikavirta 2006; Egenhofer and Fujiwara 2008; Sawa 2008). Much research has focused on policy design options for a sectoral approach (e.g., Baron 2006; Bradley, Baumert, Childs, Herzog, and Pershing 2007). Numerous bottom-up approaches to developing sector-based emission reduction targets have been proposed; other proposals adopt a policies-and-measures approach in which individual countries make binding or nonbinding commitments to adopt certain domestic policies and measures to reduce greenhouse gas (GHG) emissions (e.g., Philibert and Pershing 2001; Aldy, Barret, and Stavins 2003; Sawa 2007).

The following points have often been offered as reasons for focusing on sectoral approaches in envisaging a post-Kyoto framework[1]:

A sectoral approach encourages the participation of a wider range of countries

Given forecasts of future global emissions, meaningful action to mitigate GHG emissions on the part of non–Annex I countries that are experiencing dramatic rates of economic growth is indispensable to achieving an effective international climate policy. However, these countries have been unwilling to accept economy-wide emission caps out of concern that such caps would constrain their economic development. Moreover, even if these countries were willing to accept caps, their ability to collect reliable emissions data and monitor compliance could be insufficient to verify the results of their mitigation actions. Depending on the design of the program and the incentives it provides for participation, a sectoral approach that aims to mitigate emissions in specific sectors may serve to facilitate developing country participation while arguably also helping to address "measurability, reportability, and verifiability" issues.

A sectoral approach mitigates competitiveness issues

Sectoral approaches have the potential to resolve two issues concerning competitiveness. First, the Kyoto Protocol encompasses a mixture of countries, some with carbon emissions restrictions and others without such limits. This raises a concern about imposing unfair competitive conditions on firms in different countries, particularly energy-intensive industries in regulated jurisdictions. Second, the Kyoto Protocol establishes an economy-wide cap, but leaves the method of achieving that cap to individual countries to decide; therefore, if a country supports particular industries or imposes less stringent restrictions to protect domestic industries, comparable firms in other countries will not be able to compete on a level playing field. Sectoral approaches will enable industries to make cross-border commitments to equitable targets, thus mitigating disparities in the

---

[1] See METI 2004; Berk, den Elzen, and Gupta 2005; Watson, Newman, Upton, and Hackmann 2005; Bodansky 2007; Bradley, Baumert, Childs, Herzog, and Pershing 2007; Baron, Reinaud, Genasci, and Philibert 2007; Neuhoff and Droege 2007 regarding 1) and 2).

carbon restrictions or domestic regulations that apply in different countries.

Furthermore, sectoral approaches can help to address leakage issues by removing the incentive for energy-intensive industries to relocate from countries with strict carbon restrictions to countries that are free of such restrictions to escape a competitive disadvantage.

A sectoral approach promotes consensus by contributing to the establishment of equitable economy-wide reduction targets

Some well-known approaches include the triptych approach, which served as a basis for negotiations within the European Union (EU) in 1997 on the sharing of emission-reduction burdens among member countries (Groenenberg, Phylipsen, and Blok 2001), and the multi-sector convergence approach that differentiates emission standards among sectors with the aim of eventually equalizing per capita emissions in all countries (Jansen, Battjes, Sijm, Volkers, and Ybema 2001). Recently, the Government of Japan officially proposed that the technologically feasible emission reduction potential of all emitting sectors be aggregated in a bottom-up approach to set quantified national GHG reduction targets for the major emitting countries (Government of Japan, 2008).

By applying a technology analysis to determine reduction potentials, the process of setting national emissions targets can become more credible to stakeholders and pressure groups, thus facilitating diplomatic negotiations and increasing the chance of achieving consensus. Furthermore, compared to using a top-down approach for setting economy-wide emissions targets, there is the practical advantage that uncertainty about abatement costs as a result of uncertainty about future economic growth can be reduced because individual sectors, under their own targets, will be able to forecast their own costs irrespective of the overall economic situation, in part if not entirely (Philibert 2005).

Finally, because the number of parties concerned is small under a sectoral approach that involves mainly energy-intensive industries, the target-setting negotiation process can be substantially simplified, compared to the negotiation process of the United Nations Framework Convention on Climate Change (UNFCCC), and hence increase the likelihood of reaching agreement (e.g., Bodansky 2007; Bradley, Baumert, Childs, Herzog, and Pershing 2007).

A sectoral approach achieves effective emissions reductions through the promotion of technology development and technology transfer

To achieve significant emissions reductions in the long-term, innovative technology development is indispensable (Barrett 2003; Sugiyama and Sinton 2005; Justus and Philibert 2005; Barrett 2007). In the short- and mid-term, with properly designed incentives, direct emission reductions can be achieved by identifying energy conservation technologies that will improve energy efficiency in each sector and by transferring these technologies to countries with large emissions reduction potential, especially developing countries that are undergoing rapid economic growth. Once equipment that uses relatively inefficient carbon-intensive technology is installed in facilities with long operating lives, such as power generation plants, the opportunity for further emission reductions is lost until the next round of equipment replacements.

Although carbon prices may indeed have significant implications in promoting technology development, there is not evidence enough for the relationship to be proven true; furthermore, it will be difficult for companies to construct a technology portfolio in the likely case that carbon prices are unstable over time. Because the application of a certain technology is often limited to a single sector, sectoral approaches should provide an effective means to identify and impose mandatory standards in sectors where emissions trading is not relevant (transport, building, appliances, etc.) (De Coninck, Fischer, Newell, and Ueno 2007). The MARPOL Convention (International Convention for the Prevention of Marine Pollution from Ships, 1973, as modified by the Protocol of 1978 relating hereto) is a successful example of a multinational agreement that imposed technology standards on a specific sector to achieve a shared environmental objective, and it provides a model that can be applied in the climate change context also (Barrett 2003).

Sector-specific carbon or energy intensity targets and R&D agreements can also accelerate technology development and advance emission-reduction efforts (Watson, Newman, Upton, and Hackmann 2005). By contrast, emissions trading may undermine incentives for technology development because of uncertainty about future carbon prices and the potential for prices to be inconsistent over time (OECD 2008).

On the other hand, the viability of sectoral approaches has also been questioned, for reasons that are summarized below (e.g., Watson,

Newman, Upton, and Hackmann 2005; Philibert 2005b; Berk, den Elzen, and Gupta 2005; Baron 2006; Baron, Reinaud, Genasci, and Philibert 2007; Bradley 2007; Egenhofer and Fujiwara 2008).

A sectoral approach faces barriers in providing an international framework to replace the Kyoto Protocol

A sectoral approach requires information exchange and sector-specific negotiations and thus entails immense transaction costs. Negotiators in the UNFCCC process are reluctant to accept new approaches. Also, countries that have already introduced robust policies, such as the EU Emission Trading Scheme (EU ETS), will try to avoid approaches that risk introducing uncertainties into their domestic programs. Furthermore, a sectoral approach may create openings for countries to slip onto the negotiation table other competitiveness issues that concern their domestic industries, but bear no direct relevance to carbon restrictions, thus complicating negotiations.

Bradley, Baumert, Childs, Herzog, and Pershing (2007) describe several options for designing a final agreement based on sectoral approaches, including the "Sector-Only" model, the "Addition" model, the "Complementary" model, the "Carve-Out" model, and the "Integration" model. But these authors also conclude that it is in reality "difficult to envision" a multinational agreement based only on sectoral approaches, because this would involve a sizeable number of independent agreements and thus entail complex negotiations.

Furthermore, Kulovesi and Keinanen (2006) contend that, from the perspective of international law, implementing agreements concluded by representatives of industry sectors or between states and industry sectors will call for a new legal framework that is unprecedented except at the regional level.

A sectoral approach reduces cost-effectiveness

Because they cover all sectors, economy-wide approaches to achieving emissions targets can exploit abatement opportunities with minimum costs and thus are generally regarded as the ideal option in terms of cost-effectiveness. On the other hand, a sectoral approach forces reductions upon specific sectors and will thus be less cost-effective unless a mechanism to reduce marginal abatement costs, such as an emissions-trading scheme, is implemented. Marginal reduction costs may end up not being equalized across sectors, in which case a sectoral approach would contribute to protecting a particular industry sector. The importance of cost-effectiveness was noted in the Bali Action Plan and measures to address this issue will need to be contrived if a sectoral approach is pursued.

A sectoral approach will not be effective from an environmental standpoint

A sectoral agreement only provides for emissions reductions in specific sectors, assuming they succeed in achieving target agreements, and does not necessarily induce mitigation actions from other sectors. By comparison, an agreement based on economy-wide targets will involve all sectors.

In addition, many proposals for a sectoral approach envisage intensity targets. Because they allow emissions to grow with increased output, intensity targets may be inferior to absolute targets in terms of reducing GHG emissions.

In addition, when a low-carbon product is exposed to inter-sectoral competition, sectoral agreements and differences in the stringency or form of government regulations used to enforce them may alter competitiveness conditions and thereby risk driving low-carbon products out of the market in favor of more carbon-intensive alternatives that are produced by sectors not subject to climate-based agreements and regulations.

A sectoral approach entails government intervention

A sectoral approach is likely to increase opportunities for government intervention in two respects. First, given the prevailing asymmetry of information between the private and public sectors, the government may need new authority to collect data from firms about technology, production forecasts, and emission-reduction costs in order to set sectoral targets that will achieve substantial environmental results. In that case, government intervention in corporate activities will be aggrandized. Second, as long as the current international law regime prevails and only governments and intergovernmental organizations are eligible to become parties to international agreements, governments would need to pledge compliance in order for a consensus reached within a particular sector to gain legal status under international law. Governments would then need to take domestic action to legally bind the relevant industries within their borders.

A sectoral approach faces challenges in data collection

Several major data-related issues have been identified in connection with implementing a sectoral approach (Baron, Reinaud, Genasci, and Philibert 2007; Bradley 2007; Egenhofer and Fujiwara 2008):

- In developing countries especially, a lack of reliable data and limited monitoring capacity reduce the potential efficacy of sectoral approaches.
- No agreement has yet been reached concerning standard boundaries for defining sectors.
- The data needed for benchmarking could be confidential corporate information, in which case data collection would be complicated.
- Verification should be performed by a third party to assure transparency and reliability; this in turn may call for new institutional capacities.
- How should data marked by high uncertainty—such as data concerning prospects for future technologies and production forecasts where this information is required for baseline setting—be acquired and managed?

A sectoral approach faces challenges with antitrust laws

Successful sectoral approaches will encompass the majority of companies belonging to a particular sector and thus cover the greater part of that sector's total production volume. The mutual exchange of information on production, technology, and costs could constitute a violation of antitrust laws (Egenhofer and Fujiwara 2008).

Based on the aforementioned studies, the shared view of sectoral approaches within the academic community at present can be outlined as follows:

1. A sectoral approach may potentially play a significant role in overcoming challenges that are intractable within the current Kyoto framework, such as involving developing countries in mitigation actions and using technology assessments of emission-reduction potential as a basis for diplomatic negotiations, which would make politically acceptable national targets for individual countries easier to set. In order to realize these potential advantages of a sectoral approach, however, proper incentive policies (in terms of financial and technology transfer) should be designed to promote developing-country participation, and data problems, like setting common benchmarks, should be solved.

2. Given remaining questions regarding their cost and environmental effectiveness, it is not yet clear that sectoral approaches are superior to the existing Kyoto-type framework, in which a top-down approach to target setting for individual countries is coupled with flexibility mechanisms.

3. Furthermore, taking into account data collection issues and the need for numerous sector-specific negotiations, reaching agreement on a sectoral approach will be substantially painstaking. Therefore, sectoral approaches can only be complementary or additional to the Kyoto Protocol; they are not sufficiently cost-effective to replace the Protocol as the international framework for global warming measures that require agreement in a limited amount of time.

Practical application of sectoral approaches

Just as progress has been made in the theoretical analysis of sectoral approaches, efforts by the International Aluminium Institute (IAI), the Cement Sustainability Initiative/World Business Council for Sustainable Development (CSI), the International Iron and Steel Institute (IISI), and the Asia-Pacific Partnership on Clean Development and Climate (APP) provide opportunities to observe how sectoral approaches may be applied. To give an example, the APP's accomplishments to date are summarized below.[2]

The APP is an initiative for regional cooperation launched in July 2005 at the behest of the United States. Its membership comprises seven countries, namely, the United States, Australia, South Korea, China, India, Japan, and Canada. The purpose of the APP is to pursue the development, deployment, and transfer of clean and effective energy technologies in particular.

Given that the seven APP countries collectively account for more than half of the world's economic output, energy consumption, and GHG emissions, the Partnership's work promises to lead to substantial progress in climate change measures.[3] APP task forces have been

---

[2] For efforts in the IAI, CSI, and IISI, refer to Egenhofer and Fujiwara (2008) main text and appendix.

[3] According to one of the Asia Pacific Partnership studies, "...modeling indicates that accelerated adoption of world–best practice for thermal power generation alone would reduce global emissions by 1.5 percent by 2010..." Available at: asiapacificpartnership.org/PowerGeneration-TransmissionTF.aspx.

established for eight sectors to identify and implement technologies and flagship projects that are strategically important in the climate change arena and that promote efficient energy use and the sharing of technological information and best practices.

The APP's task forces on power generation and transmission, steel, and cement, in particular, have made the most progress in practically applying a sectoral approach. In the Power Generation and Transmission Task Force, inefficient power plants have received peer-review visits, followed by workshops and on-site guidance on operational improvements so that best practices can be shared and actual emissions reductions be implemented. The Steel Task Force has developed a handbook on state-of-the-art clean technologies for that industry and is engaged in establishing a common methodology for calculating GHG–reduction potential and performance indicators.

The Partnership's joint work to date has fostered a common awareness that there is great emissions reduction potential in China and India. Furthermore, direct corporate participation has facilitated the identification of energy- and environment-related investment barriers, including barriers related to intellectual property rights and tax systems in developing countries that governments could eliminate to improve the investment and business environment for effective and continued technology transfer. The accumulation of successful undertakings by the APP provides developing countries with a model for pursuing sustainable development through cooperation with developed countries and promises the smoother involvement of developing countries in a post-Kyoto framework.

The case for a policy-based sectoral approach

A post-Kyoto framework based on a sectoral approach

There are many advocates for a post-Kyoto framework based on the global linkage of emissions-trading schemes on grounds that these schemes provide an effective means to achieve given reduction targets at minimal cost (notwithstanding the fact that this cost-effectiveness advantage is not fully realized because of the Protocol's so-called supplementarity principle[4]). However, more attention should be directed to the process for deciding emission targets themselves.

---

[4] Because "any such trading shall be supplemental to domestic action for the

Sectoral approaches may have no advantage over emissions-trading schemes and environmental taxes from the standpoint of providing the most cost-effective means to achieve a given target. However, they should be evaluated in terms of their effectiveness as an approach for allocating reduction targets among countries in a way that minimizes the generation of hot air—that is, setting an emissions target that is likely to *exceed* actual emissions even if no abatement actions are undertaken. This aspect of sectoral approaches has been correctly recognized in the European Union, where sectoral approaches are being considered for benchmarking—that is, as an effective method for allocating allowances among the actors in the EU ETS. By enabling the allocation of allowances with minimized risks of hot air, sectoral approaches promise to increase the stability of both domestic and international emissions-trading markets already in place.

A second reason why sectoral approaches should play a role in the negotiation of a post-Kyoto framework is that they could provide a contingency framework for tentative agreement to prevent delays in implementing global warming countermeasures. If sectoral agreements can be reached when countries fail to agree on Kyoto-type, economy-wide national targets, some continued progress in mitigation actions can still be expected.

Policy-based sectoral approach

This section proposes a framework that employs sectoral approaches in national target setting and involves international commitments by governments to implement policies to achieve those targets. In the discussion that follows, this idea is termed the "policy-based sectoral approach." The commitment period under this sectoral approach should be long enough, say ten years, to allow governments and industries the time required for investments in long-term technology research and development.

purpose of meeting quantified emission limitation and reduction commitments" (Article 17, Kyoto Protocol), countries with stringent emission targets (in the sense that marginal reduction costs for the country as a whole exceed the world market price for carbon) are not permitted the full use of flexibility mechanisms and thus reductions in those countries cannot be achieved with minimal costs.

Basic structure of a policy-based sectoral approach

Sectors would be divided into three groups according to their features and sectoral negotiations would be held within each group. This would allow for negotiations to be conducted by experts who are more familiar with sector-specific concepts, circumstances, and technologies, than would be the case in a single negotiation for agreements across all sectors.

The first group of sectors would comprise energy-intensive industries that are exposed to trade and leakage issues (hereafter Group I). The second group would include sectors that are basically domestic, such as electricity generation and road transport and for which benchmarks (generation efficiency, vehicle fuel efficiency, etc.) and best practices can be relatively easily identified, but which are also susceptible to resource availability, geographic, and natural factors and domestic policies and measures (e.g., rate of deployment of renewable energy technology, traffic measures, etc.) and thus need to be unilaterally adjusted with government policies and measures (hereafter Group II). The third group (hereafter Group III) would be composed mainly of the household and commercial sectors, or sectors that encompass a wide range of technologies, thus complicating the ability to set and compare indicators at the international level, though it is worth noting that energy efficiency comparisons are possible for some products like household appliances.

In all groups of sectors, it would be preferable to have technical experts from industrial and academic circles participate to provide insights on issues like benchmarking and calculating efficiency indicators and to promote negotiations. Through this process, the generation of hot air can be avoided to the maximum extent.

As indicated by Table 7.1, each group of sectors would negotiate numerical targets and government policies and measures to achieve them. The conclusions reached through this process would be compiled into a policy template, which will constitute the new Protocol. Governments would pledge to implement agreed policies and measures and achieve numerical targets. Legally binding numerical targets refer to numerical targets for industries exposed to international competition in Group I *and* national reduction targets. In Annex I countries, policies and measures would be limited to legal regulations, government budgets and tax systems, and other measures that involve resource allocation for the primary objective of reducing GHG

Table 7.1 *Policy template to be negotiated*

| | | Energy-intensive industries | | | | Electricity | | Road transport | | Household/Commercial | | Projected amount of GHG reductions |
| | | Iron and steel | | Cement | | | | | | | | |
		Target & projected reductions	Policies & measures	Target & projected reductions	Policies & measures	Target & projected reductions	Policies & measures	Target & projected reductions	Policies & measures	Target & projected reductions	Policies & measures	
Annex1	US	binding		binding		non-binding		non-binding		non-binding		binding
	Japan											
	EU											
	UK											
	Germany											
	France											
	...											
non-Annex1	China	binding or nonbinding		binding or nonbinding		non-binding		non-binding		non-binding		binding or nonbinding
	Brazil											
	India											
	...											
	Reference value for reduction potential derived from Method 1 or 2											Projected amount of global reductions

emissions. Nonlegal measures, like national campaigns for mitigation that are not supported by government funding, would not be included.

In the case of non-Annex I countries, both numerical targets for Group I and national reduction targets may become nonbinding as a result of negotiations. Furthermore, policies and measures in developing countries would not be limited to those with the primary objective of reducing GHG emissions but may be expanded to include a wider range of policies and measures that serve to reduce GHG emissions as a co-benefit.

National reduction targets would not be represented by national emission caps for a particular point in time, rather they would reflect *total reductions projected for a certain period of time as a result of implementing policies and measures*. This is to avoid the inequities introduced by choosing a particular base year[5] and reflects the fact that it would be close to impossible to guarantee compliance with a specific emissions cap for a certain point in time unless economic changes can be precisely forecasted. Carbon dioxide (CO_2) emissions are naturally susceptible to fluctuations in the economy-wide volume of activity, especially over short time horizons in which technological structures do not change. By constructing targets as total reductions, a higher level of certainty about the efficacy of reduction efforts can be expected (Baumert and Goldberg 2006).

Countries would be able to stay in compliance with binding pledges to national emissions reductions by purchasing emissions allowances or credits, but policymakers should recognize that leaving room for such options could delay national progress toward a low-carbon society. Therefore, it may be desirable to incorporate limits on the use of these mechanisms to meet reduction goals; on the other hand, limiting the use of such flexibility mechanisms would also tend to increase abatement costs and reduce the overall cost-effectiveness of the policy.

There are three reasons to include policies and measures in future international climate negotiations: (1) to address the oft-noted disadvantage of sectoral approaches with respect to providing a clear

---

[5] The issue of what year should be set as the base year was officially raised in the UNFCCC negotiation recently by the Government of Japan, which believes that setting 1990 as the base year is too advantageous to the EU where extensive fuel switching from coal to natural gas occurred before the Kyoto Protocol took effect for reasons that had nothing to do with GHG mitigation efforts.

explanation of what role governments will play in ensuring compliance with multinational sectoral agreements, which in turn creates the need for governments to identify and pledge internationally to undertake certain domestic measures; (2) to encourage broader participation by making it more widely known to the international community that developing countries are also engaged in global warming countermeasures, as well as by providing support for policies and measures to which developing countries are committed (Lewis and Diringer 2007); and (3) to develop a built-in mechanism for promoting compliance and to encourage information sharing on effective and efficient policies and measures and policy best practices by applying the regular UNFCCC review process to relevant national policies and measures.

As envisaged for this proposal, participants in these negotiations would include not all countries but only major emitting countries. If, as a result of incentive measures for developing countries described elsewhere in this chapter, other countries wish to join, they can be welcomed as well. Countries that are not engaged in the policy template would be treated as non–Annex I countries under the Kyoto Protocol.

On the other hand, if a non–Annex I country decides to participate, different parameters consistent with the principle of "common but differentiated responsibilities and respective capabilities" may be applied with respect to the timing and extent of policies and measures. Furthermore, if negotiations conclude that further differentiation between Annex I and non–Annex I countries is required, then sectoral reduction targets for Group I industries exposed to international competition in developing countries may be determined to be nonbinding (see BASIC 2006).

Deriving reference values for the negotiation of reduction targets

Reduction potentials calculated by international organizations and research institutions should be inserted in the final row of the policy template to provide an idea of the reference level of numerical targets to be sought in negotiations. Then, the sum of national reduction targets provided in the right-most column of the final row can be compared with whatever mid- to long-term overall target has been agreed in prior negotiations. In the event that aggregated sectoral targets fall short, the distribution of the remaining reduction burden would be subject to further negotiation. If coupled with a Kyoto-type,

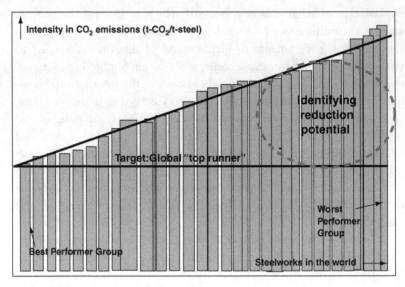

Figure 7.1. Method 1: Global Top-Runner

top-down approach from the beginning, repetitious negotiations may be avoided, but it must be noted that Kyoto-type negotiations always run the risk of generating hot air as mentioned above.

Reference numerical targets would generally be derived by using a bottom-up approach and/or by using model simulation. Method 1 calculates projected reductions for each sector assuming that best available technologies (BAT) and best practices (BP) are deployed. Method 2 calculates projected sectoral reductions in each country for the given common level of marginal abatement cost based on economic models with consideration for existing and future technologies. Sectoral numerical targets would be negotiated with reference to the values derived using these two methods.

An example of reference values determined using Method 1 is provided in Figure 7.1 which shows carbon intensity in the iron and steel industry (Okazaki 2008). As technology improves, the carbon intensity achieved by "top-runner" or industry-leading firms will change. As a result, reduction potentials and benchmarking will need to be periodically reviewed—at five-year intervals, for example.

Although Method 1 needs to be improved so that it incorporates other factors (such as regional differences in the accessibility and use of energy sources and materials and raw data on CO_2 or energy intensities at individual plants), it can provide a tentative marker for where subsequent negotiations should be headed.

An example of Method 2 is shown in Table 7.2 which employs research results generated by the Systems Analysis Group of the Research Institute of Innovative Technology for the Earth (RITE)[6].

This study assumes that marginal reduction costs will be homogenized across countries and sectors to generate estimates of reduction potential based on the energy or carbon intensities that are achievable using the latest technology, equipment, and products. The timing assumed for making capital investments in new technology should take into consideration the vintage of the existing stock.

Using this research method, it should be possible to calculate specific energy or carbon intensity values for each country and sector for any given year up to 2050. By way of example, Table 7.2 presents calculations for the United States in 2020. The study divides the world into fifty-three countries and regions and data are compiled accordingly.

Each cell provides a quantitative indication of what each country can do, to what extent, and in which sectors, to introduce the kind of technology and equipment needed to meet the requirement of equalizing marginal reduction costs. In general terms, accelerated rates of improvement should be achievable for countries and sectors that are currently marked by low energy efficiency and can make significant improvements at a relatively limited cost. Method 2 can provide important reference values not only for Group I negotiations but also for negotiations in other sectors.

Measures to ensure compliance

Measures to ensure compliance and deter noncompliance need to be considered in two dimensions: namely, failure to achieve numerical targets and failure to implement policies and measures.

As in the current Kyoto Protocol, a new Protocol should stipulate that if a party is in noncompliance with national emission targets, it must compensate for excess emissions by purchasing credits from

---

[6] The model employed for the analysis was based on work undertaken for the Assessment of Mitigation Frameworks after 2013 (Beyond 2010), a project commissioned by the New Energy and Industrial Technology Development Organization (NEDO). See the appendix of Sawa 2008 for the details of the model assumptions.

Table 7.2 *Method 2: Equalizing marginal abatement cost (US 2020)*
Part 1: Manufacturing

Negotiated agreement item / technological and policy responses		Improved energy intensity	Reduced carbon contribution due to fuel diversification	Energy efficiency improvements	Projected CO_2 reductions [Mt CO_2/yr]
Aluminum		0.964		Increased deployment of Prebake method (BaU: 8→9 kton/day)	0.281
Chemical	Ethylene-propylene	0.865		Increased deployment of current BAT (BaU: 0→48 kton/day)	5.483
	Ammonia	1.010			
	Chemical pulp	1.020	Reduced purchased power due to CHP (BaU: 115→64 TWh/yr)		4.197
Pulp and paper	Paper/paper-board	0.931			

Cement		1.185	Increased large-scale SP/NSP (current BAT) technology (BaU: 10→97 kton/day)	2.420
Iron and steel	Blast furnace/converter	0.981	Increased DRI production (Share BaU: 1.8→2.4%)	0.488
	Scrap-based electric furnace	0.996		
Other industries				8.047

Table 7.2 (*cont.*)
Part 2: Power generation*

Negotiated agreement item / technological and policy responses	Reduced carbon contribution due to fuel diversification	Energy efficiency improvements	Innovative technology development	Projected CO_2 reductions [Mt CO_2/yr]
Energy savings		Increased high efficiency gas-fired power generation (high-temperature NGCC)	Increased high-efficiency coal-fired power generation (2,278 TWh/yr)	242.405
Biomass				0.000
Photovoltaic				0.000
Wind				0.000
Hydro and geothermal	Increased hydro and geothermal power generation (2000: 248→268 TWh/yr)			1.544
Nuclear	Increased nuclear power generation (2000: 756; BaU: 433→756 TWh/yr)			380.498
Hydrogen				0.000

Conversion among fossil fuels	Increase gas-fired power generation (Share among fossil fuel-fired power generation: 2000: 22%; BaU: 0→3%)		28.201
CCS			−14.629
Other energy conversion and errors			43.669

*Improved CO_2 intensity for all energy sources: 1.397

Table 7.2 (*cont.*)
Part 3: Transportation, and household and commercial

Negotiated agreement item / technological and policy responses		Improved energy intensity	Reduced carbon contribution due to fuel diversification	Energy efficiency improvements	Projected CO$_2$ reductions [Mt CO$_2$/yr]
Transportation	Light passenger cars	0.725		More hybrid cars	
	Heavy passenger cars	0.585	Increased share of bioethanol (Share among automobile fuel: 27%)	More hybrid cars	179.815
	Buses	0.884			
	Light-duty trucks	0.879			
	Heavy-duty trucks	0.907			
Transportation, other than automobiles					0.000
Household and commercial					32.561
Total CO$_2$ emissions under BaU [Mt CO$_2$/yr] (Parts 1–3)			7680.5	Projected CO$_2$ reductions under BaU [Mt CO$_2$/yr]	914.980

other countries within the adjustment period that succeeds each commitment period. This provision would not apply to a non–Annex I country in cases where that country's national emissions target is determined to be nonbinding. To provide incentives for the implementation of policies and measures, emissions in excess of the target may be discounted in the event that sectoral policies and measures pledged in the policy template have been fully implemented, as judged from reports of the regular UNFCCC review process.

When a binding target is not achieved in Group I, emission permits must be purchased to cover emissions in excess of the target whether or not the country is in compliance with its national reductions target. Therefore, if a country has also failed to achieve its national reductions target, it would have to purchase twice the permits equivalent to its emissions in noncompliance with the Group I binding target. If not economically rational, this "double-binding" rule will ensure that the international agreements negotiated with respect to the politically sensitive Group I sources are implemented. After an adjustment period to allow countries to purchase emission permits, countries still in noncompliance would be required to accomplish additional reductions based on a certain penalty rate combined with its national reductions target for the subsequent commitment period.

To address noncompliance with respect to the implementation of policies and measures by an Annex I country, the new Protocol should establish a panel under the auspices of the UNFCCC so that legal procedures can be taken against the government(s) in question, or it should incorporate the provisions on dispute settlement articulated in Article 14 of the UNFCCC. In the latter case, considering the global characteristics of the climate issue, conflicts are unlikely to be bilateral—therefore, the following options can be conceived: (1) establish a new "objection system" where any country that believes another country is in violation of the new Protocol can make a submission to the legal panel described previously; or (2) create a totally new "dispute settlement scheme" that takes into account the global nature of the issue.

In the event that a non–Annex I country is in noncompliance, on the other hand, that country should not be exposed to penalty-oriented procedures; rather, new procedures should be developed to encourage compliance and maximize the contribution from non–Annex I countries based on assistance from developed countries in capacity building and the exchange of information about best practices.

How to proceed with sectoral negotiations

Group I

As described above, many institutions have begun to compile extensive data regarding Group I, and benchmarking methods for these industries are also increasingly being standardized. Thus, it is relatively easy for this sector to enter into negotiations. Data collection has often been raised as a challenge for implementing sectoral approaches, but the agreement reached at the Group of Eight Summit of the Leaders of the Main Industrialized Countries held in Toyako in July 2008 to exchange information on mitigation opportunities and sectoral efficiency has paved the way for addressing this issue. In the industrial and power generation sectors, the APP is engaged in identifying high-efficiency technologies, examining technology diffusion rates, and calculating emission-reduction potential. In the iron and steel, cement, and aluminum sectors, international industrial groups have been working with data on energy-efficiency indicators and best available technology (BAT) and best practices (BP). The World Business Council for Sustainable Development (WBCSD) has launched a standardized GHG protocol. The International Energy Agency (IEA) has estimated sectoral reduction potentials for the iron and steel, cement, power generation, and petrochemical/chemical industries. Negotiations can indeed be promptly initiated in Group I by employing these and other findings and analyses that are already available.

Existing data and methodologies can serve as a basis for developing the next generation of internationally standardized boundary-setting methodologies, emissions-calculation procedures, and performance indicators. Cooperation from institutions that establish international standards, such as the International Organization for Standardization (ISO) and International Electrotechnical Commission (IEC), will become essential. If these types of organizations can assume the role of certifying sectoral agreements, then the complex technical issues involved in negotiating sectoral approaches can be significantly simplified.

In developing numerical targets for Group I, negotiators would need to debate between intensity targets—either energy intensity or CO_2-emissions intensity—or targets based on absolute quantity reductions (tons). The two indicators represent different forms of commitment, and thus discussions over which is the more stringent in general terms are irrelevant. Which form should be adopted depends in part on what level of uncertainty regarding future production is acceptable. In times of stagnant economic activity, intensity-based regulations could be more environmentally effective (Ellerman and Wing 2003; Kolstad 2005; Herzog, Baumert, and Pershing 2006; Jotzo and Pezzey 2005). Another approach that may be feasible, depending on industrial circumstances, is to negotiate targets for the minimum efficiency of equipment to be installed after a given year, the ratio of existing facilities that have to install state-of-the-art technologies and equipment for efficiency improvements, and the energy efficiency of products and product standards. Whatever type of target is adopted, however, total emissions reductions must be calculated and provided in the policy template.

In the event that international consensus is reached on numerical targets for a certain industrial sector, domestic measures implemented by each government to ensure compliance by the relevant firms and facilities will constitute Group I policies and measures. EU countries may formulate such policies and measures in the form of participation in an emissions-trading scheme (presumably the EU ETS), whereas Japan and China may opt to enact laws setting technology standards that would improve energy intensities of manufacturing processes and/or enter into formal agreements with domestic industries. An internationally-shared understanding that policies and measures can be diversified to suit national circumstances should be maintained for some time in order for agreement on an initial, policy-based sectoral framework to be reached without delay. With mutual learning about the efficacy of various climate policies and measures over time, however, participating countries would be expected to accelerate their efforts toward an internationally coordinated or harmonized framework, such as a system of international linkages among emissions-trading schemes.

Group II
The most effective option for reducing GHG emissions from power generation (besides reducing end-use power consumption) is to shift the power mix to low-carbon resources. Target-setting negotiations for this group, however, would have to reflect national circumstances, given the disparities that exist in domestic resource availability, energy security policies, and equipment vintage. As many countries have recently adopted targets for introducing renewable energy, these commitments should be reflected in numerical targets.

Compared with Group I, however, it is much more difficult to designate targets in terms of CO_2 intensity in Group II because the targets will affect the power mix as a whole. Nevertheless, the power sector accounted for 41 percent of total global energy-derived CO_2 emissions in 2005, and therefore efficiency improvements in the power sector—especially improvements in thermal power plants that combust fossil fuels—have significant potential to reduce GHG emissions. The reduction potential associated with efficiency improvements in coal-fired power plants alone has been estimated to range from 1.4Gt-CO_2 to 2.0Gt-CO_2 (IEA 2008). Thus, the most appropriate commitment to numerical targets would be to increase the average conversion efficiency of coal-fired power plants—which in 2005 ranged from 33 percent in China to 42 percent in Japan (IEA 2008a)—to the highest viable level.

Since transferring technology and know-how from private companies in developed countries, extending information on best practices, and providing on-site diagnosis and guidance would hold the key to such performance, financial support for such activities by private companies should be a major option for government policies and measures.

Emissions from the road transport sector include those from automobile producers, automobile users, fuel producers, and governments—thus target-setting negotiations for this sector must also engage each actor to fulfill their separate roles.

Emissions from the road transport sector can be calculated using the following equation:

CO_2Emissions = Emissions Intensity × Activity Volume
= On-road Fuel Efficiency × CO_2 Emissions
Coefficient × Total Distance Traveled
= Certified Fuel Efficiency (km/l)-1 × Traveling
Coefficient × CO_2 Emissions Coefficient
(gCO_2/l) × Total Distance Traveled (vehicle-km)

Individual terms in this equation can be influenced by different actors. For example, automobile manufacturers can improve certified fuel efficiency (km/l)−1, while government measures to relieve traffic jams and eco-friendly changes in driver behavior can influence the traveling coefficient. Similarly, changes in the CO_2 emissions coefficient (gCO_2/l), can be achieved by fuel producers and automobile manufacturers in response to government regulations while total distance traveled (vehicle-km) can be reduced through policies to encourage mode shifting (e.g., increased use of public transit) or by the users' choice of transportation means.

Of these terms, benchmarks and technologies can be identified for certified fuel efficiency (km/l)-1 and the CO_2 emissions coefficient (gCO_2/l)—thus, these are the factors that lend themselves to specific numerical targets in a policy template. Other indicators can constitute targets for policies and measures, if associated emissions reductions can be quantified. Thus, in order for sectoral approaches to function in Group II, data collection and a standardized accounting methodology will be essential (JAMA 2008).

Group III

Group III is closely related to lifestyles and working styles and basically with the level of development in domestic service industries. Therefore, it is questionable to what extent government policies and measures that may restrain individual freedom of choice can be justified in this group. On the other hand, indicators of efficiency for household appliances in domestic markets and policies and measures that address construction standards for houses and buildings can serve as numerical targets in Group III. In Japan, the household and commercial sectors are bound by mandatory energy efficiency regulations under the Law Concerning the Rationalization of Energy Use (Energy Saving Law). In developing countries as well, governments can implement tariff reductions and usage regulations to promote the diffusion of household appliances of the highest efficiency in domestic markets; thus, such options can be considered as policies and measures to be pledged in a policy template.

Incentives to encourage developing country involvement and measures to ensure cost effectiveness

Sectoral crediting mechanism

To involve developing countries in sectoral approaches, they must be presented with financial or technological incentives that are more attractive than those related to the conventional project-based Clean Development Mechanism (CDM). Without such incentives, developing countries are more likely to devote their negotiation resources to maintaining the Kyoto Protocol, and thus they will not be economically motivated to take part in sectoral approaches to begin with. A diversity of incentive options can be conceived; these options may vary among Groups I, II, and III.

If an industry belonging to Group I is subject to an agreed emissions intensity target, credits can be granted for efforts to deviate from the baseline emissions intensity projected for that industry in a developing country. The advantage of this method is that wider coverage is possible compared to project-based CDM. A major example of this mechanism involves pledging a "no lose" target of GHG intensity. Further intensity reductions below the target can then be recognized as credits (Schmidt and Helme 2005; Schmidt, Helme, Lee, and Houdashelt 2006). To implement this concept, however, a number of challenges must be resolved (Ellis and Baron 2005; Baron and Ellis 2006):

1) How can the policy avoid motivating developing countries to deliberately set moderate baseline intensity indicators or no-lose targets? Pledged targets would have to undergo expert third-party assessment, the quality of which could risk being undermined by data collection problems in developing countries. CDM/EB or ISO could assume the role of the third party. Baseline-setting methods need to be consistent with those in the conventional CDM program in terms of environmental rigor.

2) Should the mechanism address the retrofitting of existing equipment, should it be limited to the installation of new equipment, or should it include both? If existing equipment is included, the cost and institutional capacity needed to administer the mechanism will be greater.

3) When the credits generated are issued to governments instead of individual companies, as is the assumed case, there is the question of whether domestic incentives are designed to appropriately reflect the efforts of individual companies. For example, if a portion of revenues is granted to inefficient companies—essentially as a subsidy to protect domestic industries—companies that have devoted much effort to improving their performance would be put at a competitive disadvantage and effectively penalized. Competitive circumstances would be distorted from the viewpoint of developed countries as well. In that case, the original objective for adopting sectoral approaches would be undermined.

Would developing countries tolerate restricting conditions on the use of credit-based revenue? If negotiations conclude that numerical targets should be binding for developing countries as well and if companies in developing countries directly participate in international emissions trading, such problems will be eliminated.

Other alternatives for generating incentives are worthy of full consideration. One approach known as the Dual Intensity Targets Mechanism (Samaniego and Figueres 2002) is centered on national emission intensities and gives each country dual intensity targets, namely a "compliance target," a target which, if not achieved, will constitute formal noncompliance, and a "selling target," which—if successfully exceeded—can serve as the basis for awarding salable credits. A second idea is the Technology CDM, proposed by Fei Teng, Wenying Chen, and Jiankun He in another chapter of this book. This proposal puts emphasis on the transfer of new technologies rather than incumbent ones. Teng, *et al.* contend that compared to the current project-based CDM, a Technology CDM would better meet developing countries' need for access to low-carbon technologies that are not domestically available and relieve competitiveness concerns on the part of technology providers.

A third alternative is as follows: if the established numerical target is not represented by emission intensity but by a minimum efficiency requirement for newly installed equipment, then incentive measures could include funds from international financial institutions or preferential treatment in trade insurances and export credits to be granted in the event that new equipment surpasses these minimum efficiency requirements. Also, if products manufactured at plants that meet minimum efficiency standards could receive an internationally recognized label, measures to expand trade could also be considered to provide incentives for both climate change countermeasures and economic growth.

It should be noted, however, that as long as credits are issued to developing countries under the aforementioned sectoral crediting mechanism for policies and measures undertaken in Group I, Group I policies and measures—unlike those in Groups II and III—should not be given any further incentives.

In Group II as well, credits could be issued based on a sectoral crediting mechanism for the entire power sector that rewards emissions reductions generated by capital investments in the efficiency of thermal power plants that go beyond minimum efficiency requirements. In addition, given that projects to diagnose operations and maintenance performance at thermal power plants were among the most appreciated of all APP activities in developing countries, support from developed country governments to continue such projects could constitute incentives for developing country participation. This type of incentive would increase practical opportunities for technology transfer and provide energy-security benefits.

In the road transport sector, automobiles with low-carbon technology can be widely deployed through the implementation of fuel-efficiency regulations in the domestic markets of developing countries. The wider recognition of demand side management (DSM)-type CDM projects could help accelerate such trends: DSM-type CDMs attach incentives such as cash-back rebates (partial refunds of sales price) to increase the market penetration of energy efficient products relative to "BAU sales"; this in turn reduces power (energy) consumption and can be used to generate Certified Emission Reductions (CERs). The same kind of approach can be applied to household appliances in Group III as well.[7]

More general incentives for policies and measures in Groups II and III can be provided through programmatic CDM under the current Kyoto Protocol. CDM/EB32 Annex 38 provides that, "A programme of activities (PoA) is a voluntary coordinated action by a private or public entity which coordinates and implements any policy/measure or stated goal (i.e. incentive schemes and voluntary programmes) which leads to anthropogenic GHG emission reductions or net anthropogenic greenhouse gas removals by sinks that are additional to any that would occur in the absence of the PoA." Going through programmatic CDM can help mitigate the approval procedures or requirements developing countries face in seeking credit for participation in a policy template.

Finally, the definition for programmatic CDMs can be further relaxed to cover also general Sustainable Development Policies and Measures (SD-PAM). This would invite the wider participation of developing countries. However, in that case, a determination must be made about what kind of SD-PAMs should be included in a policy template. Decisions concerning the inclusion of policies and measures

---

[7] This method was put into practice in a project to promote the replacement of incandescent lamps with compact fluorescent lamps (CFL) with Japan's cooperation in China's Shijiazhuang City in Heibei Province in 2005.

related to Groups II and III, such as traffic measures and energy, industry, and urban policies, could pose problems. A government's fiscal or regulatory actions including mandates, standards, or sectoral reforms—or other initiatives with formal status that can be numerically represented and generate GHG reductions, direct or indirect—could generally be included whether or not their primary objective is emissions mitigation. Definitions and boundaries of SD-PAM are already discussed in several studies. (Heller and Shukra 2002; Bradley and Baumert 2005; Ellis, Baron, and Buchner 2007).

Trade and investment related measures

One of the objectives of sectoral approaches is to mitigate international competitiveness issues. Therefore, it is only natural that the introduction of trade measures as incentives for compliance with agreements based on sectoral negotiations, or as penalties against noncompliance, should be a subject of debate. Such measures have been explicitly included in legislative proposals, such as the Lieberman–Warner bill for a domestic emissions-trading system in the United States and the EU ETS reform plan that is currently under discussion.

The relationship between the World Trade Organization (WTO) and multinational environmental agreements (MEA) embraces many issues yet to be debated (Cosbey and Tarasofsky 2007). Acknowledging that further talks are needed among the WTO and international-climate-agreement negotiators, a number of options for trade-based incentives can be contrived in support of sectoral approaches:

i. Introduce trade restriction measures against imports from nonparties to sectoral agreements
ii. Incorporate better treatment for imports from parties to sectoral agreements
iii. Raise tariffs or collect credits for imported goods and services from relevant sectors or parties in noncompliance
iv. Reduce tariffs or issue credits for imported goods and services from relevant sectors of compliant parties
v. Impose a process tax—that is, a tax against underperforming manufacturing processes that fail to meet agreed benchmarks—as a border tax adjustment

vi. In the automobile and household appliance sectors, impose import restrictions and unfavorable treatment in government procurement for products that do not comply with labeling and technology standards agreed upon in sectoral negotiations.

Furthermore, industries and institutional investors could introduce common codes of conduct, such as those that have been developed for green procurement, to address transactions with companies from sectors in countries (not limited to developing countries) that are in noncompliance with numerical targets or are not implementing agreed policies and measures.

Measures to ensure cost-effectiveness

The issue of cost-effectiveness, often noted as a weak point of sectoral approaches, can be resolved to a certain point by establishing an intensity-based market for emissions trading. Because the proposal described in this chapter assumes that governments will legally ensure compliance with sectoral agreements, at least in Annex I countries, cross-border emissions-trading markets could be easily established within a single industrial sector where common measurement, reporting, and verification methods have been stipulated and shared in the sectoral agreement (Philibert 2005a). In order to take full advantage of emissions trading, linkages with cross-sectoral transactions; with different emissions-trading markets, including markets that operate under absolute caps or reduction requirements; with the CDM that already exists under the Kyoto Protocol; and with the new crediting mechanism proposed here must be envisaged. Although domestic emissions-trading markets may or may not be arranged in countries other than the European Union, it would be necessary to conceive of the emergence of an international trading market to achieve sectoral agreements with minimal costs.

The general idea here is to establish both an absolute reductions-based market and an intensity-based market, setting a gateway between the two markets to restrict the net flow of allowances from the latter into the former. This is necessary because participants in an intensity-based, emissions-trading market will otherwise increase production to acquire more allowances, resulting in excess production and undermining economic efficiency (De Muizon and Glachant 2004).

Conclusion

Challenges for a policy-based sectoral approach to a post-Kyoto framework

The sections above have demonstrated that a post-Kyoto framework based on sectoral approaches can be designed to equitably allocate reduction efforts among developed countries and at the same time engage developing countries. However, in order to actually implement this idea, a number of challenges must be overcome in addition to the issues presented in Section 2.

1) Political challenges: As can be guessed from the policy template, negotiations for a post-Kyoto framework based on sectoral approaches involve procedures—including setting the forum for negotiations and incorporating UNFCCC negotiations—that are substantially more complex compared to Kyoto-type negotiations which substantively address only reduction targets for developed countries. By including policies and measures in negotiations, there would be a higher chance of achieving real GHG reductions compared to the compliance scheme under the Kyoto Protocol, which relies on legal commitments that allow for simply purchasing allowances instead of physically reducing emissions. However, the United States, in particular, could be disinclined to accept a framework in which options for domestic measures could also constitute binding international commitments (this would represent an important change from the Kyoto Protocol, which left domestic measures to be decided by each government). Such resistance would be magnified in request-and-offer-type negotiations; thus, to overcome resistance to the framework, governments may have to be given the freedom to select which policies and measures they will pledge.

2) Economic challenges: The sectoral approach proposes to facilitate participation for each country by expressing national targets in terms of total emissions reductions instead of an emissions cap or limit at a certain point in time. This has the advantage that it reduces the risk of countries not fulfilling their commitments because of uncertainties in economic growth. However, it may not be sufficient to answer initial questions regarding the volume of emissions reductions to be assigned to each country.

Sectoral approaches aim to determine national reduction targets

using a bottom-up approach and thus can better reflect national circumstances than top-down methods, which tend to decide questions of
mid- and long-term targets and burden sharing in a diplomatic game
among countries. However, efforts to distribute the burden equitably
based on the principle of equalizing marginal abatement costs could
be undermined by uncertainties in the parameters required to calculate
those costs. Even estimates of marginal abatement cost developed at
the national level by research institutions such as the Intergovernmental
Panel on Climate Change (IPCC) vary widely. Therefore, top-down
negotiations may be called for at the final stage, after reduction potentials have been assessed for each country and each sector.

Also, if sectoral crediting is to be incorporated as an incentive
measure to involve developing countries, then the issue of determining the volume of credits to be issued and the coverage of policies and
measures eligible for credits is inextricably linked to the decision about
what constitutes an acceptable target for overall reductions among
developed countries. An issue that further complicates matters is the
scope of the market for credits. If credits become widely distributed,
the marginal costs of emissions reduction can be fully equalized across
different markets, thus achieving maximum economic efficiency from
emissions-trading schemes. However, allowance prices could decline,
provoking a negative reaction from parties that look to emissions-
trading markets for promising financial and business opportunities
and from companies holding allowances as assets.

3) Technological challenges: One of the main objectives of sectoral approaches is to increase developing country involvement by
promoting technology transfer. However, it is extremely difficult to
mandate technology transfer to private companies. Therefore, technology transfer based on sectoral agreements must be accompanied
by incentives that will drive companies to participate. These incentive
measures should be included in the policies and measures identified in
policy templates, but may give rise to political concern about technology transfer to future or present competitors in developing countries.
This could be especially problematic for developed countries that
regard their possession of state-of-the-art technologies as an important element of their continued global competitiveness. In addition, if
bilateral measures aimed at providing financial support to developing
countries are implemented as untied loans, then financial leakage—the
risk that a country could provide financial aid but still lose a project

funded with that aid to a company from another country—could also pose political problems. Furthermore, from an intellectual property perspective, industries in developed countries may apply pressure on their governments to formulate sectoral agreements that limit the scale and/or range of technology transfer. Yielding to such pressures will jeopardize the involvement of developing countries. Thus, there is a need to consider expanding the export insurance system to cover infringements of intellectual property rights in preparation for such obstacles.

References

Aldy, Joseph E., John Ashton, Richard Baron, Daniel Bodansky, Steve Charnovitz, Elliot Diringer, Thomas C. Heller, Jonathan Pershing, P. R. Shukla, Laurence Tubiana, Fernando Tudela, and Xueman Wang (2003). *Beyond Kyoto: Advancing the International Effort against Climate Change.* Arlington, VA: Pew Center on Global Climate Change.

Aldy, Joseph, Scott Barrett, and Robert N. Stavins (2003). "Thirteen Plus One: A Comparison of Global Climate Policy Architectures," Working Paper No. RWP03-012, Cambridge, MA.: Kennedy School of Government, Harvard University.

Baron, Richard (2006). "Sectoral Approaches to GHG Mitigation: Scenarios for Integration," OECD/IEA information paper, COM/ENV/EPOC/IEA/SLT(2006)8, Paris: OECD/IEA.

Baron, Richard and Jane Ellis (2006). "Sectoral Crediting Mechanisms for Greenhouse Gas Mitigation: Institutional and Operational Issues," OECD/IEA information paper, COM/ENV/EPOC/IEA/SLT(2006)4, Paris: OECD/IEA.

Baron, Richard, Jullia Reinaud, Matt Genasci, and Cedric Philibert (2007). *Sectoral Approaches to Greenhouse Gas Mitigation: Exploring Issues for Heavy Industry.* Paris: OECD/IEA.

Barrett, Scott (2003). *Environment & Statecraft: The Strategy of Environmental Treaty-Making.* New York: Oxford University Press.

(2007). "Proposal for a New Climate Change Treaty System," *The Economists' Voice*: 4(3), available at: www.bepress.com/ev/vol4/iss3/art6.

BASIC Project (2006). "The Sao Paulo Proposal for an Agreement on Future International Climate Policy," Discussion Paper for COP12 and COP-MOP2, Nairobi, Kenya, available at www.basic-project.net/data/SP_prop_rev_nairobi.pdf.

Baumert, Kevin A. and Donald M. Goldberg (2006). "Action Targets: A New Approach to International Greenhouse Gas Controls," *Climate Policy*: 5: 567–81.

Berk, M. M, M. G. J. den Elzen, and Gupta, J. (2005). "Bottom Up Climate Mitigation Policies and the Linkages with Non-Climate Policy Areas" in M. T. J. Kok and H. C. de Coninck (eds.), *Beyond Climate: Options for broadening climate policy*. Netherlands, RIVM report 500019001/2004 and NRP-CC report 500036/01, pp. 201–20.

Bodansky, Daniel (2003). "Climate Commitments: Assessing the Options," in Aldy, Ashton, Baron, Bodansky, Charnovitz, Diringer, Heller, Pershing, Shukla, Tubiana, Tudela and Wang, pp. 37–60.

    (2007). *International Sectoral Agreements in a Post-2012 Climate Framework*. Arlington, VA: Pew Center on Global Climate Change.

Bodansky, Daniel, Sophie Chou, and Christie Jorge-Tresolini (2004). *International Climate Efforts beyond 2012: A Survey of Approaches*. Arlington, VA: Pew Center on Global Climate Change.

Bosi, Martina and Jane Ellis (2005). "Exploring Options for 'Sectoral Crediting Mechanisms,'" OECD/IEA information paper, COM/ENV/ EPOC/IEA/SLT(2005)1, Paris: OECD/IEA.

Bradley, Rob and Kevin A. Baumert, eds. (2005). *Growing in the Greenhouse: Protecting the Climate by Putting Development First*. Washington DC: World Resources Institute.

Bradley, Rob, Kevin A. Baumert, Britt Childs, Tim Herzog, and Jonathan Pershing (2007). *Slicing the Pie: Sector-Based Approaches to International Climate Arrangements, Issues and Options*. Washington DC: World Resources Institute.

Cosbey, Aaron and Richard Tarasofsky (2007). "Climate Change, Competitiveness and Trade," Chatham House Report, London: Chatham House.

De Coninck, Heleen, Carolyn Fischer, Richard G. Newell, and Takahiko Ueno (2007). "International Technology–Oriented Agreements to Address Climate Change." Discussion Paper 6-50, Washington, DC: Resources for the Future.

De Muizon, Gildas and Matthieu Glachant (2004). "The UK Climate Change Levy Agreements: Combining Negotiated Agreements with Tax and Emission Trading," in Baranzini, Andrea and Philippe Thalman (eds.), *Voluntary Approaches in Climate Policy*. Cheltenham, UK: Edward Elgar Publishing Limited.

Egenhofer, Christian and Noriko Fujiwara (2008). *Global Sectoral Industry Approaches to Climate Change: The Way Forward*. CEPS Task Force Reports, Brussels: Center for European Policy Studies.

Ellerman, A. Denny and Ian Sue Wing (2003). *Absolute vs. Intensity-Based Emission Caps.* Report No.100, Cambridge, MA: MIT Joint Program on the Science and Policy of Global Change.

Ellis, Jane (2006). "Issues Related to Implementing 'Programmatic CDM'." Draft Paper prepared for the OECD/IEA Project for the Annex 1 Expert Group on the UNFCCC (AIXG), Paris: OECD/IEA.

Ellis, Jane and Richard Baron (2005). "Sectoral Crediting Mechanisms: An Initial Assessment of Electricity and Aluminium," OECD/IEA information paper, COM/ENV/EPOC/IEA/SLT (2005) 8. Paris: OECD/IEA.

Ellis, Jane, Richard Baron, and Barbara Buchner (2007). "SD-PAMs: What, Where, When and How?" OECD/IEA information paper, COM/ENV/EPOC/IEA/SLT(2007)5, Paris: OECD/IEA.

Government of Japan (2008). "Views Regarding the Work Programme of the Ad Hoc Working Group on Long-term Cooperative Action under the Convention," available at: http://unfccc.int/resource/docs/2008/awglca1/eng/misc01a01.pdf.

Groenenberg, Heleen, Dian Phylipsen, and Kornelis Blok (2001). "Differentiating Commitments World Wide: Global Differentiation of GHG emissions Reductions Based on the Triptych Approach-A Preliminary Assessment," *Energy Policy*, 29:1007–30.

Heller, Thomas C. and P.R. Shukra (2002). "Development and Climate: Engaging Developing Countries," in Aldy, Ashton, Baron, Bodansky, Charnovitz, Diringer, Heller, Pershing, Shukla, Tubiana, Tudela and Wang, pp. 111–40.

Herzog, Timothy, Kevin A. Baumert, and Jonathan Pershing (2006). *Target: Intensity; an Analysis of Greenhouse Gas Intensity Targets.* Washington DC: World Resources Institute.

IEA (2008). *Energy Technology Perspectives 2008.* Paris: IEA.

(2008a). *Worldwide Trends in Energy Use and Efficiency: Key Insights from IEA Indicator Analysis.* Paris: IEA.

IPCC (2007). "Summary for Policymakers," in Metz, B., O. R. Davidson, P. R. Bosch, R. Dave, L. A. Meyer (eds.), *Climate Change 2007: Mitigation. Contribution of Working Group III to the Fourth Assessment Report of the Intergovernmental Panel on Climate Change*, Cambridge and New York: Cambridge University Press.

JAMA (2008). JAMA Proposal for the Establishment of an Asia-Pacific Partnership Road Transport Sector Task Force. Tokyo, Japan: Automobile Manufacturers Association, Inc.

Jansen, J. C., J. J. Battjes, J. P. M. Sijm, C. H. Volkers, and J. R. Ybema (2001). "The Multi-Sector Convergence Approach: A Flexible Framework for Global Rules for National Greenhouse Gas Emissions Mitigation Targets," ECN-C-01-007/CICERO. Working Paper 2001:4. Petten, Amsterdam:

Energy Research Centre of the Netherlands, and Oslo, Norway: Center for International Climate and Environment Research, Oslo.

Jotzo, Frank and John C. V. Pezzey (2005). "Optimal Intensity Targets for Emissions Trading under Uncertainty," Economics and Environment Network Working Paper EEN0504, Canberra: Australian National University.

Justus, Debra and Cedric Philibert (2005). "International Energy Technology Collaboration and Climate Change Mitigation Synthesis Report," OECD/IEA information paper, COM/ENV/EPOC/IEA/SLT(2005)11, Paris: OECD/IEA.

Kolstad, Charles D. (2005). "The Simple Analytics of Greenhouse Gas Emission Intensity Reduction Targets," *Energy Policy*, 33: 2231–6.

Kulovesi, Kati and Katja Keinanen (2006). "Long-term Climate Policy: International Legal Aspects of a Sector-Based Approach," *Climate Policy*, 6: 313–325.

Lewis, Joanna and Elliot Diringer (2007). *Policy-Based Commitments in a Post-2012 Climate Framework*. Arlington, VA: Pew Center on Global Climate Change.

METI (2004). "Sustainable Future Framework on Climate Change, Interim Report, Global Environmental Sub-Committee Industrial Structure Council," Ministry of Economy, Trade, and Industry of Government of Japan, available at: www.meti.go.jp/english/information/data/c Framework2004e.pdf.

Neuhoff, Karsten and Susanne Droege (2007). "International Strategies to Address Competitiveness Concerns," Working Paper July 6, Cambridge: Electricity Policy Research Group, University of Cambridge.

OECD (2008). *Policy Instruments to Address Climate Change*, OECD Preliminary Report, March, Paris: OECD.

Okazaki, Teruo (2008). Presentation at the International Workshop on Sectoral Approach by the Government of Japan, Paris.

Pew Center on Global Climate Change (2005). *International Climate Efforts beyond 2012: Report of the Climate Dialogue at Pocantico*. Arlington, VA: Pew Center on Global Climate Change.

Philibert, Cedric (2000). "How Could Emissions Trading Benefit Developing Countries," *Energy Policy*, 28: 947–56.

    (2005). "Approaches for Future International Co-operation," OECD/IEA information paper, COM/ENV/EPOC/IEA/SLT(2005)6, Paris: OECD/IEA.

    (2005a). "New Commitment Options: Compatibility with Emissions Trading," OECD/IEA information paper, COM/ENV/EPOC/IEA/SLT(2005)9, Paris: OECD/IEA.

    (2005b). "Climate Mitigation: Integrating Approaches for Future

International Cooperation," OECD/IEA information paper, COM/ENV/EPOC/IEA/SLT(2005)10, Paris: OECD/IEA.

Philibert, Cedric and Jonathan Pershing (2001). "Considering the Options: Climate Targets for all Countries," *Climate Policy*, 1: 211–27.

Samaniego, Joseluis and Christiana Figueres (2002). "A Sector Based Clean Development" in Baumert *et al.* (eds.), *Building on the Kyoto Protocol: Options for Protecting the Climate*. Washington DC: World Resources Institute.

Sawa, Akihiro (2007). "Proposal for a Post-Kyoto Framework," Interim Report of the research project Japan's Strategy and International Cooperation for a Post-Kyoto Framework, Tokyo: The 21st Century Public Policy Institute, available at: www.21ppi.org/english/pdf/071112.pdf.

(2008). "Sectoral Approaches as a Post-Kyoto Framework: A Proposal of Japan's Sectoral Approach" Tokyo: The 21st Century Public Policy Institute, available at: www.21ppi.org/english/pdf/080321.pdf.

Schmidt, Jake and Ned Helme (2005). *Operational Issues for a Sector-Based Approach: Questions and Answers*. Washington DC: Center for Clean Air Policy.

Schmidt, Jake, Ned Helme, Jin Lee, and Mark Houdashelt (2006). *Sector-Based Approach to the Post-2012 Climate Change Policy Architecture*. Washington DC: Center for Clean Air Policy.

Siikavirta, Hanne (2006). "Long-term Climate Policy: Sectoral Approaches and Proposals," Ministry of the Environment, Finland, available at: www.environment.fi/download.asp?contentid=59527&lan=en.

Sugiyama, Taishi and Jonathan Sinton (2005). *Orchestra of Treaties*, Tokyo: Central Research Institute of Electric Power Industry.

Watson, Clinton, John Newman, Rt Hon Simon Upton, and Petra Hackmann (2005). "Can Transnational Sectoral Agreements Help Reduce Greenhouse Gas Emissions?," SG/SD/RT(2005)1, Document Prepared for the Round Table on Sustainable Development, Paris: OECD.

Winkler, Harald, Mark Howells, and Kevin A. Baumert (2007). "Sustainable Development Policies and Measures: Institutional Issues and Electrical Efficiency in South Africa," *Climate Policy*, 7: 212–29.

8 | *A portfolio system of climate treaties*

SCOTT BARRETT[+][*]

Introduction

Climate change is so fundamental a challenge that it may be best addressed from a multiple of perspectives, using a multiple of approaches.

This is a radically different concept from the arrangement developed thus far. Under the Kyoto Protocol, emission reduction obligations apply to entire economies, not to individual sectors; reforestation (which sequesters and therefore removes carbon dioxide or CO_2 from the atmosphere) is allowed to substitute for abatement (which reduces greenhouse gas [GHG] additions to the atmosphere, relative to "business as usual"); the emissions of different countries can be traded; and increases in the emission of one gas can be offset by reductions in the emission of another. This approach has one great virtue: it promotes cost-effective abatement.

Unfortunately, this approach has also (so far, at least) failed to address the more important objective, which is to reduce GHG emissions and ultimately to stabilize atmospheric concentrations. There may be different explanations for this. My diagnosis is that this failure is due to a lack of robust enforcement. So, why not add an enforcement capability? As I shall explain in this chapter, it may not be possible to enforce the current treaty design.[1] If enforcement is important—and I shall argue here that it is essential—then a better strategy may be to break up the problem, treating different sources and types of gases separately. This strategy may succeed better at reducing emissions overall.

[+] Lenfest-Earth Institute Professor of Natural Resource Economics, Columbia University School of International and Public Affairs.

[*] I am grateful to Joseph Aldy, Robert Stavins, and an anonymous referee for very helpful comments on earlier versions of this chapter.

[1] For a discussion of the possible trade off between cost-effectiveness and enforcement, see Barrett and Stavins (2003).

Of course, in breaking things up, cost-effectiveness may be compromised—but this is why the different approaches need to be linked. We don't simply need a number of agreements; we need a *system* of agreements.

The existing regime is, by design, linear. The United Nations Framework Convention on Climate Change (UNFCCC) establishes a collective, long-run goal and lasts indefinitely (of course, this treaty, like all treaties, can always be revised or dissolved or replaced). The Kyoto Protocol, by contrast, establishes short-term, individual-country emission targets and lasts only through 2012. Kyoto was supposed to be succeeded by a series of follow-on agreements—one that established individual country targets for 2013–2017; followed by another that established targets for 2018–2022; and so on *ad infinitum*. The ultimate aim of this series of protocols was to meet the collective goal expressed in the Framework Convention: to ensure that concentrations would be stabilized "at a level that would prevent dangerous anthropogenic interference with the climate system."

There are a number of problems with this design. The short-term nature of each protocol creates little incentive for countries to innovate and invest. Also, by not promoting R&D, Kyoto fails to generate the knowledge that will be needed to reduce emissions dramatically in the future. Investments in R&D and emissions reductions are complements. Not only are both needed; both need to be considered jointly.

A focus on emissions alone is also inappropriate because of climate change uncertainty. We don't know the GHG concentration level that will prevent "dangerous interference." We might guess wrong. We might guess right but, for the reasons already mentioned, be unable to use Kyoto to stop the world from exceeding the target concentration level. The objective of a climate change policy regime should be to reduce climate change *risk*.

Of course, limiting emissions will reduce risk, but there is more we can and should do. Perhaps most importantly, countries must be made less vulnerable to the climate change that is not or cannot be avoided by reducing emissions. One way to do this is by adapting to climate change. Many countries are capable of adapting on their own, but many are not, and those that are not must be helped. The Framework Convention and the Kyoto Protocol both acknowledge this need, but neither adequately addresses it.

Another approach to reducing climate change risk is not even mentioned in these agreements. This is "geoengineering," which involves the use of technologies for scattering solar radiation to counteract the effect of rising atmospheric GHG concentrations on the climate. Geoengineering has the potential to limit climate change risk, but its use will introduce new risks. We may therefore also want to reduce the risks associated with deploying geoengineering measures. One way to do this, of course, is to limit GHG concentrations so that geoengineering need never be attempted. However, it may not be possible to reduce the probability of abrupt and catastrophic climate change to zero. Another way to reduce risk is to develop the capability to reduce concentrations rapidly after geoengineering has been tried and found, possibly, to be wanting. We can potentially do this by means of another new technology: "air capture," which involves removing GHGs from the atmosphere directly. Finally, many of the approaches to reducing emissions entail risks of their own—examples include long-term storage of nuclear waste and long-term sequestration of CO_2 in underground geologic formations. The current regime does not provide a means for balancing these risks. To do that requires a *portfolio* of agreements.

These, then, are my three main conclusions: first, that a different treaty design, comprising a system of agreements, could potentially achieve greater emission reductions overall than the current design; second, that these individual agreements must be coordinated to promote cost-effectiveness; and third, that this coordination must also manage overall risk, by developing a portfolio of approaches to climate change. In short, and as the title of this chapter indicates, my proposal is for a portfolio system of climate treaties. Subsequent sections of this chapter develop the analysis behind these conclusions.

Overview

I begin with a critical review of the Kyoto Protocol. It may be widely believed today that Kyoto is inadequate and that there is no need, therefore, for further critiques. However, even if there were widespread agreement that Kyoto has failed, there may be many incompatible explanations for *why* it has failed. If we misunderstand the reasons for Kyoto's failure, we may end up repeating the same mistakes. In the next section of this chapter I argue that enforcement is the most essential challenge for an international climate agreement and that Kyoto's greatest flaw is that it lacks effective enforcement.

I am not alone in making this diagnosis. The most popular suggested remedy is to leave the basic architecture of Kyoto unchanged and to incorporate trade restrictions as the primary means for enforcement in a post-2012 agreement. In a later section I explain why this remedy may not work—and why a different architecture may work better.

The problem, as I see it, is that a treaty's architecture and its enforcement mechanism need to be *co-determined*. Not every desirable outcome can be enforced internationally. Kyoto's architecture may be commendable, provided enforcement can be assured. But if Kyoto's architecture makes enforcement difficult, then we may be better off using a different architecture—even one that would be theoretically inferior in a world in which enforcement was assured.

This chapter begins to outline an alternative architecture for a post-2012 agreement. The focus here is on the logic of negotiating sector-specific agreements rather than a single, all-encompassing, economy-wide agreement. Later sections extend this argument to propose having different agreements for different gases and return to the earlier topic of trade restrictions. I explain here that while trade restrictions may fail to enforce economy-wide targets of the type prescribed by Kyoto, they may be effective in enforcing sector- and gas-specific agreements.

To reduce emissions dramatically, new technologies are needed; and, to develop these new technologies, increased spending on R&D is needed. In the second half of this chapter I explain how R&D agreements should be structured, and how they ought to relate to other agreements within a broader system of agreements.

I then discuss other components of a portfolio system of agreements for limiting climate change risk, including adaptation, geoengineering, and air capture. The last section of the chapter concludes with some final thoughts.

Kyoto's enforcement challenge

The Framework Convention on Climate Change was negotiated years before Kyoto, but because it is linked to Kyoto, parties to the Convention have sought to define its collective goal in terms that are compatible with Kyoto. At the G8 summit held in Hokkaido, Japan in July 2008, the G8 members agreed that they would "share with all Parties to the UNFCCC the vision of, and together with them to consider and adopt in the UNFCCC negotiations, the goal of achieving at least 50% reduction of global emissions by 2050..."[2]

Climate negotiations have been going on for so long that history is beginning to repeat itself. In 1988, at a quasi-political conference held in Toronto, participants concluded that global CO_2 emissions should be reduced 20 percent from the 1988 level by 2005. Through 2004, however, global emissions *increased* 32 percent.[3] The UNFCCC's framing of the challenge, thus, has not helped. Of course, from the perspective of the climate, only global emissions matter, and so there is a logic to expressing the collective goal in these terms. The problem is that this approach creates no incentives for countries to limit their emissions. It is easy to reach agreement on a collective goal. If everyone is responsible for meeting it, no single country is responsible for meeting it. This is why the Kyoto Protocol was needed: its purpose was to establish individual country emission limits.

Setting a global emissions target only helps if a way can be found to disaggregate the overall target and to enforce country- or source-specific emission limits. This is how Title IV of the US Clean Air Act Amendments of 1990 is designed. This law establishes a total cap on sulfur dioxide emissions for all large power plants in the United States (the initial cap was set to about 50 percent of the levels emitted in 1980).[4] It then allocates this total to individual plants. Finally, it allows the operators of these plants to trade sulfur dioxide allowances. Trading creates an incentive for operators to meet the overall emissions target at minimum cost.

Though the trading arrangement in this law inspired Kyoto's design, other features of the US sulfur dioxide program are more important. Participation in Title IV is mandatory and non-compliance is penalized severely. Indeed, the penalty for non-compliance is so severe that, in 2006, compliance was 100 percent.[5] Title IV is successful because it is enforced centrally, by the US government.

[2] www.mofa.go.jp/announce/speech/un2008/un0810-2.html.
[3] See http://cdiac.ornl.gov/ftp/ndp030/global.1751_2005.ems.
[4] For a summary of the acid rain program, see www.epa.gov/airmarkets/progsregs/arp/index.html.
[5] See www.epa.gov/airmarkets/progress/docs/2006-ARP-Report.pdf, p. 11.

An international climate change treaty cannot be enforced in the same way. There is no world government—there are, instead, nearly 200 governments, each accorded sovereign equality in international law. Under the rules of international law, states participate in a treaty (such as Kyoto) on a voluntary, not mandatory, basis. Customary law says that states must comply with their treaty obligations, but this does not create an incentive for compliance. It creates an incentive to negotiate obligations that countries will want to meet anyway, treaty or no treaty. If a treaty is to sustain international cooperation, it must create incentives for parties to comply. Of course, to be effective, it must also create incentives for states to participate.

Kyoto lacks both arrangements. It provides no incentive for participation, which explains why the United States is a non-party. It also provides no incentive for compliance, which is why Canada—a party to the Protocol— has declared that it will emit much more than allowed by Kyoto.

The problem is not with these individual countries but with the design of the agreement. China is a party to the Kyoto Protocol and it will comply, but that is only because Kyoto does not require that China reduce its emissions. Russia is a party and it will also comply, but that is only because Russia's Kyoto limits are so generous that they do not bite. Other parties, like Japan and New Zealand, face emission limits that do bite, but it is not yet clear whether these countries will ultimately comply. They could comply by purchasing surplus credits from countries like Russia, but then their compliance would not help to reduce global emissions. What would be the point? They could comply at some cost, but why should they do that when other countries (like the United States, Canada, China, and Russia) are not reducing their emissions? Compliance by some members of the European Union also appears challenging. Spain has the largest gap between actual emissions and its Kyoto limit of any country. Denmark is well off its individual target. However, thanks to the European "bubble" and substantial reductions by other EU member states (in part for reasons having nothing to do with their climate change policies), Spain and Denmark are not bound by their individual limits so long as the original fifteen members of the European Union meet their collective limit. Australia recently ratified the Kyoto Protocol, but because of the Protocol's provisions for land use, land-use change, and forestry (known to climate insiders as LULUCF), Australia is within its Kyoto limit and will have to do very little, if anything, to comply.[6]

One current strategy is to make Kyoto's emission-reduction obligations more stringent, but if that is all that is changed, the effect will be the same. A means must also be found to enforce a new agreement.

Trade restrictions in a post-2012 agreement?

President Sarkozy of France has suggested that trade restrictions be considered for enforcing a new international climate agreement. Nobel-prize-winning economist Joseph Stiglitz (2006) has likewise recommended this approach. Should it be used?[7]

Trade restrictions can serve two purposes. They can be used to correct leakage. They can also be used to promote participation (that is, deter free riding).

For example, leakage can be addressed by "border tax adjustments." Parties to a new treaty would agree to impose a tariff on imports from non-parties and give a rebate on exports to non-parties, where the tariff and rebate would equal the cost of meeting treaty obligations, as embodied in the price of traded goods. How would these values be determined? Calculating the emissions released in the manufacture of a particular good is difficult. Two identical products, manufactured in the same country, might have very different "carbon footprints" (depending, for example, on how the electricity used as an input to the manufacturing process was generated). Cruder calculations might be contemplated (and most policy proposals have simplified the issue by focusing on the most trade-sensitive and energy-intensive sectors), but sector-specific taxes aimed at reducing leakage would also be hard to calculate.[8] Moreover, as trade restrictions became cruder, they would be less effective at reducing leakage.[9] Finally, crude border tax adjustments could serve as a disguise for protectionist measures.

[6] LULUCF is normally treated differently from emissions because of various accounting and incentive problems. For example, carbon accumulated in forestry may later be released.

[7] See Jeffrey Frankel's paper on this subject in the same series for the Harvard Project on International Climate Agreements. See also Houser et al. (2008).

[8] For example, Hoel (1996) shows that there is no simple relationship between fossil-fuel intensity and the optimal sector-specific carbon tax.

[9] See Oliveira-Martins et al. (1992).

Trade restrictions intended to promote participation can be blunt. Indeed, ideally, they would not need to be imposed at all—the credible threat to impose them would suffice to make all countries want to participate. Better still, if trade restrictions impelled all countries to participate, not only would free riding be eliminated, but so too would leakage.

Unfortunately, blunt punishments cannot be relied upon to work this way. To make countries want to participate, trade restrictions would have to be severe. But the threat to impose them would also have to be credible. That is, participating countries would have to be better off imposing the punishment than not imposing it in a situation where participation is less than full. The reason this may not be credible is that trade restrictions harm the countries that impose them as well as those on the receiving end. Worse, punishments typically become less credible as they become more severe.[10]

The legitimacy of using trade restrictions to enforce an agreement may also be challenged. Who should decide what a particular country should be required to do? Who should decide the punishment that is appropriate should that country fail to fulfill this obligation? Suppose trade restrictions were to be imposed against the United States for not ratifying Kyoto. Might not the United States claim that Kyoto's base year (1990) favored Europe, or that its own efforts to promote R&D were at least as helpful in addressing climate change? Suppose that China were to be the target of trade restrictions. Might not China argue that its economic development is the greater priority or that the rich countries are primarily responsible for the accumulation of GHGs to date? Trade restrictions that lack legitimacy may only spur retaliation—and lead to trade wars. Britain's efforts to bring the topic of climate change up for debate at the United Nations Security Council in 2007 hints at the reactions that might follow the inclusion of trade punishments in a climate change treaty. Countries without permanent representation on the Security Council felt that the issue should have remained with the General Assembly, where every country has one vote. The meeting ended without even a statement, let alone a resolution. Were one group of countries to seek to impose a climate agreement on others, backed by the threat of trade restrictions, an even stronger response would seem possible if not likely.

[10] See Barrett (2005).

To be effective, trade restrictions would need to enforce compliance as well as participation. Otherwise, countries could participate and then choose not to comply to avoid both the trade restrictions and the need to reduce emissions. Will parties to a future climate treaty agree to this? Would Kyoto's current parties agree to trade restrictions as an enforcement mechanism when some of them are already at risk of not complying?

Finally, it cannot be assumed that every other aspect of a treaty would remain unaltered if trade restrictions were used for enforcement. Countries might insist that their obligations be weakened as the price for accepting trade restrictions. If so, then the adoption of trade restrictions will not have achieved very much.

I want to conclude here by saying that the case for (or against) incorporating trade restrictions is far from obvious. We have seen what happens when there is no enforcement mechanism—global emissions have kept on rising. But we haven't seen what happens if trade restrictions are used for this purpose. It might be that they will improve matters. It might be that they will make no difference. Or it might be that they will make matters worse—failing to help the climate while at the same time depriving countries of some of the gains from trade.

Indeed, I shall argue later that trade restrictions may be more helpful in enforcing a different kind of agreement—one that focuses on limiting the emissions of individual sectors rather than of whole economies.

The logic of sectoral agreements

Earlier I explained that it makes scientific but not political sense to limit global emissions. It makes scientific sense because only global emissions matter for the climate. It does not make political sense because there is no world government able to enforce a global limit. Now I want to extend this argument to say that it may not make political sense to limit emissions at the national level either. This is because national, economy-wide limits are difficult for a state to enforce. It is easier for states to enforce limits on the emissions of individual sectors.

Consider how states have chosen to implement Kyoto. No country has a single, economy-wide policy for meeting its Kyoto obligations, even though those obligations apply to entire economies. The

European Union Emission Trading Scheme (EU ETS), for example, covers less than half of EU emissions.[11] Sweden arguably has the most well developed climate change policy of any country, but its approach involves both "sector integration" (every sector plays a part towards meeting the overall goal) and "sector responsibility" (different sectors have different obligations). In other words, even Sweden's economy-wide policies differentiate by sector. Its carbon tax, for example, offers relief for energy-intensive industrial operations.[12] The mismatch between the approaches taken to implement Kyoto and the way in which the Protocol's obligations were expressed hints that a different design, focused on individual sectors, would work better.[13]

To be sure, it is *feasible* to limit an economy's total emissions. Proposals in the United States for an upstream cap-and-trade program are economy-wide in their reach. However, other proposals in the United States target individual sectors (as was done in the previously mentioned Title IV program for sulfur dioxide emissions), and it is not obvious which type of proposal will eventually become law. A key issue is likely to be the possible vulnerability of trade-sensitive industries under an economy-wide cap. If firms that compete with US firms are based in countries that do not limit emissions, comparative advantage my shift towards these countries, harming the "competitiveness" of US companies. This means that the emissions of these other countries may increase as a consequence of the United States restricting its own emissions—a phenomenon known as "leakage." Concern about leakage is the reason that Sweden offers its energy-intensive industries relief from its carbon tax.

To be clear, an economy-wide policy would be cost-effective, but it would not be efficient from the perspective of a country acting to limit emissions unilaterally—not if leakage were significant.

Though Kyoto is an economy-wide agreement, it makes exceptions.

[11] It is worth noting that Title IV, discussed previously, is also a sectoral policy.

[12] See Ministry of Sustainable Development (2005). *The Swedish Report on Demonstrable Progress Under the Kyoto Protocol*. Available at www.sweden. gov.se/content/1/c6/05/47/62/24057533.pdf.

[13] The American Clean Energy and Security Act of 2009, which was approved by the United States House of Representatives, contains an economy-wide, cap-and-trade component, but also numerous sectoral policies, such as performance standards for new coal-fired power plants, investment in an electric vehicle infrastructure, efficiency standards for appliances, emission standards for automobiles, and so on.

It excludes emissions from aviation and marine transport. One reason is that it isn't obvious how the responsibility for lowering these emissions should be allocated. Take the case of ocean shipping. Should the state where a ship refuels be responsible? Or should the responsible state be the one in which the operator is based, or the owner resides, or the ship is registered (these are often three different states)? Another reason for excluding aviation and marine transport is that, no matter how responsibility is assigned, restricting emissions at the country level creates an incentive for unwanted behavioral change—for ships to re-register with a non-party, for example. This is an extreme version of trade leakage.

Article 2.2 of the Kyoto Protocol says that emissions from aviation and marine transport should be reduced, but through arrangements made outside the Protocol, by the parties "working through the International Civil Aviation Organization and the International Maritime Organization, respectively." So far, parties to both organizations have failed to act, but the motivation for treating marine and aviation emissions outside of Kyoto remains compelling. These are international transportation *systems*. In systems it is imperative that different parts be compatible. The reason the above two organizations were formed in the first place was to provide a forum for choosing global standards. (Under rules established by the International Civil Aviation Organization, for example, pilots flying internationally must speak either the local language or English, while controllers must be able to speak both languages. This rule ensures that pilots and controllers can always communicate in the same language.) Both organizations could play a role in choosing standards for reducing GHG emissions from their respective sectors.

For example, Farrell, Keith, and Corbett (2003) have suggested that marine transport may offer attractive opportunities for switching to hydrogen fuel. One reason for this is that ports are often located near refinery operations, where hydrogen is already produced and where cargo vessels already refuel. Such network effects have already transformed other aspects of ocean shipping, such as standards for oil tankers, which initially required separate oil and ballast water tanks but later evolved to require double hulls (Barrett 2007a). Parties to the International Maritime Organisation could establish a new standard for hydrogen-powered container ships. This would require that ports make the fuel available and that individual governments ban ships (above a certain size) that are not powered by hydrogen. As more countries impose this standard, the incentives for others to do likewise would increase.

Notice that marine transport can be made carbon neutral in this way (assuming that hydrogen production is carbon-free) without needing to agree on an allocation of property rights. Even more importantly, so long as the network effects are strong, the arrangement described above will be self-enforcing. We have some assurance that this arrangement can work in the marine shipping context because it has worked to limit damage to the oceans from deliberate and accidental releases of oil.

The same logic can apply to those parts of the economy that *are* included under Kyoto emission caps, such as road transport. The economics of hydrogen for automobile transportation are currently unattractive because of the need to change transportation infrastructure—especially the fuel distribution system, refuelling stations, and vehicles. Currently, electric vehicles seem to have the edge, especially as the plug-in hybrid could possibly act as a bridge to an all-electric future. Plug-in hybrids are similar to hybrids on the road now insofar as they run on electricity and gasoline. The difference is that plug-in hybrids have bigger batteries that can be recharged from the grid. People with garages can charge them at home now. In contrast to the all-electric car (which, given current battery technology, continues to suffer from restricted driving range between charges), plug-in hybrids can be driven long distances, making use of the existing refuelling infrastructure. Some people (depending on relative prices) may want to purchase these cars now. As plug-in hybrids penetrate the market, the number of electrical outlets for recharging will increase. The incentive to improve batteries for extended travel in electric mode will also increase. Both of these developments will improve the economics of the all-electric car.

As with international marine and aviation transport, the road transportation systems of different (especially contiguous) countries must be compatible. Plug-in hybrids are compatible with existing infrastructure. Their use can spread to new geographic regions under current conditions. Wider adoption by more countries will allow economies of scale and learning to be exploited, helping to increase market penetration further. In short, the adoption of plug-in hybrid vehicles may spread without the need for international cooperation. By contrast, the all-electric vehicle may fail to take off without an international agreement. At minimum, an international agreement may be needed to facilitate the transition to an all-electric vehicle future.[14] Note as well that technical standards create an automatic trade restriction that is legal (so long as the standards are non-discriminatory) and easily administered. This also helps to encourage the proliferation of common standards. It is by this means that the catalytic converter coupled with the use of unleaded gasoline became a global standard.

Of course, a switch to electric (or hydrogen) vehicles makes it even more imperative that emissions from electricity generation be cut very substantially. I discuss the electric sector later in this chapter.

Another sector excluded by Kyoto is deforestation. This is an important omission since deforestation is estimated to be responsible for around 18 percent of global GHG emissions (Bradley *et al.* 2007: 44). There is wide agreement that the deforestation "loophole" needs to be closed, and there are proposals for doing so by creating "credits" for avoided deforestation.[15] However, there are also good reasons why avoided deforestation was left out of the Kyoto Protocol in the first place. Forest loss is sometimes beyond the control of individual parties (as in the case of forest fires), the potential for leakage is huge, the benefits of avoided deforestation are reversible, and establishing a baseline for the purpose of calculating credits is fraught with difficulties. Policies to reduce deforestation are needed, but they will be imperfect.

Indeed, while afforestation and reforestation (tree planting, essentially) are counted by Kyoto, "trade" in forestry-based credits between developing (non-Annex I) countries and developed (Annex I) countries under the Clean Development Mechanism (CDM) has been very limited. So far, only one such project has been approved, and this project has been unable to find a buyer. As noted by Basu (2009: 146), "Because of their uncertain environmental value, forest-generated

---

[14] We already have an agreement for harmonizing automobile standards—the Agreement Concerning the Establishing of Global Technical Regulations for Wheeled Vehicles, Equipment and Parts which can be Fitted and/or Used on Wheeled Vehicles. See www.unece.org/trans/main/wp29/wp29wgs/wp29gen/wp29glob/globale.pdf. An agreement on new automobile standards could be negotiated as an amendment to this agreement.

[15] See, for example, Scott L. Malcomson, "Leafonomics," *New York Times*, 20 April 2008, at www.nytimes.com/2008/04/20/magazine/20wwln-essay-t.html?partner=rssnyt&emc=rss. The UN's Reduced Emissions from Deforestation and Forest Degradation Program, or UN-REDD, also creates emission "credits."

credits are expected to fetch only $4–$5 apiece in the global markets, compared with the $20–$25 fetched by carbon credits from other offset schemes." The EU currently does not allow forestry credits such as these to be traded within its Emission Trading Scheme, thus voting with its feet, as it were, to ring-fence forestry, so as not to allow forestry activities to contaminate other efforts to reduce net emissions (other CDM projects are allowed).

To sum up this section, the Kyoto Protocol's limits are not truly economy-wide, and while there have been proposals to develop a more comprehensive agreement, there was a logic in the original design, which treated different sectors—notably marine and aviation transportation, and deforestation—differently. This logic could also be extended to other sectors that are presently included in Kyoto's emission caps. I take up the question of whether a more fragmented approach should substitute for a broader agreement, or be additional to a broader agreement, in a later section.

Separate agreements for different gases

The logic of breaking the global mitigation challenge up into pieces can also be extended to the different types of GHGs. Indeed, one of the six gases controlled by Kyoto has already been addressed under a different agreement—the Montreal Protocol, which was created to protect the ozone layer, not to limit climate change.

Protection of the ozone layer has both positive and negative implications for climate change, but a 2007 study concluded that, overall, the Montreal Protocol has been very effective in mitigating climate change.[16] Indeed, the study calculates that the Montreal Protocol has done more to address global climate change than the Kyoto Protocol, even assuming that Kyoto worked as originally intended. Already, this study estimates, the Montreal Protocol has reduced GHG emissions by four times as much as the Kyoto Protocol planned to do.

In late 2007, months after the above study was published, the Montreal Protocol was revised again. This time, an earlier agreement to phase out hydrochlorofluorocarbons (HCFCs) was accelerated. HCFCs

---

[16] See Velders *et al.* (2007). Ozone-depleting substances also have a warming effect in the atmosphere, but so does stratospheric ozone itself and so do many of the substitutes for ozone-depleting substances.

are a category of GHGs, though they are not regulated by Kyoto (for the reason that they were already controlled by the Montreal Protocol). However, the manufacture of HCFCs produces HFCs (hydrofluorocarbons) as a byproduct, and HFCs (which are a GHG but *not* an ozone-depleting substance) *are* controlled by Kyoto. This new agreement thus adds to the Montreal Protocol's earlier achievement.

The implication is that, had HFCs been addressed in a separate agreement, they could have been cut dramatically and perhaps phased out—not only by Kyoto's Annex I countries, but *globally*. By pooling HFCs with the other GHGs within Kyoto's structure, less was achieved.[17]

Why has the Montreal Protocol succeeded where the Kyoto Protocol has failed? An important reason is that climate change and ozone depletion are different problems. Ozone depletion threatens human health directly, and can be avoided at relatively low cost. There are, however, other reasons—reasons having to do with the design of these treaties and how these designs address the underlying challenges.

Four observations are especially important. First, Montreal requires that *all* countries cut their emissions, whereas Kyoto only limits the emissions of Annex I countries. Second, Montreal controls production *and consumption* whereas Kyoto only limits the emissions arising from production. By restricting consumption (defined as production plus imports minus exports), Montreal dampens the potential for emissions leakage through trade. Third, the Montreal caps are *permanent*, whereas Kyoto's last only five years. Permanent limits create an expectation of a fundamental shift in global demand, stimulating innovation. Finally, Montreal created strong incentives for both participation and compliance—"carrots" in the form of financial payments from rich to poor countries, and "sticks" in the form of trade restrictions between parties and non-parties to the agreement. Kyoto only offers financial assistance through the faulty CDM; as discussed earlier, it lacks an enforcement mechanism.

The lesson is not that an international climate agreement ought to have the features of the Montreal Protocol. These are different prob-

---

[17] Indeed, there is evidence that Kyoto might actually have created incentives for HFC production to *increase*. According to Michael Wara (2007: 596), producers of HCFCs can earn more from Clean Development Mechanism (CDM) credits for the HFCs produced as a byproduct than from the HCFCs themselves. This is an illustration of one problem with the CDM—establishing a baseline.

lems; they will have different solutions. The lesson is that, by pooling all gases and sources together, Kyoto loses the leverage that can be brought to bear in controlling, in this instance, one type of GHG independently of others. Montreal has shown us that a different design would have achieved much more.

Sectoral agreements again

Although the Montreal Protocol's production and consumption limits are economy-wide, they are determined with a view to how individual sectors can substitute away from controlled chemicals, and they take into account the benefits to be derived from these changes. For example, the adjustments agreed in late 2007 were grounded in a very detailed analysis of individual sectors, including refrigeration and air conditioning, foams, medical aerosols, and fire protection.[18] The Technology and Economic Assessment Panel (TEAP) that advises parties to the Montreal Protocol includes members who are "influential in technical standards organizations, industry associations, and private and public regulatory authorities" (Anderson and Sarma 2002, p. 441). The members from environment ministries "use knowledge of emerging technology to time regulatory approval with commercialization," while industry experts are "influential in crafting regulatory incentives necessary to stimulate investment and rapidly achieve economies of scale" (Anderson and Sarma 2002, p. 441).

A consequence of this process is that, by the time treaty parties approve TEAP recommendations, the political, economic, and technical feasibility of their implementation is virtually assured. As explained by Parson (2002), Montreal's "success was not achieved by the control measures in the original treaty. Instead, it was achieved by rapid adaptation of the controls and the flood of innovations that followed. The protocol's novel process of assessing alternatives to ozone-depleting chemicals was central to this adaptation." Parson adds, "These linked processes of assessment, innovation, and diffusion were so powerful they almost made the regulations appear superfluous, as private reduction efforts stayed consistently ahead of regulatory requirements."

---

[18] See http://ozone.unep.org/teap/Reports/TEAP_Reports/TEAP-TaskForce-HCFC -Aug2007.pdf.

For climate change, Parson suggests that more progress might be made if technology-based assessments were undertaken in key industrial sectors such as steel, smelting, chemicals, and pulp and paper, and in other areas that offer significant abatement potential, such as improving the fuel efficiency of vehicles; developing power-plant carbon capture and storage; and reducing industrial emissions of HFCs, perfluorocarbons (PFCs), and sulfur hexafluoride (SF_6).

This process of technology assessment was made effective by structural features of the Montreal Protocol. Several of these features could—and, I would argue, should—feature in a new climate treaty regime.

First, a climate treaty's obligations, whether for an individual sector or a particular type of gas, should apply globally. Developing countries should not be exempted from meeting new global standards, as they were from reducing their emissions under Kyoto (though, as with the Montreal Protocol, it may be desirable in some cases to establish a different transition path for developing countries).

Second, developing countries should be offered financial assistance to reward their participation and aid their compliance. This assistance should be based on the principle of "incremental cost," meaning that developing countries should not be made worse off for participating and complying as compared with an alternative scenario where the agreement did not exist. In contrast to Kyoto, payments would not be made for "hot air." Nor would surpluses be paid (as they are, except at the margin, under a trading system). This arrangement will lower the cost to rich countries of achieving emission reductions in poor countries and thus encourage greater action to limit emissions.

Third, trade restrictions should be used to enforce agreements for trade-sensitive sectors. Since developing countries would be compensated for participating in and complying with these agreements, and since the aim of the agreements would be to create universal standards for a "level playing field," the use of trade restrictions in this context would have legitimacy. The threat of trade restrictions should also have a high chance of being credible, since parties to such sectoral agreements would not want non-parties to have an "unfair" advantage in international trade. Moreover, the trade-sensitive sectors are, by definition, especially vulnerable to leakage. Applying trade restrictions to non-parties would help to reduce leakage, thus making credible the threat to apply restrictions (Barrett 2005).

Finally, treaty obligations should be expressed in terms of consumption and not only production. Importing countries should agree to import only goods that were produced by methods that meet global standards. This measure reduces the market for non-participants and increases the market for participants. It thus encourages participation.

The aluminum sector is a prime candidate for a sectoral agreement.[19] It is a concentrated industry: twelve countries account for 82 percent of global production; ten companies produce more than half of world output. The industry employs just two smelting technologies, and emissions can be reduced substantially by re-melting aluminum scrap, which is 95 percent less GHG-intensive than primary aluminum production. Finally, twenty-six companies, making up 80 percent of world output, belong to the International Aluminium Institute, which has already adopted voluntary energy intensity targets. There exists a basis here for negotiating new global standards for the industry, in a manner similar to the TEAP, backed by international enforcement.

The precise nature of such an agreement would need to be worked out by the parties, in association with the industry—demonstrating the value, again, of technology assessment. One possibility is to require that all smelters employ the more efficient Prebake smelting technology (some facilities in developing countries still rely on the less efficient Söderberg technology). Another possibility is to limit upstream emissions associated with electricity inputs to the production process. A final possibility is for an agreement to reduce emissions of PFCs. There is tremendous variation among aluminum plants in the amount of this gas that is emitted—and opportunities, therefore, for the lower emission rates to serve as an industry standard.[20] Other obvious candidates for sectoral agreements include steel and cement.[21]

A final question is whether sectoral and individual gas agreements should substitute for an economy-wide, multi-gas agreement or whether the different types of agreement should coincide. The latter possibility may be more cumbersome, but it has the advantage of being more evolutionary. Over time, we can shed the agreements that prove superfluous or ineffective.

[19] I am drawing here from the excellent study by Bradley *et al.* (2007), especially pp. 37–8.
[20] Watson *et al.* (2005) p. 12.
[21] Again, see Bradley *et al.* (2007).

R&D

An area where linkage is certainly needed concerns policies to reduce emissions and promote R&D.

The Kyoto Protocol lasts just five years—too short a period to provide incentives for firms to make major investments in new technologies for reducing emissions. Patents typically last 20 years. If a treaty is to create incentives for industry to innovate, its obligations must last at least as long.

Preferably, and as noted previously, the obligations expressed in a treaty should hold indefinitely and thus prevent backsliding. Future adjustments and amendments can ratchet up the actions required. It may be difficult for a climate treaty to do this if the goals are expressed as emission limits—in that case the question arises, would permanent limits be credible? It may be easier if goals are expressed in some other way—as technology standards, for instance. It is sometimes claimed that technology standards have the opposite problem of "locking in" a given level of performance. However, there is evidence to counter this claim. The oceans have been protected from oil releases by a succession of technology agreements, each one more demanding than the last.[22]

The Kyoto Protocol has the additional shortcoming that it creates little incentive for countries to invest in R&D. The product of basic research is knowledge, and knowledge (by social choice) cannot be patented. Instead, the production of basic research must be stimulated by public financing—by national laboratories undertaking research directly, by research grants being awarded on a competitive basis to universities, by research subsidies being paid to industry, or by prizes being awarded for research success. Energy R&D spending was flat after the UNFCCC was adopted in 1992; it changed little after Kyoto was negotiated; and it has remained steady since Kyoto entered into force.[23] Kyoto's design does not promote R&D directly.

Failure to stimulate R&D makes long-term progress in reducing emissions difficult. Basic knowledge and technology development are complements. The returns to each activity increase in the level of the other activity. Both activities are also crucial to addressing climate

---

[22] Barrett (2007a).
[23] See Doornbosch and Upton (2006).

change. Reducing emissions dramatically will require a technological revolution.

Knowledge is a global public good. Countries—especially large, rich countries—have incentives to invest in R&D, individually in some cases and collectively in others. However, in the case of climate change, the returns to supplying one global public good (knowledge) depend on the returns to supplying the other (using the knowledge to reduce GHG emissions).

We know that the incentives to conduct research into nuclear fusion are strong, because countries have already cooperated in this research.[24] Fusion power, however, promises to yield benefits unrelated to climate change, in addition to climate benefits. The incentives to undertake R&D into carbon capture and storage, by contrast, are much weaker. They depend entirely on the prospects of the knowledge emerging from this research being embodied in new technologies that are actually diffused, and these prospects depend in turn on the strength of future incentives for countries to cut their GHG emissions (Barrett 2006). As noted previously, these incentives are likely to remain weak even with an international climate agreement unless a way can be found to address the enforcement challenge.

Electricity is not usually traded (that is, it is mostly generated in the country where it is consumed), and so the emissions from this sector cannot be controlled in the same way as emissions from sectors like aluminum and transport. This, of course, is another reason why it makes sense to break the larger problem up to accommodate different approaches for different sectors.

Though trade restrictions cannot be used to enforce an agreement on electricity generation, at least we do not need to worry about leakage compounding free rider incentives. Recall that Title IV of the Clean Air Act Amendments of 1990, which limits power plant emissions of sulfur dioxide, was adopted as a US law. It was incorporated within a bilateral agreement with Canada, but only after being passed as domestic legislation. This law did not make any provision for trade restrictions because leakage was not a problem. Nor was free riding, because the domestic benefits of Title IV outweighed the costs.

---

[24] The International Thermonuclear Experimental Reactor, being built now in France, is a cooperative endeavour, supported by the European Union, China, India, Japan, South Korea, Russia, and the United States—the same countries that will need to cooperate in addressing climate change.

A climate change treaty requiring, say, that all new coal-fired power stations be fitted with carbon capture and storage would need to overcome free rider incentives.

How might this be done? One possibility is to make the policies of different countries contingent. For example, an agreement could require that all new coal-fired power stations be fitted with carbon capture and storage, with this obligation being binding on individual countries only so long as the treaty's minimum participation condition was met. This arrangement would address one of the motivations for free riding—the fear that, should your country cooperate, others will not, with the consequence that your country helps free riders but is made worse off itself compared with a situation in which cooperation fails completely (Barrett 2005). To provide additional reassurance that other parties really will adopt the new standard, the agreement could require that parties adopt domestic legislation mandating the technology standard. This would shift the compliance burden onto domestic institutions (participation would still need to be enforced internationally, but that would be the purpose of the minimum participation clause noted above).

Two problems with carbon capture and storage cannot be avoided. The first is that it is more costly and results in more local pollution emissions than an equivalent plant without carbon capture (this is because capture requires energy). It will never be something countries implement on a major scale unilaterally. A way must therefore be found to enforce participation in an agreement that mandates the use of this technology (or that prescribes emissions constraints that can only be met using carbon capture and storage). Second, geologic storage will introduce new risks, particularly if done on a substantial scale. Some of these risks are local (harm to groundwater, for example). Some are global (leakage of CO_2 into the atmosphere). (Deep ocean storage introduces other risks.)

A priority for action now must be to advance both carbon capture and geologic carbon storage. R&D must demonstrate the economics of large-scale, integrated power plants with carbon capture, and find ways to lower costs and improve efficiency. It must also demonstrate the safety of underground storage. Because the benefits of this R&D lie entirely in supplying the global public good of climate-change mitigation, this research will need to be coordinated. Indeed, there is almost certainly a need for international cooperation in financing R&D in this area. The Carbon Sequestration Leadership Forum (with twenty-one member states) is a "framework for international cooperation in research and development for the separation, capture, transportation and storage of carbon dioxide."[25] The Forum does not undertake R&D. Its purpose is to share information. About twenty large-scale carbon capture and sequestration demonstration projects are now being planned, but as noted by the International Energy Agency (IEA 2008: 276), the list of such plants is "changing rapidly... due to a number of project cancellations as well as new projects being announced."[26] We should be able to rely more on R&D in this vital area.

R&D agreements do not require universal participation or even a high level of participation. They can involve a small number of countries. The ITER nuclear fusion project, for example, is supported by the European Union and six other countries. Countries contribute to an effort like this when they benefit from the fruits of the research and their contributions are pivotal to the project going ahead. They also contribute so that their scientists can learn from colleagues based in other countries—a greater benefit when a country is engaged in complementary research programs. In these situations, other countries may free ride, but their free riding need not undermine the provision of knowledge-based public goods (Barrett 2007a). High participation levels are important only for agreements that aim to reduce emissions.

Adaptation

Countries have exceptionally strong incentives to adapt. They have incentives to adapt in *response* to climate change, to limit the damage from climate change, and they have incentives to adapt in *anticipation* of climate change, to insure against future damage.

---

[25] See www.cslforum.org/publications/documents/CSLFcharter.pdf.
[26] The United States had planned to build a "clean coal" pilot project called FutureGen. The plant was to produce hydrogen and electricity from coal while using carbon capture and storage to sequester the CO_2 underground. The initiative was launched in 2003. In December 2007, a site was selected. A month later, the project was cancelled, ostensibly because the cost had risen from $1 billion to $1.8 billion. See M. L. Wald, "Higher Costs Cited as U.S. Shuts Down Coal Project," *New York Times*, January 31, 2008; available at www.nytimes.com/2008/01/31/business/31coal.html?ref=environment&pagewanted=all. Recently, the Obama adminstration reversed this decision.

In contrast to mitigation, the benefits of adaptation are excludable—they need not be shared with outside parties. Much adaptation will therefore be done "automatically" by the market. Much of the rest will require governments to invest in local public goods (such as augmenting the Thames Barrier), the benefits of which will be largely internal to the countries that supply them.

Poor countries are especially vulnerable to climate change. This is partly because of their geography (Mendelsohn, Dinar, and Williams 2006). It is also because poor countries lack the capability to adapt. Adaptation requires the same institutions as development. Poor countries have weaker market institutions, and their governments routinely undersupply basic local public goods (like immunization). Poor countries are also less accustomed to cooperating with each other to address cross-border challenges like malaria, which may become an even greater threat with climate change.

Mitigation will depend mostly on the efforts of the richest countries (not only as regards their own abatement but also their willingness to finance abatement by other countries). However, these countries are also more capable of adapting. The rich countries may, therefore, substitute the local public good of adaptation (the benefits of which are captured locally) for the global public good of mitigation (the benefits of which are distributed globally), leaving poor countries more vulnerable still. Climate change thus has the potential to widen existing inequalities.

Compassion might move rich countries to offer assistance to the poor: but there is a more powerful motive: the rich countries are *responsible* for the poor needing to adapt.

Rich countries have already accepted that they are obligated to assist poor countries with adaptation. Article 3 of the UNFCCC says that rich-country parties to the Convention shall "assist the developing country Parties that are particularly vulnerable to the adverse effects of climate change in meeting costs of adaptation to those adverse effects." However, the agreement does not say how much money the rich countries ought to provide or the basis for determining this amount. Nor does it mention burden sharing. How much should each rich country contribute?

The Kyoto Protocol made a first attempt to define and implement the obligation of rich countries to assist the poor. It established an adaptation fund, financed by a levy on CDM transactions (the CDM allows rich countries to fulfill their emission-reduction obligations by obtaining credit for emission reductions they finance in poor countries). However, there are three problems with this arrangement. First, the amounts of money that will be needed for adaptation bear no relation at all to the amounts raised by CDM transactions. Second, taxing CDM transactions penalizes efforts to supply the global public good of mitigation. Finally, since the United States is not a party to the Kyoto Protocol, its obligation to assist developing countries (an obligation it accepted under the UNFCCC) cannot be fulfilled by the CDM. For all three reasons, a different approach is needed.

What form this new approach might take is presently unclear. The priority at this time should be to make investments in development that will reduce future vulnerability. An obvious area for investment is agriculture. The Consultative Group on International Agricultural Research (CGIAR) is currently undertaking research that could reduce future vulnerability dramatically. This includes developing "climate-ready" crops capable of withstanding climate change—examples include heat-tolerant crops, "drought-escaping" rice (varieties that can grow over a shorter cycle), and "waterproof" rice (varieties that survive prolonged flooding). Industrialized countries pay about 70 percent of the CGIAR's budget (multilateral and regional development organizations finance most of the balance). They should increase their contributions to finance an expanded climate-related research program.

Another obvious area for investment is tropical medicine. The link between climate change and infectious diseases is complex and uncertain but there are reasons to be concerned. For example, the relationship between temperature and the number of days it takes for the malaria parasite to develop within a mosquito is non-linear. Small changes in temperature can thus lead to large changes in malaria incidence.[27] Of course, even leaving direct climate-disease interactions aside, we can be sure that countries will be better able to adapt to the myriad impacts of climate change if they are relieved of their crushing disease burden. Much of this burden can be erased using existing medical products, but R&D into the tropical diseases has also been lacking. One way to help developing countries adapt is thus to invest in R&D on infectious diseases.

---

[27] See Patz and Olson (2006). Of course, rainfall patterns are also important, and the phenomenon of "biological amplification" described here depends on a number of things, including the existing level of transmission.

The important design question is whether and how contributions to adaptation and R&D should be linked to other actions in the treaty system. Much future climate change can be attributed to historical emissions. Even more climate change will be due to future emissions. The more we succeed in reducing emissions, the less we will need to spend on adaptation. This suggests that a component of each country's contribution to adaptation should be linked to its role in reducing future emissions.

Geoengineering

Two fundamental forces determine the Earth's climate: the amount of solar radiation that reaches the surface and the amount of this radiation that is trapped by GHGs in the atmosphere. So far, international negotiations have focused on addressing the latter—that is, the concentration of GHGs. Geoengineering is a radically different approach. Its aim is not to limit climate change by limiting GHG concentrations but to limit climate change by altering the amount of solar radiation that reaches the Earth.

There are many different ideas for how this might be done. The most prominent option involves throwing particles (sulfates or particles engineered specifically for this purpose) into the stratosphere. This would have a similar effect to some volcanic eruptions—the particles would scatter sunlight, cooling the Earth. Of course, this is a Band-Aid, not a solution that gets at the root of the problem; but there are other problems. Putting large volumes of particles in the atmosphere fails to address the allied problem of ocean acidification. It may not maintain the current distribution of climate. It may increase stratospheric ozone depletion. It may create other risks as yet unknown. There are many reasons why geoengineering should never be tried.

Geoengineering is also the only available option for lowering global temperature quickly. Reducing (net) GHG emissions takes decades to translate into temperature changes. Geoengineering could cool the Earth within months. Suppose, then, that a low-probability but high-consequence climate event started to unfold. Would we want to have the option to use geoengineering then? Certainly many people would say yes—as a last resort.[28]

---

[28] See, for example, Stephen Schneider's (2008) recent paper on this question.

Two other aspects of geoengineering are crucial. First, geoengineering is relatively cheap in financial terms. How cheap? According to David Keith (2000: 263), the cost is sufficiently low that "it is unlikely that cost would play any significant role in a decision to deploy stratospheric scatterers..." Second, geoengineering can be undertaken as a discrete action—in other words, a number of countries could deploy this option unilaterally.

This means that an international agreement is not really needed to finance deployment (alternatively, such an agreement should be easy to reach). If getting countries to reduce their emissions is "too hard," getting countries to try geoengineering may be "too easy." Indeed, the international challenge is not to get countries to use geoengineering but to get them *not* to use it if other countries object.[29]

The situation in which "abrupt and catastrophic" climate change appears imminent and can only be prevented by geoengineering is easy to analyze. Under these circumstances, many countries will want to use this technology. Since no country is likely to gain from abrupt and catastrophic climate change, few if any countries at that point are likely to oppose deployment. We can expect that geoengineering will be used under these circumstances, and that this will be desirable, at least from an *ex ante* perspective.

The situation in which "gradual" climate change is occurring is more complicated. William Cline (2007) has shown that the effects of gradual change on agriculture, within this century, are likely to be mixed. Some countries will probably lose substantially. In Cline's analysis, a "business as usual scenario" that leads to an increase in mean global temperature of 3 degrees Celsius by around the year 2080 causes India's agricultural capacity to fall by nearly one-third. This is a huge loss for a country where many millions of people rely on agriculture for their livelihood. The losses in equatorial Africa are even larger—over 50 percent. However, other countries gain. Agricultural capacity in China rises nearly 7 percent. In Russia it rises 6 percent; in the United States, 8 percent. The overall or aggregate effect of climate change in 2080 is small—global agricultural capacity falls by only

---

[29] For a discussion of this challenge, see Barrett (2008a). An anonymous referee suggested that an expectation that geoengineering could stimulate conflict may create an additional motivation for states to reduce their emissions. Others have suggested the opposite—that the possibility of geoengineering reduces the incentive for states to cut their emissions.

about 3 percent, an amount so small as to be within the "noise" given the uncertainty in these estimates and the number of things that can change over a period of 75 years. What stands out is the variation of impacts across countries.

India already has space and nuclear programs. It would certainly have the capability to use geoengineering in an attempt to reverse damages caused by "gradual" climate change, should it choose to do so. But, plainly, other countries might object, perhaps strongly, if India were to attempt this approach. In this situation, conflict seems likely. How will it get resolved? That is hard to say, but given that conflict can be anticipated, an incentive exists for making it less likely to emerge—another reason why it is essential that rich countries not only reduce their GHG emissions but also help poor countries adapt by making investments in areas like agriculture. Potentially, agricultural improvements resulting from such investments could more than offset productivity declines caused by climate change.

What else to do now? R&D in the area of geoengineering is certainly needed—to explore whether this approach is likely to work, how it should be deployed, and what the harmful consequences may be. Because individual countries may have the incentive to deploy geoengineering, they have an incentive to undertake related R&D unilaterally. However, because the consequences of geoengineering would be global, my view is that R&D on this option should be undertaken cooperatively and openly.

Air capture

Of course, R&D cannot tell us everything we need to know about geoengineering—only after this option were used at scale and over a sustained period of time would we learn its full consequences.

Suppose, then, that geoengineering is deployed in the hope that it will reduce the chances of imminent catastrophe. Suppose further that, upon deploying this technology, we learn that geoengineering works and does not result in serious adverse consequences. Then we can continue to use it. Suppose, however, that we discover geoengineering is effective at lowering global mean temperature but that it has other, adverse consequences—perhaps consequences that were previously unforeseen—then what? At this point we will want to reduce atmospheric GHG concentrations, so that we can slowly wean ourselves away from geoengineering. We could do this more quickly and at lower cost if we invest much earlier in R&D to advance new low-carbon technologies. Even so, however, reducing GHG emissions is a slow way to reduce atmospheric concentrations.

A faster approach is "air capture." This involves removing CO_2 directly from the air. Of course, the process of photosynthesis does this naturally, which is why Kyoto acknowledges the role of afforestation and reforestation. However, there are limits to reducing concentrations in these ways.

Another approach is to fertilize iron-limited regions of the oceans, to stimulate phytoplankton blooms. This has already been done on an experimental basis, but the potential for this kind of air capture is also limited. Moreover, there are concerns about the consequences of attempting ocean fertilization on a large scale—in fact, parties to the London Convention, an international treaty for the protection of the oceans, recently cautioned against large-scale experiments of this kind.[30]

Industrial air capture involves bringing air into contact with a chemical "sorbent"—an alkaline liquid that would absorb the CO_2 in the air. The CO_2 could then be sequestered in the same way as CO_2 removed from a power plant's stack gases. This technology can be scaled up to any level and would offer the fastest way to reduce atmospheric concentrations.

Air capture is also extremely expensive, however. In contrast to geoengineering, it is very unlikely that any country would choose to deploy this technology on a massive scale unilaterally. It is possible that a number of countries would be willing to do so collectively, but only if the damages avoided were at least as large as the cost—a

[30] In 2007, the eighty-four parties to the London Convention/Protocol endorsed a "statement of concern" about ocean fertilization, and urged parties "to use the utmost caution when considering proposals for large-scale ocean fertilization operations." (See OSPAR Decision 2007/02 on Storage of Carbon Dioxide Streams in Geological Formations, June 2007.) They also agreed that they would consider regulating this technology. This should be of concern to parties to the UNFCCC. Restricting ocean fertilization may be to the benefit of the oceans, which are the primary concern of parties to the London Convention. However, the choice is not whether to allow such an experiment; it is whether to allow such an experiment or to do *something else* to reduce concentrations, or to accept the damage from climate change that could have been avoided by implementing ocean fertilization. The parties to the Framework Convention must surely play a role in making this judgment.

situation that is most likely to arise when the case for implementing geoengineering is also strong and when air capture can be deployed to directly reduce atmospheric GHG concentrations so that geoengineering interventions can be scaled back or stopped. Currently, our knowledge of this technology is in its infancy. R&D should be undertaken now to develop air capture and lower its costs, so that we will be ready to deploy this technology should we feel the need to do so in the future.[31]

Conclusions

In this chapter I have outlined a different approach to addressing climate change, building on my earlier proposal for a "multitrack climate treaty system" (Barrett 2007b). I have provided more details about how the individual parts of such a treaty system might be developed and I have examined their potential interconnections, including their implications for managing climate change risk. I am not claiming here that my approach is ideal. Plainly, it is not. My proposal should be judged relative to the viable alternatives. In making this comparison, it is essential that the alternatives be shown to be self-enforcing. Proposals that either ignore the need for enforcement, or that assume that enforcement will appear out of thin air, do not offer viable alternatives.

There are two fundamental problems with the approach taken so far to reduce GHG emissions. The first is that it lacks an effective enforcement mechanism. The approach outlined here allows us to use different means to enforce different parts. We know this alternative approach could do better because we have seen it do better—the latest adjustment to the Montreal Protocol is proof. We also know that this approach could not do worse than the existing arrangement, since separate agreements for individual sectors and gases could be developed as supplements or additions to the approach tried thus far.

The second problem with the approach taken thus far is that it largely neglects other opportunities for reducing climate change risk.

[31] In a recent analysis of a similar but not identical situation, Baker, Clarke, and Weyant (2006: 173) conclude that, "from a policy perspective, the more likely we believe dramatic emissions reductions will be necessary, the more R&D funding should be pushed toward technologies that will reduce the costs of these reductions."

Adaptation is also important. So, ultimately, may be geoengineering and air capture. We need a portfolio of approaches, one that allows for changes in the mix of measures used to manage climate change as we learn more about the problem and our ability to address it.

References

Anderson, S. O. and K. Madhava Sarma (2002). *Protecting the Ozone Layer: The United Nations History*. London: Earthscan.

Baker, E., L. Clarke, and J. Weyant (2006). "Optimal Technology R&D in the Face of Climate Uncertainty," *Climatic Change* 78: 157–79.

Barrett, S. (2005). *Environment and Statecraft: The Strategy of Environmental Treaty-Making*. Oxford: Oxford University Press (paperback edition).

(2006). "Climate Treaties and 'Breakthrough' Technologies," *American Economic Review, Papers and Proceedings* 96(2): 22–5.

(2007a). *Why Cooperate? The Incentive to Supply Global Public Goods*. Oxford: Oxford University Press.

(2007b). "A Multi-Track Climate Treaty System," in Joseph E. Aldy and Robert N. Stavins (eds.), *Architectures for Agreement: Addressing Global Climate Change in the Post-Kyoto World*. Cambridge: Cambridge University Press.

(2008a). "The Incredible Economics of Geoengineering," *Environmental and Resource Economics* 39: 45–54.

(2008b). "Climate Treaties and the Imperative of Enforcement," *Oxford Review of Economic Policy* 24(2): 239–58.

Barrett, S. and R. Stavins (2003). "Increasing Participation and Compliance in International Climate Change Agreements," *International Environmental Agreements: Politics, Law, and Economics* 3(4): 349–76.

Basu, Paroma (2009). "A Green Investment," *Nature* 457: 144–6.

Bradley, R., K. A. Baumert, B. Childs, T. Herzog, and J. Pershing (2007). *Slicing the Pie: Sector-Based Approaches to International Climate Agreements*, Washington, DC: World Resources Institute.

Cline, W. R. (2007). *Global Warming and Agriculture: Impact Estimates by Country*. Washington, DC: Peterson Institute for International Economics.

Doornbosch, R. and S. Upton (2006). "Do We Have the Right R&D Priorities and Programmes to Support the Energy Technologies of the Future?" Round Table on Sustainable Development, OECD, SG/SD/RT(2006)1.

Farrell, A. E., D. W. Keith, and J. J. Corbett (2003). "A Strategy for Introducing Hydrogen into Transportation," *Energy Policy* 31: 1357–67.

Hoel, M. (1996). "Should a Carbon Tax Be Differentiated across Sectors?" *Journal of Public Economies* 59: 17–32.

Houser, T., R. Bradley, B. Childs, J. Werksman, and R. Heilmayr (2008). *Leveling the Carbon Playing Field: International Competition and US Climate Policy Design.* Washington, DC: Peterson Institute for International Economics.

International Energy Agency (2008). *Energy Technology Perspectives In Support of the G8 Plan of Action: Scenarios and Strategies to 2050.* Paris: International Energy Agency.

Keith, D. W. (2000). "Geoengineering the Climate: History and Prospect," *Annual Review of Energy and Environment* 25: 245–84.

Mendelsohn, R., A. Dinar, and L. Williams (2006). "The Distributional Impact of Climate Change on Rich and Poor Countries," *Environment and Development Economics* 11: 159–78.

Oliveira-Martins, J., J. M. Burniaux, and J. P. Martin (1992). "Trade and the Effectiveness of Unilateral CO_2 Abatement Policies: Evidence from GREEN," *OECD Economic Studies* No. 19:123–40.

Parson, E. A. (2002). "The Technology Assessment Approach to Climate Change," *Issues in Science and Technology*, 18(4): 65-72, available at www.issues.org/18.4/parson.htm.

Patz, J. A. and S. H. Olson (2006). "Malaria Risk and Temperature: Influences from Global Climate Change and Local Land Use Practices," *Proceedings of the National Academy of Sciences* 103(15): 5635–6.

Schneider, S. H. (2008). "Geoengineering: Could We or Should We Make It Work?" *Philosophical Transactions of the Royal Society A, 366.*

Stiglitz, J. E. (2006). "A New Agenda for Global Warming," *The Economists' Voice* 3(7): Art. 3. Available at www.bepress.com/ev/vol3/iss7/art3.

Velders, G. J. M., S. O. Anderson, J. S. Daniel, D. W. Fahey, and M. McFarland (2007). "The Importance of the Montreal Protocol in Protecting Climate," *Proceedings of the National Academy of Sciences* 104: 4814–19.

Wara, M. (2007). "Is the Global Carbon Market Working?" *Nature* 445: 595–6.

Watson, C., J. Newman, S. Upton, and P. Hackmann (2005). "Can Transnational Sectoral Agreements Help Reduce Greenhouse Gas Emissions?" Round Table on Sustainable Development, OECD, SG/SD/RT(2005)1.

PART II

Negotiation, assessment, and compliance

9 | *How to negotiate and update climate agreements*[*]

BÅRD HARSTAD

Executive summary

Climate change is a dynamic problem with uncertain consequences. As we learn more about the benefits and costs of abatements over time, any agreement made today is bound to be renegotiated and updated in the future. Anticipating such negotiations, every country may try to influence its future bargaining power to be able to negotiate a more favorable deal. Increasing the bargaining power can be done by (i) investing less than optimally in R&D, (ii) adapting more to climate change than what is socially optimal, (iii) signaling reluctance by delay, or (iv) delegating bargaining authority to representatives that are less in favor of an agreement. Such strategic behavior makes an efficient agreement less likely. In fact, the situation with an agreement can be worse than a situation without any agreement at all. Thus, it is immensely important to determine in advance the rules governing how the countries should negotiate and update future climate change agreements.

This chapter presents and discusses five such rules. First, the negotiations may be more efficient, and less strategic, if harmonization of contribution-levels is required across countries, or if the contribution-shares are pre-determined by some formula that itself is not subject to renegotiation. Second, the time horizon of an agreement should be long enough to prevent the above-mentioned strategies from being too influential. The larger the number of participants, the longer the time horizon should be. Third, the default (the outcome to which one reverts if the negotiations fail) should be the previous agreement or,

[*] I am grateful to the participants at the 2008 workshop of the Harvard Project on International Climate Agreements, in particular the detailed comments by Joe Aldy and an anonymous referee. This chapter does not contain original theoretical results, but draws on several papers that are (or may become) published elsewhere.

even better, a very ambitious agreement. This provides an efficient starting point from which one may renegotiate the agreement. Fourth, the unanimity requirement should be replaced by majority rules (or supermajority rules) when it comes to updating the agreement. Fifth, a minimum participation requirement should specify the lowest number of countries that has to ratify the treaty before it becomes binding to anyone. Each rule can be employed even if the other rules are not. In fact, the rules are "strategic substitutes" in the sense that each of them is more important if the other rules are *not* implemented. For example, it is more important to subsidize trade in abatement technology if the time horizon of the agreement is short. The rules can also be modified and used to regulate the entry of new participants.

While each of these rules may help in mitigating the hold-up problems described above, they may fail to be credible if countries are tempted to opt out of the agreement. Such exits are less likely to be attractive if the climate change treaty is bundled with a trade agreement, and the threat to exit is then less likely to be credible. Thus, linking trade and environmental agreements complements all the rules above. In addition, bundling trade and environmental agreements makes it possible to sanction non-compliance in a credible way.

Introduction

As a dynamic problem, climate change requires a dynamic solution. The future is uncertain and today we know neither the costs nor the benefits of reducing emissions in the future. Therefore, we cannot and should not hope for an "evergreen" agreement that specifies commitments for all future dates. Instead, we must accept that any agreement will need to be updated and renegotiated later on, and perhaps eventually be completely replaced.

At the same time, the outcome of a bargaining game depends on the bargaining rules. Anyone hoping for good environmental agreements should thus pay attention to the rules governing the negotiation process.

There are several rules and norms that govern international negotiations. Some of these are informal, like the norm against threatening an opponent with war unless a trade agreement is signed. Other rules are explicit, like the voting rules in the United Nations (UN): important decisions require a two-third majority, while other decisions require only a simple majority. Multilateral trade negotiations take place under the "reciprocity" and "most favored nation" principles of the World Trade Organization (WTO) (Bagwell and Staiger 2003).

Do we need rules for negotiating and updating climate agreements? Without rules, the outcome will be determined by countries' relative bargaining powers. A country is likely to have more bargaining power, and be a tougher negotiator, if it is reluctant to join a climate agreement and this is publicly known. To improve its bargaining position, a country may thus be tempted to signal reluctance by, for example, delaying negotiations or repeatedly rejecting other countries' proposals. Countries may also want to appoint negotiators that are recognized as being ambivalent about or even opposed to climate treaties. More importantly, national governments may think twice before investing heavily in abatement technology when climate negotiations are coming up in the near future. A superior technology can easily become a liability if other parties to the negotiation use it to argue that the high-tech country should be required to bear the lion's share of the burden. By not investing in technology, on the other hand, a country faces larger costs when entering a climate agreement and it may expect to be partly compensated for these costs. Underinvestment in abatement technologies is thus one of the big costs associated with international negotiations.

The purpose of this chapter is, first, to better explain these costs of negotiation. Second, the chapter suggests and discusses five bargaining rules. Each rule can help to reduce bargaining costs and induce countries to invest more in abatement technology. It may be necessary to commit to the rules by letting the climate agreement specify the procedure for future negotiations. The suggested rules are "strategic substitutes," meaning that each rule becomes more important to implement if the other rules are not implemented. I also discuss linkages to trade agreements. It turns out that linking to trade agreements can complement the proposed rules, making each of them more effective and credible.

The first rule is to require some kind of harmonization of policies or use formulas when deriving country-specific abatement commitments. Under this rule, it is hard for a country to exploit its bargaining position, and countries cannot be held up and required to contribute more simply because they have already paid the price of investing in abatement technologies. With agreement on the use of formulas, therefore, countries are likely to invest more in R&D.

The second rule is to aim for a long time horizon. If the time horizon is short, frequent negotiations are necessary and investing in bargaining power becomes important. To motivate countries to instead invest in abatement technology, it is thus crucial that the time horizon of each commitment period be long.

The third rule concerns the outcome if future negotiations should fail. Notice that if current climate negotiations fail, the outcome is no agreement at all, since existing emission commitments are set to expire. By contrast, when international trade negotiations fail, the outcome is that the previous set of trade agreements remains in force, not that there is *no* agreement. This is, as argued below, a much more efficient default outcome. Future climate negotiations should also revert to an existing or pre-specified agreement if they fail to be updated in negotiations.

Fourth, when updating future climate agreements, the unanimity requirement should be relaxed, since it gives the most reluctant countries a disproportionate amount of bargaining power.

I also discuss minimum participation rules and how they may govern the exit and entry of participants.

The relationship to trade agreements is relevant for two distinct reasons. First, a weak system for the international protection of intellectual property rights (patents) contributes to the underinvestment problem. Not only should patents on abatement technology be enforced to encourage innovations, but tariffs on trade in such technologies should be eliminated and replaced by subsidies to induce countries to invest more. Such policies are particularly important if the suggested rules are not followed, since then underinvestment in R&D is likely to be even more severe. R&D should be subsidized more for short-term agreements than for long-term agreements, for example.

The main problem with the suggested rules is that countries may be tempted to opt out of an agreement if the rules are strictly followed (e.g., if contributions are dictated by a formula, the time horizon is very long, or unanimity is not required). This threat makes each of the rules less likely to be credible and effective. To make the rules work, therefore, it is important to reduce the temptation to opt out. This can be done by linking participation in a climate agreement to the benefit of getting most favored nation status in international trade. Despite the obvious drawbacks, such a linkage may be necessary to encourage participation and compliance.

To simplify the discussion in this chapter, I am abstracting from firms and private investors. The private sector is, of course, going to be pivotal for the effectiveness of an agreement, and it is the private sector that for the most part is going to invest in abatement technology. However, each firm is relatively small compared to the size of a country, and thus firms may not think strategically about how their actions can affect their home country's bargaining power. On the other hand, firms do respond to rules, regulations, and incentives provided by the government. Using such instruments, governments can influence firms' choices to a large degree, and governments are, in contrast to individual firms, generally concerned with their future bargaining power. For simplicity, therefore, I will often say that *government* decides the level of investment in abatement technology, even though it may be the private sector that implements these investments in practice.

The next section argues that any agreement will need to be renegotiated, or updated, over time. The problem is that without any rules governing this process, a new or revised agreement can be worse than no agreement at all. Motivated by this claim, the third section of this chapter discusses the use of formulas to structure negotiations, the optimal time horizon of agreements, the best default outcome, the voting rule, and minimum participation requirements. I also discuss how these rules can be modified to regulate the entry of new participants and how a link to trade agreements would complement each of these rules.

Do we need rules for negotiating and updating treaties?

Why update in the first place?

Current commitments under the Kyoto Protocol expire in 2012, and subsequent commitments have yet to be negotiated. The form of a future agreement has not been specified, though several proposals have been made. Most of these proposals have a limited time horizon, and no serious proposal suggests commitments that will remain unchanged forever. Thus, we can expect climate negotiations to continue to take place more or less frequently in the future.

Is such updating necessary? Could we instead make an agreement that is "evergreen," specifying commitments for all future periods, such that no further negotiations are needed later? There are several reasons why updating agreements over time is both beneficial and necessary.

First, technology changes over time. Most likely, it is going to be cheaper to abate in the future than it is today. If so, the optimal abatement level should increase. If an emission tax is used, it should decline over time.[1] But the future abatement level (or tax) cannot be specified today, since we do not yet know how much better the new technology is going to be or what it will cost.

Second, the social cost of climate change is highly uncertain. The Intergovernmental Panel on Climate Change (IPCC, 2007) presents a variety of scenarios for how much global average temperature may increase, and each is associated with very uncertain social costs. Thus, we are most likely going to learn what actual costs will be only gradually and over time. Several decades from now, it may turn out that modern agriculture can easily adapt to a new climate, or we may instead realize that important ecosystems are going to collapse unless we reduce emissions drastically. Then, and not before, is the best time to determine future emission levels. If the problem becomes more severe over time, then abatement levels should increase, and, if an emission tax is used, the level of the tax should rise. But the future optimal abatement level (or the tax) cannot be specified in advance, since the social cost is still to be learned.

Third, differences between countries may change over time. If a country discovers large coal reserves, or anticipates rapid economic growth, it may no longer be satisfied with the emissions quota or share assigned to it. Even if a country could purchase more emission permits to meet its new demand, it may be tempted to instead exit the entire agreement. To prevent this, agreements may need to be renegotiated, or updated.

Ideally, an agreement could be updated "automatically," in that future commitments could be a specified function of technology levels, the social cost of climate change, and the preferences of different countries. However, these parameters are going to be hard to measure and verify, so "automatic" updating may not be enough. Notice that the need to renegotiate and update exists no matter the choice of policy instrument (quotas, tradable permits, or emission taxes) used to implement the agreement—though, as discussed in the Appendix,

---

[1] The Appendix discusses these arguments in detail.

certain policy instruments may need to be updated more frequently than others.

Given the necessity to update, it is surprising that basically no proposal or analysis of climate agreements addresses *how* commitments are to be negotiated or updated in the future.[2] This is a severe flaw, since it is certainly possible to let a treaty specify the rules that will govern future decisions. As argued in the next subsection, if no rules govern the future bargaining and updating process, the outcome can be detrimental to everyone. The following sections discuss five rules that can mitigate these problems.

The costs of bargaining

Suppose every country expects that at some point in the future, countries will be getting together to negotiate. They may then negotiate a new agreement, or they may renegotiate an existing agreement. Suppose, further, that no rules are in place to structure these negotiations. Then, the bargaining outcome is going to be determined by the relative bargaining powers of the countries. But what, in turn, determines the distribution of bargaining power?

In negotiations, bargaining power typically depends on how eager or "keen" a country is to arrive at agreement. The more eager a country is, the more it is willing to "pay" to get an agreement finalized. And, the more it is willing to pay, the more other countries will *require* it to pay—in this case by making a larger contribution to total abatement. Thus, a country is in a bad bargaining position if it has a lot to gain from completing the agreement, or if it has a lot to lose should negotiations fail. Such countries can expect to bear the lion's share of the abatement burden. These predictions are in line with standard bargaining theory (going back to Nash 1950 and Rubinstein 1982), and they explain why Russia, which may in fact benefit from global warming, ended up with emissions targets that exceeded its historical emissions levels under the Kyoto agreement. Europe, fearing that climate change could cause a catastrophic change in vital ocean circulation patterns, ended up bearing a relatively large share of the burden. The fact that Europe could better afford abatement further contributed to this outcome.

---

[2] Schelling (2007) addresses this problem. For an overview of alternative proposals, see Aldy, Barrett and Stavins (2003) or Aldy and Stavins (2007).

Anticipating international negotiations, a country may want to keep an eye on how its bargaining power can be affected by domestic policies. In fact, concern about future bargaining power may induce countries to distort their domestic policies in several ways.

Underinvestment in R&D

Technologies that can reduce abatement costs are obviously beneficial once an agreement is signed and more stringent emissions limits take effect. However, possessing superior technologies also makes it tempting for other countries to "hold up" the high-tech country, which already has paid much of the costs associated with abatement, and require that country to take a leading role in the collective agreement. This is possible if the high-tech country agrees to undertake more domestic abatement than other countries, or if it lends its technology cheaply to the others. This creates a "hold-up problem" that may give countries second thoughts before investing heavily in R&D, particularly if negotiations are around the corner. Thus, countries may invest less in abatement technology if they anticipate future international negotiations than if they do not. This reasoning draws on Harstad (2009), where a formal analysis shows that such strategic considerations can be immensely costly relative to the value of environmental agreements. Such costs may in fact outweigh the gains from an agreement itself, making it better to have no agreement at all.

Overinvestment in adaptation

If, after serious investments in agriculture and infrastructure, a country is in a position to adapt successfully to climate change, then no one can expect that country to be willing to pay a lot to avoid climate change. Such a country will be able to arrive at a good deal without costly abatement commitments at home. Hence, to increase its bargaining power ahead of international negotiations, a country may end up investing *too much* in adaptation (as opposed to mitigation). These predictions are, again, in line with standard bargaining theory.

Delay and reluctance in negotiations

A third way of gaining bargaining power exists if one country's valuation of the costs and benefits of reaching agreement is only vaguely known to the negotiators representing other countries. In this context, a country's representative may want to pretend that she places a low value on reaching agreement, or that the cost to her country of implementing an agreement is high. If this can be signaled credibly, other participants will understand that they may need to offer the country a better deal to ensure it agrees. Countries can signal reluctance by delaying before making serious offers or by proposing a less ambitious agreement (Harstad 2007). If emission permits are tradable, countries (or firms) may want to purchase more than they actually need, to signal that they deserve a larger allocation in the future (Harstad and Eskeland 2008). These incentives to signal reluctance may lead to a less ambitious agreement than what is optimal or, in the worst case, may result in no agreement at all.

Strategic delegation

A related strategy is to strategically appoint the individual who will represent the country in international negotiations (Schelling 1956). If this representative is well-known to be less concerned with climate change, she may be a tougher negotiator and capable of landing a deal under which the country contributes less than it would otherwise. Obviously, if every country acts this way, the round table of reluctant representatives will be unlikely to set ambitious collective goals, and the citizens in every country may be worse off.

To summarize, a country can increase its bargaining power by investing relatively little in abatement technology; by undertaking substantial adaptation to climate change; by pretending to be reluctant to join an agreement; or by appointing a representative who is personally reluctant to reach agreement. These strategies have in common that they are intended to improve a country's bargaining position; the problem is that they can both distort domestic policies and make an efficient international agreement less likely. This outcome is potentially worse than if there were no agreement at all. It is therefore immensely important to think hard about rules that could govern the bargaining game and mitigate these strategic effects.

Rules for negotiating and updating treaties

This section discusses several rules, each of which has the potential to mitigate the inefficiencies described above. The rules are independent in the sense that one rule can be employed even if the others are not.

In fact, the rules are "strategic substitutes," meaning that each rule is *more important* to implement if the other rules are *not* implemented.

This chapter recommends that nations commit to one or more of these rules before future climate treaties are negotiated, renegotiated, or updated. Such a commitment may be included in the rules of the treaty itself. As discussed in a later section, however, the danger is that countries may later be tempted to opt out or exit the treaty unless the rule is abandoned. This can make it necessary to complement the bargaining rules discussed below with certain linkages to trade agreements.

Harmonization and formulas

Bargaining costs arise when countries seek to improve their bargaining power to get a better deal. This can be avoided, however, if it is required that treaty obligations or the allocation of burdens be distributed according to a particular formula. Trade negotiations, for example, typically apply various formulas along with a requirement that each country's tariff reduction should be of the same magnitude when the formula is applied. To take an environmental example, the initial goal in the Kyoto negotiations was that every developed country should reduce its emissions by the same fraction relative to a 1990 baseline. This formula is similar to a requirement that policies should be "uniform" or "harmonized" across various countries. If such formulas pin down the contribution or share of my country, there is no point in strategically distorting domestic policies to gain bargaining power. In particular, if my opponents cannot require high-tech countries to contribute more, the hold-up problem vanishes and I dare to invest more in R&D.

Where bargaining costs result from delay and asymmetric information, the reasoning is quite similar. If there is no harmonization requirement, every country may try to signal to the others that it attaches a low value, or a high cost, to participating in the treaty (Harstad 2007). After learning of this reluctance, other participants are likelier to give in and offer the country a better deal with less costly obligations. Anticipating this dynamic, every country may want to pretend that it is not *that* interested in agreement, and may try to signal this reluctance by seeking delay or by proposing inefficient agreements. On the other hand, if policy harmonization is required, countries need only negotiate over how ambitious the common policy should be. In that case, it is less rewarding to signal bargaining power, and negotiations will proceed in a much more effective manner—that is, with less delay and signaling of reluctance—than if uniformity and harmonization were not required. A similar argument holds if permits are tradable (Harstad and Eskeland 2008) and if representatives are strategically appointed (Harstad 2008a).

The disadvantage of harmonization is, of course, that countries are heterogeneous and have different needs. If the heterogeneity is large, the cost of imposing uniformity is likely to dominate the gains associated with a more efficient negotiation process (Hoel 1992; Alesina, Angeloni and Etro 2005). However, the benefits of harmonization can be exploited without requiring completely uniform policies. If it is efficient (or fair) that developed countries contribute more than less developed ones, this could be captured by a well-designed formula, stating that rich countries should reduce emission levels by twice as much as developing ones, for example. The formula could also build in automatic responses, such as assigning emission-reduction obligations on the basis of countries' wealth (GDP), economic growth, or energy consumption. Then, the formula could automatically distribute—and redistribute—abatement burdens over time in a way that is considered to be efficient or fair. In this case, it would still be hard for a country to influence its individual burden by investing in bargaining power, so domestic policies are not likely to be very distorted by strategic considerations. Such formulas are further discussed by Frankel (2007, 2008).

As mentioned at the start of this section, it is important that the formula for distributing burdens is specified and committed to (by inclusion in the treaty) before it is applied in the negotiations. Otherwise, the choice of formula will itself be subject to negotiations, and countries will, in anticipation, distort domestic policies to get a better bargaining position.

A longer time horizon

The emission commitments of the Kyoto Protocol took effect in 2008 and expire in 2012—thus, they had a time span of only five years. As argued above, it is neither desirable nor feasible that a fixed set of commitment levels remains in place forever. How long should commitments under an international climate agreement last?

The arguments above pull in opposing directions. On the one hand, I have argued that because the future is uncertain, with aggregate and country-specific preferences and shocks that are realized only gradually over time, any agreement should be updated periodically. This may be easiest to do if an agreement is set to expire, making it natural to negotiate a successor. On the other hand, I have also argued that frequent negotiations tend to distort countries' strategic policies, since getting a better bargaining position then becomes relatively more important for each country. The more frequently an agreement is renegotiated, or the shorter its time horizon, the more domestic policies become distorted. This implies, for example, that countries are going to invest less in abatement technologies if an agreement is short-lived. To mitigate this problem, agreements should last longer.

The choice of time horizon should balance these two concerns. For example, if the future is highly uncertain, the first argument dominates and the time horizon should be shorter. If investment in R&D and technology development is perceived to be crucial, the second argument dominates and the optimal time horizon is longer. The optimal time horizon may also depend on other aspects of the situation. For a detailed analysis, see Harstad (2009), Frankel (2007) and Guriev and Kvasov (2005).

The choice of a time horizon is also related to the number of countries that participate. If every single country is participating, the optimal time horizon should be long, to make it harder for countries to opt out at the next turning point and to mitigate the hold-up problem described previously. If, instead, only a few countries participate, the time horizon should be shorter to facilitate the entry of new participants. If a country is one of only a few participants, then it may be motivated to invest in R&D by the possibility that, with new and better technology, outsiders may find it worthwhile to enter the agreement later on. So, where participation is limited, a short time horizon may increase incentives for investment in R&D.

There is also a reverse causality to be considered in the sense that a pre-specified time horizon may affect the number of participants. Suppose that every potential participant realizes that if only a few countries show up, the agreement is going to be short-term, just as recommended and predicted above. This fact makes it less tempting to opt out: with a shorter time horizon, the hold-up problem is large, and it will not take long before every country is called upon to participate once again. By coming to the negotiation table immediately, the time horizon may end up being longer, solving the underinvestment problem and leading to a more efficient agreement.

This effect can be further exploited when designing a climate treaty. If the time horizon of the treaty is a fixed, increasing function of the number of participants, countries are motivated to participate not only to reduce pollution, but also to reduce the future costs of bargaining. For this reason, it may be wise to commit to such a rule in advance, making clear to everyone that increased participation will be rewarded and will result in a more efficient agreement.

What if negotiations fail?

It happens again and again: international negotiations do break down. The effect of a break-down varies, however. When the Doha-round trade negotiations appeared to break down in July 2008, the outcome was simply the continuation of an existing set of trade agreements. If, instead, current international climate-change negotiations break down, the outcome is going to be no agreement at all, since the Kyoto Protocol commitments are set to expire. Thus, the "default outcomes" for the two bargaining games are quite different.

Is the default outcome of importance even if negotiations succeed? Yes—because it determines the allocation of bargaining power. The explanation relates to the reasoning outlined previously. If current climate negotiations break down, a country that has poor abatement options has less to lose since it would, in any case, find it quite costly to implement its obligations. And, as discussed above, a country that is comfortable with the status quo ("status-quo-biased") has a better bargaining position. If, instead, the default outcome were today's commitment levels, a participating low-tech country would not necessarily be in a better bargaining position, since it would still face costly abatement obligations, whether or not current negotiations succeed. Thus, if the default outcome is the continuation of existing agreements, instead of no agreement at all, a country cannot increase its bargaining power simply by investing relatively little in R&D. Similarly, investments in climate-change adaptation will not boost a country's bargaining power, because adaptation does not make a country relatively better prepared for a default outcome that consists of returning to the previous agreement (instead of no agreement at all).

This argument suggests that the default outcome should be the continuation of previous agreements, rather than no agreement at all. The policy recommendation is thus to update agreements by renegotiating them, not by letting them expire and negotiating a new agreement from scratch. This approach has worked well for international trade agreements, and is likely to work for climate agreements also.

What is the very best default outcome? This question is studied in the literature on "renegotiation design" (see e.g. Aghion, Dewatripont and Rey 1994). For climate politics, Harstad (2009) shows that the ideal default outcome is a very ambitious agreement. Then, countries are likely to renegotiate the agreement towards a weaker set of commitments. In this bargaining game, it is the low-tech countries that are most eager to reach agreement, since they would find it very costly to comply under the default outcome. Thus, the high-tech countries are in a better bargaining position, and can expect to have the upper hand when negotiating a new, more reasonable, agreement. Under these conditions, a country that is concerned with its future bargaining position should invest *more* in R&D, not less. These investments are going to be larger the more ambitious the default agreement is. Since investments in R&D should, from a social point of view, be larger if there are large spillovers between countries, the default agreement should be more ambitious if international patent protections are imperfect (Harstad 2009).

The optimal default outcome for a climate treaty is also related to its time horizon, as discussed above. If the time horizon is short, the countries will be particularly eager to distort their policies in order to gain bargaining power. It is then especially important that the default outcome is ambitious.

Majority rules

Unanimity is typically required for the implementation of international treaties. Trade treaties, for example, are often stymied by just a couple of countries that resist the external pressure to reach agreement. At first sight, the unanimity requirement is fairly natural, and perhaps inevitable when it comes to international cooperation, since there is no third party (or world government) that could coerce sovereign countries to implement decisions they do not like. On the other hand, unanimity is by no means *always* required for international decisions.

The UN applies majority rules for several types of decisions. The EU has, over time, replaced the unanimity requirement with majority rules for more and more types of decisions (Nugent 2003). Hence, it is not at all obvious that every agreement should be approved unanimously, particularly not when it comes to *modifying* or *updating* existing agreements. Countries may agree unanimously today that decisions in the future should be made according to weaker majority requirements. In fact, the Kyoto Protocol (Article 20) explicitly states that amendments can be adopted by a three-fourths majority vote.

It is the unanimity requirement that creates the bargaining costs discussed above. As argued previously, each country may try to influence its future bargaining power by (1) investing little in R&D, (2) focusing more on adaptation, (3) signaling reluctance to join a climate agreement, or (4) strategically delegating negotiation decisions to status-quo-biased representatives. These strategies enhance a country's bargaining power when every vote is needed for the treaty to be implemented, setting up the expectation that countries reluctant to join the agreement will be somehow compensated by those that desire agreement more. On the other hand, if unanimity were not required, this strategy would not work. A yes-vote from the most reluctant country would not be necessary, and it would be easier to get the necessary votes from less reluctant countries. The countries that have the least to gain from an agreement would thus be excluded from the "majority coalition"—the group of countries that get together in an attempt to pass the proposal.[3] Underinvesting in R&D then becomes a risky strategy: it may be wiser for a country to invest more to ensure that its vote and voice are taken seriously when a majority coalition forms among the most enthusiastic countries or representatives. Using a formal model, Harstad (2005) shows it is better to be part of the majority coalition when the majority required to reach agreement is small, because then majority parties do not have to compensate all the "losers." This in turn creates incentives for a country to invest more in R&D in preparing for the collective project, in hopes that it will not be excluded from the majority coalition. If the majority requirement is small enough, countries will invest the socially optimal amount.

For similar reasons, relaxing the unanimity requirement is also helpful when countries strategically appoint their representatives to

---

[3] This is a well-known result from e.g. Ferejohn, Fiorina and McKelvey (1987).

improve their bargaining position (Harstad 2008b). Schelling (1956) suggested that, in a situation where unanimity is required, it may be wise for a country to appoint a status-quo-biased representative (less worried about climate change), since such a tough negotiator will enhance the country's bargaining power. If all countries appoint reluctant negotiators, the resulting agreement, if any, will certainly not be very ambitious (Buchholtz, Haupt and Peters 2005). If the majority requirement is smaller, however, a reluctant delegate may be excluded from the majority coalition, and it may be wiser to appoint a representative that is somewhat more enthusiastic about the project, since she is going to have a greater chance of playing an important role in the majority coalition.

Note that using majority rule, instead of requiring unanimity, is a *strategic substitute* to the other rules above: it is particularly important to encourage R&D by reducing the majority requirement if the agreement otherwise would lead to underinvestment in R&D. This is the case, as already noticed, if (1) no formulas (or harmonization) are required, (2) the time horizon is short, and (3) the default outcome is no agreement at all. Thus, while a long-term agreement may do fine with a unanimity requirement, short-term agreements should relax this requirement.

Minimum participation rules

A minimum participation rule specifies how many countries have to ratify a treaty before it becomes binding on anyone. If the number of countries that end up ratifying the treaty is larger than the minimum, then the agreement enters into force; if not, no one needs to comply. Most environmental agreements do have a minimum participation rule, although the specified threshold varies quite a lot (Barrett, 2005). The Kyoto Protocol, for example, entered into force only if 55 percent of the countries, responsible for 55 percent of total CO_2 emissions, ratified the treaty.

There are two main rationales for including a minimum participation rule in an environmental treaty. First, it may serve as a coordination device. It may simply not be worthwhile for only a few countries to implement policies that are radically different from those of other countries. Developing and introducing new technologies, for example, may require substantial expenditures that are independent of the number of countries that end up using the technologies, and this may be worthwhile only if the number of participants is sufficiently large. A minimum participation rule could then work as a form of insurance for countries that fear to bear these costs alone. The use of minimum participation rules as a coordination device is further discussed by Barrett (2005).

Another rationale for adopting minimum participation rules is to discourage free riding (Carraro, Marchiori and Oreffice 2004; Harstad 2006). If a country realizes that unless it ratifies a treaty domestically, other countries are not committed either, it becomes impossible to free ride on other countries' participation. Thus, the minimum participation rule can make each potential member pivotal for an agreement to enter into force. This was the situation for Russia when it contemplated whether to ratify the Kyoto Protocol. If it were not to have signed, too few countries would have ratified, and the Protocol's emission commitments would not have been binding for anyone.

What should the minimum participation requirement be? The trade-off is the following: if the requirement is small, the outcome may be that only a small number of countries end up participating, since the agreement will then enter into force even if other countries decide to free ride. On the other hand, it is very likely that such an agreement will enter into force for at least some countries. If the participation requirement is too large, the problem could be that this threshold may not be possible to reach and, consequently, the agreement will not end up being binding on anyone. Clearly, this possibility is less likely if potential members find the agreement very attractive for various reasons. For example, if only ratifying countries can obtain favorable trading partner status, participation would be more attractive and the minimum participation rule could be larger.

Rules for entry and exit

The rules above can govern not only how an agreement should be negotiated or updated, but can also govern "collective" decisions related to the entry of new participants and the exit of current participants. For example, should entry of new participants be allowed at any point in time, or only at points in time when the current agreement expires or must be updated? The question may sound trivial: a first guess is that one should clearly welcome new participants at any point in time. It is certainly better for the existing participants if more countries choose to contribute to abatement efforts. This appreciation for new participants is also, of course, going to be reflected when the potential entrant negotiates its entry conditions. Since every existing member welcomes new members and the default outcome (if negotiations fail) is likely going to be the continuation of the current agreement, new entrants are in a great bargaining position and may realize that they can manage to negotiate quite attractive entry conditions. In fact, entry conditions for a new participant may be much better than if participation had been negotiated at the point in time when other countries first signed the agreement, since at that time the default outcome would not asymmetrically favor the current entrant. Hence, an individual country, instead of signing initially, may be better off waiting until a later point in time before negotiating its entry. Thus, anticipating easy entry later on makes it tempting not to enter at the initial negotiation stage. How can this kind of free riding be prevented? It may help to apply the rules discussed above.

Suppose the time horizon of the treaty defines the points in time at which entry is possible. If the time horizon is long and a country cannot expect to enter at any earlier point in time, that country may think twice before opting out at the initial bargaining stage. The default outcome is also important: if all parties revert to the existing agreement if negotiations with a potential entrant fail, then the potential entrant is in a good bargaining position, since the default outcome for that country is quite attractive as well. In this case, the entrant is likely to get a good deal in the bargaining process, and postponing its entry is indeed going to prove worthwhile. If instead the default outcome is no agreement at all, a new entrant may be willing to contribute more to ensure that negotiations succeed; it may then not end up with a better deal than if it had chosen to participate from the outset. If unanimity is required for a new entrant to be able to participate, the full set of participants is going to require more from the entrant than if only a majority were enough to allow entry. Thus, if only a small majority is required to permit new members to enter, it is more attractive to enter later. Finally, if harmonization is required, or a formula is used, the conditions for entry are not negotiable. In this case, there is no point to postponing participation.

To summarize, the new potential entrant has low bargaining power if it can enter only at certain (infrequent) points in time; if the default is no agreement at all rather than the existing agreement; if every participant can veto a potential entry; and if a specified formula determines all contribution levels. In these cases, countries may not benefit much (if at all) by postponing their entry into the agreement. The drawback of these rules, however, is that late entry is less desirable—thus, a country may not be willing to enter later if, for some reason, it did not enter at the very first stage.

It may be less relevant to define the rules for exit. In international politics, nothing may prevent a sovereign country from leaving an agreement at any point in time, should it desire to do so. Moreover, a country may be more tempted to opt out if the time horizon is long (and the agreement cannot be updated to meet countries' new demands); if the default is an ambitious agreement; if a decision was taken by a majority and not consensus; and if a formula is used (particularly if harmonization is required). Hence, each of the rules recommended above makes it more likely that someone will be tempted to exit the agreement. For this reason, it is immensely important to find ways to discourage exit and make participation more attractive.

Linkages to trade agreements

Should environmental agreements be linked to trade agreements? This is a controversial issue. Exchanging favors to overcome differences on political issues is often known as horse-trading, logrolling, or bundling agreements. This process can be perceived negatively as a way of opening the door to threats, hold-ups, or even corruption—or it can be viewed positively as an opportunity to share favors and inject efficiency-enhancing "oil in the negotiation machinery." There are several possible types of linkages, and there are a number of arguments for and against each of them. This section discusses three possibilities and relates them to the discussion above.

Enforcing patents and subsidizing technology

Since a major cost of anticipating negotiations is that countries under-invest in R&D, it is important to encourage such investments directly. One way of doing this is to enforce intellectual property rights: if other countries must pay the innovator to learn and benefit from potential technological spillovers, the innovator is rewarded—anticipating this, every country invests more in R&D. Furthermore, it may be possible to subsidize R&D investments directly. Clearly, this must be done at the international level, since each national government probably does not perceive its own chosen investment level as being too low. A difficulty with such subsidies is that it may be hard to verify domestic investment levels and thus how much a country should be granted in subsidies. However, if a country did in fact invest a lot, it may end up exporting abatement technology to other countries, and these export flows are simpler to measure and verify. By subsidizing trade in abatement technology, one may be able to encourage R&D. To be specific, all countries may benefit by collectively removing tariffs and adding subsidies on low-carbon technologies, such as solar panels, while at the same time enforcing intellectual property rights for such technologies. This would make it more attractive to develop new technology, since one can expect a better price when selling the resulting products to other countries. To some extent, therefore, such subsidies mitigate the underinvestment problem emphasized previously. The underinvestment problem is particularly severe if the rules I have recommended are not followed—that is, if (1) harmonization is not required, (2) the time horizon is short, (3) the default outcome is no agreement at all, and (4) unanimity is required. In these circumstances, it is particularly important to enforce intellectual property rights, eliminate tariffs on trade in abatement technology, and subsidize such trade or subsidize R&D investments directly. In other words, these policies are "strategic substitutes" to the rules discussed in the foregoing section.

Trade linkages and participation

The most straightforward type of linkage may be "joint membership"—if you sign here, I sign there. In other words, a country may be allowed to participate in a certain trade agreement (or in a certain free-trade area) only if it also participates in a particular climate-change agreement. This would make it more costly to not participate in the latter, and would thus tend to increase the number of signatories. As is well-known, Russia's ratification of the Kyoto Protocol was not unrelated to its entry into the WTO and the EU's support for this. The disadvantage of bundling trade and environmental agreements is, of course, that countries that nevertheless choose to opt out of a climate agreement are going to be subject to distorted and socially costly trade barriers. Undermining international trade could then be an additional and costly price for a failed climate agreement.

On the other hand, linking trade and environmental agreements makes it less attractive to opt out of an existing climate agreement (Carraro and Marchiori 2004; Cesar and de Zeeuw 1996). This is important, since increasing the temptation to opt out is the main drawback of enforcing any of the rules described previously. If uniformity is required, or if the treaty uses formulas to specify a certain distribution of the costs, individual countries may threaten to exit (Hoel, 1992). No matter how complicated the formula, it may be unable to accommodate a country's sudden need for a higher (less stringent) emissions quota. If other participants insist, in such a situation, that the formula be applied nevertheless, the country that is affected by the shock may credibly threaten to exit the entire agreement. If, instead, other participants give in by offering a better deal to the affected country, the formula becomes less effective and, because countries anticipate future exceptions, has less value as a mechanism for discouraging individual countries from focusing on their relative bargaining positions.[4] Relatedly, with a long time horizon, certain countries may eventually find the agreement unattractive, unless it can be renegotiated, and they may threaten to opt out. If the default outcome is an ambitious agreement, it may be that countries—seeking to renegotiate—would rather opt out than participate in the default agreement. The *effective* default, in this case, might be the current agreement minus the country that is leaving the agreement. Or, if the exit of one participant causes everything to unravel, it may be no agreement at all. Thus, the problem with an ambitious default agreement is that countries may prefer to opt out, making the default outcome less credible. Relaxing the unanimity requirement may also induce countries to opt out. Suppose the United States, for example, casts its vote against a proposed update of an existing climate agreement. Is it reasonable to think that the other participants can nevertheless force the United States to ratify the modification? If the modification is perceived to be major, the United States may threaten

---

[4] This second route was taken in the negotiation of Kyoto commitments, where several countries ended up being exempted and the target for industrialized countries varied between –8 percent and +10 percent of the 1990 emission levels.

to leave the agreement entirely should the update be adopted. If such a threat were credible, unanimity is in effect required for the update to take place, no matter the requirement formally specified by the treaty (Maggi and Morelli 2006).

For all of these proposed rules to work, it is thus crucial to reduce the temptation to opt out. If participation is more attractive because it is linked to trade agreements, the rules discussed above are more likely to be credible. In that case, exemptions from specified formulas may not be necessary to induce participation; the time horizon can be long without fear that countries will opt out part-way; negotiating countries may take seriously an ambitious default agreement; countries may obey collective decisions even if they are not unanimous; and the minimum participation requirement can be large and still be met. In short, linking participation in a climate treaty to trade agreements complements the rules discussed above, making each of them more credible and effective. Without such linkages, the rules above might be impossible to use, and the drive for bargaining power could undermine the value of climate agreements.

Trade sanctions and compliance

Before closing, it is worth mentioning another advantage of bundling trade and environmental agreements. One issue largely overlooked in this chapter is compliance. After an agreement is signed, it may be tempting for a country to break its promises, particularly if the consequences of doing so are negligible. Indeed, the consequences for non-compliance are likely to be small, since, as mentioned already, no third party is in a position to enforce agreements signed by sovereign countries. One may at best try to impose some ad hoc sanctions on those not complying. Under the Kyoto Protocol, for example, a country that fails to comply in the first commitment period is required to make up the difference plus an additional 30 percent. However, such a rule only delays the compliance problem; for what prevents a country from failing to comply with the penalty as well as with the original obligation? Ultimately, the sanctions for non-compliance must be more credible than they were in the case of Kyoto. In international politics, relatively few sanctions are available. Fortunately, trade sanctions have already proved effective in motivating countries to comply with trade commitments, at least to some degree. Trade sanctions could similarly be used to threaten countries that fail to comply with environmental treaties (Barrett 1997). Certain environmental agreements, like the Montreal Protocol, do indeed refer to such sanctions. Trade sanctions may, in the end, be the only way of ensuring that ambitious environmental commitments are worth complying with—even after the deal is signed.

Conclusions

Climate change agreements should and will be updated over time. If no rules govern this negotiation process, bargaining power is crucial, and countries are induced to under-invest in R&D, overinvest in adaptation, signal reluctance to participate, or appoint representatives that are known to be reluctant to participate in climate agreements. These strategies create costs associated with the negotiation process—costs that can potentially be larger than the benefits of reaching an agreement in the first place. The lesson from this is *not* that agreements should not be negotiated, but that one should pay attention to the *rules* governing the negotiation process.

This chapter has discussed five such rules. Requiring harmonization or applying certain formulas for allocating commitments under an agreement is one way of improving the bargaining game. If a formula is used to determine the distribution of emission quotas, it is hard for an individual country to affect its share of the burden, and strategic concerns are not likely to be very detrimental. Harmonization obviously imposes its own costs if countries are heterogeneous, but formulas can be cleverly designed (to depend on GDP and growth, for example) to mitigate these costs.

Rule number two is that a treaty should have a long time horizon. This reduces the frequency with which the agreement needs to be renegotiated and means that countries' strategic motives are less distortionary. The time horizon should also be longer if a larger number of countries are participating in the agreement.

The third rule concerns the default outcome: what should happen if (re)negotiations fail? If the default outcome in this case is a return to the previous agreement (as is generally true for trade agreements), then countries' incentives to gain bargaining power are less distortionary than if the default is no commitment at all (as is true for current climate negotiations). The ideal default outcome is actually a more ambitious agreement, since this would give high-tech countries the most bargaining power and induce countries to make advance investments in R&D as a means of gaining bargaining strength.

Unanimity means that everyone must agree, and it is exactly this requirement that allows individual countries to benefit from greater bargaining power. If unanimity were to be replaced by majority rule (or some supermajority requirement) when it came to updating agreements, the strategic considerations would be mitigated and could vanish entirely. Finally, a minimum participation requirement, specifying the number of countries that must ratify the treaty before it enters into force, is capable of reducing free riding and encouraging participation.

Each rule can be implemented even if the others are not. In fact, the rules proposed in this chapter are "strategic substitutes" in that each rule is *more* important if the other rules are *not* implemented. For example, it is more important to apply formulas to allocate burdens if the time horizon of each commitment period is short.

For all these rules, the chief problem is that they may not be credible *ex post*, if a country later threatens to exit the agreement unless it gets a better deal. To reduce the likelihood (and the credibility) of such threats, it may be necessary to bundle the environmental agreement with a trade agreement. If a country cannot exit one without exiting the other, it will be less tempted to opt out, implying that the rules discussed above become more credible and effective. Thus, linking to trade agreements complements each of the rules above. Despite their obvious drawbacks, such linkages may therefore be necessary to credibly commit to a long time horizon, an ambitious default outcome, the best voting rule, and the optimal formula for burden sharing. In addition, linking to trade agreements may be the only way of ensuring that participants prefer to comply with their commitments—even after an agreement is signed.

Appendix: The need for updating and economic instruments

Any agreement will need to be updated over time, no matter the choice of policy instrument used to implement the agreement. Suppose, for instance, that abatement technology improves over time. Since the cost of abatement decreases, it becomes optimal, from a social point of view, to further reduce emissions. With a quota system, the total number of emission permits should decline from q to q', say. This

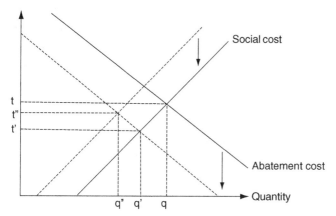

Figure 9.A1 If the social cost of pollution increases while abatement costs decrease, the total number of quotas should decrease (from q to q"), but an emission tax may not change much (only from t to t")

change is illustrated in Figure 9.A1 above, where the horizontal axis measures the quantity of emission. If, instead, emission taxes are used, the optimal tax decreases from t to t' in the same figure. The reason for this is that with better abatement technology, pollution declines, and the social marginal cost of pollution is likely to decline. Suppose, next, that the climate problem becomes more severe. Since the social cost of pollution jumps up, it is optimal to reduce pollution. Under a quota system, the total number of permits should decline from q' to q". If emission taxes are used, the optimal tax increases from t' to t". Thus, the policy needs to be updated whether or not changes take place in technology, severity of pollution, or the use of emission taxes or quotas (or changes in whether or not the permits are tradable).

Nevertheless, the choice of instrument may be crucial for how often and how much the agreement ought to be updated. It may be reasonable to expect that, over time, the climate problem will become more severe *and* abatement technology will improve. By combining the suggestions in the previous paragraph, the total emissions quota should be reduced by quite a lot, from q to q". If a tax is used, however, it may increase or decrease, depending on which of the two forces is strongest. In Figure 9.A1, the tax should change only slightly, from t to t". Thus, a tax system might be in less need of updating than a quota system. Non-tradable permits may be the most in need of updating over time, since the optimal distribution of quotas ought to change as soon as different countries develop different capacities to abate.

References

Aghion, Philippe, Mathias Dewatripont, and Patrick Rey (1994). "Renegotiation Design with Unverifiable Information," *Econometrica* 62: 257–82.

Aldy, Joseph E., Scott Barrett, and Robert N. Stavins (2003). "Thirteen Plus One: A Comparison of Global Climate Policy Architectures," *Climate Policy* 3: 373–97.

Aldy, Joseph E. and Robert N. Stavins (eds.) (2007): *Architectures for Agreement: Addressing Global Climate Change in the Post-Kyoto World*. New York: Cambridge University Press.

Alesina, Alberto, Ignazio Angeloni, and Federico Etro (2005). "International Unions," *American Economic Review*, 95(3): 602–15.

Bagwell, Kyle and Robert W. Staiger (2003): *The Economics of the World Trading System*. Cambridge, MA: MIT Press.

Barrett, Scott (1997). "The Strategy of Trade Sanctions in International Environmental Agreements," *Resource and Energy Economics* 19: 345–61.

(2005). "The Theory of International Environmental Agreements," In K. G. Mäler and J. R. Vincent (eds.), *Handbook of Environmental Economics* 3: 1457–1516.

Buchholtz, Wolfgang, Alexander Haupt, and Wolfgang Peters (2005). "International Environmental Agreements and Strategic Voting," *Scandinavian Journal of Economics* 107 (1): 175–95.

Carraro, Carlo and Carmen Marchiori (2004). "Endogenous Strategic Issue Linkage in International Negotiations," in C. Carraro and V. Fragnelli (eds.), *Game Practice and the Environment*. Cheltenham, UK: Edward Elgar Publishing, pp. 65–86.

Carraro, Carlo, Carmen Marchiori, and Sonia Oreffice (2004). "Endogenous Minimum Participation in International Environmental Treaties," CEPR Discussion Paper No. 4281, London.

Cesar, Herman and Aart de Zeeuw (1996). "Issue Linkage in Global Environmental Problems," in A. Xepapadeas (ed.), *Economic Policy for the Environment and Natural Resources: Techniques for the Management and Control of Pollution*. Cheltenham, UK: Edward Elgar Publishing, pp. 158–73.

Ferejohn, John, Morris Fiorina, and Richard D. McKelvey (1987). "Sophisticated Voting and Agenda Independence in the Distributive Politics Setting," *American Journal of Political Science* 31: 169–93.

Frankel, Jeffrey (2007). "Formulas for Quantitative Emission Targets," in Aldy and Stavins (eds.), pp. 31–56.

  (2008). "An Elaborated Proposal for Global Climate Policy Architecture: Specific Formulas and Emission Targets for All Countries in All Decades," Mimeo, for *The Harvard Project on International Climate Agreements*.

Guriev, Sergei and Dmitriy Kvasov (2005). "Contracting on Time," *American Economic Review*, 95(5): 1369–85.

Harstad, Bård (2005). "Majority Rules and Incentives," *Quarterly Journal of Economics*, 120 (4): 535–68.

  (2006). "Flexible Integration? Mandatory and Minimum Participation Rules," *Scandinavian Journal of Economics* 108 (4): 683–702.

  (2007). "Harmonization and Side Payments in Political Cooperation," *American Economic Review* 97(3): 871–89.

  (2008a). "Do Side Payments Help? Collective Decisions and Strategic Delegation," *Journal of the European Economic Association* 6: 2–3.

  (2008b). "Strategic Delegation and Voting Rules," CMS-EMS Discussion Paper 1442, Northwestern University.

  (2009). "The Dynamics of Climate Agreements," CMS-EMS Discussion Paper 1474, Northwestern University.

Harstad, Bård and Gunnar Eskeland (2008). "Trading for the Future: Signaling in Permit Markets," CMS-EMS Discussion Paper 1429, Northwestern University.

Hoel, Michael (1992). "International Environment Conventions: The Case of Uniform Reductions of Emissions," *Environmental and Resource Economics* 2 (2): 141–59.

IPCC (2007). "The Physical Science Basis," Working Group I. IPCC's Fourth Assessment Report, Climate Change 2007.

Maggi, Giovanni and Massimo Morelli (2006). "Self-Enforcing Voting in International Organizations," *American Economic Review* 96 (4): 1137–58.

Nash, John (1950). "The Bargaining Problem," *Econometrica* 18: 155–62.

Nugent, Neill (2003). *The Government and Politics of the European Union*. Houndmills, UK: Palgrave MacMillan.

Rubinstein, Ariel (1982). "Perfect Equilibrium in a Bargaining Model," *Econometrica* 50 (1): 97–109.

Schelling, Thomas C. (1956). "An Essay on Bargaining," *American Economic Review* 46 (3): 281–306.

  (2007). "Epilogue: Architectures for Agreement," In Aldy and Stavins (eds.), pp. 343–9.

UNFCCC (2008). Report of the Conference of the Parties on its thirteenth session, held in Bali, December 3–15, 2007.

10 Metrics for evaluating policy commitments in a fragmented world: the challenges of equity and integrity

CAROLYN FISCHER AND
RICHARD D. MORGENSTERN[1]

Executive summary

Despite uncertainties about the nature and stringency of commitments in future climate change agreements, some things are clear: the international negotiations not only will include national targets and timetables, but also will have to take account of diverse policies and measures undertaken by individual nations, including developing countries. The international community will face twin challenges of judging the equity and integrity of various national proposals.

Ex post, determining whether particular policies have been implemented is a relatively simple matter, even though assessing their effectiveness is not always straightforward. *Ex ante*, however, the integrity of the international process requires at least some evaluation of the policies and measures proposed by individual nations to estimate their likely impacts. The absence of such evaluation may handicap the negotiators in reaching credible agreements.

The current system for reporting national actions to the international community is highly non-uniform and insufficient to understand differences among countries' policies and their effectiveness. Thus, a first order of business should be the development of a much tighter,

[1] The authors are Senior Fellows at Resources for the Future, Washington, D.C. Portions of this chapter are drawn from an unpublished manuscript by Fischer, Jacoby, and Morgenstern (2005) that was presented at a meeting of the Climate Policy Network in Sardinia, Italy, on September 7, 2005. Capable research assistance was provided by Danae Wethmann. The authors are grateful to Joe Aldy, Rob Stavins, Richard Baron, Aaron Cosbey, Peter Wooders, and an anonymous reviewer for helpful comments.

narrowly defined set of guidelines designed to reflect genuine differences in activities among nations.

The problem with evaluating equity is that clear metrics are rarely fair, and fair metrics are rarely clear. Certain metrics, like emissions per unit of Gross Domestic Product (GDP), population, or historical emissions, are straightforward to calculate and generally informative but they are imperfect indicators of burden. Other metrics, like emissions reductions or total costs of policies undertaken, are unlikely to be reported reliably. The metric of marginal abatement costs—at least among market-based policies—has the advantage of indicating the cost-effectiveness of the international distribution of effort. It is also an important indicator of the competitiveness impacts of climate policies *vis-à-vis* trading partners. We recommend greater focus on this measure, but note the difficulty in attributing the marginal costs of nonmarket-based policies, especially inefficient measures. The key question is what carbon price would achieve the same reductions as the suite of policies selected, either by sector or for the whole economy. This would be analogous to the calculation of the level of effective protection applied in analyses of trade disputes.

Evaluating the integrity of the commitments involves both *ex post* verification of performance—essentially compliance—and the *ex ante* challenges faced by international negotiators in comparing dissimilar policies and measures. For *ex post* verification, the simplicity of an aggregate, economy-wide emissions target, or even one expressed as emissions intensity, is quite appealing. Existing data and reporting systems are certainly compatible with such approaches. When subnational or specific regulatory or voluntary policies are used, the commitment should be expressed as a transparent, verifiable goal, such as a fuel efficiency standard or level of technology deployment. However, while such goals may be clear, their effects on emissions are less transparent. Therefore, descriptive, institutionally oriented information must be supplemented with detailed data on the actual implementation and performance of these measures. Focusing on specific emissions goals as opposed to regulatory standards can help avoid excessive reliance on model-based counterfactuals. Research and development (R&D) programs are by their long-term nature difficult to compare with near-term emissions targets, but these activities should at least be made more comparable across countries. We see no alternative to relying on actual expenditure and deployment data, although care should be taken to link such data to specific program activities and to include transparent baseline information.

Assessment of the integrity of *ex ante* commitments is, perhaps, the most important but also the most problematic area. The greatest challenges are associated with the unavoidable need to model counterfactuals against which efforts can be measured, with all the attendant complexities. New guidelines should focus on greater transparency in methods, models, and data and emphasize standardization in methodologies to improve the consistency of analysis across sectors, policies, and countries. Another priority is the strengthening of the mandate of the international experts who evaluate the submissions. The current practice of peer review by the UN Framework Convention on Climate Change (UNFCCC) is far too loose an arrangement for the reports to be credible inputs to climate negotiations. Other international processes may provide lessons for evaluating the quality, consistency, and value of the estimates of *ex ante* commitments, but the UNFCCC process arguably requires a stronger framework than exists in these precedents. A strengthened and improved reporting and evaluation framework should harness and empower independent institutions, international organizations, academic researchers, and other third-party actors. The reporting and review mechanism should include more specific obligations, independent peer reviews using consistent methodologies for quantitative as well as qualitative analyses, publicly available reports and data, and a mechanism for periodic review of the process. The collection of information must be expanded beyond emissions to include a variety of objective, quantitative measures and data on implementation, as well as guidelines for and transparent descriptions of the modeling and analysis to judge the effectiveness of the activities. Since agreement on a single metric of national contributions is unrealistic, agreement on a common, consistent, and credible set of indicators should be prioritized to build the foundation of trust and transparency needed to underpin multifaceted commitments.

Introduction

Effective strategies to address global climate change require collective effort on the part of many countries over an extended time and across a range of activities. The Bali Action Plan, for example, calls for action on mitigation, adaptation, technology, and finance—with each implying a different suite of policies and contributions. In the early stages of policy development, nations and groups of nations may take action more or less independently of one another, as is happening now. The specific policies and measures that have already been adopted to address climate change in different countries or regions are quite diverse; they include cap-and-trade programs to cover at least a major portion of greenhouse gas (GHG) emissions, as well as additional regulatory, voluntary, technology, and information-oriented activities. Over the longer term, however, progress toward any GHG stabilization goal is going to require increasing levels of international burden sharing and a more formal structure. Agreement will be worked out in a sequence of international negotiations, within which the twin issues of equity and integrity will be central features.

The challenges of moving ahead in a world of diverse policies are illustrated by a simple story:

Two individuals are approached on the street by a sympathetic homeless person seeking assistance. Individual A, an established professional with a relatively high income, proposes to rent the homeless person an apartment for six months. Individual B, a younger, struggling academic, offers to donate $100. Regrettably, neither one can make good on the offer immediately. However, they both agree to return to the same location at an appointed time the following year to complete the transactions.

How can one evaluate the fairness of the relative contributions of individuals A and B? If A provides free apartment rental, should B give more than $100? Are the income differences between them the only or even the most important determinant of their relative contributions? How about differences in wealth, health, family responsibilities, life expectancy, prior support of similar causes, or other factors? In the sixteen years since the phrase "common but differentiated responsibilities" was adopted in Article 3 of the United Nations Framework Convention on Climate Change (UNFCCC), little consensus has emerged on either the concepts or the metrics of fairness to be used in future international climate negotiations.[2]

---

[2] See Cazorla and Toman (2001) for a review of a dozen alternative equity criteria for climate change policy. See Baer *et al.* (2000) for a defense of an equal per capita emisons approach and Bodansky (2004) for a survey of approaches.

A second issue, involving the integrity or credibility of the commitments countries accept as part of a post-Kyoto climate regime, has
two elements. On the one hand, we must be able to ascertain whether
agreed-upon pledges are fulfilled. Transactions should be monitored
ex post to verify that individuals A and B showed up at the appointed
time and made their stated contributions without added conditions.
Similarly, the Bali Action Plan calls for activities to be "measurable,
reportable, and verifiable," although the precise meanings of those
terms have yet to be defined (Ellis and Larsen 2008). Credible international reporting systems must verify that particular policies were, in
fact, put in place and/or that overall emissions targets have been met,
either domestically or with the assistance of trade in credits supplied
and verified abroad.[3]

On the other hand, the process lacks integrity without at least some
ex ante evaluation of the likely impact of policies and measures proposed by individual nations. Yet such an evaluation requires making
difficult assumptions and using complex modeling techniques. How
can one compare the proposal to rent an apartment made by A with
the $100 offered by B? Although we can readily determine the average
rent of an apartment in the area, absent additional information we
don't really know what A had in mind. A rooming house in a slum?
A luxury unit in a high-rent area? Similarly, as we move away from
a strict targets-and-timetables framework for structuring mitigation
commitments toward an approach that emphasizes a portfolio of
policies—presumably those around which there is a domestic consensus—the specifics of the proposed policies loom larger and the need for
an *ex ante* assessment of their emissions implications becomes greater.

In a world of diverse policies, the challenge for the international
community will be to judge the comparability and integrity of various
national proposals. Over time, proposed policies may become more
uniform, thus diminishing the need for such analyses, but at least
in the current phase of international negotiations, a useful input
to the process would be some means of talking in a coherent and
widely accepted fashion about what individual nations or nation
groups are doing or proposing to do to help reduce climate risk.
Unfortunately, the current reporting framework, designed to support

---

[3] For example, credits may be available from the Clean Development Mechanism,
Joint Implementation, or Assigned Amount Units.

Kyoto commitments to national-level emissions targets, is inadequate to evaluate the effectiveness of policies and measures other than a cap (Ellis and Larsen 2008).

In this chapter, we explore various metrics that may provide a framework for evaluating policy commitments, short of (or in addition to) a fixed GHG quantity target. As noted, our focus is on the twin challenges of assessing equity and integrity with respect to climate mitigation commitments. Although many of the lessons that emerge from this analysis also apply to evaluating commitments related to adaptation, technology, and finance, our focus is on commitments to reducing emissions.

The next section provides relevant background. We then address the issue of equity in some depth and consider alternative approaches for evaluating and comparing efforts at the national level. A subsequent section focuses on the integrity of commitments, including a discussion of the relatively straightforward issue of *ex post* verification, as well as the more complex problem of *ex ante* assessment. Also included in this section is a review of current experience with national reporting on policies under the UNFCCC framework. The final section offers recommendations for reform of the current system.

Background

The Berlin Mandate, adopted by parties to the UNFCCC in the first Conference of the Parties (COP 1), called for the elaboration of policies and measures and the setting of quantified emissions limitation and reduction objectives over specific timeframes. The implication was that these policies and measures would be common or uniform across nations. That is, parties to an agreement would be instituting roughly the same kinds of policies, and the quantified emissions limitation and reduction objective that was accepted for each country would be the main indicator of effort.

Under the Kyoto Protocol, the concept of formally crediting policies was abandoned, but the idea of fixed national emissions quantity targets and timetables was maintained as the principal indicator of country-level effort or contribution. Indeed, countries' willingness to accept more or less demanding mitigation obligations—whether reflected in future emissions targets or in the nature and stringency of policies that may substitute for fixed national quantity targets—is the main question at issue in the potential negotiation of a second Kyoto commitment period. Although a nation's Kyoto obligation can be met by increasing carbon sinks and purchasing credits from countries outside the boundaries of participating Annex B nations, the current Protocol has no provisions to credit specific policies and measures that nations may undertake. Nor is there evidence of planning among international agencies about how this would be done. Yet the issue of how to quantify diverse or uncommon policies is likely to become a significant issue in future international discussions.

Despite numerous uncertainties about the nature and stringency of commitments in future climate change agreements, one characteristic of coming discussions seems clear: the negotiations may include national targets and timetables, but they also will have to take account of specific policies undertaken by individual nations, including those inside the current Kyoto group, as well as developing countries and others outside the group. Indeed, countries with different perceptions of the issues may agree in good faith that global warming poses a danger. Yet even apart from concerns about the global public good nature of the problem, they may prefer vastly different approaches. These preferences may diverge because of the different socioeconomic characteristics of nations; the uncertain nature of the costs, benefits, and feasibility of strategies for reducing GHGs; and individual negotiators' perceptions of the risks. For example, a country that is optimistic about future technological potential may prefer to engage in less near-term mitigation in favor of more R&D now and stricter caps later. A country that is more risk averse about dampening economic growth and more pessimistic about the speed of technological progress may be willing to accept intensity-based targets. A country that has different expectations about the marginal benefits of mitigation may be willing to accept a certain carbon tax (or safety valve), but may not be willing to risk a sharp run-up in energy costs.

Almost all nations, including developing countries, are currently taking some action on GHG mitigation, and each will seek credit for what it is doing. For example, policies being undertaken now by Annex B nations include the following:

- pricing carbon emissions and energy (usually differentiated by sector) through GHG or fuel taxes, cap-and-trade systems for carbon dioxide (CO_2) or GHGs, or through the removal of fuel subsidies;

- subsidies to low-GHG energy supply technologies (e.g., biofuels, wind) or end-use products (e.g., hybrid cars);
- regulatory policies (always differentiated by sector and/or device), such as consumer device performance standards (e.g., fuel economy standards for vehicles, building and equipment efficiency standards) or portfolio standards (e.g., for electricity generation);
- voluntary programs for industry (e.g., Climate Leaders, in the United States) or consumer products (e.g., Energy Star labeling, also in the United States);
- expenditures on research, development, and demonstration of low-carbon technologies for energy production or end use; and
- aid to other countries, which can take the form of financial transfers, technology assistance and transfer, capacity building, and support for adaptation.

Note that with the exception of the price measures (carbon tax or cap-and-trade system), the United States already has at least some programs in all of these areas. Furthermore, the United States has consistently argued that it is carrying its proper share of the needed global commitment. Assuming eventual enactment of a policy that somewhat resembles recent congressional proposals for carbon-pricing programs, which are less ambitious than current or expected European policies but broader in scope, the United States is likely to make that assertion in even stronger terms. Most other non–Annex B nations also have activities underway in many of these domains. The big question is whether these diverse activities can be compared in any meaningful way.

Evaluating equity

Equity is a major concern in international climate negotiations, which are fundamentally about burden sharing. For this reason, there is a strong desire to compare efforts and assess whether countries are contributing their fair share. Yet comparing efforts involves two kinds of exercises, neither of which lends itself to clear and fair metrics. The first exercise is to compare a portfolio of disparate national policies according to a consistent measure that reflects effort—for example, cost burden incurred or emissions reduction achieved. The second exercise requires placing the level of effort in an appropriate context (e.g., in proportion to GDP, population, or some measure of capacity) that reflects countries' individual socioeconomic and other circumstances and their ability to undertake emission reductions. The basic problem is that clear metrics are not always fair and fair metrics are not always clear.

Although indicators related to effort do exist (and we discuss some below), none can be translated into total cost burden or expected emissions reduction without extensive modeling using a range of assumptions that reduce the transparency of the exercise. Most of these evaluations are conducted *ex ante* as part of the negotiating process, which requires making judgments about future actions and circumstances. *Ex post*, much of the information is observable, but attempting to evaluate equity or effort at that point still requires making assumptions about unobservable counterfactuals, such as what GDP or emissions would have been in the absence of the policies. Even seemingly straightforward metrics can have important definitional issues in practice that affect their comparability. And even reasonable measures of effort can be poor indicators of fairness.

We consider four alternative approaches to measuring climate policy efforts: emissions performance, reductions, total costs, and marginal costs. Each can provide some valuable information, but none by itself is terribly satisfying as a reliable measure of effort or equity.

Measurement options

Emissions performance

Inevitably, Kyoto-style fixed quantity targets involving emissions reductions from a specified baseline will remain part of future international discussions, whether or not commitments are negotiated in these terms. Measures of this type are straightforward to calculate at the national level with available data, at least for industrialized countries, and several comprehensive proposals have been developed (e.g., Frankel 2007).

However, emissions targets can be a poor indicator of effort, since different countries have different reduction potentials and different needs for emissions growth. For example, under the metric used in the Kyoto Protocol, the EU emissions target—at 20 percent below 1990 levels—may look much more ambitious than a US target of reducing 2020 emissions to 1990 levels. However, the United States has much higher baseline emissions growth, which makes the reduction burden larger. At the same time, the United States has higher income and GDP growth rates, which could make reductions look more affordable. Developing countries that place a priority on economic growth may find emissions intensity of GDP or emissions per capita to be more acceptable indicators, but even these measures ignore costs and other circumstances related to reduction potential. More complex methodologies for setting or evaluating targets may also be devised, such as methodologies that account for differences in historical emissions paths or reductions undertaken outside the country, such as through the Clean Development Mechanism (CDM) or other activities. Such alternative approaches were pursued during the Clinton administration in various attempts to encourage non–Annex B nations to adopt national targets. Still, all these efforts rely on some measure of aggregate emissions, which by itself is a poor indicator of burdens. Even though the standard for evaluation may depend on other metrics, nations are likely to have different views on what kinds of adjustments to relative emissions targets produce an appropriate measure of fairness.

Emissions reductions

Emissions reductions, as opposed to emissions outcomes, are more closely tied to notions of effort. However, they are much more difficult to measure. Estimating the emissions reduction effects of policies typically requires projecting a counterfactual baseline and comparing it with actual emissions (or, in the case of an *ex ante* evaluation, to projected emissions assuming the policies are in place). This task is conceptually similar to certifying emissions reductions under the CDM and confronts the same challenges in terms of positing a credible baseline. But whereas the CDM involves discrete projects, policy initiatives are generally wider in scope and involve more actors— making them harder to evaluate. As discussed below in a section on current reporting practices under the UNFCCC, the norm has been *not* to report emissions reductions for individual policies.

Assessing the reductions associated with a portfolio of policies raises additional challenges. Estimates of the emissions performance of individual policies are difficult to aggregate in a simple fashion, since some policies may overlap with each other—or with a sector-wide quantity target. Care must be taken to avoid double counting and to recognize leakage. Currently, a few countries have attempted to make adjustments for overlapping effects in their national reporting, although most have ignored the issue.

In addition to problems estimating reductions, it is unclear how to relate reductions (whether measured in absolute terms or as a percentage of total emissions) to the actual mitigation costs incurred by a country. Different countries achieving the same percentage reduction from baseline could incur very different cost burdens, depending on their relative capacities for low-cost reductions.

Total cost

Another possible metric for comparing efforts is to calculate the total cost of mitigation activities, perhaps as a share of GDP. This measure can be quite straightforward for individual policies that involve direct fiscal expenditures, such as subsidies for technology deployment or R&D. It can also allow for spending on non-mitigation activities like adaptation or international assistance. However, assessing the cost of non-fiscal policies like regulations (market-based or otherwise) and voluntary programs is often difficult and may require modeling to ascertain overall economic impacts (not to mention environmental effects).

Nor is total cost necessarily a good measure of the quality of the activities being undertaken. For mitigation policies, fiscal expenditures can be associated with varying degrees of effectiveness in terms of emissions outcomes (ethanol subsidies may be a good case in point). One must also account for baseline spending levels, preexisting energy taxes, and other factors to understand the additional costs associated with the country's policy commitments. Furthermore, the many uncertainties involved raise questions about the quality and reliability of cost measures. Not surprisingly, estimates of the total cost of regulation tend to vary more widely in most modeling analyses than estimates of marginal cost (Fischer and Morgenstern 2006).

Marginal costs

An easier measure to compare across countries may be the explicit or implicit *marginal cost* of emission reductions. In the case of an upstream cap-and-trade system or a universal GHG tax, the appropriate measure is straightforward: the market price of emissions permits (or allowances) in the former case or the level of the tax in the latter instance. However, if the price-based policy is not implemented in an economy-wide manner, then using marginal cost as a measure of effort is confounded by the question of scope: is a country with a low economy-wide carbon tax making more or less of an effort than a country with a high-price cap-and-trade system applied only to certain sectors? Once measures move beyond price-based instruments, several potential difficulties must be addressed to estimate an implicit price. How does one average across different sector-specific policies? How does one estimate the effective cost imposed by non-price emissions measures?

In some ways, the concept of calculating implicit marginal costs is analogous to that of calculating the level of effective protection in analyses of trade disputes. In the trade case, effective protection represents the difference between the domestic price of a good and the international price it would garner in the absence of trade barriers. Effective protection is a function of the tariff and nontariff barriers facing that good and all of its inputs—it can be expressed as an equivalent tariff, though doing so often requires some difficult calculations. Analogously, the effective impact of some non-price measure can be stated in terms of the emissions price that would have the equivalent mitigating effect on current emissions. However, trade calculations are typically made on the basis of specific goods. In a climate context, while one could also compare marginal abatement costs on a sector-by-sector basis and while this could be highly relevant for assessing competitiveness impacts, for comparing overall country efforts with respect to GHG mitigation, some kind of national, multi-sector metric is required. This brings with it the associated challenges of aggregating across a variety of policies and sectors.

Another question is how well marginal cost serves as a proxy for policy effectiveness. Inefficient policies can have high implicit prices but low effectiveness (e.g., over-subsidization of wind or ethanol). Many policies also raise issues of additionality, uncertainty, and credibility that need to be considered. Should one account for differences in emissions or marginal costs among nations where those differences are the result of policies imposed for reasons other than GHG control (e.g., energy, fiscal measures) or reflect national characteristics or resource endowments (e.g., geography, natural resource base)? How should expenditures on R&D be credited? For example, one may estimate what emissions price would elicit a similar amount of R&D effort, but the emissions reductions induced by a direct R&D policy are not comparable to those that would result from imposing that equivalent emissions price.

Measurement uses

It is unlikely that any single measure of effort will be acceptable to all countries. Commitments to emissions targets can be straightforward to verify, but they may have no clear relationship to actual burdens. Meanwhile, measures more related to economic burdens may not be readily verifiable. Evaluating a measure of burden or effort in terms of its fairness requires an arbitrary decision about which country-specific metrics to use in making that evaluation.

Ultimately, fairness is subjective: "There are no 'neutral' metrics: different metrics will show different countries in a good (or less good) light" (Ellis *et al.* 2008, p. 6). Furthermore, subjective views may change: whatever seems fair at one time may well be perceived differently in the future. For example, although reduction commitments relative to a 1990 emissions baseline might have seemed fair in 1997, when the Kyoto Protocol was first signed, subsequent strong differences in economic performance have changed some parties' views on the equity of the original formula.

That is not to say that it is not useful for negotiators to attempt to gather measures of effort. Each country will form its own opinion of the comparability of different proposals based on such indicators. However, the goal of negotiations is to obtain agreement on climate policy commitments, and those may not be determined by a single rule for allocating burdens.

Evaluating integrity

Effectiveness is the most important element of any climate agreement. Evaluating the integrity of a collection of country commitments requires two levels of analysis. First, are the commitments themselves credible? That is, do we believe the countries will undertake them and can they be monitored and verified? Second, are the effects of the commitments credible? That is, do we reasonably expect the set of policies being undertaken to result in the achievement of stated emissions goals? A concern with environmental integrity necessarily shifts the focus to emissions. The first question, about the credibility of the commitments themselves, requires an *ex post* analysis: metrics must be chosen in support of enforcing the agreement and countries must be willing to engage in commitments that have such metrics, be they levels of emissions, regulations, or budgetary measures. The second question, about the credibility of claimed impacts on emissions, requires primarily *ex ante* analysis—that is, estimating the expected effects of policies prior to implementation.

Credibility of commitments

The difficulty of verifying a nation's performance *ex post* depends to a great extent on how performance is actually defined. If it is defined in terms of an aggregate emissions target or a reduction from a well-established baseline, the task is relatively straightforward. Reporting requirements established under the UNFCCC already call for the development and updating of an emissions inventory for all covered GHGs. As a cross-check, the International Energy Agency routinely reports CO_2 emissions by country, as does the US Energy Information Agency. Under the terms of both the UNFCCC and the Kyoto Protocol, institutional arrangements have been established to make *ex post* assessments of compliance with aggregate emissions targets, including accounting for transactions with non–Annex B nations. It is only slightly more complex to verify an emissions intensity target, since information on GDP is readily available.

Not surprisingly, the challenge of assessing performance *ex post* is greater when the focus is on subnational or policy-specific measures as opposed to aggregate targets. This is clear in the case of sectoral emissions targets, and even more so in the case of policies that are not directly tied to an emissions target, such as voluntary programs or regulatory standards.

The principal issue with sectoral targets is that data on fuel use by sector may not be available on a current basis in all countries. In the United States, for example, the Manufacturing Energy Consumption Survey is conducted only every three years, although it is possible to extrapolate from published sources to estimate sector-specific emissions for major sectors. At the same time, nonconventional fuels, such as biomass, pose special data problems, as do some of the non-CO_2 gases. Other countries may face similar or possibly greater challenges in developing sector-specific emissions data. Currently, the only reporting requirements for sectoral emissions are the inventories and national communications required under the UNFCCC. As discussed below, in the section on current practices, the data to support these reports are sparse in many countries and are often plagued by omissions, double counting, and other problems.

In the case of policies that are not tied to emissions targets, the challenges of verifying performance *ex post* can be even greater. The difficulty arises from the fact that one needs information on the effectiveness of the policies, not simply on whether the institutional arrangements have been established. For example, in the case of voluntary programs, most of the publicly available data are descriptive in nature, covering such aspects as the number of firms or plants enrolled in the programs, what goals have been established, and whether firms have set up internal training or information activities to support the voluntary programs. Little information is available on what firms actually do to reduce their emissions and even less is known about how these actions compare with actions taken by firms that have not joined the programs. Thus, it is extremely difficult to assess the contribution of voluntary programs relative to a realistic baseline.

Recent research on selected voluntary programs in the United States, Europe, and Japan suggests that, at best, the contribution of voluntary energy or GHG reduction programs is in the order of a 5 percent reduction from baseline, plus or minus 5 percent (Morgenstern and Pizer 2007). However, because of the sparse reporting on performance, it is virtually impossible to estimate the effectiveness of most individual programs in operation today. That is not to deny the possibility of building in additional reporting requirements relevant for evaluation purposes, but few programs have done so. Of course, most economists would agree that voluntary programs are inherently limited in their ability to deliver the sizable emissions reductions or technical change needed to effectively address climate change; one may then require a stronger burden of proof for the inclusion of such measures in any international reporting of effort.

Mandatory regulations and policies generally involve verifiable compliance mechanisms. For example, one can verify the share of energy derived from renewable energy sources by a given date, the enactment (and enforcement) of energy efficiency standards, the enactment of legislation requiring certain pollution control devices (such as for methane or nitrous oxide), or the reduction of consumer subsidies for fossil fuels. However, the effectiveness of mandatory policy mechanisms may not be uniform within or across individual sectors in a single country, or even within the same sector if different programs are managed by different government agencies. Thus, regulations on new vehicle performance, for which extensive data and analysis are available, may be more (or less) effective than rules issued by the same agency covering existing stationary emissions sources, especially if the technical information for that industry is limited. Cross-national differences can further complicate the situation. Even when compliance is assured, environmental effectiveness may be an issue. In the case of policies that mandate the purchase of energy-efficient capital equipment—such as new source performance standards for power plants, fuel economy standards for vehicles, or efficiency standards for appliances—it is usually possible to obtain information on the sales volumes and performance attributes of different types of equipment. The difficulty comes in keeping track of the actual use of the equipment and in determining what old equipment is being retired in favor of the new equipment. For example, although a new, fuel-efficient vehicle can reduce energy use per mile, the lower driving cost can lead to more vehicle miles traveled (the so-called rebound effect), and higher purchasing costs can reduce vehicle turnover, thereby offsetting some of the expected gains.[4] Similarly, one can verify the installed capacity of renewable energy, but credibly calculating the emissions it offsets is a more difficult task. Carbon capture and storage equipment may be installed on a power plant, which is simple to verify, but the associated energy penalty makes it expensive to use, requiring more costly monitoring to assess the true environmental effectiveness of this measure.

In sum, *ex post* verification is most plausible at the aggregate level, especially when performance is defined in terms of a quantity-based target such as total emissions or emissions intensity. Problems of a higher order stalk efforts to verify the effectiveness of a subnational target or of specific regulatory or voluntary programs, although some of these problems may be alleviated by instituting requirements for

---

[4] Wooders (2006) offers a comprehensive review of methods for evaluating energy efficiency policies.

additional data gathering. When the targets are expressed as a change in emissions against a future, as-yet-undetermined baseline, the need for a modeled counterfactual is unavoidable. Yet gaining consensus on such a counterfactual can be quite challenging.

We would summarize the bottom line regarding *ex post* verification as follows: engage in commitments that are clearly verifiable and focus on aggregate targets whenever possible. When subnational policies or programs are adopted, collect relevant micro-level data and information and avoid metrics that require extensive reliance on modeled counterfactuals.

Credibility of claims regarding environmental effectiveness

A national emissions target represents a commitment to achieve a specified environmental outcome. Yet in the absence of information on the specific policies to be adopted, one cannot evaluate whether the target is likely to be achieved. If a country commits to a set of policies without a specific target, the need for a detailed evaluation of the proposed policies is even greater.

Some countries that are unwilling to take on fixed aggregate emissions targets at this point in time may be willing to accept targets in individual sectors where they have sound strategies in place or perceive a level playing field. Such efforts may be motivated in whole or part by fears that nations that adopt mandatory policies will implement trade sanctions against nations that do not. Indeed, even many countries with aggregate emissions targets are adopting separate targets for certain covered sectors.

Evaluating the contribution of a portfolio of policies raises difficult issues of aggregating across sectors or policies over time. Even within sectors, a host of challenges bedevil any effort to compare the effects of different policies. Many of the issues are familiar because they have already arisen in the context of crediting programs—some of the most important involve baselines, uncertainty, credibility of current and future efforts, and the secondary effects of measures or offsetting actions (e.g., crowding out, rebound effects, offsetting tax reductions, overlap with other policies). As for the crediting programs, sound guidelines are needed to develop estimates of the primary effects of individual policies, to account properly for secondary effects, and to aggregate when multiple policies are adopted at the same time.

Perhaps the most difficult challenge is to deal adequately with policies that have multi-period effects and to facilitate the comparison of long-term commitments. For example, subsidies for R&D, demonstration, and learning by doing (actual production) will influence the future cost of mitigation, with less effect on current emissions. However, given the uncertainty involved in research processes and the interdependence of success with GHG pricing or other regulatory policies, it is difficult to equate current research efforts with a reliable quantity of emissions mitigation in the future. The issue is further complicated by the fact that some policies and measures, like a carbon price, can induce private R&D efforts, thereby generating multi-period effects themselves.

In principle, one could compute the impacts of various measures—including R&D and subsidies—that would be expected to achieve the same level of emissions reduction as a specified increase in the carbon price (e.g., Fischer and Newell 2008). However, any measure of equivalency will be heavily influenced by modeling assumptions, including the expected effectiveness of R&D or learning by doing, the effectiveness of the policy program in promoting R&D, the expected duration of the R&D program, the timing of technological change, discounting, domestic and international spillovers, and so forth.

Such modeling exercises can be revealing—if not about the exact trade-offs among policies—then about the assumptions required for the proposed indirect efforts to lead to desired emissions (or cost) reductions. Understanding those conditions can help policymakers assess how realistic a predicted range of effects is likely to be. Not surprisingly, comparing across R&D (and other similar) programs may require resorting to fairly gross measures—spending, installed capacity, and the like. Even those evaluations, however, still need to account for baseline activities and choose verifiable output measures.

Thus, although expected emissions should be the primary metric, alternative measures may be more appropriate for different types of policies, especially in nations with weak reporting systems. Greater effort should be put into standardizing the use and implementation of reporting and evaluation methodologies. In the absence of detailed assessments in some countries, it may be reasonable to apply the results from well-designed studies in other nations. Hopefully, the use of such practices will encourage nations to undertake more detailed research on their own policies.

Reporting and evaluation in practice

Current UNFCCC practices

Annex I countries are currently required to submit two reports annually to the UNFCCC: a national GHG inventory and a national communication. The latter includes a chapter on the inventory but also describes policies and measures undertaken by the reporting nation and provides emissions projections. The UNFCCC has established guidelines for calculating and reporting GHG inventories, as well as for the structure and content of national communications.[5] In this section, we briefly review these practices for insight into further steps with regard to reporting and evaluation that may support a future international climate policy framework.

Under the UNFCCC guidelines, a country may report planned, adopted, and implemented policies, but must specify the status of the measure. The main intention of a policy does not have to be reducing GHGs for the policy to be listed. The reporting format calls for distinguishing among the sectors to which policies apply (energy, industrial, etc.), and the GHGs affected (CO_2, methane, etc.). Each country must explain which monitoring and evaluation systems are in place according to the objectives and/or activities affected, type of GHG affected, type of policy instrument used (economic, fiscal, voluntary or negotiated agreements, regulatory, information, education, research, and other), implementation status, and implementing entity. Where possible, countries are required to provide a numerical estimate of the expected emissions reductions. They are also asked to provide a brief description of the methodology used to make the calculations.

For emissions projections, Annex I countries are required only to report projections with policies and measures, though they may also report projections without policies and measures. To estimate the aggregate effect of a set of policies and measures, the guidelines require that a country's "with" policies and measures projection be compared to a "without" scenario. Thus, the UNFCCC guidelines call for countries to attempt to calculate cumulative emissions reductions

---

[5] Guidelines for the UNFCCC national communications were adopted during the second and fifth Conferences of the Parties (COP 2 in Geneva in July 1996 and COP 5 in Bonn in October–November 1999).

and compare them with a business-as-usual scenario. Specifically, each country should report net emissions avoided or sequestered for the years 2005, 2010, 2015, and 2020. The guidelines do not prescribe any particular model or approach, but they request that countries provide an explanation of the chosen methodology that is sufficient to give the reader a "basic understanding." A description of the method used to estimate impacts should include specifying the GHGs involved, the type of model or approach used and its characteristics (e.g., top-down versus bottom-up), the original purpose of the model and how it may have been modified to fit the purpose, the strengths and weaknesses of the model, and how it accounts for overlap among policies. Submitting nations should include references to more detailed explanations for these criteria and describe any changes in methods from their previous national communication. Basic national-level information employed in the calculations, such as GDP growth and population growth, should be included in the report.

Every national communication is reviewed by a team of UNFCCC experts, which conducts an in-country visit and an appraisal of the report. The reviews are published, usually in advance of required report revisions. They are designed to facilitate comparisons across national reports and make those comparisons more transparent, but no common metric is applied to individual country submissions.

Although a comprehensive examination of past national communications is not feasible, this section reviews the results from selected countries to gain a sense of how well or poorly the guidelines are being implemented. Specifically, we review the most recent national submissions for five Annex I parties (the United States, Australia, the United Kingdom, the European Union, and Japan), classifying their reported policies and measures into the eight categories used by the UNFCCC:

- education and outreach (E)
- economic/fiscal (F)
- information (I)
- regulatory (R)
- research, development, and deployment (RD&D)
- technical (T)
- voluntary (V)
- various/other (O)

Table 10.1 *Examples of policies and measures*

Major policies and measures	United States	Australia	United Kingdom	European Union	Japan
Framework policies and cross-sectoral measures					
Integrated climate program	Voluntary reporting of GHGs (1605(b)) (V); Climate Leaders to help companies develop long-term climate change strategies (V)	Market-based allocation of grants to abatement opportunities (E); Greenhouse Challenge Plus partnerships between government and industry to abate GHG emissions (R, F, V); National Framework for Energy Efficiency (R, I, E)	UK Climate Change Programme		Kyoto Protocol Target Achievement Plan

			Emissions trading	
			Domestic schemes since 2002 (E); EU ETS since 2005 (E)	ETS for EU

Energy sector

Renewable energy supply	Develop clean, competitive power technology using renewable sources (wind, solar, geothermal, biomass) (RD&D)	Mandatory Renewable Energy Target for power supplies (R); RD&D and early-stage commercialization of renewable energy projects, including solar cities (RD&D, E)	Renewables Obligation with 10% target for electricity supplied from renewable energy sources by 2010 (R); subsidy for biomass heat (F)	Increase contribution of renewables to primary energy supply by 2010 (R); increase biomass use for production of electricity, heat, and transport fuels; promote biofuels (R); support activities to promote renewables and energy efficiency (I)	Promote nuclear energy (V); promote new energy sources (biomass, photovoltaic) (V); promote cogeneration and fuel cells (RD&D)

Table 10.1 (*cont.*)

Major policies and measures	United States	Australia	United Kingdom	European Union	Japan
Energy efficiency improvement in industrial sector	EnergySTAR to promote cost-effective energy reduction, improve productivity, reduce waste, and save energy (V, I, RD&D)	Stimulate large energy-using businesses to take rigorous approach to energy management (R); assist industry in efficient use of energy, innovation, and capacity building (V)		ETS covers combustion plants > 20MW (F); improve energy performance of new (and partially existing) buildings (R)	Energy conservation through cooperation among multiple businesses (V)

| Energy efficiency improvement in commercial sector | EnergySTAR to promote energy performance (V); Commercial Building Integration (R, RD&D) to promote energy efficiency through whole-building system approach for new construction and renovation | Minimum energy efficiency and performance requirements (R) | Energy efficiency loan scheme for small and medium-sized enterprises (F); 2002 and 2005 regulations on energy efficiency in new and refurbished buildings (R) | Improve energy performance of new (and partially existing) buildings (R) | Energy management based on Energy Conservation Law (commercial and other) (R); improve energy performance of commercial buildings (V); promote energy management systems for buildings (V) |

Table 10.1 (*cont.*)

Major policies and measures	United States	Australia	United Kingdom	European Union	Japan
Energy efficiency improvements in residential sector	EnergySTAR to promote energy performance (V); Residential Building Integration (V, RD&D, E) for housing that integrates energy-efficient technologies and practices	Minimum energy efficiency and performance requirements (R)	Energy efficiency commitment to require energy suppliers to make homes more efficient (R); measures to encourage consumer choices and establish product standards (V)	Improve energy performance of new (and partially existing) buildings (R)	Improve energy performance of residential buildings (V); promote home energy management systems (V)

Energy efficiency in appliances	Conduct analyses, develop reviews, and update efficiency standards for most major household appliances and major commercial building technologies and equipment (R)	Energy performance codes and standards for domestic appliances and commercial and industrial equipment (R)	Market Transformation Program (V) to encourage higher product performance standards	Improve minimum boiler efficiency (R); labeling and minimum efficiency requirements for household appliances (R); promote use of CFLs by nonresidential consumers (V)
Assistance to impoverished to improve energy efficiency	Enable low-income families to reduce energy bills by making homes more energy efficient (E, RD&D)	Warm Front and fuel poverty programs (F, grants to poor)		

Table 10.1 (*cont.*)

Major policies and measures	United States	Australia	United Kingdom	European Union	Japan
Combined heat and power (CHP) generation	CHP Partnership to remove market barriers to cleaner energy supply (V)		Good Quality CHP target of 10 GWe by 2010 (E)	Promote generation of heat from renewables	
Transportation					
Car fuel efficiency Policies	Corporate average fuel economy standards to raise efficiency for light trucks from 20.7 to 22.2 mpg by 2007 (R)	National Average CO_2 Emissions Target (V); Fuel Consumption Labelling Scheme (R); Green Vehicle Guide (I)	EU fuel efficiency (V); press EU for targets beyond 140g/km after 2008	Reduce average CO_2 emissions of newly sold cars to 140 g/km until 2008–09 against 1995 baseline (V)	Increase fuel efficiency according to top-runner standards (V); promote clean-energy cars (V)

Vehicle fuel policies	Renewable Fuel Standard to increase renewable fuel supplies to 7.5 billion gallons by 2012 (R); RD&D on advanced technology to make biofuels affordable	Alternative Fuels Conversion Program (F, subsidies); compressed natural gas infrastructure (F, subsidy); reduce incentive to switch from alternative fuel to diesel (F, grants); grants for expanded biofuels production (F); production grants for ethanol and biodiesel (F)	Incentives to use bioethanol and biodiesel (F); Renewable Transport Fuel Obligation (R) requiring fuel suppliers' sales be 2.5% renewable by 2008–09	Increase use of liquid and gaseous biofuels (R)	Introduce sulfur-free fuel (and cars that use it) (V)

Table 10.1 (*cont.*)

Major policies and measures	United States	Australia	United Kingdom	European Union	Japan
Agreements and partnerships	FreedomCAR and Fuel Partnership, and Vehicle Technologies Program for fuel cells, hybrid propulsion systems, etc. (RD&D); SmartWay Transport Partnership (V,T, I,E) for fuel-saving technology in transport and freight operations	Low Emissions Technology Demonstration Fund (RD&D, F); market-based allocation grants to cost-effective abatement opportunities (F)		Promote modal shift in freight transport away from road (F); promote modal shift to lower congestion (F)	Improve environmental performance of marine transport and efficiency of trucking (V)

Integrated transport planning	Strategic transport planning initiatives to improve sustainability of passenger and freight transport (O)	Local authorities given more power to decide on public transportation and road systems and bike lanes (F); pricing policy to manage congestion (R, F)	Infrastructure charging to recover costs of roadways (F)	Design of CO_2-saving transport systems (promote intelligent transport systems, public transport, eco-driving, transport alternatives) (V); transport demand management (V)
Efficiency in aviation	Improve aircraft fuel efficiency technology (T, RD&D)	Control GHG emissions and develop sustainable strategies (V); push to make aviation part of EU ETS scheme (R)		Energy efficiency in aviation (V)

Table 10.1 (*cont.*)

Major policies and measures	United States	Australia	United Kingdom	European Union	Japan
Industry and industrial processes	Reductions in methane emissions from coal mining operations and natural gas systems (I, E, V)	Capture waste coal mine gas (R)	National and EU ETS (F); climate change levy for nondomestic energy use (F); grants for specific industrial branches (F); climate change agreements (V)	ETS (F); IPPC directive for integration of pollution permits for plant operation based on BAT (R); energy efficiency in noncore areas of industry (V)	Promote blended cement in public projects (V)
Reducing ozone-depleting chemicals and fluorinated gases	Phase out ozone-depleting chemicals to reduce HFCs, PFCs, SF_6, HFC-23 (R, I, V)	Reduce ozone-depleting substances and synthetic GHG emissions (R); develop guidelines to reduce emissions of SF_6 (R, V)		Directive on Fluorinated Gases (R, V) to improve monitoring, verification, and containment and restrict use	Abate N_2O and HFC emissions (T); recover and destroy fluorinated gases (V); promote new substitute materials and technologies (RD&D)

Agriculture	Conservation programs to encourage conservation and conversion of erodible cropland to native land (T, E); incentives to encourage bioenergy production and renewable energy systems (E)	Build capacity to reduce emissions from agriculture (I, RD&D); support for primary producers to improve environmental and natural resource management outcomes (F, V)	Common Agricultural Policy and rural development programs to reduce livestock production, enhance soil organic matter production, Catchment Sensitive Farming Program to prevent water pollution (V, R); research on methane production from different sources (R)	Common Agricultural Policy to promote sustainable agriculture by removing direct payments for production, carbon credits for energy crops (R); Rural Development Policy to promote food quality schemes, support organic farming and agri-environmental measures (F)

Table 10.1 (*cont.*)

Major policies and measures	United States	Australia	United Kingdom	European Union	Japan
Waste management					
Landfill policy to reduce landfill gases	Stringent landfill rule to reduce methane and landfill gas emissions (R)	Reduce and capture methane emissions (V, R, F)	EU Landfill Directive to reduce methane and landfill gas emissions (R)	EU Landfill Directive to reduce landfill waste and recover landfill gas (R)	
Recycling, reuse, and recovery policies	WasteWise to encourage recycling, source reduction, etc. (V, T, I, RD&D)		Waste Strategy 2000 to reduce quantity of waste produced; landfill tax with constantly rising rate (F)	Recovery rates for waste packaging (R); recovery of waste electrical and electronic equipment (R); acceptance of used vehicles and recovery by their producers (R)	Waste Disposal Law and Recycling Plan to promote waste reduction, reuse, and recycling (V)

Incineration policies				Reduce negative impacts of incineration and coincineration of waste (R)	Upgrade combustion in incineration facilities (V)
Forestry	Build capacity to enhance forest sinks (I, RD&D); encourage environmental plantings (F, I); remove impediments to plantation establishment (F, I); reduce land-use change emissions from clearing of native vegetation (R)	Forest Land Enhancement Program to help private landowners meet explicit carbon sequestration goals (T, E) .	UK Forestry Standard (R, I); woodland grants scheme for England (F); woodland planting for reforestation in Scotland (F, grant)	Sustainable forestry (R); prevent damage to forests by fires and tropical deforestation (R)	Promote appropriate forest management practices (V); establish new forests; Urban Greening to create city parks

Types of policies and measures: E = education and outreach, F = economic/fiscal, I = information, R = regulatory, RD&D = research, development, and deployment, T = technical, V = voluntary, O = various/other.
ETS = Emissions Trading Scheme (European Union). BAT = Best Available Technology.

The results are summarized in Table 10.1. Overall, the five parties report a broad range of individual policies and measures. Only the European Union has established a formal emissions trading scheme; the other four parties all report integrated climate programs of one type or another. The United States focuses on its voluntary reporting under the 1605(b) program, and both the United Kingdom and Japan refer to their comprehensive plans.

Within the energy sector, all five parties report extensive activities, ranging from regulatory programs for renewable energy and energy management to voluntary, information, and education programs. In the transportation sector, all report programs involving both vehicles and fuels. These programs rely on a variety of mechanisms, including regulatory requirements, voluntary efforts, RD&D, and financial initiatives. Beyond vehicles and fuels, most also have some activities in the areas of integrated transport planning, efficiency in aviation, and agreements or partnerships.

In the industrial and agricultural sectors, several programs focus on CO_2 while others specifically address the non-CO_2 gases. As in the other sectors, these policies involve many different activities, including information, education, and technical support. All five parties also report a broad range of policies in the areas of waste management and forestry.

Our examination of these national communications, along with the comments prepared by the UNFCCC reviewers and others, reveals several problems. Overall, it is difficult to ascertain the quality of the reports because important information for evaluating the effectiveness of individual policies is often lacking. Many policies and measures are presented in the absence of clear baselines and the reports generally suffer from a lack of transparency. A number of the national communications emphasize proposed or planned policies rather than providing an evaluation of existing policies or programs. Whether these omissions are strategic or simply reflect missing information is difficult to determine. Nonetheless, the extent of these problems calls into question the credibility of the programs.

Some of these observed problems could be easily remedied. For example, more information on the additionality of the policies could be provided, and the methods and assumptions used to project the emissions reductions associated with individual policies could be presented more clearly. Other problems are more serious and would likely be more difficult to correct, such as the potential for double counting reductions and the use of inconsistent baselines across policies, sometimes even within a single sector or program.

In the area of R&D, at least one country labels its efforts as financial instruments without providing information on the types of research activities being undertaken. In other cases, where some descriptive information is provided, there appear to be inconsistencies in the data. Information on the additionality of the policies is often missing, and some of the national communications do not indicate whether reported activities are newly implemented or represent activities that have been previously counted or reclassified.

In the area of voluntary programs, which are among the most popular of the policies and measures reported, the focus is almost exclusively on program descriptions, with very little quantification of resulting emissions reductions compared with a realistic baseline. In many cases, the reductions are compared with base-year emissions, without accounting for the likely progress that would have occurred even in a business-as-usual scenario. Also, only a few parties made an effort to address the potential for double counting. When the problem is addressed, it is often only in the form of an aggregate "guesstimate" rather than a program-specific analysis. Australia, which has devoted considerable resources to creating methodologies for evaluating and reporting its climate policy efforts and maintaining comparability across sectors, provides perhaps the clearest exception to these observations. Australia has developed separate methodological guidelines for each sector that detail how to accurately monitor, report, and verify emissions. In May 2005, the Australian Greenhouse Office initiated the Australian Greenhouse Emissions Information System to combine all emissions data and reporting processes into one unit to increase the transparency and accessibility of the inventory. This system integrates all the sector methodologies and incorporates quality control procedures into the process, using the Guideline Key Tier 1 quality assurance/quality control (QA/QC) procedures of the UN's Intergovernmental Panel on Climate Change (IPCC). This information is made public through an interactive website.

To ensure accuracy, Australia's National Greenhouse Gas Inventory Committee reviews all emissions inventories before they are released. The Australian Greenhouse Office examines the performance of individual policies and measures and updates its projections yearly. The report clearly distinguishes between policies that are existing, new, or reclassified. The emissions projections include both business-as-usual scenarios and scenarios with policies and measures, and a consensus forecasting approach is used for the calculations. Sector projections are published yearly and reviewed biannually. The Australian Greenhouse Office also publishes individual papers that provide more detail on some of the methodologies. The national communication provides a web link to those papers and a brief overview of the sector-specific projections; it also includes a summary of major assumptions, a graph showing emissions projections with policies and measures and under the business-as-usual scenario, an assessment of the impact of current measures, and a description of the models used.

Although non-Annex I nations are not obligated to provide reports as comprehensive as those of the Annex I countries, China, India, and several other nations have gone beyond the minimum reporting requirements. However, these efforts generally do not include an attempt to project current or future emissions, either with or without the implementation of policies and measures. What quantitative analysis is presented is often based on outdated information. As with the information displayed in Table 10.1 from developed nations, it is not possible to determine whether such practices are strategic or reflect genuine data gaps.

Other practices

Other international processes may provide lessons for evaluating the quality, consistency, and value of *ex ante* estimates of commitment. Several multilateral organizations conduct national policy reviews. However, most existing international peer- and expert-review processes are also relatively weak, designed for offering qualitative advice rather than for enforcing commitments, and no one process provides an ideal template.

Several established review processes give attention to energy and environmental concerns. For example, the International Energy Agency conducts an in-depth review of each member country's energy policies and sectors every five years, using a standard assessment process and offering nonbinding suggestions for policy improvements. Although the agency gathers data and technical information about projections, these reviews are primarily qualitative rather than quantitative. The UN Economic Commission for Europe has a purely voluntary Environmental Performance Review, conducted to meet the needs of the country being reviewed. The Energy Charter Protocol on Energy Efficiency and Related Environmental Aspects (PEEREA) requires members to formulate clear policy aims (as opposed to obligations) for improving energy efficiency and mitigating environmental impacts associated with energy. PEEREA provides a forum for information exchange and policy advice, in part through peer reviews of energy-efficiency policies and programs. These peer reviews involve consultations with national governments and information gathering and overlap to a significant extent with the national communications prepared in accord with UNFCCC requirements; thus, the PEEREA efforts may in part rely on, and in part reinforce, the UNFCCC process. PEEREA reports are made available to the public, although they are primarily designed for the reviewed country.

Other review processes focus on different economic policies. For example, the International Monetary Fund (IMF), in its country surveillance program, conducts annual consultations with member countries about exchange rate and financial sector policies, as well as about the overall economic situation. These reports are also primarily qualitative. Findings and recommendations are reported to the executive board, which transmits its views back to governmental authorities in the country being reviewed, which are also the primary consumers of review results. Most member countries agree to allow publication of these IMF reports, but public dissemination is not required. A more voluntary review that is open to developing countries is the United Nations Conference on Trade and Development (UNCTAD) Investment Policy Review, which is intended to offer policy advice and support, not to monitor any commitments.

The World Trade Organization (WTO) has its Trade Policy Review Mechanism, developed by agreement in the Uruguay Round, which offers regular, comprehensive reviews of individual members' trade policies and practices and their impacts on the functioning of the multilateral trading system. Although the review is mandatory, it is not intended as an enforcement mechanism; rather, it is expected to foster greater adherence to obligations by improving transparency and providing information about each country's practices and circumstances. The review mechanism itself is also subject to appraisal and improvement over time, which is a laudable feature. However, like most existing international review processes, the Trade Policy Review

Mechanism offers a primarily qualitative appraisal rather than a quantitative assessment of impacts on trade. The same kinds of quantitative assessments are made under WTO auspices during dispute settlement, but in those cases the evaluations are narrowly focused on the traded good in question. Furthermore, most of these calculations are conducted by the disputing parties and therefore reflect their obvious interests (although the Subsidies and Countervailing Measures Agreement prescribes the methods for calculating financial benefits conferred by certain subsidies). Although the WTO dispute resolution process does seem to offer the main example of quantitative, model-based analysis, it may be a poor guide for designing processes intended to foster cooperation and negotiate consensus.

Indeed, although the multilateral trading system offers some lessons in negotiating and supporting international agreements, the circumstances are quite different for a climate framework. In trade, countries negotiate the removal of barriers to foreign goods in exchange for the benefits of greater access to foreign markets. In climate change, there is no such exchange; negotiations center on how to share a global burden, and the benefits are far removed in time and not excluded from nonparticipants. Perceptions of fairness and effort thus play a greater role, even though global outcomes are ultimately what matter.

Conclusion

As the focus in international negotiations moves beyond sole reliance on national emissions targets to include specific policies and measures, there is a clear need to improve the current reporting system so that it provides greater confidence to negotiators about the credibility of countries' activities. Most importantly, reported activities need to be presented in a relatively uniform, consistent fashion. Current guidelines attempt to accommodate the metrics used in different countries, but the breadth of different reporting practices in use today can mask genuine differences among countries. Thus, a first order of business should be the development of a much tighter, narrowly defined set of guidelines that reveal the actual differences in activities among nations. Of course, no single metric can adequately address the complex issues of equity and integrity that are central to a successful international agreement on climate change mitigation. Still, some approaches are likely to be more effective than others.

First, regarding the fairness of country-level commitments, certain metrics—such as emissions as a share of GDP, population, or historical emissions—are straightforward to calculate and provide generally informative, albeit imperfect, indicators of burden. Other metrics, like emissions reductions or total costs of policies undertaken, are unlikely to be reported reliably. The metric of marginal abatement costs at least has the advantage of indicating the cost-effectiveness of the effort undertaken across different countries. It is also an important indicator of the controversial competitiveness impacts of climate policies *vis-à-vis* trading partners. We recommend greater focus on this measure but note the difficulty of attributing the marginal costs of nonmarket-based policies, especially inefficient measures. The big question is what carbon price would achieve the same reductions as the suite of policies selected, either by sector or for the whole economy. This would be analogous to calculating the level of effective protection applied in analyses of trade disputes.

Second, regarding the integrity of country-level commitments, we see related but distinct issues associated with *ex post* efforts to verify performance (essentially compliance) and the *ex ante* challenges faced by international negotiators in comparing often quite dissimilar policies and measures. For *ex post* verification, the simplicity of an aggregate, economy-wide emissions target, or even of an emissions-intensity target, is quite appealing. Existing data and reporting systems are certainly compatible with such approaches. When commitments involve subnational or specific regulatory or voluntary programs, they should be expressed in terms of a transparent, verifiable goal, such as a fuel efficiency standard or level of technology deployment. However, while such goals may be clear, their effects on emissions are less transparent. Therefore, descriptive, institutionally-oriented information must be supplemented with concrete data on the actual implementation and performance of these measures. Focusing on specific emissions goals as opposed to regulatory standards can help avoid excessive reliance on model-based counterfactuals. Because of their long-term nature, R&D programs are difficult to compare with near-term emissions targets, but these activities should at least be made more comparable across countries. We see no alternative to relying on actual expenditure and deployment data, but care should be taken to link such data to specific program activities and to include transparent baseline information.

Third, *ex ante* assessment of the integrity of commitments (in terms of whether they are likely to achieve claimed emissions reductions) is, perhaps, the most important but also the most problematic area. The greatest challenges are associated with the unavoidable need to model counterfactuals, with all the attendant complexities. New guidelines should focus on the need for greater transparency in methods, models, and data, plus the need for greater standardization in methodologies to improve the consistency of analysis across sectors, policies, and countries. Another priority is strengthening the mandate of the international group of experts who evaluate country submissions. The current practice of UNFCCC peer review is far too loose an arrangement for the reports to be credible inputs to climate negotiations.

National governments may not provide the objective evaluation that is essential to make a serious comparison between national mitigation proposals. Therefore, independent institutions, international organizations, academic researchers, and other third-party groups must play a greater role. A strengthened and improved reporting and evaluation framework should harness and empower these other actors. Indeed, this framework should go beyond the mandates of most existing review mechanisms in the following ways:

- Evaluation should be a condition for participation in multilateral negotiations and agreements.
- Reports and data should be publicly available, to inform not only the countries being reviewed but also their negotiating partners.
- Peer reviews should be independent and use consistent methodologies to promote harmonized reporting.
- Evaluations should include quantitative as well as qualitative analyses.
- A mechanism for periodic review of the evaluation process should be established.

Even with a strengthened reporting and evaluation framework, however, the thorny question remains: What exactly will be reported, monitored, verified, and evaluated? The current focus on emissions inventories must be expanded to better allow for the verification and evaluation of policies, measures, and other activities. This effort requires collecting objective quantitative measures and data on implementation (besides just emissions); it also requires conducting consistent modeling and analyses to judge the effectiveness of the activities being implemented. Toward that end, transparent documentation and clear guidelines for evaluation efforts can improve the comparability and credibility of the entire process.

Furthermore, in the spirit of common but differentiated responsibilities, a future reporting and evaluation framework may not require the same levels of sophistication for developing countries as for technically advanced countries. The review mechanism needs to be adequate and appropriate to underpin evolving commitments and proposals in the negotiating process. It should also offer developing countries the kinds of technical and policy support seen in many existing international voluntary review mechanisms, albeit targeted to the climate change challenge.

Addressing global climate change will be a long process of ongoing negotiations, compliance verification, and performance evaluations—all continually feeding back into each other. The complexity of the task requires much-improved information collecting, sharing, and review. Since agreement on a single metric of national contributions is unrealistic, agreement on a common, consistent, and credible set of indicators should be prioritized to build the foundation of trust and transparency needed to sustain multifaceted commitments.

References

Aldy, Joseph E. and Robert N. Stavins, eds. (2007). *Architectures for Agreement: Addressing Global Climate Change in the Post-Kyoto World*. New York: Cambridge University Press.

Baer, Paul, John Harte, Barbara Haya, Anthony V. Herzog, John P. Holdren, Nathan E. Hultman, Daniel M. Kammen, Richard B. Norgaard, and Leigh Raymond (2000). "Equity and Greenhouse Gas Responsibility," *Science* 289 (September 29): 2287.

Bodansky, D. (2004). *International Climate Efforts beyond 2012: A Survey of Approaches*. Washington, DC: Pew Center on Global Climate Change.

Cazorla, Marina V. and Michael A. Toman (2001). "International Equity and Climate Change Policy," in Michael A. Toman (ed.), *Climate Change Economics and Policy*. Washington, DC: Resources for the Future Press.

Ellis, Jane, Jan Corfee-Morlot, and Bruno Guay (2008). "Metrics to Measure Mitigation Potential and to Compare Mitigation Effort: Exploring the Fundamental Questions," draft, May 7, Paris, France: OECD.

Ellis, Jane and Kate Larsen (2008). *Measurement, Reporting and Verification of Mitigation Actions and Commitments*. Paris: OECD/IEA.

Fischer, Carolyn, Henry Jacoby, and Richard Morgenstern (2005). "Comparing National Commitments in a Fragmented Policy World: A Draft Research Outline," draft paper presented at the Climate Policy Network, Sardinia, Italy, September 14.

Fischer, Carolyn and Richard D. Morgenstern (2006). "Carbon Abatement Costs: Why the Wide Range of Estimates?" *Energy Journal* 27(2): 73–86.

Fischer, Carolyn and Richard Newell (2008). "Environmental and Technology Policies for Climate Mitigation," *Journal of Environmental Economics and Management* 55(2): 142–62.

Frankel, Jeffrey (2007). "Formulas for Quantitative Emission Targets," in Aldy and Stavins (eds.), pp. 31–56.

Morgenstern, Richard and William Pizer (2007). *Reality Check: The Nature and Performance of Voluntary Environmental Programs in the United States, Europe and Japan*. Washington, DC: Resources for the Future Press.

Wooders, Peter (2006). *Evaluating Energy Efficiency Policies and Measures*. Brussels: Energy Charter Secretariat. Background paper, designated CS(06)1064; PEEREA 109, prepared by Environmental Resources Management (ERM) for the Energy Charter Meeting of the Working Group on Energy Efficiency and Related Environmental Issues, 14–15 June 2006.

11 | Justice and climate change: the unpersuasive case for per capita allocations of emissions rights

ERIC A. POSNER* AND
CASS R. SUNSTEIN**

Introduction

Many people believe that the problem of climate change should be handled by an international cap-and-trade system. Under this approach, participating nations, and perhaps the entire world, would create a "cap" on greenhouse gas (GHG) emissions. Nations would be allocated specified emissions rights, which could be traded in return for cash. Other people have doubts about whether such a system is practical, and it is becoming increasingly likely that some other approach will be used—for example, a cap-and-trade system in the north along with technical and financial assistance and general targets for the south.

Both types of system raise broad questions of welfare and justice. Consider, for example, the cap-and-trade system. The proposal for such a system does not answer a crucial question: how should emissions rights be allocated? It is tempting to suggest that the status quo, across nations, provides the appropriate baseline. According to one view, emissions might be frozen at existing levels, so that every nation has the right to its current level of emissions. Taking a more aggressive view, all or most signatory nations should have to reduce their emissions levels by a specified percentage, again taking the status quo as the foundation for reductions. The status quo might seem to have intuitive appeal, but it is also somewhat arbitrary and raises serious questions from the standpoint of equity. Why should climate change policy take

* Kirkland & Ellis Professor, University of Chicago Law School.
** Felix Frankfurter Professor of Law, Harvard Law School. Thanks to Joe Aldy, Robert Hahn, Robert Stavins, David Weisbach, and an anonymous referee, for comments and Sung Eun Jung and Adam Wells for research assistance.

existing national emissions, and to that extent existing national patterns of energy use, as a given for policy purposes? Should a nation with 300 million people be given the same emissions rights as a nation with 1 billion people, or 40 million people, simply because the emissions of the three nations, at the current time, are roughly equal?

Raising these questions, many observers have strenuously urged that in an international agreement, emissions rights should be allocated by reference to population, not to existing emissions.[1] The intuition here is that every person on the planet should begin with the same emissions right; it should not matter whether people find themselves in a nation whose existing emissions rates are high. Those concerned about the welfare of developing nations are especially interested in per capita allocations of emissions rights. Why should a poor nation, with a large population, be required to stick close to its current emissions level, when wealthy nations with identical populations are permitted to emit far more? Why should existing distributions of wealth, insofar as they are reflected in current emissions, be taken as the foundation for climate change policy? More bluntly: why should the United States be given emissions rights that dwarf those of China and India, which have much larger populations?

This argument might well be connected with a general "right to development" (United Nations General Assembly 1986). If the status quo is the baseline for allocating emissions rights, poor nations are likely to have great difficulty in achieving the levels of development already attained by wealthy nations. Perhaps an imaginable climate change agreement, one that would be based on existing national rates, would violate the "right to development" even if it were both effective and efficient.

These questions and controversies are relevant for alternative proposals that do not advocate a global cap-and-trade regime. If the North is to

---

[1] See, e.g., National Development and Reform Commission, People's Republic of China (2007), p. 58; Bodansky (2004) (describing several per capita approaches); Agarwal (1999); Agarwal and Narain (1991); Athanasiou and Baer (2002); Kinzig and Kammen (1998); Altamirano-Cabrera and Finus (2006); Sagar (2000); Singer (2002); Kokott (1999); Ott and Sachs (2002) ("The equal right of all world citizens to the atmospheric commons is therefore the cornerstone of any viable climate regime."); Aslam (2002); Brown (2002); Bode (2003). See also Roberts and Parks (2007) for a description of international support for the per capita approach; and Frankel (2007) for discussion of developing world demand for a per capita system.

give financial assistance to the South, how great should this assistance be? If the South is to agree on targets, how ambitious should these targets be? Although we will focus on the cap-and-trade approach, which has been more widely discussed and is therefore better understood, our general conclusions apply to the alternative proposals as well.

The relationship between climate change and questions of justice is exceedingly large, and our goal in this chapter is relatively narrow. We aim to make some progress on the broader question by identifying the problems with the per capita system, in terms of both principle and feasibility, and to suggest that its current prominence and popularity are undeserved. We suggest that advocates of per capita allocations are correct on one point: in principle, there is little to be said for basing emissions rights on existing emissions levels. The most plausible defense of this approach is pragmatic. Nations are unlikely to sign an international agreement if they will be significant net losers (Goldsmith and Posner 2006), and wealthy nations might lose a great deal from any approach that does not use existing emissions as the baseline for reductions. But this pragmatic point shows only that powerful nations might well veto approaches that are better in principle; it does not show that those nations are correct to do so. As a matter of principle, an approach based on per capita emissions rights seems preferable to one based on existing emissions, and there are strong intuitive claims, rooted in welfarist and other arguments, on behalf of such an approach. One of our principal purposes is to cast those claims in a sympathetic light.

As we shall also see, however, a per capita approach runs into powerful objections. We demonstrate this point by comparing that approach to several others, above all those based on existing emissions and those with explicitly redistributive aims. Most fundamentally, per capita allocations will help some rich nations and hurt some poor ones. The reason is that some rich nations are highly populated, and some poor nations are not. In fact there is no correlation between population size and wealth per capita. If global redistribution or international justice is the goal, the per capita approach is a highly imperfect means.

Many people support the per capita approach not on redistributive grounds, but on the basis of a simple and plausible appeal to fairness.[2] The atmosphere's carbon-absorbing features are naturally thought of

---

[2] See, e.g., Grubb *et al.* (1992), pp. 318–19 (and citations therein).

as a common resource. Perhaps a common resource should be divided among all the people in the world on the ground that all people enjoy a right to equal opportunity or to equal human dignity.[3] Indeed, the same type of argument has been made about mineral resources discovered under the high seas: as no particular state "owns" these resources, they should be divided on a per capita basis.[4] And given the constraints of national sovereignty, the resources should be given to national governments on the basis of their state's share of the global population rather than divided up among individuals directly.

We will show that the analogy to common property is at best incomplete and obscures the relevant moral concerns. If we compare a climate treaty and a treaty that provides for the exploitation of an underwater mineral deposit, we immediately see that there is a crucial difference between the two settings. A climate treaty, by reducing global warming, will have differential benefits and costs for people around the world. While some people will benefit a great deal, others will benefit much less and perhaps not at all. By contrast, exploitation of mineral deposits has minimal differential effects. Per capita distribution of GHG emission permits would distribute the revenues from the abatement program on an equal basis, but would not equalize the overall effects of that program.

In principle, the appropriate way to distribute permits is on the basis of the aggregate effects of the climate treaty in light of standard normative theories—emphasizing, for example, distributive justice, welfare, or fairness.[5] From the standpoint of those theories, and in particular on welfarist grounds, the per capita approach does have major advantages over an approach based on existing emissions, because it would provide significantly greater benefits to poor people. But the per capita approach would also have some unfortunate incen-

---

[3] Universal Declaration of Human Rights, Art. 1.

[4] The Law of the Sea Convention provides that such resources be divided "equitably"; however, that term has multiple meanings and is left undefined. See United Nations Convention on the Law of the Sea, Art. 140.

[5] We do not explore the important controversy over historic responsibility—the claim that wealthier nations should play a special role in a climate change agreement because of their past, cumulative contributions; that therefore, developing nations should benefit from grandfathering and similar approaches; or that industrialized nations should be rewarded to the extent that they have generated benefits for others; and so forth. For discussion of these issues, see Posner and Sunstein (2008).

tive effects, which complicate the inquiry. Even if those effects are put to one side, a per capita approach is far inferior to an approach that focuses more concretely on what the right normative theory requires.

Our conclusions are that on welfarist grounds, the per capita approach is at most a crude second-best, and that it faces decisive objections from the standpoint of feasibility. Insistence on that approach would endanger and very possibly doom an international effort to reduce the risks associated with climate change.

Despite the narrowness of our conclusions, we hope that the analysis bears on some broader questions of justice, which are playing an important role in discussions of climate change. It is increasingly clear that distributive issues are crucial as a matter of both principle and practice. The allocation of effort across countries is relevant whatever the world does—and the distribution of benefits and burdens is a serious challenge in any international agreement that seeks mitigation efforts among the participants. As and when adaptation is necessary in developing nations, it remains possible to reject the per capita approach while also arguing that wealthy countries should help fund adaptation. Some of our arguments bear on that possibility. In our view, a clear understanding of the problems with the per capita approach should help to cast light on other, more plausible approaches for reducing the risks of climate change in a way that meets the requirements of justice.

The effects of a per capita permit system

Aggregate emissions vs. per capita emissions

An international agreement might allocate emissions rights in many different ways. One possibility would be to begin with existing emissions rates and freeze them or require a percentage reduction. If existing rates are the baseline, the ranking across nations would look one way, with China and the United States at the top.[6] But if we look on a per capita basis, the ranking is altogether different. Because of explosive emissions growth in developing nations, any particular ranking will change over time, but some of the basic conclusions are clear (World Resources Institute). For example, the United States ranks

---

[6] See, e.g., Netherlands Environmental Assessment Agency (2008).

toward the top of the world's emitters on a per capita basis as well as in the aggregate, but India ranks very low in a per capita basis. Perhaps the most striking point is that while China has become the world's leading national emitter of GHGs, its per capita contributions remain fairly modest, ranking it well below the top fifty contributors.

With dramatic growth in emissions from China and India, some of these conclusions will change over time; per capita emission rates in China, in particular, will be far higher in ten years. But it is clear that per capita allocations would produce radically different distributional effects from allocations based on the national status quo. With per capita emissions rights, the world's largest nations—China and India—would be significant net gainers. Indeed, their emissions rights would probably be worth hundreds of billions of dollars. The principal losers would be the nations that now have high per capita emissions. The biggest loser, by far, would probably be the United States. Because of their high per capita emissions, Canada and Australia would lose a great deal as well.

With this background, we should be able to glimpse the intuitive argument on behalf of per capita allocations. Nations are not people; they are collections of people. A citizen of India should not be given emissions rights that are a small fraction of those of a citizen of the United States. Nor should a citizen of China be given emissions rights that are a small fraction of those of a citizen of Japan. Each person should count for no more and no less than one. As we shall see, this intuition might be grounded in concerns of either welfare or fairness. But before we investigate these issues, it is necessary to untangle some complexities. An initial task is to obtain a better understanding of the effects of a per capita approach.

A simple example

Suppose that a firm consumes energy (and other inputs) to create goods that it sells on the market. Let us suppose that for every unit of energy (however defined) that the firm consumes, it generates GHG emissions that have a social cost of $10.

One approach to GHG regulation would involve taxation. In this example, the optimal tax would be $10 per unit of energy—the amount necessary to ensure that the firm uses a unit of energy only when the private benefit exceeds the social cost. Alternatively (and

Table 11.1 *An example*

	Aggregate energy consumption	Population	Energy consumption per capita
Rich State	100	5	20
Poor State	20	20	1

identically), the firm could be prohibited from consuming energy unless it bought a permit from the government. The permit would have a price of $10. Let us stipulate that if the permit is traded, the price will be $10 as well.

The tax system and the permit system would raise revenue as well as deter the emission of GHGs. In this example, each system would generate revenue of $10 per unit of energy. That money could be spent in any way: for example, the revenue could go into the treasury of the government that levied the tax or sold the permit, and then be used for ordinary budget expenditures or to lower general taxes. Note that the revenue raised would partially but not fully offset the immediate loss to consumer welfare. Firms would pass the tax along to consumers, who would either pay the higher price (and have less money to buy other things) or buy fewer energy-intensive goods. However, we assume that in the aggregate people are better off: the environmental benefits exceed the welfare losses from reduced consumption. Otherwise, there would be no reason to negotiate a climate treaty.

Now imagine that the world consists of two nations, Rich State and Poor State. Rich State has a large economy and relatively few people, while Poor State has a small economy and relatively many people. (For concreteness, we might assume that Rich State is analogous to the United States and that Poor State is analogous to India.) Suppose that Rich State consumes 100 units of energy at the time that the climate treaty goes into force, while Poor State consumes 20 units of energy. (For simplicity, we assume that Rich State and Poor State do not trade; citizens of each country consume the output of firms in that country.) Rich State has 5 citizens, while Poor State has 20 citizens. Thus, Rich State consumes 20 units of energy per citizen; Poor State consumes one unit of energy per citizen. Table 11.1 displays this information.

The tax system would require the government of each country to levy a $10-per-unit tax on each firm. Rich State would tax 100 units of

Table 11.2 *Taxes versus permits*

	Aggregate energy consumption	Tax per unit of energy	Tax revenues	Equivalent permits at $10/permit
Rich State	100	$10	$1000	100
Poor State	20	$10	$200	20

energy and receive revenues of $1,000, while Poor State would tax 20 units of energy and receive revenues of $200. Under the permit system, the treaty would authorize Rich State to sell 100 permits and Poor State to sell 20 permits. As Table 11.2 shows, the distributive effects would be the same: Rich State would raise $1000 in revenue and Poor State would raise $200 in revenue.

We will call this *the status quo approach* because it takes as its baseline the relative use of energy in the status quo. If one thinks of the treaty as "creating" permits, then the treaty would distribute more permits to Rich State than to Poor State, just because Rich State consumes more energy than Poor State. The treaty would create 120 permits, and give 100 permits to Rich State and 20 permits to Poor State. Note that the effect of this treaty is identical to the tax approach described above.

Alternative approaches

As noted, the status quo approach to distribution is based on the amount of energy consumption at the time the treaty enters into force. Because Rich State consumes five times as much energy as Poor State, Rich State receives five times as many permits as Poor State. And because wealthy countries consume more energy than poor countries, the status quo approach seems to favor wealthy countries. Of course, any judgment about whether particular nations are "favored" depends on a baseline. Rich State will surely point out that its own firms pay the revenue that it obtains from its extra permits, so that the effects wash out. It is a nice puzzle why a uniform emissions tax is not generally or intuitively taken to be unfair while the status quo approach to emissions rights is often found objectionable—even though the two are identical in their effects. But at least it can be said that the status quo approach will generally give more permits to wealthy nations than to poor ones, holding population constant, simply because wealthy nations tend to emit more GHGs.

Other approaches are possible. For example, under the *per-nation approach*, the treaty would distribute equal numbers of permits to every nation. Rich State and Poor State would each receive 60 permits. This approach also does not seem intuitively fair. All nations receive the same number of permits, but they must spread the revenues from the permits among different numbers of citizens. In effect, Poor State's 20 citizens receive 3 permits each; Rich State's 5 citizens receive 12 permits each (though it is unlikely that the government would directly hand out permits to citizens).

The *per capita approach* seems much better on this score. Each nation receives permits in proportion to its population. In our example, Poor State has four times as many citizens as Rich State, so Poor State receives 96 permits and Rich State receives 24 permits. Each citizen in both countries receives, in effect, 4.8 permits.

A final approach that we will consider will be called the *redistributive approach*. Under this approach, all the permits are given to whichever country is poorer, at least up until the point where their wealth is equalized. If we assume that Poor State is sufficiently poorer than Rich State, the redistributive approach would require that all 120 permits be given to Poor State. Poor State would then sell 20 permits to its own firms and 100 to Rich State's firms, thus acquiring all the revenue from the permit system. Table 11.3 displays this information.

Note that other approaches are possible, including mixed approaches that fall between the various approaches described above. For example, one could allocate permits on the basis of a formula that weights both population size and poverty (Frankel 2007). For simplicity, however, we will confine our discussion to the four approaches described above: status quo, per-nation, per capita, and redistributive.

A note on ex post efficiency

From what we will call the "*ex post* efficiency" perspective (our reasons for using this term will become clear later), all of these approaches are identical (assuming that the trading system works as planned). *Ex post* efficiency requires that energy users bear the social (climate) cost of energy use. If that cost is $10 per unit of energy, then

Table 11.3 *Four permit allocation schemes*

	Status quo		Per nation		Per capita		Redistributive	
	Permits	Per capita	Permits	Per capita	Permits	Per capita	Permits	Per capita
Rich State	100	20	60	12	24	4.8	0	0
Poor State	20	1	60	3	96	4.8	120	6

Note: Calculate revenues in aggregate and per capita by multiplying by $10

either a $10 tax should be used, or states should create the number of permits such that the market price is $10. All of our approaches allow states to set the price of the permits at $10 or whatever the optimal price is, so they are all equally efficient.

The only differences between the approaches are distributive. As we saw, under the status quo approach, Rich State's government would receive 100 permits and Poor State's government would receive 20 permits. Rich State would sell those 100 permits to the Rich State firms, and Poor State would sell the 20 permits to the Poor State firms. Under the per-state approach, Poor State would sell 20 of the permits to Poor State firms and 40 of its permits to the remaining Rich State firms that were unable to purchase the 60 permits distributed to the Rich State government. Under the per capita approach, a similar outcome would occur. If Poor State receives 96 permits, its government would sell 76 of the permits to Rich State firms. The same is true for the redistributive approach.

Distribution

We have seen that under the status quo system, Rich State would raise revenues of $1,000 while Poor State would raise revenues of only $200. By contrast, the per-nation system would give Rich State revenues of $600 and Poor State revenues of $600. The per capita system, where Poor State is four times as large as Rich State, gives Poor State revenues of $960 and Rich State revenues of $240. And under the redistributive system, Poor State would receive $1,200 and Rich State would receive $0.

These figures summarize the redistribution that occurs across nations. But it is also important to understand the per capita redistributive effect of the various policies. Under the status quo system, Rich State receives $200 per capita, while Poor State receives $10 per capita. Under the per-nation system, Rich State receives $120 per capita, while Poor State receives $20 per capita. Under the per capita system, Rich State receives $48 per capita, as does Poor State. Under the redistributive approach, Rich State receives $0 per capita, while Poor State receives $60 per capita (see Table 11.4).

To obtain a full understanding of the distributive effects of the alternatives, we need to take into account the benefit side of the climate treaty. The permit system would reduce GHG emissions, resulting

Table 11.4 *Distributive effects of permit allocation schemes*

System	Permit Distribution	Aggregate Revenue	Aggregate Net Benefits R: $2000 P: $0	R: $0 P: $2000	R: $1000 P: $1000
Status quo	100/20	1000/200	3000/200	**1000/2200**	2000/1200
Per-nation	60/60	**600/600**	2600/800	600/2600	**1600/1600**
Per capita	24/96	240/960	2240/960	240/2960	1240/1960
Redistrib.	0/120	0/1200	**2000/1200**	0/3200	1000/2200

System	Per Capita Permit Distribution	Per Capita Revenue	Per Capita Net Benefits R: $400 P: $0	R: $0 P: $100	R: $200 P: $50
Status quo	20/1	200/10	600/10	200/110	400/60
Per-nation	12/3	120/30	520/30	**120/130**	320/80
Per capita	4.8/4.8	**48/48**	448/48	48/148	248/98
Redistrib.	0/6	0/60	**400/60**	0/160	**200/110**

in mitigation of climate change. These benefits could be the same for Rich State and for Poor State, or different. It is well known that the benefits of reducing climate change are not constant across nations.[7] Some nations have far more to lose than others from (say) an increase in global average temperature of 2.5 degrees Celsius, while some nations are likely to experience net gains from this level of warming. Under prominent projections, India and African nations are especially vulnerable, and the United States and China have significantly less to lose; Russia might even gain. Here again we might consider both aggregate and per capita effects. Suppose that the mitigation benefits of a climate treaty produce benefits of $2,000 for one state and $0 for the other state, or $1,000 for both states. If the benefits accrue to Rich State in the first case, then each of its few citizens receive a benefit of $400; if the benefits instead accrue to Poor State, then each of its many citizens receive a benefit of $100. In the second case, each Rich State citizen receives benefits worth $200 and each Poor State citizen receives benefits of $50. Table 11.4 summarizes the discussion so far. The first panel displays aggregate figures; the second panel displays

---

[7] See, e.g., Nordhaus and Boyer (2000), p. 91; and Anthoff *et al.* (2007).

per capita figures. The first figure in each cell displays Rich State's (or Rich State citizens') gain; the second figure does the same for Poor State. The Permit Distribution column displays the distribution of permits, as depicted in Table 11.3. The Aggregate Revenue column multiplies these numbers by 10 to calculate revenues from the sale of permits. The final three columns display net treaty benefits (revenue plus climate benefits) under the three different assumptions about how the beneficial impacts of an effective climate treaty are distributed between the Rich and Poor State. The cells with bold figures show outcomes that are most nearly equal for the two states.

One can immediately see that there is a large difference between equalizing revenue (Column 3) and equalizing the net benefits of the treaty (Columns 4–6). Focusing on per capita effects (Panel 2), we can see that the per capita approach equalizes revenues, but it does not equalize treaty benefits under any of the three assumptions. Indeed, equalization of revenues can occur amidst gross disparities in treaty benefits—a point that raises serious questions about the idea that per capita distributions are fair.

The per capita approach in principle

From a welfarist perspective

The case for the per capita approach

In discussions about climate treaties, defenders of the per capita approach argue that this approach is fairer than likely alternative approaches, such as the status quo approach. This argument is especially prominent in the developing world, where it is asked: why should wealthy nations be given an entitlement to their existing emissions rights? This question seems to be one of fairness, to which we will turn in due course. But it can also be translated into a plausible welfarist argument. It makes sense to begin with that argument, which is in some ways more tractable, and which will illuminate the fairness questions as well.

Welfarists care about two things: maximizing the size of the pie and distributing it equally. The larger the pie, the more that is available for everyone to consume, and all else equal, welfare should rise with consumption. At the same time, most welfarists believe that the welfare, or utility, that is obtained from each additional good declines as consumption rises.[8] If you have zero apples, you are willing to pay a lot for one apple. If you have ten apples, you are willing to pay much less, or zero, for an eleventh. We can easily see that if disincentive effects are small, welfarists would advocate redistribution of resources from wealthy nations to poor nations, or at least from wealthy people in wealthy and poor nations to poor people in wealthy and poor nations.

With respect to maximizing the size of the pie, we observed above that the per capita approach is no less *ex post* efficient than any other approach. Thus, the welfare effects of different schemes depend entirely on their distributional effects; other things being equal, distribution to those who are poor will increase welfare. To the extent that the larger countries tend to be poorer, the per capita approach will help poor people, and because poor people have the highest marginal utility for a dollar, helping poor people will maximize global welfare. Certainly compared to the status quo approach, per capita allocations seem supportable on welfarist grounds; at first glance, they seem to be the right way to proceed. The examples of the United States on the one hand, and China and India on the other, are highly salient, because the former is rich and the latter two are poor by comparison. To the extent that the per capita approach would require the United States to give hundreds of billions of dollars to China and India, it might seem desirable on welfarist grounds.

At the outset, of course, there is a serious complicating factor, which has to do with the fact that future generations, including currently poor people, will almost certainly be wealthier than current generations.[9] Emissions reductions will help poor people in the future, not poor people in the present, and it is not obvious that policymakers in wealthy nations should attempt to help future poor people, who are likely to be far less poor than present poor people. If the goal is redistributive, current poor people almost certainly deserve priority. This point greatly complicates the claim that emissions reductions are justified on redistributive grounds. Note, however, that we are speaking of emissions rights, not emissions reductions, and emissions rights will benefit people who are now living. For this reason, the redistributive

---

[8] See Adler and Posner (2005). Note that this approach assumes that interpersonal comparisons of utility are possible.

[9] This claim has been made by many people in many places, above all Thomas Schelling. See, e.g., Schelling (1997).

argument, grounded in welfarist considerations, has considerable intuitive appeal.

Objections and Concerns

We have said that welfarists care about equal distribution, believing that money has diminishing marginal utility. From their perspective, the per capita approach has three serious defects. First and most fundamentally, the per capita approach is attractive from a welfarist perspective only insofar as larger states tend to be poorer. Not all large states are poor, and not all small states are rich; indeed, the opposite is frequently the case. The United States has a population of 301 million and per capita GDP of $46,000. Bhutan has a population of 2 million and per capita GDP of $1,400. The per capita approach seems to be a crude and even arbitrary way to redistribute wealth, certainly compared to the pure redistributive approach that gives few or no permits to rich states and all or most of the permits to poor states, regardless of size. We assumed away this problem in our example above because we stipulated that Poor State was both bigger and (as befits its name) poorer. But that assumption (driven perhaps by the examples of the United States, China, and India) is incorrect.

Indeed, the relationship between population and wealth turns out to be essentially zero. For a demonstration, consider Figure 11.1.[10]

Clearly, there are rich small states (upper left), and poor big states (lower right), and everything in between. There is no statistically significant correlation between population and GDP per capita.

Second, the permits—in the scheme that we describe—are distributed to both GHG winners and losers. Some poor states will become far poorer as a result of climate change; others are less vulnerable. Some rich states will face serious adverse effects from climate change; others are less vulnerable. Some poor states, and some rich states, may even be net gainers from climate change. Ideally, permits should be distributed in light of these consequences, but the per capita approach fails to take them into account. If distribution is our concern, why should two highly populated poor nations receive the same number

[10] The figure shows the natural logs of per capita GDP and population averaged over the years 1980 to 2000. Taking the natural log of the variables makes the data points easier to see in a manageable figure. The correlation coefficient between per capita GDP and population is −0.045 and is not statistically significant. The data are taken from Heston *et al.* (2006).

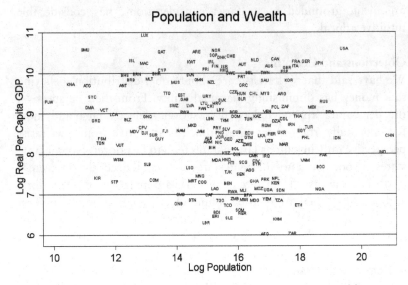

Figure 11.1. Relationship between population and per capita wealth

of permits from a program from which one gains a lot and another a little—or from which one gains a lot and another actually loses?

Third, the permits are allocated to the governments of poor states, not to the citizens of poor states. This distinction matters because nearly all poor states have a class of wealthy elites, and these wealthy elites usually control the government or have considerable influence over it. Given that the governments in these states already are unenthusiastic about redistributing wealth from the elites to the poor, it is questionable that they will use the wealth generated by a permit scheme to help the poor. They may well prefer to help the rich.

The first two problems were illustrated in Table 11.4, above. The key point is that the intuitive attractiveness of the per capita approach depends on seeing it in isolation from all of the effects of a climate treaty. Once we take these factors into account, the per capita approach appears far less attractive, and on plausible assumptions, indefensible from the standpoint of the very accounts that would seem, at least at first sight, to justify it most.

We agree that as a matter of actual practice, these defects are not necessarily fatal to the per capita approach. Everything depends on the alternatives. One might argue in response not that the per capita approach is ideal, but that it is superior to a system that is its most likely alternative—one that uses status quo energy consumption as the baseline and thus favors people living in wealthy and wasteful countries. Perhaps this response is correct. But it must acknowledge the underlying problem, which is that the per capita system is only indirectly connected to the underlying normative goal—indeed, so indirectly that it is conceivable in principle (although most unlikely in practice) that it has worse distributive effects than the status quo approach.

A welfarist should favor redistribution to the world's poor to the extent that doing so is feasible and does not excessively reduce aggregate global welfare. But if one is a welfarist, there is no reason to think that the per capita approach to climate regulation is the right way to redistribute wealth and thus to increase global welfare. It would be much better to redistribute all resources than to redistribute shares of the atmosphere's capacity to absorb GHGs; it would be much better to redistribute resources to poor people rather than to poor nations; and it would be better to redistribute to the poor nations rather than to the large nations. And if redistribution is to occur in the specific context of a climate treaty, the redistributive approach, sketched above, would be much better than the per capita approach.

These points bear directly on the "who pays" question for both emissions reductions and for adaptation. Suppose that we take distributive justice seriously. If so, we might conclude not that the per capita approach is best, but that wealthy nations should pay poor ones for emissions reductions, for adaptation, or for both. This claim itself runs into serious objections, which we cannot explore here;[11] but it is more plausible than the claim for per capita emissions allocations.

Arguments in favor of per capita distribution have, so far, focused on what we have called *ex post* efficiency effects, and neglected the possible *ex ante* effects of the distribution scheme. The *ex ante* effect of a climate treaty refers to its effect on future programs, including those that have nothing to do with GHGs. Any treaty will establish a precedent on which states will rely, at least in part, as they negotiate additional treaties in the future. For example, if the per capita approach is used for a climate treaty, then it will suggest itself as a basis for allocating the costs of a terrorism treaty.

---

[11] For further discussion, see Posner, Sunstein, and Weisbach (forthcoming 2009).

Suppose, then, that a climate treaty based on the per capita approach established a precedent. How might such a precedent influence behavior, compared to the baseline status quo approach? It would create two perverse incentives.

First, the per capita principle would establish that the most highly populated states would obtain the greatest benefits from international cooperation. Governments would be rewarded for pursuing fertility policies that maximize the size of the population. This incentive is especially perverse from the perspective of climate change, because more people will consume more of the earth's resources (though, conceivably, more efficiently). Second, to the extent that the per capita approach favors poorer countries (and that is its only normatively attractive feature), the principle would establish that poorer states would obtain the greatest benefits from international cooperation. Governments that adopt sensible policies that promote economic growth would be penalized by this principle. This incentive is also perverse.

What system, then, is optimal for *ex ante* efficiency? The ideal principle would give states an incentive to identify global problems in advance and negotiate treaties to solve them, and otherwise not affect their incentives to control their populations, invest in institutions, and so forth. Such a principle would be, at a minimum, a form of International Paretianism, so that states believe that they will not be made worse off by a legal solution, a belief that would discourage states from entering treaty negotiations.

But treaties that solve problems generate surpluses beyond the amount necessary to make states indifferent between entering and not entering a treaty. What should be done with the surplus? It is tempting to think that one can distribute the surplus without affecting incentives *ex ante*, but this is highly implausible. (If one can, then one would probably want to distribute the surplus to the poorest countries rather than on a per capita basis, which, as we have been arguing, is morally arbitrary.)

From an efficiency perspective, the best use of the surplus would be to reward the states that had taken steps in advance of the treaty to abate GHG emissions.[12] These states would probably be the

---

[12] Hence the scholarly support for banking systems under which any future climate treaty would reward states that make abatements efforts prior to treaty ratification. See, e.g., Kinzig and Kammen (1998).

European states that accepted binding reductions under the Kyoto Protocol, though there are complexities here, since not all European states accepted meaningful reductions and others were simply taking advantage of independent technological and demographic changes in their country.[13] The larger point is that such a distribution would establish a precedent to the effect that when a global problem exists, states that respond quickly and in advance of a treaty will not be penalized.

It emerges that from the standpoint of *ex ante* efficiency, the per capita approach has serious drawbacks, even when compared with the seemingly unattractive status quo approach. As we have indicated, these drawbacks cannot be evaluated without knowing the magnitude of the effects. If, for example, a climate change agreement had small consequences for population growth, and had little effect on incentives in the context of other international agreements, the drawbacks would not be a substantial concern. Our only point is that they must be investigated in order to obtain a full account of the welfare effects of the per capita approach.

Fairness

Fairness can be specified in multiple different ways. We venture three specifications here in an effort to see whether the per capita approach can be defended on fairness grounds.

Fairness and the veil of ignorance

Many people reject the idea that questions of global justice should be approached in welfarist terms (Pogge 1989; Nussbaum 2006). In their view, the goal is not to promote aggregate social welfare; it is instead to do what fairness requires. Arguments of this kind often posit a veil of ignorance, or "original position," from which allocations might be chosen (Rawls 1999). In the standard version of this argument, people behind the veil do not know various circumstances of their lives; they do not know their place in society, their social status, their class position, or even their natural assets (such as intelligence and strength) (Rawls 1999). The central claim is that the principles that

---

[13] See Harrison and Sundstrom (2007) for a description of the differential effects of the Kyoto Protocol on European countries.

would be chosen behind the veil qualify as fair, because they ensure that outcomes are not a product of factors or considerations that are irrelevant from the moral point of view.

Many people who are attracted to this claim also want to suppose that choosers are made ignorant of the nation in which they might find themselves (Pogge 1989). If deprived of that information, what distributive principles would they select? It is possible that in the international context, as in the domestic one, they would select welfarist ones. Perhaps people would choose to maximize overall welfare, if placed behind the veil.[14] But it is also possible that they would take particular care to protect the least well-off, perhaps through a version of Rawls' difference principle, which permits inequalities only to the extent that they operate to the benefit of the least advantaged (Rawls 1971). There is a vigorous debate over the application of that principle, or imaginable variations of that principle, to the international domain.[15]

We need not pause over the philosophical complexities here. The basic point is that welfarism is rejected by many people who believe that severe deprivation for some cannot be justified by large welfare benefits for many, and that fairness is often taken to require attention to those who face such deprivation, whatever is suggested by the welfarist calculus.[16]

Consider a common sense specification of this claim, adapted to the climate change problem. Some nations are much richer than others, in a way that violates the requirements of justice. Perversely, the status quo approach creates a kind of entitlement to the continuation of practices that violate those requirements. No such entitlement can be defended. A climate change agreement would be unacceptably unfair if it makes it more difficult for poor nations to develop—especially because development is designed to remove their citizens from difficult conditions and to achieve something closer to the threshold or to equality with wealthy nations. A per capita approach is the most fair, because it allows every citizen to count for no less and no more

---

[14] See Harsanyi (1975) for an argument that people would choose to maximize average utility, behind the veil of ignorance.

[15] For varying perspectives, see Pogge (1989); Nussbaum (2006), at 273–324.

[16] It will also be rejected by those who believe that principles of justice do not extend across borders. See, e.g., Rawls (1971); and Nagel (2005).

than one, in a way that respects the moral irrelevance of national boundaries.

We do not intend to challenge these general points about fairness here. Our basic claim is that if they are taken as a defense of the per capita approach, they run into serious difficulties. The reason is that the central objections to the welfarist argument rematerialize when fairness, understood in the stated way, is our guide. To the extent that some of the most populous states are wealthy, the per capita approach is not fair at all; to that extent, it has some of the same vices as the status quo approach. Per capita allocations also have the disadvantage of giving numbers of permits to highly populated nations that have relatively little to lose from climate change. And it remains true that permits are allocated to the governments of poor states, not to the citizens of poor states, and allocations to such governments may not help those who are most in need. If fairness requires redistribution across national boundaries, the status quo approach runs into significant trouble, and the per capita approach is better; but those interested in global redistribution would hardly choose that approach among a menu of possibilities.

The atmosphere as common property

There is another type of fairness argument, to the effect that the atmosphere, with its beneficial carbon-absorbing characteristics, is common property, belonging to everyone in the world.[17] A climate treaty closes a commons, converting it into private property. It is only fair to distribute the parcels of property to the former users of the commons, namely, everyone in the world, on a per capita basis. One might draw an analogy to minerals discovered in the sea bed under the high seas, which are outside the sovereignty of any country. The Convention on the Law of the Sea provides that revenues from exploitation of these minerals should be distributed "equitably."[18]

But the analogy is at best partial and in fact reveals the limits of this argument. A climate treaty, like a treaty that allows for the exploitation of minerals, has two effects of present interest. First, both treaties generate revenues—for permit sellers, in the climate case, and for mining companies, in the mineral case. Second, both treaties

---

[17] See, e.g., Grubb *et al.* (1992), at 318–19; and Ott and Sachs (2002).
[18] See United Nations Convention on the Law of the Sea, Art. 140.

generate benefits for consumers—people who benefit from abatement of climate change, and people who benefit from the lower price of, say, oil. Because virtually everyone benefits from lower oil prices, the effect is spread around the world. Thus, the only remaining question in the case of the mineral treaty is how to distribute revenues fairly. In the climate case, the climate effects are extremely variable—hurting some people very badly, others not all, and benefiting still others. From the standpoint of fairness, it would be stranger to ignore these latter effects while considering only the revenue effects. The analogy to property is not helpful; it distracts from the relevant question, which is the distribution of all treaty effects across the world's population.

Feasibility issues

Thus far our focus has been on issues of principle. But any climate change agreement must be feasible. The poignant irony is that insistence on the first-best outcome, as a matter of principle, may make the climate change problem intractable, in a way that could lead to disaster from the standpoint of the very nations that are poorest and most vulnerable.

State consent and International Paretianism

Treaties require the consent of treaty partners, and so states must believe that by entering a treaty, they are serving their national interest. Of course, the idea of national interest can be specified in many different ways. But as a first approximation, nations care about the welfare of their own citizens—the welfare of citizens in other places is not a primary consideration and may not matter greatly.[19] A workable climate treaty will have to be one that serves the interests of the United States and other major industrial nations, including developing nations such as China and Brazil. We use the term *International*

---

[19] The best evidence for this proposition is the pattern of foreign aid. Poor countries, understandably, do not provide foreign aid, but middle-income countries also do not seem to feel that they have a responsibility to help people living in poorer countries. Rich countries provide foreign aid but are not generous, and scholars have shown that much (but not all) foreign aid can be traced to specific strategic interests. See, e.g., Alesina and Dollar (2000).

Paretianism to refer to this pragmatic constraint on treaty-making: A treaty is not possible unless it makes all its signatories better off.

It should be clear, from the foregoing discussion, that we reject International Paretianism in principle. From a welfarist perspective, a step such as genocide prevention might be justified even if its national benefits are exceeded by its national costs, so long as the global benefits exceed the global costs. The only point is that domestic self-interest imposes a significant limitation on what is feasible, and that nations should not be expected to sign a climate change agreement from which they are large-scale net losers. China is not likely to sign an agreement that would cost it, on net, hundreds of billions of dollars each year; the same is true of the United States. An important question, then, is whether a proposed allocation of emissions rights will require one nation to give a great deal, in monetary terms, to others.

The pragmatic virtue of the status quo approach is that it takes seriously these political constraints on treaty-making. The corresponding problem with the per capita approach is that it would require smaller industrial states to buy permits from larger developing states, violating International Paretianism.[20] There is little reason that the rich states would be willing to agree to such an approach. The behavior of the United States, with respect to the Kyoto Protocol, is revealing in this regard. The United States would have had to spend a great deal to comply with its obligations; it is no accident that no member of the US Senate, Democratic or Republican, supported ratification.

To be sure, most wealthy nations send foreign aid to developing nations, and so it would be a mistake to define their national interests in purely economic terms. We have noted that nations are capable of being altruistic. A country's national interest might be understood as some combination of altruistic and economic interests, a combination already reflected in their foreign aid as well as economic policies. The nature of the combination will vary with domestic political pressures. To the extent that powerful domestic constituencies want to assist those in other nations, the altruistic elements will be magnified. One might argue that, given the current level of altruism, nations would be willing to adopt the per capita approach.

---

[20] To be sure, various transition measures could be used to ease the burden of states up until some future period at which a per capita system would go into effect.

The problem is that the existing level of foreign aid is probably not greatly lower than the amount that rich states are willing to pay in order to be altruistic. Such nations are unlikely to agree to massive increases in the redistribution of wealth by entering a climate treaty that requires them to bear most of the cost of GHG abatement. To insist on the per capita approach, then, is most likely to subvert the best chance for a climate treaty and hence to render the climate change problem intractable—a special problem for poor nations that are particularly vulnerable to climate change impacts.

Defective government and alternative means to redistribute

As is well known in the development literature, redistributing wealth to poor nations is not easy or obvious.[21] Large cash grants to governments are often siphoned off by corrupt officials. Loans are similarly abused and often not repaid. Grants and loans not lost to corruption are nonetheless often wasted because the donee government lacks the expertise and institutional capacity to identify problems, monitor the disbursement of funds, and use them effectively.[22] Donors have devised numerous means for monitoring and controlling the use of funds, but these often fail and frequently generate resentment. In some cases, donors misunderstand the needs of the countries they are donating to and squander funds on projects that do not help the people who live there; in other cases, donors impose conditions that are politically controversial and even destabilizing (Djankov, Montalvo, and Reynal-Querol 2005). Donors have also tried to circumvent corrupt or inept governments by directing aid to individuals and NGOs rather than governments. But small donees are hard to monitor and control, they may have limited impact, and aid programs involving multiple recipients are hard to coordinate.[23]

Now consider a climate treaty, which most likely would require the allocation of valuable permits to the governments of poor states—the same corrupt or ineffective governments that have misused foreign

---

[21] For pessimistic empirical assessments of the relationship between aid and economic growth, see Djankov, Montalvo, and Reynal-Querol (2006); Easterly, Levine, and Roodman (2004); and Barro and Lee (2002).

[22] See, e.g., Easterly (2006).

[23] See, e.g., Acharya et al. (2004) (pointing out the costs to donee countries from dealing with multiple donors).

aid. It seems highly likely that some of these governments will misuse these permits as well—transferring them to cronies, for example. Even if the governments of developing countries are not corrupt, they will still not necessarily use revenues from permits in the way that donor countries, motivated by altruism, would want them to. Recall that the per capita approach was justified by redistributive concerns: all else equal, a climate pact that favored developing nations would be desirable. If large countries tend to be poor, then the per capita approach has attractive redistributive features. The redistributive approach is even better than the per capita approach, according to this view. But if the redistributive approach is not practicable, the per capita approach might be second best.

Any realistic climate treaty will do no more than allocate permits to the governments of developing nations. After these nations sell the permits, they will be free to use the revenue however they want to. But the governments of developing nations are not particularly generous to their poor. In a state like Guatemala, for example, taxes are low, apparently because wealthy people disproportionately influence the political process.[24] It seems unlikely that the Guatemalan government, if it receives a windfall of permits, will redistribute the revenues to the poor.

The point for present purposes is that it would be hazardous to repeat the errors of development policy by using a climate treaty as an opportunity to engage in foreign aid. The distribution of permits on a per capita basis, by favoring poor states, would represent just such an effort. If giving piles of cash to poor states has failed to help them, then giving them piles of permits will also fail to help them. To the extent that this is so, such states should receive no more permits than are necessary to cause them to internalize the external climate effects of polluting activity.

Conclusion

We have urged that claims from both welfare and fairness fail to provide strong support for the per capita approach. A central problem is that some wealthy nations have large populations and some poor nations have small populations. Per capita allocations of emissions

[24] See, e.g., United Nations (2007).

rights would result in substantial benefits for China and India, both of which are poor. But many nations are significantly poorer than those nations, and a directly redistributive approach would be a far more effective way of assisting those who need help. Moreover, any international agreement will benefit some nations more than others and cost some nations more than others. In these circumstances, the per capita approach gives the appearance, not the reality, of fairness.

It remains true that from the standpoint of welfare and fairness, per capita allocations would be far better than the status quo approach. But here as elsewhere, the best is the enemy of the good. A climate treaty that included the optimal level of emissions would be good. A climate treaty that included the optimal level of emissions reductions and the optimal level of redistribution would be better still. But it is much less likely to be possible. On welfarist grounds, and putting incentive effects to one side, the redistributive approach is superior to the per capita approach, which is in turn superior to the status quo approach. Unfortunately, the best approaches in principle are also least likely to be feasible in practice. Insisting on the best approaches would likely defeat current efforts, themselves admittedly fragile, to take significant steps to reduce GHG emissions, and in the process harm poor nations, which are most vulnerable to the climate change problem.

Our discussion has focused on per capita allocations, not on other approaches to addressing current disparities of wealth across nations in a climate policy context. It would be possible to accept our conclusions while urging that wealthy countries should pay for emissions reductions in poor nations, or should help fund the costs of adaptation. But even here, our analysis raises some cautionary notes: in practice, such approaches may run afoul of International Paretianism, and it must be asked whether the relevant payments are, in principle, an effective or instead a crude way of assisting those who need help. More recent proposals, which combine financial and technical assistance to the South, plus soft targets for developing countries, run the risk of failing to address the climate problem (because developing countries will eventually be the worst emitters, whether they receive assistance or not) or failing to comply with the feasibility criterion (because wealthy nations will not spend more than they gain from a climate treaty). At least it can be said, however, that targeting adaptation assistance to poor nations, or to poor people in poor nations, would be far better than many other current proposals for combining climate change policy with distributive justice.

References

Acharya, Arnbab, Ana Fuzzo de Lima, and Mick Moore (2004). "Aid Proliferation: How Responsible Are the Donors?" IDS Working Paper 214. Brighton, UK: Institute of Development Studies, January.

Adler, Matthew and Eric A. Posner (2005). *New Foundations for Cost-Benefit Analysis*. Cambridge, MA: Harvard University Press.

Agarwal, Anil (1999). "Making the Kyoto Protocol Work: Ecological and Economic Effectiveness, and Equity in the Climate Regime," *CSE Statement* (working paper), Centre for Science and Environment, New Delhi. Available at www.cseindia.org/html/eyou/climate/pdf/cse_stat.pdf.

Agarwal, Anil and S. Narain (1991). *Global Warming in an Unequal World: A Case of Environmental Colonialism*. New Delhi: Centre for Science and Environment.

Alesina, Alberto and David Dollar (2000). "Who Gives Foreign Aid to Whom and Why?" *Journal of Economic Growth* 5(1): 33–61.

Altamirano-Cabrera, Juan-Carlos and Michael Finus (2006). "Permit Trading and Stability of International Climate Agreements," *Journal of Applied Economics* 9: 19–48.

Anthoff, David, Cameron Hepburn, and Richard S. J. Tol (2007). "Equity Weighting and the Marginal Costs and Benefits of Climate Change," FEEM Working Paper 43.2007. Milan, Italy: Fondazione Eni Enrico Mattei, April. Available at http://papers.ssrn.com/sol3/papers.cfm?abstract_id=983032.

Aslam, Malik Amin (2002). "Equal Per Capita Entitlements: A Key To Global Participation on Climate Change?" in Kevin A. Baumert (ed.), *Building on the Kyoto Protocol: Options for Protecting the Climate*. Washington, DC: World Resources Institute, pp. 175–202.

Athanasiou, Tom and Paul Baer (2002). *Dead Heat: Global Justice and Global Warming*. New York: Seven Stories Press.

Barro, Robert J. and Jong-Wha Lee (2002). "IMF Programs: Who Is Chosen and What Are the Effects?" NBER Working Paper No. 8951. Cambridge, MA: National Bureau of Economic Research, May.

Bodansky, Daniel (2004). *International Climate Efforts Beyond 2012: A Survey of Approaches*. Arlington, Virginia: Pew Center on Global Climate Change.

Bode, Sven (2003). "Equal Emissions per Capita over Time: A Proposal to Combine Responsibility and Equity of Rights," Discussion Paper Series

26240, Hamburg Institute of International Economics. Available at
http://papers.ssrn.com/sol3/papers.cfm?abstract_id=477281.

Brown, Donald (2002). *American Heat: Ethical Problems with the United States' Response to Global Warming*. Lanham, MD: Rowman & Littlefield.

Djankov, Simeon, Jose G. Montalvo, and Marta Reynal-Querol (2005). "The Curse of Aid," Universitat Pompeu Fabra Working Paper.

(2006). "Does Foreign Aid Help?" *Cato Journal* 26(1): 1–28.

Easterly, William (2006). *The White Man's Burden*. New York: Penguin Press.

Easterly, William, Ross Levine, and David Roodman (2004). "New Data, New Doubts: A Comment on Burnside and Dollar's 'Aid, Policies, and Growth,'" *American Economic Review* 94: 253–9.

Frankel, Jeffrey (2007). "Formulas for Quantitative Emissions Targets," in Joseph E. Aldy and Robert N. Stavins (eds.), *Architectures for Agreement: Addressing Global Climate Change in the Post-Kyoto World*. New York: Cambridge University Press, pp. 31–56.

Goldsmith, Jack and Eric A. Posner (2006). *The Limits of International Law*. Oxford: Oxford University Press.

Grubb, Michael, James Sebenius, Antonio Magalhaes, and Susan Subak (1992). "Sharing the Burden," in Irving M. Mintzer (ed.), *Confronting Climate Change: Risks, Implications and Responses*. Cambridge, UK: Cambridge University Press.

Harrison, Kathryn and Lisa McIntosh Sundstrom (2007). "The Comparative Politics of Climate Change," *Global Environmental Politics* 7: 1–18.

Harsanyi, John (1975). "Can the Maximin Principle Serve As a Basis for Morality? A Critique of John Rawls's Theory," *American Political Science Review* 69: 594–606.

Heston, Alan, Robert Summers, and Bettina Aten (2006). Penn World Table Version 6.2, Center for International Comparisons of Production, Income, and Prices at the University of Pennsylvania, September 2006. Available at http://pwt.econ.upenn.edu/.

Kinzig, Ann P. and Daniel M. Kammen (1998). "National Trajectories of Carbon Emissions: Analysis of Proposals to Foster the Transition to Low-Carbon Economies," *Global Environment Change* 8(3): 183–208.

Kokott, Juliane (1999). "Equity in International Law," in Ferenc L. Tóth (ed.), *Fair Weather? Equity Concerns in Climate Change*. London: Earthscan, pp. 173–88.

Nagel, Thomas (2005). "The Problem of Global Justice," *Philosophy & Public Affairs* 33: 113–47.

National Development and Reform Commission, People's Republic of China (2007). China's National Climate Change Programme, June.

Netherlands Environmental Assessment Agency (2008). "Global CO_2 Emissions: Increase Continued in 2007," available at www.mnp.nl/en/publications/2008/GlobalCO2emissionsthrough2007.html.

Nordhaus and Boyer (2000). *Warming the World: Economic Models of Global Warming*. Cambridge, MA: MIT Press.

Nussbaum, Martha C. (2006). *Frontiers of Justice: Disability, Nationality, Species Membership*. Cambridge, MA: Harvard University Press.

Ott, Hermann E. and Wolfgang Sachs (2002). "The Ethics of International Emissions Trading," in Luiz Pinguelli-Rosa and Mohan Munasinghe (eds.), *Ethics, Equity, and International Negotiations on Climate Change*. Cheltenham, UK: Edward Elgar, pp. 159–68.

Pogge, Thomas (1989). *Realizing Rawls*. Ithaca, NY: Cornell University Press.

Posner, Eric A. and Cass R. Sunstein (2008). "Climate Change Justice," *Georgetown Law Journal* 96: 1565–612.

Posner, Eric A., Cass R. Sunstein, and David Weisbach (forthcoming 2009). "Climate Change Justice."

Rawls, John (1971). *A Theory of Justice*. Cambridge, MA: Harvard University Press.

  (1999). *A Theory of Justice*. Cambridge, MA: Harvard University Press (new edition).

Roberts, J. Timmons and Bradley C. Parks (2007). *A Climate of Injustice: Global Inequality, North-South Politics, and Climate Policy*. Cambridge, MA: MIT Press.

Sagar, A. D. (2000). "Wealth, Responsibility, and Equity: Exploring an Allocation Framework for Global GHG Emissions," *Climatic Change* 45: 511–27.

Schelling, Thomas C. (1997). "The Cost of Combating Global Warming: Facing the Tradeoffs," *Foreign Affairs* 76: 8–14, November/December.

Singer, Peter (2002). *One World: The Ethics of Globalization*. New Haven, CT: Yale University Press.

United Nations (2007). Report of the Special Rapporteur on Extrajudicial, Summary or Arbitrary Executions, UN Doc. A/HRC/4/20/Add.2 (2007).

United Nations General Assembly (1986). "Declaration on the Right to Development," Res. 41/28.

World Resources Institute, Climate Analysis Indicators Tool, available at http://cait.wri.org/cait.php?page=yearly.

12 | Toward a post-Kyoto climate change architecture: a political analysis

ROBERT O. KEOHANE AND
KAL RAUSTIALA[1]

Reports of the Intergovernmental Panel on Climate Change (IPCC) make it clear that the risks of global climate change are even greater than previously realized.[2] Yet commensurate progress in negotiating a meaningful future agreement remains elusive. Since maintenance of a stable climate is a public good, both theory and history suggest it will be undersupplied. Furthermore, the costs of climate change will largely fall on politically weak developing countries, whereas the costs of emissions reduction will largely fall on industrialized countries. Consequently, agreement on any meaningful international regulatory system has been and will continue to be very difficult. With the 1997 Kyoto Protocol coming to an end in 2012, however, the design of a new regulatory regime is essential.

Any international regime aimed at the mitigation of climate change must solve three problems: (1) secure sufficient participation to be effective; (2) achieve agreement on rules that are meaningful, so that if they were followed, climate change would indeed be mitigated; and

---

[1] The authors are indebted for comments on earlier drafts of this chapter to the organizers of this project, Rob Stavins and Joe Aldy, to Deborah Avant, Scott Barrett, Dan Bodansky, Peter Gourevitch, Jeffrey Frankel, Diana Liverman, Michael Oppenheimer, Josh Rigs, David Victor, Jonathan Wiener, and an anonymous referee. We also thank participants in the Harvard Project on International Climate Agreements Workshop, March 13–14, 2008, particularly Scott Barrett, Daniel Bodansky, Richard N. Cooper, Denny Ellerman, Nathaniel Keohane, William Pizer, and Kenneth Richards; and to helpful commentators in audiences at Cambridge University, Oxford University, UCLA, UC Irvine, and NYU, especially Richard Stewart and Benedict Kingsbury, convenors of the NYU seminar on Global Administrative Law. We appreciate research assistance from Ranee Adipat.
[2] For the reports, see the website of the Intergovernmental Panel on Climate Change (IPCC): www.ipcc.ch.

(3) ensure compliance with the rules.[3] That is, it must solve problems of *participation, effectiveness,* and *compliance.* Solving all three problems simultaneously is particularly difficult, since these goals are often in tension. The most direct trade-off is between participation and the strictness of the rules, since as rules become stricter, reluctant states become even more reluctant to be bound by them.[4] Similarly, as participation becomes wider, agreement may only become possible on lax rules.

These problems require careful institutional design. But they cannot be solved without political commitment by national leaders. In democracies this means that the broader public must share that commitment. Gaining public commitment is a necessary condition for effective action, but it too is not sufficient. Commitment that leads to a poorly designed institutional structure—which fails to provide sufficient incentives to reduce emissions of greenhouse gases (GHGs)—will not solve the problem. Social scientists cannot create political commitment: climate scientists, NGOs, the media, and politicians have to play the principal roles. But we can think about ways to design institutions that contribute to effectiveness, contingent on the requisite political commitment. The standard that should be applied to an institutional design such as that proposed in this chapter is whether, given a level of political commitment, it will increase the likelihood of a satisfactory solution to the tripartite requirements of an effective regime: participation, sufficiently strict rules, and a robust compliance system.

Our goal in this chapter is to sketch such a design, particularly its compliance system, with careful attention to the realities of world politics. The first section discusses participation. Without participation by major emitters, no regime will be effective. The next section analyzes the problem of compliance and argues that a system of buyer liability under a cap-and-trade regime for limiting emissions is essential. We offer a unique version of buyer liability, in which emissions permits are annual and all permits from a given jurisdiction receive the same value. The last two sections of the chapter discuss the critical problem of assessing compliance with emissions caps and address potential weaknesses of the system we propose, including providing responses

---

[3] Barrett 2003.

[4] Downs, Rocke and Barsoom, 1996; Raustiala and Slaughter 2002; Raustiala 2005.

to these criticisms. Throughout, we write from the standpoint of the politics of international cooperation; our policy recommendations for a post-Kyoto system take into account the more technical literatures on compliance and liability but flow directly and primarily from our political analysis.

The attractions of a cap-and-trade architecture for participation

Only a cap-and-trade architecture is likely to make it politically possible to secure sufficient participation to get a climate-change mitigation regime up and running. Recently, there has been some disillusionment with comprehensive approaches to cap and trade on the part of climate analysts attuned to political issues.[5] Critics of proposals for a comprehensive regime point to many problems, in particular the difficulties of negotiating national emissions quotas, linking domestic regulatory systems coherently, monitoring implementation, avoiding renegotiation, and ensuring compliance with international obligations.

In light of these difficulties, a variety of proposals have been put forward for other architectures, including both carbon taxes and a more eclectic approach that the editors of this volume characterize as "harmonized domestic policies." These more decentralized architectures avoid the formidable negotiation problems involved in setting up a comprehensive cap-and-trade accord. They also would prevent the need for large financial transfers among countries, which raise political problems in sending countries and give rise to possible adverse effects resulting from corruption or economic distortions in recipients. We will briefly consider harmonized policies and then turn to carbon taxes.

In our view, true harmonization of national policies is extremely difficult—as even the experience of the European Union shows—and a non-integrated patchwork of national "policies and measures" will prove insufficient to deal with the climate change problem. Moreover, neither strategy adequately addresses the wide variance among states in political commitment to addressing climate change. That is, neither provides sufficient incentives for governments whose publics are indifferent to the climate problem to contribute to this global public

---

[5] See the articles by Scott Barrett, Thomas Schelling, and David Victor in Aldy and Stavins (2007).

good. In other words, these approaches lack the *institutionalized transmission belts* that we believe are critical to long-term success on a global scale. If only a few countries implement effective policies and measures to mitigate climate change, the overall response will surely be inadequate. What is needed is a system that will draw in many states, or at least the most important set of major emitters.

Advocates of harmonized policies and measures typically respond to this objection by proposing some form of project-by-project aid to countries that are reluctant to act. But this raises a second key problem. Each such project will encounter high transaction costs—the costs of negotiating and enforcing agreements—which will cumulate across projects in a way that will tax the institutional capacity even of wealthy countries. Thousands of projects would have to be designed, agreed upon, and ultimately enforced. The existing evidence on implementation gives little reason to believe that this is possible.

Indeed, we have ample experience from foreign aid conditionality to counsel great caution. The dilemma of conditionality is that if the project has high priority for the government, the government will do it anyway, so that aid simply makes resources available for other projects. If the project has low priority, the government is likely not to devote the high-quality personnel and other inputs, complementary to the foreign aid, to assure that it will work. Compensatory efforts, when engaged in, for example, by the International Monetary Fund (IMF), have led to a proliferation of conditions without improving compliance.[6] New conditions generate new efforts to evade them; and as conditions multiply, it becomes more difficult to insist on any one of them as crucial. As a result, transaction costs increase without corresponding improvements in performance. Moreover, determining that a project actually mitigated emissions as compared with "business as usual" is extremely difficult. Such a determination of "additionality" involves constructing a counterfactual baseline: what would have happened in the absence of the aid. Since this baseline is unobservable, it is impossible to determine it with a high degree of confidence: This is what is known as the "fundamental problem of causal inference."[7] The complexity of such projects will compound

---

[6] Mosley, Harrington, and Toye 1991: 61; Leandro, Shafer, and Frontini 1999; Stone 2002; Barnett and Finnemore 2004.

[7] Holland 1986; King, Keohane, and Verba 1994: 79–80.

this problem, as will the inevitable political inference with efforts to evaluate them.

The Clean Development Mechanism (CDM) of the Kyoto system illustrates these problems. The CDM funds projects as part of an emissions credit system: Members of the European Union Emission Trading System (EU ETS) purchase these credits in a growing market that even in 2006 was on the order of $30 billion.[8] The CDM experience to date supports our pessimism. Host governments seek certification of proposed credits and deal with verifiers who are dependent on the host governments for future business; furthermore, purchasers do not have a stake in assuring that projects are genuine, as long as they are certified. Normally, buyers limit the opportunism of sellers because they care about the quality of products or services, but in the case of the CDM, the buyers only care that *someone else* has certified the product they are buying as valid (Wara and Victor 2008). The CDM also produces perverse incentives—indeed, it "reduces the incentives of developing country governments to enact policies reducing emissions," since by doing so they would reduce the credits they could earn from projects that, in a particular situation, correct the results of bad incentives.[9]

To summarize, project-oriented mechanisms for mitigating climate change, which will likely be attached to any harmonization-oriented policy scheme, have three disadvantages: they fail to send a comprehensive price signal to investors and governments; they incur very high transaction costs; and they require counter-factual determinations to assess additionality. Cap-and-trade approaches are markedly superior on all three counts. Before moving to abandon them, we should try to make them politically and institutionally feasible.

Global carbon taxes also avoid these varied problems, and there are strong purely economic arguments for them. For this reason many prominent economists favor carbon taxes.[10] But taxes face major political hurdles. Most significant is the effect on reluctant states. Taxes would impose economic burdens on the industries of developing states without offering the offsetting gains of being able to sell emissions permits under a cap that made allowance for their much

---

[8] Hepburn 2007: 377.
[9] Hepburn 2007: 386.
[10] Cooper 2008.

lower historic and *per capita* emissions. It therefore seems unlikely that developing countries, including China and India, would agree to such an arrangement, since these countries have refused to be bound by binding caps even when they would be compensated for doing so. Cap and trade has the enormous advantage that permits can be set in excess of future business-as-usual emissions for those reluctant to join the system. In other words, reluctant countries can be given "hot air."

Although granting hot air is essential to obtaining the participation of reluctant states, this will shift more of the burden of real abatement to committed states. However, as a political matter this cuts both ways. Those who want to see swift and aggressive emissions reductions will resist giving out hot air; but the enterprises and other entities in the industrialized democracies that will actually be taking on the largest commitments will favor it, as it will reduce the price of permits they will need to buy in a cap-and-trade system. None of this vitiates the major problem with hot air, which is that, by definition, hot air does not represent real emissions reductions. We recognize this, but believe that some hot air is essential to jumpstart the trading system. Over time, as we discuss below, it is equally essential that hot air allocations be eliminated. That is, any cap-and-trade system needs to chart a path toward genuinely binding caps on all significant emitters of GHGs.

Cap and trade is also a more likely global approach than carbon taxes because the EU has committed to it after a long period of resistance. Once the EU has gone through the painful process of reaching internal agreement, it is notably averse to change. Moreover, the political system of the United States, the world's second largest emitter, is famously hostile to new taxes. Indeed, even the relatively trivial energy (BTU) tax suggested by the Clinton Administration went nowhere, in part because of this aversion to taxes. For all these reasons we believe that a global carbon tax is less politically feasible than an emissions trading system, and we therefore assume—as a basis for our discussion of compliance—a cap-and-trade regime such as has been discussed in this volume and in earlier work by Jeffrey Frankel.[11] We recognize that other policy elements will likely be present in any future regime,

[11] Frankel 2007 and this volume.

such as technology transfer provisions and adaptation measures. At the core, however, will likely be some form of trading.

Despite all these advantages, the task of negotiating a comprehensive cap-and-trade system will be daunting. Incentives for the most reluctant countries—or those that can bluff being most reluctant—to hold out for a better deal would be very great.[12] Although it would in principle be desirable to maintain the existing United Nations process of negotiating a universal treaty, and although the legitimacy of such a regime would be enhanced by its universality, it would be foolish to commit so irrevocably to an arrangement that gives potential hold-outs veto power. The option of beginning with a smaller "club" of major contributors to global warming, plus any other states that chose to join, or of linking various different cap-and-trade systems (Jaffe and Stavins 2008) should be maintained.

Any club-like arrangement should, like the Kyoto Protocol itself, be open to the accession of all countries on generally known terms. A club with attractive incentives to join—for example, the prospect of substantial revenues from permits—would exert a strong magnetic pull. Whatever the ultimate structure, climate institutions must be designed to attract participants—such that, for example, the thirty largest Indian industrialists are motivated to meet with the Prime Minister and demand that India join the cap-and-trade system so that they can sell into it.[13]

In short, we favor cap and trade as the basic approach, but do so cognizant of the many problems it faces. We are not confident that such a system will work. However, we think it has the best political prospects of any plausible climate system, and we believe that careful institutional design can help ensure feasibility. For these reasons we view our proposal for a cap-and-trade regime coupled to buyer liability much like Churchill viewed democracy—the worst imaginable system, but for the alternatives.

The political logic of a buyer liability system

The fundamental problem of compliance in world politics is that it is virtually impossible to force powerful states to comply with interna-

---

[12] On such bargaining problems see Fearon 1998.
[13] Personal conversation, Nathaniel Keohane, September 2008.

tional rules through a collective process. Rules that purport to ensure compliance lack credibility *ex ante*. Even where sovereignty has been curtailed, as in the EU, it remains very difficult to enforce international rules externally. In 2005 the EU could not even enforce, against France and Germany, its elaborate system of fines against states that exceeded its fiscal deficit limits—despite the fact that Germany had been the principal advocate of this disciplinary system in the first place.[14]

Difficulties of enforcement yield two common outcomes with regard to international agreements. One is the negotiation of weak or vague international commitments that largely match existing behavior. This outcome is particularly common in the environmental realm, where agreements have often been struck that exhibit high compliance—because they are carefully tuned to the status quo—yet do little to influence actual change in behavior.[15] An equally undesirable outcome is the negotiation of ambitious (but sometimes vague) rules that are frequently violated. When untethered to any meaningful monitoring and compliance system, ambitious international rules run the risk of substantial non-compliance. This pattern of over-ambition followed by widespread non-compliance has been observed with respect to human rights treaties. Some have argued that such agreements actually make the underlying problem the treaty was intended to address worse.[16]

More specifically, there are at least three major political constraints on compliance provisions for a comprehensive cap-and-trade regime. Proposals that ignore these constraints will either not be implemented or will be ineffective if implemented.

1. *Post-hoc penalties on powerful sellers are infeasible.* Non-compliant sellers whose participation in the regime is essential for its efficacy could renegotiate emissions limits in their favor, wielding the threat of exit from the regime. Non-compliant sellers with other sources of political power could use those sources of power to punish or threaten states that seek to impose sanctions for non-compliance.
2. *Any system that requires interstate negotiations to determine arrangements for compliance will be subject to political strategy and pressure.* The point here is the one that Randall Stone makes about the International Monetary Fund (IMF) in *Lending*

---

[14] See www.eubusiness.com/Finance/ecofin-council.06.
[15] Victor, Raustiala, and Skolnikoff (1998) provide many examples.
[16] Hathaway 2002.

Credibility.[17] The IMF relaxed the rules on powerful states such as Russia under pressure from Russia's supporters, particularly the United States. Another possible result of interstate negotiations is deadlock, so that no rules are agreed.

3. *Any system that can be manipulated, or "gamed," will be.* The stakes are too high for such manipulation to be avoidable.

The Kyoto Protocol nonetheless contains compliance provisions built around the idea of external enforcement. States that violate the caps on emissions can in essence "borrow" emissions from the next commitment period with a 30 percent penalty. As a response to sudden fluctuations beyond the control of states that are genuinely committed to meeting their long-term targets, this approach makes some sense. But it does not constitute an effective enforcement mechanism. Since states have yet to negotiate those future limits they can build the "penalty" into their future allocation.[18] Moreover, as in many international treaties the Kyoto Protocol permits any party to exit at will. As a result, the Kyoto arrangements are akin to requiring homeowners who default because they cannot afford their mortgage payments to pay a higher interest rate next year, without any provision for foreclosure but with the opportunity for the borrower, in the future, to reset the terms of the loan or simply walk away largely unscathed. In other words, they open the door to renegotiations and exit threats and introduce a serious problem of moral hazard.

The unrealistic nature of these provisions suggests the futility of a collective system for external enforcement. One alternative could be tariffs based on carbon or GHG content, imposed against countries that failed to adhere to an agreed international cap-and-trade regime.[19] If followed universally, authorization to impose such tariffs could provide incentives for states to enter, and abide by, a climate regime. But if the offender were a powerful state, many countries would hesitate to impose tariffs, weakening the incentives for compliance. In states that did impose trade sanctions, on the other hand, decisions on the level of these tariffs would be subject to manipulation.

---

[17] Stone 2002.

[18] See Article XV(5)a in *Procedures and Mechanisms Relating to Compliance Under the Kyoto Protocol,* FCCC/CP/2001/L.21, available at http://unfccc.int/resource/docs/cop7/l21.pdf.

[19] We thank an anonymous referee for this suggestion.

Indeed, protectionist interests would surely seek to use them for their own purposes. (There are also likely to be complex issues relating to the rules of the World Trade Organization, if any of its more than 150 member states is involved.) We propose below a system of buyer liability for permits that has desirable incentive effects without either requiring weak states to punish strong ones or creating opportunities for protectionist manipulation.

No system will be perfect. But fortunately, perfect compliance with a cap-and-trade regime is not required.[20] Compliance merely has to be strong enough to sustain trading in the near term and to make states' commitments to reduce emissions sufficiently credible to create significant price signals over the medium term, because the most significant action to address climate change is likely to come from technological innovation rather than from trading per se. In the longer term, the regime will surely have to be adjusted as a result of the extensive learning from experience that is bound to occur.

To summarize, in designing a cap-and-trade system we must not put great weight on external enforcement systems. Some alternative system of enforcement must exist to ensure that, over time, permits are allocated in ways that represent real reductions. Below, we advocate a system of buyer liability in which buyers of emissions permits are liable for those emissions should the permits not prove fully valid. We couple that recommendation to two other key features: an annual emissions assessment process and what we call "jurisdiction equality," meaning that all permits sold from a given jurisdiction (e.g. China) will have the same value.

The roles of states and enterprises

Seven years ago, David Victor proposed that the enforcement system under a cap-and-trade regime should be built on the principle of buyer liability.[21] He argued for buyer liability on political grounds: "Buyer liability enforces compliance through rule-based markets, whereas seller liability requires weak and politicized international institutions to identify and penalize sellers that have not complied." Victor's

[20] Hypothetically, enforcement could even be too strong, deterring participation. However, typically there is weak enforcement of multilateral obligations and many loopholes, so this is unlikely to be a practical problem.
[21] Victor 2001: 69–74.

arguments, though compelling, have not been adequately incorporated into the recent literature on the design of climate institutions or into the provisions for implementing the Kyoto Protocol agreed in the Marrakesh Accords of 2001.[22] In this section we revive and amplify his arguments for buyer liability, since we believe that only such a system will be robust to the political constraints that we have just discussed. Technical critiques of this approach, while raising important points, are outweighed by the political benefits of a buyer-based system.[23] First we briefly introduce the basic features of our system. Then in later sections we delve into the details of buyers, sellers, incentives, and assessment.

Under either a comprehensive cap-and-trade architecture or linked regional cap-and-trade systems, each party creates, or adapts, a national regulatory system to meet its agreed emissions target.[24] Many states that expect to find it difficult to meet their target (buyer countries, or "permit-short" countries) will enact legislation authorizing enterprises operating within their jurisdictions to purchase emissions permits from suppliers abroad in countries that are also members of the regime. (We expect there to be trading between enterprises within these permit-short jurisdictions as well.) In the near term the permit-short countries will likely include the United States, members of the EU, Japan, Australia, Canada, Norway, and New Zealand, as well as some others. Enterprises such as power companies or industrial firms in these states, or in other states that accept stringent emissions caps, will frequently need to purchase permits from entities abroad in order to meet their domestic emissions obligations.[25] We advocate that these permits be issued annually.

Consistent with most analyses, we anticipate that some parties to any future climate accord will successfully negotiate overall emissions

[22] Bluemel 2007.
[23] See OECD 2000. For analyses of buyer liability that explicitly recognize the enforcement problems entailed in seller liability, see Nordhaus *et al.* 2000a and 2000b and Zhang 1999. None of these papers emphasizes the political asymmetry that we stress between the commitments to action of buyer and seller countries.
[24] Tickell (2008) proposes allocating permits directly to individuals rather than states. But the political impediments to agreement and the administrative difficulties to implementation seem debilitating.
[25] In most national legislation, including proposed laws in the United States, trading is limited to a small fraction of the overall entity cap. We anticipate that feature continuing for some time.

limits that exceed their projected emissions. These seller, or "permit-long," countries are likely to include China, Russia, India, and other developing countries for some period into the future; obtaining hot air will be the *sine qua non* of their participation in the regime. Through their own national processes, states that are permit-long will sell or assign permits to enterprises or other entities within their jurisdiction. If permit prices are cheaper than the buying entity's internal cost of reductions, purchasing permits will be attractive and markets for emissions trading will emerge. These emissions markets already exist in various, often limited, forms.[26]

Although caps on overall emissions will be established at the national level, it is important to emphasize that in our scheme actual trading will take place between *enterprises*, whether private or state-controlled. For example, Duke Power in the United States might purchase Chinese-denominated permits from Xian Electric Power to cover its anticipated excess emissions in 2010, and it could re-sell these permits if it turned out to have more than it needed. States are nonetheless crucial to our proposal. States will have responsibility for overall emissions targets and will issue or sell permits to enterprises as they decide. States will also enforce compliance with national caps domestically. Most significantly in this regard, we advocate that all permits from a given jurisdiction be assigned the same value if sold.

In other words, under our system permit trading on the world market would be *"jurisdiction-equal."* By this we mean that permit validity will be assessed on a national basis and permits will be discounted on a national basis as well. (We discuss assessment at length below.) Consequently, the validity of permits sold by entities will depend on the *aggregate* validity of permits sold from a particular national jurisdiction, as decided by the assessment process. Hence all permits emanating from a given jurisdiction in a given year would ultimately be assigned the same validity.

Sellers will seek to command the highest price for their permits by ensuring that permits represent true reductions. Buyers will in turn seek the cheapest permits, adjusting for risk. Buyers of emissions permits that turned out to be invalid would be liable to make up the difference in some way. By invalid we mean permits that do not represent the full

[26] Examples include the European Union Emission Trading Scheme and the Chicago Climate Exchange.

amount of carbon reduction their face value implies. Buyers who hold insufficient valid permits at the end of the budget period would need to purchase more permits or engage in further internal reductions. Again, it is national governments that would enforce this commitment against private actors.

This system thus rests on the incentives of buyers, which will largely be in industrialized democracies, to comply with domestic emissions controls and the incentives of sellers, largely outside these states, to command and maintain the highest price in the market. It is therefore very important to note, as Victor does, that the likely permit-short countries, in which enterprises will be net buyers of permits, on balance have stronger and less corrupt national legal institutions than the likely permit-long countries. Furthermore, the permit-short countries are overwhelmingly democratic. We therefore rely on *internal* structures and incentives, such as democracy and the rule of law, to ensure that permit-short countries comply with the system. Indeed, the *political asymmetry*—in rule of law and democracy—between buyer and seller countries is central to our advocacy of buyer liability. Another way of expressing this point is to say that incentives for compliance for net buyer countries are exogenous to the institutional system that we propose.

By contrast, our system is designed to generate endogenous incentives for compliance on the part of permit-long, or seller, countries. These governments will gain economically from maintaining a high value for the permits that their enterprises sell, and will therefore seek to act in a way that maintains their reputations for compliance. This system, unlike many of the most prominent alternatives, provides "institutionalized transmission belts" for compliance to flow from the advanced industrial democracies, which have the strongest commitment to climate-change abatement, to the wide range of likely selling jurisdictions, which tend to have weak commitments to abatement. Below we flesh out some of the details of this process.

Buyers and incentives for prudence

As in all cap-and-trade systems, under our proposal emissions permits would trade on public markets. Their value would depend on buyers' *ex ante* estimates of validity. Shortly after the end of the year for which permits were issued, a comprehensive assessment would decide their value. For instance, Indian-jurisdiction permits for the year 2010 might be evaluated by June 30, 2011, when all entities subject to caps on their 2010 emissions would be held accountable for their emissions, taking into account valid permits bought or sold.

Since *ex post* assessment problems are difficult and complex, we devote all of the next section to that topic. Here we focus on the incentives of buyers. In many respects a buyer liability system is broadly akin to the existing international bond market. After being issued by states, bonds trade on international markets, just as emissions permits would trade on such markets. Permits would trade at prices that would reflect market participants' confidence that, when they came due for redemption, they would be valid. They would likely trade at discounts if their validity was viewed as questionable. Buyers of emissions permits that were invalid, like buyers of bonds whose issuers default, will incur losses at the end of the process; and market prices will reflect prevailing expectations of eventual validity or invalidity. Like buyers of bonds, therefore, buyers of permits will have strong incentives to assess quality *ex ante*, price the permits accordingly, and hedge to some degree by purchasing excess permits.

Market participants would in turn have incentives to create or engage ratings agencies or other entities to evaluate the quality of permits *ex ante*, just as we see bonds rated by existing agencies as a way to express and monetize the risk of default. In a world of perfectly functioning markets, reliable ratings agencies would come into being endogenously, as a result of demand for their services; and to a considerable extent we expect this to happen.[27] The recent financial crash, however, illustrates the pitfalls of ratings. Ratings agencies themselves can have perverse incentives and therefore exhibit systematic bias.

One advantage of ratings on GHG emissions permits as compared to long-term bond ratings is that the feedback would, under our system, be annual: each year the *ex post* assessment system would evaluate permits, which would provide information about the validity of permits for future years from the same issuer. It would probably be necessary also to take some measures preventing highly leveraged large banks and bank-like entities from speculating in permits since, as we have seen in the recent housing crisis, these activities generate risks that governments may be required to socialize if financial collapse occurs. Perhaps a non-profit "watchdog" to evaluate the ratings

---

[27] See Sinclair 2005.

agencies could be created. The watchdog institution could closely scrutinize a random sample of the ratings of each ratings agency, and itself provide a rating of their reliability, which investors could use in evaluating permit ratings and issuers could use in deciding which ratings agency to employ. We are agnostic about the precise structure of such a system, but we believe it is essential that permit rating works reasonably well.

In the US cap-and-trade system under Title IV of the Clean Air Act, sellers are liable for the value of their permits, and this liability is legally enforceable. Scott Barrett reports that "the penalty for non-compliance is so severe that in 2006, compliance was 100 percent."[28] But as we have seen, no such enforcement is available at the international level. At this level a major advantage of a system of buyer liability is that buyers face incentives to monitor and assess the behavior of sellers: private markets, therefore, would carry out extensive informational tasks that might otherwise be left to governments.

Accurate assessment and pricing are thus key to permit markets working smoothly. If assessments *ex ante* are accurate, buyers can simply discount permits appropriately and buy more nominal permits than they require to meet emissions limits set by their governments. As in other markets, actors will hedge against risk. Insurance markets may also arise to cover the risk of permit invalidity. We expect that buyers will also police the actions of other buyers, for they will eventually have a large economic stake in the permit system. Those who abide by the rules and accurately assess and pay for quality permits will not want competitors to gain by purchasing cheaper, riskier permits. All these features push toward compliance in the permit-short jurisdiction. However, if riskier permits fail, the buyers of those permits, now facing a shortfall, may in severe situations seek political renegotiation of their domestic emissions restrictions rather than purchase more permits. This is a serious problem—of moral hazard—that we address in a later section of this chapter.

Sellers and incentives for validity

If buyers bear the liability for invalid permits, what incentives do sellers have to ensure that the permits they sell are backed by real

---

[28] Barrett 2008: 4–5.

emissions reductions at the national level? Permits that lacked full validity would have a reduced value, with the loss borne by buyers that held the permits at that time. How would this give *sellers* incentives to follow the rules?

Under our proposal (and indeed under nearly all trading systems) emissions trading would be structured to continue for many years. Such an ongoing market creates an economic incentive for sellers to ensure quality. More specifically, if the rate at which states that are net sellers of permits discount future gains is sufficiently low, and the magnitude of expected future permit sales is sufficiently high, states will seek reputations for selling valid permits.[29] Michael Tomz (2007) has shown that such national-level reputation effects are very strong in international bond markets, and there seems no reason to believe that they would not be equally strong in emissions markets.

Sellers of fully valid permits would also have an incentive to cooperate with and even support credible monitoring systems, so that their permits would be regarded *ex ante* as valid and could command their full price. That is, the "market for lemons" logic famously outlined by George Akerlof would prevail.[30] Indeed, support by sellers for independent monitoring would be a signal of being honest, and therefore valuable in itself. In short, buyer liability makes seller incentives largely *economic* rather than *political*. Seller incentives would not rest on concern about climate change; they would rest on an ongoing desire for profit.

Reputation (for high value permits) is consequently at the center of this self-enforcement mechanism. It is therefore crucial to design the allocation system so that sellers of permits would face the prospect of a substantial stream of revenue many years into the future. If the "shadow of the future" is too short, incentives for compliance will tend to vanish.[31] In the long run, of course, the caps will have to "bite" even on those countries who were net sellers of permits when they originally joined. Our expectation is that over time, countries such as China would increasingly recognize their stake in mitigating climate change; that is, at the state level incentives would become political as well as economic, even if private entities continued to

[29] Axelrod 1984; Tomz 2007.
[30] Akerlof 1970.
[31] Axelrod 1984.

be primarily motivated by profit. Having been part of a cap-and-trade system, these governments would also have developed the institutions necessary for effective participation, and acceptance of meaningful caps would therefore create a less uncertain prospect for them. In other words, ideally the period of being large net sellers of permits would be a transition phase, easing countries' way into full membership.

There are many potential problems with this system, as we discuss below. However, the cardinal virtue of a buyer liability system is that it would not require that an international organization ensure compliance with international commitments—a condition that, as we have seen, cannot be met. This system would instead be self-enforcing.

The problem of assessment

To be effective, any cap-and-trade regime, whether involving buyer or seller liability, requires an accurate and prompt *ex post* assessment of permit quality. In view of our assumption that any system that can be gamed for strategic advantage will be gamed, any technically complex system of assessment should be examined closely from a political standpoint. As in liability systems, complex technical arrangements can be strategically manipulated in ways that are not transparent. If so, their very complexity may be self-defeating.

Permit assessment rests on the measurement of aggregate emissions in selling jurisdictions. Measuring the use of some globally-traded fuels is relatively straightforward (at the aggregate national level) but other fuels and emissions sources pose greater problems. Most problematic of all are land-use changes, where measurement is fraught by issues such as the relevant time period that a new forest can be said to be sequestering carbon, and what to do in the event of a fire later on. But a cap-and-trade system has the decisive advantage over project-based systems that it does not have to evaluate what would have happened in the absence of a given project. The assessors simply calculate actual emissions and subtract them from the agreed cap, which is public knowledge. They only have to assess a factual situation—actual emissions—rather than both a factual and a counter-factual. One promising way to simplify this process is to focus on "upstream" emissions—to measure the carbon inputs into the energy system—which enter at relatively few points—rather than emissions from thousands or millions of sources.[32]

The most serious problem of measurement, however, is political: As we noted above, any system that can be gamed will be gamed. An international assessment process will be vulnerable to political pressure and, like judges on international courts, individuals responsible for conducting an assessment may feel strong pressures to support the positions of their national government.[33] As a result, strenuous efforts must be undertaken to insulate the assessment process from political pressure.

One way to do so would be to employ a structure like the IPCC, which is run by scientists whose judgments are not directly subjected to override by politicians and diplomats. Another would be for private foundations to endow a non-profit entity to carry out the assessment process. Neither is foolproof. However, the politics of assessment in a buyer liability system will be fundamentally different from those in a seller liability system, and much more benign. In a seller liability system, sellers have every incentive to obstruct assessment. In the absence of clear proof of cheating they are unlikely to be punished. Obstruction generally will pay. In a buyer liability system, by contrast, the reputation of any seller that obstructed assessment would fall, and the value of the permits that it issued would fall accordingly. Doubt about the validity of permits would have a similar effect: markets hate uncertainty. Sellers would therefore have strong economic incentives to accept and even welcome thorough assessment, to remove such doubts and therefore raise prices.[34]

Jurisdiction-equality and assessment

As we have seen, the Kyoto CDM faces a serious assessment problem. The key flaw is the lack of a clear counterfactual baseline in devel-

---

[32] Tickell 2008: 90–92. A carbon tax would also be relatively simple to administer but founders on likely political resistance from developing countries, who will refuse to join a system that does not offer them credible compensation. Allocating them excess permits on a temporary basis does this; a carbon tax does not.

[33] Posner and de Figuerido 2005.

[34] For a similar argument in the context of arms control, see Schelling 1960: 146–50.

oping countries that sell CDM permits.[35] The CDM therefore fails
to solve the fundamental problem of such emissions markets—that
sellers and buyers alike face incentives to collude and claim high
reductions even where none exist. This devastating objection does
not apply to the system we propose; under our system all states in
the system will have emissions caps. Hence the baseline will be established by treaty.

The need for a clear jurisdiction-wide baseline demonstrates the
importance of our proposal that permit validity be assessed (and
discounted) on a national basis. Under our proposal for "jurisdiction
equality," governments of permit-long jurisdictions will seek to assure
that the permits their domestic enterprises offer for sale are valid,
because if they fail to do so future permits *from any enterprise within
their jurisdiction* will be devalued. Discounting all permits from a
given jurisdiction at the same rate may appear unfair, since it penalizes
those seller entities that scrupulously abate emissions but whose counterpart entities, in the same jurisdiction, fail to meet their obligations.
But this unfairness is essentially a national problem, since it could only
be the result of lax enforcement at the national level and can best be
fixed via national action.

Furthermore, jurisdiction-equality has two very important virtues.
First, it avoids creating very thin markets for thousands of permits
from often obscure entities whose permit quality might be impossible to assess by outsiders. Such a system would lead to very high
transactions costs and very thin markets. Second, and perhaps most
important, unfairness is a political virtue. Enterprises that meet their
emissions targets have strong incentives to press their governments to
correct internal compliance problems; in other words, to enforce the
system against shirkers. Governments themselves will also face incentives to seek low (or zero) discount factors, since aggregate national
sales and, relatedly, tax revenue will turn on permit price. The system
therefore generates *endogenous* domestic political pressures for measures to assure permit validity. Since the issuing country as a whole
would suffer from having devalued permits—permits are, after all, a
valuable commodity—the government would have multiple incentives
to avoid and correct these problems.

---

[35] See in particular Wara and Victor 2008; and Wara 2007.

Assessment: an evaluation

It is extremely difficult to insulate any assessment system against political pressures. Indeed, the central thrust of this discussion does not concern the merits of any particular arrangement, but the necessity of undertaking a careful political analysis that considers strategies that opportunists could follow to manipulate the system.

A well-functioning cap-and-trade system would likely require regular assessments, in-country and on-site inspections (perhaps done randomly), and a "true-up" period for states to work out shortfalls. Our proposal, with annual assessments of permit validity, certainly requires significantly more resources than have been allocated to the Kyoto Protocol review process to date. But the basic structure and approach is complementary. And while direct inspections of major emissions sites by an international organization will surely raise sovereignty concerns among many parties, there is substantial precedent for this model in the Chemical Weapons Convention, which permits inspections on national territory of chemical production sites, including so-called "challenge inspections" by the treaty secretariat.[36] The much less intrusive review we envision for a post-Kyoto system thus falls within established norms in international law.

But the most important point is one already made: buyer liability will give sellers incentives to facilitate assessment and show that they have done so. This is not true of other assessment processes involving developing countries that have failed or been heavily resisted, such as IMF surveillance and the WTO Trade Policy Review Mechanism.[37]

Potential weaknesses of buyer liability

Any attempt to get around what often appear as insuperable problems of agreement and compliance will have potential weaknesses. So before discussing the weaknesses of a buyer liability system, it is important to emphasize that alternative systems run directly afoul of the political constraints enumerated earlier. Seller liability is unlikely to work because there simply is no credible set of institutions available

---

[36] Convention on the Prohibition of the Development, Production, Stockpiling, and Use of Chemical Weapons, at www.opcw.org.

[37] On the WTO TPRM see Ghosh 2008.

in world politics to enforce sanctions against even moderately important states.[38] Therefore, any effective system cannot be one of pure
seller liability.

The only real question is whether it is preferable to have pure buyer
liability or a hybrid system, such as the one proposed by Nordhaus
et al. (2000a). We prefer pure buyer liability because it is the only
system that is robust to state non-compliance—if the shadow of the
future is sufficiently long—and that does not require frequent state
negotiations. Such negotiations inevitably raise issues of renegotiation, gaming, and non-transparency. Hybrid systems will typically be
subject to at least one of these three problems. To prefer a hybrid
system over pure buyer liability, it would have to be shown that the
net benefits of the hybrid system are superior, not merely that buyer
liability raises some potential problems. We doubt this is possible, and
hence favor pure buyer liability.

With these fundamental political constraints in mind, we mention
three potential weaknesses of our system. For each of the weaknesses
that we identify, we make a counter-argument that alternative schemes
are less promising.

Information and sudden changes in expectations

A common objection to a buyer liability system is that it would create
too much risk, and high transaction costs, as a result of insufficient
information about the future validity of permits. There is some basis
for this concern. Yet from a "markets for lemons" perspective, this
informational problem is two sided. On the one hand, Akerlof shows
that asymmetrical information can prevent otherwise mutually profitable trades from taking place. Cautious buyers will refrain from purchasing permits in the face of this uncertainty and the market as a result
will be very thin. Abatement costs will consequently be higher because
foregone trades will require the utilization of more expensive local
options. On the other hand, the market for lemons argument suggests
that institutions will develop to correct the market failure, if there are
financial incentives to do so. In a tradable permit regime, there would

---

[38] Bluemel (2007, at note 64) says: "Most analysts agree that a pure seller-liability
rule, in combination with a weak enforcement regime, will result in overselling
under the Kyoto Protocol."

be such incentives: buyers can gain enormously by credibly evaluating tradable permits just as they evaluate and rate government bonds. These ratings will help to determine prices in a global carbon market.

That said, our buyer liability model rests to some degree on assumptions about the ability of such an incentive system to generate and widely distribute accurate information, and the system will work well only if accurate information about permit validity is widely dispersed. However, if information about validity is not widely dispersed—if it is largely private and/or secret—and if this situation is not widely appreciated, we may see many mistakes by buyers. The ongoing mortgage crisis suggests that even in well-established markets it is surprisingly easy for sophisticated participants to misprice goods. For the system to work, the *ex post* monitoring system will have to be sufficiently reliable, credible, and prompt that adjustments can be made quickly, and fairly smoothly, in the event that permit-settling countries fail to fulfill emissions requirements. Again, we stress the annual nature of assessment. Such a system provides a steady stream of information, albeit inevitably somewhat imperfect, about emissions and permit validity.

In the end, however, the objection that buyer liability generates transaction costs that are too high founders on the false premise that seller liability has lower transaction costs. On the contrary, the defense of seller liability on the grounds of lower transaction costs is spurious: It simply "achieves" lower costs by ignoring the problem of compliance. its efficacy depends on imposing penalties on sellers of bogus permits. But neither internal enforcement under seller liability nor external enforcement is likely to be effective. We cannot count on internal enforcement since many sellers of climate change permits will be entities in jurisdictions, such as China and Russia, with weak internal regulatory systems and little domestic public pressure for effective action. We cannot count on external enforcement because these same states are strong and sensitive to issues of sovereignty. Hence, as we indicated at the outset, systems of externally enforced legal liability are unlikely to work. For these reasons a seller liability system is far more likely to break down at the compliance stage.

Negative cascades

A second potential problem relates to negative "cascades." If enterprises in a country that is "permit-short" overvalue permits *ex ante*—buying permits that turn out to be worth less than expected—then the state where the buyers reside could miss its international target. The worst-case result would be a cascade or contagion effect, in which the devaluing of one seller's permits (say, Russian permits) then triggers noncompliance in other states whose enterprises hold Russian permits. Market expectations would eventually adjust. But in that particular year shortfalls in compliance would occur, if two additional features exist: entities both did not hedge adequately and could not buy sufficient new permits from other sellers.

For several reasons we do not think this scenario is likely. We expect hedging to take place for the reasons given above. There is also reason to think that permits will be available in the event of a shortfall, albeit at higher prices. Third, under our proposed system the cascade problem would be alleviated by the fact that permits that are not fully valid would suffer only percentage reductions, not complete invalidation. Fourth, the problem would also be limited to the year in question. Finally, a work-out period could be arranged so that the full impact of holding partially invalid permits was not immediate for the buyers. Likewise, it might be desirable to have "banking and borrowing" provisions that allow the buying jurisdiction, which suffered from holding invalid permits, to make up the deficit in future years.

Consistent with our argument about the comparable Kyoto provisions above, such measures would make sense as a way to smooth out burdens arising from sudden changes in conditions, but they are not enforcement provisions. However, as Robert Stavins argues with respect to the United States, "credible mechanisms need to be established to ensure that the use of borrowed allowances is offset through future emission reductions."[39] For this reason we advocate using such banking measures only cautiously.

Moral hazard and seller default

Despite the reputational incentives to maintain the future value of their permits, some sellers may sell permits that turn out to be worth less than their nominal value, either due to opportunism or misjudgment. Buyers of these devalued permits would have to engage in further internal reductions or buy additional permits to reach their

[39] Stavins 2008: 8.

nationally-mandated caps. The consequence of seller defaults would therefore be *increases* in the price of carbon as buyers (typically) go into the market to cover shortfalls. This is actually a great advantage of the system, since without such a mechanism, overselling of permits would lead to a lower effective price of carbon by increasing permit supply.

To maintain the incentive for buyers to avoid buying invalid permits, the buyers must not be able to renegotiate their domestic emissions caps, or otherwise receive compensation from their governments, in the event that their purchased portfolio of permits is insufficient to reach their cap. That is, governments of permit-short countries need to protect against "moral hazard," similar to the moral hazard problems of bailing out banks that engage in risky lending practices and later seek government bailouts. This is probably the most serious weakness of our system, though it is a weakness shared by nearly every alternative model as well.

We cannot guarantee that authorities will not, under pressure, engage in activities that create moral hazard in a climate change permit system. Indeed, in response to the prospect of bank failures set off by the recent financial crisis, the US Federal Reserve System and the Treasury have taken radical measures to prevent bank failures. These measures have raised serious issues of moral hazard.

Explicit legislative provisions to prohibit *post hoc* subsidies and renegotiation will consequently be essential, and the media and non-governmental environmental organizations will have to be alert to the danger; but these measures are unlikely to be sufficient if the invalidity of seller permits threatened a banking crisis in the buyer country. One aid to resisting *post hoc* adjustments is likely to be pressure from buyers of valid permits, who will seek to ensure that the value of their investments is not squandered by the state. They will likely constitute a powerful interest group with a stake in the integrity of the system. Another source of resistance to moral hazard lies in the accountability of governments to their publics, and the commitment by those publics to compliance with a meaningful international climate regime. Publics will need to understand that succumbing to pressure to compensate buyers for invalid permits will destroy the climate change mitigation system.

However, neither reliance on competitors nor reliance on publics would be likely to suffice if very large banks or bank-like entities were faced with insolvency as a result of having purchased large quantities of invalid permits. Regulation will have to occur *ex ante* to ensure that such a situation does not arise. That is, regulation will have to assure, as noted above, that banks and bank-like entities cannot speculate in emissions permits with highly leveraged debt.

Conclusion

In world politics, strong commitment by states is essential to effective multilateral action. States must prefer participation to non-participation. We therefore began this chapter by reviewing reasons why a cap-and-trade regime is the most likely to induce sufficiently widespread participation among significant emitters to create the possibility of effectiveness. Proposals for assistance with projects and policies carry enormous transaction costs and have little prospect of being sufficiently effective; and an international carbon tax is unlikely to be acceptable to reluctant developing countries and the major industrialized states as well. In the end, a cap-and-trade regime must rest on strong preferences in democratic states to mitigate climate change. These are demanding political conditions, but we see no alternative arrangement that could generate sufficiently effective and timely action. And we observe around the world recent actions that counsel some optimism, in Australia, the EU, and even the United States.

Yet any cap-and-trade regime at the international level will encounter pressures toward non-compliance. As with participation, for global regulatory regimes to work well, states must, on the whole, choose compliance over violation. Since there is no external enforcer, arrangements such as that in the Kyoto Protocol for seller liability will not work. Compliance will neither reliably occur *ex post* or be expected to occur *ex ante*. The severity of the global climate problem does not by itself entail meaningful action under these conditions: for many states the costs of abatement are higher than the benefits of a more stable climate, and for some states climate change itself may even be welcome.

Our proposed system for a post-Kyoto regime rests instead on a model of buyer liability coupled to annual *ex post* assessments and jurisdiction-equal discounting of invalid permits. This system is incentive-compatible for two reasons: buyers have incentives to monitor the system and price permits according to perceived validity, and sellers have incentives, if allocations are correct, to maintain their reputations for reliability. The system will not operate automatically: in particular, institutions will need to be created to assure that *ex post* assessment is reliable and, *ex ante,* that ratings agencies are also reliable. Indeed, one of the major conclusions of this chapter is the urgent need for social scientists to think more carefully about assessment institutions that could be effective in a climate change regime with buyer liability.

Some non-compliance in climate change cooperation is inevitable. Yet the system that we propose is the least bad choice, because it is consistent with the fundamental features of world politics we have described. For this reason, it provides at least the outline of a political foundation for a working international system not doomed by enforcement problems. It could therefore contribute to effective regulation of GHG emissions and, most importantly, help to generate the technological innovation that is widely agreed to be essential if climate change is to be brought under control.

References

Akerlaf, George A. (1970). "The Market for 'Lemons': Quality Uncertainty and the Market Mechanism," *Quarterly Journal of Economics* 84(3): 488–500.

Aldy, Joseph and Robert Stavins, eds. (2007). *Architectures for Agreement: Addressing Global Climate Change in a Post Kyoto World.* New York: Cambridge University Press.

Aldy, Joseph and Robert Stavins (2008). "Designing the Post-Kyoto Climate Regime: Lessons from the Harvard Project on International Climate Agreements," Working Paper, December.

Axelrod, Robert (1984). *The Evolution of Cooperation.* New York: Basic Books.

Barnett, Michael and Martha Finnemore (2004). *Rules for the World: International Organizations in Global Politics.* Ithaca, NY: Cornell University Press.

Barrett, Scott (2003). *Environment and Statecraft: The Strategy of Environmental Treaty-Making.* Oxford: Oxford University Press.

(2008). "A Portfolio System of Climate Treaties," The Harvard Project on International Climate Agreements, Discussion Paper 08-13, October.

Bluemel, Erik B. (2007). "Unraveling the Global Warming Regime Complex: Competitive Entropy in the Regulation of the Global Public Good," *University of Pennsylvania Law Review* 155(6): 1981–2049.

Cooper, Richard N. (2008). "The Case for Charges on Greenhouse Gas Emissions," The Harvard Project on International Climate Agreements, Discussion Paper 08-10, October.

Downs, George W., David M. Rocke, and Peter N. Barsoom (1996). "Is the Good News about Compliance Good News About Cooperation?" *International Organization* 50(3): 379–406.

Fearon, James (1998). "Bargaining, Enforcement, and International Cooperation," *International Organization* 52(2): 269–306.

Frankel, Jeffrey (2007). "Formulas for Quantitative Emissions Targets," in Aldy and Stavins (eds.), pp. 31–56.

(2008). "An Elaborated Proposal for Global Climate Policy Architecture: Specific Formulas and Emissions Targets for All Countries in All Decades," The Harvard Project on International Climate Agreements, Discussion Paper 08-08, October.

Ghosh, Arunabha (2008). *See No Evil, Speak No Evil? The WTO, the Trade Policy Review Mechanism, and Developing Countries,* Unpublished Ph.D. dissertation, Oxford University.

Guzman, Andrew T. (2008). *How International Law Works.* Oxford and New York: Oxford University Press.

Hathaway, Oona (2002). "Do Human Rights Treaties Make a Difference?" *Yale Law Journal* 111(8): 1935–2042.

Hepburn, Cameron (2007). "Carbon Trading: A Review of the Kyoto Mechanisms," *Annual Review of Environment and Resources* 32: 375–93.

Holland, Paul W. (1986). "Statistics and Causal Inference," *Journal of the American Statistical Association* 81, 396: 945–60.

Jaffe, Judson and Robert N. Stavins (2008). "Linkage of Tradable Permit Systems in International Climate Policy Architecture," The Harvard Project on International Climate Agreements, Discussion Paper 08-07, September.

King, Gary, Robert O. Keohane, and Sydney Verba (1994). *Designing Social Inquiry.* Princeton, NJ: Princeton University Press.

Leandro, José E., Hartwig Shafer, and Gaspar Frontini (1999). "Towards a More Effective Conditionality: An Operational Framework," *World Development* 27(2): 285–300.

Mosley, P., J. Harrington, and J. Toye (1991). *Aid and Power: The World Bank and Policy-Based Lending. Volume 1: Analysis and Policy Proposals.* New York: Routledge.

Nordhaus, Robert R., Kyle W. Danish, Richard H. Rosenzweig, and Britt Speyer Fleming (2000a). "International Emissions Trading Rules as a Compliance Tool: What is Necessary, Effective, and Workable?" *Environmental Law Reporter* 30: 10837–55.

(2000b). "A Framework for Achieving Environmental Integrity and the Economic Benefits of Emissions Trading Under the Kyoto Protocol," *Environmental Law Reporter* 30: 11061–70.

OECD 2000. Organization for Economic Cooperation and Development, International Energy Agency. An Assessment of Liability Rules for International GHG Emissions Trading. Available at: www.iea.org/textbase/papers/2000/ghget.pdf.

Posner, Eric and Miguel de Figueiredo (2005). "Is the International Court of Justice Biased?" *Journal of Legal Studies* 34(3): 599–630.

Raustiala, Kal (2005). "Form and Substance in International Agreements," *American Journal of International Law* 99(3): 581–614.

Raustiala, Kal and Anne-Marie Slaughter (2002). "International Law, International Relations, and Compliance," in Carlsnaes *et al.* (eds.), *Handbook of International Relations*. London: Sage.

Schelling, Thomas C. (1960). *The Strategy of Conflict*. Cambridge, MA: Harvard University Press.

Sinclair, Timothy J. (2005). *The New Masters of Capital*. Ithaca, NY: Cornell University Press.

Stavins, Robert N. (2008). "Addressing Climate Change with a Comprehensive U.S. Cap-and-Trade System," ENRP Discussion Paper 2008-01. Belfer Center for Science and International Affairs, John F. Kennedy School of Government, Cambridge, MA, January.

Stone, Randall (2002). *Lending Credibility: The International Monetary Fund and the Post-Communist Transition*. Princeton, NJ: Princeton University Press.

Tickell, Oliver (2008). *Kyoto 2: How to Manage the Global Greenhouse*. London: Zed Books.

Tomz, Michael (2007). *Reputation and International Cooperation*. Princeton, NJ: Princeton University Press.

Victor, David G. (2001). *The Collapse of the Kyoto Protocol and the Struggle to Slow Global Warming*. Princeton, NJ: Princeton University Press.

(2007). "Fragmented Carbon Markets and Reluctant Nations: Implications for the Design of Effective Architectures," in Aldy and Stavins (eds.), pp. 133–60.

Victor, David G. and Danny Cullenward (2007). "Making Carbon Markets Work," *Scientific American*, 297(6): 70–7, December.

Victor, David G., Kal Raustiala, and Eugene Skolnikoff, eds. (1998). *The Implementation and Effectiveness of International Environmental Commitments*. Cambridge, MA: MIT Press.

Wara, Michael (2007). "Is the Global Carbon Market Working?" *Nature*, 445: 595–6, February 8.

Wara, Michael W. and David G. Victor (2008). "A Realistic Policy on
    International Carbon Offsets," Stanford University Program on Energy
    and Sustainable Development, Working Paper #74, April.
Zhang, Zhong Xiang (1999). "International Greenhouse Gas Emissions
    Trading: Who Should be Held Liable for the Non-Compliance by
    Sellers? *Ecological Economics* 31: 323–29.

PART III

The role and means of technology transfer

13 | *International climate technology strategies*

RICHARD G. NEWELL

Introduction

There is widespread agreement that achieving the very substantial reductions in greenhouse gas (GHG) emissions necessary to stabilize atmospheric carbon dioxide (CO_2) concentrations at 450–550 parts per million (ppm) will require innovation and large-scale adoption of GHG-reducing technologies throughout the global energy system (IPCC 2007). The set of necessary technologies includes those for increased energy efficiency, renewable energy, nuclear power, and CO_2 capture and storage. Alongside strategies aimed at reducing GHG emissions—such as emission targets in an international context or domestic GHG cap-and-trade systems or taxes—much discussion has therefore focused on policies that also target technology directly, including research and development (R&D)[1] activities and technology-specific mandates and incentives. The associated policy debate is not so much over the importance of new technology *per se* in solving the climate problem, but rather over what the most effective policies and institutions are for achieving the dramatic technological changes necessary to stabilize GHG concentrations.

The scale of the system to be reoriented is immense. The International Energy Agency (IEA), in its most recent assessment of energy investment, projects that about $22 trillion of investment in energy-supply infrastructure will be needed over the 2006–2030 period, or almost $900 billion annually, on average (IEA 2007b). Note that this does not include expenditures on energy demand-side technologies (e.g., transportation, appliances, and equipment), which will measure in the trillions of dollars each year. Relative to this baseline investment, the Secretariat of the United Nations Framework

---

[1] For simplicity the term "R&D" is intended to include initial "first-of-a-kind" demonstration projects focused on generating new knowledge.

Convention on Climate Change (UNFCCC) estimates that an additional $200 billion in global investment and financial flows will be required annually by 2030 just to return GHG emissions to current levels (UNFCCC 2007).

What are the most important international and domestic actions necessary to technologically alter energy systems in a direction that can achieve GHG stabilization targets while also meeting other societal goals? Growing attention has turned to the possible role of international technology-oriented agreements as part of the architecture of an international climate change policy (de Coninck *et al.* 2008). Specific activities under such agreements could include knowledge sharing and coordination; joint R&D; technology transfer; and technology deployment mandates, standards, or incentives.

Interest in these efforts is attributable to a number of factors, generally related to the idea that if we can lower the costs of mitigation technologies, the likelihood that countries will implement significant GHG reductions will be higher. Agreements to further R&D can increase the international exchange of scientific and technical information while also improving the cost-effectiveness of R&D through cost sharing and reduced duplication of effort. Provisions for technology transfer, on the other hand, originate primarily in the need to help developing countries follow a less GHG-intensive development path by providing access to climate-friendly technologies and the funding to cover their additional cost. As such, technology transfer efforts can help to increase incentives for developing-country participation in international climate agreements and at the same time advance goals beyond global climate mitigation (e.g., economic development, local air quality improvement, energy security). The Bali Action Plan therefore identified technology development and transfer as one of five central issues for consideration during development of a post-2012 international climate policy agreement (alongside a long-term emissions goal and actions on mitigation, adaptation, and financing) (UNFCCC 2008).

This chapter considers opportunities for improved and expanded international technology development and transfer strategies within the broader context of international agreements and institutions for climate, energy, trade, development, and intellectual property. The next section characterizes the economic scale of the climate change technology challenge, while subsequent sections review the pattern of public and private R&D and the economic rationales for R&D policies within the global innovation system; clarify the importance of options for inducing technology market demand through domestic GHG pricing, international trade, and international development assistance; and discuss upstream innovation strategies, including international coordination and funding of climate technology R&D, and knowledge transfer through intellectual property. A concluding section summarizes the main international technology issues and actions identified for consideration within the post-2012 dialogue.

The climate change technology challenge

Since its adoption in 1992, the UNFCCC has been ratified by virtually all the world's 190-plus countries. The treaty's principle objective is "stabilization of greenhouse gas concentrations in the atmosphere at a level that would prevent dangerous anthropogenic interference with the climate system." Although there is much debate about what level of GHG concentrations would prevent dangerous anthropogenic interference, one thing is clear: Stabilizing GHG concentrations *at any level* implies eventually reducing net GHG emissions to near zero.

While the idea of balancing the atmospheric GHG stock by reducing the net GHG flow to zero is simple enough, the technological reality of what it will take to do this is far from simple. Currently, 69 percent of global anthropogenic GHG emissions come from fossil fuels such as oil, coal, and natural gas, which together satisfy 81 percent of global energy demand (IEA 2007b, 2007d). The remainder of global energy is supplied by renewable energy (13 percent) and nuclear power (6 percent) (IEA 2007b).

Stabilizing GHG concentrations therefore requires large-scale and widespread substitution toward energy technologies with low to zero net GHG emissions throughout the global energy system. However, under existing policies and expected market trends, the IEA forecasts that world energy consumption will grow 55 percent and energy-related CO_2 emissions 57 percent between 2005 and 2030, with the fossil-fuel share *rising* slightly from 81 to 82 percent (IEA 2007b). Although there is substantial uncertainty over longer timeframes, recent estimates suggest that, without additional policy actions, global annual CO_2 emissions will increase by a factor of about three by the end of this century (Weyant *et al.* 2006; Fisher *et al.* 2007; Clark *et al.* 2007). These and other forecasts underscore the fact that the energy-economic system has a tremendous predisposition toward fossil-fuel-based technologies and would require substantial domestic and international policy actions to encourage change.

Economic scale of the technology challenge

To gauge, in economic terms, the magnitude of the innovation challenge presented by climate change, it is helpful to consider possible GHG emission targets and the projected costs of achieving these targets. These projected costs, most commonly measured in terms of reduced gross domestic product (GDP), indicate the scale of the benefit that could come from innovations that significantly reduce (or eliminate) the cost disadvantage of climate-friendly technologies relative to the competition. If such low-cost alternatives also made it feasible and desirable to undertake more significant reductions than otherwise would be taken, then there would also be a benefit from the further climate damages avoided. In fact, lowering the cost disadvantage of climate-friendly energy technologies relative to conventional fossil-fuel technologies—and thereby increasing the incentive to comply with international climate obligations—could play a major role in improving the long-run robustness of international frameworks (Barrett 2003).

Many proposals, and most analyses, have centered on emission paths that are consistent with ultimate stabilization targets in the range of 450–550 ppm CO_2 (530–670 ppm CO_2-equivalent, or CO_2e, if all GHGs are included). Modeling scenarios of cost-effective global climate mitigation policy suggest that, for targets in this range, the cost of GHG mitigation through 2050 is trillions or tens of trillions of dollars of discounted GDP, or an annualized cost in the tens to hundreds of billions of dollars per year (Newell 2008). Longer-term total costs through 2100 are approximately double this amount. While these estimates are based on numerous economic and policy assumptions, they give a sense of the magnitude of the payoff from technology innovations that could significantly lower the cost of achieving various GHG emission goals.

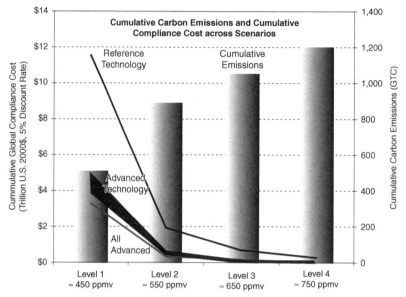

Figure 13.1. Cumulative global mitigation costs under alternative technology scenarios. Source: Clarke *et al.* (2006).

Importance of advanced technology for lowering costs and expanding options

Many studies find that the availability and cost of advanced energy technologies plays a central role in determining the cost of achieving various GHG emission targets (IPCC 2007). Virtually all studies find that a cost-effective technology solution entails a mix of energy efficiency, low-GHG energy supply, as well as reductions in non-CO_2 GHG emissions. Thus, R&D to support the necessary transition to a low-carbon energy system must also be broad-based, covering a wide range of technological opportunities. For example, one study finds that if we were limited to technologies available in 2005, the present-value cost of achieving stabilization at 550 ppm CO_2 would be more than $20 trillion greater than the estimated cost taking into account expected developments in energy efficiency, hydrogen energy technologies, advanced bioenergy, and wind and solar technologies (Edmonds *et al.* 2007). The models used in these studies typically presume that the significant innovative efforts in R&D, learning, and

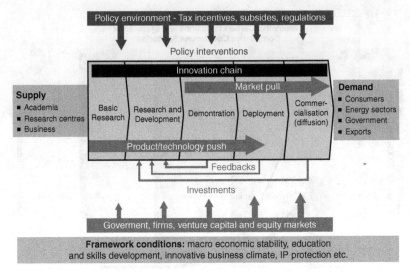

Figure 13.2. Schematic of the innovation system. Source: IEA (2008a).

new-technology diffusion needed to underpin these assumed technological improvements will be forthcoming.

Other studies have found that accelerated technology development
offers the potential to dramatically reduce the costs of stabilization,
with advanced technology scenarios reducing the cumulative costs of
stabilization by 50 percent or more, which in turn yields economic
benefits of hundreds of billions to trillions of dollars globally (Figure
13.1) (Newell 2008). While one might reasonably argue over the
details of the modeling assumptions, these and other results demonstrate that technological advances have the potential to significantly
reduce the costs of attaining societal goals for climate-change mitigation. The challenge is to structure policy to maximize the likelihood
that we will harness these technological opportunities as effectively
and efficiently as possible.

The global innovation system

Technological improvement through the creation and deployment of
new product and process innovations is one of the most important
underpinnings of economic development as well as of broader societal prosperity, including environmental protection. The complex set

of institutions, markets, and governing processes that comprise this innovation system includes private firms and consortia, their products, their production processes, and the markets within which they operate; government research institutions and public policies; universities and colleges; and other non-profit research institutions (Figure 13.2).

Patterns of global innovative effort

Nations spend about $1 trillion globally each year on R&D, with over 95 percent occurring in the OECD countries, Russia, and China—and 80 percent in countries represented in the G8 (see Table 13.1). The focus here is on overall R&D; private and public energy-related R&D is discussed in subsequent sections. Although innovation activities are not limited to R&D, R&D remains one of the few well-tracked indicators of innovative activity and is highly correlated with other indicators.

Industry is by far the largest player in R&D effort, funding over 60 percent and performing almost 70 percent of R&D globally in 2006 (the most recent year for which complete data are available). Industrial R&D focuses on applied research and especially development, stimulated by market demand for technologically advanced products and processes. Government is the second largest funder of R&D globally (30 percent). About half of government funding is transferred to universities, other non-profit research institutions, and industry, which perform the associated R&D within a system of contracts, grants, and other arrangements. Government funding tends to focus more on basic and applied research.

In addition to creating new knowledge upon which further technological development can draw, university-based R&D supports the production of young researchers. Most of these researchers eventually move into the private sector—thus they represent an important link within the overall innovation system. Ensuring a stream of scientists, engineers, and other research professionals trained in areas relevant to clean-energy technologies will be an important element in increasing the necessary innovative effort and moderating its cost. The capacity of a country's workforce to absorb and apply new know-how and technology is also essential for development, and it is one of the main impediments to more rapid technology transfer to developing countries (World Bank 2008c). By supporting researchers and graduate students,

Table 13.1 *International R&D expenditures in 2006 (units as indicated)*

Country	All sources (US$ billions)	Percent world R&D	Percent financed by Industry	Government	Percent performed by Industry	Universities	Government	Researchers (1000 FTEs)
United States	344	35.8	65	29	70	14	11	1,388
Japan	139	14.4	77	16	77	13	8	710
Germany	67	6.9	68	28	70	16	14	282
France	41	4.3	52	38	63	18	17	204
United Kingdom	36	3.7	45	32	62	26	10	184
Canada	24	2.5	48	33	54	36	9	125
Russia	20	2.1	29	29	67	6	27	464
Italy	18	1.8	40	51	50	30	17	82
Other EU-27	82	8.5	51	37	60	25	14	199
G-8 total	770	80.0	62	29	68	17	12	3,637
Korea	36	3.7	75	23	77	10	12	200
Australia	12	1.2	53	41	54	27	16	81
Mexico	6	0.6	47	45	50	27	22	48
Turkey	5	0.5	46	49	37	51	12	43
Switzerland	7	0.7	70	23	74	23	1	25
Norway	4	0.4	46	44	54	30	16	22
New Zealand	1	0.1	41	43	42	33	26	17
OECD total	818	85.0	64	30	69	17	11	3,979

OECD + Russia	838	87.1	62	30	69	17	11	4,443
China	87	9.0	69	25	71	9	20	1,223
Chinese Taipei	17	1.8	67	31	68	12	20	95
Israel	8	0.8	69	23	78	13	5	—
Singapore	5	0.5	59	36	66	24	10	25
South Africa	4	0.4	44	38	58	19	21	17
Argentina	2	0.2	29	67	30	27	41	35
Romania	1	0.1	30	64	49	18	32	21
World total*	962	100.0	63	30	69	16	13	5,859

Source: OECD (2008). Non-U.S. totals are based on purchasing power parity (PPP) exchange rates.

* *Note:* Non-OECD total covers only select non-OECD countries and thus the non-OECD and world totals may represent underestimates; however, almost all R&D occurs in the included countries.

public funding for research affects an economy's capacity to generate and assimilate scientific advances, technology innovations, and productivity improvements. This linkage has made research funding a priority among many who are concerned about the long-term competitiveness of national economies and has led to increased support for expanded R&D spending generally, including in the United States and the European Union. At an international level, programs that facilitate the international exchange of graduate students, postdocs, and more senior scholars in areas relevant to climate-mitigation research can help to expand human-capital-related spillovers.

Innovation market problems and policy strategies

The explanation for current R&D patterns is well-known. The gains from innovative activity are in general difficult for firms to appropriate, as the benefits tend to "spill over" to other firms and customers, without full compensation. While positive knowledge spillover is a good thing—other things equal—it leads to a level of private investment in innovative effort that is too low from a broader societal perspective. Moreover, this problem tends to become greater the further up the innovative chain one goes: from development, to applied, and then to basic research (See Newell 2008, IEA 2008a). When confronted with limited resources, it is sensible for public funding to focus first and foremost on the part of the innovation problem that is least likely to be addressed adequately by the private sector. Overall, public funding for pre-commercial research therefore tends to receive widespread support among experts. In situations where there is a missing market for the technology—as is currently the case for GHG mitigation in much of the world—climate policy that places a price on emissions can serve as the most cost-effective means of encouraging technology deployment.[2]

Technology demonstration projects occupy a middle ground between technology development and deployment. Arguments for public support of technology demonstration tend to point to the large expense; high degree of technical, market, and regulatory risk;

---

[2] For a more complete discussion of the role and design of technology deployment policies see Newell (2007b) in a domestic context and de Coninck *et al.* (2008) in an international context.

and inability of private firms to capture the rewards from designing and constructing first-of-a-kind facilities (Newell 2007a). Most compelling, from an economic perspective, is the fact that there may be non-appropriable returns to knowledge generated in the process of undertaking first-of-a-kind demonstration projects. For example, knowledge gained through such projects can help improve the design of future technology, lower technical risks, and serve as a basis for well-designed regulations. On the other hand, caution is required because—despite good intentions—many of the most notable failures in government energy R&D funding have been associated with large-scale demonstration projects (Cohen and Noll 1991).

While experience suggests that it should not be the focus of climate-mitigation technology investments by the public sector, public support for a limited number of first-of-a-kind demonstration projects could be valuable, so long as the purpose is to generate substantial new knowledge. Given the dominant role of coal in the energy systems of both industrialized and developing countries, demonstrating technologies for carbon capture and storage has particular salience at the international level. The 2008 G8 Hokkaido Summit Leaders Declaration, for example, supported the launch of twenty large-scale CCS demonstration projects globally by 2010. Approaches for coordinating such projects at an international level are considered in a later section of this chapter.

Technology development and transfer through market demand

GHG emission pricing through domestic emission commitments

There are many excellent treatments of the advantages of economy-wide, long-term, multi-gas, flexible emission policies that attach a cost to—or "put a price" on—GHGs. The Kyoto Protocol, the EU Emission Trading System, and the legislative proposals with the most traction in the United States have embraced this approach. Establishing a GHG emission price (through policies such as cap-and-trade or emission taxes) is essential *from a technology perspective* for two primary reasons. First, because the GHG price attaches a financial cost to GHGs and—just as people will consume less of something expensive than something given away for free—will induce households and firms to buy technologies with lower GHG emissions (a more efficient appliance, for example). Ideally, the GHG price is designed to encourage the adoption of the most cost-effective technologies for reducing emissions by sending a consistent financial signal to households and businesses across the economy.

The second reason the GHG price is essential from a technology perspective is because it creates a demand-driven, profit-based incentive for the private sector to invest effort in developing new, lower-cost climate-friendly innovations. Market-demand pull will encourage manufacturers to invest in R&D and other innovative efforts to bring new lower-GHG technologies to market, just as they do for other products and processes (for surveys see Jaffe *et al.* 2003 and Popp *et al.*). Members of the US Climate Action Partnership (USCAP 2007)—a coalition of major US companies and environmental organizations—agreed when they concluded that "the most efficient and powerful way to stimulate private investment in research, development, and deployment is to adopt policies establishing a market value for GHG emissions over the long term."

National policies that encourage GHG mitigation will therefore play an essential role in stimulating demand for, and innovation in, necessary new technologies. Conveniently, the vast majority of innovative effort globally takes place in developed countries that are expected to take the most significant initial steps to mitigate GHG emissions. In addition, agreements for the removal of existing subsidies for fossil fuels and related technologies would further move the global energy system in a more climate-friendly direction, while at the same time having broader economic benefits (UNEP 2008).

International carbon markets—employing flexibility mechanisms such as international linkage of domestic emission programs, offsets, and the Clean Development Mechanism—represent an important mechanism for financing emission reductions in developing countries, technology transfer, and cost-effective GHG mitigation. Depending on numerous assumptions, including assumptions about aggregate GHG targets as well as about burden sharing between developed and developing countries, international demand for emission credits from developing countries is estimated to total in the tens of billions of dollars up to about $100 billion annually through 2050 (UNFCCC 2007). To facilitate technology transfer and create incentives for technology development at a global level, international agreements and domestic policies should consider establishing clear rules and minimizing unnecessary barriers to the use of these market mechanisms.

Innovation generated by policies that establish a GHG emission price is sure to come from a wide array of businesses currently engaged in the development and use of energy producing and consuming technologies, especially in the provision of electricity and transportation services. It will also come from the agro-biotech sector (assuming there are incentives for biological sequestration), from companies that produce and consume other non-CO_2 GHGs (e.g., chemical companies), and from less obvious sectors such as the information technology industry (e.g., in the context of energy management and conservation). Estimates suggest that private-sector investments in energy R&D, however, have fallen significantly in real terms since peaking around 1980, in tandem with declines in energy prices and public energy R&D spending. Nonetheless, while the *trend* appears to have been downward over this period, current private-sector R&D investments relevant to energy technology are extremely difficult to assess, and these estimates provide a poor indication of the overall *level* of private-sector R&D investment that could and likely will be brought to bear on the climate technology challenge (Newell 2008).

In fact, many of the industrial sectors and individual companies that are likely to be most engaged in creating the innovations necessary to reduce GHG emissions have substantial R&D capacity. Given expected levels of energy investment over the next several decades, and assuming the level of associated private R&D investment is measured in terms of a few percent of sales, as is typical, this implies private-sector innovative efforts on energy measured in tens of billions of dollars per year. This is consistent with a recent IEA (2008a) estimate that places current global private-sector spending on energy technologies at $40–$60 billion annually, far exceeding public-sector spending of about $10 billion annually.

This is illustrated in Table 13.2, which shows 2006 R&D expenditures (including as a percent of sales) for the 1,250 companies that globally have the highest levels of R&D investment (U.K. Department for Innovation, Universities and Skills 2007). The list includes producers of transportation technologies—such as Ford, DaimlerChrysler, Toyota, Boeing, and Rolls-Royce—which have individual company R&D budgets measured in billions of dollars per year and which

Table 13.2 *R&D expenditures for top R&D-spending companies worldwide (for 2006, units as indicated)*

Sector (number of companies)	R&D US$ (millions)	Percent of sales
All sectors (1,250)	478,129	3.5
Aerospace & defence (39)	21,160	4.9
Automobiles & parts (78)	80,284	4.1
Chemicals (91)	22,341	3.1
Construction & materials (23)	2,374	0.9
Electricity (16)	2,918	0.9
Electronic & electrical equipment (102)	35,150	4.5
Forestry & paper (8)	573	0.5
Gas, water & multiutilities (7)	738	0.3
General industrials (36)	11,583	2.1
Household goods (24)	5,011	2.3
Industrial engineering (70)	11,737	2.7
Industrial metals (23)	3,201	0.8
Industrial transportation (6)	440	0.3
Mining (3)	604	0.7
Oil & gas producers (18)	6,465	0.3
Oil equipment, services & distribution (10)	1,748	1.9
Pharmaceuticals & biotechnology (157)	92,881	15.9
Software & computer services (113)	34,359	10.1
Technology hardware & equipment (207)	84,517	8.6

Note: Table includes sectors that may be relevant to GHG innovation, as well as certain very large R&D-performing sectors, from the *R&D Scorecard's* 1,250 companies globally with the highest R&D expenditures (U.K. Department for Innovation, Universities and Skills 2007). These 1,250 companies account for about 80 percent of global industry R&D.

together contribute to a global R&D budget for the automotive sector of $80 billion annually. Electronic and electrical equipment companies spent over $35 billion in R&D in 2006, including companies like Siemens and Samsung, and general industrial companies, like Mitsubishi Heavy Industries and General Electric, which have annual R&D budgets of over $11 billion globally.

Chemical and agro-biotech companies, such as Bayer, BASF, DuPont, and Dow each have R&D budgets above $1 billion per year; these companies will be active in finding substitutes for GHGs and in engineering low-GHG biofuel alternatives. While elements of the energy sector focused on fossil-fuel extraction have relatively low R&D intensities, they still have substantial R&D budgets in aggregate. Furthermore, firms in the oil services sector that are likely to play an important role in developing geologic carbon storage, such as Schlumberger, spend hundreds of millions of dollars annually on R&D and have higher R&D intensities than the large oil companies.

In addition, many smaller firms and start-up companies have benefited from a recent surge in venture capital investment in clean energy technology. For example, early-stage venture capital investments directed to clean energy in the United States totaled about $350 million in 2007, approximately double the figure for the prior year and starting from a negligible level just 10 years ago (Newell 2008; also see UNEP and New Energy Finance 2007). While relatively small, such companies can be an important source of productive innovative effort (Kortum and Lerner 2000).

Two main messages emerge from this discussion. First, substantial R&D capacity exists in the principal sectors and companies relevant to GHG innovation. Evidence indicates that this private-sector innovative capacity will be directed to developing and commercializing low-GHG technologies—if increased demand is spurred by a price on GHG emissions. The second message is that the private-sector level of R&D spending on relevant products and processes is so substantial that failure to align private-sector profit incentives with societal GHG goals means that any public R&D spending will likely push against an insurmountable tide. Pervasive incentives for GHG mitigation throughout the major economies will be necessary to reorient investment and innovation in a more climate-friendly direction. Nonetheless, such reorientation is not free and can be particularly costly if it comes at the expense of other R&D. Increased demand for specialized R&D without a complementary increase in the supply of relevant R&D professionals runs the risk of displacing or crowding out other valuable research activities, or of increasing salaries rather than effort. Education and international scholarly exchange is therefore an important element of a balanced innovation strategy.

For a GHG policy to provide an effective inducement to innovation, however, it is critical that the private sector views the policy as credible over the long term. Given the sometimes substantial time lags between initial discovery and profitable market penetration, companies must be confident that there will indeed be sufficient demand once their innovations reach the market. Such confidence would be increased by domestic policies and international agreements that put in place GHG emission targets whose stringency is spelled out for many decades in advance, and that provide stable financial incentives across a wide array of technological solutions.

Technology transfer through international trade and development assistance

Domestic actions for emissions mitigation will be a critical feature of any internationally coordinated response to climate change that induces the necessary long-term innovation. Nonetheless, transferring the resulting technological knowledge and equipment internationally—and ensuring that technologies develop that are appropriate to different countries—will require additional actions at an international level. While technology transfer strategies must address typical impediments to technology adoption, such as information availability and technological maturity, they also must address financing barriers specific to developing countries. The degree of protection afforded to intellectual property rights and other conditions related to the rule of law, regulatory transparency, and market openness are also critical and can present impediments that bear on technology transfer. Intellectual property issues are discussed in the next section on upstream innovation strategies.

The two principle mechanisms for promoting technology transfer between countries are international trade and international development assistance. In both cases, the rules and resources that underpin these mechanisms could be enhanced to enable a more effective response to global climate change. International trade and foreign direct investment are the main means by which new know-how and equipment are transferred among countries (World Bank 2008c), with private-sector investments constituting 86 percent of global investment and financial flows (UNFCCC 2007). To enhance investment and financial flows to address climate change, it is therefore crucial to focus on private-sector investments. In addition to domestic actions that foster a positive environment for technology transfer investments through regulatory flexibility, transparency, and stability, specific international actions could be taken to reduce barriers to trade in environmental goods and services. A recent study on trade and climate change found that varied levels of tariffs and non-tariff barriers are a very significant impediment to the transfer of energy technologies to developing countries (World Bank 2008d). It estimated that eliminating these barriers could increase trade in four basic clean-energy technologies (wind, solar, clean coal, and efficient lighting) with high-GHG-emitting developing countries by 14 percent (World Bank 2008d). Note that the persistence of trade barriers—despite the desire expressed by many developing countries for greater technology transfer—highlights the political challenge associated with development strategies that may have as their objective the acquisition of knowledge, but not products.

The World Trade Organization (WTO), with 153 members that include all the largest GHG emitters (except Russia, which is in the process of accession), is the principle international forum for negotiating trade agreements. The ongoing Doha Round of trade negotiations explicitly covers trade in environmental goods and services, and in 2007 the United States and the European Union put forward specific proposals covering over $600 billion of annual trade in environmental goods. They also proposed to prioritize negotiations on climate-friendly and energy-efficient technologies.

A trade agreement specific to climate-friendly technologies could be constructed as a subcategory within a larger negotiated package on environmental goods or in a separate agreement, and could be structured to come into force when members representing a minimum percentage of trade in climate-friendly products joined (this is similar to the approach taken with the Information Technology Agreement). Or a trade pact for climate-related technologies could be formulated as a plurilateral agreement—like the Agreement on Government Procurement—and could come into effect immediately and even independent of the conclusions of the Doha Round negotiations. Progress may also be possible within the WTO Working Group on Trade and Transfer of Technology (WGTTT), which was established as part of the Doha process to examine and make recommendations on WTO steps to increase flows of technology to developing countries (the WGTTT has so far produced no recommendations). Ongoing development and harmonization of technical standards relevant to climate mitigation technologies could also help facilitate trade and technology transfer; in fact, international professional associations have shown increased interest in examining the role for standards related to climate change and GHG management.[3] Just as standards development can help reduce impediments to technology transfer and accelerate the development and adoption of new innovations, disparate, uncoordinated standards can impede such progress.

The largest source of public-sector support for cross-border finance is trade finance in its various forms. Export Credit Agencies (ECAs), such as the US Export-Import Bank and US Overseas Private Investment Corporation, are often used by governments to support exports from domestic producers, usually through insurance, guarantees, favorable loan terms, or direct finance for export and overseas investment. As ECAs often provide support for energy-related technologies and can leverage significant private-sector funds, it is important that their investments are consistent with climate policy goals. The OECD has been the primary venue for discussing and coordinating international standards on the incorporation of environmental requirements for ECA support. In 2007, OECD countries agreed to stronger environmental rules for ECAs, including project environmental review and benchmarking to international (e.g., World Bank) standards (OECD 2007). Achieving these goals in the context of climate change mitigation will require implementation and ongoing review of these standards, development of specific guidelines related to climate impacts, and the extension of these rules to the ECAs of non-OECD countries such as China, Brazil, and India.

Lastly, although Official Development Assistance (ODA) funds are currently less than 1 percent of investment globally, ODA represents a larger share of investments (6 percent) in the least developed countries (UNFCCC 2007). Therefore, bilateral and multilateral development assistance has an important role to play in climate change mitigation, especially if such assistance can be used to leverage private technology investments in a more climate-friendly direction. As the official financial mechanism of the UNFCCC, the Global Environment Facility

---

[3] For example, the International Organization for Standardization has also begun cooperating with the IEA in identifying gaps and opportunities for standards to facilitate technology development and transfer (IEA 2007e), and the Institute of Electrical and Electronics Engineers Standards Association has launched a climate change study group. It could also be productive to coordinate these efforts with standards-related discussions within the WTO Committee on Trade and the Environment and the WTO Committee on Technical Barriers to Trade.

(GEF) has been the main source of climate-specific ODA funding to date. Cumulative GEF investments since 1991 have totaled about $3.3 billion for action on climate change in developing countries, with an additional $14.4 billion leveraged through co-financing from bilateral ODA, recipient countries, and the private sector. More recently, the World Bank joined with regional development banks to approve a pair of climate investment funds in support of the Bali Action Plan: the Clean Technology Fund and the Strategic Climate Fund. These funds, for which the World Bank is seeking at least $5 billion in support over the next three years (World Bank 2008a, 2008b), will provide resources for demonstration, deployment, and transfer of low-carbon technologies. They will also serve as a vehicle for testing innovative approaches to climate change, including adaptation.

Complementary upstream technology innovation strategies

The two most important international strategies for supporting the upstream supply and transfer of new climate technology innovations are (1) promoting increased and more effectively coordinated public funding of R&D, and (2) resolving any impediments to knowledge transfer through intellectual property. To implement these strategies, the UNFCCC should consider establishing an Expert Group on Technology Development to focus on activities related to technology innovation. This group would complement the existing Expert Group on Technology Transfer, which is focused primarily on technology deployment and related financial mechanisms. Together, these expert groups would serve as the UNFCCC focal point for interactions with the IEA, WTO, and other international institutions. In that capacity they could provide advice to, and develop recommendations for, the Subsidiary Body for Scientific and Technological Advice concerning specific issues related to the development of innovative technologies and the transfer of related knowledge for climate mitigation.

International coordination and augmentation of climate mitigation R&D

While private-sector effort dominates overall R&D spending and performance—particularly for product and process development—public funding of research is a significant and essential component of

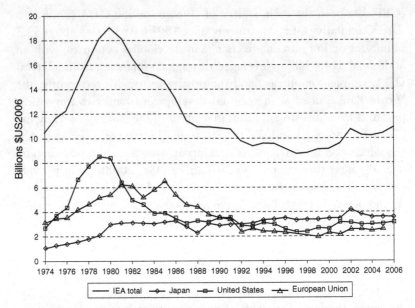

Figure 13.3. Public energy R&D spending in IEA countries (1974–2006)
Data source: IEA (2007a). Other IEA governments spend less than $500 million
annually on energy R&D

the overall innovation system for climate mitigation, in part because
of the role it plays in building capacity by training future researchers.
IEA member countries, which together account for about 85 percent
of overall global R&D expenditures, spent an estimated $11 billion on
publicly funded energy R&D in 2006 (IEA 2007a)—or about 4 percent
of overall public R&D spending by these countries in the same year
(Figure 13.3).

In real terms, this is about the same level of expenditure as in 1974,
but it is a substantial reduction since 1980, when public spending by
IEA countries on energy R&D peaked at about $19 billion in real
terms (or over 11 percent of overall public R&D funding). Public
energy R&D budgets declined in every country except Japan over
this period (that is, 1980–2006), and remain especially low in many
European countries. Low fossil-fuel prices, deregulation of the natural
gas and electric utilities industries in several countries, and a lack of
political interest led to tandem declines in both private and public
energy R&D spending. In recent years, however, the new energy
technology challenges posed by global climate change, combined with

heightened concerns over energy security, have significantly increased the prospective value of increased public funding for energy-related research. In response, funding levels have stabilized and the trend has been changing, with the most recent budgets in some countries, such as the United States, measurably increasing public funds directed to energy R&D. Priorities for public energy R&D budgets have also shifted significantly, with most energy research being reoriented in a direction that supports GHG mitigation, either by supporting nuclear, renewable, and energy efficiency R&D, or by supporting fossil energy R&D to facilitate carbon capture and storage.

Given the current level of energy R&D spending relative to the magnitude of the climate technology challenge and the magnitude of the potential payoff from innovative technology (likely measured in the hundreds of billions of dollars), it seems clear that a significant expansion of public spending on energy R&D by developed nations is warranted—in tandem with expanded private R&D in response to market demand. For example, recent IEA (2008a) and UNFCCC (2007) assessments of financial requirements to respond to climate mitigation needs conclude that it will be necessary to at least double clean-energy R&D to stabilize or significantly reduce GHG emissions within the next several decades.[4] Many innovations that address climate concerns also address energy security and local pollution concerns, in addition to yielding broader economic benefits. Studies find that accounting for these non-climate benefits further increases the value of energy R&D, often significantly (Newell 2008). It will therefore be valuable to target funding at areas that hold promise for addressing multiple energy challenges at the same time. Innovations that increase energy efficiency have this potential, as do supply-side innovations for renewable energy, advanced nuclear power, and

---

[4] Suggestions that what we really need is a "Manhattan Project" or "Apollo Project" approach to climate mitigation R&D are misguided, however, for several reasons. For both of those efforts the government was the sole customer for a single, well-defined project. This is in contrast to energy markets that are driven by millions of diverse users of a multitude of technologies. Cost was also not a key concern for the Manhattan or Apollo projects, whereas with climate technology innovation cost-competitiveness is the central issue. Those efforts also gave rise to a relatively short-lived burst of spending to solve a discrete problem, whereas what is likely to be required for climate technology innovation is steady incremental improvement over many decades. See Yang and Oppenheimer (2007) for a related discussion.

carbon capture and storage that increase fuel diversity while reducing multiple pollutants.

While the case for expanding domestic R&D on climate mitigation technologies is compelling, and the potential benefit of international cooperation seems clear, the question remains as to what specifically would be valuable and feasible to coordinate and agree to at an international level. The possibilities include agreements for knowledge sharing and coordination of R&D, joint collaboration and funding of R&D, and commitments on increased domestic R&D funding. Given the centrality of the IEA to international energy-technology cooperation, the IEA should also consider means to more regularly and deeply involve non-OECD countries such as Brazil, China, India, South Africa, and Russia in IEA programs, including accelerating the accession of such countries to the IEA (either in conjunction with or in advance of accession to the OECD).

International agreement on R&D knowledge sharing, coordination, and joint collaboration and funding

Activities undertaken under knowledge-sharing and coordination agreements can include meeting; planning; exchanging information; coordinating and harmonizing research agendas and measurement standards; and engaging in some degree of integrated, cooperative R&D (de Coninck et al. 2008, IEA 2008a). In addition, other agreements have emerged in recent years, including the Carbon Sequestration Leadership Forum, the Asia Pacific Partnership on Clean Development and Climate, and the International Partnership for a Hydrogen Economy. Energy science and technology agreements that feature a higher degree of joint, collaborative R&D are less common, and appear to be most successful in research that is more fundamental and that has not yet attracted a critical mass of commercial interest. Examples include the ITER fusion reactor and European Organization for Nuclear Research (CERN) (de Coninck et al. 2008). In addition to expanding the international exchange of scientific and technical information, joint R&D can more directly increase cost-effectiveness through cost sharing and reduced duplication of effort.

Most existing international agreements relevant to climate mitigation technology have been developed as so-called Technology Implementing Agreements under the auspices of the IEA, organized under its Committee on Energy Research and Technology (Figure 13.4).

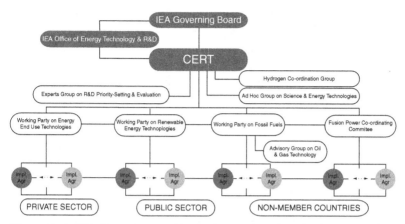

Figure 13.4. IEA Committee on Energy Research and Technology (CERT)
Source: IEA (2007c).

IEA Implementing Agreements use two primary mechanisms: task sharing and cost sharing. In task sharing, a joint program is pursued within participating countries, but each country funds and implements its own contribution to the project. In cost sharing, participating countries pool funding for a single contractor to perform a research task. There are forty-one existing IEA Implementing Agreements, all of which incorporate task sharing and about half of which have cost sharing. They cover the fields of renewable energy and hydrogen (10), end-use energy efficiency (13), fossil-fuel technologies (6), nuclear fusion energy (9), and cross-cutting activities (3) (IEA 2007f). Membership in these agreements is not restricted to governments or to IEA or OECD countries—indeed, a number of organizations from non-OECD countries have participated. Activities under these agreements are funded and conducted primarily through domestic R&D programs and budgets, and pooled funds often go to bundling research results and providing a platform for information exchange and learning (i.e., desk studies rather than primary research).

Invigorated and expanded international agreements on the coordination of public R&D in the area of climate technology could be very valuable, particularly as countries increase R&D efforts and seek maximal impact in addressing this global problem. The IEA is the best-positioned international institution to support agreement(s) related to energy technology, although it may be more appropriate to engage other international institutions for non-energy technologies. One concern with the existing IEA implementing agreements, however, is that they each have their own secretariats, operate independently, and have not undergone regular systematic review. While this approach eases the need for more central administration, it may also suffer from overlap across agreements and a lack of overall coordination and strategic vision. Another concern is that countries that have formal IEA membership—which is currently limited to OECD countries— may have greater control over decision processes. One approach for addressing that concern is to explicitly include the new UNFCCC Expert Group on Technology Development recommended above within the decision-making processes of agreements that may be supported by the IEA. Another approach is to formally broaden IEA membership to include key emerging economies in concert with, or aside from, OECD membership.

G8 countries, other major R&D-performing countries, and likely major developing-country technology users should therefore consider agreeing to an overall framework for knowledge sharing and coordination of public R&D efforts in the area of climate mitigation. This framework could include a process whereby parties regularly submit climate-technology development plans that cover R&D funding levels, current and future program plans, pertinent R&D policies, and other relevant information. One way to think of these plan submissions is as supply-side counterparts to the Technology Needs Assessments that have been prepared by many developing countries under the UNFCCC (2007). In addition to country-level plan submissions, the overall framework could provide for an evaluation of existing climate technology agreements—with an eye toward identifying best practices and expanding, integrating, or suspending particular agreements— and draw from other related national-level and international efforts by the European Union (European Commission 2007b), Japan (METI 2008), and the United States (USDOE 2006) as well as from IEA work in support of the G8 and other processes (IEA 2008b).

At a minimum, participants would work together to monitor progress, share information on individual national efforts in an integrated manner, and identify where overlaps and gaps exist across countries. This framework could also provide for the development of road maps to assess the current status of particular technologies, systems, and relevant areas of underlying science, including the identification of appropriate milestones and necessary public R&D funding levels. It would also provide a more systematic means for improving the cost-effectiveness of public R&D by identifying particular areas where it makes sense for individual countries to focus on sub-parts of an integrated overall package and areas where joint funding is sensible. For example, such a framework could be used to organize and fund joint projects to demonstrate carbon capture and storage technology. An agreement could also set out general guidelines outlining expectations with regard to the scope and magnitude of task and cost sharing across countries in the context of collaborative R&D projects. Finally, this framework could highlight the importance of human talent to both knowledge development and transfer, by helping to identify high-priority areas for scholarly exchange—including from developing to developed countries.

In addition to the traditional approach of using research contracts as the means to award joint R&D funding, another option is to offer internationally coordinated prizes for achieving specific advances in climate-related science and technology. The idea is to offer financial or other rewards for achieving specific innovation objectives that have been specified in advance (in contrast to *ex post* awards like the Nobel Prize) (Newell and Wilson 2005, National Research Council 2007).[5] Prize-like approaches have also gained traction within the private sector: Firms like Innocentive match "seekers" (organizations that wish to address challenging problems) with "solvers" (innovators with solutions) by offering them cash awards. Among other things, Innocentive has a philanthropic subprogram that is devoted to clean technology and renewable energy and that offers prizes supported by a private foundation.

Although inducement prizes are not suited to all research and innovation objectives, they have the potential to play a larger role alongside research contracts and grants. In contrast to these other instruments, prizes target and reward innovation outputs rather than inputs: the prize is paid only if the objective is attained. This can help

---

[5] Recently proposed prizes relevant to energy and climate policy include "Prizes for Achievement in Grand Challenges of Science and Technology" authorized in the US Energy Policy Act of 2005; the H-Prize (for hydrogen) and Bright Tomorrow lighting prizes authorized in the US Energy Independence and Security Act of 2007; the privately-funded Progressive Automotive X-Prize; and the Earth Challenge Prize announced by British financier Richard Branson. Only the last two private prizes have been funded.

encourage maximal research effort per dollar of research funding. Prizes or awards can also help focus efforts on specific high-priority objectives, without specifying how the goal is to be accomplished. Because prize competitors select themselves based on their own knowledge of their likelihood of success—rather than being selected in advance by a research manager—prizes can also attract a more diverse and potentially effective range of innovators from the private sector, universities, and other research institutions.

In an international context, a prize approach could have the advantage that the winner of R&D funding does not have to be chosen in advance, thus avoiding a selection process that can become politically charged when researchers and research institutions reside in particular countries. Just as the Olympics engender a spirit of both international cooperation as well as competitive record-breaking, technology prize competitions could play an important role in international climate R&D. Prizes could be particularly useful for advancing innovation relevant to the mitigation and adaptation technology needs of developing countries, given the relatively low levels of market-driven inducement for innovation that may be present in those countries. For similar reasons, the use of innovation prizes has been advocated for medical advances particularly relevant to developing countries (e.g., anti-malaria drugs) (Love and Hubbard 2007).

The detailed process of selecting appropriate prize topics and crafting prize-specific rules (e.g., the type of contest, size of award, criteria for winning, method of choosing the winner) requires extensive consultation with experts and potential participants (National Research Council 2007). Identifying particular technical and scientific challenges in GHG mitigation that could be fruitfully addressed through an inducement prize approach could be identified as part of the above systematic assessment. Then the best institutional arrangements for administering the prize would need to be determined. Consideration would need to be given to the treatment of intellectual property arising from associated innovations (as with any joint R&D project), and to the development of terms for related licensing.[6] An international climate technology prize fund would also need to be established, with contributions potentially coming from national governments, as well

---

[6] Note that while, in theory, prizes are often conceived as a substitute for patents, in practice, inducement prizes often do not preclude patenting.

as foundations, individuals, and corporations. While contributions for such a fund could be sought on an as-needed basis for specific projects, it would probably be advantageous to have larger-scale general funds that could then be prioritized to specific prize topics.[7]

International agreement on domestic climate technology R&D funding

An international agreement could also be fashioned to increase domestic funding of climate technology R&D, analogous to internationally agreed emission targets for each country. An international agreement on the necessary level of R&D funding and reasonable burden sharing of R&D efforts across parties could be valuable. Such an agreement could, for example, target a level of climate technology R&D as a percentage of GDP, or as a percentage increase from recent levels, with those levels set to reflect a significant expansion of R&D. The general idea is not without precedent: in 2002, the European Union set the goal of increasing its relatively low level of overall R&D spending—currently at 1.8 percent of GDP (OECD 2008)—to 3 percent of GDP by 2010. The goal is EU-wide rather than country-specific and applies jointly to both public and private R&D funding. However, there is little evidence of measurable progress toward the goal thus far, although ongoing discussions among government representatives and major R&D-performing companies have illuminated many of the key impediments. A more detailed example—albeit in the medical rather than climate arena—is the 2005 proposal to the World Health Organization for a Treaty on Medical Research and Development.[8] The core country obligations in the proposal are for minimum levels of support for qualified medical R&D (both general and "priority"

---

[7] An important consideration for any joint fund of this type is the incentive for entities to contribute, rather than free ride on the contributions of others. Barrett (2003) suggests an approach whereby individual country contributions to an R&D fund would depend on the other countries participating. The incentives for participation and compliance are increased by a mutually enforcing participation clause, while a cap on the total fund ensures that countries know their maximum costs. If one country accedes, then all the other parties would increase their funding by a specified amount; alternatively, if that country withdraws, the others lower their funding. While not a panacea, this approach merits consideration.

[8] A copy of the proposal can be found at www.cptech.org/workingdrafts/rndtreaty.html. See Love and Hubbard (2007) for a related background discussion.

areas), measured as a share of GDP, according to a schedule that varies by national income. Among other things, the proposal also identifies methods of qualified R&D financing (e.g., direct public support, tax expenditures, philanthropic expenditures, and certain business R&D).

Specifically with regard to energy, the IEA already collects annual data on public energy R&D spending by IEA countries, a process that could be adjusted if necessary to serve a more formal purpose. To operationalize such a commitment, it would probably have to exclude private-sector climate-related R&D expenditures, which are difficult to distinguish from other R&D. Such an agreement could incorporate a "pledge and review" structure, and the necessary reporting on funding levels could be integrated with the regular climate-technology development plans described above. Targets could be structured as a share of GDP, as a percentage increase from recent levels, or some other metric. The IEA could serve as the review body—either directly or as an assistant to a UNFCCC Expert Group on Technology Development. The process could also include a broader energy innovation policy review element: The IEA already conducts regular reviews of the energy policies, including energy-technology policies, of IEA member countries and other major energy consumers and producers (see, for example, IEA 2006).

Knowledge transfer through intellectual property

Protecting intellectual property through patents is one of the principal means by which innovators can capture value associated with developing new GHG-reducing technologies. By providing a mechanism for appropriating the value of innovation beyond the boundaries of a firm, patents and other forms of intellectual property protection (e.g., industrial designs, trademarks, copyrights) can stimulate innovative activity that might not otherwise take place, or at least not be pursued as intensely. In return, patents require that the invention be disclosed to the public, which allows future innovators to build on that knowledge and ensures that new knowledge is freely available after the patent expires (usually in twenty years). In a related manner, the ability to secure a patent can also increase technology transfer—whether to industry from a university or government laboratory, or from one country to another—by rewarding the innovator (or subsequent patent owner) for taking the necessary steps to move ideas to ultimate users.

Otherwise innovators may keep their inventions secret, thereby stifling the application of those innovations as well as follow-on innovation.

On the other hand, patents assign a temporary monopoly right, which tends to lead to higher prices and which could impede the near-term diffusion of products or processes that embody the patent. In addition, obstacles to follow-on innovation could arise in the process of securing licenses for foundational patents or if there is a "thicket" of overlapping patents that must be cleared. Firms may simply be unwilling to grant licenses out of concern that intellectual property rights will not be respected in certain countries. In the context of climate change, therefore, developing-country parties have often held that intellectual property rights are a barrier to technology transfer and that options such as compulsory licensing and greater access to technologies in the public domain should be considered. Others counter that intellectual property protection encourages technology development and transfer, that intellectual property costs are a small portion of overall technology costs, and that many existing climate-friendly technologies are no longer protected by patents. Research to examine these competing claims in the specific context of climate-friendly technologies has so far been limited (Reichman *et al.* 2008). In an analysis of existing solar, wind, and biofuel technologies, for example, Barton (2007) found that intellectual property has elicited innovation without significantly impeding technology transfer, although problems could arise if new, very broad patents were granted that impede the development of future, more efficient technologies. Views on these issues are diverse, however, and probably warrant further discussion and possible action at an international level, a discussion that has only recently begun among the relevant international institutions.[9]

The two key international institutions for developing and implementing intellectual property policies are the World Intellectual Property Organization (WIPO), a specialized agency of the United Nations that administers numerous intellectual property treaties,

---

[9] The current state of this discussion is illustrated by presentations at the workshop "Life Sciences Symposium on Patent Landscaping and Transfer of Technology under Multilateral Environmental Agreements," sponsored by the World Intellectual Property Organization, Geneva, August 2008 (www.wipo. int/meetings/en/2008/lifesciences/ip_lss2_ge/) and the "European Patent Forum 2008: Inventing a Cleaner Future," Ljubljana, Slovenia, May 2008 (www.epo. org/about-us/events/archive/2008/epf2008/forum-1/details2_fr.html).

and the WTO, through the Agreement on Trade-Related Aspects of Intellectual Property Rights (TRIPS). To improve dialogue; better integrate climate-related and other ongoing discussions where they interface with intellectual property, environment, and sustainable development issues; and identify productive solutions, the UNFCCC, WIPO, and WTO should consider seeking observer status with the other institutions. Within WIPO, the UNFCCC, through its Expert Groups on Technology, would actively engage the recently launched Committee on Development and Intellectual Property (WIPO 2008a, 2008b). As existing observers to the WTO Committee on Trade and Environment, the UNFCCC and WIPO should consider engaging with the WTO TRIPS Council and, if useful, the UNFCCC should seek observer status specifically with the TRIPS Council. Coordination with the WTO WGTTT may also be desirable.

These bodies would work jointly to identify technology development and transfer opportunities and impediments associated with the intellectual property system; advance recommendations for harnessing opportunities and reducing impediments; identify best practices; and expand technical assistance and capacity-building activities to facilitate the development and transfer of innovations for climate-change mitigation. Parties to the UNFCCC and WIPO should consider establishing a fund within the WIPO for these purposes; another possibility would be to use the new Strategic Technology Fund at the World Bank (although the immediate focus of that fund appears to be adaptation). Among other purposes, such a fund could potentially be used to purchase intellectual property rights (which could be placed in the public domain) and cover licensing fees, royalties, and other costs related to intellectual property (e.g., application, examination, registration fees), if and where this would be an effective means of increasing technology transfer. It is also worthwhile to consider whether conditioning the receipt of such support on the implementation of best practices in a particular country would increase the leverage of this approach—in terms of both promoting technology transfer and enhancing the willingness of developed countries to contribute to such a fund.

Conclusion

The range of opportunities for improving and expanding international climate technology development and transfer extends well beyond the usual boundaries of environmental decision makers to the broader context of international agreements and institutions for energy, trade, development, and intellectual property. Recognizing that any successful effort to accelerate and then sustain a higher rate of climate-technology development and transfer must harness a diverse set of markets and institutions, the following specific issues and actions should be considered within the post-2012 dialogue:

- Given the centrality of private-sector trade, investment, and innovative effort in technology, widespread global demand for low-GHG technologies will be essential to move the energy system in the desired direction. Long-term national commitments and policies for emission mitigation are crucial to providing the necessary private-sector incentives for technology development and transfer.
- For developing countries, financial assistance for technology transfer and capacity building is also necessary. At the same time, GHG-related guidelines for financing by ECAs and multilateral development banks can help ensure that investments in trade and development assistance are consistent with climate mitigation goals.
- In addition to increased incentives, barriers to the transfer of climate-friendly technologies could be reduced through a WTO agreement to reduce tariff and non-tariff barriers to trade in environmental goods and services. Efforts to develop and harmonize technical standards—by international standards organizations in consultation with the IEA and WTO—could help reduce impediments to technology transfer and accelerate the development and adoption of climate-friendly innovations.
- A framework for coordinating and augmenting climate-technology R&D could be organized through a UNFCCC Expert Group on Technology Development, supported by the IEA. Broadening IEA participation to large non-OECD energy consumers and producers could also facilitate such coordination. An agreement could include a process for reviewing country submissions on technology development, along with a process for identifying redundancies, gaps, and opportunities for closer collaboration. A fund for cost-shared R&D tasks and international prizes could be established to provide financing for innovative efforts to advance science and technology objectives that are best accomplished in a joint fashion.

The agreement could also include explicit targets for increased domestic R&D spending on GHG mitigation.

- A UNFCCC Expert Group on Technology Development, WIPO, and the WTO could work jointly to develop recommendations for addressing technology development and transfer opportunities and impediments associated with the intellectual property system. A fund could be established in WIPO or another appropriate body for related technical assistance, capacity building, and possibly to purchase intellectual property or cover its costs.

Climate-technology policy must complement rather than substitute for policies that provide a direct financial incentive for emission mitigation. R&D without market demand for the results would ultimately have limited impact, while stimulating market demand for emissions mitigation without supportive technology policies misses longer-term opportunities for significantly lowering mitigation costs and expanding opportunities for greater GHG mitigation. Impediments to the international transfer of know-how and equipment also should be reduced. The scale of the technology problem we confront in effectively managing climate risks while simultaneously addressing other major energy issues is such that it requires a portfolio of strategies for reducing barriers and increasing incentives across multiple international institutions and agreements. This is also the only way to maximize the impact of the scarce resources that are available for addressing climate change and other critical societal challenges.

References

Barrett, Scott (2003). *Environment and Statecraft*. Oxford: Oxford University Press.

Barton, John S. (2007). "Intellectual Property and Access to Clean Energy Technologies in Developing Countries: An Analysis of Solar Photovoltaic, Biofuel and Wind Technologies," Issue Paper 2, Trade and Sustainable Energy Series, Stanford Law School, Stanford University, Palo Alto, CA.

Clarke, Leon E., James A. Edmonds, Henry D. Jacoby, Hugh M. Pitcher, John M. Reilly, and Richard G. Richels (2007). "Scenarios of Greenhouse Gas Emissions and Atmospheric Concentrations," Synthesis and Assessment Product 2.1a Report by the US Climate Change Science Program and the Subcommittee on Global Change Research, Washington, DC.

Cohen, Linda R. and Roger G. Noll (1991). *The Technology Pork Barrel.* Washington, DC: Brookings.

de Coninck, Helen, Carolyn Fischer, Richard G. Newell, and Takahiro Ueno (2008). "International Technology-Oriented Agreements to Address Climate Change," *Energy Policy* 36: 335–56.

Edmonds, Jae A., M. A. Wise, James J. Dooley, S. H. Kim, S. J. Smith, Paul J. Runci, L. E. Clarke, E. L. Malone, and G. M. Stokes (2007). *Global Energy Technology Strategy: Addressing Climate Change.* College Park, MD: Joint Global Change Research Institute.

European Commission (2007a). "Limiting Global Climate Change to 2 degrees Celsius: The Way Ahead for 2020 and Beyond," Communication from the Commission to the Council, the European Parliament, the European Economic and Social Committee, and the Committee of the Regions, Brussels: European Commission.

(2007b). "European Strategic Energy Technology Plan," Brussels: European Commission.

Fisher, B. S., N. Nakicenovic, K. Alfsen, J. Corfee Morlot, F. de la Chesnaye, J.-Ch. Hourcade, K. Jiang, M. Kainuma, E. La Rovere, A. Matysek, A. Rana, K. Riahi, R. Richels, S. Rose, D. van Vuuren, R. Warren (2007). "Issues Related to Mitigation in the Long Term Context," in *Climate Change 2007: Mitigation.* Contribution of Working Group III to the Fourth Assessment Report of the Inter-governmental Panel on Climate Change [B. Metz, O. R. Davidson, P. R. Bosch, R. Dave, L. A. Meyer (eds.)], Cambridge, UK and New York: Cambridge University Press.

IEA (International Energy Agency) (2006). *Energy Policies of IEA Countries: 2006 Review.* Paris: OECD/IEA.

(2007a). *Energy Technology RD&D Budgets 2007.* Paris: OECD/IEA.

(2007b). *World Energy Outlook 2007.* Paris: OECD/IEA.

(2007c). "CERT Strategic Plan 2007–2011," Paris: OECD/IEA.

(2007d). *CO2 Emissions from Fuel Combustion: Emissions of CO2, CH4, N2O, HFC, PFC, FS6, Vol 2007 release 01.* Paris: OECD/IEA.

(2007e). "International Standards to Develop and Promote Energy Efficiency and Renewable Energy Sources," Paris: OECD/IEA.

(2007f). "Energy Technologies on the Cutting Edge," Paris: OECD/IEA.

(2008a). *Energy Technology Perspectives 2008.* Paris: OECD/IEA.

(2008b). *Towards a Sustainable Energy Future: IEA Programme of Work on Climate Change, Clean Energy and Sustainable Development.* Paris: OECD/IEA.

IPCC (Intergovernmental Panel on Climate Change) (2000). *Methodological and Technological Issues in Technology Transfer: Summary for Policymakers,* A Special Report of IPCC Working Group III of the Intergovernmental Panel on Climate Change, Geneva: IPCC.

(2007). *Climate Change 2007: Synthesis Report*, Contribution of Working Groups I, II and III to the Fourth Assessment Report of the Intergovernmental Panel on Climate Change [Core Writing Team, Pachauri, R. K and Reisinger, A.(eds.)], Geneva: IPCC.

Jaffe, A. B., R. G. Newell, and R. N. Stavins (2003). "Technological Change and the Environment," in K.-G. Mäler and J. Vincent (eds.), *Handbook of Environmental Economics*, Vol. 1, pp. 461–516. *Handbooks in Economics* series, K. J. Arrow and M. D. Intriligator, series eds. Amsterdam: North-Holland/Elsevier.

Kortum, Samuel and Josh Lerner (2000). "Assessing the Contribution of Venture Capital to Innovation," *RAND Journal of Economics* 31(4): 674–92.

Love, J. and T. Hubbard (2007). "The Big Idea: Prizes to Stimulate R&D for New Medicines," *Chicago-Kent Law Review* 82(3): 1519–54.

METI (Ministry of Economy, Trade, and Industry) (2008). "Cool Earth: Innovative Energy Technology Program," Tokyo: METI.

National Research Council (2007). *Innovation Inducement Prizes at the National Science Foundation*. Washington, DC: National Academies Press.

National Science Board (2008). *Science and Engineering Indicators*. Arlington, VA: National Science Foundation.

Newell, Richard G. (2007a). "Climate Technology Research, Development, and Demonstration: Funding Sources, Institutions, and Instruments," Issue Brief 9 in Raymond J. Kopp and William A. Pizer (eds.), *Assessing U.S. Climate Policy Options*. Washington, DC: Resources for the Future, pp. 117–32.

(2007b). "Climate Technology Deployment Policy," Issue Brief 10 in Kopp and Pizer (eds.), pp. 133–46.

(2008). "A U.S. Innovation Strategy for Climate Change Mitigation," Discussion Paper 2008–15, Hamilton Project, Washington, DC: Brookings Institution.

Newell, R. G. and N. Wilson (2005). "Technology Prizes for Climate Mitigation," Discussion Paper 05–33, Washington, DC: Resources for the Future.

OECD (Organization for Economic Cooperation and Development) (2007). "Revised Council Recommendation on Common Approaches on the Environment and Officially Supported Export Credits," TAD/ECG(2007)9, Working Party on Export Credits and Credit Guarantees, Paris: OECD.

(2008). *Main Science and Technology Indicators*. Paris: OECD.

Popp, David, Richard G. Newell, and Adam B. Jaffe. "Energy, the Environment, and Technological Change," Manuscript in preparation for the *Handbook of Economics of Technical Change*. Oxford: Elsevier.

Reichman, Jerome, Arti K. Rai, Richard G. Newell, and Jonathan B. Weiner (2008). "Intellectual Property and Alternatives: Strategies for a Green Revolution," Energy, Environment, and Development Programme Paper 08/03, London: Chatham House.

U.K. Department for Innovation, Universities and Skills (2007). *The 2007 R&D Scoreboard*. London: U.K. Department for Innovation, Universities and Skills.

UNEP (United Nations Environment Programme) (2008). "Reforming Energy Subsidies: Opportunities to Contribute to the Climate Change Agenda," Geneva: UNEP.

UNEP and New Energy Finance (2007). "Global Trends in Sustainable Energy Investment 2007," Geneva: UNEP.

UNFCCC (United Nations Framework Convention on Climate Change) (2007). "Investment and Financial Flows to Address Climate Change," Bonn: UNFCCC.

(2008). *Report of the Conference of the Parties on its thirteenth session, held in Bali from 3 to 15 December 2007. Addendum. Part Two: Action taken by the Conference of the Parties at its thirteenth session*, Bonn: UNFCCC.

USCAP (US Climate Action Partnership) (2007). "A Call for Action," Washington, DC: USCAP.

USDOE (US Department of Energy) (2006). *U.S. Climate Change Technology Program Strategic Plan*. Washington, DC: US DOE.

Weyant, John P., Francisco C. de la Chesnaye, and Geoff J. Blanford (2006). "Overview of EMF-21: Multigas Mitigation and Climate Policy," *The Energy Journal 27:1–32*; Special Issue: *Multi-Greenhouse Gas Mitigation and Climate Policy*.

WIPO (World Intellectual Property Organization) (2008a). "Initial Working Document for the Committee on Development and Intellectual Property (CDIP)," Geneva: WIPO.

(2008b). "Summary by the Chair, Committee on Development and Intellectual Property (CDIP) Second Session, July 7–11, 2008," Geneva: WIPO.

World Bank (2008a). "The Clean Technology Fund," Washington, DC: The World Bank.

(2008b). "The Strategic Climate Fund," Washington, DC: The World Bank.

(2008c). *Global Economic Prospects: Technology Diffusion in the Developing World*. Washington, DC: The World Bank.

(2008d). *International Trade and Climate Change: Economic, Legal, and Institutional Perspectives*. Washington, DC: The World Bank.

Yang, C. and M. Oppenheimer (2007). "A 'Manhattan Project' for Climate Change?" *Climatic Change* 80: 199–204.

14 | Mitigation through resource transfers to developing countries: expanding greenhouse gas offsets

ANDREW KEELER AND
ALEXANDER THOMPSON[1]

Introduction

Both developing and developed countries hold a central view in common in international climate negotiations: each thinks the other should be doing more to mitigate greenhouse gas (GHG) emissions. To date, international negotiations and agreements on climate change have not been particularly successful in creating significant changes in either the commitments or actions being adopted by developing countries with respect to GHG mitigation. Our proposal in this chapter is to build on existing offset policies to enhance efforts by developing countries to combat climate change.

For a variety of environmental and political reasons, focusing on developing countries is crucial at this stage in the climate regime's evolution (Frankel 2007). Most obviously, large developing countries —especially India and China—account for an increasingly important share of global emissions as a result of rapid population and GDP growth (Stern 2007: 169). The International Energy Agency forecasts that three-quarters of the increase in global energy use over the next two decades will come from developing countries (IEA 2007). A successful climate architecture will have to include mitigation in these parts of the world. At the same time, the world's largest emitter, the United States, has made participation in binding emissions reduction

[1] We are grateful for insightful comments from Joe Aldy, Dan Bodansky, Rob Stavins and an anonymous reviewer. We also received helpful feedback from participants at the Harvard Project on International Climate Agreements Research Workshop in March 2008. We would like to acknowledge the financial support of the Mershon Center for International Security Studies at Ohio State University.

contingent on actions by large emitters in the South. Thus developing country participation has emerged as the lynchpin of progress in global climate negotiations.

One possibility is to encourage developing countries to participate by assuming mitigation commitments, just as their richer counterparts do. While this is a potentially viable strategy in the long run, it is unrealistic and not essential in the short term. It is unrealistic because these governments have categorically rejected the option of binding targets, appealing to the historical responsibility of the industrialized world, the "common but differentiated responsibility" principle in the 1992 United Nations Framework Convention on Climate Change (UNFCCC), and their overriding concern with unfettered economic development. When the Group of Eight (G8) recently pledged to halve their emissions by 2050, a group of large developing countries refused to sign on—even though the commitment is aspirational and nonbinding. Fortunately, we argue, developing country emissions commitments are not essential given that there are other ways—both politically viable and environmentally effective—to achieve progress in GHG reduction in the developing world.

We propose to succeed the Clean Development Mechanism (CDM) with a much more expansive approach to the use of carbon offsets in the developing world as a way to reduce GHG emissions. We call for less emphasis on strict ton-for-ton accounting, with its high transaction costs, and increased reliance on a broader range of activities and policies that go beyond the relatively narrow set of projects currently pursued under the CDM. We also recommend establishing a minimum percentage of developed-country commitments that should be met by funding developing-country actions. Our proposal seeks to incentivize long-term investments and policy changes relative to short-term measures designed to meet largely artificial targets. The focus is thus on effectiveness rather than on politically derived goals. We identify which elements of the enhanced offsets mechanism would have to be negotiated by governments and suggest how existing international organizations might be adapted to manage it.

We do not claim that our proposal is a complete solution, but only that it offers one avenue for improving the current situation and may help international policy evolve in a productive direction. We also do not believe that this is the only path for progress in enhancing the participation of developing countries in international efforts to reduce GHG emissions—there are other policies or foci of negotiation that could be as or more effective (or achieve the same ends with different institutions than we propose). The attractiveness of what we are proposing is that it can be seen as an evolution of current policies and has characteristics that may overcome political and diplomatic barriers that prevent alternatives from being implemented. In any event, there is nothing we advocate that precludes other approaches if they prove to be financially, politically, and diplomatically viable.

Our proposal contains five elements:

1. Change the criteria for offsets from "real, verifiable, and permanent reductions" to "actions that create real progress in developing countries toward mitigation and adaptation."
2. Make a significant share of industrialized-country commitments (whether international or domestic) achievable through offset payments to developing countries.
3. Put a specific or minimum quantity of offset credits in a fund *ex ante*; the expenditures of the fund would then be governed by principles and institutions described later in this chapter.
4. Make the principles used to qualify actions taken in developing countries as offsets the specific focus of negotiation among state parties.
5. Delegate clearly delineated tasks to existing international organizations and new institutions for the purpose of managing and safeguarding the offsets program, consistent with negotiated guidelines.

We proceed by first giving a sketch of the problem of negotiating agreements and implementing policies and investments. We discuss the theory and experience with offsets as a part of the international regime. We then present each of these five elements in turn. We conclude with an assessment of how this proposal could be useful in enhancing developing country actions in the context of climate change negotiations and agreements.

The problem as we see it

The efficient and the possible

Any discussion of how to structure international climate agreements is permeated by the tension between two policy perspectives:

- A technical policy design perspective that seeks to meet goals of efficiency, cost-effectiveness, and equity; and
- An international relations/political economy perspective that tempers the technical perspective with the notion that nation-states will only make, participate in, and comply with agreements that are in their own self-interest (or a weaker form that says they will be strongly influenced by their own self-interest).

Proposals and supporting arguments for a particular approach to addressing climate change focus on both the characteristics of proposed policy architectures (and policies) and on the reasons why they might actually be adopted and followed. The most promising climate policy is the one with the best combination of technical merit and probability of adoption and implementation—and even then it is unclear how to weight these two factors.

A clear lesson from the international relations literature is that international institutions are most likely to thrive when they are self-regulating—that is, when states have an individual incentive to create and maintain them (Keohane 1988: 387). This logic extends to the design and rules of institutions, which must be incentive compatible in order to elicit ongoing participation and implementation (Koremenos, Lipson and Snidal 2001). The issue of political feasibility requires that we take domestic and international political considerations into account if we want to produce a robust architecture to manage climate change at the global level.

Making this even more difficult, policy architectures cannot be evaluated in a short-term sense but need to be evaluated in terms of what kinds of future agreements and actions they lead to (and with what probability). A "bad" agreement in the short run, if it leads to developing country participation, for example, ultimately will be judged better than a "good" agreement (e.g., one with strict targets and accountability) that results in lesser participation and commitment in the future. In other words, path dependence dynamics must be taken into account when making current decisions about institutional design. With this long-term perspective in mind, some analysts have advocated more flexible and adaptable approaches to complex problems such as climate over rigid, short-term commitments (Pizer 2007; Raustiala and Victor 1998; Thompson 2006).

Given the global public good nature of emissions reductions, free-rider and prisoner's dilemma logic implies that almost any policy that requires real resources is not rational. However, there are good reasons to believe that this narrow interpretation of the collective action problem at hand is too pessimistic. First, we have seen not just agreements (Kyoto) but actions (the EU's Emission Trading Scheme) where countries take on costly programs. Second, nation-states are not unitary actors—their preferences and negotiating strategies are derived from competing domestic interests, which in some cases include precautionary publics and influential NGOs (Moravcsik 1997; Sunstein 2003; Betsill and Corell 2007). Finally, international negotiations and institutions can provide a transparency and assurance mechanism, whereby rational actors are willing to move forward if they know that others are cooperating as well and that they will be interacting into the future (Axelrod and Keohane 1985; Mitchell 1998).

We base our arguments on the premise that self-interest limits the range of policies that governments are willing to pursue. However, we also assume that this does not rule out international cooperation, costly changes in behavior, and far-sighted policies if agreements are designed to be sensitive to political needs at the international and domestic levels.

Arguments about desirable international architectures and agreements are therefore based on past experience, logic, and analysis of self-interested behavior. Given the lack of success to date, the elements of international agreements that have the best combination of technical merit and broad enough appeal to achieve widespread support remain unknown until such time as an agreement is actually ratified. As an example of this, we note that in the predecessor volume (Aldy and Stavins 2007), all authors appeal to self-interest but advocate a wide and differing array of general GHG mitigation architectures. Some authors advocate efficient mechanisms and are optimistic that diplomatic and self-interest problems will not continue to prevent such agreements (for example, Frankel 2007 and Cooper 2007), while some are considerably more pessimistic about the possibilities of

achieving efficient international GHG reduction through broad commitment to price- or quantity-based policies (Victor 2007 and Barrett
2007).

From the perspective of economically efficient policy design, having
developing countries take on targets creates a set of coherent and
efficient incentives. The targets could be negotiated in such a way
that developing countries bear no costs, and rather stand to gain from
allowance sales to industrialized countries.[2] However, developing
countries have overwhelmingly rejected this path, so this particular
efficient design does not offer—at least in the short run—a plausible
path forward.

Our view of plausible combinations of efficiency and implementa-
bility for offset policy is based on the following sketch of the interests
of industrialized countries and developing countries in negotiations.
We focus both on the outcomes about which countries care the most
and on the kinds of accountability that are likely to be preferred.

Priorities for self-interested action

The good news from a political perspective is that large majorities in
most countries view climate change as a serious problem that must be
addressed. A 2006 poll of thirty countries found that, on average, 90
percent believe climate change to be a "serious problem," with concern
rising sharply over the last several years (Globescan 2006). According to
a 2007 BBC survey of twenty-one countries, both developed and developing, substantial majorities in all but a few populations agree that it is
"necessary to take major steps very soon" to combat global warming
(BBC World Service 2007).[3] These sentiments extend to the official positions of most governments. The 1992 UNFCCC and the 1997 Kyoto
Protocol, both of which call on governments to reduce emissions, enjoy
near universal participation (192 and 186 ratifications, respectively).

To be clear, nominal support by governments does not always
translate into concrete action and, except for Annex B parties to

---

[2] Proposals along these lines have employed business-as-usual or headroom (more
than projected business-as-usual) targets for developing countries. Frankel
(2007) offers a specific scheme based on this concept.

[3] Important exceptions are India and Russia, where only 37 percent and
43 percent, respectively, agree. In both countries, however, only tiny minorities
feel that it is not necessary to take any steps to address climate change.

Kyoto, these multilateral treaty commitments do not impose specific and binding commitments. Moreover, these broad concerns and professed commitments regarding climate change mask significant variation in underlying interests and preferences with respect to the details of how to address the problem. We consider these interests from the perspective of both industrialized and developing countries.

Priorities of industrialized countries

Industrialized countries have both a short-term and a long-term interest in reducing GHG emissions. Their more immediate concern is to reduce emissions in a way that contributes to achievement of their Kyoto and/or domestic policy targets,[4] and to do so in the most cost-effective way (in both an economic and a political sense). This helps explain the appeal of the CDM as an alternative to potentially costly emissions reductions at home, which face resistance from industry and energy lobbies. It also explains why, in existing offset policies, industrialized countries have focused on real and verifiable emissions reductions that allow them to maintain that they have met (or will meet) emissions targets. This has contributed to the high transaction costs and limited scope of projects the CDM has funded to date.

More broadly, industrialized countries also care about emissions reductions in the longer run from developing countries. This is not the primary focus of offset policy but is a vital and overarching concern in terms of the collective global response to climate-change risks. Developing country reductions are crucial for reasons of environmental effectiveness, given that these countries will soon account for a majority of global emissions (Wiener 2007: 69; IEA 2006: 78–83). Indeed, in 2007 China surpassed the United States as the world's leading emitter of energy-related carbon dioxide (CO_2) emissions (IEA 2007: 11), and by some measures non-Annex I countries have surpassed Annex I countries in terms of GHG emissions.[5] This implies that industrialized countries ought to care about the efficacy

---

[4] Industrialized countries also have a near-term interest in meeting targets from various regional arrangements, such as the European Trading Scheme, and from unilateral policy pronouncements on emissions reductions like Australia's emissions trading program.

[5] This is true if one takes into account GHG emissions from land-use change. These calculations are based on the World Resources Institute's Climate Analysis Indicators Tool, available at http://cait.wri.org/.

of offset policies in creating changed conditions—not just immediate reductions—in energy systems and other GHG emission and sequestration systems. It also implies that industrialized countries should care about how actions taken now affect the eventual ability and willingness of developing countries to commit to targets or to policies and measures that are comparable to those of the industrialized countries. This goal is crucial in the long run to address the concerns of companies in developed countries that compete with developing-country firms and to prevent excessive leakage of emissions. Leakage occurs when carbon-intensive activities relocate to nonparticipating countries to avoid regulation or when reduced demand from developed countries depresses fuel prices, leading to more consumption—and therefore higher emissions—in unregulated economies (IPCC 2001: 542–3).

It should also be noted that many developed countries have a separate interest in promoting economic development in the global South, for both political and principled reasons (Lumsdaine 1993; Milner 2006). To the extent that these countries promote technology transfer, infrastructure improvement, and employment in the developing world, offset activities have additional political appeal. Indeed, when asked if wealthy countries should provide aid to poorer ones that agree to limit emissions, large majorities in Australia (84 percent), Canada (84), Britain (81), France (78), Russia (77), Italy (77), Spain (76), Germany (75) and the United States (70) agreed (BBC World Service 2007). Combined with the cost-savings and flexibility advantages of cutting GHGs emission in the developing world, where smaller investments produce larger reductions, this could help industrialized-country governments build a broad-based domestic coalition in favor of climate strategies that involve the developing world.

Priorities of developing countries

Developing countries care most about economic development—improving the livelihood opportunities and welfare of their populations—and will not want to accept commitments that might now or in the future limit attractive development choices. They have thus far been unwilling to trade off any progress in this area in order to mitigate GHG emissions. Both industrialized and developing countries have recognized the primacy of economic development in developing-country decision making. Such concerns have been largely sidelined for the last several years as industrialized nations focused on negotiating commitments and the mechanisms for meeting them. However, the theme of sustainable development is clearly enshrined in the UNFCCC and Kyoto Protocol and has been resurgent lately as developing countries face increasing pressure to participate in an international climate regime (Najam, Huq and Sokona 2003). Energy systems are integral to economic development, both in terms of providing electricity for industry, commerce, and residential use, and for transportation. Changes that have the potential to expand energy availability and/or lower costs matter to developing countries.

A number of studies demonstrate that developing countries are more vulnerable to climate change impacts (Nordhaus and Boyer 2000; Cline 2007; IMF 2008: Chap. 4). For this reason, adaptation to climate change is a more pressing concern for most developing countries, although the state of knowledge about policies and investments that are most effective in aiding adaptation is limited (IPCC 2007: Chap. 17). However, relative to mitigation, adaptation expenditures benefit the location where investments are made, and not the entire planet. Therefore such expenditures may have more appeal to poor countries than mitigation actions, whose benefits are a global public good.

GHG mitigation is at the low end of developing country priorities. Reducing carbon emissions is seen—at least in the short run—as an industrialized country obligation and a low-payoff action. In large developing countries this has become a diplomatic issue, and there is some evidence that investments are beginning to be influenced by an expectation of future carbon constraints or economically and technologically transformed energy systems.

Accountability and effectiveness in reducing GHG risks

"Accountability" is used here to refer to the ways that mitigation activities are measured, credited, and assessed. Accountability is often treated as a matter of degree: a regime may contain more or less accountability. We also make a qualitative distinction between two broad approaches to accountability. *Strict* accountability typically requires specific, binding targets against which government actions are measured. An advantage of this approach is that it entails a readily observable "output" measure that can be used to evaluate compliance. However, these outputs may or may not be associated with environmentally beneficial *outcomes* if the regime is not well designed. A second approach to accountability is what we refer to as *progress-oriented* accountability. Here a government's actions are judged not by whether a specific target is attained but instead by whether there is evidence of progress—in terms of investments and policies—toward long-term reductions in emissions. Policy "inputs" become more central for evaluating performance.[6] In practice, it is likely that these two approaches to accountability should be combined, as each has strengths and weaknesses.

Industrialized countries

Political constituencies in industrialized countries care about strict accountability for offsets to maintain the environmental integrity of trading systems as a way to reach emissions targets. We discuss in a later section why we think strict accountability in this context is counterproductive.

A legitimate concern is putting poorer countries on a path to real mitigation over the long run, a version of accountability distinct from strict accountability. This form of accountability focuses less on verifying tons as additional and more on evidence that positive and productive steps are being taken as a result of resources expended. It is undeniably a less "objective" standard, and we have more to say on this below.

A harder-to-quantify goal is movement towards an outcome where commitment to an international agreement becomes more in the self-interest of developing countries. The fact that this is a hard-to-predict and somewhat unverifiable outcome does not subtract from its importance. Defining and measuring accountability in regards to this goal is inherently difficult and uncertain.

Developing countries

Developing countries will generally have a preference for less—or at least less strict—accountability when it comes to their own activities. Their view will be that they are the best judges of how to use resources to meet their goals. Developing countries are especially wary of strict accountability because they often lack the capacity to control

---

[6] Advocates of an inputs approach, rather than one based on outcomes and targets, include Barrett (2007) and Plantinga and Richards (2008).

outcomes and compliance, even when their efforts are sincere.[7] However, the magnitude of resource transfers will be tied in some way to accountability to satisfy industrialized country objectives, so the concept remains important.

One kind of accountability is to verify that resources are being used for their intended purpose—that they are not being misappropriated or used for goals unrelated to climate-change risks. This is the same challenge faced by multilateral development agencies and it is especially acute when dealing with less transparent (usually less democratic) governments. The more difficult accountability question is whether, and to what extent, resources are being used efficiently to achieve climate-related goals. This type of accountability can only be achieved with more intrusive monitoring and auditing, which most governments will resist on sovereignty terms.

The bottom line is that a broader range of metrics will have to be used to achieve accountability and assess effectiveness in the context of developing-country actions. At least in the foreseeable future, these actions should be evaluated more indirectly in terms of meaningful effort and tangible progress, defined by such activities as investments, policy reforms and spending priorities (Pizer 2007).

Assessing environmental effectiveness

There are (at least) three ways of judging how well policies and investments affect climate-change risks. First, the simplest and least informative is the effect on short-run emissions, such as the reductions called for in Kyoto's first commitment period. A second option is to assess the effect on long-run GHG concentrations in the atmosphere. This is arguably a more relevant metric, but it is also difficult to quantify given the long-run economic, technical, and political dynamics and feedbacks of current actions. Moreover, the choice of a threshold at which concentrations are safe is likely to be arbitrary, and the very notion of a single global target implies a sense of collective responsibility among nations that is unrealistic (Barrett 2007).

A final option is to use an economic metric—how do policies affect the total benefits and costs of climate change (and their distribution across time and within and among nations)?—that is directly related

---

[7] On government incapacity as a source of noncompliance with international rules, see Chayes and Chayes (1995).

to the effects of policies on long-run concentrations. Benefits and costs also depend, however, on the level of effort and efficacy of resources devoted to adaptation specifically and economic development generally. Resources expended on adaptation and development may have a greater effect in reducing welfare losses than GHG mitigation, particularly in developing countries. The weight given to each of these three metrics will affect the desirability of alternative policies and institutions.

All three of these metrics are useful. Short-term emissions are a fairly objective measure and can be used to evaluate the level of effort and success of short-run policies. Long-run emissions can be linked directly to atmospheric concentrations and thus provide—with great uncertainty—some evaluation of how policies and levels of effort contribute to long-term risks. The economic metric is the most uncertain and hardest to measure but remains conceptually important because it allows simultaneous consideration of both mitigation and adaptation actions and also encompasses a recognition that choosing any given concentration target implicitly requires trading off risk against the costs of action. The chapter by Morgenstern and Fischer in this volume contains a much fuller and more detailed discussion of the metrics available for assessing policies and actions.

Offsets and targets—a means, not an end

The theory of offsets in emissions trading is fairly straightforward. Entities outside an emissions cap can earn offset credits by undertaking (voluntary) activities that produce real emissions reductions or corresponding environmental improvements (e.g., carbon sequestration). These offset credits are sold into the emissions trading market, increasing the supply of allowances (and thus reducing allowance prices) without affecting overall emissions.

This straightforward theory is beset by a host of well-documented problems when put into practice. The biggest problem is *additionality* —the determination of exactly how large a reduction is caused by a specific offset action or policy. This requires knowing a counterfactual baseline—how many tons would have been emitted in the absence of the offset action or policy—which is impossible to estimate with certainty (IPCC 2001: 427). One must "estimate the unknown" (OECD 2000). Estimating emissions reductions also requires accounting for *leakage*—the process by which reductions from a given project are offset by increases caused elsewhere (for example, if shutting down a high-emissions cement factory causes a new cement factory to be built elsewhere to meet market demand for cement). The Marrakesh Accords require that, as part of a project design, participants must implement a plan for monitoring leakage effects (FCCC/CP/2001/13/Add.2: 19). Various proposals for how to account for leakage make clear just how difficult a challenge it is (Geres and Michaelowa 2002; Vöhringer *et al.* 2004). In the case of sequestration projects, there is also the problem of *permanence*: does the GHG reduction remain in place in perpetuity, or will sequestered CO_2 be released later (through harvesting or burning, for example), thus fully or partially reducing the GHG reduction benefits?

These concerns gave rise to a set of demanding and expensive rules and processes to ensure that offset credits produced by the CDM were "real, additional, and verifiable." Surveying the various transaction costs and delays that beset CDM projects in practice, a World Bank study concludes that "Procedural inefficiencies and regulatory bottle-necks have strained the capacity of the CDM infrastructure to deliver [emission credits] on schedule" (Capoor and Ambrosi 2008: 4). In the context of forest carbon sequestration projects, Richards and Andersson (2001) catalogue a dizzying array of measurement and implementation obstacles that make the CDM's project-based approach highly impractical.

Offsets are valuable in theory not just for reducing the cost of meeting an emissions cap, but also because they provide incentives to those not covered by that cap to take actions that ameliorate the underlying environmental problem. While in a strict accounting sense these actions are emissions neutral, they serve to bring unregulated entities within the general emissions control structure and to get these entities on a less emissions-intensive path. We argue that in the case of GHGs, emissions-neutral cost reduction gets too much attention—both because adherence with the cap is not in and of itself a solution, and because project-based offsets suffer from incurable measurement difficulties. Instead, it is the engagement of those outside the cap—with an eye toward long-term mitigation—that is the key virtue of offset policies.

Therefore, we argue that a rigid focus on ensuring that offset policies do not undermine the sanctity of targets is misplaced. Advocates of such strict accountability—under the Kyoto Protocol or under domestic programs, as reflected in the current debate over national policy within the United States—have focused too much on targets as solutions and not enough on target-based policies as part of a complex and long-term transition to a reduced GHG future. The practical manifestation of such views has been to create implementation policies as if meeting the target meant that the climate change problem were solved, and every ton over the target was a nail in the global climate coffin.

Given that worldwide emissions over long time periods, together with the effectiveness of adaptive responses, are the true underlying drivers of climate risk and damage, this emphasis is misplaced. It is particularly problematic as a guide for policies toward developing countries. Insistence that strict standards of additionality be met in CDM and other offset policies has raised the financial and non-financial costs of offset transfers.

The CDM has clearly been designed with additionality and accountability very high on the list of priorities, a focus we believe is inherently limiting. The emphasis on ton-for-ton emissions accounting has kept transaction costs high, limited innovative projects, and particularly prevented policy-based changes from being funded with offset resource transfers. This is unfortunate since there are countless policies—in areas such as taxation, technology, subsidies, and building codes—that could promote emission reductions in the long run but that cannot easily be categorized as "projects" in the CDM sense (Aldy and Stavins 2008: 7).

CDM administrators and participants have been well aware of these limitations and have worked hard to develop standardized methodologies and simplified procedures. These measures have improved the situation but cannot work around the fundamental limitation of strict accountability. The CDM has been characterized by relatively low volumes of offset credits, concentration on a few large projects to reduce hydrofluorocarbon (HFC) emissions (HFC reductions accounted for 37 percent of total credits issued through early 2008), and high transaction costs that have, to a large degree, excluded small countries and small projects. Nonetheless, language focusing attention on strict environmental integrity—and guarantees thereof—have made their way into the offset provisions of the most widely discussed US legislation and continue to be a political focus of NGOs.

The developments in Bali implicitly recognized this problem and generated proposals for granting credits for avoided deforestation that are consistent with the approach recommended here. It will never be possible to precisely define what actions prevent deforestation relative to a future counterfactual baseline, but this makes avoiding deforestation no less valuable an endeavor.

A proposal for enhancing offsets

We propose a mechanism that allows industrialized countries to meet part of their emissions reductions commitments by funding activities in developing countries. This mechanism has some significant differences from the CDM. It could supplant the CDM in a post-Kyoto agreement or serve as an institution that governs and coordinates the use of offsets in separate or partially integrated industrialized-country emissions trading programs.

Change the criteria for offsets from "real, verifiable, and permanent reductions" to "actions that create real progress in developing countries toward mitigation and adaptation."

This is the part of our proposal that diverges most from the design of offset programs historically. The theoretical justification for recognizing offsets has centered on "carbon neutrality"—the idea that global net emissions will be exactly the same with and without the offset project.

Part of the problem with this model is the basic fallacy that offsets are ever really carbon-neutral in any strict sense. Issues of permanence, leakage, and additionality are endemic and insurmountable. Offsets suffer from a version of the fallacy of misplaced concreteness. Another problem with strict ton-for-ton accounting is that the transaction costs—economic and political—of meeting requirements for real, verifiable, and quantifiable reductions prevent many useful activities from qualifying for implementation—in spite of the fact that there is widespread agreement that massive increases in resource transfers are necessary to change developing-country emissions pathways.

We propose modifying the underlying concept of what is being offset. In adopting and implementing specific mitigation targets, industrialized countries are taking on an obligation to make progress on reducing the risks of climate change. Their targets are a means to that end and provide a useful metric for signaling commitment to a level of financial and policy effort. Offsets would make a greater contribution to industrialized country goals if they focused less on offsetting specific tons of GHG emissions and more on funding, implementing, and evaluating activities in developing countries that are effective in reducing overall climate-change risk.

This proposal does not exclude the activities covered by the existing CDM, but rather tries to broaden the kinds of activities covered by that program and change the criteria for measurement and verification. This in turn requires a new set of tasks and judgments to choose activities and evaluate their effectiveness. In subsequent sections we outline how negotiation and institutional design could work to make such judgments.

Make a significant share of industrialized-country commitments (whether international or domestic) achievable through offset payments to developing countries.

The CDM and the cap-and-trade programs that have been adopted or proposed in a number of industrialized countries already contain provisions for transfers to developing countries in return for specified actions. We propose to expand the flow of resources available through this mechanism by setting a reference level of industrialized-country targets that will provide funding for developing country actions. Industrialized countries would aim to purchase credits equal to this reference level—we propose at least 10 percent of a country's overall GHG target. Credits generated by this mechanism would be accepted on par with the allowances used for compliance in international or participating national emissions trading markets. For example, if the United States were to adopt a target of 5,000 million metric tons (MMT) of CO_2 equivalent emissions for a given year, it would attempt to purchase 500 MMT of offset credits.

These credits would make it easier for industrialized countries to meet their targets, while sales of credits in industrialized-country emissions trading markets would provide financial resources for developing-country actions. Some part of this commitment would be devoted to a fund that would make *ex ante* investments and the rest would be available to projects and actions that qualified for credits *ex post*. Our recommendations for how to set criteria for actions and determine credit amounts are described in later sections of this chapter.

Current levels of transfers under the CDM have been (a) low, (b) concentrated in a limited number of countries, and (c) not concentrated in the energy sector or sequestration. The CDM is not quantitatively limited in the Kyoto Protocol, but it is limited in practice by the cost and difficulty of getting projects credited through the process. The European Union Emission Trading Scheme (EU ETS) does place limits on the number of CDM (and Joint Implementation) credits that can be used to meet EU obligations. The most widely discussed US cap-and-trade legislative proposal (S.2191) contained a rough target of 5 percent for non-forestry offsets from developing countries, with provisions for expanding that percentage if domestic offsets did not meet a threshold.

As a standard of comparison for the potential size of our proposed mechanism, we calculate the magnitude of resources in 2012 if the United States were to adopt an overall emissions target of 4 percent below 2005 levels (as in S.2191) and make 10 percent of this target available to fund developing-country activities, and if the original fifteen members of the EU ETS (EU-15) similarly pegged 10 percent of one year of its Kyoto target as eligible under this sort of mechanism. Based on an assumed allowance price of $25 per ton, the amount of money available to fund developing-country actions in 2012 would be $24.2 billion. The quantity of allowances devoted to funding in this example would be 969 $MMTCO_2$ in 2012. By way of comparison, a total of 189 MMTCO2 have been registered from the inception of the CDM through early 2008. The 10 percent figure is offered as an example and reasonable benchmark. Our point is that under anything like the current CDM rules, developing countries are unlikely to see resource transfers of this magnitude.

In theory, increased resource flows could come from government tax revenues as required through some international commitment, rather than by selling credits into industrialized-country emissions trading markets. Our proposal is based on a judgment that—given the existence of multinational and/or national cap-and-trade programs—political realities make credit sales a more politically palatable funding mechanism in the short run. We also think that such a mechanism is less prone to diminution or cancellation in difficult economic times than funding developing-country activities out of general revenues, and thus is more stable over the long run.

We also recognize that expanding the number of credits generated by developing country activities will reduce the price signal and level of effort in the energy-production and end-use sectors of industrialized countries, *ceteris paribus*. Our judgment is that—given the existence of widespread target-and-price policies like cap-and-trade programs in the industrialized countries—the importance of changing the overall portfolio of responses to climate-change risk in developing countries makes such an outcome an acceptable tradeoff. It is also possible that awareness of this outcome will allow the adoption of more ambitious targets in the industrialized countries.

Put a specified or minimum quantity of offset credits in a fund *ex ante*, where subsequent expenditures from the fund would be governed by negotiated principles and institutions.

We propose that some share of offset credits generated by the above-described mechanism—we recommend 50 percent of the total—be sold to provide the resources for an investment fund in developing-country risk reduction. Instead of granting credits after a project has been approved and carried out, credits devoted to this fund would be issued and then sold to provide an *ex ante* funding stream. How much of the total allowable quantity of offset credits would go to this fund, and how much would be awarded through more traditional means (that is, awarded after the fact for projects or policies that achieve demonstrated progress toward climate-mitigation objectives based on measurement and accountability criteria), is a policy decision that would need to be determined through negotiation.

The main strength of a fund is that it allows much greater flexibility in supporting large-scale or nonstandard mitigation options and thus would allow for a wider range of policy experiments. It also bypasses a significant hurdle in the use of existing crediting mechanisms to finance mitigation actions in developing countries: the time gap between deciding and implementing an action and obtaining verification that project or policy standards are being met. An *ex ante* fund could also help spread the benefits of offsets if geographical diversity were part of the criteria for selecting activities for investment; in contrast, CDM projects have tended to benefit only a handful of larger developing countries that are able to attract private investment (Banuri and Gupta 2000: 79). To date more than three-quarters of registered CDM projects have been implemented in just four countries: China, India, Brazil, and Mexico. Many smaller developing countries simply lack the capacity and expertise to successfully navigate the complicated and administratively onerous project cycle of the CDM (Yamin and Depledge 2005: 185).

Consider the investment required to advance a large-scale wind project, a liquid natural gas terminal, or an urban transportation project: having resources to support such projects will make a decision to move ahead more likely than in a situation where no credits will be granted until the project is approved, constructed, and producing results. An *ex ante* offsets fund reduces the need to find private-sector financing, which can be a significant impediment, and it can be used to promote policies and build capacity in ways that are not linked to specific projects, such as reducing energy subsidies, implementing appliance efficiency standards, or investing in renewable energy. It also makes for a more activist institution that is looking to spend money productively, rather than one that functions purely as an intermediary.

Another significant advantage of a fund approach is the potential for reducing transaction costs for small projects. A fund could invest in a series of small photovoltaic or wind projects at various locations in a developing country without incurring the significant documentation and submission costs that are required under the CDM.

One potential objection is that accountability becomes a much more difficult concept *ex ante* than *ex post*. If resources are committed out of a fund, what recourse is there if the funded actions are poorly managed or fail to produce desired results? To the extent that industrialized countries retain a significant focus on verifying and quantifying developing country actions, this may move the mechanism far enough away from traditional offset programs to make it incompatible with their political and diplomatic needs. This is a justifiable concern. We believe progress requires that industrialized countries should be willing to incur risk for at least some share of their offset expenditures. The amount of risk that might be considered reasonable depends on the performance of, and basis for trust in, the fund's governing institutions, but strong risk aversion is inextricably linked to limited actions and lost opportunities. In a later section of this chapter we also suggest a mechanism to at least partially address accountability concerns related to this specific proposal, and in general to provide for *ex post* adjustment. We also note that unlike single CDM projects, a fund can spread risk across a variety of activities—a single investment might fail, but the portfolio of funded activities could still produce significant progress toward climate-change mitigation and/or adaptation.

Another criticism of the idea of using offset credits to create a fund is that it is really no different than putting resources into a fund from general revenues. Governments could simply agree to put an amount of money equal to that produced by devoting a given quantity of offset credits (or could expand their emissions target by the same amount of credits, auction the additional permits or allowances generated by this expansion, and devote those resources to such a fund). This is technically true, and we think that either of those two funding options would constitute a perfectly fine outcome. Our belief that linking funding for developing-country actions to an offset program is a viable alternative is based on the proposition that it is politically easier to devote a set of additional allowances than to use general revenues. The additional allowances do reduce domestic costs (holding the target constant). It is also politically more acceptable to provide offset credits in return for actions that lower climate-change risks than it is to simply relax the target to produce general revenues—and our proposed structure does maintain that connection (to actual mitigation), if less rigidly than do traditional offset programs. Our mechanism provides stable funding that does not depend on annual appropriations, and it also maintains at least some connection between the additional allowances made available and the underlying problem that multinational or national cap-and-trade systems are set up to address: reducing atmospheric concentrations of GHGs.

Climate investment funds have been gathering increasing support. The World Bank, after a number of smaller funds designed to produce CDM credits, announced two new funds in July of 2008 that would have the flexibility to pursue both technology-oriented initiatives as well as new and innovative approaches to mitigation and adaptation. The World Bank is hoping to capitalize these new funds at a total value of $5 billion. Mexico recently proposed a multilateral climate-change investment fund that specifically does not include additionality as a criterion for funding and that would invest in both mitigation and adaptation. Our proposal is very much in the spirit of these funds, although we believe that providing capital through our proposed mechanism has the potential to create a larger and more stable source of investment capital than sovereign government contributions. We also believe that the specific operational principles of a fund can best be worked out through the process we describe below.

We note that we do not propose that the entire commitment of offset credits be devoted to an *ex ante* fund. The more familiar mechanism of awarding offset credits for actions that meet program criteria should still be used for as large a share of overall offset credits as is desired (we propose half). We do believe that the flexibility offered by a fund argues that at least some share of allowances be used in this way.

Make the principles used to qualify actions taken in developing countries as offsets the specific focus of negotiation among state parties.

One of the core principles of our proposal is that multilateral and bilateral negotiations—key ingredients of an international climate-policy architecture—should determine the kinds of activities, policies, and investments eligible for receiving resources. Industrialized countries have a number of goals for offset policy: reducing the cost of meeting domestic obligations, promoting carbon neutrality, and moving developing countries toward progress in GHG mitigation are broad categories that apply. Developing countries are a highly heterogeneous group, but have in common a primary focus on economic development and on the principle that industrialized countries should transfer resources that allow developing countries to make progress on reducing climate-change risk in a way that does not (at least in the short run) entail broad quantifiable commitments.

The principles that need to be negotiated would encompass the standard accountability criteria—additionality, leakage, and permanence—but should move beyond the current ton-for-ton accounting framework. Major energy-sector investments and policies, forestry and agricultural programs and investments, and technology adoption and implementation should be on the table. There is also no reason why adaptation actions and investments should not be included—if they are of interest to developing countries, then they should be on the table as a means of offsetting other ways of reducing climate-change risk. Economic development is widely recognized as an essential part of adaptation strategies, and the contribution of mitigation and adaptation actions to broader economic welfare should be part of this negotiation as well.

The principles that need to be negotiated are:

1. What kinds of activities, investments, policies and programs are eligible (projects, policies, infrastructure, adaptation, etc.)?

2. What kinds of documentation or accountability are required before resources are committed?
3. What kinds of documentation or accountability are required during and after resources have been used?
4. What procedures and agreements are available *ex post* to adjust credits granted *ex ante* (related to points 2 and 3, above)?
5. Are there minimum or maximum percentages of available resources that should be set aside for specific uses (e.g., wind energy or HCFC phase-out projects)?
6. Are criteria needed for the distribution of total funds among nations and among recipient groups? In other words, is there a share of total expenditures that should be reserved for the "best" projects and actions, and is there a share that should be divided among developing countries on a per capita basis or by some larger combination of criteria including stage of development and effort on climate-change mitigation?

We also propose an additional axiom that should apply as a matter of principle:

7. Be willing to take risks, make mistakes, and accept that some actions will fail or only partially succeed.

Delegate clearly delineated tasks to existing international organizations and new institutions for the purpose of managing and safeguarding the offsets program, consistent with negotiated guidelines.

Institutional framework

We recognize that any agreement resulting from the kind of principles discussed above will not give clear and unequivocal guidance on a wide range of specific decisions. We propose adapting the CDM oversight institutions to create a new body whose job is to make specific decisions about how to (a) use resources and (b) evaluate resulting actions, investments, and policies.

The existing climate regime includes a broad and impressive framework of intergovernmental and private institutions. Our proposal for an enhanced offsets mechanism can build effectively on these existing institutions, though with some modifications and novel structures. We recommend that the World Bank and the Climate Secretariat in Bonn play a central role, the former taking the lead on implementation and the latter emphasizing information sharing and decision making in conjunction with governments. While the World Bank specializes in economic development, the Climate Secretariat's main concern is with the environmental integrity of programs—that is, their contribution to reduced emissions. The two entities therefore complement each other well.

The World Bank has enormous experience with offsets activities and currently manages ten carbon funds, many of which emphasize sustainable development. The Community Development Carbon Fund, in particular, is designed to allow the world's poorest countries to benefit from emissions markets. The Climate Secretariat's main contribution would be in the areas of coordination and information sharing. Because we are recommending a much broader range of emissions reduction activities in a wider set of countries, policy information will be of enormous importance in our scheme. The national reports submitted regularly to the Secretariat by governments contain information on national circumstances and the status of emissions, with additional compliance information required of Annex I countries. We propose that these reports be expanded to contain more information on policy experiences and "best practices" to be shared among governments. This information should be compiled and analyzed by the Secretariat in conjunction with input from NGOs and other sources of research and analysis, thereby creating a new sort of information clearinghouse that will facilitate learning and allow offsets activities to be fine-tuned in an adaptive process over time.

One difference between our proposal and the current structure is that existing carbon funds are all project-based and largely focus on the compliance interests of Annex B parties in the first commitment period (Carr and Rosembuj 2007), whereas we propose funding a broader range of policy changes designed to produce longer-term benefits. This move away from ton-for-ton accounting, and the corresponding need to decide what new kinds of actions can count for offsets credits and how they will be evaluated, will have to be driven by negotiations and coordinated by some multilateral institution (or institutions).

To oversee this new structure and a new offsets program more generally, we propose the establishment of a ten-member oversight committee, composed of parties to the UNFCCC and ultimately responsible to the Conference of the Parties (COP). To make certain that a broad range of interests are represented, membership on such a committee should be distributed along similar lines as the current ten-member CDM Executive Board, with one member from each of the UN's regional groups, two other Annex I members, two other non-Annex I members, and one other member from among the least developed countries to ensure that sustainable development concerns are reflected. Since three of the five regional groupings are composed almost entirely of developing countries, they would normally enjoy a six-to-four majority on the board. A two-thirds majority voting rule would ensure that no group dominates decision-making, but would also avoid the gridlock that could result from a consensus requirement.

Finally, as our proposal is designed to reflect the interests of both industrialized and developing countries, and to include a wider range of policies, the issue of "coherence" across international regimes is likely to arise. To make sure that environmental needs do not clash with the economic interests of both developed and developing countries, we propose the creation of an informal contact group of secretariat officials, to be chaired by the UNFCCC Executive Secretary, across major relevant multilateral institutions, including the World Bank, International Monetary Fund (IMF), World Trade Organization (WTO), Organisation for Economic Co-operation and Development (OECD), United Nations Conference on Trade and Development (UNCTAD), United Nations Environment Programme (UNEP), and World Meteorological Organization (WMO). This informal contact group would raise issues concerning conflicting rules and incentives and would also share data on best practices. A useful model in this regard is the Global Environment Facility, whose complex mandate requires it to work closely with a variety of UN agencies and regional development banks (Porter *et al.* 2008: 12).

Ultimately, the institutions responsible for performing these functions will have to decide (1) which actions or projects to fund based on the specific technology or sector involved, the amount of investment required, and the contribution to non-GHG objectives (economic development, income distribution, access to energy); and (2) how much credit to grant to a specific action or project (and how much money to spend on it).

Ex post accountability
One idea we propose for a new offsets regime is the ability to make adjustments *ex post*. Expanding offset activities beyond strict

ton-for-ton accounting, and transferring resources in advance of realized progress on reducing climate-change risks, increases the uncertainty associated with quantifying benefits. This creates a problem for accountability in the way resources are used.

Giving the institution (or institutions) charged with overseeing an expanded offsets program, the responsibility to evaluate the efficacy of expenditures after projects or policies are implemented can help to ameliorate this situation. We can see two separate kinds of *ex post* adjustments—those between the oversight institution and the recipients of resource transfers, and those involving voluntary retirement of allowances by the oversight institution.

As an example, take the case where a large resource transfer takes place to fund photovoltaic and wind generation in rural areas, and the technologies fail to be implemented and/or maintained, causing continued use of diesel generators. The oversight institution could have the authority to require remediation actions from the host-country government (or business or NGO) that has responsibility for the project—including implementing corrective actions at the government's expense or undertaking some other set of GHG mitigation actions. If these remediating efforts fail to materialize, then the oversight institution could restrict access to resources in the future. The focus here should be on whether resources were used as intended and managed well, and not on whether the benefits were as large as predicted. There remains an unavoidable task of evaluation and judgment in making this determination, so performing these oversight functions will never be perfect or free of conflict.

The oversight institution should also make *ex post* corrections based on how well its portfolio of activities meets specified objectives. If funded projects or activities significantly underperform expectations about mitigating GHG risk, then retiring some quantity of the credits allocated to provide resources for our proposed fund (i.e., not selling them into industrialized-country emissions trading programs) could compensate for the gap between expected and realized benefits. Similarly, reducing the quantity of offset credits sold into industrialized-country emissions markets would have the effect of reducing industrialized-country emissions to compensate for (some part of) the failure of developing-country actions. The operational details of such an *ex post* adjustment would depend on what participants negotiate about the nature and role of accountability in a new offsets regime.

This proposal for an *ex post* correction mechanism also has its problematic aspects: it goes against the financial interests of the over-sight institution to deny itself resources and it depends on complex and uncertain evaluations. A separate institution may be required to judge the efficacy of the portfolio of activities sponsored through the fund. Nevertheless, our proposal does have the virtue of creating a mechanism that allows for *ex post* evaluations to affect the future use of resources, however imperfectly.

International agreement or coordination mechanism

The mechanism we have proposed could function under a single unified international carbon cap like that envisioned by the Kyoto Protocol. It is currently far from clear whether a unified cap approach will be agreed upon in Copenhagen, or whether a more bottom-up (or fractured) set of national-level policies for industrialized countries will characterize the post-2012 period. The elements of our proposal are of value in either scenario, and in the latter case could serve as a mecha-nism for coordinating both rules and prices among diverse national and regional emissions trading programs (Jaffe and Stavins 2007). If there were to be separate EU and US cap-and-trade systems with independent targets, for example, collective negotiation and insti-tutional innovation of the kind proposed here could serve to arrive at a common, or at least coordinated, set of rules and standards for developing country offsets. Depending on the regulations and quantity limits applied to the use of international offsets for domestic compli-ance purposes, this would tend to bring allowance prices in industrial-ized countries closer together.

Conclusion

We begin with the premise that serious participation by large devel-oping countries is a *sine qua non* for any successful climate regime in the post-Kyoto world. Our proposal for improving the international framework for addressing climate-change risks is partly an evolution of current elements. It builds on and expands the idea of the CDM and offset policy in general. It recognizes that developing countries will do significantly more if resources are available, and that industri-alized countries require accountability for the resources they provide. It further recognizes that offset policy has attractive attributes for industrialized countries from a political economy standpoint and that these attributes are likely to make offsets more viable than other mechanisms for sustaining resource transfers to developing countries.

Overall, we take into account the distinct interests of both industrialized and developing countries by emphasizing environmental and development needs simultaneously. By steering away from strict ton-for-ton accounting and project-based approaches to offsets, our proposal provides the flexibility necessary to accommodate variable interests, capabilities, and compliance costs. Such flexibility and incentive compatibility has been crucial in the past for making progress in climate negotiations and will only grow more important if serious engagement by developing countries is to be achieved (Victor 2007; Thompson in press).

It is certainly not necessary that all elements of this proposal be adopted together in order to improve on the current situation. The idea of accepting more uncertainty and experimentation in exchange for a wider and more creative portfolio of actions can be achieved in many ways. Expanding funding for offsets from target-based emission-trading programs in industrialized countries is only one of a number of possible mechanisms—albeit one that has some significant advantages. There are many possible institutional structures for handling these proposed resource transfers. We believe the one proposed here combines functionality and realism to offer a promising way forward through the daunting technical and political difficulties that confront efforts to expand resource transfers to developing countries, efforts that are essential to reduce global climate-change risks.

References

Aldy, Joseph E. and Robert N. Stavins (eds.) (2007). *Architectures for Agreement*. New York: Cambridge University Press.

(2008). "Economic Incentives in a New Climate Agreement," Prepared for The Climate Dialogue, Hosted by the Prime Minister of Denmark, May 7–8, 2008, Copenhagen, Denmark. Cambridge, MA: Belfer Center for Science and International Affairs.

Axelrod, Robert and Robert O. Keohane (1985). "Achieving Cooperation under Anarchy: Strategies and Institutions," *World Politics* 38: 226–54.

Banuri, Tariq and Sujata Gupta (2000). "The Clean Development Mechanism and Sustainable Development: An Economic Analysis," in Prodipto

Ghosh (ed.), *Implementation of the Kyoto Protocol: Opportunities and Pitfalls for Developing Countries.* Manila: Asian Development Bank, pp. 73–101.

Barrett, Scott (2007). "A Multitrack Climate Treaty System," in Joseph E. Aldy and Robert N. Stavins (eds.), *Architectures for Agreement.* New York: Cambridge University Press, pp. 237–59.

BBC World Service (2007). "All Countries Need to Take Major Steps on Climate Change: Global Poll," September 25, available at www.globescan.com/news_archives/bbc_climate/bbcclimate.pdf.

Betsill, Michele M. and Elisabeth Corell, eds. (2007). *NGO Diplomacy: The Influence of Nongovernmental Organizations in International Environmental Negotiations.* Cambridge, MA: MIT Press.

Capoor, Karan and Philippe Ambrosi (2008). *State and Trends of the Carbon Market 2008.* Washington, DC: The World Bank.

Carr, Christopher and Flavia Rosembuj (2007). "World Bank Experiences in Contracting for Emissions Reductions," *Environmental Liability* 2: 114–19.

Chayes, Abram and Antonia Handler Chayes (1995). *The New Sovereignty: Compliance with International Regulatory Agreements.* Cambridge, MA: Harvard University Press.

Cline, William (2007). *Global Warming and Agriculture: Impact Assessments by Country.* Washington, DC: Center for Global Development.

Cooper, Richard N. (2007). "Alternatives to Kyoto: The Case for a Carbon Tax," in Aldy and Stavins (eds.), pp. 105–15.

Frankel, Jeffrey (2007). "Formulas for Quantitative Emissions Targets," in Aldy and Stavins (eds.), pp. 31–56.

Geres, Roland and Axel Michaelowa (2002). "A Qualitative Method to Consider Leakage Effects from CDM and JI Projects," *Energy Policy* 30: 461–3.

Globescan (2006). "30-Country Poll Finds Worldwide Consensus that Climate Change is a Serious Problem," available at www.worldpublic opinion.org/incl/printable_version.php?pnt=187.

IEA (2006). *World Energy Outlook 2006.* Paris: International Energy Agency.

  (2007). *World Energy Outlook 2007.* Paris: International Energy Agency.

IMF (2008). *World Economic Outlook 2008.* Washington, DC: International Monetary Fund.

IPCC (2001). *Climate Change 2001: Mitigation.* New York: Cambridge University Press.

  (2007). *Climate Change 2007: Impacts, Adaptation and Vulnerability.* New York: Cambridge University Press.

Jaffe, Judson and Robert Stavins (2007). *IETA Report on Linking GHG Emissions Trading Systems,* International Emissions Trading Association.

Keohane, Robert O. (1988). "International Institutions: Two Approaches," *International Studies Quarterly* 32(4): 379–96.

Koremenos, Barbara, Charles Lipson, and Duncan Snidal (2001). "The Rational Design of International Institutions," *International Organization* 55(4): 761–99.

Lumsdaine, David Halloran (1993). *Moral Vision in International Politics: The Foreign Aid Regime, 1949–1989.* Princeton, NJ: Princeton University Press.

Milner, Helen V. (2006). "Why Multilateralism? Foreign Aid and Domestic Principal-Agent Problems," in Darren Hawkins *et al.* (eds.), *Delegation and Agency in International Organizations.* New York: Cambridge University Press, pp. 107–39.

Mitchell, Ronald B. (1998). "Sources of Transparency: Information Systems in International Regimes," *International Studies Quarterly* 42: 109–30.

Moravcsik, Andrew (1997). "Taking Preferences Seriously: A Liberal Theory of International Politics," *International Organization* 51(4): 513–53.

Najam, Adil, Saleemul Huq, and Youba Sokona (2003). "Climate Negotiations beyond Kyoto: Developing Country Concerns and Interests," *Climate Policy* 3(3): 221–31.

Nordhaus, William D. and Joseph Boyer (2000). *Warming the World: Economic Models of Global Warming.* Cambridge, MA: MIT Press.

OECD (2000). *Emission Baselines: Estimating the Unknown.* Paris: Organisation for Economic Cooperation and Development.

Pizer, William A. (2007). "Practical Global Climate Policy," in Aldy and Stavins (eds.), pp. 280–314.

Plantinga, Andrew J. and Kenneth R. Richards (2008). "International Forest Carbon Sequestration in a Post-Kyoto Agreement," Discussion Paper 08–11, October, Cambridge, MA: Harvard Project on International Climate Agreements.

Porter, Gareth, Neil Bird, Nanki Kaur, and Leo Peskett (2008). *New Finance for Climate Change and the Environment.* Washington, DC: Heinrich Boll Foundation and WWF.

Raustiala, Kal and David G. Victor (1998). "Conclusions," in David G. Victor, Kal Raustiala, and Eugene B. Skolnikoff (eds.), *The Implementation and Effectiveness of International Environmental Commitments: Theory and Practice.* Cambridge, MA: MIT Press, pp. 659–708.

Richards, Kenneth and Krister Andersson (2001). "The Leaky Sink: Persistent Obstacles to a Forest Carbon Sequestration Program Based on Individual Projects," *Climate Policy* 1: 41–54.

Stern, Nicholas (2007). *The Economics of Climate Change: The Stern Review*. New York: Cambridge University Press.

Sunstein, Cass R. (2003). "Beyond the Precautionary Principle," *University of Pennsylvania Law Review* 151: 1003–58.

Thompson, Alexander (2006). "Management under Anarchy: The International Politics of Climate Change," *Climatic Change* 78: 7–29.

(in press). "Rational Design in Motion: Uncertainty and Flexibility in the Global Climate Regime," *European Journal of International Relations*.

Victor, David G. (2007). "Fragmented Carbon Markets and Reluctant Nations: Implications for the Design of Effective Carbon Markets," in Aldy and Stavins (eds.), pp. 133–60.

Vöhringer, Frank, Timo Kuosmanen, and Rob Dellink (2004). "A Proposal for the Attribution of Market Leakage to CDM Projects," HWWA Discussion Paper 262, Hamburg Institute of International Economics.

Wiener, Jonathan B. (2007). "Incentives and Meta-Architecture," in Aldy and Stavins (eds.), pp. 67–80.

15 | Possible development of a technology clean development mechanism in a post-2012 regime

FEI TENG, WENYING CHEN AND JIANKUN HE

Introduction

Technology is central to the transition to a low-carbon society and to global efforts to cope with climate change. Many technologies that could mitigate greenhouse gas (GHG) emissions exist, but most have not been widely deployed in developing countries. In many of these countries, economic development is producing unsustainable growth in energy demand. Therefore, the transfer of climate-friendly technologies and additional investment flows from developed to developing countries is vital to solve the global climate problem. The importance of technology transfer has been recognized since the Earth Summit in Rio de Janeiro—indeed it is emphasized in both the United Nations Framework Convention on Climate Change (UNFCCC) and the Kyoto Protocol. Yet investment in technology transfer activities remains weak considering the gravity of the issue. After the 2007 Conference of the Parties in Bali, this issue has become increasingly important in the context of negotiations on a future climate regime, even as significant disagreements persist between developing and developed countries.

Article 12 of the Kyoto Protocol established the Clean Development Mechanism (CDM) to serve a two-fold objective: first, to help Annex I countries meet their emission targets in a cost-effective way and second, to support non-Annex I countries in achieving the goal of sustainable development. Though technology transfer is not required for projects that receive CDM credit, experience shows that this program may contribute significantly to technology transfer. However, it is difficult to induce large-scale technology transfer through the CDM in its present form. The project-specific nature of the CDM leads to high transaction costs and makes it difficult to create economies of scale and pool risks across projects of the same type. This chapter aims to address these shortcomings through proposing an enhanced CDM regime that places greater emphasis on technology transfer from developed countries to developing countries.

The remainder of this chapter is organized as follows: Section 2 surveys possible ways to enhance the CDM by drawing on the recent literature and ongoing climate talks, with a focus on the relationship between technology transfer and the CDM; Section 3 presents a case study involving the transfer of natural gas turbine technology to China and suggests a new CDM regime based on technology transfer; Section 4 analyzes operational issues and options for the international governance of CDM-based technology transfer; and Section 5 concludes the chapter.

Possible development of the CDM

The CDM is the only market mechanism in the Kyoto Protocol that is open to the participation of developing countries. Since the Marrakech Accords of 2001, this program has proved surprisingly effective in promoting sustainable development in developing countries and generating a large volume of credits. As of September 2008, 3,909 CDM projects were in the pipeline with 1,152 projects already registered and 200 projects in the stage of requesting registration. If all projects in the pipeline are registered and certified emission reduction credits (CERs) are issued as expected, then total CDM-issued CERs would amount to 528.6 million tons of carbon dioxide equivalent per year (UNEP Riso, 2008). This is more than Australia's national emissions in 2005[1] and it equals 2.8 percent of aggregated 2005 emissions from all Annex I countries. In the most optimistic scenario, these CERs will generate income of $5 billion (assuming a CO_2 permit price of $10 per ton) for project developers in non-Annex I countries. According to the International Energy Agency (IEA), the investment in clean energy technologies and energy efficiency needed to achieve a 50 percent reduction in global GHG emissions by 2050 is dramatically higher than the current level of investment (IEA, 2008). At its current scale,

---

[1] In 2005, Australia's national inventory of GHG emissions, excluding emissions from land use, land-use changes, and forestry, totaled 525.41 million tons in carbon dioxide-equivalent terms.

the CDM market can only meet 0.5–0.75 percent of annual investment needs in non-OECD countries.

Baseline determination and additionality are two important concepts in the CDM program, as it is currently structured. The emissions baseline for a CDM project is defined as the emissions that would have occurred in the absence of the proposed project. The difference between baseline emissions and actual emissions following project implementation is the estimated emission reduction. A CDM project is "additional" only if GHG emissions are reduced below the baseline level—that is, if emissions are reduced below what they would have been if the project had not been implemented.

The existing CDM is project-based, which means that baselines and additionality are determined on a project basis. This results in substantial transaction costs and time delays. The complete cycle for receiving CDM credits, from the preparation of a detailed project design document (PDD) to project registration, takes almost one year and costs about $500,000 per project (Ellis and Kamel 2007). Thus, the CDM needs to move from a project-based approach to a more "wholesale" approach to achieve the scales needed to meaningfully effect technology transfer from rich to poor countries (Stern 2008). Several proposals have been put forward for enhancing the current CDM; they include programmatic CDM, policy CDM, and sectoral CDM.

Programmatic CDM

Typically the CDM registers individual projects that belong to a single owner. If an owner has several similar CDM projects, they can be "bundled" to simplify the application process and reduce transaction costs. However, some emission reduction activities involve many different owners and geographic locations. At present, such mitigation activities are difficult to undertake as CDM projects: the emission reduction potential of each unit is relatively low and the overall transaction cost is very high. The programmatic CDM or pCDM offers a framework to realize the enormous emission-reduction opportunities offered by numerous small-scale projects, distributed over space and time, and across a large number of owners.

At Montreal in 2005, Parties to the UNFCCC agreed that "a program of activities can be registered as a single clean development mechanism project activity...provided that CDM methodological requirements are met."[2] To implement pCDM, a two-level framework is needed. One level would be designed to recognize a program of activities (PoA), defined as "a voluntary coordinated action by a private or public entity which coordinates and implements any policy/ measure or stated goal, which leads to GHG emission reductions or increases net GHG removals by sinks that are additional to any that would occur in the absence of the PoA..."[3] An individual project undertaken as part of a program of activities would be defined as a CDM program activity (CPA).

The pCDM has several important benefits. First, it would allow for the aggregation of emission reductions in some program areas, such as energy efficiency, that could yield large benefits but that would otherwise face high transaction costs if reductions had to be tracked on a project-by-project basis. Second, the pCDM can help to even out the distribution of CERs over small and least developed countries, thereby addressing a serious concern for those countries that have been largely absent as participants in the CDM. The smallest and least developed countries, which may lack opportunities for single projects with large-scale reduction potential, can participate in, and benefit from, CDM programs that span multiple nations and numerous facility or project owners.

Policy-based CDM

It is not surprising that climate change is not at the top of all countries' priority lists. Developing countries confront a number of urgent challenges that vary from country to country, but that typically include priorities such as reducing poverty and providing general services, education, and energy security. Nevertheless, developing countries' rapidly growing contribution to global GHG emissions means that they need to integrate climate policies and climate-change considerations in their national development strategies. At the twelfth Conference of the Parties (COP-12) in Nairobi in 2006, South Africa submitted a proposal to the UNFCCC negotiation process on sustain-

[2] Decision 7/CMP1, see also http://unfccc.int/resource/docs/2005/cmp1/eng/ 08a01.pdf#page=93.
[3] EB32, Annex 38, paragraph 1, see also http://cdm.unfccc.int/EB/032/eb32_ repan38.pdf.

able development policies and measures (SD-PAMs). This proposed approach[4] was not built on specified emission reductions (tons CO_2), but rather on policies and measures. SD-PAMs can be regarded as voluntary "commitments" by developing countries. If they result in emission reductions that can be shown to be additional and can be measured and financed by developed countries, these SD-PAMS can constitute a policy-CDM.

A policy-CDM could be used to recognize sectoral and national targets, efficiency standards, and regulation. As distinct from the regular CDM, CERs generated under a policy-CDM would flow to governments rather than to project owners. For example, the government of China may adopt a mandatory regulation for the fuel efficiency of vehicles. If such a regulation can be shown to result in additional emission reductions, in the sense that the regulation would not have been adopted without the financial incentives supplied by the carbon market, and if baseline emissions can be well established, then the Chinese government can sell these CERs into the international carbon market and receive compensation for the additional cost imposed by its regulatory action.

Both SD-PAMs and the policy-CDM can be regarded as "the middle road" between voluntary-qualified commitments for developing countries (as Russia has proposed)[5] and Kyoto Protocol-style binding commitments. Neither the former nor the latter are acceptable to many developing countries because, they argue, both violate the principle of "common but differentiated responsibility." The policy-CDM may provide an option for moving forward, not only because the CDM is well-accepted by many developing-country Parties to the UNFCCC, but also because it may expand the mitigation activities available to developing countries and result in a larger market for CERs.

---

[4] Submission by the Government of South Africa to the second workshop of the "Dialogue on long-term cooperative action to address climate change by enhancing implementation of the Convention," held in Nairobi, November 15–16, 2006. See also http://unfccc.int/files/meetings/dialogue/application/pdf/working_paper_18_south_africa.pdf.

[5] In the Russia Proposal, a developing country may commit to an absolute or relative GHG reduction target. These voluntary commitments are a no-lose proposition—that is, if a party has not achieved its target, it does not enter the non-compliance regime or pay penalties. If a party does achieve its target, it can gain carbon credits and sell them in international carbon markets for a profit.

It is still not clear what kinds of policies and measures should be regarded as additional and thus be eligible for processing through a crediting mechanism. The difficulties mainly stem from applying the additionality test in the context of SD-PAMs. First, a wide range of energy-efficiency policies that have ancillary GHG-reducing benefits have already been put into place in developing countries. Presumably, these policies and measures will continue in the future. Second, applying the additionality test to many government policies is almost impossible (Baumert and Winkler, 2005), as climate change is often not the primary target of these policies. In some cases, they have macroeconomic benefits that are difficult to accurately measure, such as the benefit of reduced demand for oil imports as a result of vehicle fuel-efficiency regulations. Third, large financial transfers to a developing country government may arouse political concerns in some developed countries. Fourth, CERs that are awarded to governments may be transferred to private companies that bear the cost of the policy or measure being credited. The efficiency of the system will depend on the way the government delivers price signals to firms throughout the economy with this redistribution. For example, a government may choose to subsidize private companies for costs incurred under the policy, but the efficiency of this approach will depend on how the subsidy policy is designed.

Sectoral CDM

There are at least two definitions for "sectoral CDM." The first version involves applying sectoral baselines or benchmarks to individual projects. Once a sectoral benchmark or baseline is defined, any facility or company in that sector with emissions below the baseline can earn CERs subject to the usual validation and verification requirements. For example, if the baseline emissions rate for the power sector is 0.8 tons of CO_2 per megawatt-hour (MWh), then any generating unit with CO_2 intensity less than 0.8 tons/MWh can receive CERs equal to the difference between its actual emissions and the sectoral baseline.

The second version of sectoral CDM is similar to the sectoral policy CDM. A sectoral baseline is developed at the national level and the government implements policies and measures to reduce average sectoral emissions below that baseline. The government can then receive

CERs for any difference between actual sectoral emissions going forward and the pre-determined baseline. For example, if, as above, the baseline CO_2 emissions rate for the electric power sector is 0.8 tons/ MWh, the government can adopt policies and measures—such as a renewable portfolio standard (RPS) or feed-in tariff—to increase the share of renewable energy and reduce sectoral emissions. If, as a result of these policies, the actual emission rate declines to 0.7 tons/MWh, then the host country will earn 0.1 tons of CO_2 credits for each MWh of electricity generated during the credit period. The CERs will flow to the government, but the government may decide to distribute them to private companies according to a cost-sharing formula (e.g., to reflect the fact that some or most of the cost of implementing the RPS may be borne by electricity distribution companies). Whatever form a sectoral CDM takes, it may be possible to abolish the additionality standard in this context.

Many authors regard the move from current project-based CDM to sectoral CDM as a way to facilitate the scaling-up of the carbon credit market (e.g., Stern 2008). However, sectoral CDM also shares the drawbacks associated with the policy CDM discussed before.

Technology transfer and CDM

In the Kyoto Protocol, CDM aims to help Annex I countries comply with their commitments while also contributing to sustainable development in Non-Annex I countries. It does not have to fulfill the technology transfer objectives of the Protocol. In practice, CDM may facilitate technology transfer by providing a funding mechanism for projects in developing countries that use technologies imported from developed countries.

A UNFCCC survey of 2,293 projects in the CDM pipeline as of September 2007 (Seres 2007) shows that technology transfer is more common in the larger projects. These include a number of projects that rely heavily on imported technology, mainly in the form of equipment, coupled in some cases with the import of related knowledge or expertise.

Does CDM induce new technology transfer or does it simply extend the scope of existing technology transfer activities? Although both potential outcomes are interesting, the first one is more attractive. If CDM can induce the adoption of new technologies, then it will lead to dynamic improvement in the technology standards of host developing countries. If not, then CDM activities are likely to focus on just "picking low-hanging fruit."

Technology transfer under the existing CDM regime is more or less passive. In most cases, technology transfer has already occurred before the CDM project is implemented, such that the project only serves to extend the scale of technology transfer, not to induce new transfers. For example the transfer of wind power technology to China began in 1986 and was further expanded in 1996 under the Chinese government's "Ride the Wind Program." The leading Chinese wind turbine manufacturer, Goldwind, has a 31 percent share in the domestic market and a 2.8 percent share in the global market. Goldwind started production by buying a license for a 750 kW turbine from Repower, a small German wind turbine manufacturer, and a 1.2 MW turbine from Vensys (Lewis 2007). The local content of wind turbines installed in China has since increased from 33 percent in 1998 to almost 100 percent today, and unit costs have declined dramatically— from more than 10,000 yuan/kW in 1996 to 4,000 yuan/kW in 2006 for a 750kW unit (Figure 15.1). The cost reduction is mainly due to the lower cost of labor and domestic-made components in China. It is still not clear if the CDM induced new technology transfer to China in the case of wind turbines. But it does contribute to the expansion of wind power in China by making wind power projects financially more attractive to investors. Almost 90 percent of the non-Concession[6] wind parks that have been built in China have been registered, or are in the process of being registered, for CDM credits (GWEC 2008b).

It is interesting to note that there is also some technology transfer involved in all nitrous oxide (N_2O) and hydrofluorocarbon (HFC) mitigation projects in China. Although such projects have been criticized as making "no contribution to sustainable development," the CDM mechanism has actually induced technology transfer through these projects. HFC23, for example, is an inevitable by-product of manufacturing HCFC 22; it has a global warming potential (GWP) of 11,700. HFC23 can be destroyed through a thermal oxidation process. VICHEM, a French company, is the major technology pro-

---

[6] Concession is a bidding process for a new wind park in which the bidder who quotes the lowest price will win the right to construct and operate the wind project.

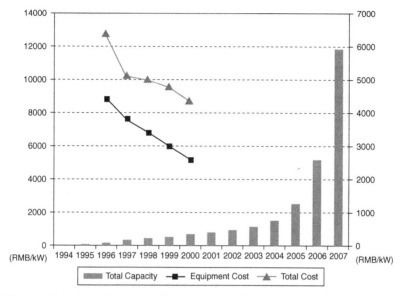

Figure 15.1. Cumulative installed capacity and cost trends for 600–750 kW wind turbines in China (1994–2007) (GWEC, 2008a)

vider for most HFC23 destruction projects in China. There is no compulsory regulation of HFC23 emissions in China and, absent the CDM, there are no other financial incentives for companies to set up HFC23 decomposition facilities. In the process of implementing a CDM project, one Chinese company even improved the original VICHEM design, which enabled the company to substantially reduce the use of alkali. "Credit sharing" between project owners and the host country government can further leverage technology transfer activities. For example, the Chinese government collects a 65 percent and 35 percent levy on CDM revenues generated by HFC23 and N_2O projects, respectively. Revenues collected from these levies have been put into a CDM fund to finance renewable energy and energy efficiency projects, support energy research and development, and increase public awareness of climate change.

The case of wind power in China shows that the CDM mechanism can contribute to technology transfer in two ways: (1) by inducing replicable technology transfer and (2) by accelerating the process of learning by doing and shortening the time to reduce cost. The objective of a technology-oriented CDM should not be to motivate com-

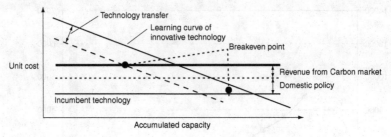

Figure 15.2 The importance of technology transfer for early action in developing countries

panies or governments to go after low-hanging fruit (i.e., low-cost mitigation options), but to spur *new* and *replicable* technology transfer from developed to developing countries. Neither the current CDM regime nor the enhanced CDM regimes that have been proposed, like programmatic CDM, policy CDM, or sectoral CDM, are sufficient to induce new and replicable technology transfer. Thus, incentives for technology transfer remain an open issue in the ongoing debate about potential CDM reforms.

Technology-oriented CDM

Success in reducing GHG emissions is highly dependent on the timing and scale of introduction of new technologies. New, climate-friendly technologies are often more expensive than existing technologies (Figure 15.2). Without innovative mechanisms to spur technology transfer, developing countries may be "locked in" to a huge amount of carbon-intensive energy infrastructure. To avoid this "lock-in" effect, early investment and accelerated application of low-carbon technology in developing country contexts is extremely important for the success of a future climate regime. Such a regime should provide sufficient and timely incentives for developing countries to invest in the most important low-carbon technologies as soon as possible. These incentives may include international efforts to lower initial investment costs, increase returns available through international carbon markets to compensate for higher costs, and support domestic policies to encourage low-carbon technology (Figure 15.2). Past experience with technology transfer in the case of gas turbines shows how the combination of these three factors can encourage low-carbon investment in developing countries and help avoid the carbon "lock-in" effect.

The case of natural gas combined-cycle (NGCC) technology transfer to China

The transfer of gas turbine technology to China has relied on a model of "binding bids." This means that the Chinese government organizes investors interested in building a gas-fired plant and bundles their equipment needs before allowing vendors to bid to supply those needs. The tendering enterprise should include a Chinese partner and a foreign partner. In addition, the foreign partner promises to transfer gas turbine technology to its Chinese partner and achieve a specified goal for local content. All major domestic and international power-plant equipment producers submitted binding bids for gas turbine technologies to the Chinese government, including Dongfang Electric in partnership with Mitsubishi, Shanghai Electric in partnership with Siemens, and Haerbin Power Equipment in partnership with GE.

Initially, Dongfang Electric contacted Alstom, GE, and Mitsubishi; it finally signed a licensing agreement with Mitubishi in April 2002 to produce and install gas turbines in China. The agreement provides for Mitsubishi to receive a royalty for each machine produced and includes a local content goal of 67 percent. The remaining 33 percent of content that does not have to be domestically produced includes core turbine components, such as the combustion chamber and turbine blades. In addition, the technology to produce high-temperature components is not transferred to the Chinese partner but to a joint venture company controlled by Mitsubishi (with a 51 percent stake). The major technology content transferred to the Chinese partner under this arrangement includes manufacturing drawings, purchase and test specifications, specific technology standards, manufacturing reference processes, and corresponding training and capacity building.

The first gas turbine produced by the Dongfang Electric was installed in Beijing with a local content of 0.2 percent. Local content increased to 46.5 percent and 58.5 percent in turbines subsequently produced by Dongfang Electric for three liquefied natural gas (LNG) projects in Guangdong. The company expects to achieve the 67 percent local content target by the end of the project.

In total, the Chinese government has conducted three binding bids for an aggregate capacity of 2.05 GW, which includes fifty-one F-type turbines[7] and four E-type[8] turbines. The unit cost of gas turbines in the third bundle has decreased by about 20 percent compared to the first bundle, mainly due to an increase in the availability of domestic components.

Although technology transfer has greatly reduced the cost of gas turbines, this lower-carbon technology still cannot compete with coal-fired power in China. The higher initial investment required for gas turbines and the higher relative price of natural gas in China makes gas-fired power plants unprofitable. Following the introduction of market reforms to the Chinese electricity sector, the National Development and Reform Commission (NDRC) forces most generators to compete with coal-fired power plants in the spot electricity market. The specific situation in the gas market also makes gas-fired power projects more risky: most operators of gas-fired power plants hold a take-or-pay contract for natural gas but they do not have any guarantees in the electricity market.

Additional income from the CDM has become a major solution for these investors to increase their profits to an acceptable level. It has been estimated that more than 20 million tons of CO_2 emissions per year[9] (approximately 1 ton of CO_2 per kW per year) could be avoided if all the gas-fired power plants planned for China are built. Almost all the projects included under the government's "binding bid" have applied for CDM credits. Four of them have registered successfully while others are still in the pipeline. Unlike the coordinated "binding bid" process for obtaining gas turbine technology, the CDM application process is more fragmented as it is conducted separately by each plant owner.

---

[7] F-type turbine has a capacity of around 250MW.
[8] E-type turbine has a capacity of around 100MW.
[9] This figure assumes 3500 hours of operation annually and 0.388 tCO_2/MWh for electricity from a gas-fired plant and 0.675 tCO_2/MWh for the baseline emission factor (the lowest grid build margin in China). Given a carbon price of $10/$tCO_2$, the extra income from CERs would be equivalent to a subsidy of about 2 cents/kWh.

The idea of a technology CDM

The Chinese gas-turbine case provides some important lessons about technology transfer. First, the whole process is technology-oriented and has as a clear goal the transfer of technology to local firms to increase the local content in gas turbines. Second, the process involves a public-private partnership, with the government as auctioneer and private firms as bidders. Third, it addresses the competitiveness concerns of developed-country firms in that the core technology is still controlled by the technology provider through a joint venture company. Fourth, scale economies have been achieved by bundling similar projects. Finally, this approach accelerates the learning curve of domestic producers. If mitigation benefits, such as CDM credits, are considered at the very beginning of projects like this, then technology transfer can be advanced, producing greater emission-reduction benefits while helping to avoid the lock-in effect.

A successful technology transfer program should do a number of things:

1. Define technology transfer priorities;
2. Establish a partnership between public and private stakeholders;
3. Address the concerns of both technology providers and recipients;
4. Bundle similar projects to achieve economies of scale; and
5. Bundle similar projects in applying for credit for carbon reductions to reduce transaction costs and further offset project costs.

A technology CDM should include all the five elements listed above; in addition, it should not only focus on the final stage of CER acquisition but on the whole technology transfer process.

The basic idea of programmatic CDM (pCDM) is that a program is a "project," while the idea of policy CDM and sectoral CDM is that a policy or a sector is a "project." The idea of a technology CDM can also be explained by viewing technology transfer as a "project." Bundling together projects that use similar technologies has two advantages: first, it produces economies of scale; second, experience shows that replicable technology transfer is likelier to occur with larger CDM projects and that bundling projects together has the effect of increasing project size.

The technology CDM also shares some of the key characteristics of pCDM. First, it can lead to a reduction in anthropogenic GHG emissions compared to the baseline emissions that would occur in the absence of the program. Second, all the projects in a "program" that adopt one type of technology (e.g., NGCC) could use the same baseline and the same monitoring methodology.[10] The whole "binding bid" could be regarded as a PoA, and each natural gas power plant under this "binding bid" could be regarded as a CPA. Once the PoA is registered successfully, a new natural gas power plant can be automatically included in the approved PoA as soon as it begins operation. Such inclusion will greatly simplify the whole process and reduce transaction costs and registration risks.

Although similar to the pCDM, the technology CDM is also unique in some respects. The most important difference is that the pCDM is solely focused on acquiring CERs, while the technology CDM would focus on the whole technology transfer process, including defining technology transfer priorities; helping stakeholders to form partnerships and collaborate; addressing the concerns of both technology providers and recipients; and facilitating the bundling of similar projects. These steps are considered not only in designing and implementing the "technology transfer program" but also in the final stage of crediting.

First, goals for technology transfer should be clearly identified based on an assessment of needs by the host country. The goal may call for a specified quantity or scale of transferred technology (e.g., 2 GW of NGCC power plant capacity or 20,000 hybrid vehicles) or it could be expressed in terms of cost reduction (e.g., a 20 percent reduction in technology cost). These goals would be used to assess whether a new project or activity can be included. Second, technology providers would be listed as participants in the technology CDM, and only projects using the technology transferred under the program could apply for CERs. This provision will help in resolving intellectual property (IP) issues. For example, if NGCC technology is successfully transferred with the participation of Siemens and Mitsubishi but without the participation of GE, then a project using GE technology can't be included in the same technology CDM, though it could apply for a regular CDM. Also, a project using domestic technology

---

[10] Such as the AM0029 methodology that has been approved by the CDM Executive Board for calculating credits for low-carbon generation technologies, including NGCC.

Table 15.1 *Comparison between pCDM and tCDM*

	pCDM	tCDM
Technology transfer	Without obligation for technology transfer	With a well-defined goal for technology transfer
Project Participants	Coordinating entities are participants. No role for technology provider if any	Technology provider should be included as participant
Project boundary	May cross countries	Within a country
Termination condition	No clear termination condition	Once the predefined goal for technology transfer is achieved or the technology is no longer eligible
Baseline	Project specific baseline	Multi-project baseline
Additionality	Based on additionality tools approved by EB	A *de facto* list approach
Credit sharing	NA	Can be shared by host countries and technology providers

couldn't be included in the technology CDM. CERs awarded under the technology CDM can be regarded as a form of guarantee for IP protection in developing countries, as the investor will prefer to be included in the technology CDM to reduce transaction costs and registration risk. Third, CERs from the technology CDM may also be shared by the government of the host country and by the technology provider if they provide enabling support for technology transfer (e.g., through policies such as feed-in tariffs) and discounted or free licensing. The "credit sharing" arrangement can be decided through negotiation. Table 15.1 summarizes the distinction between programmatic CDM (pCDM) and technology CDM (tCDM).

Advantages of tCDM

Best available technology
The tCDM can facilitate technology transfer and push it ahead of schedule. The assumed baseline for a tCDM program is not that

technology transfer would never happen, but that it would happen with a delay. The tCDM would encourage developed countries to transfer "best available" technologies to developing countries. The program can ensure that additionality is certified only for the transfer of the best available technologies.

Measurable, reportable and verifiable

The Bali Action Plan calls for the consideration of "nationally appropriate mitigation actions by developing country Parties in the context of sustainable development, supported and enabled by technology, financing and capacity-building, in a measurable, reportable and verifiable manner" (UNFCCC 2007). By promoting accelerated technology development and transfer, the tCDM can fulfill the requirements of the Bali Action Plan in the following respects. First, the tCDM creates a direct linkage between technology transfer and financing by developed countries and mitigation actions taken by developing countries. CERs from the tCDM can be shared by a technology provider or traded in the carbon market. These CERs can be regarded as a metric for measuring the technological and financial support provided by developed countries; similarly, developed countries can translate their technology transfer commitments into concrete CERs using the tCDM mechanism. Second, the whole process will follow the regular CDM process, from the submission of a project design document to validation, verification, and issuance of CERs.

Less risk for low-carbon investment

Under the regular CDM, few investors will want to pay real money for unregistered emission units, as the probability of successful registration is uncertain. Under a tCDM, by contrast, once a technology is determined to be eligible, all projects using the same technology will be automatically accepted. With less uncertainty about the future flow of CERs, project owners can sell their credit options to raise capital before the project is complete. Technology providers can also discount their prices or licensing fees in exchange for a share of the CERs that will be awarded under the tCDM for an established project activity. Reduced equipment costs will make the transferred technology more attractive.

Other issues related to the tCDM

Some methodological issues related to the tCDM

Given the particular characteristics of tCDM activities, some methodological issues will need to be considered in practice:

Baseline

Currently, the procedure for determining CDM credits is cumbersome: it requires precise calculation of baseline emissions and emissions with the project, irrespective of data availability, monitoring capacity, and incremental costs. For example, owners of a renewable electricity generation project using biomass as fuel need to include emissions associated with transporting the biomass from collection sites to the plant in calculating project emissions. Theoretically, the inclusion of such data is warranted, but collecting it has very high costs. For a 25 MW biomass generation plant, the project owner may need to document more than 20,000 pieces of data, including the type of each truck used, distance covered, fuel used, and truck efficiency to calculate overall feedstock transport emissions, even though these emissions may account for less than 1 percent of the total project impact on emissions. For this reason, the tCDM should switch from a project-specific baseline to a "multi-project" baseline (Ellis and Bosi 2000) that is aggregated at the technology level and is equivalent to an "activity standard." For example, in the case of an NGCC project, the tCDM baseline could be simply a base emissions rate, expressed in tCO_2/MWh, that reflects the baseline technology mix in the host country. Although there remain some outstanding issues for calculating multi-project baselines, this approach will undoubtedly simplify the overall process.

Additionality

Additionality is the most controversial concept in the CDM. Most project participants complain that the additionality test is the most resource-intensive part of the project approval cycle, and that criteria for additionality are not transparent—and can even be inconsistent. But without an additionality test, the environmental basis for awarding CERs will remain in question. The additionality test for tCDM could be simpler and more constructive. As in pCDM, a two-tier approach could be used to prove the additionality of technology transfer programs and individual projects. In tCDM, the technology is the project. The managing entity must demonstrate that, absent the CDM, the proposed technology transfer activity would not be implemented or would be implemented on a smaller scale. Additionality criteria for technology transfer could be applied using a "list approach," instead of the "principle approach." The list approach would identify in advance which technologies are not available in the host country and therefore which technologies would qualify as *de facto* additional. Such a list might be based on a technology needs assessment (TNA). In the case of NGCC technology in China, additionality can be established by the fact that the transfer of this technology would not otherwise happen, at least in the near term, under current market conditions. Alternatively, NGCC could be identified as additional simply by being on the "list." At the project level, it will be easier to establish additionality by using the technology barrier analysis, one of the "additionality tools" approved by the CDM Executive Board (EB),[11] if the technology to be used is not available before the implementation of the project.

Additionality can also be established based on "signaling." The difficulty of applying an additionality test stems from asymmetric information. The host country and the project owner have better information about their project than the Designated Operational Entities (DOEs) or CDM EB. The EB may question the additionality of proposed projects if EB members feel concerned about the information they don't have. The current system of dealing with this problem, which is to require that all the information be contained in the project design document, is costly, time-consuming, and controversial.

Many developing countries have special policies for preferred low-carbon technologies. These policies may include feed-in tariffs, lower taxes or subsidies, and low-interest financing. Such preferential policies should be regarded as evidence to prove additionality since they signal that the market alone will not support mitigation technologies in host countries. Also, host countries have no incentives to abuse these preferential policies.

---

[11] The CDM-EB issued a standardized tool which can be used to illustrate the additionality of a proposed project.

Participants

Both the project owner and the technology provider should be listed as participants for purposes of the tCDM. This can help safeguard the provider's intellectual property in the host country by offering him a competitive edge. The technology provider can also play the role of sole participant and CER recipient. In that case, the provider may transfer the technology to the developing country for free but ask for all or part of the CERs from associated projects in return.

Crediting period

In the tCDM, a project may join the program even after the starting time of the program; in addition, the crediting period for projects may vary.

Governance issues related to the tCDM

Defining technology transfer

There are many definitions of technology transfer, and a host country should have the discretion to choose among them based on its own national interests, as long as its definition is stated clearly. Since the tCDM would not cover multi-national projects and programs, different definitions of technology transfer in different countries won't cause confusion.

Defining the technology list

As already noted, additionality under the tCDM could be established using a *de facto* "technology list"—that is, all technologies on the list would be regarded as additional. Such technology lists can be submitted by the host country for approval by the CDM Executive Board, or the technology list can be negotiated at future Conferences of the Parties. Some parties may not accept certain choices on the technology lists submitted by other parties. For example, the Brazilian delegation strongly opposes the inclusion of carbon capture and storage (CCS) technology in the CDM. If China submits a technology list with CCS, then Brazil may oppose the list. This second approach is more time-consuming than relying on the Executive Board, as it may take years to negotiate a technology list. In any case, the list should be renewed periodically as new technologies appear and old technologies may not be considered "additional" any more.

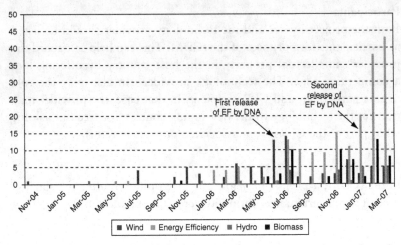

Figure 15.3. Influence of published emission factors (EFs) on the number of CDM projects in pipeline

Approval of a "multi-project" baseline

Once a technology list has been defined, a baseline would need to be established for technologies in the list. A multi-project baseline based on existing methodologies would greatly simplify the process of baseline setting. For example, the Chinese government has developed and maintained a multi-project baseline for renewable generation projects using the ACM0002 method. Publishing these baseline emission factors could greatly facilitate CDM activities (see Figure 15.3). This example also illustrates how a simplified process can contribute to further realizing a given technology's emissions reduction potential (Teng, forthcoming).

Monitoring and verification

Once the baseline is determined, the only thing that needs to be monitored is the project activity level. In most cases, monitoring and verifying project activity levels is relatively simple (e.g., metering the generation output of a natural gas power plant). If the technology is distributed and involves small appliances, like high-efficiency electric motors, then sampling should be conducted accordingly.

Conclusion

This chapter explores several possible enhancements to the CDM in a post-2012 international climate policy regime. In particular, it reviews several alternatives that have been suggested in the literature and in climate policy negotiations, including programmatic CDM (pCDM), policy CDM, and sectoral CDM. These alternatives focus on scaling up the CDM market, thereby increasing associated financial flows in international carbon markets. Technology transfer is not an explicit objective of the CDM, but it has been recognized as a possible benefit of the CDM. Although developing and developed countries differ on how to deal with technology transfer, both groups agree that technology transfer should be enhanced in a post-2012 regime.

Transferring low-carbon technologies from developed to developing countries should be a continuous process that is replicable. The concept of a tCDM offers the opportunity to strengthen technology transfer through the CDM in the near term without redesigning the whole system. A tCDM can spur the transfer of climate-friendly technology through a number of means. First, it can provide incentives for developed countries to transfer the best available technologies to developing countries and thereby avoid the possible "lock in" of carbon-intensive infrastructure. Second, the inclusion of technology providers as participants gives them a competitive advantage and thus helps to address concerns about IP protection. Third, aggregating projects on the basis of common technology can reduce project risk and transaction costs and thus can attract more low-carbon investments. Another significant advantage of the tCDM over other alternatives is the relative ease of proving additionality, as the transfer of best available technology is almost always impossible or highly unlikely in the absence of additional finance support.

The focus of this chapter is not to design a new and comprehensive solution for a post-2012 climate regime but to try to improve the existing regime. Based on experience from several rounds of climate negotiations, the authors believe that the negotiation of international climate agreements is an evolutionary and path-dependent process. A breakthrough idea is needed, but it should be arrived at through a series of gradual changes. As the old Chinese saying tells us: "Without accumulating small steps, one cannot get miles away."

References

Baumert, K. and H. Winkler (2005). "Sustainable Development Policies and Measures and International Climate Agreements," in R. Bradley and K. Baumert (eds.), *Growing in the Greenhouse: Protecting the Climate by Putting Development First*. Washington, DC: World Resources Institute, pp. 15–23.

Ellis, J. and M, Bosi (2000). *Options for Project Emission Baseline*. Paris: Organization for Economic Co-operation and Development and International Energy Agency, Pub. No. COM/ENV/EPOC/IEA/SLT(2000)8.

Ellis, J. and S. Kamel (2007). *Overcoming Barriers to Clean Development Mechanism Projects*. Paris: Organization for Economic Co-operation and Development and International Energy Agency, Pub. No. COM/ENV/EPOC/IEA/SLT(2007)3, May.

GWEC (Global Wind Energy Council) (2008a). *China Wind Power Report 2007*, available at www.gwec.net/uploads/media/wind-power-report.pdf.

(2008b). *Global Wind 2007*, available at www.gwec.net/index.php?id-90.

IEA (2008). *Energy Technology Perspective 2008: Scenarios and Strategies to 2050*. Paris: Organisation for Economic Co-operation and Development.

Lewis, J. I. (2007). *A Comparison of Wind Power Industry Development Strategies in Spain, India and China*, available at www.resource-solutions.org/lib/librarypdfs/Lewis.Wind.Industry.Development.India.Spain.China.July.2007.pdf.

Seres, S. (2007). *Analysis of Technology Transfer in CDM Projects*, prepared for the UNFCCC Registration & Issuance Unit CDM/SDM, December, available at http://cdm.unfccc.int/Reference/Reports/TTreport/report1207.pdf.

Stern, N. (2008). *Key Elements of a Global Deal on Climate Change*. London: London School of Economics, available at www.lse.ac.uk/collections/granthamInstitute/publications/KeyElementsOfAGlobalDeal_30Apr08.pdf.

Teng, F. (forthcoming). "Clean Development Mechanism Practice in China: Current Status and Possibilities for Future Regime," *Energy, The International Journal*.

UNEP Risoe Center (2008). *CDM/JI Pipeline Overview Page*, http://cdm-pipeline.org/overview.htm.

UNFCCC (2007). *Bali Action Plan*, available at http://unfccc.int/meetings/cop_13/items/4049.php.

PART IV

Global climate policy and
international trade

16 | Global environment and trade policy

JEFFREY FRANKEL[1]

The global climate regime, as represented by the Kyoto Protocol, may be on a collision course with the global trade policy regime, as represented by the WTO (World Trade Organization). Environmentalists fear that international trade will undercut efforts to reduce greenhouse gas (GHG) emissions as carbon-intensive production migrates to non-participating countries—a phenomenon known as leakage. Meanwhile businesspeople fear the adverse effects of disparate climate policies on their own competitiveness. These fears have now become prominent in the policy-making process. In early 2008, legislation to enact long-term targets for reduced GHG emissions included provisions for possible barriers against imports from countries perceived as non-participating—both in Washington, DC (where climate legislation has not yet passed) and in Brussels (where the EU Commission Directive has gone into effect). Such provisions could be interpreted as violating the rules of the WTO, which poses the nightmare scenario of a WTO panel rejecting a major country's climate change legislation. In light of the hostile feelings that such a collision would unleash, it would be a disaster for supporters of the WTO and free trade as much as for supporters of the Kyoto Protocol and environmental protection.

The clash of trade and climate policy is just the latest and largest instance of fears among many environmentalists that the WTO is an obstacle to their goals in general. The issue transcends institutions. For its critics, the WTO is a symbol of globalization, and their concerns attach also to that larger phenomenon.

Fears of a collision need not be realized. Global environmental goals and trade goals can be reconciled. Globalization and multilateral

[1] The author acknowledges useful input from Joe Aldy, Scott Barrett, Thomas Brewer, Steve Charnovitz, Gary Sampson, Rob Stavins, and an anonymous reviewer. The author would further like to thank for support the Sustainability Science Program, funded by the Italian Ministry for Environment, Land and Sea, at the Center for International Development at Harvard University.

institutions can facilitate environmental protection rather than obstruct it, if they are harnessed in the right way. Perhaps most urgent is that negotiators working on a sequel to the Kyoto Protocol agree on guidelines to govern precisely how individual countries can and cannot use trade measures in pursuit of carbon mitigation.

The first part of this chapter discusses the broader issue of whether environmental goals in general are threatened by free trade and the WTO. The second half of the chapter focuses exclusively on the narrower question of how nations' efforts to implement climate change policy will affect trade and whether they are likely to come into conflict with the WTO.

The environmental Kuznets curve

Conceptually, we must begin with the effect of economic growth on the environment, before we can address the independent effect of open trade *per se*.

Economic growth has both harmful effects on environmental quality (via the scale of industry) and beneficial effects (via shifts toward cleaner sectors and cleaner production techniques). What is the net outcome of these conflicting effects? A look at data across countries or across time allows some rough generalizations. For some important measures of environmental quality, an inverted U-shaped relationship appears: at relatively low levels of income per capita, economic growth leads to greater environmental damage, until it levels off at an intermediate level of income, after which further growth leads to improvements in the environment. This empirical relationship is known as the environmental Kuznets curve. The World Bank (1992) and Grossman and Krueger (1993, 1995) first published this statistical finding for a cross section of countries.[2] Grossman and

***

[2] Grossman and Krueger (1993, 1995) found the inverted U-shaped pattern for urban air pollution (SO_2 and smoke) and several measures of water pollution; Selden and Song (1994) found it for SO_2, suspended particulate matter (PM), oxides of nitrogen (NOx), and carbon monoxide; Shafik (1994) for deforestation, suspended PM, and SO_2; Hilton and Levinson (1998) for automotive lead emissions; Bimonte (2001) for land; and Bradford, Fender, Shore and Wagner (2005) for arsenic, chemical oxygen demand (COD), dissolved oxygen, lead, and SO_2 (but not for PM and some other measures of pollution).

Krueger (1995) estimated that sulfur dioxide (SO_2) pollution peaked when a country's income was about $5,000–$6,000 per capita (in 1985 dollars). Most developing countries have not yet reached this threshold.

For countries where a sufficiently long time series of data is available, there is also some evidence that the same inverted U-shaped relationship can hold across time. The air in major industrialized cities was far more polluted in the 1950s than it is today. A similar pattern has typically held with respect to water pollution and deforestation in rich countries.

The idea behind the environmental Kuznets curve is that, although growth is bad for air and water pollution during the initial stages of industrialization, prosperity later leads to reduced pollution as countries become rich enough to pay to clean up their environments. It would be inaccurate to portray the environmental Kuznets curve as demonstrating that if countries promote growth, the environment will eventually take care of itself. Only if pollution is largely confined within the home or within the firm does that Panglossian view apply.[3] Most conventional types of air pollution—such as SO_2, oxides of nitrogen (NOx), and so forth—are external to the home or firm. For such externalities, higher income and a popular desire to clean up the environment are not enough. There must also be effective government regulation, which usually requires a democratic system to translate popular will into action (something that was missing in the Soviet Union, for example), as well as the rule of law and reasonably intelligent mechanisms of regulation. The empirical evidence confirms that the participation of well-functioning democratic governments is an important part of the process. These requirements apply to environmental regulation at the national level. The requirements for dealing with cross-border externalities are greater still.

Another possible explanation for the Kuznets curve pattern is that it works naturally via the composition of output. In theory, the usual stages of economic development could produce the same

---

[3] Chaudhuri and Pfaff (2002) find an inverted U-shaped relationship between income and the generation of indoor smoke, across households. In the poorest households, rising incomes mean more cooking and more indoor pollution. Still-higher incomes allow a switch to cleaner fuels. Government intervention is not required.

pattern as societies transition from an agrarian economy to manufacturing, and then from manufacturing to services (Arrow *et al.* 1995; Panayotou 1993). In contrast to the conventional view, this explanation suggests that environmental improvement is less likely to require the mechanism of effective government regulation. If the Kuznets curve in practice resulted solely from this composition effect, however, then high incomes should lead to a better environment even when externalities arise at the international level, such as emissions of GHGs. Importantly, no Kuznets curve has yet appeared for carbon dioxide (CO_2), as we will see below (see, e.g., Holtz-Eakin and Selden 1995). Even though carbon emissions *per unit of gross domestic product (GDP)* do tend to fall as countries become more prosperous, this is not enough to reduce overall carbon emissions.

A third possibility is that rich countries reduce their pollution only by importing manufactured goods from lower-income countries, which become pollution havens. In this case the environmental Kuznets curve would apply only to individual countries, not to the world in the aggregate. Furthermore the pollution haven effect, to the extent it operates, is explicitly enabled by trade, the subject to which we now turn directly.

Effects of openness to trade

This chapter focuses on the implications of international trade for the global environment. Some effects come via economic growth, and some are independent of a country's level of income. In both cases, the effects can be either beneficial or detrimental. Probably the strongest effects of trade are in the first category—that is, they are directly related to growth. Much like saving and investment, technological progress, and other sources of growth, trade tends to raise income. As we have seen, higher income in turn has environmental effects that are initially adverse even though, according to the environmental Kuznets curve, they eventually turn favorable in the case of some measures of environmental quality, such as SO_2 emissions.

What about effects of trade that do not operate via economic growth? They can be classified in three categories: average global effects that are adverse (the "race to the bottom" hypothesis), average global effects that are beneficial (the "gains from trade" hypothesis), and effects that vary across countries depending on local "comparative advantage" (the "pollution haven" hypothesis).

Race to the bottom

The *"race to the bottom"* hypothesis provides perhaps the strongest basis for concerns that international trade and investment specifically (rather than industrialization generally) will put downward pressure on countries' environmental standards and thus damage the global environment. Leaders of industry, and leaders of labor unions whose members are employed in industry, are always concerned about competition from abroad. When domestic regulation raises their costs, they fear that they will become less competitive with respect to firms in other countries. They warn of a loss of sales, employment, and investment to foreign competitors.[4] Thus domestic producers often sound the competitiveness alarm as a way of applying political pressure on their governments to minimize the burden of regulation.

The "race to the bottom" concern is that, to the extent countries are open to international trade and investment, environmental standards will be lower than they would otherwise be. But how important is this dynamic in practice? Some economic research suggests that environmental regulation is not one of the most important determinants of firms' ability to compete internationally. When deciding where to locate, multinational firms seem to pay more attention to such issues as labor costs and market access than to the stringency of local environmental regulation.[5]

Once again, it is important to distinguish, first, the fear that globalization will lead to a race to the bottom in regulatory standards from, second, fears that the environment will be damaged by the very process of industrialization and economic growth itself. Opening national economies to international trade and investment could play a role in both cases, but the two possible channels for adverse environmental impacts are very different. In the race to the bottom hypothesis, the claim is that openness undermines environmental standards even for a given path of economic growth. This would be a damning conclusion

[4] Levinson and Taylor (2001) find that those US industries that have experienced the largest increase in environmental control costs have indeed also experienced the largest increases in net imports.

[5] See Jaffe, Peterson, Portney, and Stavins (1995); Grossman and Krueger (1993); Low and Yeats (1992); and Tobey (1990). Other researchers, however, have found that environmental regulation has more of an effect on direct investment decisions; see, for example, Smarzynska and Wei (2001).

from the standpoint of globalization, because it would imply that by limiting trade and investment in some way, we might be able to attain a better environment for any given level of GDP. In the second case, the implication would be that openness only affects the environment in the same way that investment, or education, or productivity growth, or any other source of growth affects the environment: by moving the economy along the environmental Kuznets curve. Trying to restrict trade and investment would be a less attractive strategy in this case, because it would amount to deliberate self-impoverishment.

Gains from trade

While the hypothesis that exposure to international competition might have an adverse effect on environmental regulation is familiar, less widely recognized and more surprising is the possibility that trade might have beneficial effects, which we will call the *gains from trade* hypothesis. Trade allows countries to attain more of what they want, which includes environmental goods in addition to market-measured outputs.

How could openness to trade have a positive effect on environmental quality, once we set aside the possibility of accelerating progress down the beneficial slope of the environmental Kuznets curve? A first possibility concerns technological and managerial innovation. Openness encourages ongoing innovation.[6] This suggests that openness could encourage innovation beneficial to environmental improvement as well as economic progress. A second possibility is an international ratcheting up of environmental standards.[7] The largest political jurisdiction can set the pace for others. Within the United States, this is called the "California effect"—when the largest state sets high standards for auto pollution-control equipment, the end result may be similar standards in other states as well. The United States can play the same role globally.

---

[6] Trade speeds the absorption of frontier technologies and management best practices. This explains why those countries that trade more than others are observed to experience higher sustained growth, rather than just a one-time increase in the level of real income, as predicted by classical trade theory.

[7] See, for example, Vogel (1995) and Braithwaite and Drahos (2000). This ratcheting up may be more effective for product standards than for standards regarding processes and production methods.

Multinational corporations are often the vehicle for these effects. They tend to bring clean state-of-the-art production techniques from high-standard countries of origin, to host countries where these techniques are not yet known. The claim is not that all multinational corporations apply the highest environmental standards when operating in other countries. Rather the claim is that their standards tend on average to be higher than if the host country were undertaking the same activity on its own (Esty and Gentry 1997, pp. 157, 161, 163; and Schmidheiny 1992).

Corporate codes of conduct offer a new way that residents of some countries can pursue environmental goals in other countries (Ruggie 2002). Formal international cooperation among governments is another way that globalization/interdependence can lead to higher environmental standards rather than lower ones (Neumayer 2002).

Evaluating the overall effects of trade on the environment

If a set of countries opens up to trade, is this development on average likely to have a positive or negative effect on the environment (for a given level of income)? In other words, which kind of effects tend, in practice, to dominate: the unfavorable "race to the bottom" effects or the favorable "gains from trade" effects? Econometrics can help answer the question.

Statistically, some measures of environmental quality are positively correlated with the level of trade. For example, countries more open to international trade, on average, experience lower levels of SO_2 pollution. But the causality is complex, running in many directions simultaneously. One would not want to claim that trade leads to a cleaner environment if, in reality, trade and environmental quality were both responding to some other, third factor, such as economic growth or democracy.

A number of studies have sought to isolate the independent effect of openness.[8] None of these studies makes allowances for the possibility

---

[8] Lucas *et al.* (1992) study the toxic intensity implied by the composition of manufacturing output and find that trade-distorting policies increase pollution in rapidly growing countries. Dean (2002) finds, on net, a beneficial effect of liberalization for a given level of income. Antweiler, Copeland, and Taylor (2001) and Copeland and Taylor (2001, 2003a) also conclude that the net effect of trade liberalization on SO_2 concentrations is beneficial.

that trade may be the *result* of other factors rather than the cause. Antweiler *et al.* (2001) point out this potential weakness. Frankel and Rose (2005) attempt to disentangle the various causal relationships by focusing on exogenous variation in trade across countries where this variation is attributable to factors such as geographical location. They find trade effects on several measures of air pollution (particularly SO_2 and NOx concentrations), for a given level of income, that are more good than bad. This suggests that the "gains from trade" effect may be at least as powerful as the "race to the bottom" effect.[9] The findings are different for emissions of CO_2, however, which appear, if anything, to be exacerbated by trade.

It is not hard to explain why carbon emissions might rise continuously with trade and growth, even while local measures of pollution improve. National governments, given the will and the money, can address local pollution because even though it is external to the household or firm, it is internal to the country. A cross-border environmental problem like global climate change, however, cannot be addressed by individual countries acting on their own, due to the free rider problem. Multilateral cooperation is required.

Cross-border institutions for cross-border problems

Even someone who does not care about trade at all should appreciate the role of international agreements and institutions given the increasing importance of major sources of environmental damage that cross national borders, and given the fact that these cross-border impacts would exist even if there were no such thing as international trade. Some externalities have long spilled over from individual countries to their neighbors; examples include SO_2 pollution, which is responsible for acid rain, or water pollution, which flows downriver. Many cross-border environmental problems can be addressed by negotiations between the two countries involved (e.g., the United States and Canada). An increasing number of environmental externalities are truly global, however. The best examples are GHGs. A ton of CO_2

---

[9] The question of whether openness has a negative effect on countries' regulatory standards overall (the race to the bottom) is distinct from the question of whether openness results in some countries becoming cleaner and others dirtier (the pollution haven hypothesis). For a review of evidence on the latter, see the pollution havens section of Frankel (2009).

creates the same global warming potential in the atmosphere regardless of where in the world it is emitted. Other good examples of direct global externalities are stratospheric ozone depletion, depletion of ocean fish stocks, and threats to biodiversity.

Processes and production methods

Even localized environmental damage, such as deforestation, is increasingly seen as a valid object of international concern. In a trade context, a distinction is traditionally made between trade measures that target specific undesirable products, such as tobacco, and those that target *processes and production methods* (PPMs), such as the use of prison labor in the manufacture of the commodity in question. It is clear that a country concerned about its own health or environment has the right to tax or ban products that it regards as harmful, such as asbestos, so long as it does not discriminate against foreign producers. Such bans are less liable to become a vehicle for surreptitious protectionism than are attempts to pass judgment on other countries' production methods that are unrelated to the physical attributes of the product itself. But is it legitimate for importing countries also to discriminate according to how a given product was produced? Some ask: what business is it of others whether the producing country wants to use its own prison labor, or cut down its own forests, or pollute its own environment?[10]

Often an international externality can be easily identified. Forests act as carbon sinks because they absorb CO_2 (through a process called sequestration)—as a result, logging contributes to global climate change. An endangered species may contain a unique genetic element that someday could be useful to international scientists. Desertification can lead to social instability and political conflict, which can in turn produce problems for international security. Thus environmental damage in one country can have indirect effects on others.

---

[10] See Charnovitz (2003a) on the history, law, and analysis of PPMs. He argues that the public failure to understand environment-friendly developments in the late 1990s within GATT/WTO jurisprudence regarding PPMs is now an obstacle to further progress (e.g., in the WTO Committee on Trade and Environment; p. 64, 103-04).

WTO *panel cases*

Environmentalists are keen to interject themselves into the WTO. Those who live in the world of international trade negotiations tell those who live in the world of environmental advocacy that their concerns may be valid, but that they should address them outside the WTO, in their own, separate negotiations, and under the auspices of their own multilateral agencies.[11]

In the post-war period, the vehicle for multilateral negotiations that succeeded in bringing down trade barriers in many countries was the General Agreement on Tariffs and Trade (GATT). The GATT organization in 1995 was replaced with a real agency, the World Trade Organization (WTO). One reason why the change was important is that the new institution featured a dispute settlement mechanism, whose findings were to be binding on the member countries. Previously, a party that did not like the ruling of a GATT panel could reject it.

Why do so many environmentalists apparently feel that the still-young WTO is a hostile power? The allegation that the GATT and WTO are hostile to environmental measures could conceivably arise from the core provisions of the GATT, which prohibit a member country from discriminating against the exports of another country in favor of "like products" made either by a third country (that is, the Most Favored Nation provision of Article I) or by domestic producers (the national treatment provision of Article III). But Article XX allows for exceptions to the non-discrimination principle for environmental reasons (among others), provided that the measures in question do not represent "a means of arbitrary or unjustifiable discrimination" or a "disguised restriction on international trade."

Under the GATT, there was ambiguity of interpretation as to what was to happen when Article XX conflicted with the non-discrimination article. To clarify the matter, in the preamble of the Articles that established the WTO, language was added to specify that the new organization's objectives were not limited to promoting trade but included also optimal use of the world's resources, sustainable development, and environmental protection. Environmental objec-

---

[11] The most prominent and articulate spokesperson for the view that trade should *not* be linked to unrelated issues is Jagdish Bhagwati (2000).

tives are also specifically recognized in WTO agreements that deal with product standards, food safety, intellectual property protection, and so on.

Given these provisions, how does one explain the common view in the anti-globalization movement that the WTO is actively harmful to the environment? When members of the protest movement identify specifics, they usually mention past rulings of WTO panels under the dispute settlement mechanism. The panels are quasi-judicial tribunals, whose job is to rule in disputes about whether parties are abiding by the rules that they have already agreed to. Like most judicial proceedings, the panels themselves are not intended to be democratic. But WTO rulings to date do not show a pattern of having been dominated by any particular country or interest group. There have been three or four fairly prominent WTO panel rulings that concern the environment in some way. Many observers within the environmentalist and non-governmental organization (NGO) community have at some point become convinced that these rulings told the United States, or another defendant country, that their attempts to protect the environment must be repealed. The mystery is why this impression is so widespread, because it has little basis in fact.

The four WTO cases that will be briefly reviewed here involve Canadian asbestos, Venezuelan reformulated gasoline, US hormone-fed beef, and Asian shrimp and turtles. We will also touch on the Mexican tuna–dolphin case. Each of the cases involves an environmental measure that the producer-country plaintiff alleged to have trade-distorting effects. None of these complaints, however, was based on the allegation that the goal of the measure was not valid, or that protectionism was the original motivation. In most of the cases, the allegation was that discrimination against foreign products was an incidental, and unnecessary, feature of the environmental measure.

Canadian asbestos
The case of Canadian asbestos was a clear win for environmental advocates. The WTO Appellate Body in 2001 upheld a French ban on asbestos products against a challenge by Canada, which had been exporting to France. This ruling made real the WTO claim that its charter gives priority to health, safety, and environmental requirements insofar as GATT Article XX explicitly allows exceptions

to the Most Favored Nation and national treatment rules for these purposes.[12]

Venezuelan reformulated gasoline

In this case, Venezuela successfully claimed that US law violated the national treatment rule—that is, it discriminated in favor of domestic producers. The case was unusual in that the intent to discriminate had, at the time the law was passed, been made explicit by US administration officials seeking to please a domestic interest group. If the WTO had ruled in favor of the United States, it would have been saying that it was fine for a country to discriminate needlessly and explicitly against foreign producers so long as the law came under an environmental label.

The United States was not blocked by this ruling from implementing its targets under the Clean Air Act, as commonly charged. Rather, the offending regulation was easily changed so as to be nondiscriminatory and thus to be permissible under the rules agreed by members of the WTO. This case sent precisely the right message to the world's governments: namely, that environmental measures should not and need not discriminate against foreign producers.

Shrimp–turtle

Perceptions regarding the WTO panel ruling on a dispute about shrimp imports and the protection of sea turtles probably vary more widely than on any other case. The perception among many environmentalists is that the panel ruling struck down a US law to protect sea turtles that are caught in the nets of shrimp fishermen in the Indian Ocean. (The provision was pursuant to the US Endangered Species Act.) In reality, the dispute resembled the gasoline case in the sense that the American ban on imports from countries without adequate regulatory regimes in place was unnecessarily selective and restrictive. The WTO panel and appellate body decided that the US application of the law, in a complex variety of ways, was arbitrarily and unjustifiably discriminatory against the four plaintiff countries. The United States had unilaterally and inflexibly banned shrimp imports from countries that did not have in place, for all shrimp production, a specific turtle-protection regime to the United States' own liking.

[12] *New York Times*, July 25, 2000.

The case could in fact be considered a victory for environmentalists, in that the WTO panel and appeals body in 1998 explicitly stated that the United States could pursue the protection of endangered sea turtles against foreign fishermen. The United States subsequently allowed more flexibility in its regulation and made good-faith efforts to negotiate an agreement with the Asian producers, which it could have done in the first place. The WTO panel and appellate body in 2001 found the new US regime to be WTO-compliant (Charnovitz 2003a). The case set a precedent in clarifying support for the principle that the WTO rules allow countries to pass judgment on other countries' processes and production methods, even if it means using trade controls to do so, provided only that the measures are not unnecessarily discriminatory.[13]

Tuna–dolphin

In an earlier attempt to protect another large, flippered sea animal, the United States had banned imports of tuna from countries that allowed fishermen to use nets that also caught dolphins. Mexico brought a case before the GATT, as this dispute pre-dated the WTO. The GATT panel ruled against the US law, in part due to features that discriminated unnecessarily against Mexican fishermen in favor of US fisherman. The GATT report was never adopted. Instead, the parties in effect worked out their differences bilaterally, "out of court." The case was considered a setback for trade-sensitive environmental measures, at least unilateral ones. But the setback proved temporary.[14] That the GATT ruling in the tuna case did not affirm the right of the United States to use trade bans to protect dolphins shows how much the environmentalist cause has progressed under the WTO, as was borne out in the subsequent gasoline, shrimp–turtle, and asbestos cases.

[13] For a full explanation of the legal issues, see Charnovitz (2003a). Also Michael Weinstein, "Greens and Globalization: Declaring Defeat in the Face of Victory," *NY Times*, April 22, 2001. Charnovitz and Weinstein (2001) argue that the environmentalists fail to realize the progress they have made in recent WTO panel cases, and may thereby miss an opportunity to consolidate those gains. It is not only environmentalists who are under the impression that the GATT rules do not allow PPMs: some developing countries also claim that PPMs violate the GATT. The motive of the first group is to fight the GATT, while the motive of the second group is to fight PPM measures.

[14] A system for labeling tuna in the US market as either "dolphin safe" or not was later found to be consistent with the GATT. The American consumer response turned out to be sufficiently great to accomplish the desired cessation of non-dolphin-safe imports.

The Kyoto Protocol and the leakage/competitiveness issue

The Kyoto Protocol on Global Climate Change, negotiated in 1997, is the most ambitious attempt at a multilateral environment agreement to date. The task of addressing climate change while satisfying the political constraints of the various factions (particularly, the United States, European Union, and developing countries) was inherently a near-impossible task. Most economists emphasize that the agreement, as it was written at Kyoto, would impose large economic costs on the United States and other countries, while making only a minor dent in the problem. The Clinton Administration's interpretation of the Protocol insisted on so-called flexibility mechanisms, such as international trading of emission permits, to bring the economic costs down to a modest range. Without the flexibility mechanisms, the United States would be out of the Protocol, even if the subsequent administration had been more environmentally friendly than it was. Ironically, when European and other countries went ahead without the United States, they found that they could not manage without such trading mechanisms.

Even those who, for one reason or another, do not believe that Kyoto was a useful step, should acknowledge that multilateral agreements will be necessary to tackle effectively the problem of global climate change. The administration of George W. Bush, even after it got past its resistance to the science, was reluctant to face up to this. The point for present purposes is that a system in which each country insists, based on an appeal to national sovereignty, that it be left to formulate environmental policies on its own, would be a world in which global externalities like climate change would not be effectively addressed.

The issues of leakage and competitiveness

Among countries making legislative attempts to limit GHG emissions, many are increasingly obsessed with twin problems related to international trade: the problems of leakage and competitiveness (Frankel 2005a, 2005b). Assume that a core of rich countries is able to agree on a target GHG emissions pathway for the remainder of the century, following the lead of Kyoto, or alternatively, is able to agree on other measures to cut back on emissions, and assume further that the path is aggressive enough at face value to go some way to achieving the atmospheric GHG concentration goals that the environmental scientists say are necessary. Even under a business–as-usual (BAU) scenario—that is, the path along which technical experts forecast that countries' emissions would increase in the absence of a climate change agreement—most of the emissions growth is expected to come from China and other developing countries. If these countries are not included in a system of binding commitments, overall global emissions will continue to grow rapidly. But the problem of leakage is worse than it may appear. Leakage means that emissions in the non-participating countries would actually rise above where they would otherwise be, thus working to undo the environmental benefits of the abatement measures adopted by rich countries. Furthermore, not wanting to become less "competitive" and pay economic costs for minor environmental benefits, the rich countries would probably lose heart and the entire effort would unravel. Thus it is essential to find ways to address concerns about competitiveness and leakage.

Developing countries

Developing countries need to be inside whatever international climate policy regime is the successor to Kyoto, for several reasons.[15]

First, as already noted, the developing countries will account for the largest share of emissions growth in coming years according to BAU projections. China, India, and other developing countries will account for as much as two-thirds of global CO_2 emissions over the course of this century, vastly exceeding the expected contribution from member countries of the Organisation for Economic Co-operation and Development (OECD), which are projected to account for roughly one-quarter of global emissions. Without the participation of major developing countries, emissions abatement by industrialized countries will not do much to mitigate global climate change.

---

[15] An additional reason that developing countries need to be included is to give the United States and other industrialized countries the opportunity to buy relatively low-cost emissions permits, which is crucial to managing the economic cost of achieving any given stabilization goal. Elaboration of this point is available from Aldy and Frankel (2004), Frankel (2007), Seidman and Lewis (2008), and many other sources.

If a quantitative international regime is implemented without the developing countries, their emissions are likely to rise even faster than current BAU projections, due to the problem of leakage. This phenomenon could come about through several (interrelated) channels. First, energy-intensive industries could relocate production from countries with emissions commitments to countries without such commitments. This could happen either if firms in these sectors relocate their plants to unregulated countries, or if firms in these sectors shrink in the regulated countries while their competitors in the unregulated countries expand. A particularly alarming possibility is that a plant in a poor unregulated country might use dirty technologies and so emit more than a plant producing the same output in a rich country with stricter environmental standards—in that case, aggregate world emissions could actually go up rather than down.

Another channel for leakage involves world energy prices. If participating countries succeed in cutting back their consumption of high-carbon fossil fuels such as coal and oil, demand will fall and prices for these fuels on world markets will decline (other things equal). This is equally true whether the initial policy is a carbon tax that raises the price of fossil fuels to rich-country consumers or if other measures are used to reduce demand. Non-participating countries would naturally respond to declining world oil and coal prices by increasing consumption.

Estimates of the likely extent of leakage (in terms of how many tons of increased emissions from developing countries would be expected for every ton abated in an industrialized country) vary. Two important studies of leakage, and of the size of border adjustments or "green tariffs" that would be necessary if countries were legitimately to counteract the problem of leakage, conclude that these impacts would be small on most traded goods.[16] But one authoritative survey reaches a less sanguine conclusion: "Leakage rates in the range 5 to 20 per cent

---

[16] And therefore that "benefits produced by border adjustment would be too small to justify their administrative complexity or their deleterious effects in trade" (McKibbin and Wilcoxen 2008). The other study is Hauser *et al.* (2008). Researchers at the OECD, however, have produced larger estimates of leakage and corresponding necessary border taxes, especially on the part of the European Union if it is the only region that is seriously taxing carbon domestically, which is more or less the current state of affairs (Brathen 2008).

are common" (International Panel on Climate Change, 2001, Chapter 8.3.2.3, pp. 536–54). Another study reports estimates of leakage ranging from 8 to 11 percent.[17]

Even more salient politically than concern about leakage is the related issue of competitiveness: specifically, the concern that domestic industries that are particularly intensive in energy or in other GHG-generating activities will be placed at a competitive disadvantage to firms in the same industries operating in non-regulated countries. Firms in such sectors as aluminum, cement, glass, paper, steel, and iron will point to real costs in terms of lost output, profits, and employment if they are subject to a GHG regulatory regime and their competitors are not (Hauser *et al.* 2008). They understandably will seek protection and are likely to get it.[18]

Measures in climate change legislation to address competitiveness and leakage

The result of environmentalists' leakage concerns and industry's competitiveness concerns is that much of the climate legislation recently proposed at the national level in the United States and elsewhere includes provisions to apply certain trade measures to imports of carbon-intensive products from countries that are deemed not to be making sufficient efforts themselves to address climate change.

---

[17] Bordoff (2008, fn. 4). One of the estimates cited by Bordoff is from McKibben *et al.* (1999), who find that if the United States had adopted its Kyoto target unilaterally, leakage would have been 10 percent. Ho, Morgenstern, and Shih (2008) also find that the imposition of a price on carbon in the United States would produce substantial leakage for some industries, especially in the short run; they conclude that petrochemicals and cement are the most adversely impacted, followed by iron and steel, aluminum, and lime products. Demailly and Quirion (2008a) and Reinaud (2008) do not find large leakage effects from the first stage of the EU Emissions Trading System; but this tells us little about the next, much more serious, stage.

[18] It is not meaningful to talk about an adverse effect on the competitiveness of the American economy in the aggregate. Those sectors low in carbon intensity would in theory *benefit* from an increase in taxes on carbon relative to everything else. This theoretical point is admittedly not very intuitive. Far more likely to resonate publicly is the example that producers of renewable energy, and of the equipment used to tap renewable energy, would benefit.

What is the right name for measures against imports from unregulated countries?

There are a variety of names for the sort of protection that carbon-intensive sectors are likely to get against imports from non-participating countries. The phrases vary widely in their connotations. A bit, but not all, of the variation is semantic.

- *Border adjustment taxes*. Technically, this phrase applies not just to import tariffs alone but to a combination of import tariffs and export subsidies. Export subsidies do not, however, seem to be under active contemplation.
- *Green tariffs*. "Import tariffs" are the most accurate description of what we are talking about; the adjective "green" converts a negative-sounding term into a positive one.
- *Import barriers*. The phrase "import barriers" also has the pejorative flavor of protectionism. It clearly includes the option—likely to be adopted in practice—of requiring importers to buy emission permits, or "international reserve allowances" in the language of the Lieberman-Warner bill introduced in the US Congress. For economists such requirements are precisely equivalent to import tariffs—the cost of the permit is the same as the tariff rate. Others would not so readily make this connection, however. International law may well defy economic logic by treating import tariffs as impermissible but permit requirements for imports as acceptable (Pauwelyn 2007; Brewer 2008; and Fischer and Fox 2009).
- *Import penalties*. The term "penalties" is a bit like the term "barriers" in its generality. Both terms have the added advantage of connoting a tie to behavior in the exporting country—in this case, insufficient action on climate change—while yet sounding less extreme than "sanctions."
- *Import measures*. "Measures" is the term that maximizes generality and neutrality.
- *Carbon-equalization taxes*. A well-designed policy to target leakage and competitiveness concerns could be described as equalizing the effective tax on the carbon content of goods produced domestically versus goods imported from abroad. One hopes that "carbon equalization" is not used as a euphemism for domestic subsidies or rebates.

- *Trade sanctions.* An alternative function of import measures is to encourage those countries not participating in a post-Kyoto multi-lateral climate policy architecture to enlist.
- *Trade controls.* Trade controls fall only on environmentally rel-evant sectors. Trade sanctions, on the other hand, target products that are arbitrary and unrelated to the non-compliant act. They are used multilaterally only by the WTO and United Nations Security Council, and are not currently under consideration as a mechanism for addressing climate change (Charnovitz 2003b, p. 156).

Pauwelyn (2007) compares some of these options more carefully, from a legal standpoint. Fischer and Fox (2009) compare four of them from an economic standpoint: import tax alone, export rebate alone, full border adjustment, and domestic production rebate. Hufbauer, Charnovitz, and Kim (2009, Chapter 3) are more exhaustive still. Recent papers that compare the options in a European context include Demailly and Quiron (2008b), Reinaud (2008), and Alexeeva-Talebi, Loschel and Mennel (2008).

Possible application of trade barriers by the United States

Of twelve market-based climate change bills introduced in the 110th Congress, almost half called for some border measures: typically a requirement that importers of energy-intensive goods surrender permits corresponding to the carbon emissions embodied in those goods (which is equivalent to a tariff on these imports).[19] The Bingaman-Specter "Low Carbon Economy Act of 2007" would have provided that "If other countries are deemed to be making inad-equate efforts [in reducing global GHG emissions], starting in 2020 the President could require importers from such countries to submit special emission allowances (from a separate reserve pool) to cover the carbon content of certain products." Similarly the Lieberman-Warner bill would have required the president to determine what countries have taken comparable action to limit GHG emissions; for imports of covered goods from covered countries, starting in 2020, it would have required the importer to buy international reserve allowances

---

[19] Source: Resources for the Future; or Hufbauer, Charnovitz and Kim (2009, Table 1.A.2).

(S. 2191: "America's Climate Security Act of 2007," Sections 6005–6006). These requirements would be equivalent to a tax on covered imports. The major candidates in the US presidential election campaign of 2008 supported some version of these bills, including import measures in the name of safeguarding competitiveness vis-à-vis developing countries.

In addition, a different law that has already passed and gone into effect poses similar issues: "The Energy Independence & Security Act of 2007" explicitly "limits US government procurement of alternative fuel to those from which the lifecycle greenhouse gas emissions are equal to or less than those from conventional fuel from conventional petroleum sources."[20] Canada's oil sands are vulnerable. Since Canada has ratified the Kyoto Protocol and the United States has not, the legality of this measure strikes this author as questionable.

Possible application of trade barriers by the European Union

It is possible that many in Washington don't realize that the United States is likely to be the victim of legal sanctions before it is the wielder of them. In Europe, where firms have already entered the first Kyoto budget period of binding emission limits, competitiveness concerns are well-advanced and the non-participating United States is an obvious target of resentment (Bhagwati and Mavroidis 2007; Bierman and Brohm 2005; and Government of Sweden 2004).

After the United States failed to ratify the Protocol, European parliamentarians proposed a "Kyoto carbon tax" against imports from the United States.[21] The European Commission had to make a decision on the issue in January 2008, when the European Union determined its emission targets for the post-Kyoto period. In preparation for this decision, French President Nicolas Sarkozy warned:

... if large economies of the world do not engage in binding commitments to reduce emissions, European industry will have incentives to relocate to such countries... The introduction of a parallel mechanism for border compensation against imports from countries that refuse to commit to binding reductions therefore appears essential, whether in the form of a tax adjustment or an obligation to buy permits by importers. This mechanism

[20] Section 526. Source: *FT*, Mar. 10, 2008.
[21] *FT*, Jan. 24, 2008.

is in any case necessary in order to induce those countries to agree on such a commitment.[22]

The envisioned mechanism sounds similar to that in the Bingaman-Specter and Lieberman-Warner bills in the United States, with the difference that it could go into effect soon, since Europe is already limiting emissions whereas the United States is not.

In the event, the EU Commission included instead the following provision in its Directive:

Energy-intensive industries which are determined to be exposed to significant risk of carbon leakage could receive a higher amount of free allocation or an effective carbon equalization system could be introduced with a view to putting EU and non-EU producers on a comparable footing. Such a system could apply to importers of goods requirements similar to those applicable to installations within the EU, by requiring the surrender of allowances.[23]

The second of the two options, "carbon equalization" sounds consistent with what is appropriate (and with the sort of measures suggested by Sarkozy and spelled out in detail in the US bills). The first option, however, is badly designed. Yes, it would help European industries that are carbon-intensive and therefore vulnerable to competition from non-members by giving them a larger quantity of free emission permits. Given the market in tradable permits that already exists in the European Union, giving a firm free permits is the same as giving them a cash subsidy. According to simple microeconomic theory, however, these subsidies would do nothing to address leakage. Because carbon-intensive production is cheaper in non-participating countries, the European firms would simply sell the permits they receive and pocket the money, while carbon-intensive production would still move from Europe to non-participants.[24] Recipient firms might even use the money to buy or develop their own subsidiaries in unregulated countries.[25]

[22] Letter to EU Commission President Jose Manuel Barroso, January 2008.

[23] Source: Paragraph 13, Directive of the European Parliament & of the Council amending Directive 2003/87/EC so as to improve and extend the EU greenhouse gas emissions allowance trading system; Brussels, Jan. 2008.

[24] This logic presumes that the subsidies are tied to past production, rather than ongoing production. But this is the idea of course: a system of granting permits based on future production would encourage emissions rather than the reverse.

[25] One important study, Hauser *et al.* (2008) tends to favor such domestic subsidies, and opposes border measures, in part because the latter are judged to be

Admittedly there might in practice be some effects from granting free allowances to affected industries: for example, an infusion of liquidity might keep a firm operating that otherwise would go bankrupt. But overall there would probably be almost as much leakage as if there had been no policy response at all. Perhaps the purpose behind this subsidy option is not to minimize leakage, for which free allowances are the wrong remedy, nor even to punish non-participating countries, but simply to buy off domestic interests so that they will not oppose action on climate change politically. But in this case it is important to make sure politicians understand that this is what they are doing, because the rhetoric is different and the economic logic is subtle.

Would trade controls or sanctions be compatible with the WTO?

Would measures that are directed against CO_2 emissions in other countries, as embodied in electricity or in goods produced using electricity or other carbon-emitting forms of energy, be acceptable under international law? Not many years ago, most international experts would have said that import barriers against carbon-intensive goods, whether in the form of tariffs or quantitative restrictions, would necessarily violate international agreements. Under GATT, although countries could use import barriers to protect themselves against environmental damage that would otherwise occur within their own borders, they could not use import barriers to affect how goods are produced in foreign countries—that is, they could not impose barriers on the basis of processes and production methods (PPMs). A notorious example was the GATT ruling against US barriers to imports of tuna from Mexico on the basis of dolphin-unfriendly fishing practices. But things have changed, as explained in the previous section summarizing WTO panel cases.

The WTO came into existence, succeeding the GATT, at roughly the same time as the Kyoto Protocol. The drafters of each treaty showed more consideration for the other than do the rank and file among envi-

Footnote 25 (*cont.*)
   more likely to run afoul of the WTO. I come to the opposite conclusion, for the reasons stated and also because subsidies to sectors facing international competition run contrary to the WTO as import tariffs do.

ronmental and free-trade advocates, respectively. The WTO regime is more respectful of the environment than was its predecessor. Article XX allows exceptions to Articles I and III for purposes of health and conservation. The Preamble to the 1995 Marrakech Agreement that established the WTO seeks "to protect and preserve the environment;" while the 2001 Doha Communiqué that sought to start a new round of free trade negotiations declared: "the aims of...open and non-discriminatory trading system, and acting for the protection of the environment...must be mutually supportive." The Kyoto Protocol text is equally solicitous of the trade regime. It says that Parties to the Protocol should "strive to implement policies and measures...to minimize adverse effects...on international trade..." The United Nations Framework Convention on Climate Change (UNFCCC) features similar language.

GHG emissions are the result of processes and production methods. Is this an obstacle to the application of trade measures to address these emissions at the border? I don't see why it has to be. Three precedents can be cited: sea turtles, stratospheric ozone, and Brazilian tires.

The true import of the 1998 WTO panel decision on the shrimp–turtle case was missed by almost everyone. The major significance of this decision was its pathbreaking ruling that environmental measures can target not only exported products (under Article XX), but also the processes and production methods (PPMs) used by trading partners in supplying these products—subject, as always, to the non-discrimination provisions of Articles I and III. The United States was, in the end, able to seek to protect turtles in the Indian Ocean, provided it did so without discriminating against Asian fishermen. Environmentalists failed to notice or consolidate the PPM precedent, and (to the contrary) were misguidedly up in arms over this case.[26]

Another important precedent for harmonizing trade and environmental goals was established by the Montreal Protocol on stratospheric ozone depletion, which contained controls on trade in ozone depleting substances (ODSs) and products that contain ODSs. These controls had two motivations:[27]

---

[26] For a full explanation of the legal issues, see the references cited in footnote 13.

[27] Brack (1996). Barrett (1997) shows theoretically how multilateral trade sanctions can enforce a multilateral environmental treaty.

1. to encourage countries to join, and
2. to minimize leakage (if major countries had remained outside
   the Montreal Protocol, the controls would have minimized the
   migration of production of banned substances to nonparticipating
   countries).

In the event, (1) worked, so (2) was not needed.

These two examples—the shrimp–turtle decision and the Montreal
Protocol precedent—go a long way towards establishing the legitimacy of trade measures against PPMs. Many trade experts, including
economists and international lawyers, let alone representatives of
India and other developing countries, are not yet convinced[28] of the
legitimacy of such measures. I personally have come to believe that
the Kyoto Protocol could have followed the Montreal Protocol by
incorporating well-designed trade controls aimed at non-participants.
One aspect of climate change that strengthens the applicability of the
precedent is that we are not talking about targeting practices in other
countries that harm solely the local environment, where the country
can make the case that this is nobody else's business. Depletion of
stratospheric ozone and endangerment of sea turtles are global externalities. (It helped that these are turtles that migrate globally.) So is
climate change from GHG emissions. A ton of carbon emitted into the
atmosphere hurts all residents of the planet.

In case there is any doubt that Article XX, which uses the phrase
"health and conservation," applies to environmental concerns such
as climate change, a third precedent is relevant. In 2007, a new
WTO Appellate Body decision regarding Brazilian restrictions on
imports of retreaded tires confirmed the applicability of Article
XX(b), which accords "considerable flexibility to WTO Member
governments when they take trade-restrictive measures to protect
life or health. . .[and] apply equally to issues related to trade and
environmental protection. . .including measures taken to combat
global warming."[29]

---

[28] Some experts believe that even multilateral trade penalties against non-members
   might not be permissible under the WTO. See Sampson (2000), p. 87. Of
   course, countries wishing to participate in such a system could always withdraw
   from the WTO.
[29] Source: Brendan McGivern, Dec. 12, 2007.

Some principles for designing legitimate penalties on carbon-intensive imports

While the shrimp–turtle case and the Montreal Protocol help establish the principle that well-designed trade measures can legitimately target PPMs, they also suggest principles that should help guide drafters as to what is good design.

First, the existence of a multilaterally negotiated international treaty such as the Kyoto Protocol conditions the legitimacy of unilateral trade controls. On the one hand, that leakage to non-members could negate the goal of the Protocol strengthens the case for (the right sort of) trade controls. Trade controls imposed in this context are stronger, for example, than in the shrimp–turtle case, which was primarily a unilateral US measure.[30] On the other hand, the case for unilateral controls on the basis of climate concerns is weaker than it was for the Montreal Protocol, where the Protocol itself defined multilaterally-agreed trade controls. (Multilateral initiatives like the latter are on firmer ground than unilateral initiatives.) The Kyoto Protocol could have made explicit allowance for multilateral trade controls, but its negotiators chose not to. The case would be especially weak for American measures if the United States has still not ratified the Kyoto Protocol or a successor agreement. The Europeans have a relatively good case against the United States, until such time as the United States ratifies. But the case would be stronger still if a future multilateral agreement, for example under the UNFCCC, agreed on the legitimacy of trade controls and on guidelines for their design.

Second, there is the question of the sorts of goods or services that would be subject to penalty. It would certainly be legitimate to apply tariffs against coal itself, assuming domestic taxation of coal or a domestic system of tradable permits were in place. It is probably also legitimate to apply tariffs to the carbon content of electricity, though this requires acceptance of the PPM principle. The big question is whether it is legitimate to impose trade measures on the basis of the

---

[30] Webster (2008) explains that unilateral measures more likely acceptable if in pursuit of an existing multilateral agreement such as the Kyoto Protocol. Even sea turtles are, however, given some protective status by their inclusion in Appendix 1 of the Convention on International Trade in Endangered Species of Wild Fauna and Flora.

carbon or energy content of manufactured goods. Trade sanctions would probably not be legitimate when applied solely as punishment for free riding against unrelated products of a non-member country or, in a more extreme case, on clean inputs—e.g., a ban on US turbines used for low-carbon projects (unless perhaps there was multilateral agreement among UNFCCC members on economy-wide sanctions—an unlikely prospect).[31]

Paradoxically, the need to keep out coal-generated electricity or aluminum from non-members of the Kyoto Protocol is greater than the need to keep out coal itself. The reason is that the Protocol already puts limits on within-country emissions. If one assumes the limits are enforced, then the world community has no particular interest in how a country goes about cutting its emissions. But if the country imports coal-generated electricity or aluminum from non-members, the emissions occur outside its borders and the environmental objective is undermined.

Unfortunately, it is difficult to determine the carbon content of manufactured goods. The best option would be to focus on the half-dozen largest-scale, most energy-intensive industries—a category that probably includes aluminum, cement, steel, paper, and glass. Even here there are difficult questions, however. What if the energy used to smelt aluminum in another country is cleaner than in the importing country (Iceland's energy comes from hydro and geothermal power) or dirtier (much of Australia's energy comes from coal)? How can one distinguish the marginal carbon content of the energy used for a particular aluminum shipment from the average carbon content of energy in the country of origin? These are questions that will have to be answered. Pauwelyn (2007) proposes that the US Customs Bureau assign imports an implicit carbon content based on the production techniques that are dominant in the United States, as a back-up when the foreign producer does not voluntarily provide the information needed to calculate carbon content; apparently there is precedent for this approach.

As soon as one goes beyond a half-dozen industries, however, it becomes too difficult for even a good-faith investigator to discern the

---

[31] Charnovitz (2003b, 156) emphasizes the distinction between trade controls, which fall on environmentally relevant sectors, versus trade sanctions, where the targeted products are arbitrary and unrelated to the noncompliant act (and are used multilaterally only by the WTO and UN Security Council).

effective carbon content. This approach is also too liable to abuse. One would not want to attempt to levy tariffs against car parts that are made with metal produced in a carbon-intensive way, or against the automobiles that use those car parts (which could include efficient, high-mileage hybrids) or against the products of firms that bought the cars, and so on.

The big danger

Just because a government measure is given an environmental label does not necessarily mean that it is motivated primarily—or even at all—by *bona fide* environmental objectives. To see the point one has only to look at the massive mistake of American subsidies to ethanol (and concurrent protection against competing imports of biofuels from Brazil). If each country on its own imposes border adjustments for imports in whatever way suits its national politics, those adjustments will be poorly targeted, discriminatory, and often covertly protectionist. When reading the language in the US Congressional bills or the EU decision, it is not hard to imagine that special interests could manipulate, for protectionist purposes, the process whereby each government decides whether other countries are doing their share, and what foreign competitors merit penalties.[32] If so, the competitiveness provisions may indeed run afoul of the WTO, and would in that case deserve to be struck down.

It is important who makes the determinations regarding what countries are abiding by carbon-reduction commitments, who can retaliate against the non-compliers, what sectors are fair game, and what sorts of barriers are appropriate. One policy conclusion is that these decisions should be delegated to independent panels of experts, rather than be left to politicians.

The most important policy conclusion is that we need a multilateral regime to guide climate-related trade measures. Ideally the regime

---

[32] The Congressional language imposing penalties on imports from countries that do not tax carbon was apparently influenced by the International Brotherhood of Electrical Workers, which regularly lobbies for protection of American workers from foreign competition. Alan Beattie, *FT*, Jan. 24, 2008. Simultaneously, the European Trade Union Confederation urged the EU Commission to tax imports from countries that refuse to reduce GHG emissions. "Unions back carbon tax on big polluting nations," AP and *Wall Street Journal*, Jan. 16, 2008.

would be negotiated along with a successor to the Kyoto Protocol that sets emissions targets for future periods and brings the United States and developing countries inside. But if that process takes too long, it might be useful in the shorter run for the United States to enter negotiations with the European Union to harmonize guidelines for border penalties, perhaps in consultation with the secretariats of the UNFCCC and the WTO (Sampson 1999).

Why take multilateralism seriously?

"Why should WTO obligations be taken seriously?" some may ask. Three possible answers may be ventured, based on considerations of international citizenship, good policy, and realpolitik.

Regarding international citizenship, the broader question is whether the United States wants to return to the highly successful post-war strategy of adherence to international law and full membership in— indeed leadership of—multilateral institutions. This course does not mean routinely subordinating American law, let alone American interests, to international law. There will be cases where the United States wants to go its own way. But efforts to address climate change surely do not (or should not) represent one of those cases. Among other reasons is the fact that GHG emissions are inherently a global externality. No single country can address climate change on its own, due to the free rider problem. While there is a role for unilateral action on climate change—for example, by the United States as part of a short-term effort to demonstrate seriousness of purpose and begin to catch up with the record of the Europeans—in the long term, multilateral action offers the only hope of addressing the problem. The multilateral institutions to do so are already in place—specifically the UNFCCC, the Kyoto Protocol, and the WTO—and all of them were created with strong US leadership.

Moreover, the basic designs and operations of these institutions happen to be relatively sensible, taking political realities as given. They are more sensible than most critics of international institutions and of their alleged violations of national sovereignty typically believe. This applies whether the critics are on the left or the right of the political spectrum, and whether their main concern is the environment or the economy. One can place very heavy weight on economic goals, and yet realize the desirability of addressing externalities, minimizing leakage, dealing with competitiveness concerns, and so forth. Likewise, one can place very heavy weight on environmental goals, and yet realize the virtues of market mechanisms, non-discrimination, reciprocity, addressing international externalities *cooperatively*, preventing special interests from hijacking environmental language for their own financial gain, and so forth.

The third reason why the United States should be prepared to modify the sort of "international reserve allowances" language of the Lieberman-Warner bill and move in the direction of multilateral coordination of guidelines for climate-related trade measures is grounded in hard-headed self interest. Section 6006 of Lieberman-Warner originally envisioned these measures going into effect only in 2020. This was as it should be, since any such bill must give the United States time to start playing the game before it can presume to punish other players for infractions.[33] But the EU language could be translated into penalties against US products any day. It is in the American interest to have any border penalties governed by a sensible system of multilateral guidelines. The Europeans might welcome US participation in joint negotiations to agree on guidelines, as part of a process of negotiations over a Kyoto-successor regime. The argument is stronger than an argument based on historical examples of US import barriers that led to subsequent emulation and retaliation, which eventually came back to hit US exports (e.g., the Smoot Hawley tariff in 1930, anti-dumping cases in the 1980s, etc.). Here the United States has an opportunity to influence other countries' barriers against its goods, probably more than ten years before the United States would be erecting barriers against others' goods.

Concluding recommendations

The issues raised in this chapter need further study. Both the economics and the law are complicated. Nevertheless, the chapter is able to offer a central message: border measures to address leakage need not necessarily violate the WTO or sensible trade principles, but there is a very great danger that in practice they will.

---

[33] The revised version of the bill, which the Senate voted on in the spring of 2008, would have moved the import measures much closer to the present. One hopes that any version of the bill that might pass in 2009 would recognize that the United States cannot very well set itself up in judgment of other countries before it has begun to take any steps of its own to fulfill the Kyoto agreement.

I conclude with some subjective judgments as to principles that could guide a country's border measures—if its goal were indeed to reduce leakage and avoid artificially tilting the playing field toward carbon-intensive imports of non-participating countries. Based on their characteristics, I classify possible border measures into two categories, which I will name by color (for lack of better labels):

1. The "Black" category—measures that seem to me very dangerous, in that they are likely to become an excuse for protectionism; and
2. The "White" category—measures that seem to me reasonable and appropriate.[34]

The Black (inappropriate) border measures include:

- Unilateral measures applied by countries that are not participating in the Kyoto Protocol or its successors.
- Judgments as to findings of fact that are made by politicians, vulnerable to political pressure from interest groups seeking special protection.
- Unilateral measures that seek to restrict trade with particular partners more broadly, rather than targeting narrowly-defined, energy-intensive sectors.
- Import barriers against products that are further removed from the carbon-intensive activity, such as firms that use inputs that are produced in an energy-intensive process.
- Subsidies—whether in the form of money or extra permit allocations—to domestic sectors that are considered to have been put at a competitive disadvantage. (One must note that the aversion to subsidies is based on economists' logic. International lawyers may have the opposite ranking.)

The White (appropriate) border measures could include either tariffs or (equivalently) a requirement for importers to surrender tradable permits. Guiding principles for inclusion in this category include:

[34] Hufbauer, Charnovitz and Kim (2009, Chapter 5) call this category "the green space" and present a list of desirable attributes which is more authoritative than the one I had drawn up, at least from a legal standpoint. Green is the more familiar color, but I had thought to avoid it because of possible confusion with the "green box" of the WTO's Agreement on Agriculture.

- Measures should follow some multilaterally-agreed set of guidelines among countries participating in the Kyoto Protocol and/or its successors.
- Judgments as to findings of fact—for example, what countries are complying or not, what industries are involved and what is their carbon content, what countries are entitled to respond with border measures, or what is the nature of allowable responses—should be made by independent panels of experts.
- Measures should only be applied by countries that are reducing their emissions in line with the Kyoto Protocol and/or its successors, against countries that are not participating, either due to their refusal to join or to their failure to comply.
- Import penalties should target fossil fuels, electricity, and a half-dozen of the most energy-intensive major industries (e.g., aluminum, cement, steel, paper, glass, iron and chemicals).

If countries follow these guidelines, the border penalties they enact are more likely to be consistent with the avowed goals of preventing leakage and undue loss of competitiveness and less likely to fall afoul of the WTO. If countries do not follow these guidelines—which may be the more likely outcome—the trade measures they devise will more probably be inconsistent with environmental and competitiveness goals, and with the WTO as well.

References

Aldy, Joseph, Scott Barrett, and Robert Stavins (2003). "Thirteen Plus One: A Comparison of Global Climate Architectures," *Climate Policy* 3(4): 373–97.

Aldy, Joseph, and Jeffrey Frankel (2004). "Designing a Regime of Emission Commitments for Developing Countries that is Cost-Effective and Equitable," *G20 Leaders and Climate Change*, Council on Foreign Relations.

Alexeeva-Talebi, Victoria, Andreas Loschel, and Tim Mennel (2008). "Climate Policy and the Problem of Competitiveness: Border Tax Adjustments or Integrated Emissions Trading?" Discussion Paper 08-061, Zentrum fur Europaische Wirtschaftsforschung GmbH, Mannheim, Germany.

Antweiler, Werner, Brian Copeland, and Scott Taylor (2001). "Is Free Trade Good for the Environment?" *American Economic Review* 91(4): 877–908.

Arrow, K., R. Bolin, P. Costanza, P. Dasgupta, C. Folke, C. S. Holling, B. O. Jansson, S. Levin, K. G. Maler, C. Perrings, and D. Pimentel (1995). "Economic Growth, Carrying Capacity, and the Environment," *Science* 268: 520–1.

Barrett, Scott (1997). "The Strategy of Trade Sanctions in International Environmental Agreements," *Resource and Energy Economics* 19: 345–1.

   (2003). "Trade Leakage and Trade Linkage," *Environment and Statecraft: The Strategy of Environmental Treaty-Making*. Oxford: Oxford University Press.

Bhagwati, Jadgish (2000). "On Thinking Clearly About the Linkage Between Trade and the Environment," *The Wind of the Hundred Days: How Washington Mismanaged Globalization*. Cambridge, MA: MIT Press, pp. 189–200.

Bhagwati, Jagdish and Petros C. Mavroidis (2007). "Is Action Against U.S. Exports for Failure to Sign the Kyoto Protocol WTO-Legal?" *World Trade Review* 6: 299–310.

Bierman, F. and R. Brohm (2005). "Implementing the Kyoto Protocol Without the United States: The Strategic Role of Energy Tax Adjustments at the Border," *Climate Policy* 4(3): 289–302.

Bimonte, Salvatore (2001). "Model of Growth and Environmental Quality, A New Evidence of the Environmental Kuznets Curve," Universita degli Studi di Siena, Quaderni, no. 321, April.

Bordoff, Jason (2008). "International Trade Law and the Economics of Climate Policy: Evaluating the Legality and Effectiveness of Proposals to Address Competitiveness and Leakage Concerns," *Climate Change, Trade and Investment Conference: Is a Collision Inevitable?*. Washington DC: Brookings Institution.

Brack, Duncan (1996). *International Trade and the Montreal Protocol*. London: The Royal Institute of International Affairs and Earthscan Publications, Ltd.

Bradford, David, Rebecca Fender, Stephen Shore, and Martin Wagner (2005). "The Environmental Kuznets Curve: Exploring a Fresh Specification," *Contributions to Economic Analysis & Policy*, Berkeley Electronic Press 4 (1): 1073–1073. Revised version of David Bradford, Rebecca Schlieckert and Stephen Shore, 2000, "The Environmental Kuznets Curve: Exploring a Fresh Specification," NBER Working Paper no. 8001.

Braithwaite, John and Peter Drahos (2000). *Global Business Regulation*. Cambridge, UK: Cambridge University Press.

Brathen, Nils Axen (2008). "Carbon-Related Border Tax Adjustments," Comments at conference *on Climate Change, Trade and Investment: Is a Collision Inevitable?* June 9, 2008, Brookings Institution, Washington, DC, organized by Lael Brainard.

Brewer, Thomas L. (2003). "The Trade Regime and the Climate Regime: Institutional Evolution and Adaptation," *Climate Policy* 3(4): 329–41.

(2004a). "Multinationals, the Environment and the WTO: Issues in the Environmental Goods and Services Industry and in Climate Change Mitigation," in S. Lundan, A. Rugman and A. Verbecke (eds.), *Multinationals, the Environment and Global Competition.* Oxford: Elsevier, p. 195.

(2004b). "The WTO and the Kyoto Protocol: Interaction Issues," *Climate Policy* 4(1): 3–12.

(2008). "U.S. Climate Change Policy and International Trade Policy Intersections: Issues Needing Innovation for a Rapidly Expanding Agenda," Paper Prepared for a Seminar of the Center for Business and Public Policy Georgetown University, February 12.

Charnovitz, Stephen (2003a). "The Law of Environmental 'PPMs' in the WTO: Debunking the Myth of Illegality," *The Yale Journal of International Law* 27(1): 59–110.

(2003b). "Trade and Climate: Potential Conflicts and Synergies," in *Beyond Kyoto: Advancing the International Effort Against Climate Change,* Pew Center on Global Climate Change, pp. 141–67.

Charnovitz, Steve and Michael Weinstein (2001). "The Greening of the WTO," *Foreign Affairs* 80(6): 147–56.

Chaudhuri, Shubham and Alexander Pfaff (2002). "Economic Growth and the Environment: What Can We Learn from Household Data?" Columbia University, February.

Copeland, Brian and Scott Taylor (2001). "International Trade and the Environment: A Framework for Analysis," NBER Working Paper No. 8540, October.

(2003a). *Trade and the Environment: Theory and Evidence.* Princeton, NJ: Princeton University Press.

(2003b). "Trade, Growth and the Environment," NBER Working Paper No. 9823, July.

Daly, Herman (1993). "The Perils of Free Trade," *Scientific American* (November): 51–55.

Dean, Judy (1992). "Trade and the Environment: A Survey of the Literature," in Patrick Low (ed.), *International Trade and the Environment,* World Bank Discussion Paper No. 159.

(2001). "Overview," in J. Dean, (ed.), *International Trade and the Environment,* International Library of Environmental Economics and Policy Series, UK: Ashgate Publishing.

(2002). "Does Trade Liberalization Harm the Environment? A New Test," *Canadian Journal of Economics* 35(4): 819–42.

Demailly, D. and P. Quirion (2008a). "European Emission Trading Schemes and Competitiveness: A Case Study on the Iron and Steel Industry," *Energy Economics* 30: 2009–27.

(2008b). "Leakage from Climate Polices and Border Tax Adjustment: Lessons from a Geographic Model of the Cement Industry," forthcoming in Roger Guesnerie and Henry Tulkens (eds.), *The Design of Climate Policy.* Cambridge, MA: MIT Press.

Dua, Andre and Daniel Esty (1997). *Sustaining the Asia Pacific Miracle: Environmental Protection and Economic Integration.* Washington DC: Institute for International Economics.

Ederington, Josh, Arik Levinson, and Jenny Minier (2003). "Footloose and Pollution-Free," NBER Working Paper No. 9718, May.

Esty, Daniel (1994). *Greening the GATT: Trade, Environment, and the Future.* Washington DC: Institute for International Economics.

(2001). "Bridging the Trade-Environment Divide," *Journal of Economic Perspectives* 15(3): 113–30.

Esty, Daniel and Bradford Gentry (1997). "Foreign Investment, Globalisation, and the Environment," in Tom Jones (ed.), *Globalization and the Environment.* Paris: Organization for Economic Cooperation and Development, pp. 141–72.

Esty, Daniel and Michael Porter (2001). "Measuring National Environmental Performance and Its Determinants," Yale Law School and Harvard Business School, April.

Fischer, Carolyn and Alan Fox (2009). "Comparing Policies to Combat Emissions Leakage: Border Tax Adjustment versus Rebates," Discussion Paper, February.

Frankel, Jeffrey (2004). "Kyoto and Geneva: Linkage of the Climate Change Regime and the Trade Regime," for Broadening Climate Discussion: The Linkage of Climate Change to Other Policy Areas, FEEM/MIT conference, Venice.

(2005a). "Climate and Trade: Links Between the Kyoto Protocol and WTO," in *Environment* 47(7): 8–19.

(2005b). "The Environment and Globalization," in Michael Weinstein (ed.), *Globalization: What's New.* New York: Columbia University Press, pp. 129–69. Reprinted in R. Stavins (ed.), *Economics of the Environment: Selected Readings,* Fifth Edition. New York: W.W. Norton.

(2007). "Formulas for Quantitative Emission Targets," in Joe Aldy and Robert Stavins (eds.), *Architectures for Agreement: Addressing Global Climate Change in the Post Kyoto World.* New York: Cambridge University Press, pp. 32–56.

(2008). "Addressing the Leakage/Competitiveness Issue In Climate Change Policy Proposals," *Climate Change, Trade and Investment: Is a Collision Inevitable?* Brookings Institution, Washington, DC, organized by Lael Brainard.

(2009). *Environmental Effects of International Trade*, Expert Report No. 31 to Sweden's Globalisation Council, Government of Sweden, Stockholm.

Frankel, Jeffrey and Andrew Rose (2005). "Is Trade Good or Bad for the Environment? Sorting out the Causality," *Review of Economics and Statistics* 87(1): 85–91.

Goulder, Lawrence and Robert Stavins (2002). "An Eye on the Future," *Nature* 419: 673–4.

Government of Sweden, Kommerskollegium (2004). *Climate and Trade Rules—Harmony or Conflict?.*

Grossman, Gene and Alan Krueger (1993). "Environmental Impacts of a North American Free Trade Agreement," in Peter Garber (ed.), *The Mexico-U.S. Free Trade Agreement.* Cambridge, MA: MIT Press, pp. 13–56.

(1995). "Economic Growth and the Environment," *Quarterly Journal of Economics* 110(2): 353–77.

Hanley, Nick, Jason Shogren, and Ben White (1997). *Environmental Economics in Theory and Practice.* New York: Oxford University Press.

Hauser, Trevor, Rob Bradley, Britt Childs, Jacob Werksman, and Robert Heilmayr (2008). *Leveling the Carbon Playing Field: International Competition and US Climate Policy Design.* Washington DC: Peterson Institute for International Economics.

Hilton, F. G. Hank and Arik Levinson (1998). "Factoring the Environmental Kuznets Curve: Evidence from Automotive Lead Emissions," *Journal of Environmental Economics and Management* 35: 126–41.

Ho, Mun, Richard Morgenstern, and Jhih-Shyang Shih (2008). "Impact of Carbon Price Policies on U.S. Industry," Discussion Paper No. 09-37, Resources for the Future, Washington DC, December.

Holtz-Eakin, Douglas and T. Selden (1995). "Stoking the Fires? CO_2 Emissions and Economic Growth," *Journal of Public Economics* 57: 85–101.

Hufbauer, Gary, Steve Charnovitz, and Jisun Kim (2009). *Global Warming and the World Trading System.* Washington DC: Peterson Institute for International Economics.

Hufbauer, Gary, Daniel Esty, Diana Orejas, Luis Rubio, and Jeffrey Schott (2000). *NAFTA and the Environment: Seven Years Later (Policy Analyses in International Economics)*, No. 61. Washington DC: Institute for International Economics.

International Panel on Climate Change (2001). *Third Assessment Report: Climate Change 2001*, Working Group III.

Jaffe, Adam, S. R. Peterson, Paul Portney, and Robert Stavins (1995). "Environmental Regulation and the Competitiveness of U.S. Manufacturing: What Does the Evidence Tell Us?" *Journal of Economic Literature* 33: 132–63.

Levinson, Arik and Scott Taylor (2001). "Trade and the Environment: Unmasking the Pollution Haven Effect," Georgetown University and University of Wisconsin.

Low, P. and A. Yeats (1992). "Do 'Dirty' Industries Migrate?" in P. Low (ed.), International Trade and the Environment, Washington, DC: The World Bank, pp. 89–104.

Lucas, Robert E. B., David Wheeler, and Hememala Hettige (1992). "Economic Development, Environmental Regulation and the International Migration of Toxic Industrial Pollution: 1960–1988," in Patrick Low (ed.), International Trade and the Environment, World Bank Discussion Papers no. 159, Washington DC: The World Bank.

McKibbin, Warwick, and Peter Wilcoxen (2008). "The Economic and Environmental Effects of Border Adjustments for Climate Policy," Brookings Conference on *Climate Change, Trade and Competitiveness: Is a Collision Inevitable?*, Washington, DC.

McKibbin, Warwick J., Martin T. Ross, Robert Shackleton, and Peter J. Wilcoxen (1999). "Emissions Trading, Capital Flows, and the Kyoto Protocol," *The Energy Journal*, Kyoto Special Issue.

Neumayer, Eric (2002). "Does Trade Openness Promote Multilateral Environmental Cooperation?" *The World Economy* 25(6): 812–32.

Panayotou, Theo (1993). "Empirical Tests and Policy Analysis of Environmental Degradation at Different Stages of Development," Working Paper WP238, Technology and Employment Programme, Geneva: International Labor Office.

Pauwelyn, Joost (2007). "U.S. Federal Climate Policy and Competitiveness Concerns: The Limits and Options of International Trade Law," Working Paper No. 07-02, Nicholas Institute, Duke University, April.

Reinaud, Julia (2008). "Issues Behind Competitiveness and Carbon Leakage—Focus on Heavy Industry," IEA Information Paper, International Energy Agency, Paris, October.

Ruggie, John (2002). "Trade, Sustainability and Global Governance," *Columbia Journal of Environmental Law* 27: 297–307.

Sampson, Gary (1999). "WTO Rules and Climate Change: The Need for Policy Coherence," in Bradnee Chambers (ed.), *Global Climate Governance: A Report on the Inter-Linkages Between the Kyoto*

Protocol and Other Multilateral Regimes. Tokyo: United Nations University.

(2000). *Trade, Environment, and the WTO: The Post-Seattle Agenda*, Baltimore, MD: Johns Hopkins University Press.

Seidman, Laurence and Kenneth Lewis (2008). "Compensation and Contributions Under an International Carbon Treaty," University of Delaware, February.

Selden, Thomas and Daqing Song (1994). "Environmental Quality and Development: Is There a Kuznets Curve for Air Pollution Emissions," *Journal of Environmental Economics and Management* 27: 147–62.

Shafik, Nemat (1994). "Economic Development and Environmental Quality: An Econometric Analysis," *Oxford Economic Papers* 46: 757–73.

Smarzynska, Beata and Shang-Jin Wei (2001). "Pollution Havens and Foreign Direct Investment: Dirty Secret or Popular Myth?" NBER Working Paper No. 8465, September.

Suri, Vivek and Duane Chapman (1998). "Economic Growth, Trade and Energy: Implications for the Environmental Kuznets Curve," *Ecological Economics* 25(2): 147–60.

Tobey, James (1990). "The Effects of Domestic Environmental Policies on Patterns of World Trade: An Empirical Test," *Kyklos* 43: 191–209.

Vogel, David (1995). *Trading Up: Consumer and Environmental Regulation in a Global Economy*, Cambridge, MA: Harvard University Press.

Webster, D. G. (2008). *Adaptive Governance: Dynamics of Atlantic Fisheries Management*. Cambridge, MA: MIT Press.

World Bank (1992). *Development and the Environment*, World Development Report.

17 A proposal for the design of the successor to the Kyoto Protocol[1]

LARRY KARP AND JINHUA ZHAO

Introduction

The primary design objectives for a successor climate agreement to the Kyoto Protocol are to promote nations' participation in and compliance with a global framework for reducing greenhouse gas (GHG) emissions. If nations do not sign the treaty, or if they sign it and then honor it only in the breach, other design details are irrelevant. The treaty must also set goals that at least approximately balance the costs and benefits of action, and must provide mechanisms to reach these goals efficiently. The design of a successor agreement should be simple, so that it presents nations with a clear choice. Ultimately, solutions to the global problem of climate change will require a measure of compulsion; therefore, it is important that nations view a new treaty as fair.

Achieving this objective begins with the recognition that managing climate change is a global public good. Because nations are sovereign, the possibilities for compelling them to join an agreement—or for compelling them to comply after they have joined—are limited. This constraint makes it necessary to design an agreement so that it is in nations' interest to participate and to comply. It is also necessary to set the stage for compelling participation in the future, should this be required.

The design proposed in this chapter includes a number of key ingredients:

- Developed-country participants face mandatory, country-specific ceilings on GHG emissions, as under the Kyoto Protocol.
- The agreement contains country-specific commitments for approximately a decade, and it sets out broad goals for subsequent periods.
- Developing countries are not required to make costly changes during the first decade of a new regime, but face restrictions

[1] This chapter benefited from the comments of an anonymous referee.

530

and incentives to ensure that they do not undercut the measures that developed countries take to reduce emissions. The agreement notifies developing countries that they will face obligations—not only opportunities—at the next round of climate change negotiations.

- The successor agreement protects signatories from unexpectedly high abatement costs by allowing them to exercise an escape clause. The availability of this clause also promotes participation in the treaty and helps to solve the problem of enforcement.
- Exercise of the escape clause requires payment of a monetary fine, or it triggers trade sanctions by other signatories—as would be consistent with current World Trade Organization (WTO) law.
- The escape clause acts as a safety valve, putting a cap on the cost of compliance with treaty obligations.
- The treaty accepts the principle that by the next round of climate negotiations (after the first decade of treaty implementation), WTO-consistent trade measures will be introduced to prevent non-signatories from undermining the actions of signatories, and possibly also as a means of inducing non-signatories to join the next agreement.
- The treaty supports the continued development and use of the Clean Development Mechanism (CDM) and Joint Implementation (JI). It also encourages the creation of a new mechanism to achieve broader developing-country participation at the sectoral rather than the project level.
- The allocation of internationally tradable permits is not used as a means of providing side payments to induce membership (as was done under the Kyoto Protocol to induce Russia's membership). The CDM and JI, or sectoral agreements, provide the primary means of taking advantage of opportunities for low-cost emissions reductions.
- In view of the randomness of abatement costs, the treaty allows international trade in emissions permits to achieve efficiency. The treaty also recognizes the potentially perverse effects of such trade.
- Together with the CDM, JI, and international purchases or sales of permits, signatories can use any combination of domestic policies—e.g., command and control, cap-and-trade, and taxes—to achieve their targets. This decision is a domestic issue.

• The treaty encourages voluntary steps and agreements among
parties outside the treaty, but recognizes that these are not substitutes for a multinational agreement with mandatory reductions.

Our objective is to provide an outline for a successor to the Kyoto
Protocol, without attempting an exhaustive description. For example,
we do not discuss the evolution of the CDM, although we recognize
the importance of reforming this mechanism and probably extending
its reach in a new agreement. Other topics, such as carbon sinks and
the development of biofuels, are also important. These issues will
likely be addressed by a reformed CDM or by the development of sectoral agreements; we do not discuss them here. Other proposals for a
post-Kyoto regime provide greater detail on issues that we ignore.

Mandatory ceilings

A post-Kyoto agreement must impose mandatory country-specific
ceilings on GHG emissions *to guarantee the environmental outcome
of the agreement*. The objective is to achieve meaningful reductions in
these emissions, not to provide politicians with an opportunity for self-
congratulation. Our collective ability to reach this objective is uncertain, but we should pursue it as long as there is a chance for success.

We recognize that voluntary methods and agreements among small
groups of countries—as exemplified by recent US efforts to promote
technology transfers outside the Kyoto Protocol—have a role. Similar
efforts should be encouraged, but they should not become substitutes
to the kind of concerted, multinational action needed to address the
problem of climate change. Without mandatory emission ceilings (or
caps) for individual nations, there will be less incentive to engage in voluntary reductions, technology transfers, and other worthwhile goals.

Pessimists conclude that such a collective effort is doomed because
of nations' inability to cooperate. Optimists think that a mandatory
effort is unnecessary, either because the danger of climate change has
been exaggerated, or because win-win alternatives will make it cheap
to deal with the problem. The scientific consensus finds a high probability that the risks posed by climate change are significant. Adoption
of cost-effective and energy-efficient technologies may lead to low-cost
reductions in GHG emissions. These kinds of win-win situations are
far more likely to be identified and exploited if policymakers' minds
are concentrated by mandatory ceilings.

We do not understate the difficulty of negotiating, ratifying, and enforcing a meaningful agreement on mandatory emission ceilings. The bulk of our design proposal addresses these difficulties.

The length of the agreement: response to new information

A new international climate agreement should emphasize country-specific obligations and the development of needed institutions during the next decade. This period is long enough to achieve real gains, but it is also short enough to provide two major advantages, as well as several minor ones. First, it takes into account *uncertainty* and the probability that *new information* will emerge surrounding both climate change and the cost of reducing GHG emissions. Second, it recognizes that there will likely be changing responsibilities across the developed and developing countries.

Climate science has improved over the past decade, but there is still disagreement about safe levels of GHG concentrations. Businesses making investments that last several decades need to adopt a planning horizon much longer than a decade, and they would like to know the future pecuniary costs of carbon emissions. However, it is not possible for an international agreement to determine those distant costs. Instead, a post-Kyoto agreement should provide a convincing signal that the world community is capable of taking measures to combat this global danger. An international agreement with precise and enforceable commitments during a short period sends a more powerful signal of this ability than does an agreement that emphasizes longer-term goals. It is better to establish the principle that the world community can respond to science, rather than to attempt to predict today what the science will be ten years from now.

The cost of achieving any given level of GHG abatement depends on the development of new technologies and on the success of institutions (e.g., markets). There is perhaps as much uncertainty about these future economic costs as there is about the environmental costs caused by the accumulation of GHGs. The optimal trajectory of GHG emissions depends on the balance of economic and environmental costs.

The best that the current generation can do is to use current estimates of these costs, and of the uncertainty surrounding them, to calculate an optimal trajectory of emissions. Many integrated assessment models (IAMs) have undertaken this exercise, typically with a time step of a decade. These models can be useful in determining emissions objectives for the next decade.

While focusing on behavior in the near term, a new international agreement must recognize that abatement efforts will have to continue in the future. For indicative purposes only—not as a commitment—the agreement should specify the target level of GHG concentrations in 50 and in 100 years associated with this first step. This information promotes transparency and helps firms make long-run plans; it is analogous to the kind of information that the US Federal Reserve provides.

The second major reason for an emphasis on the short run is that it makes it easier to incorporate changing responsibilities between the developed and the developing countries. For reasons discussed in a later section of this chapter, developing countries are exempt from commitments during the first decade of a new treaty, but this exemption does not extend beyond that time. A post-Kyoto agreement should establish the principle that developing countries will have to become engaged in the future, but not be too specific about the details of that engagement. An agreement that emphasizes the short run makes it easier to establish this principle and retain the ambiguity needed to win developing-country support.

There are secondary reasons for emphasizing the short run. Climate change arises from the stock of GHGs in the atmosphere, not from emissions in any single period. The central role of stocks rather than flows makes the climate problem inherently dynamic: the optimal policy will target a trajectory of emissions, rather than the level of emissions in a given period. This dynamic feature might appear to militate in favor of emphasizing the long run, contrary to our proposal. However, the commitment (or time consistency) problem creates an overwhelming argument for concentrating on the short run. Society's tendency to procrastinate in solving difficult problems is even greater than that of individuals: witness the inability of the US political system to reform social security or Medicare.

An agreement with a long time horizon magnifies society's temptation to defer emissions reductions. In some cases this delay is socially optimal—for example, when it results from the anticipation of improved technology. However, we want to design an international agreement to resist the tendency to procrastinate. Instead of viewing the problem of controlling climate change exclusively as a dynamic optimization problem, it is useful to also think of it as a dynamic game amongst a succession of generations (Karp 2005; Karp and Tsur 2007). The current generation can choose its own actions. By altering the stock of GHGs in the atmosphere and the institutional infrastructure bequeathed to subsequent generations, the current generation can influence future actions, but it is not able to choose those actions. Emphasis on the short run in a new agreement is a means of forcing the current generation to recognize its limited influence on the actions of future generations. A short-duration treaty makes it impossible to score political points or to salve our consciences by promising to undertake costly actions in the future. Instead, we can only decide what actions we will take in the present.

An agreement that emphasizes short-run goals is easier to negotiate and allows nations to learn and improve the design of future agreements. In theory, an agreement that specifies what will be done in future contingencies may be attractive. However, this degree of detail is not practical and it also undermines the objective of simplicity. We can envisage many different dimensions across which we might achieve simplicity. For example, we could focus on particular sectors or provide targets for particular types of fuel or offer certain kinds of taxes and subsidies. The uncertainty and time-consistency problems described above, however, favor achieving simplicity by concentrating on short-run goals. Within that constraint, we should be as ambitious as is politically feasible, consistent with current estimates of costs and uncertainty.

Several rounds of negotiations under the General Agreement on Trade and Tariffs (GATT) preceded the establishment of the WTO. The benefit of international trade has so far probably been more widely accepted than has the importance of action on climate change. The GATT rounds achieved limited objectives and created the institutional infrastructure that led to a more ambitious trade agreement. Several Kyoto-style rounds of negotiation will likely precede the establishment of a comprehensive and long-lasting agreement to manage climate change. We think that an architecture that is designed to achieve specific short-run goals offers the best chance of leading to a comprehensive climate agreement.

Fairness and distributional equity

Industrialized countries should bear most of the near-term costs of reducing GHG emissions, for three reasons. First, climate change arises from the accumulation of GHG stocks in the atmosphere, which are a by-product of industrialization and other processes that led to current levels of wealth. Second, rich countries are better able to pay for needed emission reductions, whether they achieve those reductions domestically or in developing countries (through the CDM or sectoral agreements).

Third, climate change policy requires a two-pronged approach: abatement to reduce potential climate-related damages, and adaptation to reduce the consequences of those climate changes that will occur even with abatement efforts. Abatement costs will arise in the near term, while the bulk of the adaptation costs will arise in the future, when and if major climate change actually occurs. The inability of the current generation to commit to future policies means that it is impractical for the rich countries to promise to discharge their moral obligation by requiring their children and grandchildren to pay for adaptation in developing countries in the future. The current generation in the rich countries must bear the cost today of reducing emissions. For this reason, our proposed design includes mandatory ceilings on emissions levels, but it does not include mandatory steps with respect to adaptation (e.g., building sea walls).

A focus on adaptation efforts at this time would be a distraction from the goal of achieving emissions reductions. It might give some countries political cover, tempting them to agree to contribute to future adaptation efforts while rejecting mandatory emissions ceilings. Introducing negotiations on adaptation complicates an already complicated agenda. We want to help simplify this agenda by focusing on the most urgent goals.

The emphasis on fairness has a practical implication. The acceptance of primary responsibility for causing the problem does not imply an open-ended commitment to bear all the costs, for all time, of implementing a remedy. A new climate agreement must set the stage for achieving the cooperation from developing countries needed to stabilize atmospheric GHG stocks at a safe level. The rich countries should reaffirm their primary responsibility for the problem and accept that they are best able to pay to begin solving it—a recognition explicit in the Kyoto Protocol. However, unlike the Protocol, a successor treaty should establish the principle that developing countries will (1) be obliged to undertake actions to reduce GHG emissions in the future and (2) take current actions to support abatement efforts in developed countries by avoiding carbon leakage.

The asymmetry is striking. Rich countries have the responsibility to act immediately to reduce climate-related risks. However, they retain considerable bargaining power in the negotiating "game" that will determine the form and the extent of developing countries' cooperation. By taking action today—as distinct from making unenforceable promises to act in the future—rich countries position themselves to strongly influence the institutional structure that will promote future participation and compliance by all countries, and also to prevent non-participants from undermining the agreement (leakage). These institutional changes will involve the use of trade policy, as discussed in a later section of this chapter.

Diplomats will find more agreeable language in which to couch this asymmetry, but there should be no doubt of its existence. The United States in particular has made developing country participation a *sine qua non* of its own engagement. The Obama administration might soften that stance, but Congressional approval will likely still require developing-country participation. In any case, success in managing climate change does require developing-country participation, and there is little prospect that rich countries would agree to the large transfers that would be needed in order to buy this participation.

Developing countries, particularly China, India, and Brazil, should be signatories to a new international climate agreement, in a special category as under the Kyoto Protocol. The primary cost of participation to developing countries in the short run is their acceptance of the principle of future obligations to reduce emissions. A secondary cost is that they bind themselves to rules of international trade (referred to as "trade disciplines") needed to prevent leakage. Membership also entails the responsibility to establish national carbon accounts. These accounts will be useful in setting future emission ceilings, assisting in monitoring compliance with current disciplines, and as part of the process of developing regulatory infrastructure.

Participation confers three types of benefits on developing countries: it gives them a seat at the table in determining their future involvement and the current trade disciplines; it provides them with immediate benefits, including benefits derived from technology transfer; and it enhances the prospect of an agreement that will reduce the risk they face of climate-related damages in the future (especially given their low adaptation abilities). In keeping with our recommendation to focus on current actions rather than long-term commitments, our proposal requires that developing countries accept the principle that they will reduce emissions in the future, without stating specific emissions ceilings.

The agreement can link development and climate objectives. The international community set Millennium Development Goals (www.un.org/millenniumgoals) in 2000, and rich countries made commitments to help developing countries achieve these goals. Developing countries' future climate-related actions can be conditioned on rich countries' efforts to reach the Millennium Goals. The trade disciplines necessary to prevent leakage can be conditioned on technology transfers. The developing countries can influence these outcomes only if they participate in post-Kyoto negotiations with a view to becoming signatories to a successor agreement. Participation in the CDM or in sectoral agreements and technology transfer under such an agreement should be available only to signatories, thus creating an immediate benefit for joining. China, India, and Brazil account for 63 percent of current CDM projects and 75 percent of the expected annual Certified Emissions Reductions (CERs) (http://cdm.unfccc.int/Statistics/index.html). Under a new treaty with expanded membership from rich countries and stricter emission ceilings, the value to developing countries of having the right to participate in the CDM market or in sectoral agreements should increase substantially.

In summary, rich countries need to acknowledge their responsibility for current stocks of GHGs and their greater ability to take the first steps to deal with climate risks. It is not, however, in the interest of developing countries to claim that their lack of responsibility for existing GHG stocks and their relative poverty exempt them from all obligations; those facts merely defer their obligations. With an emphasis on fairness, a new agreement should establish the principle that developing countries will have to reduce their emissions in the future, and in the meantime they cannot undermine efforts made by developed countries.

Participation and compliance

Nations' sovereignty limits the world's ability to design an international agreement that compels participation and compliance. Here we suggest how to design an agreement at the negotiation stage, in order to promote participation and compliance. We interpret the participation that actually occurs as the equilibrium outcome of a participation "game" in which nations act out of self-interest in deciding whether to join a previously negotiated agreement. The absence of a supranational institution with the ability to punish non-participants means that a non cooperative Nash equilibrium is a reasonable equilibrium concept for the participation game. In addition, we think that a simple multistage game, rather than a supergame or a complicated dynamic game, provides the most useful framework. Our choice of a multistage game is consistent with our recommendation that a post-Kyoto treaty emphasize short-run goals. There are also technical reasons for adopting this formulation.[2]

The basic proposal

Our central recommendation is to include an escape clause in a new agreement (Karp and Zhao 2007). A nation that invokes the escape clause is exempt from fulfilling either all or part of the GHG abatement stipulated by the agreement. As a practical matter, a partial escape, which exempts a signatory from fulfilling only a portion of its agreed abatement, is likely to be more useful than a total escape, which exempts the signatory from all abatement obligations. However, the extent of the escape is a secondary design issue. We want to explain why the escape clause in general provides an important ingredient in the design of an agreement. Therefore, for simplicity only, we explain the policy assuming that it involves a total rather than a partial escape.

In order to have any effect, an international agreement with a (total) escape clause has to attach a cost to invoking the clause. Here, for the purpose of a simple illustration, we take this cost to be a monetary fine, which we denote as F. Nations with different characteristics (e.g., wealth, population, carbon intensity) are likely to have different agreed levels of abatement and correspondingly different fines for invoking the escape clause. This heterogeneity complicates the actual

---

[2] The Folk Theorem of supergames shows that there are typically many non-cooperative equilibria based on punishment strategies when the game is (possibly) repeated an infinite number of times. Some of these equilibria have outcomes that are close to or equal to the outcome under perfect cooperation. We do not think that setting an infinite horizon provides the best modeling framework, both because of our emphasis on the short duration of a post-Kyoto agreement and because requiring an agreement to provide "renegotiation proofness" can undo the cooperation achieved in punishment equilibria.

negotiation process, but it adds little to understanding the role of the escape clause. Therefore, we consider here the case where potential signatories are homogenous; we have in mind the participation game amongst developed countries, those who will incur costs during the initial post-Kyoto period.

The combination of escape clause and fine has an obvious and important role in providing insurance against unexpectedly high costs, similar to the role of a safety valve in emissions trading. Nations who sign the agreement know at the outset that the economic cost of compliance does not exceed the magnitude of the fine. (A more sophisticated menu of partial escape clauses provides even better insurance.) One reason for US opposition to the Kyoto Protocol was the uncertain and possibly large cost of compliance. There is substantial variation in estimates of the economic cost of reducing GHG emissions at the regional, national, and international levels (Aldy *et al.* 2008). Some estimates, particularly those advanced by industry groups, find very high costs. Other estimates assume that win-win policies abound, leading to low abatement costs. The escape clause eliminates, or at least greatly reduces, one reason for non-participation. No nation can refuse to participate on grounds that the costs may be unimaginably large; with the escape clause, the costs cannot exceed F. This insurance property is important, but there are other ways of achieving insurance; the chief virtues of the escape clause are that it promotes participation and compliance.

If there are n signatories, and if m of these signatories invoke the escape clause, total fine payments equal mF. An essential feature of our proposal is that this revenue is returned to all signatories. In the case under consideration, where signatories are identical, each signatory receives revenue in the amount of mF/n. Here we ignore transaction costs, such as those arising from the costs of collecting the fine. The receipt of a fraction of revenue from the fine is an inducement to join the agreement. More importantly, a nation that invokes the escape clause is reimbursed by the amount F/n, so the actual cost of invoking the escape clause is $(n-1)F/n$. The actual fine increases with n, the number of signatories. The important consequence of this design is that by choosing to participate in the agreement, a nation unilaterally increases the fine that any other signatory must pay in order to invoke the escape clause. Although negotiations that precede country-level decisions about participation determine the nominal fine, F, each potential signatory can influence other signatories' actual fine, and thus their abatement decisions. A larger number of signatories increases the actual fine, making it less attractive to invoke the escape clause, and therefore more attractive to abate.

Nations participate in international agreements primarily to influence other nations' behavior, rarely their own.[3] Abatement of GHGs is a global public good. Each country would like other countries to abate. The endogeneity of the actual fine gives a potential signatory leverage over other signatories. The desire to exercise this leverage can provide a powerful incentive to participate in the agreement.

The combined escape clause and fine encourage compliance by converting a rather esoteric obligation (GHG abatement) into a familiar one, for which international compliance structures already exist. The Kyoto Protocol requires signatories to not exceed emissions ceilings, but its lack of an effective enforcement mechanism appears (at least up to this point in time) to have led to highly imperfect compliance. There is no effective sanction for not achieving a target level of abatement. The Kyoto Protocol's short duration compounds the enforcement problem, because it eliminates the ability to punish current breaches by reducing future emissions allowances. The fine converts the unfamiliar obligation, reduction of GHG emissions, into a familiar obligation: payment of an international debt. The default of sovereign debt shows that the mechanism for enforcing repayment of this debt is not perfect, but perhaps the surprise is that it works as well as it does. For example, it appears likely that Canada will not meet its Kyoto Protocol obligation, and this event does not seem to cause great consternation either within Canada or the rest of the world. Canada is less likely to default on an international debt, and certainly would not do so in a casual manner.

An important feature of the combined fine and escape clause is that other signatories actually want to enforce the fine when a partner invokes the escape clause.[4] Thus, although the fine does not

---

[3] There are, of course, counterexamples to this claim. By signing an agreement a nation can to some extent tie its own hands regarding its own future behavior. In this case, the treaty serves as a commitment device.

[4] A signatory might not want to enforce the fine if it anticipates invoking the escape clause and if it believes that its lack of enforcement will weaken the agreement to such an extent that it will in turn not be liable to pay the fine. However, our proposal requires only that some countries do want to enforce the fine.

completely solve the compliance problem, it greatly reduces that problem. We anticipate that there will be some circumstances when a nation does want to exercise the escape clause. Therefore, it must be possible to collect the fine.

Trade sanctions as an alternative to the fine

A monetary fine is probably the simplest way to limit a signatory's incentive to invoke the escape clause, but trade sanctions provide an attractive alternative. Because these sanctions are imposed against a partner who willingly entered into the environmental agreement, the sanctions are consistent with WTO law. For example, the trade sanctions in the Montreal Protocol are WTO-consistent (United Nations Environmental Programme 1999). The WTO dispute resolution mechanism also provides a (nearly) ready-made structure for adjudicating potential disputes. WTO dispute resolution panels have not previously sat in judgment on exactly this kind of dispute, but they have considered many cases involving environmental restrictions.

Under this alternative, all signatories are entitled to impose trade sanctions, of prescribed magnitude, against a signatory that invokes the escape clause. WTO law and GATT/WTO negotiations refer to a reduction in tariffs or some other trade liberalization as a concession that the member country offers other signatories. Violation of WTO law entitles the injured party to withdraw a concession from the offending party, both as a means of punishment and of compensation. The use of the term concession and the mindset of many politicians suggest that countries often do view their trade liberalization as imposing a cost upon themselves and conferring a benefit to their trading partner. Some countries are reluctant to take advantage of their right to withdraw concessions, but withdrawal sometimes occurs for an extended period, e.g., in the US-EU beef hormone dispute.

The use of trade sanctions has most of the ingredients of a monetary fine. An increase in the number of signatories increases the cost of invoking the escape clause, because the addition of a signatory increases the number of countries that can legally impose trade sanctions. Signatories have an incentive to demand payment, in the form of withdrawing concessions. Trade sanctions convert an esoteric obligation, for which there is no obvious penalty for non-compliance, into an obligation with a familiar penalty. There is an existing institutional framework, the WTO dispute resolution mechanism, for adjudicating disputes.

A minor difference is that the monetary fine puts an absolute cap on the cost of joining, equal to the cost of the nominal fine. The actual cost of exercising the escape clause approaches this nominal fine, as the number of members increases. The use of trade sanctions, in contrast, puts a flexible ceiling on the dollar cost of exercising the escape clause. If more countries join, and each signatory can impose a trade sanction of prescribed value on any country that exercises the escape clause, the actual cost of exercising the escape clause can grow large. This difference is minor, however, because the prescribed value of the trade sanctions can depend on the number of members, in order to prevent the total cost of the trade sanctions from exceeding a given limit.

The alternative of using trade sanctions has two real disadvantages relative to a monetary fine. First, regardless of whether nations think that they benefit by withdrawing a concession, in most cases this action harms them. In contrast, receiving a portion of the revenue from fine payments clearly makes a nation better off. Thus, using trade sanctions creates a net welfare loss, whereas the fine is simply a transfer payment. Second, trade sanctions are more complicated than a monetary fine, partly because disputants can question the monetary value of the trade sanction. However, the dispute resolution panels have practice in dealing with this issue.

Two other considerations offset these disadvantages. First, there is a psychological/political factor. In the event that a nation does want to exercise the escape clause, it might be difficult for its population and politicians to accept that it must pay the monetary fine. Even though the nation had willingly entered into the contract that requires this payment, there may be too much domestic opposition for the payment to actually be made.[5] Moreover, even if the nation does pay the monetary fine, it might compensate by reducing other contributions to global public goods or to development assistance. Thus, the fine may

---

[5] There is an important difference in the political difficulty of concluding an agreement that requires payments of fines to signatories in certain contingencies, and the political difficulty arising from making transfers to developing nations to induce them to reduce emissions. The latter transfer is asymmetric and certain at the time of the agreement. In contrast, at the time of the agreement the former transfer is only a possibility. Moreover, there is symmetry because in some contingency the country receives fine payments.

not involve a real cost to the nation. Trade sanctions carry their own baggage, but they may be psychologically and politically easier to tolerate compared to a monetary fine.

The second advantage of this approach is that it introduces trade policy as a means of promoting environmental objectives. Importantly, it does so in a manner that is legal under existing WTO rules. Thus, using the trade alternative during the post-Kyoto years will help set the stage for a more ambitious and more contentious use of trade policy.

Other considerations

Other features of the proposed agreement will also promote one or more of the goals of efficiency, participation, and compliance. These are noncontroversial, so we merely mention them.

GHGs are stock pollutants, so actual damages or risks depend on aggregate emissions over an extended period, rather than emissions within a period. When abatement costs fluctuate over time, it is efficient to allow countries to bank and borrow emissions credits. Therefore, we support the creation of an intertemporal market, for the same reason that—as discussed in a later section of this chapter—we support an international market in emissions permits. Intertemporal markets might lead to excessive emissions in early periods (Kling and Rubin 1997), so it is important that policymakers choose the right intertemporal trading ratio for emission credits (Yates and Cronshaw 2001; Feng and Zhao 2006). These markets provide limited benefits when governments and firms have symmetric information about abatement costs. To avoid the obvious moral hazard problem, a nation that owes emissions credits is not allowed to sell credits on the international market.

The Kyoto Protocol entered into force only after reaching a ratification threshold. This kind of conditionality is a means of encouraging participation. We are not opposed to using a similar device in a post-Kyoto agreement, but we are skeptical of its efficacy. We discuss Russia's contribution to reaching the Kyoto threshold in a later section.

A similar but perhaps more useful device is to condition the level of abatement to be undertaken by members on the actions of non-members. The European Union is using this strategy in an attempt to encourage US participation. There appears to be little risk to this strategy, but we do not expect it to make a substantial contribution to the success of a new international agreement. However, a viable strategy may be to link the actions of non-members during a next agreement to the design of future agreements. For instance, participants in a post-Kyoto agreement might commit to joint efforts, as a group, to link participation in the next (post-post-Kyoto) agreement with trade sanctions if there is sufficiently severe carbon leakage during the post-2012 period.

Extending the role of trade policy

The next international agreement should recognize the importance of trade reform in achieving climate-related objectives. This reform has two themes. First, it encourages the liberalization of markets for green products and technology. Second, it provides levers that promote membership and compliance while discouraging non-signatories from undercutting the agreement. There is an obvious tension between the two reforms, because one discourages trade restrictions and the other permits the extension of these restrictions. Therefore, it is important to be clear that the objective of both reforms is to achieve an economically efficient climate change agreement. The negotiations leading to a successor agreement to Kyoto may make only modest progress in achieving these reforms, but the agreement should clearly state the underlying principle.

The benefits of liberalizing markets for green products and technologies are non-controversial and potentially large. It may be difficult to achieve this liberalization, for the same reason that it is difficult to reform other sectors where significant distortions remain, such as agriculture. Support for the principle of open markets in a new climate treaty should include a criticism of the infant industry argument and other justifications for trade restrictions. For example, the US tariff on biofuels is a component of US agricultural policy, although supporters of this tariff invoke the infant industry argument. Removal of the tariff would make it easier to achieve a sensible policy for biofuels, in addition to benefiting exporters like Brazil. In the developing countries, removing trade restrictions on clean energy technologies could lead to substantial economic gains and to reductions in GHG emissions (World Bank 2008).

The second type of reform, which would make it easier to use trade as a lever to achieve climate objectives, is controversial. Environmentalists and trade economists have debated for years whether the mandate of the WTO should be extended in an attempt to influence environmental policy (Guzman 2002, Cone 2002). Until recently at least, trade economists have broadly opposed such an extension. Under WTO rules, the agreement of all members would be required, an unlikely outcome given the opposition of many developing countries. Even if such WTO members could reach a consensus, economists' general view has been that the gains from trade are so great, and so vulnerable to erosion, and that the dangers of climate change are so modest, that the environmental tail should not try to wag the trade dog. As long as this perception persists, it makes sense to quarantine environmental objectives from trade policy. An alternate view is that globalization of world markets is on a sound footing and that the risks of climate change are substantial. Under this view, it makes sense—even to an economist who understands the Principle of Targeting—to use trade policy to achieve environmental goals.[6]

Trade policy can be linked to environmental policy in order to encourage participation in a climate agreement; it can also be used to encourage signatories to comply and to prevent non-signatories from undermining an agreement. The most aggressive use of trade policy— requiring participation in a climate agreement in exchange for access to markets—is unlikely to be productive at this time and should be discouraged. It is better to use positive incentives, such as the right to participate in the CDM market and easier access to green technology, as means of encouraging membership. However, the agreement should allow trade taxes that discourage nations from undermining carbon reductions achieved elsewhere. In 2007 EU politicians proposed a Kyoto tax, aimed primarily at the United States. EU Trade Commissioner Mandelson opposed this tax, partly on grounds that it would be politically counterproductive. World Bank simulations show that the tax would have led to a substantial reduction in US exports to the European Union (World Bank 2008). We support a Kyoto tax, largely for political reasons, as discussed below.

Carbon leakage is the process by which stricter emissions standards in one place encourage higher emissions elsewhere, as production of

---

[6] The Principle of Targeting emphasizes the importance of matching policy instruments with their objectives. In particular, it implies that trade policy is rarely the best instrument for correcting market failures such as environmental externalities.

GHG-intensive goods moves to places with weaker environmental standards (Kallbekken 2007). The magnitude of carbon leakage is uncertain, but some estimates put it at less than 20 percent (Intergovernmental Panel on Climate Change 2001). Carbon leakage is an example of the pollution haven effect; the empirical evidence for this effect is mixed but generally quite weak (Copeland and Taylor 2003, 2004). The weakness of the evidence may be partly because the magnitude of past changes in environmental policy has not been great enough to have an appreciable effect on the location of industry, and partly because of statistical and measurement problems. It would be rash to conclude, based on evidence to date, that the policies needed to achieve substantial GHG emissions reductions would cause only modest leakage of emissions. Politicians in signatory countries would be reluctant to undertake the experiment needed to obtain stronger statistical evidence.

Trade policy provides the best hope of encouraging countries to join a climate change agreement and of persuading policymakers in signatory countries that they can achieve substantial reductions in GHG emissions without significant leakage and accompanying job losses (Stiglitz 2006). This reorientation of trade policy carries with it the well-recognized risk of protectionist policies disguised as environmental policies (environmental protectionism), for which there is no simple inoculation. The extent of this risk is a matter of dispute. The evidence of the past thirteen years shows that the WTO is capable of taking a nuanced view of the relationship between trade and environmental protection (Neumeyer 2005). WTO dispute resolution panels have been willing to designate as disguised protectionism some policies ostensibly aimed at environmental health, e.g., in the disputes between the United States and the European Union involving hormone-fed beef and genetically modified organisms (GMOs). However, the WTO does not instinctively regard environmental policies that restrict trade as disguised protectionism. The Appellate Board's 1998 decision in the shrimp and turtle case recognized the legality of trade restrictions used to protect the global environmental commons. Some trade economists were concerned that this decision would lead to environmental protectionism against developing countries (Bhagwati 2004), but there is little evidence of this occurring.

The shrimp-turtle decision provides modest but insufficient scope for using trade policy to achieve environmental goals within the confines of existing WTO law. Moreover, precedence has little force in

WTO and other international law. Other aspects of WTO law directly oppose using trade policy for environmental goals. The WTO allows countries to make border tax adjustments (BTAs) to offset domestic taxes, including those designed to achieve environmental goals. However, BTAs can offset only direct taxes. For example, a carbon tax could be offset if carbon were directly exported, but it is questionable whether adjusting the price of a product that embodies carbon is legal under WTO. Pauwelyn's (2007) detailed review of this legal question suggests that border tax adjustments do not offer a reliable means of guarding against carbon leakage.

One route to introducing trade policy as a lever for international climate policy is to revise the WTO. Most developing countries would probably oppose this revision. The developed countries succeeded in including intellectual property protection (TRIPS) in the WTO, and they failed to obtain a multinational investment agreement (MIA). Both measures faced developing-country opposition. Thus, reforming the WTO to accommodate trade policies that prevent carbon leakage and encourage reductions in GHGs is likely to be difficult. On the other hand, these measures are arguably more important to developed countries than either TRIPS or the MIA, and they benefit developed countries, even if the benefit/cost ratios are different for the two groups.

Developed countries would argue that expanding the legal use of trade policies increases the prospect of a successful climate change agreement, and that developing countries will be among the principal beneficiaries of a successful agreement. Developing countries are likely to regard this argument as paternalistic, and to think that the expansion harms them. The situation with TRIPS was analogous, but the evidence on the side of the developing countries' position in that case was stronger. During the Uruguay Round, which negotiated the WTO, developed countries made concessions in their agricultural policies partly to persuade the developing countries to accept TRIPS. For the reform that we advocate, the *quid pro quo* could be other changes that promote reductions in GHGs. Perhaps the best example of such a change is the relaxation of licensing restrictions for technologies that reduce carbon emissions.

An alternate and probably more practical way to introduce the trade lever is to include it in a new climate agreement rather than as part of WTO reform. We noted above that the use of trade sanctions would be legal under current WTO law, provided that the sanctions are imposed against a signatory to the climate agreement and are consistent with that agreement. We propose that the agreement entitles signatories to impose a border tax adjustment against other signatories in order to offset a cost disadvantage, above some minimal level, caused by stricter climate policies. Climate change policies might lead to small cost increases over much of the primary and secondary sectors, but the inclusion of a minimum threshold (below which costs increases are ineligible for a border tax adjustment) will prevent a general increase in tariffs. In practice, the few sectors that face substantially higher costs because of environmental measures receive offsetting subsidies designed to protect those sectors. These offsetting subsidies must be included in the calculation of the border tax, so that this tax provides compensation for the environmental policy's net costs to the domestic industry. This modification limits the ability to use the border tax adjustment as a means of disguised protectionism. Signatories would have the right to object to border tax adjustments using the WTO dispute resolution process. Thus, the border tax adjustment protects against carbon leakage for only those sectors that face the greatest costs of complying with climate policy.

In view of the requirement to include offsetting subsidies, and the discipline imposed by the WTO process, the aggregate effect of the border tax adjustment might be quite small—as we would hope. However, the political effect could still be substantial, by making it harder to argue that carbon leakage undercuts domestic reductions in GHG emissions and harms domestic industries.

Under our proposal, a signatory can impose border tax adjustment only against other signatories. It would most likely be used when trading partners have very different climate-related obligations, as with trade between developed and developing countries. This fact makes it particularly important to obtain developing country participation. Although developing countries are not required to reduce their emissions in the initial post-Kyoto period, the border tax adjustment limits their ability to take advantage of emissions-reduction activities undertaken by developed countries.

Tradable emissions

International trade in emissions permits can provide a means of transferring income from one signatory to another (McGinty 2007) and it can increase efficiency when there is uncertainty about abatement costs (Webster *et al.* 2007). However, the use of tradable permits has an ambiguous effect on the incentive to impose strict emissions limits and it can discourage participation in an agreement. We discuss these trade-related issues here.

Emissions trade as an indirect side payment

When abatement costs are known with certainty, the correct allocation of permits achieves efficient abatement without trade. Trade can still be useful because, together with the allocation of permits, it provides a means of making a side payment, or bribe, to induce more countries to join the agreement. It is unlikely that Russia would have joined the Kyoto Protocol in the absence of this kind of transfer.

There may be future cases where permit allocation and the option to trade can encourage membership. However, we think these inducements should not play an important role in promoting participation in a post-Kyoto agreement; rather, we recommend using the CDM or sectoral agreements as means of achieving efficient reductions in developing-country emissions. The CDM achieves GHG reductions on a project-by-project basis, limiting its ability to achieve reductions on the scale needed to address climate change. Sanchez (2008) and Niederberger (2008) discuss the possibility of scaling up the CDM in transportation and energy efficiency. Ward (2008) discusses the use of "sector no-lose targets," which set sectoral emissions targets in developing countries and reward the host country for exceeding the goal. Baron *et al.* (2007) describe sectoral approaches for iron and steel, aluminum and cement. Victor (2008) doubts that the CDM has a useful role in the post-Kyoto period, and proposes instead a sectoral approach he calls the "climate access deal." Due to space limitations, we do not attempt to summarize and evaluate these proposals here. However, we agree with the general point that, as currently constituted, the CDM is not adequate either to achieve the necessary scale of reductions or to induce developing-country participation in a broader agreement.

A simple example shows why the CDM (or sectoral agreements) can achieve the same outcome as that obtained using side payments via trade. Suppose that two groups of countries, *A* and *B*, would each produce 200 units of emissions under business-as-usual (BAU) conditions, and that the efficient way to reduce emissions by 100 units is for each group to reduce emissions by 50 units. Members of group *A* (the developed countries) agree to set a ceiling of 100 units of emissions, thereby achieving a 100-unit reduction. Under the CDM or a sectoral agreement, group *A* can pay group *B* (the developing countries) to achieve a 50 unit reduction, and achieve the balance of the target domestically. In the interest of specificity, assume that group *A* captures all of the surplus from this exchange. Alternatively, suppose that the two groups both join the agreement, and they split the total allocation of 300 units of emissions permits in such a way that, after trade, members of group *B* have the same level of welfare as under business as usual.

In this example, the first alternative has only group *A* agree to reduce emissions, and it uses the CDM or a sectoral agreement to achieve the efficient allocation; the second alternative uses the allocation of permits together with trade to bribe group *B* to agree to reduce emissions. The outcome is the same. This example assumes that, under both alternatives, group *A* captures all the surplus from achieving the emissions reduction efficiently. Of course, there is no reason to assume that the division of surplus is the same under the two alternatives, but neither is there a presumption that one alternative leads to a division of surplus more favorable for one of the groups.

This example shows that the CDM or sectoral agreements can achieve the same efficient outcome as using allocation and trade to induce membership. One might argue that there is an inherent advantage in having group *B* commit to a binding emissions ceiling, possibly as a means of promoting increased participation in the future. There are offsetting reasons, however, for preferring continued reliance on the CDM or on a mechanism based on sectoral agreements. There is considerable uncertainty about the level of permits that would be required to compensate developing countries for agreeing to an emissions ceiling, because neither the developing nor the developed countries know the future price of permits or future abatement costs within the developing countries. There is much less uncertainty about the costs of a collection of CDM projects, because these are negotiated individually and over a period of time (rather than at the time that a new post-Kyoto treaty is signed). Therefore, it is simpler to negotiate developing-country participation in a collection of CDM projects, compared to inducing them to participate as full members in a successor agreement. Similarly, proposals such as sector no-lose targets do not subject the developing country to risk. The environmental benefit of reduced emissions is uncertain, regardless of the mechanism that achieves this reduction.

Inducing membership by means of permit allocation and trade is also a bad idea because it obfuscates what should be kept clear, and it makes transparent what should be left vague. The extent of a nation's sacrifice should be kept clear. Russia did not make a sacrifice by ratifying the Protocol, but it scored political points from the European Union by joining. (One hypothesis is that Russia's adherence to the Protocol was a *quid pro quo* for EU support of Russia's accession to the WTO.) The European Union wanted Russia to join in order to achieve the threshold necessary for the Protocol to come into force, thereby increasing pressure on the United States. If it is worth including a threshold level of membership in the terms of the agreement, then it should not be possible to reach the threshold by legerdemain.

The extent to which a climate treaty results in transfers from rich to developing countries should be kept vague. If developing countries are induced to join by means of the allocation of permits and trade, it will be apparent to citizens and politicians in the rich countries that they are paying the developing countries for the right to emit GHGs. This recognition will undercut popular support for the agreement. To the extent that developing countries obtain surplus in a CDM transaction or sectoral agreement, there is also a payment from the rich to the developing country. This kind of payment is not as likely to produce a public outcry in rich countries.

The discussion above contemplates the possible use of permit allocations and trade to induce developing countries to agree on emissions reductions. Some countries may be on the cusp between joining and not joining, and the allocation of permits together with trade might be enough to persuade them to join. However, JI can be used with these countries to achieve efficiency, just as the CDM is used with developing countries. For the reasons given above, it is better to induce these countries to join by giving them an allocation of permits acceptable to them, rather than manipulating the allocation so that they will gain from trade.

Emissions trade to account for cost uncertainty

Thus far we have considered the role of tradable emissions in inducing membership; we recommend, however, that emissions trading not be used for this purpose. The other role of trade is to achieve efficiency *ex post* (after negotiation and ratification). Even if the allocation was chosen so that, in expectation, trade balances are zero, there would still be scope for trade because actual marginal abatement costs are random. We favor allowing international trade in permits in order to take advantage of the potential efficiency gains that arise from this randomness. Of course, to the extent that commodity trade is a substitute for factor trade (i.e., to the extent that the factor price equalization theorem holds), trade in emissions permits is not necessary to achieve efficiency. There are two other points concerning emissions trade.

The effect of emissions trade on the incentive to abate

Although our proposal for a successor agreement to Kyoto requires that ceilings on emissions are determined at the negotiation stage, prior to ratification, we recognize that there may be some adjustment in ceilings once membership has been determined.[7] How does the ability to trade permits affect participants' incentive to adjust their abatement levels? An instinctive answer (for an economist) is that because trade enhances efficiency, making it cheaper to achieve any given level of abatement, trade is likely to encourage greater levels of abatement. This answer is correct if society has a budget for abatement and chooses the highest level of abatement consistent with that budget. The answer is not correct in general if society chooses the optimal level of abatement by balancing marginal benefits and costs. Although trade certainly lowers total and average costs (when countries have different costs), it can either lower or increase marginal costs. Thus, the effect of trade on the incentive to abate is ambiguous in general (Karp 2008).

A simple example (based on our work in progress) shows why trade might reduce the incentive to abate. Suppose that each country has the ability to abate at most one unit. Marginal costs in each country are constant, up to the one-unit capacity. Each country obtains one unit

---

[7] Standard models in the theoretical literature on international environmental agreements assume that the level of abatement is chosen only after countries have decided whether to join (Barrett 2003, Carraro and Siniscalco 1993). The basis for this timing assumption is the belief that countries cannot make commitments at the negotiation stage that would not be in their interest to honor once they had ratified. We think that this is too extreme a view of countries' inability to make commitments, but there is some truth to it. Hence, we recognize that there may be adjustments after ratification occurs.

(e.g., $100 billion) of benefit for one unit of abatement, regardless of where abatement occurs, because the pollutant is global. Each country's cost is a random variable with support greater than 1 and expected value equal to 2. (Costs are in the same units as benefits, so 2 represents $200 billion.) To keep the example simple, suppose that the costs are independently distributed.

After having decided whether to participate in the agreement, a country learns its own costs, but this information is not verifiable, so the group decision cannot be conditioned on realizations about individual cost. (Countries would have an incentive to exaggerate their costs, in order to be assigned a lower required level of abatement.) Since the benefit to a country of abatement is 1 and the actual cost is always greater than 1, it is not in any country's self-interest to abate.

Suppose that there are three signatories and that an agreement requires each signatory to abate at its maximum level. We are now at the adjustment stage where the signatories decide collectively whether to modify or even eliminate the target. Suppose that, as with most participation games in this literature, a supranational agent who wants to maximize the collective welfare of the signatories while ignoring the welfare of non-signatories makes the adjustment decision.

First, consider the case where international trade in permits is not permitted, because, for example, the countries did not develop the institutional structure needed to govern this trade. In this case, it is in the collective interest of the signatories to carry out the agreement: the expected total costs are $3 \times 2 = 6$ and the total benefits are $3 \times 3 = 9$.[8] Suppose instead that the countries are able to trade permits amongst themselves. In this situation, the statistical problem is a bit more complicated. The collective marginal benefit of a unit of abatement is 3 (since each participant obtains the marginal benefit of 1). If the expectation of the highest cost (the third order statistic) is greater than 3, and the expectation of the second-highest cost (the second order statistic) lies between 2 and 3, then it is optimal for the countries to agree on only two units of abatement. Since costs are not verifiable, the group requires each country to achieve two-thirds of one unit of abatement,

---

[8] The assumption of constant marginal costs and constant marginal benefits means that in the absence of trade it is always in the interest of countries that ratify the agreement to either abate to capacity or not to abate at all.

and allows them to trade in order to achieve this target. In this example, the ability to trade reduces the total level of abatement by 33 %.

The effect of emissions trade on the incentive to join

The anticipation that a supranational agent will adjust the required level of abatement—conditional on actual membership—and that emissions permits will be tradable, has a more subtle effect on incentives to join an agreement. The Nash equilibrium to the participation game requires that participants do not want to leave the agreement, and non-participants do not want to join. These calculations involve the different payoffs of participation to members and non-members.

Moving from a regime that prohibits trade in permits to one that allows trade changes the payoffs to both members and non-members. In an earlier paper we conjectured that this change would reduce the equilibrium membership (Karp and Zhao 2007), and work-in-progress confirms that conjecture. Because world welfare is very sensitive to the aggregate amount of abatement, and much less sensitive to whether countries achieve this abatement in the most efficient manner, allowing trade is likely to reduce aggregate welfare as well as aggregate abatement.

The previous subsection noted that trade can reduce the amount of abatement, conditional on the level of participation, and this subsection notes that trade can also reduce the level of participation. These theoretical possibilities—together with the reasons for not using emissions trading to provide a mechanism for side payments to induce membership—are strong enough to make us skeptical that international trade in permits will contribute significantly to the design of a post-Kyoto climate agreement. However, trade does have a place in achieving the efficient reduction of emissions, and we support its use for that limited purpose.

The optimal form of regulation

Several papers examine the optimal form of regulation for stock pollutants such as GHGs when regulators are imperfectly informed about firms' abatement costs (Hoel and Karp 2001, 2002; Newell and Pizer 2003; Karp and Zhang 2006). The usual comparison is between taxes and cap-and-trade programs. The consensus from this literature is that taxes are more efficient than cap-and-trade policies for controlling

GHGs. There are several reasons for this conclusion, but the most fundamental is that the evidence supports a relatively flat marginal damage curve for GHGs. Although the qualitative conclusion that taxes are more efficient than cap and trade is quite robust, the magnitude of the gain from using taxes depends on the variance of the cost uncertainty, a parameter that is itself very uncertain. A more complicated policy, e.g., an optimal two-part tax (equivalent to a cap-and-trade system with a price ceiling), could obviously dominate either a simple tax or a cap-and-trade policy with no price ceiling.

Based on this research, we encourage nations to use a tax rather than cap-and-trade approach to achieve their national targets. Other authors, examining the same evidence, prefer a cap-and-trade policy to a tax policy (Stavins 2008). Public distaste for taxes, the lack of public understanding of the price effects of the two types of policies, and the political power of carbon-intensive industries are such that most countries are likely to opt for a cap-and-trade policy—or even worse, a command-and-control policy. This choice is of second-order importance when considering the goal of obtaining an agreement that imposes mandatory ceilings on national GHG emissions. Nations should be allowed to choose how to comply with these ceilings.

If, as in our view, taxes are more efficient than quantity restrictions, why do we support an agreement that uses country-specific emissions targets, rather than a global carbon tax? In fact, a global carbon tax is probably a more efficient means of achieving emissions reductions (Norhaus 2007). However, we think that an agreement that uses quantity restrictions has a much better chance of being negotiated and ratified than one based on a global tax. Perhaps a second successor to Kyoto will use taxes.

Conclusion

Our design for a new, post-2012 international climate agreement includes many of the important features of the Kyoto Protocol. We regard it as absolutely essential that a next agreement involve mandatory emissions ceilings. We support the continued development and use of the CDM and JI, and the likely extension to sectoral policies. To maintain flexibility, the specific requirements under a new treaty should apply to the next decade. The next agreement should acknowledge that it is one of a sequence of projected agreements.

Our proposal departs from the Kyoto Protocol in two main respects. First, our design includes an escape clause, which has three desirable features. The two most important features are that it encourages membership and it helps to solve the enforcement problem. The escape clause also caps the potential cost of joining the agreement.

The second departure is that our design recognizes that trade policy must eventually be used in order to prevent leakage and possibly also to induce countries to join the agreement. Trade economists may blanch at this proposal, but the changing relative costs of weakening the trade order versus risking environmental catastrophe make it a necessity. All countries, including developing countries that are not responsible for existing GHG stocks but that are partly responsible for increasing stocks, must also come under the discipline of an international climate agreement.

References

Aldy, J., A. Krupnick, R. Newell, I. Parry, and W. Pizer (2008). "Climate Economics and Policy," RFF Working Paper.

Aldy, J. E. and R. N. Stavins (2007). *Architectures for Agreement: Addressing Global Climate Change in the Post-Kyoto World*. Cambridge, UK: Cambridge University Press.

Baron, R., J. Reinaud, M. Genasci, and C. Philbert (2007). "Sectoral Approaches to Greenhouse Gas Mitigation: Exploring Issues for Heavy Industry," IEA Information Paper.

Barrett, S. (2003). *Environment and Statecraft*. Oxford: Oxford University Press.

Bhagwati, J. (2004). *In Defense of Globalization*. Oxford: Oxford University Press.

Carraro, C. and D. Siniscalco (1993). "Strategies for the International Protection of the Environment," *Journal of Public Economics* 52: 309–28.

Cone, S. M. (2002). "The Environment and the World Trade Organization," New York Law School working paper.

Copeland, B. and M. Taylor (2003). *Trade and the Environment: Theory and Evidence*. Princeton, NJ: Princeton University Press.

(2004). "Trade, Growth and the Environment," *Journal of Economic Literature* 41(1): 7–71.

Feng, H. and J. Zhao (2006). "Alternative Intertemporal Permit Trading Regimes with Stochastic Abatement Costs," *Resource and Energy Economics* 28: 24–40.

Guzman, A. (2002). "Global Governance and the WTO," UC Berkeley School of Law Research Paper No. 89.

Hoel, M. and L. Karp (2001). "Taxes and Quotas for a Stock Pollutant with Multiplicative Uncertainty," *Journal of Public Economics* 82: 91–114.

    (2002). "Taxes Versus Quotas for a Stock Pollutant," *Resource and Energy Economics* 24: 367–84.

Intergovernmental Panel on Climate Change (2001). *Climate Change 2001: Mitigation Working Group III contribution to the IPPC 3rd assessment report*, available at www.ipcc.ch/ipccreports/tar/wg3/index.php?idp=0.

Kallbekken, S. (2007). "Why the CDM Will Reduce Carbon Leakage," *Climate Policy* 7: 187–211.

Karp, L. (2005). "Global Warming and Hyperbolic Discounting," *Journal of Public Economics* 89: 261–82.

    (2008). "Correct (and Misleading) Arguments for Using Market-Based Pollution Control Technologies," http://are.berkeley.edu/~karp.

Karp, L. and Y. Tsur (2007). "Time Perspective, Discounting and Climate Change Policy," Unpublished working paper; http://are.berkeley.edu/~karp/.

Karp, L. and J. Zhang (2006). "Regulation with Anticipated Learning about Environmental Damage," *Journal of Environmental Economics and Management* 51: 259–80.

Karp, L. and J. Zhao (2007). "A Proposal to Reform the Kyoto Protocol: Escape Clauses and Foresight," http://are.berkeley.edu/~karp.

Kling, C. L. and J. Rubin (1997). "Bankable Permits for the Control of Environmental Pollution," *Journal of Public Economics* 64: 101–15.

McGinty, M. (2007). "International Environmental Agreements Among Asymmetric Nations," *Oxford Economics Papers* 59: 45–62.

Neumeyer, E. (2005). "The WTO and the Environment: Its Past Record is Better than Critics Believe, but the Future Outlook is Bleak," *Global Environmental Politics* 4: 1–8.

Newell, R. and W. Pizer (2003). "Regulating Stock Externalities Under Uncertainty," *Journal of Environmental Economics and Management* 45: 416–32.

Niederberger, A. A. (2008). "Scaling Up Energy Efficiency under the CDM," in K. H. Olsen and J. Fenhann (eds.), *A Reformed CDM: Including New Mechanisms for Sustainable Development*, UNEP Riso Center, pp. 127–45.

Nordhaus, W. D. (2007). "To Tax or Not to Tax: Alternative Approaches to Slowing Global Warming," *Review of Environmental Economics and Policy* 1(1): 26–44.

Pauwelyn, J. (2007). "U.S. Federal Climate Policy and Competitiveness Concerns: The Limits and Options of International Trade Law," Nicholas Institutute for Environmental Policy Solultions.

Sanchez, S. (2008). "Reforming CDM and Scaling-Up: Finance for Sustainable Urban Transport," in Olsen and Fenhann (eds.), pp. 111–24.

Stavins, R. (2008). "Addressing Climate Change with a Comprehensive US Cap-and-Trade System," Cambridge, MA: John F. Kennedy School of Government.

Stiglitz, J. E. (2006). "A New Agenda for Global Warming," *Economists' Voice* 3(7): 1–4.

United Nations Environmental Programme (1999). *Environment and Trade—a Handbook*, United Nations.

Victor, D. G. (2008). "Climate Accession Deals: New Strategies for Taming Growth of Greenhouse Gases in Developing Countries," Discussion Paper 2008–18, Harvard Project on International Climate Agreements.

Ward, M. (2008). "Sector No-Lose Targets: A New Scaling Up Mechanism For Developing Countries," in Olsen, and Fenhann (eds.), pp. 147–60.

Webster, M., S. Paltsev, and J. Reilly (2007). "The Hedge Value of Emissions Trading Under Uncertainty," Working paper MIT Joint Program on the Science and Policy of Global Change.

World Bank (2008). *International Trade and Climate Change*, World Bank.

Yates, A. J. and M. B. Cronshaw (2001). "Pollution Permit Markets with Intertemporal Trading and Asymmetric Information," *Journal of Environmental Economics and Management* 42: 104–18.

PART V

Economic development, adaptation, and deforestation

18 Reconciling human development and climate protection

A Multistage Hybrid Climate Policy Architecture

JING CAO*

Introduction

Human activity is causing irreversible harm to the climate system and the global environment. According to the Intergovernmental Panel on Climate Change (IPCC 2007), the earth's average surface temperature has increased by 0.7 degrees Celsius (°C) in the last century. Observable indicators of this change include rising sea level, declining snow cover, glacier melt, and so forth. Avoiding a future catastrophic climate crisis will require the global community to establish a valid and effective global climate policy architecture. Global emissions will have to be brought rapidly under control to stabilize atmospheric greenhouse gas (GHG) concentrations at roughly 450 parts per million (ppm) carbon dioxide (CO_2) equivalent—the stabilization target thought to be necessary to prevent global mean temperatures from exceeding the widely endorsed 2°C threshold (Scientific Expert Group 2007; Stern 2006). To achieve this target, any international climate regime ought to balance considerations of efficiency and equity—that is, it ought to

* This chapter is supported and funded by Harvard Project on International Climate Agreements. I would like to thank Prof. Robert Stavins and Dr. Joseph Aldy for their support in this project, and Fondazione Eni Enrico Mattei (FEEM) for sponsoring me to participate in the post-2012 international policy architecture for global climate change in Venice. I would also like to give thanks for some of the partial funding from the SEI and Chinese Economist 50 Forum on my relevant climate change studies. I am grateful for Joseph Aldy, Robert Stavins, Gernot Wagner, and an anonymous reviewer for comments on a first draft, as well as comments from Harvard/FEEM Workshop on Global Architecture in Venice, Italy. I would also like to especially thank Wang Zigan and Su Min for their excellent assistance work.

solve the emission reductions, economic growth, and humanitarian problems of climate change at the same time.

As the first step in the international community's battle with climate change, the Kyoto Protocol—after endless negotiations over the last two decades—has failed to deliver aggressive emission reductions; on the contrary, global emissions are still rising. Given the lessons from past Kyoto negotiations, we can lay out the key challenges for a new post-Kyoto climate regime.

First, a successful climate agreement will require that actions to reduce GHG emissions take place in both the developed and developing world, thus achieving efficiency by equalizing the marginal cost of abatement and avoiding carbon leakage. Engaging developing countries in a cooperative effort to mitigate climate change in turn requires giving them incentives to commit to undertaking emission reductions that are aligned with their self-interests.

Second, a credible climate agreement ought to reconcile economic development and equity considerations. Developed countries should accept their historical responsibility for the current stock of GHGs in the atmosphere. Developing nations should be able to safeguard a right to balance sustainable development needs with climate protection.

Finally, successful treaties must create adequate incentives for compliance, bring about significant technological change, stimulate substantial financial transfers to facilitate low-carbon actions, rely on practical measures and realistic negotiating processes, and build on existing institutional and legal architectures.

Currently, discussions of a promising international climate policy architecture that addresses the design challenges mentioned above have focused on three major categories of policies: (1) a "Kyoto successor" approach that incorporates key characteristics from the existing Kyoto framework with some modifications; (2) a brand new approach that replaces the Kyoto framework completely; or (3) a portfolio of international treaties that link multitrack climate agreements to address various sectors, gases, and key issues. In addition, since climate change poses such fundamental and complicated challenges, numerous studies have focused on specific design details, including issues such as targets and timetables, burden sharing, choice of policy instrument (e.g., harmonized carbon tax vs. linked cap-and-trade systems), technology transfer, geo-engineering, enforcement mechanisms and sanctions, sectoral approaches, and so forth.

In this chapter we describe a multistage hybrid climate policy architecture, which provides a top-down structure, in the sense that it establishes an overall global binding target, but also includes bottom-up elements in the form of a hybrid "climate club" framework to facilitate real-world climate negotiations and encourage the engagement of developing countries. This proposal conserves but improves some aspects of the Kyoto Protocol, including fair burden-sharing principles reconciling efficiency and equity, and other design details that are likely to be important from the perspective of developing countries, as well as how these building materials can be coherently embedded into the big picture of multistage hybrid climate architecture.

The chapter is structured as follows. In the next section we introduce and more thoroughly explain the overall structure of the multistage hybrid climate policy architecture we propose. In the third section we lay out key design issues, including a modified Greenhouse Development Rights framework originally developed by Baer *et al.* (2007) to reconcile human development and climate protection; and issues related to technology and financial transfer, penalty for noncompliance, and adaptation. Before concluding, in the fourth section we use China as an example to shed some light on how developing countries may coordinate their balanced path reconciling economic growth and climate protection, by reforming domestic policies, institutional and enforcement mechanisms, and coordinating with the global community on abatement efforts.

A multistage hybrid climate policy architecture: an overview picture

In this section, we provide an overview of our proposed multistage hybrid climate policy architecture. First, we sketch out a multistage timetable for negotiating differentiated long-run and short-to-medium run commitments based on countries' unique characteristics, historical emissions, and stage of development. In particular, we discuss why an incremental evolution involving intermediate transition stages is necessary and what criteria for graduation thresholds are under discussion in academic circles. Then we focus on the hybrid organizational and institutional framework, and discuss how it might work in practice.

A *multistage approach*

Climate change is a long-term challenge characterized by uncertainty in both science and economics. Thus, climate change negotiations should not focus on a short-term fix but rather on long-term concepts. However, it is not realistic to negotiate an agreement over 50 or 100 years or even a longer time frame. Thus, a realistic climate change policy structure would ideally provide for multiple stages with a long time horizon but accessible and relatively short-term targets for each stage.

Currently, many researchers have proposed that international climate change negotiations be structured in multiple stages, featuring differentiated targets and commitments, with countries participating either through a continuous process of graduation and deepening (Michaelowa 2007) or in discrete stages. The latter approach was first developed by Gupta (1998) and has subsequently been elaborated further, both quantitatively and qualitatively, by numerous researchers (see, for example, Berk and den Elzen 2001, Blanchard *et al.* 2003, CAN 2003, Criqui *et al.* 2003, den Elzen *et al.* 2003, Gupta 2003, Höhne *et al.* 2003, Ott *et al.* 2004, Blok *et al.* 2005, den Elzen 2005, den Elzen *et al.* 2007, Höhne *et al.* 2005, Michaelowa *et al.* 2005, den Elzen *et al.* 2006, Höhne 2006).

A long-term, multistage international climate negotiation framework can easily be adapted to changing circumstances as we resolve uncertainties in the future with respect to scientific knowledge on climate change, mitigation, and/or adaptation costs, and technology breakthroughs. In addition, by dividing countries into groups with different targets and timetables, and different levels of mitigation efforts, such a proposal can engage more countries to participate, and ensure that countries with similar circumstances in terms of development capacity and emission responsibilities face comparable requirements.

To engage more developing countries, reconcile economic development and equity considerations, create adequate incentives for compliance, and initiate a more realistic negotiation process based upon existing institutions and mitigation practices, a promising future climate architecture should include the following stages:

1. *In the first stage, all member countries would agree on a path of future global emissions that leads to an acceptable long-term stabilization goal.* Developed countries ought to increase the stringency

of their binding Kyoto emissions reduction commitments and achieve concrete emission reductions. The developing countries, in particular low and lower-middle income developing countries, and some upper-middle income developing countries,[1] would continue to follow their unconstrained emission path during this stage.

2. *In the second stage, developing countries would focus on "no regrets" mitigation options that prioritize local sustainable development.* Sustainable development measures should include gradual phase-out of inefficient and energy-intensive equipment, "no regrets" GHG mitigation options, and new investment and standards aimed at both economic development and environmental objectives. At this stage, developing countries would still be exempted from quantitative emissions targets, but policy commitments on emission reductions would be strongly encouraged to mitigate carbon leakages, along with further expansion of CDM[2] projects with moderate financial and technological flows from developed countries.

3. *In the third stage, developing countries would take on moderate emissions targets that are only binding in one direction.* Based on a globally agreed credible burden-sharing mechanism and graduation threshold, developing countries would take on moderate targets based on their capacities and responsibilities. These targets would be binding in only one direction—that is, if emissions are below the target (reductions are greater than expected), the excess allowances can be sold in the global emission trading market, but if the target is not achieved, no allowances have to be bought (Höhne 2006). Or as Aldy, Baron, and Tubiana (2003) have suggested, developing countries could adopt non-binding or "no lose" targets to experiment with emission mitigation efforts. In practice, if developing countries undertake some abatement efforts, such as implementing a domestic carbon tax, and thereby achieve a lower carbon emissions path than the forecast baseline, they can sell the "excess" allowances to countries with binding commitments.

---

[1] The income classifications for developing countries referenced here have been developed by the World Bank; see http://siteresources.worldbank.org/DATASTATISTICS/Resources/CLASS.XLS.

[2] The CDM is one of the flexible mechanisms established under the Kyoto Protocol to assist developing countries in achieving sustainable development, while also contributing to the stabilization of GHG concentrations in the atmosphere.

4. *In the final stage, all countries would agree to binding, absolute emissions targets.* These targets would be binding in both directions, which means failure to achieve stated targets would trigger stringently enforced penalties.

Setting up interim stages as part of this framework has a number of merits:

- *A phased approach can help break the political impasse between the North and the South in international climate negotiations,* while another round of one-stage *ad hoc* negotiations toward ultimate binding targets for all countries might only put the world in an inescapable deadlock over the issue of climate change.
- *Through the interim stage, as Baer et al. (2008) have suggested, actions and preparations can move forward to build trust between the North and the South in a sequential manner.* With efforts from both sides, the transition period can be shortened to move countries forward to subsequent stages with more stringent targets and more substantial emission reduction efforts.
- *During the interim transition stage, design details of the overall climate architecture can be further improved in a learning-by-doing manner.*

Another important factor implicit in the proposed multistage approach is the need to design metrics for graduation to more stringent commitments. A reasonable graduation threshold could be based on a consensus about the level of income per capita that represents a capacity to take on mitigation burdens; alternatively, it could be based on a per capita cumulative emission threshold that represents historic responsibility for the current build-up of GHGs. Yet another option is to apply a composite metric—the capacity-responsibility (CR) index—that accounts for both of these factors. Ultimately, the choice of a graduation threshold will be a political one, and its outcome will depend on how rule-based global commitments can be broadened and deepened. Once there is consensus about graduation thresholds, it will be necessary to regularly review each country's profile and assess whether it has met the threshold for graduation to the next stage. This will inevitably require a well-designed institution to organize and undertake these reviews and assessments—a possible structure for such an institution is described in the next sub-section.

A hybrid organizational structure

To facilitate smooth negotiations and a feasible and flexible approach to enforcement, we propose a hybrid top-down and bottom-up organizational structure for implementing the proposed multistage climate policy architecture. The overall hierarchy or structure can be decomposed into three levels, with a global authority at the top; regionally-coordinated multinational treaties among groups of countries (or 'clubs') to achieve collective goals in the middle; and single countries implementing national-level policies at the base.

The top level—a global climate agency

Ideally, a post-2012 climate policy would be supported by a top-down, independent international institution that could determine targets, emissions reduction pathways, and multitrack timetables in the climate change negotiating process, taking into account the most recent scientific findings and abatement technology innovations. This is a crucial step. We can see that part of the failure of the Kyoto Protocol lies in its overly modest targets and weak enforcement mechanisms. In the post-2012 era, countries will continue to have every incentive to push for a modest overall target and to make their own emissions allotment (or cap) as large as possible to minimize their mitigation obligations. Efforts to develop future emissions reduction pathways would have to rely on frequently updated IPCC assessment reports, which provide a common basis for projecting a global reference trajectory and the currently widely endorsed emergency pathway for limiting global average warming to 2°C. Certainly, this could bring with it an intense politicization of the IPCC process and scaled-up UN authority on climate negotiation issues.

A credible global climate change agreement must be practical, and ideally it will build upon existing institutions. Thus, the UNFCCC provides a good start as the main vehicle for international climate negotiation diplomacy. It might be very difficult, however, to set a global deal to cover all countries. However, a central institutional authority can help provide the multinational coordination needed to establish a lower level climate club structure (in this instance by further dividing the current Annex I and non-Annex I categories in the Kyoto Protocol and UNFCCC), and can facilitate an effective climate action agenda in a number of ways. First, it can enable the development of institutional

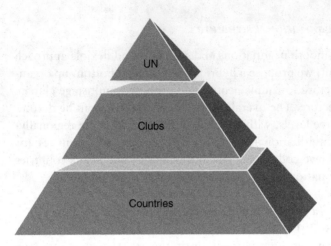

Figure 18.1. A top-down and bottom-up post-2012 climate policy enforcement framework

arrangements for collective decision making with respect to climate change, such as integrating global long-run goals with multitrack short-to-medium run objectives for individual countries. Secondly, the top-down regime can help coordinate and scale up special climate funds to promote large-scale financial and technological flows. Finally, the central authority of the UNFCCC might be leveraged to provide for financial penalties and other sanctions to induce compliance as well. A top-down review and assessment of burden sharing for each club of countries and for overall projects can be undertaken every five or ten years.

The middle level—clubs of countries
Once agreement has been reached on long-term emissions reduction targets and multitrack timetables, countries would decide what means they will use, depending on their own endowments and existing policy and institutional frameworks, to achieve the targets. Countries would be encouraged to join other countries in forming smaller groups or "climate clubs" to advance negotiations in a bottom-up manner. This was roughly the format used in the Group of Eight plus Five (G8+5) "Gleneagles" process, the Bush Administration's Major Economies Meetings (MEM), and the US-China Strategic Dialogues. A number of characteristics could be used as the basis for grouping countries in clubs:

1. **Geography:** Because countries in the same region often share similar political systems, history, and development status, it may be easier to reach consensus in regional negotiations. So, for example, one could have a European Club, a Northeast Asia Club, an Arab Club, etc.
2. **Development Level:** Countries at similar levels of development often have similar capabilities and responsibilities. So a club organization based on development level, such as a high-income club or a low-income club, could fit well into a multistage climate framework, in particular allowing developing countries to begin with voluntary carbon abatement efforts and then, at a later stage, accede to moderate or even more stringent binding commitments.
3. **Economic or Fiscal System:** For practical reasons, it will be easier for countries with similar economic and fiscal systems to bind together, to decide whether they will adopt a unified carbon trading market or a harmonized regional carbon tax regime, or opt for a hybrid system with safety valves. Then, between clubs, various market-based programs can be sewn together: cap-and-trade systems can be linked with the CDM and other emission-reduction-credit systems, emission permits can be traded against carbon tax obligations, or absolute emissions caps can be linked to intensity-based trading programs (Pizer 2007; Hall *et al.* 2008; Jaffe and Stavins 2008).
4. **Other factors:** Major emitting countries like the United States and China, which together account for about 45 percent of global carbon emissions, are important players in the climate change arena. Therefore, China and the United States can shape their own club, build upon the current US–China Strategic and Economic Dialogue (S&ED) and coordinate with other clubs.

The bottom-up formation of climate clubs would encourage participation in a future international agreement by attracting countries with similar interests and backgrounds in a simplified negotiation process. Some regional climate forums, such as the Asia-Pacific Partnership on Clean Development and Climate, can scale up from sector-by-sector action to more broadly defined and coordinated climate actions. Mitigation obligations and timetables for each country within the same club would be established through the UN's top-down allocation process. But the choice of policy regimes to meet targets and timetables can be discussed and decided among club members. In addition, countries may benefit from within-club technology transfer of the best practices of other club members.

The bottom level—countries

At this level, each country can set up its own national climate strategy using existing environment ministries or other domestic institutions to develop policies that reconcile sustainable development goals and plans with the achievement of negotiated emissions reduction obligations. Before taking on binding commitments in later stages of the proposed climate agreement, developing countries would be encouraged to join a portfolio of international treaties, such as sectoral agreements. In addition, if a country were part of a club that opted for a harmonized carbon tax regime or an auction-based emission trading regime, while the level of the tax or cap might be set by the club, each country would decide how to use the tax or permit auction revenues based on its own policy objectives, domestic conditions and background, and pre-existing fiscal systems.

Key design factors for the proposed climate architecture

Besides relying on a multistage negotiation scheme and hybrid institutional structure, a realistic multistage framework would also incorporate the following key elements: (1) a fair and efficient burden-sharing rule, which is central to our proposed architecture; (2) a portfolio of policy instruments to achieve cost-effective mitigation; (3) financial mechanisms and technology transfer; (4) penalty scheme for non-compliance; and (5) issues regarding adaptation.

Burden sharing: reconciling human development and climate protection

Defining an internationally fair and effective way to distribute the burden of reducing climate change risks has been a core issue in multilateral climate negotiations. The distribution of burdens across individual countries should be tailored to fulfill the UNFCCC principle of "common but differentiated responsibilities and respective capacities." The ideal burden-sharing formula ought to broaden participation and program coverage, support meaningful mitigation goals, and provide for feasible and self-enforcing compliance mechanisms.

Although there has been an enormous amount of work and negotiation over these issues, little progress has been achieved toward a global climate deal that substantially reduces GHG emissions and advances climate stabilization goals. The root of the difficulty lies in some basic differences of perspective between the North and the South when it comes to an equitable and fair allocation of burdens. Developing countries have tended to emphasize the issue of historical responsibility for current levels of GHG accumulation in the atmosphere, and have resisted any commitments they view as jeopardizing their ability to develop economically. Developed countries, on the other hand, are suspicious of developing countries' real motives on absolute emission reductions, and emphasize that any climate policy will be ineffective with the carbon leakage from the South. Thus, breaking the current political impasse and designing a widely accepted burden-sharing rule that both (1) reconciles the objectives of human development and climate protection; and (2) resolves the different perspectives of the North and South would be key to providing the foundation for a multistage hybrid climate architecture.

In attempting to design a "fair and equitable" scheme for burden sharing that can be accepted by all or at least most countries, a number of factors need to be considered: (1) the size of economy; (2) historical contribution to current warming; (3) the right to safeguard development; (4) controlling carbon leakage; and (5) considering other country-specific factors.

Recent proposals for an international burden-sharing formula have tended to focus mostly on per capita emission rights, or historical emissions responsibility. However, these equity-based proposals may not be as "fair" as they claim to be, and both run into powerful objections. Posner and Sunstein (2008) criticize the per capita approach, emphasizing instead a distributive justice perspective and pointing out that some rich nations are highly populated and some poor nations are not. This means that a per capita approach could reward some populous countries that are also rich, while giving an insufficient allocation to poor countries with a small population. Similarly, the proposal put forward by Brazil in 1997 focuses on historical responsibility only, but fails to consider developing countries' capacity to mitigate their own increasingly significant emissions (Brazil 1997).

This proposal takes an alternative path in that it focuses more on a combination of these two factors (per capita emissions and historical emissions) while also emphasizing the principle of distributive justice.

Specifically, it builds on an idea first described by Baer *et al.* (2007, 2008) that quantitatively links the "right to development" with measures of both capacity and responsibility at individual level, and then attempts to work out an appropriate national aggregate target on that basis. We adopt a Cobb-Douglas weighted composite index for capacity and responsibility, termed the "Responsibility and Capacity Indicator" (RCI) in the "Greenhouse Development Rights" (GDR) framework in Baer *et al.* (2007). The RCI is defined as:

$$RCI = R^a C^b \tag{1}$$

In this burden-sharing formula, C represents responsibility, defined as the integral of individual income (income below a minimum threshold is excluded) over a log-normal income distribution $f(y,\bar{y},G)$ for a given country, as described in equation (2):

$$C = P \int_{y_{DT}}^{\infty} dy (y - y_{DT}) f(y, \bar{y}, G) \tag{2}$$

where P is the population, y_{DT} is the development threshold, $\bar{y}$ is per capita income, G is the Gini coefficient, and the variance is denoted in equation (3) with N^{-1} as the inverse of the cumulative normal distribution:

$$\sigma^2 (G) = 2[N^{-1}((1 + G)/2)]^2 \tag{3}$$

Similarly, national responsibility (R) is defined as:

$$R = P \int_{y_{DT}}^{\infty} dy (e(y) - e_{DT}) f(y, \bar{y}, G) \tag{4}$$

where $e(y)$ denotes emissions at a given level of income (y) and e_{DT} is equal to the emissions of a person whose income is precisely equal to the development threshold. The emission quantity e_{DT} behaves analogously to the development threshold, in that only emissions above this emissions threshold contribute to R.

In this framework, capacity (C) says something about a country's ability to pay for GHG mitigation without sacrificing basic societal necessities, while responsibility (R) indicates a country's historic contribution to the climate problem. The exogenous weighting parameters a and b represent an ethical judgment on the relative importance of capacity versus historic responsibility.

Unlike national emission allocations at the country level, or GHG intensity targets focused at the sector level, the allocation rule proposed in Baer *et al.* (2007) as part of their GDR framework is defined in individual terms and *"implicitly accounts for the distribution of income and emissions—inequality—within countries."* Thus a combination of per capita income and per capita emissions, above a threshold, are implicitly taken into account. This obliges people with incomes and emissions above the threshold, no matter where they are, to bear a share of the costs of mitigation and adaptation, while also allowing people with incomes and emissions below the threshold to maintain their right to development. In this chapter, we select a development threshold or so called "subsistence income" of $9,000 as suggested in Baer *et al.* (2007), which means that any income below this threshold[3] is waived for purposes of determining a country's climate obligations.

This chapter makes some amendments to the calculations described in Baer *et al.* (2007, 2008). First, we use a more comprehensive record of historic carbon emissions data (from 1850 to 2004).[4] This reflects the fact that the build-up of GHGs in the atmosphere—which is what matters in terms of climate change impacts—dates back to the Industrial Revolution (at that time, the concentration of CO_2 in the atmosphere was about 280 ppm, today it is about 430 ppm). Therefore, accounting for past emissions starting in 1990, which is the approach taken by Baer *et al.* (2007, 2008), fails to take into account historical responsibilities before the 1990 era, when the economies of most developed countries had already shifted away from energy-intensive manufacturing toward a greater role for less energy- and pollution-intensive service industries. Though all GHGs would in principle be covered by a new international agreement, this chapter only addresses fossil-fuel based carbon emissions, which account for about 76 percent of the total global warming contribution from all sources and gases worldwide (USEPA, 2006). The same methodology can easily be extended to other GHGs to the extent that historical emissions data are available at the country level.

Another change from Baer *et al.* in this chapter is that we add a carbon sink component to the framework, as an indicator of responsibility.

---

[3] Baer *et al.* (2007) point out that $9,000 is slightly above the global average income (of about $8,500) and thus represents a "global middle class" income level.

[4] Carbon emissions data for the period 1850–2004 were taken from the Climate Analysis Indicators Tool (CAIT) Version 5.0 (Washington, DC: World Resources Institute, 2008).

For many years, mainstream scientific and policy studies focused only on CO_2 emissions from fossil fuel combustion—as a result, most GHG mitigation policies have concentrated on the energy sector. However, atmospheric composition and climate change are also affected, through various bio-geophysical and bio-geochemical mechanisms, by land cover and land-use changes, as well as by non-CO_2 GHGs. Land-use changes, mainly deforestation, account for about 20 percent of global emissions and related GHG abatement activities, and are expected to play an important role in combating future climate change—indeed their role may be greater than that of emissions mitigation efforts in the global transport and industrial sectors (Lagos, Wirth, and El-Ashry 2007). To address this issue, we revise the original GDR framework by including a carbon sink calculation. Quantifying carbon stock changes associated with land use is a very complicated task, so for this preliminary study we only account for forest-based carbon stocks and sequestration.[5]

The carbon stock data used for this analysis are based on a recent study by the Food and Agriculture Organization of the United Nations (FAO)—specifically the FAO's Global Forestry Resources Assessment 2005 (FRA 2005).[6] The FRA 2005 is the most comprehensive assessment of the current status of the world's forests and recent trends with respect to the extent, condition, uses, and value of forests and other wooded land. Of particular interest, it provides estimates of the accumulated flow of carbon stocks[7] in forestry and other wooded land for the year 2005. Since the missing data issue is more prominent for the carbon stocks of other wooded land, our focus is only on forestry.

As for the other data, we use the GDR version 2.0.0 database with updated information on income class categories, per capita incomes (2005 prices with PPP adjustment), Gini coefficients, and national incomes. A summary of the raw data along with the results of this

---

[5] Terrestrial carbon sinks absorb CO_2 via a number of mechanisms: the ocean's biological bump, which transports carbon from the surface euphotic zone to the ocean's interior, or the photosynthetic processes by which plants and other organisms remove carbon from the atmosphere and release oxygen. The process by which these sinks remove CO_2 from the atmosphere is known as "carbon sequestration." In this chapter we account only for carbon sequestration from changes in land use and forest carbon stocks for purposes of our calculation.

[6] Source: www.fao.org/forestry/fra2005/en/page.jsp.

[7] The FAO defines "carbon stock" as indicating the contribution of "Forest" and "Other wooded land" to the carbon cycle, and it reports carbon stocks for the years 1990, 2000, and 2005. We use data for 2005 only, which includes accumulated carbon stocks from sequestration in prior years (that is, before 2005).

Table 18.1 *Global percentage share of population, income, capacity, cumulative emissions, carbon sink, responsibility, and global RCI for selected countries and groups*

Country	Population	Income (2005 PPP Adjusted)	Global Capacity	Cumulative Emissions 1850–2004	Carbon Sink	Global Responsibility	Global RCI*
United States	4.7	22.2	33.7	29.5	8.04	43.3	39.3
United Kingdom	0.9	3.4	4.7	6.2	0.04	8.8	6.4
Germany	1.3	4.5	6.1	7.2	0.49	10.0	7.8
France	0.9	3.3	4.5	2.9	0.43	3.9	4.5
Russia	2.2	3.0	2.0	8.2	16.77	2.8	2.4
Japan	2.0	6.9	9.4	3.9	0.70	5.2	7.8
South Korea	0.8	1.8	2.1	0.8	0.11	0.9	1.6
China	20.4	10.0	2.3	8.1	2.78	1.8	2.2
India	17.0	4.2	0.1	2.3	0.97	0.0	0.0
Brazil	2.9	2.8	2.2	0.8	19.46	0.0	0.0
South Africa	0.7	0.7	0.5	1.2	0.74	0.8	0.7
All High Income	15.6	59.1	83.4	62.1	15.70	86.7	86.9
All Middle Income	47.7	33.5	16.5	33.7	62.97	13.2	13.0
All Low Income	36.7	7.4	0.2	4.2	21.34	0.1	0.1

* Here we assume the capacity weight a = 0.6 and responsibility weight b = 0.4.

revised GDR calculation for selected countries and groups of countries
is given in Table 18.1.

From our calculation, the United States has the highest share of
global capacity, the largest share of global responsibility and therefore also the largest combined RCI. Taking into account forest-based
carbon sinks and new cumulative carbon emissions, our calculation of
the US share is 5 percent higher than the results in Baer *et al.* (2007).[8]
Following the United States (which has an RCI of 39.3 percent),
Germany, Japan, and the United Kingdom will need to contribute
about 7.8 percent, 7.8 percent, and 6.4 percent, respectively. So,
under this approach, these four countries together count for about 60
percent of the overall global bill for climate change abatement. We
also calculated current obligations using this method for developing
countries. Based on the new data set, China's obligation is about 2.2
percent, India and Brazil would have no obligations, and South Africa
has a tiny obligation of 0.7 percent.

Table 18.2 provides the results of GDR calculations based on different assumptions. The first column gives the original calculation of RCI
share in Baer *et al.* (2007), only with the updated GDR 2.0.0 version
data set, so results are slightly different from their original results. For
example, GDR for China is only 2.7, not 7.0 in Baer *et al.* (2007),
because the new data set utilized updated PPP estimates for China
from the World Bank. In the second column, we expand the data set
for cumulative carbon emissions from 1990–2005 to 1850–2004. We
can see that this increases the US share by 2 percent and the EU share
by 4 percent, while on the other hand slightly reducing the shares of
developing countries. This is because most of the industrialization that
occurred fifty years ago occurred in western countries. Counting more
historical emissions increases the responsibility, and hence the shares,
assigned to those countries that industrialized earlier.

In the third column of Table 18.2, we keep the time horizon for
accumulated emissions to 1990–2005, but incorporate carbon sink
data from the FAO. Due to extensive forestry cover in the United
States, the US RCI drops by one-third, while the EU's share increases
to about 39 percent, and China's share also increases slightly.

Our preferred calculation (last column of table 18.1) is also given in
the fourth column of Table 18.2. These results suggest that the United

---

[8] Baer, Athanasiou and Kartha (2007) estimated the US share at 34.3 percent.

Table 18.2 *Share of global rci in different scenarios*

	Share of Global RCI (%)					
	2005 Baseline				2020 projection	
Historical CO2 Emissions	1990–2005	1850–2004	1990–2005	1850–2004	1990–2020	1850–2020
Capacity Weighting	0.6	0.6	0.6	0.6	0.6	0.6
Responsibility Weighting	0.4	0.4	0.4	0.4	0.4	0.4
Estimation Scope	No Carbon Sink	No Carbon Sink	Consider Forestry Sink	Consider Forestry Sink	Consider Forestry Sink	Consider Forestry Sink
United States	36.0	38.0	24.6	39.3	20.5	33.7
EU (27)	30.1	34.0	38.8	35.6	34.3	32.6
- United Kingdom	4.3	6.0	7.1	6.4	6.1	5.6
- Germany	5.9	7.4	8.4	7.8	7.3	7.0
Russia	2.9	2.9	0.0	2.4	0.0	4.5
Japan	8.4	7.5	11.8	7.8	10.2	7.0
Brazil	1.7	1.4	0.0	0.0	0.0	0.0
China	2.7	2.1	3.4	2.2	14.2	9.4
India	0.1	0.0	0.1	0.0	1.3	1.0
South Africa	0.8	0.7	0.0	0.7	0.0	0.7

Table 18.2 (cont.)

	Share of Global RCI (%)					
LDCs	0.0	0.0	0.0	0.0	0.0	0.0
All High Income	82.3	84.2	87.0	86.9	74.8	76.1
All Middle Income	17.6	15.6	12.9	13.0	23.9	22.8
All Low Income	0.1	0.1	0.1	0.1	1.3	1.1
World	100.0	100.0	100.0	100.0	100.0	100.0

States and European Union need to assume about 39 percent and 36 percent of the overall cost burden respectively. Overall, high-income countries at the current time need to contribute 87 percent of the total, while the share for middle-income countries is about 13 percent. Low-income countries are basically exempted, with only a tiny (0.1 percent) share for the time being. Our estimate for high-income countries is about 8–9 percent higher compared to Baer *et al.* (2007), and 7–8 percent lower for all the middle-income countries. These differences are due to revised estimates of cumulative emissions and carbon sinks and some other data changes in the new version of the GDR dataset.

Although the developing country share is very small at the outset, it would be expected to grow—especially as countries such as China and India begin to "catch up" with annual GDP growth rates at 8–10 percent and an increasing number of people above the poverty threshold. As these countries take on more responsibilities, the share of the burden assigned to developing countries will increase accordingly. To illustrate this point, the last two columns of Table 18.2 project future obligations as a share of the overall mitigation burden if one assumes that GDP in some developing countries like China and India continues to grow at an average rate of about 7 percent annually, while the rest of the developed countries and middle-income countries keep to annual GDP growth rates of approximately 2 percent. Estimates are given for both the 1990–2020 and 1850–2020 scenarios. Future projected carbon emissions are assumed to follow the same growth trajectory as GDP. By 2020, this reduces the share for high-income countries by roughly 11–12 percent. At the same time, developing countries take more responsibility, with China's share rising to about 9.4 percent, India's share increasing to about 1.0 percent, and South Africa to about 0.7 percent for the 1850–2004 scenario.

The proposed GDR framework can be used to calculate each committed country's share of total emissions reductions from a benchmark emissions pathway (as a reference point). Alternatively, if—as stated in the Stern report (2006)—the world needs to devote 1 percent of gross world product to climate mitigation, then each country will need to pay its share of this total amount either to achieve its own domestic reductions or to purchase credits generated by other countries that exceed their emission reduction quotas. Developing countries, like China and India, are more likely to make a profit by exceeding their emission reduction targets, especially if their abatement costs are relatively low compared to those of developed countries.

Much work would still need to be done to assign each country a binding allocation by applying this modified GDR framework in a dynamic manner. To fit this formula into our multistage hybrid climate architecture, we propose that a top-down climate authority take responsibility for deciding country-level targets. Such targets would apply to developing countries only in later stages, when they reach the graduation thresholds for taking on moderate non-binding or binding targets. Before that, countries still in transition would be exempted from quantitative obligations. To be more specific, during the early stages when non-committed countries are not counted, the shares for committed countries would be recalculated as follows:

$$RCI\_share_j^* = \frac{RCI\_share_j}{\sum_j RCL\_share_j} \quad (j \in \{\text{country with commitments}\}) \quad (5)$$

This idea of allowing emissions to increase in developing countries to accommodate development is similar to the concept of "growth budgets" proposed by Frankel (2008a) and "clean investment budgets" proposed by Wagner *et al.* (2008). Pan *et al.* (2008) have proposed a "carbon budget" model focused on per capita cumulative emissions, which is somewhat similar to our defined responsibility index, though the GDR framework combines both responsibility index and capacity factor.

A portfolio of policy instruments to achieve cost-effective mitigation

In our proposed multistage hybrid climate architecture, cost-effective implementation is key to the choice of policy options for achieving emissions reduction targets by individual countries or climate clubs. Those policy options could include cap-and-trade systems, harmonized carbon taxes, credit mechanisms such as the CDM, sectoral policies, or carbon offset projects. Countries with similar backgrounds, facing similar obligations and constraints in parallel timetables are more likely to group together in a climate club. For example, the European Union and United States might link their national and regional tradable permit systems; China and India may start with carbon offset projects in their transition period, then move on to reduction commitments; or countries facing similar risks from sea-level-rise may work together to address common adaptation issues. Thus a framework that can accommodate different policy approaches can also accommodate countries' own self-interests better, and allow negotiations to proceed more smoothly among a much smaller number of countries. Sectoral approaches are likely to be harmonized across climate clubs, as a supplementary program between both developed and developing countries in certain sectors; and possibly to cover countries in different stages, as well. A pact that allows for different policy portfolios is unlikely to maximize economic efficiency, but it could offer advantages by combining different policy options in a more feasible way.

Financial mechanisms and technology transfer

The burden-sharing GDR framework provides a formula for calculating financial flows from developed countries to developing countries (Baer *et al.* 2008; pp. 76–9). When rich nations have reduction obligations larger than the reductions they can plausibly achieve domestically, they need to buy credits from the developing countries. One way to provide incentives for developing countries to graduate is to allow quotas for offset credits proportional to their stage of commitment. That is, if one developing country commits to a binding target sooner, it can be allowed to receive disproportionate financial rewards for a given level of emissions reductions since the quotes to trade would be higher in this case. Conversely, countries eligible for receiving offset credits that have not yet graduated to binding targets could be allowed to trade those credits with developed countries, but in a disadvantaged manner with less market quotas to trade.

The bargaining problem associated with technology transfer has long been a barrier to progress and consensus in dealing with environmental problems. Disputes usually center on intellectual property rights and historical responsibility. Developed country governments argue that because they are democratic and because intellectual property rights belong to private companies, they have no power to compel the transfer of technology. However, within the framework of climate clubs, it is easier to have technology transfer protocols between different clubs. For some technologies that are unlikely to transfer at high cost, multiple countries in one climate club can buy in a collective way and share the costs. In addition, within each club, policies can be designed that allow countries to share carbon abatement or adaptation technologies with member countries, or to discount costs so as to facilitate technology transfer among club members.

Penalty scheme for non-compliance

An effective agreement must ensure that each country implements and complies with its commitments. The Kyoto Protocol has an enforcement mechanism, but it is not likely to be binding in practice. Countries that exceed their emission targets during one period are required to reduce emissions enough in the next period to make up for the excess plus an additional 30 percent. However, a country that fails to achieve its target in the first period may also fail to meet its commitments in the second period—and indeed may have no intention of ever fulfilling its treaty commitments. Thus, more stringent sanctions for non-compliance and more effective penalty schemes are necessary in a post-Kyoto agreement. The problem is that more stringent sanctions might deter countries from participating in the first place. In our proposal, the ability to graduate to the next stage of commitments, say from non-binding to binding targets, also gives countries access to greater financial flows as rewards. This positive inducement can help to offset some of the disadvantages of participation and graduation. Using trade sanctions to induce participation has the disadvantage that it may, by introducing trade distortions, conflict with efficiency goals; in addition, this approach could put free trade and climate regimes on a collision course, as suggested in Frankel (2008b).

Issues regarding adaptation

As emphasized by the Bali Roadmap, "adaptation" is vital for developing countries. Failure to address adaptation also endangers the local goals of poverty alleviation. Therefore, adequate consideration must be given to adaptation issues in the design of the future climate regime. Important questions include first, what is the best combination of mitigation and adaptation efforts, and second, how do adaptation measures fit with other pieces in the proposed policy architecture?

When country-specific estimates of adaptation costs are available they should be included in the burden-sharing formula, since they affect the resources available to build capacity for mitigation activities. Recognizing adaptation costs will also attract more developing countries to accept the proposed framework. The revised formula for financial transfers can be written as:

$$M_j' = M_j - C_j \text{ (adaptation)} \tag{6}$$

where M_j and M_j' denote each country j's monetary liability toward a global climate fund before and after adaptation adjustments and C_j denotes the local adaptation cost of country j.

Since adaptation measures are usually mostly local in scope and can often be implemented in a relatively short time frame, adaptation policies can be drafted and implemented at a lower level of the hybrid structure. For example, some small coastal countries could form a coastal climate club to deal with cross-border adaptation and infrastructure building needs. Vulnerable developing countries and major emitting countries can prioritize different policy goals and use different measures to meet their own special needs and self-interests. In addition, without a common measure to evaluate adaptation strategies, a bottom-up structure can allow countries to better integrate climate change adaptation with their plans for national development and poverty alleviation, and to partner with other countries on disaster prevention by linking with other international frameworks as well.

In summary: advantages and challenges

Compared to other post-2012 climate policy proposals, our proposal aims to engage developing countries in carbon abatement while safeguarding their right to development by adopting a staged approach with graduation. We also propose a hybrid top-down and bottom-up institutional framework to guide a realistic negotiation process. Finally, our proposal provides for a global allocation principle based on greenhouse development rights, applied at the country or club level, which reconciles human development and climate protection objectives. Our framework also allows different climate clubs and countries to enter into policy pacts that will enable individual countries to tailor their emission reduction strategies to maximize cost-effectiveness while accommodating specific domestic needs and characteristics.

Despite the advantages of this approach in an ideal, hypothetical case, many political and economic pitfalls could jeopardize support for this type of climate architecture in practice. The biggest challenge currently is linking a multistage, hybrid architecture with the existing negotiation process in a way that illuminates the structure of the necessary solution and garners more political acceptance from both developed and developing countries. In addition, a successful climate architecture will be a self-enforcing one that brings the North and the South together by building trust through coordinated actions. With no time to waste in dealing with the emerging climate crisis, it will be important to ensure that the actions of any one country don't cause the whole architecture to fail. Therefore, although climate change is a long-term issue, what is really needed is a near- and medium-term commitment to breaking the current negotiation impasse and overcoming the barriers to a concrete agreement that can successfully cut future GHG reductions on the scale and in the timeframe needed to achieve key stabilization objectives.

The role of developing countries: opportunities and challenges

Facing the prospect of a future climate catastrophe, it is urgent and necessary to get developing countries on board a global effort to reverse current trends. Even if all developed countries make best efforts to reduce their emissions, they will not be able to offset the increase in emissions that will occur if most developing countries follow old patterns of energy-intensive production with dramatically higher per capita use of fossil-fuel energy. Obviously, developed countries played the key role in the pre-2012 era. But in the post-2012 era, developing countries will need to play a gradually more important role. In this section we focus on China as a case study to illustrate some of the potential opportunities and challenges of engaging developing countries generally; to highlight some lessons and policy suggestions for China specifically; and to develop insights that may also be applicable for other developing countries.

The case of China

China's economic boom has lasted for thirty years. Its annual GDP growth rate averaged 9.6 percent over the period 1979–2006 and 11.4 percent in 2007. As a result China's total GDP was $3.4 trillion in 2007—more than twelve times higher than in 1980. This tremendous economic success has, however, been accompanied by severe environmental impacts. China's CO_2 emissions rocketed to 1,366 million metric tons in 2004—about 3.4 times its 1980 emissions, and about 80 percent higher than emissions in 1990.[9]

Climate change has already had impacts on agriculture, water resources, coastal zones, and other natural ecosystems in China. The Chinese Academy of Agriculture Sciences and other partner agencies have conducted a technical report[10] on the national-level impacts of climate change on cereal production in China. Their findings, which incorporate assumptions based on the IPCC's A2 and B2 scenarios, suggest that climate change alone, without technological progress, is likely to lead to a decline in total cereal production. Even with technological progress to offset the adverse impacts of climate change, per capita production would be expected to decline for all scenarios—with or without carbon fertilizing effects. Another study by the Natural Resources Defense Council (NRDC), an environmental advocacy organization, (the study is titled "China's National Climate Change Programme" [NDRC 2007]) also estimated that climate change would cause glaciers in western China, which play a key role in the country's water supply, to decline 27 percent by the year 2050. A declining trend in glacier runoff has already been observed over the past forty years in China's six main rivers, including the famous Yangtze River and Yellow River. At the same time there has been an observed rise in sea level along the Chinese coast, which has resulted in increased coastal erosion and seawater intrusion.

To curb negative impacts from climate change, the Chinese government has already put forward concrete efforts to address this issue domestically, though most of these efforts to date consist of promulgating guidelines, principles, and plan targets. A more ambitious plan for reducing emissions would require further capacity building, technology transfer, and financial assistance from developed countries along with a harmonized strategy for promoting continued economic development with simultaneous climate mitigation efforts. Currently, most of the mandatory policies and quantitative targets China has adopted are not driven by climate considerations—rather they are mostly motivated by domestic environmental pressures and energy security and resource conservation concerns.

---

[9] Data Source: Carbon Dioxide Information Analysis Center, Oak Ridge National Laboratory.

[10] The full technical report can be found at www.china-climate-adapt.org.

Energy intensity target in 2010

The Chinese government set several goals in its eleventh Five Year Plan, one of which was to reduce the energy intensity of the economy by 20 percent in 2010 compared to a 2005 baseline. The most prominent actions undertaken to achieve these targets so far have involved shutting down many inefficient power plants and industrial facilities and promoting end-use energy efficiency. To enforce this policy more effectively, central authorities have also linked their evaluation of local officials' performance to progress on achieving local energy reduction targets. Such energy saving regulations implemented under China's eleventh Five Year Plan have since achieved significant compliance effects. Compared to 2005, China's energy intensity declined by 3.83 percent in 2006 and by an even more significant amount—11.4 percent—in 2007.[11] Compared to other countries, China's total energy intensity (adjusted for PPP and including primary energy use in both the manufacturing and residential sectors) has also improved substantially: it is currently lower than US and Russian energy intensity, and is converging to the intensity level of Japan's economy.

Renewable energy policies

The Chinese government has set a target to increase the use of primary energy from renewable sources from 7 percent in 2008 to 16 percent in 2020. In 2004, NDRC launched the first China Medium–to–Long Term Energy Conservation Plan, and in the subsequent year, the National People's Congress adopted the Renewable Energy Law of the People's Republic of China, which sets out policy instruments options, such as total volume control, provisions for mandatory grid connections, differentiated pricing, a special fund, and favorable tax treatment, among others (NDRC 2007). The renewable energy law took effect on January 1, 2006.[12]

The government of China has supported numerous scientific studies and research initiatives on climate change to build capacity and public awareness of this issue. But a still relatively low level of economic development, a huge population, and a coal-dominated energy mix present enormous challenges for the Chinese government. Like many

---

[11] Author's own calculation based on total energy use and constant price GDP data in the China Statistical Yearbook (2008).
[12] www.gov.cn/ziliao/flfg/2005-06/21/content_8275.htm

other developing countries, China lacks many of the institutions, policies, technologies, and enforcement mechanisms needed to foster a low-carbon economy without jeopardizing local development and economic growth.

Current international climate negotiations, though now at a political impasse, pose a great opportunity for large developing countries like China to play the leadership in designing a post-2012 climate architecture that accommodates both human development and climate protection objectives. Ideally such an agreement would allow developed and developing countries both to pursue a "win-win"—as opposed to "lose-lose"—trajectory.

As a first step it will be important to emphasize the development needs of the South and to give priority to domestic sustainable development efforts that are also consistent with climate change mitigation. Second, a gradual timetable for engagement with global mitigation efforts would be more realistic for developing countries: from no emission reduction commitments, to voluntary contributions, to moderate targets, and eventually to binding and more stringent targets. Over time, as per capita incomes in developing countries converge to the world average level, it will be fair to ask those countries to take on more stringent targets and commitments. In addition, incentives in the form of financial and technological transfers might be used to encourage developing countries to take on more stringent targets or to graduate sooner. Finally, developing countries are the most vulnerable to negative impacts from climate change. Thus, efforts should be made through regional clubs and/or collaboration with developed countries to improve their capacity for climate change adaptation and to promote technology transfer with the support of a climate trust fund.

As the largest carbon emitter in the world, China has realized that climate change is a challenge it will need to cope with from both global political and domestic sustainable development perspectives. China has already played an important role in the global CDM market. We are confident that, with appropriately designed policies and global institutions, developing countries—and China in particular—can benefit from a post-2012 global climate architecture. The following elements are important for China to play a future leadership role by setting examples in reconciling carbon abatement with domestic sustainable development and capacity building toward a low-carbon economy:

- Political leadership will be a key determinant of success in global- and national-level efforts to cope with climate change. China can play a vital role in determining timetables, organizing a developing country club, negotiating for particular "survival income" or "survival emissions" thresholds, identifying specific elements of a climate trust fund to promote financial flows and technology transfer, and designing incentives to facilitate faster graduation by developing countries, and so forth.
- Translating the global issue of climate change into a local priority is also important for China. It often noted that sometimes the central government's objectives are not well aligned with those of local governments. If local governments still prioritize economic growth over energy saving and carbon mitigation, national-level guidelines and policies will usually fail to achieve satisfactory outcomes. In 2007, China launched the National Leading Group on Climate Change (NLGCC), headed by premier Wen Jiabao. Provincial governments followed suit by creating counterpart organizations, as did prefectural governments. Since then, local governments seem to have become more responsive toward climate change objectives (Qi *et al.* 2008). Likewise, a GDR framework can be applied at the provincial or even prefectural level as well. Finally, a new system of official evaluations can help to hold local governments accountable for environmental and climate change policies and can work to complement local abatement initiatives.
- Reconciling both local pollution and climate change concerns may bring large co-benefits at the local or regional level. In particular, policies that target local pollutants such as total suspended particles (TSP) and sulfur dioxide (SO_2) can often also deliver substantial GHG reductions. Environmental tax policies and local energy conservation standards and sustainable development policies can easily be revised to take into account both conventional pollution control and climate change mitigation to achieve "co-control" objectives.
- Environmental laws should be implemented strictly to ensure effective enforcement. Although the Chinese government has passed numerous environmental and energy conservation laws, these are often difficult to implement in practice because they merely set forth principles or objectives without specifying actions or concrete policies for immediate action. In addition, one-size-fits-all guidelines for energy efficiency or environmental quality often need to be differentiated to

accommodate regional differences, either through intergovernmental processes (Teng and Gu 2007) or by giving local governments more authority over the use of local revenue and capacities.

- Non-governmental organizations (NGOs) can play a useful role in improving public awareness of climate change and educating people about options for reducing climate change risks and adapting to likely impacts. To break the current international political impasse and advocate for solutions from a developing country perspective, climate change NGOs can play important complementary roles in addition to government efforts. For example, the World Wildlife Fund, Energy Foundation, Environmental Defense Fund, and many other organizations all have local offices in China and have been working with the Chinese government and universities on climate change research; public education; energy efficiency programs; and community-level efforts to build adaptation capacity, transfer low-carbon technologies, promote clean production, and so forth.

- As of the end of 2008, some 1,797 CDM projects[13] had been approved in China; indeed, China has become the largest supplier of CDM-based certified emission reductions. Still, the scale of the CDM program is inadequate to achieve meaningful levels of emissions reduction worldwide. In particular, as Wagner *et al.* (2008) have suggested, in some cases CDM is a very expensive way to reduce emissions in the developing world, and the continued existence of the CDM might actually discourage developing countries from voluntarily limiting their own emissions in order to preserve existing monetary incentives from the CDM market. For this reason, directing financial flows and technology transfer through other trading mechanisms as countries gradually move from one stage to the next might be desirable to get around these CDM issues. Alternatively, a full-scale reform of the current CDM program, such as extending credits to sectoral or policy level actions, might be preferable. It would be in the interest of developing countries to extend the scope of current CDM projects such that they can directly address the need for technology transfer and enhanced learning-by-doing in a domestic context (Teng 2008).

- Last but not the least, the US-China Strategic Dialogue might provide further opportunities to let the world's two biggest carbon emitters

[13] http://cdm.ccchina.gov.cn/WebSite/CDM/UpFile/File2123.pdf

work together on encouraging the production and consumption of low-carbon products, promoting increased investment in renewable or low-carbon technologies, and so forth. A cooperative approach can also help China and the United States find a balanced way to navigate the current global economic downturn. On the Chinese side, this may involve pursuing a new development path, one that shifts from production-led growth to consumption-led growth and increases investment in non-tradable sectors such as health, education, finance, and other services. Greater access to energy-saving, low-carbon technologies can also help China avoid lock-in effects from continued investments in coal-based technologies—a change that would benefit the whole world. For the US side, such shifts in China's economic structure can also help to lessen long-running trade imbalances and tensions between the two countries. In sum, transitioning to an alternative low-carbon path is difficult and urgent. It can nevertheless represent a win-win strategy for China, the United States, and the rest of the world—but China will need help to get around the barriers that stand in the way of such a transition.

Though this discussion has analyzed these issues from the specific perspective of China, many of the issues and principles at stake are common to other developing countries as well. In sum, although climate change poses challenges, it also provides opportunities to help developing countries pursue a better development path. This will only be possible, however, if the countries of the North and South build trust and work together to design and implement a credible post-2012 climate architecture.

Conclusion

Climate change is one of humanity's most urgent and difficult challenges. Scientific research has already indicated that the economic costs of unchecked global warming will be very severe. Without the engagement of large developing countries, in particular China, the world will experience rapid and possibly catastrophic global warming even if all Annex I countries fulfill their Kyoto commitments and continue to deepen their mitigation efforts in the post-2012 era. Thus, a feasible, flexible, accessible, and agreeable post-2012 climate policy framework remains key to solving the climate crisis.

This chapter proposes a new, multistage hybrid climate policy architecture based on a revised approach—grounded in the concept of Greenhouse Development Rights—to burden sharing. In addition, we have discussed some key design elements for a new agreement, such as allowing climate clubs to adopt policy pacts that meet their different needs, providing mechanisms for financial assistance and technology transfer, devising penalty schemes, and addressing adaptation issues. Although this proposal needs further refinement, it may provide a useful starting point for further discussions about how to break the current North–South political impasse on climate change. Specifically, it may give negotiating parties an opportunity to build trust and encourage developing countries to gradually move from their current position of no commitments to acceptance of the eventual need for binding commitments, provided there are incentives in place for developing countries to graduate to more stringent targets, along with safeguards to assure they can meet their development needs.

Finally, we emphasize that an effective international regime for containing climate change can also provide opportunities for developing countries. We use China—the world's biggest carbon emitter and largest developing country—to illustrate these opportunities. By taking the leadership of post-Kyoto climate policy architecture designing; reconciling local sustainable development and climate mitigation; bridging central and local institutions by translating global issues into local priorities; reconciling regional differences through domestic policies; working closely with NGOs; reforming the CDM; implementing domestic carbon tax policies or participating in international or regional cap-and-trade markets; strengthening its dialogue with the United States; and pursuing an alternative low-carbon development path, China can play a leadership role and help bring other developing nations together in support of a fair and effective post-2012 climate architecture.

References

Aldy, J., R. Baron, and L. Tubiana (2003). "Addressing Cost: the Political Economy of Climate Change," Pew Center on Global Climate Change. Available at www.pewclimate.org/docUploads/Addressing%20Cost.pdf.

Baer, P., T. Athanasiou, and S. Kartha (2007). "The Right to Development in a Climate Constrained World: The Greenhouse Development Rights Framework," Heinrich Böll Foundation, Christian Aid, EcoEquity and the Stockholm Environmental Institute, Berlin, November. Available at www.ecoequity.org/GDRs.

Baer, P., T. Athanasiou, S. Kartha, and E. Kemp-Benedict (2008). "The Greenhouse Development Rights Framework—The Right to Development in a Climate Constrained World," Revised 2nd edition, Heinrich Böll Foundation, Christian Aid, EcoEquity and the Stockholm Environmental Institute, Berlin, November.

Barrett, S. (2007). "A Multitrack Climate Treaty System," in J. Aldy and R. Stavins (eds.), *Architectures for Agreement: Addressing Global Climate Change in the Post-Kyoto World.* New York: Cambridge University Press, pp. 237–59.

Baumol, W. and W. Oates (1971). "The Use of Standards and Prices for the Protection of the Environment," *Swedish Journal of Economics* 73: 42–54.

Berk, M. and M. den Elzen (2001). "Options for Differentiation of Future Commitments in Climate Policy: How to Realize Timely Participation to Meet Stringent Climate Goals," *Climate Policy* 1(4): 465–80.

Blanchard, O., C. Criqui, A. Kitous, and L. Vinguier (2003). "Combining Efficiency with Equity: A Pragmatic Approach," in I. Kaul, P. Conceição, K. Le Goulven, and R. U. Mendoza (eds.), *Providing Public Goods: Managing Globalization.* Oxford, UK: Oxford University Press, pp. 280–304.

Blok, K., N. Höhne, A. Torvanger, and R. Janzic (2005). *Towards a Post-2012 Climate Change Regime.* Brussels: 3E nv. Available at http://europa.eu.int/comm/environment/climat/pdf/id_bps098.PDF.

Brazil (1997). "Proposed Elements of a Proposal to the UNFCCC," presented by Brazil in response to the Berlin mandate, FCCC/AGBM/1997/MISC.l/Add.3, Bonn: UNFCCC.

CAN (Climate Action Network) (2003). "Preventing Dangerous Climate Change," CAN position paper presented at COP 9, Milan: Climate Action Network. Available at www.climnet.org.

Cao, J., M. Ho, and D. Jorgenson (2008). "'Co-benefits' of Greenhouse Gas Mitigation Policies in China—An Integrated Top-Down and Bottom-Up Modeling Analysis," Environment for Development Discussion Paper Series, Efd DP 08–10, April.

Claussen, E. and L. McNeilly (1998). "Equity and Global Climate Change: The Complex Elements of Global Fairness," Table of models. Pew Centre on Global Climate Change, Arlington, Virginia. Available at www.pewclimate.org/docUploads/pol_equity.pdf

Cooper, R. (2008). "The Case for Charges on Greenhouse Gas Emissions," Discussion Paper 08–10, Cambridge, MA: Harvard Project on International Climate Agreements, October.

Criqui, P., A. Kitous, M. M. Berk, M. G. J. den Elzen, B. Eickhout, P. Lucas, D. P. van Vuuren, N. Kouvaritakis, and D. Vanregemorter (2003). "Greenhouse Gas Reduction Pathways in the UNFCCC Process up to 2025,"—*Technical Report*. No. B4-3040/2001/325703/MAR/E.1 for the DG Environment. Grenoble, France: CNRS-IEPE. Available at http://europa.eu.int/comm/environment/climat/pdf/pm_techreport2025.pdf.

den Elzen, M. (2005). "Analysis of Future Commitments and Costs of Countries for the 'South-North Dialogue' Proposal using the FAIR 2.1 world model," No. MNP-report 728001032 (www.mnp.nl/en) Netherlands Environmental Assessment Agency (MNP), Bilthoven, Netherlands.

den Elzen, M., M. Berk, P. Lucas, B. Eickhout, and D. van Vuuren (2003). "Exploring Climate Regimes for Differentiation of Commitments to Achieve the EU Climate Target," No. MNP-report 728001023. Netherlands Environmental Assessment Agency (MNP), Bilthoven, Netherlands.

den Elzen, M., N. Höhne, B. Brouns, H. Winkler, and H E. Ott (2007). "Differentiation of Countries' Future Commitments in a Post-2012 Climate Regime: An Assessment of the 'South-North Dialogue' Proposal," *Environmental Science and Policy* 10(3): 185–203.

den Elzen, M., P. Lucas, M. Berk, P. Criqui and A. Kitous (2006). "Multi-Stage: A Rule-Based Evolution of Future Commitments Under the Climate Change Convention," *International Environmental Agreements: Politics, Law and Economics* 6(1): 1–28.

Frankel, J. (2007). "Formulas for Quantitative Emission Targets," in Aldy and Stavins (eds.), pp. 31–56.

(2008a). "An Elaborated Proposal for Global Climate Policy Architecture: Specific Formulas and Emission Targets for All Countries in All Decades," Discussion Paper 08-08, Cambridge, MA: Harvard Project on International Climate Agreements, October.

(2008b). "Global Environmental Policy and Global Trade Policy," Discussion Paper 08–14, Cambridge, MA: Harvard Project on International Climate Agreements, October.

Gupta, J. (1998). "Encouraging Developing Country Participation in the Climate Change Regime," Discussion Paper E98-08, Amsterdam, Netherlands: Institute for Environmental Studies, Free University of Amsterdam.

(2003). "Engaging Developing Countries in Climate Change: KISS and Make-Up!" in D. Michel (ed.), *Beyond Kyoto: Meeting the Long-Term Challenge of Global Climate Change*, Johns Hopkins University Center for Transatlantic relations, Transatlantic Dialogue on Climate Change.

Hall, D., M. Levi, W. Pizer, and T. Ueno (2008). "Policies for Developing Country Engagement," Discussion Paper 08–15, Cambridge, MA: Harvard Project on International Climate Agreements.

Höhne, N. (2006). *What is Next After the Kyoto Protocol? Assessment of Options for International Climate Policy Post 2012.* Amsterdam. Netherlands: Techne Press.

Höhne, N., B. Kornelis, J. Harnisch, D. Phylipsen, and C. Galleguillos (2003). "Evolution of Commitments under the UNFCCC: Involving Newly Industrialized Countries and Developing Countries," No. Research-report 20141255, UBA-FB 000412, Berlin: ECOFYS Gmbh.

Höhne, N., S. Moltmann, M. Jung, C. Ellermann, and M. Hagemann (2007). "Climate Change Legislation and Initiatives at International Level and Design Options for Future International Climate Policy," 2004IP/A/CLIM/ST/2007-03, Germany.

Höhne, N., D. Phylipsen, S. Ullrich, and K. Blok. (2005). *Options for the second commitment period of the Kyoto Protocol, research report for the German Federal Environmental Agency,* Climate Change 02/05, ISSN 1611-8855, Berlin: ECOFYS GmbH. Available at www. umweltdaten.de/publikationen/fpdf-l/2847.pdf.

IPCC (2007). "Climate Change 2007—The Physical Science Basis," Working Group I Contribution to the Fourth Assessment Report of the IPCC, Intergovernmental Panel on Climate Change.

Jaffe, J. and R. Stavins (2008). "Linkage of Tradable Permit Systems in International Climate Policy Architecture," Discussion Paper 08-07, Cambridge, MA: Harvard Project on International Climate Agreements, September.

Lagos, R., T. Wirth, and M. El-Ashry (2007). "Framework for a Post-2012 Agreement on Climate Change," A Proposal of the Global Leadership for Climate Action (GLCA). Available at www.GlobalClimate.Action. com.

McKibbin, W. and P. Wilcoxen (2007). "A Credible Foundation for Long-Term International Cooperation on Climate Change," in Aldy and Stavins (eds.), pp. 185–208.

Michaelowa, A. (2007). "Graduation and Deepening," in Aldy and Stavins (eds.), pp. 81–104.

Michaelowa, A., S. Butzengeiger, and M. Jung. (2005). "Graduation and Deepening: An Ambitious Post-2012 Climate Policy Scenario," *International Environmental Agreements: Politics, Law and Economics* 5: 25–46.

National Development and Reform Commission (NDRC) (2007). "China's National Climate Change Programme," Beijing: P. R. China.

NBS (2007). "China Development Report 2007: Eliminating Poverty in Development," China Development Research Foundation, Chinese Statistics Publishing House, Beijing.

Nordhaus, W. (2007). "A Review of the Stern Review on the Economics of Climate Change," *Journal of Economic Literature* 45(3): 686–702.

Ott, H., H. Winkler, B. Brouns, S. Kartha, M. Mace, S. Huq, Y. Kameyama, A. P. Sari, J. Pan, Y. Sokona, P. M. Bhandari, A. Kassenberg, E. L. La Rovere, and A. Rahman (2004). "South-North Dialogue on Equity in the Greenhouse: A Proposal for an Adequate and Equitable Global Climate Agreement," S. Eschborn, Gesellschaft für Technische Zusammenarbeit. Available at www.wupperinst.org/uploads/tx_wiprojekt/1085_pro-posal.pdf.

Pan, J., Y. Chen, W. Wang, and C. Li (2008). "Carbon Budget Proposal— Global Emissions under Carbon Budget Constraint on an Individual Basis for an Equitable and Sustainable Post-2012 International Climate Regime," Working Paper, Research Centre for Sustainable Development, Chinese Academy of Social Sciences.

Pizer, W. (2007). "Practical Global Climate Policy," in Aldy and Stavins (eds.), pp. 280–314.

Posner, E. and C. Sunstein (2008). "Justice and Climate Change," Discussion Paper 08-04, Cambridge, MA: Harvard Project on International Climate Agreements.

Qi, Y., L. Ma, H. Zhang, and H. Li (2008). "Translating a Global Issue into Local Priority," *Journal of Environment & Development* 17(4): 379–400.

Sawa, A. (2008). "A Sectoral Approach as a New Post-Kyoto Framework," Presented at Harvard-FEEM conference on the post-2012 international policy architecture for global climate change, Venice, May 15, 2008.

Scientific Expert Group on Climate Change (2007). "Confronting Climate Change: Avoiding the Unmanageable, Managing the Unavoidable," Research Triangle Park, NC: Sigma Xi and the United Nations Foundation.

Stern, N. (2006). "The Stern Review on the Economics of Climate Change," London: Government Economics Service. Available at www.sternreview.org.uk.

Teng, F. (2008). "A Measurable, Reportable, and Verifiable Post-2012 Climate Framework," Presented at Harvard-FEEM conference on the post-2012 international policy architecture for global climate change, Venice, May 15, 2008.

Teng, F. and A. Gu (2007). "Climate Change: National and Local Policy Opportunities in China," FEEM working paper, Italy. Available at www.feem.it/Feem/Pub/Publications/Wpaper/default.htm.

USEPA (2006). "Global Emissions of Non-CO_2 Greenhouse Gases: 1990–2020," Office of Air and Radiation, Washington, DC: US Environmental Protection Agency (USEPA).

Victor, D. (2004). *The Collapse of the Kyoto Protocol and the Struggle to Slow Global Warming*. Princeton, NJ: Princeton University Press.

(2007). "Fragmented Carbon Markets and Reluctant Nations: Implications for the Design of Effective Architectures," in Aldy and Stavins (eds.), pp. 133–60.

Wagner, G., N. Keohane, A. Petsonk, and J. Wang (2008). "Docking into a Global Carbon Market: Clean Investment Budgets to Encourage Emerging Economy Participation," New York: Environmental Defense Fund.

Weyant, J. (2008). "A Critique of the Stern Review's Mitigation Cost Analyses and Integrated Assessment," *Review of Environmental Economics and Policy* 2(1): 77–93.

19 What do we expect from an international climate agreement? A perspective from a low-income country[1]

E. SOMANATHAN[2]

The non-marginal nature of the climate problem and the importance of technological change

Allowing Earth's global mean temperature to rise by more than 1–2 degrees Celsius above its current level carries significant risk of triggering positive feedbacks that further raise temperature and lead to catastrophic climatic changes (Hansen, Sato *et al.* 2006; Lenton, Held *et al.* 2008). To limit warming to such a small rise in temperature, when current greenhouse gas (GHG) concentrations already commit us to an increase of 0.3–0.9 degrees Celsius above a reference level equal to global average temperatures over the period 1980–1999 (IPCC 2007a), will require massive cuts in carbon dioxide (CO_2) emissions by the middle of the century. The climate problem cannot be tackled by tinkering at the margins.

Eliminating CO_2 emissions is difficult for the simple reason that it is cheaper to obtain energy by burning coal, oil, and gas than by harnessing the sun, the wind, or atomic nuclei. The 2007 report of the Intergovernmental Panel on Climate Change reviewed the scientific literature and concluded that there are currently available, low-cost or even profitable opportunities for reducing CO_2 emissions, mainly through the installation of energy-conserving equipment and techniques in industry, building, and transport. However, tapping low-cost reduction opportunities can achieve at most a cut of a few percentage points below business-as-usual (BAU) emissions (IPCC

---

[1] Chapter prepared for the Harvard Project on International Climate Agreements. I am grateful to Joe Aldy for very helpful comments.
[2] Planning Unit, Indian Statistical Institute.

2007). With current technologies, deeper cuts can come only by raising the cost of energy.

Since low- and middle-income countries, including China and India, will soon account—due to their rapid economic growth and large populations—for about half of global CO_2 emissions (EIA 2008), tackling the climate problem requires that they have incentives to substantially reduce their emissions.

The general public in low-income and even middle-income countries, however, is almost entirely unaware of the seriousness of the threats posed by global warming. Those few who have heard of the problem, also know that it is—so far—largely a consequence of the industrialization of the North. The now developed countries emitted three times as much fossil-fuel CO_2 between 1850 and 2002 as did the now developing countries (Baumert, Herzog et al. 2005).[3] Since the developing countries have a much larger population, this means that on a per capita basis, developed countries are responsible for most of the problem. Therefore, at least until the developing countries get rich, their citizens are not going to be willing to pay more than a very small share of the cost of forestalling climate change. There is no political support for paying more for energy in these countries—a reality that is very unlikely to change substantially in the near future. This implies that the only way to get developing countries to lower their CO_2 emissions substantially below their BAU path is by making it economically attractive for them to do so.

Given the present unwillingness of rich countries to bear the costs of reducing even their own emissions by very much, it would be highly optimistic to assume that they will be willing to pay for substantial reductions in Chinese, Indian, and other developing-country emissions. We are left with technological change as the only hope for drastically cutting global emissions so as to avoid the dangers of disastrous temperature feedbacks.

Technological change to replace carbon-intensive activities with carbon-neutral ones can be stimulated by raising the expected returns to investment in research and development (R&D) and by increasing public-sector R&D and/or subsidizing private-sector R&D.

---

[3] The share of rich countries ("Annex I" countries in the Kyoto Protocol) is calculated to be 55 percent when land-use change is taken into account (Müller, Höhne et al. 2007).

An international climate agreement may increase expected returns to R&D, so I will discuss this channel first.

The logic of international emissions trading

The economic logic of international emissions trading may be summarized as follows. Economic growth in developing countries will require a large expansion of energy supply. The annual CO_2 emissions of non-OECD[4] countries are projected to rise from 17.3 gigatons (Gt) to 22.3 Gt between 2010 and 2020 (EIA 2008). This expected increase can be avoided by building power plants fired by non-carbon sources of energy instead of fossil fuels. Although costly, this will nevertheless be cheaper than scrapping existing fossil-fuel power plants and replacing them with carbon-neutral plants. Suppose high-income countries set themselves an annual carbon emission cap that is well below their *present* emissions, and developing countries set themselves a cap that is *above* existing emissions, but no higher than their BAU path. Then, to achieve the total world cap, it will be cheaper to abate emissions in developing countries by *more* than the amount demanded by their cap, and thus to abate *less* in developed countries than their cap demands. Allowing emission permits to be traded between developed and developing countries will then mean that the latter end up as sellers of permits, while rich countries will be buyers. Thus, rich countries will pay for emissions to be lower in developing countries than they would have been in the absence of the cap-and-trade system. In other words, by selling permits to rich countries, developing countries will make a profit on any cuts that they make below their cap. Provided the cost of reducing emissions below BAU levels is less than the revenues gained from selling excess permits, developing countries will end up making a net profit from entering such a system.

Why would rich countries enter such a system? Since the political pressure to do something about climate change originates almost wholly from the public in these countries, their governments are the ones with an interest in addressing the problem. Thus, for any *given* limit on global CO_2 emissions, this argument suggests that it will be cheaper to achieve the limit if developing countries enter a

---

[4] OECD stands for the Organisation for Economic Cooperation and Development; it comprises thirty high-income countries.

cap-and-trade system. Since rich countries will be paying for emissions reductions, they have an interest in making sure the global limit is achieved as cheaply as possible.

A second reason for rich countries to enter into a cap-and-trade system with developing countries is so-called "leakage." If some countries cap their emissions and other countries either do not cap their emissions or set a less stringent cap, energy prices in the countries with tighter caps will rise higher than in the non-capped countries. As a result, energy-intensive industries, to the extent that they are mobile, will tend to move to countries without emissions caps, thus undoing the environmental benefits gained from imposing caps in the first place. A cap-and-trade system will equalize emissions prices and tend to make energy prices converge across participating countries, thus preventing leakage.

If all concerned are to agree to such a cap-and-trade system, however, several conditions must hold. First, emission caps in rich countries must be sufficiently tight that it becomes cheaper to pay low-income countries to abate on their behalf. At present, it is not clear that there is sufficient public demand for emission reductions in rich countries for this condition to be met, even if low-income countries were to take on commitments to cut their own emissions below their BAU paths.

Second, the fast-growing, lower-income countries have to be willing to risk taking on emission-reduction commitments in the hope that they will end up making a net profit. The problem is that it is very difficult to forecast profits from the sale of emission permits since the value of those permits will depend on the relative costs of abatement in the various countries under different caps, and on the amount by which emissions would grow in the BAU scenario. Economic growth is highly uncertain, as are changes in the future energy intensity (energy used per dollar of Gross Domestic Product or GDP) of an economy. While the emission caps applied in low-income countries can be set by agreement to rise when GDP grows faster than expected (Frankel 2007), this sort of built-in adjustment cannot be made without taking away the incentive to conserve energy. From the rich countries' point of view, bringing developing countries into an agreement will undercut emissions reductions unless the developing countries agree to quotas that are below their BAU emissions. Because future BAU emissions cannot be known with certainty, developing countries will not agree to any cap that is not close to the upper limit of what BAU emissions could conceivably turn out to be so as to avoid ending up worse off by entering into an agreement. If the result is that the cap for developing countries is set higher than their actual BAU emissions, then rich countries could end up paying developing countries for so-called "hot air"—that is, for avoiding emissions that would not have happened anyway. Developed countries will, of course, be reluctant to agree to such an arrangement, especially since it would result in world emissions being higher than they would have been in the absence of the agreement.

Finally, the profits that low-income countries stand to realize from selling excess permits have to be net of the costs of monitoring and implementation if the whole exercise is to be worth it from their perspective. It should be recognized, however, that some of the factors that may seem to lower the chances of instituting an international emissions trading system could actually create positive drivers for reaching agreement. Businesses that stand to gain from the creation of a new commodity exchange will lobby for it. Governments that participate will have to decide how to allot emissions permits within their respective countries, but these permits will constitute valuable assets that politicians can allocate in ways they find congenial. This may give politicians a strong pecuniary incentive to enter an agreement, especially in countries where they are not tightly constrained by political institutions and public opinion. Of course, the political hazard of entering into such an agreement is that it will raise energy prices, which could be damaging for politicians, especially if the sale of permits does not raise enough revenue to compensate politically relevant losers.

Global cap and trade and human welfare

The discussion so far has touched on the factors that make an international cap-and-trade regime with developing country participation more or less likely, but it has not addressed the consequences for human welfare. From a welfare standpoint, the prospective benefits of an international agreement are twofold: in the first instance, developing country participation will result in larger overall emission reductions (compared to BAU). This may be amplified by the adoption of more stringent quotas in rich countries, since the cost of achieving a given quota will be lower if emission permits can be bought from developing countries at a price below the cost of emission reductions in the rich country. Thus, rich country governments may be willing to tighten their own quotas if the ability to buy permits from developing countries helps to cushion their own firms and consumers from too great an increase in the price of energy. By preventing "leakage," the agreement may make rich countries more willing to tighten their caps.

Second, a more stringent global cap on CO_2 emissions will expand the market for carbon-neutral and low-carbon energy and increase expected returns to R&D on climate-friendly technologies. As argued above, it is this dynamic effect that is most important in terms of actually reducing the risks of climate change.

Would an international cap-and-trade agreement add credibility to individual countries' announcements about emissions caps in future years? If so, this would be a strong argument in favor of such an agreement. Uncertainty about whether governments will follow through on their commitments to cap carbon emissions constitutes a major disincentive to private R&D investments in low-carbon technologies. If governments renege, then the market for carbon-free technologies will shrink, and earlier investments in developing those technologies will have been unprofitable.

Is an international cap-and-trade agreement involving developing countries likely to be credible? Keohane and Raustiala (2008) argue that only wholly self-enforcing agreements are viable, since sovereign states can and do renege when it suits them. If a country does not enforce domestic quotas properly, there is not much that other countries can do to punish it. Keohane and Raustiala argue in favor of a system of buyer liability to address this potential problem. In short, if an *ex post* determination is made—either by an international body or by the government of the buyer country—that a seller country had emitted more than it had agreed to, then emissions permits originating from that seller country would be devalued accordingly (that is, firms in developed countries that bought these permits could count only a suitable fraction of their face value toward their compliance obligations). This would give issuing countries that are net sellers of permits on the international market an incentive to enforce their own emission caps or quotas so as not to drive down the market price of their permits. Again, this structure depends on the willingness of rich countries to set emission quotas that are sufficiently stringent to generate a net demand for permits from developing countries.

Ultimately, therefore, the basis for any international agreement is the political demand for emission cuts emanating from rich countries, and it is expectations about the size of those cuts that will be crucial in terms of driving the market for carbon-free technologies. If rich countries are willing to sign an agreement that calls for them to make steep emissions cuts this would send a positive signal to firms contemplating R&D investments in low-carbon technologies. Of course, firms would have to be convinced of the integrity of such an agreement. It would have to be self-enforcing, or credibility would be lost.

To summarize, a cap-and-trade agreement with developing countries can only be credible if the developed countries first demonstrate their willingness to pay for it. They can do this only by adopting cap-and-trade systems themselves and committing themselves to cut emissions significantly in the years immediately following the end of Phase I of the Kyoto Protocol. These must be actual cuts, not just slower emissions growth, or else there are unlikely to be significant gains from international emissions trading.[5] Having taken this first step, developed countries can then ask developing countries if they wish to opt in to the system by taking on emission caps that reflect small cuts relative to BAU.[6] At this stage, some of the developing countries may find it profitable to join the system.

All of this assumes that developing countries have or will acquire the capacity to set up their own credible domestic cap-and-trade systems. That assumption, however, is unlikely to hold in many developing countries with corrupt governments and weak institutional capacity. Implementing a cap-and-trade system will raise energy prices, and unless there is a credible way to share the profits from selling permits to foreigners with domestic constituencies affected by higher energy prices, there will be opposition within developing countries to joining

[5] As explained earlier, it is cheaper to prevent emissions from growing than to reduce emissions below current levels because the former can be achieved by installing new equipment that emits less GHGs while the latter entails scrapping old equipment before the end of its useful life, in addition to installing new equipment. Once developed countries have stopped their emissions growth and are at the point where they are reducing emissions below current levels, it will become cheaper to pay developing countries to slow their emissions growth instead.

[6] These cuts would eventually have to get much bigger once a country grew sufficiently rich or reached a sufficiently high per capita emissions quota. The determination of just how this "graduation" should occur would, of course, be subject to conflicting interpretations of fairness, and therefore to bargaining.

an international agreement. Unless at least those groups with political influence can be credibly compensated, or more than compensated, for energy price increases, a government may find it impossible to adopt, or follow through on adopting, a cap-and-trade system.

The problem, of course, is that low-income country governments are mostly characterized by high levels of corruption and low institutional capacity. This is at least a part, and very likely a large part, of the reason why they are poor. In fact, matters could get much worse than merely having energy prices increase. During the course of writing the last few pages, sitting here in my office in New Delhi, the power supply has failed several times, and the campus has switched to a back-up diesel generator. This is a symptom of a badly governed and poorly regulated electric supply and distribution system dominated by extensive political interference. India as a whole suffers from chronic power shortages and blackouts. In this context, power companies (whether public or private—India has both) faced with an incentive to supply less electricity, because this would mean they have more emission permits to sell, may end up actually rationing consumers even more. Outcomes such as this may make it politically untenable for the government to continue with a cap-and-trade system.

Turning to the distributional impact of a cap-and-trade system, I first note that higher prices for fossil fuels will, on the whole, be quite progressive in many developing countries because commercial fuels in these countries (in contrast to the situation in most developed countries) account for a higher share of expenditures for higher-income households (Datta 2008).

This pattern exists because the poor in a low-income country are too poor to use mechanized transport much and because the goods that the poor consume are less energy-intensive, on the whole, than goods consumed by those who are better off. This progressivity should make it easier to protect the poor. If the government cut indirect taxes that fall more heavily on the poor, then this could compensate for the rise in fuel prices. It is, of course, not at all clear whether this or any other effort at compensation would actually happen.

Figure 19.1 shows that coal accounts for less than 2 percent of the budget of the average Indian consumer. Since cap-and-trade schemes are likely to focus on coal, it may appear at first glance that an increase in the price of coal would not have a very large impact on the welfare of Indian consumers. But this is not the whole story. Most Indian

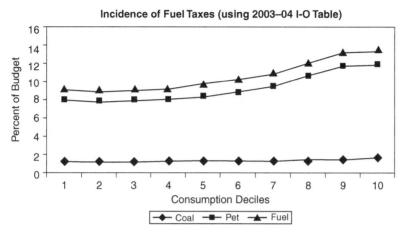

Figure 19.1. Budget shares of fuel in India in 2004–05 by consumption expenditure decile, accounting for its use as an intermediate input. Reproduced from Datta (2008). "Pet" denotes Petroleum.

households still use traditional solid fuels like firewood for cooking. In 2000, about 70 percent of Indians used such fuels (Gangopadhyay, Ramaswami *et al.* 2006). The use of these traditional fuels with traditional stoves, however, releases fine particles and gases that have significant adverse health effects. One review of the evidence on this subject concluded that indoor air pollution from the use of solid fuels for cooking results in about half a million excess deaths of women and children per year in India (Smith 2000). With economic growth and rising incomes, households can be expected to transition to sources of energy, such as cooking gas and electricity, that do not emit particulate matter and other local and regional air pollutants. To the extent that participation in a cap-and-trade system delays or prolongs this transition by raising energy prices and creating incentives for electricity rationing, it will contribute to excess deaths and ill health.

In addition, solid fuel is used to such an extent in India that it generates regional climate effects from the production of particulate matter and leads to the formation of a brown cloud of aerosols that may be up to three kilometers thick. More than 40 percent of the black carbon in the atmosphere over South Asia is estimated to come from cooking fires (Venkataraman, Habib *et al.* 2005). The aerosol cloud has been estimated to reduce the summer monsoon and, consequently, rice harvests in India by 10 percent (Auffhammer, Ramanathan *et al.* 2006). Soot in the aerosol cloud heats the upper atmosphere (Ramanathan, Ramana *et al.* 2007) and some of it is deposited in Himalayan snow and glaciers. Although firm evidence is lacking, it seems likely that upper atmospheric heating will contribute to glacial and snowpack melt, as will deposits of soot. The latter has contributed to the melting of the Greenland icepack even though there is far less particulate pollution in that region than in South Asia (Hansen and Nazarenko 2004). If Himalayan snowpack and glacier melt driven both by global GHG accumulation and by regional particulate pollution continues for more than a few decades, it will lead to a sharp reduction in winter flows in northern Indian rivers. This could cause major declines in agricultural production in a region that is not only already poor and densely populated, but that is projected to add hundreds of millions of people to its population during the course of this century.

There is thus the distinct possibility that a cap-and-trade agreement involving India—by delaying the reduction in atmospheric black carbon that would follow a transition away from traditional fuels—could end up making a majority of Indians, especially the poor, worse off. Although the details of such indirect effects are specific to India, similar concerns apply to many low-income countries.

Concerns about unintended consequences also apply to the possibility of linking emissions markets in developed countries to markets for emission credits from reduced deforestation and degradation in tropical countries. Nongovernmental organizations (NGOs) have already warned that logging companies could use the threat of clear-cutting to extract any rents that arise from such trading. Politically weak forest dwellers and indigenous peoples may face eviction from forest lands if these lands acquire value as a consequence of the creation of emissions markets (FOEI 2008).

On the other hand, markets for reduced emissions from deforestation and degradation (REDD), as well as markets for afforestation, may have a better chance of working than markets for industrial emissions reductions, simply because monitoring can be done relatively cheaply using modern satellite imagery, supplemented by ground surveys. If emission trading agreements are based on buyer liability, then agencies external to the seller countries will evaluate effectiveness as well as impacts on the rights of vulnerable groups. The same NGOs that are today protesting the introduction of these markets may then perform the valuable function of monitoring these markets to prevent land grabs and other injustices. It is not clear whether this would afford sufficient protection to vulnerable groups, but it is a possibility. It is certainly true that in some high-profile cases, activist groups in the North have succeeded in forcing the World Bank to withdraw from financing projects that would have displaced vulnerable populations in poor countries. This happened with the Narmada dam in India, although in that case, the government went ahead with the dam using domestic funds. Where projects rely on external financing, however (as would largely be the case for tropical countries participating in a REDD market), the threat of pullout by buyer countries would presumably provide stronger incentives for seller countries to abide by fairness conditions and other stipulations.

Similar external intervention to protect the poor from the consequences of higher energy prices or other indirect effects (such as energy rationing) that may be occasioned by participation in a cap-and-trade scheme for fossil-fuel emissions seems far less likely. The victims in those cases will be neither easy to identify nor as picturesque.

What should an agreement aim for?

Given that emissions trading could have significant downsides for vulnerable populations in poor countries, it is pertinent to ask whether the prospective benefits are large enough to justify this approach. From the foregoing discussion, the answer would seem to be in doubt. Under BAU assumptions, annual energy-related CO_2 emissions in the OECD countries are projected to increase from 14 Gt to 16 Gt between 2010 and 2030 (EIA 2008). Abating even this 2 Gt increase would very likely ensure quite a large market for new technologies; moreover, many OECD countries are likely to set more ambitious targets, thus ensuring an even larger market for new technologies. If they do not adopt more stringent targets, then the ability to trade emission reductions with developing countries would, in any case, be irrelevant.

I conclude that an international climate agreement involving the developing countries is of secondary importance to solving the climate problem. Of primary importance is the creation of markets for carbon-neutral technologies in the OECD countries—whether by tax, tradable permits, or traditional regulation—and an increase in direct financial incentives for R&D. Global public investment in energy R&D has fallen by half in real terms since its peak in 1980, following the second oil shock (Stern 2007, Chapter 16). This means, of course, that as a share of GDP, the decline in energy R&D investment has been even greater. In the case of the United States, the largest spender, public investment in energy R&D as a share of GDP in 2005 was less than one-third of what it had been in 1980. Meanwhile, private investments in energy R&D have also declined, though not as sharply. Indeed, the evidence suggests that public investment in R&D stimulates private investment in R&D rather than crowding it out (Nemet and Kammen 2007). This is, of course, exactly what we would expect basic research to do. Nemet and Kammen argue that a five- to ten-fold increase in spending on energy R&D in the United States is both feasible and desirable.

There is, as yet, little public support for the price signals that economists advocate as the efficient method of dealing with the carbon externality. The American public, for example, doesn't like higher taxes on gasoline if the object is to reduce energy consumption. But a majority does support higher taxes on gasoline, *if* the revenues are used to develop new non-polluting energy sources (New York Times 2004). Given this pattern of public opinion, it seems difficult to argue that raising energy prices through a cap-and-trade system or any other tax (disguised or not) should be the main instrument of public policy. As noted above, if the objective is to stimulate private investment in R&D on low-carbon alternatives, certainty about the future market value of avoided emissions is desirable. Relying solely on price incentives in the face of opposing public opinion does not appear to be a realistic way of providing that certainty. By contrast, expanded funding for energy R&D is a policy that is more likely to receive consistent public support, simply because it is a mechanism the public understands. This can take the form of an increase in funds allocated through the usual tried and tested peer-review process to universities and government research laboratories for basic research across the whole gamut of technologies that may contribute to emissions reduction and sequestration. It should also include support for large projects that may require collaboration with the private sector, such as carbon capture and storage or new electric power transmission systems.

Anderson (2006), in a background paper for the *Stern Review*, reviews a range of carbon-neutral technologies and suggests that some are likely to become cheaper than the competing fossil-fuel option by

2050 and possibly sooner. Several are expected to become economic at modest carbon prices and some, such as nuclear power, are already in use on a large scale. It is relevant to observe that the probability that some subset of low-carbon alternatives—and, in particular, at least one of them—will become cheaper than the fossil-fuel option is greater than any of the individual probabilities. Anderson, moreover, suggests that his estimates are conservative.[7] As Goodstein (2002) shows, prior estimates of the cost of achieving any given environmental target usually prove high. This is because policies introduced to achieve the target very often stimulate the development of new technologies that are unanticipated when the target is announced.

I conclude that government support for increased R&D can reasonably be expected to deliver lower costs for alternatives to CO_2-emitting energy sources. Support for R&D also has the advantage that resources are truly committed because they are spent now, rather than being promised in the future. Technology innovation induced by appropriate policies is thus a realistic way to make it economical for all countries, including developing countries, to reduce their CO_2 emissions. It accomplishes what is necessary: a transfer from rich to developing countries to induce the latter to cut emissions, albeit with some delay, in a manner that is most likely to be acceptable to the public in the developed world.

A new agreement will take advantage of those domains where there is public support for domestic action in the various countries. In developed countries, this means cap-and-trade, a greatly increased financial commitment to R&D, and the expansion of existing labeling programs and standards to promote energy efficiency.

In developing countries where there are chronic shortfalls of electricity, and where the import bill for petroleum is rising, there is considerable interest in improving energy efficiency.[8] An international agreement can facilitate information and technology flows in this

---

[7] Anderson has already been proven correct in at least this part of his story. His baseline estimates assume an oil price of $30/barrel, with another scenario using a price of $50/barrel. The price at the time of writing is about $70/barrel.

[8] For example in 2001, India passed an Energy Conservation Act creating a Bureau of Energy Efficiency that is supposed to advise government regulators and disseminate information. The Bureau has adopted a labeling program for the energy efficiency of appliances that is being expanded to cover more domains.

domain. A formal agreement for the exchange of expertise and information between agencies in each country that are responsible for regulating energy, GHGs, and associated pollutants could improve the quality of regulation in many countries. Labeling, smart metering and billing, and other information programs to promote efficient appliances and reduced energy consumption have been widely used in the United States and the European Union and are estimated to have had a considerable impact on energy consumption (Stern 2007).

One issue that arises immediately is the prospect of shifting baselines. Countries that anticipate being net sellers of permits in a global cap-and-trade scheme may want to postpone emission reductions until they can be paid for them (Narain and van't Veld 2008). With regard to energy efficiency, this may not be a serious problem in practice because postponing energy-saving improvements is immediately costly for the countries concerned, while the prospect of profits from emissions trading is highly uncertain. Developed countries could encourage early action by committing not to disadvantage countries that put energy-efficiency measures in place before other countries do.

In the case of equipment and appliances, technology is largely embodied in machines. An information problem arises because consumers find it hard to evaluate the energy costs that will accrue after they purchase the machine.[9] Labeling programs and standards can address this problem. In the building sector, however, technology has to be disseminated to builders and architects—in addition to information being given to consumers. Therefore funds are needed for information dissemination in this sector. The Government of India has proposed a technology fund (GOI 2005), to be financed by all countries, that could be used for this purpose, among others.[10]

Urban transport is another sector in which information sharing

[9] Consumers appear to systematically under-estimate costs they will incur in the future. See Stern (2006, Section 17.2) and the references therein. In other contexts, firms take advantage of consumer myopia by locking them in to future purchases of supplies after offering a discount on the up-front purchase of equipment; see, for example, Gabaix and Laibson (2006).

[10] The Government of India's proposal is for a fund to finance technology transfer to developing countries. It leaves open the issue of relative contributions to the fund. It also proposes a new network of research institutes for energy issues modeled on the CGIAR (Consultative Group for International Agricultural Research) network to be financed by developed and developing countries.

and financial support to local authorities may make a significant difference in future carbon emissions. The world's urban population is expected to increase from 3 billion to 5 billion by 2030, with nearly all the increase occurring in developing countries (UN 2004). Improved planning and design of public transport systems could greatly reduce attendant growth in carbon emissions and help avoid locking in motor-vehicle intensive patterns of development. While urban governance in developing countries is often dismal, there is a felt need for reducing traffic congestion and pollution. For example, the Confederation of Indian Industry has been trying to promote public transport improvements in many Indian cities, since traffic congestion is proving to be very costly for its members (CII 2007). Creation of an international body that would provide information and expertise to local authorities on these issues could promote the diffusion of successful approaches to urban transport planning.[11] Financial support for demonstration projects would accelerate the process. The emphasis should be on financing of public projects that are very well-monitored and can be modified after study and then scaled up.

Perhaps the most important sector in which international information exchange and technological cooperation is needed is in agriculture. Developing country governments have stressed the importance of adaptation to climate change as an issue in any international agreement because they will be affected earlier and more severely than developed countries, even if emissions mitigation measures succeed in holding the global mean temperature increase to 2 degrees Celsius or less—a target that appears increasingly unlikely (GOI 2008). Agriculture is the sector in which, perhaps more than in any other, research has a public good characteristic. With the exception of a few inputs such as hybrid seeds and fertilizers, technology is disembodied rather than embodied in products. Firms are farms—and in developing countries, typically very small farms. As a result, the externalities associated with a new disembodied technology can be enormous. Moreover, when the use of improved technologies entails adopting a set of complementary new practices, diffusion and learning may not be easy. Thus the public sector takes on a crucial role.

As the climate changes, farmers will be able to adapt only to a

---

[11] Diffusion of "best practice" policies is discussed in Aldy and Stavins (2008).

limited extent with existing technologies, and, in much of the tropics, conditions will become much less favorable. In these circumstances, technological progress in agriculture that anticipates future conditions is critical (Brown and Funk 2008). Food security in South Asia and Africa is most seriously threatened by climate change, so international funding and technology transfer for these regions' crops should be an important part of any international agreement (Lobell, Burke *et al.* 2008).

Research is also needed to address the potential for reducing GHG and black carbon emissions from agriculture. Such emissions are significant in South Asia (Venkataraman, Habib *et al.* 2006). Agriculture's "economic potential" for GHG reductions by 2030 is estimated to be comparable to that associated with changes in energy supply and is second only to the emissions-reduction potential of the buildings sector (IPCC 2007). For example, recent research (Marris 2006) suggests that adding charcoal to soil can increase fertility. Since charcoal is a stable form of carbon, it can also be used to sequester carbon from biomass that would otherwise be returned to the atmosphere. In sum, efforts to expand the mission of international agricultural research to include climate mitigation must be well-funded, otherwise adding this new focus could actually divert resources away from the original and primary objective of raising food output.

An international climate agreement can require developed countries to increase the funding they provide for international agricultural research through, for example, the CGIAR[12] group of institutions that was so important for the Green Revolution. It can require developing countries to make matching investments in their own national agricultural research systems and in their agricultural extension services so that new farming technologies and techniques can diffuse faster.

To summarize, it is not at all clear that it is either necessary, desirable, or realistic for developing countries to agree to binding emissions cuts in the next phase of an international agreement. At this stage, it is probably more realistic to try to get an agreement that will institutionalize technical cooperation between all countries and provide for financial support from the developed world for the

---

[12] CGIAR stands for Consultative Group on International Agricultural Research. More information on this organization is available at www.cgiar.org.

spread of technologies and practices that would cut emissions in developing countries. Energy conservation in buildings, transport, and industry, and technical progress in agriculture are areas where developing countries would see significant co-benefits from emissions cuts, so these are areas that should be included in an agreement. While an agreement need not bind developing countries to specific cuts, it could bind them to specific *policies* (on energy efficiency, for example) and require them to monitor the impacts of such policies on emissions.

Huge emissions reductions will be necessary over the next few decades to address global climate change. The major action needed to realize those reductions involves promoting research and development that will make low-carbon and carbon-neutral energy sources competitive vis-à-vis fossil fuels. Developed countries will have to support this development not only through domestic regulation, taxes, and tradable permits for fossil-fuel use, but also by committing more government funds to R&D on non-carbon energy sources.

References

Aldy, Joseph E. and Robert N. Stavins (2008). "The Role of Technology Policies in an International Climate Agreement," Prepared for The Climate Dialogue, Hosted by the Prime Minister of Denmark, September 2–3, 2008, Copenhagen, Denmark. Cambridge, MA: The Harvard Project on International Climate Agreements.

Anderson, Dennis (2006). "Costs and Finance of Abating Carbon Emissions in the Energy Sector," Background Paper for the Stern Review of the Economics of Climate Change, Imperial College London, October 20.

Auffhammer, M., V. Ramanathan, *et al.* (2006). "Integrated Model Shows That Atmospheric Brown Clouds and Greenhouse Gases Have Reduced Rice Harvests in India," *Proceedings of the National Academy of Sciences* 103(52): 19668–72.

Baumert, K. A., T. Herzog, *et al.* (2005). *Navigating the Numbers: Greenhouse Gas Data and International Climate Policy*. Washington, DC: World Resources Institute.

Brown, M. E. and C. C. Funk (2008). "Food Security Under Climate Change," *Science* 319(5863): 580–1.

Confederation of Indian Industry (2007). "Communique," *Journal of the Confederation of Indian Industry*. Special Issue. November.

Datta, A. (2008). *The Incidence of Fuel Taxation in India*. Economics Discussion Paper 08-05 Delhi: Indian Statistical Institute.

Energy Information Administration (2008). *International Energy Outlook*,
    EIA, Washington, DC: US Department of Energy.
Friends of the Earth (2008). Press Release. FOEI. Available at www.foei.
    org/en/media/archive/2008/land-grab-threat-at-un-climate-talks.
Frankel, Jeffrey (2007). "Formulas for Quantitative Emission Targets," in
    Aldy and Stavins (eds.), *Architectures for Agreement: Addressing Global
    Climate Change in the Post-Kyoto World*, New York: Cambridge
    University Press, pp. 31–56.
Gabaix, X. and D. Laibson (2006). "Shrouded Attributes, Consumer
    Myopia, and Information Suppression in Competitive Markets,"
    Quarterly Journal of Economics 121(2): 505–40.
Gangopadhyay, S., B. Ramaswami, *et al.* (2006). "Reducing Subsidies on
    Household Fuels in India: How Will it Affect the Poor?" *Energy Policy*
    33: 2326–6.
Goodstein, E. (2002). "Money, Markets and Priorities: An Economic
    View of Climate Change," in S. Spray (ed.), *Climate Change: An
    Interdisciplinary Approach*. Lanham, MD: Rowman and Littlefield.
Goodstein, E. and H. Hodges (1997). "Polluted Data," *The American
    Prospect* 35: 65–9, Nov–Dec.
Government of India (2005). "Dealing with the Threat of Climate Change,"
    India Country Paper, prepared for the Gleneagles Summit Meeting
    of the Group of Eight, July 6–8. Available at www.meaindia.nic.in/
    speech/2005/07/07ss02.pdf.
    (2008). *National Action Plan on Climate Change*. New Delhi: GOI.
    Available at http://pmindia.nic.in/Pg01-52.pdf.
Hansen, J. and L. Nazarenko (2004). "Soot Climate Forcing Via Snow and
    Ice Albedos," *Proceedings of the National Academy of Sciences* 101(2):
    423–8.
Hansen, J., M. Sato, *et al.* (2006). "Global Temperature Change,"
    Proceedings of the National Academy of Sciences 103: 14288–93.
IPCC (2007). "Summary for Policymakers," in Metz, B., O. R. Davidson,
    P. R. Bosch, R. Dave, L. A. Meyer (eds.), *Climate Change 2007:
    Mitigation. Contribution of Working Group III to the Fourth
    Assessment Report of the Intergovernmental Panel on Climate Change*.
    Cambridge and New York: Cambridge University Press.
    (2007a). "Summary for Policy Makers," in Solomon, S., D. Qin, M.
    Manning, Z. Chen, M. Marquis, K. B. Averyt, M. Tignor, and H. L.
    Miller (eds.), *Climate Change 2007: The Physical Science Basis.
    Contribution of Working Group I to the Fourth Assessment Report of
    the Intergovernmental Panel on Climate Change*. Cambridge and New
    York: Cambridge University Press.

Keohane, R. O. and K. Raustiala (2008). "Toward a Post-Kyoto Climate Change Architecture: a Political Analysis," Discussion Paper 08-01, Cambridge, MA: Harvard Project on International Climate Agreements.

Lenton, T. M., H. Held, *et al.* (2008). "Tipping Elements in the Earth's Climate System," *Proceedings of the National Academy of Sciences* 105(6): 1786–93.

Lobell, D. B., M. B. Burke, *et al.* (2008). "Prioritizing Climate Change Adaptation Needs for Food Security in 2030," *Science* 319(5863): 607–10.

Marris, E. (2006). "Putting the Carbon Back: Black is the New Green," *Nature* 442(7103): 624–6.

Müller, B., N. Höhne, *et al.* (2007). *Differentiating (Historic) Responsibilities for Climate Change: Summary Report.* Oxford: Oxford Climate Policy.

Narain, U. and K. van 't Veld (2008). "The Clean Development Mechanism's Low-hanging Fruit Problem: When Might it Arise, and How Might it be Solved?" *Environmental and Resource Economics* 40(3): 445–65.

Nemet, G. F. and D. M. Kammen (2007). "U.S. Energy Research and Development: Declining Investment, Increasing Need, and the Feasibility of Expansion," *Energy Policy* 35(1): 746–55.

New York Times (2004). New York Times/CBS News Poll. Available at www.nytimes.com/polls.

Ramanathan, V., M. V. Ramana, *et al.* (2007). "Warming Trends in Asia Amplified by Brown Cloud Solar Absorption," *Nature* 448(7153): 575–8.

Smith, K. R. (2000). "National Burden of Disease in India from Indoor Air Pollution," *Proceedings of the National Academy of Sciences* 97(24): 13286–93.

Stern, N. (2007). *The Economics of Climate Change: The Stern Review.* Cambridge: Cambridge University Press.

United Nations (2004). "UN Report Says World Urban Population of 3 Billion Today Expected to Reach 5 Billion by 2030," UN Population Division Press Release. Available at www.un.org/esa/population/publications/wup2003/pop899_English.pdf.

Venkataraman, C., G. Habib, *et al.* (2005). "Residential Biofuels in South Asia: Carbonaceous Aerosol Emissions and Climate Impacts," *Science* 307: 1454–6.

(2006). "Emissions from Open Biomass Burning in India: Integrating the Inventory Approach with High-Resolution Moderate Resolution Imaging Spectroradiometer (MODIS) Active-fire and Land Cover Data," *Global Biogeochemical Cycles* 20: GB2013.

20 | *Climate accession deals: new strategies for taming growth of greenhouse gases in developing countries*

DAVID G. VICTOR[1]

Effective strategies for managing the dangers of global climate change are essential yet difficult to design and implement. One of the greatest difficulties is in devising a policy that will engage developing countries in the global effort. Those nations, so far, have been nearly universal in their refusal to make credible commitments to reduce growth in their emissions of greenhouse gases. Most put a higher priority on economic growth—even at the expense of distant, global environmental goods. And most have little administrative ability to control emissions in many sectors of their economy. Even if they adopted policies to control emissions it is not clear that firms and other actors within their countries would follow. To be successful, a strategy for engaging developing countries must create stronger incentives for these countries to adjust their development patterns while also fixing (or navigating around) the administrative barriers that would make it difficult for these governments to honor international commitments.

Such problems are hardly new in international affairs. Diplomats have considerable experience designing instruments to address situations where countries have little interest in cooperation or are unable to implement their commitments. Those instruments have included sticks (e.g., trade sanctions) and carrots (e.g., subsidies for projects

[1] This chapter is part of a larger book project on more effective "post-Kyoto" strategies for managing climate change that the author has under way. Thanks to Joe Aldy and Rob Stavins for the invitation to contribute this part of the research to the Harvard Project on International Climate Agreements; they, Robert Keohane and an anonymous reviewer provided particularly helpful critical comments on a draft. A special thanks to Xander Slaski for terrific research assistance and Michael Wara for joint research on the troubles with the Clean Development Mechanism (CDM). The ideas discussed here are elaborated in fuller detail in Victor (2009).

that reduce emissions and for administrative capacity building). So far, however, the sticks and carrots that have been mobilized in the area of climate change have not had much impact on investment and behavior in developing countries. All the sticks that have been considered are costly to deploy in the real world. Trade sanctions and border tariffs, for example, have been widely discussed and included in some draft legislation.[2] Yet in practice such border measures probably would be an administrative nightmare to design and apply and actually threatening or deploying them would undermine the already political fragile consensus for liberal trade policies in the World Trade Organization (WTO) and other trade-promoting institutions.[3]

Because sticks have proved difficult and costly to brandish, especially in these early years of developing an effective global regulatory regime where a tone of cooperation is essential, most practical efforts to engage developing countries have focused on carrots. The industrialized countries have created new funds and programs to help pay the extra cost of new low-emission technologies and to ease the process of adapting to a changing climate. In practice, however, these explicit funds have been very small when compared with the magnitude of the task because it has been exceptionally difficult to muster the political support for large and visible income transfers—especially if such funds were to subsidize activities in the most rapidly developing economies that are also the West's most formidable economic competitors.

Because explicit fund transfers are politically toxic, most diplomatic effort has instead focused on the Kyoto Protocol's Clean Development Mechanism (CDM)—a carrot that is politically more popular among donor countries in part because the income transfers that it mobilizes are less visible and not directly on government budgets. While the CDM has encouraged investment in a large pipeline of projects and

---

[2] For example, Morris and Hill (2007) propose a sanctions-like mechanism targeted against developing countries that could be included in US legislation; in parallel, the French government discussed possible sanctions against the United States for failure to adopt meaningful limits on emissions.

[3] The WTO legality of such sanctions is hotly contested (for a review, see, e.g., Pauwelyn 2007). My assessment here is based on the extreme challenge of devising a sanctioning system that would account for difficult to observe differences in production methods and the likelihood that such a system would violate the spirit and probably also the letter of the Article XX exceptions in the General Agreement on Tariffs and Trade (GATT)/WTO trade law system.

investments, the mechanism is running into serious trouble. There is growing evidence that many (probably most) CDM projects do not represent real reductions in emissions. And the majority of actual credits issued under the CDM represent investments for which the rewards under the CDM far exceed the actual cost of implementing the projects.[4]

Certainly it is possible, in theory, to improve the existing toolbox of sticks and carrots. Fundamentally, however, these tools are unlikely to offer a full strategy for engaging developing countries. It is hard to envision how governments could craft more effective trade sticks without seeding nasty trade disputes that, eventually, would require rewriting the expectations of WTO members in an era when the WTO is already unable to forge consensus on its existing agenda.[5] Tightening the CDM so that credits were issued only to *bona fide* projects would necessarily laden the mechanism with higher operational cost and would probably relegate the CDM to a niche role that, while valuable, would hardly deliver the massive investment scheme that developing countries had envisioned when they embraced the CDM as their favored way to engage with the global effort to regulate emissions.[6] And even

---

[4] See, e.g., Wara (2007) on over-compensation for the industrial gas projects that are the majority of actual emission credits issued under the CDM to date as well as Wara and Victor (2008) and Schneider (2007) who question whether significant fractions of the CDM pipeline represent real reductions in emissions. Those papers and others have triggered a wave of investigative reports on particular projects and echoed such concerns about false crediting.

[5] The WTO system has blessed trade restrictions in a few areas, such as the waiver for the Kimberley Process that allows countries to bar imports of diamonds from countries that do not adhere to the Kimberley norms (Jojarth 2009). These are important exceptions, but they arise in special circumstances where exporters are unwilling or unable to challenge the restrictions; significant border tariffs or other restrictions linked to greenhouse gases are likely to be different.

[6] A large effort to tighten the rules is important, but I do not explore its modalities further here. A better CDM could be a pivotal element of a strategy that would encourage integration of the many different emission-trading systems "bottom-up" through linkages around high quality emission credits. Such integration would yield more cost-effective and global emission-trading systems and would also create stronger incentives to price emission offsets according to their underlying quality. I have explored that issue elsewhere (Victor 2007) and others have explored trading linkages and the CDM in more detail (e.g., Jaffe and Stavins 2008). My view on the CDM is that credibility and integrity are paramount goals and should be pursued even at the expense of a large and liquid trading system; for an opposite perspective that offers a strategy that would probably lower the integrity of the CDM, but increase the flow of emission credits and thus integration with the emerging markets see Keeler and Thompson (2008).

a reformed CDM will not solve the problems that plague most offset systems. Offset systems are easiest to administer when they reward marginal changes in technology and behavior that are easy to measure and assign as truly "additional." Even more problematic is that offset systems are rife with incentives for project sponsors to hide the truth about actual investment plans because, by design, offset schemes only reward investments that deviate from existing plans. These plagues are a problem because truly engaging developing countries will require fundamental changes in technology and behavior that are deeply integrated into countries' investment strategies for which it is impractical to parse marginal from fundamental incentives.[7]

Some analysts have imagined avoiding these problems by engaging developing countries in a full-blown system of emission trading rather than a CDM-like system of offsets. But realizing that outcome is little different from inventing a new form of currency. It requires solving the politically difficult task of setting acceptable emission targets in developing countries—which those countries have studiously rejected in the past—as well as devising the mechanisms for monitoring and enforcing compliance with trading systems that will require exceptional administrative capabilities. Integrating those systems with markets in the Western countries, such as the European Union Emission Trading Scheme (EU ETS), may also introduce new sources of volatility in prices and financial flows due to the large swings in emission trajectories present in developing countries. (The last decade, for example, has seen a huge upward revision in expected emissions from China and India. The last quarter of 2008 has seen a huge downward revision as those economies, notably China's, have suffered in the world financial meltdown.) New safeguards on permit flows and pricing floors and caps may be needed, although there has been neither serious effort to devise those mechanisms nor testing of how they could function in the real world. To be sure, these problems may be easier to address by focusing on just a few of the better administered sectors of developing country economies; moreover, a much tighter and more predictable CDM could facilitate some linkages. Such efforts should be pursued, but they are likely to yield isolated and fragmented efforts that do not, on their own, encourage investment in the large array of opportunities

---

[7] Elsewhere, I have explored the problems and remedies for CDM in more detail (Wara and Victor 2008; Victor 2009).

to reduce emissions from developing countries and to engage those countries diplomatically.

In short, all the main strategies for engaging developing countries do not appear to be poised to work. Some, such as sanctions, are stillborn. Others, such as the CDM, create the appearance of action, but mask the underlying reality that they do not have much impact on investment and behavior. Full-blown emissions trading is a fantasy.

This chapter suggests a new strategy that looks beyond the sticks and carrots that are the mainstay of today's debate. While existing sticks and carrots can play a role, neither is well suited to encourage large-scale adjustment in developing country technologies and behavior.

First, I will outline some examples of such large-scale changes in policy and practice that align with developing countries' own interests and could have a substantial (and growing) impact on emissions. Self-interest is the crucial starting point for these discussions because it assures that these initiatives are largely self-enforcing and likely to become integrated within the host developing country's core policies and investment plans. Here, I discuss just a few illustrations, and elsewhere I have detailed many more (Victor 2009). The discussion here is quite similar to the burgeoning literature on "co-benefits"—a literature that has documented the many opportunities for developing countries to pursue local goals while also contributing to global aims (Smith and Haigler 2008; Creutzig and He 2009; Cordeiro *et al.*, 2008). That literature, as with the argument here, is that there are many opportunities for such shifts that align with the interests of critical developing countries and which also, fortuitously, allow big reductions in greenhouse gases. However, much of the co-benefits literature has merely posited that these opportunities exist; the present chapter focuses on the actors and organizations that would need to change behavior and offers a vision for how that could be achieved.

The task for the industrialized nations—who are presently more enthusiastic and able to pursue the mission of slowing climate change—is to identify the areas where they can play a constructive role in crafting the policy reforms and investments needed to encourage these changes within the developing countries. In this chapter, I will call these "Climate Accession Deals" (CADs) because of their similarity to the accession arrangements that are made when countries join the World Trade Organization (WTO).

Most of these deals will require external resources—such as technology, money, administrative training, security guarantees, or other actions that the enthusiastic nations and international institutions can provide. Mobilizing such resources—especially if they include politically sensitive income transfers—will be politically challenging; thus, there is a special premium on minimizing and tailoring such resources to the needs of the particular deal. By focusing, first, on host country interests each CAD can be tailored to gain maximum leverage on emissions while minimizing the need for external resources.[8]

Because CADs will be complex to design and implement, they must be small in number and therefore focused in areas with extremely high potential for leverage. This approach is nearly opposite to the CDM, which prizes large numbers of broadly distributed projects based on a few cookie-cutter methodologies. Unlike the CDM—which requires that project sponsors demonstrate, for purposes of asserting "additionality," that their investments are not otherwise in the interest of the host country—CADs are based on aligning external compensation with host country interests. Such an approach, I argue, will create a scheme that is more stable, scalable, and self-enforcing. Moreover, alignment with host country interests will also make it politically easier to extinguish external compensation as the developing countries become more enmeshed in the global institutions for addressing climate change and as they learn more about the dangers of unchecked climate change and become more willing to devote their own resources to controlling emissions. CADs do not eliminate the long-term need for developing country regulation of greenhouse gases to converge with the stricter efforts in industrialized countries; rather, they create the right incentives for that convergence to occur quickly, effectively, and with minimal provision of external resources.

Second, I offer a design for the institutions that could facilitate this deal-oriented approach to engaging the reluctant nations. Those institutions include a bidding scheme so that the suppliers of deals are

---

[8] By contrast, external compensation in the CDM is largely not determined by the size of resources needed because the value of CDM emission credits is priced in markets—mainly the EU ETS—that bear little relationship to the actual need for compensation. Thus, most of the CDM credits issued to date have concerned industrial natural gas projects that have yielded huge infra-marginal rents for their sponsors (Wara 2007), but those rents have not generated any additional reduction in emissions.

forced to compete and thus minimize the need for external resources. They also include a much stronger international mechanism for scrutinizing potential deals to ensure that they represent genuine additional effort.

The international institutions that I outline here will seem complex and intrusive in the eyes of scholars of international environmental diplomacy, but they are not much different from the institutions that govern the most important areas of international economic coordination, such as trade and some macroeconomic policy. Relying on the WTO model is instructive. All WTO members subscribe to common norms and principles and new members negotiate a transition—often extending over a long period of time—to that common core. Accession talks are complex, intrusive, and especially time-consuming when the stakes are large. Applied to the problem of climate change, accession deals would prescribe the norms that would apply when new members were full members of the institutions that govern climate change while also tailoring the compensation—which could extend over many decades—that would ease the path to full membership.

While I rely on the WTO experience as a guide, other international economic institutions offer similar models—such as the policy-review process in the Marshall Plan and the Organisation for Economic Co-operation and Development (OECD); the macroeconomic reviews of countries under Article IV of the International Monetary Fund (IMF) Agreement; and accession to the European Union. In all, incentives—initially carrots but eventually also sticks—are tailored to encourage a transition into full regime membership. None of these models is perfect, but they are reminders that the problems of climate change—especially those related to mismatched interests and administrative capabilities—are matters of economic coordination and wholly new playbooks for managing such problems need not be invented. Yet most diplomacy on this issue has been guided by lessons from environmental cooperation where the toolbox is stuffed with instruments and experiences that are not adequate to the magnitude of the tasks in building an effective climate change regime.

Climate accession deals

Briefly, my overall argument is that a series of deals must be struck with the main developing countries. Each deal must be crafted with attention to two attributes. First, the deals must align with the interests of the host country because commitments that reflect national interests tend to be self-enforcing and easier to replicate on a large scale. At the international level, there is a special premium on such commitments because effective enforcement mechanisms are rare—especially in the early stages of building a regulatory regime, as in the case of climate change today. Second, these deals must minimize the need for external resources—especially on-budget income transfers—because such resources are especially costly to mobilize. In this section, I provide four examples of deals that illustrate these attributes. Elsewhere, I have outlined more than a dozen other examples (Victor 2009). These arrangements are unlike the CDM, which attempted to engage developing countries by altering incentives at the *margins* and sought to avoid the political sensitivity of resource transfers by shifting resources through less visible (yet more difficult to regulate) credit-trading schemes.

China

We start with China because that country's emissions are the largest and its growth the highest, which offers the potential of large leverage. Those high emissions stem from the country's heavy dependence on coal, which accounts for 69 percent of its primary energy system (EIA 2006). Throughout the 1990s, structural reforms in China caused a decoupling of energy demand from economic growth, with the former growing at about two-thirds of the rate of the latter. All that changed around 2000 as Chinese economic growth turned more aggressively to heavy industry and thus hinged, to a greater degree, on energy (Rosen and Houser 2007). Since then, the country's stellar economic growth has driven a similar rise in energy demand which has in turn caused shortages in energy supply and upward pressure on energy prices that has been felt worldwide. (Since October 2008 the pendulum has swung in the opposition direction—steep declines in economic growth have caused surpluses of commodities and energy supplies. Most analysts expect these surpluses to be short-lived, but they could radically slow the growth in Chinese emissions for a year or two.) Chinese officials know that this rapid growth poses a danger for their economic health and thus have initiated a broad program with the aim of, once again, decoupling economic growth from energy consumption. Those efforts include pressure on power generators to install more efficient coal-fired power plants (and now that the power supply is growing in tandem with demand, incentives to close older inefficient plants), standards on energy-using appliances from refrigerators to automobiles, and an aggressive economy-wide goal of reducing energy intensity 20 percent by 2010. These efforts are underway on their own logic and will also reduce growth in carbon dioxide (CO_2), although the ambitious 20 percent goal may not quite be met.

In addition to what China is already doing, what more could be achieved with a fuller focus on the effort and perhaps external assistance? I concentrate here on the power sector because it is still under strong direction from the central government and the governments of the major provinces. There are many opportunities, notably in improving the efficiency of power plants and the grid. Here, I focus on natural gas. Given the extremely low cost of coal, it seems unlikely that China will make a strong turn to natural gas in the foreseeable future. It has already indicated that it wants to shift to a greater share of natural gas to help balance its power generation portfolio away from its high reliance on coal, but so far it has fallen short on its own goals for natural gas due to rising costs for the fuel (most natural gas that the country would import has been offered on terms that are linked to the price of increasingly costly oil) and due to fears of insecure supplies.

China has little natural gas of its own except in its far west—that the country's first major natural gas supply project was a long and uneconomic pipeline from its western supplies is a sign of the priority that the country places on energy security. China can speed its shift to natural gas by tightening local air pollution rules—a move it already favors to clear the skies in polluted cities—since tighter rules also tilt the balance away from coal (which requires costly pollution clean-up equipment) toward cleaner fuels. It can also build a network of liquefied natural gas (LNG) reception terminals with a diversity of foreign suppliers, which would give the country more options in case a particular supply was curtailed. It can also work to reduce transit interruptions in natural gas supply such as those from pirates or through interdiction on the sea lanes. With other large LNG importers (and countries that depend on safe sea lanes), there could be joint exercises, confidence building, and anti-piracy squads in crucial transit choke points such as the Strait of Malacca. China must also engage more directly with the fact that its most cost-effective natural gas supplies come from neighboring Russia. To date, Sino-Russian wariness along with Russian natural gas monopoly Gazprom's vision that it should export its natural gas to Western Europe for the best price has made China wary of depending on Russia. Outsiders cannot fix this problem, but they can make it easier to strike deals that will be self-enforcing once new pipelines are in operation, just as the big Soviet pipelines built in the 1970s and 1980s to Western Europe have been remarkably reliable suppliers of natural gas once they had been put into operation.[9] A compact with Russia, China, and Europe may be needed to give Russia and China, alike, the confidence they need to develop a bilateral natural gas supply arrangement. Western nations offering diplomatic assistance provide a degree of assurance that would not otherwise be possible. Because natural gas emits about half the CO_2 per unit of electricity generated, there is huge potential leverage in shifting to natural gas. Elsewhere, we have calculated that just one province in China (Guangdong) could cut its annual CO_2 emissions 100 million tons by 2025 if it tightened local air pollution regulations (Jiang *et al.* 2008).

India

Like China, India's energy system hinges on coal. Thus, like China, the greatest leverage on India's emissions lies with finding ways to use coal more efficiently or supplanting coal. Beyond those similarities, however, the details of a viable engagement strategy in India vary markedly because the organization of India's energy system is distinct and thus so are the challenges and opportunities for engagement.

The greatest opportunity for leverage on India's emissions lies in boosting the efficiency of converting coal to electricity. (As with China, there is great theoretical opportunity in boosting efficiency

[9] Russia's less reliable supplies in 2006 and 2009 are rooted in pricing disputes with Ukraine. When the Soviet Union existed, natural gas exports crossed few transit countries before they reached lucrative Western markets. The collapse of the Soviet Union yielded many more independent transit countries, notably Ukraine, and is a lesson that China knows it must heed. A direct gas export route from Russia is likely to be much more reliable than one that depends on transit countries. That logic helps explain China's interest in circumventing Mongolia with a possible natural gas pipeline from Russia and also its keen interest in direct export of natural gas and other products from Kazakhstan, which borders China to the west.

for direct coal combustion, such as its use in brick kilns, but it is hard to see how outsiders could have much impact since the Indian government itself is barely able to administer such uses.) Electricity is interesting not only because it is the largest single user of coal, but also because nearly all of the coal-fired power system is owned by the state. India has a federal system of governance, and in the power sector, competence is shared between the central government and the states. The single largest operator of coal-fired power plants is the centrally owned National Thermal Power Corporation (NTPC); I will focus there since it offers the greatest potential for leverage, though similar opportunities may also exist in some of the so-called State Electricity Boards (SEBs)—the regional state companies that also build and operate power plants. The SEBs are more challenging partners for controlling emissions leverage, though, as all are technically bankrupt and pulled in many directions by local political priorities, and most are badly managed. NTPC, by contrast, is remarkably well-managed for a government-owned corporation; it is in touch with technological opportunity, attentive to cost, and steeped in competence.

NTPC, while the most efficient of India's government-owned power generators, is notable for sitting far back from the world technological frontier. It is building the nation's first "supercritical" coal-fired plant—a less efficient version of the "ultrasupercritical" plants that are the world's most efficient conventional coal-fired power units. NTPC has realized that it has a strong incentive to find more efficient ways to burn coal because the era of cheap coal is over, but NTPC has little experience with these more efficient plants. Its counterparts in developed nations, such as equipment suppliers, can assist in this process.

Nearly all coal in India is supplied from a consortium of government-owned coal-mining companies held by the behemoth Coal India Ltd (CIL). The consortium members of CIL vary radically in their performance, but all are running into trouble as they dig into more difficult to mine coal seams, produce lower quality coal, and depend on a creaking transport infrastructure of railroads that is barely able to keep up with demand. Over the last two years, the stockpile of coal on hand at key power plants has dwindled to a few days. Efforts to reform the coal supply system—such as by allowing private ownership of mines, forcing better accountability in CIL, rationalizing rail rates—are making only halting progress due to massive political obstacles. Even seemingly obvious steps such as encouraging more washing of coal have been difficult. Coal washing removes impurities before shipping so that the product actually moved contains more useable content; by some estimates perhaps as much as one-third of the "coal" that is moved in India is actually rocks that do not burn. Yet a pricing system that is based on weight rather than British thermal units (BTUs) does not reward use of this process.

These problems in coal supply are hard and slow to fix. Part of the solution is to allow coal prices to reflect scarcity and to encourage a shift to more reliable supplies of imported coal. Efforts on both fronts are underway—for example, a rising share of India's coal is priced in electronic auctions rather than through the government's central planning system of "linkages"—and that means that coal is becoming much more expensive. Imported coal, too, is much costlier than it was a decade ago, and the fundamentals in international coal supply portend high prices into the future. For NTPC, these supply trends put a premium on efficiency. A program to rebuild old coal-fired power plants with advanced supercritical units and to test deployment of ultrasupercritical plants could help the country lift its average coal combustion efficiency from 29 percent to perhaps 35 percent over two decades. Looking to 2025, such a program could avoid about 600 million tonnes of CO_2 annually (Victor, 2009). The Indian government has already removed the most serious obstacle to this approach by dismantling in the 1990s the requirement that coal-combustion technologies be supplied only by Indian vendors. A viable plan to work with NTPC (and perhaps some of the better managed SEBs) to apply new technologies could work on two tracks—one with outside vendors (perhaps using export-import financing from countries keen to export the technology) and the other in consortium with India's main equipment manufacturer (Bharat Heavy Electrical, Ltd.) so that the two ventures compete. NTPC would be a welcome partner not only because this aligns with its severe problems in coal supply but also because the firm is suffering some reputational harm from being the world's third largest source of CO_2. Scrutiny of its carbon footprint on the planet is already growing in India since that news was first reported in April 2008.

Such a program would operate under the useful shadow of competition from private investors in power plants as India has just embarked on a program to build up to fourteen "ultra mega power projects"—all based on private investment for power parks that would rely partly on captive coal mines and mainly on imported coal. All of the ultra mega power parks are expected to use supercritical technology; it would be useful to explore whether some may even use ultrasupercritical technology or even Integrated Gasification Combined Cycle (IGCC) a decade or so down the road when the technology is further along.

Indonesia

After Brazil, Indonesia is the world's biggest deforester by area (FAO 2005, Chapter 2). A deal to stem deforestation could be crafted along terms similar to those outlined elsewhere for Brazil (Victor, 2009). Uncomfortable choices will be needed to help arm the Indonesian police; assurances will be needed so that such resources are actually used for enforcement. Corruption, long rampant in the forest regions of Indonesia, will need special scrutiny. The challenges to such a deal will be many, but such is the nature of getting a grip on CO_2 emissions.

Indonesia offers a special opportunity because its deforestation occurs in many different types of soils, and one type of deforestation—by fire on peat soils—is the country's main source of CO_2 emissions. Peat soils are a particular concern because they are especially rich in carbon and while any clearing will release some carbon, fires are particularly intensive in their carbon release. In the past, regional efforts in Southeast Asia have attempted to ban all land clearing by fire, the main cause of a haze that appears across the region—reducing visibility and causing severe health effects. The clearing season during the dry years of 1997–1998 was particularly bad and animated such regional attempts. So far, however, they have not had much impact because they run contrary to the interests and capabilities of pivotal players—notably Indonesia, which hosts most of the peaty fires. A fresh attempt, animated not just by regional haze but also by global climate change, could navigate around this problem by focusing first on the fires that have the largest externality (i.e., peat consumption) while posing less threat to the underlying agricultural and palm plantation activities that give rise to the need for forest clearing. With success, a peat-focused effort could expand to other soils.[10]

In practice, focusing on peat probably would require external assistance. Help is needed to build Indonesian capacity to map the country's

---

[10] This proposal for a peat-focused program is inspired by Tacconi *et al* (2008).

soils and understand the major sources of fire threat. Monitoring and technical assistance, in the context of a broader engagement with international scientists, could be essential. A better police force could, in time, enforce a ban on clearing peat lands. There may be places where such a ban would be impractical because it would be seen as an effort to ban commercially productive use of the land altogether. In those cases, a fund could be established to pay the extra cost of manual non-fire clearing. (Clearing by fire is preferred by land owners when there are no constraints on their actions because it costs about one-fourth of the amount of manual clearing.) While the exact emissions are difficult to calculate, an analysis of the 1997 wildfires in Indonesia found that the emissions from that event were approximately equal to 13–40 percent of worldwide annual emissions from fossil fuels.[11]

Gulf states

Finally, I speculate whether the countries that have been most wary of climate policy—the oil-exporting Persian Gulf states such as Kuwait and Saudi Arabia—may be engaged in useful ways. These are not reluctant nations—rather, many are hostile to the mission of cutting CO_2 emissions. Engaging them, if feasible at all, will require measures that strictly align with their interests. Their largest sources of emissions come from consuming oil, and unlike most other countries—which are becoming more efficient in their oil consumption thanks to higher international prices—the Gulf states generally insulate their populations from the real cost of oil. Higher oil prices beget much higher emissions. Certainly the petro states could raise internal prices for oil and also build more effective natural gas supply systems (which would reduce the need for oil in power generation and also, fortuitously, allow deep cuts in CO_2 emissions). But outsiders will have little influence on this process except to discuss the need for such reforms and to provide advice, where useful, on ways to shift toward more efficient and lower-carbon energy systems.

Outsiders could have more leverage in the Gulf petro states on deployment of carbon-storage systems, however. If successful, carbon storage could help lower that region's emissions, accelerate deployment

---

[11] The paper estimates that between 0.81 and 2.57 Gt of carbon were released during the 1997–1998 forest fires. See Page (2002).

of the technology worldwide, and squarely advance the interests of
the Gulf states because the most interesting niche for testing carbon
storage at scale is in enhanced oil recovery. BP, plc (the former British
Petroleum) is far advanced in the region's first demonstration plant—
an enhanced oil recovery and carbon-storage venture in Abu Dhabi.
The Gulf, by virtue of its rich oil production, is well endowed with
empty pore space suitable for carbon capture and storage. Other Gulf
states may follow suit after Abu Dhabi's demonstration, and the West
should be willing to help clear roadblocks and share technology where
needed although most of these projects will probably proceed on their
own commercial merits. It is hard to assess how much CO_2 could be
stored through such ventures, but a Gulf-wide initiative in this area
may scale up over the lifetime of large new investments in the power
sector and new oil production fields (i.e., about 15–20 years) and
the level of effort could be on the order of magnitude of 100 million
tonnes CO_2 per year. An effort on that magnitude would involve
50–100 projects on the scale of the large CO_2-injection projects
already being tested in Norway or Algeria and is roughly comparable
with all planned CO_2-injection projects worldwide today.[12]

Institutions for engagement

The previous section outlined a set of opportunities for deep cuts in
CO_2 emissions across a relatively small number of efforts. All these
share a few essential attributes:

- They are anchored in host countries' interests and capabilities and
  thus do not require the extremely difficult task of crafting international agreements that run contrary to a country's core interests;
- They are limited in number, and all yield large leverage—each
  on the order of 100 million tonnes of annual emissions within a
  decade, growing as the investments become more pervasive in the
  host economy and society;
- All involve a complex array of interests and institutions, notably in
  the host country, and thus must engage private enterprise and government ministries that are far beyond the environmental and foreign
  affairs ministries that have dominated climate diplomacy to date;

[12] Injection rates for particular projects and for the totality of world efforts in
carbon storage are reported in Rai *et al.* (2008).

- All are replicable and scalable. Where they succeed, they offer paths for similar "deals" (at lower cost) in other countries and are self-reinforcing in the original host country. This self-reinforcing attribute makes them the opposite of the CDM logic, which rewards only reductions below a baseline. These "deals" are about changing the baseline, not crediting against it.

How could such deals be crafted in a way that did not simply replicate the problems of the CDM—in which efforts are made and resources transferred without much impact on underlying behavior? Once industrialized and developing countries focused on such deals, what would sustain cooperation so that the deals expanded in scale and scope? And how could these deals help pave the way for fuller regulation of greenhouse gases in the developing countries? This section answers those questions.

My answers are rooted in new international institutions that would elicit "bids" from the developing countries on possible CADs and then assess those bids as well as performance in actually implementing CADs. That process can also, in time, manage the convergence between the reluctant countries (who engage in the collective effort only through CADs) and the enthusiastic countries (who engage by spending their own resources on policies such as applying a price on carbon in their home economies, supporting novel technologies, and providing the external resources needed to make CADs work). The rest of this section addresses those three functions—bidding, assessment, and convergence.

Bidding

The process of assembling CADs must begin with the host country—in particular, its government. This is due to the fact that the host government has four advantages that no other actor enjoys. First, it can make the most credible long-term commitments on behalf of its territory and thus is the best locus for accountability. Second, nearly always, the host government is able to mobilize the most reliable and widely accepted information about the actual baseline of policies and efforts that are planned, and it can best contemplate how those may be adjusted as part of a CAD. Third, the host government knows the most about what it can actually implement in different sectors of its economy. And fourth, there is rarely any other actor that can better assemble the complex array of stakeholders needed for high-leverage CADs—the industrial and economic development ministries, state-owned power corporations, etc. Thus, the bidding must begin with the host government.

To make these CADs feasible, outsiders—the enthusiastic nations—will be expected to offer incentives that combine with real efforts by governments in the reluctant nations to alter development trajectories. The previous section outlined the incentives that may be required—such as financial resources in some cases, access and special licensing incentives for technology, or provision of security guarantees needed to assure reliable delivery of low-carbon fuels such as natural gas. But the central question remains: what can be done to elicit accurate information from the host governments (in the reluctant nations) on exactly what they really need? CDM has faltered on exactly this front because it has encouraged host governments and project investors to claim incentives that they did not actually need for the policies and investments that they pursued.

This problem is not new in international cooperation—it is analogous to the accession problem in international institutions. The key task in accession is to entice a new member into the club (and thus create broader benefits for the club) while not overpaying (or under-charging) the new member. When the terms of accession *ex ante* are relatively straightforward and vary in only a few important dimensions, the problem can be fixed readily. An auction, for example, can be used to force new entrants to compete and obtain the best price for entry. When the terms are more complex, broad competition is less feasible. The CDM has tried to operate on the former philosophy, and most proposals for CDM reform envision an even larger market and thus more effective commodity-style competition. In reality, almost every interesting mode for engaging developing countries involves efforts and investments of the latter type.[13]

The WTO offers a model through its accession process.[14] Potential new members assemble bids of promises that they will offer in exchange

---

[13] The many visions for new international funds to invest in developing countries also, in general, seem to be based on the former philosophy and thus may be prone to fail unless their backers develop more sophisticated visions of the bidding and assessment process.

[14] Here, for simplicity, I will speak of the "WTO" although the relevant experience extends much earlier than the formal creation of the WTO in 1995.

for external benefits. In the WTO case, those external benefits are particular tariff concessions and, ultimately, most–favored-nation status and the other core benefits afforded to all WTO members.[15] Negotiations then proceed with any interested WTO member allowed to join the "working party" that shapes the final accession agreement, which includes transition provisions and other concessions that often require radical changes in host-government policy.[16] For small countries with clear benefits and few interested parties, the negotiations can proceed over a brief period; for larger countries, the effort requires years. On average, WTO accession negotiations require about five years. In the case of CADs, the benefits may come in two forms— general benefits afforded to all good-standing members of the global climate regime and then specific benefits tailored to each member. The general benefits, akin to the general benefits of WTO membership, could include access to the carbon markets in the enthusiastic nations for CDM-like offset trading as well as access to general-purpose funds (such as those being established at this writing within the World Bank) for emission-abatement projects, adaptation, and capacity building. The particular benefits, where I will focus the rest of this chapter, would include the external elements needed for the efforts under the CAD to proceed. While the WTO model is imperfect because it concentrates mainly on the negotiations that yield a transition to the general benefits of membership, it is nonetheless apt because the WTO experience reveals that the international community can organize such bidding and sustained negotiation.[17] In every significant case of WTO

---

[15] On WTO accession broadly, see Michalopoulos (2002).

[16] The most recent and important example of such large changes is China. For reviews of the accession process and its real impact internally in China, see, e.g., Farah (2006).

[17] In other ways, the WTO model is also not ideal. For example, open access rules for joining access working parties allow, in effect, veto membership. The climate process may eventually arrive at that state, but when launching the first round of accession deals, it would probably be better to limit the number of negotiating forums by establishing voting rules that are more permissive—for example, countries that account for half of the enthusiastic countries' emissions could block approval of a country's accession deal. (This approximates the rule adopted in the Kyoto negotiations, and such rules are important because they protect the enthusiastic countries from adopting strict emission controls only to find that their most important economic competitors do not face such regulations.) Such a rule would force the industrialized countries to negotiate in blocks rather than singly. It would also tilt the balance, initially, in favor of encouraging expansion of membership and then, as the rules tighten, toward

accession, those first bids are not accepted—rather, each interested WTO member begins bilateral negotiations with the candidate and, through the normal process of bargaining, arrives at a final, agreed package. The negotiation process focuses on both what the host country is willing to concede and also what the WTO members think the host country is actually able to deliver.

A key to success with CADs will be the rules of transition. If CADs are seen by the reluctant governments as single one-off deals, then they will be reluctant to make the investments and adjustments needed for the deals to help put the country on a different development trajectory. Moreover, a series of one-off deals probably will be more costly for donors because they could actually create incentives for reluctant nations to avoid making internal adjustments such as imposing a positive price on carbon and beginning to regulate sectors of the economy toward lower emissions. A solution to this problem is to ensure that the individual, tailored elements of each CAD are coupled to a broader set of expectations and a clear transition path for the country to adhere to general norms. (Those general norms may be codified into the United Nations Framework Convention on Climate Change, or UNFCCC, or a protocol—akin to the general norms that were codified into the GATT.) That transition process could include milestones as well as visible commitments to extinguish external support as a country develops. By combining these transition commitments into a broader agreement their enforceability will rise because the commitments will be connected to a broader set of membership benefits.[18]

The reluctant countries would bid packages of efforts such as those outlined here. Some of those efforts may be grand and interlocking— requiring a major intervention by a complex array of other countries.

Footnote 17 (*cont.*)
   more demanding accession talks. Encouraging larger early membership would help broaden the climate regime in helpful ways. The WTO, back in the 1960s when it was still the GATT, also had accession rules that tilted much more strongly in favor of approving new members when compared with today's rules (which are not only tighter, but also cover a much broader spectrum of trade-related activities).
[18] Such a broader norm-based process may make it easier, eventually, to apply stronger sticks in future, including trade sanctions. A general agreement on climate change and the negotiated transition with each of the new entrants would create higher legitimacy (and expectation) of future enforcement than a series of one-off deals.

For example, China may bid the creation of an East Asian natural gas pipeline grid that connected Russia's continental natural gas supplies with markets in China and South Korea. (That grid, in turn, would facilitate the greater use of natural gas for power generation and thus lower CO_2 emissions.) Initially, however, most bids would probably rest on proposals that are less complex and thus more tractable for single donor countries or small groups of countries because those deals would be easier to organize and less fragile politically. For example, India may bid to test and deploy ultrasupercritical power plants through its state-owned power company. Enthusiastic countries that harbor the relevant technologies would then negotiate—and compete—to provide financing, training, and other elements that help realize a greater deployment of these advanced power plants. (Those countries are numerous and include the European Union and Japan and, for some of the equipment, the United States. A useful competition between suppliers could help lower the cost of technology demonstration.) Many countries may bid a wide array of possible CADs to ensure that donor countries compete across a variety of opportunities. Those negotiations would then codify the expectations for both parties as well as milestones that can be used to judge progress.

To a small degree, these kinds of investments are already underway through the normal process of bilateral and multilateral development assistance. The CADs approach is different for two reasons. First, CADs would include an explicit transition to more general norms and thus reduce the most costly (for donor countries and the climate) perverse effects of one-off deals. (One-off deals discourage reluctant countries from policies that change their baselines because they offer the promise of a stream of payments for continued avoidance of serious emission control policies.) Second, by integrating CADs into a broader "general agreement on climate change" the CAD system more readily gives donor countries credit for their efforts. Under the present Kyoto-style system of targets and timetables, the enthusiastic countries earn credit for investments in the reluctant nations only when those investments are monetized as an emission reduction under the CDM. Part of the CAD negotiation, by contrast, would include the appropriate credit that the enthusiastic nation would earn—in some cases, that credit may be quantified and monetized, but in others it would simply be part of the explicit package of commitments that the enthusiastic nation makes to its peers. For example, the European Union (led by the

United Kingdom) has a project under way to develop advanced coal combustion technology in China. The only forces that hold that project together are British altruism and Chinese tolerance. If both countries gained credit for the effort as part of broader commitments to address climate change, then the odds would be much higher that the effort would be focused on activities of real utility. As the collective effort to address climate change becomes more demanding, it will become increasingly important to offer flexibility for nations—reluctant and enthusiastic—to tailor their efforts to their interests and capabilities rather than requiring all effort to be measured along a single (often difficult to control) dimension of quantified emission reductions.

I have focused here on the WTO accession process as a model, but of course there are many other examples that offer similar guidance. EU accession occurs through a similar process of negotiation, although the resources mobilized are much larger and the scrutiny much more intense because much more is at stake. Indeed, the European Union itself arose from a core group of countries that focused on collective management of a few of the "commanding heights" of the 1950s economy (coal and steel) and then expanded to address other topics with new members.[19] The original formation of the OECD arose through a process of negotiation among recipient states—the war ravaged economies of Western Europe—for the Marshall Plan funds provided by the United States. Each European member bid for a share of the pie by proposing a complex array of policy reforms that it would implement; its peers evaluated the bids and negotiated a full package of resources and policy efforts that all the members would implement.

Assessment and Monitoring

What keeps countries from promising much more than they actually deliver? That question is a shadow over all efforts to negotiate effective solutions to the climate problem. Simply measuring compliance with output targets—such as emission targets and timetables—reveals little

---

[19] Much of this thinking goes back to what used to be called "functionalism"— the argument that deep integration arises through technocratic cooperation between governments that then spills over into a broader need for cooperation. For an origin along those lines, see Haas (1958) and for an assessment of the broader array of domestic political forces that shape which countries are willing to integrate (and under which terms) see Moravcsik (1998).

because even the enthusiastic countries can simply move the goalposts (and move them again, such as through the use of offsets of dubious quality). What is really needed is an assessment of whether countries are honoring the *efforts* that they have promised. (Governments can influence efforts; they have a harder time controlling emissions—and governments with poor administrative apparatus, which is true across most of the reluctant nations, have an especially difficult time controlling emission outputs rather than more tightly specified effort inputs.) In time, that assessment process can make it easier to negotiate more meaningful commitments. The monitoring and assessment has always been a weak link in international environmental governance. While there are some decent precedents in environmental cooperation, those cases mostly arise in instances where the implementation effort needed by governments is fairly simple and thus monitoring and assessment are relatively easy to organize.[20]

The answer to this question comes in two parts. First, the negotiation of commitments can help ensure that governments promise genuine efforts that they are likely to implement. A process focused on CADs, along the lines I suggest here, is designed to elicit negotiations over whether the host governments are actually willing and able to implement their commitments and to demand external resources only in the area needed. For the reluctant countries, these negotiations will concentrate on the carrots needed, and failure to honor commitments will put the carrots in jeopardy. (I discuss sticks later.) For the enthusiastic countries—who are expected to make donations and other contributions to the carrots—these negotiations will concentrate on minimizing the demand for resources while maximizing the leverage on emissions because the CADs that they sponsor will be part of their overall effort toward managing the climate change problem. And the enthusiastic countries will also negotiate with their peers about the proper credit that they should earn from supporting CADS toward broader, collective goals of managing global emissions and exposure to climate change. Falling short (or overpaying) for CADs will require additional effort on other fronts.

Second, a new institution is needed to provide regular assessments of implementation. Such institutions are rare in environmental

[20] See, generally, Part I on "systems for implementation review" in Victor *et al.* (1998).

negotiations but increasingly common in areas of economic cooperation.[21] The creation of the WTO in 1995 included an agreement to
launch a trade-policy-review mechanism (TPRM) that would regularly
review nations' compliance with WTO commitments. That model is
imperfect, however, because its architects could not agree on whether
the TPRM would connect to the WTO's real enforcement system (its
dispute resolution process); thus, there is no connection, and TPRM
has withered in its practical influence (Price 2007). Better precedents
are probably found in the OECD, International Energy Agency (IEA)
and the IMF. From the outset, the OECD included an intensive review
process because the original members wanted to hold each other
accountable to the commitments that they had made collectively.
(Some of those commitments—such as on public budgets, exchange
rates, and customs—were interdependent and prone to deteriorate
unless each country had confidence that the others were in compliance.) OECD's review process continues today with regular reviews of
its members' economic policies, science and technology policies, and
environmental policies. While the economic reviews have atrophied
in importance, OECD's environmental reviews remain an area where
the institution has particularly high visibility and, in many cases, influence. IEA, an independent arm of OECD, conducts regular reviews
of its members' energy policies that are also, often, influential.[22] The
IMF's Article IV process includes an intensive review of policies when

[21] Such institutions are also increasingly common in collective arms-control
agreements—especially agreements that require complex (and often contested)
implementation efforts. Examples include the increasingly complex monitoring
systems under the International Atomic Energy Agency (IAEA). But the security shadow over arms control agreements is so strong that I am wary about
drawing too many parallels.

[22] For example, see IEA's review of the European Union's energy policy—which
is an extraordinary event in revealing the extent to which large, industrialized
economies will allow intrusive reviews of their policies by institutions that they
trust for an even-handed assessment (e.g., IEA 2008). OECD's reviews occur
in a much wider array of issue-areas—such as innovation and competition
policy—which reflects OECD's origins and functioning as a general purpose
agency for international cooperation. The United States is noticeably less
engaged in OECD policy reviews than most other members, and one of the
important challenges will be the design of an institution that is tolerable to
the United States—a problem that arises in nearly every area of international
institution-building. OECD, increasingly, even reviews policies (by invitation)
of nonmembers, notably China, where OECD has reviewed innovation policy
(in 2008) and other policies, such as investment policy (OECD 2003).

members are allowed to suspend some of the institution's norms. Through an intensive process of review, the IMF (and its members) learns about the political and economic forces that lead to a member's noncompliance and works with the target country to outline a path back to compliance (Chayes and Chayes 1991).

Applied to the climate problem—in particular, creating a role for CADs in a general agreement on climate change—these experiences suggest an assessment institution that could look broadly at a country's promised efforts (as in the WTO, OECD, and IEA policy reviews) and then probe in detail where those efforts seem to be falling short (as in the IMF Article IV reviews). Benchmarks and milestones promised during the negotiation process could be used to measure broad compliance, but the real value in this review would lie with the detailed assessments and negotiations with host governments that would determine (and make transparent) the factors that are blocking fuller implementation. With experience and demonstrated competence, the review process may also make assessments of the degree to which donor efforts have fallen short (and thus external donors should not earn credit for their contributions) and also where efforts have exceeded expectations (thus leading, perhaps, to bonuses). As a practical matter, this under- and over-compliance may not take the form of quantified emissions, but would be an assessment of effort that could feed into negotiations among the enthusiastic countries about whether each is meeting its obligations.

Converging to global norms

The scheme proposed here—CADs as part of a broad general negotiation on climate change, backed by new institutions to assess and shape the efforts—will seem cumbersome. But that is intrinsic to the climate problem for two reasons. First, serious strategies for addressing climate change will require a complex array of national policy efforts; thus, international collective action will be much more complex (and time consuming) to organize than evident in the experiences under the UNFCCC and the Kyoto Protocol. Second, important players in that process presently do not have an interest in spending their own resources; thus, mechanisms must be created to compensate (and punish) these countries. These countries will have low or zero prices on carbon in their economies; thus, normal economic pressures to reduce emissions will be absent. CADs are an effort to address that problem of reluctance.

The first problem is intrinsic to the issue of climate change and will not go away. The institutions for negotiating and assessing collective efforts will always be complex and multidimensional—they will always have characteristics more like the WTO than the simple targets and timetables negotiated under the auspices of the UNFCCC and the Kyoto Protocol. If the complexity is managed well, then such a broader negotiation can actually lead to more effective management because it will allow deal making on a broader set of dimensions.

The second problem, however, is transient. It will disappear as the reluctant countries converge with the enthusiastic ones. The speed with which that transition occurs will drive the increased efficiency of the global effort and reduce the difficulty, politically, for the enthusiastic countries to maintain the system of resource transfers and special arrangements that their populations will find difficult to tolerate. The question I address here is how to shape and accelerate that convergence. International environmental agreements offer few good models for convergence because none of the major international environmental regimes has actually converged. The major agreements of the 1970s applied similar norms to all members, but since the late 1980s essentially all international environmental agreements have, at their core, a permanent distinction between industrialized and developing countries. Essentially all expect the former to compensate the latter for the "agreed incremental cost" of all efforts to comply.[23] Even in obvious cases—such as Mexico and South Korea, both of which are OECD members yet have traditionally been included in the ranks of developing countries—it has been extremely difficult to undo this norm in environmental diplomacy. Convergence is difficult to orchestrate when the founding principles of a cooperative regime enshrine the exact opposite—two worlds, permanently distinct, with developing countries not expected to spend their own resources to help solve global problems.

Better models for convergence are found in the international regimes for economic cooperation. In the WTO system and the IMF, for example, all members subscribe to common norms. Accession packages (and Article IV negotiations in the case of the IMF) are

[23] The experience with the Montreal Protocol was most pivotal in establishing this approach to developing-country compensation and the permanent "two worlds" division between industrialized (donor) and developing (recipient) countries. See, generally, DeSombre and Kauffman (1996).

extended negotiations and performance reviews focused on tolerable breaches from those common norms. The core idea behind these cooperative regimes is commonality in basic obligations; the practical political and administrative efforts concentrate on achieving such convergence—even if, as is notable for the IMF, the alignment takes decades.

Applied to the climate problem, the core principles could be numerous and complex. Here I focus on a few that probably matter most:

- Pricing of carbon (through trading or taxation) and linkage of carbon markets;
- Direct support for low-carbon technologies;
- Minimal trade and other barriers to application of low-carbon technologies;
- Transparency in policies and their expected effects on emissions and deployment of technology so that all members of the agreement can learn from and scrutinize the efforts of others;
- "Most favored" treatment for all members so that any concession offered to others—such as linkage of a trading system or reduction in a tariff for low-carbon technologies—is available to all other members;
- Good faith participation in regular reviews of the performance and adequacy of the regime and each member's efforts to implement the regime's norms;
- Good faith in research on the causes, consequences, and remedies to the problem of climate change.

These norms will seem abstract and general, but meaningful common norms often arise through particular applications of common understandings. Some have already attracted widespread agreement although such agreement is highest where ambition and effort are the least. Each nation—through bidding and assessment along the lines discussed earlier—would then make commitments to "opt out" of some norms (e.g., economy-wide carbon pricing) for delineated periods of time. The review process, as in IMF Article IV reviews, would then assess regularly whether avoidance of compliance with those norms is acceptable.

The final task is to explore why any nation—in particular in the developing world, which has been wary of becoming entangled in climate commitments—would ever agree to this scheme. The answer lies in conditionality and contingency. The enthusiastic nations have large resources to offer—technology, funding, linkages to valuable carbon markets, and the like—that will be available only to members in good standing. And the enthusiastic nations will also threaten the eventual use of sticks—such as trade sanctions—to large countries that avoid such commitments. (Eventually, depending on how the climate and trade regimes evolve, the two could merge in some respects.) And the regime would evolve as quickly as possible to a system that includes linkages between carbon-pricing systems and technology markets so that the "most favored" provisions have real value. The deeper that the linkages are, the greater the benefits from membership.

The effort to craft such a regime requires rejecting the principle of universality that has guided essentially all international environmental negotiations (and all efforts under the auspices of the United Nations). Universality is a liability because, by design, it does not encourage discrimination between countries based on their level of effort; it means that countries that invest few of their own resources have as much influence on the rules and procedures in international organizations as those that have a lot more at stake. Combined with the difficulty in enforcing international obligations and the permanent "two worlds" approach that pervades environmental negotiations, a system that is unable to discriminate is rarely able to achieve outcomes that require massive efforts by countries that have very different interests. Instead of universality, a better approach starts small—with a "club" of countries that matter most to the climate problem (i.e., the large emitters) and who are willing to make concessions. The core agreements crafted in that club can then be replicated and extended. To the extent that those agreements can be made conditional on like-minded efforts by other members of the club, membership in good standing will offer big benefits that countries will be keen to obtain. This kind of evolution exactly mirrors the origins of the WTO which began as a club of willing countries that made reciprocal (and thus self-enforcing) agreements with each other that then deepened and expanded with experience and confidence. Political scientists and anthropologists have long studied such evolutionary regimes using simple permissive "tit-for-tat" models and shown that a regime with built-in enforcement and gains from membership can evolve into wider and full-blown cooperation (Axelrod 1984; Seabright 2005).

Conclusions

For too long, analysts and practitioners in the field of international environmental cooperation have had a blind spot on how to solve the problem of developing-country participation in a global climate regime.

Analysts have imagined two ideal worlds that do not exist. In one ideal world, all countries would apply carbon pricing such as through a global system of emission trading. That world does not exist because most countries (and soon most of the world economy) have neither the interest nor the ability to apply effective carbon pricing. In another ideal world, the industrialized countries would simply compensate developing countries for the full cost of compliance. But that world does not exist because the industrialized nations are hardly ready to mobilize the tens or hundreds of billions of dollars needed for such a compensation scheme when official development assistance stands at just $100 billion for all purposes—such as reconstruction in Iraq—and the countries that would get the most compensation (e.g., China) are also the most potent economic competitors. The politics of mobilizing resource transfers under these circumstances are probably impossible to organize successfully. These two worlds have combined into imaginary schemes such as global allocation of emission credits and full-blown global trading.

The practitioner, meanwhile, is painted into a box—a world that exists, but is dangerous for the planet's climate system. Well-tested tools such as financial transfers along the lines of the Montreal Protocol are not available because the scale of transfer is much too large to be politically tolerable. Climate diplomacy has avoided that problem through the Clean Development Mechanism (CDM)—a scheme that offers, in theory, to pay developing countries the full cost of cutting emissions while also laying a theoretical foundation for global-emission trading. The funds paid are kept off the public budget and thus less vulnerable to political backlash. The credits issued are legal tender in the countries (mainly Europe) that are most enthusiastic to cut global emissions.

This chapter has argued that the current approach to engaging developing countries is a dead end. The CDM has done little to cut emissions, and its flaws are so fundamental that it will never amount to a serious strategy. And the existing norms and practices in international environmental diplomacy are a poor guide for solving the problems that arise as enthusiastic countries (mainly the industrialized world) attempt to coax reluctant nations (mainly the developing world) into a common global effort. Huge potentials for emission reductions remain untapped.

The solution, I suggest, is to look to the GATT/WTO, IMF, OECD, and other international economic regimes. All have had to contend with this problem of differential interests and capabilities. The most apt solution to the problem would create a common set of norms that apply to all member countries and then focus negotiations on the terms of accession. Reluctant countries would bid a variety of policies and programs that make sense for their development trajectory, and their bids would include information on the barriers (funding, technology, windows to carbon-trading markets, access to international institutions, etc.). The negotiations that follow would determine the resources that enthusiastic nations would provide and the metrics for assessing compliance. Those negotiations would also determine the role that support for CADs could play as part of an enthusiastic nation's contribution to the collective goal of managing climate change. And, if managed well, the CAD process could also accelerate the reluctant countries down the path of adhering to global norms on the need to control emissions.

References

Axelrod, R. (1984). *The Evolution of Cooperation*. New York: Basic Books.

Chayes, A. and A. H. Chayes (1991). "Managing the Transition to a Global Warming Regime, or What to Do 'til the Treaty Comes," in J. Mathews (ed.), *Greenhouse Warming: Negotiating a Global Regime*. Washington, DC: World Resources Institute, pp. 61–7.

Christine, J. (2009). *Crime, War and Global Trafficking: Designing International Cooperation*. New York: Cambridge University Press.

Cordeiro, M, L. Schipper, and D. Noriega (2008). *Measuring the Invisible: Quantifying Emissions Reductions from Transport Solutions, Querétaro Case Study*. Washington, DC: Embarq and World Resources Institute.

Creutzig, F. and D. He (in press). "Climate change mitigation and co-benefits of feasible transport demand policies in Beijing," *Transportation Research Part D: Transport and Environment* 14:2, March: 120–31.

DeSombre, E. and J. Kauffman (1996). "The Montreal Protocol Multilateral Fund: Partial Success Story," in R. O. Keohane and M. Levy (eds.), *Institutions for Environmental Aid: Pitfalls and Promise*. Cambridge, MA: MIT Press, pp. 89–126.

EIA (2006). *China Energy Brief: Coal.* Washington, DC: Energy Information Administration, United States Department of Energy.

FAO (2005). "Chapter 2: Extent of Forest Resources," in *Global Forest Resources Assessment 2005: Progress toward sustainable forest management.* Rome: Food and Agriculture Organization, pp. 11–36.

Farah, P. D. (2006). "Five Years of China's WTO Membership," *Legal Issues of Economic Integration,* 33: 263–304.

Haas, E. (1958). *The Uniting of Europe: Political, Social, and Economic Forces, 1950–1957.* Palo Alto, CA: Stanford University Press.

IEA (2008). *IEA Energy Policies Review—The European Union 2008.* Paris: International Energy Agency.

Jaffe, J. and R. Stavins (2008). "Linkage of Tradable Permit Systems in International Climate Policy Architecture," Discussion Paper 08-07. Cambridge, MA: Harvard Project on International Climate Agreements Discussion, September.

Jiang, B., C. Wenying, Y. Yuefeng, Z. Lemin, and D. G. Victor (2008). "The future of natural gas consumption in Beijing, Guangdong and Shanghai: An assessment utilizing MARKAL," *Energy Policy* 36: 3286–99.

Jojarth, C. (2009). *Crime, War, and Global Trafficking: Designing International Cooperation.* Cambridge, UK: Cambridge University Press.

Keeler, A. and A. Thompson (2008). "Industrialized-Country Mitigation Policy and Resource Transfers to Developing Countries: Improving and Expanding Greenhouse Gas Offsets," Discussion Paper 08-05. Cambridge, MA: Harvard Project on International Climate Agreements, September.

Lanchbery, J. *et al.* (1998). "Part I: Systems for Implementation Review" in D. G. Victor *et al.* (eds.), *The Implementation and Effectiveness of International Environmental Commitments.* Cambridge, MA: MIT Press, pp. 47–305.

Michalopoulos, C. (2002). "Chapter 8: WTO Accession," in B. M. Hoekman, P. English and A. Mattoo (eds.), *Development, Trade and the WTO: A Handbook.* Washington, DC: World Bank, pp. 61–70.

Moravcsik, A. (1998). *The Choice for Europe: Social Purpose and State Power from Messina to Maastricht.* Ithaca, NY: Cornell University Press.

Morris, M. and E. Hill (2007). "Trade is the Key to Climate Change," *Energy Daily.* February 20.

OECD (2003). *OECD investment policy reviews—China.* Paris: Organisation for Economic Co-operation and Development.

Page, S. E. (2002). "The amount of carbon released from peat and forest fires in Indonesia during 1997," *Nature* 420: 61–5.

Pauwelyn, J. (2007). "US Federal Climate Policy and Competitiveness Concerns: The Limits and Options of International Trade Law," Working Paper 07-02. Durham, NC: Nicholas Institute for Environmental Policy Solutions.

Price, V. (2007). "GATT's New Trade Policy Review Mechanism," *The World Economy* 14: 227–38.

Rai, V., N. Chung, M. Thurber, and D. G. Victor (2008). "PESD Carbon Storage Project Database," Working Paper #76. Stanford, CA: Program on Energy and Sustainable Development.

Rosen, D. and T. Houser (2007). *China Energy: A Guide for the Perplexed.* Washington, DC: Peterson Institute for International Economics.

Seabright, P. (2005). *The Company of Strangers: A Natural History of Economic Life.* Princeton, NJ: Princeton University Press.

Schneider, L. (2007*). Is the CDM Fulfilling its Environmental and Sustainable Development Objectives? An Evaluation of the CDM and Options for Improvement.* Berlin: Oko-Institute, available at www.oeko.de/oekodoc/622/2007-162-en.pdf.

Smith, K. R. and E. Haigler. (2008). "Co-Benefits of Climate Mitigation and Health Protection in Energy Systems: Scoping Methods," *Annual Review of Public Health* 29: 11–25.

Tacconi *et al.* (2008). "Local causes, regional co-operation and global financing for environmental problems: the case of Southeast Asian Haze pollution," *International Environmental Agreements.* 8: 1–16.

Victor, D. G. (2007). "Fragmented Carbon Markets and Reluctant Nations: Implications for the Design of Effective Architectures," in J. Aldy and R. Stavins (eds.), *Architectures for Agreement: Addressing Global Climate Change in the Post-Kyoto World.* New York: Cambridge University Press, pp. 133–60.

(2009). "Global Warming Policy After Kyoto: Rethinking Engagement with Developing Countries," Working paper #82. Stanford, CA: Program on Energy and Sustainable Development.

Victor, D. G., K. Raustiala and E. B. Skolnikoff (eds.) (1998). *The Implementation and Effectiveness of International Environmental Commitments.* Cambridge, MA: MIT Press.

Wara, M. 2007. "Is the Global Carbon Market Working?" *Nature* 445: 595–6.

Wara, M. and D. G. Victor (2008) "A Realistic Policy on International Carbon Offsets," Working Paper #74. Stanford, CA: Program on Energy and Sustainable Development.

21 | Policies for developing country engagement

DANIEL S. HALL,
MICHAEL A. LEVI, WILLIAM A. PIZER,
TAKAHIRO UENO*

Introduction

Much of the debate surrounding global climate policy focuses on the appropriate role for developing countries in mitigating global emissions—and on how industrialized countries can best support and encourage that role. Climate change is a global problem that requires all major emitting countries to undertake mitigation efforts; moreover, developing countries account for most of the emissions growth projected over the next century. If current developing countries are going to make significant progress towards greater prosperity while the world simultaneously seeks to stabilize atmospheric greenhouse gas (GHG) concentrations at somewhere between 450 and 750 parts per million carbon dioxide-equivalent (ppm CO_2e), developing countries are going to have to develop in a less GHG-intensive fashion than the already-industrialized economies did (Clarke *et al.* 2007).

Yet developing countries face considerable obstacles: they lack resources and place greater priority on economic development relative to environmental protection. At the same time, industrialized countries like the United States are well aware that their own efforts to reduce emissions can be thwarted if, through trade in goods and services, their emitting activities shift to non-participants in a climate agreement, or if their GHG cuts are simply overwhelmed by growth elsewhere.

* Authors are Research Assoicate, Resources for the Future; Senior Fellow, Council on Foreign Relations; now with the US Treasury Department; and Researcher, Central Research Institute of the Electric Power Industry (Japan). The authors greatly appreciate helpful comments from Joe Aldy and Rob Stavins, as well as other participants in the Harvard Project for International Climate Agreements.

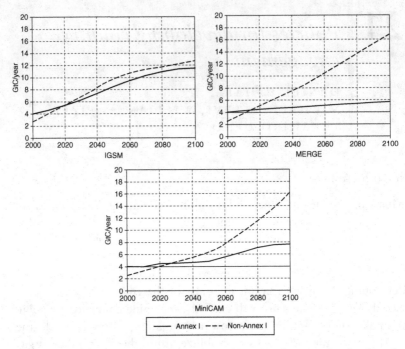

Figure 21.1. Fossil fuel and industrial CO_2 emission forecasts for developed (Annex I) and developing (non-Annex I) countries

"Emissions of fossil fuel and industrial CO_2 in the non-Annex I countries exceed Annex I emissions for all three reference scenarios by 2030 or earlier. The MERGE and MiniCAM reference scenarios exhibit continued relative rapid growth in emissions in non-Annex I regions after that, so that emissions are on the order of twice the level of Annex I by 2100. The IGSM reference scenario does not show continued divergence, due in part to assumptions of relatively slower economic growth in non-Annex I regions and faster growth in Annex I than the scenarios from the other modeling groups. The IGSM reference scenario also shows increased emissions in Annex I as those nations become producers and exporters of shale oil, tar sands, and synthetic fuels from coal."

Source: Clarke et al (2007), Figure 3.16.

The focus of this chapter is on the intersection of interests between developing and developed countries. How can developed countries—with more resources and, for the most part, a greater sense of urgency—engage developing countries in a cooperative effort to mitigate climate change? Part of the answer is an increasing awareness among developing countries that they themselves are vulnerable to the impacts of climate change, which will tend to make them more willing to seek cooperative solutions. But engaging developing countries as partners in a global mitigation effort will require more than just the threat of physical impacts: it will require increased attention to sensible domestic policies within developing countries, an increase in financial support from developed countries, and creative diplomacy to carefully integrate different tools.

The bulk of this chapter looks at each of these areas in more detail.

Domestic policy improvements

There is an emerging consensus that developing countries will need to pursue mitigation actions under any new climate agreement.[1] Chief among these actions would be policy reforms which developing countries could take that would have domestic political, economic, and environmental benefits while simultaneously providing global climate benefits. Opportunities for "win-win" policies often remain unexploited for a variety of reasons, including domestic political realities, mismatches between the pattern of costs and benefits over time, or limited technical expertise or institutional capacity. To realize emissions benefits from these opportunities, developed and developing countries will have to find the right mix of domestic political will and international funding and expertise that can deliver effective policy reforms. While we address the structure of this funding and the diplomatic effort necessary to find the right mix in later sections, here we focus on the domestic policy opportunities themselves.

Reforming energy subsidies

Many non-OECD[2] countries currently subsidize energy, and particularly fossil fuels, thereby creating an opportunity for subsidy reform or elimination that would have a variety of domestic benefits while also reducing GHG emissions. Energy subsidies encourage the over-consumption of fuels and lead to higher CO_2 emissions. Yet many countries pursue these policies to accomplish specific domestic policy objectives with respect to

---

[1] The Bali Action Plan agrees to consider "nationally appropriate mitigation actions by developing country Parties."

[2] OECD stands for the Organisation for Economic Co-operation and Development. The membership of the OECD includes the largest developed economies; hence the term "non-OECD" is frequently used as shorthand for the world's developing countries.

social stability, access to cleaner cooking fuels, increased electrification, or industrial policy. In some cases these are worthy objectives, but the energy subsidies have significant domestic costs (UNEP 2008).[3]

Table 21.1 provides information on the level of energy subsidies in the eight non-OECD countries with the largest total subsidies in 2005. Combined these countries accounted for about $185 billion of the $220–$280 billion in total energy subsidies provided in all non-OECD countries in 2005.[4] For comparison, a 2002 report (UNEP/IEA 2002) estimated that gross energy subsidies in OECD countries totaled $20–$30 billion, with most of this total directed towards R&D and production subsidies. Further, in most OECD countries gross subsidies are outweighed by taxes on fuels (Morgan 2007). These data suggest that reforming energy subsidies in non-OECD countries would slow the growth of a significant portion of global emissions. The eight nations in Table 21.1 accounted for just over one-third of global CO_2 emissions in 2005 and over the long term their contribution is expected to increase strongly, particularly as a result of growth in China. Subsidies to fossil fuels act as a "negative tax" on carbon emissions. The right-most panel in Table 21.1 reports the effective negative CO_2 price that is implied by energy subsidies in a few of these countries. Thus, for example, eliminating subsidies for transport fuels in China would be equivalent to imposing a CO_2 tax of $11 per ton on gasoline—or $25 per ton on diesel—relative to current fuel prices.[5] Previous studies have suggested there would be significant emissions benefits to eliminating subsidies. Modeling work from the OECD in 2001 suggested that the immediate removal of all subsidies in the industrial and power sectors worldwide would reduce global CO_2 emissions by 6 percent in 2010 relative to business as usual (OECD 2001). An earlier study from the International Energy Agency (IEA) suggested that the removal of consumption subsidies in eight of the largest non-OECD countries would have lowered global CO_2 emissions by 4.6 percent relative to (then)

---

[3] Energy subsidies also often help the urban middle class far more than the rural poor.

[4] These figures represent the net economic value of subsidies as estimated using a price-gap approach (described in IEA 2006). They do not necessarily represent the budgetary cost of subsidies, as they include both direct interventions (such as grants or soft loans) and indirect interventions such as price ceilings or the free provision of energy infrastructure. For more recent discussions, see Bradsher (2008), Hargreaves (2008), and Paulson (2008).

[5] Note that these specific numbers could have changed significantly since 2005.

Table 21.1 *Energy subsidies in developing countries*

Country	Emissions (2005) [1]			Subsidies, total (2005, $B) [2]					(Consumption) Subsidy CO$_2$ price equivalent in 2005 ($/mt CO$_2$) [3]			
	MtCO2	% global emissions	% non-OECD emissions	Coal	Oil	NG	Electricity	Total	Coal	Gasoline	Diesel	NG
China	5101	18.8%	35.9%	7.8	7.0	3.8	7.0	25.6	$4.76*	$10.98	$24.90	NA
Russia	1544	5.7%	10.9%	0.0	0.4	25.4	14.7	40.5	$0.00	$0.00	$0.00	$33.34
India	1147	4.2%	8.1%	0.0	6.9	2.2	10.1	19.2	$0.00	$0.00†	$0.00†	NA
Iran	407	1.5%	2.9%	0.0	24.2	9.4	2.7	36.3	No IEA energy price data.			
Indonesia	341	1.3%	2.4%	0.5	14.0	0.0	1.7	16.2	NA	$62.91	$115.55	NA
Saudi Arabia	320	1.2%	2.2%	0.0	10.0	4.3	5.5	19.7	No IEA energy price data.			
Ukraine	297	1.1%	2.1%	0.5	0.2	12.4	2.4	15.4	No IEA energy price data.			
Egypt	148	0.5%	1.0%	0.0	9.2	1.2	1.8	12.2	No IEA energy price data.			
Total	9304	34.3%	65.4%	8.8	71.9	58.7	45.7	185.1				
World	27136											
Non-OECD	14226							Estimated 220–280				

* Calculated from 2004 coal price.
† Consumption subsidies for refined oil products in India are focused on kerosene and LPG.
[1] IEA Key World Energy Statistics 2007 (data for 2005)
[2] IEA WEO2006 (Figure 11.7)
[3] Calculated from IEA WEO2006, Table 11.1, and IEA Energy Prices & Taxes 1st Quarter 2008 (2005 end-use energy prices)

current emissions (IEA 1999). Although the precise magnitude of current subsidies is uncertain, there can be no doubt that cutting subsidies would have salutary effects in terms of reducing global emissions.

This leaves the question of how to convince nations to eliminate fuel subsidies. Recent high global energy prices made the case easier in many respects, as subsidies designed to maintain low prices became much more expensive, but countries still will want to minimize the impact of high energy prices on low-income consumers, particularly to allow access to cleaner cooking fuels and electricity. These objectives could frequently be pursued more efficiently by allowing energy prices to rise to market rates while directly supporting consumers with lump-sum distributions (such as per capita rebates) and/or (in the case of electricity) by subsidizing the cost of connections rather than energy (UNEP 2008). This raises the possibility of an agreement where the developed world provides financing and technical assistance for these types of programs in exchange for subsidy reforms.

Enhancing energy efficiency

Many developing countries have made significant strides in recent decades toward using more energy-efficient technologies and practices throughout their economies. In general, however, most remain behind Europe, Japan, and North America on this front. The Fourth Assessment Report of the Intergovernmental Panel on Climate Change (IPCC) estimated that energy efficiency improvements in the residential and commercial building sector—which includes end-use devices such as appliances—could reduce CO_2 emissions in non-OECD countries by 1.5 billion metric tons, or gigatonnes ($GtCO_2$), per year in 2020 at zero marginal cost (Levine *et al.* 2007). Meanwhile, efficiency improvements offer additional benefits to developing nations: they can dampen the need for new infrastructure, reduce local environmental pollution, and increase energy security.

Given these local benefits, most countries—developed and developing—already have a national program or plan that specifies objectives for energy efficiency improvements, often with a national agency or ministry designated as responsible for related policies.[6] But

[6] See Annex 2 of WEC 2008 for a thorough survey of national-level energy efficiency agencies and programs.

these agencies tend to be understaffed and underfinanced, particularly in developing countries, and often lack the capacity to effectively implement policies (Sugiyama and Ohshita 2006). This has led to a variety of proposals for providing international funds to support efficiency policies in developing countries, either through direct funding for national agencies, through partnerships with national agencies to implement efficiency policies or projects, or through technical assistance and capacity building.[7]

The kinds of developing country policies that might be targeted by these efforts include public procurement of efficient products, efficiency labeling and standards, and support for energy services companies. Public procurement of more efficient products is perhaps the easiest to implement and can provide an important demand-side stimulus to the development of markets for efficient products. For example, China's Ministry of Finance has directed government agencies to preferentially procure high-efficiency products (Caifeng and Tienan 2006). Public procurement is relatively easy because it does not require institutional capacity for regulation or enforcement.

Labeling programs, which require manufacturers to provide information about the energy efficiency of a product, are one step up and help resolve information problems that hinder the adoption of more efficient products, especially in the case of consumer items. While labeling programs require the institutional capacity to rate products, such schemes may be a low-cost way to increase end-use energy efficiency because they do not attempt to regulate actual production.

The next step up is to mandate energy efficiency standards for products—a policy that remains relatively less common in developing countries. Whether these kinds of standards are economically efficient can depend on how they are designed and whether they resolve a market failure (Jaffe *et al.* 2001). However, even if they are not the best policy tool to address a market failure, efficiency standards may be attractive to governments if more economically efficient policies such as pollution taxes or other market-based regulations are not

---

[7] For example, the UN Foundation has called for a policy push to promote energy efficiency on the part of the Group of Eight (G8) industrialized nations and the so-called "+5" countries (Brazil, China, India, Mexico, and South Africa). The proposed effort would include establishing a facility to provide loan guarantees for commercial energy efficiency projects (Expert Group on Energy Efficiency 2007).

politically or institutionally feasible. A recent study published by the Collaborative Labeling and Appliance Standard Program found that non-OECD emissions could be reduced by 0.4 $GtCO_2$ in 2020 if energy efficiency standards were implemented in 2010 for a range of residential and commercial appliances (McNeil *et al.* 2008).

Finally, developing country governments can also improve energy efficiency by encouraging certain private-sector activity. This may occur directly through work with large energy users, or indirectly through energy services companies (ESCOs) which offer financing and expertise for energy efficiency projects. (Such companies are also sometimes referred to as energy management companies, or EMCs, especially in China.) ESCOs arrange financing, internally or through third-parties, to implement efficiency improvements, with loans typically guaranteed by projected cost savings for energy. In this way they can help other firms overcome barriers to efficiency investments such as credit constraints, lack of technical knowledge, and transaction costs. A recent study by Zhao Ming (2006) noted the rapid growth of ESCOs in China, from a handful of companies in the late 1990s to more than 100 in 2006. This study pointed out that government policy can encourage further growth.

Promoting technology diffusion and deployment

Even with substantial improvements in energy efficiency, dealing with climate change will require the diffusion and deployment of technologies that are less emissions-intensive than their historical counterparts. Over time, these "climate-friendly technologies" are the only way developing countries can raise their incomes and standards of living—which remain a fraction of those in developed countries—without simultaneously putting global GHG stabilization out of reach.

Widespread diffusion takes time. How can governments encourage more rapid and more thorough technology diffusion? Policy levers for influencing the speed and depth of adoption can target a number of factors; these include information, input prices, regulation, credit, subsidies, investment in human and physical capital, and protection of intellectual property rights (Blackman 2001).

While multilateral funds can provide subsidies for higher-cost climate-friendly technologies in developing countries (this is a topic we address in the next section), the domestic policy environment in developing countries provides the enabling conditions for technology transfer and diffusion and greatly influences the effectiveness of incremental financing from developed countries. To this end, developing country governments can facilitate the formation of human and institutional capacities; encourage the development of supporting infrastructure; provide a supportive legal environment, including secure property rights and appropriate intellectual property protection; and support R&D (Metz *et al.* 2000). Some of these policies can have broad social benefits apart from facilitating technology transfer and so may be particularly attractive first steps for domestic policies; examples include investments in human capital, energy infrastructure, and R&D (Blackman 2001).

To be sure, establishing some enabling conditions will be politically contentious. Protection for intellectual property has been one sticking point in recent global negotiations. Trade agreements are another politically contentious lever for influencing technology transfer: compared to OECD countries, developing countries retain relatively high tariffs on many climate-friendly technologies, thereby creating a barrier to the diffusion of those technologies (Iturregui and Dutschke 2005).

Table 21.2 summarizes policy actions available to developing countries that could provide local benefits while also reducing GHG emissions. The table also lists the types of support from developed countries that would facilitate these policy changes. This external support can be crucial: even policies that may be in the long-term interest of developing countries can remain unutilized due to a lack of (near-term) funding, technical expertise, or private-sector experience. The table also suggests that developing and developed country actions are linked and need to be coordinated.

International financial mechanisms

Recent IEA estimates (2008b) indicate that if global emissions are to be stabilized at current levels by 2050—an emissions trajectory that could still allow significant warming—there would need to be an additional $10 trillion of cumulative investment in non-OECD countries by mid-century.[8] If global emissions are to be brought down to

[8] There would also need to be $7 trillion in additional investment in the OECD.

Table 21.2 *Summary of actions for domestic policy improvements in developing countries*

Policy arena	Action by developing countries	Areas for support from developed countries
Subsidy reform	• Reduce subsidies • Establish alternative programs or policies to accomplish objectives, e.g., subsidize connections for electricity rather than power	• Technical assistance and funding for alternative programs, e.g., subsidized electricity connections, expanding access to cleaner stoves, etc.
Energy efficiency	• Establish national plan or program • Labeling programs • Energy efficiency standards • Public procurement of EE products • Improved operation and maintenance • Enabling environment for ESCOs (access to capital, public procurement, etc.)	• Funding for EE programs • Technical assistance and training • Regional or agency-level partnerships to support energy efficiency standards
Technology diffusion	• Establish enabling conditions: fund R&D and infrastructure, and invest in human capital • Reduce trade barriers (e.g., tariffs) • Improve IP laws and/or enforcement	• Technology funds • Capacity building for establishing IP laws and enforcement • Soft loans and/or export guarantees for exports

less than half of current levels—as has been proposed by Europe and Japan—the level of additional investment needed rises to $27 trillion. It is unclear how much of this incremental cost in developing countries will be paid for by developed countries. Even if the resources involved totaled only a fraction of these estimates, the magnitude of the challenge should be sufficient to encourage us to rethink our use of the international financial mechanisms used to support such investments.

There are two key questions associated with the design of such mechanisms: the size of the transfer and the form of delivery. On the first matter, at one extreme, one could offer payments equal to the full environmental value of additional emission reductions under one or another existing market-based CO_2 regulatory program (e.g., the market value of reductions under the European Union Emission Trading Scheme [EU ETS]). At another extreme, one could seek to cover all or even just part of the (lower) incremental cost of lower-emissions technologies.

In addition to the level of payment, the other key question is what form it takes. Possible financial mechanisms include grants, concessional loans, loan guarantees, or credits that can be sold into a regulated GHG market or tax system. The remainder of this section looks at the question of form in greater detail. Given their significant differences, we organize this discussion around offset mechanisms and international public funds.

Offset mechanisms

Arguably, the most critical distinguishing feature of offset mechanisms is their capacity to channel potentially large flows of private financial resources, rather than depending on more limited government appropriations or on a more obvious diversion of public monies. For example, the suggestion, in a recent US legislative proposal,[9] that up to 15 percent of a facility's compliance obligation under a domestic CO_2 cap-and-trade program could be met with international offsets translates into potentially tens of billions of dollars in financing for developing country mitigation—a level of funding equal to roughly 40 percent of the entire non-military US foreign assistance budget. And

[9] The specific proposal referenced here was introduced in the US Congress by Senators Lieberman and Warner.

while foreign aid–style financing *competes* for scarce public funds, the use of offsets *complements* the desire to match environmental ambition with economic practicality.[10]

Of equal importance, various offset proposals are both blurring the strict focus on tons and the distinction between offsets and linked trading systems. A useful way to organize a discussion of these proposals is through the lens of proposed reforms to the Kyoto Protocol's Clean Development Mechanism (CDM), the leading GHG offset mechanism in developing countries. Through the CDM, Annex B Parties to the Protocol can comply with their mitigation obligation using credits—referred to as certified emissions reductions (CERs)—that are issued for emissions offset projects in developing countries.[11] This has created market demand for CERs as governments seek to use offsets as part of their strategies for complying with the Kyoto Protocol. More importantly, the EU ETS allows participants to meet their obligations with CERs, creating widespread private demand.

On the one hand, the CDM is frequently highlighted as a particularly successful aspect of the Kyoto Protocol in the sense that it has generated a large quantity of CERs and lowered the cost to developing countries of meeting their emissions reduction targets under the Protocol. The CDM has been operational since the Marrakech Accords were reached in late 2001; by July 2008, 1,151 projects were registered, 183 million tons of credits had been issued, and more than 1 billion tons of CERs were expected to be issued by 2012, according to the Secretariat of the United Nations Framework Convention on Climate Change (UNFCCC).[12]

On the other hand, there have been many criticisms of the CDM. First, a relatively small number of non-CO_2 project types initially dominated the array of registered projects and projected credits. More recently, wind power and other renewable projects have gained traction and now represent more than 30 percent of expected credits through 2012. However, as shown in Figure 21.2 energy efficiency projects still account for a very small share of expected credits.

---

[10] According to an analysis by the US Environmental Protection Agency (2008), the use of offsets would have been necessary to keep the price of CO_2 allowances under the proposed Lieberman-Warner legislation at $40 per ton rather than $77 dollars per ton. Unlimited use of offsets could lower the CO_2 allowance price to $11 per ton.

[11] A unit of CER is issued for each reduction of one ton of CO_2 equivalent.

[12] See the UNFCCC's website cdm.unfccc.int/index.html.

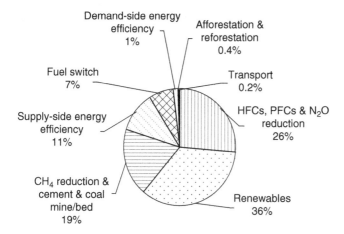

Figure 21.2. Distribution of CERs issued from each project type
Source: UNEP/RISO Centre (2009)

Second (and related to the first point), the CDM is frequently criticized for providing "excessive subsidies" for low-cost projects (Wara 2006). The incremental costs of projects that reduce emissions of high global-warming-potential (GWP) industrial gases are typically very low compared to the market price of CERs, which have frequently exceeded $20 per ton. This discrepancy upsets constituents in developed countries, who dislike sending large excess payments to firms in developing countries. And there is also a dynamic inefficiency, as these subsidies may cause firms that generate high-GWP industrial gases to enter the market, with the perverse effect of raising emissions, in the hope that future reductions can be profitable.

Third, some have criticized the regional distribution of CDM projects for being highly unbalanced and thus failing to bring the benefits of sustainable development to the least developed countries. As shown in Figure 21.3, four big countries account for more than 60 percent of the credits generated under the CDM, while less than 5 percent of credits have come from projects in African countries.

Finally, and most fundamentally, the CDM creates perverse incentives for developing country governments. Specifically, developing countries may hesitate to enact domestic policies—even policies in their own self-interest—if they believe doing so may adversely affect future CDM financing. Efforts to remove such perverse incentives by excluding the influence of new policies on baseline emissions simply shift the problem

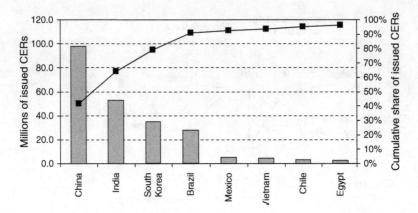

Figure 21.3. Regional distribution
Source: UNEP/RISO Centre (2009)

from one of domestic inaction to one of paying for non-additional efforts.

Numerous proposals for reforming the CDM have emerged to address these criticisms, providing guidance for both the CDM and offset mechanisms more generally.[13] Most proposals fall into one of two categories: (1) adjusting crediting rules to address the distribution of projects and the level of subsidy, or (2) moving beyond projects to provide credits for programs, policy reforms, or sectoral targets. Proposals that fall in the former category attempt to address the first three concerns, while proposals in the latter category generally aim to begin providing incentives for developing countries to change their own policies.

Changing the rules for project credit

Responding to criticism over project types, excessive subsidies, and regional distribution, parties to the Kyoto Protocol are engaged in negotiations on possible CDM reforms. They have proposed a wide range of ideas for managing the project pipeline, including:

- positive and/or negative lists of project types (i.e., automatic registration and/or rejection of certain types of projects)
- loose application of rules for specific project types (e.g., less strict criteria for energy efficiency projects)

---

[13] Proposals for CDM reform by the Parties to the Protocol are summarized in UNFCCC (2008).

- multiplication factors to increase or decrease the number of credits issued for specific project types (e.g., discount for industrial gas projects, favorable multiplication factors for emerging technologies)[14]
- limit countries eligible for hosting CDM projects (e.g., only least developed countries [LDCs] are eligible for CDM)
- minimum quotas for specific project types (e.g., 10 percent of all credits used for compliance by developed countries must be from renewable energy projects)
- minimum quotas for specific regions (e.g., 5 percent of all credits used for compliance by developed countries must be from projects in African countries)[15]

A variety of concerns surround these proposed reforms, in particular, the potential economic inefficiency of discriminating among reductions from different regions or activities. In addition, there is the risk that non-additional emission reductions (that is, reductions that would have happened anyway) will be credited if looser rules are imposed for certain types of projects. Finally, even if adopted, reforms may not achieve the declared goal of boosting financial flows to certain project types or regions because other barriers related to market failures, institutional capacity, and/or enabling environments, may be limiting offset project development.

Offsets for programs, policies, and sectoral targets

The limitations of a project-based approach have led to proposals to expand the CDM to include credit for programs of bundled activities, policy reforms, and even sectoral targets.[16] Because generating these credits requires substantial efforts, they can require idiosyncratic

---

[14] While there is a tendency for economists to look at such multiplication factors as distorting efficiency, placing different per-ton values on different activities is, in reality, a form of price discrimination. Given the monopsony power of countries purchasing CDM credits, it may make sense for them to pay less for identifiably less costly activities. Or, given spillovers associated with new technology developments, it may make sense to for them to pay more for new technologies.

[15] These ideas are briefly analyzed in the UNFCCC's Technical Paper (UNFCCC/TP/2008/2).

[16] Parties to the Kyoto Protocol have been hesitant to allow policy-level activities to be registered under the CDM.

negotiations, generating an opportunity and incentive for domestic policy reform.

The most limited form of CDM expansion, referred to as programmatic CDM (pCDM), would grant credits for program-level activities as opposed to the project-level activities already recognized under the conventional CDM. Frequently, these programs would consist of dispersed small-scale efforts that collectively generate large reductions (e.g., a program to replace incandescent lamps with compact fluorescent lamps). The pCDM may offer a promising way to overcome barriers to end-use energy efficiency, one of the most underdeveloped project types and one with vast potential for emissions reduction (Levine *et al.* 2007).[17] Examples of programmatic activities that might be credited under a pCDM could include demand-side management (DSM) programs that decouple utility profits from kilowatt-hour sales, thus reorienting utility incentives to favor energy efficiency rather than power production, and subsidizing energy-efficient products.[18] Nonetheless, substantial technical challenges exist in attributing specific emissions reductions to program activities.

Alternatively, one could imagine expanding the notion of pCDM such that, beyond recognizing a specific initiative in a given sector or area of activity, it could also cover an entire suite of efforts to influence product penetration in a particular sector. This might include sectoral policies, in which credits would be issued for reductions from sectoral baselines, and crediting for the achievement of agreed sectoral targets—collectively referred to as sectoral crediting (Bosi and Ellis 2005, UNFCCC 2008; Schmidt *et al.* 2006). The negotiation of country-specific terms for sectoral crediting, even more than pCDM, would begin to remove—or at least reduce—perverse incentives that discourage developing countries from taking proactive mitigation

---

[17] On the underdevelopment of energy efficiency CDM, see Arquit Niederberger (2007) and Arquit Niederberger and Fecher (2006).

[18] California Energy Efficiency Evaluation Protocols and International Performance Measurement & Verification Protocols are frequently mentioned as prototype methodologies on which a crediting methodology for pCDM should be built. The former was developed by the California Public Utilities Commission, the latter by the US Department of Energy. On technical and methodological work to apply demand-side management (DSM) methodologies to pCDM, see Figueres and Philips (2007) and Figueres (2005).

action. In the end, a sectoral target for offsets could begin to look a lot like a linked cap-and-trade program.

For precisely this reason, sectoral targets are likely to face strong opposition from developing countries that fear that even limited, no-lose targets will eventually lead to binding caps in the future—an outcome that the vast majority of developing countries are strenuously seeking to avoid. Sectoral crediting is also likely to require differentiation among developing countries as it is appealing mainly for a small number of large-emitting, middle-income countries that collectively account for a large share of global emissions, and not for the bulk of developing countries. Such differentiation, however, will also be opposed by at least some countries that may see it as an effort to undermine the unity of developing nations.

International public funds

Regardless of how offset programs in general—and CDM reforms in particular—progress, there are obvious funding gaps that need to be addressed. Offsets are not well suited to support core capacity building and technical assistance, more targeted financial products, and efforts in countries with weak institutions. They also require sufficient demand from large and robust market-based regulatory programs or quantitative commitments. Finally, offsets have been criticized for failing to provide reductions additional to the regulated emissions cap or mitigation commitment that creates the demand for offsets—though such criticism ignores the endogeneity of offsets noted previously.

Exactly these shortcomings are addressed by several advantageous features of international public funds, where support need not be tied to the timing and price of reductions delivered to an existing market and where delivered reductions can be additional to any existing emission cap. While offsets provide payment when reductions occur based on the market price of those reductions somewhere else, funds can make payments earlier and with more attention to incremental cost rather than market price. Currently, international public funds are supported by government contributions; however, future funds could be supported by auctioning credits into an existing market-based system, with these credits established within, or in addition to, the system's cap. Reductions financed in this way would clearly be additional if the credits are within the cap; to the extent the financed cost of reductions is less than the market price, they would be additional even if credits were created beyond the system's cap.[19]

Funds can also make it possible to more closely tailor the level of financing to the additional incentive required to just make viable an otherwise un-viable GHG-reducing investment or activity—a characteristic not shared by offset programs, which are focused squarely on tons. In particular, emissions trading typically generates a surplus—in terms of permits or offsets—for both buyers and sellers. From the buyer perspective, a tailored approach can shift surplus from sellers (developing countries) to buyers (developed countries), allowing developed countries to pay the cost—or even just part of the cost—rather than the full market price for emission reductions in developing countries. It also allows developed countries to pay *more* than the market price in some instances, if there is potentially a longer-term or coincidental benefit, as in the case of early technology development or conservation efforts with non-climate global benefits.

Equally important, the fund approach is more flexible in terms of the forms of support it can provide. Rather than crediting emission reductions when the reductions occur, funds can provide upfront grants, loans, loan guarantees, or other risk mitigation products. In particular, funds may be able to encourage mitigation activities where the obstacle does not involve a straight calculation of cost and benefit, but rather a market failure that relates to risk or borrowing. Despite these advantages, however, funds too can be problematic.

There has been an explosion of international public funds over the past year, including several funds established at the World Bank;[20] in addition, a number of bilateral funds have been proposed (Porter *et al.* 2008). These funds differ from the most prominent existing fund—the Global Environment Facility (GEF)—in a variety of ways, including scale, governance, and focus. Some are much larger—with Japanese, US, and UK commitments to some funds totaling several times the GEF's annual spending on climate change. Perhaps most important, they also shift the governance structure away from the heavily negotiated GEF model, where project approval requires a 60 percent vote of a governing council and a 60 percent vote of donors, towards a more

---

[19] That is, selling an extra 1-ton credit into a capped market in order to raise perhaps $25 that is then spent on 5 tons of developing country reductions costing perhaps $5 each yields a net reduction of 4 tons.

[20] See www.worldbank.org/cif.

donor-centric model (this is especially the case for many of the bilateral funds). Governance of public funds is an extremely contentious issue. On the one hand, variations in donor support and governance are undoubtedly related: countries that make larger contributions typically want more control over their funds. On the other hand, developing countries also want control and have argued that funds should be established under the UNFCCC, guided by the Conference of the Parties (COP), and governed by a board whose members are appointed by the COP—all because this means their representation will be enhanced.[21] This suggests a trade-off: if developing countries want more control over public funds, this may reduce the amount of money they can receive because developed countries tend to contribute more to funds over which they have greater control.

The Kyoto Protocol's Adaptation Fund offers an interesting alternative model for both financing and governance. Resources for this fund come from a 2 percent levy on CDM projects when the UNFCCC issues CERs. Meanwhile, developing countries are well represented with ten members on the board of the Adaptation Fund, compared to six members from developed countries. While some countries see this model (or a related model of just auctioning allowances[22]) as providing a potentially significant source of revenue for public funds, the governance of such market-financed funds may depend on whether allowances are issued domestically or internationally. National governments manage sales of domestic allowances and control how they are used, while sales of international allowances are currently managed by the UNFCCC. Perhaps more to the point, developing country offsets originate in developing countries, where developing-country governments clearly have the capacity to tax them. While the governance model of the Adaptation Fund may only be relevant for this last circumstance, where developing countries have the most leverage, even this venue may come under pressure from donors if there is a significant scaling up of financial flows.

To the extent that international public funds begin focusing on the private sector, become standardized (e.g., support a renewable energy subsidy program in a particular country), and have access to

---

[21] See the proposal for financial mechanisms under the Convention put forward by the Group of 77 (G77) and China (Phillipines 2008).
[22] See Carbon Finance (2008), NRDC (2008b), EC (2008), and Norway (2007).

a steady funding source (e.g., a transaction tax or allocated share of allowances), they begin to look more like offsets. And, to the extent that offset programs begin using multiple or fractional crediting to target some activities while avoiding the over-subsidization of others, offset programs begin to have the more nuanced capacity of funds. At that point, the distinction we have drawn so far may blur, and the more important design questions center on the predictability and stability of funds, flexibility and simplicity of financial products, and balance of control among donors and recipients. Here, funds may retain an advantage in terms of providing more flexible financing (as offsets tend to provide funds only once mitigation occurs), and offsets may retain an advantage in terms of offering a stable funding source (by contrast, public funds—regardless of the source of revenue—will always be similar to an appropriation and will therefore be more vulnerable to disruption).

Private and public diplomacy

The potential for domestic policy improvements on the part of developing countries and increased financing by developed countries is inextricably tied to diplomatic efforts—including efforts that tie policy improvements and financing together, as well as efforts aimed at securing additional commitments to policy improvements and financing independently. How can developed countries encourage developing countries to adopt GHG-reducing domestic policy improvements? How does the world negotiate for financing mechanisms that best serve environmental goals while leveraging developing country commitments?

This section addresses two dimensions of climate diplomacy that help answer those questions. First, it discusses various sources of leverage that might be used in climate negotiations, including, in particular, sources of leverage that go beyond the financing mechanisms discussed so far. Wielding these levers may help the United States and other developed countries encourage both domestic action and favorable financing arrangements in developing countries. Second, we discuss various institutional arrangements that might be used for climate diplomacy. Although economists often think in terms of leverage, bargaining, and trades that benefit all parties, institutions—both in terms of their participants and their rules—can have an enormous impact on the success or failure of climate negotiations. Even without significant leveraging of additional domestic action, it will be necessary to at least coordinate certain efforts.

Sources of leverage

The last section discussed two approaches to financing emissions reductions in developing countries that might be used to alter decisions in those countries: private-sector financing through offset markets and public-sector financing through international funds. Historically, financial inducements have been used—not just to promote emission reductions—but as a primary means of influencing developing country decisions. While financial assistance remains an important focus of international climate negotiations, many other tools for encouraging participation are available. This section discusses four of them.

Energy security as a lever.
In many countries, energy security—including security of access to supplies of fuel for power generation, industrial needs, and transportation—is as important as economic considerations in driving energy policy decisions. A state might adopt policies that promote the use of alternative fuels in order to diversify its set of suppliers even if those alternatives are more expensive. Conversely, a state might avoid shifting to economically attractive alternative sources of energy if those sources are also unreliable or expose the state to intolerable influence from fuel suppliers. Altering a country's energy security calculus can thus be an effective way of influencing its decisions on fuel supply and, as a result, its GHG emissions.

Consider an example.[23] China and India might hesitate to increase their use of nuclear power, a zero-emission energy source, due to worries that the need to import nuclear fuel would subject them to excessive outside influence. Moreover, this barrier could persist even in the face of special economic incentives for switching to cleaner energy sources. To address it, developed countries might take steps to ease Chinese and Indian concerns about the reliability of nuclear fuel supplies, such that these countries could increase their use of nuclear energy in a way that also enhances their energy security and diversifies

---

[23] For more on this example, see Victor (2007).

their energy portfolios. To be certain, clearing the way for increased use of nuclear power in developing countries introduces challenges with respect to proliferation, waste storage, and safety. Nonetheless, such arrangements are being actively considered, most prominently in discussions concerning the US-India nuclear cooperation agreement. Meanwhile, Chinese officials have also expressed interest in gaining international support for a more robust expansion of nuclear power in their country.

Financial penalties

The threat of sanctions has long been used as a way to induce compliance with international regimes, including environmental regimes—most notably the Montreal Protocol on Ozone Depleting Substances.[24] The possible use of trade sanctions against exports from countries that do not take appropriate steps to reduce GHG emissions has become a prominent topic in discussions concerning climate legislation in the US Congress; in addition, this concept has received favorable attention from many leaders in the European Union.

The threat of sanctions has the potential, in theory, to motivate action in key emerging economies, where governments and firms might take steps to avoid economic disadvantage. That said, many have argued that any feasible sanctions would not rise to the level where they would be significant enough to induce any major shifts.[25] Even if that were true, on the other hand, the mere willingness of developed countries to raise the prospect of trade sanctions might facilitate climate action by buying political support for domestic action among key constituencies in countries that might be targeted by sanctions.

Regardless of their practical leverage in climate diplomacy, sanctions would introduce other problems. To be legal, they would need to be designed to equalize an economic playing field that would otherwise be distorted by uneven GHG regulations. Practically speaking, however, it would be technically difficult to establish whether sanctions were in fact leveling the playing field or were instead thinly disguised economic protectionism. The use of sanctions would also introduce political problems, putting strains on world trade at a

---

[24] Because non-signatory countries could negate global efforts to reduce the production of ozone-depleting chemicals, the Montreal Protocol introduced trade sanctions as an incentive for participation.

[25] See Houser *et al.* 2008.

time when global trade regimes are already in dire straits. Here in particular, an important distinction must be drawn between sanctions imposed unilaterally and sanctions that are agreed to in advance as part of an international climate regime. (In the latter case, sanctions would essentially be used as enforcement mechanisms, as they were under the Montreal Protocol.) It would likely be difficult, however, to get major developing countries to agree in advance to the legitimacy of sanctions that might be used against them.

Support for adaptation efforts

Addressing climate change will require not only reducing emissions but also adapting to the climate changes that are inevitable, even with future mitigation efforts. Poorer countries will generally be more vulnerable to climate change, and wealthier countries are expected to provide them with some support as they adapt. How that support for adaptation is realized will play a role in mitigation diplomacy.

There is considerable debate as to what role support for adaptation should play in diplomatic efforts to promote emissions mitigation; there is also debate as to how influential support for adaptation might be. Some argue that the link is strong, contending that the main trade-off in climate negotiations will be between commitments from developing countries to undertake emissions reductions and commitments from developed countries to provide assistance with climate adaptation. This is problematic, however, because the countries most in need of adaptation assistance are generally not the countries from which the greatest emission-reduction commitments will be required. For example, countries in sub-Saharan Africa will need help with adaptation, but have very low emissions and hence are unlikely to face significant reduction requirements. In contrast, China is not only a large emitter, it is among the countries most likely to need persuasion on the mitigation front. At the same time, however, it is difficult to envision an international agreement that provides China with large amounts of outside support for adaptation.

Others see the diplomatic link between adaptation and mitigation as more indirect. The developing world has consistently shown solidarity against any efforts to promote restrictions on GHG emissions by any of its members. Some argue that if developed countries make adaptation assistance for the poorest developing countries part of a deal that also requires mitigation commitments from the wealthier developing countries, the poorest countries are less likely to provide political cover for countries like China. While this dynamic is almost certain to emerge, its importance is debatable. Countries like China and India are sensitive to political pressure—both in their regions and more broadly from the developing world—but it is unclear how much such pressure can sway their decision making on broader climate deals that have large implications for economic growth and energy security.

Broader issue linkage

Developed countries may seek linkages that go beyond the climate sphere to press developing countries to reduce their emissions. This would allow developed countries to offer a wider variety of incentives in exchange for mitigation actions by developing countries. The clearest precedent for this approach is the deal made to obtain Russia's ratification of the Kyoto Protocol. Russia had previously been blocked from membership in the World Trade Organization (WTO) by EU leaders, who were concerned about Russia's high-priced natural gas exports (among other things). Worried that Russia's failure to ratify would doom the Kyoto Protocol, however, EU leaders offered Russia a deal: in exchange for ratification, EU leaders would ease Russia's entry into the WTO. To be certain, there has since been much legitimate debate about whether this was a good deal, particularly given the lax emission caps Russia ultimately signed up to. Nonetheless, this example illustrates how progress can be made by linking climate commitments to other major foreign policy issues.

Such linkages can be specific, as in the Russian case, but they can also be more diffuse. In particular, if major developing countries can be brought to believe that taking domestic actions to restrain GHG emissions will speed their integration into the class of great powers (with the broad benefits that would confer for them internationally), this perception could promote greater action on their part to reduce emissions. So long as countries such as China are seen as out of the global mainstream in a wide variety of ways, they suffer little damage for also being outliers on climate issues. In addition, so long as there are key developed countries that are not taking sufficient action to address climate change, it will be difficult to equate global stature with a responsible stance on this issue. But as both of those pieces change, there is likely to be increasing pressure for developing countries to take mitigation action for its own sake. This is not likely to be a significant issue for many of the key developing countries—notably China and India—in the very near term, but it is likely to become increasingly relevant over time.

Institutions

Efforts to exploit the aforementioned sources of leverage will unfold in a variety of forums, including through bilateral and regional relationships. However, global negotiations, at least among key countries, will be necessary to significantly advance prospects for addressing the climate challenge. Failing a grand deal, other coordination among key countries will be necessary to make sure various efforts reinforce each other and to minimize potential conflicts. Cooperation is needed to ensure comparability of effort among developed countries; to coordinate domestic policies as necessary, including harmonizing carbon trading systems and financing; to develop a common understanding on the roles of different negotiating forums; and to reach agreement on the role of trade sanctions. With these needs in mind, we turn to the two main types of forums for global negotiations: first, the United Nations and second, so-called minilateral climate-focused groups, such as the Group of Eight plus Five (G8+5) "Gleneagles" process and the Bush administration's Major Economies Meetings, which have been succeeded by the Obama administration's Major Economics Forum (MEF).

United Nations Framework Convention on Climate Change

All major countries have emphasized the centrality of the process established under the UNFCCC as the main vehicle for international climate diplomacy, including efforts to promote action on the part of developing countries. There are three basic arguments for working within the UNFCCC. Because GHG emissions have the same effect on the climate regardless of their source, a global forum in principle provides the greatest possible set of opportunities to reduce them. In addition, because free riding by even small numbers of countries can undermine progress toward the environmental objective and introduce competitiveness concerns, a forum that leaves out even a relatively small number of countries may be unable to deal with such issues effectively. Meanwhile, the UNFCCC has become associated in many circles with serious action on climate change—conversely, alternatives to it have become associated by many with a lack of ambition.

As a result, emphasizing the centrality of the UNFCCC has become symbolically important.

Within the UNFCCC, there are two basic models for how an agreement might be reached. One would be a self-contained agreement, where different countries make different commitments with trade-offs acceptable to all. This is similar to the Kyoto deal but would be enlarged to include other key emitters. Alternatively, a deal might be reached within the UN process but only as the result of many other trade-offs and bargains made outside of that forum. There is widespread concern, however, that no comprehensive deal of either variety will be reached within the UNFCCC. It was already very difficult to reach agreement on the Kyoto Protocol, which only required mitigation commitments from a small number of advanced countries. Adding several rapidly emerging economies to the mix, as is likely to be necessary to sell a deal in many of the developed countries, will make things far more difficult—and embedding this negotiation within a forum involving nearly 200 countries only exacerbates the challenges. All of these problems are reflected in the recent failure of the Doha round of trade negotiations—negotiations that involve far fewer countries than the UNFCCC and that are, in other ways, simpler (and certainly more familiar) than climate negotiations.[26]

The UN process is also distinguished by its emphasis on legal arrangements. This is helpful in that such agreements often provide a stronger basis for collective action of the sort required for dealing with climate change, where inaction (or recidivism) by one country can undermine the viability of action by others. At the same time, treaty-focused negotiations can often drive states to focus on committing to the weakest possible actions; the resulting treaties can then become rallying points for national-level actors who do not wish to go beyond what their countries have formally committed to. This in turn undermines those who advocate more ambitious efforts to cut emissions. To achieve a strong outcome, it is essential that negotiators keep the above dynamic in mind and aim to conclude a deal that promotes the greatest emissions reductions from developing countries, not merely the strongest *form* of commitment to reduce emissions.

---

[26] See, for example, comments in Stephen Castle, "For Global Trade Talks, the Stakes Have Risen," *New York Times*, July 19, 2008.

Minilateral forums

There has been a move in recent years—pushed particularly by the United States and the UK, but supported by several other key countries—toward using smaller groups for climate negotiations, whether as complements or alternatives to the UN process. The most prominent of these small groups have been the G8+5 "Gleneagles" process established by Prime Minister Tony Blair in 2005, and the Major Economies Meetings (MEM) established by President Bush in 2007 and succeeded by the Obama administration's Major Economics Forum in 2009. By reducing the number of participants in negotiations while including major emerging economies, these efforts aim to simplify discussion while still encompassing the majority of global GHG emissions.[27] The MEM/MEF effort has also emphasized the inclusion of government officials outside environment and foreign ministries, on the premise that many of the most powerful actors in national climate and energy policy often come from elsewhere in government.

It is difficult to judge whether the MEM/MEF effort was successful. The perception that the Bush administration was unwilling to engage seriously on climate change until recently undermined the effectiveness of any US-sponsored forum, including the MEM. The MEM initiative was also distinguished by the fact that it was not aimed at establishing independent agreements, but at laying the groundwork for a global post-Kyoto deal. This means that many of the same impediments that face UNFCCC negotiations—in particular, the difficulty of finding a legal arrangement (either a treaty or a protocol to an existing treaty) acceptable to all key developed and developing countries—applied to the MEM. This is not a necessary feature of all minilateral efforts, but it was required in order for the United States to gain acceptance by reassuring other parties that it did not intend to sideline the UN process. The MEF, established as a successor to the MEM, has been more warmly received internationally; it is still impossible, however, to determine its effectiveness.

The G8+5 effort, in contrast, has not only been aimed at feeding into the post-Kyoto negotiations but is also attempting to establish complementary agreements, such as a recent agreement to jointly

---

[27] Eight countries or groups of countries—the United States, the European Union, Japan, Russia, China, India, Brazil, and Indonesia—are responsible for roughly three-quarters of the world's GHG emissions.

pursue carbon capture and sequestration demonstration projects.[28] Such agreements indirectly support diplomacy and negotiations by building countries' confidence that they can meet promises to control emissions; moreover, this approach also takes advantage of the greater ease with which political (rather than legal) agreements can be reached. The G8+5 process has, however, aroused concerns on the part of some key developing countries about what they perceive as their second-class status in the forum, and has suffered from that. Its focus on non-binding commitments also means that promises may be more likely to go unfulfilled.

In addition to these two types of global efforts, regional forums can play important roles. The most prominent currently is the Asia-Pacific Partnership on Clean Development and Climate, which is focused squarely on sector-by-sector action on the ground and on implementing emission reductions. By working in a regional grouping, it simplifies interactions, and by focusing on concrete cooperation, it removes some of the difficulties associated with higher-level negotiation. At the same time, the Asia-Pacific Partnership has been criticized for its focus on aspirational rather than binding goals; it has also suffered from a lack of political attention and additional public funding for the implementation of projects.

Conclusions

Over the next few years, as the United States returns to a more prominent role on the international stage and as the end of the first Kyoto commitment period draws near, there will be increasingly intensive efforts to reach a new global climate arrangement. Such an arrangement would have enormous value both in addressing the need to mitigate rapidly increasing developing country emissions and in addressing the need for financial support from developed countries (of course, an agreement would also address the need for further mitigation efforts on the part of developed countries themselves). If no arrangement can be found that reduces emissions *and* provides the right support for developing countries, there will be virtually no chance of stabilizing atmospheric GHG concentrations at an acceptable level while simul-

---

[28] "G8 Declaration on Environment and Climate Change," July 8, 2008, accessed at www.nma.org/pdf/misc/070808_g8e/pdf, September 9, 2008.

taneously and fully promoting increased economic prosperity in the developing world.

Much of the effort to find a workable global solution is likely to focus on a kind of "grand bargain," with developing countries offering some form of commitments in exchange for emission mitigation commitments and significantly increased financing from developed countries. On the one hand, a grand bargain will not be reached easily; the contentiousness that has characterized both domestic debates within countries like the United States and international debates within the UNFCCC negotiating tracks demonstrates the difficulty of the challenge. On the other hand, the emergence of new ideas about commitments and financing, as well as less formal and less inclusive negotiating efforts, suggests growing interest in pursuing a variety of approaches.

It is difficult to judge now exactly what approach, what diplomatic and financing tools, and what forum are going to prove most successful—only experience will reveal precisely what approaches work best. In this situation, betting on a single "silver-bullet" strategy is not a good idea: the climate problem is too urgent to admit a narrow focus that might turn out to fail. Instead, the United States and the world will need to pursue a variety of policy reform efforts, financing approaches, and diplomatic venues in parallel.

References

Arquit Niederberger, A. (2007). "Energy Efficiency Projects in the CDM," Issue Paper prepared for the Seminar on Energy Efficiency Projects in CDM and JI, organized by UNIDO, Vienna, Austria, March.

Arquit Niederberger, A. and R. S. Fecher (2006). "Demand-Side Energy Efficiency Promotion under the Clean Development Mechanism: Lessons Learned and Future Prospects," *Energy for Sustainable Development* 10(4): 45–58.

Blackman, A. (2001). "The Economics of Climate-Friendly Technology Diffusion in Developing Countries," in M. A. Toman (ed.), *Climate Change Economics and Policy: An RFF Anthology*, Washington, DC: Resources for the Future, pp. 248–252.

Bosi, M. and J. Ellis (2005). "Exploring Options for Sectoral Crediting Mechanisms," COM/ENV/EPOC/IEA/SLT(2005)1, Paris: OECD/IEA.

Bradsher, K. (2008). "Fuel Subsidies Overseas Take a Toll on U.S.," *New York Times*, July 28, 2008, available at www.nytimes.com/2008/07/28/business/worldbusiness/28subsidy.html?ex=1374984000&en=f388c8c4c

e149ceb&ei=5124&partner=permalink&exprod=permalink.
Accessed August 30, 2008.

Caifeng, L. and L. Tienan (2006). *Chinese Government Procurement Policy for Energy-Efficient Products*. Beijing: China Standard Certification Center, available at http://mail.mtprog.com/presentations/session_H/H4LinCaifeng/pdf. Accessed August 30, 2008.

Carbon Finance (2008). "Germany earmarks EUA revenue for emissions projects," June 25, 2008, available at www.carbon-financeonline.com/index.cfm?section=europe&action.=view&id=11344. Accessed January 20, 2009.

Clarke, L., J. Edmonds, H. Jacoby, H. Pitcher, J. Reilly, and R. Richels (2007). *Scenarios of Greenhouse Gas Emissions and Atmospheric Concentrations*. Sub-report 2.1A of Synthesis and Assessment Product 2.1 by the US Climate Change Science Program and the Subcommittee on Global Change Research, Washington, DC: US Department of Energy, Office of Biological & Environmental Research.

Council on Foreign Relations (2008). *Confronting Climate Change: A Strategy for U.S. Foreign Policy*. Washington, DC: Council on Foreign Relations.

de Coninck, H., C. Fischer, R. G. Newell, and T. Ueno (2008). "International Technology-Oriented Agreements to Address Climate Change," *Energy Policy* 36: 335–56.

Energy Information Administration (2008). *Federal Financial Interventions and Subsidies in Energy Markets 2007*, SR/CNEAF/2008-01, Washington, DC: Energy Information Administration.

Expert Group on Energy Efficiency (2007). *Realizing the Potential of Energy Efficiency: Targets, Policies, and Measures for G8 Countries*. Washington, DC: United Nations Foundation.

Figueres, C. (2005). "Study on Programmatic CDM Project Activities: Eligibility, Methodological Requirements and Implementation," paper prepared for the Carbon Finance Business Unit of the World Bank.

Figueres, C. and M. Philips (2007). "Scaling Up Demand-Side Energy Efficiency Improvements through Programmatic CDM," ESMAP Technical Paper 120/07, Carbon Finance Unit, World Bank.

Hall, D. (2007). "Offsets: Incentivizing Reductions While Managing Uncertainty and Ensuring Integrity," in R. Kopp and W. Pizer (eds.), *Assessing U.S. Climate Policy Options*. Washington, DC: Resources for the Future, pp. 189–98.

Hargreaves, S. (2008). "Bye-Bye Gas Subsidies," *CNNMoney.com*, July 7, 2008, available at money.cnn.com/2008/07/02/news/international/gas_subsidies/index.htm?postversion=2008070214. Accessed August 30, 2008.

Houser, T., R. Bradley, B. Childs, J. Werksman, and R. Heilmayr (2008). *Leveling the Carbon Playing Field*. Washington, DC: Peterson Institute.

IETA (2007). "2007 State of the CDM," IETA Position on the CDM for COP/MOP3.

International Energy Agency (IEA) (1999). *World Energy Outlook Insights, Looking at Energy Subsidies: Getting the Prices Right*. Paris: OECD/IEA.

(2006). *World Energy Outlook 2006*. Paris: OECD/IEA.

(2007). *Key World Energy Statistics*. Paris: OECD/IEA.

(2008a). *Energy Prices & Taxes: Quarterly Statistics, First Quarter 2008*. Paris: OECD/IEA.

(2008b). *Energy Technology Perspectives 2008: Scenarios and Strategies to 2050*. Paris: OECD/IEA.

Iturregui, P. and M. Dutschke (2005). *Liberalisation of Environmental Goods & Services and Climate Change*, HWWA Discussion Paper 335, Hamburg: Hamburg Institute of International Economics (HWWA).

Jaffe, A. B., R. G. Newell, and R. N. Stavins (2001). "Energy-Efficient Technologies and Climate Change Policies: Issues and Evidence," in M. A. Toman (ed.), *Climate Change Economics and Policy: An RFF Anthology*. Washington, DC: Resources for the Future, pp. 171–81.

Levine, M., D. Ürge-Vorsatz, K. Blok, L. Geng, D. Harvey, S. Lang, G. Levermore, A. Mongameli Mehlwana, S. Mirasgedis, A. Novikova, J. Rilling, and H. Yoshino (2007). "Residential and Commercial Buildings," in *Climate Change 2007: Mitigation. Contribution of Working Group III to the Fourth Assessment Report of the Intergovernmental Panel on Climate Change*. Cambridge, UK: Cambridge University Press.

McNeil, M. A., V. E. Letschert, and S. de la Rue du Can (2008). *Global Potential of Energy Efficiency Standards and Labeling Programs*. Washington, DC: The Collaborative Labeling and Appliance Standards Program.

Metz, B., O. R. Davidson, J.-W. Martens, S. N. M. van Rooijen, L. Van Wie McGrory, eds. (2000). *Methodological and Technological Issues in Technology Transfer*, A Special Report of Working Group III of the Intergovernmental Panel on Climate Change, Cambridge, UK: Cambridge University Press.

Morgan, T. (2007). *Energy Subsidies: Their Magnitude, How they Affect Energy Investment and Greenhouse Gas Emissions, and Prospects for Reform*. Bonn, Germany: UNFCCC Secretariat, Financial and Technical Support Programme.

Nadel, S., J. Thorne, H. Sachs, B. Prindle, and N. Elliott (2003). "Market Transformation: Substantial Progress from a Decade of Work," Report Number A036, Washington, DC: American Council for an Energy-Efficient Economy.

Natural Resources Defense Council (2008a). The Boxer-Lieberman-Warner Climate Security Act Substitute Amendment, NRDC, available at www.nrdc.org/legislation/factsheets/leg_07121101A.pdf.

(2008b). NRDC Comments to CARB on Offsets—April 18, 2008, available at www.arb.ca.gov/cc/scopingplan/pgmdesign-sp/meetings/040408/NRDC_Comments_on_offsets_040408.pdf. Accessed September 9, 2008.

Norway, Ministry of Finance (2007). "Finance Minister Kristin Halvorsen:—We need a global contract." Press release 82/2007, available at www.regjeringen.no/en/dep/fin/Press-Center/Press-releases/2007/--We-need-a-global-contract.html?id=493747. Accessed January 20, 2009.

Organisation for Economic Co-operation and Development (OECD) (2001). Environmental Effects of Liberalising Fossil Fuels Trade: Results from the OECD Green Model, Unclassified Document No. COM/TD/ENV(2000)38/FINAL, Paris: OECD.

(2005). Opening Markets for Environmental Goods and Services. OECD Policy Brief, September 2005, Paris: OECD.

Paulson, H. M. Jr. (2008). "A Strategic Economic Engagement," Foreign Affairs, Sep/Oct 2008, New York: Council on Foreign Relations.

Phadke, A., J. A. Sathaye., and S. Padmanabhan (2005). Economic Benefits of Reducing Maharashtra's Electricity Shortage through End-Use Efficiency Improvement, LBNL-57053, Berkeley, CA: Lawrence Berkeley National Laboratory.

Philippines (on behalf of the Group of 77 and China) (2008). "Proposal: Financial Mechanism for Meeting Financial Commitments under the Convention," submission to the Ad-hoc Working Group on Long-term Cooperative Action under the Convention, available at http://unfccc.int/files/kyoto_protocol/application/pdf/g77_china_financing_1.pdf. Accessed January 20, 2009.

Porter, G., N. Bird, N. Kaur, and L. Peskett (2008). "New Finance for Climate Change and the Environment," Washington, DC: World Wildlife Fund, available at http://assets.panda.org/downloads/ifa_report.pdf. Accessed January 20, 2009.

Regional Greenhouse Gas Initiative (2007). "Overview of RGGI CO_2 Budget Trading Program," available at http://rggi.org/docs/program_summary_10_07.pdf. Accessed September 9, 2008.

Schmidt, J, N. Helme, J. Lee, and M. Houdashelt (2006). "Sector-Based Approach to the Post-2012 Climate Change Policy Architecture," Washington, DC: Center for Clean Air Policy.

Sugiyama, T. and S. Ohshita, eds. (2006). *Cooperative Climate: Energy Efficiency Action in East Asia*. Winnipeg, Canada: International Institute for Sustainable Development.

United Nations Environment Programme (UNEP) (2008). *Reforming Energy Subsidies: Opportunities to Contribute to the Climate Change Agenda*. Paris: UNEP Division of Technology, Industry, and Economics.

UNEP/IEA (2002). *Reforming Energy Subsidies: An explanatory summary of the issues and challenges in removing or modifying subsidies on energy that undermine the pursuit of sustainable development*. Paris: UNEP Division of Technology, Industry, and Economics.

UNEP/RISO Centre (2009). "CDM pipeline overview," available at www. uneprisoe.org.

UNFCCC (2008). "Analysis of Possible Means to Reach Emission Reduction Targets and of Relevant Methodological Issues," FCCC/TP/2008/2, available at http://unfccc.int.

US Environmental Protection Agency (2008). "EPA Analysis of the Lieberman-Warner Climate Security Act of 2008: S. 2191 in 110th Congress," Washington, DC: EPA, available at www.epa.gov/ climatechange/economics/economicanalyses.html.

Victor, David (2007). "Fragmented Carbon Markets and Reluctant Nations: Implications for the Design of Effective Architectures," in Joseph E. Aldy and Robert N. Stavins (eds.), *Architectures for Agreement*, Cambridge: Cambridge University Press, pp. 133–60.

Wara, M. (2006). "The Performance and Potential of the Clean Development Mechanism," PESD Working Paper #56, available at http://pesd.stanford.edu/.

World Energy Council (WEC) (2008). *Energy Efficiency Policies around the World: Review and Evaluation*. London: WEC.

Zhao Ming (2006). *EMCA and China's ESCO Industry*, Presentation at the 2006 Conference on Energy Conservation in Buildings, Energy Performance Contracting and Financial Guarantee for Energy Efficiency Projects, Beijing, China, July 25–26, 2006.

22 | International forest carbon sequestration in a post-Kyoto agreement

ANDREW J. PLANTINGA AND
KENNETH R. RICHARDS[1,2]

Introduction

Forest carbon management must be an important element of any international agreement on climate change. Forest carbon flows comprise a significant part of overall global greenhouse gas (GHG) emissions. While global forests as a whole may be a net sink (Nabours and Masera 2007), global emissions from deforestation contribute between 20 and 25 percent of all GHG emissions (Sedjo and Sohngen 2007, Skutsch *et al.* 2007). The size of the total global carbon pool in forest vegetation has been estimated at 359 gigatonnes[3] of carbon (GtC), which compares to annual global carbon emissions from industrial sources of approximately 6.3 GtC (IPCC 2000). The potential impact on the global carbon cycle of both natural and anthropogenic changes in forests is enormous.

An effective international forest carbon management regime must not only provide landowners and governments with incentives to protect and expand stocks of carbon, but must induce countries to enroll in the forest agreement in the first place. Ideally, a multilateral forest carbon program would also impose relatively low transaction costs even as it encourages decision makers to seek low-cost opportunities for sequestration.

The current international regime, the Kyoto Protocol, has proven ineffective in this regard. There are three primary problems. First, the

[1] Department of Agricultural and Resource Economics, Oregon State University, Corvallis and School of Public and Environmental Affairs, Indiana University, Bloomington, respectively. The authors would like to thank Elizabeth Baldwin, Naomi Pena, Stephanie Richards, Robert Stavins, and an anonymous referee for useful comments.
[2] Corresponding author—kenricha@indiana.edu, telephone: 812-855-5971.
[3] One gigatonne is one billion (10^9) metric tonnes.

Annex I (industrialized) countries are required to include afforesta-tion, reforestation, and deforestation in their national accounting.[4] However, Article 3.3 of the Kyoto Protocol limits that accounting to changes that are "human-induced," inviting endless arguments about which changes should be included. For example, one can make reasonable arguments both for and against, say, Canada's inclusion of continued northern forest growth as a "human-induced" change in its national carbon account. By considering only human-induced changes, the Kyoto approach discourages countries from accepting the responsibility for, and the benefit of, all carbon changes under their authority.

Kyoto has also failed to provide non-Annex I countries with incen-tives to reduce carbon emissions through forest management. Forestry-related carbon gains in non-Annex I countries, which are included under the Clean Development Mechanism (CDM) of Article 12, are limited to afforestation and reforestation projects only (Santilli *et al.* 2005). The CDM thus excludes potentially beneficial projects, includ-ing those that could reduce deforestation. In addition, the carbon effects of *individual* forestry projects are difficult to measure. This makes the CDM a poor tool for providing incentives for individual forestry projects, even though the aggregate potential of such projects is significant. Perhaps predictably, the CDM mechanism as currently constituted has certified only one forestry project.

Finally, the current approach under the Kyoto Protocol may actually accelerate deforestation by shifting timber harvesting from Annex I to non-Annex I countries (Silva-Chavez 2005). This inter-country leakage cannot be addressed by a system that does not include global accounting of changes in forest use.

The impending expiration of the Kyoto Protocol in 2012 invites a reexamination of how the global community can address forest carbon management in the context of an international climate change agreement. There has also been growing interest in identify-ing a mechanism for including avoided tropical deforestation under the Kyoto Protocol or its successor (Skutsch *et al.* 2007, Nepstad *et al.* 2007, Gullison *et al.* 2007). At the ninth Conference of Parties

---

[4] Afforestation refers to the conversion of non-forested land to forest, whereas reforestation refers to the replanting of forest land following harvest. Deforestation is the destruction of forests.

meeting (COP9), a proposal for "compensated reduction" (CR) in deforestation was advanced by a group of Brazilian NGOs (Santilli *et al.* 2005) and endorsed by Papau New Guinea and Costa Rica (UNFCCC 2005).[5] Subsequently, participants at the COP11 meeting initiated a two-year study on reduced emissions from deforestation and degradation (REDD) to address the expansion of the Kyoto Protocol to include this major source of emissions (Sanz 2007, UNFCCC 2005).

The purpose of this chapter is to consider alternative approaches to forest management that will reduce net global carbon dioxide (CO_2) emissions more effectively than the current Kyoto Protocol. We suggest that there are attractive alternatives to the Kyoto Protocol approach, particularly the national inventory (NI) approach first described by Andersson and Richards (2001). While the CR proposals contain some of the attractive features of the NI approach, they also have a number of shortcomings that make them less promising than the NI system.

The next section provides a brief description of assumptions regarding how energy-related emissions are addressed in the successor to the Kyoto Protocol. Subsequent sections discuss the range of terrestrial carbon sequestration activities that might ideally be addressed by a carbon management regime; design issues for a forest carbon management regime, including alternative program structures and the intertemporal nature of carbon flows; and alternatives to the Kyoto Protocol approach to forests. Specifically, we explore two options: a scheme that provides emission allowances in proportion to national accomplishments and an aid-based approach that is not linked to a carbon trading program. The chapter concludes with a discussion of the alternatives, suggesting that the NI approach, when linked to an international emissions trading system, appears most promising.

Assumptions about policy context

To provide a complete description of a forest carbon sequestration program, it is important to be explicit about the assumed institutional context for program implementation. The framework for this analysis

---

[5] Refinements and critiques of the CR approach are found in Schlamadinger *et al.* (2005), Skutsch *et al.* (2007), Myers (2007), and Sedjo and Sohngen (2007).

is a treaty under which countries are obligated to meet specified emissions reductions targets. We assume that the treaty establishes an international cap-and-trade program for CO_2 emissions from energy sources. This raises the possibility, but not the requirement, that a forest carbon program could be linked to the emissions cap-and-trade program.

We assume also that the international agreement is developed under the United Nations Framework Convention on Climate Change (UNFCCC). There are currently 191 parties to the UNFCCC, and we assume that broad participation will be an objective of the international agreement. As a result, an effective agreement will accommodate a large range of countries that differ in terms of size, geographic location, stage of development, extent of forest resources and land opportunities, and sophistication of forest management. As we will discuss, broad participation by countries will be important to limit leakage effects from the carbon sequestration program.

Also important is the current political context, which will shape the negotiations over any forestry proposal. It is evident from the current interest in REDD that some countries and interest groups favor a comprehensive national approach such as we propose here, while it is likely that others will advocate for the present system of project-by-project (PBP) accounting. Moreover, there may be some actors who oppose, in general, the inclusion of carbon sinks under a new treaty, while others may favor expanding the range of eligible sinks. Given space constraints, we cannot provide the treatment that these issues deserve. We focus here on presenting the NI approach, leaving for a future paper an assessment of how our proposal is likely to be viewed by the climate change community.

Range of forestry activities involved

All terrestrial carbon sequestration removes CO_2 from the atmosphere and stores it in organic material. A broad range of potential activities can contribute to terrestrial carbon sequestration. As Table 22.1 suggests, activities can be organized according to (1) the strategy or objective of individual practices and (2) the land type on which the practices are implemented. Terrestrial sequestration strategies fall into three broad categories, which appear as columns in Table 22.1: expansion of carbon stocks, conservation of stocks, and offsite sequestration/

Table 22.1 *Terrestrial sequestration practices to increase carbon stocks or reduce greenhouse gas emissions*

	Strategy/Objective		
Land type	Conservation of stocks	Expansion of stocks	Offsite sequestration or emissions reduction
Forest	Modified harvesting practices Preventing deforestation Change to sustainable forest management Fire suppression and management	Reforestation Modified management e.g., fertilization, improve stocking, biotechnology, species mix, extended rotations	Wood fuel substitution Expanded wood products Extended wood product life Displace concrete/ steel Recycling wood and paper products
Crop	Soil erosion and fertility management Water management Maintain perennial crops Residue management	Afforestation Agroforestry Improved cropping systems Improved nutrient and water management Conservation tillage Crop residue management Restoration of eroded soils Conversion to grass or other permanent vegetation	Biofuels substitution Fertilizer substitution or reduction Other bioproducts substitution
Grazing	Improved grazing systems	Afforestation Change in species mix, including woody species Restoration of riparian zones Fertilization Irrigation	Livestock dietary changes

Source: Richards *et al.* (2006)

emissions reductions. Each of these strategies can be carried out on different land types (rows in Table 22.1): forestlands, croplands, and grazing lands.

One objective of terrestrial carbon sequestration is to prevent the loss of carbon that is already stored in natural and man-made ecosystems. On forestland this might include modifying harvest practices to reduce soil disturbance, preventing deforestation, and managing fire more effectively to avoid catastrophic loss. On cropland it could include reducing soil erosion to avoid carbon loss. Another objective of sequestration is to expand carbon stocks by reforesting harvested forestland and implementing new management methods such as extended rotations, afforesting croplands, implementing agro-forestry practices, and converting grazing lands to forest stands. Finally, forest practices can also affect carbon emissions by changing the way resources are used offsite. For example, when structural wood products and wood fuels displace concrete, steel and fossil fuels, net carbon emissions will be reduced.

Two important observations emerge from this very brief discussion.[6] First, most of the practices that increase terrestrial sequestration are familiar activities that are already integral to land-use management. The goal of an international terrestrial carbon sequestration program is not so much to induce landowners to engage in "new" activities, but rather to expand the adoption of established practices that protect and expand carbon stocks. This raises two intertwined issues: causality and additionality.

First, according to Article 3.3 of the Kyoto Protocol, countries must differentiate changes in land use that are human-induced from those that are natural in their national reports. The need to determine causality raises important issues. The Intergovernmental Panel on Climate Change (IPCC) Special Report on Land Use, Land-Use Change and Forestry (Section 2.3.3.1) acknowledges that while "carbon stock changes can be measured directly with a variety of techniques, attributing a given change in carbon stocks to a particular cause can be much more challenging." The IPCC Special Report nonetheless asserts that accounting for causality is a necessary element of an international forest carbon sequestration program for reasons of interannual variation and consistency with objectives.

---

[6] For more detail on terrestrial sequestration practices see Paustian *et al.* (2006) and Richards *et al.* (2006).

Second, the project-based approach in the CDM requires parties to establish not only that humans induced a change in carbon sequestration, but why. The key issue is *additionality*—would the activity have taken place in the absence of the program, or does it represent additional reductions in emissions? As discussed below, national-level accounting addresses both causality and additionality concerns while circumventing the problems raised by the requirement to differentiate between human-induced and natural changes.

The second issue raised by Table 22.1 is that because the range of terrestrial activities is so broad, it has been challenging to find one simple approach that will suffice to encourage all of these practices. Two alternatives suggest themselves. First, the international community could develop a large number of programs, evaluation approaches, and incentives, each designed to address a subset of these practices. Indeed, some proposals have, for example, suggested separate programs for afforestation/reforestation and deforestation (Santilli *et al.* 2005). Alternatively, an international agreement could pragmatically focus instead on aggregate results, attempting to cover as many of the practices and results as possible under one seamless program. While all of the practices listed in Table 22.1 warrant consideration, it is beyond the scope of this chapter to examine all of them in detail. This report focuses solely on forest carbon, specifically on programs to encourage afforestation, reforestation, deforestation, low-impact logging, forest management, fire management, and related forestry activities.

Broad issues for program design

As the international community considers how to incorporate forest management into the next climate change agreement, it must make several choices about program design. These include (1) the basic unit of analysis—individual forestry project, national forest inventory, or some other intermediate level—upon which the program will focus; (2) the linkage, if any, with a broader international GHG emissions trading program; and (3) appropriate methods for determining a baseline or reference case, which in turn will vary depending on the unit of analysis.

Unit of analysis

A critical feature of a policy is the scale at which carbon sequestration is measured and rewarded. This design element has important impacts on the way forest management is valued and on the parties responsible for implementation. For example, under the CDM provision of the Kyoto Protocol, the unit of analysis is the individual project. Carbon sequestration activities are undertaken by a project developer, who defines a project for a particular parcel (or parcels) of land and for a specific time period. Changes in the terrestrial carbon stock are then measured for the duration of the project.

Alternatively, the unit of analysis could be the territory under the jurisdiction of a nation or other political entity. In this case, measurement would be made of a nation's entire carbon stock (or changes therein). The national carbon inventory would include, but would not be limited to, stocks associated with specific carbon sequestration activities. Under this approach, national governments would be responsible for developing domestic programs to encourage carbon sequestration. Unlike the project-based approach, this system can include multiple carbon sequestration practices under the umbrella of one seamless program. In addition, this approach avoids the definitional problems associated with the current requirement to distinguish between anthropogenic and natural forest changes. Instead, the NI system fully values the potential for forestry policies to contribute to national carbon mitigation by considering the aggregate impact of all forestry changes.

Measurement issues and linkage

Another important feature of the policy design is the relationship of carbon sequestration to an international allowance trading program. The presence of linkage will determine whether measurement focuses on inputs or outcomes. The first possibility is a linked system whereby carbon sequestration offsets can be redeemed in the permit market. Offset credits would be defined for increments of sequestered carbon that are additional relative to a specified reference case. A project developer or nation could sell these offset credits in the permit market, thereby allowing carbon sequestration to substitute for emissions reductions. This approach necessarily focuses on outcomes by measuring changes in the carbon stock, either as the result of an individual project or on a nationwide basis. The metric of interest concerns carbon flows—namely, the flow of carbon into the terrestrial system over a defined period. Carbon offsets need to be measured in flow terms to allow substitution for emissions reductions, which are also measured as a flow. Of course, the flow of carbon is functionally related to the stock of carbon, being equal to the difference in the stock at two points in time.

If carbon sequestration is not linked to allowance trading, then one need only measure inputs into activities, such as the number of acres afforested or the expenditures on programs to deter deforestation. Incentives for carbon sequestration could be provided by sponsoring organizations, including national governments, non-governmental organizations, and international agencies. As with a program linked to allowance trading, the unit of analysis for these programs can be either individual projects or the nation. This approach might be favored if reliably measuring changes in the carbon stock over time proves too difficult.

Baseline

Under a linked policy, offset credits would be granted for carbon sequestration that is additional relative to a baseline reference case. The reference case can be defined either as a flow or a stock. In the latter case, credits would be based on the difference between the actual stock and the reference stock. There are two basic ways to specify the reference case. One is to define it as the carbon stock that would have resulted in the absence of the carbon sequestration activity. Because this is the counterfactual scenario, the reference stock cannot be observed and must be estimated. One simple estimation approach is to apply extrapolation methods to historical data. For example, the rate of forest loss in the reference case might be set equal to the rate during a recent historical period (Schlamadinger et al. 2005). Alternatively, future forest conditions can be predicted with structural economic and forest inventory models, similar to what is done for assessments under the Resources Planning Act in the United States (US Department of Agriculture, Forest Service 2000).

The second way to specify the reference case is through a negotiation process. While these negotiations could be informed by historical trends or modeling results, there would be no presumption that the reference case is an estimate of the stock in the absence of the policy. This approach makes more sense if national inventories are the basis for defining offset credits, as the costs of negotiating baselines for numerous individual projects would likely be prohibitive.

Negotiated baselines offer several advantages. First, they avoid the difficult task of estimating unobservable counterfactuals. Second, they allow negotiators to address equity and fairness issues related to nations' historical uses of forests. For example, developing countries may be given more generous baselines—including, in some cases, baselines that are actually below known carbon stocks—to address the argument that developed nations have contributed more to the climate change problem and, therefore, should shoulder more of the burden. Finally, disassociating target stocks from baseline stocks may mitigate the adverse selection problem whereby countries with historically declining carbon stocks refuse to participate in the agreement.

Negotiated baselines also have potential pitfalls. Reliance on the negotiation process introduces the possibility that nations with more bargaining power will be able to negotiate less stringent targets. While this will not be inefficient if the permit market equalizes national sequestration costs on the margin, some countries may perceive it to be unfair and refuse to participate. It should be recognized that the threat of non-participation actually acts as a check on the unrestrained use of bargaining power. Further, the logical alternative—use of historical or predicted baselines—may also discourage participation because of the adverse selection problem discussed above. An intermediate approach is to use historical baselines as a starting point for negotiating target stocks. This may lessen the influence of bargaining power while avoiding the adverse selection problem.

Summary of design issues

This discussion has provided an overview of a few of the important design issues involved in developing an international carbon sequestration program. There are several important implications. First, it is beneficial to minimize implementation costs, particularly for developing nations. One way to minimize costs is to unify the treatment of forest carbon under one seamless program to the extent possible.

It is also important to assure that the measurement and monitoring requirements of the program are manageable.

Second, the program should encourage parties, whether private or governmental, to find an efficient balance between the abatement of energy-related emissions and forest carbon sequestration. It is important, then, for the program to provide appropriate incentives at the margin to undertake all types of forestry practices that protect and expand forest carbon stocks. At the same time it is important to recognize that it may be necessary to provide side payments, or "infra-marginal inducements," to get countries or other parties to sign up initially. These payments could be in the form of financial inducements or they could take the form of more generous allocations of emissions allowances. In the latter case, it will be necessary to account for the additional allowances when setting targets and determining the overall distribution of allowances among countries.

Finally, it is important that the system not encourage adverse selection. For example, it will be critical to the program's success to ensure that countries with diminishing carbon stocks are not discouraged from participating.

The preceding discussion points to three basic policy designs: (1) a project-level program linked to a cap-and-trade system, (2) a national-level program linked to a cap-and-trade system, and (3) a system to promote national policies and practices (i.e., input-based programs) that are not linked to the trading program. The CDM falls in the first category; the NI approach falls in the second category; and an input-based national aid approach falls in the third category.

National inventory approach

The problems associated with project evaluation under the PBP or project-by project approach, as embodied in the CDM,[7] have prompted a search for alternatives. Andersson and Richards (2001) first recommended a National Inventory (NI) approach that would change the unit of analysis from individual projects to gains in carbon inventories at the national level. The NI and compensated reduction (CR)

---

[7] For a discussion of the problems associated with the PBP approach to carbon sequestration program design, see, for example, Richards and Andersson (2001).

approaches are similar in that they both measure changes in carbon stocks relative to a national baseline.[8] However, NI is broader in that it applies to all participating countries and accounts for any measurable changes in terrestrial carbon (not just changes from avoided deforestation in tropical countries). In this sense the NI approach is more consistent with, and provides specificity for, the concept of "full carbon accounting." The CR proposals are largely developed within the basic framework of the Kyoto Protocol (Santilli *et al.* 2005). For example, the CR proposals define different responsibilities for Annex I and non-Annex I countries, whereas the NI approach does not.

In this section, we describe and evaluate the NI approach for promoting expansion of global forest carbon stocks, regardless of the type or source of change. NI is an alternative approach to carbon management that eliminates or mitigates many of the serious problems encountered with the PBP accounting of the CDM. The NI approach is based on the observation that to the extent possible, all forest carbon conservation and augmentation practices should be included in a seamless program. In contrast, while the CR approach provides an attractive mechanism to encourage countries to slow deforestation, it appears limited to tropical countries and incorporates an artificial distinction between slowing deforestation and other practices, like afforestation, that increase carbon.

In the next subsection, we provide an overview of the NI approach. This is followed by an evaluation of the performance of NI relative to the PBP approach. In the two final subsections, we consider in further detail the measurement technologies available for national inventories and options available for the domestic implementation of carbon sequestration activities. Whenever possible, we compare and contrast NI with CR.[9]

Defining the national inventory approach

The defining feature of the NI approach is that changes in terrestrial carbon stocks are measured at the level of nations, rather than at the

---

[8] Some proposals have been based on a change in deforestation rates. Others have focused on changes in deforested acres per year. With sufficient data, both of these metrics can be translated into changes in forest carbon stocks.

[9] Further discussion of the NI approach is found in Andersson and Richards (2001) and Andersson *et al.* (2009).

level of projects. Specifically, the focus is on the change in a nation's *entire* carbon stock rather than the change associated with identified carbon sequestration projects. Similar to the negotiation of emissions reduction targets, we envision countries negotiating changes in national carbon stocks. At the start of the process, countries will have conducted a national forest carbon inventory, yielding an estimate of S_0, the carbon stock at time 0. In addition, countries will have assembled available information on historical forest trends.[10] This estimate would be used only to inform the negotiation process—it has no specific or binding effect on the setting of countries' baselines.

The process starts with a negotiation to determine each country's baseline carbon stock or reference case, which we denote NS_0. Then each nation's carbon stock is assessed periodically, say every five years. The new stock level at the end of the first period is denoted S_1. If S_1 exceeds the negotiated reference stock, then S_1-NS_0 offsets are awarded to the participant country. Conversely, if the actual stock at the end of the first period is below the negotiated reference stock, the country must cover its deficit by submitting NS_0-S_1 credits. At the end of the second time period the process is repeated and S_2-S_1 additional allowances are awarded to the participating nation (or debited if the number is negative).[11]

Two assumptions are implicit in this design. First, a country can opt into the forest sector program even if it has not agreed to a cap on its energy- and industry-related emissions. Second, once a country has enrolled in the international forest carbon program, it is fully responsible for changes in its forest carbon stocks relative to its negotiated reference case. Some countries might not have annual allocations of allowances because they are not participating in an emissions trading program under a cap. If those countries experience a reduction in their estimated carbon stocks, S_1, relative to their negotiated baseline reference case, NS_0, they will have to surrender allowances to cover the difference. Presumably countries in that position would purchase those allowances from the international emissions trading market.

[10] Bird (2005) notes that prior to the negotiations in Kyoto, each Party had to provide data on emissions from fossil fuel use and forecasts of future emissions under different scenarios. He recommends a similar process for the negotiation of targets for CR.

[11] It is also possible to imagine a system under which a new reference case stock would be negotiated at the beginning of each period.

Much recent attention has focused on rewarding countries for avoided deforestation (Moutinho *et al.* 2005). In the CR proposals, there is a reluctance to hold tropical countries liable when they fail to meet targets. One concern is that penalties for non-compliance will deter these countries from participating (Schlamadinger *et al.* 2005). Nonetheless, Santilli *et al.* (2005) argue that host country liability is the only viable option with national-level accounting, thus rejecting the principle of investor liability used under the CDM.[12] Under their proposal, countries would be allowed to make up unmet obligations during the subsequent commitment period.[13] It is unclear whether there would be any repercussions if a country failed to do so. Schlamadinger *et al.* (2005) propose that credits be awarded on a sliding scale. As emissions from deforestation increase above a lower target, a declining number of credits are awarded until finally, when emissions exceed an upper target, no credits are given. Similarly, under the Joint Research Centre proposal (see Skutsch *et al.* 2007), countries receive credits for reducing emissions below their target but are not penalized for emissions above the target.

The basic problem with these proposals is that they attempt to use one instrument—credits for avoided deforestation—to influence two types of decisions: the initial decision to participate in the international sequestration program and on-going land-use management decisions. The NI approach recognizes that these are two distinct goals—inducing countries to enroll and providing them incentives to make efficient choices about sequestration once they are enrolled. The concern raised by Schlamadinger *et al.* (2005) that countries will not enroll if they know they will be held responsible for losses can be addressed by recognizing that it is possible to provide *ex ante* inducements for countries to enroll—perhaps in the form of a relatively generous reference case— and still hold them strictly responsible for their *ex post* performance.

An important feature of NI is the use of a negotiated reference stock. The CR proposals emphasize the construction of historical baselines against which future performance is evaluated.[14] While historical data

---

[12] Afforestation and reforestation projects under the CDM generate temporary Certified Emissions Reduction credits. If the carbon sequestered under the project is released, the buyer of the credits is liable for an equivalent reduction in emissions.

[13] Sedjo and Sohngen (2007) propose a similar mechanism.

[14] An exception is Bird (2005), who proposes negotiated targets similar to those envisioned for the NI approach (Andersson and Richards 2001).

would be a logical starting point for negotiating NI targets, there is no presumption that the negotiated reference stock is functionally related to either the actual historic or projected baseline stock (i.e., the stock that would result in the absence of domestic carbon sequestration activities). As noted above, by avoiding the difficult task of forecasting baselines, negotiations can better address perceived fairness and equity concerns and mitigate adverse selection problems.[15]

Some authors have worried that if the reference case or baseline set for each country does not reflect the actual level of activity, or in the case of the NI approach, the actual carbon stock, it could lead to "hot air," i.e., a condition under which countries are receiving allowances or payments without actually making any changes (Morgan *et al.* 2005, Skutsch *et al.* 2007). A further concern is that if countries are given allowances, while in fact effecting no change, the integrity of the environmental goal will be undermined.

These concerns are both valid and resolvable. The key is first to recognize that "hot air" allowances serve as an inducement for reluctant countries to enroll at the outset. They provide a way to overcome the necessary severity of the payback requirement for countries that actually reduce their stocks. Second, it is important to assure that any of these hot air allowances are balanced with corresponding emissions reductions in the developed world. In this sense, hot air allowances are equivalent to an indirect financial transfer from countries that adopt lower emission targets to those that agree to enroll in the carbon sequestration program.

In contrast to the PBP approach, national governments, rather than project developers, have the responsibility for managing terrestrial carbon stocks. Accordingly, under the NI approach, governments replace project developers in the offset allowance market. We envision governments pursuing a suite of domestic policies to augment carbon stocks as well as to satisfy other national objectives. While the financing of domestic activities would be the ultimate responsibility of a national government, funds could originate with the sale of offset credits from a previous evaluation period, or from the sale of carbon bonds at the start of an evaluation period (Santilli *et al.* 2005).

---

[15] Osafo (2005) notes that Ghana has experienced little past deforestation, but that its deforestation rate has recently been increasing. He suggests that a target rate be set higher than the historical rate to encourage participation.

National inventories would be performed using verifiable methodologies, consistently applied across participating countries. To help ensure that measured changes in stocks are due to actions by a country, and not to changes in methodology, the same measurement protocol would be used within a country to estimate carbon stocks at the beginning and end of an evaluation period. However, over successive evaluation periods, new technologies could be employed to increase accuracy and reduce costs. Because NI requires measurement of changes in the entire carbon stock, we anticipate that remote sensing (e.g., satellite images of land cover) will need to be extensively used.

Performance of the NI approach relative to the PBP approach

The NI approach mitigates the problems of additionality, leakage, and permanence that arise under the PBP approach (Richards and Andersson 2001). By design, NI gives credit only for carbon sequestration that is additional to the negotiated target stock. The target stock is, in effect, a national reference case against which a country's carbon sequestration activities are measured. It is still possible that a national government may pay for non-additional projects when it pursues domestic policies to sequester carbon; however, only additional carbon will be credited under the carbon accounting mechanism of the international treaty.

Because a country's entire carbon stock is measured under NI, there is explicit accounting for intra-country leakage and inter-country leakage among participating countries. The problem of inter-country leakage to non-participating countries persists; however, this is not a problem particular to NI. Whenever there is less than full participation in an international treaty, there is the potential for unregulated actions by non-participating countries to counteract the treaty's objectives. Finally, as long as the mechanism for tracking national inventories continues, permanence is not an issue. If carbon sequestered today is released later on, it will be explicitly accounted for in a future national inventory.

In addition to mitigating the problems encountered under PBP accounting, the implementation of a carbon offset program is simplified under the NI approach. Instead of thousands of projects and project developers, the number of parties is reduced to the number of participating countries. Currently, there are 191 parties to the UNFCCC, a number that includes some countries with negligible terrestrial carbon stocks. A smaller number of parties increases the verifiability of carbon stock measurements. Rather than thousands of project-level measurements, fewer than 200 national inventories would need to be verified. This enhances prospects for the application of open and consistent methodologies. A smaller number of parties should also lead to lower transaction costs, though Skutsch *et al.* (2007) note that income generated nationally must still be distributed to domestic actors. Nepstad *et al.* (2007) suggest the use of three separate funds to channel offset payments to public and private entities in the Brazilian Amazon.

While the NI approach has many advantages over the PBP approach, it also has several disadvantages. Foremost among these is that the scope of carbon sequestration activities that can be considered may be limited by the feasibility of measuring changes in the forest carbon stock, particularly in the initial stages. Remote sensing must be an integral component of the NI approach because of the need for national-scale measurements. With current satellite imagery, changes in forest cover can be detected which, when combined with ground-level measurements, can be used to estimate associated changes in forest carbon stocks. Higher-resolution instruments can detect forest characteristics and, thus, measure carbon stock changes associated with forest management. However, with current technology some carbon sequestration activities are too costly to measure on a comprehensive basis, including changes in the stock of carbon stored in agricultural soil carbon and wood products.

Even with these present limitations, the NI approach can account for the most important terrestrial carbon sources and sinks. According to the IPCC (2000), deforestation releases approximately 1.8 GtC per year, compared to a potential uptake of 0.4 GtC per year from cropland and grazing land management. Further, applying the NI approach to forest carbon stocks does not preclude the use of an alternative mechanism for crediting changes in agricultural and other stocks. The fact that some components of national carbon stocks cannot be measured accurately under the NI approach at present should not prevent this approach being applied to stocks that can be measured reliably.

The fact that all changes in carbon stocks, whether deliberate or accidental, are treated the same under the NI approach may lead to the perception that some countries are making greater sacrifices than others. These beliefs may influence subsequent negotiations over reference case carbon stocks, and perhaps the decision by some countries to participate in the treaty. While this concern is valid, we feel that attempts to differentiate between policy-induced and naturally-occurring changes would impede efforts to accurately and objectively measure changes in carbon stocks.

Under the NI approach, incentives for carbon sequestration arise from government policies rather than from private project developers. This is a relative disadvantage of the NI approach to the extent that a country lacks strong governmental institutions, government agencies are corrupt or poorly run, and the domestic policy-making process is captured by special interest groups. As well, CDM-type projects, whereby investors in one country fund carbon sequestration projects in another, are unlikely to occur because credits are given on a national, rather than on a project, basis.[16] On the other hand, the NI approach gives national governments a great deal of flexibility in developing policies that are tailored to specific domestic conditions and that satisfy other domestic objectives besides climate change. For example, an afforestation policy may sequester carbon at the same time that it reduces soil erosion and enhances wildlife habitat.

Some commentators on the CR approach worry that credits from avoided deforestation will "flood the market" for emissions allowances, thereby lowering prices and discouraging long-term investments in clean energy technologies (Silva-Chavez 2005, Vera-Diaz and Schwartzman 2005, Morgan *et al.* 2005, Skutsch *et al.* 2007). A common suggestion is to impose limits on the use of deforestation offsets, similar to those placed on offsets from CDM projects. If offsets from carbon sequestration are equivalent to those from emissions reductions[17] and the market for allowances is efficient, then these concerns are misplaced. For a given time-profile of emissions caps, agents have the incentive to minimize the cost of satisfying these targets. If carbon sequestration offsets are available, they will only be purchased

---

[16] As we will discuss later, international agencies and non-governmental organizations may want to provide support for national policies and measures.

[17] The use of the term "tropical hot air" by some commentators suggests they consider offsets to be less legitimate than emissions reductions.

if they are less expensive than reducing actual emissions. Thus, on efficiency grounds, the use of offsets should be allowed without limit and low allowance prices should be seen as a welcome sign of cost reductions. Of course, our assumption about efficiency would need to apply to the actual market and policy environment for this conclusion to be valid.

Measurement technologies

Signatories to the UNFCCC and the Kyoto Protocol are required to report the results of periodic national inventories of GHG emissions and removals that include inventories of forest carbon. In practice, however, national communications about countries' GHG status have been sporadic or, in some cases, non-existent. Moreover, the reporting that has occurred has not been characterized by transparency. Andersson et al. (2009) were unable to identify the methods and data sources used in each of the reports submitted by Annex I countries. Nor were they able to document the exact manner in which the UNFCCC expert review team assessed the reliability and validity of the methods used in these reports.

For changes in national stocks of terrestrial carbon to be successfully linked to a permit trading program, frequent inventories will be needed for all participating countries. Given the high stakes that will be involved, the process of estimation will need to be highly transparent to garner broad support. Finally, these measurements will also need to be highly accurate to generate confidence among the participants that carbon allowance allocations correspond to actual increments in carbon. Accuracy is also important because of the linkage of carbon stocks to the permit trading market. Given the sheer magnitude of the carbon flows involved, even small errors in the measurement of the global forest carbon stock could exceed the total emissions reductions stipulated under a treaty.[18] Clearly, this uncertainty could undermine efforts to reduce net emissions if countries erroneously estimate that they have met their emissions reduction targets based on changes in carbon stocks alone.

---

[18] When estimates based on existing carbon inventory techniques are subject to uncertainty analysis, it is not uncommon to see 15 percent or greater standard error in estimates of a country's forest carbon pool (Jonas et al. 1999, Nilsson et al. 2000, Balzter and Shvidenko 2000).

Tradeoffs clearly exist between the frequency, transparency, accuracy, and cost of national inventories. With massive expenditures on field-based sampling, it would be possible to develop highly accurate national carbon inventories. In contrast, low-cost inventories could be done through the processing of low-resolution satellite imagery using existing field data. However, this low-cost option is unlikely to provide a level of accuracy that is acceptable to the policy community (Andersson *et al.* 2009). Applying a single measurement protocol in all countries would increase transparency, but given the tremendous variety of geographic, topographic, and ecological conditions among countries, this would likely entail prohibitively high costs.

An intermediate approach will be needed to achieve a reasonable balance of cost, frequency, transparency, and accuracy. Because field-based inventories are time-consuming and expensive, remote sensing would need to play a central role in the NI approach. Two basic methods can be used to link remote sensing to the assessment of biomass and carbon stocks. First, using the land-cover approach, raw images can be classified into distinct land-cover categories whose biomass properties are well understood. If there is relatively little within-category variation in biomass measures, this method can produce reasonable carbon assessments. An alternative, the forest variable approach, uses remote-sensing tools to directly measure stand-level variables such as species, leaf area index, and canopy height. These measurements are then used in allometric equations to estimate total carbon in the stand.

Many remote-sensing instruments can contribute data to the carbon inventory estimation process. Sensors fall under two main categories: active sensors and passive sensors. Passive sensors, including satellite-based instruments such as the Landsat Thematic Mapper (TM) and the Moderate Resolution Imaging Spectroradiometer (MODIS), measure solar radiation reflected from the Earth's surface. Active sensors, including the Synthetic Aperture Radar (SAR) and Light Detection and Ranging (LIDAR) instruments, transmit radiation that is reflected from Earth's surface and then measured. In general, the instruments with moderate resolution (e.g., Landsat TM) are well suited for land classification, while those instruments with higher resolution and more specialized functions (e.g., LIDAR) are better adapted for measuring forest variable inputs for the allometric models.

For all types of instruments, the data collected via remote sensing have to be correlated to the characteristics of sites sampled via field measurements. Once these relationships are established, it becomes possible to infer land-use and forest characteristics based on the remote-sensing data alone. This places a premium on initially undertaking a high-quality inventory. Thereafter, remote-sensing techniques can be used to identify changes in the spatial extent and characteristics of forests relative to their initial state. In this regard, costs might be further reduced by concentrating resources on the forest areas that are changing most rapidly. Whatever measurement approach is adopted, certain technologies will favor some countries over others in terms of which stocks can be included and how accurately they can be measured. This could have distributional consequences that would shape negotiations over the adoption of measurement protocols.

Not all countries will have the financial resources or institutional capacity to conduct regular and credible national inventories. This is especially true for developing countries, with Brazil and India being important exceptions (Skutsch *et al.* 2007). This suggests a role for an international organization, acting perhaps through the IPCC, in providing assistance to countries in developing their national inventories and documenting the results.[19] This organization might also play a role in verifying inventories and in increasing transparency by serving as a clearinghouse for data and other information. Non-governmental organizations might also be funded to act as third-party auditors.

Domestic implementation

Under the NI approach, nations would have responsibility for developing domestic policies to increase carbon sequestration. A wide variety of land management practices will increase the stock of terrestrial carbon, including tree planting on non-forest lands (afforestation), avoiding deforestation, modifying forest management practices to increase carbon uptake, and fire suppression and management. As

---

[19] Skutsch *et al.* (2007) indicate that the World Bank, among others, have indicated an interest in providing upfront financing for national inventories. These authors also suggest that Annex I Parties, as the beneficiaries of deforestation offsets, might provide funding for forest inventories and related domestic policies.

noted above, however, some carbon stocks (e.g., carbon in agricultural soils and wood products) would have to be excluded, at least initially, under NI due to the cost of measuring the entire national stock. One possible remedy is to allow countries to generate credits for selected projects that credibly provide additional and permanent carbon storage. An example might be a new use of wood products in the construction of long-lived structures.

Countries have a range of policy instruments at their disposal to create incentives for carbon sequestration, including subsidies, contracts, and government production. In some tropical countries, carbon sequestration might be increased by removing policies that promote deforestation (Santilli and Moutinho 2005, Silva-Chavez 2005). The success of domestic carbon sequestration policies will depend to a large degree on the soundness of a country's governmental institutions. International aid organizations may have a role to play in helping countries strengthen property rights and by providing financial assistance for domestic programs. Santilli and Moutinho (2005) note as an example the G7 Pilot Program for the Protection of the Brazilian Rainforests. As well, a mechanism exists under the UNFCCC for Annex I countries to provide financial and technical assistance to developing countries (Morgan *et al.* 2005).

While the NI approach mitigates the problems of additionality, leakage, and permanence with respect to carbon accounting for the international treaty mechanism, these problems resurface when countries pursue domestic policies. For example, if a national government provides subsidies for afforestation, it will be difficult to ensure that payments are given only for additional carbon sequestration. Likewise, there may be intra-country leakage associated with an afforestation program. Problems of this nature arise with many types of domestic policies.[20] Although problems with additionality, leakage, and permanence may raise the costs borne by national governments, the NI approach helps to ensure that they do not undermine international efforts to combat climate change.

Countries will gain valuable experience as they seek to implement domestic carbon sequestration policies. It will be important to have a mechanism for sharing this information among nations

[20] For example, see Wu (2000) for an analysis of leakage from the Conservation Reserve Program, a large-scale land conservation program in the United States.

so that policymakers can adapt and improve policies over time. National reporting requirements have already been established by the UNFCCC.

Input-based approaches

While the PBP and NI approaches described above are linked to the emissions allowance trading system, the international community could choose to adopt a system in which the forest carbon program and the emissions allowance system are not linked. This is exactly what the German Advisory Council on Global Change (Grassl *et al.* 2003) advised when it recommended a "protocol for the conservation of carbon stocks."

One such approach would be for countries to set goals for reducing emissions (Morgan *et al.* 2005) or to target other metrics of improvement such as reductions in deforestation, increases in forest acreage or biomass, a beneficial change in management practices, or improvement in forest health. Rather than focusing primarily on carbon credits, the program would focus on inputs, such as policies to discourage deforestation, programs to encourage the conversion of marginal agricultural land to forests, projects to better manage under-stocked forests, and efforts to enhance technical capacity within forest-rich countries. The Global Initiative on Forests and Climate established by Australia[21] employs this approach.

These commitments would be incorporated in the national plans required under the UNFCCC; they could be financed through overseas development aid, international institutions such as the World Bank or through a separate fund established under the successor to the Kyoto Protocol.

There are also variations on this delinked approach. Grassl *et al.* (2003) describe a delinked approach that would involve a "world-wide system of non-utilization obligations." Under this system, first developed by Sedjo (1991), countries would accept obligations to protect either their own natural forest systems or pay for certificates from other countries that exceed their non-utilization or protection quotas.

The Carbon Finance Mechanism in the World Bank's Forest Carbon Partnership Facility illustrates another variation. Under that system,

[21] www.ausaid.gov.au/hottopics/topic.cfm?ID=4755_6308_104_9400_7292

"countries would receive payments for reducing emissions below a reference scenario. Payments would only be made to countries that achieve measurable and verifiable emissions reductions" (Myers 2007).

There are several advantages to a delinked forest carbon sequestration program. First, it would save on transaction costs (Andersson and Richards 2001). The focus would be on implementing policies, programs, and projects—at both the national and local levels—rather than on issues of measurement, enforcement, and crediting. This is not to say that estimation of carbon effects would not be important for program evaluation, but rather that implementation and policing would be simpler.

Second, if negotiations over international forest sequestration and energy emissions proceed on separate tracks, delays in one need not hold up the other. Whereas there is at least some experience and precedent for the next round of negotiations on energy-related emissions, an agreement on targets and rules for the inclusion of carbon sinks would "have to start practically from scratch" (Grassl *et al.* 2003).

Third, separating the forest carbon program from carbon trading would ameliorate the problems associated with dealing with issues of liability for carbon losses due to fire, pests, or natural disaster.

There are two particularly serious disadvantages to a delinked approach, however. First, a delinked approach that shifts the focus from accomplishments (outcomes) to encouraging policies, programs, and projects (inputs) dulls the incentives for the protection and expansion of carbon stocks relative to either the NI or PBP approach. Participating countries may shift their attention from assuring positive carbon outcomes to attracting more dollars for more projects, regardless of efficacy. Also, decoupling the forest carbon program from the cap-and-trade program removes one of the best sources of funding to promote changes in land use: emitters seeking lower-cost options to reduce their net emissions.

Conclusions

The Kyoto Protocol has not been fully effective, as demonstrated by continuing disagreements over what constitutes human-induced changes in carbon stocks; by the small number of approved CDM forestry projects; and by the lack of provisions to address tropical deforestation, the largest source of forest-based emissions. The Kyoto

Protocol establishes national-level accounting for Annex I countries with the stipulation that, to count toward Protocol commitments, all changes in carbon inventories must be human-induced. The CDM established for non-Annex I countries requires PBP accounting for afforestation and reforestation activities. The expiration of the Kyoto Protocol in 2012 invites a reexamination of how to address terrestrial carbon management within the framework of an international climate change treaty. This chapter has described three mechanisms to encourage reductions in net emissions of CO_2 from the forest sector. A large number of general policy design issues arise when one contemplates mechanisms for including forests in an international climate change treaty. These include scale, linkage to allowance trading, and baseline measurement. Based on our discussion of these issues, we identify three basic policy approaches: (1) PBP accounting linked to the permit market, (2) national-level accounting linked to the permit market, and (3) an unlinked input-based approach.

Past experience with PBP accounting, which is the approach used under the CDM, reveals a number of serious challenges. Foremost among these is the difficulty of establishing a reference case against which to measure project benefits, especially when the carbon stock is dynamic due to biological processes or human activity. In the absence of a credible reference case, it is impossible to know if carbon offsets are additional and, thus, deserving of compensation through the permit market. The additionality problem is compounded by problems of leakage (the off-site effects of projects), permanence (the potential for stored carbon to be released in the future), and a host of adverse selection problems. Our conclusion is that PBP accounting has fundamental flaws and should not be a central component of the forestry mechanisms adopted in a post-2012 agreement.

We find linked national-level accounting to be a much more promising approach. Under the NI approach, nations conduct periodic inventories of their entire forest carbon stock. The measured stock is compared to a negotiated baseline to determine the quantity of offset credits that can be redeemed, or debits that must be covered, in the permit market. With the NI approach, it is the nation, rather than the project developer, who pursues carbon sequestration activities through the development of domestic policies. To circumvent the difficult task of forecasting future stocks in an unobservable reference case, we favor a negotiation process to determine the reference case stock.

These negotiations could be used to address fairness and equity issues as well as to provide incentives for countries—especially countries with historically declining stocks—to participate in the agreement.

The NI approach offers many advantages relative to the primary objective of achieving real, global reductions in GHG emissions. It greatly reduces the problems of additionality, leakage, permanence, and adverse selection that plague the PBP approach and the CDM. It also provides comprehensive coverage of all forest carbon stocks and accounts for all changes in these stocks, whether they have human or natural causes. Unlike the forestry provisions of the Kyoto Protocol, the NI approach can be implemented as a seamless program that applies equally to all participating countries and to all measurable changes in forest carbon stocks.

National-level accounting is also included in a number of recent proposals for compensating reductions in tropical deforestation. While the CR proposals contain some of the attractive features of the NI approach, they also have shortcomings. First, they are essentially an appendage to the Kyoto Protocol; thus, while they bring tropical deforestation under the Framework Convention, they leave in place other problematic features like the CDM. Second, these proposals emphasize reference cases based on historical trends in forest area, giving rise to an adverse selection problem whereby countries with declining forest area refuse to participate. The various schemes proposed to address this problem all dilute the incentives for carbon capture. Under the NI approach, participation is induced through a separate wealth-transfer mechanism (e.g., a lower negotiated reference case stock) while appropriate marginal incentives for reducing deforestation are retained. In the literature on CR, some authors express concern that excessive offsets for avoided deforestation will create "tropical hot air," thereby leading to artificial reductions in permit prices. In our view, it is appropriate to create additional offsets to induce participation, provided that reductions are made elsewhere to maintain the overall emissions reduction goal.

The NI approach also has disadvantages that need to be acknowledged. First, because of the need to conduct national inventories, the scope of carbon sequestration activities is limited to those that can be measured with relative ease. Even so, nothing prevents the development of an alternative mechanism to provide incentives for activities that are excluded from the NI program. Second, incentives for carbon sequestration activities must arise from domestic policies initiated by national government rather than from private project developers, a relative disadvantage in countries with weak institutions, corruption, and a domestic policy-making process captured by special interest groups. On the other hand, the NI approach gives national governments a great deal of flexibility in developing policies that are tailored to specific domestic conditions and that satisfy other domestic objectives besides climate change. It will be important to establish a reporting mechanism so that information on policy experiences can be shared among nations. Third, problems with additionality, permanence, etc. may resurface with—and reduce the effectiveness of—domestic carbon sequestration policies pursued by national governments, though this does not compromise the performance of the international treaty. Finally, while we favor negotiated forest carbon baselines and targets, we recognize that the negotiation process can fail for a number of reasons, including unequal bargaining power among nations. Nevertheless, our assessment is that the alternatives, such as these that require the development of historical baselines, give rise to an even more difficult set of problems.

The feasibility of the NI approach hinges on whether it is possible to conduct regular and reliable national forest inventories for a large group of countries. We have briefly reviewed some of the important technical issues, but this is clearly an area that requires further inquiry.[22] An appropriate balance would need to be found between costs, frequency, transparency, and accuracy. Inventories will need to be accurate because small errors in national inventories could generate large numbers of offsets, potentially swamping the permit market. If current measurement technologies are inadequate, then we would recommend that an input-based approach be used as an interim measure while the scientific community works to overcome the measurement challenges.

References

Andersson, K., T. P. Evans, and K. R. Richards (2009). "National Forest Carbon Inventories: Policy Needs and Assessment Capacity," *Climatic Change* 93: 69–101.

Andersson, K. and K. R. Richards (2001). "Implementing an International Carbon Sequestration Program: Can the Leaky Sink be Fixed?" *Climate Policy* 1: 173–88.

[22] See Andersson *et al.* (2009) for a more in-depth treatment.

Balzter, H. and A. Shvidenko (2000). *Map accuracy report—Siberia forest cover map*. Siberia Working Note 58, Laxenburg, Austria: International Institute for Applied Systems Analysis.

Bird, N. (2005). "Considerations for Choosing an Emission Target for Compensated Reduction," in P. Moutinho and S. Schwartzman (eds.), *Tropical Deforestation and Climate Change*. Belém, Brazil, and Washington, DC: Amazon Institute for Environmental Research, and Environmental Defense, pp. 87–92.

Grassl, H., J. Kokott, M. Kulessa, J. Luther, F. Nuscheler, R. Sauerborn, H.-J. Schellnhuber, R. Schubert, and E.-D. Schulze (2003). *Climate Protection Strategies for the 21st Century: Kyoto and Beyond*. Special Report, Berlin, Germany: German Advisory Council on Global Change (WBGU).

Gullison, R. E., P. C. Frumhoff, J. G. Canadell, C. B. Field, D. C. Nepstad, K. Hayhoe, R. Avissar, L. M. Curran, P. Friedlingstein, C. D. Jones, and C. Nobre (2007). "Tropical Forests and Climate Policy," *Science* 316: 985–6.

IPCC (2000). *Land Use, Land-Use Change, and Forestry*, Special Report, Geneva, Switzerland: IPCC.

Jonas, M., S. Nilsson, M. Obersteiner, M. Gluck, and Y. Ermoliev (1999). *Verification Times Underlying the Kyoto Protocol: Global Benchmark Calculations*, Interim Report IR-99062, Laxenburg, Austria: International Institute for Applied Systems Analysis.

Morgan, J., C. Maretti, and G. Volpi (2005). "Tropical Deforestation in the Context of the Post-2012 Climate Change Regime," in Moutinho and Schwartzman (eds.), pp. 101–10.

Moutinho, P., S. Schwartzman, and M. Santilli (2005). "Introduction," in Moutinho and Schwartzman (eds.), pp. 9–12.

Myers, E. (2007). *Policies to Reduce Emissions from Deforestation and Degradation (REDD) in Tropical Forests*, Discussion Paper 07-50, Washington, DC: Resources for the Future.

Nabours, G. and O. Masera (2007). "Forestry," in *Climate Change 2007: Mitigation of Climate Change*, Working Group III Contribution to the Fourth Assessment Report of the IPCC, Cambridge University Press, pp. 541–84.

Nepstad, D., B. Soares-Filho, F. Merry, P. Moutinho, H. O. Rodriques, M. Bowman, S. Schwartzman, O. Almeida, and S. Rivero (2007). *The Costs and Benefits of Reducing Carbon Emissions from Deforestation and Forest Degradation in the Brazilian Amazon*. Falmouth, MA: The Woods Hole Research Center.

Nilsson, S., A. Shvidenko, V. Stolbovoi, M. Gluck, M. Jonas, and M. Obersteiner (2000). *Full Carbon Account for Russia*, Interim Report

IR-00-021, Laxenburg, Austria: International Institute for Applied Sciences.

Osafo, Y. B. (2005). "Reducing Emissions from Tropical Forest Deforestation: Applying Compensated Reduction in Ghana," in Moutinho and Schwartzman (eds.), pp. 63–72.

Paustian, K., J. Antle, J. Sheehan, and E. Paul (2006). *Agriculture's Role in Greenhouse Gas Mitigation*. Arlington, VA: Pew Center on Global Climate Change.

Richards, K. R. and K. Andersson (2001). "The Leaky Sink: Persistent Obstacles to a Forest Carbon Sequestration Program Based on Individual Projects," *Climate Policy* 1: 41–54.

Richards, K., N. Sampson, and S. Brown (2006). *Agricultural and Forestlands: U.S. Carbon Policy Strategies*. Arlington, VA: Pew Center on Global Climate Change.

Santilli, M. and P. Moutinho (2005). "National Compacts to Reduce Deforestation," in Moutinho and Schwartzman (eds.), pp. 125–30.

Santilli, M., P. Moutinho, S. Schwartzman, D. Nepstad, L. Curran, and C. Nobre (2005). "Tropical Deforestation and Kyoto Protocol: An Editorial Essay," *Climatic Change* 71: 267–76.

Sanz, M. (2007). *Reducing Emissions from Deforestation in Developing Countries (REDD)*, Presentation to COM+ Media Training, Vienna, Austria, August 29, 2007.

Schlamadinger, B., L. Ciccarese, M. Dutschke, P. M. Fearnside, S. Brown, and D. Murdiyarso (2005). "Should We Include Avoidance of Deforestation in the International Response to Climate Change?" in Moutinho and Schwartzman (eds.), pp. 53–62.

Sedjo, R. A. (1991). *Implications of a Tradable Obligations Approach to International Forest Protection*, Report to the US Environmental Protection Agency, Washington, DC: Resources for the Future.

Sedjo, R. A. and B. Sohngen (2007). *Carbon Credits for Avoided Deforestation*, Discussion Paper DP 07-47, Washington, DC: Resources for the Future.

Silva-Chavez, G. A. (2005). "Reducing Greenhouse Gas Emissions from Tropical Deforestation by Applying Compensated Reduction to Bolivia," in Moutinho and Schwartzman (eds.), pp. 73–86.

Skutsch, M., N. Bird, E. Trines, M. Dutschke, P. Frumhoff, B. H. J. de Jong, P. van Laake, O. Masera, and D. Murdiyarso (2007). "Clearing the Way for Reducing Emissions from Tropical Deforestation," *Environmental Science and Policy* 10: 322–34.

UNFCCC (2005). *Reducing Emissions from Deforestation in Developing Countries: Approaches to Stimulate Action*, UNFCCC: FCCC/CP/2005/MISC.1.

US Department of Agriculture, Forest Service (2000). *2000 RPA Assessment of Forest and Range Lands*, FS-687, Washington, DC: US Department of Agriculture, Forest Service.

Vera-Diaz, M. D. C. and S. Schwartzman (2005). "Carbon Offsets and Land Use in the Brazilian Amazon," in Moutinho and Schwartzman (eds.), pp. 93–100.

Wu, J. (2000). "Slippage Effects of the Conservation Reserve Program," *American Journal of Agricultural Economics* 82: 979–92.

PART VI

Modeling impacts of alternative allocations of responsibility

23 | Modeling economic impacts of alternative international climate policy architectures: a quantitative and comparative assessment of architectures for agreement

VALENTINA BOSETTI, CARLO CARRARO,
ALESSANDRA SGOBBI, AND
MASSIMO TAVONI

This chapter is part of the research work being carried out by the Climate Change Modeling and Policy Research Programme of the Fondazione Eni Enrico Mattei and by the Climate Impacts and Policy Division of the EuroMediterranean Center on Climate Change. The authors are grateful to Rob Stavins, Joe Aldy and the Harvard Project on International Climate Agreements for many helpful comments and enduring support. William Nordhaus and participants to the 3rd Atlantic Workshop on Energy and Environmental Economics also provided precious comments and suggestions. The collaboration with Scott Barrett, Jeff Frankel and David Victor has been fundamental for the successful development of the research project whose results are presented in this chapter. Any remaining errors are the authors' sole responsibility.

Introduction

According to the latest report of the Intergovernmental Panel on Climate Change (IPCC) there is unequivocal evidence that the climate system is warming, which is expected to affect both ecosystems and socio-economic systems to varying degrees (IPCC, 2007). Changes in atmospheric concentrations of greenhouse gases (GHGs) are deemed responsible for the observed increase in average global temperature, which has risen by 0.76°C since 1850—mostly in the last fifty years. The IPCC also points to widespread agreement in the scientific community that such changes in the climate system may be spurred by global GHG

715

emissions from human activities, which increased by 70 percent between 1970 and 2004. If emissions continue unabated, the Earth's average global surface temperature is likely to rise by a further 1.8°C −4.0°C this century (IPCC, 2007). A temperature increase between 2°C and 3°C is thought to be a threshold beyond which irreversible and possibly catastrophic changes in the climate system may take place.

After many decades of debate, climate change has now become a central topic in the policy agenda of all industrialized nations, and is becoming increasingly critical for developing countries as well. Policies and actions to control climate change have already been implemented around the globe—from the European commitment to cut GHG emissions at least 20 percent by 2020, to international and local adaptation strategies, such as the effort led by the Organisation for Economic Co-operation and Development (OECD) for mainstreaming adaptation in Official Development Assistance.

It is clear, however, that a global, coordinated effort is needed to keep temperature change below dangerous levels, as illustrated by Figure 23.1. While it is true that industrial emissions from fossil fuels have been and continue to be mostly attributable to industrialized nations, it is also true that soon non-Annex I countries will overtake Annex I countries in terms of their total carbon dioxide (CO_2) emissions (top panel). At the same time, per capita emission levels will remain much lower in developing countries, given differences in population growth and initial lifestyles (bottom panel).

The implication of such emission projections is therefore twofold: on the one hand, global action is needed; at the same time, such action is likely to entail differentiated targets and levels of effort. Negotiations are already underway to define a climate control agreement for the post-Kyoto world, and a number of proposals have appeared in both the academic and policy literature (see, for instance, IEA 2002, Aldy and Stavins 2007, Stern 2008). To date, however, there has been no attempt to compare and contrast different architectures for an international agreement on climate policy using a common framework. Such an exercise would enable a better understanding of the implications of different designs and make more transparent the trade-offs that exist between different criteria deemed important for international agreements.

Therefore, the main objective of this chapter is to provide a quantitative comparison of the main architectures for an international climate agreement that have been put forward in the literature.

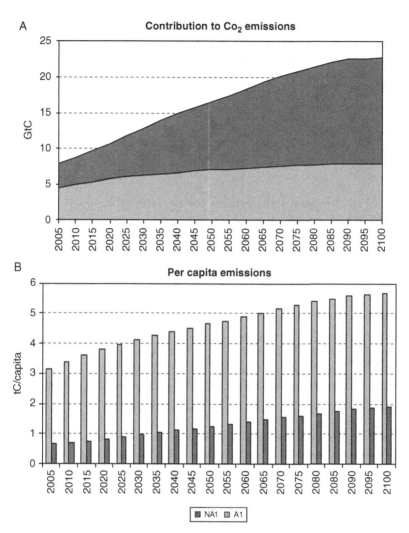

Figure 23.1. Projected fossil-fuel CO_2 emissions from the WITCH model in the business-as-usual scenario

Proposals are assessed using WITCH[1]—an energy-economy-climate model—and compared according to four criteria: economic efficiency; environmental effectiveness; distributional implications; and political acceptability, as measured in terms of feasibility and enforceability.

[1] www.feem-web.it/witch

The ultimate aim is to derive useful policy implications that could provide insights for designing the next agreement on climate change.[2]

The chapter is organized as follows. We begin in the next section by briefly describing the underlying model and then present, in the next section, the features that characterize the architectures for agreement being examined. The main (fourth) section of the chapter compares and contrasts eight different architectures, according to the four criteria noted above. The final section of the chapter summarizes key lessons and policy implications.

A tool to compare architectures for agreement: the WITCH model

WITCH (Bosetti, Carraro *et al.* 2006) is a climate-energy-economy model designed to assist in the study of the socio-economic dimensions of climate change. It is structured to provide information on the optimal responses of world economies to climate damages and to identify impacts of climate policy on global and regional economic systems. An appendix provides a short introduction to the model. A thorough description and a list of related papers and applications are available at www.feem-web.it/witch.

WITCH is a hybrid model because it combines features of both top-down and bottom-up modeling: the top-down component consists of an intertemporal optimal growth model in which the energy input of the aggregate production function has been expanded to yield a bottom-up description of the energy sector. The model provides a fully intertemporal allocation of investments in energy technologies and R&D that is used to evaluate optimal and second-best economic and technological responses to different policy measures.

Countries are grouped in twelve regions that cover the world, and strategic interactions between those regions are modeled through a dynamic game. The game theory set-up accounts for interdependencies and spillovers across regions of the world, while equilibrium strategies

---

[2] The analysis presented in this chapter originates within the context of the Harvard Project on International Climate Agreements (http://belfercenter.ksg. harvard.edu/project/56/harvard_project_on_international_climate_agreements. html) which aims at identifying the key features to design scientifically sound, economically efficient and politically feasible post-2012 international policy architectures for global climate change.

reflect inefficiencies induced by global strategic interactions. This allows us to analyze both fully cooperative equilibria (all regions of the world sign a climate agreement) and partial/regional coalitional equilibria (only a subgroup of regions signs the agreement or different groups of regions sign different agreements).

In WITCH, technological progress in the energy sector is endogenous, thus enabling us to account for the effects of different stabilization policies on induced technical change, via both innovation and diffusion processes. The role of endogenous technical change has been shown to be very important in model analyses of climate policies. We do not tackle this issue in this chapter because of space constraints and because our aim is to compare different policies. The interested reader is referred to a recent OECD working paper (Bosetti, Carraro *et al.* 2009) for a more exhaustive analysis of the role of technical change for climate policy featuring the WITCH model. Feedbacks from economic variables to climate variables, and vice versa, are also accounted for in the model's dynamic system.[3]

Several features of the model allow us to investigate a number of issues in greater detail than most of the studies in the existing literature. First, though quite rich in its energy modeling and close in spirit to bottom-up energy models, WITCH is based on a top-down framework that guarantees the coherent, fully intertemporal allocation of investments under the assumption of perfect foresight. Second, the model can track all actions that have an impact on the level of mitigation—R&D expenditures, investment in carbon-free technologies, purchases of emission permits, or expenditures for carbon taxes— and we can thus evaluate equilibrium responses stimulated by different policy tools. This leads to a transparent evaluation of abatement costs and to a clearer quantification of the uncertainties affecting them.

Diffusion and innovation processes are modeled to capture advancements in carbon mitigation technologies, through both learning-by-doing and research. The model also explicitly includes the effects of international technology spillovers and captures innovation market failures. The detailed representation of endogenous technical change and the explicit inclusion of spillovers in technologies and knowledge

---

[3] The model is solved numerically in GAMS/CONOPT for thirty five-year periods, although only twenty are retained as we do not impose terminal conditions. Solution time for the Baseline Scenario is approximately thirty minutes on a standard Pentium PC.

are crucial to understanding and assessing the impact of policy architectures that combine climate and R&D policies.

Architectures for agreement

We explore eight policy architectures, which have been discussed in the literature or have been proposed as potential successors to the Kyoto agreement. These architectures are inspired by the proposals put forward by the Harvard Project on International Climate Agreements.[4] All of them are assessed against a scenario without climate policy (business as usual or BAU). Table 23.1 summarizes the key distinguishing features of the architectures that we compare and contrast in this chapter.

In Table 23.1, we emphasize two main features of any policy architecture that have important implications for its cost and feasibility, namely scope and timing. Universal agreements involve all regions, while partial agreements only require cooperation among a subset of regions. Agreements may require immediate efforts from participating countries, or they may take into account differential abilities to undertake abatement and, therefore, involve incremental participation, where some regions—usually transition economies and developing countries—are allowed to enter the agreement at a later point in time, when they satisfy some pre-defined criteria. A further distinction across architectures is the type of policy instrument involved: most schemes use a cap-and-trade approach, but carbon taxes and R&D policies are also considered.

Two key aspects of the architectures considered in this chapter should be pointed out at this stage in order to make the results of our analysis clear. First, all proposed architectures focus on CO_2 mitigation only, excluding other GHGs. Although it is widely recognized that including other GHGs would improve the efficiency of any climate agreement, most of the proposals investigated in the present context intentionally concentrate only on CO_2 emissions in order to keep the analysis as simple as possible. Therefore, we assume (consistent with all the architectures analyzed here) an exogenous path for all GHGs other than CO_2. Secondly, as issues of emissions leakage and incentives for free riding are likely to be substantial for less than a global agreement,

---

[4] Most architectures considered in this chapter are carefully described in Aldy and Stavins 2007 and Aldy, Stavins *et al.*, 2007.

Table 23.1 *Architectures for agreement*

Name	Key feature	Policy Instrument	Scope	Timing
Cap and Trade (CAT) with redistribution	Benchmark cap and trade	Cap and Trade	Universal	Immediate
Global Carbon Tax	Global tax recycled domestically	Carbon Tax	Universal	Immediate
REDD	Inclusion of REDD	Cap and Trade	Universal	Immediate
Climate Clubs	Clubs of countries	Cap and Trade and R&D	Partial	Incremental
Burden Sharing	Delayed participation of DCs	Cap and Trade	Universal	Incremental
Graduation	Bottom up targets	Cap and Trade	Partial	Incremental
Dynamic Targets	Political feasibility	Cap and Trade	Universal	Incremental
R&D Coalition	R&D cooperation	R&D	Universal	Immediate

all the proposed architectures envisage all countries committing—at a minimum—to not exceeding their projected emissions under the BAU scenario. This may seem restrictive, but it is less so if we consider that regions do benefit from committing to the BAU, since they then have the option of participating in the market for carbon permits, undertaking cheap abatement measures, and receiving financial resources for doing so.

We begin by providing a short description of each climate policy proposal.

Cap-and-Trade (CAT) policy with redistribution

In this benchmark scenario, a standard cap-and-trade policy is implemented, there is a global carbon market, and complete and immediate cooperation exists among regions as they seek to attain a climate stabilization goal. The goal is to stabilize atmospheric concentrations of CO_2 at 450 parts per million (ppm) by 2100, which equals roughly 550 ppm CO_2-equivalent, taking into account all GHGs.

As shown above, today's average per capita emissions vary substantially across countries. In the United States, for instance, emissions are around 5.5 metric tons carbon (tC) per capita, compared to 0.06 tC per capita in sub-Saharan Africa and 1.3 tC per capita in China. It is often argued that a fair long-term agreement for tackling climate change would require a move from the common practice of allocating allowances on the basis of historical emissions towards the adoption of an equal per capita rule, based on the Rawlsian principle of equal entitlement to pollute. Thus, permits in this scheme are distributed according to an equal per capita rule (EPC). It should be noted that, because the modeling analysis assumes a perfect global carbon market, marginal abatement costs are equalized and the allocation scheme has a negligible effect on global variables. It does however have important distributional implications as it implies significant wealth transfers through the global carbon market.

Global tax recycled domestically

The second architecture we analyze does not envisage an explicit emission target, but exogenously sets a global carbon tax consistent with a CO_2 emission path leading to stabilization at an atmospheric concentration of 450 ppm. While this approach requires global cooperation in deciding upon the path of the carbon tax and its implementation, it is autarchic in the sense that there is no global market for emission trading: rather, the revenues from the tax are recycled domestically in the national budgets of countries that impose the tax.

The assumed carbon tax starts at around $3 per ton of CO_2, but rises rapidly to provide incentives for substantial emission reductions: in 2050, the tax reaches $500 per ton of CO_2, and it increases to over $1000 per ton by the end of the century. In a very broad sense, this architecture is inspired by the work of McKibbin and Wilcoxen (2007), who emphasize the absence of international carbon trading as one of the key features of their proposed policy architecture.[5]

---

[5] A large increase in the carbon tax rate over time is necessary to induce the short-run investments required to reduce GHG emissions in the long run. This may

Reducing Emissions from Deforestation and Degradation (REDD)

One proposal is to allow tropical forest countries to set aside forest land that would otherwise be cleared in exchange for payment from industrialized countries looking to reduce their carbon emissions in order to meet targets set under international agreements like the Kyoto Protocol. According to Ebeling (2006), the inclusion of REDD in a climate agreement would significantly lower the costs of meeting a given environmental target. Similar proposals to include the Clean Development Mechanism (CDM) and other programs to avoid deforestation in international climate agreements have been put forward by Plantinga and Richards (see, e.g., Plantinga and Richards 2008).

This architecture for agreement entails essentially the same instruments as the cap-and-trade-with-redistribution proposal discussed previously. However, it also includes avoided deforestation as a potential mitigation option, with CO_2 abatement from avoided deforestation in the Amazon forest included in the global permit market.

Although the Bali Action Plan explicitly addresses the need for *"policy approaches and positive incentives on issues relating to reducing emissions from deforestation and forest degradation in developing countries,"* there are still many unresolved issues, ranging from the definition of forestry to the issue of additionality and the definition of baselines. For this reason we make here the very conservative assumption that only Brazil is allowed to get credits for avoided emissions from deforestation. Indeed, Brazil is the only country that already has a monitoring and enforcement system in place.

Results on the economic efficiency of including REDD would be strengthened if the crediting system were open to other countries, such as the Democratic Republic of Congo or Papua New Guinea, although time would be needed to have a crediting system in place in those countries.

raise an issue of time inconsistency for this policy architecture (as well as for all architectures based on cap and trade) as noted by Montgomery and Smith (2005). However, the implicit assumption here is that reputation effects are strong enough to get rid of policy time inconsistency.

Specific abatement costs[6] for the avoided-deforestation mitigation option were considered, with the opportunity costs of developing forested land under alternative land uses as a proxy.

Climate clubs

This architecture for an international agreement is inspired by the proposal put forward by Victor (2007). Differentiated effort is expected from different regions of the world, depending on their ability to abate. A group of virtuous regions—"the climate club"[7]—agrees to abide by their Kyoto target, reducing GHG emissions by 70 percent below their emission levels in the 1990s by the year 2050. Their effort is to some degree compensated by joint cooperation in technology development, which increases the knowledge spillovers generated by energy efficiency improvements and R&D efforts to develop new, carbon-free technologies across regions that belong to the climate club.

Fast-growing countries or regions—like China, India, Latin America, the transition economies, and the Middle East—are also part of the global deal, but their effort is gradual. These countries face increasingly stringent targets[8] to reduce their CO_2 emissions below what they would emit in a BAU scenario. In the second half of the century, fast-growing countries agree to increase their abatement effort to converge towards the effort of the climate club. The rest of the world does not have any binding target.[9]

---

[6] Data on REDD supply curves comprise estimates of the opportunity costs of reducing deforestation emissions in the Brazilian Amazon only and are based on data from the Woods Hole Research Center (Nepstad *et al.* 2007). Supply estimates from the tropical Asian region will also be included once available.

[7] The members of the Climate Club are the United States, Europe, Canada, Japan, New Zealand, Australia, South Korea, and South Africa.

[8] The target is to reduce industrial CO_2 emissions by 5 percent with respect to BAU by 2020, by 10 percent with respect to BAU by 2030, by 20 percent with respect to BAU by 2040, and by 30 percent with respect to BAU by 2050.

[9] Different versions of the climate club architecture were simulated to test sensitivity to a number of parameters—including the definition of the club (e.g., having the Middle East within the Rest of the World group), assumptions about global emission trading, and the definition of enhanced spillovers within the climate club—and to measure the penalty imposed by the club structure as opposed to an agreement characterized by full and immediate participation.

There is a global market for carbon permits, in which all regions may participate. Regions that do not have an explicit emission reduction target must commit to not exceeding their BAU emissions level in order to participate in the carbon market: this expedient encourages abatement from non-signatories, and thus reduces the incentive to free ride.

Burden sharing

A key feature of this post-Kyoto architecture is the delayed participation of non-Annex I countries. While the group of Annex I countries commit to undertake abatement efforts immediately, with the burden shared on an equal per capita basis, non-Annex I countries are initially required to commit to not emitting more than their projected emissions under the BAU scenario, in order to avoid incentives for free riding and carbon leakage. Indeed, although non-Annex I countries already have higher total emissions than Annex I countries, differences in per capita terms are still very significant: per capita emissions in developing non-Annex I countries are still very low and may justify a delay in these countries' participation in a global agreement to control climate change.

After an initial phase in which only Annex I countries cooperate to control CO_2 emissions, binding abatement targets are extended to the whole world in 2040, except for sub-Saharan Africa where the level of development remains well below the world average.

This architecture is inspired by the policy proposal developed by Keeler (see, for instance, Keeler and Thompson 2008) and by results in Bosetti, Carraro, and Tavoni (2008).

Graduation

Inspired by Michaelowa's proposal (Michaelowa 2007), this policy architecture entails differentiated efforts among signatory countries, with differentiation based on the satisfaction of bottom-up graduation criteria and with the ultimate objective of stabilizing atmospheric CO_2 concentrations at 450 ppm.

The idea of bottom-up targets is that they can account for regions' differing abilities to undertake abatement efforts and their differing contributions to the climate change problem. Graduation to binding targets is based on the satisfaction of two criteria based on per capita income and emissions relative to the world average.[10]

Annex I countries do not graduate, but rather enhance their abatement effort in order to compensate for the emissions of non-Annex I countries and ensure the achievement of the 450 ppm stabilization target.

Dynamic targets

This policy architecture is notable for being deeply rooted in political reality and in statements made by political leaders. Inspired by the proposal developed in Frankel 2007, bottom-up targets are based on progressive cut factors—initially applied to a 1990 baseline for the first period, and subsequently applied to projected emissions under the BAU scenario, corrected by a Lieberman-Lee "latecomer catch-up" factor for countries that have not yet ratified Kyoto.

Progressive cut factors take into account historic emissions relative to the emissions of the European Union in 1990, current and projected emissions in the BAU scenario, income per capita relative to the EU average, and population. The target-setting rule thus explicitly accounts for the fact that emissions from developing countries will soon overtake those of industrialized countries on an absolute—though not necessarily on a per capita—basis.

Targets are defined for all regions, with the world divided into three broad groups. The first group of early movers includes Europe, the United States, Canada, Japan, New Zealand, Australia, South Korea, and South Africa and takes action from 2010 to 2015 and from 2015 to 2025. The second group, late comers, includes China and Latin America—which face binding emission reduction targets starting in

[10] The first graduation step is reached when the average of the two criteria is satisfied, that is, emissions per capita match average world per capita emissions, and income per capita increases to $5,000 (2005 value). When countries reach the first graduation level, their abatement target is equivalent to a 5 percent reduction with respect to 2005 emissions. The second graduation period is reached when emissions per capita are 1.5 times the world average and income per capita is $10,000. This second step entails a reduction in emissions of 10 percent with respect to 2005 levels. The only exception is China, which reduces emissions gradually, starting from 2050, in order to cut its emissions 50 percent below its 2005 baseline. Sub-Saharan Africa never graduates, and therefore faces no binding targets. This region does, however, commit to keeping emissions at or below BAU levels, in order to be able to participate in the carbon market.

2035—and India, which faces binding targets starting from 2050. The third group includes all other regions; it faces no binding targets but agrees not to exceed BAU emissions and can thus take part in the international market for carbon permits. Sub-Saharan Africa does not face any emission target until 2030, after which it enters the market for carbon permits by committing not to exceed its BAU emissions.

R&D and technology development

This last policy architecture is very different in nature from the previous ones because it does not entail any emission reduction target. Inspired by the proposal developed in Barrett 2007, its main concern is to ensure the acceptability of the global agreement. It therefore focuses on R&D policies only, because they are characterized by a different incentive structure—that is, they provide a club good rather than a public good.

In this architecture for a global deal, all regions of the world agree to contribute a fixed percentage of their gross domestic product (GDP) to establish an international fund to foster the advancement of climate-related technologies. The share of GDP devoted to technology improvements is roughly equal to double the level of public expenditures on energy R&D in the 1980s, which amounts to about 0.2 percent of regional GDP (see Bosetti, Carraro *et al.* 2007a for an analysis of optimal energy R&D investment strategies).

The financial resources of the fund are redistributed to all regions on an equal per capita basis, and they are equally split to foster the deployment of two key categories of low-carbon technology—(1) wind and solar energy and (2) carbon capture and sequestration—and to promote innovation in a breakthrough zero-carbon technology for the non-electric sector. The subsidy to new technologies lowers their costs, favors their deployment, and leads to emission reductions as a by-product of transitioning to a lower-carbon technology mix.

Assessing architectures for agreement

Climate effectiveness

The first and most important objective of a climate treaty, most would argue, is its environmental effectiveness—that is, the degree to which the problems associated with climatic change are addressed.

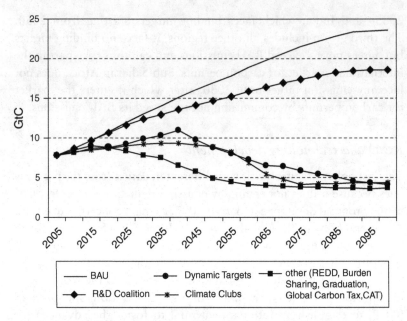

Figure 23.2. Global energy CO_2 emissions paths

Figure 23.2 shows the path of industrial CO_2 emissions implied by the eight architectures for agreement described briefly above and by the BAU scenario. In the BAU scenario, global atmospheric carbon emissions are projected to continue increasing from the current level of slightly less than 8 gigatonnes (or billion metric tons) carbon (GtC) to over 22 GtC by 2100. The more stringent architectures lead to a stabilization of emissions at well below 5 GtC by the middle of the century. These more stringent architectures all assume global participation using different policy instruments to implement reductions: cap and trade, with and without avoided deforestation, and a global carbon tax. These three architectures are characterized by an explicit, top-down target for stabilizing atmospheric CO_2 concentrations, which is set at 450ppm. Interestingly, one of the architectures based on bottom-up targets—the graduation architecture—also leads to the stabilization of CO_2 concentrations at 450 ppm.

A second set of architectures which rely on either universal participation with incremental, rather than immediate, effort, or on partial participation, achieve the same level of emissions at the end of the century, but through a different transition path. These architectures

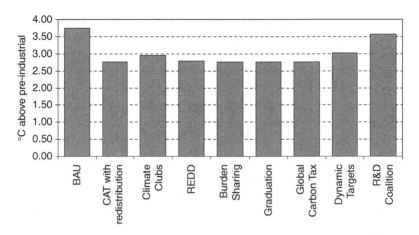

Figure 23.3. Temperature change above pre-industrial levels in 2100

are Dynamic Targets and Climate Club with late comers. Their emissions paths are less smooth than those for reducing emissions from deforestation and degradation (REDD) or cap and trade (CAT), reflecting the different dates at which regions start to face binding constraints. Consequently, these two architectures would achieve a less stringent stabilization target: atmospheric CO_2 concentrations stabilize at about 550 ppm rather than around 450 ppm.

Finally, the architecture that envisions a global coalition cooperating on energy R&D does not achieve the stabilization of CO_2 emissions— and consequently of atmospheric concentrations —even though emissions are lower than for BAU. Over the century, cumulative emissions are only 17 percent lower than in the BAU trajectory, as opposed to an average of 62 percent lower for the other policy architectures. Let us recall, however, that the crucial feature of this policy architecture is its focus on providing adequate incentives for cooperation; it is not designed to achieve a given stabilization target with high costs and limited incentives.

Figure 23.3 shows the expected temperature increase above pre-industrial levels as a result of the different architectures in 2100.[11] Even though the magnitude of the increase implied by each of the

---

[11] We used the MAGICC model to relate emissions and concentrations to temperature changes.

proposed architectures is to be taken as a rough estimate, given the many scientific uncertainties involved in projecting climate impacts, this comparison provides a relative ranking of the proposals with respect to their effectiveness in mitigating global temperature change.

In the BAU scenario, where no international policy to curb CO_2 emissions is implemented, temperature change is expected to reach 3.7 degrees Celsius (°C) above pre-industrial levels in 2100. When cooperation on low-carbon technologies and zero-carbon breakthrough innovation is pursued in the absence of any emission reduction targets, the expected temperature increase is only slightly lower, at 3.5°C. The more environmentally aggressive policy architectures yield a temperature change of around 2.7°C, whereas intermediate efforts lead to a temperature increase of around 3°C.

It is thus clear that none of the policy architectures analyzed in this chapter are able to keep global average temperature change below the 2°C threshold advocated by more proactive parties like the European Union.[12] On the other hand, stabilizing emissions below 5 GtC keeps temperature change below 3°C, the less stringent upper limit often called for by the United States (Newell and Hall 2007). However, we must recognize that some proposals (e.g., dynamic targets or climate clubs) do not explicitly refer to a single stabilization target and could be modified to account for more ambitious stabilization scenarios (i.e., scenarios that aim to achieve the 2°C target with a higher degree of probability).

In order to check whether different proposals entail different paths of temperature change, we also consider the rate of temperature change over the century. Even though it is difficult to know what path of temperature change is best, given our ignorance about the existence of potential threshold effects, it is reasonable to think that more gradual temperature changes will entail lower costs—if not economic, then at least environmental, as more gradual changes imply more time for ecosystems to adapt. To that end, in addition to quantifying the total temperature increase expected by the end of the century under different scenarios, we also count the number of five-year periods for which the predicted temperature increase is

[12] One should keep in mind that the carbon signal that would be generated by such policies would imply significant abatement in other GHGs as well, if they were to be included in the policy agreement. This would reduce the expected increase in global average temperature by roughly an additional 0.2°C.

Table 23.2 *Number of times that five-year temperature change is greater than 0.1°C*

BAU	CAT with redistri- bution	Climate Clubs	REDD	Burden Sharing	Gradua- tion	Global Carbon Tax	Dynamic Targets	R&D Coalition
19	12	14	12	12	12	12	14	19

greater than 0.1°C with respect to the previous five-year period, as shown in Table 23.2. The effect of the different policy architectures on the rate of temperature change is very similar to their overall effect on temperature—that is, more stringent architectures result in fewer periods with a predicted temperature change greater than 0.1°C over the previous period. Similarly, the least stringent architecture, R&D Coalition with no explicit emission target, produces results similar to the BAU scenario.

Economic efficiency

Different emissions paths resulting from the eight policy architectures imply different streams of costs. We therefore adopt a simple criterion for comparing the cost implications of the post-Kyoto proposals: we compute the difference in gross world product (GWP) under each one of the proposed policies in comparison to the BAU scenario.[13] This global indicator is defined as the discounted sum of GDP losses over the next century, aggregated across world regions and subject to a 5 percent discount rate (a rate which is close to the average market interest rate). To avoid the debate on the appropriate assessment of damages (e.g., whether the focus should be on gross costs or on costs net of adaptation and related costs), we consider here the pure cost of climate policy without taking into account the benefits from avoided climate damage, which are separately measured through the

---

[13] Although it is widely recognized that policy costs depend crucially on basic assumptions behind the BAU scenario (which in turn drive estimates of BAU emissions and GDP), in the present analysis the *relative* cost of different archi- tectures is what we are mostly interested in. Therefore, we do not perform a sensitivity analysis of the impact of different baseline assumptions.

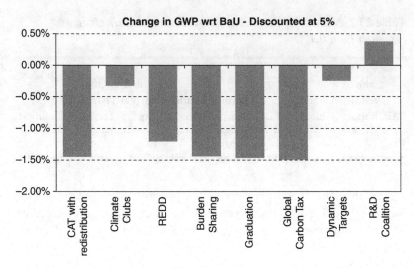

Figure 23.4. Implications for GWP

environmental effectiveness indicator. Policymakers can aggregate GWP losses with temperature increases *ex post* and compute the ranking using the range of weights they believe should be applied to both metrics.

While temperature change varies less across the eight architectures considered for this analysis because of the inertia in the climate system, the economic costs of the different set-ups vary considerably. Figure 23.4 shows that more stringent policy architectures imply a higher GWP loss. Stabilizing atmospheric CO_2 concentrations at 450 ppm would cost between 1.2 percent and 1.49 percent of GWP. The most costly architecture would be the autarchic global tax implemented domestically, and the least costly would be the global cap and trade with emission reduction from avoided deforestation as an option (REDD). The inclusion of avoided deforestation as a mitigation option reduces the costs of meeting the environmental target from 1.49 percent of GWP to slightly above 1.2 percent.

Climate clubs and dynamic targets—which stabilize CO_2 concentrations at about 490 ppm and 500 ppm respectively—entail moderate costs: around 0.32 percent and 0.24 percent of GWP respectively.

Finally, the R&D Coalition is the only architecture that leads to gains at the global level of about 0.37 percent of GWP. These gains are explained by the positive effects of R&D cooperation that reduces

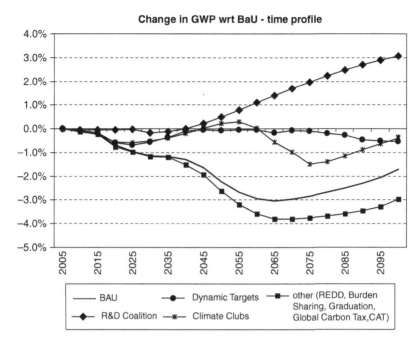

Figure 23.5. Temporal distribution of the policy costs

free-riding incentives on knowledge production.[14] By internalizing international and intertemporal knowledge spillovers, the R&D Coalition policy architecture leads to higher levels of GWP after an initial period of net losses due to the increased investments in R&D (see Figure 23.5 on the temporal distribution of policy costs).

When we look at the temporal distribution of costs associated with the different architectures (see Figure 23.5) we see that the stringent architectures that require universal and immediate action imply an immediate loss of GWP, rising up to 4 percent by the middle of the century. Gradual effort implies, on the other hand, less costly intervention at the beginning of the century. Also, the progressive inclusion in the agreement (and in the international carbon market) of some non-Annex I countries alleviates the global burden. Only the global coalition based on R&D cooperation leads to gains starting in

---

[14] See Bosetti, Carraro *et al.* 2007b for a detailed analysis of knowledge spillovers.

2040—though it too implies short-term costs due to the diversion of resources to replenish the global R&D fund.

Equity and distributional impacts

The distribution of costs and benefits from climate change and climate-change policy is of paramount importance in determining both the feasibility and desirability of a specific architecture for agreement. The analysis of how GDP changes over time for different world regions in the different scenarios may offer some indications as to what the distributional implications of climate policies are and can serve to highlight winners and losers under each scenario. This information is likely to be important for policymakers and negotiators.

Several criteria have been proposed in the literature for measuring the equity and distributional implications of climate change agreements (see, e.g., Goulder 2000). Examples of such criteria include responsibility for the problem, ability to pay, or distribution of the benefits from controlling climate change. While the first two criteria would seem to indicate that industrialized countries should bear most of the burden of controlling climate change, the last criterion would imply that developing countries—who would be the largest beneficiaries from controlling climate change—should bear a relatively higher share of the burden (Aldy, Barrett *et al.* 2003).

In principle, the best way to address equity and distributional issues in the context of climate change would be to undertake a full cost-benefit analysis, assuming cooperation among countries and changing the set of weights used to aggregate different countries to account for equity concerns. The main difficulty in applying this approach stems from the fact that damage functions are still far from being well-defined, particularly at the regional level. In addition, adaptation policies and their trade-offs with mitigation policies would become a crucial component of the analysis.

For the purpose of our assessment, we abstract from the current debate and use a compact measure of distributional equity to characterize the eight policy architectures and the BAU scenario. We compute the Gini Index for GDP in 2100 to show the concentration of income in different regions of the world and measure inequality in income distribution (the lower the value of the Gini index, the more equal the distribution of income).

Table 23.3 *Gini index in 2100*

BAU	CAT with redistri- bution	Climate Clubs	REDD	Burden Sharing	Grad- uation	Global Carbon Tax	Dynamic Targets	R&D Coalition
0.200	0.198	0.158	0.197	0.196	0.158	0.178	0.156	0.181

In all scenarios, there is an improvement in the distribution of income across the world's regions with respect to the current situation. However, Table 23.3 also reveals some differences: three policy architectures emerge as being more egalitarian, since they distribute the effort in a fair way according to per capita income and average per capita emissions. These are the Dynamic Targets approach, which uses historical emissions and projected BAU emissions to determine regional efforts, and the Climate Clubs and Graduation approaches.

By comparing the two global architectures with a stabilization target, immediate participation, and implementation through a cap-and-trade system—with redistribution in one case and with REDD in the other case—we can observe that including avoided deforestation among the mitigation options leads to an improvement in the distribution of income across regions. This reflects the fact that avoided deforestation is mostly an option in developing and tropical countries. Finally, notice that the Carbon Tax policy is an intermediate one in terms of distributional effects.

Enforceability and feasibility

In the context of international agreements, enforceability and compliance become a critical issue: the national sovereignty of individual states may lead to strategic behavior, free-riding incentives, and to countries not complying with the agreement they have signed. Ideally, a global deal for climate change would sustain full participation and compliance, while ensuring an efficient level of emission reduction. Yet, because of the lack of a supranational institution able to enforce a climate policy, achieving global agreement on controlling GHG emissions may be very difficult if not impossible (Barrett, 2003).

When analyzing the feasibility and enforceability of proposed architectures for agreement, one should therefore assess whether different set-ups limit incentives to free ride, and whether they would be enforceable. Debate about the feasibility and enforceability of post-Kyoto architectures so far has been limited to qualitative analysis; there has been no attempt to quantify the degree to which each architecture deters free-riding behavior. In this chapter, we borrow concepts from game theory to derive quantitative measures of enforceability and political acceptability for all policies, at global and regional levels respectively.

We use the concept of "potential internal stability" (see Carraro, Eyckmans, and Finus 2006 for a definition and discussion of this term) as a proxy for the theoretical enforceability of the agreement. This is a weak stability concept in the sense that an agreement is said to be potentially internally stable if the aggregate payoffs are at least as large as the sum of the regional payoffs in the BAU scenario. If this condition is satisfied, all coalition members could be at least as well off as under BAU through suitably designed transfer schemes. Global welfare is computed as the sum of welfare for each region.[15]

From the first column of Table 23.4, it is clear that all but one of the architectures imply an *improvement* in global welfare over the status quo: if one could design appropriate transfer schemes, then all regions could be made at least as well off as under the BAU scenario. The only exception is the autarchic coalition, where all countries, including developing countries, are required to undertake emission reductions domestically by imposing a carbon tax. In particular, if global welfare is the only metric, then Cap-and-Trade with redistribution is the policy to be preferred. Notice however that most of the welfare gains are experienced in developing countries (and depend on the allocation of the burden of climate policy). Hence, the stability of the agreements would require the transfer of resources from developing to developed countries—which is unlikely to be politically acceptable and feasible.

---

[15] Most of the agreements result in a global welfare improvement. It should, however, be noticed that global welfare is here measured by using a utilitarian approach (no specific weights are used to aggregate welfare over regions). The positive global welfare improvement in some cases depends on the fact that very few countries are largely better off whereas most countries are worse off. For this reason we use a second indicator defined by the number of regions that are better off.

Table 23.4 *Potential enforceability and political acceptability*

	Potential stability World welfare	Feasibility
	% change wrt BAU	No. of countries with +ve variation in welfare
CAT with redistribution	0.681%	3
Climate Clubs	0.183%	6
REDD	0.456%	4
Burden Sharing	0.243%	3
Graduation	0.085%	3
Global Carbon Tax	−0.168%	0
Dynamic Targets	0.202%	5
R&D Coalition	0.103%	12

How to aggregate welfare across regions is a challenging question that is far from being resolved. For this reason we complement the potential internal stability metric with an indicator of the potential enforceability of the architectures, as summarized in the second column of Table 23.4. If we consider the policy that maximizes the number of regions with an improvement in welfare then Climate Clubs would be the preferred agreement and Cap and Trade with redistribution would be ranked fourth.

While at the global level almost all architectures for agreement seem to be potentially enforceable, the picture is very different when we move down to explore the feasibility of the proposals at the regional level. The last column of Table 23.4 shows the likely political feasibility of each policy architecture, approximated by the number of regions whose welfare under the specific climate policy architecture is higher than in the BAU scenario. Thus, the higher the number of countries that find a specific coalition profitable from an individual perspective, the more likely it is that the architecture is politically acceptable. Notice that individual profitability is only a necessary condition for stability if the latter is defined in the usual manner—that is, using the concept of cartel stability proposed in industrial organization (see Carraro and Siniscalco 1993). However, individual profitability may become a sufficient condition for stability if a concept of farsighted stability is adopted (Chew 1994) or if a minimum participation constraint is imposed (Carraro, Marchiori, and Oreffice 2003).

It is clear that in the R&D Coalition and Climate Clubs architectures, both of which involve some form of cooperation on R&D, a large share of countries find the agreement profitable (*all* and *half* of the countries are better off, respectively). The result on the Climate Club architecture is particularly interesting, as it seems to support a role for issue linkage in generating scope for gains from cooperation. The universal but incremental coalition based on Dynamic Targets is also likely to be politically feasible, as five out of twelve regions find it profitable: it is quite likely that a careful revision of the criteria for setting binding emission reduction targets could lead to a redistribution of welfare so that all countries would be better off.

The above analysis of the political acceptability and potential enforceability of proposed post-2012 climate policy architectures is clearly a simplification and can be criticized on various grounds, such as (1) the choice of the welfare indicator or (2) the fact that other important factors, which may determine ultimately whether an international agreement can be accepted at the national level, are overlooked. Our results do, nonetheless, provide a good starting point for assessing the enforceability dimensions of the proposed architectures for agreement.

Summary of the comparison analysis

Table 23.5 summarizes the performance of the different post-Kyoto architectures we considered according to the criteria discussed in foregoing sections. Significant differences are reported, which makes an unequivocal ranking of different architectures impossible. Some clear indications emerge nonetheless. The architectures have been ordered by increasing environmental performance. Notice, however, that this produces the same result as ordering by decreasing economic cost— that is, increasing costs (the second column). It also corresponds to declining scores for enforceability.

There is therefore evidence of a perfect trade-off between environmental effectiveness and economic efficiency and enforceability.

Among the environmentally more efficient architectures—Cap and Trade, reducing emissions from deforestation and degradation (REDD), Burden Sharing, Graduation, and Global Carbon Tax—results for the

Table 23.5 *Assessment criteria for the different policy architectures*

	Environmental Effectiveness (T°C above pre-industrial)	Economic Efficiency (GDP change wrt BAU, 5% d.r.)	Distributional Impact (Gini 2100)	Enforceability (Countries with positive welfare change, out of 12)
BAU	3.75	–	0.200	–
R&D Coalition	3.58	0.37%	0.181	12
Dynamic Targets	3.02	–0.24%	0.156	5
Climate Clubs	2.95	–0.32%	0.158	6
REDD	2.76	–1.20%	0.197	4
Burden Sharing	2.76	–1.44%	0.196	3
CAT with redistribution	2.76	–1.45%	0.198	3
Graduation	2.76	–1.47%	0.158	3
Global Carbon Tax	2.76	–1.49%	0.178	0

REDD approach show that the inclusion of deforestation in a climate agreement can significantly improve the economic efficiency of the policy, and also its enforceability, since recognizing forestry changes provides additional incentives for participation to some developing countries. Note however that for all these architectures GWP losses are above 1 percent. Graduation reports the fairer distribution of income within this group.

Dynamic Targets and Climate Clubs are policies that come at a very low economic cost, though obviously at the expense of foregone climate effectiveness. They both perform well in terms of distribution and feasibility. Finally, the R&D Coalition architecture actually improves world economic performance, which suggests that all regions should be willing to participate, but it achieves very little in terms of climate protection.

Multi-criteria techniques could be used to provide a more precise ranking of the climate policy architectures analyzed in this chapter.

As an example, one can apply the min-max criterion to identify the architecture that minimizes the maximum possible loss across all dimensions considered. According to this criterion, the R&D Coalition is to be preferred to all other architectures. Given the uncertain nature of the issues at stake, though, a deterministic approach could lead to misleading conclusions. Further investigation based on stochastic data envelopment analysis and other probabilistic multi-criteria approaches could help in identifying the most robust climate policy architectures.

Conclusions and policy implications

In this chapter, we have evaluated eight policy architectures that can be briefly described as follows:

1. *Global Cap-and-Trade system with redistribution*: All nations participate immediately in a global cap-and-trade system designed to stabilize atmospheric CO_2 at 450 ppm by 2100. Permits are allocated to all countries on an equal per capita basis.
2. *Global Tax recycled domestically*: All countries apply a globally consistent carbon tax designed to achieve the same stabilization trajectory as above. Revenues from the tax are recycled domestically and implementation begins immediately.
3. *Reducing Emissions from Deforestation and Degradation (REDD)*: Same as the first scenario, except credits from avoided Amazon deforestation are included in the permit market.
4. *Climate Clubs*: In this scenario, a group of mostly advanced economies agrees to abide by its Kyoto target and reduce GHG emissions 70 percent below 1990 levels by 2050. Other fast-growing countries and regions begin gradual efforts to reduce emissions below BAU, but converge to the same level of reductions as the first group after 2050. All remaining countries face no binding targets, but their emissions are limited to BAU.
5. *Burden Sharing*: Developed (Annex I) countries commence abatement immediately, with the burden shared on an equal per capita basis. Binding emissions targets are extended to all other countries, except those in sub-Saharan Africa, in 2040.
6. *Graduation*: Countries adopt binding emission targets as they reach specified criteria for income and emissions. Annex I countries

compensate for the delayed entry of non-Annex I countries by undertaking additional reductions as required to achieve a 450 ppm stabilization trajectory.

7. *Dynamic Targets*: Different countries adopt different targets over time depending on current and projected emissions, income, and population.

8. *R&D and technology development*: No binding emissions targets; instead all countries contribute a fixed percentage of GDP to an international fund for developing low-carbon technologies.

The quantitative comparison of these architectures has focused on the following four features:

- *Relative environmental effectiveness*, measured as temperature change above pre-industrial levels in 2100;
- *Economic efficiency*, measured as change in GWP compared to projected GWP under BAU conditions;
- *Distributional implications*, assessed by the Gini index at the end of the century; and
- *Potential enforceability*, measured by changes in global and regional welfare with respect to the BAU scenario.

These indicators are meant to provide policymakers with a clearer picture of the various implications of some of the policy options currently on the table in international climate negotiations.

We draw on the comparative analysis presented in the previous sections to offer a series of general recommendations.

First, limiting warming to 2°C, as envisaged by the IPCC and the European Commission, requires more drastic measures than those indicated in all the policy architectures considered in this chapter.

Second, non-CO_2 gases should be included among the mitigation options in an international agreement: not only would their inclusion lead to lower temperature increases for a similar concentration of CO_2 in the atmosphere, it would also lower the cost of meeting a given stabilization target.

Third, a clear trade-off between environmental effectiveness and economic efficiency emerges from our analysis, as does another clear trade-off between environmental effectiveness and political enforceability.

Fourth, the inclusion of avoided deforestation reduces the cost of a policy and improves enforceability.

Fifth, an international climate policy can achieve a fairer distribution of income worldwide, but the global economic loss is small only for policies that aim at intermediate stabilization objectives, in the range of 650 ppm CO_2-equivalent for all GHGs (550 ppm for CO_2 only). This stabilization target is shown to have little impact on economic activity, but may not provide sufficient climate protection.

Finally, policies to promote R&D cooperation that do not involve any carbon constraints or taxes are shown to have a marginal effect on climate, though a positive one on economic activity. Thus, they are likely to be the only ones that lead to a global, self-enforcing agreement.

Far from providing a final and unique answer, this analysis is intended as a starting point for other critical comparisons of proposals for climate policy agreements. Further research may adopt more sophisticated analytical tools to account for the public perception of climate change and for varying priorities among the different dimensions considered.

References

Aldy, J., S. Barrett, and R. N. Stavins (2003). "Thirteen Plus One: A Comparison of Global Climate Policy Architectures," *Climate Policy* 3(4): 373–97.

Aldy, J. and R. N. Stavins, eds. (2007). *Architectures for Agreement: Addressing Global Climate Change in the Post-Kyoto World.* Cambridge, UK: Cambridge University Press.

Aldy, J. and R. N. Stavins (2008). "Climate Policy Architectures for the Post-Kyoto World," *Environment* 50: 6–17.

Aldy, J., R. N. Stavins, C. Carraro, and W. A. Pizer (2007). "Architectures for Agreement: Issues and Options for Post-2012 International Climate Change Policy," paper presented at Conference of the Parties, Cambridge, MA: Harvard Project on International Climate Agreements, Bali, Indonesia.

Barrett, S. (2003). *Environment and Statecraft*, Oxford: Oxford University Press.

(2007). "A Multitrack Climate Treaty System," in Aldy and Stavins (eds.), pp. 237–59.

Bosetti, V., C. Carraro, M. Galeotti, E. Massetti, and M. Tavoni (2006). "WITCH: A World Induced Technical Change Hybrid Model," *The Energy Journal*, Special Issue on Hybrid Modeling of Energy-Environment Policies: Reconciling Bottom-up and Top-down: 13–38.

Bosetti, V., C. Carraro, E. Massetti, and M. Tavoni (2007). "International Energy R&D Spillovers and the Economics of Greenhouse Gas Atmospheric Stabilization," *Energy Economics* 30 (2008): 2912–29.

Bosetti, V., C. Carraro, E. Massetti, A. Sgobbi, and M. Tavoni (2008a). "Optimal Energy Investment and R&D Strategies to Stabilize Greenhouse Gas Atmospheric Concentrations," *Resource Energy Economics* 31(2) (May 2009): 123–7.

Bosetti, V., C. Carraro, and M. Tavoni (2008b). "Delayed Participation of Developing Countries to Climate Agreements: Should Action in the EU and US be Postponed?" FEEM Nota di Lavoro 70.08 and CEPR Working Paper 6967 and CESifo Discussion Paper 2445.

Bosetti, V., C. Carraro, R. Duval, A. Sgobbi, and M. Tavoni (2009). "The Role of R&D and Technology Diffusion in Climate Change Mitigation: New Perspectives Using the WITCH Model," OECD Economics Department Working Paper, No. 664, OECD publishing.

Carraro, C., J. Eyckmans, and M. Finus (2006). "Optimal Transfers and Participation Decisions in International Environmental Agreements," *Review of International Organizations* 1(4): 379–96.

Carraro, C., M. Marchiori, and S. Oreffice (2003). "Endogenous Minimum Participation in International Environmental Treaties," FEEM Nota di Lavoro 113.03 and CEPR DP 4281.

Carraro, C. and D. Siniscalco (1993). "Strategies for the International Protection of the Environment," *Journal of Public Economics* 52(3): 309–28, October.

Chew, M. S.-Y. (1994). "Farsighted Coalitional Stability," *Journal of Economic Theory* 63: 299–325.

Ebeling, J. (2006). "Tropical Deforestation and Climate Change: Towards an International Mitigation Strategy," University of Oxford, Oxford.

Frankel, J. (2007). "Formulas for Quantitative Emission Targets," in Aldy and Stavins (eds.), pp. 31–56.

Goulder, L. H. (2000). "Central Themes and Research Results in Global Climate Change Policy," Paper prepared for the Intergovernmental Panel on Climate Change, Working Group III, Third Assessment Report, Stanford, California.

IEA (2002). *Beyond Kyoto: Energy Dynamics and Climate Stabilization*. Paris: IEA.

IPCC (2007). "Climate Change 2007: Synthesis Report," Geneva: IPCC.

Keeler, A. and A. Thompson (2008). "Rich Country Mitigation Policy and Resource Transfers to Poor Countries," paper presented at the Harvard Project on International Climate Agreements First Workshop, Cambridge, MA, March 15–16.

McKibbin, W. J. and P. J. Wilcoxen (2007). "A Credible Foundation for Long-Term International Cooperation on Climate Change," in Aldy and Stavins (eds.), pp. 185–208.

Michaelowa, A. (2007). "Graduation and Deepening," in Aldy and Stavins (eds.), pp. 81–104.

Montgomery, D. W. and A. E. Smith (2005). "Price, Quantity and Technology Strategies for Climate Change Policy," Boston, MA: CRA International.

Nepstad, D., B. Soares-Filho, F. Merry *et al.* (2007). "Reducing Emissions from Deforestation and Forest Degradation (REDD): The Costs and Benefits of Reducing Carbon Emissions from Deforestation and Forest Degradation in the Brazilian Amazon." Falmouth, MA: Woods Hole Research Center. www.whrc.org/resources/published_literature/pdf/WHRC_REDD_Amazon.pdf.

Newell, R. and D. Hall (2007). "U.S. Climate Mitigation in the Context of Global Stabilization," Washington DC: Resources for the Future.

Plantinga, A. J. and K. R. Richards (2008). "The Role of Terrestrial Carbon Sequestration in a Post-Kyoto International Climate Change Treaty," paper presented at the Harvard Project on International Climate Agreements First Workshop, Cambridge, MA, March 15–16.

Stern, N. (2008). "Key Elements of a Global Deal on Climate Change," London: The London School of Economics and Political Science.

Victor, D. (2007). "Fragmented Carbon Markets and Reluctant Nations: Implications for the Design of Effective Architectures," in Aldy and Stavins (eds.), pp. 133–60.

Wigley, T. M. L., R. Richels, and J. A. Edmonds (1996). "Economic and Environmental Choices in the Stabilization of Atmospheric CO_2 Concentrations," *Nature* 379: 240–3.

Appendix: Description of WITCH

Full details on the WITCH model can be found in Bosetti, Carraro *et al.* 2006. The description below focuses on the overall model structure, and on the specification of endogenous technical change processes.

Overall model structure

WITCH is a dynamic optimal growth general equilibrium model with a detailed ("bottom-up") representation of the energy sector, thus belonging to a new class of hybrid (both "top-down" and "bottom-up") models. It is a global model, divided into 12 macro-regions. A reduced form climate module (MAGICC) provides the climate feed-back on the economic system. The model covers CO_2 emissions but does not incorporate other GHGs, whose concentration is typically added exogenously to CO_2 concentration in order to obtain overall GHG concentration—a 450 ppm CO_2 concentration scenario is roughly assumed to correspond to a 550 ppm overall GHG concentration scenario in the simulations below. In addition to the full integration of a detailed representation of the energy sector into a macro model of the world economy, distinguishing features of the model are:

- *Endogenous technical change.* Advancements in carbon mitigation technologies are described by both diffusion and innovation processes. Learning by Doing and Learning by Researching (R&D) processes are explicitly modeled and enable identification of the "optimal"[16] public investment strategies in technologies and R&D in response to given climate policies. Some international technology spillovers are also modeled.
- *Game-theoretic set up.* The model can produce two different solutions, a cooperative one that is globally optimal (global central planner) and a decentralized, non-cooperative one that is strategically optimal for each given region (Nash equilibrium). As a result, externalities due to global public goods (CO_2, international knowledge spillovers, exhaustible resources, etc.) and the related free-riding incentives can both be accounted for, and the optimal policy response (world CO_2 emission reduction policy, world R&D policy) can be explored. A typical output of the model is an "optimal" carbon price path and the associated portfolio of investments in energy technologies and R&D under a given environmental target.[17]

Endogenous Technical Change (ETC) in the WITCH model

In the basic version of WITCH, technical change is endogenous and is driven both by learning-by-doing (LbD) and by public energy R&D

---

[16] Insofar as the solution concept adopted in the model is the Nash equilibrium (see below), "optimality" should not be interpreted as a first-best outcome but simply as a second-best outcome resulting from strategic optimization by each individual world region.

[17] A stochastic programming version of the model also exists to analyze optimal decisions under uncertainty and learning. However, it was not used within the context of this chapter.

investments.[18] These two drivers of technological improvements display their effects through two different channels: LbD is specific to the power generation industry, while energy R&D affects overall energy efficiency in the economy.

The effect of technology diffusion is incorporated based on experience curves that reproduce the observed negative empirical relationship between the investment cost of a given technology and cumulative installed capacity. Specifically, the cumulative installed world capacity is used as a proxy for the accrual of knowledge that affects the investment cost of a given technology:

$$SC\,(t+1) = A \sum_n K\,(n,t)^{-\log_2 PR} \tag{1}$$

where SC is the investment cost of technology j, PR is the so-called progress ratio that defines the speed of learning, A is a scale factor, and K is the cumulative installed capacity for region n at time t. With every doubling of cumulative capacity, the ratio of the new investment cost to its original value is constant and equal to $1/PR$. With several electricity production technologies, the model is flexible enough to change the power production mix and modify investment strategies towards the most appropriate technology for each given policy measure, thus creating the conditions to foster the LbD effects associated with emission-reducing but initially expensive electricity production techniques. Experience is assumed to fully spill over across countries, thus implying an innovation market failure associated with the non-appropriability of learning processes.

R&D investments in energy increase energy efficiency and thereby foster endogenous technical change. Following Popp (2004), technological advances are captured by a stock of knowledge combined with energy in a constant elasticity of substitution (CES) function, thus stimulating energy efficiency improvements:

$$ES(n,t) = \left[\alpha_H(n)HE(n,t)^\rho + \alpha_{EN}\,(n)EN(n,t)^\rho \right]^{1/\rho} \tag{2}$$

where $EN(n,t)$ denotes the energy input, $HE(n,t)$ is the stock of knowledge and $ES(n,t)$ is the amount of energy services produced by

---

[18] Due to data availability constraints, only public R&D is modelled in the current version of WITCH. However, private R&D would be expected to respond in a qualitatively similar way to climate change mitigation policies.

combining energy and knowledge. The stock of knowledge $HE(n,t)$ derives from energy R&D investments in each region through an innovation possibility frontier characterized by diminishing returns to research, a formulation proposed by Jones (1995) and empirically supported by Popp (2004) for energy-efficient innovations in the United States:

$$HE(n,t+1) = aI_{R\&D}(n,t)^b \, HE(n,t)^c + HE(n,t)\left(1-\delta_{R\&D}\right) \qquad (3)$$

where $\delta_{R\&D}$ is the depreciation rate of knowledge, and b and c are both between 0 and 1 so that there are diminishing returns to R&D both at any given time and across time periods. Reflecting the high social returns from energy R&D, it is assumed that the return on energy R&D investment is four times higher than that on physical capital. At the same time, the opportunity cost of crowding out other forms of R&D is obtained by subtracting four dollars of private investment from the physical capital stock for each dollar of R&D crowded out by energy R&D, $\psi_{R\&D}$, so that the net capital stock for final good production becomes:

$$K_C(n,t+1) = K_C(n,t)\left(1-\delta_C\right) + \left(I_C(n,t) - 4\Psi_{R\&D}I_{R\&D}(n,t)\right) \qquad (4)$$

where δ_C is the depreciation rate of the physical capital stock. New energy R&D is assumed to crowd out 50 percent of other R&D, as in Popp (2004).

The WITCH model has been extended to carry out the analysis presented in this chapter to include additional channels for technological improvements, namely learning through research or "learning-by-searching" (LbS) in existing low carbon technologies (wind and solar electricity, electricity from integrated gasifier combined cycle (IGCC) plants with carbon capture and storage (CCS)), and the possibility of developing breakthrough, zero-carbon technologies for both the electricity and non-electricity sectors.

Breakthrough technologies

In the enhanced version of the model used for this chapter, backstop technologies in both the electricity and non electricity sectors are developed and diffused in a two-stage process, through investments in R&D first and installed capacity in a second stage. A backstop technology can be better thought of as a compact representation of a portfolio of advanced technologies. These would ease the mitigation burden away from currently commercial options, but they would become commercially available only provided sufficient R&D investments are undertaken, and not before a few decades. This simplified representation maintains simplicity in the model by limiting the array of future energy technologies and thus the dimensionality of techno-economic parameters for which reliable estimates and meaningful modeling characterization exist.

Concretely, the backstop technologies are modeled using historical and current expenditures and installed capacity for technologies which are already researched but are not yet viable (e.g., fuel cells, advanced biofuels, advanced nuclear technologies, etc.), without specifying the type of technology that will enter into the market. In line with the most recent literature, the emergence of these backstop technologies is modeled through so-called "two-factor learning curves," in which the cost of a given backstop technology declines both with investment in dedicated R&D and with technology diffusion (see, e.g., Kouvaritakis, Soria *et al.* 2000). This formulation is meant to overcome the limitations of single factor experience curves, in which the cost of a technology declines only through "pure" LbD effects from technology diffusion, without the need for R&D investment (Nemet 2006). Nonetheless, modeling long-term and uncertain phenomena such as technological evolution is inherently difficult, which calls for caution in interpreting the exact quantitative results and for sensitivity analysis (see below).[19]

Bearing this caveat in mind, the investment cost in a technology *tec* is assumed to be driven both by LbS (main driving force before adoption) and LbD (main driving force after adoption), with $P_{tec,t}$, the unit cost of technology *tec* at time *t*, being a function of the dedicated R&D stock $R\&D_{tec,t}$ and deployment $CC_{tec,t}$:

$$\frac{P_{tec,T}}{P_{tec,0}} = \left(\frac{R\&D_{tec,T-2}}{R\&D_{tec,0}}\right)^{-e} * \left(\frac{CC_{tec,T}}{CC_{tec,0}}\right)^{-d} \tag{5}$$

---

[19] This is especially true when looking at the projected carbon prices and economic costs at long horizons—typically beyond 2030, while the short-run implications of long-run technological developments are comparatively more robust across a range of alternative technological scenarios (see below).

where the *R&D stock* accumulates with the perpetual inventory method and CC is the cumulative installed capacity (or consumption) of the technology. A two-period (10 years) lag is assumed between R&D capital accumulation and its effect on the price of the backstop technologies, capturing in a crude way existing time lags between research and commercialization. The two exponents are the LbD index (*d*) and the learning by researching index (*-e*). They define the speed of learning and are derived from the learning ratios. The learning ratio *r* is the rate at which the generating cost declines each time the cumulative capacity doubles, while *lrs* is the rate at which the cost declines each time the knowledge stock doubles. The relation between *d,-e,lr* and *lrs* can be expressed as follows:

$$1 - lr = 2^{-d} \text{ and } 1 - lrs = 2^{-e} \tag{6}$$

The initial prices of the backstop technologies are set at roughly 10 times the 2002 price of commercial equivalents. The cumulative deployment of the technology is initiated at 1000 TWh, an arbitrarily low value (Kypreos 2007). The backstop technologies are assumed to be renewable in the sense that the fuel cost component is negligible. For power generation, it is assumed to operate at load factors (defined as the ratio of actual to maximum potential output of a power plant) comparable with those of baseload power generation.

This formulation has received significant attention from the empirical and modeling literature in the recent past (see, for instance, Criqui, Klassen *et al.* 2000; Barreto and Kypreos 2004; Klassen, Miketa *et al.* 2005; Kypreos 2007; Jamasab 2007; Söderholm and Klassen 2007). However, estimates of parameters controlling the learning processes vary significantly across available studies. Here, averages of existing values are used, as reported in Figure 23.1. The value chosen for the LbD parameter is lower than those typically estimated in single factor experience curves, since here technological progress results in part from dedicated R&D investment. This more conservative approach reduces the role of "autonomous" learning, which has been seen as overly optimistic and leading to excessively low costs of transition towards low carbon economies.[20]

---

[20] Problems involved in estimating learning effects include: *i)* selection bias, i.e., technologies that experience smaller cost reductions drop out of the market and therefore of the estimation sample; *ii)* risks of reverse causation, i.e.,

Backstop technologies substitute linearly for nuclear power in the electricity sector, and for oil in the non-electricity sector. Once backstop technologies become competitive thanks to dedicated R&D investment and pilot deployments, their uptake is assumed to be gradual rather than immediate and complete. These penetration limits are a reflection of inertia in the system, as presumably the large deployment of backstops would require investment in infrastructures and wide re-organization of economic activity. The upper limit on penetration is set equivalent to 5 percent of the total consumption in the previous period by technologies other than the backstop, plus the electricity produced by the backstop in the electricity sector, and 7 percent in the non-electricity sector.

Spillovers in knowledge and experience

In addition to the international LbD spillovers mentioned above, WITCH also features international spillovers in knowledge for energy efficiency improvements. The amount of spillovers entering each world region is assumed to depend both on a pool of freely available world knowledge and on the ability of each country to benefit from it. In turn, this absorption capacity depends on the domestic knowledge stock, which is built up through domestic R&D according to a standard perpetual capital accumulation rule. The region then combines knowledge acquired from abroad with the domestic knowledge stock to produce new technologies at home. For details, see Bosetti, Carraro *et al.* 2008.

Footnote 20 (*cont.*)

cost reductions may induce greater deployment, so that attempts to force the reverse may lead to disappointing learning rates *a posteriori*; *iii)* the difficulty to discriminate between "pure" learning effects and the impact of accompanying R&D as captured through two-factor learning curves; *iv)* the fact that past cost declines may not provide a reliable indication of future cost reductions, as factors driving both may differ; *v)* the use of price—as opposed to cost—data, so that observed price reductions may reflect not only learning effects but also other factors such as strategic firm behavior under imperfect competition.

Appendix References

Barreto, L. and S. Kypreos (2004). "Endogenizing R&D and Market Experience in the 'Bottom-up' Energy-Systems ERIS model," *Technovation* 2: 615–29.

Bosetti, V., C. Carraro, M. Galeotti, E. Massetti, and M. Tavoni (2006). "WITCH: A World Induced Technical Change Hybrid Model," *The Energy Journal*, Special Issue on Hybrid Modeling of Energy-Environment Policies: Reconciling Bottom-up and Top-down: 13–38.

Bosetti, V., E. Massetti, and M. Tavoni (2007). "The WITCH Model: Structure, Baseline, Solutions," FEEM Working Paper Series, Milan, October 2007, FEEM.

Criqui, P., G. Klassen and L. Schrattenholzer (2000). "The Efficiency of Energy R&D Expenditures: Economic Modeling of Environmental Policy and Endogenous Technical Change," Amsterdam, November 16–17.

Edenhofer, O., N. Bauer, and E. Kriegler (2005). "The Impact of Technological Change on Climate Protection and Welfare: Insights from the Model MIND," *Ecological Economics* 54: 277–92.

Gerlagh, R. and B. C. C. van der Zwaan (2004). "A Sensitivity Analysis on Timing and Costs of Greenhouse Gas Abatement, Calculations with DEMETER," *Climatic Change* 65: 39–71.

Hansen, L., D. Epple, and W. Roberds (1985). "Linear Quadratic Duopoly Models of Resource Depletion," in T. J. Sargent (ed.), *Energy, Foresight, and Strategy*. Washington DC: Resources for the Future, pp. 101–142.

Jamasab, T. (2007). "Technical Change Theory and Learning Curves: Patterns of Progress in Electric Generation Technologies," *The Energy Journal* 28(3): 51-71.

Jones, C. (1995). "R&D Based Models of Economic Growth," *Journal of Political Economy* 103: 759–84.

Klassen, G., A. Miketa, K. Larsen, and T. Sundqvist (2005). "The Impact of R&D on Innovation for Wind Energy in Denmark, Germany and the United Kingdom," *Ecological Economics* 54(2–3): 227–40.

Kouvaritakis, N., A. Soria, and S. Isoard (2000). "Endogenous Learning in World Post-Kyoto Scenarios: Application of the POLES Model under Adaptive Expectations," *International Journal of Global Energy Issues* 14(1–4): 228–48.

Kypreos, S. (2007). "A MERGE Model with Endogenous Technical Change and the Cost of Carbon Stabilization," *Energy Policy* 35: 5327–36.

Nemet, G. F. (2006). "Beyond the Learning Curve: Factors Influencing Cost Reductions in Photovoltaics," *Energy Policy* 34(17): 3218–32.

Nepstad, Daniel, Britaldo Soares-Filho, Frank Merry, Paulo Moutinho, Hermann Oliveira Rodrigues, Maria Bowman, Steve Schwartzman, Oriana Almeida, and Sergio Rivero (2007). "The Costs and Benefits of Reducing Deforestation in the Brazilian Amazon," Woods Hole, MA: The Woods Hole Research Center, available at. www.whrc.org/policy/BaliReports/index.htm.

Nordhaus, W. D. and J. Boyer (2000). *Warming the World*. Cambridge, MA: MIT Press.

Popp, D. (2004). "ENTICE: Endogenous Technological Change in the DICE Model of Global Warming," *Journal of Environmental Economics and Management* 48: 742–68.

Söderholm, P. and G. Klassen (2007). "Wind Power in Europe: A Simultaneous Innovation-Diffusion Model," *Environmental and Resource Economics* 36(2): 163–90.

24 Sharing the burden of GHG reductions

HENRY D. JACOBY,
MUSTAFA H. BABIKER, SERGEY PALTSEV,
AND JOHN M. REILLY

Introduction

In response to the ever-clearer threat posed by climate change, the Group of Eight (G8) large industrialized countries have adopted a goal of reducing global greenhouse gas (GHG) emissions 50 percent by 2050. Together with existing developed-country commitments and proposals, and equity principles written into various climate agreements, this target provides a starting point for consideration of a post-2012 international climate agreement. Success in upcoming negotiations should be aided by a clear-eyed view of the implications of simultaneously pursuing emissions targets and equity goals, and this analysis is intended as a contribution to this important international process.

While references to a 50 percent global GHG reduction target can be found in the statements of the major industrialized countries, it is clear that meeting this target will require the participation of countries beyond that small group.[1] The United Nations Framework Convention on Climate Change (UNFCCC) and its subsidiary agreements lay out broad terms of reference for sharing the task. For example, the Convention and the Kyoto Protocol divide the world into a set of developed countries (Annex I) and developing countries (non-Annex I) with "common but differential responsibilities." The Bali Action Plan, in setting out guidelines for long-term cooperative action in the post-2012 period, reflects this equity principle and

---

[1] A 50 percent reduction in global emissions is closest to the most stringent target considered in a 2007 study by the US Climate Change Science Program (US CCSP 2007), which analyzed the reductions necessary to achieve atmospheric carbon dioxide (CO_2) stabilization at 450 parts per million by volume (ppmv).

emphasizes the need for "positive incentives for developing country Parties for the enhanced implementation of national mitigation strategies and adaptation action." Developed countries, in turn, have the responsibility to provide financial and other resources to "meet the specific needs and concerns of developing country Parties arising from adverse effects of climate change and/or *the impact of the implementation of response measures*" (UNFCCC, Article 4.8, italics added). Note that the language stipulates that developed countries should cover not only the direct costs of mitigation measures within developing countries, thereby creating incentives to take on commitments, but also provide compensation for the indirect effects of emissions mitigation undertaken elsewhere.

We analyze this set of objectives in the context of a global emissions trading scheme. One attraction of emissions trading is that the allowance allocation mechanism provides a means for altering the distributional effects of an emissions target, while the ability to trade equalizes marginal costs of reduction among participants. Thus, in principle, an international emissions trading regime can be designed so that allowance allocations take care of developing country concerns about costs while still ensuring the adoption of least-cost abatement opportunities. Note, however, that the insights drawn from this analysis are not limited to a policy architecture based on universal cap-and-trade. For example, reductions could be achieved as well with a harmonized carbon tax, augmented by side payments equal to the level of the financial flows we show as necessary to meet burden-sharing objectives. While strictly speaking the analysis is based on the implementation of a highly efficient policy mechanism such as cap-and-trade or a carbon dioxide (CO_2) tax, the results might still be used to inform negotiations on levels of international compensation in a context where countries are allowed to implement reductions using policy mechanisms of their choice. In that case, welfare costs and CO_2 prices would differ from the results shown here, though these results would still provide insights into the scale of the task.

While an actual post-2012 international climate agreement may fall short of ideal solutions, analyzing different policies can help inform judgments about the nature of the challenge ahead. To explore possible burden sharing in this context we employ a technique for endogenously estimating the allowance allocations necessary to achieve predetermined distributional outcomes, implemented within the MIT

Emissions Prediction and Policy Analysis (EPPA) model. We then apply these allocation results to abatement scenarios that bring global GHG emissions to 50 percent below year 2000 emissions by 2050. We consider a variety of possible policy architectures and explore the allowance allocations, and associated financial flows under a trading regime, that are consistent with achieving particular distributional goals.

Our exploration stands in a long tradition of efforts to analyze options for burden sharing among nations in the context of climate-change mitigation. Previous work in this literature includes Beckerman and Pasek (1995); Jacoby *et al.* (1997); Reiner and Jacoby (1997); Rose *et al.* (1998); Jacoby, Schmalensee, and Wing (1999); Babiker, Reilly, and Jacoby (2000); Winkler *et al.* (2002); McKibbin and Wilcoxen (2004); Perrson, Azar, and Lindgren (2006); and a survey of approaches by Bodansky (2004). Several other articles in this volume also touch on this topic. Our contribution here is to analyze the implications of currently proposed emissions targets when imposed in the context of the equity principles articulated in the Bali Action Plan and earlier international agreements.

Note that our focus is on mitigation costs only. The UNFCCC also specifies that developed countries are responsible for helping developing countries adapt to climate change. If achieved, the mitigation goal proposed by the G8 would avoid some of the projected warming and thereby lessen the need for adaptation assistance. Our estimate of financial flows to compensate developing countries does not include amounts that might be needed to provide adaptation assistance, or to cope with the effects of residual climate change itself. Also, our analysis does not take account of the potential for welfare-enhancing reductions in energy subsidies, which are particularly prominent among energy-exporting countries.

We begin by describing the EPPA model and the endogenous instruments used in this analysis to simulate the impacts of mitigation policies that also achieve distributional goals. Next we describe the reference scenario of GHG emissions that underlies the analysis and summarize the policy scenarios to be considered. The discussion then moves to a comparison of costs and financial flows under the different allowance allocations implied by several current policy proposals. We begin with a simple burden-sharing rule implicit in current developed-country targets, and then analyze alternatives based on population and gross domestic product (GDP). Our simulations find that these alternatives yield distributional implications that are inconsistent with notions of equity among nations. Another result is that different burden-sharing arrangements have an effect on the difficulty of the task, through income effects.

The analysis then turns to cases where allowances are allocated endogenously to compensate developing-country parties—either fully or partially—for the burdens they incur in the global effort, including both direct costs (mitigation expenses) and indirect costs (e.g., terms-of-trade effects).[2] This analysis highlights the scale of the implied international financial transfers, which far exceed any historical experience. We also explore different assumptions about the distribution of mitigation and compensation burdens among developed regions, comparing an allocation based on proportional reductions to one that imposes the same welfare loss on all. The results from this portion of the analysis suggest that the distribution of burdens among Annex I parties is no less complicated than that between Annex I and non-Annex I parties. Finally, we summarize our findings and speculate about their implications for the negotiation of a post-2012 international policy architecture.

The EPPA model and endogenous allocation

The EPPA model

The Emissions Prediction and Policy Analysis (EPPA) model is a general equilibrium model of the world economy developed by the MIT Joint Program on the Science and Policy of Global Change (Paltsev *et al.* 2005). It divides the world into sixteen individual countries and regional groups and is designed to provide scenarios of anthropogenic GHG emissions and estimates of the economic impact of climate change policies, either as a stand-alone model or as part of a larger Integrated Global Simulation Model (IGSM) of the climate system (Sokolov *et al.* 2005). For economic data the EPPA model relies on the Global Trade Analysis Project (GTAP) dataset

---

[2] The terms of trade are defined as the prices of a country's exports in relation to the prices of its imports. In this analysis a main concern is the effect on energy exporters of a reduction in oil, gas, and coal prices, leading to deterioration in their terms of trade.

(Dimaranan and McDougall 2002), which accommodates a consistent representation of regional macroeconomic consumption, production, and bilateral trade flows. Energy data in physical units are based on energy balances from the International Energy Agency (IEA). Additional data for the most important anthropogenic GHGs (carbon dioxide [CO_2], methane [CH_4], nitrous oxide [N_2O], hydrofluorocarbons [HFCs], perfluorocarbons [PFCs], and sulfur hexafluoride [SF_6]) are from inventories maintained by the US Environmental Protection Agency. For data on other air pollutants (sulfur dioxide [SO_2], nitrogen oxides [NO_x], black carbon [BC], organic carbon [OC], ammonia [NH_3], carbon monoxide [CO], and non-methane volatile organic compounds [VOC]) we rely on the global EDGAR data (Olivier and Berdowski 2001). Different types of GHGs are aggregated using global warming potentials (GWPs) specified by the Intergovernmental Panel on Climate Change (IPCC). Biofuels are assumed to be from cellulosic sources and their contribution to the overall fuel supply for given inputs of land and other inputs is net of the energy required for crop production, transport, and processing. Potential effects of indirect land-use change (see Melillo *et al.* 2009) are not considered.

Regions, sectors, and primary factors are shown in Table 24.1. For the most part, regional groupings attempt to include contiguous areas. The sectors and primary factors are disaggregated to focus on energy demand, supply, resource use and depletion, and key technology alternatives to fossil-fuel use. The model can be solved recursively or dynamically at five-year time steps. Solving the model as a fully dynamic problem requires some sacrifice of detail and so we solve it here recursively. Production and consumption sectors are represented in the EPPA model by nested constant elasticity of substitution (CES) production functions (or the Cobb-Douglas and Leontief special cases of the CES). The model is written in the GAMS software system and solved using the MPSGE modeling language (Rutherford 1995). It has been used in a wide variety of policy applications (e.g., Babiker *et al.* 2004; US CCSP 2007; Paltsev *et al.* 2007; Paltsev *et al.* 2008).

Endogenous instruments for policy targets and distributional goals

The GAMS-MPSGE algorithms applied in the EPPA model conveniently allow constrained solutions. Thus the shadow value of a CO_2

Table 24.1 *Regions, sectors, and primary factors in the EPPA model*

Country or Region[†]	Sectors	Factors
Developed	*Non-Energy*	Capital
United States (USA)	Agriculture (AGRI)	Labor
Canada (CAN)	Services (SERV)	Crude Oil
Japan (JPN)	Energy-Intensive	Natural Gas
European Union+	Products (EINT)	Coal
(EUR)	Other Industries Products	Shale Oil
Australia & New	(OTHR)	Nuclear
Zealand (ANZ)	Transportation (TRAN)	Hydro
Former Soviet Union	Household Transportation	Wind/Solar
(FSU)	(HTRN)	Land
Eastern Europe (EET)	Other HH Consumption	
Developing	*Fuels*	
India (IND)	Coal (COAL)	
China (CHN)	Crude Oil (OIL)	
Indonesia (IDZ)	Refined Oil (ROIL)	
Higher Income East	Natural Gas (GAS)	
Asia (ASI)	Oil from Shale (SYNO)	
Mexico (MEX)	Synthetic Gas (SYNG)	
Latin America (LAM)	Liquids from Biomass	
Middle East (MES)	(B-OIL)	
Africa (AFR)	*Electricity Generation*	
Rest of World (ROW)	Fossil (ELEC)	
	Hydro (HYDR)	
	Nuclear (NUCL)	
	Solar and Wind (SOLW)	
	Biomass (BIOM)	
	Coal with CCS	
	Adv. gas without CCS	
	Gas with CCS	

[†] Details of regional groupings are provided in *Paltsev et al.* (2005).

emissions constraint can be interpreted as the price that would result if the CO_2 target were implemented by a cap-and-trade system. The EPPA model is set up so that caps can be specified separately for each country, each sector within a country, and for each major GHG. The option then exists to create markets that allow trading of allowances among any of these separately capped regions, sectors, or gases where trading equilibrates the marginal cost of abatement as observed by the trading entity.[3] Trading among gases occurs at GWP exchange rates which can be set to other values if desired or as GWPs change. For this analysis, we enforce the cap on total GHG emissions with trade among all sources, sectors, and regions except where we exclude some regions from the policy. Land-use emissions and/or sinks are not explicitly capped, and no incentives are provided to enhance sinks.

This analysis assumes that any allowance revenue is returned to the representative consumer in each region in a lump-sum manner. This assumption is consistent with a cap-and-trade system under competitive conditions where allowances are distributed free or are auctioned with the revenue distributed as a lump sum. Under these conditions, the way in which allowances are distributed within a country does not affect production (or abatement) decisions.[4] For example, lump-sum free distribution to firms provides a windfall gain to recipients: the value of any allowances given to firms will increase the equity value of those firms or otherwise be distributed to shareholders and therefore increase the value of stocks held by households (our representative consumer). But that distribution will not affect a firm's abatement decisions—those decisions will be based on the GHG price observed in the allowance market recognizing the opportunity cost/value of any free allowances it has received. If allowances are instead auctioned, the firm would see the same price and abate the same amount. This approach does not consider other uses of funds such as using revenue from an allowance auction to replace existing distortionary taxes, support energy R&D, eliminate possible market failures in energy use, or alter within-country distributional outcomes of the policy.

---

[3] GAMS-MPSGE solves the model as a mixed complementarity problem—that is, it finds equilibrium in markets for factors and goods. Under idealized conditions—perfect competition, small open economy or a closed economy, no market distortions—this is consistent with welfare maximization. In the presence of distortions—taxes, terms-of-trade effects and the like, the solution represents a market solution: consumers and producers are optimizing on the basis of distorted prices and without considering the economy-wide impact of their actions on the terms of trade. Thus, in the presence of distortions it is possible that there is a solution that is better in welfare terms than an unfettered emissions trading system.

[4] As noted below, different allocations among countries lead to differences in global price and cost because of income effects.

Emissions targets and distributional objectives are jointly implemented in the EPPA model through the use of an endogenous procedure implemented for this study. These instruments allocate emissions allowances among parties in such a way that the targeted mitigation and distributional goals are achieved simultaneously. Two forms of endogenous instruments are used to simulate the policy cases. One such internal procedure is needed to simulate the allocations (and resulting financial transfers from emissions trading) required to compensate the mitigation-related costs of developing countries. Another must be employed to simulate the requirement that the same percentage welfare burden be imposed across developed regions. While these two approaches differ from a technical standpoint, they both use mechanisms that (re)allocate allowances to achieve specific welfare targets in different regions.

Though a full description of this technique is beyond the scope of this discussion, a brief summary is provided here. The first endogenous instrument starts from a given global allocation of allowances among countries and then reallocates such that the welfare cost of mitigation in developing countries is capped at a pre-determined level while global emissions meet the desired reduction target. Technically, implementing this scheme involves two components, one to determine the allowances needed by each participating developing country to achieve the distributional objective, and a second to scale back developed countries' allowance allocation so that the overall global emissions reduction target remains fixed. We apply this procedure by scaling back emissions allowances proportionally in each developed country; thus, the economic consequences depend on the original distribution of allowances.

Another potential outcome simulated for this chapter involves equating the welfare cost of mitigation in percentage terms across developed countries while again limiting costs in developing countries. To achieve this result we apply a second, global allowance-allocation instrument that starts from a global emissions reduction target and allocates the reduction requirement across individual countries in a way that meets both developed and developing country objectives. The technical implementation of this scheme in EPPA makes use of one endogenous instrument to allocate emission allowances among parties, and a second to ensure that the overall reduction target is exactly met.

Reference projection and policy scenarios

A reference projection

Figure 24.1 shows reference projections for developed (Annex I) and developing (non-Annex I) parties. Estimates of abatement costs to meet a specific policy target depend strongly on the choice of baseline or "reference" case emissions levels. A decade or so ago, a reference projection that assumed no climate policy was considered a reasonable "business-as-usual" scenario. We are moving into an era where some mitigation measures are already in place, so differences emerge between a reference case with no policy and a reference case that includes policies and measures already on the books. Where climate policies are explicit and underway, such as the European Union's Emission Trading Scheme (EU ETS), or where national-level Kyoto commitments are in place, it is fairly clear that they should be considered for inclusion under a business-as-usual projection. If, however, the focus is on estimating the full cost of GHG mitigation, and calculating what carbon prices may be in the future, the analysis needs to start from a counterfactual or reference case absent the commitments and policies already in place. For purposes of this study, which aims to examine various scenarios of policy development, the appropriate reference case for comparison is one without existing mitigation measures. Accordingly, our reference emissions projections do not include the effect of the EU ETS and other commitments made within or outside the Kyoto Protocol.[5] Also, our measures of welfare cost include the influence of policies that have already been undertaken.

The reference projection developed for this analysis is similar to the one that underlies the EPPA-derived results in a multi-model study conducted for the US Climate Change Science Program (US CCSP 2007). That study has emissions growing relatively rapidly through 2050, not unlike the central forecasts of the International Energy Agency (IEA) and the US Energy Information Administration (EIA). Its estimates of economic and emissions growth for the United States are closer to the EIA projections in 2007. In 2008, EIA revised its projection of

---

[5] Reference-case emissions for 2050 are shown in Figure 24.1 as totaling 83 million metric tons CO_2 equivalent (MtCO_2-e). If existing commitments under the Kyoto protocol were taken into account, and maintained for 2008-2050, the 2050 projection would be reduced to 73 MtCO_2-e.

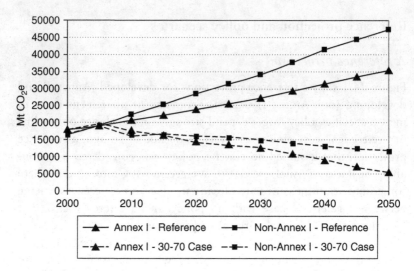

Figure 24.1. Annex I and Non-Annex I emissions, reference and 30-70 cases

US economic growth downward, leading to lower estimates of future energy use and emissions. Hence emissions growth in the developed-country EPPA aggregate is somewhat more robust than other projections that either include emissions mitigation actions already on the books or have been subject to recent revision. On the other hand, projections for China from earlier this decade appear to be below the growth actually experienced in the past few years.[6] All these projections are well within the range of uncertainty about future growth in emissions to 2020 and even more clearly for 2050 (Webster *et al.* 2009).

Finally, all fuel and energy prices in EPPA are determined endogenously and so reflect underlying long-term factors. The rapid increase in oil prices that occurred in recent years and appears to have peaked in 2008 is not simulated or reflected in the model results. Since the model solves on a five-year time step, 2008 is not a solution year;

---

[6] Analysis by Blanford *et al.* (2009) suggests that many modeling exercises underestimate the near-term rate of increase in China's emissions. On the other hand, if the 2008–2009 global recession turns out to be deeper and/or longer than the experience of the past half-century would indicate (and thus deviate from the recessions already built into the growth assumptions that underlie this analysis), then welfare effects and financial transfers could be somewhat smaller than calculated here.

thus, the model cannot represent energy price volatility over days or months, or even interannually. That said, the EPPA model projects that oil prices, in the absence of climate policy, will nearly triple between 2005 and 2050—reaching about $145 per barrel (in 2005 dollars) by mid-century. The model projections show oil prices rising gradually such that they do not exceed $100 per barrel until 2025.

Scenarios of allocation and compensation

This analysis considers seven scenarios, shown in Table 24.2, for an international agreement that either implicitly or explicitly allocates the economic cost of abatement. All the scenarios assume universal participation. The first three apply simple rules, like fixed percentage reductions for Annex I vs. non-Annex I parties (Case 1) and allocations based on population or ability to pay (Cases 2 and 3). Later we explore the implications of an agreement among developed countries to compensate developing countries for all costs associated with emissions mitigation; we also consider different ways to distribute the burden of this responsibility. The final two scenarios are designed to reveal the effects of only partly compensating developing countries—the first of these scenarios allows all countries to experience a welfare loss of up to 3 percent; the second compensates energy exporting countries for the direct costs of mitigation but does not compensate them for indirect costs (e.g., through terms-of-trade effects).

Several assumptions apply to all of these scenarios. First, emission caps are formulated to cover all GHG emissions and are relative to 2000 emissions. Further, we assume that an efficient cap-and-trade system within each country includes all sectors and all GHGs. In addition, all cases involve international emissions trading. The one category of activity that is not included is land use—either with respect to emissions or the possible enhancement of carbon sinks. In principle, creating incentives for enhancing sinks could reduce policy costs, but an important contributor to abatement in our analysis is the use of cellulosic ethanol, which we credit as a zero-carbon fuel. Including land-use emissions would raise the cost of that abatement option even as it might lead to additional abatement opportunities through sink enhancement or avoided deforestation. Exactly how sinks and land-use emissions might be included in an international agreement is a critical topic identified under the Bali Action Plan, but it is beyond the scope of this analysis.

Table 24.2 *Scenarios of allocation and compensation*

Allocation Rule	
1. 30–70	2050 allocation with developed at 30 percent and developing at 70 percent of 2000 emissions
2. Pop based	Allocations based on share of 2000 population
3. GDP based	Allocations based on inverse share of year 2000 GDP per capita
Full Compensation of Developing Countries	
4. Full comp-equal alloc	Full compensation of all costs in developing countries with developed countries given equal allowances as a percentage of their year 2000 emissions
5. Full comp-equal cost	Full compensation of all costs in developing countries with developed bearing equal percentage costs
Partial Participation of Developing Countries	
6. 3% cost cap	Compensation so that no developing country region's welfare costs exceeds 3 percent, with developed countries given equal allowances as a percentage of their year 2000 emissions
7. Direct only	Compensation to developing countries for the cost of their participation but not for the indirect costs of developed country mitigation through terms of trade effects

Note: All scenarios achieve the global goal of 50 percent reduction of emissions from 2000 levels by 2050, linearly falling from 2015.

This analysis also does not investigate the implications if full participation is not achievable. It has been suggested that negotiations would be easier if fewer countries were involved so talks could focus on the larger developed economies and major developing-country emitters like China and India. Unfortunately, if only a few of the smaller developing countries are omitted the goal of reducing emissions 50 percent below 2000 levels becomes infeasible—in part because of emissions leakage to those outside the agreement.

Results

Simple allocation rules

The first three cases in Table 24.2 involve simple allocation rules derived from existing proposals for sharing the abatement burden among parties to a universal agreement. All three are intended to require greater effort by the developed Annex I countries and so they allocate a disproportionate share of allowances (relative to actual 2000 emissions) to the non-Annex I developing countries. The *30–70* scenario gradually reduces the allowances allocated to developed countries such that, by 2050, their allocation totals just 30 percent of their year 2000 emissions (thus implying a 70 percent reduction below 2000 emissions). Willingness to assume a disproportionate share of the global 50 percent reduction goal can be seen as an offer implicitly put on the table by developed countries.[7]

Given this stringent level of control by developed countries a smaller abatement burden falls on developing countries: they are required to reduce emissions to 70 percent of 2000 levels by 2050 (thus implying a 30 percent reduction below 2000 emissions). This non-Annex I result is independent of the projection of future emissions—rather, it simply reflects the near equality of the year 2000 emissions of the two nation groups. Allocations over this time period are shown in Figure 24.1. With a trading system, a common global price for CO_2-equivalent emissions will emerge, as shown in Figure 24.2. Actual emissions for developing and developed countries will not necessarily follow the 30 percent and 70 percent reduction paths that form the basis for their respective allocations; instead future emissions will depend on where abatement actually occurs, which in turn will be determined by the market as firms take advantage of allowance trading to seek out the lowest-cost abatement options. To the extent that actual emissions diverge from the initial allocation there will be a corresponding flow of net financial payments among countries.

---

[7] Proposals for a national GHG policy in the US Congress, like the Waxman-Markey-Warner bill, and targets suggested in a number of state initiatives, aim to cut GHG emissions by 70 or 80 percent in the 2050 timeframe. Similar proposals have been put forward in Europe—an example is the "Factor 4" proposal, which targets a four-fold reduction in emissions by 2050 and is supported by ministries of the French government.

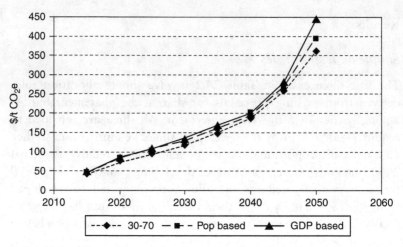

Figure 24.2. CO_2-e. prices under alternative allocation rules

Generous though the *30–70* offer may appear, many developing countries would experience a larger percentage welfare loss (approximately, the reduction in national consumption) than would developed countries, as shown in the first column of Table 24.3. Among the non-Annex I parties, all but China experience welfare losses greater than does the United States, and most carry a larger cost burden in percentage terms than do the rest of the Annex I countries. The larger welfare costs among developing countries are largely a result of their more rapidly-growing emissions. The use of a historical-year benchmark will, over time, impose tighter constraints on countries with more rapid emissions growth. This phenomenon is familiar from experience with the Kyoto Protocol, which imposed tighter constraints on countries like Canada and Australia that had rapidly growing emissions, while posing less of a challenge for Europe, where emissions were growing more slowly. In fact, relative to the benchmark year of 1990, emissions in the Former Soviet Union—principally in its largest component, Russia—have actually fallen. The United States and China see relatively small costs under a *30–70* rule because both use a substantial amount of coal for power generation and can achieve large emission reductions through the application of CO_2 capture and storage. The United States also tends to gain through improvements in the terms of trade.

Notably, the large energy exporters—the Middle East (MES), Africa, Canada, Central and Latin America (LAM), and the Former Soviet

Table 24.3 *Welfare effects in 2020 & 2050, universal participation*
(percent change from reference)

	Allocation Rule			Full Compensation	
	30–70	Pop based	GDP based	Full comp-equal alloc	Full comp-equal cost
2020					
Annex I					
USA	−0.1	−2.8	−3.7	−1.3	−1.9
CAN	−2.7	−6.0	−5.9	−4.2	−1.9
JPN	−0.2	−0.8	−1.5	−0.7	−1.9
ANZ	−1.4	−4.9	−4.1	−3.0	−1.9
EUR	−1.2	−2.3	−3.5	−2.1	−1.9
EET	0.0	−5.0	5.4	−4.5	−1.9
FSU	−2.0	−8.4	−6.7	−7.7	−1.9
Non-Annex I					
MEX	−2.4	−2.9	1.2	0.0	0.0
ASI	−0.4	−3.4	−5.0	0.0	0.0
CHN	−0.1	5.3	−2.7	0.0	0.0
IND	−4.9	20.9	39.0	0.0	0.0
IDZ	−4.8	7.0	56.1	0.0	0.0
AFR	−9.1	7.6	14.3	0.0	0.0
MES	−18.2	−21.6	−18.8	0.0	0.0
LAM	−2.7	−1.7	−5.6	0.0	0.0
ROW	−1.9	10.2	12.2	0.0	0.0
2050					
Annex I					
USA	−2.6	−5.5	−7.2	−7.4	−9.4
CAN	−11.8	−15.6	−16.0	−18.1	−9.4
JPN	−2.6	−3.0	−4.3	−4.5	−9.4
ANZ	−6.3	−10.0	−9.1	−12.5	−9.4
EUR	−5.2	−6.3	−8.6	−8.9	−9.4
EET	−8.5	−11.6	3.4	−25.0	−9.4
FSU	−21.6	−24.5	−22.5	−41.0	−9.4
Non-Annex I					
MEX	−7.4	−11.2	−3.7	0.0	0.0
ASI	−4.3	−11.0	−14.0	0.0	0.0
CHN	−0.4	2.2	−7.7	0.0	0.0
IND	−11.4	21.0	48.9	0.0	0.0
IDZ	−15.8	−3.7	63.2	0.0	0.0
AFR	−28.5	−7.5	4.7	0.0	0.0
MES	−51.7	−61.0	−56.8	0.0	0.0
LAM	−12.2	−13.2	−20.0	0.0	0.0
ROW	−9.8	5.1	10.2	0.0	0.0

Note: Entries in **bold** indicate pre-specified welfare outcomes.

Union (FSU)—suffer large losses, because GHG constraints change their terms of trade in the other direction. Welfare losses in the Middle East are dramatic—over 18 percent in 2020 rising to over 50 percent in 2050. This result is not surprising because the economies of this region are heavily dependent on oil production, and a stringent emissions target extracts much of the rent associated with exploitation of their oil resources.

Table 24.4 shows the net financial transfers between nations as allowances are redistributed through emissions trading, following the initial allocation, to reflect an efficient distribution of actual reductions. Results for the *30–70* case are provided in the first column. The last line for 2020 and 2050, labeled "AnxI net," is the total financial flow to developing countries. A *30–70* allocation might be expected to always lead to net purchases of allowances by developed countries, creating a flow of revenue to developing countries to provide some of the financial assistance agreed in international treaties. In fact, this "deal" actually results in some developing countries *purchasing* allowances. The modeling results indicate that several non-Annex I parties are purchasing allowances in 2020, and Indonesia (IDZ) and Latin America are still net purchasers in 2050. Because of its ability to abate emissions from coal relatively inexpensively in this scenario, China is the largest seller of allowances, and those sales substantially offset its abatement costs. Interestingly, the Middle East (MES) is a net seller of allowances in 2050, but the revenue is not enough to overcome the direct costs of the policy and its unfavorable impact on the region's terms of trade.

For comparison with this *30–70* case, two commonly-discussed alternatives are of interest. The first reflects the notion that all global citizens have an equal right to the absorptive capacity of the atmosphere—thus our *population-based* scenario allocates allowances in proportion to year 2000 population. Other proposals hold that a fair allocation of burden would be based on ability to pay. To investigate the latter idea, we examine a *GDP-based* scenario that allocates according to the inverse of per capita GDP in the year 2000. This policy gives the most allowances to the poorest countries.[8] Table 24.5 (second and third columns) shows the distribution of allowances

---

[8] The share based on the inverse of per capita GDP (pcgdp) for region r is calculated by the formula: share(r) = (1/pcgdp(r))/sum(r, 1/pcgdp(r)). The underlying GTAP data base on which the EPPA model relies converts all economic data for all regions to US dollars using market exchange rates prevailing in the base year.

Table 24.4 *Net financial transfers, 2000 US$ billions, resulting from allowance trade in 2020 & 2050, universal participation (+ is sale, – is purchase)*

	Allocation Rule			Full Compensation	
	30–70	Pop based	GDP based	Full comp- equal alloc	Full comp- equal cost
2020					
Annex I					
USA	−30.3	−368.7	−483.5	−196.7	−264.5
CAN	−2.7	−36.2	−36.4	−20.0	4.5
JPN	−13.1	−47.4	−92.6	−44.8	−118.9
ANZ	−5.2	−32.3	−29.2	−18.5	−8.8
EUR	−12.3	−127.7	−270.1	−116.9	−86.3
EET	8.6	−9.3	36.9	−9.9	3.2
FSU	41.0	−27.1	−9.1	−26.7	44.6
Non-Annex I					
MEX	0.1	−3.8	22.9	16.4	14.6
ASI	−23.7	−87.9	−122.8	−13.8	−14.9
CHN	69.4	222.5	26.7	73.9	74.4
IND	10.1	232.7	439.7	51.8	52.3
IDZ	−10.1	33.1	238.6	8.0	8.2
AFR	−10.8	154.9	220.0	81.2	79.3
MES	−32.3	−59.5	−40.2	119.4	116.5
LAM	−0.8	23.6	−57.1	62.7	61.3
ROW	12.2	133.1	156.0	33.9	34.4
AnxI net	14.0	648.7	883.9	433.5	426.2
2050					
Annex I					
USA	−179.6	−668.8	−1024.0	−1239.4	−1715.5
CAN	−35.7	−87.2	−93.6	−148.8	2.1
JPN	−172.8	−187.3	−288.6	−358.6	−942.1
ANZ	−30.1	−72.7	−70.3	−120.5	−78.6
EUR	−195.9	−299.9	−715.6	−866.1	−985.3
EET	−9.1	−15.5	119.4	−146.9	7.1
FSU	−44.2	−58.8	0.8	−434.3	299.9
Non-Annex I					
MEX	31.5	−9.2	66.7	108.4	110.1
ASI	130.5	−131.2	−241.3	355.8	363.8
CHN	484.0	577.1	80.8	589.0	578.3
IND	14.7	513.9	1056.3	176.4	189.5
IDZ	−40.9	32.9	574.1	85.0	91.2
AFR	43.4	373.1	609.7	543.0	558.7
MES	77.4	−15.4	51.1	761.1	797.3
LAM	−81.9	−158.6	−428.3	536.8	556.7
ROW	8.6	207.6	302.9	159.1	167.0
AnxI net	667.3	1390.3	2071.9	3314.6	3412.5

Table 24.5 *Allowance allocations in 2020 & 2050 (% change relative to 2000 emissions)*

	Allocation Rule			Full Compensation	
	30–70	*Pop based*	*GDP based*	*Full comp-equal alloc*	*Full comp-equal cost*
2020					
Annex I					
USA	80	20.5	1.7	49.3	37.3
CAN	80	21.2	21.7	49.3	92.0
JPN	80	48.4	8.1	49.3	−20.8
ANZ	80	20.9	29.6	49.3	71.7
EUR	80	44.2	3.6	49.3	57.7
EET	80	49.1	110.1	49.3	67.7
FSU	80	49.0	56.5	49.3	80.5
Non-Annex I					
MEX	98	88.3	144.7	134.2	129.8
ASI	98	56.5	33.3	104.4	103.6
CHN	98	130.8	78.9	98.1	97.6
IND	98	265.4	405.2	127.6	127.5
IDZ	98	200.0	668.1	142.3	142.3
AFR	98	219.2	266.9	168.1	165.8
MES	98	71.0	92.3	263.8	259.6
LAM	98	108.5	49.0	139.4	137.9
ROW	98	193.1	211.0	114.4	114.1
Global	89	89	89	89	89
2050					
Annex I					
USA	30	11.4	0.9	−8.3	−22.5
CAN	30	11.8	12.0	−8.3	44.4
JPN	30	26.8	4.5	−8.3	−113.4
ANZ	30	11.6	16.4	−8.3	12.3
EUR	30	24.5	2.0	−8.3	−12.3
EET	30	27.2	61.0	−8.3	32.7
FSU	30	27.1	31.3	−8.3	58.7
Non-Annex I					
MEX	70	48.9	80.2	101.9	99.7
ASI	70	31.3	18.4	96.8	94.9
CHN	70	72.5	43.7	71.2	68.7
IND	70	147.1	224.6	93.3	93.5
IDZ	70	110.9	370.3	133.8	133.6
AFR	70	121.5	147.9	143.3	141.3
MES	70	39.4	51.1	238.6	234.8
LAM	70	60.1	27.2	152.2	150.7
ROW	70	107	117.0	95.1	94.6
Global	50	50	50	50	50

under these rules. All but a few developing countries receive a larger allocation than under a *30–70* rule (first column), and as a general pattern this leads to large sales of allowances from non-Annex I to Annex I parties (shown in Table 24.4)—in other words, a *population-* or *GDP-based* allocation will short the developed countries to a much greater extent than will the *30–70* allocation.

For this reason, population or GDP-per-capita allocation rules also impose greater welfare costs on developed countries than does a *30–70* rule, as seen in Table 24.3. Moreover, these simple rules have widely varying effects among developing-country regions. Welfare is improved in some regions, India and Indonesia most notably. There the scheme goes well beyond compensating for mitigation costs and turns the GHG mitigation policy into an instrument for global income redistribution. On the other hand these rules impose greater burdens on the Middle East exporters (MES); they also impose greater burdens on the higher-income Asian countries (ASI) and Latin America (LAM), albeit to a lesser extent. Also, which of the two rules is used makes a big difference for some regions. Indonesia realizes a large increase in welfare under the *GDP-based* allocation, but suffers a loss of nearly 4 percent if the allocation is based on population. With such wildly different economic outcomes, these two proposals cannot be justified on equity or responsibility grounds when they penalize some developing countries while redistributing sums to others that go well beyond compensating for mitigation costs. Indeed, one conclusion from these simulations is that no simple allocation formula can deal with the huge variation in circumstances among countries.

Another aspect of the burden-sharing issue, which can be seen even in the context of these simple rules, is the effect of the allocation on allowance price. Given the assumption of global emissions trading one might expect allowance prices to be unaffected by the allocation rule as long as the global constraint remains the same. In fact, as shown in Figure 24.2, the variation in allowance prices under different allocation rules is surprisingly large. In 2020, the *GDP-based* scenario results in a price of more than \$8 per ton CO_2 (tCO_2)—this is 10 percent higher than the projected allowance price in the *30–70* case. By 2050 the difference in allowance prices is still most pronounced for these two cases—in fact, by mid-century it has risen to \$82 per ton, a 23 percent difference. This result is due to a differential income effect in developing vs. developed countries. The *GDP-based* case leads, especially in later years, to large income transfers to developing countries. Higher income in developing countries spurs an increase in fuel consumption to a degree that exceeds the reduction in fuel use expected as a result of income losses in developed countries. Thus, an interesting indirect effect of this particular equity-driven proposal is that it actually raises the marginal cost of abatement, thereby making it more expensive to achieve the overall global objective than a partial equilibrium analysis would indicate.

The economic impacts modeled for this study, particularly among developing countries (and developed energy exporters) may appear large compared with the global cost estimates in the literature. For example, the IPCC has surveyed studies of the global macroeconomic cost of achieving a target level of atmospheric GHG stabilization at 445–535 parts per million (ppm) CO_2-e. It finds that the range of estimates for expected GDP loss lies below 3 percent in 2030 and below 5.5 percent in 2050 (IPCC 2007, Tables SPM.5 and SPM.6), substantially below our estimates. One obvious difference is that we estimate costs in welfare terms (lost consumption) rather than GDP. While there are some important technical differences between these measures, at the level of this discussion they are broadly comparable. Several other factors help to explain the difference. First, many studies do not include targets as tight as those proposed by the G8: some of the most aggressive mitigation scenarios in the recent literature achieve reductions equal to just one-third below 2000 levels by 2050. Also, the literature includes some older scenarios that significantly underestimate the actual emissions growth that occurred over the years since the analyses were done—further, our analysis cannot take account of the benefit of these intervening years and start a mitigation program in 2000 or 2005. And, of course, much of the work reports global average cost (or the results of individual country studies) and thus fails to deal with the complex issue of dividing up the global mitigation burden.

A factor that also contributes to higher costs in developing countries is the fact that energy is a larger share of GDP than in developed regions; in addition, some developing countries have large emissions of non-CO_2 GHGs from agriculture that are difficult to control. As a result, their mitigation costs are larger as a share of the overall economy than is the case in richer nations. Abatement costs, in absolute terms, are not necessarily larger in developing countries (our model assumes they have access to the same technology as developed countries), but because these countries are poorer abatement costs constitute a larger share of their income. Also, the developing economies are growing relatively rapidly in the EPPA reference case; moreover many of them are in the midst of a structural transition that involves energy-intensive infrastructure development, increased consumption of energy-using goods or services (more automobiles, air conditioning, appliances, etc.), and the replacement of traditional fuels such as firewood with commercial fuels.

Allocations that fully compensate developing countries

Scenarios 4 and 5, summarized in Table 24.2, are designed to achieve the same 50 percent global emissions reduction target, again with universal participation, but they include provisions to protect developing countries from "the impact of the implementation of response measures," as required under the UNFCCC. Here the "impact" to be avoided is defined in terms of the welfare cost in Table 24.3 (that is, in terms of the expected loss in national consumption). The two cases differ according to how they allocate burdens among the developed nations: in the *equal allocation* case, each developed country gets an equal fraction of its year 2000 emissions, whereas in the *equal cost* case, the allocation is set to impose the same welfare burden on each developed country. The allowance price paths for these two cases lie between the *population-based* and *GDP-based* scenarios in Figure 24.2, indicating the relative influence of the income effect from financial transfers associated with allowance trading and the differential effect of these financial transfers on the rates of growth in more- and less-developed regions.

The analysis assumes that allowance allocation is the instrument used to achieve equity goals. With the model we determine just that allocation that would, in each year, leave the non-Annex I parties with zero welfare cost.[9] In the *equal allocation* case the Annex I parties take an equal proportional reduction from year 2000 emissions. The resulting allocations for 2020 and 2050 are shown in the fourth column of Table 24.5. While the notion of differential

---

[9] Such a calculation can be done within a model setting. Applying the same calculation in the context of real negotiations is problematic because one needs to rely on a projection of reference emissions and costs. Agreeing on the particulars of such a projection would obviously be a highly contentious issue, even if the principle of compensation were fully accepted by some group of developed countries.

responsibilities between developed and developing countries is a key principle in international negotiations, individual national circumstances also figured into the negotiation of commitments under the Kyoto Protocol, which applied emission reduction targets only to developed regions. If each developed country is responsible for providing compensation in proportion to its reference emissions (the *equal allocation* case) strong differences emerge between countries, particularly in later decades of the period studied. Developed countries would need to set a target for themselves that is more on the order of a 49 percent reduction in 2020, as shown in Table 24.5. In 2050, moreover, each developed country would start not with a positive allocation but with an allowance *deficit* equal to 8.3 percent of its 2000 emissions (shown here as an allocation of −8.3 percent). The idea of a negative allocation may seem odd, but in a trading system the idea is not that the developed countries would achieve negative emissions. Rather, they would be required to purchase allowances for *all* of their emissions *plus* an additional quantity of allowances equal to 8.3 percent of their 2000 emissions levels.

One way to view the burden on Annex I parties under the *equal-allocation* scheme is to break down the aggregate welfare cost by separating the direct cost of emissions reductions *plus* terms-of-trade effects from the cost of allowance transfers to non-Annex I parties. The results of this disaggregation for 2020 and 2050 are shown in the left-hand columns of Table 24.6: there, the sum of direct cost and terms-of-trade effects (denoted Direct+ToT) and allowance transfers equals the total welfare cost of the *full compensation–equal allocation* case in Table 24.3. For example, the estimated welfare cost to the United States of 7.4 percent in 2050 is comprised of direct cost plus gains from terms of trade totaling a net cost of 2.5 percent, plus an additional 4.9 percent loss attributable to financial transfers to developing countries as a result of allowance trading. Note that direct costs differ somewhat under the two compensation schemes—this difference is due to income effects.

Under a *full compensation–equal allocation* agreement the energy exporting countries in Annex I would bear heavy welfare costs, as can be seen in Tables 24.3 and 24.6, with the economic burden falling disproportionately on Canada and the Former Soviet Union (FSU). The poorer of the developed regions—Eastern Europe (EET) and again the FSU—also face high costs as a percent of GDP compared with richer

Table 24.6 *Breakdown of welfare effects on Annex I parties of full compensation (% change from reference level)*

	2020				2050			
	Full comp-equal alloc		Full comp-equal cost		Full comp-equal alloc		Full comp-equal cost	
	Direct + ToT	Transfers	Direct + ToT	Transfers	Direct + ToT	Transfers	Direct + ToT	Transfers
USA	0.4	−1.7	0.4	−2.3	−2.5	−4.9	−2.6	−6.8
CAN	−1.9	−2.3	−2.4	0.5	−10.4	−7.7	−9.5	0.1
JPN	0.3	−1.0	0.7	−2.6	−1.2	−3.3	−0.7	−8.7
ANZ	−0.2	−2.8	−0.6	−1.3	−4.6	−7.9	−4.3	−5.1
EUR	−1.0	−1.1	−1.1	−0.8	−5.0	−3.9	−5.0	−4.4
EET	−2.1	−2.4	−2.7	0.8	−10.7	−14.3	−10.1	0.7
FSU	−4.9	−2.8	−6.6	4.7	−23.5	−17.5	−21.5	12.1

countries such as the United States and Japan. Nevertheless, costs for Japan, because it is so energy- and GHG-efficient per dollar of GDP, remain a very small percent of GDP in any allocation scheme based on present emissions.

In the *full compensation–equal cost* case allowances are allocated so that an equal welfare burden is imposed on all Annex I parties. As can be seen in the far right column of Table 24.5, this leads to similar allocations among the non-Annex I parties but very different allocations to Annex I countries. Table 24.3 shows that the bottom-line average cost of this approach to developed countries totals 1.9 percent in 2020, rising to 9.4 percent by 2050. Again, the breakdown of costs to Annex I parties is shown in Table 24.6.

A striking result in the *full compensation–equal cost* scenario is the large negative allowance allocation it implies for Japan: -113 percent of 2000 emissions in 2050 (Table 24.5). Again, this result reflects Japan's relatively low level of GHG emissions given the size of its economy. In a sense, if a fair rule is thought to be based on income levels, then GDP or GDP per capita is the direct measure we should use for dividing up responsibility. Benchmarking the allocation to historical emissions means we are using past emissions as a proxy for GDP. But if economies have very different GHG intensities, then emissions are a very poor proxy for GDP, and the differentiation of burdens under an allocation based on historical emissions must be very large. Thus, for Japan to bear an equal share of the cost burden of compensating developing countries for their mitigation costs, its allowance allocation in 2050 must be nearly 200 percent below its year 2000 emissions.[10]

If the initial allocation is as assumed in these last two cases, where financial transfers from allowance trading provide the mechanism for compensating developing countries, then the net transfers from and to each EPPA region as a result of the purchase and sale of allowances are as shown in the two right-most columns of Table 24.4. With full compensation, the total net flow of funds (in the form of allowance sales) from the developed to the developing countries is over $400 billion in 2020 and reaches over $3 trillion (annually) in 2050. The largest recipient region is the MES, accounting for nearly one-quarter of the total.

We can put these flows in perspective. If they are viewed as aid to developing countries then one comparison is to Official Development Assistance (ODA). In recent years, ODA transfers have totaled about $80 billion per year. So relative to current ODA levels, these allowance transfers imply a five-fold increase in assistance by 2020 and a nearly forty-fold increase by 2050. Transfers under a global climate policy might also be compared to current market flows—as allowance purchases will add to developed countries' import bill. To maintain current trade balances, countries that import allowances or permits will need to offset these purchases by reducing other imports or increasing exports. US exports totaled about $120–$155 billion per month in 2007–2008. Assuming US exports maintain the same relation to (projected) GNP, they would be expected to rise to $175–$225 billion per month in 2020 and $385–$500 billion in 2050. To offset projected allowance purchases in those years and maintain its current trade balance (taking the *full compensation-equal cost* case as an example), the United States would need to increase exports by 10–13 percent in 2020 and 29–37 percent in 2050.

---

[10] This rule for dividing up compensation costs is mostly about sharing the burden of mitigation costs in the poorer countries and so the size of the economy is a relevant measure. When it comes to compensating developing countries for adaptation or damage costs, a case can be made that Japan should not bear such a large share of the burden because its low emissions mean that Japan is not responsible for as much of the damage.

Allocations that partly compensate developing countries

Allocations that fully cover all developing-country costs likely represent an extreme interpretation of the principle of "common but differentiated responsibilities" in the context of an international climate agreement. Therefore it is useful to look at scenarios where some costs go uncompensated. For this analysis we explore the implications of an agreement under which developing countries accept some level of uncompensated welfare cost—in this case 3 percent. We also consider a case where developing countries are compensated for the direct costs of emissions mitigation but not for losses, mainly through terms-of-trade effects, resulting from mitigation actions by developed countries. Estimated allowance prices for these cases are not substantially different from the *full compensation–equal allocation* case in Figure 24.2.

Table 24.7 presents estimated welfare effects in the case where developing country costs are held to a maximum welfare loss of 3 percent (this case is denoted *3% cost cap* in the table). In 2020, the compensation cap is not yet binding on several of the developing countries (that is, welfare losses from the policy are below 3 percent), but by 2050 it constrains the welfare loss on all developing countries with the exception of China. A policy that only partly compensates developing countries is obviously less costly to developed countries than one that offers full compensation. The savings to Annex I regions can be seen by comparing welfare costs in Table 24.7 to those for the *full compensation–equal allocation* case in Table 24.3. The comparison reveals that partial compensation substantially reduces welfare costs to developed countries: for example, the welfare cost to the United States in 2020 drops from 1.3 percent to 0.7 percent, while the estimated cost in 2050 is reduced from 7.4 percent to 6.5 percent. Though the cost difference is smaller in percentage terms in 2050 than it is in 2020, it is larger in absolute value given the growth in the overall US economy projected by mid-century. Partial compensation provides similar cost savings to other Annex I regions. Overall, financial transfers to non-Annex I parties are reduced by about $200 billion in 2020, and by more than $500 billion in 2050.

The other potential partial-compensation case we explore would exclude compensation for the indirect costs of developed-country actions, an issue which has generally been debated separately from incentives for participation. The welfare results for this case, denoted as *direct only*,

Table 24.7 *Welfare effects in 2020 and 2050, partial compensation (percent from reference)*

	2020		2050	
	3% Cost cap	Direct only	3% Cost cap	Direct only
Annex I				
USA	−0.7	−1.1 (−0.3)	−6.5	−7.1 (−3.0)
CAN	−3.5	−3.9 (−1.8)	−16.8	−17.6 (−10.3)
JPN	−0.5	−0.6 (−0.4)	−4.1	−4.3 (−4.5)
ANZ	−2.3	−2.7 (−1.3)	−11.3	−12.0 (−7.9)
EUR	−1.7	−1.9 (−1.2)	−8.1	−8.6 (−7.4)
EET	−2.3	−3.6 (−0.8)	−21.7	−23.9 (−9.5)
FSU	−4.9	−6.5 (−1.1)	−37.0	−39.7 (−15.2)
Non-Annex I				
MEX	−2.3	−0.5 (−0.5)	−3.0	0.0 (1.0)
ASI	−0.5	0.0 (0.5)	−3.0	0.0 (1.2)
CHN	−0.1	0.0 (0.1)	0.1	0.0 (0.8)
IND	−3.0	0.0 (0.8)	−3.0	0.0 (5.5)
IDZ	−3.0	−0.6 (−0.6)	−3.0	0.0 (0.9)
AFR	−3.0	−2.1 (−2.1)	−3.0	−0.6 (−0.6)
MES	−3.0	−5.4 (−5.4)	−3.0	−9.0 (−9.0)
LAM	−2.6	−0.4 (−0.4)	−3.0	−0.1 (−0.1)
ROW	−1.9	0.0 (0.6)	−3.0	0.0 (7.7)

Note: Entries in **bold** indicate pre-specified welfare outcomes.
Figures in parentheses are the welfare effects of when Annex I countries only pursue
the cut, showing gains in some non-Annex I regions. The pre-specified losses are
those welfare losses from the Annex I only policy that are not compensated.

are shown in Table 24.7. To generate these estimates we first simulate a
case where only the Annex I regions undertake reductions, meeting the
allocation of the *30–70* case. (The actions of developing countries will
also result in some indirect costs, but this more limited calculation is a
good way to get a feel for the magnitude of the indirect cost of developed
country actions.) The welfare consequences of this Annex I-only policy
scenario are shown in parentheses in the table. Previous studies of this
issue (e.g., Babiker, Reilly, and Jacoby 2000) have shown that by far the
main indirect effect is on the oil exporting regions. Therefore we focus
on those regions in the EPPA aggregation that capture a good deal of this
effect: the Middle East (MES), Africa (AFR), Indonesia (IDZ), Mexico
(MEX), and Latin America (LAM). These regions or countries experience estimated welfare losses of 5.4 percent, 2.1 percent, 0.6 percent, 0.5

percent, and 0.4 percent respectively even in a scenario where they face no direct mitigation obligations—in other words, these welfare losses are solely attributable to the indirect effects of actions undertaken by Annex I nations. Comparing this scenario to one where all countries undertake mitigation actions, we offer compensation to developing countries only to the extent that their welfare costs under the full-participation scenario exceed their costs under the Annex I-only scenario. The effect of this approach is to compensate developing countries only for their direct mitigation costs, excluding losses that arise from the indirect effects of mitigation actions undertaken by developed countries (such as actions that reduce developed countries' demand for oil). Compensating developing countries for their direct mitigation costs only would lower the welfare cost of the policy to Annex I parties somewhat, as can be seen by comparing the results in Table 24.7 with the figures for *full compensation–equal allocation* in Table 24.3. The welfare loss experienced by the United States, for example, would fall from 1.3 percent to 1.1 percent in 2020 and from 7.4 percent to 6.5 percent in 2050. Interestingly, the uncompensated *indirect* welfare loss to the Middle East is larger than the cost to all parties or regions except Former Soviet Union (FSU) in 2020, and it remains larger than the cost to the United States, Europe, and Japan in 2050. Compared to the case where all developing countries are fully compensated for all costs, annual financial transfers from these three regions, if indirect effects are not compensated, are lower by $77 billion in 2020 and $108 billion in 2050.

Conclusions

The G8 has proposed, as a global goal, reducing GHG emissions 50 percent by 2050, though the proposal does not provide detail on how this would be accomplished, nor does it even specify the base year to which the percentage reduction applies. For purposes of this analysis, we have represented the G8 goal as a reduction from year 2000 emissions, which is between the Kyoto benchmark year of 1990 and the 2005 benchmark years in some US climate proposals. Whatever specific target emerges in international negotiations, there is a general sense that developed countries will assume a disproportionate share of the global reduction burden. In line with that expectation, recent federal and state legislative initiatives in the United States and proposals from a number of other developed countries have included domestic reduction targets on the order of 70–80 percent by mid-century. Assuming that abatement commitments are extended to include developing countries and that the global goal remains a 50 percent reduction from year 2000 emissions by mid-century, this implies that developing countries would be required to achieve a roughly 30 percent reduction below their 2000 emissions in the same timeframe. While this *30–70* proposal for dividing the abatement burden may appear to constitute a generous offer from the developed countries, it turns out that it would result in some developing countries making net purchases of allowances from the developed countries, in effect partially compensating richer countries for their mitigation efforts. This is contrary to the equity principles articulated in existing international climate agreements and in the Bali Action Plan.

Other allocation proposals advanced by developing countries would distribute allowances on an equal per capita basis or in inverse proportion to GDP per capita. Either of these approaches would shift costs toward the richer countries but would also raise other difficulties. For example, some developing countries would realize large net benefits that go well beyond the costs they can expect to incur for GHG mitigation, while for other developing countries a *population-* or *GDP-based* allocation would be less advantageous (i.e., more costly) than a simpler *30–70* allocation. In addition, this analysis finds that the use of population or GDP as a basis for allocation would result in highly divergent cost impacts among the Annex I countries.

One perhaps not surprising conclusion from this analysis, therefore, is that simple rules for distributing the overall abatement burden are incapable of dealing with the highly varying circumstances of different countries. Sometimes the results are peculiarly perverse, with richer countries faring very well while poorer ones bear particularly large costs. Moreover, even among developed countries, simple allocation rules can lead to differences in relative cost burdens that likely are unacceptable as well. Further discussion of these simple rules thus seems a waste of time, for they likely will generate little support, even as a starting point for negotiations between the G8 and the G77 that might eventually lead to a middle-ground compromise.

A second point highlighted by these simulations is that reducing global emissions 50 percent below 2000 levels by mid-century is a very ambitious goal. If it could be attained and sustained beyond 2050 there would be a good chance of keeping atmospheric CO_2 concentrations below 450 ppm, which—combined with reductions in other types of GHGs—might limit long-term radiative forcing to around 3.4 Watts per square meter (W/m^2) (US CCSP 2007). This in turn would yield something like 50-50 odds that global average temperature rise could be kept within the 2°C range—consistent with the underlying policy target endorsed by several European governments and environmental groups. Absent near-universal participation, however, a 50 percent global emissions reduction goal is not achievable given our projection of economic growth in various regions and the potential for emissions leakage if some regions do not take part. Even if all nations take on commitments, however, there are substantial costs to be shared, and meeting a global target at this level of stringency will require a complex web of transfers to share the burden.

Two interacting equity concerns would have to be dealt with to have any hope of meeting the 50 percent reduction goal. First, incentives and compensation for developing country participation will be required; moreover, the fact that these financial transfers will have income effects increases the magnitude of the task. No one really expects developing countries to bear the full burden of achieving their own reductions. But easing the burden on developing countries substantially increases the costs imposed on developed countries, so an acceptable sharing of the burden among richer nations will also be essential. The policy scenario designed to explore this possibility in our study is the *full compensation–equal cost* case, which holds the welfare costs imposed on non-Annex I parties to zero while imposing an equal welfare cost on all the Annex I parties. This case is perfect in its compensation and burden-sharing features—but, perhaps in part for this reason, it is also unlikely to emerge from international negotiations. Still, this scenario does give an impression of the challenge implicit in solving equity problems while simultaneously minimizing costs.

Even under this ideal agreement the welfare costs imposed on developed countries are substantial: around 2 percent in 2020 rising to a bit less than 10 percent in 2050.[11] In addition, this approach would result in large international financial transfers, modeled here as allowance flows from emissions trading. We estimate that the net transfer to

[11] To put these costs in context, under this policy US welfare increases by 62 percent between 2005 and 2020 (and by 222 percent between 2005 and 2050), rather than 65 percent and 255 percent, respectively, under the reference case.

developing countries ranges from nearly $500 billion per year in 2020 to over $3 trillion per year in 2050. Implied transfers from the United States alone total more than $1 trillion in 2050, though in 2020 the total is only around $200 billion.

Of course, it is an extreme assumption that developing countries will demand complete compensation. If, as is more likely, they are willing to bear some costs, then the welfare burden on the developed countries is reduced, along with implied financial transfers. The burden is further reduced if rich countries cover only the direct mitigation costs incurred by developing countries and not other losses associated with the policy, such as losses that might come from terms-of-trade effects. Even with less than full compensation, however, the welfare burden on the developed countries remains substantial, and the scale of the implied international financial transfers remains unprecedented.

Naturally, all these projections are subject to uncertainty. The task could turn out to be easier than our analysis suggests. Global growth could be lower than projected. If oil prices turn out to be higher than assumed in our analysis, this would take some pressure off the required CO_2 price and mitigation effort, as would a breakthrough agreement on forest destruction and degradation. Technological change could be more rapid than represented in the EPPA model, lowering mitigation costs. On the other hand, many features of these simulations could turn out to be optimistic, especially as regards the ease of emissions control. Growth, oil prices, and technological change could be less favorable than we assume. Importantly, the model assumes that CO_2 capture and storage technology will be demonstrated and the needed regulatory structure will be put in place, so that this abatement option can begin to take market share in 2020. Based on recent history this assumption is questionable. Also, a model like EPPA implements mitigation in cost-minimizing ways, equalizing reduction costs at the margin across all sources. In practice, domestic policies and international agreements are messier and less efficient than the calculation implies, leading to higher costs. On balance, then, we believe the results shown here provide a sound basis for forming judgments about the challenge of meeting targets like the one the G8 has proposed.

Negotiations on a post-2012 agreement will be difficult. New evidence as described in recent IPCC reports and elsewhere suggests that the risks of climate change are more serious than previously thought, and robust economic growth, especially in developing countries, has spurred growth in energy use and emissions over the past decade at rates faster than was previously projected. Economic growth is a good thing, especially for developing countries, but the evidence on growth, energy use, and emissions suggests that the belief that emissions growth could naturally or easily be decoupled from economic growth were highly optimistic. A recent MIT analysis also confirms that, absent a strong policy response, the climate change risk is great (Sokolov *et al.* 2009).

The G8 countries, spurred by scientific evidence that points to greater climate risks, have called for an aggressive global emissions goal. The Bali Action Plan and previous climate change agreements provide a framework for discussing developing country participation, including solutions that involve the developed countries providing incentives for participation and perhaps compensation for other costs of a global effort. These transfers could come in different guises, but it would seem the magnitude of the incentives offered must be on the scale of the mitigation costs that would be borne by developing countries in achieving their own reductions. Putting all these things together suggests not only that there will need to be an increased willingness on all sides to reach agreement, but also that the selection of targets in recent proposals is not well conditioned by an understanding of the complexities involved in finding a mutually acceptable way to share the economic burden.

Acknowledgements

We thank Jennifer Morris for research assistance. Development of the EPPA model used has been supported by the US Department of Energy, US Environmental Protection Agency and US National Science Foundation, and by a consortium of industry and foundation sponsors of the MIT Joint Program on the Science and Policy of Global Change.

References

Babiker, M., J. Reilly, and H. Jacoby (2000). "The Kyoto Protocol and Developing Countries," *Energy Policy* 28: 525–36.
Babiker, M., J. Reilly, and L. Viguier (2004). "Is Emissions Trading Always Beneficial?" *The Energy Journal* 25(2): 33–56.
Beckerman, W. and J. Pasek (1995). "The Equitable International Allocation of Tradable Carbon Emission Permits," *Global Environmental Change* 5: 405–13.

Blanford, G., R. Richels, and T. Rutherford (2009). "Revised Emissions Growth Projections for China: Why Post-Kyoto Climate Policy Must Look East," in this volume.

Bodansky, D. (2004). "International Climate Efforts Beyond 2012: A Survey of Approaches," Washington, DC: Pew Center on Global Climate Change, November.

Dimaranan, B. and R. McDougall (2002). "Global Trade, Assistance, and Production: The GTAP 5 Data Base, Center for Global Trade Analysis," West Lafayette, IN: Purdue University.

IPCC [International Panel on Climate Change] (2007). Policymakers Summary, Climate Change, Mitigation of Climate Change, B. Metz, O. Davidson, P. Bosch, R. Dave and L. Meyer (eds.), Working Group III of the Fourth Assessment Report of the Intergovernmental Panel on Climate Change, Cambridge, UK: Cambridge University Press.

Jacoby, H., R. Eckaus, A. D. Ellerman, R. Prinn, D. Reiner, and Z. Yang (1997). "CO_2 Emissions Limits: Economic Adjustments and Distribution of Burdens," *The Energy Journal* 18(3): 31–58.

Jacoby, H., R. Schmalensee, and I. Sue Wing (1999). "Toward a Useful Architecture for Climate Change Negotiations," Report 49, MIT Joint Program on the Science and Policy of Global Change.

McKibbin W. and P. Wilcoxen (2004). "Estimates of the Costs of Kyoto: Marrakech versus the McKibbin-Wilcoxen Blueprint," *Energy Policy* 32: 467–79.

Melillo, J., A. Gurgel, D. Kicklighter, J. Reilly, T. Cronin, B. Felzer, S. Paltsev, C. Schlosser, A. Sokolov, and X. Wang (2009). "Unintended Environmental Consequences of a Global Biofuels Program," Report 168, MIT Joint Program on the Science and Policy of Global Change.

Olivier, J. and J. Berdowski (2001). "Global Emissions Sources and Sinks," in J. Berdowski, R. Guicherit, and B. J. Heij (eds.), *The Climate System*. Lisse, Netherlands: Swets and Zeitlinger, pp. 33–78.

Paltsev, S., J. Reilly, H. Jacoby, R. Eckaus, J. McFarland, M. Sarofim, M. Asadoorian, and M. Babiker (2005). "The MIT Emissions Prediction and Policy Analysis (EPPA) Model: Version 4," Report 125, MIT Joint Program on the Science and Policy of Global Change.

Paltsev, S., J. Reilly, H. Jacoby, A. Gurgel, G. Metcalf, A. Sokolov, and J. Holak (2008). "Assessment of US GHG Cap-and-Trade Proposals," *Climate Policy* 8(4): 395–420.

Paltsev, S., J. Reilly, H. Jacoby, and K. Tay (2007). "How (and Why) Do Climate Policy Costs Differ among Countries?" in M. Schlesinger *et al.* (eds.), *Human-Induced Climate Change: An Interdisciplinary Assessment*. Cambridge, UK: Cambridge University Press, pp. 282–293.

Persson, T., C. Azar, and K. Lindgren (2006). "Allocation of CO_2 Emissions Permits—Economic Incentives for Emissions Reduction in Developing Countries," *Energy Policy* 34: 1889–99.

Reiner, D. and H. Jacoby (1997). "Annex I Differentiation Proposals: Implications for Welfare, Equity and Policy," Report 27, MIT Joint Program on the Science and Policy of Global Change.

Rose, A., B. Stevens, J. Edmonds, and M. Wise (1998). "International Equity and Differentiation in Global Warming Policy," *Environmental and Resource Economics* 12(1): 25–51.

Rutherford, T. (1995). "Extension of GAMS for Complementary Problems Arising in Applied Economic Analysis," *Journal of Economic Dynamics and Control* 19(8): 1299–324.

Sokolov, A., A. Schlosser, S. Dutkiewicz, S. Paltsev, D. Kicklighter, H. Jacoby, R. Prinn, C. Forest, J. Reilly, C. Wang, B. Felzer, M. Sarofim, J. Scott, P. Stone, J. Melillo, and J. Cohen (2005). "The MIT Integrated Global System Model (IGSM) Version 2: Model Description and Baseline Evaluation," Report 124, MIT Joint Program on the Science and Policy of Global Change.

Sokolov, A., P. Stone, C. Forest, R. Prinn, M. Sarofim, M. Webster, S. Paltsev, A. Schlosser, D. Kicklighter, S. Dutkiewicz, J. Reilly, C. Wang, B. Felzer, and H. Jacoby (2009). "Probablistic Forecast for 21st Century Climate Based on Uncertainties in Emissions (without Policy) and Climate Parameters," *Journal of Climate*, in press.

US CCSP [United States Climate Change Science Program] (2007). "CCSP Synthesis and Assessment Product 2.1, Part A: Scenarios of Greenhouse Gas Emissions and Atmospheric Concentrations," L. Clarke *et al.*, US Climate Change Science Program, Department of Energy, Washington, DC.

Webster, M., S. Paltsev, J. Reilly, and H. Jacoby (2009). "Uncertainty in Greenhouse Emissions and Costs of Atmospheric Stabilization," Report 165, MIT Joint Program on the Science and Policy of Global Change.

Winkler, H., R. Spalding-Fecher, L. Tyani (2002). "Comparing Developing Countries under Potential Carbon Allocation Schemes," *Climate Policy* 2: 303–18.

25 When technology and climate policy meet: energy technology in an international policy context

LEON CLARKE, KATE CALVIN,
JAE EDMONDS, PAE KYLE,
AND MARSHALL WISE[1]

Introduction

International efforts to stabilize atmospheric greenhouse gas (GHG) concentrations will ultimately rest on two pillars of climate policy: (1) the architecture and stringency of international agreements to reduce emissions and (2) efforts to speed the development and diffusion of climate-friendly technology. Although emissions mitigation writ large is the central focus of international climate negotiations, technology deployment is a primary means of achieving emissions reductions. The development of cheaper and more effective technologies will be critical for reducing costs and increasing the social and political viability of deep and widespread emissions reductions. Hence, it is important to understand the international context in which new technologies might be used to achieve mitigation and the implications of technological improvements for policy-relevant issues such as regional mitigation costs, the evolution of regional energy systems, and the associated likelihood and extent of national and international mitigation actions.

One avenue for exploring these issues is to conduct experiments using long-term, global, energy-economy-climate models. This is the approach used in this chapter. Although there is an extensive literature that explores international policy issues and technology issues individually using these

[1] The authors are researchers at the Pacific Northwest National Laboratory's Joint Global Change Research Institute (JGCRI), a collaboration with the University of Maryland at College Park. The authors are grateful to the US Department of Energy and the Electric Power Research Institute for research support and to an anonymous reviewer for helpful comments on an earlier draft. The opinions expressed here are the authors' alone.

models, efforts to explore these issues in tandem are more recent. One set of authors has focused on the interaction between international policy and the rate or direction of technological change, building on a recent tradition of incorporating stylistic representations of technological change in formal energy-economy models (see, for example, Goulder and Schneider 1999; Goulder and Mathai 2000; Nordhaus 2002; Popp 2004; Manne and Richels 2002; Messner 1997). For example, Bosetti *et al.* (2007) and Bosetti *et al.* (2008), use the WITCH model, which includes endogenous representations of technological change, including international spillovers, to explore the interactions between international policy architectures and technological change.[2]

A second avenue of research explores the interactions between international policy and *technology availability*, as opposed to the rate and direction of technological change, without commenting on the sources of technological change or the costs of bringing about technological change. This approach builds on a long line of research that has explored the relative benefits and characteristics of various exogenous portfolios of technology developments (e.g., Clarke *et al.* 2008b; Clarke *et al.* 2007a; Edmonds *et al.* 2007; GTSP 2000; IEA 2008), often for use in research and development (R&D) planning activities, and to inform broader discussions on the role of technology in addressing climate change more generally (Pacala and Socolow 2004; Hoffert *et al.* 2002). For example, Richels *et al.* (2007) explore the value of technology in an inefficient international context by considering first-best and second-best policy structures under two sets of exogenous technology assumptions: one that limits the deployment of nuclear power and another that limits the deployment of carbon capture and storage (CCS) technology.

This chapter follows the path set out in Richels *et al.* (2007). The technologically-detailed MiniCAM integrated assessment model (Kim *et al.* 2006; Clarke *et al.* 2007a; Clarke *et al.* 2008b) was used to create eight climate action scenarios based on four possible exogenous

---

[2] In general, these representations of technological change have remained highly stylistic because the processes of technological advance are enormously complex, context specific, and highly resistant to the sorts of simplifications needed to incorporate them into formal economic models (see, for example, Grubb *et al.* 2002; Clarke and Weyant 2002; Loschel 2002; Clarke *et al.* 2006; and Clarke *et al.* 2008a for discussions about capturing endogenous technological change in formal energy–economy models).

technology futures and two possibilities for international mitigation: full global participation and delayed participation by developing regions. All scenarios lead to a target atmospheric carbon dioxide (CO_2) concentration of 500 parts per million by volume (ppmv) in 2095. These scenarios provide a window into issues surrounding the national and international benefits of new technologies, the regional distribution of technology deployment, and the interactions between technology availability and regional mitigation actions.

With regard to the value of technological developments, these scenarios support the argument that the global benefits of new and improved technologies are probably larger when international participation is incomplete. Further, developed regions benefit disproportionately because more of the abatement burden falls on them, particularly in the near term, if participation by developing regions is delayed.

The scenarios in this study also reinforce the importance of technology diffusion in evaluating national R&D and other technology development programs. The mitigation cost benefits of technology development investments (e.g., R&D investments) in individual regions are strongly linked to the ability to deploy these technologies internationally. By accelerating technology diffusion, the likelihood and extent of international mitigation actions is increased, reducing the abatement burden on the countries that developed the technology. This perspective on the indirect value of investments in technology development is important; many analyses of the mitigation benefits that accrue to domestic R&D expenditures look only at reductions in the domestic cost of mitigation for a given, invariant national emissions pathway.

This analysis also supports the assertion that there are a range of near-term technology-related actions in developing regions—actions that are not formally tied to emissions mitigation—that could be seen to constitute near-term action in a global climate regime. Many climate-friendly technologies provide benefits even absent climate change concerns and might therefore be deployed for non-climate reasons. Improved energy end-use technologies; advances in nuclear power that alleviate concerns over waste, safety, or proliferation; and improvements in the cost and performance of renewable energy technologies such as wind and solar power fall into this category. Under the scenarios that assume delayed climate action by developing countries, increased deployment of these technologies leads to near-term mitigation.

Finally, the scenarios help elucidate the relationship between near-term abatement and expectations about technology availability in the long run. In particular, the scenarios highlight the interactions between mitigation technologies such as bioenergy with CCS that could be used in the long term to achieve negative emissions and global emissions pathways in which concentrations temporarily exceed long-term targets ("overshoot" pathways). Overshoot pathways are beneficial because they expand the range of very low concentration targets that are feasible, and the availability of negative emissions technologies increases the degree of overshoot that is possible. On the other hand, overshoot pathways are troubling because they lead to concentrations that exceed, at least for some period of time, the concentration target to be achieved at a later date. They are therefore associated with potentially greater environmental damage than pathways in which concentrations never exceed the long-term target. In addition, allowing emissions to follow an overshoot pathway in the near term leaves open the possibility that once the concentration target is exceeded, the necessarily steeper emissions declines required later in the century to reach the target may never materialize.

The remainder of this chapter proceeds as follows. The next section discusses the approach to the analysis and provides background on important issues that influence this approach. Subsequent sections discuss the implications of technology development and international participation in terms of emissions and concentrations, the relationship between near-term mitigation and technology deployment, and the uncertain character of future global and national energy systems. The last two sections discuss the value of technology availability in reducing mitigation costs and provide a brief summary and several closing thoughts.

Approach

The scenarios in this chapter are constructed using the MiniCAM integrated assessment model. They combine four alternative sets—or "suites"—of assumptions concerning technology evolution over the course of the century with two alternative hypothetical international policy architectures, both of which aim to limit the atmospheric concentration of CO_2 to 500 ppmv in the year 2095.

MiniCAM

MiniCAM (Brenkert *et al.* 2003; Kim *et al.* 2006) combines a technologically detailed global energy-economy-agriculture-land-use model with a suite of coupled gas-cycle, climate, and ice-melt models, integrated in the Model for the Assessment of Greenhouse-Gas Induced Climate Change (MAGICC). MiniCAM is directly descended from a model developed by Edmonds and Reilly (1985).

MiniCAM is a global, partial equilibrium model disaggregated into fourteen geopolitical regions. Energy, agriculture, forestry, and land markets are integrated with representations of unmanaged ecosystems and the terrestrial carbon cycle. MiniCAM thus produces outputs that include not only emissions of fifteen GHGs and aerosols but also agricultural prices, land use, and stocks of terrestrial carbon. The model does not attempt to address international trade in goods and services other than energy and agriculture and does not consider bilateral trade issues.

MiniCAM is solved on a fifteen-year time step and is designed to examine long-term, large-scale changes in global and regional energy systems, with a focus on the impact of energy technologies.[3] It provides substantial energy-sector detail in comparison to other integrated assessment models. Of particular relevance to this study, MiniCAM takes the availability of technology to be exogenous. This means that the scenarios considered here do not address important issues associated with the relationship between mitigation and technological change. The exogenous technology assumption can be interpreted as assigning the majority of technological change to sources that are not particularly influenced by mitigation actions and to associated changes in markets for technology (see Clarke *et al.* 2006 and Clarke *et al.* 2008a for more on this subject).

The scenarios in this chapter were developed using the version of MiniCAM that was used to examine scenarios of GHG emissions and concentrations as part of the United States Climate Change Science Program (CCSP). Extensive documentation of the energy demand and technology assumptions can be found in Clarke *et al.* (2007a) and Clarke *et al.* (2007b). Of particular interest for the purposes of

---

[3] Documentation for MiniCAM can be found at www.globalchange.umd.edu/models/MiniCAM.pdf/.

Table 25.1 *Definitions for four technology suites*

Technology Suite Components*	Technology Suites			
	Reference (REF)	Advanced (ADV)	Bioenergy, CCS & Storage, Hydrogen (BIO/CCS)	Renewable, Nuclear, and Efficiency (RNE)
Carbon dioxide capture and storage (CCS)	Reference (not allowed)	Advanced	Advanced	Reference (not allowed)
Bioenergy	Reference (no purpose-grown bioenergy crops)	Advanced	Advanced	Reference
Hydrogen	Reference	Advanced	Advanced	Reference
End-use Energy Efficiency	Reference	Advanced	Reference	Advanced
Wind Power	Reference	Advanced	Reference	Advanced
Solar Power	Reference	Advanced	Reference	Advanced
Nuclear Power	Reference (no new builds)	Advanced	Reference (no new builds)	Advanced
Geothermal Power	Reference	Advanced	Reference	Advanced

* Technology descriptions are similar to those documented and discussed in Clarke *et al.* (2008b).

this chapter, the scenarios assume—as do many current scenarios—a gradual shift of economic activity and emissions from the developed to the developing world over the course of the century.

Technology suites

Four technology evolution pathways, or technology suites, are explored in these scenarios (Table 25.1). Each of the four suites is defined by developments in eight different technology domains. Each technology domain is associated with a reference technology case and an advanced technology case. The approach to the advanced and reference cases varies among the technology domains. For solar power, geothermal power, wind power, and hydrogen, the reference and advanced cases are distinguished by different assumptions about technology cost and performance. The advanced cases assume greater and more rapid cost and performance improvements over the century than the reference cases.

Nuclear power and CCS are treated differently. Under reference case assumptions, neither is allowed to deploy beyond today's levels; under advanced case assumptions both technologies play a greater role based on mainstream evolutions of cost and performance over time. Several studies have concluded that both of these technologies would be deployed at significant levels under any reasonable range of cost and performance assumptions if a long-term climate goal such as the goal modeled in this chapter is adopted. The issues surrounding these technologies have less to do with cost and performance, *per se*, and more to do with their fundamental availability, which in turn is based on technology and institutional structures. For example, although there are uncertainties regarding the cost of nuclear power, the main concerns regarding widespread deployment (and cost) are associated with waste, safety, and security. The uncertainties regarding CCS revolve around the long-term reliability of underground storage, but perhaps more importantly stem from the infrastructural and institutional issues that will have to be addressed to develop an entirely new infrastructure for transporting and injecting gas streams underground.

Bioenergy is treated in a similar fashion to nuclear power and CCS. The reference technology case assumes no dedicated bioenergy crops, while the advanced technology case assumes that large-scale production from dedicated cellulosic feedstocks is viable over the long term. Without technology for using cellulosic feedstocks, the negative consequences of bioenergy production—particularly taking into account the effect of deforestation to clear land for production—could put a significant long-term brake on this option. Hence, the reference case captures a world without breakthroughs in bioenergy production and therefore highly limited deployment.

Bioenergy can be considered a zero emissions fuel with respect to direct emissions. However, several authors, including Searchinger *et al.* (2008) and Crutzen *et al.* (2008) have raised questions about the indirect effect of bioenergy production on deforestation rates, crop prices, and non-CO_2 GHG emissions. Indirect emissions are addressed in MiniCAM, which accounts for agriculture, land use, land cover, and terrestrial carbon stocks and flows.[4] In this analysis, all anthropogenic carbon emissions, be they from fossil fuel and industrial sources or land-use change, are treated equally—that is, they receive the same carbon price (Wise *et al.*, 2009). Thus, in all of the policy regimes considered in this analysis, afforestation programs are an important component of the technology response. Since energy-sector technology is the focus of this chapter, discussion of the potential roles of non-energy technologies is left for future papers.

When both CCS and bioenergy are available technology options they can be applied in combination to provide electric power with negative emissions. Since biofuels derive their carbon from the atmosphere, applying CCS technology to a power plant that uses biofuels[5] has the net effect of removing CO_2 from the atmosphere. In a context where the potential exists to temporarily overshoot target concentration levels, this combination of technologies can have important implications for emissions trajectories over time.

Energy end-use technologies are treated differently. The reference and advanced technology cases assume different rates of exogenous improvement in the relationship between end-use service demands in the transport, buildings, and industry sectors—irrespective of policy or prices. Hence energy consumption is lower in the advanced technology scenarios than in the reference scenarios, irrespective of policy. A large literature argues that end-use technology choices are rife with market failures—the advanced technology scenarios assume an ability to overcome some of these barriers, as well as to improve technology.

Based on these reference and advanced technology cases across technology domains, the four technology suites can be described as follows. The reference technology suite (REF) is based on reference case assumptions in all technology domains. This is a pessimistic scenario since it assumes that GHG reductions must be achieved using currently expensive technologies such as wind and solar power along with reductions in energy services. The advanced technology suite (ADV) is

---

[4] Note that we do not consider non-CO_2 GHG emissions in this chapter, though these are tracked in MiniCAM. Similarly, MiniCAM tracks agricultural and forest product prices, which are also not reported in this chapter.

[5] This option assumes that biomass can be gasified and burned in an integrated combined cycle power plant with CCS.

based on advanced assumptions in all technology domains. It represents the most optimistic view of the future. Between the reference and advanced technology suites are two intermediate suites. One of them (RNE) assumes advances in technologies that are broadly in use today, such as energy end-use technologies, nuclear power, solar power, and wind power; it might be thought of as a "known technologies" suite. A second (BIO/CCS) uses reference case assumptions in these technology areas, but allows for the deployment of newer, largely untested technologies such as advanced bioenergy, CCS, and hydrogen.

The technology assumptions in the scenarios are exogenous. In other words, the analysis is silent on the means by which each of these technology suites emerges. It is agnostic as to whether technology advances, relative to the reference technology suite, represent the fruits of intensive and potentially expensive research campaigns, learning-by-doing, spillovers from other industries, or a serendipitous process of scientific discovery.[6] If technology advances depend on intensive R&D efforts, then all associated costs would have to be added to the direct mitigation costs computed in the scenarios to obtain the total cost of achieving a desired emissions mitigation result. In this exercise, however, no attempt is made to associate research investments with particular technology outcomes.

Hypothetical international policy architectures

This analysis focuses on a single potential climate goal: namely, limiting the concentration of atmospheric CO_2 to 500 ppmv in the year 2095. As none of the technology suites considered in this chapter by themselves result in an atmospheric concentration that is 500 ppmv or less in the year 2095, policies that explicitly limit emissions are required to achieve this outcome.

The scenarios do not require that the concentration limit be binding before 2095: that is, concentrations can exceed 500 ppmv at any time prior to 2095. Emissions pathways that allow atmospheric CO_2 concentrations to exceed the long-term goal for some portion of the time between the adoption of the target and the target date are known as "overshoot" trajectories. By contrast, most mitigation sce-

---

[6] Again, see Clarke *et al.* 2006 and Clarke *et al.* 2008a for a discussion of the implications of different modeling approaches.

narios in the literature are constructed so that the atmospheric CO_2 concentration limit that applies in the final period is never exceeded (see, for example, the scenarios developed in Clarke *et al.* 2007a). In such a "not-to-exceed" framing of the concentration limit, emissions are constrained such that the atmospheric concentration rises to the limit and is maintained at that level in perpetuity thereafter (note that any scenario in which concentrations *fall* is, by construction, an overshoot trajectory since it implies that concentrations must, for at least some period of time, have exceeded the level they will reach in the long term). The implications of overshoot for these scenarios will be discussed in more detail later in this chapter.

Two hypothetical policy architectures are used in this analysis to reach the 2095 goal. One approach reflects an idealized setting in which a price is imposed on all carbon emissions, from all sources everywhere, and raised at a rate that minimizes the total cost to the world economy of achieving that goal. While such a scenario is not likely, it provides a benchmark against which to compare other, less perfect international policy architectures. Scenarios based on this architecture are referred to as FULL participation scenarios.

A more realistic policy architecture is one in which different nations take different levels of action to mitigate carbon emissions, leading to pricing that varies across regions over time. In the DELAY scenarios, nations included in Annex I to the United Nations Framework Convention on Climate Change (UNFCCC) (United Nations 1992) as well as South Korea, begin efforts to mitigate emissions in 2012, but other regions do not follow suit until later. Table 25.2 shows the dates when emission limits first apply to each of the MiniCAM's fourteen regions in the DELAY scenarios.

Stabilization of CO_2 concentrations implies a rising price of carbon. It is assumed that the Annex I plus South Korea group, and other regions as they join, share a common price of carbon and apply that price to all emissions from all sources. Since the coalition price is doubling regularly, new members of the coalition would experience an economic shock if they introduced a carbon price that was instantaneously set at the same level as the then current price in the mitigating coalition. Therefore this analysis assumes that the initial carbon price in a region that begins emissions mitigation after the year 2012 is below the price shared by the original members of the coalition. It is further assumed that the initial price assigned to a new entrant is based on gross

Table 25.2 *Year in which carbon emissions limitations are first imposed in each of the 14 MiniCAM regions*

MiniCAM Region	Year in which carbon emissions limitations are first imposed
United States	2012
Australia & New Zealand	2012
Canada	2012
Western Europe	2012
Eastern Europe	2012
Japan	2012
Former Soviet Union	2012
Korea	2012
China	2020
Latin America	2035
Middle East	2035
Other South and East Asia	2035
India	2050
Africa	No emissions limitations are imposed

Table 25.3 *Combinations of technology suites and hypothetical policy architectures examined in this chapter*

		Alternative Technology Suites			
		REF	RNE	BIO/CCS	ADV
Alternative Emissions	FULL	•	•	•	•
Limitation Regimes	DELAY	•	•	•	•

domestic product (GDP) per capita relative to the United States in the year 2000. The price of carbon in regions that accept emissions limitations later in the century gradually rises to that of the Annex I group.

Summary of the scenarios

Combining the two policy architectures with four technology suites leads to eight scenarios (Table 25.3). By comparing and contrasting scenarios, it is possible to observe the relative influences of international participation and technology in shaping the future development of the global energy system and in determining the cost of meeting the hypothetical atmospheric CO_2 limit in 2095.

Emissions and concentrations: the implications of technology, participation, and overshoot

A brief overview of the implications of overshoot

Before discussing the implications of technology and participation in an international regime, it is useful to first discuss the implications of overshoot for the scenarios. These implications are important because overshoot pathways create the potential for greater variation in emissions and concentration pathways, and greater variation in climate impacts, than is possible with a not-to-exceed formulation.[7]

The potential impacts and role of overshoot pathways can be perceived in two ways. On the one hand, overshoot pathways are troubling because they lead to concentrations that exceed, at least for some period of time, the concentration target to be achieved at a later date. They are therefore associated with potentially greater environmental damage during the period in which concentrations are above the eventual goal. In addition, allowing emissions to follow an overshoot pathway leaves open the possibility that once the concentration target is exceeded, the necessarily steeper emissions declines required later in the century to reach the target may never materialize.

On the other hand overshoot pathways can facilitate the adoption of lower long-term concentration limits than would be achievable under a not-to-exceed approach. For some stringent concentration limits, overshoot pathways may be the only realistic option for meeting the long-term goal. The 350 ppmv emissions concentration pathway developed by Wigley, Richels, and Edmonds was an overshoot pathway that featured negative global carbon emissions in some years. Work by Van Vuuren *et al.* (2007) shows that limiting long-term radiative forcing to 2.6 watts per square meter (W/m^2) entails limiting atmospheric CO_2 concentrations in the year 2100 to below current levels. Van Vuuren *et al.* achieve this outcome by first overshooting

---

[7] However, it must be remembered that even with a not-to-exceed formulation, variation in emissions, concentrations, and climate change exist (Wigley, Richels, and Edmonds 1996). Furthermore, there are limits to overshooting a goal, depending on the options for reducing emissions in the second half of the century. The degree of overshoot therefore depends on the suite of technologies that is anticipated to be available in the future, especially in the post-2050 future, as we discuss in more detail below.

the long-term target and then employing steep reductions in the late 21st century through the large-scale deployment of biomass-based electricity production with CCS to achieve negative global emissions.

If technologies capable of delivering negative global carbon emissions—such as the combination of bioenergy and CCS explored in these scenarios—become available, human society will have the option to move atmospheric CO_2 concentrations arbitrarily down. This potential capability raises still more questions about the long term: namely, at what concentration should humankind choose to maintain the atmosphere? Should emissions trajectories be compared in terms of the maximum GHG concentration level or temperature increase they produce rather than in terms of a long-term stabilization goal? No attempt is made to answer this question here; it is left for a deeper exploration of the implications of overshoot pathways. The key for interpreting the scenarios in this chapter is that overshoot pathways allow for greater intertemporal flexibility in emissions reductions than not-to-exceed scenarios.

Overshoot, technology, and global emissions and concentrations

This section focuses on the emissions and concentration pathways that emerge from the FULL participation scenarios. Economic implications generally are addressed in a later section, but it is useful here to briefly touch on the carbon prices associated with different scenarios because of their relationship to emissions and concentration pathways over time. Limiting the atmospheric CO_2 concentration to 500 ppmv in 2095 is accomplished by imposing an exponentially rising price on carbon in all regions and all emitting activities in the FULL participation scenario, where all nations join in global mitigation efforts from the outset. Not surprisingly, the price path is highest for the REF technology suite and lowest for the ADV technology suite with costs for the other two technology suites falling in between (Figure 25.1).[8]

---

[8] The carbon prices provide some insight into the contrasting arguments about whether it is possible to achieve climate goals with today's technology. Without CCS, new nuclear power plants, or dedicated bioenergy crops, the REF technology suite can roughly be interpreted as a "known technologies" suite. Hence, the scenarios support the argument that climate goals can be met with "known technologies" (Pacala and Socolow 2004). However, the economic

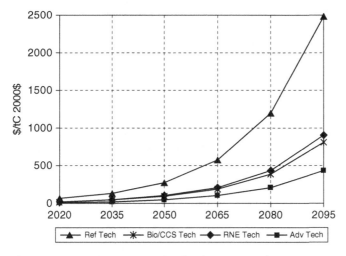

Figure 25.1. Carbon price paths that limit atmospheric CO_2 concentrations to 500 ppmv for four alternative technology suites under FULL international participation from 2012 onward

These results illustrate the importance of expectations regarding technology availability in shaping near-term carbon prices. Because limiting atmospheric CO_2 concentrations involves limiting global carbon emissions over the entire century, the long-term future and present are tightly coupled. The assumption of intertemporal cost-effectiveness along with complete foresight leads to a simple inter-temporal carbon price pathway with the price in each period directly linked to the price in the previous period by the rate of interest. The implication is that near-term prices depend as much on expected technology availability in the long term as they do on actual technology availability in the near term. While it is impossible to anticipate technology availability a half century or more into the future—or indeed to predict with certainty any of the other variables that define our scenarios—it is clear that near-term actions depend on *expectations* about the long term in a way that distinguishes climate change from other environmental issues, such as acid deposition or local air

cost is substantially higher than if more advanced technologies become available. Therefore, the scenarios also support the argument that the development of advanced energy technologies is important to the success of the enterprise (Hoffert *et al.* 2002).

quality, with which society has dealt in the past. There are, of course, other interactions between near-term mitigation and carbon prices, on the one hand, and long-term technology expectations on the other. For example, near-term mitigation actions can influence technology development through induced R&D and learning-by-doing (Goulder and Mathai 2000; Grubb *et al.* 1995). Nonetheless, emissions reductions are not the only drivers of improvement in carbon-friendly technologies, and the relationship between mitigation and technology development will not alter the fundamental linkage between long-term expectations and near-term action.

Technology influences not only carbon prices, of course, but also the global emissions and concentration pathways that might be followed to meet a particular long-term target (Figures 25.2 and 25.3). To understand the influence of technology on near-term emissions, it is useful to distinguish between the influence of near-term technology availability and long-term technology availability. The influence of long-term technology in these scenarios is highlighted by the presence of CCS coupled with bioenergy production. The assumption that a radical technology option such as this one will be available in the future puts less pressure on near-term abatement efforts and allows for higher near-term emissions: the more that can be done cheaply in the future, the less it makes sense to do today. The combination of CCS and bioenergy technology allows for negative emissions in the far future, and thus diminishes pressure on near-term emissions reductions in both the ADV and BIOCCS technology suites.[9]

Near-term technology advances have the opposite effect. Lower near-term technology costs and greater availability imply larger near-term reductions. In these scenarios, the major near-term options are improved energy end-use technologies and nuclear power. The advanced end-use assumptions are based on the notion that (1) improvements to end-use technologies will be deployed irrespective of climate policy and (2) many options can provide meaningful near-term emissions

---

[9] The presence of CCS alters the way in which bioenergy is used. A great deal of research has focused on the use of bioenergy to produce liquid fuels, primarily for transport. At lower carbon prices, this approach proves to be dominant. However, when CCS is available and carbon prices rise, bioenergy is predominantly deployed in conjunction with electric power generation. Such market forces could emerge if CCS is available and the net negative emissions of the bioenergy and CCS technology combination were appropriately rewarded.

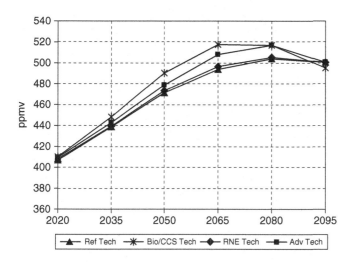

Figure 25.2. CO_2 concentration paths for four alternative technology suites under FULL international participation from 2012 onward

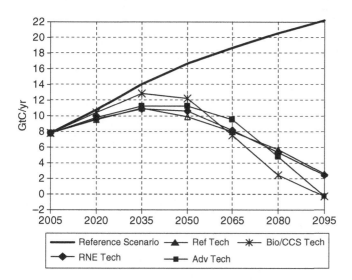

Figure 25.3. Carbon emissions paths that limit atmospheric CO_2 concentrations to 500 ppmv for four alternative technology suites under FULL international participation from 2012 onward

reductions. The advanced nuclear assumptions are based on the notion that waste, security, and safety concerns do not limit the near- or long-term deployment of nuclear power. These assumptions result in lower near-term emissions in both the RNE and ADV scenarios.

The resulting emissions pathways reflect the interactions between near- and long-term technology availability. The BIOCCS scenario has the highest near-term emissions because emissions reductions are pushed to the future. In contrast, near-term emissions are lower in the ADV scenario because of low-cost, near-term end-use options. The REF scenario has neither of these options. Its near-term emissions are on the low side because the lack of improved mitigation options results in higher carbon prices that push emissions down through more costly means.

Delayed participation, technology, and regional emissions mitigation

Previous sections discuss the role of technology assuming full international participation in a global GHG control regime. This section compares the results from these idealized scenarios with outcomes under a hypothetical international control regime with delayed participation. We focus here on three observations. First, the variation in global carbon emissions across technology regimes is significantly larger than the variation across different international regimes for achieving a given concentration goal (Figure 25.4). This is a consequence of the discipline that the carbon cycle imposes on possible pathways to a given concentration target. While some flexibility exists in shifting emissions forward and backward in time—with a given technology regime, that ability is limited. Emission shifts across time depend on available technology. That is, the ability to sharply reduce emissions in the BIOCCS technology suite implies higher near-term emissions as compared with other technology suites. It is worth noting that the ability to overshoot and return to the long-term concentration target brings the time-shift of emissions into relief, but the effect is present even with a not-to-exceed formulation of the concentration limit.

Second, although the global emissions pathway for achieving a given concentration target is less sensitive to the international policy environment than to technology availability, the same is not true at the regional scale. With REF technology, the DELAY international policy architecture results in India having higher emissions relative to the "no

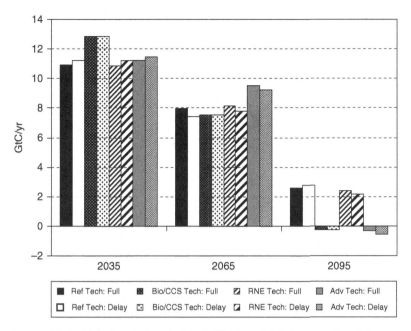

Figure 25.4. Global emissions in 2035, 2065, and 2095 across the eight atmospheric CO_2 concentration limitation scenarios

climate policy" reference scenario (Figure 25.5). This is the result of emissions leakage from participating regions: their mitigation efforts result in lower demand, and hence lower international prices, for fossil fuels. This in turn leads to increased fuel use and higher emissions in non-participating regions. Only after India joins the set of emissions mitigating regions do its emissions begin to decline. In contrast, emissions in the United States decline almost linearly to zero by 2065 under the DELAY international policy architecture (Figure 25.6). This outcome is dramatically different than the outcome modeled under the FULL participation international policy architecture. In that scenario, which assumes India and all other regions of the world begin emissions mitigation in 2012, United States emissions are approximately two-thirds of 2005 levels in 2065. These results follow from the earlier observation that for a given technology suite there is relatively little ability to shift global emissions mitigation over time. Thus, participating regions are forced to compensate for the emissions mitigation that is not forthcoming from non-participating regions. The availability of

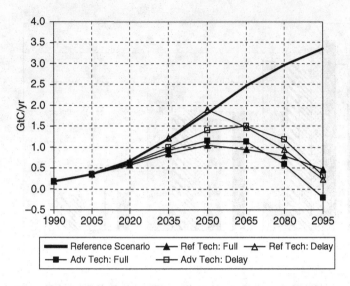

Figure 25.5. Emissions pathways in India for selected scenarios

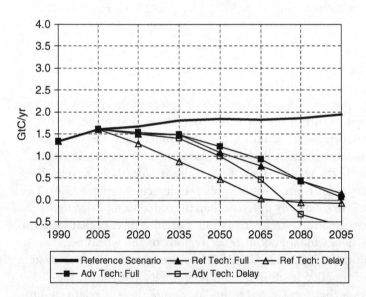

Figure 25.6. Emissions pathways in the United States for selected scenarios

improved abatement options over time in the ADV technology suite does substantially mute the shift in burden.

Third, the availability of near-term abatement options such as nuclear power and end-use technology options allows for some mitigation even in non-participating countries. When the ADV technology suite is modeled, Indian emissions are lower relative to the no-climate-policy reference scenario, even though India is not participating in a climate regime. Under these technologies assumptions, the United States benefits from lower costs to meet a given domestic emissions target, plus some relief in terms of the stringency of that target due to Indian reductions. This result highlights the point that not all mitigation needs to be a function of climate policy—as researchers have noted repeatedly in calling attention to the technological improvements already embodied in reference or "no-policy" scenarios. Although technology cannot solve the challenge of climate mitigation without the impetus of climate policy, accelerated diffusion of currently available technologies could provide a means for achieving near-term emissions reductions in developing countries that are not inclined toward accepting explicit emission-reduction commitments. The mitigation effect in these scenarios is somewhat artificial, due to the construction of the reference and advanced technology assumptions for nuclear power and end-use technologies. Nonetheless, the results highlight the potential benefits that could be achieved if developing countries were able to overcome barriers and failures in markets for energy efficiency; develop the technological or institutional structures needed to allow for greater penetration of nuclear power; and take advantage of near-term advances in wind and solar power along with associated technologies for facilitating system integration, such as batteries.

The composition of technology deployment in the near term and long term

Long-term technology evolution

To meet the sorts of long-term goals explored in this chapter, fossil fuel technologies that freely emit carbon must be virtually removed from the energy system by the end of the century. A view of the Chinese and United States energy systems in 2095 under all eight of the mitigation scenarios along with the reference scenario (Figure 25.7 and

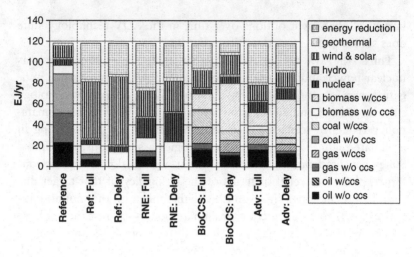

Figure 25.7. Primary energy, United States, 2095 for four alternative technology suites under FULL and DELAY international policy architectures

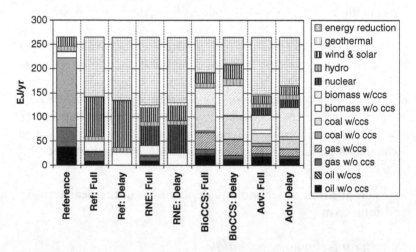

Figure 25.8. Primary energy, China, 2095 for four alternative technology suites under FULL and DELAY international policy architectures

Figure 25.8) illustrates this requirement. However, though all the scenarios share this common feature, they lead to otherwise dramatically different energy systems, for reasons that have to do with the evolution of both technology and international policy over the course of the century. This variation illustrates the inherent uncertainty in attempting to forecast how technology might evolve and be deployed to meet a climate goal. Although it is well understood that dramatic change is necessary, the nature of that change is highly uncertain, especially in the far future.

Technology deployment varies in the long run due to both of the dimensions explored in this study: the evolution of technology availability and the evolution of international participation in global mitigation efforts. That deployment varies depending on technology availability is not surprising. In general, the absence of any single technology requires greater contributions from other technologies and additional reductions in energy use. Scenarios with improved end-use technologies rely to a greater extent on energy-use reductions (RNE and ADV), as do higher cost scenarios (REF). On the other hand, scenarios with greater options for low-carbon supply allow for less emphasis on energy-demand reductions (RNE, BIOCCS, and ADV).

International participation influences the long-term composition of energy systems through several avenues. For one, delay increases long-term carbon prices, leading to greater long-term deployment of low or negative emissions technologies across all of the technology suites. Delay also affects long-term technology deployment through any continued differences in participation that may persist through the end of the century. Those countries participating in mitigation will see still higher carbon prices than those that do not participate (Africa in 2095) or those that participate at lower relative carbon prices (India and Latin America in 2095). Finally, the path of investments in technology over the course of the century is influenced by international participation, and some of these effects will linger. Note, for example, the earlier and continued deployment of bioenergy in the REF DELAY scenario relative to the REF FULL scenario (Figures 25.7 and 25.9).

Near-term technology deployment in a long-term context

Figure 25.9 and Figure 25.10 show the United States and Chinese energy systems in 2035 under the reference scenario and the eight

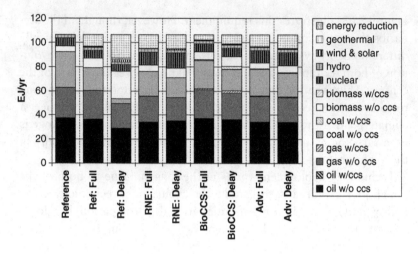

Figure 25.9. Primary energy, United States, 2035 for four alternative technology suites under FULL and DELAY international policy architectures

mitigation scenarios. Recall that China has a lower carbon price in 2035 than the United States due to its delayed entrance into the global coalition. In contrast to the results for 2095, which show dramatic variation in the energy supply mix for different scenarios and include widespread deployment of low-carbon energy sources, the results for 2035 reflect the continued influence of the capital stocks, infrastructure, and institutions that existed in 2005. The 2035 composition varies primarily in terms of total production from fossil fuels, which continue to dominate in all scenarios regardless of the technology suite that ultimately becomes available. The contribution from low-carbon energy sources remains small relative to the total size of the energy system.

The primary effects of technology are similar to those observed in the FULL participation scenarios and discussed in a previous section. Expectations regarding future abatement options influence the carbon price, and higher carbon prices lead to greater near-term emission reductions. Given turnover rates in the energy system, much of this near-term mitigation is achieved through energy demand reductions and fuel switching. More effective near-term options also lead to near-term adjustments, particularly energy demand reductions

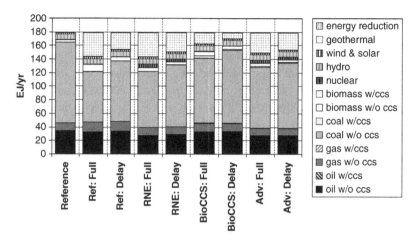

Figure 25.10. Primary energy, China, 2035 for four alternative technology suites under FULL and DELAY international policy architectures

achieved through the increased availability and use of more efficient end-use technologies.

Several interactive effects related to delayed participation bear discussion here. First, mitigation efforts are simply more aggressive in the participating countries, and this leads to obvious differences in energy demand reduction and low-carbon technology deployment. Second, asymmetric emissions mitigation will lead to a drop in global fossil fuel prices, pushing consumption toward those countries that are taking no action or little action. This leakage effect is manifest in higher emissions for non-participating countries compared to the reference case (see, for example, Figure 25.5). Third, the results point to increased use of bioenergy in participating nations relative to a full participation scenario. Bioenergy is produced around the world, but it is the participating nations that will demand bioenergy for climate purposes. To the extent that bioenergy production is associated with emissions from land-use changes, this means that delayed participation involves substantial emissions leakage—not simply through asymmetric fuel prices, but also through the exporting of land-use change emissions for bioenergy production to non-participating countries.

The contrasting composition of energy systems in 2095 and 2035 informs questions regarding the nature and aggressiveness of required near-term technology deployments for meeting the sorts of long-term goals similar to the long-term goal explored in this chapter. It is not surprising that the long-term composition of the energy system is highly uncertain and dependent on the availability, cost, and performance of future technology and on the architecture of emissions mitigation policies. How should decision makers *today* respond to this uncertainty and what near-term actions should they take with regard to technology policy, from basic science through deployment policies? What does it mean to begin to lay down the foundation for the future energy system today?

All pathways to stabilization include a gradual movement toward a new and differently composed energy system. Given uncertainty about the long-term character of that system, it should be remembered that the goal of near-term technology-related actions is not simply to reduce emissions through technology deployment. Additional goals of near-term action are (1) to promote investments that will maximize the number of long-term options for mitigation, including R&D and technology deployment to spur innovation and learning; (2) to ascertain which will be the most effective long-term options; and (3) to build the social, institutional, and physical infrastructure needed to support the dramatic changes of the future. Put another way, in addition to mitigating emissions, the near-term focus must be on preparing for a dramatic long-term transformation of the energy system about which we are not fully informed today. The question from the perspective of technology deployment is how long this period of uncertainty might last: how long do we have until the deployment of energy technology must truly reflect the character of the long-term energy system?

The length of this near-term period will depend on a range of factors, including the stringency of the long-term climate goal— clearly it would be shorter for more aggressive long-term goals than those considered in this chapter. Though the level of action by 2035 in all the mitigation scenarios here is substantial, and though changes at investment margins increasingly reflect the nature and evolving character of new technology options, much of the near-term action is focused on energy-demand reductions. The deployment of new low-carbon energy sources over the next quarter century remains far below the levels that will eventually be required for long-term stabilization.

On the surface, comparing the level of technology deployment in 2035 to the level in 2095 indicates a large degree of flexibility to alter course moving forward from 2035. In some sense, the die has not been cast with respect to the character of the long-term energy system by 2035. However, this does not mean that the sorts of near-term actions needed to prepare for a long-term transformation have not been undertaken. For any of the long-term futures modeled in this study to emerge beyond 2035, near-term actions must have laid the necessary technological and scientific foundations, resolved some uncertainty regarding optimal choices for future energy systems, and established the social and institutional structures that would allow for dramatic transformations to emerge. An analysis such as this can only hint at the magnitude of these efforts. What it does show, however, is that it is these foundation-laying efforts, along with the deployment of effective near-term technologies such as those associated with energy-use reductions, that constitute near-term action.

Technology, policy, and the cost of emissions mitigation

A range of studies have demonstrated that technology is critical for lowering the costs of addressing climate change. Indeed, technology was identified as perhaps the most important driver of differences in mitigation costs in the mitigation scenarios generated by the United States CCSP (Clarke *et al.* 2007a). Mitigation costs are important not just because they drive welfare impacts for achieving any given long-term climate goal, but also because of their influence on the long-term goals that might be considered socially and politically feasible. The degree of action that countries take to mitigate GHG emissions is in large part a function of the perceived costs associated with different levels of action, regardless of whether that calculation is made qualitatively or using rigorous cost-benefit analysis. This section explores the cost implications of different assumptions about technology availability based on results from the scenarios at both the global and regional levels.

The global benefits of technology

The scenarios in this chapter indicate that the global economic benefits of improved technology, in terms of reduced mitigation costs, are greater when policy regimes are less than ideal. Figure 25.11 shows discounted global mitigation costs over the course of the century across four alternative technology suites under FULL and DELAY international policy architectures. The value of technology can be measured as the difference between mitigation costs with reference technology and mitigation costs with more advanced technology suites. The global cost reduction from advanced technology under a regime of delayed participation approaches twice the magnitude of the global cost reduction when international participation is complete and immediate. In other words, technology development and deployment is an even more important component of the climate policy portfolio if markets for climate mitigation are not fully formed.

Two factors influence this differential impact on mitigation cost. First, in less efficient regimes, costs will be higher irrespective of technology because participating regions will have to exercise abatement options with higher marginal cost earlier than under a more efficient regime. This means costs to achieve any given abatement target will be higher. A second, and more ambiguous, factor is that higher marginal costs in participating regions interact with the suite of technologies that is available for deployment. It is possible that some technologies provide larger benefits for lower or intermediate reductions while others provide larger benefits for deep reductions. This chapter has not focused on this dynamic (see Baker *et al.* 2006 for a lengthier discussion of this issue). Here we simply note that the global economic benefits of improved technology are higher when the international policy architecture deviates from full participation.

The regional benefits of technology

Although global costs are important, most technology R&D activities are conducted at the *national* or *regional* level, and the national benefits to technology advances are usually the basis for justifying these expenditures. Furthermore, though global costs are an important indicator of the social value of technology, the distribution of mitigation costs across regions has an important influence on the degree and distribution of action. Hence, the regional benefits of technology are a relevant unit for analysis.

Unfortunately, it is impossible to determine the ultimate financial

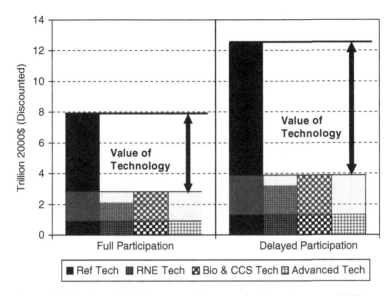

Figure 25.11. Total global present discounted mitigation costs, 2005 through 2095, for four alternative technology suites under FULL and DELAY international policy architectures

effects for any country participating in an international mitigation regime, even within the rarefied environment of an integrated assessment model, without considering the allocation of burdens across regions. The precise mechanisms that are used internationally, from offset crediting programs such as the Clean Development Mechanism (CDM), to technology deployment incentives, to full carbon trading, will determine the final burdens carried by individual countries and regions. This analysis is silent on these distributional issues, noting only the global costs.

At the same time, though, it is clear that the value of technology will be higher in the developed regions under delayed participation, assuming a given long-term goal as is assumed in this study. Early participants in a global mitigation regime, generally assumed to be the developed regions, must undertake more abatement to meet a given climate goal under delayed participation than they would under idealized conditions with full participation. As a result, they incur higher costs, because of the larger emissions reductions they must achieve and because achieving these larger reductions requires implementing mitigation options with higher marginal costs. As early participants are expected to be developed countries, they are unlikely to be on the receiving end of financial transfers (such as permit trades or CDM), so they will bear the bulk of near-term global costs. By contrast, developed regions may bear something less than the total global cost in a full participation scenario. In that case, developing regions would bear some costs, although perhaps not their full in-country mitigation costs, depending on the particulars of the burden-sharing regime. Even if the developed countries were to fully compensate developing regions for their mitigation costs under a full participation regime, their near-term costs would still be lower than under a delayed participation regime in which developed countries have to exercise less efficient domestic mitigation measures while the developing regions are delaying participation.

A second element of regional technology value derives from the public goods nature of technology development and diffusion and the public goods nature of reductions in global stock pollutants such as GHGs. There are two mechanisms—a direct effect and an indirect effect—by which domestic R&D activities can alter mitigation costs for the nation conducting them. The direct effect is to reduce the costs of meeting any national mitigation goal, irrespective of international efforts. The indirect effect—the emissions burden effect—is to reduce the mitigation effort required at the national level to meet any given long-term global concentration target by inducing greater emissions reductions internationally; if technology makes mitigation cheaper internationally, it will lessen the national mitigation requirement to meet any long-term climate goal.

The relationship between direct and indirect effects is important because many national-level investments in climate-related R&D are supported by analyses of direct effects. This approach tends to downplay the benefits of international technology deployment and diffusion in justifying domestic R&D activities.

To illustrate the importance of this indirect effect, we conducted an experiment in which we applied the advanced technology assumptions, first only inside the United States and then only outside the United States. The experiment was conducted under the assumption of full global participation, and only the reference technology and advanced technology suites were considered. Comparing global mitigation costs in these two cases (and leaving aside the distribution of

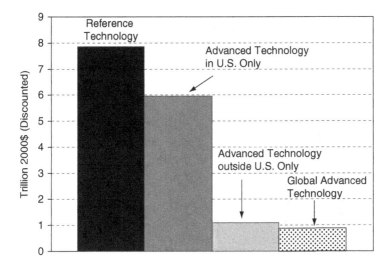

Figure 25.12. Global discounted mitigation cost, 2005 through 2095, under varying deployment assumptions

burdens) illustrates the relative impacts of US versus international technology deployment.

Not surprisingly, if advanced technology is available everywhere but the United States, the total global costs of abatement are smaller than if advanced technology is only available in the United States (Figure 25.12). Although the United States has historically been among the largest GHG emitters, it does not account for the majority of global emissions; moreover, the United States share of global emissions will decline over time as emissions from the developing countries continue to grow more rapidly than those in developed countries. Hence, deploying advanced technologies outside the United States allows these technologies to be applied to a larger quantity of global emissions, reducing global costs.

The United States results provide more direct insight into the domestic impacts of domestic and international technology deployment (Figure 25.13). When deployment is limited to the United States, mitigation costs to the United States, under full participation, are higher. With increased technological capacity to mitigate, the United States is called on to do more than other countries. In this case, the indirect effect—a higher domestic mitigation burden—is larger than the direct cost savings from access to improved technology. In contrast,

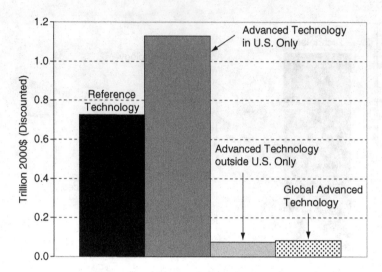

Figure 25.13. Discounted mitigation cost in the United States, 2005 through 2095, under varying deployment assumptions

when technology is deployed only outside the United States, domestic costs are dramatically lower even though there has been no change in United States technology. To meet a particular long-term environmental goal—in this case limiting atmospheric CO_2 concentrations to 500 ppmv by the end of the century—greater options for mitigation outside the United States lead to a lower United States emissions reduction requirement.

The caveat to these results is that it is impossible to determine the ultimate financial effects for any country participating in an international mitigation regime, as discussed above, without considering the allocation of burdens across regions. The results shown in Figure 25.12 and Figure 25.13 were developed assuming a global carbon tax or, equivalently, a global cap-and-trade regime in which emissions quantities are perfectly allocated to achieve the least costly overall distribution of mitigation efforts so that there will be no trading. In reality, the net burden on any region will not be the same as its mitigation costs. Permit allocations, wealth transfers, and other financial flows associated with mechanisms such as emissions trading or CDM can shift the economic burden across regions.

This caveat notwithstanding, the experiment makes a strong case for the public goods nature of technology investments in addressing climate change. If countries were to choose targets independently, without considering the international context, then international diffusion and the associated indirect effect of technology development—the emissions burden effect—are not relevant to domestic R&D decisions. On the other hand, to the degree that countries such as the United States are looking toward a long-term environmental goal and are interacting with other countries to meet that goal, there is strong evidence that the international diffusion of technology is a larger driver of *domestic costs* than domestic deployment. This argues strongly for domestic incentives to promote the international deployment of climate technologies, and it also argues strongly for considering the effects of international deployment when analyzing the benefits of domestic investments, such as R&D investments, to develop technology. Simply put, the international benefits of climate change R&D can be as or more important than the domestic benefits.

Concluding thoughts

This chapter has explored how international policy architectures and technology availability interact and how they influence the degree and character of emissions mitigation actions that individual countries and the global community must take in both the near term and the long term. The analysis uses the MiniCAM integrated assessment model to explore these issues in the context of a long-term concentration goal of limiting atmospheric CO_2 concentrations to 500 ppmv in the year 2095. It adds to recent research that applies formal energy-economy-climate models to explore these issues (see, for example, Richels *et al.* 2007; Bosetti *et al.* 2007; Bosetti *et al.* 2008). The results touch on, and reinforce, a range of themes relating to the availability of new and improved technology and international participation in climate mitigation. We conclude here by summarizing three main insights that emerge from this work.

First, there is nothing in this analysis that contradicts the ever-growing body of research indicating that technology is fundamental to the costs, and therefore the political viability, of achieving climate mitigation. Indeed, this research suggests that technology is even more valuable—from a global perspective and from the perspective of individual nations—if international participation is less than perfectly efficient, which will undoubtedly be the case.

Second, national-level activities to promote technology development should be viewed not only from a national perspective, but also from an international perspective. It is widely understood that if mitigation is to occur, nations may benefit by establishing leadership in related technology areas, while a failure in this regard could adversely affect their competitiveness. This study has highlighted another, equally important, international dimension to the rationale for domestic technology investments. Any country that places priority on achieving a long-term climate goal understands that international mitigation efforts are fundamental for meeting this goal: the more other countries contribute to abatement, the less must be done domestically. Technology diffusion is therefore not simply a competitiveness issue, it is fundamental for fostering international mitigation efforts. Hence, assessments of the benefits from domestic technology development activities should be based not simply on improved national mitigation options, but also the potential for increased mitigation internationally, which in turn means a lower national burden on participating countries to meet any given long-term climate goal. Indeed, even without explicit climate policies in many nations, there are improvements to technology, or policies to better take advantage of existing technologies, that could lead to emissions reductions.

Finally, investments in technology development must be viewed from a long-term as well as a near-term perspective. R&D activities, and technology policies for climate change more generally, should certainly focus on the near term to facilitate action at the national and international levels, but they must also continue to lay a foundation for the deeper and wider reductions in emissions that will be required decades into the future. Regardless of international participation in the near term, global emissions must ultimately move toward zero to achieve any long-term stabilization goal. This will require the participation of all nations, and it will require energy systems that are far different than those of today. Tomorrow will ultimately turn into today, and without the scientific and technological foundations for achieving and sustaining a long-term transformation of the world's energy systems, the deep reductions necessary for stabilization may not be socially and politically viable.

References

Baker, E., L. Clarke, and J. Weyant (2006). "R&D as a Hedge Against Climate Damages," *Climatic Change* 78(1): 157–79.

Bosetti, V., C. Carraro, E. Massetti, and M. Tavoni (2007). "Optimal Energy Investment and R&D Strategies to Stabilize Atmospheric Greenhouse Gas Concentrations," CEPR Discussion Paper 6549 and CESifo Working Paper N. 2133, FEEM Nota di Lavoro 95.07.

Bosetti, V., C. Carraro, and M. Tavoni (2008). "Delayed Participation of Developing Countries to Climate Agreements: Should Action in the EU and US be Postponed?" CEPR Working Paper 6967 and CESifo Working Paper N. 2445, FEEM Nota di Lavoro 70.08.

Brenkert, A., S. Smith, S. Kim, and H. Pitcher (2003). *Model Documentation for the MiniCAM*, PNNL 14337, Pacific Northwest National Laboratory, Richland, Washington.

Clarke, L., J. Edmonds, H. Jacoby, H. Pitcher, J. Reilly, and R. Richels (2007a). *Scenarios of Greenhouse Gas Emissions and Atmospheric Concentrations*, Sub-report 2.1A of Synthesis and Assessment Product 2.1 by the US Climate Change Science Program and the Subcommittee on Global Change Research, Department of Energy, Office of Biological & Environmental Research, Washington, DC.

Clarke, L., J. Edmonds, S. Kim, J. Lurz, H. Pitcher, S. Smith, and M. Wise (2007b). *Documentation for the MiniCAM CCSP Scenarios*, Battelle Pacific Northwest Division Technical Report, PNNL-16735.

Clarke, L., P. Kyle, M. Wise, K. Calvin, J. Edmonds, S. Kim, M. Placet, and S. Smith (2008b). *CO_2 Emissions Mitigation and Technological Advance: An Updated Analysis of Advanced Technology Scenarios*, Technical Report PNNL-18075, Pacific Northwest National Laboratory.

Clarke, L. and J. Weyant (2002). "Modeling Induced Technological Change: An Overview," in A. Grubler, N. Nakicenovic, and W. Nordhaus (eds.), *Technological Change and the Environment*. Washington, DC: Resources for the Future, pp. 320–63.

Clarke, L., J. Weyant, and A. Birky (2006). "On Sources of Technological Change: Assessing the Evidence," *Energy Economics* 28: 579–95.

Clarke, L., J. Weyant, and J. Edmonds (2008a). "On Sources of Technological Change: What do the Models Assume?" *Energy Economics* 30: 409–24.

Clarke L., M. Wise, S. Kim, A. Thomson, R. Izaurralde, J. Lurz, M. Placet, and S. Smith (2006). *Climate Change Mitigation: An Analysis of Advanced Technology Scenarios*, Technical Report PNNL-16078, Pacific Northwest National Laboratory.

Crutzen, P. J., A. R. Mosier, K. A. Smith, and W. Winiwarter (2008). "N_2O Release from Agro-Biofuel Production Negates Global Warming

Reduction by Replacing Fossil Fuels," *Atmospheric Chemistry and Physics* 8: 389–95.

Edmonds, J. and J. Reilly (1985). *Global Energy: Assessing the Future*, New York: Oxford University Press.

Edmonds, J., L. Clarke, J. Lurz, and M. Wise (2008). "Stabilizing CO_2 Concentrations with Incomplete International Cooperation," *Climate Policy* 8: 355–76.

Edmonds, J. A., M. A. Wise, J. J. Dooley, S. H. Kim, S. J. Smith, P. J. Runci, L. E. Clarke, E. L. Malone, and G. M. Stokes (2007). *Global Energy Technology Strategy Addressing Climate Change: Phase 2 Findings from an International Public-Private Sponsored Research Program*, College Park, MD: Joint Global Change Research Institute.

Goulder, L. and K. Mathai (2000). "Optimal CO_2 Abatement in the Presence of Induced Technological Change," *Journal of Environmental Economics and Management* 39(1): 1–38.

Goulder, L. and S. Schneider (1999). "Induced Technological Change and the Attractiveness of CO_2 Abatement Policies," *Resource and Energy Economics* 21: 211–53.

Grubb, M., J. Kohler, and D. Anderson (2002). "Induced Technological Change in Energy and Environmental Modeling," *Annual Review of Energy and the Environment* 27: 271–308.

Grubb, M., T. Chapuis, and M. Ha-Duong (1995). "The Economics of Changing Course: Implications of Adaptability and Inertia for Optimal Climate Policy," *Energy Policy* 23(4/5): 417–32.

GTSP (2000). *Global Energy Technology Strategy: Addressing Climate Change*, Global Technology Strategy Program.

Hoffert, M. I., K. Caldeira, G. Benford, D. R. Criswell, C. Green, H. Herzog, A. K. Jain, H. S. Kheshgi, K. S. Lackner, J. S. Lewis, H. D. Lightfoot, W. Manheimer, J. C. Mankins, M. E. Mauel, L. J. Perkins, M. E. Schlesinger, T. Volk, and T. M. L. Wigley (2002). "Advanced Technology Paths to Global Climate Stability: Energy for a Greenhouse Planet," *Science* 298(1): 981–7.

IEA (2008). *Energy Technology Perspectives 2008*. Paris: IEA.

Keppo, I. and S. Rao (2006). "International Climate Regimes: Effects of Delayed Participation," *Technology Forecasting & Social Change* 74: 962–79.

Kim S. H., J. A. Edmonds, J. Lurz, S. J. Smith, and M. A. Wise (2006). "The ObjECTS: Framework for Integrated Assessment: Hybrid Modeling of Transportation," *The Energy Journal* (Special Issue No. 2 2006): 63.

Loschel, A. (2002). "Technological Change in Economic Models of Environmental Policy: A Survey," *Ecological Economics* 43: 105–26.

Manne, A. and R. Richels (2002). *The Impact Of Learning-By-Doing on the Timing and Cost of CO$_2$ Abatement*, Working paper, AEI-Brookings Joint Center for Regulatory Studies.

Messner, S. (1997). "Endogenized Technological Learning in an Energy Systems Model," *Evolutionary Economics* 7: 291–313.

Nordhaus, W. (2002). "Modeling Induced Innovation in Climate-Change Policy," in A. Grubler, N. Nakicenovic, and W. Nordhaus (eds.), *Technological Change and the Environment*. Washington, DC: Resources for the Future, pp.182–209.

Pacala, S. and R. Socolow (2004). "Stabilization Wedges: Solving the Climate Problem for the Next 50 Years with Current Technologies," *Science* 305: 968–72.

Popp, D. (2004). "Entice: Endogenous Technological Change in the DICE Model of Global Warming," *Journal of Environmental Economics and Management* 48: 742–68.

Richels, R., T. Rutherford, G. Blanford, and L. Clarke (2007). "Managing the Transition to Climate Stabilization," *Climate Policy* 7: 409–28.

Searchinger, Timothy, Ralph Heimlich, R. A. Houghton, Fengxia Dong, Amani Elobeid, Jacinto Fabiosa, Simla Tokgoz, Dermot Hayes, and Tun-Hsiang Yu (2008). "Use of U.S. Croplands for Biofuels Increases Greenhouse Gases Through Emissions from Land-Use Change," *Science* 319: 1238–40.

United Nations (1992). *Framework Convention on Climate Change*. New York: United Nations.

Van Vuuren, D. P., M. G. J. den Elzen, P. L. Lucas, B. Eickhout, B. J. Strengers, B. van Ruijven, S. Wonink, and R. van Houdt (2007). "Stabilizing Greenhouse Gas Concentrations at Low Levels: An Assessment of Reduction Strategies and Costs," *Climatic Change* 81: 119–59.

Wigley, T. M. L., R. Richels, and J. A. Edmonds (1996). "Economic and Environmental Choices in the Stabilization of Atmospheric CO$_2$ Concentrations," *Nature* 379(6562): 240–3.

Wrse, M., K. Calvin, A. Thomson, L. Clarke, B. Bond-Lamberty, R. Sands, S. J. Smith, A. Janetos, J. Edmonds (2009). "Implications of Limiting CO$_2$ Concentrations for Land Use and Energy," *Science* 324: 1183–6.

26 | Revised emissions growth projections for China: why post-Kyoto climate policy must look east

GEOFFREY J. BLANFORD,
RICHARD G. RICHELS, AND
THOMAS F. RUTHERFORD*

Introduction

Growth rates in energy-related emissions of carbon dioxide (CO_2) in developing countries, particularly the People's Republic of China, have increased rapidly in recent years. Emissions from the original signatories to the Kyoto Protocol (known as "Annex B countries")— essentially the developed world and economies in transition—will almost certainly be surpassed by emissions from non-Annex B countries before 2010. Previous analyses projected that this crossing point would occur in 2020 or later (Weyant *et al.* 1999). The main source of unexpected emissions growth is China. According to the historical record provided by Marland *et al.* (2008), since 2000 the average annual growth rate in China's emissions has exceeded 10 percent, compared to 2.8 percent in the 1990s. Globally, the average growth rate since 2000 has been 3.3 percent, compared to 1.1 percent in the 1990s.[1]

Raupach *et al.* (2007) decompose emissions growth in several regions into the factors of the Kaya identity: population, per capita income, energy intensity of gross domestic product (GDP), and carbon intensity

* We thank participants in a workshop at the Pacific Northwest National Laboratory, as well as Joe Aldy, Rob Stavins, and an anonymous reviewer for helpful comments. This research was funded by the Electric Power Research Institute (EPRI). The views presented here are solely those of the individual authors, and do not necessarily represent the views of EPRI or its members.

[1] Apart from the lower rate in China, global emissions growth in the 1990s was also anomalously slowed by the contraction of former Soviet and Eastern European economies after the collapse of the Soviet Union.

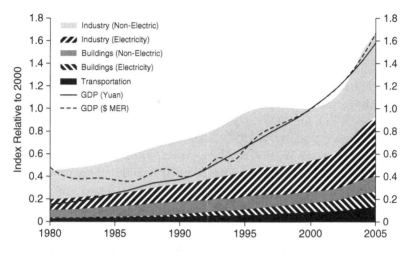

Figure 26.1. Primary energy consumption in China relative to economic growth

Real GDP grew faster than primary energy consumption in China between 1980 and 2000. Since 2000, energy use has grown faster than the economy. Dollar figures are converted using market exchange rates (MER). Growth in constant dollars converted using purchasing power parity (PPP) rates coincides with growth in constant local currency. (Economic data from IMF World Economic Outlook [2008] database, energy data from IEA World Energy Statistics [2007a])

of energy. In China, the first and last factors have been stable: population growth is slow and carbon intensity has remained consistently high due to heavy reliance on coal. Emissions growth has been driven by a combination of rapid economic development and the reversal of the past trend of declining energy intensity. Between 1980 and 2000, energy intensity in China had been falling faster than in any other major economy. This decline has been attributed to efficiency improvements at the firm level as market reforms privatized formerly state-operated enterprises (Fisher-Vanden *et al.* 2004). Since 2000, however, energy use—driven primarily by industrial demand and coal-fired electric generation—has not only kept pace with, but has slightly exceeded aggregate economic growth (IMF 2008; IEA 2007a) (Figure 26.1). The International Energy Agency (IEA) reports that China added over 100 gigawatts (GW) of new electric generation capacity in 2006, of which at least 90 GW was coal-fired (IEA 2007b). While this rate may not be indicative of an annual average, it represents coal plant construction in a single year equivalent to one quarter of the entire US coal fleet. Despite some uncertainty about the accuracy of Chinese data sources, China has likely become the world leader in carbon emissions, surpassing the United States in 2006 (Gregg *et al.* 2008).

Baseline (i.e., business-as-usual or BAU) projections of emissions growth in China over a near- to medium-term timeframe (e.g., through 2030) have, until very recently, been modest. The IEA's World Energy Outlook (WEO) for 2000 reported an average growth rate of 3 percent in its reference case over a 1997–2020 time horizon (IEA 2000).[2] The 2005 edition of the WEO revised the expected growth rate downward to 2.4 percent between 2003 and 2030 (IEA 2005). This projection likely seemed plausible at the time, given the one-to-two year lag in accurate observations and the anomalous dip in emissions totals in the late 1990s (Marland *et al.* 2008). However, as a pattern of rapid growth became evident, the 2007 WEO, in a special report focused on China, projected a 2030 emissions total over 50 percent higher than the figure given in the 2005 edition (IEA 2007b).

The IEA's projections are significant because many modeling studies use them to calibrate baseline emissions paths, either formally or informally. A prominent example in the United States was a report commissioned by the federal government's Climate Change Science Program (CCSP) that compared reference case and coordinated stabilization scenarios by three economic modeling teams (Clarke *et al.* 2007).[3] Two of the models used year 2000 emissions as a starting point, while the third used 2005, but all three models assumed emission growth rates for China that matched the IEA's unadjusted projections of the 2000–2005 era. Figure 26.2 shows the various IEA reference forecasts, along with the CCSP report range, in the context of observed historical emissions as reported by the Oak Ridge National Laboratory (ORNL) (Marland *et al.* 2008) [including the Netherlands Environmental Assessment Agency (MNP) figure for 2007 (MNP 2008)].

Other recent estimates have been even more aggressive. Auffhammer and Carson (2008) present econometric forecasts of China's emissions path through 2010 using a province-level dataset up to 2004

[2] The US Energy Information Administration (EIA) projected a 4.1 percent annual growth rate over the same period in its 2000 forecast.
[3] These included the MERGE model, the MiniCAM model, and the IGSM/EPPA model. The report was released in 2007, but the analysis was conducted in 2006.

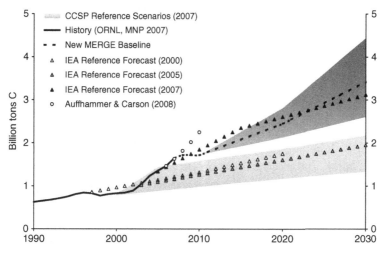

Figure 26.2. Energy-related CO_2 emissions in China
China's emissions began increasingly rapidly after 2001. IEA forecasts did not reflect the acceleration until after 2005, and projections in the 2007 CCSP report reflected earlier forecasts. A 2008 econometric study projects an exponential extrapolation of the current annual growth rate through 2010. The new MERGE baseline projections, which account for a near-term recession, reach 3.4 GtC by 2030 (dashed line) in the reference growth scenario, 2.6 GtC in the low scenario, and 4.4 GtC in the high scenario (bounds of the gray shaded region).

and applying a variety of alternative model structures. The models with the best dynamic fit to the sample data indicate the potential for annual fossil-fuel emissions to reach 2.25 billion metric tons of carbon (GtC) by 2010 (also depicted in Figure 26.2)—a sharp increase from the MNP's reported total of 1.65 GtC for 2007. This estimate for 2010 is almost double the IEA's 2005 forecast of 1.25 GtC for the same year, and significantly larger than the linearly interpolated 2010 level of 1.87 GtC from the 2007 forecast. However, the econometric results reflect an assumption that emissions for 2008–2010 will follow the same pattern as the preceding years in the sample, which now appears doubtful in light of the current global financial crisis.

Model calibration

These observations warrant an update to assumptions about future growth used by the economic modeling community in climate policy studies. Accordingly, we have recalibrated one of the models used in the US CCSP report, the MERGE model (Manne and Richels 2005; Richels *et al.* 2007). MERGE is an intertemporal optimization model with a top-down general equilibrium representation of the economy and a bottom-up process representation of energy technologies. In each region, exogenous trajectories for population and reference economic growth are used to derive a growth scenario for labor productivity (equivalent to per capita income). A nested production function is used to describe how aggregate economic output depends upon inputs of capital, labor, and electric and non-electric energy. Energy prices are determined endogenously in the model as a result of resource scarcity, technological change, and policy constraints. For more details about the treatment of technology in MERGE, please see Appendix A.

The rate of increase in energy demand relative to economic growth is determined both by price-induced shifts among inputs to production (as determined by elasticities in the production function) and by autonomous (i.e., non-price-induced) changes in energy intensity. Such changes can occur due to both technological progress (e.g., end-use efficiency) and structural changes in the economy (e.g., shifts away from manufactured goods toward services). All sources of non-price-induced changes in energy intensity are summarized in MERGE by a single "autonomous energy efficiency index" (AEEI) parameter, which operates as a scaling factor on the energy input to production. The exogenous choices of growth rate and AEEI are the key parameters for incorporating updated assumptions about development patterns and energy use in emerging economies.

MERGE operates in ten-year time steps with 2000 as the base year. To ensure that the model replicates observed growth since 2000, as well as the latest near-term projections for the remainder of the decade, we use GDP projections from the International Monetary Fund (IMF 2008) for 2010 to determine the average annual growth rate since 2000.[4] However, neither the IMF nor any other major data source has updated projections to account for the impacts of the still-unfolding global recession. Therefore we adjust the average economic

---

[4] To best capture real growth as a driver for energy demand, we observe the rate of growth in terms of constant local currency. For aggregated regions, observed growth rates are calculated using purchasing power parity (PPP) weights. However, the relative size of economies in the model's base year is measured in terms of market exchange rates.

growth rates for the current decade according to a simple rule: the effect of the current recession is assumed to be two years of zero net growth in output, applied uniformly in all regions. For example, in China the average growth rate since 2000 has been nearly 10 percent. Using our rule, we assume average growth of roughly 8 percent per year for the 2000–2010 period. Although it is very difficult to predict the severity of the current situation, preliminary observations suggest that some deceleration is unavoidable. Our adjustment is a straightforward way to represent one plausible scenario.[5]

After 2010, we consider three possible growth scenarios for developing countries: a reference scenario and two outliers. Table 26.1 shows annual average growth rates in aggregate GDP, population, and labor productivity/per capita income through 2030 in China and India for the three scenarios. Although the economic component of MERGE runs on a 100-year timescale, we focus here on the next two decades.

Growth rates in the reference scenario are roughly consistent with the latest IEA projections (IEA 2007b). In the case of China, the high growth rates shown in Table 26.1 match those used by modelers in that country (e.g., Jiang and Hu 2006) to represent continued achievement of the government's goals. The low growth scenario reflects the possibility of a (relative) slowdown, perhaps due to short-term bottlenecks in material inputs as capacity expands, or perhaps due to lingering effects of the current crisis. Population growth rates are based on the most recent central United Nations (UN) estimate. Over the remainder of the century, we assume that growth rates gradually decline, reaching 1 percent for both aggregate and per capita GDP with a stabilized population.

Choosing appropriate values for the AEEI parameter is less straightforward. The autonomous component of energy intensity change can be difficult to separate from price effects in the observed record. For developed economies such as the United States, previous work has supported the assumption of roughly 1 percent per year decline in energy intensity due to non-price-induced changes. This decline is the net effect of several factors: a shift toward less energy-intensive industries, improvements in end-use energy efficiency (energy requirement per service unit), and increases in service demand with wealth (a

---

[5] According to China's National Bureau of Statistics, GDP growth in the first half of 2009 was around 7 percent, suggesting that our recession scenario may be too pessimistic. If this recovery is robust, our reference emissions path may yet be underestimating the challenge of stabilization.

Table 26.1 *Exogenous annual growth rates in MERGE*

		Aggregate GDP			Population			Labor Productivity		
		2000 – 2010	2010 – 2020	2020 – 2030	2000 – 2010	2010 – 2020	2020 – 2030	2000 – 2010	2010 – 2020	2020 – 2030
China	Low	7.8%	4.5%	3.6%	0.6%	0.5%	0.3%	7.2%	4.0%	3.3%
	Ref		6.0%	4.8%					5.5%	4.5%
	High		7.5%	6.0%					7.0%	5.7%
India	Low	6.0%	4.9%	4.1%	1.5%	1.2%	0.9%	4.4%	3.6%	3.2%
	Ref		6.5%	5.5%					5.2%	4.6%
	High		8.1%	6.9%					6.8%	5.9%

diminishing effect at high income levels). For economies in earlier stages of development, the pattern could be very different. A casual observer might conclude that because developing countries tend to rely on energy-intensive industries to begin building their economies, and tend to increase service demand more rapidly as incomes rise, these two effects will dominate efficiency improvements initially, leading to an autonomous *increase* in energy intensity during this stage rather than a decline. On the other hand, it has also been proposed that faster economic growth leads to a higher turnover rate in the capital stock, which in turn accelerates the introduction of end-use efficiency improvements. The latter proposal has been applied in previous MERGE studies, which assume a faster rate of autonomous decline in China and India than in the United States.

The reality is that each country's experience is unique. China and India provide two very distinct pictures. As discussed above, changes in China's institutions in recent decades allowed a correction from very inefficient industrial practices in the 1990s. This correction overwhelmed all other effects and drove a steep decline in energy intensity from very high levels (similar to current trends in the former Soviet Union). With the saturation of this effect and the emergence of strong growth in energy-intensive industries in China, the current decade has seen an abrupt return to the more conventional model of rising energy intensity. Meanwhile, in India, energy intensity prior to the current decade had remained fairly constant, rising slightly but remaining much lower than in China. During this decade, by contrast, India's energy intensity has fallen rapidly, driven by a different and less energy-intensive industry mix. In choosing the AEEI parameter for developing countries, we have attempted to take into account current trends as well as judgments about the relevant stage and patterns of development in different countries.

The combined implications of our AEEI choices, elasticities, and energy prices in a no-policy baseline are reflected in Table 26.2, which shows average annual rates of change in primary energy and energy intensity for the decades in question in China and India. Note that while primary energy diverges across the three growth scenarios, energy intensity changes very little. There is no doubt that the future path of energy intensity is uncertain, but we have elected to hold the AEEI parameter fixed and let the variation in economic growth rates determine the range of growth in primary energy use and therefore emissions.

Table 26.2 *Annual rates of change in total primary energy and intensity*

		Total Primary Energy			Energy Intensity		
		2000 – 2010	2010 – 2020	2020 – 2030	2000 – 2010	2010 – 2020	2020 – 2030
China	Low		2.4%	2.1%		-1.9%	-1.3%
	Ref	7.7%	3.8%	3.4%	-0.1%	-2.1%	-1.3%
	High		5.1%	4.5%		-2.3%	-1.4%
India	Low		2.8%	2.8%		-1.9%	-1.2%
	Ref	3.0%	4.2%	4.4%	-2.8%	-2.1%	-1.1%
	High		5.4%	6.0%		-2.5%	-1.0%

Figure 26.2 shows new baseline projections for energy-related carbon emissions in China, allowing for a range of possible growth rates. In the new projections, emissions level off at 1.7 GtC by 2010, but rise to between 2.6 and 4.4 GtC by 2030—around twice as high as the range in the CCSP study released in 2007. The IEA's 2007 forecast, which does not include any consideration of a near-term recession, falls in the middle of our projected range. These projections illustrate the likelihood that China will become the overwhelming world leader in emissions. US baseline emissions in our scenarios fall slightly from current levels to 1.5 GtC by 2030; the European Union's emissions, even without further policies, are also projected to remain roughly constant at 1.1 GtC. Although India is often placed in the same category as China with respect to growth, its current emissions are one-quarter the level of China's, and that fraction is likely to fall in the next few decades. In comparison to previous MERGE studies, total baseline emissions projections from non-Annex B countries in the year 2030 have nearly doubled with the new reference specification; 80 percent of this increase is due to the revised treatment of China.

Historical comparison

While current observations inform modeling choices about the beginning of the time horizon, it can be instructive to use historical experience in similar countries as a guide in judging the plausibility of results for future periods. Key variables are the rate of economic growth and

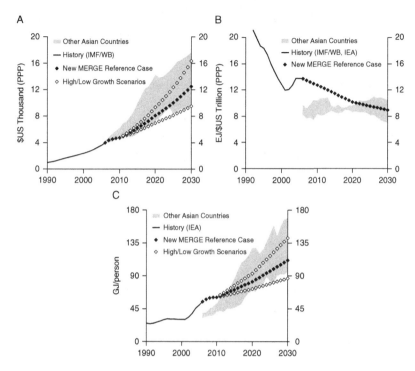

Figure 26.3. MERGE projections relative to historical experience in Asia. (**A**) Growth paths for per capita income (measured in constant 2000 PPP dollars) in other Asian countries were similar to current projections for China. (**B**) Energy intensity changes—the net effect of structural shifts in the economy, improvements in end-use energy efficiency, and increases in service demand with wealth—were minimal in other Asian countries while an overall decline is projected for China (only one scenario is considered). (**C**) Per capita energy use has risen sooner with respect to per capita income levels in China, but it is projected to follow historical patterns as energy intensity declines.

changes in energy intensity. In the case of China, we consider time series for per capita income, energy intensity, and per capita energy use from four of the wealthiest Asian economies (Japan, Taiwan, Korea, and Malaysia).[6] The data are lagged so that per capita income in the starting year matches China's 2006 income level of roughly $4,000

[6] There are seven Asian countries whose per capita income currently exceeds that of China: Singapore, Hong Kong, Japan, Taiwan, Korea, Malaysia, and Thailand. However, we eliminated Singapore and Hong Kong as special cases and Thailand as too recent.

(in constant 2000 dollars using the World Bank's recently updated PPP exchange rates) (IMF 2008; IEA 2007a; Heston *et al.* 2006). Per capita income in Malaysia reached this level in 1979, Korea in 1977, Taiwan in 1973, and Japan in 1959.[7] We use the subsequent twenty-four years of observations to provide a comparison for our projections for China from 2006 through 2030. Figure 26.3 shows model projections for per capita income, energy intensity, and per capita energy use compared to the range of experience in these four countries.

From the starting level of $4,000, annual per capita incomes in the sample countries grew over the subsequent twenty-four years to between $10,000 and $18,000, with Taiwan representing the high end of the range and Malaysia the low end. The central MERGE projection for China rises to just over $12,000 by 2030, and the outliers of its range correspond closely to the sample range. Thus the economic growth rates underlying our updated specification are consistent with the historical Asian experience, which includes some recession years for Korea and Malaysia around the time of the 1997 financial crisis, as well as a minor recession in Japan after the 1973 energy crisis.

As discussed above, China's energy intensity was in decline prior to 2000, after which it rose slightly. The sample countries all had lower energy intensity than China did in 2006 in the year their per capita income level stood at $4,000. However, during the subsequent period of growth, energy intensity did not decline in any of the sample countries. This observation reinforces the expectation that China may be entering a pattern of energy-fueled development. On the other hand, China's government has stated its goals for rebalancing her economy toward a less intensive mix (Jiang and Hu 2006; He and Kuijs 2007), and energy prices for the foreseeable future (though subsidized in China) will likely be higher than in the period captured by the sample data. Some early projections for 2006 and 2007 indicate that energy intensity in China has in fact begun to decline again. Using estimates of total primary energy from the 2008 BP Statistical Review (BP 2008) and the IMF's estimates for GDP (IMF 2008), intensity fell by roughly

[7] Economic data from IMF (2008), which are based on the World Bank's 2006 estimates of the PPP value of GDP, only extend back to 1980. For earlier years, we have used Penn World Table 6.2 (PWT) data, scaled so that the two data series are equal in 1980. Although China's PPP value of GDP was significantly reduced in the 2006 revision relative to estimates used in PWT, the adjustment for the other four countries was minimal.

3 percent between 2006 and 2007. Therefore we assume a small net decline from 2000 in the current decade, followed by a continued decline afterwards so that by 2030 China is in line with the historical range. Thus the very rapid growth in primary energy in the current decade may be viewed as an anomalous period of flat energy intensity combined with rapid economic growth.

Finally we compare total primary energy use per capita. This metric is attractive because it summarizes the implications of growth assumptions without relying on the conversion of economic quantities across time and space, which are often speculative and based on limited data. Although per capita energy use was lower in the sample countries in the starting year (a consequence of lower energy intensity at the same income level), growth in subsequent years was rapid. China appears to have taken off slightly earlier than its predecessors in the Asian sphere, but with a comparatively fast reduction in energy intensity, our projections to 2030 again correspond closely to the sample range. The MERGE reference case projects roughly 110 gigajoules (GJ) per capita energy use in China by 2030 (current per capita use in Japan and Western Europe is roughly 175 GJ; in the United States it is 330 GJ).

Differences in per capita energy use across countries with similar levels of wealth reflect concrete factors such as average temperature and population density, as well as cultural preferences and development patterns. Whichever model China follows in the long run, our projections for energy use in the upcoming decades are entirely plausible given the experience of its neighbors. Certainly the results would be different with a sample of countries outside of Asia. For example, recent growth in Latin American countries such as Brazil, Mexico, Chile, and Argentina has been both slower and less energy-intensive. However, the emerging Chinese economy bears a much closer resemblance to the Asian countries examined here. While not an econometric study, this comparison provides a useful check for the validity of our projections. Moreover, other recently calibrated models project similar rates of growth over this time horizon for China (McKibbin *et al.* 2008).

Policy implications

If China and other developing countries are growing much faster than anticipated, what are the implications for stabilization goals currently being discussed by policymakers in Annex B countries? The US CCSP report examined four stabilization scenarios, of which the two most stringent corresponded to stabilizing atmospheric CO_2 concentrations at 450 and 550 parts per million by volume (ppm$_v$).[8] For each scenario, modelers calculated the pathway of global carbon emissions consistent with achieving the stabilization target. The updated growth rates bring a new urgency to the question of incomplete global participation in abatement efforts. As shown in Figure 26.4, emissions from the non-Annex B countries alone meet or exceed the allowable global total for stabilization regimes in the near future, even in the apparently unlikely scenario of nearly zero growth between 2007 and 2010. Juxtaposing current and expected future rates of growth in developing countries with the proximity of the targets under discussion reveals a very narrow window of feasibility. If the price of carbon outside of Annex B is effectively zero for roughly the next decade, Annex B emissions must be completely eliminated by 2020, followed by rapid reductions outside of Annex B after 2020, in order to keep atmospheric CO_2 concentrations below 450 ppm$_v$. With a 550 ppm$_v$ target, the window is only a decade wider, and both are even smaller if growth in emissions follows the high scenario. Moreover, reductions in Annex B emissions at this pace are likely not realistic.

These results illustrate that the discussion of post-Kyoto international policy frameworks must focus on the participation of developing countries in the very near future. The remainder of this paper examines representative policy choices by applying MERGE in alternative solution modes. As a point of reference to the CCSP report (Clarke *et al.* 2007), we begin by re-calculating optimal stabilization paths for the two most stringent targets discussed above. Next we consider three scenarios that take into account constraints limiting developing country involvement. In the first scenario, we assume no developing country participation before 2050. In the second scenario, developing countries gradually adopt the first-best carbon price. In the third, countries take on quantitative emissions targets as their incomes rise, according to a rule based on the 1997 Kyoto negotiations. In each case we focus on the first half of the 21st century, although the speci-

---

[8] The two most stringent stabilization scenarios were defined in terms of limits on total radiative forcing, from the GHGs covered by the Kyoto Protocol, of 3.4 and 4.7 watts per square meter (W/m^2), respectively. These limits on forcing were chosen so that the resulting optimal atmospheric concentrations of CO_2 roughly matched the frequently discussed targets of 450 and 550 ppm$_v$.

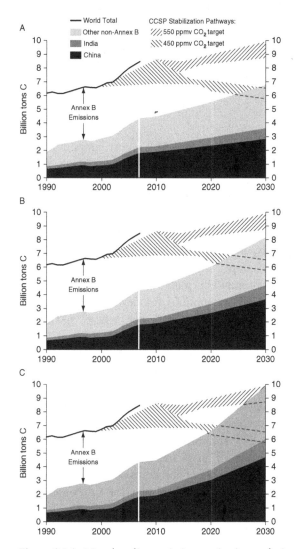

Figure 26.4. New baseline emission projections relative to stabilization pathways

Historical global emissions (including all energy and industrial sources) allocated to Annex B, China, India, and other non-Annex B countries are shown. After 2007, the data reflect new MERGE projections for baseline emissions through 2030 in non-Annex B countries, with growth rates corresponding to the low scenario (A), reference scenario (B), and high scenario (C). The range of global emissions consistent with the 450 ppmv (CO_2 only) stabilization target in the CCSP report intersects non-Annex B baseline emissions between 2020 and 2025; for the 550 ppmv target, the intersection occurs in 2025 for the high growth scenario and after 2030 for the other scenarios.

fication for the more distant future remains important.[9] Finally, we discuss the implications for cost and long-term temperature increase associated with the various scenarios.

Optimal stabilization

The most stringent target assessed in the CCSP report limits radiative forcing from all GHGs covered by the Kyoto Protocol to 3.4 watts per square meter (W/m^2), which corresponds to 525 ppm_v CO_2-equivalent (CO_2-e). Achieving this target with the optimal mix of abatement across gases results in a maximum CO_2-only concentration of 450 ppm_v. Thus our scenarios assume that commensurate abatement in other gases is undertaken simultaneously, although we focus on the implications for carbon emissions in this paper and refer to this target as the "450 target." In the newly recalibrated formulation of MERGE, following the reference growth-path assumptions for developing countries, achieving the 450 target with perfect "when" and "where" flexibility is much more costly than in the 2007 study. As shown in Figure 26.5, emissions reductions must begin immediately with a 25 percent drop from BAU by 2020. This corresponds to a carbon price in 2020 of \$335 per ton carbon (tC), or \$90 per ton CO_2, which rises over time. Even with all nations participating on an intertemporally optimal schedule, a target of this stringency would carry a substantial price tag.

The second-most stringent stabilization level discussed in the CCSP report is 4.7 W/m^2 for all gases (roughly equivalent to 670 ppm_v CO_2-e), under which CO_2-only concentrations reach 550 ppm_v (hereafter the "550 target"). The global pathway for CO_2 emissions consistent with optimal stabilization at this level consists of a slower (but still immediate) departure from the baseline with growth peaking around 2040, then returning to roughly 2005 levels by 2050 and declining quickly thereafter. While all countries undertake similar percentage reductions from their respective BAU paths in this scenario, reductions relative to 2005 differ significantly across regions. Annex B emissions, which grow very little in the BAU case, are reduced to roughly 50 percent below their 2005 level. On the other hand,

---

[9] The economic component of MERGE operates through 2100, but the climate module runs through 2200 to capture the long-term effects of accumulating atmospheric GHG concentrations on temperature.

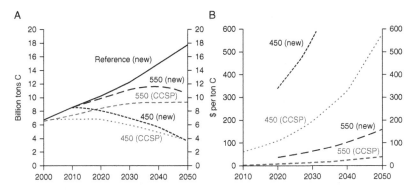

Figure 26.5. Global carbon emissions (A) and carbon price (B) for optimal stabilization pathways

The optimal stabilization scenarios from the CCSP report were re-run using the new growth rate assumptions. The dashed lines show the MERGE results from the CCSP report, while the solid lines show the new MERGE results. While the respective pathways for global emissions are similar to those depicted in Figure 26.4, stronger BAU growth and 10 years of delay result in much higher corresponding carbon prices.

emissions in the developing, non-Annex B countries, where baseline growth is rapid, are around 50 percent above their 2005 level by mid-century in the optimal stabilization scenario. The 2020 price for the 550 target is \$38/tC, or \$10/ton CO_2.

Comparing the carbon price for these two stabilization scenarios with the prices generated by MERGE in the CCSP report, both targets have become more expensive. Based on expected carbon prices, the 550 target is now much closer in stringency to our previous understanding of the 450 target, while the latter is reaching the limits of political feasibility. This shift is the result not only of our updated growth assumptions, but also of the fact that this analysis assumes no abatement activity in 2010 (beyond Kyoto Protocol compliance in ratifying countries). As emissions and concentrations have continued to climb during the current decade, we have moved closer to the target levels. Each year of unconstrained growth in emissions makes a given stabilization target more costly to reach.

With perfect "when" and "where" flexibility, abatement effort is allocated optimally across time and space. In other words, the effective carbon price in all regions is equal to a single world price, which rises smoothly at approximately the rate of interest from a starting point determined by the stringency of the target. Note that this allocation of abatement effort maximizes efficiency (i.e., minimizes total economic cost) without specifying an allocation of costs. Financial transfers in a variety of forms can be arranged to address concerns about equity and burden sharing. Still, even with the potential for incentives of this kind from developed countries, most observers familiar with the current state of international negotiations would agree that developing countries are not prepared to join a system with a single world price. The lack of sufficient institutional capital in these countries to implement effective abatement policies likely means that for at least the next decade, or longer in some cases, investments in energy supply and demand will continue to be made assuming a carbon price that is effectively close to zero.

Graduated accession

To examine alternative modes of engagement for developing countries, we hold emissions in Annex B countries constant along a path consistent with optimal stabilization at the 550 target, for which 2050 emissions are 50 percent below the 2005 level. Equivalently, we assume that the effective carbon price in Annex B is the one shown in Figure 26.5 for this stabilization target, passing through $38/tC in 2020 and rising to $160/tC in 2050. For non-Annex B, we first examine a "worst-case" policy environment in which no other countries adopt meaningful abatement measures (including hosting CDM-type projects) for several decades, so that emissions in these countries follow their baseline path at least through 2050. In such a scenario, as we have seen above, no matter how aggressive the action taken by Annex B countries, global energy-related carbon emissions will continue to rise rapidly. Figure 26.6 shows global emissions by region through 2050 when the optimal price for the 550 target is applied in Annex B immediately, but the rest of the world follows its reference path. Because Annex B represents a diminishing fraction of global emissions, this scenario results in only a slight reduction from the global reference path. Even if emissions decline rapidly after 2050, they will have peaked at a level far higher than that consistent with stabilization goals.[10]

---

[10] While "overshoot" is always possible, i.e., returning to a stabilization level after exceeding it, effects on temperature and climate will be determined by the

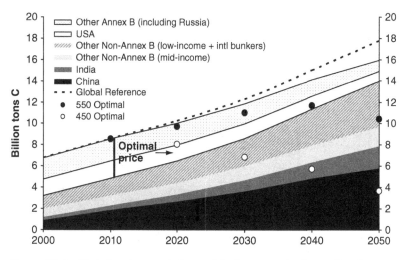

Figure 26.6. Global carbon emissions with abatement in Annex B only Annex B adopts the optimal 550 price beginning after 2010, while non-Annex B countries follow their reference path. Global emissions depart only slightly from the reference scenario. International bunker fuel emissions, which are not included in national totals by the Intergovernmental Panel on Climate Change (IPCC), are included in the "other" group.

Against this backdrop, we next consider a graduated accession scenario. China is undoubtedly the most important player in any global policy regime. While it is unrealistic to assume that China would adopt the same price regime as the Annex B countries initially, China may opt in to a global agreement in the future (Wiener 2008). In addition, several nations outside of Annex B may be willing to participate before others—these countries are grouped under the "other mid-income" category in the figures (examples include Korea, Brazil, Mexico, and South Africa; a complete regional breakdown is provided in Appendix B). In this case, to "join" the coalition means to adopt the same carbon price as Annex B under the optimal 550 stabilization path. We assume that the mid-income countries join China as participants in the global regime beginning after 2020. For lower income countries, we assume India does not join until 2040, and other poorer countries do not join at all before 2050. Figure 26.7 shows global emissions in this scenario, termed the "graduated 550 tax" scenario.

integral of the radiative forcing time path, not its ultimate equilibrium. That is, how far we exceed a stabilization target, and for how long, matters.

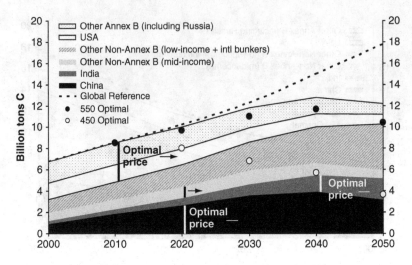

Figure 26.7. Global carbon emissions in the "graduated 550 tax" scenario. Annex B adopts the optimal 550 price beginning after 2010. Non-Annex B countries adopt the same price path in future years after following the reference path until graduation.

Since not all countries are adopting the optimal price throughout the time horizon, the resulting emissions path exceeds the optimal path. Still, emissions in this scenario have begun to decline before 2050 and the target is within reach.

In this scenario, a country follows its reference case before "graduating" to full participation in the global regime; afterwards it adopts the optimal 550 stabilization price. For participating countries, the price rises at approximately the rate of interest, which helps to create incentives for early abatement in an intertemporal optimization model such as MERGE. To simulate the lack of institutional capacity for creating abatement incentives in non-participating countries, we hold energy-related variables fixed prior to "graduation" to eliminate this anticipation effect. If graduating countries were modeled without constraints in the pre-accession time periods, so that energy technology investments were made with perfect foresight about the post-accession price, emissions prior to graduation would be only slightly higher than the optimal stabilization path. That is, if a country agrees to adopt a high carbon price in a future time period and if market participants view this announcement as credible, the effect of the policy is not far from the optimal policy of participation from the beginning. Such

Table 26.3 *Progressive emissions reduction targets*

	Per Capita Income thousands of US$(2000)				Corresponding Emissions Reduction Target below BAU			
	2005	2015	2025	2035	2020	2030	2040	2050
China	3.6	6.3	10.6	16.2	—	5%	11%	17%
Other mid-income	10.8	13.0	16.6	21.4	11%	14%	17%	21%
India	2.0	3.1	5.1	7.9	—	—	2%	7%
Other low-income	2.9	3.6	4.9	6.7	—	—	1%	5%

is the magnitude of the "shadow" that future prices cast back on investment decisions by fully rational, forward-looking actors. Many observers, however, believe this is not a fitting description of likely pre-accession behavior for developing countries, whose governments are currently unwilling and unable to set a credible future price on carbon. Instead, our scenario reflects a world in which "graduation" corresponds to the establishment of credible abatement incentives.

Progressive targets

The graduated accession scenario assumed that, as countries join the coalition, they immediately adopt the world optimal carbon price, which is growing over time at approximately the rate of interest. A more realistic political outcome may be that the stringency of the emissions target adopted by different countries gradually increases over time. Frankel (2007) observed that targets agreed to for the first commitment period of the Kyoto Protocol, when converted to implicit percentage reductions from a projected baseline, were progressively correlated with per capita income at the time of negotiation (Frankel 2007). Poorer countries were willing to adopt targets that represented smaller percentage reductions from BAU emissions than higher-income countries. This relationship suggests a simple rule that could be used to estimate reasonable targets for developing countries as their incomes rise. The threshold for accepting positive emission reduction commitments in 2010 was a per capita income of around $4,500 (in year 2000 currency) in 1996.[11] At the upper end of the range, a large group of countries with per capita incomes around $30,000 in 1996 adopted targets that were roughly 25 percent below their projected BAU emissions for 2010. Using these two points and assuming a logarithmic relationship (as indicated by the data), we construct a simple rule for determining an "acceptable" quantitative reduction target based on per capita income (with an approximate fifteen-year lag). The following table shows results for the four non-Annex B regions, using exogenous growth projections in MERGE as the basis for average income levels (which begin with the figures for 2005, in PPP terms, published by the IMF in 2008).

Based on our simple rule, only the mid-income group had an average income level high enough in 2005 to indicate that participation beginning in the next commitment period (i.e., between 2010 and 2020) is likely. China would be the next to join the coalition, but only with a 5 percent reduction from BAU by 2030 and a 17 percent reduction by 2050. In the previous scenario, when China adopted the optimal stabilization price in 2030, abatement by 2050 reached 45 percent below BAU in 2050. India and other low-income countries are unwilling to adopt targets before 2040 and still have not significantly reduced emissions by 2050. Figure 26.8 shows the projected global emissions pathway through 2050 if these targets were adopted and met (termed the "progressive targets" scenario), again assuming that the optimal carbon price for achieving the 550 target is applied in Annex B.

In this case, the progressive reduction targets modeled do not lead to a global downturn in emissions before 2050. Under such a scheme, stabilization even at the 550 ppm$_v$ level appears doubtful. This is particularly true if we assume that the same rule applies to commitments beyond 2050. In the "graduated 550 tax" scenario shown in Figure 26.7, we assumed that "graduating" countries adopted the optimal world price so that, in the long run, emissions returned to close to the stabilization path. In the "progressive targets" scenario, even if we

---

[11] We interpret this income level as representative of real purchasing power for the purposes of comparison to future income projections. If, as is more likely, it reflects a conversion at market exchange rates, the true purchasing power value of the threshold income would be higher. Thus we are potentially underestimating the level of wealth necessary for a country to accept a positive reduction target.

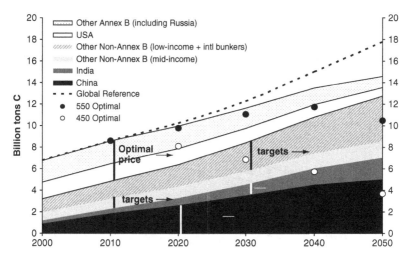

Figure 26.8. Global carbon emissions in the "progressive targets" scenario. Non-Annex B countries adopt targets as a function of per capita income levels consistent with observed outcomes in Kyoto negotiations. Annex B adopts the optimal 550 price. Global emissions do not begin to decline by 2050 in this scenario.

assume that countries begin to converge to the optimal stabilization price once they reach the $30,000 income level, the long-run global emissions path remains high. Figure 26.9 shows these two scenarios over the full 100-year time horizon. With the progressive target rule, emissions from the lowest-income countries alone rise to nearly 8 GtC, approximately equal to today's global total. If the targets are interpreted as allocations of permits and if global trading is allowed among regions above the income threshold, many developing countries would export their permits to Annex B. In this case the regional distribution of emissions would change, but the global total would not. Thus if developing countries are only willing to adopt targets commensurate with Annex B commitments during the initial Kyoto negotiations, long-term climate stabilization will likely not be possible.

Costs of alternative proposals

We now turn to an examination of the economic costs involved for the various scenarios under consideration, as well as the potential environmental outcomes.

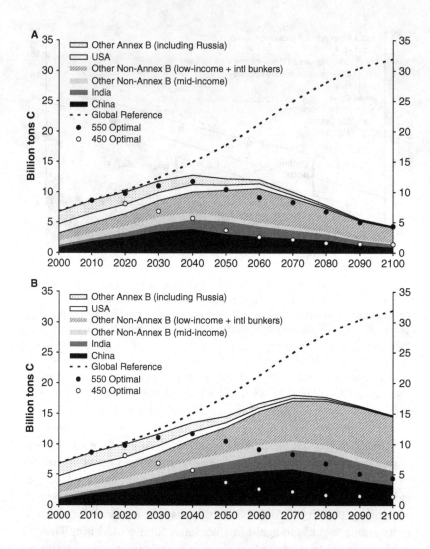

Figure 26.9. Global emissions through 2100

In the "graduated 550 tax" scenario (A), global emissions remain only slightly higher than in the optimal 550 path as countries adopt the global price. In the "progressive targets" scenario (B), the quantitative target rule does not result in an emissions path consistent with stabilization.

Abatement costs

When policies are introduced to create incentives for emissions reductions, more expensive, lower-carbon energy technologies are deployed (to the extent they are available). This shift leads to direct costs in terms of lost consumption due to higher energy expenditures, but also to deadweight loss in terms of reductions in energy use and economic activity. When more advanced low-emitting technologies are available for deployment at the necessary scale, the costs associated with achieving a particular emissions reduction goal are reduced.[12] We measure the total cost of the abatement effort at a given point in time in a given region by the loss in gross domestic product (GDP) relative to the no-policy reference scenario. Costs can also be summed across regions to measure the total burden of a particular scenario. Figure 26.10 shows the effects on gross world product (GWP) for the two optimal stabilization cases, as well as for the two alternative scenarios.

A first observation is that the policy costs of the optimal 450 stabilization scenario rise quickly to over 6 percent of global income. The costs of the 550 scenario (although considerably higher than those calculated by MERGE for the same target in the CCSP report), are lower than the 450 scenario, rising to 2 percent of global income by 2060 and to 3.5 percent by 2100. In the graduated 550 tax scenario, costs are lower initially because not all countries are undertaking abatement.[13] In the long run, however, even though emissions are not as low as in the optimal 550 case (i.e., the target is not being met), policy costs are higher because long-lived investments in carbon-emitting technologies (such as coal-fired electric power plants) made in the interim by non-participating regions have made the transition more difficult. This result helps to illustrate that not only are global environmental goals jeopardized the longer developing countries remain outside the coalition, but also the global cost burden of achieving a given target is increased by their adherence to a BAU path. Finally, global costs are lowest in the progressive targets scenario because emissions remain substantially above the levels required for stabilization at 550 ppm$_v$.

---

[12] See Richels and Blanford (2008) for an application of the MERGE model to the value of technology in development in the context of the US electric sector.

[13] Because MERGE is an inter-temporal optimization model, consumption can be shifted over time to maximize welfare. This sometimes results in negative costs in non-participating regions but it is a minor effect.

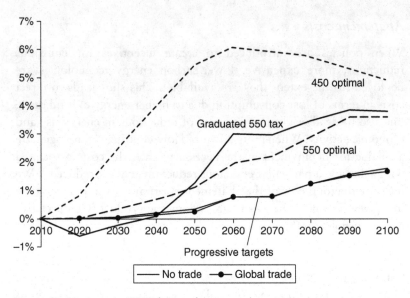

Figure 26.10. Loss in GWP from reference under various mitigation scenarios

The 450 stabilization target is excessively costly. In the graduated 550 tax scenario, non-participating countries do not anticipate joining the coalition, thus increasing costs after graduation relative to the intertemporally optimal path. The progressive targets scenario involves less stringent emissions reductions and therefore lower cost. Costs are aggregated using MERs.

If targets are allocated as globally tradable permits, total GWP losses are slightly less than if the targets reflect actual reductions realized in each region.

GDP losses in a particular region depend on both the stringency of the target adopted (i.e., the region's effective carbon price), and on physical characteristics such as the set of available low-carbon technologies and initial conditions with respect to energy use in the economy and the age of the capital stock.[14] Regional costs also depend importantly on the implementation of the policy, which can set rules for allocating the global cost burden across countries according to

[14] Because MERGE assumes an exogenous growth path, as discussed in the model calibration section, it does not include a link between energy costs and total factor productivity growth. Particularly for developing countries, abatement costs could be larger than our estimates if increased energy expenditures induce a negative feedback on productivity growth.

equity principles or the outcome of international negotiations. We do not investigate the implications of alternative burden-sharing schemes in this analysis.

However, our results do offer some insight into the way abatement effort affects regional economies independent of equity-related transfers. Figure 26.11 maps emissions reductions on the x-axis to economic cost on the y-axis for each region and each time period up until 2050 for the 550 optimal case. In the top panel of the figure (A), abatement and cost are expressed in terms of percentage reductions from the reference case, while in the bottom panel (B), reductions are expressed in absolute terms. In this first-best scenario, marginal abatement cost is equalized across regions in optimally satisfying the long-term constraint, and each country bears the cost of reducing its emissions up to the efficient price. The correlation of *total* abatement cost exhibited in Figure 26.11(B) suggests in addition that intrinsic emissions reduction opportunities are similar across regions; they vary only in scale, with China by far the largest. On the other hand, Figure 26.11(A) shows that in rapidly growing countries such as China and India, the same percentage reduction in emissions corresponds to a greater percentage reduction in GDP than in Annex B countries. It is discrepancies in this dimension that drive the need for equity-based adjustments. If such adjustments cannot be accomplished with compensating financial transfers, parity in percentage-based GDP impact can only be achieved by limiting the percentage reductions in emissions in countries like China and India, as in the progressive targets scenario. However, this approach has been demonstrated above to yield comparatively little environmental protection.

Environmental outcomes

Ultimately, society must choose an appropriate balance between the near-term economic cost of abatement and the long-term environmental risks posed by increased global temperature. We do not undertake such a benefit–cost analysis here, but we provide an estimate of how these emissions scenarios translate into environmental outcomes. In the extremely stringent optimal 450 scenario, radiative forcing from the GHGs covered by the Kyoto Protocol was, by definition, limited to 3.4 W/m². When combined with other exogenously specified forcing agents in our analysis, principally the gases regulated under

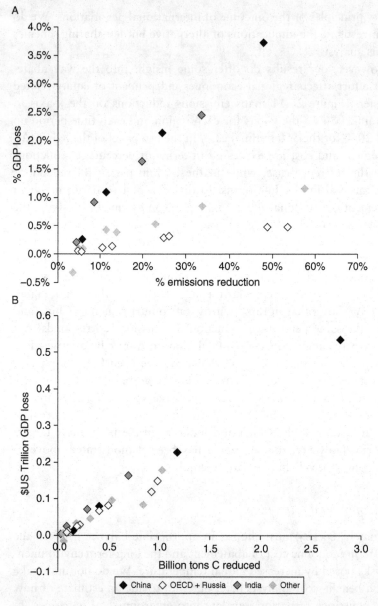

Figure 26.11. Distribution of abatement cost in 550 optimal scenario, 2020–2050.

Regional abatement and GDP loss are shown in percentage terms (A) and absolute terms (B), relative to the reference case. While regional costs are similar in the absolute dimension, abatement as a share of GDP is higher for developing countries.

the Montreal Protocol and the cooling effect (i.e., negative forcing) from sulfur aerosols,[15] total radiative forcing stabilized at approximately 3.0 W/m^2. The equilibrium temperature increase above pre-industrial associated with sustained forcing of this magnitude depends on our assumption about climate sensitivity. This parameter, the key uncertainty in understanding anthropogenic impacts on the climate system, is defined as the equilibrium temperature increase associated with a doubling of atmospheric CO_2, which corresponds to a radiative forcing of 3.7 W/m^2. The latest assessment by the IPCC (2007) reports a global average temperature increase of 3 degrees Celsius (°C) relative to pre-industrial for the median value of climate sensitivity. Accordingly, our 450 scenario leads to a median equilibrium temperature increase of 2.4°C above pre-industrial.[16]

This result implies that limiting the increase in global average surface temperature (or more precisely, our median estimate of temperature increase) to 2°C would be even more costly than the scenario illustrated here, even with optimal participation. For the 550 scenario, forcing from the Kyoto gases is held to 4.7 W/m^2, resulting in a total net forcing of 4.2 W/m^2. In this case, we observe a median temperature increase of 3.4°C by 2200. In the graduated 550 tax scenario, total radiative forcing is not stabilized: it reaches 4.5 W/m^2 by the end of the century and continues to rise. This leads to a temperature increase of 3.8°C by 2200. In the progressive targets scenario, radiative forcing is much higher at the end of the century, around 5.8 W/m^2, resulting in a median temperature increase that eventually exceeds 5°C (depending how quickly emissions are reduced after 2100). These results are summarized in Table 26.4 and Figure 26.12, which include temperature outcomes for a broad range of climate sensitivity assumptions corresponding to the IPCC's 90 percent confidence interval.

[15] The exogenous forcing from both Montreal gases and sulfur aerosols declines over time—in the former case due to enforcement of the Montreal Protocol and in the latter case due to increased use of sulfur control technologies for coal plants or, in the policy scenarios, reduced use of coal without carbon capture and sequestration.

[16] The equilibrium temperature response to forcing levels other than 3.7 W/m^2 is proportional to climate sensitivity. For example, in the 450 optimal case, equilibrium temperature is equal to (3.0 / 3.7) × 3 = 2.4°C. For median and lower climate sensitivity, the equilibrium response is realized by 2200. For higher climate sensitivities, we must assume a slower response time for consistency with current observations, so that even when forcing is stabilized by 2100 or before, equilibrium temperature is not reached by 2200.

Table 26.4 *Radiative forcing and temperature outcomes*

	Radiative forcing (W/m²) in 2100		Temperature increase (°C above pre-industrial) by 2100 (2200) with alternative climate sensitivities		
	From Kyoto gases	Total (including aerosols)	1.5 (5th %-ile)	3.0 (50th %-ile)	6.0 (95th %-ile)
450 Optimal	3.4	2.9 (stabilized)	1.2 (1.2)	2.2 (2.4)	2.6 (3.5)
550 Optimal	4.7	4.2 (stabilized)	1.7 (1.7)	3.1 (3.4)	3.3 (4.9)
Graduated 550 Tax	5.0	4.5 (not stabilized)	1.8 (2.0)	3.2 (3.8)	3.4 (5.6)
Progressive Targets	6.3	5.8 (not stabilized)	2.3 (3+)	3.7 (5+)	3.7 (7+)
Reference	7.6	7.1 (not stabilized)	2.7 (4+)	4.2 (8+)	4.1 (10+)

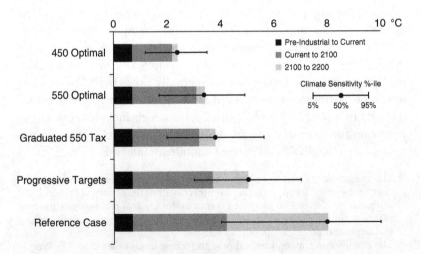

Figure 26.12. Average surface temperature increase above pre-industrial Current average surface temperatures are roughly 0.7°C above pre-industrial. Error bars are shown around total warming through 2200 corresponding to the 5th–95th percentile confidence interval for climate sensitivity. Even in the 450 optimal case, median temperature increase exceeds 2°C.

Conclusion

The recent acceleration of energy-related emissions in the developing world, particularly in China, has taken many analysts by surprise. Our results indicate that with an updated view of near-term prospects for growth and opportunities for abatement, keeping the concentration of CO_2 in the atmosphere below the 450 ppm$_v$ level would require immediate action in all countries. As little as one decade of unconstrained emissions growth in non-Annex B countries could compromise the world's ability to meet a target of this stringency. At the same time, a target in the range of 550 ppm$_v$ CO_2 has become almost as difficult to achieve as the 450 ppm$_v$ target appeared just a few years ago. This trend will continue as long as growth in global emissions continues unabated. Moreover, an impending recession, even if it effectively stops economic growth for two years, does not mitigate the severity of the climate challenge we face, nor change the fundamental reality that the majority of future emissions (and required abatement) will occur in the developing world.

Therefore a critical design element for post-Kyoto international climate policy should be the creation of incentives for abatement outside of Annex B. Global policy measures must engage developing countries, especially China, soon and in a meaningful way if stringent stabilization goals are to be achieved. Such engagement must be accompanied by emissions reductions in Annex B countries and may also require significant financial incentives from the developed world, depending on the negotiated burden-sharing scheme. It is in all nations' interests to work cooperatively to limit our interference with the global climate.

References

Auffhammer, M. and R. T. Carson (2008). "Forecasting the Path of China's CO_2 Emissions Using Province-Level Information," *Journal of Environmental Economics and Management* 55(3): 229–47, doi:10.1016/j.jeem.2007.10.002.

BP (2008). *BP Statistical Review of Energy.*

Clarke, L. *et al.* (2007). "Scenarios of Greenhouse Gas Emissions and Atmospheric Concentrations," Sub-report 2.1A of Synthesis and Assessment Product 2.1 by the US Climate Change Science Program and the Subcommittee on Global Change Research, Department of Energy, Office of Biological & Environmental Research, Washington, DC, USA.

Fisher-Vanden, K., G. H. Jefferson, H. Liu, and Q. Tao (2004). "What is Driving China's Decline in Energy Intensity?" *Resource and Energy Economics* 26(1): 77–97.

Frankel, J. (2007). "Formulas for Quantitative Emissions Targets," in J. E. Aldy and R. N. Stavins (eds.), *Architectures for Agreement: Addressing Global Climate Change in the Post-Kyoto World.* New York: Cambridge University Press, pp. 31–56.

Gregg, J. S., R. J. Andres, and G. Marland (2008). "China: Emissions patterns of the world leader of CO_2 emissions from fossil fuel consumption and cement production," *Geophysical Research Letters* 35: L08806 doi:10.1029/2007GL032887.

He, J. and L. Kuijs (2007). "Rebalancing China's Economy: Modeling a Policy Package," World Bank China Research Paper No. 7.

Heston, A., R. Summers, and B. Aten (2006). Penn World Table Version 6.2, Center for International Comparisons of Production, Income and Prices at the University of Pennsylvania.

IEA (2000). *World Energy Outlook 2000.* Paris: IEA.

(2005). *World Energy Outlook 2005.* Paris: IEA.

(2007a). *World Energy Statistics 2007.* Paris: IEA.

(2007b). *World Energy Outlook 2007: China and India Insights.* Paris: IEA.

IMF (2008). *World Economic Outlook 2008.* Washington, DC: IMF.

IPCC (2007). *Climate Change 2007: The Physical Science Basis. Contribution of Working Group I to the Fourth Assessment Report of the Intergovernmental Panel on Climate Change,* Solomon, S. *et al.* (eds.), Cambridge, UK: Cambridge University Press.

Jiang, K. and X. Hu (2006). "Energy Demand and Emissions in 2030 in China: Scenarios and Policy Options," *Environmental Economics and Policy Studies* 7: 233–50.

Manne, A. S. and R. G. Richels (2005). "MERGE: An Integrated Assessment Model for Global Climate Change," in R. Loulou, J. Waaub, and G. Zaccour (eds.), *Energy and Environment.* New York: Springer, pp. 175–89.

Marland, G. *et al.* (2008). "Global, Regional, and National Fossil Fuel CO_2 Emissions," in *Trends: A Compendium of Data on Global Change,* Carbon Dioxide Information Analysis Center, Oak Ridge National Laboratory, US Department of Energy, Oak Ridge, TN.

McKibbin, W. J., P. J. Wilcoxen, and W. T. Woo (2008). "Preventing the Tragedy of the CO_2 Commons," Brookings Global Economy and Development Working Paper 22.

MNP (2008). *Global CO_2 emissions: increase continued in 2007,* Netherlands Environmental Assessment Agency.

Raupach, M. *et al.* (2007). *Global and regional drivers of accelerating* CO_2 *emissions*, proceedings of the National Academy of Sciences.

Richels, R. G. and G. J. Blanford (2008). "The value of technological advance in decarbonizing the US economy," *Energy Economics* 30(6): 2930–46. Available at dx.doi.org/10.1016/j.eneco.2008.06.005.

Richels, R. G., T. F. Rutherford, G. J. Blanford, and L. Clarke (2007). "Managing the Transition to Climate Stabilization," *Climate Policy* 7(5): 409–28.

Weyant, J. P. *et al.* (1999). "The costs of the Kyoto Protocol: a multi-model evaluation," *Energy Journal*, Special Issue.

Wiener, J. B. (2008). "Climate Change Policy and Policy Change in China," *UCLA Law Review* 55: 1805–26.

Appendix A. Technology in MERGE

Table 26.A1 describes technological options in the electric sector. Parameter ranges reflect the improvement path over time. For Annex B countries, coal with capture and new nuclear plants are first available in 2020, with improvement beginning in subsequent decades through 2050. In other regions, we assume the same technologies become available, lagged by one decade in the case of China and other mid-income countries, and two decades in the case of India and other low-income countries. Table 26.A2 shows our assumptions for non-electric energy technologies.

Table 26.A1 *Electric generation technology assumptions*

Existing Technologies*	
Coal	LCOE° = $25 / MWh Efficiency = 33%
Natural Gas	LCOE° = $52 / MWh[#] Efficiency = 40%
Nuclear	LCOE° = $25 / MWh
Hydroelectric, etc.[†]	LCOE° = $20 / MWh
New Technologies	
Coal (without CCS)	LCOE° = $57 – $41 / MWh Efficiency = 38% – 46%

Table 26.A1 (*cont.*)

New Technologies	
Coal with CCS	First available in 2020 LCOE° = $80 – $56 / MWh Efficiency = 31% – 42% Capture rate = 90%
Natural Gas (without CCS)	LCOE° = $50 – $70 / MWh[#] Efficiency = 49% – 60%
Natural Gas with CCS	First available in 2020 LCOE° = $84 – $110 / MWh[#] Efficiency = 39% – 42% Capture rate = 90%
Nuclear (new ALWR)[‡]	First available in 2020 LCOE° = $40 – $37 / MWh Non-market cost[‡] = $10 / MWh
Wind	LCOE° = $86 – $62 / MWh
Biomass	LCOE° = $86 – $69 / MWh
Solar (thermal)	LCOE° = $144 – $66 / MWh
Solar (photovoltaic)	LCOE° = $225 – $81 / MWh

[*] Capital costs are assumed to be fully recovered for existing generation assets and hence are omitted from the levelized cost calculation.

[°] LCOE refers to full levelized cost of electricity.

[#] LCOE for existing natural gas generation is shown for the base year price for natural gas. The full range of natural gas prices reported in the model is shown in the LCOE projections for new natural gas generation.

[†] This category, while predominantly hydroelectric, includes all categories of renewables in place in the base year.

[‡] ALWR refers to advanced light water reactor. We assume that the cost of nuclear generation has a market and non-market component. The latter, which is calibrated to current usage, rises proportionally to market share and is intended to represent public concerns about security and environmental risks in the technology and associated nuclear fuel cycle. Non-market costs are not included in the LCOE calculation.

Appendix B. Scenario Descriptions

Table 26.B1 provides an overview of the scenarios presented in the policy analysis section of this paper. All scenarios use the reference assumption for growth in developing countries discussed in the earlier part of the paper.

Table 26.A2 *Non-electric energy technology assumptions*

Coal (for direct use)	Cost = $2 – $3 / GJ
Petroleum (cost rises with extraction and depends on region)	Cost = $3 – $20 / GJ
Natural Gas (cost rises with extraction and depends on region)	Cost = $4 – $20 / GJ
Synthetic (coal-based) Liquids	Cost = $11 / GJ
Biofuels	Cost = $10 / GJ
Non-Electric Backstop	Cost = $25 / GJ

Table 26.B1 *Overview of scenarios*

	450 and 550 Optimal	Graduated 550 Tax	Progressive Targets
Policies Enacted			
Annex B	Optimal price	Optimal price (550)	Optimal price (550)
Non-Annex B	Optimal price	Optimal price (550) after graduation	Quantity targets corresponding to income
Year after which participation begins			
Annex B	2010	2010	2010
China	2010	2020	2020
Other mid-income	2010	2020	2010
India	2010	2040	2030
Other low-income	2010	2050	2030

Table 26.B2 gives details of the composition of regions in the analysis. Note in particular the "rest of OECD" includes only those members of the OECD which were also parties to the Kyoto Protocol, that is, it excludes Korea, Mexico, and Turkey. The distinction between the mid-income country grouping and the low-income

Table 26.B2 *Regional composition*

Rest of OECD	Other Mid-Income	Other Low-Income
EU27 + Iceland, Norway and Switzerland	Argentina	OPEC countries
	Brazil	Other Asia
	Chile	Other Latin America
Australia	Korea	Other Middle East
Canada	Malaysia	Low-income Former
Japan	Mexico	Soviet Republics
New Zealand	South Africa	Sub-Saharan Africa
	Taiwan	
	Thailand	
	Turkey	
	Other small high- and mid-income countries	

country grouping was made on the basis of current per capita income. The dividing threshold was roughly $6,000 per capita (in year 2000 $US PPP). One exception is the wealthy oil-exporting countries of Kuwait, Qatar, and United Arab Emirates, which were placed in the low-income group along with other oil-exporters. Also, relatively high-income countries who are not members of the OECD or Annex B, such as Israel and Singapore, are placed in the mid-income group.

27 Expecting the unexpected: macroeconomic volatility and climate policy*

WARWICK J. MCKIBBIN, ADELE MORRIS
AND PETER J. WILCOXEN

Introduction

The global financial crisis, a deepening global recession, and continued turmoil in credit markets drive home the importance of developing a global climate architecture that can withstand major economic disruptions. A well-designed global climate regime and the attendant domestic policies in participating countries need to be resilient to large and unexpected changes in economic growth, technology, energy prices, demographic trends, and other factors that drive costs of abatement and emissions. Ideally, the climate regime would not exacerbate macroeconomic shocks, and would possibly buffer them instead, while withstanding defaults by individual members. Because climate policy must endure indefinitely in order to stabilize atmospheric concentrations of greenhouse gases (GHGs), all sorts of shocks will occur at some stage in the policy's existence. Anticipating such shocks may mean rejecting policies that might reduce emissions reliably in stable economic conditions but would be vulnerable to collapse—with consequent deterioration in environmental outcomes—in volatile conditions.

Macroeconomic volatility is the practical manifestation of an issue that has received considerable attention in the theoretical literature on the design of environmental policies: uncertainty about the costs and

* Prepared for the Harvard Project on International Climate Agreements (HPICA). The authors thank Waranya Pim Chanthapun for excellent research assistance and an anonymous referee for very useful suggestions. The views expressed in the chapter are those of the authors and should not be interpreted as reflecting the views of any of the above collaborators or of the Institutions with which the authors are affiliated including the trustees, officers or other staff of the ANU, Lowy Institute or The Brookings Institution.

benefits of reducing emissions.[1] In particular, macroeconomic shocks can cause the cost of regulation to be much higher or lower than anticipated. Unexpectedly stringent and costly regulations may become political lightning rods. Recent world events, for example, highlight the fact that economic surprises can subject governments to enormous pressures to relax or repeal taxes or other policies perceived to impede economic growth. For a climate policy to survive future shocks, therefore, it must not violate time consistency: it must be optimal for each government to continue to enforce the policy even when confronted with sharp departures from the conditions expected when the governments undertook the commitments. All else equal, a climate regime that exacerbates downward macroeconomic shocks or depresses the benefits of positive macroeconomic shocks would be more costly and less stable than a system that better handles global business cycles and other volatility.

The stability of the policy has important environmental implications for two reasons. First, collapse of the policy could set back progress on emissions reductions for years. Second, decisions of economic actors depend on their expectations of future policy, and this dependency affects the performance of the policy itself.[2] In the case of climate change, a system that is more robust to shocks, and is thus more likely to persist, would increase the expected payoffs of investments in new technologies and emissions reductions relative to a system that is less robust. In particular, a system of rigid and ambitious targets may seem the most environmentally rigorous approach, but if the rigidity decreases the probability the agreement would be ratified, or reduces compliance, or limits long-term participation, households and firms will take that into account in their investment decisions. They will invest too little in abatement and alternative energy technologies, causing the system to be less effective in practice than one with more flexibility. If governments try to compensate for low credibility by imposing a more stringent target, they could inadvertently worsen the incentives for investment by further reducing the program's credibility. This all points to the central importance

---

[1] See, for example, Weitzman (1974), Roberts and Spence (1976), Pizer (1997), McKibbin and Wilcoxen (1997), Pezzey (2003), von Below and Persson (2008), Hoel and Karp (2002) and Quirion (2004).

[2] Kydland and Prescott (1977) make this point more broadly.

of establishing a regime that is credibly robust to changing economic conditions.

This chapter uses the G-Cubed model to explore how shocks in the global economy propagate differently depending on the design of the climate policy regime. G-Cubed divides the world economy into ten regions: the United States, the European Union, Japan, Australia, the remaining member-countries of the Organisation for Economic Co-operation and Development (OECD), Eastern Europe and the former Soviet Union, China, India, other developing countries, and oil-exporting developing countries.[3] Using the model, we construct two reference case scenarios for policies to address climate change: a quantity-based approach similar to an international cap-and-trade system and a price-based approach similar to a harmonized carbon tax.[4] The scenarios are calibrated so that they produce identical emissions levels and marginal abatement costs in the absence of unexpected shocks. We then subject each of the policies to two kinds of shocks relevant to recent experience: (1) a positive shock to economic growth in China, India, and other developing countries, and (2) a sharp decline in housing markets and a rise in global equity risk premiums, causing severe financial distress in the global economy. We analyze the effects of each shock on key economic indicators for the first decade after the shock occurs. We compare the results from the two policy regimes and draw inferences about the strengths and weaknesses of each regime in the context of these economic disruptions. We then compare the two regimes against a hybrid policy, such as the one described in McKibbin and Wilcoxen (2002a).

A number of authors have explored the properties of different climate policies under uncertainty. Much of the work has focused on the relative advantages of intensity-based approaches in which national emissions targets are indexed to gross domestic product (GDP). For example, Ellerman and Sue Wing (2003) and Sue Wing

---

[3] The model is summarized in Appendix A and described more fully in McKibbin and Wilcoxen (1998).

[4] The quantity and price approaches we model are polar policy cases that produce the most extreme potential interactions of climate policy and macroeconomic shocks. Other policy proposals, such as a cap-and-trade system that allows banking, lie between these poles, so our results reflect the bounds of likely climate policy on the effects of interest.

et al. (2006) compare the performance of an intensity-based policy to a traditional system of fixed absolute emissions limits when future GDP growth is uncertain. They find that the intensity-based system leads to abatement that is more predictable and less volatile. Jotzo and Pezzey (2005) examine GDP-indexed intensity targets in an international context and show that by reducing uncertainty, indexing can encourage countries to adopt more stringent emissions targets than would be optimal under a traditional permit system. Fischer and Springborn (2007) add to the literature by examining the performance of intensity targets under uncertainty using a real business cycle model. They point out that although intensity-based policies provide greater stability of abatement than ordinary permit systems, it comes at the cost of increasing the variability of emissions. They also emphasize that conventional permit systems act as a form of automatic stabilizer, with permit prices (and therefore the effective stringency of the policy) increasing in economic booms and decreasing during downturns.

In this study we extend the literature in two respects: we explore how the global climate regime can affect the propagation of shocks between economies, and we use that information to evaluate the merits of a hybrid policy. We find that although quantity-based and price-based climate regimes are similar in their ability to reduce carbon emissions efficiently in the absence of shocks, they differ importantly in how they affect the transmission of economic disturbances between economies. In particular, a quantity target with an annual cap on global emissions can cause unexpectedly high growth in one country to reduce growth in other economies or even force their growth to be negative. The rise in the global carbon price caused by higher growth in one economy can have a larger negative impact on other economies than the positive spillover of growth through trade. This effect is absent in the price-based regime. However, in the case of the global financial crisis we find that the quantity-based approach works well because it is globally counter-cyclical: carbon prices fall as the world economy slows, which acts to dampen the economic slowdown. A hybrid policy, however, could achieve the best of both policies: it could provide the counter-cyclical advantages of a permit system in a downturn but also provide the flexibility of a price-based mechanism in a boom.

We discuss each climate policy system in more detail in the next section of this chapter. Subsequent sections review key sources of uncertainty in the design of climate policy and describe the particular shocks we introduce into the model, discuss our modeling results, and draw policy-relevant insights.

Alternative climate policy regimes

Analysts have offered a wide range of alternative frameworks for international climate policy once the Kyoto Protocol expires in 2012.[5] Each of these approaches has advantages and disadvantages with respect to stability in the face of shocks. Some propose an agreement similar to the Kyoto Protocol with targets and broader participation. Frankel (2007) explains that targets could be indexed to economic growth so that parties do not face unanticipated stringency with strong economic growth or benefit from international allowance sales when their emissions reductions are a result of economic downturns, rather than explicit actions on climate. Bodansky (2007) argues that targets and timetables have proven to be politically untenable for those who sat out the Kyoto Protocol and that a successor agreement should therefore be more flexible. For example, a new agreement could include an explicit range of domestic actions that parties could take, including taxes, efficiency standards, and indexed targets, with the mix chosen at the discretion of each party. Some combination of targets and timetables for industrialized countries and more flexible provisions for developing countries could emerge as parties seek to expand participation and China and India resist hard national targets.

An agreement that is tailored at least to some extent to different countries' national circumstances is likely. Nonetheless, it is useful to examine more analytically tractable policies. Analysts have paid particular attention to an international system of binding emissions caps, like the Kyoto Protocol, that reaches a specified target with certainty (at least in principle) and a system of agreed price signals on GHG emissions, such as a harmonized carbon tax, which promises a certain level of effort but leaves emissions levels uncertain. For example,

[5] See for example Aldy and Stavins (2007).

Nordhaus (2006) and others find that a price-signal approach reduces the risk of inadvertent stringency and is likely to be more efficient than a system of hard caps in the context of uncertainty over both the costs and benefits of abatement.

In addition to conventional price or quantity approaches, hybrid policies have been proposed that would combine features of cap-and-trade and a tax in a way that seeks to capture the advantages of each. The hybrid system proposed in McKibbin and Wilcoxen (2002a and 2002b) would create and distribute a set of long-term permits, each entitling the owner to emit a specified amount of carbon every year for the life of the permit. Once distributed, the long-term permits could be traded among firms, or bought and retired by environmental groups. In addition, the government would agree to sell annual permits for a pre-set but increasing fee (possibly harmonized within an international agreement). There would be no restriction on the number of annual permits sold, but each permit would be good only in the year it is issued.

Under the McKibbin-Wilcoxen hybrid system, if robust economic growth leads to more demand for emissions permits than can be satisfied by the long-term permits alone, the government would supply the difference via annual permits, and the policy would essentially function as a tax at the margin. However, during a severe downturn, the demand for permits could drop enough that it could be supplied entirely by long-term permits. In that case, the rental price of a permit would drop below the government's annual permit price, and the policy would behave like an ordinary permit system. As we discuss below, the fact that the hybrid policy can perform like a tax in a boom and like a permit system in a downturn is an important strength.

A key attribute of any climate policy is its ability to create a constituency that would oppose the repeal of the policy.[6] Any significant policy to reduce GHG emissions will have important distributional implications within the country that adopts it. Large transfers of income that involve organized sub-groups are particularly likely to affect the political dynamics of the program. Such transfers could become increasingly important as the stringency of the climate policy increases, particularly if marginal abatement costs do not fall over

[6] For a discussion of this topic, see McKibbin and Wilcoxen (2002a, 2002b).

time. For example, a carbon tax that contributes to general government revenue could generate increasingly strong political pressure for its repeal or relaxation as the tax rate rises. This could be true even if the tax is fully revenue neutral because as the effect on energy prices becomes increasingly salient, energy-intensive stakeholders would organize against it. A carbon tax that generates revenues that are earmarked for particular purposes may develop the same sort of constituency that other special-interest tax provisions do, and the political contention would then be between recipients of the revenue and those on whom the tax falls.

A hybrid system or a conventional cap-and-trade policy in which all the allowances are in the hands of private actors, such as electric utilities, produces a constituency with a strong financial stake in perpetuating the policy, which may help counteract objections from those who bear the costs of abatement, such as electricity consumers. However, a cap-and-trade policy with annual allowance auctions and revenue recycling would run some of the same political risks as a carbon tax that funds the general treasury, with the exception that holders of banked allowances and of private futures and options contracts on emissions allowances would have an incentive to preserve their asset values.

Sources of uncertainty and shocks

Many uncertainties affect the optimal climate policy and the willingness of individual countries to undertake binding international commitments. A key uncertainty is the cost of complying with any given commitment, making it risky for a country to agree to a hard target that may later prove to be infeasible. Uncertainty in economic growth, energy prices, and the development and cost of abatement technologies all contribute to uncertainty in costs.[7] Because these factors are not necessarily correlated, together they could amplify or attenuate the overall stringency of the program. For example, higher-than-expected macroeconomic growth would increase the stringency of a given cap,

---

[7] For a range of estimates of the costs of complying with the Kyoto Protocol, see Weyant (1999). Other studies include Bohringer (2001), Kemfert (2001), Buchner *et al.* (2002), Loschel and Zhang (2002), and International Monetary Fund (2008). Literature surveys appear in the Intergovernmental Panel on Climate Change (2001, 2007).

but if accompanied by the development of technologies with lower-than-expected abatement costs, the net effect of these dual shocks could be modest. But at its core, the targets-and-timetables approach requires each participant to achieve its national emissions target regardless of the cost of doing so. Even if the targets are indexed to factors correlated with the feasibility of the target, the basic approach does not bound costs.

The history of the Kyoto Protocol shows that ambitious targets do not guarantee significant reductions. Countries facing potentially high costs either refused to ratify the Protocol, such as the United States, or have so far failed to achieve an emissions level consistent with their 2008–2012 targets. The latter group is not necessarily out of compliance with the Protocol since it may be possible for those countries to acquire allowances from other Protocol participants before the end of the commitment period. However, countries that are on track to reduce emissions to match their assigned amounts have been aided by historical events largely unrelated to climate policy, such as German reunification, the Thatcher government's reform of coal mining in Britain, or the collapse of the Soviet economy in the early 1990's. This suggests that despite the sincere intentions of those countries that ratified the Kyoto Protocol, the targets negotiated in 1997 did not fully anticipate the economic expansion of the ensuing years.

The uncertainty each country faces around its own growth matters, but in a global economy—and particularly with international allowance trading—other countries' growth matters too. For example, even if a country perfectly predicts its own economic performance, higher-than-expected growth in another major economy could induce inadvertent stringency by increasing the global demand for permits. To quantify this effect and others, we explore in the next section what happens if China, India, and other developing countries experience unexpectedly high levels of growth during the tenure of a climate policy. We compare and contrast the impacts of this shock in a regime with a harmonized global price on carbon versus a global cap-and-trade system.

The experiment is highly pertinent to recent growth trends in Asia. As an example of how difficult it is to project the future even over short periods, Figure 27.1 (from McKibbin, Wilcoxen, and Woo [2008]) shows projections for Chinese energy consumption from

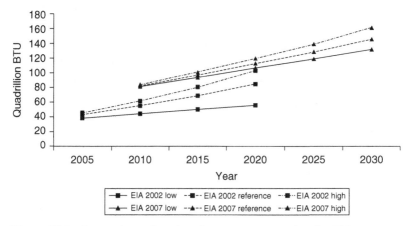

Figure 27.1. Comparison of projected energy consumption for China
Source: US Energy Information Administration *International Energy Outlook 2002*
and *2007*

the *2002 International Energy Outlook* and the *2007 International
Energy Outlook*.[8] Both reports included projections for 2010, 2015,
and 2020. The surprising fact is that, for each of those future years,
China's projected energy consumption in the 2007 report's *low*-growth
scenario was above its projected energy consumption in the 2002
report's *high*-growth scenario. For example, the 2002 high-growth
forecast for 2020 was 103 quadrillion British thermal units (BTU) and
the 2007 low-growth forecast for 2020 was 107 quadrillion BTU: that
is, the updated low-growth forecast was 4 quadrillion BTU *above* the
original high-growth forecast.

The change in the *International Energy Outlook*'s reference-case
energy consumption forecast for China underscores how much expectations changed between the two editions: the 2002 reference-case
forecast was 84 quadrillion BTU in 2020, and the 2007 reference-
case forecast was 113 quadrillion BTU in 2020—an upward revision
of 34 percent. Even more important, China's carbon dioxide (CO_2)
emissions in 2005 were 50 percent higher than predicted based on the
forecast made in 2002. A surge in energy use since 2002 is obvious
from the figure; this surge resulted from accelerated GDP growth
since 1998 as well as a rise in the energy intensity of GDP. The shift

[8] US Energy Information Administration (2002, 2007).

in the energy intensity of the Chinese economy, in turn, was driven by increased electrification, greater energy demand from manufacturing, greater energy demand by households, and increased use of cement and steel with rising infrastructure spending. The unexpected growth shock we discuss in the next section is similar to that actually experienced by China over this period.

For comparison, we also examine a second unexpected event: a financial crisis of roughly the same magnitude as the one that began unfolding in the fall of 2008. As we discuss in the next section, we impose an unexpected fall in the return to housing in each economy, with the largest drop occurring in the United States. We add to this an exogenous rise in the equity risk premium in all sectors in all economies. Together, these shocks cause a substantial financial crisis, including a sharp drop in equity markets, declines in household wealth, a sharp contraction in consumption, a jump in the required rate of return on investment, and a sharp decline in investment. These adjustments lead to a global recession.

Methodology and results

In this section we use a global economic model called G-Cubed to explore uncertainties in costs and carbon abatement under a pair of alternative climate policies. G-Cubed is a widely-used intertemporal general equilibrium model of the world economy. It divides the world into the ten regions listed in Table 27.1: the United States, Japan, Australia, Europe, a region representing the rest of the OECD (often abbreviated ROECD in the remainder of the chapter), China, India, oil exporting developing countries (OPEC), Eastern Europe and the former Soviet Union (abbreviated EEFSU), and a final region representing all other developing countries (LDC). Each region is subdivided into the thirteen industries listed in Table 27.2. The model produces annual results for trajectories running decades into the future. Appendix A provides additional details.[9]

We begin by generating a baseline projection as set out in detail in McKibbin and Wilcoxen (2008).[10] In the baseline, we assume

---

[9] See McKibbin and Wilcoxen (1998) for a complete description. The version of G-Cubed used in this chapter is 80J.

[10] See McKibbin, Pearce, and Stegman (2007) for a discussion of the importance of structural change in undertaking long-term projections.

Table 27.1 *Regions in the G-Cubed model*

Num	Name	Description
1	USA	United States
2	Japan	Japan
3	Australia	Australia
4	Europe	Europe
5	ROECD	Rest of the OECD
6	China	China
7	India	India
8	OPEC	Oil Exporting Developing Countries
9	EEFSU	Eastern Europe and the former Soviet Union
10	LDC	Other Developing Countries

Table 27.2 *Sectors in each region*

Num	Description
1	Electric Utilities
2	Gas Utilities
3	Petroleum Refining
4	Coal Mining
5	Crude Oil and Gas Extraction
6	Mining
7	Agriculture, Fishing and Hunting
8	Forestry/Wood Products
9	Durable Manufacturing
10	Non-Durable Manufacturing
11	Transportation
12	Services
13	Capital Producing Sector

that one of two canonical, market-based climate policies (discussed further below) will be implemented to constrain GHG emissions relative to business as usual. Under either policy, emissions in each country, and for the world as a whole, are initially allowed to rise along a business-as-usual path until 2028. In effect, we assume that through 2028, the baseline climate policy grants each country exactly the number of emissions permits it would need to cover its business-as-usual emissions. After 2028, however, both policies require that emissions begin to fall. By 2050, global emissions are 10 percent below 2002 levels, and by 2100 they are 60 percent below. This trajectory is consistent with the World Economic Outlook (International Monetary Fund [2008]) and provides a useful starting point for evaluating the effects of unexpected shocks that might occur after the policy is adopted.

The two climate policies we consider are a global cap-and-trade system for CO_2 emissions, which we will refer to as a quantity-based approach, and a price-based approach calibrated to induce an identical emissions trajectory. The price-based approach harmonizes the marginal cost of carbon abatement globally; it could take the form of a harmonized carbon tax, a cap-and-trade system with full banking and borrowing, or a hybrid policy along the lines of McKibbin and Wilcoxen (2002a).[11] The two regimes are normalized so that they produce identical trajectories for carbon prices and emissions absent any unforeseen shocks.

We then subject each regime to a pair of unexpected shocks: a productivity boom in developing countries and a global financial crisis. All told, there are four policy simulations: the two shocks run against two climate policies. In each case, we assume that the applicable climate regime is in place when the shock arrives.[12] Comparing the results for each shock under the two policies illustrates the strengths and weaknesses of each approach.

In each scenario, we hold climate and broader economic policy rules constant. The fiscal deficit of each economy is held at its baseline level,

---

[11] The carbon tax and the hybrid policy would not be equivalent under a more severe shock to the world economy. If the shock were sufficiently damaging, the demand for emissions permits in one or more countries might drop low enough that no annual permits would be sold in that country. In that case, carbon prices would vary across countries, and the hybrid system would have some of the counter-cyclical properties of a pure permit system. In the results presented here, however, the demand for permits is large enough that at least a few annual permits are sold under all circumstances.

[12] This approach was chosen to illustrate how each shock affects the global economy under each regime. Clearly this is not a reflection of the current state of global climate policy.

as are tax rates, so changes in tax revenues will result in corresponding changes in government spending.[13] The behavior of each region's central bank follows a region-specific Henderson-McKibbin-Taylor rule with a weight on output growth relative to trend, a weight on inflation relative to trend, and a weight on exchange rate volatility.[14] The weights vary across countries, with industrialized economies focusing on controlling inflation and output volatility, and developing countries placing a large weight on pegging the exchange rate to the US dollar.

Growth shock in developing countries

The first scenario we consider is an unexpected rise in economic growth rates in China, India, and the LDC region. The particular shock we analyze is an unexpected increase in labor productivity growth of 3 percent per year for sixteen years, after which each country's productivity growth returns to its baseline rate. The rise in productivity expands the effective supply of labor to each economy, rapidly increasing output in each sector and raising GDP. At the same time, it also increases the marginal product of capital, which causes a large rise in private investment in all three countries. The higher investment is financed partly from capital inflows, which cause each of the three currencies to appreciate and the countries' trade balances to worsen, and partly from higher domestic savings. Household consumption, as a result, rises more slowly than GDP. After growth rates return to their baseline levels, the three economies are permanently larger. After ten years, China's GDP is about 15 percent larger than it would have been in the baseline case, India's GDP is 18 percent larger, and the GDP of the LDC region is almost 20 percent higher.

Strong growth in the developing-country economies is transmitted positively to other countries. Direct transmission occurs through increased trade flows between developed and developing countries. In addition, indirect transmission occurs through higher global wealth and increased trade flows more generally. The benefits of productivity

---

[13] The assumption that fiscal deficits remain fixed is clearly at odds with the current economic situation. We hold them constant in this chapter in order to isolate the effect of the shock itself. Future research could assess the impacts of fiscal policy used to stabilize emissions and abatement costs.

[14] See Henderson and McKibbin (1993) and Taylor (1993).

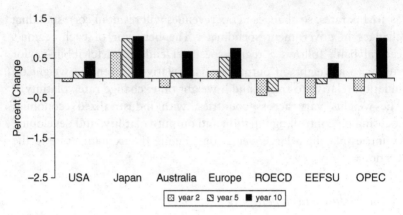

Figure 27.2. Effect of a growth shock on GDP, price policy

growth in one country are also transmitted through international capital flows responding to the return to capital. Capital achieves a higher rate of return in rapidly growing economies and the resulting capital flows raise incomes globally.

The effect of the growth shock on the GDP of other regions is shown in Figure 27.2 for the price-based climate policy. The shock eventually leads to higher GDP in every country, although the timing and magnitude of the increase varies considerably. The United States, for example, experiences a slight decline in GDP at the onset of the shock, but quickly moves above the baseline. By the tenth year, US GDP is nearly 0.5 percent larger than it would have been otherwise. Japan experiences an immediate increase in GDP of 0.6 percent and by year 10 it is more than 1 percent higher than its baseline. The outcome for Australia is similar in timing to that of the United States but larger in magnitude: its initial decline is –0.2 percent, about twice the US value, and by year 10 its GDP is 0.7 percent above the baseline. Three regions, however, experience a significant short-run reduction in GDP: ROECD, EEFSU, and OPEC. By year 10, however, GDP in ROECD has returned to baseline and GDP in EEFSU and OPEC is substantially above baseline.

The acceleration in GDP growth raises energy consumption and increases carbon emissions. China's and India's emissions grow faster than their GDPs: after ten years, China's emissions are 17 percent above baseline even though its GDP has only risen by 15 percent, and India's emissions are 23 percent above baseline while its GDP has

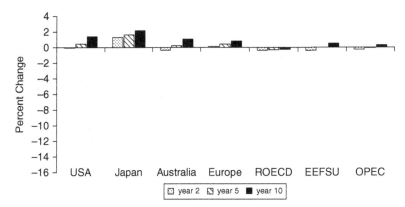

Figure 27.3. Effect of a growth shock on emissions, price policy

increased by 18 percent. For the LDC region, emissions rise roughly in proportion to GDP: after ten years, both are about 20 percent above their baseline values. The effect of the shock on emissions from other regions is shown in Figure 27.3. In all cases, the percentage change is much smaller than it was for the countries directly subject to the shock. The largest percentage change occurs in Japan, which sees its carbon emissions rise by about 2 percent after ten years. Emissions in the United States rise by a little more than 1 percent—a considerable amount in absolute terms—and by less in most other countries. After a decade, emissions are at least slightly higher in all regions other than the rest of the OECD, which essentially remains at its baseline value.

In contrast, under a quantity-based climate policy the effect of the growth shock on GDP is less positive (or more negative) for every country in every year. The shock raises demand for energy worldwide, which pushes up the price of emissions permits and effectively tightens the global emissions constraint. The permit price rises gradually and is $11 per ton of carbon ($3 per ton of CO_2) higher after ten years. The increase in productivity, which would otherwise tend to raise GDP, is thus partially offset by the tighter constraint. The overall effect varies across countries. China's GDP after ten years is about 14 percent larger than the reference case rather than 15 percent. The effect on India and the LDC region is similar: year 10 GDP in both cases is about 1 percent smaller under the quantity policy than under the price-based policy. Although the form of the climate policy affects

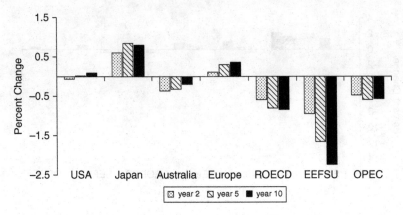

Figure 27.4. Effect of a growth shock on GDP, quantity policy

GDP in these countries, the impact is relatively small compared to the improvement due to higher productivity growth.

The effects on the remaining countries are shown in Figure 27.4. For the United States, the amplitude of the GDP effect is considerably smaller in every year relative to the price-based policy, and the shock no longer has much effect at all. For Japan and Europe, the GDP effects are also smaller but are all still positive and significant in magnitude. For Australia, in contrast, the shock is no longer bad in the short run and good in the long run: under the quantity-based policy, Australian GDP is lower in every year. For ROECD, EEFSU and OPEC, the growth shock under a quantity-based policy is bad in the short run and even worse in the long run—that is, the effect on GDP is negative and increases over time. For these three regions and Australia, a growth shock that occurs under a climate system with a hard emissions cap raises abatement costs so much that the added costs outweigh the benefit from trade and financial spillovers.

The difference in GDP outcomes under the two policies is illustrated by Figure 27.5, which shows the GDP effect in year 5 under the price-based policy, less (or minus) the GDP effect under the quantity-based policy. In terms of GDP in year 5, the United States and Japan would be better off by 0.2 percent under the price-based policy; Europe would be better off by 0.3 percent; Australia, ROECD, and LDC would be better off by 0.5 percent; OPEC, China, and India would be better off by 0.7 percent; and EEFSU would be better off by more than 1.5 percent.

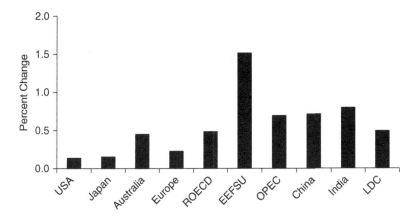

Figure 27.5. Year 5 difference in GDP, price less quantity result

The effects of the growth shock on emissions under a quantity policy differ considerably from the results under a price policy. By year 10, China's emissions are only 0.5 percent above baseline. China's emissions are sharply lower under the quantity policy because the Chinese economy's marginal abatement cost curve is relatively elastic: it is cheaper for China to keep emissions from growing than to buy additional permits on the world market. Emissions for India and the LDCs rise considerably more—by 12 and 13 percent relative to the baseline—but the increases are much smaller than under the price policy. Emissions from most of the other regions fall, as shown in Figure 27.6. The effect of the constraint on emissions is clear: in order for emissions from India and the LDCs to rise, emissions from the United States, Australia, the rest of the OECD, and Eastern Europe and the former Soviet Union fall considerably. US emissions drop by 6 percent relative to the baseline, as do emissions from ROECD. Australian emissions drop by a little less, 4 percent, while emissions from EEFSU drop by much more: nearly 14 percent. Table 27.3 summarizes emissions changes in each region in year 10 under both policies.

In summary, unexpectedly strong economic growth in one part of the world has sharply different effects under price-based and quantity-based climate policies. As would be expected from economic theory, a price-based policy accommodates the shock by allowing emissions to rise, and a quantity-based policy restrains emissions by allowing

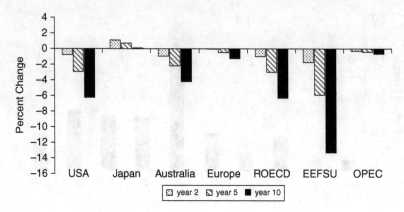

Figure 27.6. Effect of a growth shock on emissions, quantity policy

Table 27.3 *Effect of a growth shock on carbon emissions in year 10*

Region	Price-Based Policy	Quantity-Based Policy
USA	1.4%	−6.2%
Japan	2.2%	0.1%
Australia	1.1%	−4.2%
Europe	0.8%	−1.2%
ROECD	−0.2%	−6.3%
EEFSU	0.5%	−13.3%
OPEC	0.3%	−0.7%
China	16.7%	0.5%
India	23.0%	11.9%
LDC	19.0%	13.4%

the price of permits to rise. What our results emphasize, however, is the magnitude of the effect. Under a quantity-based policy, the rise in the price of permits does more than slow GDP growth marginally: for several economies, GDP actually contracts. In those regions, the rise is more than enough to completely offset positive spillovers from the productivity shock. In contrast, under a price-based policy all regions eventually share in the gains, although emissions rise as a consequence. Roughly speaking, a quantity-based policy adds a strong zero-sum element to an event that would otherwise produce gains for everyone.

Rise in global risk: a financial crisis

The second shock we consider is a global financial crisis. We chose this scenario because it differs from the growth shock in two respects: it affects every region directly (as opposed to being concentrated in a few regions with only indirect effects on the remaining regions) and it represents an adverse shock for all regions. We model the crisis as a rise in the equity risk premium in all sectors in all countries. The premium increases by 10 percent in the first year and then declines by 1 percent per year until the sixth year. From year 6 on, it remains 5 percent above baseline. In addition we introduce a permanent fall in the productivity of housing in developed countries. The reduction is 5 percent in all developed countries other than the United States and 10 percent in the United States. This is intended to simulate a housing bubble bursting.[15]

The shock to the equity premium causes the risk-adjusted required return on capital to rise. Combined with the fall in developed-country housing productivity, it leads to a portfolio reallocation in all countries away from equities and housing and into government bonds. This drives up bond prices and drives down bond yields, while also sharply lowering the prices of housing and equities. At the initial set of capital stocks, the actual return to capital is too low after the shock and thus investment collapses. As the capital stock shrinks, the marginal product of capital (and hence the rate of return) gradually rises toward its new equilibrium level. Consumption falls because of the sharp decline in real wealth and that, combined with lower investment, reduces GDP.

Figure 27.7 shows the effect of the risk shock on each region's GDP under the price-based policy. GDP drops below its baseline in all countries and all years. Initially, the largest effects are felt by China, the United States, ROECD, and Japan, which experience immediate GDP declines of 6 percent, 4.5 percent, 3.2 percent, and 2.5 percent,

---

[15] See McKibbin and Stoeckel (2006).

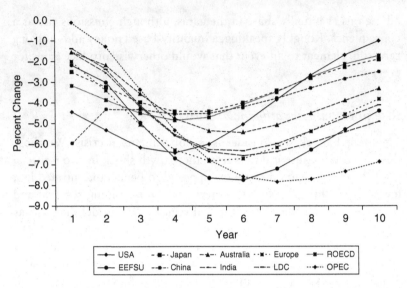

Figure 27.7. Effect of a risk shock on GDP, price policy

respectively. However, these four regions also rebound from the shock most quickly: China's GDP starts to recover in year 2, and the United States, ROECD, and Japan begin to recover in year 4. By year 10, the four regions are the closest to being back to their baseline GDPs. At the opposite end of the spectrum, OPEC is affected least in the first year, but its GDP eventually falls furthest: to 7.8 percent below baseline in year 7. After that it begins to recover gradually but by year 10, its GDP is still 6.9 percent below baseline. Results for the remaining regions—Europe, Australia, LDCs, India and EEFSU—lie between these extremes: they experience short-term declines of 1–2 percent, begin to recover in years 5 and 6, and are 3–5 percent below baseline in year 10.

Under the price-based policy, the carbon price is not affected by the shock and remains at its baseline level. As a result, it induces more abatement than planned when the economy grows more slowly than expected. As shown in Figure 27.8, emissions fall relative to the baseline in both the short and long run. For the regions other than OPEC and China, emissions drop by 1–3 percent at the onset of the shock and are down 3–8 percent by year 10. China's immediate drop in emissions is larger, a decline of 6 percent, and OPEC's emissions actually increase very slightly in the first year. Both are consistent

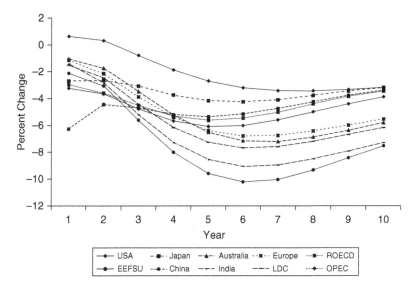

Figure 27.8. Effect of a risk shock on emissions, price policy

with the GDP effects for the corresponding countries: China's initial drop in GDP was largest and OPEC's was smallest. Over time, the largest change in emissions occurs in Eastern Europe and the former Soviet Union: by year 6, EEFSU emissions have fallen by more than 10 percent and they remain nearly 8 percent below baseline in year 10.

Under the quantity-based policy, in contrast, emissions do not change but carbon prices fall. In the short run, the risk shock would cause permit prices to be $4 per ton of carbon ($1.10 per ton of CO_2) lower than they would be in the baseline. The drop would gradually increase to $8 per ton ($2.18 per ton of CO_2) by years 5 and 6 when the effects of the shock are at their peak. By year 10, permit prices would recover somewhat and would be $5 per ton ($1.36 per ton of CO_2) below baseline.

Lower carbon abatement costs under a quantity-based policy help to moderate the decline in GDP caused by the risk shock. Figure 27.9 shows the difference in the effects of the two policies on GDP. The values plotted are the effect of the shock under the quantity policy, less the effect of the shock under the price policy: a value of 1 percent, for example, indicates that GDP would be 1 percent higher under the quantity-based policy than it would be under the price-based policy.

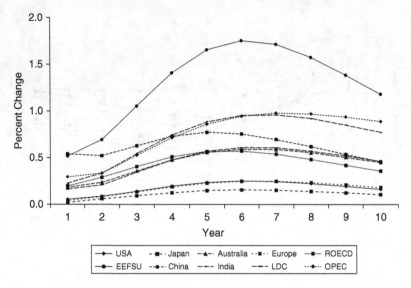

Figure 27.9. Difference in GDP, quantity less price result

Among the ten regions, EEFSU stands out: in the short run, its GDP under the quantity-based policy is 0.5 percent higher than it would be under the price-based policy; by year 6 the difference has widened to 1.75 percent; and by year 10, its GDP is still 1.2 percent higher under the quantity policy than it would be under the price policy. At the opposite pole are Japan, the United States, and Europe: all three are slightly better off under the quantity policy, but the difference is at most 0.25 percent.

Under the quantity-based policy, the risk shock does not change the total amount of emissions but it shifts their geographic distribution substantially. Figure 27.10 shows the change in emissions by region for years 2, 5, and 10. In all three years, emissions shift significantly toward China. The effect is largest during the peak of the shock, around year 5, when Chinese emissions are more than 8 percent higher than under the baseline. As noted in our discussion of the growth shock, China's abatement is very elastic with respect to the price of emissions permits.

To summarize the risk shock, we find that a price-based climate policy would tend to exacerbate the economic downturn caused by the shock. A quantity-based policy, on the other hand, tends to be

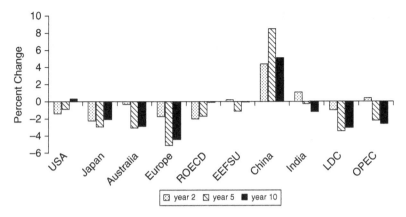

Figure 27.10. Effect of a risk shock on emissions, quantity policy

counter-cyclical. Under a quantity-based policy, the drop in permit prices during a downturn prevents GDP in most countries from falling as sharply as it otherwise would. However, a quantity-based policy does produce significant changes in the geographic distribution of emissions and hence involves international transfers of wealth.

Summary

Our results show that neither of the main market-based policies performs well in all circumstances. A pure quantity-based approach behaves poorly when confronted with good economic news: in this case, an unexpected boom somewhere in the world economy. It causes permit prices to rise by enough that GDP in some regions would actually contract. Governments in those regions would be under severe pressure to abandon the policy. A pure price-based policy would allow emissions to rise somewhat, but it would be more likely to survive the episode intact. A price-based policy, on the other hand, has a significant disadvantage when economic developments are worse than expected. It tends to exacerbate downturns by keeping the marginal cost of emissions high even in difficult economic conditions.

These results clearly demonstrate that unexpected future events may make sustaining an international climate agreement very difficult. However, a hybrid policy such as that described by McKibbin and

Wilcoxen (2002a) could avoid these problems.[16] Like a price-based policy, providing for sales of annual permits would allow emissions to increase somewhat in order to accommodate an unexpected boom somewhere in the world economy. Unlike a pure quantity-based policy, it would not cause strong growth in one country to drive down growth among other participants in the agreement. At the same time, like a quantity-based policy, it would provide counter-cyclical stabilization during downturns. A sustained drop in economic growth would cause the rental price of a long-term permit to fall below the price of an annual permit. Sales of annual permits would cease until the economy recovered.

Summary and conclusions for policy

The growth boom in China and the global financial crisis of 2008 have starkly highlighted a number of important lessons for the design of global and national climate policy. These lessons need to be considered explicitly during international negotiations on a new treaty to succeed the Kyoto Protocol after its 2008–2012 commitment period ends.

The first lesson is that a wide variety of macroeconomic shocks will undoubtedly occur over the coming decades, and a successful global climate framework would need to endure in spite of them. Thus there must be a mechanism built into the framework that directly addresses the issue of uncertainty and avoids imposing unsustainable economic costs during either an unexpected boom or bust. Otherwise, it will be much harder to negotiate a broad agreement, and the agreement may be vulnerable to collapse under adverse future shocks.

The second lesson is that it is critical to get global and national governance structures right. There must be a clear regulatory regime in each country and a transparent way to smooth out excessive short-term volatility in prices. A system that enables or even encourages short-term financial speculation in climate markets may collapse at huge expense to national economies. A hybrid system provides many of the advantages of a permit system while limiting opportunities for speculation through the annual permit mechanism. It provides a strong mix of market incentives and predictable government intervention.

---

[16] Other hybrid approaches such as a cap-and-trade system with a safety valve would also avoid these problems.

The third lesson is that since shocks in one part of the world will certainly occur, the global system needs to have adequate firewalls between national climate systems to prevent destructive contagion from propagating local problems into a system-wide failure. A global cap-and-trade system, or alternative systems such as those described by Stern (2006) or the Garnaut Review (2008), would be extremely vulnerable to shocks in any single economy. A system based on national hybrid policies, on the other hand, would be explicitly designed to partition national climate markets and limit the effects of a collapse in climate policy in one part of the world on climate markets elsewhere.[17]

This chapter has explored these issues by examining the effects of shocks that have actually occurred in the past decade: a surprising surge of economic growth in developing countries and a global financial crisis. Quantity-based approaches such as a global permit-trading regime tend to buffer some kinds of macroeconomic shocks: carbon prices rise and fall with the business cycle. However, price-based approaches such as a global carbon tax (levied at the national level) perform better during unexpected booms. A hybrid policy would offer the best of both worlds, and would provide stronger firewalls to prevent adverse events in one carbon market from causing a collapse of the global system.

Appendix A: The G-Cubed Model

The G-Cubed model is an intertemporal general equilibrium model of the world economy. The theoretical structure is outlined in McKibbin and Wilcoxen (1998).[18] A number of studies—summarized in McKibbin and Vines (2000)—show that the G-cubed modeling approach has been useful in assessing a range of issues across a number of countries since the mid-1980s.[19] Some of the principal features of the model are as follows:

---

[17] For further discussion of the advantages of this point see McKibbin and Wilcoxen (2002a, 2004, 2008).

[18] Full details of the model including a list of equations and parameters can be found online at: www.gcubed.com.

[19] These issues include: Reaganomics in the 1980s; German Unification in the early 1990s; fiscal consolidation in Europe in the mid-1990s; the formation of NAFTA; the Asian crisis; and the productivity boom in the US.

- The model is based on explicit intertemporal optimization by the agents (consumers and firms) in each economy.[20] In contrast to static CGE models, time and dynamics are of fundamental importance in the G-Cubed model. The MSG-Cubed model is known as a DSGE (Dynamic Stochastic General Equilibrium) model in the macroeconomics literature and a Dynamic Intertemporal General Equilibrium (DIGE) model in the computable general equilibrium literature.
- In order to track the macro time series, the behavior of agents is modified to allow for short-run deviations from optimal behavior either due to myopia or to restrictions on the ability of households and firms to borrow at the risk-free bond rate on government debt. For both households and firms, deviations from intertemporal optimizing behavior take the form of rules of thumb, which are consistent with an optimizing agent that does not update predictions based on new information about future events. These rules of thumb are chosen to generate the same steady state behavior as optimizing agents so that in the long run there is only a single intertemporal optimizing equilibrium of the model. In the short run, actual behavior is assumed to be a weighted average of the optimizing and the rule of thumb assumptions. Thus aggregate consumption is a weighted average of consumption based on wealth (current asset valuation and expected future after tax labor income) and consumption based on current disposable income. Similarly, aggregate investment is a weighted average of investment based on Tobin's q (a market valuation of the expected future change in the marginal product of capital relative to the cost) and investment based on a backward looking version of Q.
- There is an explicit treatment of the holding of financial assets, including money. Money is introduced into the model through a restriction that households require money to purchase goods.
- The model also allows for short-run nominal wage rigidity (by different degrees in different countries) and therefore allows for significant periods of unemployment depending on the labor market institutions in each country. This assumption, when taken together with the explicit role for money, is what gives the model its "macroeconomic" characteristics. (Here again the model's assumptions

---

[20] See Blanchard and Fischer (1989) and Obstfeld and Rogoff (1996).

differ from the standard market clearing assumption in most CGE models.)

- The model distinguishes between the stickiness of physical capital within sectors and countries and the flexibility of financial capital, which immediately flows to where expected returns are highest. This important distinction leads to a critical difference between the quantity of physical capital that is available at any time to produce goods and services, and the valuation of that capital as a result of decisions about the allocation of financial capital.

As a result of this structure, the G-Cubed model contains rich dynamic behavior, driven on the one hand by asset accumulation, and on the other by wage adjustment to a neoclassical steady state. It embodies a wide range of assumptions about individual behavior and empirical regularities in a general equilibrium framework. The interdependencies are solved out using a computer algorithm that solves for the rational expectations equilibrium of the global economy. It is important to stress that the term 'general equilibrium' is used to signify that as many interactions as possible are captured, not that all economies are in a full market clearing equilibrium at each point in time. Although it is assumed that market forces eventually drive the world economy to a neoclassical steady state growth equilibrium, unemployment does emerge for long periods due to wage stickiness, to an extent that differs between countries due to differences in labor market institutions.

References

Aldy, J. and R. Stavins, eds. (2007). *Architectures for Agreement: Addressing Global Climate Change in the Post-Kyoto World*. New York: Cambridge University Press.

Bagnoli, P., W. J. McKibbin, and P. Wilcoxen (1996). "Future Projections and Structural Change," in N. Nakicenovic, W. Nordhaus, R. Richels, and F. Toth (eds.), *Climate Change: Integrating Economics and Policy*, CP 96–1, Vienna: International Institute for Applied Systems Analysis, pp. 181–206.

Blanchard, O. and S. Fischer (1989). *Lectures on Macroeconomics*. Cambridge, MA: MIT Press.

Bodansky, Daniel (2007). "Targets and Timetables: Good Policy but Bad Politics?" in Aldy and Stavins (eds.), pp. 57–66.

Bohringer, C. (2001). "Climate Policies from Kyoto to Bonn: From Little to Nothing?" ZEW Discussion Paper No. 01–49, Mannheim.

Buchner B., C. Carraro, and I. Cersosimo (2002). "Economic Consequences of the US Withdrawal from the Kyoto/Bonn Protocol," *Climate Policy* 2: 273–92.

Castles, I. and D. Henderson (2003). "The IPCC Emission Scenarios: An Economic-Statistical Critique," *Energy & Environment* 14 (2–3): 159–85.

Ellerman, A. D. and I. Sue Wing (2003). "Absolute vs. Intensity-Based Emission Caps," *Climate Policy* 3 (Supplement 2): S7–S20.

Energy Information Administration (2002). *International Energy Outlook.* Washington, DC: US Department of Energy.

(2007). *International Energy Outlook.* Washington, DC: US Department of Energy.

Fischer, Carolyn and Michael Springborn (2007). "Emissions Targets and the Real Business Cycle," Washington, DC: Resources for the Future.

Frankel, Jeffrey (2007). "Formulas for Quantitative Emission Targets," in Aldy and Stavins (eds.), pp. 31–56.

Garnaut Review (2008). Garnaut Climate Change Review Interim Report, February.

Henderson, D. W. and W. J. McKibbin (1993). "A Comparison of Some Basic Monetary Policy Regimes for Open Economies: Implications of Different Degrees of Instrument Adjustment and Wage Persistence," *Carnegie-Rochester Conference Series on Public Policy* 39: 221–317.

Hoel, M. and L. Karp (2002). "Taxes versus Quotas for a Stock Pollutant," *Resource and Energy Economics* 24: 367–84.

IMF (2008). *World Economic Outlook,* April.

IPCC (2001). *Climate Change 2001,* 3 vols. Cambridge, UK: Cambridge University Press.

(2007). *Climate Change 2007: Synthesis Report.* Cambridge, UK: Cambridge University Press.

Jotzo, Frank and John C. V. Pezzey (2005). "Optimal Intensity Targets for Emissions Trading under Uncertainty," Centre for Resource and Environmental Studies, Australian National University, Canberra.

Kemfert, Claudia (2001). "Economic Effects of Alternative Climate Policy Strategies," *Environmental Science and Policy* 5(5): 367–84.

Kydland F. and E. Prescott (1977). "Rules Rather than Discretion: The Inconsistency of Optimal Plans," *The Journal of Political Economy* 85(3): 473–92.

Löschel, A. and Z. X. Zhang (2002). "The Economic and Environmental Implications of the US Repudiation of the Kyoto Protocol and the

Subsequent Deals in Bonn and Marrakech," *Weltwirtschaftliches Archiv—Review of World Economics* 138(4): 711–46.

McKibbin, W. J., D. Pearce, and A. Stegman (2007). "Long Term Projections of Carbon Emissions," *International Journal of Forecasting* 23: 637–53.

McKibbin, W. J. and A. Stoeckel (2006). "Bursting of the US Housing Bubble," www.EconomicScenarios.com, Issue 14, October.

McKibbin, W. J. and D. Vines (2000). "Modeling Reality: The Need for Both Intertemporal Optimization and Stickiness in Models for Policymaking," *Oxford Review of Economic Policy* 16(4): 106–37.

McKibbin, W. J. and P. J. Wilcoxen (1997). "A Better Way to Slow Global Climate Change," *Brookings Policy Brief* # 20, June, Washington DC: The Brookings Institution.

(1998). "The Theoretical and Empirical Structure of the G-Cubed Model," *Economic Modelling* 16(1): 123–48.

(2002a). *Climate Change Policy After Kyoto: A Blueprint for a Realistic Approach*. Washington, DC: The Brookings Institution.

(2002b). "The Role of Economics in Climate Change Policy," *Journal of Economic Perspectives* 16(2): 107–30.

(2004). "Estimates of the Costs of Kyoto-Marrakesh Versus The McKibbin-Wilcoxen Blueprint," *Energy Policy* 32(4): 467–79.

(2007). "A Credible Foundation for Long Term International Cooperation on Climate Change," in Aldy and Stavins (eds.), pp. 185–208.

(2008). *Building on Kyoto: Towards a Realistic Global Climate Change Agreement*, The Brookings Institution, June.

McKibbin, W. J., P. J. Wilcoxen, and W. T. Woo (2008). "Can China Grow and Help Prevent the Tragedy of the CO_2 Commons?" in L. Song and W. T. Woo (eds.), *China's Dilemma: Economic Growth, the Environment, and Climate Change*. Washington, DC: ANU Press, Asia Pacific Press, the Brookings Institution Press, and Social Sciences Academic Press (China).

Nordhaus, William (2006). "After Kyoto: Alternative Mechanisms to Control Global Warming," *American Economic Review* 96(2): 31–4.

(2007). "To Tax or Not to Tax: Alternative Approaches to Slowing Global Warming," *Review of Environmental Economics and Policy* 1(1): 26–44.

Obstfeld, M. and K. Rogoff (1996). *Foundations of International Macroeconomics*. Cambridge, MA: MIT Press.

Pezzey, J. (2003). "Emission Taxes and Tradable Permits: A Comparison of Views on Long Run Efficiency," *Environmental and Resource Economics* 26(2): 329–42.

Pizer, W. A. (1997). "Prices vs. Quantities Revisited: The Case of Climate Change," Resources for the Future Discussion Paper 98–02, Washington, DC: Resources for the Future.

Quirion, P. (2004). "Prices versus Quantities in a Second-Best Setting," *Environmental & Resource Economics* 29: 337–59.

Roberts, M. J. and A. M. Spence (1976). "Effluent Charges and Licenses under Uncertainty," *Journal of Public Economics* 5: 193–208.

Stern, N. (2006). "Stern Review: Report on the Economics of Climate Change," Cambridge, UK: Cambridge University Press.

Taylor, J. B. (1993). "Discretion Versus Policy Rules in Practice," *Carnegie-Rochester Conference Series on Public Policy* 39: 195–214.

Von Below, D. and T. Persson (2008). "Uncertainty, Climate Change and the Global Economy," Institute for International Economic Studies, Stockholm University (mimeo).

Weitzman, M. L. (1974). "Prices vs. Quantities," *Review of Economic Studies* 41: 477–91.

Weyant, John, ed. (1999). "The Costs of the Kyoto Protocol: A Multi-Model Evaluation," *The Energy Journal*, Special Issue.

Wing, I. S., A. D. Ellerman, and J. Song (2006). "Absolute vs. Intensity Limits for CO_2 Emission Control: Performance Under Uncertainty," MIT Joint Program on the Science and Policy of Global Change, Report 130, MIT.

PART VII

Synthesis and conclusion

28 | *Epilogue*

RICHARD SCHMALENSEE[1]

History's evaluation of this generation will surely depend to an important extent on its handling of the climate problem—not just on what gases we leave in the atmosphere but also on what durable climate policy architecture we leave to our heirs. This valuable collection sheds new light on what I believe to be the most difficult and important dimension of the climate policy problem. All who have had a hand in the creation of this volume deserve thanks and applause. In this brief essay I offer some thoughts on what makes the international dimension of the climate problem so difficult and important, on the history of climate policy debates, and on some key elements of policy architecture that those debates have so far produced.

The international dimension

Climate change would be a very difficult issue even without its international dimension, of course. Because much of the benefit of limiting greenhouse gas emissions would accrue to future generations, it would be both economically and politically hard to compare the costs and benefits of mitigation policies even if both were known.[2] But the future benefits of reducing emissions are highly uncertain, both because we cannot confidently predict important regional-scale climate changes and because the adaptation technologies available to future generations are unknown. Similarly uncertain are the pace of technological innovation and the quality of future climate policy design and implementation, both critical factors in determining future costs of emissions reduction.

---

[1] I am indebted to Henry Jacoby and Robert Stavins for useful comments; all errors and opinions are mine alone.
[2] To simplify exposition I generally ignore sinks and deal only with emissions sources. Essentially the same arguments apply to enhancing sinks as to reducing sources.

But these difficulties seem little more than academic puzzles when set against the international dimension of this problem. To over-simplify, there are many more poor people than rich people on this planet. Those poor people want desperately to become rich—i.e., to live as well as Americans or Europeans. Recent experience in China and elsewhere strongly suggests to them that this is possible. If the world's poor become prosperous in anything like the same way today's rich did, however, greenhouse gas emissions will increase substantially, and the consequences for the entire human race are likely to be extremely unpleasant. The world's poor will not long tolerate measures they view as slowing their emergence from poverty, but we do not yet know any way for them to become rich without substantially increasing their per capita emissions. We need both to show them a much more climate-friendly path to prosperity and to induce them to follow it. Creating such a path obviously requires developing new, climate-friendly technologies, but unless they involve both lower emissions *and* lower costs than current technologies, they will not be automatically adopted in developing nations.

A few basic numbers illustrate the magnitude of this problem. According to US Bureau of the Census and Energy Information Administration (EIA) data, the United States accounted for just over 4.5 percent of world population in 2005 and about 21 percent of global CO_2 emissions associated with fossil fuels. US per capita emissions were about 5.6 times those in the rest of the world, even though the rest of the world includes all the other rich nations.

To see what these numbers imply, suppose, to be conservative, there is no population growth anywhere and that US emissions remain constant in the future. Suppose, however, that economic development continues in the rest of the world so that per capita emissions in the rest of the world rise to become one-third of those in the United States. With today's technology, this change would correspond to a dramatic reduction in global poverty, but it would hardly be enough to give most of the human race anything like the US lifestyle they see on television. *Nonetheless, this change would also correspond to an increase of just over two-thirds in global emissions.* If the climate problem is to be addressed effectively, today's poor nations simply must go down a very different path to prosperity than that followed by today's rich nations.

Some (discouraging) history

The climate policy problem has been on the world's agenda since at least the creation of the Intergovernmental Panel on Climate Change (IPCC) in 1988. That same year, Presidential candidate George Bush promised to use "the White House Effect" to deal with the greenhouse effect. In November of the following year, in connection with the Ministerial Conference in Noordwijk, President George Bush declared that "stabilization of carbon dioxide (CO_2) emissions should be achieved as soon as possible" and that "it is timely to investigate quantitative targets to limit or reduce carbon dioxide emissions."

In this early period, the stage seemed to be set for constructive, global action, plausibly with US leadership. In February, 1990, the United States hosted—and President Bush addressed—a plenary meeting of the IPCC, and a year later it hosted the first meeting of the Intergovernmental Negotiating Committee (INC) that was drafting the Framework Convention on Climate Change (FCCC). In April, 1991, President Bush announced that "actions—recently established in law or proposed by my Administration—will hold US net emissions of greenhouse gases at or below the 1987 level through the foreseeable future." And just over two years later, in October, 1993, the Clinton Administration announced a Climate Action Plan that it contended would reduce US emissions to 1990 levels by 2000.

I first became engaged in climate policy as a Member of the Council of Economic Advisers in this lively early period. In the fall of 1989 I found myself heading an interagency task force charged with producing a report on the economics of climate change. That report was completed in March, 1990, and a slightly revised version was published that September (US Department of Energy 1990). It noted "substantial gaps in current knowledge" and, of course, called for "a coordinated economic research program."

Some of the report's more detailed findings and conclusions have been overturned by subsequent research, but many have endured. The report noted, for instance, that "climate change is not a one-gas or one-nation problem" and that "Command-and-control efficiency standards have several significant disadvantages in comparison to incentive-based systems—such as charges, user fees, and tradable emissions rights ... "

On the international front, the interagency report concluded that "Even dramatic unilateral cuts by member states of the OECD would not be sufficient to achieve widely discussed global CO_2 emissions goals unless most other nations participate fully in emissions reductions efforts." (Among those "widely discussed" goals were cuts of 20 percent below 1985 levels by 2005 and 50 percent below 1985 levels by 2025!) And, in what has proven to be rather an understatement, the report observed that "while global action is essential to limit greenhouse emissions significantly, differences among nations may make it difficult to find universally acceptable emissions targets or ways of sharing the costs involved."

In this early period, some participants in the climate debate called for substantial near-term emissions reductions, but most analysts argued that it would be more efficient to focus for at least a decade on studying the climate system and developing new technologies that could reduce the costs of emissions reductions and of adaptation to climate change.[3] This preparatory investment would permit subsequent policies both to better reflect actual risks and benefits and to impose lower net social costs.

Subsequently, of course, no substantial emissions reductions were made. US emissions rose despite the promises of the Bush and Clinton Administrations. Emissions of CO_2 associated with fossil fuels (not the same as net emissions of greenhouse gases, but an important component thereof) increased by 25 percent between 1987 and 2005 and by 12 percent between 1990 and 2000 even though as noted above the Bush and Clinton Administrations, respectively, had promised no increases. A good deal of research was subsequently done on the climate system, but much less effort was devoted to the development of mitigation and adaptation technologies than rhetoric and analysis in the early period would have led one to expect. US Department of Energy spending on research, development, and demonstration actually declined in real terms after fiscal year 1990 and remained below that year's level through fiscal year 2007 (Gallagher *et al.* 2007). It is only a bit too strong to assert that we wasted nearly two critical decades on the technology front.

Since this early period there has been considerable movement toward developing an international climate policy architecture, as I discuss below. But the fundamental, critical problem of inducing poor nations to follow climate-friendly paths to development has not yet

[3] See, e.g., IPCC 1996.

been effectively addressed. And the early-period arguments that we could wait a decade or more before making significant cuts in global emissions have passed their sell-by dates: we have in fact waited nearly two decades, and most knowledgeable observers now contend that the time for serious action is upon us—ready or not.

Thoughts on architecture

European churches were often built on top of earlier churches or temples; two or more places of worship can sometimes even be visited on the same site. A church that may have seemed ideal for decades after its construction was apparently considered inadequate somewhat later. Architectural styles and details of course differ between successive structures, often dramatically. Nonetheless, all the churches built on the same site clearly served as appropriate venues for very similar, if not identical, ceremonies over many centuries. The basic basilica scheme, in particular, has served Western Christianity well for almost two millennia.

Absent unimaginable, transformative technological breakthroughs, climate policy will be a global concern for centuries. It is not likely that our generation will create an international climate policy architecture that will remain workable in all its details for even a single century, let alone as long as the great gothic cathedrals have served as places of worship. Not only are the domestic and international political, economic, and institutional environments within which climate policy is embedded almost certain to change over the relevant horizon, probably radically, but our understanding of the climate system will advance, and the set of available technologies for mitigation and adaptation will expand considerably.

It is of course essential to focus on policy designs that can be useful today, even if they fall short of what future, more stringent mitigation efforts may require. However, one must also bear in mind that the core elements of policy architectures, once put in place, are not easily changed. It is thus important to ensure that today's policy designs embody architectural elements that can serve as foundations for better designs in the future, rather than elements that must be excised if progress is to be possible. If we cannot now build an elegant gothic cathedral, let us try for a workable, adaptable basilica design scheme.

One valuable element of the emerging architecture deserves particular mention. Early European proposals in the run-up to the first meeting of the INC in Washington in February, 1991 focused on what is called in this volume "harmonized domestic policies," except that the policies proposed were essentially all of the command-and-control variety. The basic idea was that there would be protocols on autos, on steelmaking, and so on. To those of us in the Bush Administration who had been involved in the passage of the 1990 Clean Air Act Amendments, which put in place the tradable allowance regime for control of sulfur dioxide emissions, this approach seemed fundamentally wrongheaded. At that first INC meeting, I participated in the start of a serious effort by the United States to move the focus of discussion from performance standards to emissions limits. In part as a result of that effort, the Framework Convention focuses on emissions, and, in large part because the Clinton Administration continued to push emissions trading as superior to command-and-control regulation, the Kyoto Protocol permits this approach to be used within and even between nations. It is, of course, more than a little ironic that as of this writing the EU ETS has for some time been the only large-scale working example of emissions trading as a greenhouse gas mitigation strategy.

The Framework Convention's call for "stabilization of greenhouse gas concentrations in the atmosphere at a level that would prevent dangerous anthropogenic interference with the climate system" contains two architectural elements. The focus on stabilization is a valuable reminder of the long-run nature of the climate problem. On the other hand, the assertion of a threshold that cannot be exceeded is problematic. In practice, though, this assertion may be a purely ornamental element of the policy architecture: since the Convention's critical level is unknown and possibly non-existent, it cannot be used to attack or defend any plausible policy proposal.

Architectural elements that will be of enduring value in the Convention include the coverage, in principle at least, of all anthropogenic greenhouse gases (except those being phased out under the Montreal Protocol) and of all sources and sinks thereof. In addition, the Convention and the Protocol properly stress the importance of measurement of sources and sinks and call for the creation of what seems on paper, at least, an appropriate institutional structure.

But some necessary elements are missing from these documents, and some elements that are present will need to be excised or worked around in the future. Though technology transfer is mentioned in the Convention and the Protocol, for instance, and its importance is emphasized in the Bali Action Plan, there is essentially no reflection in any of these documents of the critical need to develop *new* technologies for measurement of sources and sinks, for reducing net emissions, and for enhancing the ability to adapt. Without new measurement technologies, it will be difficult to extend international "targets-and-timetables" agreements much beyond CO_2 associated with fossil fuels, which will make stabilization of radiative forcing more difficult. Without more climate-friendly technologies to power their economies, it will be impossible for today's poor countries to become prosperous without doing serious damage to the global climate. And without serious attention to adaptation and development of new technologies to facilitate it, those same poor countries are likely to bear substantial, avoidable costs, regardless of what feasible mitigation path is followed.

The Clean Development Mechanism (CDM) plainly needs to be transformed or at least fundamentally reformed, as several contributions to this volume argue. It suffers from a deep problem that afflicts all systems based on emissions reductions rather than emissions. Emissions can be measured or at least estimated directly, while emissions reductions can only be inferred by subtracting emissions from a no-action baseline that is always unobservable and arguably generally unknowable. If one requires that proposed baselines withstand rigorous review, few projects will pass; if one relaxes the requirements, CDM-like mechanisms are likely to produce little enduring mitigation. Perhaps the CDM can be transformed into a useful mechanism for technology transfer or for some other purpose beyond limiting emissions. If not, it might as well be scrapped.

The most serious problem with the architectural elements currently in place, however, is the "deep, then broad" approach they dictate.[4] The Convention divides the world into Annex I nations, with emissions reduction obligations, and those without such obligations, and the Kyoto Protocol defines those obligations as legally binding limits on CO_2 emissions. This division is at best an imperfect reflection of relative incomes at the time the Convention was drafted; fifty non-Annex I countries now have higher per capita incomes than the poorest Annex

---

[4] For a longer version of this basic argument, written during the negotiations leading up to the Kyoto Protocol, see Schmalensee 1998.

I countries. Moreover, poor nations, naturally more concerned with alleviating today's poverty (or, sometimes, fattening today's rulers' bank accounts) than improving climate a generation or more hence, are understandably reluctant to opt-in to Annex I and thereby take on obligations that may be violated if their economic growth exceeds expectations—particularly in the absence of serious mitigation efforts by the United States.

As of this writing, it seems likely that the United States will act to reduce its CO_2 emissions from fossil fuels, probably via a cap-and-trade system. The task of developing and enacting the necessary legislation is likely to be sufficiently intellectually and politically complex that it will necessarily be "unilateral"—i.e., only loosely coupled to the international negotiation process. Serious US action seems a necessary condition for substantially broadening international participation in emissions mitigation efforts, but it will not likely be sufficient.

Since the climate problem cannot be solved without the participation of poor nations, particularly India, China, and other large and growing countries, it is thus critical to explore ways to modify the current architecture in ways that encourage their participation. The sort of long-term, income-contingent scheme discussed by Jeffrey Frankel in this volume may be a useful design element. But to the extent that accepting such a scheme involves binding emissions limits at the start, it may be unattractive even if those limits seem initially loose. Similarly, while the sort of "accession deals" discussed by David Victor in this volume could usefully be used to encourage participation in mitigation efforts, it does not seem politically realistic to expect rich countries to make large transfers for this purpose, particularly in the critical early years when they are likely to be especially worried about setting expensive precedents. Thus if poor nations are highly allergic to binding emissions limits, rich nations may be unwilling to finance the accession deals necessary to entice them to accept such limits.

I believe it would be accordingly useful to consider gentler accession on-ramps that do not involve targets and timetables. Suppose the next Protocol to the Convention were to create an Annex III category of nations: those willing to commit to some non-trivial mitigation efforts but not to binding emissions limits.[5] A nation could commit to

---

[5] Annex II is already taken; Annex II nations are a subset of Annex I nations with additional obligations. It does not seem possible to opt-in to Annex II.

non-binding emission targets, against which actual emissions would later be compared—a return to what used to be called "pledge and review." Or it could commit to particular climate-friendly domestic policies—what is still called "policies and measures." Commitments of either sort could involve land use or gases other than CO_2 and thus tend to broaden global mitigation efforts. It would be critical, of course, to monitor compliance with mitigation commitments of any sort.

It is hard to imagine non-Annex I developed nations and middle-income nations refusing to use this general sort of on-ramp, since there can be no claim that doing so amounts to limiting economic growth. If, in addition, the Convention could be modified so that only nations in either Annex I or Annex III had voting rights, participation would be further encouraged. It might be feasible to modify WTO rules so as to impose (mild) trade sanctions (perhaps above some per capita income threshold) on those nations unwilling to do *any* mitigation. There might—or might not—be an upper limit on per capita income for nations in Annex III or a limit on how long a nation could remain on the Annex III on-ramp. The result of adding an on-ramp of this general sort would be a less tidy and elegant policy architecture but, I believe, one much more likely to be effective in the long run.

The most important and difficult climate change task before the world's policymakers today is not to negotiate Annex I emissions limits for the immediate post-Kyoto period, nor even to design the policy regime for that period. The most important and difficult task is to move toward a policy architecture that can induce the world's poor nations to travel a much more climate-friendly path to prosperity than the one today's rich nations have traveled. In this volume, Joseph Aldy and Robert Stavins have assembled a set of thoughtful essays that deserve to be read by anyone engaged in this task or, indeed, anyone who takes this task seriously.

References

Gallagher, Kelly Sims, Ambuj Sagar, Diane Segal, Paul de Sa, and John P. Holdren (2007). "U.S. Government Investments in Energy Research, Development, and Demonstration Database," ETIP Fact Sheet (BCSIA), Cambridge, MA: Harvard Kennedy School, February.

Intergovernmental Panel on Climate Change (1996). *Climate Change 1995—Economic and Social Dimensions of Climate Change:*

Contribution of Working Group III to the Second Assessment Report of the Intergovernmental Panel on Climate Change, Cambridge, UK: Cambridge University Press, Ch. 10.

Schmalensee, Richard (1998). "Greenhouse Policy Architectures and Institutions," in W. D. Nordhaus (ed.), *Economics and Policy Issues in Climate Change*. Washington, DC: Resources for the Future Press, pp. 137–58.

US Department of Energy (1990). "The Economics of Long-Term Global Climate Change: A Preliminary Assessment, Report of an Interagency Task Force," DOE/PE-0096P, Washington, DC: US Department of Energy.

29 | Lessons for the international policy community

JOSEPH E. ALDY AND
ROBERT N. STAVINS

The nations of the world confront a tremendous challenge in designing and implementing an international policy response to the threat
of global climate change that is scientifically sound, economically
rational, and politically pragmatic. It is broadly acknowledged that
the relatively wealthy, developed countries are responsible for a
majority of the anthropogenic greenhouse gases (GHGs) that have
already accumulated in the atmosphere, but developing countries will
emit more GHGs over this century than the currently industrialized
nations if no efforts are taken to alter their course of development.
The architecture of a robust international climate change policy will
need to take into account the many dimensions and consequences of
this issue with respect to the environment, the economy, energy, and
development.

The Kyoto Protocol—which builds directly on the foundation laid
by the United Nations Framework Convention on Climate Change
(UNFCCC)—represented a first step toward addressing this long-
term, global problem. Now, the international policy community needs
to identify the next step, both in terms of setting sensible climate-
related goals and in designing effective policies to achieve those goals.
The Harvard Project on International Climate Agreements aims to aid
and inform that process through a diverse set of research initiatives
in Europe, the United States, China, India, Japan, and Australia. This
book is a product of that research.

Drawing upon lessons from experience with the Kyoto Protocol
(Aldy and Stavins, Chapter 1; and Schmalensee)[1] and insights from
economics, political science, international relations, legal scholarship,

---

[1] All citations to specific authors in this chapter refer, unless otherwise specified,
to the author's work in this volume. Corresponding chapters can be ascertained
from the table of contents. Where articles or books outside this volume are referenced, the usual citation is provided.

and other disciplines, the contributors to this volume have set forth a range of ideas about how best to construct a post-2012 international climate change policy regime. The targets-and-timetables approach embodied in the Kyoto agreement appears here in proposals advanced by Jeffrey Frankel, Denny Ellerman, Larry Karp and Jinhua Zhao, and Jing Cao. A second category of international climate policy architectures—harmonized domestic policies—is represented in proposals by Scott Barrett, Judson Jaffe and Robert Stavins, Richard Cooper, and Akihiro Sawa. And one proposal by Judson Jaffe and Robert Stavins falls in a third category: decentralized, bottom-up approaches that rely primarily on coordinated, unilateral national policies.

Combined with nineteen additional chapters that focus on specific design issues, these proposals cover virtually the entire spectrum of potential international climate policy architectures. This concluding chapter provides a synthesis of the exceptionally diverse set of proposals and analyses contained in this volume.[2] We begin by identifying a set of principles that our research teams have explicitly or implicitly identified as being important for the design of post-2012 international climate policy architecture. We then go on to highlight four potential architectures, each of which is promising in some regards and raises important issues for consideration. Finally, we turn to key design issues in international policy architecture, because regardless which overall architecture is ultimately chosen, certain key design issues and elements will stand out as particularly important. We conclude with a look at the path ahead.

Principles for an international agreement

A set of core principles emerges from the diverse strands of research reported in this book. These principles constitute the fundamental premises that underlie various proposed policy architectures and design elements; as such they can provide a reasonable point of departure for ongoing international negotiations.[3]

---

[2] Of the twenty-six chapters in this book from the research of the Harvard Project on International Climate Agreements, seven propose complete international policy architectures for the post-2012 period, fourteen examine key design issues and elements, and five provide quantitative modeling of alternative policy architectures or allocations of responsibility.

[3] Aldy, Barrett, and Stavins (2003) present six criteria for evaluating potential international climate policy architectures that map closely to most of these principles.

Climate change is a global commons problem, and therefore a cooperative approach involving many nations—whether through a single international agreement or some other regime—will be necessary to address it successfully. Because GHGs mix uniformly in the atmosphere, the location of emissions sources has no effect on the location of impacts, which are dispersed worldwide. Hence, it is virtually never in the economic interest of individual nations to take unilateral actions. This classic free-rider problem means that cooperative approaches are necessary (Aldy and Stavins 2008a).

Since sovereign nations cannot be compelled to act against their wishes, successful treaties should create adequate incentives for compliance, along with incentives for participation. Unfortunately, the Kyoto Protocol seems to lack incentives of both types (Barrett; Karp and Zhao; and Keohane and Raustiala).

Since carbon-intensive economies cannot be replicated throughout the world without causing dangerous anthropogenic interference with the global climate, it will be necessary for all countries to move onto much less carbon-intensive growth paths. Even reducing emissions in the currently industrialized world to zero is insufficient (see chapters in this volume by Blanford, *et al.*; Bosetti, *et al.*; Cooper; Hall, *et al.*; and Jacoby *et al.*). With appropriate negotiating rules (Harstad), more countries can be brought on board. The rapidly emerging middle class in the developing world seeks to emulate lifestyles that are typical of the industrialized world and may be willing to depart from this goal only if the industrialized world itself moves to a lower-carbon path (Agarwala; Schmalensee; and Wirth). Moving beyond the current impasse will require that developed countries achieve meaningful near-term emission reductions, with a clear view to medium- and long-term consequences and goals (Agarwala; Harstad; and Karp and Zhao).

A credible global climate change agreement must be equitable. If past or present high levels of emissions become the basis for all future entitlements, the developing world is unlikely to participate (Agarwala). Developed countries are responsible for more than 50 percent of the accumulated stock of anthropogenic GHGs in the atmosphere today, and their share of near-term global mitigation efforts should reflect this responsibility (Agarwala). In the long term, nations should assume the same or similar burdens on an equalized per capita basis (Agarwala; Cao; and Frankel, Chapter 2). However, if the goal is a more equitable distribution of wealth, approaches based on metrics other than per capita emissions can be better (Jacoby, *et al.*; and Posner and Sunstein). It is also important to recognize and acknowledge that in the short term, developing countries may value their economic growth more than future, global environmental conditions (Victor).

Developing countries face domestic imperatives for economic growth and political development. More and better research is needed to identify policies that promote both mitigation and adaptation, while accommodating development. At the same time, developing countries should not "hide behind the poor" (Agarwala): the burgeoning middle class in the developing world is on a path to exceed the population of developed countries and, as we have already noted, its lifestyle and per capita emissions are similar to those in much of the developed world. While not exclusively a problem of developing countries, tropical forests, in particular, are one important dimension of the larger interplay between development and climate change policy. Because of the enormous impacts that natural and anthropogenic changes in forests have on the global carbon cycle, it is important to provide a meaningful, cost-effective, and equitable approach to promoting forest carbon sequestration in an international agreement (Plantinga and Richards).

A credible global climate change agreement must be cost-effective. That means it should minimize the global welfare loss associated with reducing emissions (Aldy and Stavins 2008b; Ellerman; and Jaffe and Stavins), and also minimize the risks of corruption in meeting targets (Agarwala; and Somanathan).

A credible global climate change agreement must bring about significant technological change. Given the magnitude of the problem and the high costs that will be involved, it will be essential to reduce mitigation costs over time through massive technological invention, innovation, diffusion, and utilization (Blanford, *et al.*; Bosetti, *et al.*; Clarke, *et al.*; Newell; Somanathan; Wirth; and Aldy and Stavins 2008c). Rapid technology transfer from the developed to the developing world will be needed (see Hall, *et al.*; Keeler and Thompson; Newell; Somanathan; Teng, *et al.*; and Wirth).

Governments should work through a variety of channels to achieve a credible global climate change agreement that uses multiple ways to mitigate climate change risks. Although a post-2012 agreement under the UNFCCC may be at the core of a post-Kyoto regime, other venues—whether bilateral treaties, or G8+5, or L20 accords—should continue to be explored, as additional agreements and arrangements may be necessary (Hall, *et al.*; and Schmalensee).

An effective global climate change agreement must be consistent with the international trade regime. A global climate agreement can lead to conflicts with international trade law, but it can also be structured to be mutually supportive of global trade objectives (Frankel, Chapter 16; and Harstad).

A credible global climate change agreement must be practical, realistic, and verifiable. That means it needs institutional mechanisms for effective implementation (Agarwala). Because tremendous start-up costs are usually incurred in creating new institutions, consideration should be given—whenever appropriate—to maintaining existing institutions, such as the Clean Development Mechanism (CDM), and improving them rather than abandoning them (Hall, *et al.*; Karp and Zhao; Keeler and Thompson; and Teng, *et al.*). In addition, it should be recognized that most parts of the industrialized world have signaled their preference for the use of cap-and-trade mechanisms to meet their domestic emissions commitments (Jaffe and Stavins), and it would be *politically* practical to build upon these institutional and policy preferences. Whatever institutions or mechanisms are used to implement policy commitments, they should promote emission abatement consistent with realistic technological innovation or risk costly and ineffective outcomes (Agarwala; Blanford, *et al.*; Bosetti, *et al.*; and Jacoby, *et al.*). The best agreements will be robust in the face of inevitable global economic downturns (McKibbin, *et al.*). Finally, various metrics can be employed to judge the equity and integrity of national commitments, including measures of emissions performance, reductions, or cost (Fischer and Morgenstern). An international surveillance institution could provide credible, third-party assessments of participating countries' efforts.

Promising international climate policy architectures

While we have identified a number of core principles to guide the analysis and frame the proposals presented in this volume, the Harvard Project does not endorse a single approach to international climate policy. This is because we recognize that the decision to adopt a particular architecture is ultimately a political one that must be reached by the nations of the world, taking into account a complex array of factors.

We highlight four potential architectures—each with advantages as well as disadvantages—because each is promising in some regards, raises key issues for consideration, and to a considerable extent is exemplary of the types of architectures discussed in this volume.

One architecture follows a targets-and-timetables structure, using formulas to set dynamic national emissions targets for all countries. Two fall within the category of harmonized domestic policies: a portfolio of international treaties and harmonized national carbon taxes. The fourth architecture summarized below is based on a set of coordinated, unilateral national policies and involves linking national and regional tradable permit systems.

Targets and timetables: formulas for evolving emission targets for all countries[4]

This targets-and-timetables proposal offers a framework of formulas that yield numerical emissions targets for all countries through the end of this century (Frankel, Chapter 2). National and regional cap-and-trade systems for greenhouse gases would be linked in a way that allows trading across firms and sources (Jaffe and Stavins), not among nations per se (as in Article 17 of the Kyoto Protocol). Such a global trading system would be roughly analogous to the system already established in the European Union, where sources rather than nations engage in trading (Ellerman).[5]

The formulas are based on what is possible politically, given that many of the usual science- and economics-based proposals for future emission paths are not dynamically consistent—that is, future governments will not necessarily abide by commitments made by today's leaders.[6] Several researchers have observed that when participants

---

[4] This proposed architecture was developed by Frankel, supplemented by Aldy and Stavins (2008b), Harstad, Cao, Ellerman, and Jacoby, *et al.* Bossetti, *et al.* provide an economic analysis of this and several other potential architectures.

[5] For an examination of the possible role and design of cap-and-trade and other tradable permit systems as part of an international policy architecture, see Aldy and Stavins (2008b).

[6] It is worth nothing that Harstad's game-theoretic analysis in this volume supports the efficacy of using formulas to calculate national obligations or contributions. This is because if the distribution of contributions or obligations is determined by a formula it is fundamentally more difficult for a country to renegotiate its own share of the burden. Enhancing its bargaining position is then less useful, and investments in research and development increase.

in the policy process discuss climate targets, they typically pay little attention to the difficulty of finding mutually acceptable ways to share the economic burden of emission reductions (Bosetti, *et al.*; and Jacoby, *et al.*).

This formula-based architecture is premised on four important political realities. First, the United States may not commit to quantitative emission targets if China and other major developing countries do not commit to quantitative targets at the same time. This reflects concerns about economic competitiveness and carbon leakage. Second, China and other developing countries are unlikely to make sacrifices different in character from those made by richer countries that have gone before them. Third, in the long run, no country can be rewarded for having "ramped up" its emissions well above 1990 levels. Fourth, no country will agree to bear excessive cost. (Harstad adds that use of formulas can render negotiations more efficient.)

The proposal calls for an international agreement to establish a global cap-and-trade system, where emission caps are set using formulas that assign quantitative emissions limits to countries in every year through 2100. The formula incorporates three elements: a progressivity factor, a latecomer catch-up factor, and a gradual equalization factor. The progressivity factor requires richer countries to make more severe cuts relative to their business-as-usual emissions. The latecomer catch-up factor requires nations that did not agree to binding targets under the Kyoto Protocol to make gradual reductions to account for their additional emissions since 1990. This factor prevents latecomers from being rewarded with higher targets and is designed to avoid creating incentives for countries to ramp up their emissions before signing on to the agreement. Finally, the gradual equalization factor addresses the complaint that rich countries are responsible for a majority of the accumulated anthropogenic GHGs currently in the atmosphere. In the second half of the century, this factor moves national per capita emissions in the direction of the global average of per capita emissions.[7]

---

[7] This is similar to Cao's "global development rights" (GDR) burden-sharing formula and is consistent with calls for movement toward per capita responsibility by Agarwala. On the other hand, it contrasts with the analyses of Jacoby, *et al.* and Posner and Sunstein. Under Cao's GDR formula, the lion's share of the abatement burden would fall on the industrialized world in the short term, with developing countries initially accepting a small but increasing share over time, such that, by 2020, fast-growing economies such as China and India would take on significant burdens.

The caps set for rich nations would require them to undertake immediate abatement measures. Developing countries would not bear any cost in the early years, nor would they be expected to make any sacrifice that is different from the sacrifices of industrialized countries, accounting for differences in income. Developing countries would be subject to binding emission targets that would follow their business-as-usual (BAU) emissions in the next several decades.[8] National emission targets for developed and developing countries alike should not cost more than 1 percent of Gross Domestic Product (GDP) in present value terms or more than 5 percent of GDP in any given year.

Every country under this proposal is given reason to feel that it is only doing its fair share. Importantly, without a self-reinforcing framework for allocating the abatement burden, announcements of distant future goals may not be credible and so may not have desired effects on investment. The basic architecture of this proposal—a decade-by-decade sequence of emission targets determined by a few principles and formulas—is also flexible enough that it can accommodate major changes in circumstances during the course of the century.

Harmonized domestic policies: a portfolio of international treaties[9]

The second proposal we highlight is for a very different sort of architecture than that of the Kyoto Protocol. Rather than attempting to address all sectors and all types of GHGs under one unified regime, this approach envisions a system of linked international agreements that separately address various sectors and gases; as well as key issues, including adaptation and technology research and development (R&D); plus last-resort remedies, such as geoengineering and air capture of greenhouse gases.

First, nations would negotiate sector-level agreements that would establish global standards for specific sectors or categories of GHG sources. Developing countries would not be exempted from these

---

[8] Somanathan would argue against including developing countries in the short term, even with targets equivalent to BAU, as recommended in this proposal. We discuss alternative burden-sharing arrangements below.

[9] This proposed architecture was developed by Barrett and supplemented by Newell on research and development policies, by Sawa on sectoral approaches, and by economic modeling from Bosetti, *et al.*

standards, but would receive financial aid from developed countries to help them comply. Trade sanctions would be available to enforce agreements governing trade-sensitive sectors. Such a sectoral approach could have the advantage that it protects against cross contamination: if policies designed for a given sector prove ineffective, their failure need not drag down the entire enterprise. Similar arguments can be made for separate approaches to different types of GHGs.

In general, sectoral approaches in a future climate agreement can offer some advantages (Sawa). First, sectoral approaches could encourage the involvement of a wider range of countries, since incentives could be targeted at specific industries in those countries. Second, sectoral approaches can directly address concerns about international competitiveness and leakage: if industries make cross-border commitments to equitable targets, this would presumably mitigate concerns about unfair competition in energy-intensive industries. Third, sectoral approaches could be designed to promote technology development and transfer. It should also be recognized, however, that sectoral approaches have some significant problems (Sawa). First, it may be difficult to negotiate an international agreement using this approach if negotiators are reluctant to accept the large transaction costs associated with collecting information and negotiating at the sector level. Countries that are already participating in emission trading schemes may tend to avoid any approach that creates uncertainty about their existing investments. Second, a sectoral approach would reduce cost-effectiveness relative to an economy-wide, cap-and-trade system or emission tax. Finally, it is difficult for a sectoral approach to achieve high levels of environmental effectiveness, because it does not induce mitigation actions by all sectors.

Recognizing the technology challenge implicit in successfully addressing climate change, a second component of this suite of international agreements could focus on research and development. Specifically, it could require participants to adopt a portfolio of strategies for reducing barriers and increasing incentives for innovation in ways that maximize the impact of scarce public resources and effectively engage the capacities of the private sector (Newell).[10] R&D

[10] In the section below on key design issues, we focus on technology transfer as a key design issue for any international climate policy architecture. Bosetti, *et al.* analyze the costs and effectiveness of R&D strategies compared with alternative architectures.

obligations could be linked with emission reduction policies. For example, an agreement could require all new coal-fired power stations to have certain minimum thermal efficiency—and ready capacity to incorporate carbon capture and storage, as the latter becomes technically and financially feasible—with these obligations binding on individual countries as long as the treaty's minimum participation conditions were met. Such an agreement would reduce incentives for free riding and could directly spur R&D investments in areas where countries and firms may otherwise be likely to underinvest.

Third, an international agreement should address adaptation assistance for developing countries. All nations have strong incentives to adapt, but only rich countries have the resources and capabilities to insure against climate change risks. Rich countries may substitute investments in adaptation—the benefits of which can be appropriated locally—for investments in mitigation, the benefits of which are distributed globally. If so, this would leave developing countries even more exposed to climate risks and widen existing disparities. Critical areas for investment include agriculture and tropical medicine. Policy design to leverage such investment can improve developing countries' resilience to climate shocks while facilitating their economic development.

A fourth set of agreements would govern the research, development, and deployment of geoengineering and air capture technologies.[11] Geoengineering could serve as an insurance policy in case refinements in climate science over the next several decades suggest that climate change is much worse than currently believed and that atmospheric concentrations may have already passed important thresholds for triggering abrupt and catastrophic impacts. Geoengineering may turn out to be cheap relative to transforming the fossil-fuel foundation of industrial economies. While no one country can adequately address climate change through emissions abatement, individual nations may be able to implement geoengineering options. The challenge may lie

[11] Geoengineering strategies attempt to limit warming by reducing the amount of solar radiation that reaches the Earth's surface—the most commonly discussed approach in this category involves throwing particles into the atmosphere to scatter sunlight. Air capture refers to strategies for removing carbon from the atmosphere. Possible options include fertilizing iron-limited regions of the oceans to stimulate phytoplankton blooms or using a chemical sorbent to directly remove carbon from the air.

in preventing nations from resorting to it too quickly or over other countries' objections.

This portfolio approach to international agreements could avoid the enforcement problems of a Kyoto-style targets-and-timetables structure, while providing the means to prevent climate change (through standards that lower emissions), become accustomed to climate change (through adaptation), and fix it (through geoengineering). By avoiding the enforcement problems of an aggregate approach and by taking a broader view of risk reduction, the portfolio approach could provide a more effective and flexible response to the long-term challenge posed by climate change.

Harmonized domestic policies: a system of national carbon taxes[12]

This architecture consists of harmonized domestic taxes on GHG emissions from all sources. The charge would be internationally adjusted from time to time, and each country would collect and keep the revenues it generates (Cooper). Since decisions to consume goods and services that require the use of fossil fuels are made on a daily basis by more than a billion households and firms around the world, the most effective way to reach all these decision makers is by changing the prices they pay for these goods and services. Levying a charge on carbon dioxide (CO_2) emissions does that directly.

Carbon taxes could have several advantages over a cap-and-trade system (Cooper). First, the allocation of valuable emission allowances to domestic firms or residents under a cap-and-trade scheme could foster corruption in some countries. A carbon tax would avoid such problematic transfers. Likewise, a carbon tax minimizes bureaucratic intervention and the necessity for a financial trading infrastructure (Agarwala). Second, a carbon charge would generate significant revenues that could be used to increase government spending, reduce other taxes, or finance climate-relevant research and development—though it should be noted that the same is true of a cap-and-trade system that auctions allowances. Third, a carbon tax may be less objectionable

---

[12] This proposed architecture was developed by Cooper and supplemented by Fischer and Morgenstern on measurement issues, McKibbin, *et al.* on a hybrid of this approach, and economic modeling by Bosetti, *et al.*

to developing nations than an emission cap because it does not imply a hard constraint on growth (Pan 2007).[13] Fourth, any international climate regime requires some means for evaluating national commitments and performance (Fischer and Morgenstern). A carbon tax system provides a straightforward and useful metric, since the marginal cost of abatement activities is always equivalent to the tax rate itself.

Since several economies, most notably the European Union, have embarked on a cap-and-trade system, Cooper investigates whether cap-and-trade systems and tax systems can co-exist. He concludes that the answer is "yes," provided that several conditions are met. First, allowance prices under the cap-and-trade system should average no less than the internationally agreed carbon tax. Second, if the allowance price fell below the agreed global tax for more than a certain period of time, trading partners should be allowed to levy countervailing duties on imports from countries with a low permit trading price. Third, countries could not provide tax rebates on their exports, and cap-and-trade systems would have to auction all of their allowances.

The tax should cover all the significant GHGs, insofar as is practical. The initial scheme need not cover all countries, but it should cover the countries that account for the vast majority of world emissions. All but the poorest nations should have sufficient administrative capacity to administer the tax at upstream points in the energy supply chain—that is, on the carbon content of fossil fuels.[14] The level of the tax would be set by international agreement and could be subject to periodic review every five or ten years.[15]

A carbon tax treaty would need to include monitoring and enforcement measures. The International Monetary Fund could assess whether signatory nations have passed required legislation and set

[13] China's 2007 National Program on Climate Change indicated that any near-term emissions reductions in that country will be accomplished using domestic policies designed to address energy efficiency, renewable and nuclear energy, and energy security. The document also indicated that in the longer term, China may be willing to place a price on carbon emissions using more direct mechanisms such as an emissions tax or cap-and-trade system (Jiang 2008). This policy approach is reinforced in Part III of China's October 2008 White Paper on climate change (Information Office of the State Council 2008).

[14] For example, the carbon content of oil should be taxed at refineries, natural gas should be taxed at major pipeline collection points, and coal should be taxed at mine heads or rail or barge collection points.

[15] For a thorough economic assessment of the implications of a system of harmonized domestic carbon taxes, see Bosetti, et al.

up the appropriate administrative machinery to implement the tax (Agarwala). If a country were significantly and persistently out of compliance, its exports could be subject to countervailing duties in importing countries. Non-signatory countries could also be subject to countervailing duties. This possibility would provide a potent incentive for most countries to comply with the agreement, whether or not they were formal signatories.[16]

Cost-effective implementation at a global level would require the tax to be set at the same level in all countries. The abatement costs incurred by key developing countries would likely exceed, by a considerable margin, the maximum burden they would be willing to accept under an international agreement, at least in the near term. This could be addressed through transfers (side payments) from industrialized countries to developing countries, thereby enhancing both cost-effectiveness and distributional equity. These transfers would be from one government to another, raising concerns about possible corruption, as well as political acceptability in the industrialized world. Alternatively, distributional equity could be achieved by pairing the carbon tax agreement with a deal on trade or development that benefits these emerging economies.

Coordinated national policies: linkage of national and regional tradable permit systems[17]

A new international policy architecture may be evolving on its own, based on the reality that tradable permit systems, such as cap-and-trade systems, are emerging worldwide as the favored national and regional approach. Prominent examples include the European Union's Emission Trading Scheme (EU ETS); the Regional Greenhouse Gas Initiative in the northeastern United States; and systems in Norway, Switzerland, and other nations; plus the existing global emission-reduction-credit system, the CDM. Moreover, cap-and-trade systems now appear likely to emerge as the chosen approach to reducing

---

[16] In the section on key design issues, below, we discuss the relationship of climate policy architectures with international trade law and practices.

[17] This proposed architecture was developed by Jaffe and Stavins, and supplemented by Ellerman on the European approach as a potential global model, Keohane and Raustiala on buyer liability, Hall, *et al.* and Victor on the importance of domestic institutions, and by economic modeling from Bosetti, *et al.*

greenhouse gas emissions in an additional set of industrialized countries, including Australia, Canada, Japan, New Zealand, and the United States.

The proliferation of cap-and-trade systems and emission-reduction-credit systems around the world has generated increased attention and increased pressure—both from governments and from the business community—to link these systems. By linkage, we refer to direct or indirect connections between and among tradable permit systems through the unilateral or bilateral recognition of allowances or permits.[18]

Linkage produces cost savings in the same way that a cap-and-trade system reduces costs compared to a system that separately regulates individual emission sources—that is, it substantially broadens the pool of lower-cost compliance options available to regulated entities. In addition, linking tradable permit systems at the country level reduces overall transaction costs, reduces market power (which can be a problem in such systems), and reduces overall price volatility.

There are also some legitimate concerns about linkage. Most important is the automatic propagation of program elements that are designed to contain costs, such as banking, borrowing, and safety valve mechanisms. If a cap-and-trade system with a safety valve is directly linked to another system that does not have a safety valve, the result will be that both systems now share the safety valve. Given that the European Union has opposed a safety valve in its emission trading scheme, and given that a safety valve could be included in a future US emission trading system, this concern about the automatic propagation of cost-containment design elements is a serious one.

More broadly, linkage will reduce individual nations' control over allowance prices, emission impacts, and other consequences of their systems. This loss of control over domestic prices and other effects of a cap-and-trade policy is simply a special case of the general proposition that nations, by engaging in international trade through an open economy, lose some degree of control over domestic prices, but do so voluntarily because of the large economic gains from trade.

Importantly, there are ways to gain the benefits of linkage without the downside of having to harmonize systems in advance. If two cap-and-trade systems both link with the same emission-reduction-credit

---

[18] As Ellerman explains, to some degree the EU ETS can serve as a prototype for linked national systems.

system, such as the CDM, then the two cap-and-trade systems are indirectly linked with one another. All of the benefits of linkage occur: the cost-effectiveness of both cap-and-trade systems is improved and both gain from more liquid markets that reduce transaction costs, market power, and price volatility. At the same time, the automatic propagation of key design elements from one cap-and-trade system to another is much weaker when the systems are only indirectly linked through an emission-reduction-credit system.

Such indirect linkage through the CDM is already occurring, because virtually all cap-and-trade systems that are in place, as well those that are planned or contemplated, allow for CDM offsets to be used (at least to some degree) to meet domestic obligations. Thus, indirectly linked, country- or region-based cap-and-trade systems may already be evolving into the *de facto*, if not the *de jure*, post-Kyoto international climate policy architecture.

Of course, reliance on CDM offsets also gives rise to concerns, especially as regards the environmental integrity of some of those offsets.[19] Some have recommended that a system of buyer liability (rather than seller or hybrid liability) would endogenously generate market arrangements—such as reliable ratings agencies and variations in the price of offsets according to perceived risks—that would help to address these concerns, as well as broader issues of compliance (Keohane and Raustiala). These features would in turn create incentives for compliance without resorting to ineffective interstate punishments. In addition, a system of buyer liability gives sellers strong incentives to maintain permit quality so as to maximize the monetary value of these tradable assets.

While, in the near term, linkage may continue to grow in importance as a core element of a bottom-up, *de facto* international policy architecture, in the longer term, linkage could play several roles. A set of linkages, combined with unilateral emissions reduction commitments by many nations, could function as a stand-alone climate architecture. Such a system would be cost-effective, but may lack the coordinating mechanisms necessary to achieve meaningful long-term environmental results. Another possibility is that a collection of bottom-up links may eventually evolve into a comprehensive, top-down agreement. In this

[19] See section on key design issues below for an examination of ways to reform the CDM.

scenario, linkages would provide short-term cost savings while serving as a natural starting point for negotiations leading to a top-down agreement.[20] The top-down agreement may continue use of linked cap-and-trade programs to reduce abatement costs and improve market liquidity.

A post-2012 international climate agreement could include several elements that would facilitate future linkages among cap-and-trade and emission-reduction-credit systems. For example, it could establish an agreed trajectory of emissions caps (Frankel, Chapter 2) or allowance prices, specify harmonized cost-containment measures, and establish a process for making future adjustments to key design elements. It could also create an international clearinghouse for transaction records and allowance auctions, provide for the ongoing operation of the CDM, and build capacity in developing countries. If the aim is to facilitate linkage, a future agreement should also avoid imposing "supplementarity" restrictions that require countries to achieve some specified percentage of emission reductions domestically.

Key design issues in international policy architecture

Regardless which overall international policy architecture is ultimately chosen, a number of key design issues will stand out as particularly important. Based on research carried out under the auspices of the Harvard Project on International Climate Agreements, we identify key lessons for five issues and elements relevant for a post-2012 international agreement: burden sharing, technology transfer, CDM reform, addressing deforestation, and making global climate policy compatible with global trade policy. All five of these issues are relevant to the relationship between global climate policy and economic development (Wirth).

---

[20] Carraro (2007) and Victor (2007) also describe the potential for trading to emerge organically as a result of linking a small set of domestic trading programs. This evolution would be analogous to the experience in international trade in goods and services, in which a small number of countries initially reached agreement on trade rules governing a small set of goods. As trust built on these initial experiences, trading expanded to cover more countries and more goods, a process that eventually provided the foundation for a top-down authority in the form of the World Trade Organization.

Burden sharing in an international climate agreement

The most challenging aspect of establishing a post-Kyoto international climate regime will be reaching agreement on burden sharing among nations that will be explicitly or implicitly part of the adopted regime. In this context, the interface between global climate policy and economic development becomes particularly important.

One approach to thinking about this issue is to start by focusing on what is politically possible, and to identify an allocation of responsibility—with appropriate changes over time—that makes every country feel that it is doing only its fair share (Frankel, Chapter 2). A common thread in many discussions about "fair," long-term burden sharing is the desirability of gradually moving all countries toward equal per capita emissions.[21] As a long-term outcome, this would be consistent with what many people, from diverse perspectives, regard as ultimately equitable (Agarwala; Cao; and Frankel, Chapter 2), although others have noted that if the goal is greater equity in the distribution of wealth, directly targeting wealth redistribution would be more effective (Posner and Sunstein).

More broadly, the three-element formula proposed by Frankel for setting evolving country-level emissions targets has the virtue of recognizing the industrialized countries' historic responsibility for GHG emissions (Agarwala; and Somanathan) and does not reward countries for previous lack of action. Furthermore, this time-path of evolving commitments reflects the reality that, in the short term, developing countries value their economic growth more than future environmental conditions (Victor). But by providing for increased participation by developing countries over time, this approach also recognizes that it will be impossible to stabilize atmospheric GHG concentrations unless rapidly growing developing countries take on an increasingly meaningful role in reducing global emissions (Blanford, *et al.*; Bosetti, *et al.*; Clarke, *et al.*; Cooper; Hall, *et al.*; and Jacoby, *et al.*). The real test lies in whether domestic constituencies in the developed world will perceive such agreements as fair.

---

[21] Somanathan argues that although an effective solution to climate change will require the cooperation of developing countries, achieving near-term GHG reductions in these countries will be neither feasible nor desirable because of their other priorities for economic and social development.

Technology transfer in an international climate agreement[22]

Achieving long-term climate change policy goals will require a remarkable ramp-up in the innovation and deployment of energy-efficient
and low-carbon technologies in an environment that is already experiencing substantial increases in investment (Aldy and Stavins 2008c;
Newell).[23] Transitioning away from fossil fuels as the foundation of
industrialized economies and as the basis for development in emerging
economies and less developed countries will likely necessitate a suite
of policies to provide the proper incentives for technological change
(Somanathan). Two principal categories of policies are potentially
important to drive the invention, innovation, commercialization,
diffusion, and utilization of climate-friendly technologies: (1) international carbon markets and other pricing strategies and (2) non-price
mechanisms, including various means of technology transfer to developing countries and coordinated innovation and commercialization
programs.

International carbon markets and technology transfer

The most powerful tool for accelerating the development and deployment of climate-friendly technologies will be policies that affect the
current and expected future prices of fossil fuels relative to lower-
carbon alternatives. By setting a price on GHG emissions and thereby
raising the price of conventional fossil fuels and energy-intensive
production practices, these policies—which are at the core of several
proposed international climate policy architectures—will induce investment in less emissions-intensive technologies. Cap-and-trade programs;
emission reduction credit systems, such as the CDM; and harmonized
domestic carbon taxes can thus create incentives for emission mitigation projects in industrialized and developing countries alike.

---

[22] Below we address technology transfer in the context of efforts to reform the
CDM.

[23] The International Energy Agency forecasts more than $20 trillion of investment
in the global energy infrastructure between now and 2030. Some of this accelerated investment is evident in China, where one out of six coal-fired power plants
is less than three years old. But the investment is not universal—populations
in least developed countries still suffer from lack of access to power and basic
energy poverty that can inhibit advances along a variety of development measures (Aldy and Stavins 2008c).

Given the long lifetimes of many emissions-intensive capital assets—power plants may operate 50 years or more, building shells may last 100 years—long-term carbon price signals may be necessary to allow the owners of such capital to form appropriate expectations and alter the nature of their investments. Blunt policy instruments such as performance standards or bans on carbon-intensive products can also induce innovation, but such approaches are typically less efficient.

Pricing carbon can leverage foreign direct investment to promote less carbon-intensive development. For example, some CDM projects have resulted in the deployment of renewable power, such as wind farms, as an alternative to coal-fired power generation. Other CDM projects have been criticized for rewarding minor process modifications that do not involve substantial investment in new technologies, such as the manufacture of fluorinated refrigerants. Some countries may also consider CDM participation a substitute for taking further mitigation actions or even use the CDM to justify weakening policies in other areas. More broadly, reforming the CDM could facilitate more substantial transfers of technology (Keeler and Thompson; Hall, *et al.*; and Teng, *et al.*). We consider such approaches below.[24]

In any event, putting a price on carbon may not facilitate new investment flows and associated technology transfers to developing countries with weak market institutions. If a country has difficulty attracting capital generally, changing the relative prices of carbon-intensive and carbon-lean capital will not resolve this problem. In this case, additional policy interventions would be required to stimulate the transfer of technology to developing countries. Also, while putting a price on carbon will draw more resources into low-carbon technology R&D, it will not be sufficient to fully overcome the general disincentive for private-sector investments in R&D. This is because undertaking R&D effectively produces new knowledge, and this knowledge is a public good. Once the knowledge exists, it is difficult for firms to prevent others from sharing its benefits (although patent law provides some protection). Since innovating firms cannot capture all the benefits of their R&D efforts, they tend to underinvest in such activities. Thus, additional policies are needed to promote the

---

[24] An alternative to reforming the CDM that could also facilitate greater technology transfer is to establish climate accession deals with individual developing countries (Victor).

public- and private-sector innovation that will be required to ensure that a next generation of climate-friendly technologies is available for deployment.

Additional technology policy in post-2012 international climate agreements

The next international climate agreement can provide several mechanisms to facilitate the development and deployment of climate-friendly technologies (Aldy and Stavins 2008c; Newell; and Somanathan). First, the agreement can provide a venue for countries to pledge resources for technology transfer and for R&D activities (Newell). The agreement could also codify such pledges as commitments, on par with commitments to limit emissions (as in Annex B of the Kyoto Protocol). Besides negotiating a given level of financial commitment, developed and emerging countries could explicitly articulate how they mean to meet their commitments, thereby promoting credibility and trust in the agreement. This could take the form of identifying a specific revenue stream (for example, auction revenues from a cap-and-trade program) that would be adequate and reliable for supporting financial pledges.

Financing technology transfer will require coordination and agreement on principles for allocating resources. An institutional home for clean technology funds may be necessary, in which case the international policy community will need to decide whether to centralize such efforts in a new institution, rely on an existing international institution, or manage the program through a decentralized array of national institutions. Likewise, some agreement on the means for coordinating R&D activities will have to be considered in identifying the appropriate institutional design.

A framework for coordinating and augmenting climate technology R&D could be organized through a UNFCCC Expert Group on Technology Development, supported by the International Energy Agency (IEA) (Newell). Broadening IEA participation to include large non–Organisation for Economic Co-operation and Development (OECD) energy consumers and producers could also facilitate such coordination. An agreement could include a process for reviewing country submissions on technology development and for identifying redundancies, gaps, and opportunities for closer collaboration. A fund for cost-shared R&D tasks and international technology prizes could be established to provide financing for science and innovation objectives that are best pursued in a joint fashion. The agreement could also include explicit targets for increased domestic R&D spending on GHG mitigation.

An independent mechanism for reviewing policies that affect technological development and deployment may benefit these efforts. Rigorous, third-party review of all nations' policies and financing mechanisms could support coordinated, international efforts by providing an authoritative assessment of the comparability of effort among participating countries. This could include reviews of financial contributions by large countries, analyses of the effectiveness of technology transfer activities, and identification of the best policy practices being implemented around the world. Such reviews could be undertaken by an existing international institution or may require the creation of a new, professional bureaucracy focused on this single surveillance task. The same institution or mechanisms could also help to assess the comparability of efforts on mitigation, adaptation, and other elements of an international agreement.

In addition to strengthening incentives, barriers to climate-friendly technology transfer could be lowered through a World Trade Organization (WTO) agreement to reduce tariff and non-tariff barriers to trade in environmental goods and services (Newell). Development and harmonization of technical standards—which could be undertaken by international standards organizations in consultation with the IEA and WTO—could further reduce impediments to technology transfer and accelerate the development and adoption of climate-friendly innovations.

Finally, an international climate policy architecture could provide positive incentives for developing and emerging economies to pursue good policy practices. For example, conditioning access to climate technology funds on the implementation of domestic "no regrets" climate policies could substantially increase the "climate return" to technology fund resources. Alternatively, access to clean technology funds could be scaled based on the extent of policy action in developing and emerging economies—as governments implement more climate-friendly policies, they could access a larger pool of resources. Such determinations could be made on the basis of independent, expert reviews of countries' climate and energy policies.

Reforming the clean development mechanism

One of the important principles identified by our research teams is that, because there are very large start-up costs for creating new institutions, consideration should be given to maintaining existing institutions, such as the CDM, and improving them rather than abandoning them (Hall, *et al.*; Karp and Zhao; Keeler and Thompson; and Teng, *et al.*).

As we emphasized earlier, serious critiques have been leveled at the CDM in its current form: because the CDM is an emission-reduction-credit system (not a cap-and-trade system), the concern is that it may credit emission reductions that are not truly additional. There have been numerous calls to address the CDM's problems by putting in place criteria and procedures to increase the likelihood that certified offset credits represent emission reductions that are truly "additional, real, verifiable, and permanent." While such reforms would have merit if they were effective, there are a number of alternative, more dramatic changes in the CDM that merit consideration.[25]

Improved, expanded, and focused ghg offsets

One promising approach would involve less emphasis on strict ton-for-ton accounting and more emphasis on a range of activities that could produce significant long-term benefits (Keeler and Thompson). There are five key elements of this proposal. First, the criteria for CDM offsets would be changed from "real, verifiable, and permanent reductions" to "actions that create real progress in developing countries toward mitigation and adaptation." The reasoning behind this change is that strict, project-based accounting rules, while intended to protect the environmental integrity of trading programs, have increased transaction costs and thereby limited the utility of the CDM. The argument is that developing country actions are more important than the sanctity of short-term targets in making real progress on mitigating climate change risk.

---

[25] We noted above the possibility of addressing the problems of the CDM through a system of buyer (rather than seller or hybrid) liability, in order to generate market arrangements that would help address these critiques, such as reliable ratings agencies, and variations in the price of offsets according to perceived risks (Keohane and Raustiala). This approach would give sellers incentives to maintain permit quality to maximize the monetary value of these tradable assets.

Second, this proposal would make a significant share of industrialized country commitments (whether international or domestic) achievable through offset payments to developing countries. If industrialized countries aimed to purchase offset credits equivalent to at least 10 percent of their overall emissions targets, they would greatly expand the flow of resources available to support developing country actions. Third, a specified portion of offset credits (perhaps 50 percent) would be sold up front, and the proceeds would be put in a fund for supporting investments in projects throughout the developing world. By allowing greater flexibility to support large-scale or nonstandard projects, this approach could increase the geographic diversity of mitigation activities and reduce transaction costs.

Fourth, international negotiations would be focused on developing guidelines for an international offsets program. Key issues to be addressed would include criteria for eligible activities, policies, and investments; requirements for documentation or accountability; mechanisms for *ex-post* adjustment; criteria for the distribution of funds; and set-asides, if any, for particular types of projects or technologies. Fifth, clearly delineated tasks would be delegated to new and existing institutions for the purpose of managing and safeguarding the offsets program.

Such reform of the CDM could facilitate more substantial transfers of technology (Aldy and Stavins 2008c). In addition, creating a list of pre-approved technologies could lower the transaction costs of the review and certification process and thus encourage more projects. Expanding the coverage of the CDM from specific projects to an entire industry, such as the power sector, could promote the exploitation of all low-cost mitigation opportunities in that country's industry, some of which may be too small to be proposed on a project-by-project basis. Finally, modifying the CDM to include policies, as well as projects, could also stimulate further investment in low-carbon technologies. For example, credits could be awarded for implementing vehicle fuel-economy standards, reducing fossil-fuel subsidies, or enforcing land-tenure rules that slow deforestation.

On the other hand, efforts to improve the performance of the CDM as a means for transferring climate-friendly technologies to developing countries also confront some major challenges (Aldy and Stavins 2008c). First, the difficulty of demonstrating additionality in a project context may become even greater in an industry or policy context—that is, the problem of constructing a project-based counterfactual (what would have happened anyway) becomes a similar counterfactual estimation problem, only at the more complicated level of a broader industry or policy. Second, limits imposed by industrialized countries on the volume of CDM credits that can enter their carbon markets will lower credit prices and discourage some new technology investment. Third, the CDM may create disincentives for some emerging economies to take on more substantial action domestically or make commitments as part of an international agreement.

If the transfer of climate-friendly technology from developed to developing countries is necessary to address climate change, then some have argued that the objective of a revamped CDM should not be primarily to capture inexpensive mitigation opportunities ("low-hanging fruit"), but rather to spur new and replicable technology transfer from developed to developing countries. Consistent with this notion, some have proposed a "Technology CDM" under which technology transfer would be the only emissions-reducing activity for which credits would be awarded (Teng, *et al.*). This would offer the opportunity to strengthen the technology transfer effects of the CDM in the near term without redesigning the whole system.

Climate accession deals

Others have taken the early limitations of the CDM as evidence that a fundamentally different approach will be needed to make real progress. One proposal that reflects this view is for climate accession deals to be employed as a new strategy for engaging developing countries (Victor). This approach builds on two premises: first, that developing nations value economic growth far more than they value future global environmental conditions and second, that many governments of developing nations lack the administrative ability to control emissions.

Under this proposal, climate accession deals would be negotiated on a country-by-country basis. An individual accession deal would essentially consist of a set of policies that are tailored to gain maximum leverage on a single developing country's emissions, while still aligning with its interests and capabilities. Industrialized countries would support each accession deal by providing specific benefits such as financial resources, technology, administrative training, or security guarantees. Because these deals would be complex to engineer, they should be few in number and focused on nations with extremely high potential for reducing emissions.

A given developing country would bid a variety of policies and programs that make sense for its development trajectory. Its bid would include information on existing barriers (e.g. funding, technology, access to international institutions). Subsequent international negotiations would determine the resources that industrialized nations would provide to that country and the metrics for assessing compliance. Accession deals could assist developing countries in adhering to global norms for GHG abatement efforts, akin to trade accession deals that promote adherence to a consistent set of trade rules.

Compared to conventional approaches, accession deals could have several advantages (Victor). First, they would be anchored in host countries' interests and capabilities. Second, they would be limited in number and could yield a significant degree of leverage while minimizing external investment. Third, they would engage private enterprise and government ministries that are beyond the environmental and foreign affairs ministries. Fourth, such accession deals would be replicable and scalable. Where they succeed, they could offer templates for similar deals in other countries.

Addressing deforestation in an international climate agreement[26]

Forest carbon flows comprise a significant part of overall global GHG emissions, with deforestation contributing between 20 and 25 percent of net emissions. Worldwide, the amount of CO_2 sequestered in forest vegetation is approximately 1,300 billion tons, compared with annual industrial CO_2 emissions of 31 billion tons. Thus, changes to forests can have enormous impacts on the global carbon cycle, which implies in turn that forest carbon management ought to be an element of the next international agreement on climate change. A promising path forward could involve taking a "national inventory" approach, in which nations receive credits or debits for changes in forest cover relative to a measured baseline (Plantinga and Richards).

Three basic approaches could be taken to address deforestation in an international climate agreement. The first approach, currently

---

[26] This section draws on Plantinga and Richards.

used by the CDM, relies on project-level accounting. Under this system, individual landowners can apply for credits for net increases in carbon stored in forests on their land. Once the permitting authority verifies that the claimed sequestration is valid, the landowner can sell the credits in allowance markets. But experience has shown that such project-by-project accounting faces serious challenges, especially in establishing the counterfactual baseline against which to evaluate projects. This additionality problem is compounded by problems of leakage (the off-site effects of projects), permanence (the potential for future changes or events to result in the release of sequestered carbon), and adverse selection problems (the most profitable projects, which are most likely to occur anyway, are also the most likely to be credited under project-oriented CDM).

A second policy approach would "delink" forest carbon programs from emission allowance systems. Rather than focusing on carbon credits, the program would focus on inputs such as policies to discourage deforestation, programs to encourage the conversion of marginal agricultural land to forests, and projects to better manage forests in forest-rich countries. These commitments could be funded by overseas development aid, international institutions, or through a separate climate fund. A delinked system would have some advantages in terms of lower transaction costs and by virtue of opening separate negotiations over international forest sequestration and energy emissions. But this approach would also have two serious disadvantages. First, incentives for forest-based carbon sequestration would be diminished and participating countries may shift their attention from assuring positive carbon outcomes to attracting project funding. Second, decoupling the forest carbon program from cap-and-trade systems removes one of the best sources of funding to promote land-use changes—emitters seeking lower-cost options to reduce their net emissions.[27]

A third, more promising approach is national inventory accounting. Under this approach, nations would conduct periodic inventories of their forest carbon stock. The measured stock would be compared with a pre-negotiated baseline to determine the offset credits that can be redeemed, or debits that must be covered, in the permit market. With this approach, national governments, rather than project developers,

---

[27] Bosetti, *et al.* find that including credits for deforestation in a global cap-and-trade system reduces costs significantly.

pursue carbon sequestration activities through the implementation of domestic policies. International negotiations would determine the reference or baseline stock of stored forest carbon. These negotiations could be used to address equity issues, as well as provide incentives for countries—in particular, countries with declining stocks—to participate in the agreement.

A national inventory approach would greatly reduce the problems that plague the CDM's project-by-project approach. It could also provide comprehensive coverage of changes to forest carbon stocks and be applied equally to all participating countries and to all measurable changes in forest carbon stocks. There are also some reasonable concerns about this approach. First, the scope of carbon sequestration activities is limited to those that can be measured. Second, the approach provides incentives for governments, not private project developers, which may be a disadvantage in countries with weak institutions, high levels of corruption, or powerful special interest groups. Third, problems with additionality, permanence, etc. may resurface with—and reduce the effectiveness of—domestic carbon sequestration policies pursued by national governments.[28]

Making global climate policy compatible with global trade policy[29]

Global efforts to address climate change could be on a collision course with global efforts through the WTO to reduce barriers to trade (Frankel, Chapter 16). With different countries likely to adopt different levels of commitment to climate change mitigation, the concern arises that carbon-intensive goods or production processes could shift to countries that do not regulate GHG emissions. This leakage phenomenon is viewed as problematic—by environmentalists because it would undermine emission-reduction objectives and by industry leaders and labor unions because it could make domestic products less competitive with imports from nations with weaker GHG regulations.

---

[28] A delinked, input-based approach could be used as an interim strategy while the scientific community works to develop the measurement capacity necessary to support national inventories.

[29] This section draws extensively on Frankel (Chapter 16); supplemented by Karp and Zhao on trade sanctions, and Newell and Hall, *et al.* on subsidies for international transfers.

Thus, various trade measures—including provisions for possible penalties against imports from countries viewed as non-participants—have been included in some climate policy proposals in the United States and Europe, as well as in proposals for a post-2012 international policy architecture (Jaffe and Stavins; and Karp and Zhao).

The widespread impression that the WTO is hostile to environmental concerns has little basis in fact. The WTO's founding Articles cite environmental protection as an objective; environmental concerns are also explicitly recognized in several WTO agreements. Recent WTO rulings support the principle that countries not only have the right to ban or tax harmful products, but—perhaps more critically—that trade measures can be used to target processes and production methods (PPM), provided they do not discriminate between domestic and foreign producers. The question is how to address concerns about leakage and competitiveness in a way that does not run afoul of WTO rules and avoids derailing progress toward free trade and climate goals alike.

Future national-level policies to address climate change may be expected to include provisions that target carbon-intensive products from countries deemed to be making inadequate efforts. These provisions need not violate sensible trade principles and WTO rules, but there is a danger that in practice they will. The kinds of provisions that would be more likely to conflict with WTO rules and provide cover for protectionism include the following: (1) unilateral measures applied by countries that are not participating in the Kyoto Protocol or its successors; (2) judgments made by politicians vulnerable to political pressure from interest groups for special protection; (3) unilateral measures that seek to sanction an entire country, rather than targeting narrowly defined energy-intensive sectors; (4) import barriers against products that are further removed from carbon-intensive activity, such as firms that use inputs that are produced in an energy-intensive process; and (5) subsidies—whether in the form of money or extra permit allocations—to domestic sectors that are considered to have been put at a competitive disadvantage.

By contrast, border measures that are more likely to be WTO-compatible include either tariffs or (equivalently) requirements for importers to surrender tradable permits designed with attention to the following guidelines: (1) trade measures follow some multilaterally-agreed set of guidelines among countries participating in the emission targets of the Kyoto Protocol and/or its successors; (2) judgments about which countries are complying or not, which industries are involved and their carbon content, and which countries are entitled to respond with border measures are made by independent panels of experts; (3) measures are applied only by countries that are reducing their emissions, against countries that are not doing so, either as a result of their refusal to join an agreement or their failure to comply; and (4) import penalties target fossil fuels, and five or six of the most energy-intensive major industries that produce manufactured bulk goods: aluminum, cement, steel, paper, glass, and perhaps iron and chemicals.

The economics and the laws governing the interaction of trade and environmental policy are complex, and a multilateral regime is needed to guide the development of trade measures intended to address concerns about leakage and competitiveness in a world where nations have different levels of commitment to GHG mitigation. Ideally, this regime would be negotiated along with a successor to the Kyoto Protocol that sets emission-reduction targets for future periods. If that process takes too long, however, it may be useful in the shorter term for a limited set of countries to enter into negotiations to harmonize guidelines for border penalties, ideally in informal association with the secretariats of the UNFCCC and the WTO.

Conclusion

Great challenges confront the community of nations seeking to establish an effective and meaningful international climate regime for the post-2012 period. But some key principles, promising policy architectures, and guidelines for essential design elements have begun to emerge.

Climate change is a global commons problem, and therefore a cooperative approach involving many nations will be necessary to address it successfully. Since sovereign nations cannot be compelled to act against their wishes, successful treaties must create adequate internal incentives for compliance, along with external incentives for participation. A credible global climate change agreement must be: (1) equitable; (2) cost-effective; (3) able to facilitate significant technological change and technology transfer; (4) consistent with the international trade regime; (5) practical, in the sense that it builds—

where possible—on existing institutions and practices; (6) attentive to short-term achievements, as well medium-term consequences and long-term goals; and (7) realistic. Because no single approach guarantees a sure path to ultimate success, the best strategy may be to pursue a variety of approaches simultaneously.

The Harvard Project on International Climate Agreements does not endorse a single international climate policy architecture. Rather, in this concluding chapter, we have highlighted four potential frameworks for a post-Kyoto agreement, each of which is promising in some regards and raises important issues for consideration. One calls for emissions caps established using a set of formulas that assign quantitative emissions limits to countries through 2100. These caps would be implemented through a global system of linked national and regional cap-and-trade programs that would allow for trading among firms and sources. A second potential framework would instead rely on a system of linked international agreements that separately address mitigation in various sectors and gases, along with issues like adaptation, technology research and development, and geoengineering. A third architecture would consist of harmonized domestic taxes on emissions of GHGs from all sources, where the tax or charge would be internationally adjusted from time to time, and each country would collect and keep the revenues it generates. Fourth, we discussed an architecture that—at least in the short term—links national and regional tradable permit systems only indirectly, through the global CDM. We highlight this option less as a recommendation and more by way of recognizing the structure that may already be evolving as the *de facto* post-Kyoto international climate policy architecture.

Regardless of which overall international policy architecture is chosen, a number of key design issues will stand out as particularly important, including burden sharing, technology transfer, CDM reform, addressing deforestation, and making global climate policy compatible with global trade policy. All of these issues involve the relationship between global climate policy and economic development, and all are under careful investigation as part of the Harvard Project.

As the Harvard Project on International Climate Agreements moves forward, we continue to draw upon leading thinkers from academia, private industry, government, and nongovernmental organizations around the world. We also continue to work with our research teams around the world and meet in a wide variety of venues with those who can share their expertise and insights. We look forward to receiving input regarding all elements of our work—including feedback on the proposals and analyses which constitute the content of this book.

References

Aldy, Joseph E., Scott Barrett, and Robert N. Stavins (2003). "Thirteen Plus One: A Comparison of Global Climate Policy Architectures." *Climate Policy* 3(4): 373–97.

Aldy, Joseph E. and Robert N. Stavins, eds. (2007). *Architectures for Agreement: Addressing Global Climate Change in the Post-Kyoto World*. New York: Cambridge University Press.

(2008a). "Climate Policy Architectures for the Post-Kyoto World." *Environment* 50 (3): 6–17.

(2008b). "Economic Incentives in a New Climate Agreement." Prepared for The Climate Dialogue, Hosted by the Prime Minister of Denmark, May 7–8, 2008, Copenhagen, Denmark. Cambridge, MA: Belfer Center for Science and International Affairs, May 7.

(2008c). "The Role of Technology Policies in an International Climate Agreement." Prepared for The Climate Dialogue, Hosted by the Prime Minister of Denmark, September 2–3, 2008, Copenhagen, Denmark. Cambridge, MA: Belfer Center for Science and International Affairs, September 3.

Carraro, Carlo (2007). "Incentives and Institutions: A Bottom-Up Approach to Climate Policy," in Aldy and Stavins, (eds.), pp. 161–72.

Information Office of the State Council (2008). "China's Policies and Actions for Addressing Climate Change," white paper published by the government of the People's Republic of China, October 29. Available at http://china.org.cn/government/news/2008-10/29/content_16681689.htm.

Jiang, Kejun (2008). "Opportunities for Developing Country Participation in an International Climate Change Policy Regime." Draft Discussion Paper, Cambridge, MA: Harvard Project on International Climate Agreements.

Pan, Yue (2007). *Thoughts on Environmental Issues*. Beijing: China Environmental Culture Promotion Association.

Victor, David G. (2007). "Fragmented Carbon Markets and Reluctant Nations: Implications for the Design of Effective Architectures," in Aldy and Stavins, (eds.), pp. 133–60.

Appendix A: selected list of individuals consulted

We wish to thank the following individuals—and many others—who took time from their exceptionally busy schedules over the past two years to meet with us and offer their observations and insights in regard to the work of the Harvard Project on International Climate Agreements. The Project has benefitted tremendously from these meetings and exchanges. However, none of the individuals listed have reviewed, let alone approved, the content of this volume. Institutions listed are for identification purposes only and were accurate at the time of our consultation(s).

Jan Adams
First Assistant Secretary and
Ambassador
for Climate Change
Department of Climate
Change
Government of Australia

His Excellency Ban Ki-moon
Secretary-General of the United
Nations

Howard Bamsey
Deputy Secretary
Department of Climate Change
Government of Australia

Kit Batten
Senior Fellow
Center for American Progress

Peter Betts
Director, International Climate
Change
Department of Energy and Climate
Change
Government of the
United Kingdom

CHEW Tai Soo
Ambassador-at-Large
Government of Singapore

Rae-Kwon Chung
Climate Change Ambassador
Government of the Republic of
Korea

James Connaughton
Chairman, Council on
Environmental Quality
Executive Office of the President
Government of the United States

Fulvio Conti
Chief Executive Officer and
General Manager
Enel SpA

John Deutch
Institute Professor
Massachusetts Institute of
Technology

Stavros Dimas
Commissioner for
Environment
European Commission

Elliot Diringer
Vice President, International
Strategies
Pew Center on Global Climate
Change

Robert Dixon
Team Leader, Climate Change and
Chemicals
Global Environmental Facility

Paula Dobriansky
Under Secretary, Democracy and
Global Affairs
Department of State
Government of the
United States

David Doniger
Policy Director, Climate Center
Natural Resources
Defense Council

Brian Flannery
Manager, Environment and
Strategy Development
ExxonMobil

Christopher Flavin
President
Worldwatch Institute

Jody Freeman
Professor of Law
Harvard Law School

Masahisa Fujita
President and Chief Research
Officer
Research Institute of Economy,
Trade, and Industry (Japan)

Kristalina Georgieva
Vice President and Corporate
Secretary
World Bank Group

Al Gore
Former Vice President of the United
States

C. Boyden Gray
Special Envoy for European Affairs
and Eurasian Energy
Mission of the United States to the
European Union

HAN Wenke
Director General, Energy Research
Institute
National Development and Reform
Commission
People's Republic of China

Gary Hart
Wirth Chair Professor
School of Public Affairs
University of Colorado Denver

Connie Hedegaard
Minister of Climate
and Energy
Government of Denmark

Jim Heyes
Environmental and Corporate
Governance Officer
Global Environment Fund

Trevor Houser
Visiting Fellow
Peterson Institute for International
Economics

Steve Howard
Chief Executive Officer
The Climate Group

Michael Jacobs
Special Advisor to the Prime
Minister
United Kingdom

Dale Jorgenson
Samuel W. Morris University
Professor
Harvard University

Lars Josefsson
President and Chief Executive
Officer
Vattenfall

Peter Kalas
Advisor to the Prime Minister
Czech Republic

Nathaniel Keohane
Director of Economic Policy and
Analysis
Climate and Air Program
Environmental Defense Fund

Melinda Kimble
Senior Vice President
United Nations Foundation

Fred Krupp
President
Environmental Defense Fund

Brice Lalonde
Ambassador for Climate Change
Negotiation
Government of France

Jonathan Lash
President
World Resources Institute

Kevin Leahey
Managing Director
Climate Policy and Economics
Duke Energy

LI Liyan
Deputy Director, Office of the
National Coordination Committee
on Climate Change
People's Republic of China

Bo Lidegaard
Permanent Under Secretary of State
Office of the Prime Minister of
Denmark

Christine Loh
Chief Executive Officer
Civic Exchange

LU Xuedu
Deputy Head, Office of Global
Environmental Affairs
Ministry of Science and
Technology
People's Republic of China

Adrian Macey
Climate Change Ambassador
Government of New Zealand

Ichiro Maeda
Deputy General Manager
Tokyo Electric Power
Company

Michael Martin
Ambassador for Climate Change
Government of Canada

Alden Meyer
Director of Strategy and Policy
Union of Concerned Scientists

John Morton
Managing Director, Economic
Policy
Pew Charitable Trusts

Fernando Napolitano
Managing Director
Booz & Company Italia

Marty Natalegawa
Permanent Representative to the
United Nations
Republic of Indonesia

Mutsuyoshi Nishimura
Special Advisor to the Government
Government of Japan

Robert Nordhaus
Member
Van Ness Feldman

Maciej Nowicki
Minister of the Environment
Government of Poland

Marvin Odum
President
Shell Oil Company

PAN Jiahua
Executive Director, Research Centre
for Sustainable Development
Chinese Academy of
 Social Sciences

PAN Yue
Vice Minister, Ministry of
Environmental Protection
People's Republic of China

Janos Pasztor
Director, Climate Change Support
Team
Office of the Secretary-General
United Nations

Annie Petsonk
International Counsel
Environmental Defense Fund

Manjeev Singh Puri
Joint Secretary (UNES)
Ministry of External Affairs
Government of India

Nigel Purvis
Visiting Scholar
Resources for the Future

**His Excellency Anders Fogh
Rasmussen**
Prime Minister of Denmark

Janusz Reiter
Ambassador for
Climate Change
Government of Poland

Theodore Roosevelt IV
Managing Director
Barclays Capital

François Roussely
Chairman
Credit Suisse, France

Masayuki Sasanouchi
Senior General Manager
Carbon Management Group
Toyota Corporation

Phil Sharp
President
Resources for the Future

Kunihiko Shimada
Principal International Negotiator
Ministry of the Environment
Government of Japan

Domenico Siniscalco
Vice Chairman and Managing
Director
Morgan Stanley International

Nicholas Stern
IG Patel Professor of Economics
and Government
London School of Economics

Todd Stern
Senior Fellow
Center for American Progress

Björn Stigson
President
World Business Council for
Sustainable
Development

Lawrence Summers
Charles W. Eliot University
Professor
Harvard University

Nobuo Tanaka
Executive Director
International Energy Agency

Masakazu Toyoda
Vice-Minister for International
Affairs
Ministry of Economy, Trade, and
Industry
Government of Japan

Koji Tsuruoka
Director-General for
Global Issues
Ministry of Foreign Affairs
Government of Japan

Harald Winkler
Energy Research Centre
University of Cape Town

Timothy Wirth
President
United Nations Foundation

ZOU Ji
Professor and Head
Department of Environmental
Economics and Management
Renmin University of China

Appendix B: workshops and conferences*

Sponsored and Conducted by the Harvard Project:

Presentation to and discussion with policy makers
and business and NGO leaders
Hosted by Resources for the Future, Washington, DC
October 4, 2007

Presentation to and discussion with business leaders
Venue: Harvard Club of New York City
October 18, 2007

Presentation to and discussion with scholars and stakeholders
Hosted by the Harvard Kennedy School
October 24, 2007

Workshop with stakeholders from business and the NGO community
Hosted by The Centre (policy research institute in Brussels, Belgium)
November 16, 2007

Official side-event presentation
Thirteenth Conference of the Parties, Bali, Indonesia
December 10, 2007

Workshop with Japanese industry representatives
Hosted by the 21st Century Public Policy Institute (affiliated with
Keidanren), Tokyo
March 25, 2008

Presentation to scholars and government officials
Hosted by Tsinghua University, School of Economics and Management,
Beijing
March 27, 2008

---

* This list does not include the numerous meetings the Harvard Project on International Climate Agreements has held with national climate delegations, business and NGO leaders, and many others around the world.

Seminar discussion with scholars and government officials
Hosted by the Research Centre for Sustainable Development, Chinese
Academy of Social Sciences, Beijing
March 28, 2008

Presentations to and discussions with business leaders
Hosted by Resources for the Future, Washington, DC
September 5, 2008

Presentations to and discussions with NGO leaders
Hosted by Resources for the Future, Washington, DC
September 5, 2008

Official side-event presentation
Fourteenth Conference of the Parties, Poznan, Poland
December 6, 2008

Presentations to and discussions with senior business
and NGO leaders
Fourteenth Conference of the Parties, Poznan, Poland
December 10, 2008

Banking Roundtable on Post-Kyoto Climate Policy
Hosted by Barclays Capital, New York
April 30, 2009

Major Harvard Project participation in events sponsored by other organizations:
Principal presentation to and participation in roundtable on "Architectures
for Agreement," as part of the 2007 World Energy Congress, Rome
November 15, 2007

Participation in and technical presentation at a workshop hosted by the
International Emissions Trading Association
Thirteenth Conference of the Parties, Bali, Indonesia
December 10, 2007

Participation in and background technical support for the Copenhagen
Climate Dialogue on Economic Incentives in a New Climate Agreement,
attended by senior business, government, and NGO leaders, and hosted by
Prime Minister Anders Fogh Rasmussen, Denmark
May 7–8, 2008

Participation in and technical presentations to Productivity Commission
Roundtable Discussion: Promoting Better Environmental
Outcomes
Hosted by Productivity Commission, Canberra, Australia
August 19–21, 2008

Participation in and background technical support for the Copenhagen
Climate Dialogue on Role of Technology Policies in an International
Climate Agreement, attended by senior business, government, and
NGO leaders, and hosted by Prime Minister Anders Fogh Rasmussen,
Denmark
September 2–3, 2008

Provided background technical presentations for a debate between energy
and environment representatives of the US presidential campaigns
Hosted by the Progressive Policy Institute, Washington, DC
September 16, 2008

Participation in and technical presentations to group of EU officials and
business and NGO leaders
Hosted by Bruegel (policy research institute in Brussels, Belgium)
September 24, 2008

Participation in and presentation to the Global Governance Conference
Hosted by Columbia University
December 1, 2008

Participation in and technical presentation at a workshop hosted by the
International Emissions Trading Association
Fourteenth Conference of the Parties, Poznan, Poland
December 9, 2008

Participation in and presentation to new Members of Congress
Hosted by the US Congressional Research Service
January 12, 2009

Participation in and presentation to the Multi-stakeholder Conference on
the Global Issues of Energy, Environment and Development
Hosted by EnergyPact Foundation, Geneva, Switzerland
March 15, 2009

Appendix B: workshops and conferences

Participation in and presentation to the conference on Climate Change
Policy: Insights from the US and Europe
Hosted by French-American Foundation and France-Stanford Center for
Interdisciplinary Studies
March 23–24, 2009

Glossary and abbreviations

For additional definitions, see:
 www.pewclimate.org/global-warming-basics/full_glossary
 http://unfccc.int/essential_background/glossary/items/3666.php

The texts of the United Nations Framework Convention on Climate Change and the Kyoto Protocol may be found at:
 http://unfccc.int/essential_background/convention/background/items/2853.php
 http://unfccc.int/kyoto_protocol/items/2830.php

Allowance	A tradable right to emit a specified amount of a substance. In greenhouse gas markets, usually denominated in metric tons of CO_2-equivalent per year. "Allowance" is generally used interchangeably with "permit."
Annex I	An annex to the UNFCCC listing countries that would, among other things, "adopt national policies and take corresponding measures on the mitigation of climate change" (article 4, para. 2.a), upon ratification. These countries belong to the OECD or are economies in transition. The list of Annex I countries overlaps almost completely with the list of countries in the Kyoto Protocol's Annex B.
Annex B	An annex to the Kyoto Protocol listing countries that would assume legally binding commitments, upon ratification of the Protocol. Annex B also lists the actual commitments, as a percentage change in annual emissions (from which an "assigned amount" may be computed), generally from emissions in 1990. The list of Annex B countries overlaps almost completely with the list of countries in the UNFCCC's Annex I.

Assigned Amount Unit	An Annex B country's binding emissions target under the Kyoto Protocol is referred to as its "assigned amount" (Article 3, paras. 7–8). These targets are divided into "assigned amount units" (AAUs), each equal to one metric ton of CO_2 equivalent. AAUs may serve as the currency for international emissions trading under Article 17 of the Kyoto Protocol.
Banking	Saving emission permits for future use (not in the year assigned) in anticipation that these will accrue value over time. This value might be realized either through trading or through use, if emissions are anticipated to increase or become more expensive to abate.
Basket of Gases	The six greenhouse gases listed in Annex A of the Kyoto Protocol, together constituting a "basket" in which Kyoto commitments are denominated. They are: carbon dioxide (CO_2), methane (CH_4), nitrous oxide (N_2O), hydrofluorocarbons (HFCs), perfluorocarbons (PFCs), and sulphur hexafluoride (SF_6).
BAU	"Business as Usual." This refers to the projected level of future greenhouse gas emissions expected without emission mitigation policies.
Benchmark	A measurable variable used as a reference in evaluating the performance of projects or actions. Also referred to as a baseline.
BTU	The British Thermal Unit is a standard measure of the energy content of fuels. It is the amount of heat needed to raise the temperature of one pound of water one degree Fahrenheit.
Bubble	An informal term referring to a provision in the Kyoto Protocol (Article 4, para. 1) that allows a group of countries to aggregate their emissions and emissions targets, and strive to meet the latter jointly. The European Union, through its Emission Trading Scheme, has utilized this provision.
Cap	An absolute aggregate emissions limit for a country, region, subnational territory, or sector.
Cap-and-Trade	A policy that sets a cap for a particular air pollutant, issues permits (or "allowances"—see glossary terms) that sum to the cap, allocates the permits to entities

subject to regulation under the system (usually business firms), and provides for those entities to buy and sell the permits. The system does not, in general, specify the means by which participating entities achieve emissions reductions.

Carbon Dioxide Equivalent   See CO_2e.

Carbon Sequestration   The uptake and storage of carbon. Trees and plants, for example, take in carbon dioxide, release the oxygen, and store the carbon. Sometimes used in connection with CCS.

Carbon Sink   Any reservoir that takes up and stores carbon. Oceans and forests are the primary carbon sinks in the Earth's carbon cycle.

CCS   Carbon capture and storage (or "sequestration") refers to a set of technologies that remove carbon dioxide from process streams in power or manufacturing facilities and store it (generally underground) for long periods of time. Only a very small number of pilot CCS facilities have been built.

CDM   Clean Development Mechanism. Article 12 of the Kyoto Protocol establishes the CDM to assist developing countries in achieving sustainable development through project-based emissions reduction. Successful projects generate "certified emission reduction" units (CERs). (In practice, the term "credit" is often used instead of "unit.") CERs may be sold to Annex I countries, which may apply them to their emission-reduction-commitments, or into carbon markets (e.g., national or regional cap-and-trade systems), where they may be traded (in some cases subject to quantitative limitations) interchangeably with government-issued allowances. The UNFCCC, through its CDM Executive Board, evaluates projects and issues CERs. An important criterion for issuance is "additionality": The Board must determine that emissions reductions resulting from the project would not have occurred in its absence.

CER   Certified Emission Reduction. One CER unit (or credit) corresponds to one metric ton of CO_2-equivalent emission reduction generated through a Clean Development Mechanism project. (See also "CDM.")

CO_2 Carbon dioxide. CO_2 is the primary greenhouse gas emitted by human activities, through fossil fuel combustion, land-use change, and industrial processes (cement production being one of the most significant contributors).

CO_2e Carbon dioxide equivalent. The emissions of a greenhouse gas, by weight, multiplied by its global warming potential (see "GWP" in glossary).

Commitment Period   A time period during which parties to a greenhouse-gas-reduction agreement are subject to the terms of that agreement. For example, the Kyoto Protocol's first commitment period covers the years 2008 through 2012.

COP   Conference of the Parties. The "supreme body of the UNFCCC," established by Article 7 of the Convention, comprised of countries that are parties to the Convention. In practice, the Conference meets annually, in early December.

Credit   Like an "allowance" or "permit" (which are in practice nearly synonymous with each other), a tradable right to emit a specified amount of a substance. "Credit," though, generally refers to a right generated from an emission-reduction project (usually a CER from a CDM project) and may be specified more completely as an "emission reduction credit" or "offset credit."

Economies in Transition   The industrialized countries listed in Annex I or Annex B that are undergoing the process of transition to a market economy. These include some former Soviet republics, including Russia, and several central and eastern European countries.

EU ETS   The European Union Emission Trading Scheme. The EU ETS's first trading period—which was a trial period in some respects—ran from 2005 through 2007. The second period is coincident with the first Kyoto Protocol commitment period, 2008—2012.

In late 2008, the EU specified, in part, the parameters of the third commitment period, which will start in 2013. The EU ETS is the largest and most developed cap-and-trade system in the world.

GATT   General Agreement on Tariffs and Trade. The GATT was for many years the multilateral agreement for international trade policy, succeeded in 1995 by the World Trade Organization.

GEF   Global Environment Facility. The GEF is a multilateral organization established in 1991 that provides grants to developing countries for projects that address a variety of environmental problems. The GEF is also the formally designated financial mechanism for several multilateral agreements, including the UNFCCC.

GHG   Greenhouse gas. An atmospheric gas that differentially allows incoming solar radiation to pass unimpeded and absorbs outgoing long-wavelength (infrared) radiation emitted or reflected from the Earth's surface. GHGs thereby cause warming of the Earth's surface and near-surface atmosphere. Six GHGs are named in Annex A of the Kyoto Protocol.

GWP   Global Warming Potential. A GWP measures the effectiveness of a greenhouse gas in absorbing outgoing infrared radiation, relative to that of CO_2. The Kyoto Protocol (Article 5, para. 3) mandates the use of GWPs determined by the IPCC for comparing and aggregating greenhouse gas emissions with regard to Annex B commitments. See also "radiative forcing."

G8   Group of Eight. The G8 is a forum of the largest industrialized economies. Members are Canada, France, Germany, Italy, Japan, the United Kingdom, the United States, and Russia, which joined in 1998, after several years of informal participation. While the G8 was founded to address economic issues, it has increasingly focused on climate change policy and other matters over the last several years. Also of late, the annual summit has been preceded by a meeting of members' environmental ministers, who have prepared the climate change agenda for the summit.

G8+5 Climate   A discussion forum launched at the 2005 G8 meeting
Change   in Gleneagles, Scotland, incorporating the G8 countries
Dialogue   and the large emerging economies: Brazil, China, India,
               Mexico and South Africa.

G20   Group of Twenty. The G20 includes the G8 members
               and major emerging market countries, providing a
               forum for finance ministers and central bank governors
               to address international finance issues.

Hot Air   "Hot air" is an informal term referring to Kyoto or
               other targets in excess of expected (or actual) emissions,
               for a particular country or region. Within a cap-and-
               trade system, "hot air" yields excess permits that might
               be sold into the market. Russia and Eastern Europe have
               a great deal of hot air, in large part because their econo-
               mies (and hence emissions) declined significantly subse-
               quent to the 1990 baseline set by the Kyoto Protocol.

IEA   International Energy Agency. An intergovernmen-
               tal organization founded by the Organisation for
               Economic Co-operation and Development (OECD) in
               1974 that conducts analysis of energy policy and pro-
               vides guidance to its member governments.

IET   International Emissions Trading, established by Article
               17 of the Kyoto Protocol. Countries with Annex B
               commitments can participate in IET. See also "cap and
               trade."

IPCC   Intergovernmental Panel on Climate Change. The IPCC
               was created in 1988 by the United Nations Environment
               Programme and the World Health Organization to
               advise the international policy community on scientific
               research on global climate change.

JI   Joint Implementation. JI refers to emission mitigation
               projects conducted collaboratively between industrial-
               ized countries, as specified in Article 6 of the Kyoto
               Protocol. Such projects yield emission reduction units
               (ERUs) that may be traded.

Kyoto   The market mechanisms of the Kyoto Protocol: JI,
Mechanisms   CDM and IET.

Kyoto   A protocol to the UNFCCC that was adopted in
Protocol   1997 and came into force in 2005. The protocol sets

binding targets for 37 industrialized countries and the European Union for reducing GHG emissions.

Leakage	Leakage is an increase in emissions in one country as the result of a cap on emissions in another country. Leakage can occur because emission reduction caps increase costs for industry, which may lead to a shift of production to countries without caps.
Linkage	Provision for interchangeability of permits, credits, or both between and among cap-and-trade and emission-reduction-credit systems.
LULUCF	Land use, land-use change, and forestry. A potential source of emissions reductions.
L20	An analog to the G20 whose membership overlaps almost completely with the Leaders of the G20 member countries. The L20, established by former Canadian Prime Minister Paul Martin and two Canadian NGOs in 2003, addresses a variety of multinational policy issues.
MOP	Meeting of the Parties. The supreme body of the Kyoto Protocol that meets annually for negotiations, in conjunction with the UNFCCC COP.
Non-Annex I countries	All countries that are not listed in Annex I of the UNFCCC, that is, developing countries and some economies in transition.
OECD	Organisation for Economic Co-operation and Development.
Offset	A reduction in greenhouse gas emissions from one source, used to compensate for (offset) emissions elsewhere. See also "credit."
OPEC	Organization of the Petroleum Exporting Countries.
PAM	Policies and measures. Under the UNFCCC, Annex I countries should undertake policies and measures to demonstrate leadership in addressing global climate change.
Permit	See "allowance."
ppm	Parts per million; may be measured by weight or volume.
ppmv	Parts per million by volume.
Radiative Forcing	Refers to the difference between radiation coming into the atmosphere and reaching the Earth's surface, and

the radiation emitted from the Earth's surface. Positive radiative forcing increases the temperature of the lower atmosphere and the Earth's surface. Negative radiative forcing cools them. Increasing concentration of GHGs in the atmosphere increases radiative forcing. Radiative forcing is closely related to the global warming potential (GWP) of individual GHGs.

REDD — "Reducing emissions from deforestation and degradation."

RGGI — Regional Greenhouse Gas Initiative. A cap-and-trade scheme introduced in ten US Northeast and Mid-Atlantic states, beginning in 2009.

RTA — Regional trade agreement.

Targets and Timetables — Targets refer to binding emission caps, and timetables refer to the timing of the commitment period during which these caps must be met.

UNFCCC — United Nations Framework Convention on Climate Change. The multilateral agreement that provides the foundation for international climate negotiations, which entered into force in 1994.

US EIA — US Energy Information Administration, an agency of the US Department of Energy.

US EPA — US Environmental Protection Agency.

WTO — World Trade Organization.

Index

abatement. *See* mitigation
Abe, Shinzo, 53n
Abu Dhabi, 632
accession deals
  See also climate accession deals
  EU process, 638
  incentives, 634
  norm convergence, 642–3
  OECD, 638
  reporting mechanisms, 640–1
  transition rules, 636
  WTO, 622, 634–6
accountability
  mitigation activities, 447–9
  offsets, 457, 462–4
acid rain, 183
adaptation
  assessment of needs, 197
  Bali Action Plan, 10–11, 584
  developing countries, 262, 447
    support, 671–2, 908
  incentives, 261–2
  meaning, xxxiv
  mitigation and, 536
  multistage hybrid model, 584–5
  necessity, 241
  overinvestment, 280
  portfolio approach, 261–4
  research and development, 263–4
  rich countries' responsibility, 262
Adaptation Fund, 667
Africa
  emissions allocation, welfare costs,
    778–9
  emissions targets, 69, 70, 727
  greenhouse gas emissions, 722
  vulnerability to climate change, 353
Agarwala, Ramgopal, 15, 198, 901,
    902, 903, 905n, 909, 911,
    915

agriculture
  climate-ready crops, 263
  Consultative Group on International
    Agricultural Research
    (CGIAR), 194, 263, 614
  effects of global warming on, 265–6,
    278
  Green Revolution, 614
  methane production, 155
  national reports to UNFCCC, 330
  slash and burn agriculture, 158
  technology cooperation, 613–14,
    908
air capture, 242, 266–8
air traffic control, 250
Akerlof, George, 387
Aldy, Joseph, 27, 567, 897
Algeria, 632
Alstom, 479
aluminium, 218, 257, 518, 550
Anderson, Dennis, 610–11
Anderson, Krister, 451
Anderson, S. O., 255
Andersson, K., 684, 692–3, 700
Annex I countries, 254, 895–6, 939
anti-dumping, 521
anti-globalization movement, 503
architectures
  accession deals. *See* climate
    accession deals
  assessment, 903–14
  basic proposal, 539–42
    conditionality, 544–5
    elements, 530–2
    emissions trading, 549–55
    escape clause, 531, 539–42
    mandatory ceilings, 532–3, 536
    ratification threshold, 544
    role of trade policy, 545–9
    trade sanctions, 542–4